Cracking the SAT® Spanish Subject Test

15th Edition

George Roberto Pace
and the Staff of The Princeton Review

PrincetonReview.com

PENGUIN RANDOM HOUSE

The Princeton Review
24 Prime Parkway, Suite 201
Natick, MA 01760
E-mail: editorialsupport@review.com

Published in the United States by Random House LLC, New York, and simultaneously in Canada by Random House of Canada Limited, Toronto.

A Penguin Random House Company.

ISBN: 978-0-8041-2576-5
eBook ISBN: 978-0-8041-2577-2
ISSN: 1558-3406

Editor: Colleen Day
Production Artist: Deborah A. Silvestrini
Production Editor: Ali Landreau

Printed in the United States of America on partially recycled paper.

10 9 8 7 6 5 4 3 2 1

15th Edition

Acknowledgments

Para Roberto, Carmina y Enrique, sin quienes no estuviese donde estoy.

To Ernie and Bert, for helping me learn to speak English.

G.R.P.

Special thanks to Adam Robinson, who conceived of and perfected the Joe Bloggs approach to standardized tests and many of the other successful techniques used by The Princeton Review.

The Princeton Review would like to give a special thanks to Michael Giammarino for his creation of the listening practice section of the book, and to Claudia Landgrover for her review of this edition.

Contents

...So Much More Online!

Register Your Book Now!

- Get access to your Listening Drills for the *Cracking the SAT Spanish Subject Test.*
  - First, create a username and password on **PrincetonReview.com.**
  - Then, go to **PrincetonReview.com/cracking** and enter the ISBN that appears on the back cover of the book (right above the bar code). In case you can't locate it, the number is: 9780804125765. Then click "Go."
  - You'll be directed to a Shopping Cart page. Please do not be alarmed; you will not be asked for any type of payment information nor will you be charged to access your material. Once you've filled out the necessary info, go back to **PrincetonReview.com/cracking.**
  - Now, in the upper right-hand corner, click Student Tools. Then go to "My Online Content" to access your drills!

PrincetonReview.com

Look For These Icons Throughout The Book

 Proven Techniques

 More Great Books

 Applied Strategies

Part I Orientation

Chapter 1
Introduction

The SAT Spanish Subject Test is an hour-long, multiple-choice exam intended for students who have had a minimum of two years of high school-level Spanish or the equivalent. In this chapter, we explain why you've made a wise decision to prepare with The Princeton Review and discuss the reasons you should take this exam. We also present the structure of the exam.

YOU'RE ON YOUR WAY—¡VAMOS!

Congratulations! By purchasing this book, you've taken the first step toward raising your score on the SAT Spanish Subject Tests. Now you just have to read the book, practice the strategies, and take the practice tests. We know that taking a standardized test is about as exciting as watching paint dry, but we've done everything possible to make working through this book as painless and fun as possible.

To get the most out of this book, you should tackle it in bite-size pieces. You'll drive yourself crazy and lose interest if you try to read through the entire book in one sitting or one weekend. We recommend that you figure out how much time you have left before you take the actual test and come up with a game plan that makes sense. Just be sure to set aside a solid hour to take each one of the practice tests. You won't do yourself any good or get an accurate assessment of your performance if you take the practice tests in pieces or if you give yourself extra time to finish them.

WHAT IS THE PRINCETON REVIEW?

The Princeton Review is a test-preparation company with branches across the United States and abroad. We've developed the techniques you'll find in our books, courses, and online resources by analyzing actual exams and testing their effectiveness with our students. What makes our techniques unique is that we base our principles on the same ones used by the people who write the tests. We don't want you to waste your time with superfluous information; we'll give you just the information you need to improve your scores. You'll learn to recognize and comprehend the relatively small amount of information that's actually tested. You'll also learn to avoid common traps, think like the test writers, find answers to questions of which you're unsure, and budget your time effectively. You need to do only two things: trust the techniques, and practice, practice, practice.

WHY OUR BOOK?

The Princeton Review is on your side. We didn't create the tests, and we don't force anyone to take them. We simply help students do better on them. In this book, you'll find a thorough review of the content that will be covered on the test, test-taking strategies that will help you apply your existing knowledge, and enough practice tests for you to determine your own personal strengths and weaknesses.

Welcome
Remember—this test shows little of your knowledge of Spanish, only how well you do on this particular test.

WHAT ARE THE SPANISH SUBJECT TESTS?

There are two different Spanish Subject Tests: the traditional Spanish Subject Test and the Spanish with Listening Subject Test. Most of you will take the traditional Spanish Subject Test, and the majority of this book will be dedicated to that exam. However, for those of you who are planning to take the Spanish with Listening Subject Test, we provide some strategies to help you do your best, as well as online listening drills for realistic practice. See the "...So Much More Online!" page at the front of this book for instructions on accessing these drills.

Both SAT Spanish Subject Tests are hour-long, multiple-choice exams that are supposed to measure your knowledge of Spanish. Do the SAT Spanish Subject Tests really accomplish this? Absolutely not. If you really want to know how well you speak Spanish, you should try reading a Spanish newspaper, watching a Spanish television show, or speaking Spanish with a native speaker. Each of these activities will give you a better idea of how well you speak the language than the results of the SAT Spanish Subject Tests.

WHY SHOULD YOU TAKE A SPANISH SUBJECT TEST?

There are only two good reasons to take an SAT Spanish Subject Test. The first of these reasons is that one of the colleges to which you are applying either requires or strongly recommends you take several different SAT Subject Tests. If this is the case, you will want to make sure you pick the three subjects that best demonstrate your academic achievement. Evaluate your own strengths and weaknesses, and contact colleges to see which tests they suggest or require. The second reason you might take the SAT Spanish Subject Test is that one of the colleges to which you're applying plans to use the Spanish Subject Test as a placement exam.

Love Spanish?
Are you a Spanish aficionado? Are you enrolled or planning to enroll in AP Spanish? We also have a prep book for the Advanced Placement Exam! Check out *Cracking the AP Spanish Language & Culture Exam, 2015.*

WHEN SHOULD YOU TAKE IT?

The first thing you need to decide is whether to take one of the Spanish Subject Tests. These tests are appropriate for students who have completed a minimum of two years of high school Spanish or the equivalent, but are more often taken by students who have completed or are in the middle of their third year of high school Spanish.

The second thing you need to decide is whether to take the Spanish Subject Test or the Spanish with Listening Subject Test. If you have a lot of experience speaking Spanish, you might want to take the Spanish with Listening Subject Test. If you learned most of your Spanish from reading a book, you should probably take the Spanish Test that does not contain a listening section.

The Spanish Subject Test is given five times each year: October, December, January, May, and June. The Spanish with Listening Subject Test is given only once each year, in November. There is really no advantage to taking the test in a particular month, though there are plenty of rumors going around that certain administrations are easier than others. Don't pay any attention to those rumors; just take the test when you feel most ready to do so. Of course, if you decide to take the Spanish with Listening Subject Test, you don't really have much choice in the matter.

HOW DO I REGISTER FOR THE TESTS?

To register by mail, pick up the *Registration Guide for the SAT and SAT Subject Tests* at your guidance counselor's office. You can also register at the College Board website at **www.collegeboard.org**. This site contains other useful information such as the test date and fees. If you have questions, you can talk to a representative at the College Board by calling 1-888-756-7346.

You may have your scores sent to you, to your school, and to four colleges of your choice. Additional reports will be sent to additional colleges for—you guessed it—additional money. Scores are made available to students via the College Board's website. To find out about the timeline of when scores are made available, please visit sat.collegeboard.org.

HOW IS THE TEST STRUCTURED?

Both the Spanish Subject Test and the Spanish with Listening Subject Test contain 85 multiple-choice questions. You'll have one hour to complete each of the tests, but you do not necessarily need to finish either test to get a good score. The structure of each test is discussed in the pages that follow.

Spanish Subject Test: Spanish

The Spanish Subject Test contains three sections that measure different skills. Each section is weighted equally and contains approximately the same number of questions (about 28). The three sections are

- Part A: Vocabulary and Structure (Sentence Completion)
- Part B: Paragraph Completion
- Part C: Reading Comprehension

Spanish Subject Test: Spanish with Listening

The Spanish with Listening Subject Test consists of two sections: the Listening section and the Reading section. The Listening section (about 20 minutes) contains approximately 30 questions, and the Reading section (about 40 minutes) has around 55 questions. Each section contains questions that measure different skills.

Listening Section

- **Part A: Pictures**—You will be presented with a series of images (approximately 10) and asked to select the sentence that best reflects what is portrayed in the picture or what someone in the picture might say. The answer choices will be spoken to you in the listening sample rather than written in your test booklet.
- **Part B: Rejoinders**—You will listen to a short conversation and/or selection and then be asked to select the answer choice that best represents the continuation of the conversation. There are no written questions, answers, or images in your test booklet. This portion requires you to listen carefully to the conversation and answer about 10 questions.
- **Part C: Selections**—You will be asked to listen to extensive selections including conversations among a group of people, advertisements, or short stories. You will then have to answer approximately 10 questions. Unlike those in Parts A and B, the questions and answers in Part C *are* written in your test booklet.

Reading Section

- Part A: Vocabulary and Structure (Sentence Completion)
- Part B: Paragraph Completion
- Part C: Reading Comprehension

HOW IS THE TEST SCORED?

Your overall score on either the Spanish Subject Test or the Spanish with Listening Subject Test is based on the number of questions you answer correctly minus $\frac{1}{3}$ of the number of questions you answer incorrectly. You get no credit and lose no points for questions you leave blank. On the Spanish Subject Test, the result of this simple calculation (number correct – $\frac{1}{3}$ of number incorrect) represents your raw score. Raw scores can range from –28 to 85. On the Spanish with Listening Subject Test, you receive several different scores: a raw score for each section, a scaled score for each section (20–80), and an overall scaled score (200–800).

Both Spanish Subject Tests are scored on a 200–800 scale. Just like with the SAT, the lowest possible score is a 200 (even if you answer every question incorrectly) and the highest possible score is an 800 (which you can get even if you miss a question or two). The only tricky thing about the scoring is on the Spanish with Listening Subject Test. On this test, the two sections are weighted differently. Because the Reading section represents about $\frac{2}{3}$ of the overall test, your raw score in that section is multiplied by 1.12. The Listening section represents about $\frac{1}{3}$ of the overall test, so your raw score in that section is multiplied by .881. The products of each of these two calculations are added together to determine your overall raw score. This new raw score is then converted to a scaled score between 200 and 800.

You shouldn't get too worked up over the scoring. Just do your best, and follow the techniques you learn in this book.

THE SPANISH WITH LISTENING TEST

If you're fairly comfortable listening to spoken Spanish or if you speak it regularly, consider taking the Spanish with Listening Test. If not, you may be better off taking the basic Spanish Subject Test.

The Essentials

If you plan to take the Spanish with Listening Subject Test, the most important thing you need to remember is to bring a CD player with you to the test center. That's right, even though the test administrators will hand out a CD on the day of the test, they will NOT provide you with a CD player. For your CD player to be "acceptable," it must have earphones, operate on batteries (bring your own—the test administrator will not have extras), and be able to play a standard CD. Under no circumstances will you be allowed to share your CD player with another student.

The other thing to keep in mind if you're considering taking the Spanish with Listening Subject Test is that it's offered only once each year—in November. If you're planning to take the test, be sure to register in time for the November exam.

Strategies

The good news is that the strategies that apply to the Spanish Subject Test are also appropriate for the Reading section of the Spanish with Listening Subject Test. Chapters 3 to 6 contain a thorough review of the vocabulary and grammar you need for both tests, as well as a review of the reading and test-taking strategies you need for the Spanish Subject Test and the Reading section of the Spanish with Listening Subject Test. However, you need to prepare for the Listening section of the Spanish with Listening Subject Test on your own. The following are a few ways you can do this:

- Practice speaking Spanish with your friends, classmates, or family members—by speaking Spanish with others, you will get more comfortable with understanding and responding to spoken Spanish.
- Listen to a Spanish-language radio station and practice interpreting what you hear.

- Watch a Spanish-language television program and practice interpreting what you hear.
- Be sure to take our online listening drills, which can be found by going to **PrincetonReview.com/cracking** and registering your book. Once you complete the free "Checkout" process, click on "Student Tools" to access the listening drills.

The most important thing you can do to improve your score on this section of the test is to relax, take a deep breath, and focus.

IS THERE ANY OTHER MATERIAL AVAILABLE FOR PRACTICE?

The College Board publishes a book called *Official Study Guide for All SAT Subject Tests*, which contains full-length tests in almost all the SAT subjects offered. You can also go to the College Board's website, **www.collegeboard.org**, for more information and practice questions.

For book updates, links to more information, last-minute test changes, and access to our practice listening drills, visit this book's online Student Tools at **PrincetonReview.com/cracking**.

FINAL THOUGHTS

You may be concerned that you'll be at a significant disadvantage if you're not a native speaker. This is a common concern, but remember that college admissions officers aren't stupid. They will realize that non-native speakers cannot be expected to meet the same standards as native speakers.

Preparation is the key to success—not only on this test, but also in everything you do. If you want to succeed on the Spanish Subject Test or any other test, make sure you understand the content, practice the strategies, and develop an overall plan to attain your target score. In addition to working through this book, you may want to read a Spanish newspaper (looking up the words you don't know in a dictionary), listen to Spanish-language radio stations, watch Spanish-language television programs, or engage in conversations in Spanish with your classmates, friends, or family members.

Finally, RELAX. Once you've finished preparing, there's no need to stress about the tests. Just make sure you get plenty of sleep the night before the test, eat a balanced breakfast, walk into the test center with a feeling of confidence, and do your best. In the end, your score is just a number. These tests will never be able to measure the most important aspect of your academic potential: your determination.

Summary

Did you get all that?

- o There are two different Spanish Subject Tests: the traditional Spanish Subject Test and the Spanish with Listening Subject Test. Most of you will take the traditional test, but if you have a lot of experience speaking Spanish, consider taking the Spanish with Listening Subject Test. Keep in mind that the listening test is only administered in November each year.
- o The good news is that you can use the same strategies to prepare for both exams!
  - Practice speaking Spanish with your friends or family.
  - Listen to Spanish radio stations or watch Spanish TV shows.
  - Use our listening drills, which can be found in Student Tools in your online dashboard. Go to **www.PrincetonReview.com/cracking** to access the drills.
- o Don't stress! By preparing the right way and taking time to relax, you'll be able to take the test with confidence.

Chapter 2
How to Take the Test: Overall Strategies

Strategy is very important when taking a standardized exam. In this chapter, we look at overall strategies for the test, such as pacing, guessing, and Process of Elimination (POE).

In Chapters 3 through 5 you will review the Spanish that you need to know (as well as some strategies) for the different question types. Right now, let's talk about how to take a standardized test.

PACING

Since your earliest days in school, you were probably taught that when you take a test, finishing is important. Standardized tests, however, are a completely different ball game. The folks who write these tests are interested in how fast you can work, and they design the tests so that it's nearly impossible to finish on time. Because you're so accustomed to the idea that finishing is crucial, you may pressure yourself to answer every question. Have you ever stopped to consider how much sense this makes? It's not as if you get a special prize for finishing! In fact, to finish, you usually have to rush through questions, and as a result you make careless errors that could have been avoided. Doesn't it make more sense to slow down a little, answer the questions of which you're sure, and leave a few blanks? Well, let's see how pacing yourself on the Spanish Subject Tests relates to actual scores.

Pace Yourself

There is no need to do the whole test, especially because it's designed so that you can't! Use the pacing chart. Not doing all the questions gives you more time to get the ones you **are** doing right. If you walk into the test without a pacing strategy, you're basically unprepared.

Pacing Chart

Structure
60 minutes, 85 questions

To Get a Score of	Answer About	Leave This Many Blank
400	13	72
450	26	59
500	38	47
550	48	37
600	58	27
650	68	17
700	78	7
750 and up	85	0

Understand that the pacing chart assumes you'll make fewer than six mistakes, and it doesn't take guesses into account. If you take your time, pick your questions carefully, and learn to guess effectively, making fewer than six errors really isn't as tough as it might sound.

You should walk into your test with a target score in mind and a pacing strategy that reflects the score you want. Remember, this is *your* test, and that means you can answer the questions you want, when you want, how you want, and still get an excellent score. If you want to leave most (or all) of the reading comprehension questions blank and concentrate on the other questions, go ahead. If you're good at reading comprehension but not so good at grammar, then do more of the reading comprehension and fewer of the grammar sentence completions. If all the other students at your test site want to race frantically to the end of the test and make careless mistakes along the way, that's their problem. You're going to be sitting there, cool and relaxed, taking your time and getting a great score.

THE GUESSING STRATEGY

Many people talk about the "guessing penalty" on the SAT and the SAT Subject Tests. What they really mean is that there's no advantage to random guessing. The truth is, there really isn't a penalty either.

Each question on the Spanish Subject Test and the Spanish with Listening Subject Test has four answer choices. If you answer a question correctly, you will receive 1 raw-score point. If you get a question wrong, you will lose $\frac{1}{3}$ of a raw-score point. If you were to randomly guess on four questions with four answer choices each, odds are you would get one question right and three questions wrong. How would this affect your raw score?

Scoring
Raw score = # right – $\frac{1}{3}$ of # wrong, converted to an 800 point scale

1 question correct = +1 point

3 questions incorrect = $-(\frac{1}{3}) \times 3 = -1$ point

Total impact on overall score = 0

So should you guess? Sometimes. If you can eliminate one or more incorrect answer choices, the odds become more favorable. Imagine you were able to eliminate two answer choices and then randomly guess on the remaining two answer choices for four different problems. In this case, you would likely get two questions right and two questions wrong. How would this affect your raw score?

Guessing
If you can eliminate even one answer choice, guessing is to your advantage.

2 questions correct = +2 points

2 questions incorrect = $-(\frac{1}{3}) \times 2 = -\frac{2}{3}$ point

Total impact on overall score = $+1\frac{1}{3}$ points

The moral of this story is that if you can eliminate even one answer choice over several questions, guessing is to your advantage. If you can't eliminate any answer choices, there's no reason to guess. You'll just be wasting valuable time.

THE THREE-PASS SYSTEM

Because the test is written for students with varying levels of expertise in Spanish, the questions vary in difficulty. The questions in a section often get more difficult as you go along. That said, whether you find a question difficult is a personal thing; it's a matter of whether *you* know the words and/or grammar being tested.

The Three-Pass System Means...

- **First Pass**—Go through an entire section of the test from beginning to end, but answer only the easiest questions, that is, those for which you thoroughly understand all the vocabulary, grammar, and so on. Skip anything that looks as if it's going to give you grief.
- **Second Pass**—Go back to the beginning of the same section and take a shot at those questions for which you knew some, but not all, of the vocabulary.
- **Third Pass**—Use Process of Elimination on each remaining question in that section to eliminate some answers. Then take a guess. If you can't eliminate anything, leave the question blank.

Taking a section of the test using the Three-Pass System keeps you from getting stuck on a tough question early in the section and spending too much time on it.

Note: The Three-Pass System does not work on the Listening section of the Spanish with Listening Subject Test. For that section, you listen to a CD and must answer the questions in the order in which they appear (you can, of course, choose to leave some blank).

POE—PROCESS OF ELIMINATION

Process of Elimination is one of the gifts of a multiple-choice exam. The idea is simple: There are three wrong answers and only one right one; therefore, if you can eliminate answers you know are wrong, you eventually stumble upon the right answer because it's the only one left. Approaching questions in this manner also ensures that you avoid the traps the test writers set for students. You'll learn how this applies to each question type later on. POE varies based on question type, but the general idea is always the same.

Summary

- You don't need to answer every question to get a good score. Use your target score as a guide for how many questions you should answer.
- Guessing is to your advantage when you can eliminate at least one incorrect choice.
- Process of Elimination (POE) is an extremely useful strategy on this exam. The idea behind it is to eliminate choices that you know are wrong so you can get to the right answer.

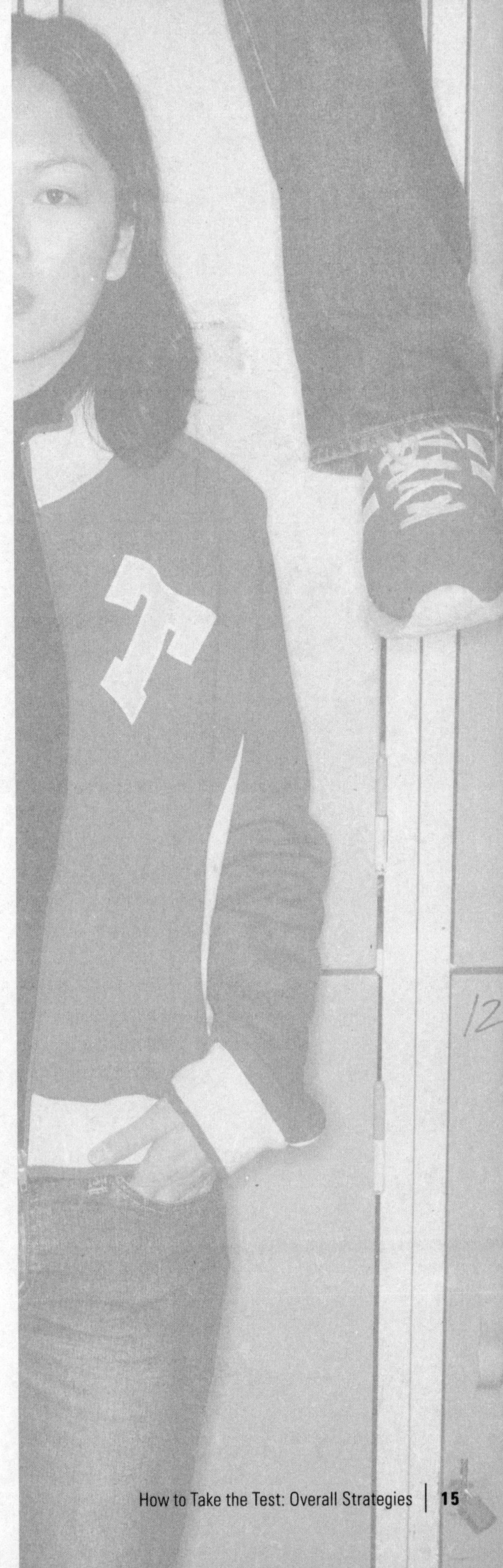

Part II Content Review and Strategies

Chapter 3
Sentence Completion: Vocabulary

Sentence completion questions on the SAT Spanish Subject Test are designed to evaluate your knowledge of both Spanish vocabulary and grammar. In this chapter, we focus on strategies for tackling this type of question and provide a comprehensive vocabulary review.

SENTENCE COMPLETION: AN OVERVIEW

The first section of the Spanish Subject Test and the first part of the reading section of the Spanish with Listening Subject Test consist of vocabulary and grammar questions tested in a format we call *sentence completion*. Each sentence is missing one or more words, and your job is to select the answer choice that best completes the sentence in terms of meaning. In other words, fill in the blank with the answer that makes the most sense. Like all the questions on the test, each of the questions in this section has four answer choices. Before you go any further, memorize the directions to this question type until you're so familiar with them, you never have to read them again.

> Part A
>
> **Directions:** This part consists of a number of incomplete statements, each having four suggested completions. Select the most appropriate completion and fill in the corresponding oval on the answer sheet.

HOW TO CRACK THIS SECTION

One of the keys to cracking sentence completion questions is to understand the vocabulary. If you know every word that appears in the section, understanding the sentences and choosing the right answers is a breeze. So, one of the things you're going to have to work on is improving your vocabulary. Later in this chapter you'll find lists of words that are most likely to appear on your test; if you think your vocabulary needs help, then start studying these lists *today*. We'll see more about vocabulary later. What else can be done to attack this question type?

To master this section, you need to combine your vocabulary and grammar reviews with some common sense. You've already read about pacing, POE, and the Three-Pass System. Now you're going to learn how these techniques, as well as some others, apply to this section in particular.

First Pass: When You Understand the Entire Sentence

It's pretty obvious that the easiest questions are the ones that don't contain unknown vocabulary words. You should do these questions first. Your approach should be to read the sentence and answer it if it's easy. If you're a little uncomfortable with some of the vocabulary, move on and come back to that question later, during your second pass.

Be careful. Just because a question is a "first-pass question" doesn't mean you should blow through it as fast as possible and risk making a careless error. Once you've decided to answer a question on the first pass, follow the steps listed on the next page.

Step 1: Think of Your Own Word The first step after reading the sentence is to fill in the blank with your own word without peeking at the answers. Your word doesn't have to be long or difficult; in fact, short and simple is best. Your word doesn't even have to be in Spanish. If it's easier for you to think in English, then write the word in English. The important thing is to choose a word that fits in terms of meaning. After you have a word, write it down next to your sentence (or in the actual blank, if there's room). Try it on the following example:

> Hoy hace mucho frío. Por eso voy a ponerme un…

What would make sense in this blank? Pretty much any article of clothing that would be appropriate in cold weather, such as a pair of gloves (**par de guantes**) or a sweater (**suéter**). You shouldn't feel that there's only one possible answer because there are usually several words that would make sense in the blank. Don't worry about picking the *right* word; just worry about picking a word that makes sense. Once you've done this, move on to the next step.

Tip:
Don't worry about picking the *right* word. Just pick a word that makes sense.

Step 2: Eliminate Answers That Are Out of the Ballpark Now you're going to look at the answers and cross out the ones that do not fall into the same category as your word. You're not looking for the right answer; you're looking to eliminate wrong answers.

Let's say you filled in the word **suéter** in the previous example. Which of the following answer choices would you eliminate?

(A) vestido
(B) abrigo
(C) zapato
(D) lápiz

Does a dress (**vestido**), shoe (**zapato**), or pencil (**lápiz**) have anything to do with cold or a sweater? No, and so the correct choice is (B). If you don't know all of the words in the answers, then eliminate the ones you can and guess from the remaining choices.

Step 3: Avoid Trap Answers Once you've filled in your own word, it's crucial that you don't just pick the first answer you see that reminds you of it. The people who write this test are very clever about creating answer choices that are tempting but incorrect. Knowing the types of traps they set will help you to avoid them. In this section, there are a couple of tricks that show up frequently.

- **Answers That Sound Alike** One way the test writers try to confuse you is by having all four answers sound alike, even though their meanings are different. You can easily avoid this trap by reading carefully and not using your ear. Remember that you're picking the best answer based on its meaning, not on how it sounds.

Try the following example:

> La mamá de Pedro no le dejó salir porque todavía no había . . . su cuarto.
>
> (A) llamado
> (B) limpiado
> (C) llevado
> (D) llenado

Why wouldn't a mom allow her son to go out? Probably because he hadn't cleaned his room. The word for clean is **limpiar** and, because we're in the pluperfect, **limpiado** is the correct form (if that doesn't make sense, don't fret—the grammar review is in the next chapter, and you don't need to be an expert on Spanish grammar to do well on this test). Notice how all the other answers sound very similar to **limpiado**. This is why it's important to take your time and concentrate on meaning.

- **Categories** Another of the test writers' favorite tricks is to give you four choices that all come from the same category, as in the following example:

> Ricardo quiere lavarse las manos, y por eso necesita . . .
>
> (A) un cepillo
> (B) una cuchilla
> (C) pasta de dientes
> (D) jabón

Each of the answer choices is something you'd find in a bathroom (**jabón** = soap, **cuchilla** = razor, **pasta de dientes** = toothpaste, **cepillo** = hairbrush). Although these words have very different meanings, seeing them all together like this may be confusing, especially if you're thinking in general terms (bathroom stuff) and not in terms of the specific word you chose for the blank. It's therefore very important that you fill in the blank with a specific word and not a general category.

Second Pass: When You Don't Understand the Entire Sentence

Let's say you've answered all of the easy questions. Now what? The strategy for first-pass questions works just fine when you have a clear understanding of the sentence, but unfortunately, there probably will be some words that you don't know. Will that keep you from answering these questions altogether? Absolutely not, but you *will* leave these questions for the second pass. The approach is different for these questions, but it works just as well as the approach for the first-pass questions. Not knowing some of the vocabulary is hardly a handicap if you are aggressive and use POE, so don't let these questions intimidate you.

One of These Things Is Not Like the Others One of the nice things about this question type (from your point of view) is that the answer choices are usually far apart in meaning. In other words, you *rarely* find two answers that are separated by subtle shades of meaning. Instead, you find four things that have nothing to do with one another, except perhaps a very general common category, similar to what you saw earlier in the "avoid trap answers" examples. Why is this so helpful? It allows you to eliminate answer choices even if you have only a minimal understanding of the sentence. If you can figure out the general context of the sentence by piecing together one or two words as clues, you can eliminate answers that are unlikely to appear in that context. You'll usually find that there's really only one word that makes any kind of sense in that context. Choose the answer that is *not* like the others.

Use POE
When you can eliminate one or more answer choices, guess.

Eduardo se monta en el automóvil y dice que . . .

(A) tiene hambre
(B) hace mucho calor
(C) el perro es grande
(D) necesita gasolina

What if the only word you understand in the above sentence is **automóvil**? Well, your next thought should be, "Which of the answers has a word that has something to do with a car?" Choice (A), which means "he's hungry," doesn't seem likely. Choice (B) talks about the weather, which isn't a car-related topic. Choice (C) probably wins the prize for most ridiculous: "the dog is big." So which answer is not like the others? Choice (D), which means "he needs gas." Notice that if you can make out some of the key words in either the sentence or the answers, you can eliminate some of the answer choices and get the correct answer.

It's important to understand that this technique will *not* always leave you with only one remaining answer, that is, the right one. Sometimes you will be able to eliminate just one or two choices and end up taking an educated guess. However, guessing one out of two is much better than guessing one out of four. Never eliminate an answer simply because you don't understand it. If you're not sure, leave it in and deal with the choices of which you are sure. Also, the technique allows you to get around some of the tough vocabulary, but you still need to know the meanings of some of the words to use the technique: If you don't know what the answers mean, you can't determine which one is not like the others. The moral of the story is *don't neglect your vocabulary work*!

Three-Pass System
Do all the easy questions first. Do the questions with moderately difficult vocabulary and grammar second. For the rest, use POE to get rid of at least one answer choice and guess, or skip them.

Third Pass: When You Hardly Understand Any Part of the Sentence

These questions should be left for last. Your goal on the third pass is to go back to each question that you skipped on the first two passes and see whether you can eliminate even one answer choice based on the word or words that you do know in the sentence, using the same approach that you used on the second pass. The only difference is you'll probably have less on which to base your decision. If you're unable to eliminate anything, no sweat—just move on to the next question.

You don't need to know the most difficult words in the sentence to knock off some of the answers. If you can determine only that the answer is going to be a feminine word based on its article (**la**), then that may be enough to help you get rid of one or two choices. So be aggressive!

VOCABULARY REVIEW

Why Work on Your Vocabulary?

In case you haven't already noticed, vocabulary is a very important part of this test. In fact, a sizeable portion of the exam is essentially a vocabulary test. You've already seen some ways to get around the tough vocabulary by using certain techniques, but that doesn't mean that you can blow off this section of the book. We know, we know—memorizing vocabulary words is about as much fun as watching grass grow. However, vocabulary work can translate into some easy points on the day of the test. If you know the words, the questions are that much easier. By not working on your vocabulary, you're blowing a golden opportunity to improve your score. We've narrowed down your work so that you have to deal only with the words that are most likely to appear on the test. Now it's up to you to memorize them.

How to Use These Lists

If you are taking the SAT Spanish Subject Test, you have probably taken at least two years of Spanish. The following vocabulary lists, like the rest of the review material in this book, are meant to be used in conjunction with your accumulated classroom material. If you feel fuzzy on a concept, by all means return to your textbooks. If there seems to be a concept or a word group that you have never really mastered, then you can set up your third pass or "skip" questions accordingly.

The vocabulary in these lists is arranged by thematic category to facilitate learning the words. At the very least, you should memorize all the words in this chapter, but you may also want to review other thematic presentations in your textbooks for any categories on which you need to brush up. One of the categories contains practical words and concepts (such as prepositional phrases and conjunctions) that you'd use if you were comfortable with Spanish. Words like these frequently appear in both the paragraph completion and reading comprehension portions of the test. At the end of the chapter we also provide a vocabulary list that contains words that the test writers might use to trap you, such as false cognates. Don't forget to add any words you don't know from the practice tests to your study list! See if you can place them into categories, as we do.

Thematic Vocabulary

Don't Forget to Use Your English Cognates

profundo	profound
participar	to participate
el automóvil	automobile
el circo	circus
el minuto	minute
el perfume	perfume
el/la dentista	dentist
la farmacia	pharmacy
la música	music
estupendo/a	stupendous
el crítico/la crítica	critic
criticar	to criticize
la ovación	ovation
el plato	plate
el programa de televisión	television program
el apetito	appetite
las vacaciones	vacation
el teatro	theater
la biología	biology
el empleado, la empleada	employee
el arte	art
el/la artista	artist
la controversia	controversy
la creación	creation
el hotel	hotel
la manifestación	manifestation
furioso/a	furious

A Cogna...WHAT?
Sounds like you may want to dance the Conga, right? Not quite! A cognate is simply a word that has the same original word or root from another language. This applies to various languages!

cordial	cordial, polite
la residencia	residence, home
practicar	to practice
la operación	operation
el estómago	stomach
falso	false, fake
decidir	to decide
el caso	case (as in "in this case," not "suitcase")
la clase	class (as in school, or society)
comparar	to compare
la justicia	justice
defender	to defend
la gloria	glory
misterioso/a	mysterious
la impresión	impression
plantar	to plant
servir	to serve
contemporáneo/a	contemporary
el verso	verse
el acto	act
la gracia	grace

Low-Tech Vocab Review

Make flash cards! Five minutes each day learning and reviewing words can make a huge difference.

Basic Words and Phrases You Should Know

por eso	that's why
la noticia	news
cada uno	each one
poner	to put
sentado/a	seated
dormido/a	asleep
llamar	to call
muy poco	very little
manejar, conducir	to drive
entrar (en)	to enter
¿Quién eres?	Who are you?
llevar	to take, to carry, to wear
tocar	to touch, to play (an instrument)
tocar a la puerta	to knock at the door
el correo	mail
el buzón	mailbox

sacar	to take out, to remove
dar la vuelta	to turn or flip over or around
la carrera	race (as in a marathon), career
el negocio	business
sin falta	without fail
terminar	to finish
la calidad	quality
la cantidad	quantity
la revista	magazine
mostrar	to show
el partido	party (as in political), game, match
el árbol	tree
devolver	to give back
el almacén	warehouse, store (as in department)
el desfile	parade, procession
advertir	to notice, observe, warn
el estilo	style
tener cuidado	to be careful
envolver	to wrap
ahorrar	to save (as in money, not a life)
algo	something
empezar	to begin
asco	disgust
falsamente	falsely
romper	to break
¿Con qué derecho?	How dare you? What gives you the right?
olvidar	to forget
sucio/a	dirty
grave	serious
a contrapelo	the wrong way

Vocabulary = Important
Make sure vocab review is a routine part of preparing for the exam. Not knowing the vocabulary is the surest way not to do as well as you could otherwise.

We Are Family

la madre	mother
el padre	father (also sometimes used for priest)
el hijo/la hija	son/daughter
el tío/la tía	uncle/aunt
el sobrino/la sobrina	nephew/niece
el primo/la prima	cousin

el nieto/la nieta	grandson/granddaughter
el niño/la niña	boy/girl (usually used for small children)
el muchacho/la muchacha	boy/girl (usually used for teenagers)
el abuelo/la abuela	grandfather/grandmother
el hermano/la hermana	brother/sister
el esposo/la esposa	husband/wife
el marido	husband
los gemelos	twins
el cuñado/la cuñada	brother-in-law/sister-in-law
el bisabuelo/la bisabuela	great-grandfather/great-grandmother
el padrastro	stepfather
la madrastra	stepmother
el suegro/la suegra	father-in-law/mother-in-law
el yerno	son-in-law
la nuera	daughter-in-law
la boda	wedding
el compromiso	engagement
casarse	to get married
el matrimonio, el casamiento	marriage
el divorcio	divorce

School Days

¡Despiértate!	Wake up!
¡Levántate!	Get up!
la escuela	school
a tiempo	on time
tarde	late
la tarde	afternoon
el trabajo	work
la tarea	homework
hacer la tarea	to do homework
leer	to read
el cuento	story
saber	to know
escribir	to write
la librería	bookstore
el libro	book
el número	number

tonto/a	boneheaded, silly
estudiar	to study
los estudiantes	students
prestar atención	to pay attention
el idioma	language
preguntar	to ask
la biblioteca	library

Feed Me

el apetito	appetite
tener hambre	to be hungry
comer	to eat
beber, tomar	to drink
la comida	food
el camarero/la camarera	waiter/waitress
la cuenta	the check, the bill
el arroz	rice
el pollo	chicken
gordo/a	fat
delgado/a	thin
el vaso	glass
el pescado	fish
la ensalada	salad
las legumbres	vegetables
las verduras	vegetables
el queso	cheese
el postre	dessert
la taza	cup
la cuchara	spoon
el cuchillo	knife
el tenedor	fork
el helado	ice cream
el olor	smell, odor, aroma
el sabor	flavor
el desayuno	breakfast
el almuerzo	lunch
la cena	dinner

The Neck Bone's Connected to the...

los dientes	teeth
las encías	gums
la muela	molar
el estómago	stomach
las manos	hands
la cintura	waist
la cabeza	head
las piernas	legs
los brazos	arms
los pies	feet
la espalda	back
el pelo/el cabello	hair
los ojos	eyes
la boca	mouth
la nariz	nose
el pecho	chest
el cuerpo	body
la rodilla	knee
la muñeca	wrist
la barba	beard
el dedo	finger
la garganta	throat
la nuca	nape of the neck
la mejilla	cheek
el hueso	bone
las caderas	hips
el cuello	neck
el codo	elbow
el cerebro	brain
el hombro	shoulder
el rostro	face
las uñas	nails
las cejas	eyebrows
los labios	lips
la lengua	tongue

Shopping Is My Life

comprar	to buy
ir de compras	to go shopping
la ropa	clothes
la camiseta, la playera	T-shirt
la cartera, la bolsa	purse
la zapatería	shoe store
la corbata	tie
el pañuelo	handkerchief
el calcetín	sock
el vestido	dress
el abrigo	coat
la billetera	wallet
el dinero	money
los zapatos	shoes
los pantalones	pants
la camisa	shirt
la blusa	blouse
la falda	skirt
las medias	pantyhose/stockings
los dólares	dollars
de lujo	expensive, luxurious
gastar dinero	to spend money

An Apple a Day

la úlcera	ulcer
diagnosticar	to diagnose
la operación	operation
la extracción	extraction
pálido/a	pale
la herida	injury, wound
enfermo/a	sick
sufrir	to suffer
el dolor	pain
el yeso, la escayola	arm or leg cast
urgencias	emergency room
el médico/la médica	doctor

el/la dentista	dentist
la salud	health
sano/sana	healthy
la receta	prescription
las muletas	crutches
la silla de ruedas	wheelchair
la aguja	needle
la vacuna	vaccine
la cicatriz	scar
la enfermedad	illness
la sangre	blood
las lesiones	cuts
las píldoras	pills
estornudar	sneeze
enfermarse	to get sick
mejorarse	to get better
respirar	to breathe

Mi Casa Es Su Casa

la casa	house
el piso	floor (a level of a building)
el suelo	floor (in a house), ground
la alfombra	rug, carpet
los muebles	furniture
la butaca	armchair, easy chair
salir (de)	to leave
volver	to return
el espejo	mirror
el jabón	soap
la silla	chair
el sillón	rocking chair, armchair
lavar	to wash
el fregadero	sink (kitchen)
el cesped, la grama	lawn
limpiar	to clean
el cuarto/la sala	room

la cocina	kitchen
el dormitorio	bedroom
el baño	bathroom
las llaves	keys

What's Your Job?

el abogado/la abogada	lawyer
el médico/la médica	doctor
el enfermero/la enfermera	nurse
el contador/la contadora	accountant
el/la comerciante	businessman/businesswoman
el banquero/la banquera	banker
el profesor/la profesora	professor
el maestro/la maestra	teacher
el/la periodista	journalist
el presentador/la presentadora	newscaster
el escritor/la escritora	writer
el ingeniero/la ingeniera	engineer
el científico/la científica	scientist
el psicólogo/la psicóloga	psychologist
el antropólogo/la antropóloga	anthropologist
el bombero/la bombera	firefighter
el vaquero/la vaquera	cowboy/cowgirl
el/la soldado	soldier
el/la marinero	sailor
el/la socorrista	lifeguard
el entrenador/la entrenadora	trainer
el pintor/la pintora	painter
el escultor/la escultora	sculptor
el sastre/la sastra	tailor
el cocinero/la cocinera	cook
el panadero/la panadera	baker
el peluquero/la peluquera	hairdresser
el vendedor/la vendedora	salesperson
el cajero/la cajera	cashier

Comparatively Speaking

antes	before
después	after
demasiado/a	too (as in too much, too late, too funny, and so on)
mayor	older
menor	younger
mejor	better
peor	worse
mediocre	mediocre
bien hecho	well done
(me) da igual	it doesn't matter (to me)

The Meaning of Life

la vida	life
cambiar	to change
con cariño	with affection
los chistes	jokes
reír	to laugh
regalar	to give as a gift
ganar	to win, to earn (money)
saber	to know (facts, how to do things)
la sabiduría	knowledge, wisdom
jugar	to play
aceptar	to accept
ofrecer	to offer
querer	to want, to love (te quiero = I love you)
amar	to love
tranquilo/a	peaceful, tranquil
reposar, descansar	to rest, relax
desear	to want
esperar	to wait
odiar	to loathe, hate
decir	to say
es decir	that is,…
tener	to have
buscar	to look for, search for
hacer	to do, to make

sentir(se)	to feel
¿Cómo te sientes?	How do you feel?
pésame, condolencias	with deepest sympathy
la pena	sorrow, trouble, pain
escoger	to choose
conocer	to know (people, places—indicates familiarity)
prestar	to lend
empeñarse	to pledge or devote oneself

Too Much Time on My Hands

la última vez	last time
el siglo	century
el centenario	centennial
despacio	slow, slowly
en cuanto	as soon as
inmediatamente	immediately
durante	during
empezar, comenzar	to begin
terminar, acabar	to finish
hace un rato	a little while ago
próximo/a	next
el próximo día	the next day
media hora	half hour
una/la hora	hour, time
¿Qué hora es?	What time is it?
de la noche	P.M. (after sunset)
de la tarde	P.M. (afternoon)
de la mañana	A.M.
apurarse	to hurry oneself
en marcha	on the move, on the go
ahora mismo	right now
la fecha	date (as in calendar)
hoy	today
mañana	tomorrow
la mañana	morning
la madrugada	early morning
ayer	yesterday

cada vez	each/every time
el año	year
en seguida	right away
de buena gana	gladly ("I'd be happy to")
a eso de	around (a eso de las ocho = around 8:00)

Places to Go, People to See

ir	to go
la esquina	street corner
la playa	the beach
la obra de teatro	the play
la taquilla	box office
cerca de	near
la calle	street
el viaje	trip
aquí	here
allí	there
el mapa	map
dondequiera	wherever
la ciudad	city
el país	country
la película	movie
el banco	bank, bench
el camino	path, route
el señor	gentleman
la señora	lady
la mujer	woman
el hombre	man
el torero	bullfighter
el cartero/la cartera	mail carrier

How's the Weather?

hacer frío	to be cold out
hacer calor	to be hot out
caliente	hot
caluroso/a	warm, hot
llover/la lluvia	to rain/rain
mojado/a	wet

oscuro/a	dark
nevar/la nieve	to snow/snow
el sol	the sun
el viento	the wind

Music Soothes the Savage Beast

la música	music
la orquesta	orchestra
tocar	to play (an instrument), to touch
cantar	to sing
practicar	to practice

Beggars and Choosers

nada más	no more, nothing more
¡De ninguna forma!	No way!
nadie	no one
¡Ya lo creo!	Absolutely! For sure!
ningún/ninguna	none, neither
tener culpa	to be at fault, guilty
sin querer	unintentionally, against your will
el mendigo/la mendiga	beggar
pedir limosna	to beg
quemar	to burn
rechazar	to push away, repel, reject
quejarse	to complain
distraído/a	absentminded
poner fin a	to put an end to
de mala gana	reluctantly
de mal humor	in a bad mood
inconveniente	unsuitable, inappropriate, inconvenient

Life's a Bowl of Cherries

perfumado/a	scented, sweet-smelling
cómodo/a	comfortable
lleno/a	full
por favor	please
el premio	prize
premio gordo	grand prize

¡Cómo no!	Of course! I'd be glad to!
empeñarse	to pledge or vow
¡Felicitaciones!	Congratulations!
cortés	courteous
cordial	cordial
estar de acuerdo	to be in agreement
Que Dios lo bendiga.	May God bless you.
el regalo	gift
el regalo de cumpleaños	birthday gift
bastante	enough
gracioso/a	cute, funny

Planes, Trains, and Automobiles

el avión	airplane
el tren	train
el carro, el coche	car
el crucero	cruise
el equipaje	luggage
la maleta	suitcase
el pasaporte	passport
la tarjeta de embarque	boarding pass
el portón	gate
la aduana	customs
la seguridad	security
el pasajero	passenger
el piloto	pilot
el agente de viajes	travel agent
la azafata	flight attendant (feminine)
el aeromozo/la aeromoza	flight attendant
el asiento	seat
el cinturón de seguridad	seatbelt
la cabina	cabin
el pasillo	aisle
el boleto, el billete	ticket
de ida solamente	one way
de ida y vuelta	round trip
el vuelo	flight
la tarifa	fare
hacer las maletas	to pack the suitcases

embarcar	to board
despegar	to take off
aterrizar	to land
arrancar	to start
la carretera	highway
el parabrisas	windshield
la llanta	tire
el volante	steering wheel

Reflexive Verbs

ponerse	to put on, to become (with verbs of emotion)
hacerse	to make oneself, to become (with nouns: **Me hice abogado.** I became a lawyer.)
acostarse	to go to bed
involucrarse	to involve oneself with
lavarse	to wash oneself
peinarse	to comb one's hair
vestirse	to get dressed
sentarse	to sit down
divertirse	to have fun
quitarse	to take off
bañarse	to bathe oneself
ducharse	to shower

Other Prepositions, Conjunctions, Adverbs, and Phrases to Remember

hacia	toward
enfrente de	in front of
frente a	in front of
dentro de	inside of
fuera de	outside of
a la derecha de	to the right of
a la izquierda de	to the left of
debajo de	underneath
encima de	above, on top of
alrededor de	around, surrounding
en medio de	in the middle of

hasta	until
tras	behind, after
cerca de	close to, near
lejos de	far from
detrás de	behind
delante de	in front of
al lado de	next to
sin	without
contra	against
junto a	next to
respecto a	in regard to
a pesar de	in spite of
en vez de	instead of
en cuanto a	as to, as regards
mientras que	while, meanwhile
aunque	although
sin embargo	nevertheless
a menos que	unless
de antemano	beforehand
ni siquiera	not even
apenas	barely
a no ser que	unless
siempre que	as long as
por más que	no matter how (much)
también	also
de repente	suddenly
en seguida	immediately
por desgracia	unfortunately
al azar	by chance
de todos modos	in any case
tarde o temprano	sooner or later
de nuevo	again
despacio	slowly
acaso	perhaps
tampoco	neither, either
mientras tanto	meanwhile
de una vez	once and for all
en fin	in short

por supuesto	of course
por lo menos	at least

Practical and Useful Nouns

el rincón	corner
el sacapuntas	pencil sharpener
el incendio	fire (as natural disaster)
el seguro	insurance
la herencia	inheritance
la inversión	investment
el salvavidas	lifejacket
el socorrista	lifeguard
la acera	sidewalk
los impuestos	taxes
el guión	script
la red	line, Web, network
el recado	message (as in "leave a…")
el despacho, la oficina	person's office
el escritorio	desk
el equipaje	luggage
la huelga	worker's strike
la superficie	surface
el silbido	whistle
la moda	fashion
el marco	frame
las joyas	jewelry
la mochila	backpack
la factura, la cuenta	bill (for services rendered)
la fecha	date
el estreno	debut
la empresa	company
el esfuerzo	effort
el/la periodista	journalist
el ordenador (in Spain)	computer
la computadora (in Latin America)	computer
la impresora	printer
el orgullo	pride
la misericordia	mercy
la temporada	season

el descubrimiento	discovery
el peso	weight
la pantalla	screen
los recursos	resources
la propina	tip
la contraseña	password

Verbs: Actions to Take

recuperarse	to recover
respirar	to breathe
dirigir	to direct
encabezar	to lead, head
superar	to overcome
lanzar	to launch
ampliar	to broaden, expand
repasar	to review
encargarse	to take charge of
imprimir	to print
fortalecer	to strengthen
resplandecer	to shine
sostener	to sustain
dar a luz (a)	to give birth (to)
negociar	negotiate
caer en cuenta, dar(se) cuenta	to realize
tener en cuenta	to take into account
hallar	to find
reciclar	to recycle
tranquilizarse	to calm (oneself) down
amueblar	to furnish (a room)
enjuagar	to rinse
rescatar	to rescue
traducir	to translate
viajar	to travel
agradar	to please
madrugar	to get up early
despegar	to take off (said of an airplane)
llevar a cabo	to finish
atreverse	to dare
acertar	to guess correctly

Traps

Different Genders, Different Meanings

el editorial	editorial
la editorial	publishing house
el mañana	the future
la mañana	morning
el orden	order
la orden	religious order
el coma (en estado de)	coma
la coma	comma
el corte	cut
la corte	court
el frente	front (as in a war)
la frente	forehead
el guía	guide
la guía	phonebook
el policía	police officer (masculine)
la policía	police force; police officer (feminine)
el capital	capital (as in money)
la capital	capital (of a country)

Feminine Nouns with Masculine Articles

el hambre	hunger
el habla	speech
el ancla	anchor
el aula	classroom
el hacha	ax
el arma	weapon

el alma	soul
el águila	eagle
el alba	dawn
el agua	water

False Cognates and Other Pitfalls

actualmente	at the present moment
sensible	sensitive
embarazada	pregnant
el éxito	success
insólito	uncanny
aterrizar	to land (said of an airplane)
el vidrio	glass (window, bottle)
grabar	to record
el desenlace	climax, denouement, finale
el frenesí	frenzy
el collar	necklace
los parientes	kin
el ámbito	field of activity, environment
cazar	to hunt
la informática	computer science
la tormenta, la tempestad	storm
estornudar	to sneeze
la tos	cough
rendirse	to surrender

Drill 1: Process of Elimination

In the following drill, each sentence is missing all but a few key words. Eliminate answers that aren't related to the words in the sentence. If you're left with more than one answer, guess the one that fits best with the words in the sentence. Answers and explanations can be found in Part III.

1. Cristina *blah blah blah* limpia *blah blah* . . .

   (A) libro
   (B) casa
   (C) huesos
   (D) lluvia

2. *Blah blah blah* revistas *blah blah blah* . . .

   (A) vacaciones
   (B) obras de teatro
   (C) conciertos
   (D) artículos interesantes

3. No *blah* salir porque *blah* mucha . . .

   (A) comida
   (B) dinero
   (C) nieve
   (D) hambre

4. *Blah* postre me *blah blah* que . . .

   (A) el agua
   (B) las vitaminas
   (C) el helado
   (D) arroz con pollo

5. La película *blah blah blah* miedo porque *blah blah* . . .

   (A) violenta
   (B) graciosa
   (C) corta
   (D) tremenda

6. La niña *blah blah* llora por que *blah blah* . . .

   (A) feliz
   (B) silla
   (C) sueño
   (D) corriendo

Drill 2: Sentence Completion

Answers and explanations can be found in Part III.

1. La camisa de mi novia es hecha de ------- .

   (A) rosas
   (B) algodón
   (C) madera
   (D) azul

2. Buscaba las medicinas para mi abuelo en la ------- de la esquina.

   (A) librería
   (B) farmacia
   (C) oficina
   (D) panadería

3. Estaba ------- porque mis empleados llegaron tarde por cuarta vez en la misma semana.

   (A) furioso
   (B) encantado
   (C) contentísimo
   (D) abierto

4. Una buena manera de mejorar las notas en la escuela es ------ mucho.

   (A) enseñar
   (B) entender
   (C) hablar
   (D) practicar

5. Es un hombre sumamente vanidoso; siempre se está mirando en el ------- .

   (A) espejo
   (B) cristal
   (C) gafas
   (D) mismo

6. Los viejos tienen más ------- que los jóvenes, porque han tenido más experiencias.

   (A) tiempo
   (B) que comer
   (C) sabiduría
   (D) apetito

7. Es bastante evidente que a Alejandro le gusta hacer sus tareas; siempre las hace ------- .

   (A) de mala gana
   (B) con entusiasmo
   (C) muy despacio
   (D) sin gusto

8. Pedro ------- muy contento cuando nació su hijo.

   (A) se cambió
   (B) se dio
   (C) se hizo
   (D) se puso

9. Quiero que ------- apuntes sobre la lectura.

   (A) tomas
   (B) tomes
   (C) tomabas
   (D) tomaste

Summary

- First Pass: When You Understand the Entire Sentence
    - Fill in your own word (short and simple, but specific).
    - Eliminate answers that are not in the same category as your word.
    - Beware of the little traps: Concentrate on meaning, not sound.
    - Out of the remaining choices, pick the answer that's closest to your word.
- Second Pass: When You Don't Understand the Entire Sentence
    - Determine the meanings of as many individual words as you can.
    - Put these words together to try to determine the general context of the sentence.
    - Eliminate any choices that don't make sense in that context.
    - Pick the choice out of the remaining choices that is most likely to appear in that context (it should be the only one left).
- Third Pass: When You Hardly Understand Any Part of the Sentence
    - Try to locate sentences in which you know at least one or two words.
    - See if any of the answers seem impossible based on those words.
    - Eliminate those answers and guess.
- Never...
    - eliminate an answer choice because you don't know its meaning—just because you don't know it doesn't mean it's wrong! Use POE on choices that have words you *do* know.
    - leave a question blank if you can eliminate even one answer—the odds are in your favor if you can eliminate one or more of the choices, so guess!

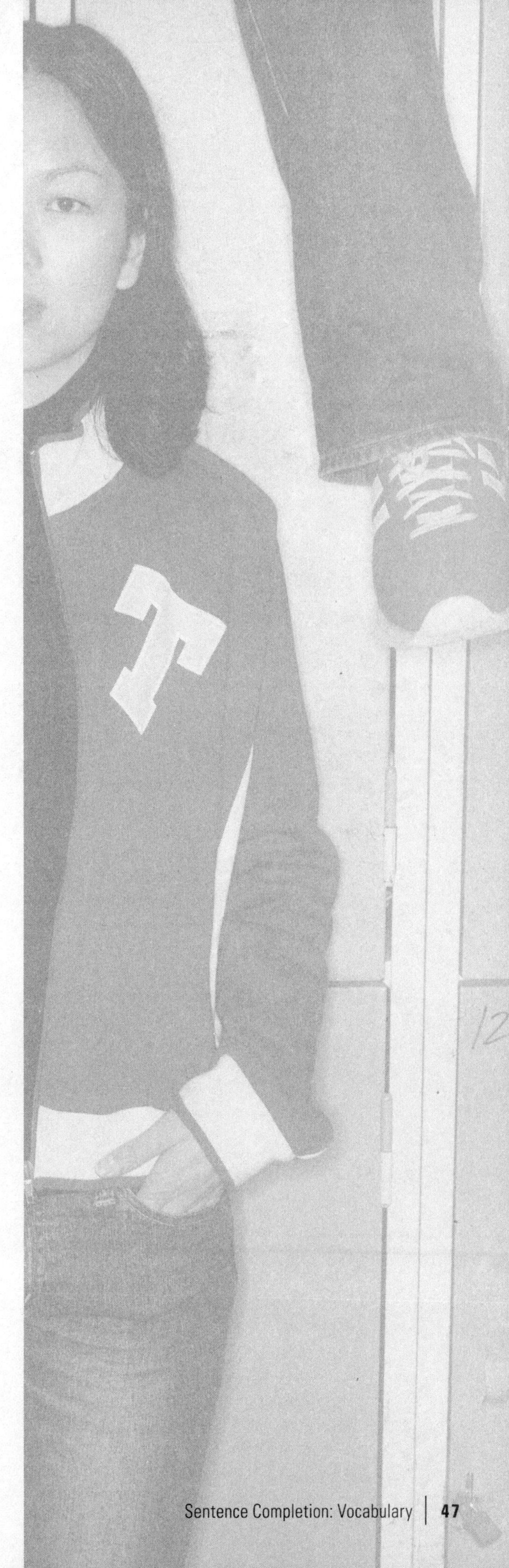

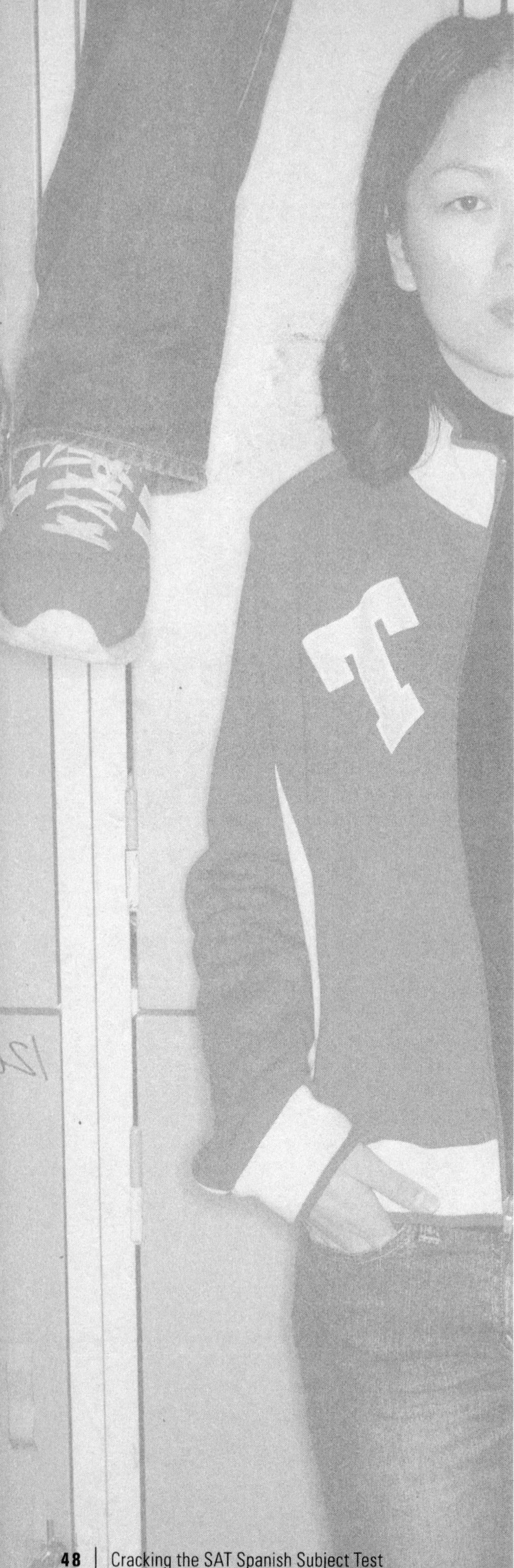

- Vocabulary is an essential component of the Spanish Subject Tests, which is why you should make a concerted effort to learn new words.
- The vocabulary lists in this chapter make up some of the most frequently tested words on the exam. Test yourself on all the words by covering the translations and see how many words you know; eventually, you will learn them all.

Chapter 4 Sentence Completion: Grammar

Grammar is another very important part of the SAT Spanish Subject Test. In this chapter, we review the most important grammar rules you should know for the exam and give you sample questions to test your knowledge of these rules. We cover basic terms, pronouns, essential verb forms, prepositions, and more.

GRAMMAR QUESTIONS: AN OVERVIEW

Memorize All Directions
Reading the directions when you take the test is a waste of precious time. Know them beforehand.

Now we're going to take a look at the grammar portion of the sentence completion questions that you'll find in Part A of the Spanish Subject Test and the first part of the reading section of the Spanish with Listening Subject Test. The good news is that you don't need to review everything you've ever learned about grammar, because only a small portion of Spanish grammar is actually tested, and our review will focus on that portion. The even better news is that the techniques you've learned in this book work very well on this section, and by combining them with a brief review of grammar, you will increase your chances of doing well on the exam. Before you get into strategies or review, memorize the instructions for this question type.

> Part A
>
> **Directions:** This part consists of a number of incomplete statements, each having four suggested completions. Select the most appropriate completion and fill in the corresponding oval on the answer sheet.

Each question will be followed by four answer choices. These differ from the vocabulary sentence completion questions because the answer choices will all have the same or very similar meanings, but only one of them will fit the blank and make the sentence grammatically correct. It's not about vocabulary; it's about verbs, pronouns, prepositions, and idioms, but don't let that scare you! After you get through this chapter, you'll know everything you need to know to master this section.

HOW TO CRACK THIS SECTION

The key to succeeding on this section is to focus specifically on the grammatical concepts that are being tested, and to spend a little time relearning them. Contrary to what the test writers would like you to believe, this section doesn't test everything you learned in Spanish class, but instead sticks to a few grammatical ideas and tests them over and over again. You probably already know and are comfortable with many of them, and even if you're not right now, you will be once you invest a little time studying.

In addition to reviewing the grammar, you will use Process of Elimination and the Three-Pass System to beat this section. You'll supplement both of these with what may be your best friend on these questions: your ear. Remember how your ear could easily steer you wrong on vocabulary sentence completions because of the way the wrong answers sometimes sounded like the right ones? Well, on this section, your ear, or the way the answers sound, can actually help you to eliminate answers right off the bat without having to worry about grammar at all. This won't work on all questions, but it certainly will on some, and you're going to take full advantage of it.

Applying the Three-Pass System

First Pass: I'm Sure I've Seen This Somewhere Before

Again, the questions are not arranged in any particular order of difficulty, but the level of difficulty of the different questions varies tremendously. Your goal on the first pass is to locate the questions that test the verb tenses, pronouns, prepositions, and idioms that you know like the back of your hand. Find the easiest questions, and do them first. How do you tell whether a question is easy? Read it, and if the structure looks familiar, go for it. If it looks as if it's going to take a little POE to crack it, leave that question for the second pass.

Tip:
Remember—you don't have to do the questions in the order in which they're presented. Do the easiest first—no matter where they are in the lineup.

Second Pass: Haven't I Seen This Somewhere Before?

If you read a question and the answer doesn't immediately jump off the page at you, don't be discouraged: Just because you don't immediately know what the answer *is* doesn't mean you can't tell what the answer *isn't.* Work backward from the answer choices and eliminate answers you know are wrong. If you understand some of the answer choices and know they're wrong, it's just as effective as knowing which ones are right.

Third Pass: I've Never Seen This Anywhere

If the grammar in both the sentence and answers is a complete mystery to you, chances are you won't be able to find the right answer using POE. Eliminate any of the choices that you can and then guess. The most important thing about the third pass (on any section) is that you don't spend too much time on these really tough questions.

GRAMMAR REVIEW

Although we won't lie and tell you that reviewing grammar rules will be fun, we can promise you that spending a little time on this material will mean easy points for you on the day of the test. Grammar is merely a bunch of rules, and once you've learned those that are tested, you'll be ready for this question type.

Basic Terms

While you won't be tested on these definitions, the following terms are important because they will come up later in the chapter. Knowing them allows you to understand the rules of grammar that you're about to review.

Grammar Refresher
While you don't need to know specific grammar terms or rules for the Spanish Subject Test, having a basic grasp of grammar can be helpful. If you have the time and want to brush up on your grammar skills, pick up a copy *Grammar Smart.*

Noun:	a person, place, or thing EXAMPLES: Abraham Lincoln, New Jersey, taco
Pronoun:	a word that replaces a noun EXAMPLES: Abe Lincoln would be replaced by "he," New Jersey by "it," and taco by "it." You'll learn more about pronouns later.
Adjective:	a word that describes a noun EXAMPLES: cold, soft, colorful
Verb:	an action word; the main action being done in a sentence EXAMPLE: Ron *ate* the huge breakfast.
Infinitive:	the original, unconjugated form of a verb EXAMPLES: to eat, to run, to laugh
Auxiliary Verb:	the verb that precedes the past participle in the perfect tenses EXAMPLE: He *had* eaten his lunch.
Past Participle:	the appropriate form of a verb when it is used with the auxiliary verb EXAMPLE: They have *gone* to work.
Adverb:	an adverb describes a verb, adjective, or another adverb, just like an adjective describes a noun EXAMPLES: slowly, quickly, happily (Adverbs often, but don't always, end in *-ly*.)
Subject:	the thing (noun) in a sentence that is performing the action EXAMPLE: *John* wrote the song.

Compound: a subject that's made up of two or more subjects or nouns
EXAMPLE: *John and Paul* wrote the song together.

Object: the thing (noun or pronoun) in the sentence to which the action is happening, either directly or indirectly
EXAMPLES: Mary bought *the shirt.* Joe hit *him.* Mary gave a gift to *Tim.*

Direct Object: the thing that receives the action of the verb
EXAMPLE: I see *the wall.* (The wall "receives" the action of seeing.)

Indirect Object: the person who receives the direct object
EXAMPLE: I wrote the letter to *her.* (She receives the letter.)

Preposition: a word that marks the relationship (in space or time) between two other words
EXAMPLES: He received the letter *from* her. The book is *below* the chair.

Article: a word (usually a very small word) that precedes a noun
EXAMPLES: *a* watch, *the* room

That wasn't so bad, was it? Now let's put all those terms together in a couple of examples.

Dominic	spent	the	entire	night	here.
subject	verb	article	adjective	dir. obj.	adverb

Margaret	often	gives	me	money.
subject	adverb	verb	indir. obj.	dir. obj.

Alison and Rob	have	a	gorgeous	child.
compound subject	verb	article	adjective	dir. obj.

Once you've spent a little time with these terms, review the grammar on which you'll actually be tested.

PRONOUNS

You already learned that a pronoun is a word that takes the place of a noun. Now you'll review what pronouns look like in Spanish, and learn how they are tested on the Spanish Subject Test.

If you can tell the difference between subject, direct object, and indirect object pronouns, you are in very good shape. Beyond those different types, there are a few odds and ends that may show up. Still, the majority of questions that test pronouns focus on these three basic types.

Subject Pronouns

These are the most basic pronouns, and probably the first ones you learned. Just take a moment to look them over to make sure you haven't forgotten them. Then spend some time looking over the examples that follow until you are comfortable using them.

yo	I	**nosotros/nosotras**	we (mas./fem.)
tú/usted (Ud.)	you (familiar/ formal)	**vosotros/vosotras/ ustedes (Uds.)**	you (pl.) (mas./fem.)
ella/él	she/he	**ellas/ellos**	they

Note that "vosotros" is a form mainly used in Spain and almost never appears on the Spanish Subject Test.

When to Use Subject Pronouns

A subject pronoun (like any other pronoun) replaces the noun that is the subject of the sentence.

Subject Pronouns
Subject pronouns aren't always necessary in Spanish sentences, because the form of the verb gives us a clue as to the subject's identity. They are used, however, for emphasis or clarification.

> *Marco no pudo comprar el helado.*
> Marco couldn't buy the ice cream.

Who does the action of this sentence? Marco, so he is the subject. If we wanted to use a subject pronoun in this case, we'd replace "Marco" with "**él**."

> ***Él** no pudo comprar el helado.*
> **He** couldn't buy the ice cream.

Direct Object Pronouns

A direct object pronoun replaces (you guessed it) the direct object in a sentence.

me	me	nos	us
te	you (*tú* form)	**os**	you (*vosotros* form)
lo/la	him, it (mas.)/her, it (fem.)/ you (*Ud.* form)	**los/las**	them (mas./fem.)/ you (*Uds.* form)

When to Use Direct Object Pronouns

Now let's see what it looks like when we replace the direct object in a sentence with a pronoun.

Marco no pudo comprar el helado.

What couldn't Marco buy? Ice cream. Because ice cream is what's receiving the action, it's the direct object. To use the direct object pronoun, you'd replace "**helado**" with "**lo.**"

*Marco no pudo comprar**lo**.* *or* *Marco no **lo** pudo comprar.*

When the direct object pronoun is used with the infinitive of a verb, it can either be tacked on to the end of the verb (the first example) or it can come before the conjugated verb in the sentence (the second example). Another example:

*Voy a ver**lo**.* I'm going to see **it.**

***Lo** voy a ver.* (Both sentences mean the same thing.)

The direct object pronoun also follows the verb in an affirmative command, for example:

*¡Cóme**lo**!* Eat **it!**

*¡Escúcha**me**!* Listen to **me!**

Finding the Direct Object

I throw the *ball.*
What do I throw?
Ellen knew the *answer.*
What did she know?
We will see the *bus.*
What will we see?
What received the action of the verb?
The answer is always the direct object.

Indirect Object Pronouns

An indirect object pronoun replaces the indirect object in a sentence. The indirect object is easy to spot in English because a preposition often comes before it. However, *this is not the case in Spanish.* In Spanish, when the object is indirect, the preposition is often implied, not explicitly stated. So how can you tell the difference? In general, the indirect object is the person who receives the direct object.

me	me	nos	us
te	you (*tú* form)	os	you (*vosotros* form)
le	him/her/you (*Ud.* form)	les	them/you (*Uds.* form)

When to Use Indirect Object Pronouns

This might seem a little strange, but in Spanish the indirect object pronoun is often present in a sentence that contains the indirect object noun.

*Juan **le** da el abrigo al viejo.*

Juan gives the coat to the old man. *or* Juan gives the old man the coat.

Notice that the sentence contains the indirect object noun (**viejo**) and the indirect object pronoun (**le**). This is often necessary to provide clarification of the identity of the indirect object pronoun or to emphasize that identity. Typically, an expression of clarification is needed with the pronouns "**le**" and "**les**" and "**se**" (see below) but is not obligatory with other pronouns.

*María **nos** ayudó.*	María helped **us.**
*Juan **me** trae el suéter.*	Juan brings **me** the sweater.

Indirect Object
I will write a letter to *her.* Who will get the letter? We tell *him* the truth. Who hears the truth? He suggested changes to *me.* Who got the changes? Essentially, who gets the noun? The answer is always the indirect object.

The identity of the indirect object is obvious with the choice of pronoun in these examples, so clarification is not necessary. An expression may be used, however, to emphasize the identity of the indirect object:

*No **me** lo trajeron a mí; **te** lo trajeron a ti.*
They didn't bring it to **me**; they brought it to **you.**

We would change our intonation to emphasize these words in English. This doesn't happen in Spanish; the expressions "**a mí**" and "**a ti**" serve the same function.

"Se" is used in place of "**le**" and "**les**" whenever the pronoun that follows begins with "**l**."

*¿**Le** estás contando la noticia a María?*	Are you telling Maria the news?
*Sí, **se** la estoy contando a María.*	Yes, I'm telling it to **her.**
*¿**Les** prestas los guantes a los estudiantes?*	Do you lend gloves to the students?
*No, no **se** los presto a ellos.*	No, I don't lend them to **them.**

Notice that "**le**" changes to "**se**" in the first example and "**les**" to "**se**" in the second because the direct object pronouns that follow begin with "**l**." Notice also the inclusion of "**a María**" and "**a ellos**" to clarify the identity of "**se**" in each example.

Prepositional Pronouns

As we mentioned earlier, there are some pronouns that take explicitly stated prepositions, and they're different from indirect object pronouns. The prepositional pronouns are as follows:

mí	me	nosotros/nosotras	us
ti/Ud.	you (fam./formal)	vosotros/vosotras/Uds.	you (plural)
él/ella	him/her	ellos/ellas	them

When to Use Prepositional Pronouns

Consider the following examples:

1. *Cómprale un regalo de cumpleaños.* — Buy **him** a birthday present.
2. *Vamos al teatro sin él.* — We're going to the theater without **him**.

Notice that in the first example, "him" is translated as "**le**," whereas in the second, "him" is translated as "**él**." What exactly is the deal with that?! Why isn't it the same word in Spanish as it is in English? In Spanish, the different pronouns distinguish the different functions of the word within the sentence.

In the first example, "him" is the indirect object of the verb "to buy" (buy the gift for whom? For him—"him" receives the direct object), so we use the indirect object pronoun "**le**." In the second example, however, "him" is the object of the preposition "without," so we use the prepositional pronoun "**él**." Here are some more examples that involve prepositional pronouns. Notice that they all have explicitly stated prepositions.

*Las flores son **para** ti.* — The flowers are **for** you.

*Estamos enojados **con** él.* — We are angry **with** him.

*Quieren ir de vacaciones **sin** Uds.* — They want to go on vacation **without** you.

In two special cases, when the preposition is **con** and the object of the preposition is **mí** or **ti**, the preposition and the pronoun are combined to form "**conmigo**" (with me) and "**contigo**" (with you).

*¿Quieres ir al concierto **conmigo**?* — Do you want to go to the concert **with me**?

*No, no puedo ir **contigo**.* — No, I can't go **with you**.

When the subject is **él, ella, ellos, ellas, Ud.**, or **Uds.**, and the object of the preposition is the **same** as the subject, the prepositional pronoun is **sí** and is usually accompanied by **mismo/a** or **mismos/as.**

Alejandro es muy egoísta. Siempre habla de ***sí mismo****.*

Alejandro is very egotistical. He always talks about **himself.**

Ellos compran ropa para ***sí mismos*** *cuando van de compras.*

They buy clothes for **themselves** when they go shopping.

POSSESSIVE ADJECTIVES AND PRONOUNS

Possessive adjectives and pronouns are used to indicate ownership. When you want to let someone know what's yours, use the following pronouns or adjectives:

Stressed Possessive Adjectives

mío/mía	mine	**nuestro/nuestra**	ours
tuyo/tuya	yours (*tú* form)	**vuestro/vuestra**	yours (*vosotros* form)
suyo/suya	his/hers/yours (*Ud.* form)	**suyo/suya**	theirs/yours (*Uds.* form)

Unstressed Possessive Adjectives

mi	my	**nuestro/nuestra**	our
tu	your (*tú* form)	**vuestro/vuestra**	yours (*vosotros* form)
su	his/hers/your (*Ud.* form)	**su**	their/your (*Uds.* form)

When to Use Possessive Adjectives

The first question is, "When do you use an unstressed adjective, and when do you use a stressed adjective?" Check out these examples, and then we'll see what the rule is:

Esta es ***mi*** *casa.*
This is **my** house.

Esta casa es ***mía****.*
This house is **mine.**

Aquí está ***tu*** *billetera.*
Here is **your** wallet.

Esta billetera es ***tuya****.*
This wallet is **yours.**

The difference between stressed and unstressed possessive adjectives is emphasis as opposed to meaning. Saying "This is my house" puts emphasis on the house, while saying "This house is mine" takes the focus off the house and stresses the identity of its owner—me. To avoid getting confused, just remember that unstressed is the Spanish equivalent of "my" and stressed is the Spanish equivalent of "mine."

In terms of structure, there is an important difference between the two types of adjectives, but it's easy to remember: A stressed adjective comes after the verb, but an unstressed adjective comes before the noun. Notice that neither type agrees with the possessor; they agree with the possessed thing.

If it's not clear to you why these are adjectives when they look so much like pronouns, consider their function. When you say "my house," the noun "house" is being described by "my." Any word that describes a noun is an adjective, even if that word looks a lot like a pronoun. The key is how it's being used in the sentence.

Possessive Pronouns

These look like stressed possessive adjectives, but they mean something different. Possessive pronouns *replace* nouns; they don't *describe* them.

When to Use Possessive Pronouns

This type of pronoun is formed by combining the article of the noun that's being replaced with the appropriate stressed possessive adjective. Just like stressed possessive adjectives, possessive pronouns must agree in gender and number with the nouns they replace.

***Mi** bicicleta es azul.* **My** bicycle is blue.	***La mía** es azul.* **Mine** is blue.

Notice how the pronoun not only shows possession but also replaces the noun. Here are some more examples.

***Mis** zapatos son caros.* **My** shoes are expensive.	***Los míos** son caros.* **Mine** are expensive.
***Tu** automóvil es rápido.* **Your** car is fast.	***El tuyo** es rápido.* **Yours** is fast.
*No me gustaron los discos **que ellos trajeron**.* I didn't like the records **they brought**.	*No me gustaron **los suyos**.* I didn't like **theirs**.

Reflexives
Many reflexive verbs can be used non-reflexively. Ask yourself—is the person doing the action the one who is receiving it? If so, the verb is reflexive. If not, the verb is normal (or transitive).

Reflexive Pronouns

Remember those reflexive verbs you saw in the vocabulary review (like **ponerse** and **hacerse**)? Those all have a common characteristic: They indicate that the action is being done to or for oneself. When one of those verbs is conjugated, the reflexive pronoun (which is always **se** in the infinitive) changes according to the subject.

me	myself	**nos**	ourselves
te	your (*tú* form)	**os**	yours (*vosotros* form)
se	himself/herself/yourself (*Ud.* form)	**se**	themselves/yourselves (*Uds.* form)

A reflexive pronoun is used when the subject and indirect object of the sentence are the same. This may sound kind of strange, but after you see some examples it should make more sense.

Alicia se pone el maquillaje.
Alicia puts on makeup.

What does she put on? **Makeup**—direct object.
Who "receives" the makeup? **Alicia**—she's also the subject.

The action is thus *reflected* back on itself: Alicia does the action and then receives it. No outside influences are involved.

Another meaning for reflexive verbs is literally that the person does something directly to or for him/herself.

*Rosa **se cortó** con el cuchillo.*
Rosa **cut herself** with the knife.

*Roberto tiene que **comprarse** una libreta nueva.*
Roberto has to **buy himself** a new notebook.

The Pronoun *Que*
Keep in mind that what follows *que* is generally an expression that further describes the noun just before it.

The Pronoun *Que*

The pronoun **que** can mean *who, that,* or *which,* depending on the context of the sentence. In other words, it can take the place of a person or a thing. Fortunately, it isn't too tough to tell which meaning is correct.

*¿Cómo se llama la maestra **que** tuvimos ayer?*
What's the name of the teacher **whom** we had yesterday?

*Ese es el equipo **que** más me gusta.*
That's the team **that** I like the most.

¿Cuál es la revista ***que*** *compraste ayer?*
Which is the magazine **that** you bought yesterday?

In the first example, **que** means "whom," because you are talking about a person. In the other examples, **que** refers to things, so it means "that" or "which."

When to Use *Que*

Although in English we sometimes leave out the pronouns *who*, *that*, and *which* (for example, "the food [that] I ate"), in Spanish you have to use *que*. **Que** always follows the noun (as in the previous examples) because it begins a clause that further describes the noun.

When referring to people, **quien** (or **quienes**) replaces **que** if the pronoun follows a preposition.

El maestro sin quien yo no pudiera haber aprendido español está aquí hoy.
The teacher without **whom** I couldn't have learned Spanish is here today.

Los tipos con quienes juego a la pelota son jugadores magníficos.
The guys with **whom** I play ball are magnificent players.

The Pronoun *Cuál*

Cuál (meaning *which* or *what*) is used when a choice is involved. It's used in place of **que** before the verb **ser**, and it has only two forms: singular (**cuál**) and plural (**cuáles**). Both **cuál** and the verb **ser** must agree in number with the thing(s) being asked about.

¿Cuál es tu ciudad favorita? — **What** is your favorite city?
¿Cuáles son nuestros regalos? — **Which** presents are ours?

Demonstrative Pronouns and Adjectives

First, learn the construction and meaning.

este/esta	this (one)	**estos/estas**	these
ese/esa	that (one)	**esos/esas**	those
aquel/aquella	that (one over there)	**aquellos/aquellas**	those (over there)

Demonstrative Adjectives
This and *these* in Spanish have Ts (este/esta and estos/estas).

Adjective or Pronoun—Which Is It?

If the demonstrative word *comes before* a noun, then it is an adjective.

Este plato de arroz con pollo es mío.	**This** plate of chicken with rice is mine.
Ese *edificio es de mi hermano.*	**That** building is my brother's.

If the demonstrative word *takes the place of* a noun, then it's a pronoun.

Dije que ***este*** *es mío.*	I said that **this one** is mine.
Sabemos que ***ese*** *es de mi hermano.*	We know **that one** is my brother's.

When used as adjectives, these words mean *this, that,* and so on. When used as pronouns, they mean *this one, that one,* and so on. Don't worry about the use of **ese** versus **aquel**. No question on this exam will ask you to pick between the two.

TIPS FOR PRONOUN QUESTIONS

Helpful Hints
When it comes to pronouns, understanding how and when to use them is key. We also encourage you to use POE and the Three-Pass System. And remember: pace yourself!

- The types of pronouns that you need to know are subject, object (direct and indirect), possessive, prepositional (which you'll see again later), reflexive, demonstrative, and a couple of odds and ends like **que** and **cuál**. We're not guaranteeing that only these types will appear, but, if you know these inside and out, you should feel confident that you'll be able to tackle most (if not all) of the pronoun questions.
- Don't just memorize what the different pronouns look like! Recognizing them is important, but it's just as important that you understand how and when to use them.
- Don't forget about POE. The test writers may try to trip you up on simple things (like the gender of a pronoun) that are easy to overlook if you're not on your toes. Before you start thinking about grammar on a pronoun question, eliminate answers that are wrong based on flagrant stuff like gender, singular versus plural, and so on.
- If all else fails, your ear can sometimes be your guide. In learning Spanish, you probably spoke and heard the language on a pretty regular basis, and so you have a clue as to what correct Spanish sounds like. You don't want to use your ear if you can eliminate answers based on the rules of grammar, but if you've exhausted the rules and you're down to two answers, one of which sounds much better than the other, guess the nice-sounding one. The fact is that many grammatical rules were born out of a desire to make the language sound good.
- Last (but not least), don't forget to pace yourself wisely and use the Three-Pass System. Look for questions that test the pronouns with which you're most comfortable, and skip the tough ones. If you're stumped by a question, leave it for the third pass, eliminate what you can, and guess, but never spend too much time on a question that tests something you don't really know.

VERBS

You probably learned what felt like a zillion different verbs and tenses in Spanish class. For the purposes of this section, you only need to know a few of the tenses you learned. What's even better is that you don't need to know how to conjugate verbs in the different tenses, nor do you need to know the names for the different tenses. You do need to know how to recognize them, however. For example, you don't need to know how or why the conditional is used; all that you need to know is what it looks like when a verb is in the conditional, and when the conditional should be used.

You should focus on recognizing clues in the sentences that suggest certain tenses, and then finding answers in the appropriate tenses. Remember, even if you don't know which answer is in the tense that corresponds with the sentence, you can still eliminate answers that definitely aren't in that tense. Use POE! A brief review of the tenses that show up in the test is probably a good place to begin, so let's get right to it.

The Present Tense (or the Present Indicative)

The present tense is the easiest, and probably the first tense you ever learned. It is used when the action is happening in the present, as in the following:

> *Yo **hablo** con mis amigos todos los días.*
> I **speak** with my friends every day.

Because the present is the most basic, and probably the easiest tense, it rarely shows up as the right answer to a question. So why go over it? Because it sometimes does show up as a right answer, and it often shows up as a wrong answer. You need to know how to recognize it to eliminate it if it's incorrect. Take a quick glance at the present tense of the following verbs just to refresh your memory.

	trabajar	**vender**	**escribir**
yo	trabajo	vendo	escribo
tú (fam.)	trabajas	vendes	escribes
él/ella/Ud.	trabaja	vende	escribe
nosotros/nosotras	trabajamos	vendemos	escribimos
vosotros/vosotras (fam.)	trabajáis	vendéis	escribís
ellos/ellas/Uds.	trabajan	venden	escriben

Remember
Usted (Ud.) and *Ustedes (Uds.)* may have the same verb forms as *él/ella* and *ellos/ellas*, but they mean the same things as *tú* and *vosotros*, respectively.

Stem-Changing Verbs

Not all verbs are created equal. When you conjugate some verbs, the endings change in the first, second, and third person. These verbs fall into three main categories: verbs that change **-e** to **-ie**, **-o** to **-ue**, and **-e** to **-i**.

	cerrar (e : ie)	volver (o : ue)	pedir (e : i)
yo	cierro	vuelvo	pido
tú (fam.)	cierras	vuelves	pides
él/ella/Ud.	cierra	vuelve	pide
nosotros/nosotras	cerramos	volvemos	pedimos
vosotros/vosotras (fam.)	cerrais	volveis	pedis
ellos/ellas/Uds.	cierran	vuelven	piden

Other verbs that follow this pattern include:

(e : ie)	(o : ue)	(e : i)
comenzar	almorzar	conseguir
empezar	costar	decir
entender	dormir	repetir
perder	poder	seguir
preferir	recordar	servir
querer	volar	

The Past Tense (AKA the Preterite)

The past tense is used to describe an action that had a *definite beginning and ending in the past* (as opposed to an action that may be ongoing), as in the following example:

> *Ayer yo **hablé** con mis amigos.*
> Yesterday I **spoke** with my friends. (The action began and ended.)

There are a bunch of different tenses that are past tenses that describe actions that took place at various points in the past. There are different tenses for saying "I spoke," "I was speaking," "I have spoken," and so on. Let's start by reviewing the most basic of these, the plain past tense.

	trabajar	vender	escribir
yo	trabajé	vendí	escribí
tú (fam.)	trabajaste	vendiste	escribiste
él/ella/Ud.	trabajó	vendió	escribió
nosotros/nosotras	trabajamos	vendimos	escribimos
vosotros/vosotras (fam.)	trabajasteis	vendisteis	escribisteis
ellos/ellas/Uds.	trabajaron	vendieron	escribieron

The easiest forms to spot are the first- and third-person singular (**yo** and **él/ella** forms) because of the accents.

The Imperfect

The imperfect is another past tense, used to describe actions that occurred continuously in the past and exhibited no definitive end at that time. This is different from the preterite, which describes one-time actions that began and ended at the moment in the past that is being described. Look at the two together, and the difference between them will become clear.

*Ayer **hablé** con mis amigos y entonces me fui.*
Yesterday **I spoke** with my friends and then left.
(The act of speaking obviously ended, because I left afterward.)

***Yo hablaba** con mis amigos mientras caminábamos.*
I spoke with my friends while we walked.
(The act of speaking was **in progress** at that moment, along with walking.)

The imperfect is also used to describe conditions or circumstances in the past that are obviously ongoing occurrences.

Era una noche oscura y tormentosa.
It was a dark and stormy night.

*Cuando **tenía** diez años…*
When **I was** ten years old…

In the first example, it didn't just start or just stop being a stormy night, did it? Was the dark and stormy night already a past event at that point? No. The dark and stormy night was **in progress** at that moment, so the imperfect is used, not the preterite.

Preterite vs. Imperfect
Think of the preterite as a self-contained unit of time (*She finished her homework*). The imperfect, in contrast, refers to something in the past that doesn't have a clear beginning or end (*She was doing her homework when the doorbell rang*).

In the second example, did I start or stop being ten years old at that point? Neither. Was being ten already a past event at the moment I am describing? No. I was simply in the process of being ten years old at that moment in the past, so the imperfect is the more precise tense to use.

Make sense? Good; now check out the formation:

Remember:
Context clues that denote a use of the imperfect tense include ***siempre, normalmente, cada año, usualmente, todos los años, de niño/a,*** and so on. Look for clues that indicate a habitual action.

	trabajar	**vender**	**escribir**
yo	trabaj**aba**	vend**ía**	escrib**ía**
tú (fam.)	trabaj**abas**	vend**ías**	escrib**ías**
él/ella/Ud.	trabaj**aba**	vend**ía**	escrib**ía**
nosotros/nosotras	trabaj**ábamos**	vend**íamos**	escrib**íamos**
vosotros/vosotras (fam.)	trabaj**abais**	vend**íais**	escrib**íais**
ellos/ellas/Uds.	trabaj**aban**	vend**ían**	escrib**ían**

Although the imperfect tense is similar to the other past tenses you've seen (such as the preterite and the present perfect) because it speaks of past actions, it looks quite different. That's the key, because half of your job is just to know what the different tenses look like. The toughest part will be distinguishing the preterite from the imperfect.

The Future Tense

The future tense is used to describe things that will *definitely* happen in the future. The reason we stress "definitely" is because there is a different verbal mode (the subjunctive) used to describe things that *may* happen in the future. In Spanish, just as in English, there is a difference between being certain ("I will go") and being uncertain ("I might go"), and different forms are used for the different degrees of certainty. You'll see the fancier stuff later. First take a look at the regular future tense.

> *Mañana yo **hablaré** con mis amigos.*
> Tomorrow I **will speak** with my friends.

Notice that what takes two words to say in English (**will speak**) takes only one word to say in Spanish (**hablaré**). The future is a nice, simple tense (no auxiliary verb, only one word) that is easy to spot thanks to the accents and the structure. The future is formed by tacking on the appropriate ending to the infinitive of the verb *without dropping the -ar, -er, or -ir.*

	trabajar	vender	escribir
yo	trabajaré	venderé	escribiré
tú (fam.)	trabajarás	venderás	escribirás
él/ella/Ud.	trabajará	venderá	escribirá
nosotros/nosotras	trabajar**emos**	vender**emos**	escribir**emos**
vosotros/vosotras (fam.)	trabajaréis	venderéis	escribiréis
ellos/ellas/Uds.	trabajarán	venderán	escribirán

Back to the Future: The Conditional

Remember, when you want to describe actions that are *definitely* going to happen in the future, use the future tense. When you want to describe actions that *might* happen in the future, use the conditional tense.

The conditional describes what could, would, or might happen in the future.

> *Me* ***gustaría*** *hablar con mis amigos todos los días.*
> I **would like** to talk to my friends every day.
>
> *Si tuviera más tiempo,* ***podría*** *hablar con ellos el día entero.*
> If I had more time, I **could** speak with them all day long.
>
> *Si gastara cinco pesos, solamente me* ***quedarían*** *tres.*
> If I spent (were to spend) five dollars, I **would have** only three left.

It can also be used to make a request in a more polite way.

> *¿Puedes prestar atención?*
> **Can you** pay attention?
>
> *¿Podrías prestar atención?*
> **Could you** pay attention?

The conditional is formed by taking the future stem of the verb (which is the infinitive) and adding the conditional ending.

	trabajar	vender	escribir
yo	trabajaría	vendería	escribiría
tú (fam.)	trabajarías	venderías	escribirías
él/ella/Ud.	trabajaría	vendería	escribiría
nosotros/nosotras	trabajar**íamos**	vender**íamos**	escribir**íamos**
vosotros/vosotras (fam.)	trabajaríais	venderíais	escribiríais
ellos/ellas/Uds.	trabajarían	venderían	escribirían

To avoid confusing the conditional with the future, concentrate on the conditional endings. The big difference is the accented **í**, which is in the conditional, but not in the future.

Future	Conditional
trabajaré	trabajaría
venderán	venderían
escribiremos	escribiríamos

The Present Perfect

This is where it gets a little weird: If something happens in the very recent past, we can also use the present perfect to show its proximity to the present. We hardly ever do this in American English.

The Present Perfect

The present perfect is used to refer to an action that began in the past and is continuing into the present (and possibly beyond). It is also used to describe actions that were completed very close to the present. Compare these sentences.

1. *Ayer **hablé** con mis amigos.*
   Yesterday **I spoke** with my friends.

   ***Decidiste** no ir al cine.*
   You decided not to go to the movies.

2. ***He hablado** mucho con mis amigos recientemente.*
   I have spoken a lot with my friends lately.

   ***Has decidido** hacerte abogado.*
   You have decided (recently) to become a lawyer.

The first examples are in the plain past tense: You started and finished talking with your friends yesterday, and you completed the process of deciding not to go to the movies. In the second examples, the use of the present perfect tense moves the action to the very recent past, instead of leaving it in the more distant past. The present perfect, then, is essentially a more precise verb form of the past, used when the speaker wants to indicate that an action happened very recently in the past.

Spotting the perfect tenses is rather easy. This is a compound tense, meaning that it is formed by combining two verbs: a tense of the auxiliary (or helping) verb **haber** (present, imperfect, future, conditional) and the past participle of the main verb.

	trabajar	vender	escribir
yo	**he** trabajado	**he** vendido	**he** escrito
tú (fam.)	**has** trabajado	**has** vendido	**has** escrito
él/ella/Ud.	**ha** trabajado	**ha** vendido	**ha** escrito
nosotros/nosotras	**hemos** trabajado	**hemos** vendido	**hemos** escrito
vosotros/vosotras (fam.)	**habéis** trabajado	**habéis** vendido	**habéis** escrito
ellos/ellas/Uds.	**han** trabajado	**han** vendido	**han** escrito

Most past participles are formed by dropping the last two letters from the infinitive and adding **-ido** (for **-er** and **-ir** verbs) or **-ado** (for **-ar** verbs). **Escribir** has an irregular past participle, as do some other verbs, but don't worry about it. This is no problem because the irregulars still look and sound like the regulars, and with respect to this tense, you still know it's the present perfect because of **haber.**

The Subjunctive

Don't give up now! Just two more verb modes (not tenses—the subjunctive is a different *manner* of speaking) and you'll be done with all this verb business (give or take a couple of special topics).

The Present Subjunctive

The present subjunctive is used in sentences that have *two distinct subjects* in *two different clauses,* generally (on this test, at least) in four situations.

1. When a *desire* or *wish* is involved

   Quiero que ***comas*** *los vegetales.*
   I want you **to eat** the vegetables.

   Deseamos que Uds. nos ***sigan.***
   We want you (pl.) **to follow** us.

2. When *emotion* is involved

   Me alegro que ***haga*** *buen tiempo hoy.*
   I am happy that the weather **is** nice today.

   Te enoja que tu novio nunca te ***escuche.***
   It makes you angry that your boyfriend never **listens** to you.

3. When *doubt* is involved

   Ellos no creen que ***digamos*** *la verdad.*
   They don't believe that **we are telling** the truth.

   Jorge duda que su equipo ***vaya*** *a ganar el campeonato.*
   Jorge doubts that his team **is going** to win the championship.

A Quick Note

If the subject is expressing a personal desire, then the infinitive is used. For example, "Quiero **ser** médico." *I want to be a doctor.*

Impersonal Expressions
Here are some of the most common impersonal expressions: *conviene, es importante, es mejor, es necesario, es posible, puede ser.*

4. When an *impersonal, subjective commentary* is made

   Es ridículo que yo no ***pueda*** *encontrar mis llaves.*
   It's ridiculous that I **can't** find my keys.

   Es importante que los estudiantes ***estudien*** *mucho.*
   It's important that students **study** a lot.

The subjunctive is formed by taking the **yo** form of the present tense, dropping the **-o**, and adding the appropriate ending.

	trabajar	vender	escribir
yo	trabaj**e**	vend**a**	escrib**a**
tú (fam.)	trabaj**es**	vend**as**	escrib**as**
él/ella/Ud.	trabaj**e**	vend**a**	escrib**a**
nosotros/nosotras	trabaj**emos**	vend**amos**	escrib**amos**
vosotros/vosotras (fam.)	trabaj**éis**	vend**áis**	escrib**áis**
ellos/ellas/Uds.	trabaj**en**	vend**an**	escrib**an**

The present subjunctive is easy to spot because certain key phrases tell you that a wish or desire, emotion, doubt, or an impersonal commentary is being made.

Commands

Commands also use the present subjunctive form because they are an obvious attempt to tell someone what to do. The one exception is the **tú** form of affirmative commands, which uses the same ending as the present indicative of **él/ella/Ud.** Let's look at the differences.

Ud.	tú
¡Trabaje con su hijo! Work with your son!	*¡Trabaja con tu padre!* Work with your father!
¡Escriba la carta! Write the letter!	*¡Escribe la carta!* Write the letter!
¡No trabaje con su hijo! Don't work with your son!	*¡No trabajes con tu padre!* Don't work with your dad!
¡No escriba la carta! Don't write the letter!	*¡No escribas la carta!* Don't write the letter!

The Imperfect Subjunctive

Here we are, at the final verb form you'll need to know for the Spanish Subject Test! This version of the subjunctive is used with the same expressions as the present subjunctive (wish or desire, emotion, doubt, impersonal commentaries), but it's used in the *past tense.*

Quería que ***comieras*** *los vegetales.*
I wanted you **to eat** the vegetables.

Me alegré que ***hiciera*** *buen tiempo ayer.*
I was happy that the weather **was** nice yesterday.

No creían que ***dijéramos*** *la verdad.*
They didn't believe that **we told** the truth.

Era ridículo que yo ***no pudiera*** *encontrar mis llaves.*
It was ridiculous that **I couldn't** find my keys.

One very important thing to notice in the previous examples is that because the *expression* is in the past, you use the imperfect subjunctive. If you're looking at a sentence that you know takes the subjunctive, but you're not sure whether it's present or imperfect, focus on the expression. If the expression is in the present, use the present subjunctive. If the expression is in the past, use the imperfect subjunctive.

The imperfect subjunctive is also always used after the expression **como si**, which means "as if." This expression is used to describe hypothetical situations:

El habla como si lo supiera todo.
He speaks as if **he knew** it all.

Gastamos dinero como si ***fuéramos*** *millonarios.*
We spend money as if **we were** millionaires.

The imperfect subjunctive is formed by taking the **ellos/ellas/Uds.** form of the preterite (which you already know, right?) and adding the correct ending.

	trabajar	vender	escribir
yo	trabajara	vendiera	escribiera
tú (fam.)	trabajaras	vendieras	escribieras
él/ella/Uds.	trabajara	vendiera	escribiera
nosotros/nosotras	trabajáramos	vendiéramos	escribiéramos
vosotros/vosotras (fam.)	trabajarais	vendierais	escribierais
ellos/ellas/Uds.	trabajaran	vendieran	escribieran

The Imperfect Subjunctive
This follows the same rules as the present subjunctive, but it is in the past tense. Look for time clues and clues for the subjunctive.

Verbs that are in the imperfect subjunctive shouldn't be too tough to spot when they show up in the answer choices. The imperfect subjunctive has completely different endings than the preterite. It's not a compound tense, so you won't confuse it with the present perfect. The stems are different from the present subjunctive, so distinguishing between those two shouldn't be a problem.

Special Topics

Irregular Verbs

Good news: you've made it through the major verb conjugations. Not-so-good-news: there are exceptions. Some verbs don't follow a set pattern, and, well, you just have to be able to recognize them. Here are some of the most common ones, in all their irregular glory. Please note that the six columns are for the verb conjugations in the **yo, tú, él/ella/Ud., nosotros/nosotras, vosotros/vosotras,** and **ellos/ellas/Uds.** forms, respectively.

dar (to give)						
present:	doy	das	da	damos	dais	dan
preterite:	di	diste	dio	dimos	disteis	dieron
imperfect:	daba	dabas	daba	dábamos	dabais	daban
future:	daré	darás	dará	daremos	daréis	darán
conditional:	daría	darías	daría	daríamos	daríais	darían
present subjunctive:	dé	des	dé	demos	deis	den
imperfect subjunctive:	diera	dieras	diera	diéramos	dierais	dieran

decir (to say, to tell)						
present:	digo	dices	dice	decimos	decís	dicen
preterite:	dije	dijiste	dijo	dijimos	dijisteis	dijeron
imperfect:	decía	decías	decía	decíamos	decíais	decían
future:	diré	dirás	dirá	diremos	diréis	dirán
conditional:	diría	dirías	diría	diríamos	diríais	dirían
present subjunctive:	diga	digas	diga	digamos	digáis	digan
imperfect subjunctive:	dijera	dijeras	dijera	dijéramos	dijerais	dijeran

estar (to be)						
present:	estoy	estás	está	estamos	estáis	están
preterite:	estuve	estuviste	estuvo	estuvimos	estuvisteis	estuvieron
imperfect:	estaba	estabas	estaba	estábamos	estabais	estaban
future:	estaré	estarás	estará	estaremos	estaréis	estarán
conditional:	estaría	estarías	estaría	estaríamos	estaríais	estarían
present subjunctive:	esté	estés	esté	estemos	estéis	estén
imperfect subjunctive:	estuviera	estuvieras	estuviera	estuviéramos	estuvierais	estuvieran

haber (to have)						
present:	he	has	ha	hemos	habéis	han
preterite:	hube	hubiste	hubo	hubimos	hubisteis	hubieron
imperfect:	había	habías	había	habíamos	habíais	habían
future:	habré	habrás	habrá	habremos	habréis	habrán
conditional:	habría	habrías	habría	habríamos	habríais	habrían
present subjunctive:	haya	hayas	haya	hayamos	hayáis	hayan
imperfect subjunctive:	hubiera	hubieras	hubiera	hubiéramos	hubierais	hubieran

hacer (to make, to do)						
present:	hago	haces	hace	hacemos	hacéis	hacen
preterite:	hice	hiciste	hizo	hicimos	hicisteis	hicieron
imperfect:	hacía	hacías	hacía	hacíamos	hacíais	hacían
future:	haré	harás	hará	haremos	haréis	harán
conditional:	haría	harías	haría	haríamos	haríais	harían
present subjunctive:	haga	hagas	haga	hagamos	hagáis	hagan
imperfect subjunctive:	hiciera	hicieras	hiciera	hiciéramos	hicierais	hicieran

ir (to go)						
present:	voy	vas	va	vamos	vais	van
preterite:	fui	fuiste	fue	fuimos	fuisteis	fueron
imperfect:	iba	ibas	iba	íbamos	ibais	iban
future:	iré	irás	irá	iremos	iréis	irán
conditional:	iría	irías	iría	iríamos	iríais	irían
present subjunctive:	vaya	vayas	vaya	vayamos	vayáis	vayan

poder (to be able)						
present:	puedo	puedes	puede	podemos	podéis	pueden
preterite:	pude	pudiste	pudo	pudimos	pudisteis	pudieron
imperfect:	podía	podías	podía	podíamos	podíais	podían
future:	podré	podrás	podrá	podremos	podréis	podrán
conditional:	podría	podrías	podría	podríamos	podríais	podrían
present subjunctive:	pueda	puedas	pueda	podamos	podáis	puedan
imperfect subjunctive:	pudiera	pudieras	pudiera	pudiéramos	pudierais	pudieran

poner (to put, to place)						
present:	pongo	pones	pone	ponemos	ponéis	ponen
preterite:	puse	pusiste	puso	pusimos	pusisteis	pusieron
imperfect:	ponía	ponías	ponía	poníamos	poníais	ponían
future:	pondré	pondrás	pondrá	pondremos	pondréis	pondrán
present subjunctive:	ponga	pongas	ponga	pongamos	pongáis	pongan
imperfect subjunctive:	pusiera	pusieras	pusiera	pusiéramos	pusierais	pusieran

querer (to want, to wish, to love)						
present:	quiero	quieres	quiere	queremos	queréis	quieren
preterite:	quise	quisiste	quiso	quisimos	quisisteis	quisieron
imperfect:	quería	querías	quería	queríamos	queríais	querían
future:	querré	querrás	querrá	querremos	querréis	querrán
conditional:	querría	querrías	querría	querríamos	querríais	querrían
present subjunctive:	quiera	quieras	quiera	queramos	queráis	quieran
imperfect subjunctive:	quisiera	quisieras	quisiera	quisiéramos	quisierais	quisieran

saber (to know)						
present:	sé	sabes	sabe	sabemos	sabéis	saben
preterite:	supe	supiste	supo	supimos	supisteis	supieron
imperfect:	sabía	sabías	sabía	sabíamos	sabíais	sabían
future:	sabré	sabrás	sabrá	sabremos	sabréis	sabrán
conditional:	sabría	sabrías	sabría	sabríamos	sabríais	sabrían
present subjunctive:	sepa	sepas	sepa	sepamos	sepáis	sepan
imperfect subjunctive:	supiera	supieras	supiera	supiéramos	supierais	supieran

salir (to leave)						
present:	salgo	sales	sale	salimos	salís	salen
preterite:	salí	saliste	salió	salimos	salisteis	salieron
imperfect:	salía	salías	salía	salíamos	salíais	salían
future:	saldré	saldrás	saldrá	saldremos	saldréis	saldrán
conditional:	saldría	saldrías	saldría	saldríamos	saldríais	saldrían
present subjunctive:	salga	salgas	salga	salgamos	salgáis	salgan
imperfect subjunctive:	saliera	salieras	saliera	saliéramos	salierais	salieran

ser (to be)						
present:	soy	eres	es	somos	sois	son
preterite:	fui	fuiste	fue	fuimos	fuisteis	fueron
imperfect:	era	eras	era	éramos	erais	eran
future:	seré	serás	será	seremos	seréis	serán
conditional:	sería	serías	sería	seríamos	seríais	serían
present subjunctive:	sea	seas	sea	seamos	seáis	sean
imperfect subjunctive:	fuera	fueras	fuera	fuéramos	fuerais	fueran

tener (to have)						
present:	tengo	tienes	tiene	tenemos	tenéis	tienen
preterite:	tuve	tuviste	tuvo	tuvimos	tuvisteis	tuvieron
imperfect:	tenía	tenías	tenía	teníamos	teníais	tenían
future:	tendré	tendrás	tendrá	tendremos	tendréis	tendrán
conditional:	tendría	tendrías	tendría	tendríamos	tendríais	tendrían
present subjunctive:	tenga	tengas	tenga	tengamos	tengáis	tengan
imperfect subjunctive:	tuviera	tuvieras	tuviera	tuviéramos	tuvierais	tuvieran

ver (to see)						
present:	veo	ves	ve	vemos	veis	ven
preterite:	vi	viste	vio	vimos	visteis	vieron
imperfect:	veía	veías	veía	veíamos	veíais	veían
future:	veré	verás	verá	veremos	veréis	verán
conditional:	vería	verías	vería	veríamos	veríais	verían
present subjunctive:	vea	veas	vea	veamos	veáis	vean
imperfect subjunctive:	viera	vieras	viera	viéramos	vierais	vieran

venir (to come)						
present:	vengo	vienes	viene	venimos	venís	vienen
preterite:	vine	viniste	vino	vinimos	vinisteis	vinieron
imperfect:	venía	venías	venía	veníamos	veníais	venían
future:	vendré	vendrás	vendrá	vendremos	vendréis	vendrán
conditional:	vendría	vendrías	vendría	vendríamos	vendríais	vendrían
present subjunctive:	venga	vengas	venga	vengamos	vengáis	vengan
imperfect subjunctive:	viniera	vinieras	viniera	viniéramos	vinierais	vinieran

Ser vs. *Estar*

The verbs **ser** and **estar** both mean *to be* when translated into English. You might wonder, "Why is it necessary to have two verbs that mean exactly the same thing?" Good question. The answer is that in Spanish, unlike in English, there is a distinction between temporary states of being (for example, "I am hungry") and fixed, or permanent states of being (for example, "I am Cuban"). Although this difference seems pretty simple and easy to follow, there are some cases when it isn't so clear. Consider the following examples:

> *El señor González ________ mi doctor.*
> *Cynthia ________ mi novia.*

Would you use **ser** or **estar** in these two sentences? After all, Cynthia may or may not be your girlfriend forever, and the same goes for Mr. González's status as your doctor. You might get rid of both of them tomorrow (or one of them might get rid of you). So which verb do you use?

In both cases, the answer is **ser** because in both cases there is no *foreseeable* end to the relationships described. In other words, even though they may change, nothing in either sentence gives any reason to think they will. So whether you and Cynthia go on to marry or she dumps you tomorrow, you would be correct if you used **ser**. When in doubt, ask yourself, "Does this action/condition have a definite end in the near or immediate future?" If so, use **estar**. Otherwise, use **ser**.

***Ser* vs. *Estar* (A Hint)**
If it's a permanent state, go with *ser*. If it's temporary go with *estar*.

Ser vs. *Estar* Drill

Fill in the blanks with the correct form of **ser** or **estar**. Answers and explanations can be found in Part III.

1. Pablo ________ muy cansado.
2. El automóvil ________ descompuesto.
3. No puedo salir de casa esta noche porque ________ castigado.
4. Mi hermano ________ muy gracioso.
5. Mis profesores ________ demasiado serios.
6. Ayer salí sin abrigo, por eso hoy ________ enfermo.
7. Los tacos que mi madre cocina ________ ricos.
8. ¡No podemos empezar! Todavía no ________ listos.
9. ________ muy enojado con el tipo que me insultó.

Don't assume that certain adjectives (like **enfermo**, for example) necessarily take **estar**. If you're saying someone is sick as in "ill," then **estar** is appropriate. If you're saying that someone is sick, as in, "a sickly person," then **ser** is correct.

Unfortunately, usage is not the only tough thing about these two verbs. They are both irregular, and they come up all over this exam. Spend a little time reviewing the conjugations of **ser** and **estar** before you move on.

estar	
present:	estoy, estás, está, estamos, estáis, están
preterite:	estuve, estuviste, estuvo, estuvimos, estuvisteis, estuvieron
present subjunctive:	esté, estés, esté, estemos, estéis, estén
imperfect subjunctive:	estuviera, estuvieras, estuviera, estuviéramos, estuvierais, estuvieran

The other tenses of **estar** follow the regular patterns for **-ar** verbs.

ser	
present:	soy, eres, es, somos, sois, son
imperfect:	era, eras, era, éramos, erais, eran
preterite:	fui, fuiste, fue, fuimos, fuisteis, fueron
present subjunctive:	sea, seas, sea, seamos, seáis, sean
imperfect subjunctive:	fuera, fueras, fuera, fuéramos, fuerais, fueran

The other tenses of **ser** follow the regular patterns for **-er** verbs.

Conocer vs. *Saber*

We hate to do this to you again, but there is another pair of verbs that have the same English translation but are used differently in Spanish. However, don't worry; these two have (for the most part) regular conjugations, and knowing when to use them is really very straightforward.

The words **conocer** and **saber** both mean "to know." In Spanish, knowing a person or a thing (basically, a noun) is different from knowing a piece of information. Compare the uses of **conocer** and **saber** in these sentences.

> *¿Sabes cuánto cuesta la camisa?*
> **Do you know** how much the shirt costs?
>
> *¿Conoces a mi primo?*
> **Do you know** my cousin?
>
> *Sabemos que Pelé era un gran futbolista.*
> **We know** that Pelé was a great soccer player.
>
> *Conocemos a Pelé.*
> **We know** Pelé.

When what's known is a person, place, or thing, use **conocer**. It's like the English, "acquainted with." When what's known is a fact, use **saber.** The same basic rule holds for questions.

> ***¿Saben** a qué hora llega el presidente?*
> **Do you know** at what time the president arrives?

> ***¿Conocen** al presidente?*
> **Do you know** the president?

Now that you know how they're used, take a look at their conjugations.

conocer	
present:	conozco, conoces, conoce, conocemos, conocéis, conocen
present subjunctive:	conozca, conozcas, conozca, conozcamos, conozcáis, conozcan

The other tenses of **conocer** follow the regular **-er** pattern.

saber	
present:	sé, sabes, sabe, sabemos, sabéis, saben
preterite:	supe, supiste, supo, supimos, supisteis, supieron
future:	sabré, sabrás, sabrá, sabremos, sabréis, sabrán
conditional:	sabría, sabrías, sabría, sabríamos, sabríais, sabrían
present subjunctive:	sepa, sepas, sepa, sepamos, sepáis, sepan
imperfect subjunctive:	supiera, supieras, supiera, supiéramos, supierais, supieran

Conocer vs. *Saber* Drill

Fill in the blanks with the correct form of **conocer** or **saber.** Answers and explanations can be found in Part III.

1. ¡Él ________ cocinar muy bien!
2. ¿ ________ el libro que ganó el premio? (tú)
3. Las mujeres ________ bailar como si fueran profesionales.
4. ¿Es verdad que ________ a Oprah? (ustedes)
5. Es importante ________ nadar.
6. No ________ cómo voy a ganar la carrera.
7. ¿Cómo puede ser que tú no ________ la casa donde viviste?
8. Los dos abogados no se ________ el uno al otro porque nunca han trabajado juntos.
9. ________ que vamos a divertirnos en el circo esta noche. (yo)

TIPS FOR VERB QUESTIONS

- The tenses you need to know are the present, past, future, conditional, imperfect, and present perfect. You also need to know the subjunctive mode (both present and imperfect) and commands. In terms of memorizing and reviewing them, we think the best approach is to lump them together in the following way:

Present Tenses	Past Tenses	Future Tenses	Subjunctive Mode/ Commands
Present	Preterite	Future	Present
	Imperfect	Conditional	Imperfect
	Present Perfect		Commands

By thinking in terms of these groupings, you'll find that eliminating answer choices is a snap once you've determined the tense of the sentence. That is your first step on a question that tests your knowledge of verb tenses: Determine the tense of the sentence (or at least whether it's a past, present, or future tense), and eliminate.

Verb Clues
Often, superficial characteristics like accent marks indicate what tense a verb is in. Clues like these can guide you to the right answer.

- When memorizing the uses of the different tenses, focus on clues that point to one tense or another.
- There are certain expressions (wish or desire, emotion, doubt, and impersonal commentaries) that tell you to use the subjunctive, and whether the expression is in the present or the past tells you which subjunctive form to use.
- To distinguish between future and conditional, focus on the certainty of the event's occurrence.
- The three past tenses are differentiated by the end (or lack) of the action and when that end occurred (if it occurred).
    - If the action had a clear beginning and ending in the past, use the regular **past tense.**
    - If the action was a continuous action in the past, use the **imperfect tense.**
    - If the action began in the past and is continuing into the present, or ended very close to the present, use the **present perfect tense.**
- Recognizing the different tenses shouldn't be too tough if you focus on superficial characteristics.
- The only compound tenses you're likely to see are the perfect tenses.
- Certain tenses have accents, others do not.
- As far as pacing goes, apply the same principles that we outlined for pronoun questions: Spend time on the easy questions and use POE and guess on the tougher ones. Keep in mind that, although the simple tenses (present, past, and future) do appear, they are seldom the correct answers. Why? Because they're the first tenses you learned, they're the easiest to use, and the test writers know that you'll guess them if you're stuck on a question. They don't want you to guess successfully, so they frequently use these basic tenses as trap answers. Careful now, we didn't say that the basic tenses were never right.

PREPOSITIONS

Prepositions are those little words that show the relationship between two other words. In English, they include words like *to*, *from*, *at*, *for*, and *about*. In Spanish, they include words such as **a**, **de**, and **sobre**.

Part of what you need to know about prepositions is what the different ones mean. That's the easy part. The other thing you need to know is how and when to use them. You need to know which verbs and expressions take prepositions and which prepositions they take. This isn't too difficult to learn either, but it can be tricky.

The good news is that only a very small number of prepositions appears on the test, so you can limit your study to those instead of trying to master every preposition in existence. Yes, it is much like doing vocabulary work, but once again, you probably already know many of these expressions, so it shouldn't be too terrible.

Remember in the beginning of this chapter, when you learned that some of the sentence completion part of the exam would focus on grammar instead of meaning, and that because of this, answer choices on a given question would mean roughly the same thing? Well, we lied (sort of), but that's actually a good thing. What we're getting at is that, with preposition questions (unlike verb and pronoun questions), the answers sometimes do have different meanings, and this makes POE a lot easier.

Common Prepositions and Their Uses

a: to; at

¿Vamos a la obra de teatro esta noche?
Are we going to the play tonight?

Llegamos a las cinco.
We arrive at 5:00.

de: of; from

Son las gafas de mi hermano.
Those are my brother's glasses.
(Literally, the glasses of my brother.)

Soy de Argentina.
I am from Argentina.

con: with

Me gusta mucho el arroz con pollo.
I like chicken with rice a lot.

sobre: on; about; over

La chaqueta está sobre la mesa.
The jacket is on the table.

La conferencia es sobre la prevención del SIDA.
The conference is about AIDS prevention.

Prepositions
Prepositions are often idiomatic, which means there are no rules for their use—they just sort of sound right. It's the same reasoning behind our use of prepositions in English.

Los Yankees triunfaron sobre los Padres en la serie mundial.
The Yankees triumphed over the Padres in the World Series.

antes de: before

Antes de salir quiero ponerme un sombrero.
Before leaving I want to put on a hat.

después de: after

Después de la cena me gusta caminar un poco.
After dinner I like to walk a little.

en: in

Regresan en una hora.
They'll be back in an hour.

Alguien está en el baño.
Someone is in the bathroom.

entre: between

La carnicería está entre la pescadería y el cine.
The butcher shop is between the fish store and the movie theater.

La conferencia duró entre dos y tres horas.
The conference lasted between two and three hours.

durante: during

Durante el verano me gusta nadar todos los días.
During the summer I like to swim every day.

desde: since; from

He tomado vitaminas desde mi juventud.
I've been taking vitamins since my childhood.

Se pueden ver las montañas desde aquí.
The mountains can be seen from here.

Para vs. *Por*

The prepositions **para** and **por** both mean "for" (as well as other things, depending on context), but they are used for different situations, and so they tend to cause a bit of confusion.

Luckily, there are some pretty clear-cut rules as to when you use **para** and when you use **por**, because they both tend to sound fine even when they're being used incorrectly. Try to avoid using your ear when choosing between these two.

When to Use *Para*

The following are examples of the most common situations in which **para** is used. Instead of memorizing some stuffy rule, we suggest that you get a feel for what types of situations imply the use of **para**, so that when you see those situations come up on your test, you'll recognize them.

The preposition **para** expresses the idea of *destination*, but in a very broad sense.

Destination in time

El helado es ***para*** *mañana.*
The ice cream is for tomorrow. (Tomorrow is the ice cream's destination.)

Destination in space

Me voy ***para*** *el mercado.*
I'm leaving for the market. (The market is my destination.)

Destination of purpose

Compraste un regalo ***para*** *Luis.*
You bought a gift for Luis. (Luis is the destination of your purchase.)

Estudiamos ***para*** *sacar buenas notas.*
We study to get good grades. (Good grades are the destination of our studies.)

Destination of work

Trabajo ***para*** *IBM.*
I work for IBM. (IBM is the destination of my work.)

When to Use *Para*
Para is almost always used to indicate some sort of destination—time, space, a person, an event, a resulting action (an effect)—so be on the lookout for this type of meaning in the sentence.

The following two uses of *para* do not indicate a sense of destination:

To express opinion

Para mí, el lunes es el día más largo de la semana.
For me, Monday is the longest day of the week.

To qualify or offer a point of reference

Para ser un niño joven, tiene muchísimo talento.
For a young boy, he has a lot of talent.

When to Use *Por*

Chances are, if you're not discussing destination in any way, shape, or form, or the other two uses of **para**, then you need to use **por**. If this general rule isn't enough for you, though, study the following possibilities and you should have all the bases covered.

To express a period of time

Trabajé con mi amigo ***por*** *quince años.*
I worked with my friend for 15 years.

To express how you got somewhere (by)

Fuimos a Italia ***por*** *barco.*
We went to Italy by boat.

Pasamos ***por*** *esa tienda ayer cuando salimos del pueblo.*
We passed by that store yesterday when we left the town.

To describe a trade (in exchange for)

Te cambiaré mi automóvil ***por*** *el tuyo este fin de semana.*
I'll trade you my car for yours this weekend.

To lay blame or identify cause (by)

Todos los barcos fueron destruidos ***por*** *la tormenta.*
All the boats were destroyed by the storm.

To identify gain or motive (for; as a substitute for)

Ella hace todo lo posible ***por*** *su hermana.*
She does everything possible for her sister.

Cuando Arsenio está enfermo, su madre trabaja ***por*** *él.*
When Arsenio is ill, his mother works (as a substitute) for him.

Ir a and *Acabar de*

Ir a is used to describe what the future will bring, or, in other words, what is going to happen. The expression is formed by combining the appropriate form of **ir** in the present tense (subject and verb must agree) with the preposition **a.**

> *Mañana **vamos a** comprar el árbol de Navidad.*
> Tomorrow we are going to buy the Christmas tree.
>
> *¿**Vas a** ir a la escuela aun si te sientes mal?*
> You're going to go to school even if you feel ill?

Acabar de is the Spanish equivalent of "to have just," and is used to talk about what has just happened. It is formed just like **ir a**, with the appropriate form of **acabar** in the present tense followed by **de.**

> ***Acabo de** terminar de cocinar el pavo.*
> I have just finished cooking the turkey.
>
> *Ellos **acaban de** regresar del mercado.*
> They have just returned from the supermarket.

Other Prepositions to Remember

Following is a list of other prepositions and prepositional phrases you should know. Notice that many of these are merely adverbs with a **de** tacked on to the end to make them prepositions.

a la derecha de	to the right of
a la izquierda de	to the left of
al lado de	next to
alrededor de	around, surrounding
cerca de	near
debajo de	underneath
delante de	in front of
dentro de	inside of
detrás de	behind
en medio de	in the middle of
encima de	above, on top of
enfrente de	in front of
frente a	in front of
fuera de	outside of
hacia	toward
hasta	until
lejos de	far from
tras	behind

TIPS FOR PREPOSITION QUESTIONS

- Much of your work with prepositions boils down to memorization: which expressions and verbs go with which prepositions, and so on. Keep in mind that preposition questions account for less than 15 percent of the questions on the sentence completion section of your exam, so don't drive yourself nuts trying to memorize every single one you've ever seen.
- You should concentrate on the boldface examples at the beginning of the preposition section because those are the most common. Once you're comfortable with them, the subsequent list should be a snap because many of those expressions are merely adverbs with **a** or **de** after them.
- Some verbs take prepositions all the time, some never do, and others sometimes do. This isn't as confusing as it may sound, though, because prepositions (or lack thereof) change the meanings of verbs. Consider the following:

  Voy a tratar ------- despertarme más temprano.

  (A) a
  (B) de
  (C) con
  (D) sin

  Which one of these goes with **tratar**? Well actually, each of them does, depending on what you are trying to say. In this case you want to say "try to," so **de** is the appropriate preposition. **Tratar con** means "to deal with," and **tratar sin** means "to try/treat without," while **tratar a** doesn't mean anything unless a person is mentioned afterward, in which case it means "to treat." None of them makes sense in this sentence. The moral of the story is to not try to memorize which verbs go with which prepositions; instead, concentrate on meaning.
- Just like you did with the vocabulary list, scan the prepositional phrase list and check off the expressions with which you are comfortable and which you are certain you'll remember on the day of the exam. You may want to review them briefly as you approach the date of the test, but for now focus your efforts on the ones with which you have trouble.

First Pass
Easy vocabulary; present, past, and future tenses; simple prepositions that you've already memorized

Second Pass
Not so obvious vocabulary; subjunctive and conditional tenses; harder prepositions

Third Pass
More obscure vocabulary and grammar; the imperfect subjunctive tense

Drill 1: Pronouns

Answers and explanations can be found in Part III.

1. Si él puede hacerlo solo, yo no ------- tengo que ayudar.

   (A) la
   (B) lo
   (C) le
   (D) los

2. Pedimos asientos cerca de una ventana, pero ------- dieron estos.

   (A) nos
   (B) les
   (C) nuestros
   (D) me

3. Cuando sus estudiantes se portan mal, la profesora ------- castiga.

   (A) las
   (B) los
   (C) les
   (D) le

4. ¿Son ------- aquellos guantes que están sobre la butaca?

   (A) mío
   (B) mía
   (C) míos
   (D) mías

5. Para tu cumpleaños ------- daré un caballo nuevo.

   (A) le
   (B) te
   (C) a ti
   (D) me

6. ¿ ------- es tu cantante favorito?

   (A) Quién
   (B) Cuál
   (C) Quiénes
   (D) Qué

7. ¿ ------- prefieres? ¿El azul o el rojo?

   (A) Qué
   (B) Cuál
   (C) Cuáles
   (D) Ese

Drill 2: Verbs

Answers and explanations can be found in Part III.

1. Cuando tenga dinero, te ------- un automóvil de lujo.

   (A) compraré
   (B) compré
   (C) compraría
   (D) compraste

2. Quiero que ------- la tarea antes de acostarte.

   (A) hiciste
   (B) hace
   (C) haga
   (D) hagas

3. Yo no ------- a la mama de mi amiga.

   (A) conoció
   (B) conoces
   (C) conozco
   (D) conozcas

4. Si tuvieran tiempo, ------- pasar el tiempo relajándose.

   (A) quieren
   (B) querían
   (C) quieran
   (D) querrían

5. ¿------- tú el numero de teléfono de la estación de trenes?

   (A) Sabes
   (B) Sabré
   (C) Sabrán
   (D) Sé

6. Carlos ------- mucho tiempo estudiando la biología últimamente.

   (A) pasó
   (B) pasaría
   (C) pasaba
   (D) ha pasado

Drill 3: Prepositions

Answers and explanations can be found in Part III.

1. Quiero llegar a la fiesta antes ------- María.
   (A) de
   (B) de que
   (C) a
   (D) sin

2. La cafetería esta ------- la biblioteca.
   (A) alrededor de
   (B) en frente de
   (C) por abajo de
   (D) sobre

3. Mi escuela esta ------- la estación de autobús.
   (A) lejos de
   (B) por
   (C) dentro de
   (D) encima de

4. ------- un poco de suerte, no va a llover el día del casamiento!
   (A) A mas de
   (B) Por
   (C) Para
   (D) Con

5. La próxima semana ellos van ------- tocar aquí.
   (A) a
   (B) de
   (C) con
   (D) por

6. No me gusta ver las películas de horror ------- la noche.
   (A) tras de
   (B) sobre
   (C) en
   (D) durante

7. Me voy en excursión a Italia ------- poder aprender el italiano mas rápido.
   (A) por
   (B) en
   (C) para
   (D) a

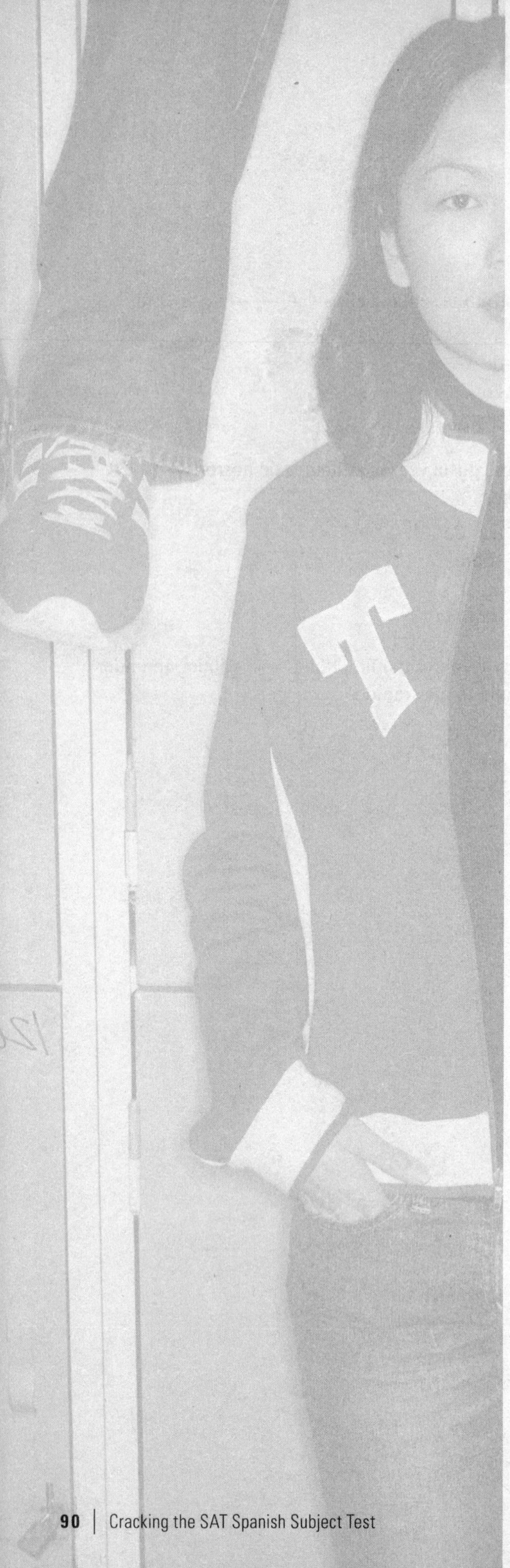

Summary

- Pronouns are commonly tested on the exam. You should be familiar with the various types (subject, direct object, indirect object, possessive, prepositional, reflexive, demonstrative) and know how and when to use them.
- There are a number of verb tenses and modes you should know (though you don't have to know all of them). The ones with which you should be familiar are present, past (preterite, imperfect, and present perfect), future, conditional, subjunctive (present and imperfect), and command.
- Prepositions are also tested, though to a lesser extent than pronouns and verbs. You simply have to know certain expressions and the prepositions they use.
- You can do a lot of POE based on grammar. Apply the grammar rules that apply to the context of the sentence to eliminate choices that aren't possible. You don't need to understand all of the words in the sentence to do this effectively.

Chapter 5
Paragraph Completion

Paragraph completion is the second section of the SAT Spanish Subject Test. The section is designed to test vocabulary and grammar within the context of an entire paragraph. In this chapter, we focus on strategies for effectively handling this question type.

PARAGRAPH COMPLETION BASICS

In this chapter we take a look at the paragraph completion questions that appear in Part B of the Spanish Subject Test and Part B of the reading section of the Spanish with Listening Subject Test. To simplify things, we simply refer to this section of each respective exam as Part B.

If you've made it this far, you've completed the review of all the grammar and vocabulary that's likely to appear on your Spanish Subject Test. We won't be presenting anymore new material (although it would probably be wise to continue reviewing anything that gave you trouble up to now). Just as you did in the last chapter, the first thing you should do is memorize the directions.

> Part B
>
> **Directions:** In each of the following passages, there are numbered blanks indicating that words or phrases have been omitted. For each numbered blank, four completions are provided. First read through the entire paragraph. Then, for each numbered blank, choose the completion that is most appropriate given the context of the entire paragraph and fill in the corresponding oval on the answer sheet.

Part B is a lot like sentence completions (Part A). You're given two to four (most likely three) brief paragraphs (roughly five to seven sentences each) with several words or phrases replaced by blanks. Your job is to fill in the blanks with the answers that are appropriate based on either meaning or grammar. How do you know whether it's a "meaning" blank or a "grammar" blank? If it's a grammar blank the answers all have the same (or very similar) meanings and you have to choose based on form or verb tense. Sound familiar? It should, because it's the same as in Part A. The meaning blank answers have different meanings, only one of which makes sense in the context of the passage. These questions are just like those in Part A.

So What's the Difference Between Parts A and B?

In Part A, if a sentence makes no sense you just skip it and go on to the next one—no sweat. In Part B, missing a sentence is a little more important, because it can make understanding the overall passage difficult. You don't need to get every single word, but getting at least the main idea of each of the sentences is definitely helpful.

As we mentioned earlier, you've already covered the material necessary to answer the questions in Part B. The vocabulary is all you need for the meaning questions, and the grammar (especially verb tenses) is all you need for the grammar questions. This does not mean you're ready to do drills! First, you need to learn the best way to approach the section.

PACING

Because the passages in Part B have different degrees of difficulty but are in no particular order, you first have to decide on the order in which to attack these questions. As in Part A, you want to start with the easiest questions and finish up with the toughest ones. In Part B this decision will be more involved and more important because if you choose a really tough passage first, you will probably waste time and throw off your pacing for the remainder of the section. We're not trying to make it sound like life or death. We're just saying that by taking on these passages in a certain order, you can make the section easier for yourself. You're eventually going to do all three, but you're going to do them in the order that you like.

Do What Works for You
Answer Part B questions in the order that you like, not the order that the test writers like!

Your decision should be based on a brief skim of the first couple of sentences of the passage. If these sentences make sense, and the writing style strikes you as being pretty clear, go for it. If you have any doubt as to whether the passage is going to be easy, go on and see what the next one looks like. Your goal is to find the easiest one and to do it first.

Don't base your decision on subject matter. The fact that a passage pertains to something you know about or find interesting doesn't mean much if you can't understand every third word. You're not going to be asked about content (that comes later in the reading comprehension section); you'll only be asked to fill in blanks. You don't need to retain the information in the passage, but you need to understand the tense that it's in and the meaning of individual sentences. In other words, topic doesn't count for much. Base your decision on writing style and vocabulary.

USING THE THREE-PASS SYSTEM

Once you've decided which passage you're doing first, what next? Answer the questions in the order that's best for you. Keep in mind that you will want to do all three passes within one passage *before* you move on to the next one.

Three Is the Magic Number
Before you move on to the next passage, do all THREE passes.

First Pass

The questions on each of the Part B passages should be done in order. Starting at the beginning will give you some sense of the passage's structure, which will probably make you more comfortable with it overall. However, on your first pass through the passage you should skip any question that looks like it *might* be tricky. Attempt only the very easiest questions on this pass. Focus on the ones for which you know the answer without using POE or anything but your knowledge of grammar or vocabulary.

Second Pass

On the second pass start using POE to eliminate and guess. Go back to the questions you left blank on the first pass and see if there are any answers that can be eliminated. Look to cancel wrong answers. You'll find (just as you did on Part A) that some of the wrong answers are pretty obviously wrong, and in some cases you'll be able to eliminate all but one—the right one.

Don't be intimidated if the sentence that contains a certain blank is difficult. You can determine what tense a verb is even if you don't understand the verb's meaning! The same goes for pronouns and prepositions. If you are pretty sure that the noun being replaced is feminine, then eliminate the masculine pronouns. You have to be aggressive if you want to take advantage of POE.

As far as *meaning* blanks are concerned, use the same technique you learned for second-pass questions on Part A. Piece together any words in the sentence that you know to try to get some sense of the context. See if any of the answers are completely wacky based on that context. This is where a general knowledge of the passage can be helpful to you as well. Any sentence in the passage, even if you don't understand it, has to make sense within the topic and intention of the overall passage. In other words, there won't be a sentence about the history of the toothpick in a passage about military strategies. Answer choices that seem to stray off the subject of the overall passage are probably wrong.

Third Pass

As before, spend very little time, eliminate what you can based on whatever clues the sentence or passage has to offer, use your ear if necessary, and guess. The same rule about not guessing holds here as well. If you can't eliminate any of the answers, then it's fine to leave a question blank.

It's very easy to fall into a mindset that says you're not done with a passage until every single question is answered, but this is a dangerous mindset. Just because a passage is easy overall doesn't mean every single question in that passage is a gift.

Don't waste your time: If you've answered all the questions that you can and there are still one or two blanks, move on to the next passage. You may never have to, but you should be prepared to skip some questions.

Let's apply some of what we've learned so far to maximize your performance.

Drill 1: Paragraph Completion

Answers and explanations can be found in Part III.

Part B

Directions: In each of the following passages, there are numbered blanks indicating that words or phrases have been omitted. For each numbered blank, four completions are provided. First, read through the entire paragraph. Then, for each numbered blank, choose the completion that is most appropriate given the context of the entire paragraph and fill in the corresponding oval on the answer sheet.

Parecía que el pasado 6 de abril todo __(1)__ listo para el __(2)__ del transbordador *Discovery* cuya missión era la de realizar investigaciones atmosféricas y estudios solares, pero una __(3)__ de última hora obligó a la Agencia Nacional de Aeronáutica y el Espacio (NASA) a abortar por __(4)__ vez consecutiva el lanzamiento de la nave.

El se apagó del motor __(5)__ antes de que los tres motores principales de la nave, alimentados por hidrógeno, fueran activados a las 2:32 de la madrugada del pasado 6 de abril, unos 6.6 segundos antes del lanzamiento.

1. (A) estaba
   (B) esté
   (C) estaría
   (D) está

2. (A) desempleo
   (B) despegue
   (C) desventaja
   (D) descanso

3. (A) negocio
   (B) testigo
   (C) retrato
   (D) dificultad

4. (A) nueva
   (B) tremenda
   (C) segunda
   (D) dos

5. (A) años
   (B) días
   (C) segundos
   (D) lugares

Drill 2: Paragraph Completion

Answers and explanations can be found in Part III.

Part B

Directions: In each of the following passages, there are numbered blanks indicating that words or phrases have been omitted. For each numbered blank, four completions are provided. First read through the entire paragraph. Then, for each numbered blank, choose the completion that is most appropriate given the context of the entire paragraph and fill in the corresponding oval on the answer sheet.

La quinceañera de Rosa (1) un día inolvidable. Todos sus (2) vinieron, incluyendo su bisabuela, a quien Rosa nunca había (3) antes. La ceremonia empezó, tradicionalmente, con la misa de acción de gracias. Rosa traía un vestido largo, color rosa. Ella se veía tan elegante que hasta su padre (4) un poco al verla. Después de la ceremonia, todos se reunieron (5) su casa para una gran fiesta. Rosa inició los bailes con su padre, luego con sus tíos y sus primos. Al final de la noche, su padre tomó un vaso y (6) a su hija querida.

1. (A) fue
   (B) fuera
   (C) sea
   (D) sería

2. (A) parabrisas
   (B) parientes
   (C) paraisos
   (D) paraguas

3. (A) conoce
   (B) conozca
   (C) conocido
   (D) conoció

4. (A) lloró
   (B) llamó
   (C) llovió
   (D) llegó

5. (A) con
   (B) para
   (C) en
   (D) por

6. (A) brindó
   (B) desconoció
   (C) asombró
   (D) guardó

Summary

- The paragraph completion section is a combination of the two that preceded it: no new information, just a different format. You should be warmed up and confident going in.
- The majority of the blanks test you on meaning. If the answer to a meaning question isn't immediately apparent, leave it for the second pass. When you come back to it, try to determine the context of the sentence and use POE.
- Determine the best order for you to attack the passages—this could make the difference between smooth sailing and a really big headache, so don't rush your decision.
- Use the Three-Pass System: Do easy questions first, do tougher questions second, eliminate what you can, and guess on whatever's left.
- Don't feel as if you have to answer every single question on a given passage. Sometimes your best move is to go on to the next passage.

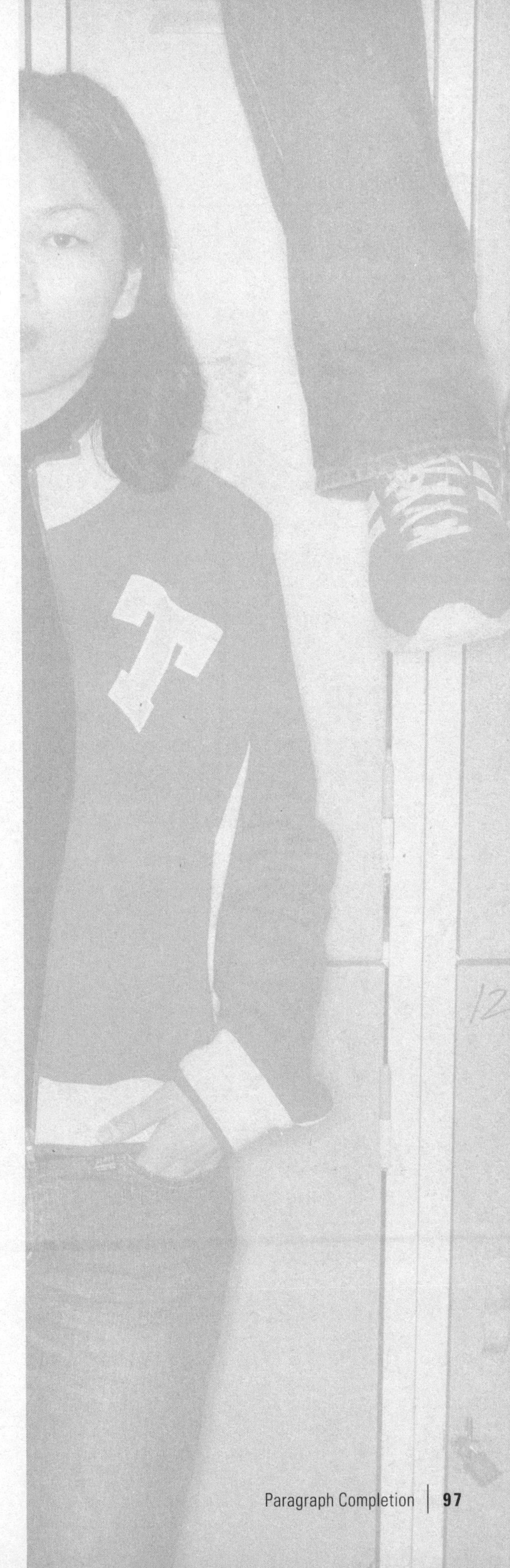

Chapter 6 Reading Comprehension

Reading comprehension questions on the SAT Spanish Subject Test are designed to evaluate your ability to read and interpret information from a piece of text. In this chapter, we focus on strategies for how most effectively to approach this section.

THE LAST SECTION: READING COMPREHENSION

Welcome to Part C. Reading comprehension is the last section of the exam, as well as the section that many consider the most difficult. Even so, there are two good reasons you shouldn't worry.

1. You can afford to leave some (or most) of the reading comprehension questions blank and still come away with a great score.
2. By carefully choosing the right question(s) to leave blank, you can make the reading comprehension section much easier.

As usual, the first step is to get acquainted with the directions.

> Part C
>
> **Directions:** Read the following texts carefully for comprehension. Each passage is followed by a number of questions or incomplete statements. Select the answer or completion that is best according to the text and fill in the corresponding oval on the answer sheet.

This section contains approximately 28 questions on the Spanish Subject Test and approximately 17 questions on the Spanish with Listening Subject Test. On each test you will have between four and nine passages or pictures (ads, announcements, menus, and so on) that contain between one and six questions each. The longer passages are usually followed by more questions. We'll get into how to choose which passages to do later, but for now realize that the length of the passage tells you nothing about its difficulty, so don't assume that the long passages are the hardest ones.

Remember...
The length of a passage tells you NOTHING about its level of difficulty!

One of the nicest things about Reading Comprehension is that you may not need to do very much of it to get your desired score. In terms of the big picture, you should *not* rush through Parts A and B to get to Part C. In fact, because the other two parts lend themselves to POE and educated guessing, you should do the opposite. Take your time on the questions that are the most "technique-able" (Parts A and B), and if this means leaving some of the reading questions blank, that's just fine. It's not that this section is impossible, but rather that it lends itself less to shortcuts and techniques.

HOW TO CRACK THIS SECTION

The first and most important step in beating the reading comprehension section is choosing which passages to do and which to skip. Luckily, you've already had an introduction to this type of decision in Part B of the exam. The idea is very similar: If the writing style is familiar (that is, you can understand it without a major struggle) and there isn't too much tough vocabulary, then you're probably looking at a passage that you should do. This doesn't mean that you must know every single word in the passage. In fact, most passages will have some words (if only one or two) that you don't know. If you can understand the gist of the overall passage, then you can answer the questions that follow.

Basic Approach for Reading Comprehension Questions

- Preview the questions to see what you're going to be asked.
- Read the passage for the big picture.
- Read a question.
- Go back to the passage to find your answer.
- Use Process of Elimination.

How to Read the Spanish Passages

Over the years, you've probably developed a reading style that includes a pace at which you're comfortable, a certain level of attention to detail, and so on. When you know that someone is going to ask you questions about what you've read, you usually change your reading style to match the situation. You read much more slowly, and you pay much more attention to detail than you would if you were reading, say, an article in a newspaper. The reason for this is simple: You assume that by reading more slowly and carefully you will better understand what you've read. Makes sense, right? Unfortunately, even though it seems logical, this approach can be disastrous when it comes to the reading comprehension section of the SAT Spanish Subject Test.

What usually happens when you try to read ultra-slowly and virtually memorize the passage is that you finish reading with no sense of what the overall passage is about. You may have picked up a few details, but who knows whether those particular details will be asked? What eventually happens is that on each question (or at least on most questions) you end up going back to the passage and rereading what you just read a minute ago. This approach is time consuming and can be very frustrating. There is a better way.

Looking back at the passage to find the answer to a question is a very good idea. The problem is the initial time wasted in trying to memorize the passage in one reading. If you're going to refer to the passage anyway, then what's the point? It doesn't make sense to read the passage slowly and carefully twice, especially if one of those two readings doesn't help you answer questions.

Reading Comprehension or Treasure Hunt?

We know that the instructions to the section ask you to read for comprehension, but we also know that those same instructions are written by the people who wrote the rest of the exam. Is this section really about reading for comprehension, or is it about answering a few silly questions? Not surprisingly, it's about answering a few silly questions. Treat the reading comprehension section like a treasure hunt; the answers to the individual questions are hidden somewhere in the passage, and your job is to find them. Here's the best way to approach that task.

Get the Big Picture

Think Big

Don't get hung up on individual words. If you don't know what a word means, try to see whether you can still get the gist of the sentence. You can spend a lot of time trying to decipher words you may not even need to know.

You've already seen that it's a waste of time to try to memorize the passage in one reading. Instead of trying to memorize the entire thing, your first reading should be dedicated to finding the *topic* and the *structure* of the passage. This means that if you finish your initial read and you know what the overall passage is about, as well as the main point of each paragraph, you've read the passage properly. Don't worry about facts or details (such as names, dates, places, titles, and the like). Focus on what the whole passage is about and, in a very general sense, what each paragraph is about. A good way to test whether you've done this well is to try to summarize the passage in a few words (no more than five or six) in English, and summarize the content of each paragraph in even fewer words. If you can do both of these things, you've definitely got a handle on the big picture, and that's going to be a big help in answering the questions.

There's no way we can tell you how long this initial reading should take, simply because everyone reads at a different pace. We can tell you that if you're stopping to try to decipher the meaning of every unknown word you come across, or if you're reading the same difficult sentence again and again, you've missed the boat. Focus on ideas, not on specific words or facts.

The point of reading this way is not to enable you to answer *all* the questions without looking back (we wish it were that easy too). The point is to give you a sense of where things are, so that when a question asks about a particular fact or detail, even if you don't know the answer, you *will* know where to look to find it.

Sample Passage

Let's take a look at a sample passage. Read through it with the aim of getting the general idea and don't get caught up with unfamiliar vocabulary. Jot down just a few words summing up each paragraph and a few words summing up the entire passage.

España, con una superficie aproximada de dos veces la del estado de Wyoming y una población de una vez y media la de California, está situada en el suroeste de Europa, separada de Francia por las montañas de los Pirineos y de África por el estrecho de Gibraltar. Su territorio está formado por la Península Ibérica, excepto Portugal, y los archipiélagos de las Islas Baleares, en el Mar Mediterráneo, y de las Islas Canarias, en el Océano Atlántico. Además, ejerce su soberanía en dos ciudades de la costa de Marruecos, Ceuta y Melilla, y no la ejerce en un peñón, en su propia costa, el Peñón de Gibraltar, que es una posesión inglesa.

El español, aunque tiene muy poco que ver en muchos aspectos con los habitantes del norte y centro de Europa, es europeo y latino, por su historia y por su cultura. A pesar de todo, algunos dicen que "África empieza en los Pirineos," y esto se debe a la influencia que tuvieron los casi ocho siglos de dominación árabe.

Para mucha gente, los españoles son personas pequeñas, morenas, que pasan la vida cantando y bailando flamenco, muy aficionadas a las corridas de toros, que les gusta mucho perder el tiempo hablando de todo en las tertulias y en la sobremesa y que cuando están contentas, que es muy frecuente, dicen "olé." Esta idea es tan falsa como la que en España mucha gente también tiene de los estadounidenses. El estadounidense típico, para ellos, es el *vaquero*, el gangster o el artista de Hollywood. Sin embargo hay españoles en los Estados Unidos que han visto, oído, cantado y bailado más flamenco aquí que en España, lo mismo que la mayoría de los estadounidenses no tienen nada que ver ni con un *vaquero*, ni con un gangster ni con Hollywood.

Here are some possible summaries.

Paragraph 1: "borders of Spain" or "Spain's territory"
Paragraph 2: "Spain's not like much of Europe"
Paragraph 3: "there are misconceptions about Spanish people"

So what's the passage about? Spain and Spanish people.

Do you see how brief and simple we're being? And there is certainly some tricky vocabulary at the end of the first paragraph—*ejerce, soberanía, peñón*—but you don't need to know what all the words mean to understand the big picture.

Mark It Up
While you're reading for the big picture, you may notice a word or phrase that stands out. Flag it. It may help when searching for the answer to a question.

Using Process of Elimination

Use POE
Wrong answers to reading comprehension questions are often lousy. Be sure to use POE to eliminate those bogus answers.

One of the biggest problems students have with this section is that they don't like any of the answer choices to some questions. It's as if on some questions the test writers forgot to include the correct answer in the choices. The key to using Process of Elimination on Part C is that, when you're stuck, you should forget about finding the right answer and concentrate on finding wrong answers. If you read all four choices and none of them looks good to you, don't panic. A couple of them probably look pretty bad to you, and those are just as helpful as the choices that look good. Eliminate the ones you know are wrong, and choose from whatever is left.

We know this is a bitter pill to swallow, but the fact is that sometimes you'll end up choosing an answer that you don't like or even understand. That's fine, though, because if you're sure three of the choices are incorrect, then you must have confidence that the last one is the right one. Too often students shy away from answer choices they don't understand or don't like. Unfortunately, this section has little to do with what you like or understand. You're looking for the answer that will earn you a point, not the one with which you agree.

TYPES OF PASSAGES AND QUESTIONS

Yes!
You can skip entire passages! After all, if you don't understand the passage, it's unlikely that you'll answer most of the questions correctly. Do the easy passages first and skip the one that's most difficult for you.

In the reading comprehension section you will primarily encounter passages based on fictional events or characters, history, or current events. However, you may also come across ads, announcements, or menus. Although subject matter has nothing to do with the difficulty of a passage, you may find that a certain passage, because it's about a familiar topic, has vocabulary that you understand. Don't take this on faith. Read a few sentences to make sure.

Although there are some general questions (main idea, or what the passage is about), most of the questions ask you about more specific things that come from a particular place in the passage. You should deal with these two types of questions separately.

There will be times when the correct answer is so obvious that it practically jumps off the page at you. Some of the time, however, it won't be quite that easy. If you know how to work through the answer choices efficiently, and understand how they might try to stump you, even the most difficult questions can be mastered.

General Questions

Once you've finished your first reading, you should go right to the questions to see if there are any general ones. Why? Because if you know the topic and structure of the passage, you can answer any general question without having to scrutinize every detail of the passage. The general questions (when they appear) ask you for general ideas. Here are some examples of general questions.

> **¿De qué se trata este artículo?**
> What is this passage about?
>
> **¿Quién narra este pasaje?**
> Who narrates this passage?

Very few of these appear on a given reading section, but when they do appear they are very easy. You may want to do the general questions first if you choose a passage that contains any.

Trap Answers

On *general questions*, the main thing to be on the lookout for is an answer that is too specific. Unlike the answer to a specific question, the answer to a general question can't be located in one particular place in the passage. This makes sense because the answer to a general question should encompass the contents of the entire passage.

General Question Traps
Be wary of answers that are too specific when you're tackling general questions.

The test writers try to trip you up by providing answers that come from one part of the passage or another, but are not general enough to be correct. These answers tend to be very tempting because they are in the passage that you just finished reading and you recognize them. If the answer to a general question is about a specific part of the passage, it's probably a trap.

Try to answer this general question about the passage you just read.

1. El pasaje se trata de
   (A) la geografía de España y los españoles
   (B) los vaqueros estadounidenses
   (C) la influencia de la dominación árabe en España
   (D) la manera en cual los españoles verdaderamente viven

Here's How to Crack It

Since this is a question about the entire passage, our correct answer should sum up all three paragraphs. Any choice that refers to just one part of the passage, even if accurate, cannot be the correct answer.

Choice (A), which translates to "the geography of Spain and the Spaniards," seems to be right on the money. Notice that each of the other choices—(B) American cowboys, (C) the influence of Arab domination in Spain, and (D) the way in which Spaniards truly live—refers to only a small part of the passage.

Specific Questions

The vast majority of reading comprehension questions require you to refer to the passage to find the answer. This is why it's so important to get a sense of structure before you attempt to answer them. Otherwise you waste lots of time looking for the part of the passage from which the question came. The approach to these questions is simple.

On *specific questions*, the most important thing to remember is that the correct answer must come from the passage. We know this seems obvious, but one of the test writers' favorite tricks on these questions is to provide answers that are reasonable and logical and gel with the contents of the passage, but are not *in* the passage. For this reason it's important that you stick to what you read when you refer to the passage. Don't think in terms of what the author might think or what you think. What's on the page in black and white is all you should go by to answer these questions.

Basic Approach for Specific Questions

- Read the question.
- Locate the source of the question by using guide words (we'll discuss guide words soon).
- Carefully read the section of the passage from where the question came.
- Go to the answers and find the one that matches what you just read.
- When you don't understand what you just read, use POE to eliminate wrong answers.

Correct answers to specific questions won't be exact quotes from the passage, but they'll be pretty darn close. They'll have the same exact meaning as the corresponding words in the passage, with maybe a couple of the words moved around or changed so that it looks a little different. In other words, the right answers are *close* paraphrases of the passage.

How Do You Know Where to Look?

Any specific question will have a word or words that tell you what the question is about. We call these *guide words* because they guide you to the place in the passage where the question originated. If you can determine the subject of the question, you should be able to tell (at least roughly) from where it came. Now all that's left is for you to read the source of the question carefully, and match it up with one of your answer choices.

Specific Question Traps
Correct answers to specific questions must be supported by the passage. Too often the wrong answer is reasonable but not actually in the passage.

Here is the passage we saw on page 103. Take a crack at some specific questions.

España, con una superficie aproximada de dos veces la del estado de Wyoming y una población de una vez y media la de California, está situada en el suroeste de Europa, separada de Francia por las montañas de los Pirineos y de África por el estrecho de Gibraltar. Su territorio está formado por la Península Ibérica, excepto Portugal, y los archipiélagos de las Islas Baleares, en el Mar Mediterráneo, y de las Islas Canarias, en el Océano Atlántico. Además, ejerce su soberanía en dos ciudades de la costa de Marruecos, Ceuta y Melilla, y no la ejerce en un peñón, en su propia costa, el Peñón de Gibraltar, que es una posesión inglesa.

El español, aunque tiene muy poco que ver en muchos aspectos con los habitantes del norte y centro de Europa, es europeo y latino, por su historia y por su cultura. A pesar de todo, algunos dicen que "África empieza en los Pirineos," y esto se debe a la influencia que tuvieron los casi ocho siglos de dominación árabe.

Para mucha gente, los españoles son personas pequeñas, morenas, que pasan la vida cantando y bailando flamenco, muy aficionadas a las corridas de toros, que les gusta mucho perder el tiempo hablando de todo en las tertulias y en la sobremesa y que cuando están contentas, que es muy frecuente, dicen: "olé." Esta idea es tan falsa como la que en España mucha gente también tiene de los estadounidenses. El estadounidense típico, para ellos, es el *cowboy*, el gangster o el artista de Hollywood. Sin embargo, hay españoles en los Estados Unidos que han visto, oído, cantado y bailado más flamenco aquí que en España, lo mismo que la mayoría de los estadounidenses no tienen nada que ver ni con un *cowboy*, ni con un gangster ni con Hollywood.

---

1. La superficie de España es de un tamaño

   (A) dos veces el tamaño de los Estados Unidos
   (B) dos veces el tamaño del estado de Wyoming
   (C) una vez y media el tamaño de California
   (D) igual al tamaño del Peñón de Gibraltar

A Handy Guide

They're called "guide words" for a reason! Look for key words that point to where you should look in the passage for the right answer.

Here's How to Crack It

The answer to this question is located in the beginning of the first paragraph. The guide word **superficie** is located only in that one area of the passage, and that's a big hint that they took the question from this area. The passage says that Spain is "dos veces la del estado de Wyoming" (twice the size of Wyoming). Choice (B) is therefore the answer.

Try this next question.

---

2. ¿Cuál de los siguientes no es territorio español?

    (A) Las Islas Canarias
    (B) El Peñón de Gibraltar
    (C) Las Islas Baleares
    (D) Ceuta y Melilla

Here's How to Crack It

Notice that here we are looking for the choice that is not a part of Spain. The answer choices are mentioned in the first paragraph, so that's where you go to find the answer. Pay close attention to the wording of the last two sentences of the paragraph:

> Su territorio está formado por la Península Ibérica, excepto Portugal, y los archipiélagos de las Islas Baleares, en el Mar Mediterráneo, y de las Islas Canarias, en el Océano Atlántico. Además, ejerce su soberanía en dos ciudades de la costa de Marruecos, Ceuta y Melilla, y no la ejerce en un peñón, en su propia costa, el Peñón de Gibraltar, que es una posesión inglesa.

Choices (A), (C), and (D) are cited as parts of Spain. Choice (B) is therefore the answer.

And finally, see if you can answer the question on the next page.

3. ¿Cuál de las ideas siguientes tienen muchos estadounidenses de los españoles?

(A) Que los españoles típicos son gangsters
(B) Que las mujeres españolas están enamoradas de los *cowboys* estadounidenses
(C) Que todos pasan el día bailando y cantando flamenco
(D) Que quisieran vivir en Hollywood

Here's How to Crack It

This question doesn't have guide words, but since the entire third paragraph is about the mutual stereotypes to which Americans and Spaniards subscribe, it isn't too tough to locate the source of the question. You *do* have to read the question carefully, though, because some of the wrong answers are misconceptions Spaniards have about Americans—choices (A), (B), and (D) are variations on this idea—and the question asks for the opposite. Therefore, (C) is correct.

Question Order

The specific questions are best done in the order in which they appear (although you want to follow the golden rule of skipping any question that looks really difficult). This is because the order of the questions usually follows the progression of the passage—early questions come from the beginning of the passage, and subsequent questions come from the middle of the passage. Something that you read in the early part of the passage can sometimes help on a later question.

As with Part B of the exam, there is a tendency on Part C to feel as if you're not done until you've answered every question that pertains to a certain passage. You're done whenever you want to be done. In other words, if you've done all the questions that you understand and to which you can easily find answers, then move on to the next passage and see if you can find a couple of easy questions there. To a certain extent, reading comprehension will be as easy (or as difficult) as you want to make it.

Drill 1: Reading Comprehension

Answers and explanations can be found in Part III.

Part C

Directions: Read the following texts carefully for comprehension. Each passage is followed by a number of questions or incomplete statements. Select the answer or completion that is best according to the text and fill in the corresponding oval on the answer sheet.

En nuestra oficina regía el mismo presupuesto desde el año mil novecientos veintitantos, o sea desde una época en que la mayoría de nosotros estába luchando con la geografía y con los quebrados. Sin embargo, el jefe se acordaba del acontecimiento y a veces, cuando el trabajo disminuía, se sentaba familiarmente sobre uno de nuestros escritorios, y así, con las piernas colgantes que mostraban después del pantalón unos inmaculados calcetines blancos, nos relataba con la misma emoción de antes y las quinientas noventa y ocho palabras de costumbre, el lejano y magnífico día en que su jefe —quien era entonces el primer oficial que le había palmeado el hombro— le había dicho: "Muchacho, tenemos presupuesto nuevo", con la sonrisa amplia y satisfecha del que ya ha calculado cuántas camisas podrá comprar con el aumento.

1. ¿Por más o menos cuánto tiempo han tenido el mismo presupuesto?
   (A) Por varias décadas
   (B) Por varios siglos
   (C) Por unas cuantas semanas
   (D) Desde ayer

2. El jefe hacía el cuento cuando
   (A) estaba triste
   (B) había tomado demasiado cerveza
   (C) el trabajo era menos de lo corriente
   (D) tenían una fiesta

3. El cuento del presupuesto nuevo que hacía el jefe
   (A) tenía calcetines blancos
   (B) siempre era diferente
   (C) era interesante
   (D) siempre era el mismo

4. ¿Cuál fue la reacción del jefe cuando su jefe le contó del presupuesto nuevo?
   (A) Se fue de la compañía.
   (B) Se puso muy contento.
   (C) Le dio un abrazo a su jefe.
   (D) Compró camisas nuevas.

Drill 2: Reading Comprehension

Answers and explanations can be found in Part III.

Part C

Directions: Read the following texts carefully for comprehension. Each passage is followed by a number of questions or incomplete statements. Select the answer or completion that is best according to the text and fill in the corresponding oval on the answer sheet.

Como haces falta, Basilio . . . Me gustaría tanto que estuvieras presente, con los ojos abiertos, a ver lo que ha pasado con tu casa. Se está desmoronando, como si la hubieras levantado con ladrillos mal cocidos; se han quebrado las tejas, permitiendo al sol y la lluvia entrar en todas partes; a las paredes ya no les caben las cuarteaduras. Y los hijos —¡qué te puedo contar de nuestros hijos!

Manuel estuvo aquí, hace unos días, verdaderamente desesperado por las deudas. A él no le pudiste quitar los vicios. Y de ser el que más tenía, se ha quedado sin nada. Me contaron que hasta su mujer y sus hijos lo corrieron.

No he visto a Néstor durante mucho tiempo. Te confieso que ya casi no veo nada. Pero creo que él está en los Estados Unidos. Como tú no les enseñaste a trabajar, aquí no pudieron hacer nada, por eso se fueron a buscar entre los mendrugos de otra patria, el pan para sus hijos.

Allá también está José.

1. ¿Qué ha pasado durante la ausencia de Basilio?
   (A) Le han contado de sus hijos.
   (B) Él ha cocido los ladrillos.
   (C) Su casa ha empezado a caerse a pedazos.
   (D) Se ha ido a otra patria.

2. ¿Quién es Basilio?
   (A) El esposo de la narradora
   (B) El hijo de la narradora
   (C) La narradora
   (D) El hombre con las deudas

3. ¿Cuál es el problema de Manuel?
   (A) No puede ver muy bien.
   (B) Se ha quitado sus vicios.
   (C) Su esposa tuvo un bebé.
   (D) Le debe mucho dinero a la gente.

4. ¿Dónde está Néstor?
   (A) Visitando a la narradora
   (B) Con los mendrugos
   (C) En otro país
   (D) Cocinando pan para sus hijos

5. ¿Quién ha tenido éxito en el pasado y lo ha perdido?
   (A) Basilio
   (B) Manuel
   (C) José
   (D) Néstor

6. ¿Qué se podría asumir de José?
   (A) A él no le gusta la narradora.
   (B) No tuvo nada en su propio país.
   (C) Enseñó a Néstor a trabajar.
   (D) Su mujer y sus hijos lo abandonaron.

Summary

- Choose the order in which you want to do the passages. Read a couple of sentences to see if the writing style is easy to follow and the vocabulary is manageable. If so, go for it. If not, look ahead for something easier.
- Read the passage for topic and structure only. Don't read for detail, and don't try to memorize the entire thing. The first read is for you to get a sense of the subject and the overall structure—that's all.
- Go straight to the general questions. If you read correctly, you should be able to answer any general questions without looking back to the passage. Very few passages have general questions, so don't expect to find many.
- Then do the specific questions in order. For these, you're going to let the guide words in the question tell you where to look in the passage. Then slowly and carefully read the area that the question comes from. Find an answer choice that basically says the same thing in slightly different language. These questions are about paraphrasing, not about comprehension.
- Avoid specific answers on general questions, and on specific questions avoid answers that are reasonable but aren't from the passage.
- Don't be afraid to leave blanks if there are questions that stump you. You're done with a passage whenever you've answered all the questions that you can answer. Instead of banging your head against a wall trying to do the last remaining question on a passage, go on to the next passage and find an easier question.

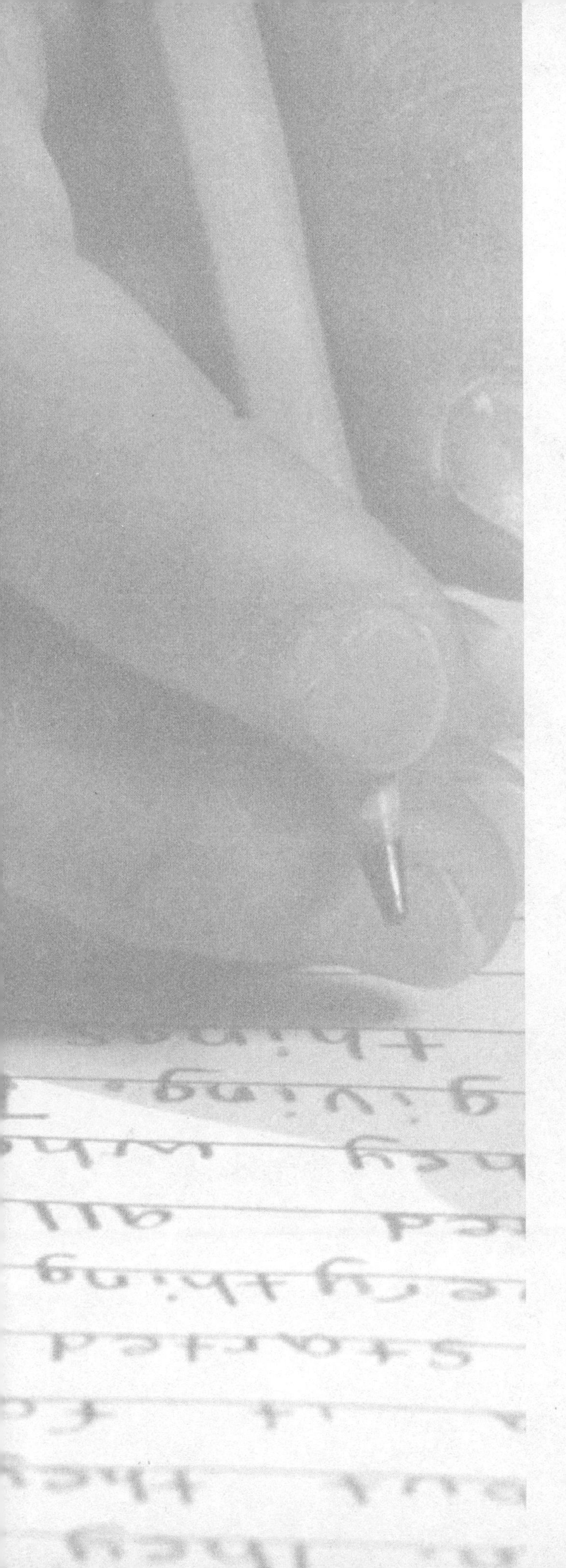

Part III
Drill Answers and Explanations

CHAPTER 3 DRILLS

Drill 1: Process of Elimination

1. **B** **Limpia** (cleans) would make **casa** (house) a very good guess. The other answers—**libro** (book), **huesos** (bones), and **rain** (lluvia)—are not clearly related to cleaning.

2. **D** **Revistas** (magazines) would match up with **artículos interesantes** (interesting articles) better than it would with any of the other choices offered (**vacaciones** = vacation, **obras de teatro** = plays, **conciertos** = concerts).

3. **C** This is a pretty tough one, but you can still take a good guess. **Salir** (to go out), combined with the **no** that precedes, gives you "not go out." Are any of the answers something that might keep you from going out? Yes, **nieve** (snow). None of the others really makes sense (**comida** = food, **dinero** = money, **hambre** = hunger).

4. **C** **Postre** means dessert, and there is only one answer that is a dessert: **helado** (ice cream). **Arroz con pollo** (chicken with rice), **vitaminas** (vitamins), and **agua** (water) are all edible, but they aren't desserts.

5. **A** If you put **película** (movie) and **miedo** (fear) together, what do you get? A scary movie! The closest guess would be **violenta** (violent). **Graciosa** means funny, **corta** means short, and **tremenda** means huge or grand.

6. **C** **Sueño** (sleepiness) would be a good fit because we know that the little girl is crying. **Feliz** (happy) and **corriendo** (running) could describe a little girl, but wouldn't make a great fit with crying. **Silla** (chair) would not fit with any of the clues.

Drill 2: Sentence Completion

1. **B** **Translation:** My girlfriend's shirt is made of ------- .

   (A) roses
   (B) cotton
   (C) wood
   (D) blue

   The key words in the sentence are **camisa** (shirt) and **hecha** (made of). **Rosas** (roses) and **madera** (wood) do not work; **azul** (blue) could describe the color of the shirt, but not what the shirt is made of. Therefore, **algodón** (cotton) is the correct answer.

2. **B** **Translation:** I was looking/looked for medicine for my grandfather in the ------- on the corner.

(A) bookstore
(B) pharmacy
(C) office
(D) bakery

The clue in this question is a cognate (remember those?), **medicinas**, so that even if the rest of the sentence was a blur you could tell that the answer had something to do with medicine. The answer also happens to be a cognate and is the only choice that relates to medicine.

3. **A** **Translation:** I was ------- because my employees arrived late for the fourth time in the same week.

(A) furious
(B) delighted
(C) very happy
(D) open

Unless you were some sort of lunatic, you'd be pretty peeved if your staff was late all the time. Although three of the answers are emotions, only one of the three is a negative emotion.

4. **D** **Translation:** A good way to improve your grades in school is ------- a lot.

(A) to teach
(B) to understand
(C) to speak
(D) to practice

The key words in the sentence are **mejorar** (to improve) and **notas** (grades). **Practicar** (to practice) is the best answer choice. **Enseñar** (to teach), **entender** (to understand), and **hablar** (to speak) all have to do with school, but they don't quite fit in with what is described.

5. **A** **Translation:** He is an extremely vain man; he's always looking at himself in the ------- .

(A) mirror
(B) glass
(C) glasses
(D) self

Vanidoso is one clue in this one, but that's a pretty tough vocabulary word (add it to your list). You've also got **mirarse** (to look at oneself) later in the sentence to tell you that the best answer is **espejo. Cristal** means plain old glass, as in a window or a bottle, or fine glass.

6. **C** **Translation:** Old people have more ------- than young people because they've had more experiences.

(A) time
(B) to eat
(C) wisdom
(D) appetite

Older people probably have more of everything than young people, but what might they have more of based on experience? Not time, food, or appetite, which leaves you with only (C). We know this is a hard word, but you could have used POE to get this question right without knowing **sabiduría**.

7. **B** **Translation:** It's evident enough that Alejandro likes doing his homework; he always does it ------- .

(A) reluctantly
(B) with enthusiasm
(C) very slowly
(D) without taste

"Likes" implies a positive answer, such as (B). The others are all negative things, and if you could determine that much, you could eliminate them without knowing their precise meanings.

8. **D** **Translation:** Pedro ------- very happy when his child was born.

(A) changed
(B) gave himself
(C) made himself
(D) became

Choices (A) and (B) are really awkward, and although (C) seems like it could work, the verb **ponerse** is generally used to indicate a change of emotions. **Hacerse** is not.

9. **B** **Translation:** I want you to ------- notes about the lecture.

(A) take (simple present)
(B) take (present subjunctive)
(C) used to take (imperfect)
(D) took (preterite)

The phrase that starts the sentence, "Quiero que," tells you that you should use the subjunctive. Choices (C) and (D) both refer to the past, so if you at least know you need to stay in the present tense, then you can eliminate two choices.

CHAPTER 4 DRILLS

Ser vs. *Estar* Drill

1. está
2. está
3. estoy
4. es
5. son
6. estoy
7. son
8. estamos
9. Estuve/Estaba/Estoy

Conocer vs. *Saber* Drill

1. sabe
2. Conoces
3. saben
4. conocen
5. saber
6. sé
7. conozcas (present subjunctive)
8. conocen
9. Sé

Drill 1: Pronouns

1. **B** **Translation:** If he can do it alone, I don't have to help ------- .

   (A) her
   (B) him (direct object)
   (C) him (indirect object)
   (D) them

   Whom do I have to help? **Him**, which is the direct object.

2. **A** **Translation:** We asked for seats near a window, but they gave ------- these.

(A) us
(B) them (indirect object)
(C) ours
(D) me

Pedimos tells you that the subject of the sentence is **nosotros**. Since you are trying to say, "they gave us these," the correct pronoun is **nos**.

3. **B** **Translation:** When her students misbehave, the professor punishes ------- .

(A) them (feminine, direct object)
(B) them (masculine, direct object)
(C) to them (indirect object)
(D) to him (indirect object)

Estudiantes is masculine and plural, so choices (A) and (D) are incorrect. (Remember that in Spanish the masculine pronoun is used whenever the gender of a group is mixed, even if the majority of the group is female. Also, when the gender of the people in the group is unknown [as it is in this question], the male pronoun is used.) Whom does the professor punish? **Them**, which is the direct object; therefore, (B) is the answer.

4. **C** **Translation:** Are those gloves that are on the armchair ------- ?

(A) mine (masculine, singular)
(B) mine (feminine, singular)
(C) mine (masculine, plural)
(D) mine (feminine, plural)

Guantes is a masculine plural word, so the correct form of the possessive adjective is **míos**, which is choice (C).

5. **B** **Translation:** For your birthday, I'll give ------- a new horse.

(A) him (indirect object)
(B) you
(C) to you
(D) me

The person whose birthday it is in the sentence is **tú**, so **te** is the correct indirect object pronoun. It is indirect in this case because it receives the direct object "horse." Choice (C) is incorrect because it is an expression of emphasis that complements an indirect object pronoun. However, there is no indirect object pronoun to complement, so it cannot be right. The indirect object pronoun itself is necessary, so (B) is the best answer.

6. **A** **Translation:** ------- is your favorite singer?

(A) **Who**
(B) Which
(C) Who (plural)
(D) What

Since the question refers to a single person (**el cantante**), **quién** is the correct pronoun.

7. **B** **Translation:** ------- do you prefer? The blue one or the red one?

(A) What
(B) Which
(C) Which (plural)
(D) That one

In this question a choice is being given, so **cuál** is used instead of **qué. Cuáles** is incorrect because the choice is between two singular things.

Drill 2: Verbs

1. **A** **Translation:** When I have money, I ------- you a luxury car.

(A) will buy (future)
(B) bought (past—*yo* form)
(C) would buy (conditional)
(D) bought (past—*tú* form)

The sentence refers to something that will happen in the future, so the correct answer will be in either the future or the conditional tense. In this case, the event is certain (I will buy you a luxury car); therefore, the future (A) is correct.

2. **D** **Translation:** I want you to ------- the homework before going to bed.

(A) did (past—*tú* form)
(B) does (present—*él* form)
(C) do (present subjunctive—*él* form)
(D) do (present subjunctive—*tú* form)

Quiero que is one of those expressions that tells you to use the subjunctive. In this case, the expression is in the present tense, so the present subjunctive is correct. If the expression were in the past (**quería que**), you'd use the imperfect subjunctive. The reason (D) is correct is that **te** is the direct object pronoun in the sentence, so you want the **tú** form of the verb.

3. **C** **Translation:** I don't ------- my friend's mother.

(A) knew (preterite—*él* form)
(B) know (present—*tú* form)
(C) know (present indicative—*yo* form)
(D) know (present subjunctive—*tú* form)

The key to answering this correctly is to look at the subject of the sentence, *I*. Since *I* is the subject, the only choice that works is (C). Even if you don't know that the verb **conocer** means "to know," you can get to the right answer simply by using POE!

4. **D** **Translation:** If they had (were to have) time, they ------- pass the time relaxing.

(A) want to (present)
(B) wanted to (imperfect)
(C) want to (present subjunctive)
(D) would want to (conditional)

Si tuvieran tells you to use the conditional tense (in fact, **si** often precedes use of the conditional because it introduces a condition that doesn't currently exist). The only answer that's in the conditional tense is **querrían** (D).

5. **A** **Translation:** Do you ------- the phone number for the train station?

(A) know (present—*tú* form)
(B) will know (future—*yo* form)
(C) will know (future—*ellos* form)
(D) know (present—*yo* form)

This sentence uses the second-person singular **tú**. Choices (B), (C), and (D) are in the wrong forms and, therefore, not correct. Choice (A) is the correct answer.

6. **D** **Translation:** Carlos ------- much time studying biology lately.

(A) spent (past)
(B) would spend (conditional)
(C) spent (imperfect)
(D) has spent (present perfect)

"Lately" suggests the past tense, but a more recent past tense. Choices (A) and (C) place the action too far in the past, while (B) is not a past tense. Therefore, (D) is the answer.

Drill 3: Prepositions

1. A **Translation:** I want to arrive at the party ------- María.

   (A) before
   (B) before (preceding a verb)
   (C) at
   (D) without

   In the original sentence, you're given **antes** followed by a blank, leaving it up to you to fill in the correct preposition. **Antes** tells you that you're going for "before," so **de** is the correct preposition. Choice (B) (**de que**) is one of those expressions that needs to be followed by a verb (in the subjunctive) because the word **que** always begins a new clause. The others are way off in terms of meaning.

2. B **Translation:** The coffee shop is ------- the library.

   (A) around
   (B) in front of
   (C) underneath
   (D) on

   We can deduce from the sentence that the coffee shop and the library are in some kind of physical relation to each other. Choice (A) does not work grammatically in this sentence, and choices (C) and (D) do not make logical sense. The correct answer is (B).

3. A **Translation:** My school is ------- the bus station.

   (A) far from
   (B) for
   (C) inside of
   (D) on top of

   As in the previous question, this sentence involves a geographical relationship between two places, the school and the bus station. Choice (B), **por**, does not make sense grammatically, and choices (C) and (D) do not make sense logically. Therefore, choice (A) is correct.

4. **D** **Translation:** ------- a little luck, it will not rain on the day of the wedding!

(A) More than
(B) For
(C) For (expressing point of reference)
(D) With

This sentence can be a little tricky, since **por** (B) and **para** (C) are both choices. However, we wouldn't say "For a little luck"; therefore, neither (B) nor (C) is correct. Choice (A) also does not work in this context. Choice (D), "With a little luck," is clear and conveys the correct meaning, so it is the correct answer.

5. **A** **Translation:** Next week they are going ------- play here.

(A) to
(B) of
(C) with
(D) for

This one is nice and easy, no tricks or traps, and it translates straight from English. This is an example of the use of **ir a**. Notice that **ir** is conjugated to agree with the subject of the sentence (**ellos**).

6. **D** **Translation:** I don't like to see horror films ------- the night.

(A) behind
(B) on
(C) in
(D) during

This one is a pretty tough call between (C) and (D) because both sound fine in the blank, but one of them makes a little more sense than the other if you think carefully about the difference in meaning. Do you see films *in* (as in, "inside") the night, or *during* the night? They're sort of close, and the exact English would be "at night," but *during* makes a bit more sense.

7. **C** **Translation:** I am going on an excursion to Italy ------- to be able to learn Italian faster.

(A) for
(B) in
(C) for (destination)
(D) to

Here we have **para** versus **por** again! In this case, the sentence states a clear purpose. Thus, choices (A) and (B) do not work. Choice (D) means "to," but the the sentence states that someone is going on a trip to Italy for a specific reason. We have to use **para**, which is choice (C).

CHAPTER 5 DRILLS

Drill 1: Paragraph Completion

Paragraph Translation:

It seemed that last April 6 everything (1) was ready for the (2) takeoff of the shuttle *Discovery*, whose mission was to conduct atmospheric investigations and solar studies, but a last-minute (3) difficulty forced the National Aeronautics and Space Administration (NASA) to abort for the (4) second time the launching of the ship.

The shutdown of the motor occurred (5) seconds before the three principal engines of the ship, fed by hydrogen, were activated at 2:32 in the morning last April 6, some 6.6 seconds before takeoff.

1. **A** (A) was
   (B) is (present subjunctive)
   (C) would be
   (D) is (present)

   The first sentence of the first paragraph mentions "el pasado 6 de abril" just before we get to our first blank, so we know that we want the past tense of **estar**. If you can recognize that choice (A) is the only one in the past tense (the imperfect, to be precise), then your work is done. Eliminate choices (B), (C), and (D), which use the present subjunctive, the conditional, and the simple present tense, respectively.

   If you had trouble determining whether the event was in the past, present, or future, don't forget to look forward—the word **obligó** later in the sentence tells you that it's in the past. There are always clues in the passage that help you fill in the blanks, but it's up to you to find them.

2. **B** (A) unemployment
   (B) takeoff
   (C) disadvantage
   (D) rest

   After a quick glance at the choices, you might realize that you don't know most of the words. If so, this is probably a question for the second or third pass.

   When you come back to it, you will want to first see what can you figure out from the context. Before the blank, we see the phrase "listo para" (ready for), and after the blank, we see "del transbordador *Discovery*." If you don't know what **transbordador** means, you might recognize that *Discovery* is a space shuttle. Putting the pieces of the puzzle together, you might come up with something like "launch" for the blank.

Let's say you know that (D) **descanso** means "rest." Does that agree with the word which you selected? No. Not sure what any of the other words mean? See if you can break down any of them to help you make an educated guess. You might be familiar with the word **ventaja**, which means advantage; therefore, you might deduce that (C) **desventaja** means disadvantage, which is the correct definition. Does that work for the blank? No. Eliminate it. Similarly, we can get rid of (A) **desempleo** (unemployment). The best answer is (B) **despegue** (takeoff).

3. **D** (A) business
(B) witness
(C) portrait
(D) difficulty

Abortar, which means the same thing in English as it does in Spanish (to abort), tells you that something went wrong with the launch, so you want a negative word for the blank. This leaves you with only choice (D). In addition, and even more simply, the word **una** tells us that we need a feminine word. Only (D) is feminine.

4. C (A) new
(B) tremendous
(C) second
(D) two

It's easiest to think of this blank as part of the larger phrase **abortar por…vez consecutiva**. In this context, only (C) **segunda** (second) makes any sense in the blank.

5. C (A) years
(B) days
(C) seconds
(D) places

If you think about the situation described in the passage, and read ahead in the last paragraph, you realize that the period of time you're looking for is very brief. Also, there is a clue earlier in the passage that helps you out on this question. **De última hora**, which appears in the first sentence, means "at the last moment." Choice (C) is the correct answer.

Drill 2: Paragraph Completion

Paragraph Translation:

Rosa's quinceañera (1) was an unforgettable day. All her (2) relatives came, including her great-grandmother, who Rosa had never (3) met before. The ceremony began, traditionally, with the mass to say thanks. Rosa wore a long, pink dress. She looked so elegant that even her father (4) cried a little when he saw her. After the ceremony, everyone met (5) at her house for a big party. Rosa began the dancing with her father, and then continued it with her uncles and cousins. At the end of the night, her father took a glass and (6) toasted his beloved daughter.

1. A **(A) was (preterite)**
 (B) was (imperfect subjunctive)
 (C) is (present subjunctive)
 (D) would be

 The quinceañera already took place. There is a clue in the second sentence: **vinieron**, which is in the preterite (simple past) tense. Therefore, (A) is correct.

2. B (A) windshield
 (B) relatives
 (C) paradises
 (D) umbrella

 Here you're presented with a group of choices that look similar. Know your definitions. The passage mentions **bisabuela**, which means great-grandmother. Choice (B) is the only one that makes any sense.

3. C (A) meet (present)
 (B) meet (present subjunctive)
 (C) met (past participle)
 (D) met (preterite)

 A key word here is **antes**. This tells us that we need a form of the verb in the past. Additionally, the auxiliary verb **había** (a form of **haber**) tells us we need a past participle to complete the past perfect. Choice (C) is the only one that works.

4. A **(A) cried**
 (B) called
 (C) rained
 (D) arrived

 What makes sense that her father might do after seeing Rosa in her lovely dress? He'd shed a tear. Even fathers cry. Thus, choice (A) is correct, as none of the other choices makes any sense.

5. C (A) with
(B) for
(C) **at**
(D) for

This answer is idiomatic. They met **at** her house.

6. A (A) **toasted**
(B) denied
(C) amazed
(D) guarded

A clue is that the father picked up a glass. Choice (A) is the only logical option. There are some tough words in these answer choices. Be sure to add any unfamiliar vocabulary to your list of words to know.

CHAPTER 6 DRILLS

Drill 1: Reading Comprehension

Passage:

En nuestra oficina regía el mismo presupuesto desde el año mil novecientos veintitantos, o sea desde una época en que la mayoría de nosotros estábamos luchando con la geografía y con los quebrados. Sin embargo, el Jefe se acordaba del acontecimiento y a veces, cuando el trabajo disminuía, se sentaba familiarmente sobre uno de nuestros escritorios, y así, con las piernas colgantes que mostraban después del pantalón unos inmaculados calcetines blancos, nos relataba con la misma emoción de antes y las quinientas noventa y ocho palabras de costumbre, el lejano y magnífico día en que su jefe —él era entonces oficial primero— le había palmeado el hombro y le había dicho: "Muchacho, tenemos presupuesto nuevo," con la sonrisa amplia y satisfecha del que ya ha calculado cuántas camisas podrá comprar con el aumento.

Translation:

In our office, the same budget was in force since the 1920s, that is, since a time in which the majority of us were struggling with geography and fractions. The boss, however, remembered the event, and at times, when the work diminished, he would sit down familiarly on one of our desks, and there, with his legs dangling, and immaculate white socks showing below his trousers, he would tell us, with all his old feeling and with his usual five hundred and ninety-eight words, of that distant and splendid day when his boss—he was head clerk then—had patted him on the shoulder and had said, "My boy, we have a new budget," with the broad and satisfied smile of a man who has already worked out how many new shirts he will be able to buy with the increase.

1. **A** **Translation:** For how long, more or less, have they had the same budget?

(A) **For many decades**
(B) For many centuries
(C) For a few weeks
(D) Since yesterday

There are a few choices—namely, (B), (C), and (D)—that are pretty silly in the context of the story, but this is more apparent as you read further into the passage. If you didn't get **novecientos veintitantos**, then you should have read on. There are lots of clues later on that give you the time frame of the budget.

2. **C** **Translation:** The boss told his story when

(A) he was sad
(B) he had drunk too much beer
(C) **the work was less than usual**
(D) they had a party

Disminuía means decreased or diminished. **Jefe** is one guide word on this question, and **cuento** is sort of another, although **acontecimiento** is the actual word in the passage.

3. **D** **Translation:** The story of the new budget that the boss told

(A) had white socks
(B) was always different
(C) was interesting
(D) **was always the same**

Palabras de costumbre (usual words) is the key to this one.

4. **B** **Translation:** What was the boss's reaction when his boss told him about the new budget?

(A) He left the company.
(B) **He became very happy.**
(C) He gave his boss a hug.
(D) He bought new shirts.

Choice (D) is a pretty nasty trap, but if you read carefully you could have avoided it.

Drill 2: Reading Comprehension

Passage:

Como haces falta, Basilio . . . Me gustaría tanto que estuvieras presente, con los ojos abiertos, a ver lo que ha pasado con tu casa. Se está desmoronando, como si la hubieras levantado con ladrillos mal cocidos; se han quebrado las tejas, permitiendo al sol y la lluvia entrar en todas partes; a las paredes ya no les caben las cuarteaduras. Y los hijos —¡qué te puedo contar de nuestros hijos!

Manuel estuvo aquí, hace unos días, verdaderamente desesperado por las deudas. A él no le pudiste quitar los vicios. Y de ser el que más tenía, se ha quedado sin nada. Me contaron que hasta su mujer y sus hijos lo corrieron.

No he visto a Néstor durante mucho tiempo. Te confieso que ya casi no veo nada. Pero creo que él está en los Estados Unidos. Como tú no les enseñaste a trabajar, aquí no pudieron hacer nada, por eso se fueron a buscar entre los mendrugos de otra patria, el pan para sus hijos.

Allá tambíen está José.

Translation:

How you are missed, Basilio...I would like it so much if you were here, with your eyes open, to see what has happened with your house. It is falling to pieces, as if you had built it with badly baked bricks; the tiles have broken, allowing the sun and the rain to enter everywhere; there's no more room for cracks on the walls. And the children—what I can tell you about our children!

Manuel was here a few days ago, truly exasperated by his debts. You could not rid him of his vices. And for being the one who had the most, he's ended up with nothing. They tell me that even his wife and children chased him away.

I haven't seen Néstor for a long time. I confess that now I see almost nothing. But I think that he is in the United States. As you didn't teach them to work, here they couldn't do anything, so they left to search for bread for their children among the crusts of stale bread of another country.

José is there too.

1. **C** **Translation:** What has happened during Basilio's absence?

(A) He has been told of his children.
(B) He has baked the bricks.
(C) His house has started to fall apart.
(D) He has gone to another country.

The passage says that Basilio's house **Se está desmoronando**—it's falling apart, so (C) is the answer. Choice (A) is incorrect because it is what the narrator is doing. We cannot assume either (B) or (D) because there is not enough information to support these answers.

2. **A** **Translation:** Who is Basilio?

(A) **The husband of the narrator**
(B) The son of the narrator
(C) The narrator
(D) The man with the debts

The narrator is talking to Basilio—(C) is out—and refers to **nuestros hijos**, which eliminates (B), so (A) is logical. The man referred to in (D) is Manuel, not Basilio.

3. **D** **Translation:** What is Manuel's problem?

(A) He can't see very well.
(B) He has gotten rid of his vices.
(C) His wife had a baby.
(D) He owes people a lot of money.

Manuel is **desesperado por las deudas**, so (D) is the proper response. Choice (B) is incorrect because it is a misreading of the passage, which says just the opposite. Choice (A) is true of the narrator and (C) simply doesn't happen.

4. **C** **Translation:** Where is Néstor?

(A) Visiting the narrator
(B) With the stale crusts of bread
(C) In another country
(D) Baking bread for his children

The passage says that **se fueron a...otra patria**, so (C) is the correct answer. The narrator complains that (A) has not happened, and (B) and (D) are silly answers.

5. **B** **Translation:** Who has had success in the past and lost it?

(A) Basilio
(B) Manuel
(C) José
(D) Néstor

This is hidden within some tricky wording—**el que más tenía, se ha quedado sin nada**—thus (B) is correct. There is not enough information about Basilio to assume that he was successful, so (A) is out, and José and Néstor have left because they couldn't find success in their own country. Therefore, (C) and (D) are incorrect as well.

6. **B** **Translation:** What could we assume about José?

(A) He doesn't like the narrator.

(B) He didn't have anything in his own country.

(C) He taught Néstor how to work.

(D) His wife and children abandoned him.

The passage ends by telling us that José went to the United States also, just like Néstor, but says nothing else. As such, (A), (C), and (D) are way too specific to be correct, and can therefore be eliminated. This leaves (B) as the proper response—it offers a plausible reason for leaving home and going to the United States.

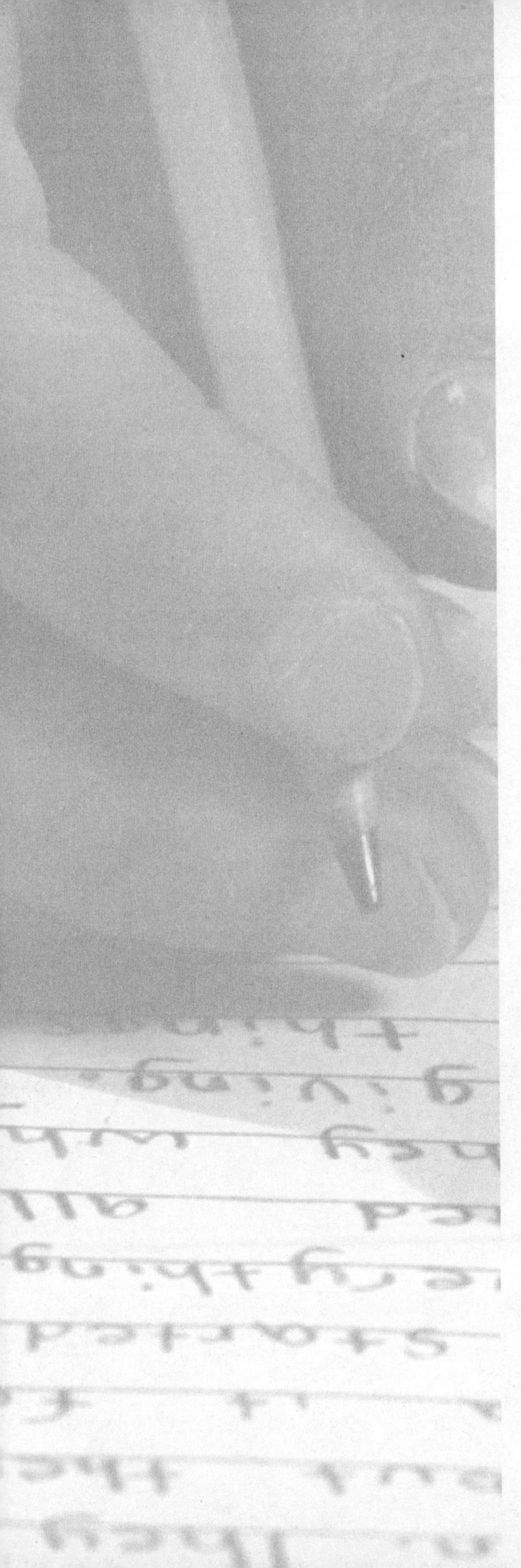

Part IV
Practice Tests

Chapter 7
Practice Test 1

SPANISH SUBJECT TEST 1

Your responses to Spanish Subject Test 1 questions must be filled in on Test 1 of your answer sheet (at the back of the book). Marks on any other section will not be counted toward your Spanish Subject Test score.

When your supervisor gives the signal, turn the page and begin the Spanish Subject Test.

SPANISH SUBJECT TEST

PLEASE NOTE THAT YOUR ANSWER SHEET HAS FIVE ANSWER POSITIONS MARKED A, B, C, D, E, WHILE THE QUESTIONS THROUGHOUT THIS TEST CONTAIN ONLY FOUR CHOICES. BE SURE NOT TO MAKE ANY MARKS IN COLUMN E.

Part A

Directions: This part consists of a number of incomplete statements, each having four suggested completions. Select the most appropriate completion and fill in the corresponding oval on the answer sheet.

1. Si quieres ver el principio de la película, llega al teatro ------- .

   (A) más tarde
   (B) sin dinero
   (C) a tiempo
   (D) por la noche

2. Cuando vivía en Nueva York, ------- mucho tiempo escuchando conciertos y visitando los museos.

   (A) pasaba
   (B) pasé
   (C) he pasado
   (D) pasaré

3. Mi abuelo quiere vivir en un sitio bien tranquilo, porque no le gusta el ruido. Por eso se ha mudado ------- .

   (A) a una calle muy ruidosa
   (B) fuera de la ciudad
   (C) al centro del mundo
   (D) sin querer

4. ¿ ------- museo prefieres, el de ciencia o el de arte?

   (A) Cuál
   (B) Qué
   (C) Cuánto
   (D) Quién

5. ¿Qué ------- cuando me llamaste al móvil esta tarde?

   (A) quisieras
   (B) querrían
   (C) querías
   (D) quieres

6. No lo conozco muy bien, pero la gente dice que ------- un tipo muy sincero e inteligente.

   (A) estamos
   (B) son
   (C) está
   (D) es

7. La invención del teléfono por Alexander Graham Bell en 1876 ------- como la gente se comunica.

   (A) cambia
   (B) cambió
   (C) cambiaron
   (D) cambias

8. Vamos a tomar el viaje en dos días en vez de uno, porque nuestro destino está muy ------- aquí.

   (A) cerca de
   (B) lejos de
   (C) junto a
   (D) en frente de

9. Mi hermano nació tres años antes que yo; por eso es ------- .

   (A) mayor
   (B) más alto
   (C) mi hermano favorito
   (D) muy aburrido

10. Si no te gusta la ley, ¿por qué ------- los últimos cuatro años trabajando como abogado?

    (A) pasas
    (B) has pasado
    (C) pasarías
    (D) pasarás

GO ON TO THE NEXT PAGE

SPANISH SUBJECT TEST–*Continued*

11. En la biblioteca se encuentran ------- .

    (A) plumas
    (B) esperanzas
    (C) preguntas
    (D) libros

12. La bandera que ondea sobre el estadio es ------- .

    (A) nuestro
    (B) nuestras
    (C) nuestra
    (D) mío

13. La sopa caliente me dio dolor de muelas. Necesito ------- .

    (A) una silla
    (B) una mesa
    (C) un dentista
    (D) un tornillo

14. La receta que Marta le dio a Verónica era difícil de leer por que ------- .

    (A) es grande
    (B) es linda
    (C) estaba borrada
    (D) estaba limpia

15. Para ir a México el ------- más rapido es este.

    (A) camino
    (B) cielo
    (C) paseo
    (D) suelo

16. Ayer tenía mucho dolor de espalda, pero hoy no ------- ninguno.

    (A) tienen
    (B) tenemos
    (C) tienes
    (D) tengo

17. La copa mundial de futbol es un ------- .

    (A) evento para espectadores
    (B) deporte local
    (C) evento nacional
    (D) partido

18. García es nuestro cliente más estimado; siempre ------- damos a él lo que quiera.

    (A) la
    (B) le
    (C) lo
    (D) les

19. Alberto se sienta y pide arroz con pollo y una copa de vino. El está en ------- .

    (A) un restaurante
    (B) un circo
    (C) un banco
    (D) una zapatería

20. ¿ ------- cuándo han estudiado la historia española?

    (A) Hasta
    (B) Durante
    (C) Desde
    (D) En

21. Este otoño que viene, ------- todos juntos a mi casa en las montanas.

    (A) vamos
    (B) vayan
    (C) voy
    (D) iremos

22. Mi tío sabe cocinar los frijoles negros bastante ------- .

    (A) bien
    (B) bueno
    (C) buenos
    (D) baños

23. El concierto que vimos anoche fue estupendo. ¡Esa ------- de verdad sabe tocar!

    (A) partido
    (B) novela
    (C) comida
    (D) orquesta

GO ON TO THE NEXT PAGE

24. Tengo miedo de que la tormenta ------- durante la boda que vamos a tener en el patio.

(A) llegue
(B) llega
(C) llegaría
(D) llegara

25. Carlos es un muchacho muy pesado que siempre está metido en algún lío. No es milagro que todo el mundo lo ------- .

(A) quiera
(B) rechace
(C) ayude
(D) conozca

26. Los libros de la biblioteca no están en buenas condiciones. La biblioteca no tiene los ------- para comprar nuevos libros.

(A) dinero
(B) fondos
(C) espacio
(D) estudiantes

27. Después de dos años de investigaciones, el médico por fin ------- la causa de la enfermedad.

(A) descubrió
(B) dirigió
(C) abrió
(D) buscó

28. Jamás hemos bailado la samba, pero sí ------- bailar la lambada.

(A) conocemos
(B) conozca
(C) sabrán
(D) sabemos

29. Se dice que José Martí, el famoso autor cubano, empezó a escribir ------- cuando tenía solamente seis años.

(A) lápices
(B) alfabetos
(C) idiomas
(D) poemas

GO ON TO THE NEXT PAGE

Part B

Directions: In each of the following passages, there are numbered blanks indicating that words or phrases have been omitted. For each numbered blank, four completions are provided. First read through the entire paragraph. Then, for each numbered blank, choose the completion that is most appropriate given the context of the entire paragraph and fill in the corresponding oval on the answer sheet.

Emma dejó caer el papel. Su primera (30) fue de malestar en el vientre y en las rodillas; luego, de ciega culpa, de irrealidad, de frío, de (31) ; luego, quiso ya (32) en el día siguiente. Acto seguido comprendió que ese deseo era inútil porque (33) muerte de su padre era lo único que (34) en el mundo, y (35) sucediendo sin fin. Recogió el papel y se fue a su cuarto. Furtivamente lo (36) en un cajón, como si de algún modo ya (37) los hechos ulteriores.

30. (A) tiempo
    (B) vista
    (C) puesto
    (D) impresión

31. (A) juventud
    (B) temor
    (C) alegría
    (D) hambre

32. (A) estar
    (B) ser
    (C) estaré
    (D) ir

33. (A) lo
    (B) el
    (C) la
    (D) las

34. (A) entraba
    (B) crecía
    (C) había terminado
    (D) había sucedido

35. (A) seguiría
    (B) pararía
    (C) cambiaría
    (D) sentiría

36. (A) sacó
    (B) guardó
    (C) encontró
    (D) quitó

37. (A) sabe
    (B) sabía
    (C) supiera
    (D) sabría

GO ON TO THE NEXT PAGE

SPANISH SUBJECT TEST–*Continued*

Después (38) haber mandado dos expediciones a explorar la costa de México, el gobernador de Cuba (39) otra expedición bajo el mando de Hernán Cortés en 1519. En las tres expediciones (40) parte un soldado que se (41) Bernal Díaz del Castillo. (42) soldado, cuando ya era casi un viejo y (43) retirado en Guatemala, (44) sus recuerdos de las guerras mexicanas, que forman la mejor narración (45) la conquista de México y que se titula "Historia verdadera de la conquista de la Nueva España."

La expedición de Cortés constaba de once navíos que (46) poco más de seiscientos hombres y dieciséis (47) . Cuando Cortés estaba listo (48) salir, el gobernador trató de quitarle el mando, pero él decidió hacerse a la mar.

38. (A) que
    (B) de
    (C) a
    (D) por

39. (A) puso fin a
    (B) ensayó
    (C) preguntó
    (D) organizó

40. (A) hizo
    (B) dio
    (C) dejó
    (D) tomó

41. (A) llamó
    (B) llama
    (C) llamaba
    (D) había llamado

42. (A) Este
    (B) Esa
    (C) Un
    (D) La

43. (A) paraba
    (B) pensaba
    (C) oía
    (D) vivía

44. (A) escribió
    (B) corrió
    (C) perdió
    (D) pidió

45. (A) encima de
    (B) junto a
    (C) sobre
    (D) en vez de

46. (A) llevaba
    (B) llevaron
    (C) llevaban
    (D) llevan

47. (A) automóviles
    (B) aviones
    (C) caballos
    (D) guantes

48. (A) por
    (B) para
    (C) en
    (D) de

GO ON TO THE NEXT PAGE

Pero hoy, en esta mañana fría, en que tenemos más prisa que nunca, la niña y yo __(49)__ de largo delante de la fila tentadora de autos parados. Por __(50)__ vez en la vida vamos al colegio . . . Al colegio, le digo, no __(51)__ ir en taxi. Hay que correr un poco por las calles, hay que tomar el metro, hay que __(52)__ luego, a un sitio determinado, para un autobús . . . Es que yo he escogido un colegio muy __(53)__ para mi niña, esa es la verdad; un colegio que __(54)__ mucho, pero está muy lejos . . . Sin embargo, yo no estoy impaciente hoy, ni __(55)__, y la niña lo sabe. Es ella ahora la que inicia una caricia tímida con su manita __(56)__ la mía; y por primera vez me doy cuenta de que su mano de cuatro años es __(57)__ mi mano grande: tan decidida, tan suave, tan nerviosa como la mía.

49. (A) pasamos
    (B) entramos
    (C) dábamos
    (D) pagamos

50. (A) ninguna
    (B) primera
    (C) siempre
    (D) costumbre

51. (A) se engaña
    (B) conocemos
    (C) se puede
    (D) sobran

52. (A) dormir
    (B) tocar
    (C) jugar
    (D) caminar

53. (A) cerrado
    (B) lejano
    (C) oscuro
    (D) difícil

54. (A) me gusta
    (B) odio
    (C) no conozco
    (D) dudamos

55. (A) vieja
    (B) alta
    (C) cansada
    (D) fresca

56. (A) dentro de
    (B) fuera de
    (C) cerca de
    (D) sin

57. (A) diferente a
    (B) igual a
    (C) cerca de
    (D) encima de

GO ON TO THE NEXT PAGE

Part C

Directions: Read the following texts carefully for comprehension. Each passage is followed by a number of questions or incomplete statements. Select the answer or completion that is best according to the text and fill in the corresponding oval on the answer sheet.

Al pasar ante una granja, un perro mordió a mi amigo. Entramos a ver al granjero y le preguntamos si era suyo el perro. El granjero, para evitarse complicaciones, dijo que no era suyo.

—Entonces —dijo mi amigo— présteme una hoz para cortarle la cabeza, pues debo llevarla al Instituto para que la analicen.

En aquel momento apareció la hija del granjero y le pidió a su padre que no permitiera que le cortáramos la cabeza al perro.

—Si es suyo el perro —dijo mi amigo— enséñeme el certificado de vacunación antirrábica.

El hombre entró en la granja, y tardó largo rato en salir. Mientras tanto, el perro se acercó y mi amigo dijo:

—No me gusta el aspecto de este animal.

En efecto, babeaba y los ojos parecían arderle en las órbitas. Incluso andaba dificultosamente.

—Hace unos días —dijo la joven— le atropelló una bicicleta.

El granjero nos dijo que no encontraba el certificado de vacunación.

—Debo haberlo perdido.

—La vida de un hombre puede estar en juego —intervine yo. Díganos, con toda sinceridad, si el perro está vacunado o no.

El hombre bajó la cabeza y murmuró:

—Está sano.

58. ¿Qué les pasó a los tipos cuando pasaron por la granja?
    (A) A uno de ellos lo mordió un perro.
    (B) Un granjero les pidió direcciones
    (C) Se evitaron complicaciones.
    (D) Perdieron su perro.

59. ¿Por qué el granjero les dijo que el perro no era suyo?
    (A) No sabía de quien era el perro.
    (B) No conocía a los tipos que vinieron a la puerta.
    (C) No quería echarse la culpa de lo que había hecho el perro.
    (D) No le gustaban los perros.

60. ¿Qué le pidió su hija al granjero?
    (A) Que sacara el perro a caminar
    (B) Que llevara el perro al médico
    (C) Que le diera comida al perro
    (D) Que no dejara que los hombres hirieran al perro

61. ¿Qué le pidieron los tipos al granjero?
    (A) Dinero para pagar un médico
    (B) El certificado de vacunación antirrábica
    (C) Un teléfono para llamar a la policía
    (D) Prueba de que verdaderamente era granjero

62. ¿Cómo parecía el perro del granjero?
    (A) Sano y de buen humor
    (B) Enfermo, como si tuviera rabia
    (C) Joven y lleno de energía
    (D) Serio y pensativo

63. ¿Qué razón dio la niña por la manera en que el perro se portaba?
    (A) Tuvo un accidente con una bicicleta.
    (B) Acaba de recibir su vacuna antirrábica.
    (C) Es un perro muy feroz.
    (D) Tenía mucha hambre.

64. En fin, ¿qué les dice el granjero a los tipos?
    (A) Que vayan al hospital
    (B) Que adopten un perro
    (C) Que se vayan de la granja ahora mismo
    (D) Que el perro no tiene ninguna enfermedad

GO ON TO THE NEXT PAGE

Hotel Marybel

Mendoza * Córdoba * Buenos Aires

¡Especiales del mes para todos! ¡Reserven con dos semanas de anticipación y reciban un descuento de 10%! Llamen al 239-7155—24 horas al día, 7 días a la semana.

Dirección de Internet: www.hotalmarybel.ar

Aire acondicionado en todos los cuartos, cafetería, bar, conexión de Internet gratis en los cuartos. No se pierdan esta oferta. Oferta vence a fin de mes.

65. ¿Este anuncio es para qué tipo de servicio?
    (A) Un hotel
    (B) Una cadena de hoteles
    (C) Una tienda
    (D) Un aviso de servicios gratis

66. ¿Cuánto dura esta oferta?
    (A) Un día
    (B) Un mes
    (C) Un año
    (D) Dos semanas

67. ¿Qué tiene que hacer el cliente para recibir un descuento?
    (A) Reservar dos semanas antes de llegar
    (B) Reservar por dos semanas
    (C) Reservar con un mes de anticipación
    (D) Reservar con una semana de anticipación

68. ¿Cuál de los siguientes servicios ofrece el hotel?
    (A) Aire acondicionado solamente en los cuartos grandes
    (B) Piscina de natación
    (C) Internet en el bar
    (D) Un lugar para comer

GO ON TO THE NEXT PAGE

Para los arqueólogos y los historiadores, la civilización maya es, sin duda ninguna, la que alcanzó un mayor nivel de desarrollo entre todas las civilizaciones que existían antes de la llegada de Colón. Aunque todavía hay muchos secretos que no se han descifrado con relación a los mayas, parece que esta civilización empezó varios siglos antes del nacimiento de Cristo. Sin embargo, se sabe que los mayas abandonaron los grandes centros ceremoniales en el siglo X de nuestra era.

Los primeros templos que construyeron son de forma de pirámide de cuatro lados con una gran escalinata. Sobre la pirámide hay un edificio de un piso normalmente, y en algunos casos de dos, y en él podemos ver relieves de arcilla y esculturas de madera y piedra caliza. Las figuras son siempre de perfil y en ellas se puede apreciar los adornos y joyas que usaban. En la clasificación que se ha hecho de las épocas de esta civilización, se llama preclásica a la época primera, que se desarrolla en Guatemala y Honduras, y que según los arqueólogos duró hasta el fin del siglo III de nuestra era.

69. ¿Qué piensan los arqueólogos y los historiadores de la civilización maya?
    (A) Que era una civilización muy avanzada.
    (B) Que los maya escribieron libros magníficos.
    (C) Que conocieron a Colón.
    (D) Que tenían muchos secretos.

70. ¿Cuándo empezó la civilización maya?
    (A) En el siglo X de nuestra era
    (B) Inmediatamente antes de la llegada de Colón
    (C) Bastante más temprano que el nacimiento de Cristo
    (D) Varios siglos después del nacimiento de Cristo

71. ¿Cómo parecían los primeros templos de los mayas?
    (A) Eran edificios muy bajos.
    (B) Eran hechos de madera y piedra caliza.
    (C) Eran pirámides de cuatro lados.
    (D) Eran casas corrientes, como las que tenemos hoy.

72. ¿Qué se puede decir de las esculturas que hicieron los mayas?
    (A) Tenían escalinatas grandes.
    (B) Dan información sobre las joyas y adornos que usaban.
    (C) Cuesta mucho comprarlas.
    (D) Se puede encontrarlas en los museos famosos.

73. ¿Aproximadamente cuanto tiempo pasó desde que terminó la era preclásica hasta que los mayas abandonaron sus centros ceremoniales?
    (A) Cien años
    (B) Tres siglos
    (C) Siete siglos
    (D) Diez siglos

74. El pasaje se trata de
    (A) la civilización y arquitectura maya
    (B) la influencia de Cristo sobre la civilización maya
    (C) las diferencias entre nuestra civilización y la de los mayas
    (D) los adornos y las joyas que usaban los mayas

GO ON TO THE NEXT PAGE

En 1992, se cumplieron cinco siglos ya del encuentro de Europa con América. Fue poco después de la medianoche del 11 al 12 de octubre de 1492, cuando Rodrigo de Triana, un tripulante de la carabela *La Niña*, la cual se había adelantado a *La Santa María*, donde iba Colón, dio el grito de "¡Tierra! ¡Tierra!" El lugar estaba muy cercano a la Florida, era una pequeña isla llamada Guanahaní que Colón llamó San Salvador y que pertenece al archipiélago de las Lucayas, o Bahamas.

Lo que Colón encontró y describe en sus cartas a los Reyes Católicos fue mucha pobreza y gente que iba desnuda, como su madre los parió, todos jóvenes, con hermosos cuerpos, cabellos gruesos como los de los caballos y cortos, que les caían por encima de las cejas y otros largos por detrás.

Pocos días después, descubrió la costa de Cuba, que llamó Juana, por la hija de los reyes. Por entonces, Martín Alonso Pinzón, que mandaba *La Pinta*, se separó de la expedición, lo cual consideró Colón como una deserción, aunque lo disimuló por mantener la unidad de la expedición. Al cabo de unos días llegó a Haití, que llamó la Hispaniola, pero debido a los muchos bajos y arrecifes que había, *La Santa María* encalló.

75. ¿Quién fue el primero que vio tierra en la expedición?
    (A) Un tripulante que se llamaba Rodrigo de Triana
    (B) Colón
    (C) *La Niña*
    (D) Guanahaní, el mejor amigo de Colón

76. ¿Cómo era la gente que Colón encontró?
    (A) Muy pobre, pero también hermosa
    (B) Violenta y agresiva
    (C) Más inteligente que los tripulantes
    (D) Muy miedosa y confundida

77. ¿Qué descubrió Colón unos días después de que descubrió San Salvador?
    (A) El archipiélago de las Bahamas
    (B) La isla que hoy se llama Cuba
    (C) Haití
    (D) Cabellos gruesos

78. ¿Cuál fue la reacción de Colón cuando Martín Alonso Pinzón se separó de la expedición?
    (A) Se puso furioso.
    (B) Empezó a llorar.
    (C) Dio la impresión de que no sabía lo que había pasado.
    (D) Mandó otra carabela tras él.

79. ¿Cómo terminó *La Santa María*?
    (A) Regresó a España.
    (B) Se perdió y nunca la han encontrado.
    (C) Se hundió.
    (D) Embarrancó como resultado de los bajos y arrecifes.

GO ON TO THE NEXT PAGE

SPANISH SUBJECT TEST–*Continued*

Si no fuera por el gusto exigente de los bebedores de café de Arabia Saudita, el pueblo guatemalteco de Cobán, al otro lado del mundo, estaría en problemas.

Cobán, capital de la región montañosa de Alta Verapaz, en Guatemala, es la fuente de la mayor parte del cardamomo que consume el mundo árabe: una especia dulce, picante y sumamente aromática que se emplea en la cocina de la India. De hecho, el café de cardamomo, conocido en el mundo árabe como *kahwe hal*, es considerado un símbolo de hospitalidad en todo el Medio Oriente.

En Cobán, famoso por su iglesia católica del siglo XVI y las ruinas mayas que se encuentran en los alrededores, prácticamente nadie habla árabe y ninguno de sus 125.000 habitantes pone cardamomo en el café. Sin embargo, todos conocen perfectamente la conexión que existe entre la especia y el mundo árabe. "El cardamomo es la base de nuestra economía, y Guatemala es el principal exportador del mundo."

80. ¿En qué país en particular toman el café de cardamomo?

(A) En Guatemala
(B) En Arabia Saudita
(C) En la Alta Verapaz
(D) En el Medio Oriente

81. ¿Qué es el cardamomo?

(A) Un tipo de café raro
(B) Una especia
(C) Un estilo de cocinar indio
(D) Un tipo de árbol

82. ¿Cómo sabe el cardamomo?

(A) Picante, pero también dulce
(B) Un poco amargo
(C) Casi no tiene sabor
(D) Sabe como el café colombiano

83. ¿Por qué es conocida la ciudad de Cobán?

(A) Por el cardamomo
(B) Por el mejor café en América del Norte
(C) Por sus ruinas, y por su iglesia del siglo XVI
(D) Por la comida india

84. ¿Cuál es la conexión entre el mundo árabe y Guatemala?

(A) En Guatemala todos hablan árabe.
(B) En los dos lugares les encanta el café de cardamomo.
(C) Guatemala exporta mucha especia al mundo árabe.
(D) De verdad no hay conexión entre los dos lugares.

85. ¿Cuál sería un buen título para el pasaje?

(A) "Cobán: la ciudad en las montañas"
(B) "La economía de Guatemala"
(C) "Los cafés del mundo"
(D) "Cardamomo: lo que une a Guatemala con el mundo árabe"

STOP

If you finish before time is called, you may check your work on this test only. Do not work on any other test in this book.

Chapter 8
Practice Test 1: Answers and Explanations

- Practice Test 1 Answer Key
- Practice Test 1 Explanations
- How to Score Practice Test 1

PRACTICE TEST 1 ANSWER KEY

Question Number	Correct Answer	Right	Wrong	Question Number	Correct Answer	Right	Wrong	Question Number	Correct Answer	Right	Wrong
1	C	____	____	33	C	____	____	65	B	____	____
2	A	____	____	34	D	____	____	66	B	____	____
3	B	____	____	35	A	____	____	67	A	____	____
4	A	____	____	36	B	____	____	68	D	____	____
5	C	____	____	37	C	____	____	69	A	____	____
6	D	____	____	38	B	____	____	70	C	____	____
7	B	____	____	39	D	____	____	71	C	____	____
8	B	____	____	40	D	____	____	72	B	____	____
9	A	____	____	41	C	____	____	73	C	____	____
10	B	____	____	42	A	____	____	74	A	____	____
11	D	____	____	43	D	____	____	75	A	____	____
12	C	____	____	44	A	____	____	76	A	____	____
13	C	____	____	45	C	____	____	77	B	____	____
14	C	____	____	46	C	____	____	78	C	____	____
15	A	____	____	47	C	____	____	79	D	____	____
16	D	____	____	48	B	____	____	80	B	____	____
17	A	____	____	49	A	____	____	81	B	____	____
18	B	____	____	50	B	____	____	82	A	____	____
19	A	____	____	51	C	____	____	83	C	____	____
20	C	____	____	52	D	____	____	84	C	____	____
21	D	____	____	53	B	____	____	85	D	____	____
22	A	____	____	54	A	____	____				
23	D	____	____	55	C	____	____				
24	A	____	____	56	A	____	____				
25	B	____	____	57	B	____	____				
26	B	____	____	58	A	____	____				
27	A	____	____	59	C	____	____				
28	D	____	____	60	D	____	____				
29	D	____	____	61	B	____	____				
30	D	____	____	62	B	____	____				
31	B	____	____	63	A	____	____				
32	A	____	____	64	D	____	____				

PRACTICE TEST 1 EXPLANATIONS

Part A

1. **C** **Translation:** If you want to see the beginning of the film, arrive at the theater ------- .

   (A) later
   (B) without money
   (C) on time
   (D) at night

   The key phrase in this sentence is **si quieres ver el principio.** If you were able to get this much, you could determine that time had something to do with the answer, and that would eliminate (B) and (D). What would make more sense in terms of seeing the beginning of something: arriving later or arriving on time? On time makes more sense, and (C) is the correct answer.

2. **A** **Translation:** When I lived in New York, I ------- a lot of time listening to concerts and visiting the museums.

   (A) spent (imperfect)
   (B) spent
   (C) have spent
   (D) will spend

   Because the sentence refers to the past, the answer must be some kind of past tense, and because **pasaré** is the future, you can immediately scratch (D). The other three choices are all past tenses, but since the action described was an ongoing one during the time the person lived in New York, the answer must be in the imperfect tense, which is (A).

3. **B** **Translation:** My grandfather wants to live in a peaceful place because he doesn't like noise. That's why he's moved ------- .

   (A) to a noisy street
   (B) outside of the city
   (C) to the center of the earth
   (D) unintentionally

   If you understood either the part about not liking noise or the part about wanting to live peacefully you could eliminate (A). Choices (C) and (D) are sort of ridiculous, and so (B) is your best bet.

4. **A** **Translation:** ------- museum do you prefer, the science one or the art one?

(A) **Which**
(B) What
(C) How much
(D) Who

Quién is used to refer to people, and since we're talking about museums, you can eliminate (D). **Cuánto** is used to inquire about quantities, so we're down to (A) and (B). **Qué** is often used in questions (**¿Qué hora es?**), but because a choice is asked for, **cuál** (A) is used instead of **qué**.

5. **C** **Translation:** What ------- when you called my cell phone this afternoon?

(A) would you have wanted
(B) would they want
(C) **did you want**
(D) do you want

Choice (B) can be eliminated because **me llamaste** tells us that we need a second person verb. The preterite, along with **cuando**, clues us into the need for the imperfect to express an action that was ongoing when something else occurred.

6. **D** **Translation:** I don't know him well, but people say that he ------- a sincere and intelligent guy.

(A) are
(B) are
(C) is
(D) **is**

Since we're talking about one person (**lo** is a singular pronoun), (A) and (B) can be easily eliminated. Now for the subtle part. If you know when to use **ser** and when to use **estar**, this question is a piece of cake. Does the sentence give us any reason to suspect that this person's admirable qualities are going to change or disappear in the near future? No. Therefore, (D) is correct.

7. **B** **Translation:** The invention of the telephone by Alexander Graham Bell in 1876 ------- how people communicate.

(A) changes (present—*él* form)
(B) **changed (preterite—*él* form)**
(C) changed (preterite—*ellos* form)
(D) change (present—*tú* form)

The year 1876 tells us that the action (inventing the telephone) happened in the past, so we need the verb **cambiar** (to change) conjugated in the past (preterite) tense. Our only options are (B) and (C), and because there is only one Alexander Graham Bell, choice (B) is the correct answer.

8. **B** **Translation:** We're going to make the trip in two days instead of one, because our destination is very ------- here.

(A) near
(B) far from
(C) next to
(D) in front of

The meaning of this sentence gives some helpful clues. In fact, since the duration of the trip is going to be twice what was expected, the only answer that makes any sense is **lejos de** (B).

9. **A** **Translation:** My brother was born three years before I was; that's why he's ------- .

(A) older
(B) taller
(C) my favorite brother
(D) very boring

Although each of the answers is something a brother could be, "born three years before" clearly suggests choice (A), which is correct.

10. **B** **Translation:** If you don't like the law, why ------- the past four years working as a lawyer?

(A) do you spend
(B) have you spent
(C) would you spend
(D) will you spend

"The past four years" tells you that we need some type of past tense, so eliminate (A), (C), and (D). The correct answer is (B).

11. **D** **Translation:** In the library one finds ------- .

(A) pens
(B) hopes
(C) questions
(D) books

This is a very straightforward question if you know the word for library. The correct answer is (D). (Be careful not to confuse **biblioteca** with **librería**, the latter of which means bookstore.)

12. **C** **Translation:** The flag that flies over the stadium is ------- .

(A) ours (masculine)
(B) ours (feminine, plural)
(C) ours (feminine, singular)
(D) mine (masculine)

The wrong answers here (as on many SAT Spanish Subject Test questions) are incorrect because they don't agree with what they're replacing, either in gender or in number. Since **la bandera** is singular and feminine, **nuestra** (C) is the correct pronoun.

13. **C** **Translation:** The hot soup gave me a toothache. I need ------- .

(A) a chair
(B) a table
(C) a dentist
(D) a screw

"Toothache" is the key word in this example. If you understood that much, you could easily have guessed (C), which is correct.

14. **C** **Translation:** The récipe that Marta gave to Veronica was difficult to read because ------- .

(A) it is big
(B) it is nice/pretty
(C) it was erased
(D) it was clean

The sentence tells us that the recipe was difficult to read. This would eliminate choices (A), (B), and (D). The only plausible answer is choice (C).

15. **A** **Translation:** To go to Mexico, the fastest ------- is this one.

(A) road
(B) sky
(C) stroll
(D) ground/floor

Only one of the choices is something that would be involved in going to Mexico, and that choice is (A). "Stroll" is a tricky choice because it sort of goes with "fastest," but it makes no sense with the first part of the sentence.

16. **D** **Translation:** Yesterday I had a lot of back pain, but today I don't ------- any.

(A) have (ellos)
(B) have (nosotros)
(C) have (tú)
(D) have (yo)

Somewhere on your exam you will probably see a question whose answer is the plain present tense, like this one. All four choices are in the present tense, so you have to pay special attention to the verb ending. "Tenía" could work with **yo, él, ella**, or **Ud.**; and since the last three are not given as choices, the answer has to be (D), which uses the **yo** form.

17. **A** **Translation:** The World Cup of soccer is a ------- .

(A) spectator event
(B) local sport
(C) national event
(D) match (sport)

The World Cup of soccer is a world event, so choices (B) and (C) are incorrect. Choice (D) is also incorrect because the World Cup is not a single match but a series of matches. Since people from all over the world watch it, both in person and on TV, it is a spectator event. So choice (A) is correct.

18. **B** **Translation:** García is our most respected client; we always give ------- what he wants.

(A) it (feminine)
(B) him
(C) it (masculine)
(D) them

Direct object or indirect object: that is the question. What do we give? *What he wants*—that's the direct object. To whom? To *him*—the singular indirect object pronoun is needed, which is (B).

19. **A** **Translation:** Alberto sits down and asks for chicken with rice and a glass of wine. He is in ------- .

(A) a restaurant
(B) a circus
(C) a bank
(D) a shoe store

If you caught any of the food words in this sentence you would guess (A). The other choices aren't even in the ballpark.

20. **C** **Translation:** ------- when have you (pl.) studied Spanish history?

(A) Until
(B) During
(C) Since
(D) In

This is another preposition question, and once again, meaning is your savior. The only choice that really works in terms of meaning is **desde** (C). **Durante cuándo** is redundant (you would just say **cuándo**), and **hasta cuándo** does not work because of the tense of the verb: we could say "until when did you study" or "until when will you study" but not "until when have you studied." Therefore, the correct answer is (C).

21. **D** **Translation:** This coming fall, ------- all together to my house in the mountains.

(A) we go (present)
(B) they go (present subjunctive)
(C) I go (present)
(D) we will go (future)

The sentence suggests "all will go together to the house in the mountains." Since the subject is in the plural first-person tense (**nosotros**), choices (B) and (C) are incorrect. Furthermore, "This coming fall" indicates that the action has not yet happened, so choice (A) is incorrect because it is in the present tense. Choice (D) is the correct answer.

22. **A** **Translation:** My uncle knows how to cook black beans pretty ------- .

(A) well
(B) good (singular)
(C) good (plural)
(D) baths

Just thought we'd sneak an "adjective versus adverb" question in for fun. **Bueno** (good) is an adjective, and because you are describing an action (*how* the black beans are made), an adverb is used. **Baños** is thrown in there to see if you're awake, as it resembles **buenos**. But (A) is correct.

23. **D** **Translation:** The concert that we saw last night was excellent. That ------- really knows how to play!

(A) game
(B) novel
(C) food
(D) orchestra

The word "concert" points to (D), which is the correct choice.

24. **A** **Translation:** I'm afraid that the storm ------- during the wedding that we're going to have on the patio.

(A) **will arrive (present subjunctive)**
(B) arrives
(C) would arrive
(D) arrived

Expressions of fear are dead giveaways that you need to use the subjunctive. Then all you have to do is check the tense of the expression to tell you which subjunctive to use. **Tengo miedo** is in the present, so this time it's present subjunctive (A).

25. **B** **Translation:** Carlos is an annoying kid who is always in some kind of trouble. It's no miracle that everyone ------- him.

(A) likes
(B) rejects
(C) helps
(D) knows

There is some tough vocabulary here. Fortunately, there are many different clues that tell you Carlos isn't a particularly likable guy, and that makes (B) the best answer.

26. **B** **Translation:** The books at the library are not in good condition. The library doesn't have the ------- to buy new books.

(A) money
(B) funds
(C) space
(D) students

The main ideas of these sentences are 1) the poor condition of the library's books and 2) the library's inability to buy new books. With this understanding, we can eliminate choices (C) and (D), which do not make sense in this context. While (A) may seem like the correct answer, the article **los** indicates a plural noun. Thus, (B) is correct.

27. **A** **Translation:** After two years of research, the doctor finally ------- the cause of the disease.

(A) discovered
(B) directed
(C) opened
(D) looked for

Choices (B) and (C) don't make much sense. Choice (D) would only make sense if the doctor hadn't yet begun his research. Choice (A) is correct.

28. **D** **Translation:** We've never danced the samba, but sure ------- how to dance the lambada!

(A) we know
(B) I know (subjunctive)
(C) they will know
(D) we know

Knowing how to do a type of dance falls under the category of facts (as opposed to people), so **saber** is the correct verb. Choice (C) is not correct because there is no reason given in the sentence either to change the subject or to change the verb to the future tense.

29. **D** **Translation:** They say that José Martí, the famous Cuban author, began to write ------- when he was only six years old.

(A) pencils
(B) alphabets
(C) languages
(D) poems

What does an author write? Well, lots of things, but out of these choices only (D) is reasonable.

Part B

Passage:

Emma dejó caer el papel. Su primera impresión fue de malestar en el vientre y en las rodillas; luego, de ciega culpa, de irrealidad, de frío, de temor; luego, quiso ya estar en el día siguiente. Acto seguido comprendió que ese deseo era inútil porque la muerte de su padre era lo único que había sucedido en el mundo, y seguiría sucediendo sin fin. Recogió el papel y se fue a su cuarto. Furtivamente lo guardó en un cajón, como si de algún modo ya supiera los hechos ulteriores.

Translation:

Emma dropped the paper. Her first *impression* was of uneasiness in her belly and in her knees, then of blind guilt, of unreality, of coldness, of *fear*; then she wanted *to* already *be* in the next day. Immediately afterwards she understood that that wish was futile because *the* death of her father was the only thing that *had happened* in the world and it *would continue* happening endlessly. She picked up the paper and went to her room. Furtively, she *saved* it in a drawer, as if somehow she already *knew* the subsequent facts.

30. **D** (A) time
(B) sight
(C) place
(D) impression

In this sentence, Emma's initial reaction to a letter is being described. The word that makes sense in the blank has to be something along the lines of "reaction." Of the choices offered, only **impresión** is even remotely similar to "reaction."

31. **B** (A) youth
(B) fear
(C) joy
(D) hunger

At this point in the paragraph, you know from the rest of Emma's reactions that she's not feeling so well, and the blank should be filled with a word that's consistent with her bad reactions. The only really negative choice is **temor.** If you weren't sure whether she was feeling good or bad, you should have skipped this and read on—later we find out that her father has died, which tells you for sure how she's feeling.

32. **A** **(A) to be (estar)**
(B) to be (ser)
(C) will be
(D) to go

So we know Emma isn't happy. It makes sense that she'd want to be in the next day. That eliminates (C) and (D), but does this situation call for **estar** or **ser**? Being in the next day is a location in time, so **estar** is correct. Another approach to this question is to use the preposition that follows the blank **(en)**. **Ir en** means to go via (as in **ir en avión**...), which makes no sense at all in this blank. Also, **quiso** (wanted to) implies the past, so **estaré** is wrong because it's in the future tense.

33. **C** (A) it
(B) the (masculine, singular)
(C) the (feminine, singular)
(D) the (feminine, plural)

Muerte is a singular feminine noun, so the proper article is **la.**

34. **D** (A) entered
(B) grew
(C) had finished
(D) had happened

It doesn't make sense that the death of her father would enter or grow, so cross out (A) and (B). **Había terminado** is possible, but if you read on, you find out that in fact Emma feels that her father's death will go on affecting her, so the best choice is (D).

35. **A** **(A) would continue**
(B) would stop
(C) would change
(D) would feel

This is sort of a continuation of the last question. The expression **sin fin** (without end) is a big clue because it tells you that Emma's going to be unhappy for a long time. The fact that her grief is on-going, without end, really only leaves one possible answer, and that's **seguiría** (A).

36. **B** (A) took out
(B) saved
(C) found
(D) took away

In this sentence, Emma does something with her letter. Because we know she already has it and has read it, (A) and (C) don't make sense. **Quitó** is just strange, so that leaves us with (B).

37. **C** (A) knows
(B) knew
(C) knew (imperfect subjunctive)
(D) would know

The saving grace on this question is the **como si** that comes just before the blank, which tells you to use the imperfect subjunctive, since it is a hypothetical event. Luckily, only choice (C) is in the imperfect subjunctive because this would be a very tough question to do based on meaning alone.

Passage:

Después de haber mandado dos expediciones a explorar la costa de México, el gobernador de Cuba organizó otra expedición bajo el mando de Hernán Cortés en 1519. En las tres expediciones tomó parte un soldado que se llamaba Bernal Díaz del Castillo. Este soldado, cuando ya era casi un viejo y vivía retirado en Guatemala, escribió sus recuerdos de las guerras mexicanas, que forman la mejor narración sobre la conquista de México y que se titula "Historia verdadera de la conquista de la Nueva España."

La expedición de Cortés constaba de once navíos que llevaban poco más de seiscientos hombres y dieciséis caballos. Cuando Cortés estaba listo para salir, el gobernador trató de quitarle el mando, pero él decidió hacerse a la mar.

Translation:

After having led two expeditions to explore the coast of Mexico, the governor of Cuba *organized* another expedition under the command of Hernán Cortés in 1519. A soldier whose *name was* Bernal Díaz del Castillo *took* part in the three expeditions. *This* soldier, when he was almost an old man and *lived* retired in Guatemala, *wrote* his memoirs of the Mexican wars, which form the best narrative *about* the conquest of Mexico and are titled "The True History of the Conquest of New Spain."

Cortés's expedition consisted of eleven ships that *carried* little more than six hundred men and sixteen *horses*. When Cortés was ready *to* leave, the governor tried to take command from him, but he decided to set out to sea.

38. B (A) that
(B) of
(C) to
(D) for

The preposition that follows **después** to mean "after" is **de** (B). It's on your list of prepositions.

39. D (A) put an end to
(B) rehearsed
(C) asked
(D) organized

The only answers that make any kind of sense in the blank are (A) and (D). How do we know whether the governor organized or put an end to the next expedition? We know a third one happened because in the very next sentence it talks about three expeditions. Therefore, the answer is (D). By skipping a question and reading on, you can sometimes find a clue that helps answer an earlier question.

40. D (A) made
(B) gave
(C) left
(D) took

Although a couple of the choices are a bit awkward in the blank—namely, (A) and (C)—it really helps on this question if you know that the expression **tomar parte** means "to take part." If you didn't know this expression, you should've eliminated (A) and (C) and guessed.

41. C (A) was named (preterite)
(B) is named
(C) was named (imperfect)
(D) had been named

Here, what you want to say is "was named." We know it's going to be some kind of past tense, but which past tense is appropriate? Well, a person's name goes on for a period of time, so it's not the regular past, which eliminates (A). Choice (D) doesn't make any sense because it implies that Castillo's name changed at some point in the past. That leaves the imperfect, which is choice (C).

42. A **(A) This (masculine)**
(B) That (feminine)
(C) A (masculine)
(D) The (feminine)

Soldado is masculine, so (B) and (D) are immediately out. The sentence goes on to discuss the soldier in question, so what you want to say is "this soldier," making choice (A) correct.

43. D (A) stopped
(B) thought
(C) heard
(D) lived

Look at the adjective that follows the blank (**retirado**). Even if you've never seen this word before, you can tell what it means because it looks like the English equivalent. Does a person *stop* retired, *think* retired, or *hear* retired? None of those makes sense, so that leaves only (D).

44. A **(A) wrote**
(B) ran
(C) lost
(D) asked for

The blank in this case precedes **recuerdos**, which can mean "memories." However, in this case it means "memoirs," which is a hint that something having to do with writing (like **escribió**) would be the correct answer, (D). If you missed **recuerdos**, the word **título** is mentioned later on, followed by a title with quotes. Look around for clues; don't just stick to the immediate area where the blank is.

45. C (A) on top of
(B) next to
(C) on; about
(D) instead of

The meaning you want for this blank is roughly "about" (C) because you're providing a preposition that describes the relationship between the memoirs and their subject (memoirs are *about* a subject). **Encima de** means "on," like "on top of" or "above," not "about." **En vez de** and **junto a** don't mean anything close to "about."

46. **C** (A) carried
(B) carried (plural)
(C) carried (plural imperfect)
(D) carry

The verb **(llevar)** in this blank refers back to the plural subject **navíos**, so you know the answer must be plural, which leaves (B), (C), and (D). If you back up just a bit earlier in the sentence, you notice that we're in the imperfect tense (**constaba** tells you). Even if you only knew it was some type of past tense, you could eliminate (D) (**llevan** is present tense) and guess. You'd have a fifty-fifty chance of guessing (C), which is correct.

47. **C** (A) cars
(B) airplanes
(C) horses
(D) gloves

The big hint on this question is that the passage deals with events that happened in the early sixteenth century (1519), before the invention of the airplane and the automobile. "Gloves" could work, but "horses" (a means of transportation) is a much more likely answer, leaving (C) as the correct choice.

48. **B** (A) for
(B) to
(C) in
(D) of

This question asks for the preposition that precedes **salir**. Although (C) and (D) do not make sense, you are still left with a decision between **para** and **por**. In this case, we are concerned with the narrator's purpose (to leave), so we should use **para** (B).

Passage:

Pero hoy, en esta mañana fría, en que tenemos más prisa que nunca, la niña y yo pasamos de largo delante de la fila tentadora de autos parados. Por primera vez en la vida vamos al colegio...Al colegio, le digo, no se puede ir en taxi. Hay que correr un poco por las calles, hay que tomar el metro, hay que caminar luego a un sitio determinado, para un autobús...Es que yo he escogido un colegio muy lejano para mi niña, esa es la verdad; un colegio que me gusta mucho, pero está muy lejos.... Sin embargo, yo no estoy impaciente hoy, ni cansada, y la niña lo sabe. Es ella ahora la que inicia una caricia tímida con su manita dentro de la mía; y por primera vez me doy cuenta de que su mano de cuatro años es igual a mi mano grande: tan decidida, tan suave, tan nerviosa como la mía.

Translation:

But today, on this cold morning, in which we're in a bigger hurry than ever, the girl and I *passed by* the tempting line of stopped cars. For the *first* time in our lives we're going to school...I tell her, *you cannot* go to school by taxi. You have to run through the streets a bit, you have to take the subway, then you have to *walk* to a specific place for a bus.... It's true that I've chosen a school that is very *far* for my daughter, a school that *I like* very much, but it is very far away. However, I'm not impatient today, nor *tired*, and the girl knows it. It is now she who initiates a timid caress with her little hand *inside* mine, and for the first time, I realize that her four-year-old hand is *the same as* my adult one: just as resolute, just as soft, and just as nervous as mine.

49. A **(A) we passed**
(B) we entered
(C) we gave
(D) we paid

The preposition **delante de** (in front of) that comes shortly after the blank is the main clue on this question. The only verb that makes sense before this expression is (A).

50. B (A) none
(B) first
(C) always
(D) habit

The word **vez** (time, occasion) immediately follows the blank, and the only choice that forms an expression in conjunction with **vez** is (B).

51. C (A) tricks herself
(B) we know
(C) one can
(D) have left over

The sentence is about getting to school by taxi. Earlier in the passage it says that they passed by a row of taxis. But that only gets rid of (A) and (D) because we don't know why they passed by the taxis. Choice (B) doesn't make sense because we'd use **saber (sabemos)**, not **conocer**, to say we know how to do something like get to school in a taxi.

52. D (A) to sleep
(B) to touch
(C) to play
(D) to walk

You wouldn't "sleep," "touch," or "play" to get to a bus stop. Walking (A), however, seems likely.

53. **B** (A) closed
(B) **far away**
(C) dark
(D) difficult

This blank describes the type of school that the mother chose for her daughter. Common sense eliminates (A) and (C). If you're stuck at this point, you just need to look forward a little to find the clue that singles out (B) as the best answer: **está muy lejos.**

54. **A** (A) **I like**
(B) I hate
(C) I don't know
(D) we doubt

The blank is followed by the expression **pero está muy lejos**. The **pero** tells you that a positive quality about the school came immediately before the expression (the word **pero** indicates a contrast, as in "strict *but* fair"). This gets rid of (B) and (D), and (C) doesn't make sense because the mother in the passage chose this school for her daughter, whom she seems to love very much. Would she send her daughter to a school she didn't know? Probably not.

55. **C** (A) old
(B) tall
(C) **tired**
(D) fresh

The verb **estar** is used in this sentence, and that eliminates **vieja** because **vieja** would be used with **ser (ella *es* vieja)**. The same is true for **alta (ella *es* alta)**. **Fresca** is a word you are more likely to use when referring to fruit or vegetables. Therefore, (C) is correct.

56. **A** (A) **inside**
(B) outside
(C) close to
(D) without

Here the daughter is making an affectionate gesture (**caricia**) toward her mom by putting her hand somewhere in relation to her mom's hand. Choices (B) and (D) suggest just the opposite, as if she were making a negative gesture. Choice (C) is fine, but it really doesn't make a lot of sense if you think about it: You wouldn't put your hand *close to* someone else's to show affection; you'd put your hand *in* someone else's. That's choice (A).

57. **B** (A) different from

(B) equal to; the same as

(C) close to

(D) on top of

The giveaway for this question follows the blank: **tan**. **Tan** by itself means "so," but the expression **tan...como** means "as…as." The correct answer, therefore, is (B).

Part C

Passage:

Al pasar ante una granja, un perro mordió a mi amigo. Entramos a ver al granjero y le preguntamos si era suyo el perro. El granjero, para evitarse complicaciones, dijo que no era suyo.

—Entonces —dijo mi amigo— présteme una hoz para cortarle la cabeza, pues debo llevarla al Instituto para que la analicen.

En aquel momento, apareció la hija del granjero y le pidió a su padre que no permitiera que le cortáramos la cabeza al perro.

—Si es suyo el perro —dijo mi amigo— enséñeme el certificado de vacunación antirrábica.

El hombre entró en la granja y tardó largo rato en salir. Mientras tanto, el perro se acercó y mi amigo dijo:

—No me gusta el aspecto de este animal.

En efecto, babeaba y los ojos parecían arderle en las órbitas. Incluso andaba dificultosamente.

—Hace unos días —dijo la joven— le atropelló una bicicleta.

El granjero nos dijo que no encontraba el certificado de vacunación.

—Debo haberlo perdido.

—La vida de un hombre puede estar en juego — intervine yo. Díganos, con toda sinceridad, si el perro está vacunado o no.

El hombre bajó la cabeza y murmuró:

—Está sano.

Translation:

Upon passing in front of a farm, a dog bit my friend. We went in to see the farmer and asked him if the dog was his. The farmer, in order to avoid trouble, said it was not his.

"Then," said my friend, "lend me a scythe to cut off his head, since I should take it to the Institute so they can analyze it."

At that moment the farmer's daughter appeared and asked her father not to let us cut off the dog's head.

"If the dog is yours," said my friend, "show me the certificate of rabies vaccination."

The man went into the farmhouse and took a long time to come back out. Meanwhile, the dog approached, and my friend said:

"I don't like the way this animal looks."

Essentially, he foamed at the mouth and his eyes seemed to burn in their sockets. He also walked with difficulty.

"A few days ago," said the girl, "a bicycle hit him."

The farmer told us that he didn't find the certificate of vaccination.

"I must have lost it."

"The life of a man may be at stake," I interjected. "Tell us, in all honesty, if the dog is vaccinated or not."

The man bowed his head and murmured:

"He's healthy."

58. A **Translation:** What happened to the men when they passed by the farm?

(A) A dog bit one of them.
(B) A farmer asked them for directions.
(C) They avoided complications.
(D) They lost their dog.

The answer to this question, (A), is in the first sentence of the passage. Normally the progression of the questions follows the progression of the passage. The earlier a question is, the earlier in the passage you'll find its answer.

59. C **Translation:** Why did the farmer tell them that the dog wasn't his?

(A) He didn't know whose dog it was.
(B) He didn't know the men who came to the door.
(C) He didn't want to take blame for what the dog had done.
(D) He didn't like dogs.

In the passage (third line) it says that the farmer wanted to **evitarse complicaciones** (avoid trouble). The answer closest to that in meaning is (C). Some of the other answers are reasonable, but they aren't in the passage.

60. **D** **Translation:** What did the farmer's daughter ask of him?

(A) That he take the dog out for a walk
(B) That he take the dog to the doctor
(C) That he give food to the dog
(D) That he not let the men hurt the dog

The guide word for this question is **hija.** The first place where **hija** appears (and the source of the answer) is toward the beginning of the passage, where you will find that (D) is correct.

61. **B** **Translation:** What did the men ask the farmer for?

(A) Money to pay for a doctor
(B) The certificate of rabies vaccination
(C) A telephone to call the police
(D) Proof that he was really a farmer

The certificate of rabies vaccination, and whether the farmer has it, is the focus of most of the passage, so (B) is the answer.

62. **B** **Translation:** How did the farmer's dog seem?

(A) Healthy and in good humor
(B) Sick, as if it had rabies
(C) Youthful and full of energy
(D) Serious and thoughtful

Most of the passage is concerned with vaccinations (**vacunas**) and whether or not to cut off the dog's head and have it inspected. You probably wouldn't do this to a happy, healthy dog (unless you're some kind of sick weirdo), so you can eliminate (A) and (C) immediately. You probably wouldn't decapitate a dog for being **serio y pensativo** either, so (D) is out. That leaves you with (B).

63. **A** **Translation:** What reason did the girl give for the way the dog behaved?

(A) It had an accident with a bicycle.
(B) It just had its rabies shot.
(C) It's a very ferocious dog.
(D) It was very hungry.

Once again, this question deals with the daughter, who is referred to as **la joven,** as well as **hija** and **niña,** in different parts of the passage. Choice (A) is the answer you're looking for.

64. D **Translation:** Finally, what does the farmer tell the men?

(A) To go to a hospital
(B) To adopt a dog
(C) That they should leave the farm right now
(D) That the dog has no disease

En fin is a pretty strong hint that the answer is toward the end. The correct choice is (D).

Advertisement:

Hotel Marybel

Mendoza * Cordoba * Buenos Aires

¡Especiales del mes para todos! ¡Reserven con dos semanas de anticipación y reciban un descuento de 10%! Llamen al 239-7155—24 horas al dia, 7 dias a la semana.

Dirreccion de Internet: www.hotalmarybel.ar

Aire acondicionado en todos los cuartos, cafeteria, bar, conneccion de Internet gratis en los cuartos. No se pierdan esta oferta. Oferta vence a fin de mes.

Translation:

Hotel Marybel

Mendoza * Cordoba * Buenos Aires

Monthly specials for everyone! Reserve two weeks in advance and receive a 10% discount!

Call 239-7155—24 hours a day, 7 days a week.

Website: www.hotalmarybel.ar

Air conditioning in all rooms, café, bar, free Internet connection in rooms. Don't lose out on this offer. Offer expires at the end of the month.

65. B **Translation:** This announcement is for what type of service?

(A) A hotel
(B) A chain of hotels
(C) A store
(D) An ad for free services

At the top of the announcement, below the name of the hotel, are three cities: Mendoza, Cordoba, and Buenos Aires. This indicates that Hotel Marybel is a chain rather than one hotel. Choice (B) is the correct answer.

66. **B** **Translation:** How long does the offer last?

(A) A day
(B) A month
(C) A year
(D) Two weeks

The announcement starts off by mentioning the hotel's "monthly specials," and at the bottom it states that the offer expires at the end of the month. Choice (B) is the correct answer.

67. **A** **Translation:** What does the client have to do in order to receive a discount?

(A) Reserve two weeks prior to arrival
(B) Reserve for two weeks
(C) Reserve with a month's notice
(D) Reserve with a week's notice

The announcement states that reservations should be made at least two weeks before arrival in order for a discount to apply, so choice (A) is the correct answer.

68. **D** **Translation:** Which of the following services does the hotel offer?

(A) Air conditioning in the larger rooms only
(B) Swimming pool
(C) Internet in the bar
(D) A place to eat

The announcement states that the hotel offers air conditioning in all rooms, as well as a café, a bar, and free Internet connection in the room. It does not mention Internet in the bar, a swimming pool, or air conditioning being available only in the larger rooms. Since a café is a place to eat, choice (D) is the correct answer.

Passage:

Para los arqueólogos y los historiadores, la civilización maya es, sin duda ninguna, la que alcanzó un mayor nivel de desarrollo entre todas las civilizaciones que existían antes de la llegada de Colón. Aunque todavía hay muchos secretos que no se han descifrado con relación a los mayas, parece que esta civilización empezó varios siglos antes del nacimiento de Cristo. Sin embargo, se sabe que los mayas abandonaron los grandes centros ceremoniales en el siglo X de nuestra era.

Los primeros templos que construyeron son de forma de pirámide de cuatro lados con una gran escalinata. Sobre la pirámide hay un edificio de un piso normalmente, y en algunos casos de dos, y en él podemos ver relieves de arcilla y esculturas de madera y piedra caliza. Las figuras son siempre de perfil y en ellas se puede apreciar los adornos y joyas que usaban. En la clasificación que se ha hecho de las épocas de esta civilización, se llama preclásica a la época primera, que se desarrolla en Guatemala y Honduras, y que según los arqueólogos duró hasta el fin del siglo III de nuestra era.

Translation:

For archaeologists and historians, the Mayan civilization is, without a doubt, the one that reached the highest level of development among all the civilizations that existed before the arrival of Columbus. Although there are still many secrets that have not been deciphered with regard to the Mayas, it seems that this civilization began many centuries before the birth of Christ. However, it's known that the Mayas abandoned their large ceremonial centers in the tenth century of our era.

The first temples they built were pyramid-shaped, with four sides and a huge outside stairway. On top of the pyramid there is an edifice that is normally one story, and in some cases two, and in it we can see clay reliefs and statues made of wood and limestone. The figures are always in profile, and in them one can appreciate the adornments and jewels that they used. In the classification that has been made of the epochs of this civilization, the first, which developed in Guatemala and Honduras, is called the pre-classic era and, according to archaeologists, it lasted until the end of the third century of our era.

69. A **Translation:** What do the archaeologists and historians think of the Mayan civilization?

(A) That it was a very advanced civilization
(B) That the Mayas wrote wonderful books
(C) That they knew Columbus
(D) That they had many secrets

Arqueólogos and **historiadores** are the guide words; use them to lead you to the correct answer, which is (A).

70. C **Translation:** When did the Mayan civilization begin?

(A) In the tenth century of our era
(B) Immediately before Columbus's arrival
(C) Quite a while before Christ's birth
(D) Many centuries after Christ's birth

It's technically not a guide word, but **cuando** tells you that you want to look for a period in time. The correct answer is (C).

71. C **Translation:** How did the first Mayan temples seem?

(A) They were very short buildings.
(B) They were made of wood and limestone.
(C) They were pyramids with four faces.
(D) They were ordinary houses, like the ones we have today.

Templos is your guide for this question, and the answer is (C).

72. **B** **Translation:** What can be said about the sculptures that the Mayas made?

(A) They had large outside staircases.
(B) They give information about the jewels and adornments that they used.
(C) It costs a lot to buy them.
(D) One can find them in famous museums.

Esculturas tells you where to look, but you still must read with care in order to determine that (B) is the correct answer.

73. **C** **Translation:** Approximately how much time passed between the end of the pre-classic era and when the Mayans abandoned their ceremonial centers?

(A) One hundred years
(B) Three centuries
(C) Seven centuries
(D) Ten centuries

The end of the pre-classic era was in the third century (see end of second paragraph), and the Mayans abandoned their ceremonial centers in the tenth century (see end of first paragraph). This puts the gap at about seven centuries (C).

74. **A** **Translation:** The passage deals with

(A) Mayan civilization and architecture
(B) Christ's influence on Mayan civilization
(C) the differences between our civilization and Mayan civilization
(D) the adornments and jewels that the Mayas used

This one's a little tricky. The passage does mention Christ (**Cristo**), whose name appears in (B), and adornments and jewels (**adornos y joyas**), which appear in answer choice (D), but it also deals with other stuff. Choices (B) and (D) are too specific. Omit them. The passage doesn't specifically compare Mayan culture to any other culture, including ours, so (C) is out. That leaves (A), a nice, general, correct answer.

Passage:

En 1992, se cumplieron cinco siglos ya del encuentro de Europa con América. Fue poco después de la medianoche del 11 al 12 de octubre de 1492, cuando Rodrigo de Triana, un tripulante de la carabela *La Niña*, la cual se había adelantado a *La Santa María*, donde iba Colón, dio el grito de "¡Tierra! ¡Tierra!" El lugar estaba muy cercano a la Florida, era una pequeña isla llamada Guanahaní que Colón llamó San Salvador y que pertenece al archipiélago de las Lucayas, o Bahamas.

Lo que Colón encontró y describe en sus cartas a los Reyes Católicos fue mucha pobreza y gente que iba desnuda, como su madre los parió, todos jóvenes, con hermosos cuerpos, cabellos gruesos como los de los caballos y cortos, que les caían por encima de las cejas y otros largos por detrás.

Pocos días después, descubrió la costa de Cuba, que llamó Juana, por la hija de los reyes. Por entonces, Martín Alonso Pinzón, que mandaba *La Pinta*, se separó de la expedición, lo cual consideró Colón como una deserción, aunque lo disimuló por mantener la unidad de la expedición. Al cabo de unos días llegó a Haití, que llamó la Hispaniola, pero debido a los muchos bajos y arrecifes que había, *La Santa María* encalló.

Translation:

In 1992, five centuries were completed since the meeting of Europe and America. It was shortly after midnight between the 11th and 12th of October in 1492 when Rodrigo de Triana, a crew member of the ship *The Niña*, which had gone ahead of *The Santa María*, where Columbus went, let out the shout of "Land! Land!" The place was very close to Florida, a small island named Guanahaní, which Columbus called San Salvador and which belongs to the archipelago of the Lucayas, or Bahamas.

What Columbus found and describes in his letters to the Catholic king and queen was much poverty and people who went about naked, as their mothers bore them, all young, with beautiful bodies, thick heads of hair like a horse's that fell over their eyebrows and that others wore long in back.

A few days later, he discovered the coast of Cuba, which he called Juana, after the daughter of the king and queen. At that point, Martín Alonso Pinzón, who captained *The Pinta*, pulled away from the expedition, which Columbus considered an act of desertion, although he overlooked it to maintain the unity of the expedition. At the end of a few days he reached Haiti, which he called Hispaniola, but because of the many sandbanks and reefs that were there, *The Santa María* ran aground.

75. A **Translation:** Who was the first to see land in the expedition?

(A) A sailor named Rodrigo de Triana
(B) Columbus
(C) *The Niña*
(D) Guanahaní, Columbus's best friend

You can knock off (C) without looking back at the passage. Once you look back, the answer, choice (A), is in the sentence containing **tierra.**

76. A **Translation:** What were the people who Columbus found like?

(A) Very poor, but also beautiful
(B) Violent and aggressive
(C) Smarter than the sailors
(D) Very scared and confused

This question doesn't really have guide words, but luckily there is an entire paragraph about this topic, so it shouldn't have been too tough to locate the answer to the question, which is (A).

77. **B** **Translation:** What did Columbus discover a few days after he discovered San Salvador?

(A) The archipelago of the Bahamas
(B) The island that today is called Cuba
(C) Haiti
(D) Thick hair

This is a tricky question, because it's easy to think that **San Salvador** is the guide, when actually **pocos días después** is your clue on this one. The correct answer is (B), but remember, if you ever have trouble locating the source of a question, just skip it and come back to it later.

78. **C** **Translation:** What was Columbus's reaction when Martín Alonso Pinzón separated from the expedition?

(A) He became furious.
(B) He started to cry.
(C) He gave the impression that he didn't know what had happened.
(D) He sent another ship after him.

The name Martin Alonso Pinzón is the guide, and it only appears once. The answer is (C).

79. **D** **Translation:** How did *The Santa María* end up?

(A) It returned to Spain.
(B) It was lost and they have never found it.
(C) It sank.
(D) It ran aground as a result of reefs and shallows.

The name of the ship is the big clue. The location of the question tells you to look toward the end of the passage, where you will find that (D) is the correct answer.

Passage:

Si no fuera por el gusto exigente de los bebedores de café de Arabia Saudita, el pueblo guatemalteco de Cobán, al otro lado del mundo, estaría en problemas.

Cobán, capital de la región montañosa de Alta Verapaz, en Guatemala, es la fuente de la mayor parte del cardamomo que consume el mundo árabe: una especia dulce, picante y sumamente aromática que se emplea en la cocina de la India. De hecho, el café de cardamomo, conocido en el mundo árabe como *kahwe hal*, es considerado un símbolo de hospitalidad en todo el Medio Oriente.

En Cobán, famoso por su iglesia católica del siglo XVI y las ruinas mayas que se encuentran en los alrededores, prácticamente nadie habla árabe, y ninguno de sus 125.000 habitantes pone cardamomo en el café. Sin embargo, todos conocen perfectamente la conexión que existe entre la especia y el mundo árabe. "El cardamomo es la base de nuestra economía, y Guatemala es el principal exportador del mundo."

Translation:

If it weren't for the demanding taste of the coffee drinkers of Saudi Arabia, the Guatemalan town of Cobán, on the other side of the world, would be in big trouble.

Cobán, capital of the mountainous region of Alta Verapaz, in Guatemala, is the source of the majority of cardamom that the Arab world consumes: a sweet, sharp, and extremely aromatic spice that is used in Indian cooking. As a matter of fact, coffee with cardamom, known in the Arab world as *kahwe hal,* is considered a symbol of hospitality in all of the Middle East.

In Cobán, famous for its sixteenth-century Catholic church and the Mayan ruins that are found in its environs, practically no one speaks Arabic, and none of its 125,000 inhabitants puts cardamom in his/her coffee. However, they all know perfectly well the connection that exists between the spice and the Arab world. "Cardamom is the base of our economy, and Guatemala is the principal exporter in the world."

80. **B** **Translation:** In which country in particular do they drink coffee with cardamom?

(A) In Guatemala
(B) In Saudi Arabia
(C) In Alta Verapaz
(D) In the Middle East

A couple of answers, namely, (C) and (D), can be eliminated right away, since they aren't countries. Choice (B) is the correct answer here.

81. **B** **Translation:** What is cardamom?

(A) A rare type of coffee
(B) A spice
(C) An Indian style of cooking
(D) A type of tree

Even if you'd never seen the word **especia,** POE works really well on this question and will help you choose (B) as your answer.

82. **A** **Translation:** How does cardamom taste?

(A) Sharp, but also sweet
(B) A bit bitter
(C) It hardly has any flavor
(D) It tastes like Colombian coffee

The answer to this one is in the paragraph that describes the spice. Choice (A) is correct.

83. C **Translation:** For what is the city of Cobán known?

(A) For cardamom
(B) For the best coffee in North America
(C) For its ruins, and for its sixteenth-century church
(D) For the Indian food

Choice (A) is an easy trap to fall for if you're lazy on this one and don't look back. For those who aren't lazy, the answer, choice (C), is right at the top of the final paragraph. Look back to the passage on the specific questions.

84. C **Translation:** What is the connection between the Arab world and Guatemala?

(A) In Guatemala everyone speaks Arabic.
(B) In both places they love coffee with cardamom.
(C) Guatemala exports much spice to the Arab world.
(D) There really is no connection between the two places.

Although the answer to this one, choice (C), is in the last paragraph (**conexión** is your guide), the relationship is mentioned earlier in the passage as well.

85. D **Translation:** What would be a good title for the passage?

(A) "Cobán: The City in the Mountains"
(B) "The Economy of Guatemala"
(C) "The Coffees of the World"
(D) "Cardamom: What Joins Guatemala with the Arab World"

Remember, the answer to a question like this must include the ideas of the whole passage. Choice (B) is only partially correct; it's not wrong, but it doesn't tell the whole story. You want to go with (D).

HOW TO SCORE PRACTICE TEST 1

When you take the real exam, the proctors take away your exam and your bubble sheet and send it to a processing center, where a computer looks at the pattern of filled-in ovals on your exam and gives you a score. We couldn't include even a small computer with this book, so we are providing this more primitive way of scoring your exam.

Determining Your Score

STEP 1 Using the answer key, determine how many questions you got right and how many you got wrong on the test. Remember, questions that you do not answer do not count as either right answers or wrong answers.

STEP 2 List the number of right answers here. (A) _____

STEP 3 List the number of wrong answers here. Now divide that number by 3. (B) _____ ÷ 3 _____ = (C) _____

STEP 4 Subtract the number of wrong answers divided by 3 (C) from the number of correct answers (A). Round this score to the nearest whole number. This is your raw score. (A) – (C) = _____

STEP 5 To determine your real score, take the number from Step 4 above and look it up in the left column of the Score Conversion Table on the next page; the corresponding score on the right is your score on the exam.

PRACTICE TEST 1
SCORE CONVERSION TABLE

Raw Score	Scaled Score	Raw Score	Scaled Score	Raw Score	Scaled Score
85	800	47	590	9	360
84	800	46	580	8	360
83	800	45	570	7	350
82	800	44	570	6	350
81	790	43	560	5	340
80	790	42	550	4	340
79	780	41	550	3	330
78	780	40	540	2	320
77	770	39	530	1	320
76	770	38	530	0	310
75	760	37	520	–1	310
74	760	36	520	–2	300
73	750	35	510	–3	290
72	750	34	500	–4	290
71	740	33	500	–5	280
70	730	32	490	–6	270
69	730	31	490	–7	260
68	720	30	480	–8	260
67	720	29	470	–9	250
66	710	28	470	–10	240
65	700	27	460	–11	230
64	700	26	460	–12	220
63	690	25	450	–13	220
62	680	24	450	–14	220
61	680	23	440	–15	210
60	670	22	430	–16	210
59	670	21	430	–17	210
58	660	20	420	–18	200
57	650	19	420	–19	200
56	650	18	410	–20	200
55	640	17	410	–21	200
54	630	16	400	–22	200
53	630	15	400	–23	200
52	620	14	390	–24	200
51	620	13	390	–25	200
50	610	12	380	–26	200
49	600	11	380	–27	200
48	590	10	370	–28	200

Chapter 9
Practice Test 2

SPANISH SUBJECT TEST 2

Your responses to Spanish Subject Test 2 questions must be filled in on Test 2 of your answer sheet (at the back of the book). Marks on any other section will not be counted toward your Spanish Subject Test score.

When your supervisor gives the signal, turn the page and begin the Spanish Subject Test.

SPANISH SUBJECT TEST

PLEASE NOTE THAT YOUR ANSWER SHEET HAS FIVE ANSWER POSITIONS MARKED A, B, C, D, E, WHILE THE QUESTIONS THROUGHOUT THIS TEST CONTAIN ONLY FOUR CHOICES. BE SURE NOT TO MAKE ANY MARKS IN COLUMN E.

Part A

Directions: This part consists of a number of incomplete statements, each having four suggested completions. Select the most appropriate completion and fill in the corresponding oval on the answer sheet.

1. Hay siete días en una semana y cuatro semanas en ------- .

(A) un siglo
(B) una estación
(C) un mes
(D) una década

2. Me gustaría realmente comprar un traje nuevo, pero ¡me encantan estos zapatos! ¿ ------- ?

(A) Cómo son
(B) Cuáles son
(C) Cuándo cuestan
(D) Cuántos cuestan

3. Mi abuela me tejía un suéter y ------- una revista a la vez.

(A) leyera
(B) leía
(C) había leído
(D) lee

4. Los pulmones están ------- del pecho.

(A) debajo
(B) arriba
(C) en medio
(D) dentro

5. Los empleados no han trabajado desde el miércoles pasado, porque ------- un incendio ese día que destruyó el edificio donde trabajan.

(A) hubo
(B) haya
(C) habría
(D) hay

6. Aunque no teníamos mucho dinero, no había ------- problema con pagar nuestra cuenta.

(A) algún
(B) alguna
(C) ninguna
(D) ningún

7. Tú ------- a Francisco en el estadio durante el partido de fútbol el sábado pasado.

(A) conociste
(B) conoces
(C) conozcas
(D) conocerás

8. ¿ ------- dónde son los Gutiérrez? Me parece que son guatemaltecos, pero no sé con toda seguridad.

(A) Para
(B) A
(C) De
(D) En

9. La música cubana fue ------- muy bien por la orquesta del Hotel Playa de Oro.

(A) oída
(B) hecha
(C) leída
(D) tocada

GO ON TO THE NEXT PAGE

SPANISH SUBJECT TEST–*Continued*

10. Después de que yo los esperé una hora y media, ------- llegaron mis hermanos a visitarme.

(A) por casualidad
(B) por fin
(C) por supuesto
(D) por favor

11. Es ridículo que las naciones del mundo no ------- vivir en paz.

(A) podían
(B) puedan
(C) pudieron
(D) pueden

12. Me alegro que Ud. esté en casa, Don Alejandro, quería ------- un favor.

(A) sacarte
(B) pedirlo
(C) pedirle
(D) prestarle

13. Uds. vivirían en una mansión gigante y espléndida si ------- millonarios.

(A) son
(B) habrían sido
(C) sean
(D) fueran

14. ------- tú no entiendes es que odio las alcachofas.

(A) Que
(B) Cual
(C) Lo que
(D) Como

15. Después de nadar un poco, Marta se secó porque estaba muy ------- .

(A) mojada
(B) molesta
(C) enferma
(D) lista

16. Nuestro primo es famoso porque ------- el papel de Don Quijote en una obra de teatro hace muchos años.

(A) tocó
(B) puso
(C) jugó
(D) hizo

17. Yo tengo diecisiete años, pero mi hermana ------- sólo tiene quince años.

(A) mayor
(B) mejor
(C) menor
(D) peor

18. Cuando vayamos de compras el lunes que viene, ------- a las tiendas más exclusivas.

(A) vayamos
(B) iremos
(C) fuimos
(D) vamos

19. Ricardo habla alemán y ruso muy ------- .

(A) malos
(B) malas
(C) mal
(D) maldad

20. Uds. están furiosos que nosotros no ------- nada de la cultura puertorriqueña.

(A) sabemos
(B) supimos
(C) hemos sabido
(D) sepamos

21. Allí está el paraguas de Alicia, pero ¿dónde está ------- ?

(A) el tuyo
(B) tuyo
(C) la tuya
(D) tuya

22. Ramón compró un anillo para su amiga y ------- dio a ella para su cumpleaños.

(A) lo
(B) le
(C) se la
(D) se lo

GO ON TO THE NEXT PAGE

SPANISH SUBJECT TEST–*Continued*

23. Ya que has pasado tanto tiempo en el campo, ahora te ------- las montanas.

    (A) encantas
    (B) encantan
    (C) encanta
    (D) encantes

24. La prestigiosa familia contrató al pintor para pintar ------- de su matriarca, la Sra. Pedregal.

    (A) un retrato
    (B) un vaso
    (C) un césped
    (D) un recado

25. Aunque Lucía y Roberto no querían hacer su trabajo, lo hicieron ------- .

    (A) de todos modos
    (B) a primera vista
    (C) al azar
    (D) por desgracia

26. Después de recibir una mala nota en su examen final, Manuel ------- muy enojado y se fue del cuarto.

    (A) se volvió
    (B) se hizo
    (C) se puso
    (D) llegó a ser

27. Las butacas mejores ------- en el fondo del teatro, porque se puede ver toda la pantalla desde allí.

    (A) son
    (B) están
    (C) hay
    (D) hayan

28. El papá de Joaquín es un abogado que se especializa en ------- de los impuestos.

    (A) la piedra
    (B) el ajo
    (C) el sótano
    (D) la ley

29. Desde que me mudé a la Argentina, paso mucho tiempo pensando ------- mis amigos en Paraguay.

    (A) de
    (B) en
    (C) que
    (D) con

GO ON TO THE NEXT PAGE

SPANISH SUBJECT TEST–*Continued*

Part B

Directions: In each of the following passages, there are numbered blanks indicating that words or phrases have been omitted. For each numbered blank, four completions are provided. First read through the entire paragraph. Then, for each numbered blank, choose the completion that is most appropriate given the context of the entire paragraph and fill in the corresponding oval on the answer sheet.

La Sra. Jensen llegó el primer día a la clase diciendo que (30) aprender español. Era obviamente una persona alerta y vivaz. Lo único que (31) distinguía de los otros estudiantes era su (32) : en ese momento tenía sesenta y nueve años. Su historia es interesante. El esposo de la Sra. Jensen (33) inesperadamente de un ataque cardíaco cuando ella tenía apenas treinta años, dejándola sola con cuatro hijos y ningún oficio para ganarse la vida. Sus padres habían muerto, los abuelos paternos de sus hijos tenían muy pocos recursos, y ella no tenía otros (34) que la ayudaran. En efecto, la muerte de su esposo (35) destruyó la vida. (36) ver bien su situación, ella (37) que tenía que volver a pensar todos sus planes y rehacer su vida sobre otras bases.

30. (A) querría
    (B) quiera
    (C) quiere
    (D) quería

31. (A) la
    (B) lo
    (C) los
    (D) le

32. (A) ropa
    (B) edad
    (C) comportamiento
    (D) mochila

33. (A) nació
    (B) murió
    (C) habló
    (D) oyó

34. (A) brazos
    (B) cuentos
    (C) mapas
    (D) parientes

35. (A) la
    (B) lo
    (C) le
    (D) se

36. (A) Al
    (B) Para
    (C) Antes de
    (D) A

37. (A) reconoce
    (B) reconozca
    (C) reconocerá
    (D) reconoció

GO ON TO THE NEXT PAGE

—Cuando te sientas mal, mi hijita, le (38) consejos al retrato. El (39) dará. Puedes rezarle, ¿acaso no rezas a los santos?

Este (40) de proceder le pareció extraño a Alejandrina. Mi vida transcurría monótonamente, pues tengo un testigo constante que me prohibe la felicidad: mi dolencia. El doctor Edgardo es la única persona que lo (41) . Hasta el momento de conocerlo, (42) ignorando que algo (43) mi organismo me carcomía. Ahora conozco todo lo que sufro: el doctor Edgardo me lo (44) . Es mi naturaleza. Algunos (45) con ojos negros, otros con ojos azules. Parece imposible que, siendo tan joven, él (46) tan sabio; (47) , me he enterado de que no es precisa ser un anciano para serlo. Su piel lisa, sus ojos de niño, su cabellera rubia, ensortijada, son para (48) el emblema de la sabiduría.

38. (A) pidas
(B) pedirás
(C) pides
(D) pediste

39. (A) me lo
(B) me las
(C) te los
(D) te la

40. (A) guante
(B) tópico
(C) modo
(D) relato

41. (A) sabe
(B) anuncia
(C) ignora
(D) muestra

42. (A) viviera
(B) viví
(C) vivo
(D) viva

43. (A) fuera de
(B) al lado de
(C) dentro de
(D) alrededor de

44. (A) ha explicado
(B) hubiera explicado
(C) habré explicado
(D) haya explicado

45. (A) salen
(B) andan
(C) mueren
(D) nacen

46. (A) sería
(B) fue
(C) es
(D) sea

47. (A) porque
(B) sin embargo
(C) además
(D) entonces

48. (A) yo
(B) mi
(C) mí
(D) mío

GO ON TO THE NEXT PAGE

Cortejar es pretender en matrimonio a una señorita. En la España del siglo XIX, y en particular, en la clase media, existían ciertas costumbres muy (49) que se observaban durante el cortejo. Así, un joven y una joven eran presentados el uno al otro en un evento (50), por ejemplo, en un baile o una fiesta. Si ellos se gustaban y querían verse otra vez, tenían que (51) una ocasión para un nuevo encuentro. Cuando se veían, a la salida de la misa, durante el intermedio de una obra de teatro, o en el paseo de la tarde, intercambiaban cartitas (52).

La mujer joven informó al pretendiente (53) la hora en la cual ella (54) al balcón para verse o hablarse calladamente o cuándo iría al paseo, con quién estaría acompañada, dónde se sentaría, y las demás señas necesarias.

Una vez que la joven pareja decidía (55), el joven hacía una cita con los padres de la novia y les pedía la mano de su hija en matrimonio. (56) ese momento, se les permitía a los novios verse más a menudo.

Pero, por supuesto, la novia siempre era acompañada de una hermana mayor, una tía, una dueña, un hermano u otra persona mayor hasta el día de (57).

49. (A) perturbadores
(B) tradicionales
(C) chocantes
(D) tontas

50. (A) social
(B) secreto
(C) sombrío
(D) inapropiado

51. (A) olvidar
(B) mencionar
(C) buscar
(D) recordar

52. (A) amorosas
(B) profesionales
(C) antiguas
(D) odiosas

53. (A) para
(B) de
(C) a
(D) con

54. (A) salga
(B) habían salido
(C) saldría
(D) saldrá

55. (A) casarse
(B) despedirse
(C) divorciarse
(D) enfadarse

56. (A) Antes de
(B) A partir de
(C) Para
(D) Con

57. (A) la fiesta
(B) la boda
(C) la muerte
(D) el baile

GO ON TO THE NEXT PAGE

SPANISH SUBJECT TEST–*Continued*

Part C

Directions: Read the following texts carefully for comprehension. Each passage is followed by a number of questions or incomplete statements. Select the answer or completion that is best according to the text and fill in the corresponding oval on the answer sheet.

Pasaron días terribles sin que llegara respuesta. Le envié una segunda carta y luego una tercera y una cuarta, diciendo siempre lo mismo, pero cada vez con mayor desolación. En la última, decidí relatarle todo lo que había pasado aquella noche que siguió a nuestra separación. No escatimé detalle ni bajeza, como tampoco dejé de confesarle la tentación de suicidio. Me dio vergüenza usar eso como arma, pero la usé. Debo agregar que, mientras describía mis actos más bajos y la desesperación de mi soledad en la noche frente a su casa de la calle Posadas, sentía ternura para conmigo mismo y hasta lloré de compasión. Tenía muchas esperanzas de que María sintiese algo parecido al leer la carta, y con esa esperanza me puse bastante alegre.

Cuando despaché la carta, certificada, estaba francamente optimista. A vuelta de correo llegó una carta de María, llena de ternura. Sentí que algo de nuestros primeros instantes de amor volvería a reproducirse . . . Quería que fuera a la estancia. Como un loco, preparé una valija, una caja de pinturas, y corrí a la estación Constitución.

58. ¿Cómo se describiría el estado mental del narrador al principio de este pasaje?
    (A) Optimista
    (B) Contento
    (C) Impaciente
    (D) Triste

59. ¿A quién le está enviando el narrador sus cartas?
    (A) Al correo
    (B) A la Srta. Posadas
    (C) A su prima en la estación Constitución
    (D) A su novia lejana

60. ¿Por qué está escribiendo el narrador estas cartas?
    (A) Quiere visitar a María en su casa.
    (B) Quiere jactarse de las cosas malas que ha hecho.
    (C) Quiere escribirle a María tantas veces como sea posible.
    (D) Quiere explicarse para que María lo entienda mejor.

61. ¿Cómo se ha sentido el narrador desde su confrontación con María?
    (A) Avergonzado
    (B) Tranquilo
    (C) Irritado
    (D) Estable

62. ¿Por qué está feliz el narrador cuando envía su carta?
    (A) Recibe una carta afectuosa de María.
    (B) Piensa que la carta le va a inspirar el amor a María.
    (C) No tiene que escribir cartas nunca más.
    (D) Sabe que María va a llorar de compasión.

63. ¿Cuál es la reacción del narrador cuando lee la respuesta de María?
    (A) Quiere pensar un largo rato en sus sentimientos.
    (B) Decide mudarse.
    (C) Sale para la estación.
    (D) Corre una milla.

GO ON TO THE NEXT PAGE

Los mayas eran oriundos de Guatemala. De Guatemala pasaron a la península de Yucatán en México, a Belice y Honduras. La cultura de los mayas era aún más avanzada que la de los aztecas, a quienes encontró Cortés cuando llegó a México. La arquitectura de los mayas era notable, como atestiguan las famosas ruinas de templos y pirámides en Palenque, Uxmal, Tikal y Copán. Se sitúa el apogeo de su cultura y civilización en el año 250 D.C. Poco antes del año 900 D.C. desaparecieron. Su desaparición ha sido un enigma. No se sabe precisamente por qué desaparecieron. Nuevos descubrimientos arqueológicos indican que existe la posibilidad de que los mayas quisieran lograr una gran expansión territorial y que las confrontaciones bélicas que acompañaban esa expansión fueran la causa más importante de la decadencia del Imperio Maya.

64. Belice y Honduras
   - (A) son partes de la cultura azteca
   - (B) son los sitios de los templos de los mayas
   - (C) están cerca de la península de Yucatán
   - (D) están en Guatemala

65. El Imperio Maya
   - (A) no existió después del año 900 D.C.
   - (B) fue una expansión territorial
   - (C) fue destruido por Cortés cuando llegó a México
   - (D) era mejor que el Imperio Azteca

66. El gran misterio de los mayas es
   - (A) su apogeo
   - (B) sus ruinas
   - (C) su éxito
   - (D) su desaparición

67. La belicosidad de los mayas se debe a
   - (A) los nuevos descubrimientos arqueológicos
   - (B) las famosas ruinas de templos
   - (C) la decadencia de su imperio
   - (D) su deseo de ampliar la extensión de su imperio

GO ON TO THE NEXT PAGE

Nos conviene pensar en los inmigrantes como miembros de tres grupos. El primer grupo consiste en los que vinieron aquí cuando eran adultos y ya hablaban su lengua materna. El segundo grupo consiste en los que nacieron aquí o vinieron aquí cuando eran niños; son hijos del primer grupo. El tercer grupo consiste en los que nacieron aquí, hijos del segundo grupo.

El primer grupo suele aprender un inglés funcional. Es decir, aprenden a expresarse y a comprender bastante bien pero casi nunca aprenden a hablar sin errores y sin acento. El segundo grupo aprende a hablar inglés perfectamente bien, sin ningún acento extranjero. Pero como hijos de inmigrantes, este grupo retiene algo de su primera lengua y muchas veces es bilingüe. El tercer grupo suele estar lingüísticamente asimilado, con poco conocimiento funcional de la lengua de sus abuelos.

La asimilación de los hispanos se ha estudiado mucho, y se ha visto repetidas veces que la gran mayoría de los inmigrantes hispanos siguen exactamente el mismo patrón que todos los demás inmigrantes. Por lo tanto, la percepción de que los inmigrantes hispanos no quieren aprender inglés es totalmente falsa. Como en el caso de cualquier grupo de inmigrantes, casi todo depende del tiempo que lleve su generación en este país.

68. ¿Qué determina el grupo al cual pertenece el/la inmigrante?

(A) Su deseo de aprender inglés
(B) El alcance de su conocimiento de inglés
(C) El país de donde vino originalmente
(D) El número de idiomas en que puede se comunicar

69. ¿Por qué no pierden sus acentos los miembros del primer grupo?

(A) Su conocimiento de su lengua nativa es más fuerte.
(B) No tienen deseo de aprender una lengua nueva.
(C) No necesitan aprender inglés.
(D) No se han asimilado bien a la cultura nueva.

70. ¿Cuál es una característica principal del segundo grupo?

(A) Aprendieron la lengua nueva de sus padres.
(B) Nacieron en este país.
(C) Tiene facilidad en dos idiomas.
(D) Han pasado muy poco tiempo en Estados Unidos.

71. ¿Cuál es la gran similitud entre el primer y el tercer grupos?

(A) No están bien asimilados lingüísticamente en este país.
(B) Solamente pueden hablar un idioma sin error.
(C) No creen que haya necesidad de aprender inglés.
(D) Son inmigrantes a este país.

72. ¿Cuál es el patrón que siguen casi todos inmigrantes?

(A) Sus oportunidades de aprender la lengua no son muchas.
(B) Se dividen en tres grupos que hablan sus propios idiomas.
(C) Tienen la misma percepción de que a ellos les falta el deseo de aprender inglés.
(D) El alcance de su asimilación lingüística depende de cuánto tiempo han vivido aquí.

73. ¿Cuál sería un buen título para este pasaje?

(A) "Generaciones de asimilación"
(B) "Dificultades con un idioma nuevo"
(C) "Inmigrantes que han aprendido inglés"
(D) "Percepciones erróneas de los inmigrantes"

GO ON TO THE NEXT PAGE

Los estudiantes se pusieron a reír. Primero, me molestaron los modales del profesor —era mi segundo día en un país extranjero— pero ahora me daba cólera que me pusiera en ridículo. No dije nada.

—¿Tal vez, continuó, nos hará el honor de tocar "Souvenir de Spa"?

Se trataba de una composición superficialmente brillante, popular en la escuela belga. Contesté que sí, que la tocaría.

—Estoy seguro de que vamos a oír algo asombroso de este joven que lo sabe todo. Pero, ¿y en qué va a tocar?

Más risa entre los estudiantes. Yo estaba tan furioso que estuve a punto de irme. Pero, recapacité. Quiera o no quiera, me dije, me va a escuchar. Le arrebaté el violoncelo al estudiante que estaba a mi lado y empecé a tocar. Se produjo un gran silencio en la sala. Cuando concluí, no se oía un ruido. El profesor me observaba intensamente, tenía una rara expresión en la cara.

—¿Quiere venir a mi oficina?—preguntó el profesor.

74. ¿Quién es el narrador?
   (A) Un músico professional
   (B) Un estudiante de un país extranjero
   (C) Alguien que está perdido
   (D) Un empleado de la escuela

75. ¿Qué es "Souvenir de Spa"?
   (A) Es una obra de música bien conocida.
   (B) Es una pieza maestra de literatura.
   (C) Es una escultura magnífica.
   (D) Es un poema clásico.

76. ¿Cuál es la actitud del maestro hacia el narrador al principio del pasaje?
   (A) Respeto profundo
   (B) Apoyo humillado
   (C) Condescendencia entretenida
   (D) Desprecio abierto

77. ¿Cómo reaccionan los estudiantes cuando oyen el narrador tocar el instrumento musical?
   (A) No dicen nada.
   (B) Empiezan a aplaudir.
   (C) Se ríen.
   (D) Salen de la clase.

78. ¿Qué característica del narrador se destaca más?
   (A) Su timidez
   (B) Su bondad
   (C) Su humildad
   (D) Su determinación

79. ¿Qué sería un buen título para esta narración?
   (A) "Una Manzana al Día Mantiene Alejado al Doctor"
   (B) "Las Grandes Mentes Piensan Igual"
   (C) "No Juzgue un Libro por Su Cubierta"
   (D) "El Amor No Tiene Precio"

GO ON TO THE NEXT PAGE

SPANISH SUBJECT TEST–*Continued*

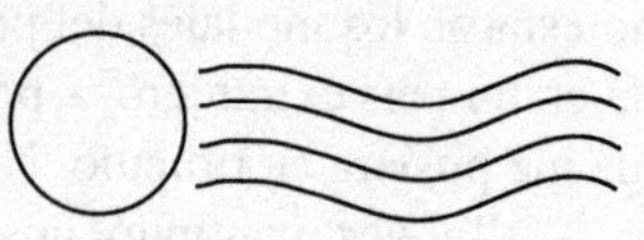

25 de Marzo de 2014
Londres, Inglaterra
Reino Unido

Querido Abuelo:

¡Hola! ¡Tanto tiempo que no te escribo! Espero que te sientas bien y que tu pierna ya se haya curado. ¡Cuidado con el hielo abuelo! Es muy resbaladizo.

Los estudios van muy bien y realmente me gusta mucho Oxford. Es una universidad muy popular pero los profesores dan mucho trabajo, y eso no me gusta. El fin de semana pasado, me tome un tren a Londres. ¡Que lindo que es! Visité los grandes museos, el palacio de Buckingham, el río Thames y las Casas de Parlamento. Realmente fue una experiencia. Las cafeterías son bastante caras, pero sin embargo me he juntado con muchos amigos para cenar. Me gusta mucho la comida. Espero poder volver el próximo año por última vez antes de volver para casa. ¿Están planeando en visitarnos el próximo año? Me gustaría verte a vos y a la abuela. Ya sé que el viaje de Alaska a Oregón no es nada fácil. A lo mejor podemos planear en encontrarnos en California.

Mañana empiezo una nueva clase de arte. Quería otro curso de arte artesanal, pero no tenían espacio. Me anoté en un curso de arte moderno. ¡Estoy muy entusiasmada! Te voy a mandar unos de mis grandes dibujos—¡algún día los podrás vender!

¡Te mando muchos abrazos y besos! Espero verte pronto. ¡Te quiero mucho!

Ana

80. ¿Qué no le gusta a Ana?
    (A) La Universidad de Oxford
    (B) La cantidad de tarea que dan los profesores
    (C) La cuidad de Londres
    (D) La popularidad de Oxford

81. ¿Cómo se lastimó la pierna el abuelo?
    (A) Fue a patinar en Alaska.
    (B) Se cayó.
    (C) Se cayó sobre el hielo.
    (D) Se quebró la pierna.

82. ¿Que se puede decir de las cafeterías?
    (A) Son caras.
    (B) No están cerca de el centro de Londres.
    (C) No aceptan reservaciones.
    (D) No le gusta la comida a Ana.

83. ¿Por qué fue a Londres?
    (A) Para estudiar
    (B) Para encontrarse con el abuelo
    (C) Para encontrarse con amigos
    (D) En excursión de turista

84. ¿Dónde y cuándo se quiere encontrar Ana con su Abuelo?
    (A) En Oregón el próximo año
    (B) En Oregón el próximo mes
    (C) En Alaska el próximo año
    (D) En California el próximo año

85. ¿Qué tipo de curso quería tomar Ana?
    (A) Un curso de arte moderna
    (B) Un curso de arte artesanal
    (C) Un curso de arte general
    (D) Un curso de arte especial

S T O P

If you finish before time is called, you may check your work on this test only.
Do not work on any other test in this book.

Chapter 10
Practice Test 2: Answers and Explanations

- Practice Test 2 Answer Key
- Practice Test 2 Explanations
- How to Score Practice Test 2

PRACTICE TEST 2 ANSWER KEY

Question Number	Correct Answer	Right	Wrong	Question Number	Correct Answer	Right	Wrong	Question Number	Correct Answer	Right	Wrong
1	C	____	____	33	B	____	____	65	A	____	____
2	D	____	____	34	D	____	____	66	D	____	____
3	B	____	____	35	C	____	____	67	D	____	____
4	D	____	____	36	A	____	____	68	B	____	____
5	A	____	____	37	D	____	____	69	A	____	____
6	D	____	____	38	B	____	____	70	C	____	____
7	A	____	____	39	C	____	____	71	B	____	____
8	C	____	____	40	C	____	____	72	D	____	____
9	D	____	____	41	A	____	____	73	A	____	____
10	B	____	____	42	B	____	____	74	B	____	____
11	B	____	____	43	C	____	____	75	A	____	____
12	C	____	____	44	A	____	____	76	C	____	____
13	D	____	____	45	D	____	____	77	A	____	____
14	C	____	____	46	D	____	____	78	D	____	____
15	A	____	____	47	B	____	____	79	C	____	____
16	D	____	____	48	C	____	____	80	B	____	____
17	C	____	____	49	B	____	____	81	C	____	____
18	B	____	____	50	A	____	____	82	A	____	____
19	C	____	____	51	C	____	____	83	D	____	____
20	D	____	____	52	A	____	____	84	D	____	____
21	A	____	____	53	B	____	____	85	B	____	____
22	D	____	____	54	C	____	____				
23	B	____	____	55	A	____	____				
24	A	____	____	56	B	____	____				
25	A	____	____	57	B	____	____				
26	C	____	____	58	C	____	____				
27	B	____	____	59	D	____	____				
28	D	____	____	60	D	____	____				
29	B	____	____	61	A	____	____				
30	D	____	____	62	B	____	____				
31	A	____	____	63	C	____	____				
32	B	____	____	64	C	____	____				

PRACTICE TEST 2 EXPLANATIONS

Part A

1. **C** **Translation:** There are seven days in a week and four weeks in ------- .

   (A) a century
   (B) a season
   (C) a month
   (D) a decade

   The key to this question is time, but all the answers are expressions for specific lengths of time. What to do? Vocabulary knowledge is important when choosing an answer. We might use POE to eliminate (B) because it's a length of time that's a little more obscure than the rest of the answers, but the only logical answer is (C).

2. **D** **Translation:** I really would like to buy a new suit, but I love these shoes! ------- ?

   (A) How are they?
   (B) Which are they?
   (C) When much are they?
   (D) How much are they?

   The implication here is that I want to buy the shoes instead of a suit. What is the most appropriate question that follows? Choice (A) sounds as if I am asking for a description of the shoes, but if I love them, I must be able to see them! Likewise, (B) does not make sense, unless I am extremely forgetful, and (C) is just silly and grammatically incorrect. The correct answer, then, is (D).

3. **B** **Translation:** My grandmother knitted/was knitting me a sweater and ------- a magazine at the same time.

   (A) read/was reading (subjunctive)
   (B) read/was reading
   (C) had read
   (D) reads

   The verb **tejía** places the action of the sentence in the past, so (D) (the present) does not correspond. Choice (C) (the pluperfect) places the act of reading the magazine before that of knitting the sweater, but the sentence says **a la vez**, so this is incorrect. Choices (A) and (B) are both in the past tense, but there is no cue for the use of the subjunctive in this sentence, so (A) is out. The correct answer is (B).

4. **D** **Translation:** The lungs are ------- the chest.

(A) under
(B) above
(C) in between
(D) inside

This is a basic anatomy question, as long as you know what the prepositions mean. Choice (D) is obviously correct.

5. **A** **Translation:** The employees haven't worked since last Wednesday because ------- a fire on that day which destroyed the building where they work.

(A) there was
(B) there is (subjunctive)
(C) there would be
(D) there is

The fire occurred last Wednesday, which is in the past, so (B) and (D) can be eliminated. The conditional tense in (C) does not apply because the fire doesn't depend on anything (it already happened), so (A) is the correct answer.

6. **D** **Translation:** Although we didn't have a lot of money, there was not ------- problem with paying our bill.

(A) any (masculine, affirmative)
(B) any (feminine, affirmative)
(C) any (feminine, negative)
(D) any (masculine, negative)

Translation doesn't really help, as you can see. Remember the double negative rule in Spanish—it's mandatory, so (A) and (B) are gone because they are affirmative words, which cannot be used in a negative sentence. The word "any" is an adjective in this sentence, and so it must agree in number and gender with the word it modifies, **problema**, which in Spanish is singular and masculine (even though it ends in an **a**), so (C) is eliminated and the correct answer is (D).

7. **A** **Translation:** You ------- Francisco in the stadium during the soccer game last Saturday.

(A) met
(B) meet
(C) meet (subjunctive)
(D) will meet

El sábado pasado indicates that the action took place in the past, so (B) and (C) (the present) and (D) (the future) are omitted. Choice (A) is correct.

8. **C** **Translation:** ------- where are the Gutiérrezes? It seems to me that they are Guatemalan, but I don't know for sure.

(A) For
(B) To
(C) From
(D) In

The sentence is speaking of the nationality of the family—their country of origin. Answers (A) and (B) imply destination, or movement toward something instead of away from it. Because these choices would also require the use of **estar** to make any grammatical sense, they are wrong. Likewise, (D) suggests their current location, and also requires the use of **estar**, so it is incorrect as well. Choice (C) is correct.

9. **D** **Translation:** The Cuban music was ------- very well by the orchestra of the Hotel Playa de Oro.

(A) heard
(B) made
(C) read
(D) played

An orchestra doesn't generally listen to its own or other people's music, so (A) makes no sense whatsoever. "To make music" would make sense in English, but it is better represented in Spanish by the verb **componer**, "to compose," so (B) is eliminated. Does an orchestra read music? Sure, and one supposes that if it reads music well, then it might be a pretty decent orchestra, but that's not the main function of an orchestra, so (C) is out. Only (D) is right on target.

10. **B** **Translation:** After I waited an hour and a half for them, ------- my brothers arrived to visit me.

(A) by chance
(B) finally
(C) of course
(D) please

The sentence indicates that the reason I was waiting was that my brothers were supposed to come, so (A) is silly, unless their visit is an unbelievable coincidence. Choice (C) indicates that there was never any doubt they would come, but I waited an hour and a half—surely I must have started second-guessing at some point. In the context of the sentence, (D) makes no sense. Only (B) puts an end to the waiting.

11. **B** **Translation:** It is ridiculous that the nations of the world ------ not live in peace.

(A) could
(B) can (subjunctive)
(C) could
(D) can

The implication of both (A) and (C) is that the nations of the world were unable to coexist only in the past (or perhaps that these nations don't even exist anymore), which is not the case, so those choices are wrong. The present tense is used in (B) and (D), but remember that the subjunctive is used with impersonal expressions that characterize the opinion of the speaker. **Es ridículo** is obviously a personal opinion, not a general truth, so the subjunctive is needed and (B) is the answer.

12. **C** **Translation:** I'm glad you (formal) are home, Don Alejandro, I wanted to ------- a favor.

(A) extract from you
(B) ask it
(C) ask you
(D) lend you

This question hinges on a student's knowledge of the indirect pronoun to use in formal situations. Choice (B) is a trap for those who attempt to match the pronoun to the direct object **favor**, which, as it's used in this context, does not need one. The correct answer is (C).

13. **D** **Translation:** You (plural) would live in a gigantic and splendid mansion if ------- millionaires.

(A) you (plural) are
(B) you (plural) would have been
(C) you (plural) are (subjunctive)
(D) you (plural) were (subjunctive)

The use of the conditional tense in combination with the word **si** tells us that we are talking about something that is not currently true—it has the condition of already being a millionaire attached. Placing the action in the present tense, then, would be incorrect, which eliminates (A) and (C). Choice (B) is simply not logical; it is awkward and grammatically incorrect. When you speak about something hypothetical in Spanish, the imperfect subjunctive is always used to indicate such situations, so (D) is correct.

14. **C** **Translation:** ------- you don't understand is that I hate artichokes.

(A) That
(B) Which
(C) What
(D) As

Choice (B) makes absolutely no sense, while (D) would make sense only if we eliminated the words **es que**. Choice (A) might seem to make sense if you translate **que** to mean "what," but this is only true when **que** has an accent mark, which indicates that it is being used as an interrogative (question) word. In this instance, **que** (no accent) is a conjunction (connecting word) that should join the two parts of the sentence together logically, which doesn't happen here. Choice (C) means literally "that which" or "the thing which," and this is correct in the context of the sentence.

15. **A** **Translation:** After swimming a little, Marta dried off because she was very ------- .

(A) wet
(B) bothered
(C) sick
(D) ready

Choice (C) is a basic word of high school Spanish and does not make sense in the context of this sentence, so it's out. Choice (B) is a pseudo-cognate that indicates someone is doing something to someone else that he/she doesn't appreciate, which does not make sense. That leaves (A) and (D). She didn't dry off because she was ready to do so but rather because of the normal reason—she was wet. The correct answer is (A).

16. **D** **Translation:** Our cousin is famous because ------- the role of Don Quijote in a play many years ago.

(A) he played
(B) he played
(C) he played
(D) he played

Translation doesn't help at all, as all these verbs mean the same thing in English; however, they have a variety of meanings in Spanish. Choice (A) means "to play an instrument," while (B) means "to play a compact disc." Choice (C) is "to play a game," while (D) carries the appropriate meaning of "to play a role" and is correct.

17. **C** **Translation:** I am seventeen years old but my ------- sister is only fifteen.

(A) older
(B) better
(C) younger
(D) worse

Many people confuse the meanings of (A) and (B) because they seem so similar in spelling, but (A) and (C) and (B) and (D) are actually pairs of opposites. Unless I regularly compare my sisters, (B) and (D) really don't make any sense here. Choice (A) defies logic, so (C) is the appropriate response.

18. **B** **Translation:** When we go shopping next Monday, ------- to the most exclusive stores.

(A) we go/are going (subjunctive)
(B) we will go
(C) we went
(D) we go/are going

Since the shopping trip will take place next Monday, a specific day in the future, we want to avoid verbs that use the present tense, such as (A) **vayamos** (present subjunctive) and (D) **vamos** (present). Likewise, we don't want to use the past tense, which leads us to eliminate (C) **fuimos**. Choice (B) is the only option that speaks of the future. Note that we could also say **vamos a ir** ("we are going to go"), which is not the same as saying simply **vamos** ("we go/we are going").

19. **C** **Translation:** Ricardo speaks German and Russian very ------- .

(A) bad (masculine, plural)
(B) bad (feminine, plural)
(C) badly
(D) evil

Choices (A) and (B) are incorrect because they modify the wrong part of the sentence—the languages. Choice (D) is way off. The answer is (C), an adverb modifying how Ricardo speaks.

20. **D** **Translation:** You (plural) are furious that we don't ------- anything about the Puerto Rican culture.

(A) know
(B) knew
(C) have known
(D) know (subjunctive)

The verb **están** places the action in the present, thus eliminating (B). Remember that the subjunctive is used with expressions of emotion, and the word **furioso** is definitely an emotion, so the use of the indicative in (A) and (C) is incorrect. Choice (D) is correctly in the present tense and the subjunctive mood.

21. **A** **Translation:** There is Alicia's umbrella, but where is ------- ?

(A) yours (masculine, plural)
(B) yours (masculine, singular)
(C) yours (feminine, plural)
(D) yours (feminine, singular)

The word **tuyo** cannot be used by itself. It is a possessive adjective and must be used in conjunction with the noun that it modifies, so (B) and (D) are incorrect. In the case of (A) and (C), the words **tuyo** and **tuya** modify **el** and **la** respectively, and are thus appropriate. Remembering that adjectives agree in number with the nouns they modify, and seeing from the sentence that **el paraguas** is a masculine noun, you can figure out that (A) is correct.

22. **D** **Translation:** Ramón bought a ring for his friend and gave ------- for her birthday.

(A) it (masculine)
(B) him/her
(C) it (feminine) to her
(D) it (masculine) to her

Choice (B) does not make sense in the context of the sentence. Choice (A) may seem correct, but it eliminates important information—gave it to whom? Choice (C) says that Ramón gave a feminine noun to his friend. Since there is no feminine noun in the sentence, (C) is wrong. Choice (D) is correct.

23. **B** **Translation:** Since you have spent so much time in the country, the mountains now ------- you.

(A) (you) enchant
(B) (they) enchant
(C) (he/she/it) enchants
(D) (you) enchant (subjunctive)

Encantar is a verb like **gustar**, which confuses many. Generally, this sentence would read, "now you love the mountains," but one loses the thread of who/what the subject is and who/what the object is with this translation. *The mountains* is the subject of the sentence, so the verb must correspond to the third-person plural conjugation, which is (B). Choice (A) is a common mistake, which comes from not understanding how this verb type functions. Choice (C) is way off base, while (D) is out because there are no cues in the sentence that require the use of the subjunctive.

24. A **Translation:** The prestigious family commissioned the painter to paint ------- of its matriarch, Mrs. Pedregal.

(A) a portrait
(B) a glass
(C) a lawn
(D) a message

Choice (B) is a relatively common vocabulary word in high school Spanish, while (C) is a little less common but still within reach. Both can be eliminated readily. Choices (A) and (D) sound very similar, but the proper response is (A).

25. A **Translation:** Although Lucía and Roberto did not want to do their work, they did it ------- .

(A) anyway
(B) at first sight
(C) at random
(D) unfortunately

This question relies on a knowledge of idioms. Choice (B) makes absolutely no sense in the context of this sentence. One would hope that (C) were simply not true, but it is actually incorrect because the conjunction **aunque** doesn't lead logically to the second part of the sentence—**porque** would make more sense. While (D) may be the opinion of Lucía and Roberto, it doesn't make any sense either. Choice (A) is the appropriate response.

26. C **Translation:** After receiving a bad grade on his final exam, Manuel ------- very angry and left the room.

(A) became
(B) became
(C) became
(D) became

Again, translating doesn't help at all, as all the verbs mean the same thing in English, though very different things in Spanish. Choice (A) means not only that he became angry, but also that he was never happy again—his anger is a permanent condition. Choices (B) and (D) are essentially interchangeable, as they mean "became" in the sense of moving to a new social position or status ("he became a doctor" or "he became a success"). Choice (C) indicates a temporary change in emotional condition, which is the intention of the sentence, and it is thus correct.

27. **B** **Translation:** The best seats ------- at the back of the theater, because one can see the entire screen from there.

(A) are
(B) are
(C) there is/are
(D) they have (subjunctive)

This sentence locates the best seats, so this question hinges around the sometimes confusing **ser** versus **estar** issue. Choice (C) is not correct because **hay** is used only to indicate the general existence of something, not its specific location. Choice (D) does not make sense at all, first because it is an auxiliary (helping) verb, which requires another verb afterward, second because there are no cues in the sentence that require the use of the subjunctive. The verb **ser** is used to describe permanent characteristics, so (A) is incorrect. **Estar** is used to locate things, so (B) is the answer.

28. **D** **Translation:** Joaquín's father is an attorney who specializes in tax ------- .

(A) stone
(B) garlic
(C) basement
(D) law

This is another vocabulary question, just to prove that no matter how much you think you know, there is always something you might *not* know. Choice (D) is the only one that makes sense.

29. **B** **Translation:** Since I moved to Argentina, I spend a lot of time thinking ------- my friends in Paraguay.

(A) of
(B) about
(C) that
(D) with

Prepositions in Spanish can often change the meaning of a verb very subtly, as is the case in this sentence. Choice (D) is obviously wrong, and we can use the literal translation to get rid of it. Choice (C) is incorrect because the word **que** must introduce a new clause. Choices (A) and (B) can both be translated as "of," but the preposition **de** can only be used with the verb **pensar** in a question. Choice (B) gives the appropriate meaning of the verb.

Part B

Passage:

La Sra. Jensen llegó el primer día a la clase diciendo que <u>quería</u> aprender español. Era obviamente una persona alerta y vivaz. Lo único que <u>la</u> distinguía de los otros estudiantes era su <u>edad</u>: en ese momento tenía sesenta y nueve años. Su historia es interesante. El esposo de la Sra. Jensen <u>murió</u> inesperadamente de un ataque cardíaco cuando ella tenía apenas treinta años, dejándola sola con cuatro hijos y ningún oficio para ganarse la vida. Sus padres habían muerto, los abuelos paternos de sus hijos tenían muy pocos recursos, y ella no tenía otros <u>parientes</u> que la ayudaran. En efecto, la muerte de su esposo <u>le</u> destruyó la vida. <u>Al</u> ver bien su situación, ella <u>reconoció</u> que tenía que volver a pensar todos sus planes y rehacer su vida sobre otras bases.

Translation:

Mrs. Jensen arrived to class the first day saying that *she wanted* to learn Spanish. She was obviously an alert and lively person. The only thing that distinguished *her* from the other students was her *age*: at that moment she was seventy-nine years old. Her story is interesting. Mrs. Jensen's husband *died* unexpectedly of a heart attack when she was scarcely thirty, leaving her alone with four children and no job in order to earn a living. Her parents were dead, the children's paternal grandparents had very few resources, and she did not have other *relatives* to help her. In effect, the death of her husband destroyed life for *her*. *Upon* looking well at her situation, she *recognized* that she had to rethink all her plans and remake her life upon other foundations.

30. **D** (A) would want
(B) wants (subjunctive)
(C) wants
(D) wanted

The action of the first sentence is in the past, so the verb **querer** must correspond, thus eliminating (B) and (C). Choice (A) does not make sense in the context of the sentence, as the conditional is most often used in hypothetical situations or situations of conjecture. The class is happening—it is not hypothetical, so (A) is incorrect. Choice (D) is in the past and is the correct response.

31. **A** **(A) her**
(B) him
(C) them (masculine)
(D) (to) her/him

Distinguished what? Distinguished *her*—Mrs. Jensen receives the action of the verb. A direct object pronoun is needed, thus eliminating (D), which is indirect. Choice (B) suggests that there is a man in this passage. Unless we're talking about the deceased Mr. Jensen being in the class, this is incorrect. Likewise, the only noun to which (C) might be referring is **los estudiantes**, which would not make sense in the context of the sentence. Choice (A) is correct.

32. **B** (A) clothes
(B) **age**
(C) behavior
(D) knapsack

The clue to the answer of this problem follows the colon: **en ese momento tenía sesenta y nueve años.** This is a pretty distinguishing characteristic, and (B) is the correct answer.

33. **B** (A) was born
(B) died
(C) spoke
(D) heard

Important words in this sentence are **ataque cardíaco** and **dejándola sola**. People are not "born" of a heart attack, so (A) is incorrect. Likewise, it hardly seems possible that Mr. Jensen unexpectedly spoke or heard of a heart attack and then left his family almost fifty years ago. Choice (B) is the only one that makes any sense.

34. **D** (A) arms
(B) stories
(C) maps
(D) relatives

The sentence before says that Mrs. Jensen was with **ningún oficio para ganarse la vida**. What are some things, then, that could help Mrs. Jensen financially following the death of her husband? Certainly not (B), and probably not (A) or (C) (unless it's a treasure map and they'll dig for the gold...), and so we are left with (D), the only choice that could offer this type of help.

35. **C** (A) her
(B) him
(C) (for) her/him
(D) itself

Destroyed what? Destroyed life—life is the direct object, receiving the action of the verb directly. We are not, then, looking for a direct object pronoun, because the direct object is already in the sentence, so (A) and (B) are incorrect. Is life destroying itself? That doesn't make much sense, so (D) is out, as well. Choice (C) is correct, as Mrs. Jensen is the person who receives the effect of the destroyed life—she is the indirect object of the sentence.

36. **A** **(A) Upon**
(B) In order to
(C) Before
(D) Let's

This question depends on a knowledge of idiomatic expressions. Choices (B) and (C) present situations that are backwards in their logic: to see (before seeing) her situation well, she has to rethink her life. It's the other way around, so both choices are out. **A ver** in Spanish means "Let's see" and does not fit in the sentence, so (D) is eliminated. Choice (A) presents a logical introduction to the situation in the sentence and is correct.

37. **D** (A) recognizes
(B) recognizes (subjunctive)
(C) will recognize
(D) recognized

The verb **tenía** tells us that we are in the past, so (A), (B), and (C) are all incorrect because they don't correspond to the proper tense. Choice (D) is the answer.

Passage:

—Cuando te sientas mal, mi hijita, le pedirás consejos al retrato. El te los dará. Puedes rezarle, ¿acaso no rezas a los santos?

Este modo de proceder le pareció extraño a Alejandrina. Mi vida transcurria monótonamente, pues tengo un testigo constante que me prohibe la felicidad: mi dolencia. El doctor Edgardo es la única persona que lo sabe. Hasta el momento de conocerlo, viví ignorando que algo dentro de mi organismo me carcomía. Ahora conozco todo lo que sufro: el doctor Edgardo me lo ha explicado. Es mi naturaleza. Algunos nacen con ojos negros, otros con ojos azules. Parece imposible que, siendo tan joven, él sea tan sabio; sin embargo, me he enterado de que no es precisa ser un anciano para serlo. Su piel lisa, sus ojos de niño, su cabellera rubia, ensortijada, son para mí el emblema de la sabiduría.

Translation:

"When you feel bad, my little girl, *you will ask* the portrait for advice. It will give *it to you*. You can pray to it—perhaps you don't pray to the saints?"

This *way* of proceeding seemed strange to Alejandrina. My life was passing monotonously, as I have a constant witness which prohibits happiness for me: my ailment. Dr. Edgardo is the only person who *knows* it. Until the time I recognized it, *I lived* ignoring that something inside my organism was consuming me. Now I know all that I suffer: Dr. Edgardo *has explained* it to me. It is my nature. Some *are born* with dark eyes, others with blue eyes. It seems impossible that, being so young, *he is* so wise; *however*, I have gotten to know that you don't need to be an old man to be wise. His smooth skin, his childlike eyes, his blond, curly head of hair are for *me* the emblem of wisdom.

38. **B** (A) you ask for (subjunctive)

(B) you will ask for

(C) you ask for

(D) you asked for

Cuando anticipates a time in the future when the narrator will feel bad (the use of the subjunctive tells us this, also), so the answer must also be in the future tense. Choice (D) is thus incorrect. You can use the present tense to speak of the near future, but it is already used in the subjunctive with **sientas** and would indicate the present if used again in a different part of the sentence, so (A) and (C) are out. Only (B) is in the appropriate future tense.

39. C (A) it (masculine) to me

(B) them (feminine) to me

(C) them (masculine) to you

(D) it (feminine) to you

Will give what? Will give advice. **Consejos**, the direct object, is replaced by the masculine plural pronoun **los**. This eliminates everything except (C), which is the answer.

40. C (A) glove

(B) topic

(C) way

(D) story

The word **este** refers to what immediately precedes it—the first paragraph, which involves someone telling the narrator to pray to the saints when she feels bad. Which word would describe this situation best? Answer (A) is obviously quite silly and can be eliminated. The answer must also be an adjective that is logical with the word **proceder**—"proceeding"—so (D) seems silly. Because the person speaking seems to be suggesting a method of reaction to illness, (C) is the most logical fit.

41. A **(A) knows**

(B) announces

(C) ignores

(D) shows

A doctor who announces patients' illnesses? Or ignores them? Choices (B) and (C) are eliminated for making no sense whatsoever. Choice (D) is a little strange—Dr. Edgardo is the only person who shows it. To whom? When? Where? Why? The most logical answer is choice (A).

42. **B** (A) I lived (subjunctive)

(B) I lived

(C) I live

(D) I live (subjunctive)

The narrator already knows that she is sick, so her life **ignorando** obviously took place in the past (before she knew), thus eliminating (C) and (D). There are no cues in the sentence that require the use of the subjunctive, so (B) is the correct answer.

43. **C** (A) outside

(B) next to

(C) inside

(D) around

Where is the illness that is consuming the narrator's body? Obviously inside the body; therefore, (C) is the correct answer. All the other choices are prepositions referring to the *outside* of the body, which is hard to imagine.

44. **A** **(A) has explained**

(B) had explained (subjunctive)

(C) will have explained

(D) has explained (subjunctive)

If the narrator now understands **todo lo que sufro**, then the doctor has already explained it to her. We need the past tense, which eliminates (C). There are no cues in the sentence that require the use of the subjunctive, thus eliminating (B) and (D), so (A) is the answer.

45. **D** (A) leave

(B) walk

(C) die

(D) are born

Dark eyes and blue eyes are relatively permanent conditions throughout one's life, so (A), (B), and (C) seem rather silly. Choice (D) establishes this permanent condition for life, and, therefore, it is the answer.

46. **D** (A) would be

(B) was

(C) is

(D) is (subjunctive)

The verb **parece** places the action in the present tense, eliminating (A) and (B). The phrase "**Parece imposible que**" is an impersonal expression of opinion on the part of the speaker (not a statement of general fact), and thus requires the use of the subjunctive. Choice (D) is correct.

47. **B** (A) because
(**B**) **however**
(C) furthermore
(D) then

Look at what's happening on either side of the semicolon: It seems impossible to be so smart / you don't have to be old to be wise. Which conjunction most logically connects these two ideas? They seem not to be saying the same thing, which eliminates (A), (C), and (D). Choice (B) gives us the proper word to show the contradiction between the two parts of the sentence.

48. **C** (A) I
(B) my
(C) me
(D) mine

Para is a preposition, and nouns in prepositional phrases are the objects of those prepositions. Choice (A) is a subject pronoun and can be eliminated. Choices (B) and (D) are out because they are types of possessive pronouns. The proper response is (C).

Passage:

Cortejar es pretender en matrimonio a una señorita. En la España del siglo XIX, y en particular, en la clase media, existían ciertas costumbres muy tradicionales que se observaban durante el cortejo. Así, un joven y una joven eran presentados el uno al otro en un evento social, por ejemplo, en un baile o una fiesta. Si ellos se gustaban y querían verse otra vez, tenían que buscar una ocasión para un nuevo encuentro. Cuando se veían, a la salida de la misa, durante el intermedio de una obra de teatro, o en el paseo de la tarde, intercambiaban cartitas amorosas.

La mujer joven informó al pretendiente de la hora en la cual ella saldría en al balcón para verse o hablarse calladamente o cuándo iría al paseo, con quién estaría acompañada, dónde se sentaría, y las demás señas necesarias.

Una vez que la joven pareja decidía casarse, el joven hacía una cita con los padres de la novia y les pedía la mano de su hija en matrimonio. A partir de ese momento, se les permitía a los novios verse más a menudo.

Pero, por supuesto, la novia siempre estaba acompañada de una hermana mayor, una tía, una dueña, un hermano u otra persona mayor hasta el día de la boda.

Translation:

Courtship is to seek a woman for marriage. In the Spain of the nineteenth century, and in particular, in the middle class, there existed certain very *traditional* customs that one observed during the courtship. Thus, a young man and a young woman were presented to each other at a *social* event, for example, at a dance or a party. If they liked each other and wanted to see each other again, they had to *look for* an occasion for a new encounter. When they saw each other, at departure from Mass, during the intermission of a play, or on an afternoon walk, they exchanged *love* letters.

The young woman informed the suitor *of* the hour at which *she would go out* onto the balcony to see him or talk to him quietly, or when she would go for a walk, by whom she would be accompanied, where she would sit, and other necessary signs.

Once the young couple decided *to be married*, the young man made an appointment with the young woman's parents and asked them for their daughter's hand in marriage. *From* that moment, they would allow the couple to see each other more often.

But, of course, the young woman was always accompanied by an older sister, an aunt, a chaperone, a brother or another older person until the day of *the wedding.*

49. B (A) annoying
(B) traditional
(C) shocking
(D) stupid

Customs are customs because of their tradition, so (B) is the answer. The other three terms would not normally be applied to customs.

50. A **(A) social**
(B) secret
(C) somber
(D) inappropriate

What kind of events are dances and parties? They involve being with other people, and thus are social, so (A) is the answer. The other three terms are not normally associated with dances and parties.

51. C (A) forget
(B) mention
(C) look for
(D) remember

If the two people want to see each other again, they have to be reasonably active in setting up another meeting. Choices (B) and (D) are a little too passive, and (A) would certainly defeat their purpose. Choice (C) makes sense—they would try to find another time to meet.

52. A **(A) love**
(B) professional
(C) ancient
(D) hateful

What kinds of letters would two people who like each other a lot exchange? The answer is understandably (A).

53. **B** (A) for
(B) of
(C) to
(D) with

This is a question regarding the use of idiomatic expressions. Luckily, the expression in Spanish is the same as that in English. You inform someone about or of something, so (B) is correct.

54. **C** (A) goes out (subjunctive)
(B) had gone out
(C) would go out
(D) will go out

The use of the verb **informaba** puts us in a tense that corresponds with the past, so (A) and (D) are eliminated. Look at the tense of the other verbs in this sentence: **iría, estaría, sentaría.** They are all in the conditional, as they are speaking of anticipated events, not events that have already happened. Choice (B) is the conditional perfect, which is only used to describe an event occurring in the past before another past event (and is thus not anticipated). Choice (C) corresponds to the other verbs in the sentence and speaks of anticipated events.

55. **A** **(A) to be married**
(B) to say good-bye
(C) to be divorced
(D) to become angry

The key phrase in this sentence is **les pedía la mano de su hija en matrimonio.** These people obviously like each other a lot. Choice (A) describes the next logical step in their relationship. The other three choices don't really describe what a couple in love would want to do.

56. **B** (A) Before
(B) From
(C) For
(D) With

Logic is important. Would the young woman's parents allow the two to see each other more often before he asks for her hand? Probably not, so (A) is out. Likewise, (C) is eliminated because it would not be for that moment only that they would allow it, especially because the sentence continues by suggesting various chaperones for their future dates. Choice (D) doesn't really make a whole lot of sense either, so (B) is the proper answer—from that moment on.

57. **B** (A) the party
(B) the wedding
(C) the death
(D) the dance

We've been clobbered over the head with the words **matrimonio** and **amor** in this passage. What's the obvious conclusion we can draw? Choice (B) is correct.

Part C

Passage:

Pasaron días terribles sin que llegara respuesta. Le envié una segunda carta y luego una tercera y una cuarta, diciendo siempre lo mismo, pero cada vez con mayor desolación. En la última, decidí relatarle todo lo que había pasado aquella noche que siguió a nuestra separación. No escatimé detalle ni bajeza, como tampoco dejé de confesarle la tentación de suicidio. Me dio vergüenza usar eso como arma, pero la usé. Debo agregar que, mientras describía mis actos más bajos y la desesperación de mi soledad en la noche frente a su casa de la calle Posadas, sentía ternura para conmigo mismo y hasta lloré de compasión. Tenía muchas esperanzas de que María sintiese algo parecido al leer la carta, y con esa esperanza me puse bastante alegre.

Cuando despaché la carta, certificada, estaba francamente optimista. A vuelta de correo llegó una carta de María, llena de ternura. Sentí que algo de nuestros primeros instantes de amor volvería a reproducirse . . . Quería que fuera a la estancia. Como un loco, preparé una valija, una caja de pinturas, y corrí a la estación Constitución.

Translation:

Awful days passed without a response arriving. I sent her a second letter and then a third and a fourth, always saying the same thing, but each time with greater distress. In the last one, I decided to relate to her all that had happened that night that followed our separation. I didn't skimp on detail or baseness, as I also didn't neglect to confess to her the temptation of suicide. I was ashamed to use that as a weapon, but I used it. I should add that, while I described my lowest acts and the desperation of my solitude on that night in front of her house on Posadas Street, I felt tenderness toward myself and I almost cried in pity. I had much hope that María would feel something similar on reading the letter, and with that hope I became quite happy.

When I sent the letter, certified, I was clearly optimistic. Once back from the post office, a letter from María arrived, full of tenderness. I felt that something of our first moments of love would start to happen again...I wished that I were at the hacienda. Like a fool, I prepared a suitcase, a box full of paints, and I ran to Constitution Station.

58. C **Translation:** How would one describe the mental state of the narrator at the beginning of this passage?

(A) Optimistic
(B) Content
(C) Impatient
(D) Sad

The guy has sent four letters to the same person and is complaining that he has not received a response yet. He is certainly not content with or optimistic about the situation, so (A) and (B) are gone. While he may be sad that María has not responded, one doesn't sense this emotion as much as his impatience (four letters?). Choice (C) is correct.

59. D **Translation:** To whom is the narrator sending his letters?

(A) To the post office
(B) To Miss Posadas
(C) To his cousin at Constitution Station
(D) To his estranged girlfriend

We know that María is receiving the letters and that the narrator once had a relationship with her that he wants to recapture. He is sending the letters from, not to, the post office, so (A) is incorrect. Posadas is the name of María's street, so (B) is wrong, and there is no cousin mentioned in the passage, so (C) is incorrect as well. Choice (D) describes the narrator's relationship with María well.

60. D **Translation:** Why is the narrator writing these letters?

(A) He wants to visit María in her home.
(B) He wants to brag about the bad things he has done.
(C) He wants to write to María as many times as possible.
(D) He wants to explain himself so that María understands him better.

The narrator does not want to visit María—he already did that when they separated, so (A) is out. He doesn't necessarily want to brag about his deeds as much as he wants to explain them to her, so (B) is not correct. While it may seem that the narrator is going for the world record in letter writing, this is not his intention in writing them either. He wants María to understand him, so (D) is the correct response.

61. **A** **Translation:** How has the narrator felt since his confrontation with María?

(A) **Ashamed**
(B) Calm
(C) Irritated
(D) Stable

In addition to seeming a little desperate, the narrator does not seem at all proud of his actions. Why else would he write four letters trying to explain himself and his actions to María? He is certainly not stable (he thought about suicide), nor is he calm (he's a nervous wreck waiting for her response), so (B) and (D) are eliminated. While he may be a little irritated that he hasn't received a response to his letters, the focus of the passage is on his motive for writing the letters, which is his shame; thus, (A) is the answer.

62. **B** **Translation:** Why is the narrator happy when he sends his letter?

(A) He receives an affectionate letter from María.
(B) He thinks that the letter will inspire María's love.
(C) He doesn't have to write letters anymore.
(D) He knows that María is going to cry in pity.

Choice (A) is incorrect because he receives the letter after he returns from the post office. Choice (D) is a misreading of the passage—it is the narrator who cried when he wrote the letter. Choice (C) is a little strange when it seems that the narrator didn't seem to mind writing four letters to get a response. The second-to-last sentence says that he hoped that María would feel tenderness toward him upon reading the letter, so (B) is the answer.

63. **C** **Translation:** What is the narrator's reaction when he reads Maria's response?

(A) He wants to think for a long while about his feelings.
(B) He decides to move.
(C) He leaves for the station.
(D) He runs a mile.

While it is true that the narrator packed his suitcase, it's not because he has decided to move (B). He also didn't need to think a long while about his feelings (A) because he knows what he feels and can't wait to see his beloved. We don't know whether he runs a mile (D), but he does leave for the station (C).

Passage:

Los mayas eran oriundos de Guatemala. De Guatemala pasaron a la península de Yucatán en México, a Belice y Honduras. La cultura de los mayas era aún más avanzada que la de los aztecas, a quienes encontró Cortés cuando llegó a México. La arquitectura de los mayas era notable, como atestiguan las famosas ruinas de templos y pirámides en Palenque, Uxmal, Tikal y Copán. Se sitúa el apogeo de su cultura y civilización en el año 250 D.C. Poco antes del año 900 D.C. desaparecieron. Su desaparición ha sido un enigma. No se sabe precisamente por qué desaparecieron. Nuevos descubrimientos arqueológicos indican que existe la posibilidad de que los mayas quisieran lograr una gran expansión territorial y que las confrontaciones bélicas que acompañaban esa expansión fueran la causa más importante de la decadencia del Imperio Maya.

Translation:

The Mayas were natives of Guatemala. From Guatemala they moved to the Yucatán Peninsula in Mexico, to Belize and Honduras. The culture of the Mayas was even more advanced than that of the Aztecs, whom Cortés encountered when he arrived in Mexico. The architecture of the Mayas was notable, as the famous ruins of temples and pyramids in Palenque, Uxmal, Tikal, and Copán prove. The apex of their culture and civilization is situated in the year 250 A.D. A little before 900 A.D. they disappeared. Their disappearance has been an enigma. One does not know precisely why they disappeared. New archaeological discoveries indicate that the possibility exists that the Mayas wanted to achieve a great territorial expansion and that the warlike confrontations that accompanied that expansion were the most important cause of the decline of the Mayan Empire.

64. C **Translation:** Belize and Honduras

(A) are parts of the Aztec culture
(B) are the sites of the Mayan temples
(C) are near the Yucatán Peninsula
(D) are in Guatemala

The passage does not focus on the Aztecs at all; therefore, (A) is incorrect. The Mayas moved from Guatemala—they left, so Belize and Honduras cannot be in Guatemala; thus, (D) is incorrect. The sites of the Mayan temples and pyramids are the four cities mentioned, not these two countries, so (B) is incorrect. That leaves (C) as the answer.

65. A **Translation:** The Mayan Empire

(A) didn't exist after 900 A.D.
(B) was a territorial expansion
(C) was destroyed by Cortés when he arrived in Mexico
(D) was better than the Aztec Empire

The Empire was not a territorial expansion and was not destroyed by Cortés, so choices (B) and (C) are incorrect. Although the passage says that "**La cultura de los mayas era aún más avanzada**" than that of the Aztecs, it doesn't say that it was better, so (D) is incorrect. Choice (A) corresponds with the time of the disappearance of the Mayan civilization and is correct.

66. **D** **Translation:** The great mystery of the Mayas is

(A) their apex
(B) their ruins
(C) their success
(D) their disappearance

Nearly the entire second half of the passage talks about the disappearance of the Mayas and says that it has been **un enigma.** Choice (D) is correct.

67. **D** **Translation:** The bellicosity of the Mayas is due to

(A) the new archaeological discoveries
(B) the famous ruins of temples
(C) the decline of their empire
(D) their desire to increase the extent of their empire

The passage says that **las confrontaciones bélicas...acompañaban esa expansión**—that is, they became more aggressive in trying to expand their empire. Choice (D) summarizes this nicely.

Passage:

Nos conviene pensar en los inmigrantes como miembros de tres grupos. El primer grupo consiste en los que vinieron aquí cuando eran adultos y ya hablaban su lengua materna. El segundo grupo consiste en los que nacieron aquí o vinieron aquí cuando eran niños; son hijos del primer grupo. El tercer grupo consiste en los que nacieron aquí, hijos del segundo grupo.

El primer grupo suele aprender un inglés funcional. Es decir, aprenden a expresarse y a comprender bastante bien pero casi nunca aprenden a hablar sin errores y sin acento. El segundo grupo aprende a hablar inglés perfectamente bien, sin ningún acento extranjero. Pero como hijos de inmigrantes, este grupo retiene algo de su primera lengua y muchas veces es bilingüe. El tercer grupo suele estar lingüísticamente asimilado, con poco conocimiento funcional de la lengua de sus abuelos.

La asimilación de los hispanos se ha estudiado mucho, y se ha visto repetidas veces que la gran mayoría de los inmigrantes hispanos sigue exactamente el mismo patron que todos los demás inmigrantes. Por lo tanto, la percepción de que los inmigrantes hispanos no quieren aprender inglés es totalmente falsa. Como en el caso de cualquier grupo de inmigrantes, casi todo depende del tiempo que lleve su generación en este país.

Translation:

It is fitting for us to think about immigrants as members of three groups. The first group consists of those who came here when they were adults and already spoke their mother language. The second group consists of those who were born here or who came here when they were children; they are children of the first group. The third group consists of those who were born here, children of the second group.

The first group usually learns a functional English. That is to say, they learn to express themselves and to understand well enough but almost never learn to speak without errors or without accent. The second group learns to speak English perfectly well, without any foreign accent. But as children of immigrants, this group retains something of its first language and is often bilingual. The third group is usually linguistically assimilated, with little functional knowledge of their grandparents' language.

The assimilation of Hispanics has been much studied, and it has been seen repeatedly that the great majority of Hispanic immigrants follows exactly the same pattern as all the rest of the immigrants. Therefore, the perception that Hispanic immigrants don't want to learn English is totally false. As in the case of any group of immigrants, almost everything depends on the time that their generation has been in this country.

68. B **Translation:** What determines the group to which an immigrant belongs?

(A) His/her desire to learn English
(B) The extent of his/her knowledge of English
(C) The country from which he/she came originally
(D) The number of languages in which he/she can communicate

The focus of this passage is on an immigrant's relative knowledge of English, as it is explained extensively in the second paragraph, so (B) is the correct answer.

69. A **Translation:** Why don't the members of the first group lose their accents?

(A) Their knowledge of their native language is stronger.
(B) They don't have the desire to learn a new language.
(C) They don't need to learn English.
(D) They haven't assimilated well in the new culture.

Choice (B) is a myth that this passage hopes to end, so it is incorrect. Choice (C) is negated by the phrase **suele aprender un inglés funcional**. If they don't need to, why bother? Choice (D) really has nothing to do with their accents, so (A) is the correct answer. Remember: When they came to this country **ya hablaban su lengua materna.**

70. C **Translation:** What is the principal characteristic of the second group?

(A) They learned the new language from their parents.
(B) They were born in this country.
(C) They have facility in two languages.
(D) They have spent very little time in the United States.

Choice (A) is incorrect because their parents speak only **un inglés funcional**. Choice (B) is not necessarily correct: They could have come here at an early age. If they were born here or came here early, then (D) is also incorrect. Choice (C) is the correct answer—**es bilingüe.**

71. **B** **Translation:** What is the great similarity between the first and third groups?

(A) They are not well assimilated linguistically in this country.
(B) They can only speak one language without error.
(C) They don't believe that there is a necessity to learn English.
(D) They are immigrants to this country.

The third group was born in the United States, so (A), (C), and (D) are all illogical, so (B) is the answer. The first group only speaks Spanish well, the third group only English.

72. **D** **Translation:** What is the pattern that almost all immigrants follow?

(A) Their opportunities to learn the language are not many.
(B) They divide themselves into three groups that speak their own languages.
(C) They have the same perception that they lack a desire to learn English.
(D) The extent of their linguistic assimilation depends on how much time they have lived here.

Again, (C) is a point the passage is trying to disprove, so it is incorrect. Choice (A) is not logical, given the fact that they have to learn **un inglés funcional** to survive in the country. Choice (B) is a misunderstanding—these are not physical groups that the immigrants themselves form. They are groups formed theoretically to allow us to understand how generations of immigrants differ. Choice (D) is the ultimate point of the passage, expressed in the final sentence.

73. **A** **Translation:** What would be a good title for this passage?

(A) "Generations of Assimilation"
(B) "Difficulties with a New Language"
(C) "Immigrants who Have Learned English"
(D) "Erroneous Perceptions of Immigrants"

The main idea of the passage is that of linguistic assimilation, so (A) is the answer. The other choices are either too narrow in scope, like (B) and (D), or completely off the map (C).

Passage:

Los estudiantes se pusieron a reír. Primero, me molestaron los modales del profesor—era mi segundo día en un país extranjero— pero ahora me daba cólera que me pusiera en ridículo. No dije nada.

—¿Tal vez, continuó, nos hará el honor de tocar "Souvenir de Spa"?

Se trataba de una composición superficialmente brillante, popular en la escuela belga. Contesté que sí, que la tocaría.

—Estoy seguro de que vamos a oír algo asombroso de este joven que lo sabe todo. Pero, ¿y en qué va a tocar?

Más risa entre los estudiantes. Yo estaba tan furioso que estuve a punto de irme. Pero, recapacité. Quiera o no quiera, me dije, me va a escuchar. Le arrebaté el violoncelo del estudiante que estaba a mi lado y empecé a tocar. Se produjo un gran silencio en la sala. Cuando concluí, no se oía un ruido. El profesor me observaba intensamente, tenía una rara expresión en la cara.

—¿Quiere venir a mi oficina? —preguntó el profesor.

Translation:

The students started to laugh. First, the professor's manner bothered me—it was my second day in a foreign country—but now it angered me that he ridiculed me. I said nothing.

"Perhaps," he continued, "you will do us the honor of playing 'Souvenir de Spa'?"

He was talking about a superficially brilliant composition, popular in the Belgian school. I answered yes, I would play it.

"I am sure that we are going to hear something amazing from this young man who knows it all. But, on what are you going to play?"

More laughter among the students. I was so furious that I was at the point of leaving. But I thought things over. Like it or not, I told myself, he is going to listen to me. I snatched the cello from the student that was at my side and began to play. A great silence came over the room. When I finished, not a sound was heard. The professor was observing me intensely; he had a strange expression on his face.

"Do you want to come to my office?" he said.

74. B **Translation:** Who is the narrator?

(A) A professional musician
(B) A student from a foreign country
(C) Someone who is lost
(D) An employee of the school

In the first paragraph, the narrator says **era mi segundo día en un país extranjero.** There is no indication that he is lost or an employee of the school, so we can eliminate (C) and (D). And although he can play a musical instrument, we do not know if he is a professional musician (A). Choice (B) is the correct answer.

75. A **Translation:** What is "Souvenir de Spa"?

(A) It is a well-known work of music.
(B) It is a masterpiece of literature.
(C) It is a magnificent sculpture.
(D) It is a classic poem.

The word **composición** may fool some people into picking (B) or (D). When we see, however, the words **violoncelo** and **tocar**, we should realize that we are talking about music, making (A) the answer.

76. C **Translation:** What is the attitude of the teacher toward the narrator at the beginning of the passage?

(A) Profound respect
(B) Humbled support
(C) Amused condescension
(D) Open disdain

The passage begins with the teacher having just ridiculed the narrator, so (A) and (B) seem unlikely. Choice (D) is a little too extreme an answer; the point is that the teacher is subtly questioning the ability of the narrator, not openly saying that he hates him. Choice (C) is the proper response.

77. A **Translation:** How do the students react when they hear the narrator play the musical instrument?

(A) They don't say anything.
(B) They begin to applaud.
(C) They laugh.
(D) They leave the classroom.

In the second to last paragraph, the narrator says that when he finished playing, **no se oía ni un ruido**. The students don't applaud, laugh, or leave the room, so (B), (C), and (D) are incorrect. Choice (A) is the correct answer.

78. D **Translation:** What trait about the narrator stands out the most?

(A) His timidity
(B) His generosity
(C) His humility
(D) His determination

To stand up to a condescending teacher is anything but timid, so that eliminates choice (A). Nothing indicates that the narrator is generous or humble, which rules out (B) and (C). Choice (D) is the best answer.

79. C **Translation:** What would be a good title for this passage?

(A) "An Apple a Day Keeps the Doctor Away"
(B) "Great Minds Think Alike"
(C) "Don't Judge a Book by Its Cover"
(D) "Love Has No Price"

Neither (A) nor (D) has any relevance to the passage. We can also eliminate choice (B); clearly the teacher and the narrator don't see eye to eye. Choice (C) is the best answer because the teacher assumes without any real basis that the narrator can't play the song.

Passage:

25 de Marzo de 2014
Londres, Inglaterra
Reino Unido

Querido Abuelo:

¡Hola! ¡Tanto tiempo que no te escribo! Espero que te sientas bien y que tu pierna ya se haya curado. ¡Cuidado con el hielo abuelo! Es muy resbaladizo.

Los estudios van muy bien y realmente me gusta mucho Oxford. Es una universidad muy popular pero los profesores dan mucho trabajo, y eso no me gusta. El fin de semana pasado, me tome un tren a Londres. ¡Que lindo que es! Visité los grandes museos, el palacio de Buckingham, el río Thames y las Casas de Parlamento. Realmente fue una experiencia. Las cafeterías son bastante caras, pero sin embargo me he juntado con muchos amigos para cenar. Me gusta mucho la comida. Espero poder volver el próximo año por última vez antes de volver para casa. ¿Están planeando con la abuela visitarnos el próximo año? Me gustaría verte a vos y a la abuela. Ya sé que el viaje de Alaska a Oregón no es nada fácil. A lo mejor podemos planear en encontrarnos en California.

Mañana empiezo una nueva clase de arte. Quería otro curso de arte artesanal, pero no tenían espacio. Me anoté para un curso de arte moderno. ¡Estoy muy entusiasmada! Te voy a mandar unos de mis grandes dibujos—¡algún día los podrás vender!

¡Te mando muchos abrazos y besos! Espero verte pronto. ¡Te quiero mucho!

Ana

Translation:

March 25, 2014
London, England
United Kingdom

Dear Grandpa:

Hello! It's been a long time since I wrote you. I hope you are feeling good and that your leg has healed. Careful with the ice, Grandpa! It's very slippery.

My studies are going really well and I really like Oxford. It's a very popular university, but the professors give a lot of work, and I don't like that. Last weekend, I took a train to London. It's so pretty! I visited the grand museums, Buckingham Palace, the Thames River, and the Houses of Parliament. It really was an experience. The cafes are very expensive, but nevertheless I met up with a lot of my friends for dinner. I really love food. I hope to be able to go back once more next year before returning home. Are you and Grandma planning on visiting us next year? I would like to see you and Grandma. I know that the trip from Alaska to Oregon is not easy. Maybe we can plan to meet up in California.

Tomorrow I start a new art class. I wanted another course on artisanal art, but there was no room. I signed up for a course on modern art. I am very excited! I will send you some of my grand drawings—someday you might be able to sell them!

I send you lots of hugs and kisses! I hope to see you soon. I love you very much!

Ana

80. B **Translation:** What does Ana not like?

(A) Oxford University
(B) The amount of work that the professors give
(C) The city of London
(D) Oxford's popularity

In her postcard, Ana makes reference to liking Oxford very much but not the amount of work that the professors give her. Choice (B) is the correct answer.

81. C **Translation:** How did the grandfather hurt his leg?

(A) He went ice skating in Alaska.
(B) He fell.
(C) He fell on the ice.
(D) He broke his leg.

At the beginning of the her letter, Ana sends her good wishes to her grandfather about his leg. She says to be cautious of ice because it's slippery. However, it's not clear whether the accident involved ice skating or whether her grandfather broke his leg, so we have to eliminate choices (A) and (D). Also, choice (B) is not specific enough, since we know ice was the cause of the incident. Therefore, choice (C) is the correct answer.

82. A **Translation:** What can be said of the cafes?

(A) They are expensive.
(B) They are not close to central London.
(C) They don't take reservations.
(D) She doesn't like the food they serve.

Ana states that the cafes are expensive. She makes no mention of the distance to central London (B) or reservations (C), and she mentions loving the food in London. Therefore, choice (A) is the correct answer.

83. D **Translation:** Why did she go to London?

(A) To study
(B) To meet up with her grandfather
(C) To meet up with her friends
(D) To go on a tourist excursion

Ana is already studying at Oxford and finishing up her studies next year. She is sending her grandfather a postcard, so we can eliminate (A) and (B). She mentions meeting up with her friends for dinner, but that does not seem to be the main reason for her trip, so we can eliminate (C). However, we know that Ana visited numerous tourist attractions, so (D) is the correct answer.

84. **D** **Translation:** Where and when does Ana want to meet up with her grandfather?

(A) Next year in Oregon
(B) Next month in Oregon
(C) Next year in Alaska
(D) Next year in California

Ana is visiting London, but she lives in Oregon. We know her grandfather lives in Alaska, as Ana mentions that the trip from Alaska to Orgeon is not easy. This probably explains why she suggests that they meet up in California next year, making choice (D) the correct answer.

85. **B** **Translation:** What type of course did Ana want to take?

(A) A course in modern art
(B) A course in artisanal art
(C) A course in general art
(D) A course in special art

Ana writes that she has started a new class. She wanted an artisan art class, but it was full, so she registered for a course in modern art instead. Choice (B) is the correct answer, as it represents what she *wanted* to take, not what she ended up taking.

HOW TO SCORE PRACTICE TEST 2

When you take the real exam, the proctors take away your exam and your bubble sheet and send it to a processing center, where a computer looks at the pattern of filled-in ovals on your exam and gives you a score. We couldn't include even a small computer with this book, so we are providing this more primitive way of scoring your exam.

Determining Your Score

STEP 1 Using the answer key, determine how many questions you got right and how many you got wrong on the test. Remember, questions that you do not answer do not count as either right answers or wrong answers.

STEP 2 List the number of right answers here. (A) ______

STEP 3 List the number of wrong answers here. Now divide that number by 3. (B) ______ ÷ 3 ______ = (C) ______

STEP 4 Subtract the number of wrong answers divided by 3 (C) from the number of correct answers (A). Round this score to the nearest whole number. This is your raw score. (A) – (C) = ______

STEP 5 To determine your real score, take the number from Step 4 above and look it up in the left column of the Score Conversion Table on the next page; the corresponding score on the right is your score on the exam.

PRACTICE TEST 2
SCORE CONVERSION TABLE

Raw Score	Scaled Score	Raw Score	Scaled Score	Raw Score	Scaled Score
85	800	47	590	9	360
84	800	46	580	8	360
83	800	45	570	7	350
82	800	44	570	6	350
81	790	43	560	5	340
80	790	42	550	4	340
79	780	41	550	3	330
78	780	40	540	2	320
77	770	39	530	1	320
76	770	38	530	0	310
75	760	37	520	–1	310
74	760	36	520	–2	300
73	750	35	510	–3	290
72	750	34	500	–4	290
71	740	33	500	–5	280
70	730	32	490	–6	270
69	730	31	490	–7	260
68	720	30	480	–8	260
67	720	29	470	–9	250
66	710	28	470	–10	240
65	700	27	460	–11	230
64	700	26	460	–12	220
63	690	25	450	–13	220
62	680	24	450	–14	220
61	680	23	440	–15	210
60	670	22	430	–16	210
59	670	21	430	–17	210
58	660	20	420	–18	200
57	650	19	420	–19	200
56	650	18	410	–20	200
55	640	17	410	–21	200
54	630	16	400	–22	200
53	630	15	400	–23	200
52	620	14	390	–24	200
51	620	13	390	–25	200
50	610	12	380	–26	200
49	600	11	380	–27	200
48	590	10	370	–28	200

Chapter 11
Practice Test 3

SPANISH SUBJECT TEST 3

Your responses to Spanish Subject Test 3 questions must be filled in on Test 3 of your answer sheet (at the back of the book). Marks on any other section will not be counted toward your Spanish Subject Test score.

When your supervisor gives the signal, turn the page and begin the Spanish Subject Test.

SPANISH SUBJECT TEST

PLEASE NOTE THAT YOUR ANSWER SHEET HAS FIVE ANSWER POSITIONS MARKED A, B, C, D, E, WHILE THE QUESTIONS THROUGHOUT THIS TEST CONTAIN ONLY FOUR CHOICES. BE SURE NOT TO MAKE ANY MARKS IN COLUMN E.

Part A

Directions: This part consists of a number of incomplete statements, each having four suggested completions. Select the most appropriate completion and fill in the corresponding oval on the answer sheet.

1. Manuel no pudo comer ------- porque estaba demasiado caliente.

(A) la naranja
(B) las medias
(C) la sopa
(D) la acera

2. Mis amigos van de compras ------- : cada lunes, jueves y sábado.

(A) a menudo
(B) de mala gana
(C) diariamente
(D) poco

3. Comeríamos mucho menos si no ------- comida en casa.

(A) hay
(B) haya
(C) habría
(D) hubiera

4. Cuando el fin de semana venga, ------- tiempo para hacer tus deberes en casa.

(A) tienes
(B) tenías
(C) tendrías
(D) tendrás

5. Como ella trabaja en Nueva York y Connecticut, tiene que pagar ------- en los dos estados.

(A) ingresos
(B) impuestos
(C) deudas
(D) luto

6. El equipo tuvo que cancelar el partido ------- la lluvia.

(A) para
(B) sin
(C) a causa de
(D) dentro de

7. Mi sofá es muy cómodo porque es viejo; ------- es nuevo y no muy cómodo.

(A) el suyo
(B) la suya
(C) los suyos
(D) las suyas

8. Mi mamá fue al dentista porque le dolían los dientes. El dentista necesitó sacarle ------- .

(A) las carteras
(B) las muelas
(C) los techos
(D) los hombros

9. Rodrigo sabe esquiar muy bien, pero yo no. Él es mejor ------- yo.

(A) que
(B) como
(C) para
(D) de

GO ON TO THE NEXT PAGE

SPANISH SUBJECT TEST–*Continued*

10. A Susana no le gusta que casi todo el mundo ------- todo lo que pasa en su vida.

(A) sabe
(B) sepa
(C) conoce
(D) conozca

11. Fue imposible sacar agua del pozo porque el pozo estaba completamente ------- .

(A) alto
(B) fresco
(C) anaranjado
(D) seco

12. El policía va a dudar que le ------- la verdad si nos detiene.

(A) digamos
(B) decimos
(C) diríamos
(D) habremos dicho

13. La tienda está en ------- de la Calle Santo Tomás y la Avenida de Toros.

(A) el pasillo
(B) la esquina
(C) la red
(D) el rincón

14. Bárbara y Nicolás siempre quieren dar su ayuda. Cuando ------- la dan a sus compañeros de clase, ellos están muy alegres.

(A) le
(B) se
(C) les
(D) lo

15. ¿ ------- cuántas horas trabaja tu esposa todos los días?

(A) Por
(B) Para
(C) Antes de
(D) Desde

16. Si Uds. no se acuestan más temprano, estarán muy ------- mañana.

(A) borrachas
(B) cansadas
(C) activas
(D) heridas

17. ¡No me ------- cuenta de que él era tu tío hasta este momento!

(A) he dado
(B) había dado
(C) habría dado
(D) habré dado

18. Roberto perdió la voz anoche, entonces no podrá ------- hoy.

(A) correr
(B) respirar
(C) cantar
(D) barrer

19. ¿No puedes encontrar tu anillo? Creo que lo ------- en la cocina cerca del fregadero.

(A) vi
(B) fui
(C) di
(D) oí

20. Si tengo un paquete, compro estampillas, y entonces se lo envío a alguien, probablemente estoy en la oficina de ------- .

(A) correos
(B) platos
(C) educación
(D) regalos

21. Cuando una película nos confunde, la ------- después para entenderla mejor.

(A) discutes
(B) discute
(C) discutimos
(D) discuten

GO ON TO THE NEXT PAGE

22. El jefe me sigue como si ------- que yo hiciera algo malo.

    (A) esperó
    (B) esperara
    (C) espera
    (D) espere

23. Cuando el profesor terminó su lección, borró ------- y se fue de la sala de clase.

    (A) la pizarra
    (B) la basura
    (C) el escritorio
    (D) a la alumna

24. ¿Necesitas tomates y lechuga en la ensalada? Te ------- traeré en seguida.

    (A) lo
    (B) la
    (C) los
    (D) las

25. ¿Le ------- a Ud. un poco extraño que ellos no llevaran zapatos en la nieve?

    (A) veía
    (B) miraba
    (C) buscaba
    (D) parecía

26. ¿ ------- quién estaban preparando un pavo grande y puré de papas?

    (A) De
    (B) Dónde
    (C) A
    (D) Para

27. Estas dos rosas huelen exactamente similares, entonces esta rosa es ------- esa.

    (A) poco aromática a
    (B) menos aromática que
    (C) más aromática que
    (D) tan aromática como

28. Nadie ------- los tambores como Tito Puente.

    (A) jugaba
    (B) hacía
    (C) tocaba
    (D) ponía

29. Cuando la compañía ------- quién ganó el premio, estoy segura que seré yo.

    (A) anuncia
    (B) anuncie
    (C) anunció
    (D) anunciara

GO ON TO THE NEXT PAGE

Part B

Directions: In each of the following passages, there are numbered blanks indicating that words or phrases have been omitted. For each numbered blank, four completions are provided. First read through the entire paragraph. Then, for each numbered blank, choose the completion that is most appropriate given the context of the entire paragraph and fill in the corresponding oval on the answer sheet.

En cada segundo, vivimos un momento nuevo y único del universo, un momento que no existió (30) y no existirá otra vez. ¿Y qué (31) enseñamos a los niños en las escuelas? Enseñamos que dos más dos es cuatro y que París es la capital de Francia. ¿Cuándo enseñamos (32) ellos son? Deberíamos decirle a cada niño: ¿Sabes lo que eres? Eres una maravilla. Único. No (33) en todo el mundo otro niño exactamente como (34). Todos debemos trabajar para hacer que este mundo (35) digno de sus niños. (36) familia es una sola. Cada uno de nosotros tiene un deber (37) sus hermanos. Todos somos (38) de un solo árbol y ese árbol es la humanidad.

30. (A) nada
(B) nunca
(C) siempre
(D) alguna vez

31. (A) los
(B) lo
(C) le
(D) les

32. (A) que
(B) cuando
(C) lo que
(D) donde

33. (A) hay
(B) está
(C) esté
(D) es

34. (A) ti
(B) tú
(C) tuyo
(D) suyo

35. (A) es
(B) sea
(C) era
(D) fuera

36. (A) Nosotros
(B) Nos
(C) Nuestra
(D) Ningún

37. (A) para
(B) con
(C) desde
(D) sin

38. (A) ruedas
(B) hojas
(C) pastillas
(D) albóndigas

GO ON TO THE NEXT PAGE

Una mañana, se levantó y fue a buscar al amigo al otro lado de la valla. Pero el amigo no (39), y cuando volvió, le dijo la madre:

—El amigo se murió. Niño, no pienses más (40) él y busca otros para jugar.

El niño se sentó en el quicio de la puerta con la cara (41) las manos y los codos en las rodillas.

"Él (42)", pensó. Porque no podía ser que allí (43) las canicas, el camión, la pistola de hojalata y el reloj que ya no andaba, y el amigo no viniera a buscarlos. Vino la noche, con (44) muy grande, y el niño no quería entrar a comer.

—Entra niño, que (45) el frío—dijo la madre. Pero (46) entrar, el niño se levantó del quicio y se fue en busca del amigo. Pasó buscándole toda la noche. Cuando llegó el sol, el niño pensó: "Qué tontos y pequeños son (47) juguetes. Y ese reloj que no anda, (48) sirve para nada." (49) tiró al pozo y volvió a la casa, con mucha hambre.

39. (A) había
    (B) era
    (C) iba
    (D) estaba

40. (A) de
    (B) en
    (C) que
    (D) sobre

41. (A) entre
    (B) arriba de
    (C) debajo de
    (D) sin

42. (A) volvió
    (B) vuelva
    (C) volviera
    (D) volverá

43. (A) estaban
    (B) estuvieron
    (C) estuvieran
    (D) están

44. (A) una estrella
    (B) un sol
    (C) una flor
    (D) un océano

45. (A) lleva
    (B) llega
    (C) llueve
    (D) llora

46. (A) además
    (B) al
    (C) a pesar de
    (D) en lugar de

47. (A) esas
    (B) esos
    (C) esa
    (D) eso

48. (A) no
    (B) nadie
    (C) nada
    (D) ninguno

49. (A) La
    (B) Lo
    (C) Le
    (D) Les

GO ON TO THE NEXT PAGE

Hoy, con la facilidad de la fotografía, tendemos a olvidarnos (50) la importancia que tenía la pintura en el pasado como modo de conservar (51) de momentos históricos. El enorme (52) , *La rendición de Breda,* fue pintado para conmemorar la victoria militar española de 1625 contra los holandeses. Velázquez (53) pintó diez años después del incidente y (54) que usar todo su ingenio para representar a personajes y un paisaje que nunca (55) . Pero, ¡qué sorpresa! No es típico de las pinturas militares, porque (56) la violencia, la guerra y el orgullo nacional para evocar, en cambio, (57) de tranquilidad y compasión humana.

50. (A) con
    (B) a
    (C) de
    (D) en

51. (A) la basura
    (B) los recuerdos
    (C) la música
    (D) las muertes

52. (A) cuadro
    (B) abrazo
    (C) español
    (D) acontecimiento

53. (A) le
    (B) la
    (C) lo
    (D) se

54. (A) tuvo
    (B) tuviera
    (C) tendría
    (D) habría tenido

55. (A) ve
    (B) verá
    (C) habrá visto
    (D) había visto

56. (A) muestra
    (B) delinea
    (C) evita
    (D) adopta

57. (A) unos hechos
    (B) una salida
    (C) un mes
    (D) un sentido

GO ON TO THE NEXT PAGE

Part C

Directions: Read the following texts carefully for comprehension. Each passage is followed by a number of questions or incomplete statements. Select the answer or completion that is best according to the text and fill in the corresponding oval on the answer sheet.

Se marchó y Luisa quedó sola. Absolutamente sola. Se sentó, desfallecida. Las manos dejaron caer el cuchillo contra el suelo. Tenía frío, mucho frío. Por el ventanuco, entraban gritos de los vencejos y el rumor del río entre las piedras. "Marcos, tú tienes la culpa . . . tú, porque Amadeo"…De pronto, tuvo miedo, un miedo extraño, que hacía temblar sus manos. "Amadeo me quería. Sí: El me quería". ¿Cómo iba a dudarlo? Amadeo era brusco, desprovisto de ternura, callado, taciturno. Amadeo —a medias palabras, ella lo entendió— tuvo una infancia dura, una juventud amarga. Amadeo era pobre y ganaba su vida— la de él, la de ella y la de los hijos que hubieran podido tener— en un trabajo ingrato que destruía su salud. Y ella: ¿Tuvo ternura para él? ¿Comprensión? ¿Cariño? De pronto, vio algo. Vio su silla; su ropa allí, sucia, a punto de lavar; sus botas, en el rincón, aún llenas de barro. Algo le subió, como un grito. "Sí, me quería . . . acaso ¿será capaz de matarse?"

58. ¿Qué siempre ha dudado la narradora?
    (A) Que Amadeo tuviera sentimientos por ella
    (B) Que Marcos tuviera la culpa por sus problemas
    (C) Que Amadeo y ella pudieran tener hijos
    (D) Que Amadeo y ella fueran a ser ricos

59. ¿Qué tipo de persona es Amadeo?
    (A) Es muy amable y extrovertido.
    (B) Es profundamente cruel y violento.
    (C) Es apasionado y sensible.
    (D) Es bastante tranquilo y no muy bien refinado.

60. Según el pasaje, ¿por qué es la personalidad de Amadeo tal como es?
    (A) La narradora no lo amaba.
    (B) Siempre peleaba con Marcos.
    (C) Tuvo una vida muy difícil.
    (D) Tiene problemas de salud.

61. ¿Adónde piensa la narradora que Amadeo fue?
    (A) Al río para pescar
    (B) A su trabajo para ganar dinero
    (C) Afuera de la casa para suicidarse
    (D) Al cuarto de sus hijos

62. ¿Cuál es el punto central de este pasaje?
    (A) La narradora no ha sabido que Amadeo la ama hasta este momento.
    (B) Marcos es la causa de los problemas entre Amadeo y la narradora.
    (C) La vida de Amadeo y la narradora es increíblemente próspera.
    (D) Amadeo y Marcos se odian.

GO ON TO THE NEXT PAGE

Muchos científicos advierten con alarma que la Tierra está calentándose. Explican que esto podría significar un gran peligro debido al efecto invernadero. Un invernadero es un edificio donde se cultivan plantas usando el techo de vidrio (cristal) que permite la entrada de los rayos del sol, pero no deja que salga todo el calor reflejado. Según esta comparación, la atmósfera de nuestro planeta funciona como el techo de vidrio.

En realidad, el efecto invernadero, en proporciones moderadas, es positivo y aun necesario. Si no tuviera esta función nuestra atmósfera, la Tierra sufriría los radicales cambios de temperatura que ocurren en la luna, con un frío espantoso de noche y un calor insoportable de día. Mirándolo así, debemos darle gracias al efecto invernadero. Sin embargo, algunos expertos temen que la acumulación del dióxido de carbono, del metano y de otros gases producidos por las actividades humanas aumente la eficiencia de nuestro "techo de vidrio" a tal punto que atrape demasiado calor.

Muchos factores, como los terremotos y las erupciones de volcanes, influyen momentáneamente en el clima, pero el gradual calentamiento de la Tierra parece casi inevitable. De acuerdo con sus cálculos, los científicos afirman que desde el año 1850, el aumento de la temperatura global ha sido de uno a cinco grados centígrados, y que hacia el año 2030, podría llegar a aumentar entre 1,5 a 4,5 grados más. Junto con esta subida, se pronostican consecuencias drásticas en las economías de muchas regiones debido a fluctuaciones en la producción agrícola, pérdida o ganancia en el negocio del turismo y otros cambios.

63. ¿Cuál es la función de un efecto invernadero?
    (A) Aumentar la temperatura de la Tierra
    (B) Tener efectos positivos en la atmósfera del planeta
    (C) Dejar que el sol entre, pero que el calor no salga
    (D) Producir gases para el beneficio de la atmósfera

64. ¿Cuál es un resultado positivo del efecto invernadero?
    (A) La temperatura de la Tierra no varía demasiado.
    (B) El frío es espantoso y el calor insoportable.
    (C) Atrapa el calor del sol para calentar el planeta.
    (D) La producción agrícola fluctúa.

65. ¿Por qué piensan algunos expertos que la atmósfera es un "techo de vidrio"?
    (A) Nos deja ver las estrellas.
    (B) Encierra el planeta de manera efectiva.
    (C) La temperatura fluctúa mucho.
    (D) Causa problemas económicos.

66. ¿Cuál es el gran temor de algunos científicos?
    (A) Que la situación empeore
    (B) Que los gases producidos por la actividad humana desaparezcan
    (C) Que no se pueda ver el universo fuera del "techo de vidrio"
    (D) Que la temperatura baje drásticamente antes del año 2030

67. ¿Cuál podría ser el aumento total de la temperatura de la Tierra hacia el año 2030?
    (A) Entre 1 y 5 grados centígrados
    (B) Entre 1,5 y 4,5 grados centígrados
    (C) Entre 2,5 y 9,5 grados centígrados
    (D) Entre 5 y 15 grados centígrados

68. ¿Por qué la economía sufriría si el efecto invernadero continuara en el futuro?
    (A) Los terremotos y los volcanes destruirían mucho del planeta.
    (B) La cantidad de comida cultivada en la tierra podría bajar mucho.
    (C) Los científicos necesitarían más dinero para investigar más este fenómeno.
    (D) Necesitaríamos más industrias que no dependan tanto del tiempo.

GO ON TO THE NEXT PAGE

LA COCINA DE TOMAS

RESTAURANTE * CLUB DE BAILE

28 Elf Street, Lee, MA * 432-888-9090

El lugar mas lindo, original, y lujoso de Massachusetts.

Comida Hispana con especialidad en: ¡empanadas y margaritas!

¡Venga a probar uno o todos los platos en el menú y quédese a bailar! ¡Música Latina para todos y mucho mas!

¡Abierto todo los días desde las 12 P.M. hasta amanecer!

¡Tenemos muchos grupos musicales que tocan todos los viernes!

La Cocina de Tomas presenta:

Junio 13: Orquesta Orlando—música de Argentina y Colombia
Junio 20: Los Lobos Locos—Mariachi
Junio 27: María Luz Roca—la Cantante Mejicana
Julio 4: Los Independientes—¡un grupo local que viene a festejar el día de la Independencia Americana! ¡Compre 2 entradas antes del 4 de julio y reciba una margarita gratis!

¡Reserve Hoy!

Mesas y asientos limitados.

69. ¿Que tipo de lugar es La Cocina de Tomas?
   (A) Cocina
   (B) Restaurante
   (C) Restaurante y bar
   (D) Restaurante y lugar de baile

70. ¿Quiénes son Los Independientes?
   (A) Grupo musical de Argentina
   (B) Grupo musical de los Estados Unidos
   (C) Grupo musical local
   (D) Grupo musical que festeja todo

71. ¿Cuándo hay que reservar y por que?
   (A) Cuando se pueda porque hay muchas mesas
   (B) Después de amanecer porque si no están cerrados
   (C) Después de el 4 de Julio porque es un día feriado
   (D) Inmediatamente porque no hay mucho lugar

72. ¿Cómo se describe el establecimiento?
   (A) Lujoso
   (B) Deo
   (C) Famoso
   (D) Lejano

GO ON TO THE NEXT PAGE

SPANISH SUBJECT TEST–*Continued*

73. ¿A que hora cerraría La Cocina de Tomas?

    (A) 12:00 A.M.
    (B) 2:00 A.M.
    (C) 6:00 A.M.
    (D) 12:00 P.M.

74. ¿Hay alguna ventaja por comprar las entradas temprano?

    (A) Si, pero hay que comprarlas el 4 de Julio.
    (B) Si, pero hay que comprarlas antes del 4 de Julio.
    (C) No, no hay ventaja.
    (D) No, no hay ninguna oferta especial.

GO ON TO THE NEXT PAGE

Un producto de enorme importancia cultural y comercial en el mundo, el café tiene una historia pintoresca y de origen incierto. Según una conocida leyenda, fue en Etiopía, por el año 850, que un pastor observó que su rebaño se agitaba tras ingerir los frutos de un arbusto misterioso, el cafeto. Él mismo probó los frutos, y le gustó tanto la sensación, que compartió los frutos con otros en su poblado.

Varios siglos más adelante, el café llegó a Venecia por medio de los turcos. Desde esta ciudad italiana, el café pasó al resto de Europa, llegando primero a París y, pocos años después, a Londres. En el año 1723, Gabriel de Clieu llevó un cafeto al Caribe, y así llegó esta deliciosa bebida a las Américas. Hoy en día, el café es la bebida más popular del mundo.

Los expertos dicen que hay cuatro factores claves en la producción del café: el clima, es decir, la proporción de sol y lluvia; la altura (cuanto mayor sea, mejor es la calidad); el terreno (el suelo volcánico es el más rico en nutrientes); y el cuidado durante la cosecha. Cada árbol tarda entre tres y cuatro años antes de dar fruto, pero una vez maduro, el árbol permanece activo y productivo durante muchas décadas.

Así, lo que conocemos como el café tuvo que pasar por una interesante historia antes de llegar a la taza que nos tomamos.

75. ¿Dónde tiene el café su origen, supuestamente?
    (A) En el Caribe
    (B) En Etiopía
    (C) En Turquía
    (D) En Venecia

76. ¿Quién descubrió el café?
    (A) Unos animales salvajes en el desierto
    (B) Agricultores musulmanes
    (C) Un pastor que observó cómo sus cabras se agitaban
    (D) Unos pintores inciertos

77. ¿Cuál fue la reacción inicial al probar los frutos del cafeto?
    (A) Repugnancia
    (B) Confusión
    (C) Satisfacción
    (D) Indiferencia

78. Se podría deducir que el mejor sitio para cultivar el café sería
    (A) la playa
    (B) el desierto
    (C) una gran ciudad
    (D) las montañas

79. El árbol de café
    (A) tiene una vida corta
    (B) produce una libra de semillas desde el primer año
    (C) puede ser productivo durante más de diez años
    (D) tarda varias décadas en dar fruto

GO ON TO THE NEXT PAGE

Nos gustaba la casa porque, aparte de espaciosa y antigua, guardaba los recuerdos de nuestros bisabuelos, el abuelo paterno, nuestros padres y toda la infancia.

Nos habituamos Irene y yo a vivir solos en ella, lo que era una locura, pues en esa casa podían vivir ocho personas sin estorbarse. Hacíamos la limpieza por la mañana, levantándonos a las siete, y a eso de las once yo le dejaba a Irene las últimas habitaciones por repasar y me iba a la cocina. Almorzábamos a mediodía, siempre puntuales; ya no quedaba nada por hacer fuera de unos pocos platos sucios. Nos resultaba grato almorzar pensando en la casa profunda y silenciosa. A veces, llegamos a creer que era ella la que no nos dejó casarnos. Irene rechazó dos pretendientes sin mayor motivo. A mí se me murió María Esther antes que llegáramos a comprometernos. Entramos en los cuarenta años con la inexpresada idea de que el nuestro simple y silencioso matrimonio de hermanos era una clausura necesaria de la genealogía asentada por los bisabuelos en nuestra casa.

Pero es de la casa que me interesa hablar, de la casa y de Irene, porque yo no tengo importancia. Me pregunto qué hubiera hecho Irene sin el tejido. No necesitábamos ganarnos la vida. Todos los meses llegaba la plata de los campos y el dinero aumentaba. Pero a Irene solamente le entretenía el tejido. Mostraba una destreza maravillosa, y a mí se me iban las horas viéndole las manos. Era hermoso.

80. ¿Cómo es la vida del narrador e Irene?
    (A) Es excitante y llena de aventura.
    (B) Es repetitiva y bastante pasiva.
    (C) Es triste y muy deprimente.
    (D) No es muy próspera.

81. ¿Cómo es la casa del narrador e Irene?
    (A) Es pequeña y básicamente cómoda.
    (B) Está mal construida.
    (C) Está muy sucia.
    (D) Es enorme y está bastante vacía.

82. ¿Por qué rechazó Irene a sus dos novios?
    (A) No hay una razón aparente.
    (B) Al narrador no le gustaban.
    (C) Ellos no querían vivir en la casa.
    (D) Los padres de Irene los rechazaron también.

83. ¿Quién es María Esther?
    (A) Otra hermana del narrador
    (B) La madre del narrador
    (C) La novia muerta del narrador
    (D) La esposa del narrador

84. ¿Cuál es el estado financiero del narrador e Irene?
    (A) Son muy pobres porque no trabajan.
    (B) Tienen una vida difícil, pero tienen pocos problemas financieros.
    (C) No se puede determinar su estado financiero en el pasaje.
    (D) Ellos son muy ricos con el dinero de su propiedad.

85. ¿Cómo pasa el narrador su tiempo?
    (A) Sale con María Esther.
    (B) Investiga la genealogía de su familia.
    (C) Teje.
    (D) Mira a Irene hacer su propio trabajo.

S T O P

If you finish before time is called, you may check your work on this test only. Do not work on any other test in this book.

Chapter 12
Practice Test 3: Answers and Explanations

- Practice Test 3 Answer Key
- Practice Test 3 Explanations
- How to Score Practice Test 3

PRACTICE TEST 3 ANSWER KEY

Question Number	Correct Answer	Right	Wrong	Question Number	Correct Answer	Right	Wrong	Question Number	Correct Answer	Right	Wrong
1	C	___	___	33	A	___	___	65	B	___	___
2	A	___	___	34	B	___	___	66	A	___	___
3	D	___	___	35	B	___	___	67	C	___	___
4	D	___	___	36	C	___	___	68	B	___	___
5	B	___	___	37	B	___	___	69	D	___	___
6	C	___	___	38	B	___	___	70	C	___	___
7	A	___	___	39	D	___	___	71	D	___	___
8	B	___	___	40	B	___	___	72	A	___	___
9	A	___	___	41	A	___	___	73	C	___	___
10	B	___	___	42	D	___	___	74	B	___	___
11	D	___	___	43	C	___	___	75	B	___	___
12	A	___	___	44	A	___	___	76	C	___	___
13	B	___	___	45	B	___	___	77	C	___	___
14	B	___	___	46	D	___	___	78	D	___	___
15	A	___	___	47	B	___	___	79	C	___	___
16	B	___	___	48	A	___	___	80	B	___	___
17	B	___	___	49	B	___	___	81	D	___	___
18	C	___	___	50	C	___	___	82	A	___	___
19	A	___	___	51	B	___	___	83	C	___	___
20	A	___	___	52	A	___	___	84	D	___	___
21	C	___	___	53	C	___	___	85	D	___	___
22	B	___	___	54	A	___	___				
23	A	___	___	55	D	___	___				
24	C	___	___	56	C	___	___				
25	D	___	___	57	D	___	___				
26	D	___	___	58	A	___	___				
27	D	___	___	59	D	___	___				
28	C	___	___	60	C	___	___				
29	B	___	___	61	C	___	___				
30	B	___	___	62	A	___	___				
31	D	___	___	63	C	___	___				
32	C	___	___	64	A	___	___				

PRACTICE TEST 3 EXPLANATIONS

Part A

1. C **Translation:** Manuel couldn't eat ------- because it was too hot.

   (A) the orange
   (B) the stockings
   (C) the soup
   (D) the sidewalk

   Generally, we don't eat articles of clothing or parts of the street, so (B) and (D) are wrong. And because oranges are not usually heated, (C) is the correct answer.

2. A **Translation:** My friends go shopping -------: every Monday, Thursday, and Saturday.

   (A) often
   (B) reluctantly
   (C) daily
   (D) little

   If my friends go shopping three days per week, we can hardly call that "reluctant" or a "little," so (B) and (D) are incorrect. Choice (C) also cannot be right because there are four days on which they *don't* go shopping, so the correct answer is (A).

3. D **Translation:** We would eat much less if ------- no food at home.

   (A) there is
   (B) there is (subjunctive)
   (C) there would be
   (D) there were (subjunctive)

   This sentence describes a situation that does not currently exist, so the present tense cannot be right—eliminate (A) and (B). The imperfect subjunctive is needed with the conditional to describe hypothetical events, so (D) is the correct answer.

4. D **Translation:** When the weekend comes, ------- time to do your chores at home.

   (A) you have
   (B) you had
   (C) you would have
   (D) you will have

   The weekend is an anticipated event in the future, so (D) is the only answer that makes sense.

5. **B** **Translation:** Since she works in New York and Connecticut, she has to pay ------- in both states.

(A) income
(B) taxes
(C) debts
(D) mourning

This is a difficult question based on a student's knowledge of difficult vocabulary. While debts are certainly paid, **trabaja** is a clue that **impuestos** are what is at issue, so the correct answer is (B).

6. **C** **Translation:** The team had to cancel the game ------- the rain.

(A) for
(B) without
(C) because of
(D) inside of

Choice (B) can be quickly eliminated, as it's unlikely a team would cancel a game because it wasn't raining. Choices (A) and (D) also don't make a tremendous amount of sense, while choice (C) is quite logical. Therefore, (C) is correct.

7. **A** **Translation:** My sofa is very comfortable because it is old; ------- is new and not very comfortable.

(A) his/hers (masculine, singular)
(B) his/hers (feminine, singular)
(C) his/hers (masculine, plural)
(D) his/hers (feminine, plural)

Translating is not a big help in this case, as all the choices mean the same thing in English. Remember that stressed possessive adjectives agree in number and gender with the words they modify. In this case, the adjective must agree with **sofá**, which is masculine and singular, so (A) is the answer.

8. **B** **Translation:** My mother went to the dentist because her teeth hurt her. The dentist needed to take out ------- .

(A) her wallets
(B) her molars
(C) her ceilings
(D) her shoulders

This is a vocabulary question. **Dentista** and **dientes** are big clues that we're looking for a type of tooth, so (B) is correct.

9. **A** **Translation:** Rodrigo knows how to ski very well, but I don't. He is better ------- I.

(A) than
(B) as
(C) for
(D) from

This is an idiomatic expression. Choices (C) and (D) are wrong because they are prepositions and would require the prepositional pronoun **mí** at the end of the sentence. **Mejor que** (A) is the proper expression.

10. **B** **Translation:** Susana doesn't like that almost everyone ------- everything that's happening in her life.

(A) knows
(B) knows (subjunctive)
(C) knows
(D) knows (subjunctive)

Our first hurdle here is the **saber/conocer** thing: Does everyone know a fact, or is everyone familiar with a person, place, or thing? **Todo lo que pasa en su vida** would be a series of *facts*, and we would thus use **saber**, which eliminates (C) and (D). Now, do we use the subjunctive or not? **No le gusta** is an expression of emotion, which always requires the subjunctive, so (B) is correct.

11. **D** **Translation:** It was impossible to take water from the well because the well was completely ------- .

(A) tall
(B) fresh
(C) orange
(D) dry

Even if you don't know what **pozo** means, the sentence has something to do with **agua**, so you should be looking for a word in the answer choices that relates to water. Choices (A) and (C) do not work. Choice (B) is possible and is a good second choice if you're unsure of the vocabulary, but it doesn't make as much sense as choice (D).

12. **A** **Translation:** The policeman is not going to believe that we ------- him the truth if he detains us.

(A) are telling (subjunctive)
(B) are telling
(C) would tell
(D) will have told

The action of the sentence will occur in the *future*, and so (C)—which is used in the past or in hypothetical situations in the present—cannot be correct. The real key to this sentence is the expression **va a dudar**, which is an expression of doubt and, therefore, always requires the subjunctive. Choice (A) is the only choice in the subjunctive tense.

13. **B** **Translation:** The store is on ------- of Santo Tomás Street and the Avenue of Bulls.

(A) the hallway
(B) the corner
(C) the net
(D) the corner

If we are out on the street, then (A) can't be correct. Likewise, because we're not playing sports, (C) is not right. The answer here is tricky because it relies on a knowledge of the difference between a corner found *outside* a building (where two streets intersect), which is an **esquina**, and a corner found *inside* a building (where two walls intersect), which is a **rincón**. Thus, choice (B) is the answer.

14. **B** **Translation:** Bárbara and Nicolás always want to give help. When they give it ------- (their classmates), they are very happy.

(A) to him/her
(B) to them
(C) to them
(D) it (masculine, singular)

What do they give? *Help*—a direct object. Who gets the help? Their *classmates*—an indirect object. (D) can be eliminated because it is not an indirect object pronoun. **A sus compañeros de clase** is the clarification of the identity of the indirect object, so we know that we need a plural pronoun, which eliminates (A). Remember that we cannot use **le** or **les** before a direct object pronoun that begins with "l," like **la**. It changes to **se** in these cases, and so (B) is correct.

15. **A** **Translation:** ------- how many hours does your wife work every day?

(A) For
(B) For
(C) Before
(D) Since

Choices (C) and (D) are not really logical in this context, which brings us to the dreaded **para** versus **por** dilemma once again. Remember that **para** is used with destinations in time, which this sentence doesn't seem to be describing, while **por** is used with durations of time, which is the correct meaning here. Therefore, (A) is the answer.

16. **B** **Translation:** If you (pl.) don't go to bed earlier, you will be very ------- tomorrow.

(A) drunk
(B) tired
(C) active
(D) injured

Vocabulary is important in this question as well. Not going to bed earlier means less sleep, which means less energy, thereby eliminating (C). Since no liquor or accidents are mentioned, eliminating (A) and (D), (B) is the only logical choice.

17. **B** **Translation:** I ------- that he was your uncle until this moment!

(A) have not realized
(B) had not realized
(C) would not have realized
(D) will not have realized

When did this lack of realization take place? In the *past*, which eliminates (D). *When* in the past, though? Before or after this moment of realization that has just passed? *Before.* The tense that places past events before other past events is the pluperfect tense, which is choice (B).

18. **C** **Translation:** Roberto lost his voice last night, so he won't be able to ------- .

(A) run
(B) breathe
(C) sing
(D) sweep

You need to know the word **voz** to be clued in on this question. Only choice (C) has anything to do with one's voice.

19. **A** **Translation:** You can't find your ring? I think I ------- it in the kitchen near the sink.

(A) saw
(B) went
(C) gave
(D) heard

This question is playing tricks with verb forms that all sound the same, which may lead to confusion. Only (A) is logical.

20. **A** **Translation:** If I have a package, buy stamps, and then send it (the package) to someone, I am probably in the ------- office.

(A) **post**
(B) plates
(C) education
(D) presents

Again, vocabulary is essential in this question. The words **paquete, estampillas,** and **envío** make it obvious that you are in the post office, so (A) is the answer.

21. **C** **Translation:** When a movie confuses us, ------- it afterward to understand it better.

(A) you discuss
(B) he/she discusses
(C) **we discuss**
(D) you (plural)/they discuss

There has been no change in the subject that is apparent in the sentence. The indirect object pronoun **nos** gives us a "backdoor entry" into finding out the subject, **nosotros,** so (C) is correct.

22. **B** **Translation:** The boss follows me as if he ------- for me to do something bad.

(A) waited
(B) **were waiting (imperfect subjunctive)**
(C) waits
(D) waits (present subjunctive)

Remember that the expression **como si** always requires the imperfect subjunctive, regardless of the tense of the sentence. The answer here is (B).

23. **A** **Translation:** When the professor finished the lesson, he erased ------- and left the classroom.

(A) **the blackboard**
(B) the garbage
(C) the desk
(D) the student (feminine)

Borró is the key word, and the entire problem hinges on knowledge of this word. Only (A) makes sense.

24. **C** **Translation:** You need tomatoes and lettuce in the salad? I will bring ------- to you immediately.

(A) it (masculine, singular)
(B) it (feminine, singular)
(C) them (masculine, plural)
(D) them (feminine, plural)

How many things am I bringing? *Two,* so I need a plural word, which eliminates (A) and (B). Remember that when a masculine and feminine noun are grouped together, the group retains the *masculine* article, so (C) is the answer.

25. **D** **Translation:** Did it ------- strange to you that they weren't wearing shoes in the snow?

(A) see
(B) look
(C) look for
(D) seem

This question is playing with the English translation of this idea: "Did it ***look*** strange to you..." While this is a proper translation, it is not correct in Spanish. Only (D) is correct.

26. **D** **Translation:** ------- whom were you preparing a big turkey and mashed potatoes?

(A) From
(B) Where
(C) To
(D) For

Think about meaning here. Only (C) and (D) are possibilities, but (D) is more appropriate.

27. **D** **Translation:** These two roses smell exactly similar, so this rose is ------- that one.

(A) little aromatic to
(B) less aromatic than
(C) more aromatic than
(D) as aromatic as

If the roses are **exactamente similares**, then (B) and (C) do not make sense. Choice (A) is just awkward and means nothing, so (D) is correct.

28. **C** **Translation:** No one ------- the drums like Tito Puente.

(A) played
(B) played
(C) played
(D) played

All of these verbs can mean "to play" in the appropriate context. Only (C) is used with musical instruments, however.

29. **B** **Translation:** When the company ------- who won the prize, I am sure it will be me.

(A) announces
(B) announces (present subjunctive)
(C) announced
(D) announced (imperfect subjunctive)

The future tense at the end of the sentence tells us what tense we're in, which eliminates choices (C) and (D). Since the event is not *currently* happening, however, we cannot use the present tense—only the present subjunctive lets us know that the event is not happening right now—it is merely anticipated at this point. Therefore, (B) is correct.

Part B

Passage:

En cada segundo, vivimos un momento nuevo y único del universo, un momento que no existió nunca y no existirá otra vez. ¿Y qué les enseñamos a los niños en las escuelas? Enseñamos que dos más dos es cuatro y que París es la capital de Francia. ¿Cuándo enseñamos lo que ellos son? Deberíamos decirle a cada niño: ¿Sabes lo que eres? Eres una maravilla. Único. No hay en todo el mundo otro niño exactamente como tú. Todos debemos trabajar para hacer que este mundo sea digno de sus niños. Nuestra familia es una sola. Cada uno de nosotros tiene un deber con sus hermanos. Todos somos hojas de un solo árbol y ese árbol es la humanidad.

Translation:

In every second, we live a new and unique moment of the universe, a moment that *never* existed and will not exist again. And what do we teach the children in the schools? We teach that two plus two is four and that Paris is the capital of France. When do we teach *what* they are? We ought to tell each child: Do you know what you are? You are a wonder. Unique. *There is* not another child exactly like *you* in the world. We all should work to make this world worthy of its children. *Our* family is one alone. Each one of us has a duty *to* his or her brothers and sisters. We are all *leaves* of a single tree and *that* tree is humanity.

30. **B** (A) nothing
(B) never
(C) always
(D) sometime

We're talking about a **momento**, which is a measure of time, so we can get rid of (A). The expression **no existió** is very important because it begins a negative clause, which means that all other words that follow must also be negative. Choice (B) is the only negative word left.

31. **D** (A) them (masculine, plural)
(B) it (masculine, singular)
(C) to him/her
(D) to them

What are we teaching? We should be teaching **lo que ellos son**, which would function as the direct object of the sentence (yes, the direct object can be more than one word). Who is receiving this teaching? **Los niños**, who are the indirect object, which is what we're looking for, so we eliminate (A) and (B). Since we know the identity of the indirect object already, we know that it is plural, so (D) is the correct answer.

32. **C** (A) that
(B) when
(C) what
(D) where

Let's look at each choice: Choice (A) can't be right because it would leave a sentence fragment. Choice (B) does not make sense. Choice (D) cannot be right because it would require the use of the verb **estar**. Choice (C) is the idiomatically correct way to say "what" in Spanish in this context.

33. **A** **(A) there is**
(B) is
(C) is (subjunctive)
(D) is

The key to this sentence is the expression **otro niño**, which is an *indefinite* expression. The verb **estar** is generally used with *definite* expressions, so (B) and (C) are not correct. **Ser** can be used with indefinite expressions, but not to express general existence, as this sentence does. The verb **haber** is used in such contexts, so (A) is the correct answer.

34. **B** (A) you
(B) you
(C) yours
(D) his/hers

When making a comparison, the sentence is understood in the following way: "There is no other child exactly like you (*are*)." Therefore, we are looking for a subject word to correspond with the verb, which is understood. Choice (B) is the only subject word among the choices.

35. **B** (A) is
(B) is (subjunctive)
(C) was
(D) was (imperfect subjunctive)

The key expression in this sentence is **hacer que,** which means "to make," as in "to ensure that," which is a way of exerting one's desire or wish over the actions of someone or something else. Such an expression requires the use of the subjunctive, so choices (A) and (C) are wrong. Because the sentence is in the present tense, the present subjunctive is appropriate, and (B) is the answer.

36. **C** (A) We
(B) Us/To us
(C) Our
(D) No

In this sentence, we are looking for an adjective to modify the word **familia**. Since (A) and (B) are not adjectives, they are wrong. Choice (D) is incorrect because it is masculine, and we are looking for a feminine adjective, which is choice (C).

37. **B** (A) for
(B) with
(C) since
(D) without

Choices (C) and (D) really don't make a tremendous amount of sense. The *destination* of our duty is our brothers, and **para** is used in contexts of destination, but, idiomatically, the preposition used with **deber** is always **con**. Choice (B) is the correct answer.

38. **B** (A) tires
(B) leaves
(C) pills
(D) meatballs

Choosing the right answer to this question all comes down to your vocabulary knowledge. Neither **ruedas** (tires), **pastillas** (pills), nor **albóndigas** (meatballs) works here, but (B), **hojas** (leaves), does.

Passage:

Una mañana, se levantó y fue a buscar al amigo al otro lado de la valla. Pero el amigo no estaba ,y cuando volvió, le dijo la madre:

—El amigo se murió. Niño, no pienses más en él y busca otros para jugar.

El niño se sentó en el quicio de la puerta con la cara entre las manos y los codos en las rodillas.

"Él volverá ", pensó. Porque no podía ser que allí estuvieran las canicas, el camión, la pistola de hojalata y el reloj que ya no andaba, y el amigo no viniera a buscarlos. Vino la noche, con una estrella muy grande, y el niño no quería entrar a comer.

—Entra niño, que llega el frío—dijo la madre. Pero en lugar de entrar, el niño se levantó del quicio y se fue en busca del amigo. Pasó buscándole toda la noche. Cuando llegó el sol, el niño pensó: "Qué tontos y pequeños son esos juguetes. Y ese reloj que no anda—no sirve para nada." Lo tiró al pozo y volvió a la casa, con mucha hambre.

Translation:

One morning he got up and went to look for the friend, on the other side of the fence. But the friend *was* not there, and when he returned, the mother said to him:

"The friend died. Child, don't think more *about* him and look for others to play."

The child sat on the door frame with his face *between* his hands and his elbows on his knees.

"He *will return*," he thought. Because it *couldn't be* that the marbles, the truck, the tin pistol, and the watch that now didn't work were there, and the friend didn't come to look for them. Night came, with a very big *star*, and the child didn't want to go inside to eat.

"Come in child, it's *getting* cold," said the mother. But *instead of* entering, the child got up from the door frame and went to look for the friend. He spent all night looking for him. When the sun came up, the child thought: "How stupid and small *these* toys are. And that watch that doesn't work—it's *no* good for anything." He threw *it* into the well and returned home, very hungry.

39. D (A) there were
(B) was
(C) went
(D) was (there)

The sentence is trying to say that the friend could not be located, which would require the use of the verb **estar**, which is choice (D).

40. B (A) of
(B) about
(C) that
(D) above

Choice (C) cannot be right because the word **que** introduces clauses, and there is no clause in the second part of the sentence. The expression **pensar de** is generally used only in questions, while (D) does not make sense. The expression **pensar en** means "to think about," and (B) is correct.

41. A (A) **between**
(B) above
(C) below
(D) without

Imagine the boy's posture: He has his elbows on his knees. What might be the relation between his face and his hands? Choice (D) is silly, and (C) is only right if he is sitting upside down. While (B) makes sense, it seems more likely that the boy's head would be *between* his hands, since his mother just told him that his friend died. Choice (A) is the best answer.

42. D (A) returned
(B) returns (subjunctive)
(C) returned (imperfect subjunctive)
(D) **will return**

The boy doesn't know where his friend is, and his friend doesn't appear in the rest of the passage, so neither the past nor the present would be logical in this sentence. Choices (A), (B), and (C) are all eliminated. The boy is hopeful that his friend will return in *the future*, so (D) is correct.

43. C (A) were
(B) were
(C) **were (subjunctive)**
(D) are

No podía ser que is an expression of *doubt*, which, you'll remember, requires the use of the subjunctive. Only choice (C) is in the subjunctive mood.

44. A (A) **a star**
(B) a sun
(C) a flower
(D) an ocean

The night came *with* something—what is something that comes with the night? Even if you've never seen the word **estrella**, the other three answers don't make any sense.

45. B (A) it's carrying
(B) **it's getting**
(C) it's raining
(D) it's crying

Does the cold rain or cry? No. Does it carry anything? Possibly, but the sentence doesn't tell us what it could be carrying. The only choice that is logical is (B).

46. **D** (A) in addition to
(B) upon
(C) in spite of
(D) instead of

Does the boy actually enter his house when his mother calls him? No, he goes to look for his friend. Choices (A), (B), and (C), which all suggest that he *has* entered the house, are wrong. Choice (D) is correct.

47. **B** (A) these (feminine, plural)
(B) these (neutral, plural)
(C) that (feminine, singular)
(D) that (masculine, singular)

We are looking for the correct demonstrative. Since the word being modified is **juguetes**, which is masculine and plural, (B) is the correct answer.

48. **A** **(A) doesn't**
(B) no one
(C) nothing
(D) none

You have to follow the logic of the sentence here: The boy is complaining about the watch, saying it doesn't work. Since he's limiting his commentary to just a watch, (C) is wrong because it implies that he's dissatisfied with *everything* in his life. Answer (D) implies that there is more than one watch that doesn't work, which isn't true. Choice (B) is silly, so (A) is correct.

49. **B** (A) It (feminine, singular)
(B) It (masculine, singular)
(C) To him/her
(D) To them

What did the boy throw? The *watch*, which is the direct object, so answers (C) and (D) are incorrect. Because **reloj** is masculine, (B) is correct.

Passage:

Hoy, con la facilidad de la fotografía, tendemos a olvidarnos <u>de</u> la importancia que tenía la pintura en el pasado como modo de conservar <u>los recuerdos</u> de momentos históricos. El enorme <u>cuadro</u>, *La rendición de Breda,* fue pintado para conmemorar la victoria militar española de 1625 contra los holandeses. Velázquez <u>lo</u> pintó diez años después del incidente y <u>tuvo</u> que usar todo su ingenio para representar a personajes y un paisaje que nunca <u>había visto</u>. Pero, ¡qué sorpresa! No es típico de las pinturas militares porque <u>evita</u> la violencia, la guerra y el orgullo nacional para evocar, en cambio, <u>un sentido</u> de tranquilidad y compasión humana.

Translation:

Today, with the ease of photography, we tend to forget *about* the importance that painting had in the past as a means of preserving *memories* of historic moments. The enormous *painting The Surrender of Breda* was painted to commemorate the Spanish military victory of 1625 against the Dutch. Velázquez painted *it* ten years after the incident and *had* to use all his genius to represent people and a landscape that he *had* never *seen*. But, what a surprise! It is not typical of military paintings because *it avoids* violence, war, and national pride to evoke instead *a sense* of tranquility and human compassion.

50. C (A) with
(B) at
(C) about
(D) in

"To forget about" is an idiomatic expression that requires the use of **de** (C). Remember, idiomatic expressions don't necessarily have a rule: You either know them or you don't.

51. B (A) the garbage
(B) the memories
(C) the music
(D) the deaths

What exactly is the garbage of an historic moment? How does a painting preserve music? Do we actually preserve the deaths of historic moments or the moments themselves? Interesting questions all, but (A), (C), and (D) are all wrong because they are not answered in this passage. An historic painting is a representation of a memory, so (B) is correct.

52. A **(A) painting**
(B) hug
(C) Spaniard
(D) event

Notice that *La rendición de Breda* is italicized. Generally, names of books, movies, ships, and, yes, paintings are italicized. Hugs, Spaniards, and events are not accorded this same special treatment, so (A) is the answer.

53. **C** (A) to him/her
(B) it (feminine, singular)
(C) it (masculine, singular)
(D) himself

What did he paint? The *painting*, which is the direct object, thus eliminating (A). (He did not paint himself, although that would have been interesting.) **Cuadro** is masculine, so (C) is the answer.

54. **A** **(A) had**
(B) had (imperfect subjunctive)
(C) would have
(D) would have had

Choice (D) suggests that Velázquez *didn't* use all his genius (he *would* have, but...), but the sentence says just the opposite, so it is wrong. Choice (B) is incorrect because there are no expressions that cue the use of the subjunctive. While (C) might sound correct in English, it is only right as an obscure, dramatic narrative technique in the past. Choice (A) is the clearest way to get the point across.

55. **D** (A) sees
(B) will see
(C) will have seen
(D) had seen

The painting was dated 1625, long ago, so (A), (B), and (C) are simply not logical. Choice (D) is the answer.

56. **C** (A) shows
(B) delineates
(C) avoids
(D) adopts

We're looking for something that *wouldn't* be typical of a military painting. Violence and war are the typical themes, and so showing, delineating, or adopting these themes would not be what we are looking for. Choice (C) is more likely.

57. **D** (A) some facts
(B) an exit
(C) a month
(D) a sense

Choice (B) doesn't make sense in context, while choice (A) changes the intended purpose of the painting. Instead of being about a moment of military history, it has become a sort of spiritual self-help painting. It is also highly doubtful that Velázquez only wanted his painting to result in one month of tranquility, and so (D) is correct.

Part C

Passage:

Se marchó y Luisa quedó sola. Absolutamente sola. Se sentó, desfallecida. Las manos dejaron caer el cuchillo contra el suelo. Tenía frío, mucho frío. Por el ventanuco, entraban gritos de los vencejos y el rumor del río entre las piedras. "Marcos, tú tienes la culpa . . . tú, porque Amadeo . . . " De pronto, tuvo miedo, un miedo extraño, que hacía temblar sus manos. "Amadeo me quería. Sí: El me quería." ¿Cómo iba a dudarlo? Amadeo era brusco, desprovisto de ternura, callado, taciturno. Amadeo —a medias palabras ella lo entendió— tuvo una infancia dura, una juventud amarga. Amadeo era pobre y ganaba su vida—la de él, la de ella y la de los hijos que hubieran podido tener —en un trabajo ingrato que destruía su salud. Y ella: ¿Tuvo ternura para él? ¿Comprensión? ¿Cariño? De pronto, vio algo. Vio su silla; su ropa allí, sucia, a punto de lavar; sus botas, en el rincón, aún llenas de barro. Algo le subió, como un grito. "Sí, me quería . . . acaso ¿será capaz de matarse?"

Translation:

He left and Luisa remained alone. Absolutely alone. She sat down, weakened. Her hands dropped the knife on the floor. She was cold, very cold. Through the window, the calls of the birds and the murmur of the river between the rocks entered. "Marcos, you are to blame...you, because Amadéo..." Suddenly, she was afraid, a strange fear that made her hands shake. "Amadeo loved me. Yes: He loved me." How was she going to doubt it? Amadeo was abrupt, lacking tenderness, quiet, sullen. Amadeo—at mid-sentence she understood it—had a tough childhood, a bitter adolescence. Amadeo was poor and earned his living—his, hers, and that of the children that they could have had—at an ungrateful job that was destroying his health. And she: Did she have tenderness for him? Understanding? Affection? Suddenly, she saw something. She saw his chair; his clothes there, dirty, ready for washing; his boots, in the corner, still full of mud. Something rose in her, like a shout. "Yes, he loved me...by any chance will he be capable of killing himself?"

58. **A** **Translation:** What has the narrator always doubted?

(A) **That Amadeo had feelings for her**
(B) That Marcos was to blame for her problems
(C) That Amadeo and she could have children
(D) That Amadeo and she were going to be rich

The narrator spends the majority of the passage convincing herself that Amadeo loved her—**Sí, me quería**—so she must not have believed it in the past. Therefore, (A) is correct.

59. **D** **Translation:** What type of person is Amadeo?

(A) He is very friendly and extroverted.
(B) He is profoundly cruel and violent.
(C) He is passionate and sensitive.
(D) **He is pretty quiet and is not very well refined.**

Amadeo is described as **brusco** and **callado**, descriptions that are paraphrased nicely in choice (D).

60. C **Translation:** According to the passage, why is Amadeo's personality like it is?

(A) The narrator didn't love him.

(B) He always fought with Marcos.

(C) He had a difficult life.

(D) His health is bad.

The narrator speaks of **una infancia dura** and **una juventud amarga**, which are hardly qualities of a happy life. Thus, the best answer is (C).

61. C **Translation:** Where does the narrator think that Amadeo went?

(A) To the river to fish

(B) To work to earn money

(C) Outside the house to kill himself

(D) To his children's room

The phrase **será capaz de matarse** at the end of the passage is a good clue of what's on the narrator's mind. The answer here is (C).

62. A **Translation:** What is the central point of this passage?

(A) The narrator hasn't known that Amadeo loves her until this moment.

(B) Marcos is the cause of the problems between Amadeo and the narrator.

(C) Amadeo's and the narrator's life is incredibly prosperous.

(D) Amadeo and Marcos hate each other.

We can look at the reasoning for question 58 to explain why choice (A) is correct.

Passage:

Muchos científicos advierten con alarma que la Tierra está calentándose. Explican que esto podría significar un gran peligro debido al efecto invernadero. Un invernadero es un edificio donde se cultivan plantas usando el techo de vidrio (cristal) que permite la entrada de los rayos del sol, pero no deja que salga todo el calor reflejado. Según esta comparación, la atmósfera de nuestro planeta funciona como el techo de vidrio.

En realidad, el efecto invernadero, en proporciones moderadas, es positivo y aun necesario. Si no tuviera esta función nuestra atmósfera, la Tierra sufriría los radicales cambios de temperatura que ocurren en la luna, con un frío espantoso de noche y un calor insoportable de día. Mirándolo así, debemos darle gracias al efecto invernadero. Sin embargo, algunos expertos temen que la acumulación del dióxido de carbono, del metano y de otros gases producidos por las actividades humanas aumente la eficiencia de nuestro "techo de vidrio" a tal punto que atrape demasiado calor.

Muchos factores, como los terremotos y las erupciones de volcanes, influyen momentáneamente en el clima, pero el gradual calentamiento de la Tierra parece casi inevitable. De acuerdo con sus cálculos, los científicos afirman que desde el año 1850, el aumento de la temperatura global ha sido de uno a cinco grados centígrados, y que hacia el año 2030, podría llegar a aumentar entre 1,5 a 4,5 grados más. Junto con esta subida, se pronostican consecuencias drásticas en las economías de muchas regiones debido a fluctuaciones en la producción agrícola, pérdida o ganancia en el negocio del turismo y otros cambios.

Translation:

Many scientists warn with alarm that the Earth is warming. They explain that this could signify a great danger because of the greenhouse effect. A greenhouse is a building where one grows plants using a glass roof that permits the entry of the sun's rays but doesn't allow all the reflected warmth to leave. According to this comparison, the atmosphere of our planet functions as a glass roof.

In reality, the greenhouse effect, in moderate proportions, is positive and even necessary. If our atmosphere didn't have this function, Earth would suffer the radical temperature changes that occur on the moon, with a frightful cold at night and an insufferable heat during the day. Looking at it in this way, we should give thanks to the greenhouse effect. However, some experts fear that the accumulation of carbon dioxide, methane, and other gases produced by human activities will increase the efficiency of our "glass roof" to the point that it will trap too much heat.

Many factors, such as earthquakes and volcanic eruptions, momentarily influence the climate, but the gradual warming of Earth seems almost inevitable. In accordance with their calculations, scientists affirm that since the year 1850, the increase of the global temperature has been from one to five degrees centigrade, and that near the year 2030, it could increase between 1.5 and 4.5 degrees more. Along with this increase, they predict drastic consequences in the economies of many regions because of fluctuations in agricultural production, loss or gain in tourism, and other changes.

63. C **Translation:** What is the function of a greenhouse effect?

(A) To increase the temperature of Earth
(B) To have positive effects in the planet's atmosphere
(C) To allow the sun to enter but not the heat to leave
(D) To produce gases for the benefit of the atmosphere

The answer, choice (C), can be found in the second sentence of the passage.

64. A **Translation:** What is a positive result of the greenhouse effect?

(A) The temperature of Earth doesn't vary much.
(B) The cold is frightful and the heat insufferable.
(C) It traps the heat of the sun to heat the planet.
(D) Agricultural production fluctuates.

The passage states that we should really **darle gracias** to the greenhouse effect because we don't have the drastic temperature shifts of the moon. Choice (A) is correct.

65. B **Translation:** Why do some experts think that the atmosphere is a "glass roof"?

(A) It allows us to see the stars.
(B) It effectively encloses the planet.
(C) The temperature fluctuates a lot.
(D) It causes economic problems.

This question requires a little careful thinking. Choice (A) is silly, while (D) is not the reason for this expression being coined—rather, that it is a result of the phenomenon. Choice (C) looks good only if you misunderstand it—the temperature would only fluctuate if we *didn't* have this "glass roof." Choice (B) is therefore the correct answer.

66. A **Translation:** What is the great fear of some scientists?

(A) That the situation will get worse
(B) That the gases produced by human activity will disappear
(C) That one will not be able to see the universe outside of the "glass roof"
(D) That the temperature will drop drastically before the year 2030

The entire last paragraph is dedicated to telling of the "doom and gloom" that the greenhouse effect promises for us in the next 25 years or so; therefore, (A) is correct.

67. C **Translation:** What could be the total increase in Earth's temperature near the year 2030?

(A) Between 1 and 5 degrees centigrade
(B) Between 1.5 and 4.5 degrees centigrade
(C) Between 2.5 and 9.5 degrees centigrade
(D) Between 5 and 15 degrees centigrade

The passage states that the temperature has increased from 1 to 5 degrees centigrade since 1850, then states that it could increase an *additional* 1.5 to 4.5 degrees before 2030. The potential totals are given in choice (C).

68. B **Translation:** Why would the economy suffer if the greenhouse effect continued in the future?

(A) Earthquakes and volcanoes would destroy much of the planet.
(B) The quantity of food grown on Earth could drop a lot.
(C) Scientists would need more money to investigate this phenomenon more.
(D) We would need more industries that didn't depend so much on the weather.

The last sentence of the passage speaks of the **consecuencias drásticas** of a continued warming of the planet, and a potential shortage of crops (B) is mentioned.

Advertisement:

La Cocina de Tomas
Restaurante * Club de Baile

28 Elf Street, Lee, MA * 432-888-9090

El lugar mas lindo, original, y lujoso de Massachusetts.

Comida Hispana con especialidad en: ¡empanadas y margaritas!

¡Venga a probar uno o todos los platos en el menú y quédese a bailar! ¡Música Latina para todos y mucho mas!

¡Abierto todo los días desde las 12 P.M. hasta amanecer!

¡Tenemos muchos grupos musicales que tocan todos los viernes!

La Cocina de Tomas presenta:

Junio 13: Orquesta Orlando—música de Argentina y Colombia
Junio 20: Los Lobos Locos—Mariachi
Junio 27: María Luz Roca—la Cantante Mejicana
Julio 4: Los Independientes—¡un grupo local que viene a festejar el día de la Independencia Americana! ¡Compre 2 entradas antes del 4 de Julio y reciba una margarita gratis!

¡Reserve hoy!
Mesas y asientos limitados.

Translation:

Thomas's Kitchen
Restaurant * Dance Club

28 Elf Street, Lee, MA * 432-888-9090

The most beautiful, original, and luxurious place in Massachusetts.

Hispanic cuisine specializing in empanadas and margaritas!

Come try one or all of our menu items and stay for dancing! Latin music for everyone and much more!

Open every day from 12 P.M. until dawn!

We have a lot of musical groups that play every Friday!

Thomas's Kitchen presents:

June 13: Orlando's Orchestra—Music from Argentina and Colombia
June 20: The Crazy Wolves—Mariachi

June 27: Maria Luz Roca—the Mexican singer

July 4: The Independents—a local group that is coming to celebrate the American Independence Day! Buy 2 entries before the 4th of July and get a free margarita!

Reserve today!

Tables and seats are limited.

69. **D** **Translation:** What kind of place is Thomas's Kitchen?

(A) A kitchen

(B) A restaurant

(C) A restaurant and bar

(D) A restaurant and place for dancing

The title of the announcement below the restaurant name describes Thomas's as a restaurant and dance club. Choice (D) is the correct answer.

70. **C** **Translation:** Who are The Independents?

(A) A music group from Argentina

(B) A music group from the United States

(C) A local music group

(D) A music group that celebrates everything

The flier lists the music groups that are playing at the venue. The Independents are a local group of musicians who are playing on the Fourth of July to celebrate American Independence Day. Therefore, choice (C) is the correct answer.

71. **D** **Translation:** When do you have to make a reservation and why?

(A) Whenever, because there are a lot of tables

(B) After dawn, because the restaurant will be closed

(C) After the 4th of July, because it's a holiday

(D) Immediately, because there is not a lot of available space.

The flier says to "reserve today," as tables and seating are limited. Choice (A) contradicts this statement, and choices (B) and (C) do not apply, making (D) the correct answer.

72. **A** **Translation:** How is the establishment described?

(A) Luxurious

(B) Ugly

(C) Famous

(D) Far

The flier states that the venue is the "most beautiful, original, and luxurious place in Massachusetts." Choice (A) is correct.

73. **C** **Translation:** At what time would Thomas's kitchen be closed?

(A) 12:00 A.M.

(B) 2:00 A.M.

(C) 6:00 A.M.

(D) 12:00 P.M.

According to the flier, Thomas's Kitchen is open from 12:00 P.M. until dawn. The only time that doesn't fall into that range in the given answer choices is 6:00 A.M., so (C) is the correct answer.

74. **B** **Translation:** Is there an advantage to buying the entries early?

(A) Yes, but you have to buy them on the 4th of July.

(B) Yes, but you have to buy them before the 4th of July.

(C) No, there isn't an advantage.

(D) No, there's no special offer.

This one requires you to read carefully! Choice (A) may seem correct, but the flier states that you will receive a free margarita if you buy your entries before July 4th. So choice (B) is correct.

Passage:

Un producto de enorme importancia cultural y comercial en el mundo, el café tiene una historia pintoresca y de origen incierto. Según una conocida leyenda, fue en Etiopía, por el año 850, que un pastor observó que su rebaño se agitaba tras ingerir los frutos de un arbusto misterioso, el cafeto. Él mismo probó los frutos, y le gustó tanto la sensación, que compartió los frutos con otros en su poblado.

Varios siglos más adelante, el café llegó a Venecia por medio de los turcos. Desde esta ciudad italiana, el café pasó al resto de Europa, llegando primero a París y, pocos años después, a Londres. En el año 1723, Gabriel de Clieu llevó un cafeto al Caribe, y así llegó esta deliciosa bebida a las Américas. Hoy en día, el café es la bebida más popular del mundo.

Los expertos dicen que hay cuatro factores clave en la producción del café: el clima, es decir, la proporción de sol y lluvia; la altura (cuanto mayor sea, mejor es la calidad); el terreno (el suelo volcánico es el más rico en nutrientes); y el cuidado durante la cosecha. Cada árbol tarda entre tres y cuatro años antes de dar fruto, pero una vez maduro, el árbol permanece activo y productivo durante muchas décadas.

Así, lo que conocemos como el café tuvo que pasar por una interesante historia antes de llegar a la taza que nos tomamos.

Translation:

A product of enormous cultural and commercial importance in the world, coffee has a history that is both picturesque and uncertain. According to popular legend, it was in Ethiopia in the year 850 that a shepherd observed that his herd of goats became excited and energetic after ingesting the berries of a mysterious shrub, the coffee tree. The shepherd tried the berries for himself, and he liked the sensation so much that he shared them with others in his village.

Several centuries later, the Turks brought coffee to Venice. From this Italian city, coffee traveled to the rest of Europe, arriving first in Paris and a few years later in London. In 1723, Gabriel de Clieu took a coffee plant to the Caribbean, and that's how this delicious beverage arrived in the Americas. Nowadays, coffee is the most popular beverage in the world.

The experts say there are four key factors in the production of coffee: the climate, that is to say, the proportion of sun and rain; the altitude (the higher the altitude, the better the quality), the land (volcanic land is richest in nutrients), and the care during the harvest. Each tree takes between three and four years to produce the first berries, but once it's mature, the tree remains active and fruitful for many decades.

So, that which we know as coffee had to go through an interesting history before arriving in our cups.

75. B **Translation:** Where did coffee supposedly originate?

(A) In the Caribbean
(B) In Ethiopia
(C) In Turkey
(D) In Venice

The passage mentions that a shepherd discovered coffee in Ethiopia in the year 850. The passage does indeed also mention Turkey, Venice, and the Caribbean in the second paragraph, but it does so only to show how coffee traveled throughout the world. The correct answer is (B).

76. C **Translation:** Who discovered coffee?

(A) Some wild animals in the desert
(B) Muslim farmers
(C) A shepherd who observed his goats in an animated state
(D) Some uncertain painters

The first paragraph indicates that **un pastor** observed his herd acting strange after ingesting the fruit of the mysterious coffee tree. The passage makes no mention of wild animals, Muslim farmers, or uncertain painters, so choice (C) is the best answer.

77. **C** **Translation:** What was the initial reaction after trying the berries of the coffee tree?

(A) Disgust
(B) Confusion
(C) Satisfaction
(D) Indifference

The end of the first paragraph also indicates that the shepherd who first tried the berries of the coffee tree liked the sensation so much that he shared the berries with others. Therefore, he did not react with (A) disgust, (B) confusion, or (D) indifference. The best answer is (C): satisfaction.

78. **D** **Translation:** One can infer that the best place to cultivate coffee would be

(A) the beach
(B) the desert
(C) a big city
(D) the mountains

In the third paragraph, experts outline the four keys to the successful production of coffee. One of these is the altitude of the coffee plants. Since mountains have the greatest altitude of the four answer choices, (D) is the best answer.

79. **C** **Translation:** A coffee tree

(A) has a short lifespan
(B) produces a pound of seeds beginning in the first year
(C) can flourish for more than ten years
(D) takes several decades to produce its first berries

According to the end of the third paragraph, the coffee tree takes three or four years to produce its first fruit. This helps us eliminate answer choices (B) and (D). The author then tells us that the coffee tree can continue to produce fruit for many decades. Now we can eliminate answer choice (A) and select answer choice (C).

Passage:

Nos gustaba la casa porque, aparte de espaciosa y antigua, guardaba los recuerdos de nuestros bisabuelos, el abuelo paterno, nuestros padres y toda la infancia.

Nos habituamos Irene y yo a vivir solos en ella, lo que era una locura, pues en esa casa podían vivir ocho personas sin estorbarse. Hacíamos la limpieza por la mañana, levantándonos a las siete, y a eso de las once yo le dejaba a Irene las últimas habitaciones por repasar y me iba a la cocina. Almorzábamos a mediodía, siempre puntuales; ya no quedaba nada por hacer fuera de unos pocos platos sucios. Nos resultaba grato almorzar pensando en la casa profunda y silenciosa. A veces, llegamos a creer que era ella la que no nos dejó casarnos. Irene rechazó dos pretendientes sin mayor motivo. A mí se me murió María Esther antes que llegáramos a comprometernos. Entramos en los cuarenta años con la inexpresada idea de que el nuestro simple y silencioso matrimonio de hermanos era una clausura necesaria de la genealogía asentada por los bisabuelos en nuestra casa.

Pero es de la casa que me interesa hablar, de la casa y de Irene, porque yo no tengo importancia. Me pregunto qué hubiera hecho Irene sin el tejido. No necesitábamos ganarnos la vida. Todos los meses llegaba la plata de los campos y el dinero aumentaba. Pero a Irene solamente le entretenía el tejido. Mostraba una destreza maravillosa, y a mí se me iban las horas viéndole las manos. Era hermoso.

Translation:

We liked the house because, aside from being spacious and old, it guarded the memories of our great-grandparents, paternal grandfather, our parents, and all of childhood.

Irene and I became accustomed to living alone in it, which was a crazy thing since in that house eight people could live without getting in each other's way. We did the cleaning in the morning, getting up at seven, and at about eleven I left the last rooms to Irene to finish and went to the kitchen. We ate lunch at noon, always punctual; there now remained nothing to do aside from a few dirty dishes. We found it pleasing to eat lunch thinking about the deep and silent house. At times, we believed that it was she (the house) that didn't allow us to marry. Irene rejected two suitors for almost no reason at all. María Esther died before we could get engaged. We entered our forties with the unexpressed idea that our simple and silent marriage of brother and sister was a necessary closure of the genealogy laid down by our great-grandparents in our house.

But it is the house about which I am interested in speaking, the house and Irene, because I am not important. I ask myself what Irene would have done without weaving. We didn't need to earn a living. Every month the money arrived from the fields and the money grew. But only weaving entertained Irene. She showed marvelous skill, and watching her hands, the hours flew by for me. It was beautiful.

80. B **Translation:** How is the life of the narrator and Irene?

(A) It is exciting and full of adventure.
(B) It is repetitive and pretty passive.
(C) It is sad and very depressing.
(D) It isn't very prosperous.

The narrator and his sister do *the same thing every day,* which pretty much amounts to nothing. The use of the imperfect tense tells us that all of the actions the narrator describes are habitual. Choice (B) is a nice summary of this description.

81. D **Translation:** What is the narrator and Irene's house like?

(A) It's small and basically comfortable.
(B) It's badly constructed.
(C) It's very dirty.
(D) It's enormous and is pretty empty.

The narrator says **en esa casa podían vivir ocho personas.** Sounds pretty big, huh? Choice (D) is the perfect answer.

82. A **Translation:** Why did Irene reject her two boyfriends?

(A) **There is no apparent reason.**
(B) The narrator didn't like them.
(C) They didn't want to live in the house.
(D) Irene's parents rejected them also.

The narrator doesn't tell us what he thought of Irene's boyfriends, so (B) is incorrect. He also doesn't say much about the boyfriends themselves, so (C) is wrong. Irene's parents are apparently not living, so their opinion is not relevant in her decision, and therefore (A) is the best answer.

83. C **Translation:** Who is María Esther?

(A) Another sister of the narrator
(B) The narrator's mother
(C) **The narrator's dead girlfriend**
(D) The narrator's wife

The narrator says that María Esther died before they could **comprometerse**, which means "to get engaged." This is a pretty serious (and strange) step for brother and sister to take [(A) is wrong], or mother and son [so is (B)]. If she died before they got engaged, they couldn't have been married, so (C) is the answer.

84. D **Translation:** What is the financial state of the narrator and Irene?

(A) They are very poor because they don't work.
(B) They have a difficult life, but they have few financial problems.
(C) One can't determine their financial state in the passage.
(D) **They are very rich with the money from their property.**

The narrator says **No necesitábamos ganarnos la vida** but that **el dinero aumentaba** anyway. Doesn't sound like too much of a struggle. Choice (D) is correct.

85. D **Translation:** How does the narrator spend his time?

(A) He goes out with María Esther.
(B) He researches the genealogy of his family.
(C) He weaves.
(D) **He watches Irene do her own work.**

The narrator says in the next to the last line **a mí se me iban las horas viéndole las manos**. Loads of fun, huh? Choice (D) is the answer.

HOW TO SCORE PRACTICE TEST 3

When you take the real exam, the proctors take away your exam and your bubble sheet and send it to a processing center, where a computer looks at the pattern of filled-in ovals on your exam and gives you a score. We couldn't include even a small computer with this book, so we are providing this more primitive way of scoring your exam.

Determining Your Score

STEP 1	Using the answer key, determine how many questions you got right and how many you got wrong on the test. Remember, questions that you do not answer do not count as either right answers or wrong answers.	
STEP 2	List the number of right answers here.	(A) _____
STEP 3	List the number of wrong answers here. Now divide that number by 3.	(B) _____ ÷ 3 _____ = (C) _____
STEP 4	Subtract the number of wrong answers divided by 3 (C) from the number of correct answers (A). Round this score to the nearest whole number. This is your raw score.	(A) – (C) = _____
STEP 5	To determine your real score, take the number from Step 4 above and look it up in the left column of the Score Conversion Table on the next page; the corresponding score on the right is your score on the exam.	

PRACTICE TEST 3
SCORE CONVERSION TABLE

Raw Score	Scaled Score	Raw Score	Scaled Score	Raw Score	Scaled Score
85	800	47	590	9	360
84	800	46	580	8	360
83	800	45	570	7	350
82	800	44	570	6	350
81	790	43	560	5	340
80	790	42	550	4	340
79	780	41	550	3	330
78	780	40	540	2	320
77	770	39	530	1	320
76	770	38	530	0	310
75	760	37	520	–1	310
74	760	36	520	–2	300
73	750	35	510	–3	290
72	750	34	500	–4	290
71	740	33	500	–5	280
70	730	32	490	–6	270
69	730	31	490	–7	260
68	720	30	480	–8	260
67	720	29	470	–9	250
66	710	28	470	–10	240
65	700	27	460	–11	230
64	700	26	460	–12	220
63	690	25	450	–13	220
62	680	24	450	–14	220
61	680	23	440	–15	210
60	670	22	430	–16	210
59	670	21	430	–17	210
58	660	20	420	–18	200
57	650	19	420	–19	200
56	650	18	410	–20	200
55	640	17	410	–21	200
54	630	16	400	–22	200
53	630	15	400	–23	200
52	620	14	390	–24	200
51	620	13	390	–25	200
50	610	12	380	–26	200
49	600	11	380	–27	200
48	590	10	370	–28	200

Practice Test Form

Completely darken bubbles with a No. 2 pencil. If you make a mistake, be sure to erase mark completely. Erase all stray marks.

1.

YOUR NAME: ____________________ (Print) Last First M.I.

SIGNATURE: ____________________ DATE: / /

HOME ADDRESS: ____________________ (Print) Number and Street

____________________ City State Zip Code

PHONE NO.: ____________________ (Print)

Practice Test 1

1. (A) (B) (C) (D) (E)
2. (A) (B) (C) (D) (E)
3. (A) (B) (C) (D) (E)
4. (A) (B) (C) (D) (E)
5. (A) (B) (C) (D) (E)
6. (A) (B) (C) (D) (E)
7. (A) (B) (C) (D) (E)
8. (A) (B) (C) (D) (E)
9. (A) (B) (C) (D) (E)
10. (A) (B) (C) (D) (E)
11. (A) (B) (C) (D) (E)
12. (A) (B) (C) (D) (E)
13. (A) (B) (C) (D) (E)
14. (A) (B) (C) (D) (E)
15. (A) (B) (C) (D) (E)
16. (A) (B) (C) (D) (E)
17. (A) (B) (C) (D) (E)
18. (A) (B) (C) (D) (E)
19. (A) (B) (C) (D) (E)
20. (A) (B) (C) (D) (E)
21. (A) (B) (C) (D) (E)
22. (A) (B) (C) (D) (E)
23. (A) (B) (C) (D) (E)
24. (A) (B) (C) (D) (E)
25. (A) (B) (C) (D) (E)
26. (A) (B) (C) (D) (E)
27. (A) (B) (C) (D) (E)
28. (A) (B) (C) (D) (E)
29. (A) (B) (C) (D) (E)
30. (A) (B) (C) (D) (E)
31. (A) (B) (C) (D) (E)
32. (A) (B) (C) (D) (E)
33. (A) (B) (C) (D) (E)
34. (A) (B) (C) (D) (E)
35. (A) (B) (C) (D) (E)
36. (A) (B) (C) (D) (E)
37. (A) (B) (C) (D) (E)
38. (A) (B) (C) (D) (E)
39. (A) (B) (C) (D) (E)
40. (A) (B) (C) (D) (E)
41. (A) (B) (C) (D) (E)
42. (A) (B) (C) (D) (E)
43. (A) (B) (C) (D) (E)
44. (A) (B) (C) (D) (E)
45. (A) (B) (C) (D) (E)
46. (A) (B) (C) (D) (E)
47. (A) (B) (C) (D) (E)
48. (A) (B) (C) (D) (E)
49. (A) (B) (C) (D) (E)
50. (A) (B) (C) (D) (E)
51. (A) (B) (C) (D) (E)
52. (A) (B) (C) (D) (E)
53. (A) (B) (C) (D) (E)
54. (A) (B) (C) (D) (E)
55. (A) (B) (C) (D) (E)
56. (A) (B) (C) (D) (E)
57. (A) (B) (C) (D) (E)
58. (A) (B) (C) (D) (E)
59. (A) (B) (C) (D) (E)
60. (A) (B) (C) (D) (E)
61. (A) (B) (C) (D) (E)
62. (A) (B) (C) (D) (E)
63. (A) (B) (C) (D) (E)
64. (A) (B) (C) (D) (E)
65. (A) (B) (C) (D) (E)
66. (A) (B) (C) (D) (E)
67. (A) (B) (C) (D) (E)
68. (A) (B) (C) (D) (E)
69. (A) (B) (C) (D) (E)
70. (A) (B) (C) (D) (E)
71. (A) (B) (C) (D) (E)
72. (A) (B) (C) (D) (E)
73. (A) (B) (C) (D) (E)
74. (A) (B) (C) (D) (E)
75. (A) (B) (C) (D) (E)
76. (A) (B) (C) (D) (E)
77. (A) (B) (C) (D) (E)
78. (A) (B) (C) (D) (E)
79. (A) (B) (C) (D) (E)
80. (A) (B) (C) (D) (E)
81. (A) (B) (C) (D) (E)
82. (A) (B) (C) (D) (E)
83. (A) (B) (C) (D) (E)
84. (A) (B) (C) (D) (E)
85. (A) (B) (C) (D) (E)

Practice Test Form

Completely darken bubbles with a No. 2 pencil. If you make a mistake, be sure to erase mark completely. Erase all stray marks.

1.
YOUR NAME: ____
(Print) Last First M.I.

SIGNATURE: ______________________________________ DATE: ___/___/___

HOME ADDRESS: ____
(Print) Number and Street

____
City State Zip Code

PHONE NO.: ____
(Print)

Practice Test 2

1. (A) (B) (C) (D) (E)
2. (A) (B) (C) (D) (E)
3. (A) (B) (C) (D) (E)
4. (A) (B) (C) (D) (E)
5. (A) (B) (C) (D) (E)
6. (A) (B) (C) (D) (E)
7. (A) (B) (C) (D) (E)
8. (A) (B) (C) (D) (E)
9. (A) (B) (C) (D) (E)
10. (A) (B) (C) (D) (E)
11. (A) (B) (C) (D) (E)
12. (A) (B) (C) (D) (E)
13. (A) (B) (C) (D) (E)
14. (A) (B) (C) (D) (E)
15. (A) (B) (C) (D) (E)
16. (A) (B) (C) (D) (E)
17. (A) (B) (C) (D) (E)
18. (A) (B) (C) (D) (E)
19. (A) (B) (C) (D) (E)
20. (A) (B) (C) (D) (E)
21. (A) (B) (C) (D) (E)
22. (A) (B) (C) (D) (E)
23. (A) (B) (C) (D) (E)
24. (A) (B) (C) (D) (E)
25. (A) (B) (C) (D) (E)
26. (A) (B) (C) (D) (E)
27. (A) (B) (C) (D) (E)
28. (A) (B) (C) (D) (E)
29. (A) (B) (C) (D) (E)
30. (A) (B) (C) (D) (E)
31. (A) (B) (C) (D) (E)
32. (A) (B) (C) (D) (E)
33. (A) (B) (C) (D) (E)
34. (A) (B) (C) (D) (E)
35. (A) (B) (C) (D) (E)
36. (A) (B) (C) (D) (E)
37. (A) (B) (C) (D) (E)
38. (A) (B) (C) (D) (E)
39. (A) (B) (C) (D) (E)
40. (A) (B) (C) (D) (E)
41. (A) (B) (C) (D) (E)
42. (A) (B) (C) (D) (E)
43. (A) (B) (C) (D) (E)
44. (A) (B) (C) (D) (E)
45. (A) (B) (C) (D) (E)
46. (A) (B) (C) (D) (E)
47. (A) (B) (C) (D) (E)
48. (A) (B) (C) (D) (E)
49. (A) (B) (C) (D) (E)
50. (A) (B) (C) (D) (E)
51. (A) (B) (C) (D) (E)
52. (A) (B) (C) (D) (E)
53. (A) (B) (C) (D) (E)
54. (A) (B) (C) (D) (E)
55. (A) (B) (C) (D) (E)
56. (A) (B) (C) (D) (E)
57. (A) (B) (C) (D) (E)
58. (A) (B) (C) (D) (E)
59. (A) (B) (C) (D) (E)
60. (A) (B) (C) (D) (E)
61. (A) (B) (C) (D) (E)
62. (A) (B) (C) (D) (E)
63. (A) (B) (C) (D) (E)
64. (A) (B) (C) (D) (E)
65. (A) (B) (C) (D) (E)
66. (A) (B) (C) (D) (E)
67. (A) (B) (C) (D) (E)
68. (A) (B) (C) (D) (E)
69. (A) (B) (C) (D) (E)
70. (A) (B) (C) (D) (E)
71. (A) (B) (C) (D) (E)
72. (A) (B) (C) (D) (E)
73. (A) (B) (C) (D) (E)
74. (A) (B) (C) (D) (E)
75. (A) (B) (C) (D) (E)
76. (A) (B) (C) (D) (E)
77. (A) (B) (C) (D) (E)
78. (A) (B) (C) (D) (E)
79. (A) (B) (C) (D) (E)
80. (A) (B) (C) (D) (E)
81. (A) (B) (C) (D) (E)
82. (A) (B) (C) (D) (E)
83. (A) (B) (C) (D) (E)
84. (A) (B) (C) (D) (E)
85. (A) (B) (C) (D) (E)

Practice Test Form

Completely darken bubbles with a No. 2 pencil. If you make a mistake, be sure to erase mark completely. Erase all stray marks.

1.
YOUR NAME: ______________________________ (Print) Last First M.I.

SIGNATURE: ______________________________ DATE: / /

HOME ADDRESS: ______________________________ (Print) Number and Street

______________________________ City State Zip Code

PHONE NO.: ______________________________ (Print)

Practice Test 3

1. Ⓐ Ⓑ Ⓒ Ⓓ Ⓔ	26. Ⓐ Ⓑ Ⓒ Ⓓ Ⓔ	51. Ⓐ Ⓑ Ⓒ Ⓓ Ⓔ	76. Ⓐ Ⓑ Ⓒ Ⓓ Ⓔ
2. Ⓐ Ⓑ Ⓒ Ⓓ Ⓔ	27. Ⓐ Ⓑ Ⓒ Ⓓ Ⓔ	52. Ⓐ Ⓑ Ⓒ Ⓓ Ⓔ	77. Ⓐ Ⓑ Ⓒ Ⓓ Ⓔ
3. Ⓐ Ⓑ Ⓒ Ⓓ Ⓔ	28. Ⓐ Ⓑ Ⓒ Ⓓ Ⓔ	53. Ⓐ Ⓑ Ⓒ Ⓓ Ⓔ	78. Ⓐ Ⓑ Ⓒ Ⓓ Ⓔ
4. Ⓐ Ⓑ Ⓒ Ⓓ Ⓔ	29. Ⓐ Ⓑ Ⓒ Ⓓ Ⓔ	54. Ⓐ Ⓑ Ⓒ Ⓓ Ⓔ	79. Ⓐ Ⓑ Ⓒ Ⓓ Ⓔ
5. Ⓐ Ⓑ Ⓒ Ⓓ Ⓔ	30. Ⓐ Ⓑ Ⓒ Ⓓ Ⓔ	55. Ⓐ Ⓑ Ⓒ Ⓓ Ⓔ	80. Ⓐ Ⓑ Ⓒ Ⓓ Ⓔ
6. Ⓐ Ⓑ Ⓒ Ⓓ Ⓔ	31. Ⓐ Ⓑ Ⓒ Ⓓ Ⓔ	56. Ⓐ Ⓑ Ⓒ Ⓓ Ⓔ	81. Ⓐ Ⓑ Ⓒ Ⓓ Ⓔ
7. Ⓐ Ⓑ Ⓒ Ⓓ Ⓔ	32. Ⓐ Ⓑ Ⓒ Ⓓ Ⓔ	57. Ⓐ Ⓑ Ⓒ Ⓓ Ⓔ	82. Ⓐ Ⓑ Ⓒ Ⓓ Ⓔ
8. Ⓐ Ⓑ Ⓒ Ⓓ Ⓔ	33. Ⓐ Ⓑ Ⓒ Ⓓ Ⓔ	58. Ⓐ Ⓑ Ⓒ Ⓓ Ⓔ	83. Ⓐ Ⓑ Ⓒ Ⓓ Ⓔ
9. Ⓐ Ⓑ Ⓒ Ⓓ Ⓔ	34. Ⓐ Ⓑ Ⓒ Ⓓ Ⓔ	59. Ⓐ Ⓑ Ⓒ Ⓓ Ⓔ	84. Ⓐ Ⓑ Ⓒ Ⓓ Ⓔ
10. Ⓐ Ⓑ Ⓒ Ⓓ Ⓔ	35. Ⓐ Ⓑ Ⓒ Ⓓ Ⓔ	60. Ⓐ Ⓑ Ⓒ Ⓓ Ⓔ	85. Ⓐ Ⓑ Ⓒ Ⓓ Ⓔ
11. Ⓐ Ⓑ Ⓒ Ⓓ Ⓔ	36. Ⓐ Ⓑ Ⓒ Ⓓ Ⓔ	61. Ⓐ Ⓑ Ⓒ Ⓓ Ⓔ	
12. Ⓐ Ⓑ Ⓒ Ⓓ Ⓔ	37. Ⓐ Ⓑ Ⓒ Ⓓ Ⓔ	62. Ⓐ Ⓑ Ⓒ Ⓓ Ⓔ	
13. Ⓐ Ⓑ Ⓒ Ⓓ Ⓔ	38. Ⓐ Ⓑ Ⓒ Ⓓ Ⓔ	63. Ⓐ Ⓑ Ⓒ Ⓓ Ⓔ	
14. Ⓐ Ⓑ Ⓒ Ⓓ Ⓔ	39. Ⓐ Ⓑ Ⓒ Ⓓ Ⓔ	64. Ⓐ Ⓑ Ⓒ Ⓓ Ⓔ	
15. Ⓐ Ⓑ Ⓒ Ⓓ Ⓔ	40. Ⓐ Ⓑ Ⓒ Ⓓ Ⓔ	65. Ⓐ Ⓑ Ⓒ Ⓓ Ⓔ	
16. Ⓐ Ⓑ Ⓒ Ⓓ Ⓔ	41. Ⓐ Ⓑ Ⓒ Ⓓ Ⓔ	66. Ⓐ Ⓑ Ⓒ Ⓓ Ⓔ	
17. Ⓐ Ⓑ Ⓒ Ⓓ Ⓔ	42. Ⓐ Ⓑ Ⓒ Ⓓ Ⓔ	67. Ⓐ Ⓑ Ⓒ Ⓓ Ⓔ	
18. Ⓐ Ⓑ Ⓒ Ⓓ Ⓔ	43. Ⓐ Ⓑ Ⓒ Ⓓ Ⓔ	68. Ⓐ Ⓑ Ⓒ Ⓓ Ⓔ	
19. Ⓐ Ⓑ Ⓒ Ⓓ Ⓔ	44. Ⓐ Ⓑ Ⓒ Ⓓ Ⓔ	69. Ⓐ Ⓑ Ⓒ Ⓓ Ⓔ	
20. Ⓐ Ⓑ Ⓒ Ⓓ Ⓔ	45. Ⓐ Ⓑ Ⓒ Ⓓ Ⓔ	70. Ⓐ Ⓑ Ⓒ Ⓓ Ⓔ	
21. Ⓐ Ⓑ Ⓒ Ⓓ Ⓔ	46. Ⓐ Ⓑ Ⓒ Ⓓ Ⓔ	71. Ⓐ Ⓑ Ⓒ Ⓓ Ⓔ	
22. Ⓐ Ⓑ Ⓒ Ⓓ Ⓔ	47. Ⓐ Ⓑ Ⓒ Ⓓ Ⓔ	72. Ⓐ Ⓑ Ⓒ Ⓓ Ⓔ	
23. Ⓐ Ⓑ Ⓒ Ⓓ Ⓔ	48. Ⓐ Ⓑ Ⓒ Ⓓ Ⓔ	73. Ⓐ Ⓑ Ⓒ Ⓓ Ⓔ	
24. Ⓐ Ⓑ Ⓒ Ⓓ Ⓔ	49. Ⓐ Ⓑ Ⓒ Ⓓ Ⓔ	74. Ⓐ Ⓑ Ⓒ Ⓓ Ⓔ	
25. Ⓐ Ⓑ Ⓒ Ⓓ Ⓔ	50. Ⓐ Ⓑ Ⓒ Ⓓ Ⓔ	75. Ⓐ Ⓑ Ⓒ Ⓓ Ⓔ	

NOTES

NOTES

NOTES

WELCOME TO

POLICING TODAY

FRANK SCHMALLEGER
JOHN L. WORRALL

The following pages introduce the features and content of the newest and best introduction to law enforcement text available, **POLICING TODAY**.

Technology is becoming ever more central to today's society. **POLICING TODAY** takes a close look at today's technology in the law enforcement world and examines why it is important.

WEB-BASED CRIME FIGHTING

Police departments are involving the public when seeking information about crimes. Surveillance tapes are being loaded on YouTube.com in order to try to help solve crimes.

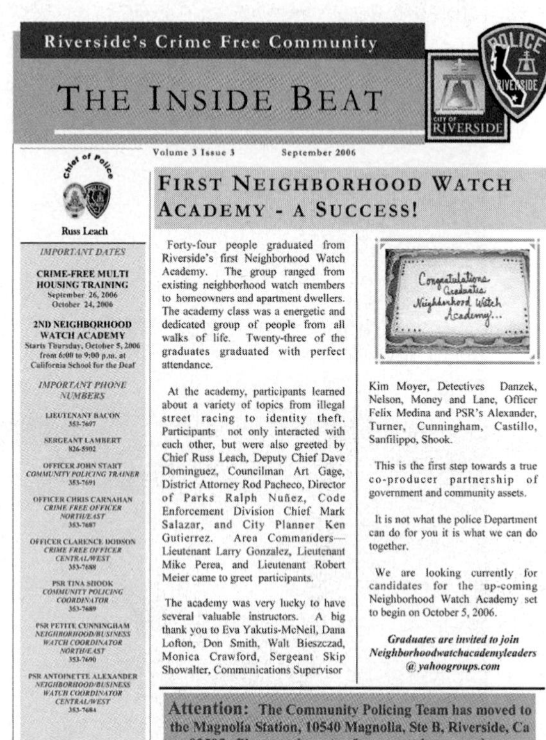

Riverside's Crime Free Community

THE INSIDE BEAT

CITY OF RIVERSIDE — POLICE RIVERSIDE

Volume 3 Issue 3 September 2006

Chief of Police
Russ Leach

IMPORTANT DATES

CRIME-FREE MULTI HOUSING TRAINING
September 26, 2006
October 24, 2006

2ND NEIGHBORHOOD WATCH ACADEMY
Starts Thursday, October 5, 2006 from 6:00 to 9:00 p.m. at California School for the Deaf

IMPORTANT PHONE NUMBERS

LIEUTENANT BACON
353-7697

SERGEANT LAMBERT
826-5902

OFFICER JOHN START
COMMUNITY POLICING TRAINER
353-7691

OFFICER CHRIS CARNAHAN
CRIME FREE OFFICER
NORTH/EAST
353-7687

OFFICER CLARENCE DODSON
CRIME FREE OFFICER
CENTRAL/WEST
353-7688

PSR TINA SHOOK
COMMUNITY POLICING COORDINATOR
353-7689

PSR PETITE CUNNINGHAM
NEIGHBORHOOD/BUSINESS WATCH COORDINATOR
NORTH/EAST
353-7690

PSR ANTOINETTE ALEXANDER
NEIGHBORHOOD/BUSINESS WATCH COORDINATOR
CENTRAL/WEST
353-7684

FIRST NEIGHBORHOOD WATCH ACADEMY - A SUCCESS!

Forty-four people graduated from Riverside's first Neighborhood Watch Academy. The group ranged from existing neighborhood watch members to homeowners and apartment dwellers. The academy class was a energetic and dedicated group of people from all walks of life. Twenty-three of the graduates graduated with perfect attendance.

At the academy, participants learned about a variety of topics from illegal street racing to identity theft. Participants not only interacted with each other, but were also greeted by Chief Russ Leach, Deputy Chief Dave Dominguez, Councilman Art Gage, District Attorney Rod Pacheco, Director of Parks Ralph Nuñez, Code Enforcement Division Chief Mark Salazar, and City Planner Ken Gutierrez. Area Commanders—Lieutenant Larry Gonzalez, Lieutenant Mike Perea, and Lieutenant Robert Meier came to greet participants.

The academy was very lucky to have several valuable instructors. A big thank you to Eva Yakutis-McNeil, Dana Lofton, Don Smith, Walt Bieszczad, Monica Crawford, Sergeant Skip Showalter, Communications Supervisor

Congratulations Graduates Neighborhood Watch Academy...

Kim Moyer, Detectives Danzek, Nelson, Money and Lane, Officer Felix Medina and PSR's Alexander, Turner, Cunningham, Castillo, Sanfilippo, Shook.

This is the first step towards a true co-producer partnership of government and community assets.

It is not what the police Department can do for you it is what we can do together.

We are looking currently for candidates for the up-coming Neighborhood Watch Academy set to begin on October 5, 2006.

Graduates are invited to join Neighborhoodwatchacademyleaders @yahoogroups.com

Attention: The Community Policing Team has moved to the Magnolia Station, 10540 Magnolia, Ste B, Riverside, Ca 92505. Please make note of our new phone numbers.

CUTTING-EDGE TECHNOLOGY

Some police agencies are now using unmanned aerial reconnaissance vehicles (UAVs). How might UAVs benefit police and sheriff's departments in our new technology age?

REAL-LIFE POLICING

POLICING TODAY accurately portrays the reality of police work and law enforcement in today's society.

THE MEDIA

Dealing with the media is an important aspect of policing today.

BECOMING A COP

What are the advantages and disadvantages of a career in law enforcement?

PRIVATE POLICING AND SECURITY

The relationship between private security and public law enforcement is of growing importance as police seek to develop intelligence about possible terrorist attacks and other forms of criminal activity.

LATEST POLICING ISSUES

POLICING TODAY spotlights important contemporary issues, techniques, and technology.

EVIDENCE-BASED POLICING

One of the hottest topics in law enforcement today, evidence-based policing quantifies how effective research is in policing today. It asks, "What works?"

DOES IT WORK?

One or Two Officer Patrols?

We have looked at several varieties of patrol in this chapter, but we have not yet looked at the number of officers engaged in such patrol. Some departments employ one-officer patrols; others employ two-officer patrols. Which is most effective?

A department's decision to adopt one- versus two-officer patrol is usually dictated by concerns like officer safety. In late 2006, for example, the Mesa, Arizona police department changed from one- to two-officer patrols[1], in part, because of a high-profile killing of a Phoenix police officer who was on patrol by himself (incidentally, Phoenix also uses two-officer patrols, as do many other large cities like Los Angeles and New York City).

Officer safety is obviously important. Some would say it's more important than crime control, but it is also interesting to look at one- versus two-officer patrols from a crime control standpoint. What does the research show? Unfortunately, most of it is now a bit dated, but there was a time when researchers were very concerned with the relationship between one and two-officer patrols and crime. The findings from several published studies[2] can be summarized thusly:

1. Patrol staffing mode has virtually no effect on police effectiveness.
2. Single-officer staffing increases patrol visibility, but the effect on crime is almost non-existent.
3. Two-officer patrols are, not surprisingly, twice as costly as single-officer patrols.
4. Patrol activity levels are compatible between both staffing methods.

Neither of these observations are expressly concerned with crime. So, does one- versus two-officer patrol make a difference in terms of crime? In particular, can police prevent crime with the added visibility of one-officer patrols? One researcher has noted: "As to the issue of prevention, the limited mathematical data....suggest that since visibility is only marginally improved by single-officer patrol, the concurrent deterrent effects should be minimal.[3] The answer, then, is that we don't know for sure.

[1] S. Scarborough, "Mesa police praise two-officer teams," Arizona Republic. Accessed 12/12/2006 from: <http://www.azcentral.com/community/tempe/articles/1209mesa-twomanpatrol1208Z10.html>.

[2] Examples include L.E. Boydstun, M.E. Sherry, and N.P. Moelter, Patrol Staffing in San Diego: One- or Two-Officer Units. Washington, DC: Police Foundation, 1977; S.H. Decker and A.E. Wagner, "The Impact of Police Patrol Staffing on Police-Citizen Injuries and Dispositions," Journal of Criminal Justice 10(1982):375–382; E.H. Kaplan, "Evaluating the Effectiveness of One-Officer Versus Two-Officer Patrol Units," Journal of Criminal Justice 7(1977):325–355; D.A. 64; National Institute of Justice, Performance Measures for Evaluating One- Versus Two-Person Cars.

IMMIGRATION

Illegal immigration and the policing of immigrant populations have become central activities in American law enforcement today.

TERRORISM AND THE FUTURE OF POLICING

Effective policing in an age of terrorism is vitally important. How has the threat of terrorism changed the face of American policing?

SPECIAL FEATURES

POLICING TODAY is filled with special features that promote a greater understanding of law enforcement. Some of those features include:

YOU DECIDE

The Second Job

You are an officer employed with the city of Fairview. Under the city's "detail system," private employers, such as hotel owners, can request services from the police department for officers to provide security services. Officers serve on a rotation system so that all have an equal opportunity to work the security service details and they are paid between $25 and $30 per hour for their services. Some private employers have elected to hire officers outside of the "detail system" to ensure they receive the services of the same officer—and so they do not have to pay the city's detail rate. You consult your department's policy manual, which states in part:

> Although officers of the force are assigned specific hours of regular duty, they shall be considered "on duty" at all times for the preservation of the public peace and the protection of life and property, and shall be prepared to take all reasonable police action to accomplish this purpose. All serious matters of public concern shall receive appropriate attention, even though an officer is not on duty at the time.

Fairview also has a policy affecting all its employees (including police officers), which states in part:

> ...municipal employees are prohibited from accepting other employment involving compensation of substantial value, the responsibilities of which are inherently incompatible with the responsibilities of his public office.*

Assuming you do not wear your uniform and accept the title "security guard," would it be ethical for you to step outside the detail system and assume this position? Would the security guard position amount to a conflict of interest?

* This scenario was adapted from an actual decision by Commonwealth of Massachusetts State Ethics Commission (Opinion EC-COI-94-8).

YOU DECIDE features, found throughout the book, present ethical dilemmas requiring critical thought.

COMING FULL CIRCLE uses discussion topics and writing assignments to help students appreciate the significance of chapter materials.

COMING FULL CIRCLE

For Discussion

Return to the questions posed at the start of this chapter. Have any of your answers changed since reading the chapter? What portions of this chapter helped you answer these questions?

Writing Assignment

Using material from this chapter and additional resources, write a 500-word essay in response to one of the questions we posed at the beginning of this chapter.

MYCRIMEKIT is an online supplement that offers book-specific learning objectives, chapter summaries, flashcards, and practice tests as well as video clips and media activities to aid student learning and comprehension.

INSTRUCTOR SUPPLEMENTS

PowerPoint Presentation	0-20-562468-5
Instructor's Manual (download only)	0-20-562467-7
Test Item File for WebCT	0-20-562456-1
Test Item File for BlackBoard	0-20-562454-5
TestGen Computerized Test Bank	0-20-562457-X

To access supplementary materials online, instructors need to request an instructor access code. Go to **www.pearsonhighered.com/irc**, where you can register for an instructor access code. Within 48 hours after registering, you will receive a confirming email, including an instructor access code. Once you have received your code, go to the site and log on for full instructions on downloading the materials you wish to use.

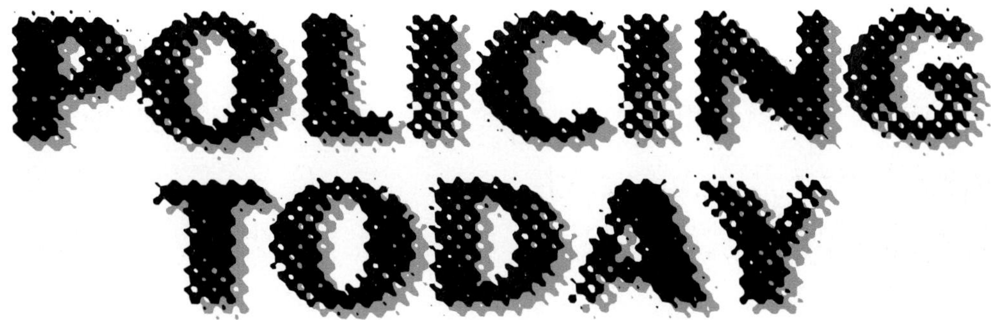

POLICING TODAY

FRANK SCHMALLEGER
Distinguished Professor Emeritus
University of North Carolina at Pembroke

JOHN L. WORRALL
Professor of Criminology
University of Texas at Dallas

Prentice Hall

Upper Saddle River, New Jersey
Columbus, Ohio

Library of Congress Cataloging-in-Publication Data

Schmalleger, Frank.
Policing today / Frank Schmalleger, John Worrall.
p. cm.
Includes bibliographical references and index.
ISBN-13: 978-0-20-551551-6 (alk. paper)
ISBN-10: 0-20-551551-7 (alk. paper)
1. Law enforcement—United States—History. 2. Law enforcement—United States. I. Worrall, John L. II. Title.
HV8139.S325 2010
363.2'30973—dc22

2008042117

Editor in Chief: Vernon R. Anthony
Acquisitions Editor: Tim Peyton
Editorial Assistant: Alicia Kelly
Production Coordination: Janet Bolton, Milford Publishing Services
Project Manager: Steve Robb
Senior Operations Supervisor: Pat Tonneman
Art Director: Diane Ernsberger
Interior Design: Candace Rowley
Cover Designer: Candace Rowley
Cover Photos: Jupiter Images (top and middle); PhotoEdit (bottom)
Manager, Rights and Permissions: Zina Arabia
Manager, Cover Visual Research and Permissions: Karen Sanatar
Image Permissions Coordinator: Cynthia Vincenti
Photo Researcher: Jerry Marshall/Truitt and Marshall
Director of Marketing: David Gesell
Marketing Manager: Adam Kloza
Senior Marketing Coordinator: Alicia Wozniak
Copyeditor: Judith M. Riotto, Ganymede Editorial Services

Chapter Opener Photo Credits: Weldon Wilson/Washington State Patrol, p. 2; Robert Brenner/PhotoEdit Inc., p. 24; Bob Daemmrich/The Image Works, p. 52; Kimball Andrew Schmidt/Stock Connection, p. 76; Rendering by Ewing Cole Digital Media Group (ECDMG), provided by the National Law Enforcement Officers Memorial Fund (NLEOMF), p. 106; © David Gard/Star Ledger/CORBIS, All Rights Reserved, p. 126; Steven Senne/AP Wide World Photos, p. 152; Roger Tully/Getty Images Inc.—Stone Allstock, p. 174; John Stillwell/PA Wire/AP Wide World Photos, p. 200; Jeff Greenberg/Alamy Images, p. 226; Jeff Greenberg/Alamy Images, p. 248; Patrick Byrd/Alamy Images, p. 276; Hemis/Alamy Images, p. 302; Dennis Oda, p. 324; Mary Altaffer/AP Wide World Photos, p. 350; Susan Meiselas/Magnum Photos, Inc., p. 376

This book was set in 10/12 Garamond by S4Carlisle Publishing Services and was printed and bound by Courier Kendallville, Inc. The cover was printed by Phoenix Color Corporation.

Pearson Education Ltd., London
Pearson Education Singapore Pte. Ltd.
Pearson Education Canada, Inc.
Pearson Education—Japan
Pearson Education Australia Pty. Limited
Pearson Education North Asia Ltd., Hong Kong
Pearson Educación de Mexico, S.A. de C.V.
Pearson Education Malaysia Pte. Ltd.

Prentice Hall
is an imprint of

www.pearsonhighered.com

10 9 8 7 6 5 4
ISBN-13: 978-0-20-551551-6
ISBN-10: 0-20-551551-7

CONTENTS

PREFACE

Our goal in writing this book was to present the *reality* of police work in the United States today. Readers of this book will see, for instance, that the primary police functions are not necessarily crime fighting and criminal investigation. They will learn, instead, that they are the much more mundane tasks of maintaining order and providing services. Readers will also learn that the police operate in a complex environment in which they must comply with myriad policies and legal constraints. All the while, they face immense pressures from diverse populations, including members of the general public, politicians, the media, interest groups, and other stakeholders. We will also look at what it takes to enter the policing profession and what the job is really like for those who make it. Finally, we will take up complex issues like discretion, police subculture, deviance, and international cooperation among police agencies.

It is likely that you are reading this book for a college course in policing or law enforcement. Perhaps you are majoring in criminal justice or criminology with the intention of entering police work in the future. Maybe you are already employed in policing and are continuing your education, or maybe you have no interest at all in working for any criminal justice agency but still find policing an interesting topic. We wrote this book to satisfy all these different kinds of readers. For veteran police officers (including, perhaps, instructors), the book covers all of the leading controversies and issues that officers face today. It will help aspiring officers think about their chosen career path and what it takes to enter the field. And for those with no current or future connection to police work, we believe that this book will help them become more informed observers and enlightened critics.

ACKNOWLEDGMENTS

Many thanks go to all who assisted in many different ways in the development and production of this textbook. Manuscript reviewers were especially helpful in giving the manuscript a clear focus and meaningful direction during its early development. We would like to thank manuscript reviewers Less Boggess, Fairmont State University; Hilary Buck, Joliet Junior College; William Carcara, American Crime Prevention Institute; Otis Grant, Indiana University–South Bend; Darrell Irwin, University of North Carolina–Wilmington; Deborah L. Laufersweiler-Dwyer, University of Arkansas–Little Rock; Kenneth Novak, University of Missouri–Kansas City; Forrest J. Nutter, Chippewa Valley Technical College; Louis A. Reeves, Indiana State University; Lorie Rubenser, Sul Ross State University; Scott Rudeen; Arnold R. Waggoner, Rose State College; and Stacey Wyland, Keystone College.

We are very grateful to the Pearson team for all their efforts in seeing this book through to production and for their many activities in getting it into the hands of students across the country. The Pearson team includes editor in chief Vernon R. Anthony, acquisitions editor Tim Peyton, editorial assistant Alicia Kelly, project manager Steve Robb, audio visual project manager Janet Portisch, senior operations supervisor Pat Tonneman, art director Diane Ernsberger, interior and cover designer Candace Rowley, Image Resource Center rights and permissions manager Zina Arabia, cover visual research and permissions manager Karen Sanatar, image permissions coordinator Cynthia Vincenti, director of marketing David Gesell, marketing manager Adam Kloza, senior marketing coordinator Alicia Wozniak, managing editor JoEllen Gohr, creative director Christy Mahon, media editor Michelle Churma, and media project manager Karen Bretz.

Thanks, too, to other production team members, especially production coordinator Janet Bolton of Milford Publishing Services, copyeditor Judith Mara Riotto, and photo researcher Jerry Marshall at Truitt and Marshall.

The authors would like to thank their colleagues inside and outside of academia, including (but not limited to) Robert Taylor, University of North Texas; Larry Gaines, California State University–San Bernardino; Dallas Police Chief David Kunkle; and Michael Scott, Center for Problem-Oriented Policing. Finally, thanks go to our families whose love and continued support inspire us to write.

FRANK SCHMALLEGER and JOHN L. WORRALL

ABOUT THE AUTHORS

FRANK SCHMALLEGER, PH.D., holds degrees from the University of Notre Dame and Ohio State University, having earned both a master's (1970) and a doctorate in sociology (1974) with a special emphasis in criminology from Ohio State University. From 1976 to 1994, he taught criminal justice courses at the University of North Carolina at Pembroke. For the last 16 of those years, he chaired the university's Department of Sociology, Social Work, and Criminal Justice. In 1991, he was awarded the title Distinguished Professor, and the university named him Professor Emeritus in 2001.

As an adjunct professor with Webster University in St. Louis, Missouri, Dr. Schmalleger helped develop the university's graduate program in security administration and loss prevention. He taught courses in that curriculum for more than a decade. Dr. Schmalleger has also taught in the online graduate program of the New School for Social Research, helping to build the world's first electronic classrooms in support of distance learning through computer telecommunications. An avid proponent of criminal justice education, he has worked with numerous schools to develop curricula at both the undergraduate and graduate levels.

Dr. Schmalleger is the author of numerous articles and many books, including the widely used *Criminal Justice Today* (Prentice Hall, 2009), *Criminology Today* (Prentice Hall, 2009), *Criminal Law Today* (Prentice Hall, 2006), and *The Definitive Guide to Criminal Justice and Criminology on the World Wide Web* (Prentice Hall, 2009).

He is also founding editor of the journal *Criminal Justice Studies*. He has served as editor for the Prentice Hall series *Criminal Justice in the Twenty-First Century* and as imprint adviser for Greenwood Publishing Group's criminal justice reference series.

Dr. Schmalleger's philosophy of both teaching and writing can be summed up in these words: "In order to communicate knowledge, we must first catch, then hold, a person's interest—be it student, colleague, or policymaker. Our writing, our speaking, and our teaching must be relevant to the problems facing people today, and they must in some way help solve those problems."

JOHN L. WORRALL, PH.D., is professor of criminology at the University of Texas at Dallas. A Seattle native, he received a bachelor's degree in both psychology and law and justice from Central Washington University in 1994. Both his master's degree in criminal justice and his doctorate in political science were received from Washington State University, where he completed his studies in 1999. From 1999 to 2006, he was a member of the criminal justice faculty at California State University, San Bernardino. He moved to Texas in the fall of 2006.

Dr. Worrall has published articles and book chapters on a wide range of law enforcement topics, ranging from legal issues in policing to community prosecution. He is the author of *Crime Control in America: What Works?* (Allyn and Bacon, 2008) and *Criminal Procedure: From First Contact to Appeal* (Allyn and Bacon, 2007), the coauthor of *Criminal Evidence: An Introduction* (Oxford University Press, 2005), and *Police Administration* (McGraw-Hill, 2003), and the coeditor of *The Changing Role of the American Prosecutor* (State University of New York Press, 2008).

In addition to teaching and writing, Dr. Worrall serves as a consultant, evaluator, and trainer for police departments and prosecutor's offices across the United States and Canada. In this capacity, he recently teamed up with the Center for Problem-Oriented Policing to author a guide for law enforcement officials on the use of asset forfeiture to combat illegal activity.

Dr. Worrall was recently elected to the executive board of the Academy of Criminal Justice Sciences, where he serves in the position of trustee at large (2008–2011). He is also editor of the journal *Police Quarterly*, the top-rated policing journal, and he serves as associate director for research for the W. W. Caruth, Jr., Dallas Police Institute, a collaborative research and training organization involving the Dallas Police Department, the Communities Foundation of Texas, the University of North Texas, and the University of Texas at Dallas.

FOUNDATIONS

SECTION I

chapter one
ORIGINS AND EVOLUTION OF AMERICAN POLICING

LEARNING OBJECTIVES

After reading this chapter, students should be able to:

1. Explain the origins of policing in America.
2. Identify and describe the main eras of policing.
3. Discuss the development of state and federal law enforcement agencies in the United States.
4. Summarize some of the controversies associated with private policing.

THINK ABOUT IT

Illegal immigration is a hot-button issue today. U.S. Customs and Border Protection (CBP) agents routinely apprehend undocumented immigrants crossing the U.S.-Mexico border, but there are not enough agents to effectively stop the massive influx of illegal immigrants. In response to this concern, citizen groups are volunteering their time and energies to help with border protection. One of these groups, the Minuteman Project,[1] rose to national prominence in the early years of the twenty-first century. Its members claim to be working in collaboration with U.S. Customs and Border Protection, but that agency has not officially teamed with or endorsed the Minuteman Project's efforts.

The Minuteman Project (and its sister organization, the Minuteman Civil Defense Corps) consists mostly of civilian volunteers who literally watch portions of the U.S.-Mexico border (employing foot, car, and helicopter patrols) and alert CBP agents to possible illegal crossings. The Minuteman Project calls itself a "vigilance operation" and says that it does not advocate altercations between volunteers and those seeking to cross the border illegally; instead, it aims to provide information to officials whose legitimate responsibility is securing the border. Some volunteers, however, work together in armed patrols and sometimes detain suspected illegal immigrants until CBP agents arrive.

Whether the Minuteman volunteers are a "vigilance" group or a "vigilante" group is open to debate. There is no shortage of critics who claim that the Minutemen are concerned with anything but "vigilance." Some have gone so far as to create Vigilante Watch, another volunteer group whose mission is to "watch the watchers."[2] The American Civil Liberties Union (ACLU) has denounced the detentions of suspected illegal immigrants by Minuteman volunteers, and some members of the ACLU ride out into the Arizona desert to keep an eye on the Minutemen.[3]

The Minuteman Project raises several interesting questions to keep in mind as you read this chapter:

1. Should *any* civilian volunteers get involved in actively patrolling our borders?
2. What should organizations like the Minuteman Project be allowed to do in terms of policing the borders?
3. Are the Minutemen vigilantes? If so, is there a place for vigilante groups in contemporary law enforcement?
4. Should civilian organizations be involved with general issues of crime prevention and security?
5. Where should the line be drawn between civilian and "official" law enforcement?
6. To what extent is private policing and security helpful or harmful to society's interests?

INTRODUCTION

The police get more attention than any other component of the criminal justice system. By some accounts, they get more attention than almost any other aspect of modern society. Consider what we see in the media. Almost every movie with a good-versus-evil theme features a law enforcement officer trying to bring wrongdoers to justice. Television shows featuring police officers have been the staple of nearly every major network since the beginning of television. Local news shows routinely start their broadcasts with coverage of high-profile crimes and police investigations. The print media thrive on reporting crimes and law enforcement activities. Sometimes, though, the police are painted in an unfavorable light. Corruption scandals quickly capture the headlines, and questionable police shootings lead to investigations, public outcries, and sometimes criminal charges against law enforcement personnel.

Police are attention getters of the first magnitude not just because of television, movies, and the news. They simply stand out. Their uniforms are distinctive, and many of their vehicles are easily identifiable. When they do anything controversial or even out of the ordinary, they are thrust into

U.S. Border Patrol agents ride along the U.S.-Canadian border near Oroville, Washington. Agents in the area ride mustangs adopted from the U.S. Bureau of Land Management's wild horse and burro program. Illegal immigration and the policing of immigrant populations have become important activities in American law enforcement today. What other important activities do law enforcement agencies engage in?

Ted S. Warren/AP Wide World Photos

the spotlight. And while some police work is not observed because it is done undercover, most police duties are performed right in front of the public. Few occupations are subject to such a high level of visibility. Consequently, police officers and police activities are the subjects of intense scrutiny by all sorts of individuals, ranging from criminals and marginalized populations to aspiring criminal justice professionals and university researchers.

The attention that the police receive does not always work in their favor. At one extreme, an officer who justifiably kills a person in the line of duty may quickly be criticized by civilians who fail to grasp the difficulties and intricacies of real police work. This is especially true when a white officer shoots a minority suspect. The same holds true for forceful arrests made in the public eye. Civilians sometimes become outraged when the police use physical force, even if the circumstances necessitate such action. At the other extreme, many people aspire to enter police work but misunderstand what the job is really like. Popular television programs like CBS's *CSI: Crime Scene Investigation* give the impression that everyone can live a fascinating life as a forensic investigator, but they fail to mention that these jobs are not only the exception in police work but not nearly as exciting as the show's writers and producers would have us believe.

THE ORIGINS OF POLICING

For students of policing, an appreciation of policing history is essential in order to understand the contemporary structure of policing in the United States today. As a result of historical circumstances, the American system of policing is nearly unique in the world. Most countries today rely on one or only a few agencies for law enforcement. In the United States, however, there are thousands of law enforcement agencies with hundreds of thousands of employees. No other country has a policing system that looks quite like ours.

The study of policing history is important for another reason: For better or for worse, history often repeats itself. History repeats itself for worse when policymakers make decisions in a vacuum, without regard for those who have faced the same problems before. In other words, the failure to appreciate what was once tried without success leads to a costly repetition of past mistakes. Some critics of recent changes in American policing, such as the shift toward community policing, for example, argue that what we are now doing signals a return to days of old, which may not be desirable.

Alternatively, a technique or program that looks totally innovative and desirable today may have been purposefully avoided in the past. An example, which we will later cover more thoroughly, is federal–local law enforcement partnerships, which some see as especially important in the fight against terrorism. Critics of such efforts suggest that we are inching toward a national police force, a notion that, to the minds of many, is antithetical to our nation's system of government.

WEB PATROL 1-1
Police History
http://www.mycrimekit.com

History can repeat itself for the better when we revisit the successful strategies of the past. The decentralization that served policing early on in our nation's history, for example, is now part and parcel of recent reforms in policing around the country.

From Private to Public Policing

frankpledge system
The ultimate outgrowth of the night watch system of social control, dating to the twelfth century, in which ten households were grouped into a tithing, and each adult male member of the tithing was held responsible for the conduct of the others.

tithing
Under the frankpledge system, a group of ten households.

parish
Under the frankpledge system, a group of ten tithings. Also referred to as a *hundred*.

shire
Under the frankpledge system, a collection of several parishes.

sheriff
The modern-day term for the Old English *shire-reeve*. In the United States today, the senior law enforcement official in a county.

shire-reeve
The Old English term for *sheriff*. Literally, "the keeper of the shire."

watchman
An early officer on foot patrol who, during the hours of darkness, watched for fires and criminal activities. Upon detecting such events, the watchman's role was to sound the "hue and cry" to evoke a defensive response from the citizenry. This style of policing dates back to the early to mid-eighteenth century in England.

Henry Fielding (1707–1754)
An English magistrate who founded what some have called London's first police force, the Bow Street Runners.

One of the earliest known methods of policing, called *kin policing*, involved families, clans, and tribes enforcing informal rules and customs. Each member of the group was given authority to enforce the established rules, and individuals who deviated from community norms were often dealt with harshly.[4] This method of policing changed during the rise of the Greek city-states and the Roman Empire, and law enforcement evolved from what was essentially a private affair to a public one.

Greece and Rome began to use appointed magistrates to enforce the law. These unpaid individuals were largely responsible for law enforcement until about the third century BC in Rome and the sixth century BC in Greece. The first *paid* law enforcement official was the *praefectus urbi*, a position created in Rome about 27 BC.[5] By AD 6, Rome had a large force of these individuals who patrolled the streets day and night. Once the Roman Empire fell, though, law enforcement became the responsibility of the individual monarchies throughout Europe.

Kings used military forces for law enforcement, but they also relied on so-called night watches, or groups of citizens who roamed the streets looking for signs of trouble. Members of the night watch were given the authority to investigate crimes and to make arrests. The night watch system eventually evolved into the **frankpledge system**, which became more formalized around the twelfth century when kings appointed individuals known as chief-pledges to ensure that the system worked.[6] In the frankpledge system, ten households were grouped into a **tithing**, and each adult male member of the tithing was held responsible for the conduct of the others. Ten tithings were known as a hundred, or **parish**, and a group of several parishes eventually came to be called a **shire**. Shires resembled modern-day counties in terms of their size. The term **sheriff** comes from the old English word **shire-reeve**, which means "the keeper of the shire." The shire-reeve was granted authority by the Norman kings to levy fines against criminals and also to levy fines against the parishes for failing to capture criminals.

In England, the Second Statute of Westminster (1285)[7] required that each parish appoint two constables.[8] Their duties were to inspect the arms of the parish and to assist the sheriff with law enforcement. Men over the age of 15 formed the *posse comitatus*, which assisted with the pursuit and capture of dangerous criminals. Magistrates, who eventually came to be known as *justices of the peace*, began to be appointed by the king or the sheriff around the thirteenth century. They had primary responsibility for adjudicating crimes, not unlike modern-day judges. In England, from which we derive many of our traditions, this was the predominant model of law enforcement until the nineteenth century.

What set early approaches to policing apart from modern policing practices is that most of the officials charged with enforcing laws were volunteers. If paid, they were not salaried as police officers are today. Sheriffs, for example, were allowed to appropriate a portion of the money collected in the king's name.[9] Even though these developments signaled a shift from private to public policing, much of the job of enforcing the law remained largely private; there simply were not enough public officials to do the job. As the years passed, though, policing took ever greater steps in the direction of becoming a governmental function.

One of the most significant steps toward fully public policing occurred in 1735, when two London parishes were given authority to pay their **watchmen** out of tax collections.[10] Then, toward the middle of the eighteenth century, John and **Henry Fielding**, two Bow Street magistrates, started to pay men to serve as constables and patrol the streets at night.[11] These **Bow Street Runners**, or **thief takers**, patrolled the city on foot and the surrounding areas on horseback. They also performed investigations, and for that reason they have been described as the first known detective unit.[12]

In 1800, the Thames River Police were paid by public monies.[13] Private police forces did not disappear, however. Outside London in more rural areas, much law enforcement was still the responsibility of churches, communities, parishes, magistrates, and a variety of other individuals. Moving beyond England, other countries also started to form public police agencies. France, Prussia (Germany), Russia, China, and India all made the gradual shift from private to public law enforcement.[14] As police officers came to be paid with public funds, the shift away from private policing became more apparent.

The Influence of the English Model

To a large extent, policing in London became the model for policing in America. Historians have called attention to various forces behind the emergence of American policing, several of which we will consider shortly, but what early American policing looked like stemmed a great deal from the English approach.

In 1822, British home secretary **Sir Robert Peel** criticized the state of policing in London. Some years later, he was responsible for passage of the "Act for Improving the Police in and Near the Metropolis," otherwise known as the **Metropolitan Police Act**. Adopted by Parliament in 1829, this legislation created the world's first large-scale organized police force in the city of London.[15] As others have noted, the Metropolitan Police Act "introduced a centralized and unified system of police in England" and constituted a revolution in traditional methods of law enforcement.[16] The legislation heralded the end of the old fragmented and ineffectual system of parish constables and represented the dawn of a whole new era of policing.[17]

Two men, Charles Rowan and Richard Mayne, were appointed to oversee development of the force. They adopted a military organizational model. This was resisted to a large degree by British citizens out of fear that the line between policing and the military would be too thin, and that police might behave like an army of occupation. Rowan and Mayne, however, went to great lengths to ensure that their officers behaved properly, and the police force eventually gained widespread acceptance.

Sir Robert Peel's contribution lies not just in the creation of the first organized police force, however. He was among the first to envision a broader role for officers than just crime fighting. Peel emphasized the *prevention* of crime. He also felt that uniforms were necessary because they would make officers stand out in a crowd and thus discourage crime.[18] Beyond that, Peel identified a series of principles that he said ought to characterize any police force (Figure 1-1).

Bow Street Runners
An early English police unit formed under the leadership of Henry Fielding, magistrate of the Bow Street region of London. Also referred to as *thief takers*.[i]

thief taker
An alternative name for Henry Fielding's Bow Street Runners.

WEB PATROL 1-2

A History of British Policing
http://www.mycrimekit.com

Sir Robert Peel (1788–1850)
A former British home secretary whose criticisms of the state of policing in London led to the passage of the Metropolitan Police Act and the establishment of the world's first large-scale organized police force in that city in 1829.

Metropolitan Police Act
The legislation adopted by the British Parliament in 1829 that established the world's first large-scale organized police force in London.

Figure 1-1 • Sir Robert Peel's Nine Principles of Policing

1. The basic mission for which the police exist is to prevent crime and disorder.
2. The ability of the police to perform their duties is dependent upon public approval of police actions.
3. Police must secure the willing co-operation of the public in voluntary observance of the law to be able to secure and maintain the respect of the public.
4. The degree of co-operation of the public that can be secured diminishes proportionately to the necessity of the use of physical force.
5. Police seek and preserve public favor not by catering to public opinion but by constantly demonstrating absolute impartial service to the law.
6. Police use physical force to the extent necessary to secure observance of the law or to restore order only when the exercise of persuasion, advice and warning is found to be insufficient.
7. Police, at all times, should maintain a relationship with the public that gives reality to the historic tradition that the police are the public and the public are the police; the police being only members of the public who are paid to give full-time attention to duties which are incumbent on every citizen in the interests of community welfare and existence.
8. Police should always direct their action strictly towards their functions and never appear to usurp the powers of the judiciary.
9. The test of police efficiency is the absence of crime and disorder, not the visible evidence of police action in dealing with it.

Source: J. L. Lyman, "The Metropolitan Police Act of 1829: An analysis of certain events influencing the passage and character of the Metropolitan Police Act in England," *Journal of Criminal Law, Criminology, and Police Science*, vol. 55, no. 1 (March 1964), pp. 141–54.

A protestor is arrested by British police for attempting to interfere with an Olympic torchbearer on Downing Street in London, England, in 2008. Scores of arrests were made as clashes between pro-Tibetan protestors and police marred the Olympic torch parade on its 31-mile-long London route. How would Sir Robert Peel's nine principles of policing apply to the policing of public demonstrations, like the one shown here?

Policing Comes to America

The first North American colonists settled along the eastern seaboard. They hailed from a number of countries, including Spain, France, Holland, Sweden, and of course England. The first of these settlements, Jamestown, was established in 1607 in what is now Virginia. The colony at Plymouth, Massachusetts, followed, set up by the Pilgrims in 1620. Swedish and Dutch citizens settled around what is today New York City. The Spanish claimed land in what is now the southern United States and in the Caribbean. All these people had visions of expanding their settlements, but given their distance from the European mainland, doing so was difficult. Expansion was particularly difficult for the English and French because Spain's presence was significant.

Early on, churches in America were heavily involved in crime control, though without a formal criminal justice system. People who strayed from acceptable forms of conduct were often shunned by their congregations. According to one historian, church congregations functioned as the "police and courts of first resort."[19] Moreover, when corporal punishments were used, they were often carried out in public. The use of stocks, floggings in the public square, and even public hangings were common methods of dealing with wayward individuals. Public punishments, often witnessed by hundreds of people, made clear to everyone the consequences of inappropriate behavior.

As more colonists moved to the New World, however, they "brought the law in their baggage."[20] That is, they brought knowledge of English criminal codes, law enforcement agencies, and methods of punishment, and they adapted them to serve the needs of their new communities.

Chaos in the Cities. As America came of age, more immigrants arrived and settled in urban areas. Cities became increasingly crowded, dangerous, and dirty. For example, from 1850 to about 1880, New York City's population grew until almost a million people were crowded into the two-square-mile center of the city. The city's East Side housed nearly 300,000 people who lacked toilet facilities, heat, fire protection, and other essentials. Unemployment levels were high, and sickness abounded. Cholera outbreaks were common, killing thousands of people at a time.

By the mid-1800s, crime had become commonplace. People stole and looted to survive. Organized gangs formed, fought for territory, and contributed to the violence and mayhem within the city. By one account, by 1850 New York City had become America's most terrifying city.[21] Other large cities like Boston, Chicago, and Philadelphia hardly fared better.

Early efforts to control crime fell on the shoulders of appointed constables and citizen volunteers. The constables patrolled during the daytime; citizens patrolled at night. But as the cities grew and became more dangerous, this system could not keep pace with crime.[22] In 1844, the first metropolitan police department was formed in the New York City area. It initially patrolled only during the daylight hours, leaving the preexisting night watch to patrol the city during darkness. The early New York City force was modeled after London's Metropolitan Police and consisted of only 16 officers appointed by the mayor.[23] The force was reorganized and expanded to 800 officers in 1845 under Mayor William Havemeyer, who divided the city into three police districts. This period also saw the elimination of the old night watch system and the construction of station houses and local courts.[24] Twelve years later, in 1857, the police in Manhattan, Brooklyn, Staten Island, Westchester County, and the Bronx were consolidated into one department under a governor-appointed board of commissioners, becoming what we think of today as the New York City Police Department (NYPD).[25] Prior to the consolidation, 18 separate police forces patrolled within the area that comprises present-day New York City.[26] Some of them were better equipped and organized than others. Lacking, however, was a centralized police mandate, good communications, and coordinated efforts.[27]

On the one hand, the combined force of 1857, which initially consisted of 6,396 members, was welcomed by people who were distressed about problems of social disorganization and crime within the city. On the other hand, there was concern that the new police force might become a standing army (recall that our nation was founded, in part, out of frustration with overreaching, centralized government).[28] Other large cities quickly followed the New York example, establishing their own police forces. They did so in response to surges in violence, conflict, multiple riots, and citizen fears that America's experiment in self-governance might not survive.

WEB PATROL 1-3

The History of the New Orleans Police Department
http://www.mycrimekit.com

London's police, as we have already seen, served as something of a model for policing in many American cities. Reformers in America were impressed with what London's **bobbies** did to prevent, and not just respond to, crime.[29] London's police stressed highly visible patrols intended to discourage crime. But the police forces of New York and other large cities differed from their English counterparts in at least two important ways. First, unlike police in London, America's first police officers were heavily involved in politics.[30] Most police officers at the time answered to political leaders or ward bosses in the areas they served. Officers' very jobs were dependent on remaining in the good favor of whatever political figure was in charge at the time. Second, in stark contrast to their counterparts in London, American police officers were more willing to use force.[31] These two unique features of American policing contributed in no small part to policing as it is known today.

bobby
The popular British name given to a member of Sir Robert Peel's Metropolitan Police Force.[ii]

The Move West. As American pioneers moved westward, they did not leave the problems of the cities behind. In fact, the frontier mentality of fending for oneself and providing one's own self-protection fueled plenty of violence. Guns, knives, and fists were commonly used to resolve disputes in newly settled areas. Sheriffs and their marshals were appointed by town leaders to provide what little law enforcement was available on the frontier. These officials' authority, though, was not always welcomed or respected. Theirs was a lonely and dangerous job, and they repeatedly became the targets of outlaws. Making matters even more difficult, prominent outlaws of the day, including Billy the Kid and Jesse James, were apparently idolized as much, if not more, than the sheriffs and marshals themselves. Law enforcement was, at best, unreliable; at worst, it was nonexistent. Indeed, some of the new "lawmen" worked both sides of the law, depending on which side offered them the best opportunities and rewards.

Consequently, communities often formed their own posses and vigilante citizen groups to confront any person or group intent on disrupting social stability.[32] Sam Walker, a criminal justice historian, puts it this way:

> Compelled by circumstance to rely on themselves, the settlers developed a highly pragmatic outlook. They regarded the law as something that should serve their immediate needs; if the law was inadequate, they simply took matters into their own hands. The result was a distinctly American style of criminal justice: informal, often rough, and highly democratic.[33]

Even these efforts eventually failed, despite support from the community. Not unlike what happened in the big cities, once populations in the West grew, something more was needed. It was inevitable that the kinds of agencies formed along the eastern seaboard would be replicated in cities throughout the West. An example was Stephen Austin's corps of fighters, a group of tough men he enlisted to protect the settlers he was bringing into the Tejas, Mexico, area. This corps of rangers eventually aided in the Texas revolution against Mexico, providing scout services for the U.S. Army during the Mexican-American War. They came to be known as the **Texas Rangers**, and their efforts

Texas Rangers
A militia originally formed by Stephen F. Austin in 1823 to protect the territory of Texas against American Indian raids, criminals, and intruders. Today, the Rangers serve as part of the Texas Department of Public Safety.

ushered in a period of enhanced border patrol in Arizona and New Mexico as well as the formation of state police forces throughout the Southwest.[34]

Organized police forces in early America were born of necessity. A single law enforcement official rapidly became inadequate as populations surged. Densely populated cities could not realistically be patrolled with one or even a few officers. But unlike the evolution of policing in other nations, Americans rejected centralized power and shunned any national police force. Law enforcement became a local effort that reflected local priorities and issues. That is why today we see thousands of distinct police agencies at various levels of government all across the United States. Even if there had been a desire during this period for a centralized police agency, it is doubtful it could have succeeded, given the size of the territory for which it would have been responsible. Early police agencies could not have survived without some connection to the communities they patrolled.

This decentralized policing model (which is discussed in more detail in Chapter 4) has been hailed as representing the American ideal, but there was a downside. As police agencies proliferated across America, they varied widely in terms of quality and professional commitment. Some may argue that policing today is not as highly regarded an occupation as it could be, but in the late nineteenth century, policing was generally viewed as routine, unglamorous work. Officers were held in low regard and, because the pay was poor, cities had difficulty recruiting qualified candidates. So desperate were some cities to hire police officers that, as one historian observed, "illiteracy, poor health, chronic drunkenness, or a criminal record were no barriers to a job as a police officer."[35] Pressure for agencies to grow, combined with close relationships between the police and politicians and others in positions of influence, resulted in poor quality police work. Worse, a commitment to crime control and community service was secondary. Nonetheless, this period of politics and ineptitude has been described as the first significant era of policing in America.

slave patrol
A crude form of private policing, often carried out by citizen volunteers. Slave patrols were created in the eighteenth century to apprehend runaway slaves and to ensure that slaves did not rise up against their owners.

due process of law
A right guaranteed by the Fifth, Sixth, and Fourteenth Amendments to the U.S. Constitution and generally understood, in legal contexts, to mean the due course of legal proceedings according to the rules and forms established for the protection of individual rights. In criminal proceedings, due process of law is generally understood to include the following basic elements: a law creating and defining the offense, an impartial tribunal having jurisdictional authority over the case, accusation in proper form, notice and opportunity to defend, trial according to established procedure, and discharge from all restraints or obligations unless convicted.

Policing the Slaves. Unique circumstances existed in the American South during this early period. There, **slave patrols** represented a crude form of policing. Slave patrols were created in the eighteenth century to apprehend runaway slaves and to ensure that slaves did not rise up against their owners. The slave patrols were largely a private activity carried out by citizen volunteers, leading to a serious lack of control of the slave patrols' actions. When they apprehended runaway slaves, they often meted out "justice" on the spot, frequently using violence.

Due process of law was a distant concern. Slave patrols could (and did) arbitrarily enter private residences for the purpose of rounding up those who fled from bondage. The patrols were largely an outgrowth of fear on the part of wealthy white landowners that slaves were a dangerous group in need of careful scrutiny and control. With the end of the Civil War came the dissolution of the slave patrols. They did, however, provide the impetus for the Ku Klux Klan, whose mission of terrorizing black families and black communities was not entirely different from that of the slave patrols.

DOES IT WORK?

An Introduction to Evidence-Based Policing

Evidence-based policing is a hot topic in contemporary law enforcement. According to Lawrence Sherman, Director of the Jerry Lee Center of Criminology at the University of Pennsylvania, evidence-based policing is "the use of the best available research on the outcomes of police work to implement guidelines and evaluate agencies, units, and officers." Put more simply, says Sherman, "evidence-based policing uses research to guide practice and evaluate practitioners."

There is little consensus about what is effective in policing. Many practitioners have an almost unshakable faith in the ability of police officers to prevent crime by simply driving around and keeping a watchful eye on the community. But as Sherman notes, "we are all entitled to our own opinions, but not to our own facts." Evidence-based policing is about the facts, about what the data and rigorous research show.

Throughout this book, you will find a number of "Does It Work?" boxes in which we summarize the literature concerning the effectiveness of various policing approaches to the crime problem. In the second "Does It Work?" box in this chapter, we will consider the effects of private policing on crime. We turn to other strategies in later chapters.

Source: L. W. Sherman, *Evidence-based policing* (Washington, DC: Police Foundation, 1998), pp. 3–4.

POLICING ERAS

As we have just seen, from the colonial period to the late nineteenth century, organized police forces of various kinds emerged across America. Like early policing on the other side of the Atlantic, law enforcement began as a private affair and eventually became public. Once police agencies were an established presence, they grew in number and influence. They also evolved in response to the demands and pressures of the time. Most researchers agree that these changes occurred in three distinct eras: the **political era**, the **reform era**, and the **community era**.[36]

WEB PATROL 1-4

Research for Police: Who Needs It?
http://www.mycrimekit.com

political era
The period of American policing during the late nineteenth and early twentieth centuries during which police forces served more to regulate crime pursuant to the wishes of corrupt politicians (who used patronage to give police jobs to handpicked loyalists) than to control crime in the interests of the public good.

reform era
The period of American policing during the early to mid-twentieth century during which efforts were made to professionalize police forces and to eliminate the influence of corrupt politicians.

community era
By most accounts, the contemporary era of U.S. law enforcement, which stresses service and an almost customer-friendly approach to police work.

The Political Era

In 1895, "the realities of patrol work mocked Robert Peel's dream of a continuous visible presence . . . police patrol barely existed at all."[37] Corruption was widespread, and some cities assigned unmanageable beats to their officers. In 1880, for example, Chicago officers patrolled more than three miles of streets—on foot. Large portions of other major metropolitan areas were not patrolled at all. Residential districts were all but ignored in most cities.[38] In addition, communication systems were inadequate, making it next to impossible for sergeants and other command officials to call officers to crime scenes.

Regulating Criminals. Historians generally agree that police officers of the political era did more to regulate criminal activity than to control it: "Officers established relationships with professional criminals, especially pickpockets, tolerating certain kinds of crime in return for information or stolen goods."[39] They were also heavily involved in providing essential services for those in need. The recently discovered diary of a Boston police officer from 1895 reveals that one of the most common services officers provided was shelter for the homeless.[40] In Cincinnati, for instance, the police station was "a place of last resort for the desperately poor."[41] Police stations came to be dirty, disease-ridden places as a result of this practice, so the sheltering of the homeless came to a halt near the end of the nineteenth century.

Many police officers, along with the politicians and ward bosses they served, were corrupt. By one account, jobs in some early police departments were sold as investment opportunities.[42] Corruption flourished at all levels of government as a result of restrictions on various "vices." Laws limiting drinking, gambling, and sex provided ample opportunity for the criminal element to provide much-desired products and services. Such illegal activities could only thrive, of course, with support from local law enforcement. The payoffs to officers who provided protection for criminals were significant. Detective Thomas Byrnes, head of the New York City Detective Bureau from 1880 to 1895, and widely said to have been corrupt, acquired a fortune of more than $350,000 by the late 1880s (that's about $5 million today).[43] Byrnes was forced to resign by Theodore Roosevelt in 1895 when Roosevelt became head of the New York City Police Commission.

Patronage Problems. To get elected, political candidates at the turn of the twentieth century made promises to the voters, especially promises of employment. Once a candidate was elected, jobs of various sorts, including police jobs, were used to reward the politician's supporters. Newly hired police officers adopted a number of measures to ensure that their "bosses" remained in power. There are many accounts of police officers, assigned to maintain order at polling stations, who pressured voters to support particular candidates.

An example of political patronage run amok was **Tammany Hall** in New York City, the name given to the Democratic Party "machine" that played a significant role in the city's politics from the late nineteenth to the early twentieth centuries. The most notorious Tammany leader was **William M. "Boss" Tweed**. Tweed's control over the political machine was so complete that he was eventually elected to the New York Senate. By most accounts, he and his cronies were corrupt and heavily involved in a wide range of criminal activities. His career eventually ended in a storm of corruption controversy, and he was ultimately sent to prison. During his heyday, though, he relied heavily on police officers to keep him in office and in control of the ward.

Tammany Hall
The corrupt Democratic Party political "machine" that operated in New York City in the late nineteenth and early twentieth centuries and that used patronage to control city operations.

William M. "Boss" Tweed (1823–1878)
A corrupt American politician who became notorious as the powerful leader of New York City's Tammany Hall.

The Reform Era

Frustrations over the likes of Boss Tweed ushered in an era of profound reform. In early 1892, Reverend Charles Parkhurst described New York City's mayor and his aides as "a lying, perjuring, rum-soaked, and libidinous lot of polluted harpies."[44] He also claimed that the police existed for no reason other than "to protect and foster crime and make capital out of it." Using his church as his forum, Parkhurst began a crusade to bring reform to the political system in New York City. He and a number of other like-minded individuals were largely responsible for the appointment of Theodore Roosevelt as commissioner of the New York City Police Department (NYPD).

Once Roosevelt took charge, he forced corrupt officers to resign and launched a series of unannounced nighttime inspections of the police department. He even took to the streets and approached officers in civilian attire. He initiated disciplinary action against officers who were asleep or away from their posts. Roosevelt resigned in 1897, claiming that the NYPD had been reformed; the reality was that little had actually changed.[45] Nonetheless, Roosevelt's efforts were quickly duplicated in a number of other cities that were experiencing similar problems. Reform efforts failed in these places, too. According to historian Sam Walker, "the reformers never came to grips with the basic problems of police administration."[46] They claimed that corrupt officers lacked moral character but ignored some of the deeper issues, such as how the department's rank structure (or absence of one) contributed to the problems reformers lamented. Reform efforts floundered for several years until police reformer August Vollmer changed their focus.

August Vollmer (1876–1955)
An early and especially effective advocate of police reform whose work with the University of California established the study of criminal justice as an academic discipline.

August Vollmer's Legacy. **August Vollmer**, the first police chief of Berkeley, California, and perhaps the foremost presence in America's police reform movement, argued that policing should be regarded as a public service, as a profession focused on improving society. During his address to the International Association of Chiefs of Police in 1919, Vollmer argued that the police had "far greater obligations than the mere apprehending and prosecution of lawbreakers." The police, he claimed, should go "up stream a little further" by trying to prevent crime by working with families, schools, and other influential institutions. He called for organizational reforms in police agencies, elevated standards of recruitment and retention, and the adoption of modern management techniques, such as those used in the business sector and military.[47]

There was something of a contradiction in Vollmer's message, however. On the one hand, he called for the expansion of the police role to include crime prevention. On the other, he called for increased crime-fighting efforts. It was crime fighting that won out in the end, leading to "a centralized, authoritarian bureaucracy focusing on crime control."[48]

Vollmer did more than call for reforms. As chief of the Berkeley Police Department during the early twentieth century, he transformed his department. He began by increasing the size of the force, from three officers to 27. He also put officers on bicycle and motorcycle patrol. He was the first to adopt fingerprinting technology to aid in criminal investigations, and he collaborated with the nearby University of California in making other advances. He was also the first police leader of note to hire officers who had obtained college degrees. The Berkeley Police School, a Vollmer creation, got started in 1908. In short, Vollmer's reforms were consistent with a reform mentality intended to move policing toward professional stature. He took his ideas beyond Berkeley by evaluating numerous police agencies around the country, including the scandal-ridden Los Angeles Police Department.[49] In 1921 Vollmer was elected president of the International Association of Chiefs of Police (IACP), a position he used to spread his ideas about police reform.

WEB PATROL 1-5
The Wickersham Commission Report
http://www.mycrimekit.com

Illinois Crime Survey
A series of influential reports, published in 1929, on homicide, juvenile justice, and justice operations in Chicago that criticized the corrupt political influence on the justice system.[iii]

Wickersham Commission
A commission appointed by President Herbert Hoover in 1929 to investigate the operations and problems of the criminal justice system. Formally known as the *National Commission on Law Observance and Enforcement.*

The Crime Commissions. As one of the authors of the 1929 **Illinois Crime Survey** (a series of influential reports on homicide, juvenile justice, and justice operations in Chicago), Vollmer criticized "the corrupt political influence exercised by administrative officials and corrupt politicians."[50] He was also the lead police consultant to the 1931 National Commission on Law Observance and Enforcement, popularly known as the **Wickersham Commission** after its head, George W. Wickersham. The commission was appointed by President Herbert Hoover in 1929 to investigate the real operations and problems of the criminal justice system. Again, Vollmer called attention to corruption, excessive political influence and meddling in criminal justice, poor leadership and management, ineffective recruitment practices, poor-quality training programs, and other issues.

The work of the Wickersham Commission and others not mentioned here, coupled with Vollmer's reformist vision, led to some consensus that a professional model of policing would greatly benefit America. It was hoped that policing would become a civil service profession divorced from politics. Reformers had faith in centralization, crime fighting, scientific investigations, and above all else police work that followed the letter of the law.

Interestingly, one of the most significant developments that fueled this change was the Great Depression. With less money to spend, many cities had to cut back on services, which included the closing of some police precincts. This brought police officers under the control of a central police station, consistent with the managerial model Vollmer had envisioned. Some have called this the *professional era*, others the *legalistic era*, and still others the *reform era*. Regardless of what it was called, what occurred was a dramatic change in the way policing was practiced in the United States. It did not happen quickly, though. The process played out over decades, leading up to the 1960s and the third of America's key policing eras: the community era.

The Community Era

The community era is, by most accounts, the era of contemporary law enforcement. It stresses service and almost a customer-friendly element to police work. Routine and traditional police functions like patrol, investigations, and the like remain, but many police agencies have changed their mission statements to reflect a new way of thinking epitomized by O. W. Wilson.

O. W. Wilson and the Limitations of Professionalism. August Vollmer's protégé, **O. W. (Orlando Winfield) Wilson**, served as chief of the Wichita (Kansas) Police Department between 1928 and 1939. As chief, he clamped down on corruption and brutality, firing 20 percent of the officers on the force. His department's mission statement, the "Square Deal Code," eventually became the template for the code of ethics of the International Association of Chiefs of Police.[51] His reforms, many of which were quite radical, were not necessarily welcomed with open arms, even by some people outside the police department. For example, his efforts to aggressively enforce vice laws met with so much resistance that he resigned in 1939.

Orlando Winfield "O. W." Wilson (1900–1972)

A progressive era reformer, professor of police administration, and protégé of August Vollmer whose writings and teachings continue to influence contemporary U.S. law enforcement.

Despite Wilson's resignation, he went on to gain national prominence. His 1938 textbook, *Municipal Police Administration*, became a leading work (its eighth edition was published in 1979). A year later, he became a professor of police administration at his mentor's old stomping grounds, the University of California, Berkeley. He remained there until 1960, during which time he started the nation's first doctoral program in criminology and wrote another successful policing text, *Police Administration*.[52] He went on to write other influential works, including a manual on how to allocate police patrols according to calls for service.[53] More importantly, he called for a shift from foot patrol (the dominant mode of patrol at the time) to automobile patrol. On top of that, he called for one- rather than two-officer patrols to maximize police resources.

Although O. W. Wilson was certainly a progressive reformer, he may have done more to usher in the community era than many realize. In 1960, during the twilight of his career, Wilson was appointed by Chicago Mayor Richard Daley to reform the city's police department in the wake of a scandal. Wilson used many of the same tools as he did in Wichita (Kansas), including reorganization of the department, widespread firings, improved personnel standards, and improved communications. Despite his best efforts, however, civil rights leaders continued to criticize the department, citing police brutality and discrimination in police employment. Wilson was defensive about the discrimination allegations because he had taken significant steps to diversify the predominantly white police department. Unfortunately, though, Wilson never gave much attention to some of the real-world aspects of police work, such as discretionary decision making and use of force. According to one source,

> [Wilson's] own textbook did not even mention the word "discretion" and said nothing about race relations. In even the best police departments, police officers on the street exercised virtually uncontrolled discretion with respect to arrests, physical force, and deadly force. . . . Officers were given few if any guidelines on when to shoot and were rarely disciplined for shooting and killing someone.[54]

These problems led to a great deal of resentment of police in the African American community, vestiges of which remain today in various cities. Wilson retired in 1968, marking the end of a notable career. What he did not, or could not, fix became abundantly clear in 1969, when some Chicago police officers appeared to run amok on national television, brutally beating protestors outside the Democratic Party's national convention. Wilson was clearly a progressive era reformer, but his actions (or, as some would say, failure to act) in Chicago started the push for something else.

WEB PATROL 1-6

Local Police Departments
http://www.mycrimekit.com

Toward Customer Service. It is perhaps a simplification to say that the community era is characterized by customer service, but at its core, this new era of policing is about connecting the community and the police in a way that was not accomplished during the reform era. Following the public outcry in the wake of the Chicago fiasco and other publicized instances of strained police-public relations, it was no mystery why a new era emerged. Research began to reveal that the police could not reduce crime by their own efforts alone, another reason the dawn of the third era was at hand.

The sentiments of the community era were expressed in a prescient article authored by University of Alaska professor John Angell at the beginning of the 1970s.[55] Angell argued that traditional police management practices were culture bound, that they were inconsistent with the humanistic democratic values of the United States, that they demanded that employees demonstrate "immature" personality traits, and that they couldn't cope with environmental pressures. In his view, a more community-centered model would (1) improve community relations, which suffered under the bureaucratic, military model of law enforcement; (2) improve officer morale by allowing them a measure of flexibility in the performance of their duties; and (3) improve interagency coordination.

Some aspects of the community era look remarkably similar to policing near the turn of the twentieth century, but without the corruption, patronage, and other problems that characterized the political era. Community era reformers have sought authorization from community members and extensive citizen support, a broad mandate that stresses the provision of services, a decentralized, responsive organizational structure, and close relations with citizens. A strong tie to citizens would be achieved through foot patrol, problem solving, the preservation of quality of life, and a host of other tactics—all of which were designed to ensure citizen satisfaction and all of which look remarkably similar to practices that were in place before the birth of the reform era.

Since, by most accounts, we are in the midst of the community era, much more needs to be said about it. Accordingly, we will devote a full chapter to this topic. In Chapter 10, we will look in depth at why the community era came to pass, what it looks like today, and what its prospects are for the future.

The Homeland Security Era?

Few people would deny that the September 11, 2001, terrorist attacks on the United States changed the world. The attacks led to one of the most dramatic reorganizations of the U.S. government, including the formation of the cabinet-level Department of Homeland Security. They also led to untold numbers of changes in America's police agencies. When, for instance, the nation's terrorist alert level is elevated, it is the local law enforcement agencies that take on most of the responsibility for increased vigilance.

A New York City Police Department officer patrols the subway at Columbus Circle in Manhattan on April 24, 2008. How has the threat of terrorism changed the face of American policing?

Matthew Roberts/ZUMA Press

Local police agencies are entering into uncharted territory with multiagency partnerships, terrorist response training, and the like. Whether the community era can survive the more militaristic style of law enforcement that followed September 11 remains to be seen. We cannot be certain a new era is upon us, but it very well could be. For the time being, however, local police agencies are struggling to fit their new antiterrorist responsibilities within their community focus and are using intelligence gathered through good community relations to further the goal of terrorism prevention.

BEYOND LOCAL LAW ENFORCEMENT

Most of our discussion of police history thus far has focused on local law enforcement: municipal police and sheriff's departments. There is also an interesting history behind state and federal law enforcement, but the story is much shorter. With the exception of the U.S. Marshals Service, which was founded in the late eighteenth century, the history of state and federal law enforcement goes back only to the nineteenth century.

WEB PATROL 1-7

State Police Agency Home Pages
http://www.mycrimekit.com

The Emergence of State Agencies

When Texas declared its independence from Mexico in 1836, the Texas Rangers were already an established law enforcement agency. As discussed earlier, they did not begin as a state-level organization. Their initial focus was defending the community, but they adopted policing responsibilities after Texas independence was declared. The early Rangers often took the law into their own hands and were not as concerned with equal treatment and due process as police are today. In 1935, Texas created the Department of Public Safety (DPS), which remains in existence to this day. The Texas Rangers are part of the Texas DPS, as are the troopers of the Texas State Patrol. Once the Rangers came under the supervision of the DPS, conduct problems, excessive force, and the like were reined in. This hasn't stopped Hollywood from giving the impression that the Rangers are very special, as evidenced by the long-running television show *Walker, Texas Ranger*. For an overview of the Texas Rangers' *real* responsibilities, see Figure 1-2.

The other states eventually formed their own state-level police agencies, but they often took unique forms. The Pennsylvania State Police, for example, was founded in 1905 in response to the difficulty local police were having resolving state-specific issues. For example, the western Pennsylvania mining region attracted scores of immigrant workers and experienced ethnic violence and labor disputes. A major coal strike in 1902 prompted President Theodore Roosevelt to appoint a commission to look into the problems of maintaining order in the mining region. This led to the establishment of the state police. Unlike the Texas Rangers and other state agencies, the Pennsylvania State Police consisted largely of men with National Guard and army experience. The Pennsylvania State Police also had their share of problems in the beginning, just like the Rangers, but they gradually assumed greater law enforcement responsibilities and adopted professional standards.

As automobiles became more common and highways were built, state police agencies shifted much of their focus toward the enforcement of traffic laws. What we see today, then, is a mixture of state agencies, some with general law enforcement responsibilities, and others with a traffic enforcement focus. Today, nearly every state has at least one state-level police agency. We will look at them in more detail when we discuss the organization of law enforcement in America in Chapter 4.

The First Federal Agencies

In 1789, President George Washington appointed the first 13 U.S. Marshals in accordance with the Judiciary Act. Until the Secret Service was established in 1865, the U.S. Marshals focused their efforts on apprehending counterfeiters. Between 1790 and 1870, the marshals were also required to take the national census every ten years, a responsibility that was eventually transferred to the Bureau of the Census. During the nineteenth century, the marshals did everything from arrest fugitive slaves to confiscate property used to support the Confederacy.

Figure 1-2 • Job Duties of the Texas Rangers

- The activities of the Texas Ranger Division consist primarily of making criminal and special investigations; apprehending wanted felons; suppressing major disturbances; the protection of life and property; and rendering assistance to local law enforcement officials in suppressing crime and violence.
- The Texas Ranger Division will, through investigation and close personal contact with all federal, state, county, and city law enforcement agencies, be responsible for the gathering and dissemination of criminal intelligence pertaining to all facets of organized crime. The Texas Ranger Division joins with all other enforcement agencies in the suppression of the same.
- Under orders of the Director, suppress all criminal activity in any given area, when it is apparent that the local officials are unwilling or unable to maintain law and order.
- Upon the request or order of a judge of a court of record, serve as officers of the court and assist in the maintenance of decorum, the protection of life, and the preservation of property during any judicial proceeding.
- When called upon, provide protection for elected officials at public functions and at any other time or place when directed to do so by a superior officer.
- Establish direct personal contact and maintain close liaison with all agencies, or branches thereof, concerned with the investigation and suppression of criminal activities. These contacts are not to be limited to the state but shall be nationwide. Every effort will be exerted to maintain a full and free flow of information on active offenders and offenses between all interested agencies.
- Participate in educational training programs and provide specialized instruction to local, state, and federal law enforcement representatives.
- With the approval of the Director, conduct investigations of any alleged misconduct on the part of other Department personnel.
- Be the primary Department investigator when a Department member is killed or suffers serious bodily injury, attributable to an intentional act.
- Provide Forensic Hypnotists for use as an investigative tool in gathering additional information.
- Provide forensic art work for use as an investigative or procedural tool in major criminal cases.
- Assist the Governor's Protective Detail in providing security for the Texas Governor during his official travel throughout the state, as well as other dignitaries.

Source: Texas Department of Public Safety, http://www.txdps.state.tx.us/director_staff/texas_rangers/#Job%20Duties (accessed June 3, 2008). Also available at http://tinyurl.com/ysffdb.

More than anything, though, in the latter part of the nineteenth century the marshals and their deputies were responsible for maintaining law and order in the Old West. On October 26, 1881, in Tombstone, Arizona, Marshal Virgil Earp and his deputies (brothers Wyatt and Morgan Earp and John H. "Doc" Holliday) gunned down Frank and Tom McLaury and Billy Clanton in a vacant lot just down the street from the O.K. Corral. Movies like *Tombstone* and *Wyatt Earp* have recounted this series of events. Since the nineteenth century, the U.S. Marshals Service has taken on a range of duties quite distinct from those of days past. We will look at both the history and the modern duties of the U.S. Marshals in Chapter 4.

Another early federal law enforcement effort involved U.S. postal inspectors, whose job it was to target crimes committed via the mail. In 1865, the Secret Service was established with the mission to suppress counterfeiting. That responsibility remains today, along with a number of others, including the protection of the president.

The Bureau of Investigation, now known as the *Federal Bureau of Investigation (FBI)*, was formed in 1908. The agency began with eight Secret Service agents, 14 newly hired investigators, and 12 accountants; their task was to investigate antitrust land fraud and similar matters. The agency grew rapidly and became the primary investigative agency for federal crimes. It ascended to a position of high visibility during the 1920s, when J. Edgar Hoover was appointed to lead the agency. Under Hoover's charge from 1924 to 1972, the FBI apprehended a number of dangerous offenders and engaged in numerous high-profile investigations, perhaps most notably the kidnapping of ace flyer Charles Lindbergh's baby.

Hoover was a controversial director. He routinely fired agents who displeased him, and it is alleged that he blackmailed political leaders and illegally disrupted the activities of the Black Panther Party, Martin Luther King, Jr.'s, Southern Christian Leadership Conference, the Ku Klux Klan, and other groups. Today, FBI directors cannot serve more than a ten-year term due to concerns that they may become too powerful. To his credit, though, Hoover did a great deal to usher in the professional policing era through his insistence on a crime-fighting role for FBI agents. The FBI is discussed in greater detail in Chapter 4.

WEB PATROL 1-8

Federal Law Enforcement Agency Home Pages
http://www.mycrimekit.com

PRIVATE POLICING AND SECURITY

The police are not the only ones in the business of crime control and prevention. Public police (municipal police officers, sheriff's deputies, state troopers, and so on) work alongside scores of private police and security officials.[56] People employed as private police officers or security personnel outnumber public police officers by three to one.[57] The number of companies engaged in providing private police or security services has been estimated at more than 10,000.[58] They employ more than 500,000 personnel, including more than 10,000 store detectives, nearly 100,000 managers and staff, and nearly 400,000 security officers.[59]

The contract security industry (consisting of companies that enter into contracts with businesses to provide security) estimated in 1999 that it employed 719,000 uniformed personnel.[60] Other estimates place the number of people involved in either private policing or security at more than 2 million.[61] Despite their numbers, private police and security professionals have largely escaped the notice of police scholars. University of California at Berkeley law professor David Sklansky notes,

> For most lawyers and scholars, private security is *terra incognita*—wild, unmapped, and largely unexplored. . . . The neglect is increasingly indefensible. The private security industry already employs significantly more guards, patrol personnel, and detectives than the federal, state, and local governments combined, and the disparity is growing. . . . If criminal procedure scholars continue to focus exclusively on the public side of law enforcement, our work is likely to become of steadily more marginal importance.[62]

WEB PATROL 1-9

ASIS Home Page
http://www.mycrimekit.com

YOU DECIDE

An Introduction to Ethics

The subject of police ethics is often relegated to a single chapter in most policing texts, but since ethical dilemmas pervade police work, we feel it is useful to integrate ethical issues throughout this book. Accordingly, in most chapters we present at least one ethical dilemma that relates to the chapter's topic.

Most professions, including law enforcement, have adopted a code of ethics. Such codes help members of the profession make appropriate decisions when ethical dilemmas develop. Here, for example, is the code of ethics of the International Association of Chiefs of Police (IACP). Most local police departments throughout the country have adopted some form of the IACP code.

> As a Law Enforcement Officer, my fundamental duty is to serve mankind; to safeguard lives and property; to protect the innocent against deception, the weak against oppression or intimidation, and the peaceful against violence or disorder; and to respect the Constitutional rights of all men to liberty, equality, and justice.
>
> I will keep my private life unsullied as an example to all; maintain courageous calm in the face of danger, scorn, or ridicule; develop self-restraint; and be constantly mindful of the welfare of others. Honest in thought and deed in both my personal and official life, I will be exemplary in obeying the laws of the land and the regulations of my department. Whatever I see or hear of a confidential nature or that is confided to me in my official capacity will be kept secret unless revelation is necessary in the performance of my duty.
>
> I will never act officiously or permit personal feelings, prejudices, animosities, or friendships to influence my decisions. With no compromise for crime and with relentless prosecution of criminals, I will enforce the law courteously and appropriately without fear or favor, malice or ill will, never employing unnecessary force or violence and never accepting gratuities.
>
> I recognize the badge of my office as a symbol of public faith, and I accept it as a public trust to be held so long as I am true to the ethics of the police service. I will constantly strive to achieve these objectives and ideals, dedicating myself before God to my chosen profession . . . law enforcement.

Notice how this short code does not (and cannot) cover every conceivable ethical dilemma a police officer may encounter. Even so, keep this code in mind as you consider the ethical dilemmas presented throughout this book.

Source: International Association of Chiefs of Police. Reprinted with permission.

DOES IT WORK?

Private Security

Given the prevalence of private policing today, the question of its effectiveness invariably arises. Surprisingly few researchers, however, have looked at how successful private police forces have been in deterring crime. In examining the question, two varieties of literature are helpful. One looks at the deterrent effect of patrol generally.[1] The other examines the effects of private policing in specific locations.[2]

Some researchers have looked at the problems of car theft and burglary in parking garages, especially when there is little monitoring of the vehicles temporarily stored there. These researchers have focused on whether the addition of guards, security attendants, and closed-circuit television (in various combinations) reduces these crimes. Their studies have shown that guards and security attendants do deter criminals, but the costs of employing attendants or security guards may raise parking fees.

Concerning the deterrent effect of patrol in general, the evidence is fairly mixed. One review of the research found that police presence was significantly associated with reduced crime in only ten of 36 studies. We consider this topic more fully in the second "Does It Work?" box in Chapter 8.

[1]T. B. Marvell and C. E. Moody, "Specification problems, police levels and crime rates," *Criminology* 34 (1996): 609–46.

[2]P. Barclay and others, "Preventing auto theft in suburban Vancouver commuter lots: Effects of a bike patrol," in *Preventing mass transit crime*, vol. 6, ed. R. V. Clarke, pp. 133–61 (Monsey, NY: Criminal Justice Press, 1996); G. Laycock and C. Austin, "Crime prevention in parking facilities," *Security Journal* 3 (1992): 154–60; B. Poyner, "Situational crime prevention in two parking facilities," *Security Journal* 2 (1991): 96–101; and B. Poyner, "Lessons from Lisson Green: An evaluation of walkway demolition on a British housing estate," in *Crime prevention studies*, vol. 3, ed. R. V. Clarke, pp. 127–50 (Monsey, NY: Criminal Justice Press, 1994). For additional findings, see N. Tilley, *Understanding car parks, crime, and CCTV: Evaluation lessons from safer cities*, vol. 42 (London: Home Office, 1993).

Private Security versus Private Policing

Security guards are highly visible to the public. They work in retail establishments, hotels, gated communities, and sports venues, just to name a few locations. These guards come immediately to mind when we consider private policing, but they represent the proverbial tip of the iceberg. In this regard, it is useful to distinguish between **private security** and **private policing.** According to Elizabeth Joh, a law professor at the University of California–Davis, *private security* refers to the industry that provides "for-profit security products and services, which include three broad categories: the provision of guards, equipment, and investigation or consulting services."[63] Homeowners who buy a home security system do so from the private security industry. *Private policing*, on the other hand, refers to "the acquisition and use of these products and services, as well as the application of specialized knowledge in areas like crime control, investigation, and risk management."[64] In other words, private police are supplied by the private security industry.

private security
"The industry that provides for-profit security products and services, which include three broad categories: the provision of guards, equipment, and investigation or consulting services."[iv]

private policing
The acquisition and use of security products and services, as well as the application of specialized knowledge in areas like crime control, investigation, and risk management by nonsworn personnel.

Our concern here is not with the private security industry per se. Rather, our interest is in private policing's provision of security, crime prevention, and crime-control functions. Whether we call it *security* or *policing* is not particularly important, but for consistency's sake, we will use the term *private policing* from here on out, knowing that private policing owes its livelihood to the private security industry. Private police could be trained personnel supplied by the private security industry or ordinary people—trained in the trade or not—who are not affiliated with any known security company but are hired to provide security services.

Private Policing versus Public Policing

Earlier in this chapter, we detailed the shift in the United States from private to public policing. One of the hallmarks of public policing is that it is funded by tax dollars. One distinguishing feature of private policing, on the other hand, is its "client-driven mandate."[65] Client-driven relationships in the world of public policing are usually regarded as unethical. For example, most people regard it as inappropriate for a store owner to offer perks (such as free merchandise or discounts) to a city police officer. An officer who receives such benefits from a citizen may be more inclined to favor that person with additional security or to ignore minor criminal offenses. Stepping over into the private policing realm, though, few people would object to a store owner who hires a private police officer for additional protection.

Private Policing Methods. Private policing can also be distinguished from public policing by its methods. South African criminologist Clifford Shearing has identified four such methods.[66] First, private police personnel focus largely on loss control and prevention. Retail security guards, for instance, are in the business of making sure their clients' products are not stolen or embezzled. The term *loss prevention* can encompass much more than lost merchandise. Some private police focus on the prevention of accidents and costly mistakes. According to Joh, "The emphasis on loss also means that private police are disengaged from the moral underpinnings of the criminal law; they focus instead on property and asset protection."[67] "Moral underpinnings" refers to the what's right/what's wrong aspect of the laws that public police are charged with enforcing. Whereas public police target situations deemed by constituents and law-making bodies to be problems, private police are not limited by these issues; they do what their clients want without regard to moral issues.

The second main private policing method is prevention: "Private police stress preventive means over detection and apprehension to control crime and disorder."[68] Their concern is not so much with the punishment of wrongdoers. Rather, it is with preventing the disruption of legitimate business activities. It is ironic, in fact, that retailers often place signs throughout their establishments warning that "shoplifters will be prosecuted to the fullest extent of the law." For one thing, retailers have limited say over whether someone will be charged with theft; prosecutors make this decision. In addition, retailers' concern with prosecution is typically incidental to their more immediate concern for making sure the business doesn't lose money.

That is why private police rely on surveillance. Casino owners, for example, go to great pains to keep an eye on things and make sure that dishonest gamblers do not line their pockets at the casino's expense.

Private policing is also distinguished from public policing by its focus on "private justice" rather than public justice. As Joh points out, private security provides a functional alternative to the public police and the criminal justice system.[69] Consider, for example, employee theft from a retail store. What would the store's owner rather do, go to the trouble of prosecuting the employee or simply fire him? The latter choice would be the easiest. What about the gambler who counts cards in a blackjack game and gets caught? She would sooner be banned from the casino than charged with any criminal violation. "In a private justice system," Joh says, "the resolution of problems is left to the control and discretion of private police and their clients, who may see some incidents as unworthy of the lost time and resources necessary to assist in a public prosecution."[70] Indeed, some businesses are willing to absorb a certain amount of loss rather than incurring the costs of pursuing formal criminal charges against a wrongdoer.

The fourth distinguishing feature of private policing is a concern with private rather than public property. Generally, public police do not have the luxury of entering private places without proper cause or an invitation. At the opposite extreme, private police generally don't care what happens in public spaces. Their job is, for the most part, protecting private property. Often they work in quasi-public places, such as privately owned malls that are open to the public, but their loyalties lie with the businesses that employ them, not the general public.

Core Responsibilities. Now that we have shown how private policing differs from public policing, it is possible to get a feel for the various responsibilities of the typical private police official. In terms of responsibility, there is at least some overlap between public and private police. Private police responsibilities include the following[71]:

1. Perimeter security.
2. Internal security.
3. Fire protection.
4. Access control.
5. Protection of employees and executives.
6. Information security.
7. Risk management, including tracking and forecasting of security threats.
8. Disaster and emergency preparedness.
9. Control of drugs in the workplace.
10. Control of workplace violence.
11. Discovery of white-collar crime.
12. Alarm monitoring.
13. Fraud detection and monitoring.
14. Investigations.
15. Crisis management.

A security guard talks on his radio at the Westroads Mall in Omaha, Nebraska, during the 2007 holiday shopping season. The mall was the scene of a horrific shooting a few weeks earlier, when 19-year-old Robert A. Hawkins opened fire with a semi-automatic rifle, killing eight people and wounding four near the Von Maur department store before taking his own life. Hawkins, apparently bent on suicide, left a note saying that he wanted to take others with him. How can private security personnel and law enforcement officers work better together?

Eric Francis/Getty Images, Inc.

The Growth of Private Policing

Three explanations have been offered for the growth in private policing witnessed during the past four decades or so.[72] One is an ideological shift, a preference for the nongovernmental provision of key services. Some people are convinced that the private sector can do better than the public sector when it comes to providing security and criminal justice services. Another explanation is that private policing has simply evolved in response to the need to police **mass private property**,[73] notably large shopping malls and other properties that attract large numbers of consumers but that have little or no public police protection. Another example is the gated housing development. As the population grows and as those who can afford it move into gated communities, they often need the services of security personnel. The third explanation for the growth of private policing is simply an outgrowth of the first two—a belief that public police are incapable of providing the volume and type of policing that people want:

mass private property Large shopping malls and other properties that attract large numbers of consumers but have little or no public police protection. It can be argued that private policing evolved to meet the protection needs of mass private property.

> As we have seen, for over two centuries privately paid entrepreneurs in both Britain and America have been filling gaps in the police protection offered by public law enforcement. Private police today, moreover, tend at least in broad outline to do the kinds of things that public police departments are faulted for not doing: patrol visibly and intensively, consult frequently with the people they are charged with protecting, and—most basically—view themselves as service providers.[74]

Controversies in Private Policing

Private security is controversial in a number of respects. First, it is important to note that private security is but one part of a larger privatization movement in criminal justice.[75] Private prisons, for instance, have emerged to provide a presumably cost-effective alternative to state-run correctional facilities. Critics charge that privatization turns criminal justice into a for-profit venture, which could translate into detrimental cost-cutting measures. Second, some people have charged that private policing is poised to replace public policing. Nothing could be further from the truth,

YOU DECIDE
The Second Job

Imagine that you are an officer employed with the city of Fairview. Under the city's "detail system," private employers, such as hotel owners, can ask the Fairview Police Department for officers to provide security services. Officers serve on a rotation system so that all have an equal opportunity to work the security service details. They are paid between $25 and $30 per hour for their services. Some private employers have elected to hire officers outside of the "detail system." This ensures that they receive the services of the same officer but without having to pay the city's detail rate. A Fairview hotel owner has asked you to work outside the detail system for $20 per hour. You consult your department's policy manual, which states, in part:

> Although officers of the force are assigned specific hours of regular duty, they shall be considered "on duty" at all times for the preservation of the public peace and the protection of life and property, and shall be prepared to take all reasonable police action to accomplish this purpose. All serious matters of public concern shall receive appropriate attention, even though an officer is not on duty at the time.

Fairview also has a policy affecting all its employees (including police officers), which states, in part:

> Municipal employees are prohibited from accepting other employment involving compensation of substantial value, the responsibilities of which are inherently incompatible with the responsibilities of his public office.

If you do not wear your police uniform, would it be ethical for you to step outside the detail system and assume a position as a hotel security guard? Would the position amount to a conflict of interest?

Note: This scenario was adapted from an actual decision by the Commonwealth of Massachusetts State Ethics Commission (Opinion EC-COI-94-8).

---

however. As Sklansky puts it, "Private policing poses no risk of supplanting public law enforcement entirely, at least not in our lifetime, and it is far from clear to what extent the growing numbers of private security employees are actually performing functions previously carried out by public officers."[76]

Perhaps the most significant controversy associated with private policing deals with constitutional concerns. In general, because private police are nongovernmental, they are not bound by the same legal requirements as public police. As Sklansky notes,

> Perhaps the most basic and invariable principle of criminal procedure is that constitutional restrictions on policing—the limitations imposed by the Fourth, Fifth, and Sixth Amendments, the prophylactic rules of evidentiary exclusion constructed to reinforce those limitations, and the analogous rules of state constitutional law—apply only to investigative action attributable to the government.[77]

The U.S. Supreme Court has yet to tackle the issue of private policing head-on. It decided one case in 1964 involving an amusement park security guard who had been "deputized" by the county sheriff,[78] ruling that the security guard was a state official and thus was bound by the same legal constraints as public police officers. Beyond that case, the Supreme Court has had little to say. State courts, however, have been much more vocal, and most of them have refused to treat private police as state actors. For example, private police have been exempted from the Fourth Amendment,[79] the *Miranda* rule,[80] and entrapment restrictions.[81] We will look at these issues from a public policing perspective in Chapter 11.

It would be a mistake to construe these decisions as granting unbridled power to private police. It is true that some private police do have more power than ordinary citizens, and deputizing private police officers gives them—briefly—the same authority as public police. Additionally, many private police officers are off-duty public police officers. Yet most private police do not enjoy the same legal powers as public police: "Many private security guards . . . possess no greater legal capabilities than do ordinary citizens to forcibly detain persons who are suspected of or have in fact committed a crime."[82] In many states, ordinary citizens can arrest people for misdemeanors committed in their presence and for felonies that they have probable cause to believe were committed.[83]

DOES IT WORK?

Citizen Patrols

Citizen crime patrols came into vogue in the 1980s as a way of allowing trained volunteers to serve as the eyes and ears of local police departments in neighborhoods. After training, volunteers drive around and "patrol" their neighborhoods looking for suspicious activity and reporting it to officers who then respond. Citizen crime patrols have been touted as creating an extra barrier to criminal activity in the community.

At least one study has been especially critical of citizen patrols, however, arguing that they lend credence to traditional, antiquated police strategies, such as routine preventive patrol.[1] One of the few studies that comes close to evaluating the effectiveness of citizen patrol reported on a survey of citizens' and police officers' attitudes toward the Guardian Angels, an unsanctioned civilian group that patrols the streets and subways of New York City. Most of the respondents felt that patrol should be performed by armed, state-sanctioned police.[2] Two other similar studies suggest that citizen patrols of this sort may exacerbate fear and have no discernible effect on crime.[3]

The topic of citizen patrol has received relatively little attention from researchers, who have concentrated their efforts on studying the effectiveness of patrol by uniformed, sworn police officers. To determine whether citizen patrol works would require a carefully crafted evaluation, ideally with treatment and control groups and a sound research methodology. Even if such a study were possible, it is doubtful that citizen patrol would be shown to be effective. Much of the literature has found that patrol—whether by public or private entities—does not effectively deter crime.

[1] W. J. Einstadter, "Citizen patrols: Prevention or control?" *Crime and Social Justice* 21 (1984): 200–12.

[2] B. B. Ostrowe and R. DiBiase, "Citizen involvement as a crime deterrent: A study of public attitudes toward an unsanctioned civilian patrol group," *Journal of Police Science and Administration* 11 (1983): 185–93.

[3] D. J. Kenney, "Crime on the subways: Measuring the effectiveness of the Guardian Angels," *Justice Quarterly* 3 (1986): 481–96; and B. Webb and G. Laycock, *Reducing crime on the London Underground: An evaluation of three pilot projects*, vol. 30 (London: Home Office, 1992).

SUMMARY

- Policing began as a private affair and became a public, or governmental, responsibility. Policing in America looks as it does today largely because it was inherited from the English, beginning with the frankpledge system, the watchman system, and Henry Fielding's Bow Street Runners.
- American policing has evolved through three distinct eras: the political, reform, and community eras. We may be on the cusp of a fourth policing era: the homeland security era.
- State and federal law enforcement agencies have their own, unique histories. With the exception of the U.S. Marshals Service, however, which was founded in the late eighteenth century, the history of state and federal law enforcement goes back only to the nineteenth century. Among the earliest organized state police agencies were the Texas Rangers and the Pennsylvania State Police.
- Private police officers outnumber sworn public police officers by roughly three to one. Private police are hired to serve a client's interests, and thus their priorities differ from those of public police. The most significant controversy in private policing is whether private police can be regarded as governmental actors for purposes of the law. The integration of private and public policing resources continues to be an ongoing challenge for public safety managers everywhere.

COMING FULL CIRCLE

For Discussion

Review the discussion of citizen patrols in the Does It Work? box above. Then return to the questions posed at the start of this chapter. Have any of your answers changed since you read the chapter? What portions of this chapter helped you answer these questions?

Writing Assignment

Using material from this chapter and additional resources, write a 500-word essay in response to one of the questions presented at the beginning of the chapter. Submit your essay to your instructor if asked to do so.

KEY TERMS AND NAMES

August Vollmer
bobby
Bow Street Runners
community era
due process of law
frankpledge system
Henry Fielding
Illinois Crime Survey
mass private property
Metropolitan Police Act
O. W. (Orlando Winfield) Wilson
parish
political era
private policing
private security
reform era
sheriff
shire
shire-reeve
Sir Robert Peel
slave patrol
Tammany Hall
Texas Rangers
thief taker
tithing
watchman
Wickersham Commission
William M. "Boss" Tweed

WEB INTERACTIVITY

The history page of the London Metropolitan Police's website begins with these words, "The word 'Police' means, generally, the arrangements made in all civilised countries to ensure that the inhabitants keep the peace and obey the law. The word also denotes the force of peace officers (or police) employed for this purpose."

Visit the Met at http://www.met.police.uk/history/definition.htm, and read about its history. You'll notice that the section "Origins of Policing" begins with these sentences: "The origin of the British police lies in early tribal history and is based on customs for securing order through the medium of appointed representatives. In effect, the people were the police." Think about those words, and then write a brief essay answering these two questions:

1. How did the history of police development in Britain influence policing in early America?
2. Is policing in the United States today true to its early origins?

Submit your essay to your instructor if asked to do so.

Metropolitan Police Service

REVIEW QUESTIONS

1. What were the major milestones in the historical development of policing in America?
2. Identify and describe the three eras of policing discussed in this chapter. Are the eras distinct or overlapping? Explain.
3. Outline the development of state and federal law enforcement agencies in the United States. How did the development of those agencies parallel the development of local police forces? How did it differ?
4. Summarize the leading controversies in private policing today.

chapter two
POLICING IN THE AMERICAN CONTEXT

LEARNING OBJECTIVES

After reading this chapter, students should be able to:

1. Describe the nature and characteristics of policing in a democracy and under federalism.
2. Identify various elements of the policing environment in America and discuss their influence on the practice of policing.

POLICE DEPARTMENT
CITY OF

THINK ABOUT IT

In late 2002, three off-duty San Francisco police officers became involved in a violent altercation with two men who turned out to be doing nothing more than carrying bags of fajitas. The three officers, one of whom was the son of the assistant chief and had reported using force 14 times in his first 13 months on the job, were indicted for felonies in a case that quickly captured news headlines. The case led to the resignation of two police chiefs and a short-lived grand jury indictment against other top officials for alleged obstruction of justice. The altercation and the ensuing events were quickly branded "Fajitagate," and the incident tarnished the San Francisco Police Department's image for years. The charged officers were eventually acquitted, but the incident left a sour taste in the mouths of many, including numerous local reporters.

An article in the *San Francisco Chronicle* claimed that the city's police department "failed to control officers who repeatedly resort to force, hitting, choking, clubbing and pepper-spraying citizens at rates far higher than fellow officers who patrol the same streets."[1] Staff writers at the *Chronicle* submitted a Freedom of Information Act request and obtained the department's complete use-of-force logs from 1996 to 2004. From the handwritten documents, they created a computerized database that allowed them to determine which officers reported using force and how often. According to the reporters' investigation, the "data showed the city has a core group of violence-prone officers—fewer than 100 in a force of 2,200."[2] They also made these observations:

1. Officers with questionable records were promoted to supervisory positions or were assigned to train rookies, putting them in position to carry forward a culture that tolerates and rewards the use of force.
2. Between 2001 and 2004, San Francisco officers were the subject of more allegations of improper use of force than officers in San Jose, Oakland, San Diego, and Seattle combined.
3. Taxpayers are exposed to high legal costs in defending lawsuits against officers who use force. From 1996 to 2005, the city paid more than $5 million in judgments and legal settlements related to the improper use of force. For that same amount of money it could have put 60 new officers on the street.
4. Public trust in the department has eroded, particularly among the city's African American residents, who department records show have disproportionately experienced the use of force by police.[3]

Most of us don't have to worry about having our dirty laundry aired before scores of concerned citizens, but the police do. The *Chronicle's* investigation of the use-of-force data landed on the front page of a newspaper that is read daily by more than 1 million people.[4] "Fajitagate" raises several interesting questions that should be kept in mind throughout this chapter:

1. Was press coverage fair in this case?
2. Should police departments be treated any differently than other public agencies when it comes to press coverage of their actions?
3. How do the goals of the media contrast with those of the police? Are they at all compatible? Are they antagonistic?
4. Did the San Francisco Police Department create or perpetuate a culture of violence that contributed to the incidents identified by the paper?

INTRODUCTION

American policing is unique in the world. Our country's style of democratic government has had a significant impact on policing. Democracy puts power into the hands of the people and forces the police to consider the interests of the populace. Federalism, another hallmark of American government, has had considerable

WEB PATROL 2-1

"Fajitagate"
http://www.mycrimekit.com

Figure 2-1 • The Police Environment

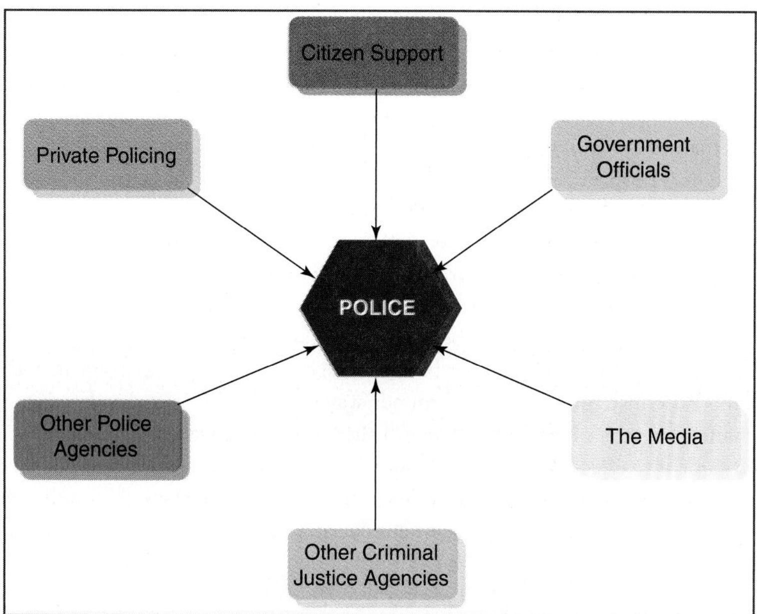

implications for the organization of policing. One result of federalism is multiple agencies serving the same areas at the same time.

Whether they like it or not, police agencies operate in a complex organizational environment (Figure 2-1).[5] This environment consists, first, of citizens who both request police services and scrutinize officers' every move. It also consists of political heavyweights, including executive officials (e.g., mayors), legislators, and the courts. Then there is the media that report regularly on everything from police scandals to high-profile drug busts. Some media coverage is favorable, but much of it is not. Consequently, the police often feel the need to develop strategies to deal with the media and ensure that the "right" message gets out. The police work in an enviroment alongside other law enforcement organizations. Finally, the work of professional associations and research organizations helps them stay connected.

POLICING IN AMERICA

The United States is a representative democracy and the world's oldest functional federation (a union consisting of several more or less self-governing states). These unique arrangements have affected the structure and organization of government agencies at all levels, including the police.

Policing in a Democracy

Democracy is usually defined as government by the people. It vests supreme authority in the citizenry, usually through free elections and the representatives they choose to elect. Other features of a democracy include equality of rights, privileges, and opportunities; open government; and due process protections against unreasonable arrest and prosecution. To many, democracy also means that people should be free from excessive government influence in their lives.

democracy
A form of government that vests supreme authority in the people, usually through their freely elected representatives.

Nearly everyone values the full exercise of democratic principles, and some express serious concern when those principles are threatened. Consider the recent outcries over electronic eavesdropping of domestic phone conversations by federal investigators as part of antiterrorism intelligence gathering. Some people feel that such eavesdropping is necessary to maintain security. Others, though, fear that it threatens core democratic values and is unreasonably intrusive.

In an effort to balance these opposing views, a police force in a democratic nation should be one that "is subject to the rule of law embodying values respectful of human dignity, rather than the wishes of a powerful leader or party; can intervene in the life of citizens only under limited and carefully controlled circumstances; and is publicly accountable."[6] In other words, most of us would likely agree that the police should be able to enforce the law, but they shouldn't go "too far" and run roughshod over people's rights.

Consequences of Democracy for Police. Robert Kennedy once pointed out that "every society gets the kind of criminal it deserves." Kennedy also said, "What is equally true is that every community gets the kind of law enforcement it insists on."[7]

There are many ways to interpret Kennedy's observations, but one is especially relevant here. With its concern over people's rights and privacy, democracy ensures that a certain amount of crime is inevitable. In other words, some of the crime problems our country has might be due to the very nature of our government. Consider those who manufacture methamphetamine in clandestine laboratories. If they know that the police can arbitrarily enter the facility at any time, they might choose an alternative pursuit. On the other hand, if they know that there are steps the police must take before they can enforce the law, they might be willing to take a chance.

We are not arguing that democracy is bad. On the contrary, it is important to realize that the traditional democratic institutions that inform our way of government make effective law enforcement more challenging than it might be under other forms of government. Likewise, the Bill of Rights, which came into effect two years after our Constitution was ratified, also has important implications for policing in a democracy. Not only does it play a key role in our country's governmental operations, but it serves as a clear symbol of democracy's core concern with human freedom and dignity. The Bill of Rights reinforces the critical notion that while our system of government is based on majority will, the government cannot go too far without answering to us. Democracy, then, is the political institutionalization of freedom. Figure 2-2 reviews democracy's core principles.

WEB PATROL 2-2

Democratizing the Police Abroad: What to Do and How to Do It
http://www.mycrimekit.com

Consider the Fourth Amendment to the U.S. Constitution. It protects people from unreasonable searches and seizures and mandates that the police meet specific legal requirements before they can enter private residences, make arrests, and seize evidence. (We look at the Fourth Amendment more closely in Chapter 11.) Few of us would want the police to dispense with constitutional requirements, but if they did, law enforcement and crime deterrence would certainly be easier to accomplish. Democracy makes police work somewhat more demanding. Officers cannot simply waltz into what they think is an illegal "meth" lab, beat confessions out of suspects, and summarily execute suspected criminals—at least, not without facing serious consequences. Instead, they must balance a clear need to control crime with respect for people's rights and privileges.

Balancing Due Process and Crime Control. Policing is an exciting topic because of the inherent tension it creates between two competing sets of interests. On the one hand, both the police and the public have an interest in controlling crime. This leads to an emphasis on catching law-

Figure 2-2 • The Pillars of Democracy

- Sovereignty of the people
- Government based on the consent of the governed
- Majority rule
- Minority rights
- Guarantee of basic human rights
- Free and fair elections
- Equality before the law
- Due process of law
- Constitutional limits on government
- Social, economic, and political pluralism
- Values of tolerance, pragmatism, cooperation, and compromise

Source: U.S. Department of State, "Defining Democracy," Web available at http://usinfo.state.gov/products/pubs/whatsdem/whatdm2.htm. Accessed January 10, 2008.

breakers and discouraging people from committing crime. On the other hand, our democratic system of government values the protection of people's rights and freedom from overbearing government authority. These competing interests have been described by Herbert Packer as the **crime-control** and **due process models**.[8]

crime-control model
One of two competing perspectives—the other is the *due process model*—described by Herbert Packer that embody the inherent tension in contemporary U.S. society regarding government's role in response to criminal behavior. Crime-control advocates argue that protecting the public is the government's primary duty, even at the expense of individual rights.

due process model
One of two competing perspectives—the other is the *crime-control model*—described by Herbert Packer that embody the inherent tension in contemporary U.S. society regarding government's role in response to criminal behavior. Due process advocates argue that protecting individual rights is the government's primary duty, even at the expense of increased threats to public safety.

You may be familiar with the due process and crime-control models (Figure 2-3). Balancing both views is an integral function of the criminal justice process. When the Supreme Court makes a controversial decision affecting police, the decision typically seeks to balance the need to control crime with people's constitutional rights. When new tough-on-crime policies are enacted, such as three-strikes legislation, the due process/crime-control debate rears its head; some feel such laws are essential to make society safer, while others are concerned that life in prison for a third felony is excessive. The point is that everyone connected in any way to criminal justice understands the need to balance these two competing perspectives.

The due process and crime-control perspectives are also familiar because they closely parallel liberal and conservative thinking. At the risk of oversimplification, liberals tend to believe that as far as criminal justice is concerned, due process protections are of paramount importance and that constitutionally ensured individual rights must be respected. In contrast, conservatives tend to believe that there is too much contemporary concern with people's rights and with due process; that the control of crime, at whatever cost, is critical; and that an obsession with people's rights will ultimately threaten our safety. Most police officers, but not all, tend to fall into the conservative camp.

The Due Process Model As mentioned, the due process model is first and foremost concerned with people's rights and liberties. Due process advocates believe that the government's job is not to control crime but rather to maximize freedom and opportunities for all citizens, which includes protecting people from undue government influence. Due process values minimize the potential for mistakes, partly because

> people are notoriously poor observers of disturbing events; . . . confessions and admissions by persons in police custody may be induced by physical or psychological coercion so that the police end up hearing what the suspect thinks they want to hear rather than the truth; witnesses may be animated by a bias or interest that no one would trouble to discover except one specially charged with protecting the interests of the accused (as the police are not).[9]

Due process advocates also believe that all suspects are innocent until proven guilty, just as most of us have been taught while growing up. Due process advocates place greater emphasis on legal guilt (whether a person's guilt can be proven under the law) rather than factual guilt (whether a person actually committed the crime with which he or she is charged). Consider how the two types of guilt affect the role of a defense attorney: The attorney might argue that the police wrongfully

Figure 2-3 • Due Process versus Crime-Control Values

Crime-Control Model	Due Process Model
Assembly line	Obstacle course
Quantity over quality	Quality over quantity
Favors informality	Prefers formality
Faith in the police	Faith in the courts
Presumption of guilt	Presumption of innocence
Seeks to benefit society	Seeks to benefit suspects
Concerned with ends, not means	Concerned with means, not ends
Maximizes police authority	Maximizes human freedom
Control crime at all costs	Protect people's rights at all costs
Emphasis on factual guilt	Emphasis on legal guilt

Source: J. L. Worrall, *Criminal procedure: From first contact to appeal*, 2nd ed. (Boston: Allyn and Bacon, 2007).

searched the defendant, rather than argue that the defendant did not commit the crime with which he is charged.

At the heart of the due process perspective are four ideals: (1) The criminal justice process looks—or should look—something like an obstacle course; (2) quality (of police work and prosecution) is more important than quantity (of arrests and prosecutions); (3) formality is preferred over informality because of the protections that it offers the accused; and (4) faith is placed in the courts, which serve as a check against enforcement agents who might attempt to circumvent due process guarantees.

The obstacle course metaphor describes a criminal justice process that is complex, that requires navigation by skilled legal professionals, and that sometimes fails to operate predictably. It is the opposite of a process that prides itself on speed and efficiency, which are values of significant importance to those who adhere to the crime-control perspective. The obstacle course metaphor also stresses that each case must pass through several complicated twists and turns before a just verdict can be rendered.

Another way to distinguish between due process and crime control is in terms of quantity and quality. The due process view favors quality, that is, fair and accurate decisions at every stage of the criminal justice process. The due process view stresses that each case should be handled on an individual basis, with special attention paid to the facts and circumstances surrounding each step in the justice process. This concern with quality is thought necessary to minimize the potential for error. Due process advocates, for example, are in favor of several death penalty appeals following every capital conviction because they feel that the possibility of executing the wrong person must be avoided at all costs.

Due process advocates do not favor informal processes and insist that the potential for human error or bias requires a highly structured adversarial process. They also believe that early intervention by judges and other presumptively objective parties is in the best interest of people who find themselves on the wrong side of the law.

Finally, the due process perspective puts its faith in the courts, not in law enforcement agencies. Due process advocates correctly point out that the job of judges is to interpret the laws and state constitutions, and (sometimes) federal laws and the U.S. Constitution. This, they argue, helps provide protection to those charged with crimes. Faith in the courts is also consistent with the insistence on formality. When guilt and innocence are determined in the courts, an air of fairness and objectivity presides.

The Crime-Control Model The crime-control model stands in contrast to the due process perspective. It emphasizes the importance of reducing crime rates, even to the detriment of civil liberties. From a cost-benefit perspective, crime-control advocates believe that the benefit to all of controlling crime outweighs the costs of infringing a person's due process protections. Another way to distinguish between the due process and crime-control perspectives is to consider the distinction between means and ends. Crime control is more concerned with the goal of eliminating crime or at least mitigating its harmful effects. By contrast, due process is concerned with the means, that is, with the methods by which people suspected of crimes are processed by the criminal justice system. The end result—either the presence or absence of crime—is not the primary concern of due process advocates.

The metaphor of an assembly line suggests that the criminal justice process should be automatic, predictable, and uniform. Ideally, everyone accused of a crime should be treated the same, with quick efficiency and minimal variation in terms of charges, processing, and sentencing. The goal of the crime-control model is to move criminals through the justice process as swiftly as possible. A full-blown, adversarial criminal justice process, replete with hearings and other "pauses" in the interest of the accused, is at odds with the crime-control view.

Unlike the due process model's focus on quality over quantity, the crime-control model favors quantity over quality. This view is consistent with the assembly line metaphor. The goal is to move as many offenders as possible through the criminal justice system with as little delay as possible. If mistakes are made along the way and someone is wrongfully charged or convicted, so be it. That is the cost of ensuring the overall goal that the accused are dealt with as efficiently as possible and that law-abiding citizens are protected from wrongdoers.

Whereas the due process perspective favors the formality of the criminal justice process, with particular emphasis on the courts, the crime-control perspective favors informality. Lengthy courtroom involvement is something to be avoided whenever possible, and justice should be meted out with no more formal processing than is necessary. Plea bargaining, for instance, is favored by advocates of crime control because of its swift behind-the-scenes nature, not to mention that it avoids the need for accused suspects to go to trial.

An insistence on informality further suggests that the law enforcement establishment should be more involved in making guilt determinations than is normally the case under the due process model. Whereas the due process perspective places a great deal of faith in the courts, the crime-control perspective puts its trust in the police. In junior high school, we are all taught that criminal suspects are innocent until proven guilty in a court of law. Clearly, courts are charged with making this kind of formal determination. However, crime-control advocates sometimes favor "street justice"—that is, giving the police vast discretion over deciding how people suspected of being involved in criminal activity should be handled. A fitting description of the crime-control perspective may be that "all criminals are guilty until proven innocent."

If you have any doubts that the crime-control model pervades American law enforcement agencies today, try to find a veteran police officer who votes Democratic in most elections and who routinely criticizes efforts to make police work more efficient. That is not to say there are no liberally minded police officers; there clearly are, but they are likely to be in the minority. We also do not mean to say that police officers have no regard for people's rights; most certainly do. In the end, though, theirs is the job of enforcing the law. Making one's superiors and the community happy requires catching criminals and controlling crime. Consequently, thinking about crime control is an inherent part of any police officer's job.

Policing and Federalism

One of democracy's most distinguishing features is policy making by majority rule, either directly by the people, as in a direct democracy, or through elected representatives, as in a representative democracy. The very term *democracy* comes from the Greek words *demos*, meaning "people," and *kratos*, meaning "rule." In other words, *democracy* means "ruled by the people." One can even go further and call ours an advanced or liberal democracy because of its concern with the rule of law, the separation of powers, and, most importantly, people's liberties. But democracy alone does not fully describe our system of government. The government structure in the United States is also characterized by **federalism**. Policing in a federalist nation is quite distinct from policing in nonfederalist nations.

federalism
A political doctrine holding that power is divided (often constitutionally) between a central governing body (the federal government, for example) and various constituent units (the states).

Features of Federalism. Federalism, often confused with democracy, is another feature of American government that has served to shape the policing apparatus in the United States. Federalism is a political doctrine wherein power is divided (often constitutionally) between a central governing body (the federal government, for example) and various constituent units, such as states.

Federalism helps facilitate democracy because it promotes participation in all levels of government. If one had ambitions to enter political office, one would likely start with the goal of becoming a county supervisor, a city council person, or an elected state official. With experience, a political veteran might then rise to ranks of U.S. senator or representative.

In a federalist system, laws are made by the central governing authority as well as by the constituent units. This is the case in the United States. The federal government makes laws for the entire nation, but federalism also gives the states power to make their own laws. In the United States, we have both the federal Constitution and individual state constitutions, consistent with the idea of shared power. The federal government and each state also have their own legal codes. This is in contrast to a unified system of government in which all power is vested in a central authority. It is also distinct from a **confederation**, which has no strong central government.

confederation
A system of government that lacks a strong central authority.

A perusal of the U.S. Constitution suggests a system of **dual federalism**, in which the only powers vested in the federal government are those explicitly listed in the Constitution; the rest are left to the states. In reality, though, ours is more of a system of cooperative federalism, meaning that some of the lines between federal and state power are blurred or at least have fluctuated over time. For example, Article I, Section 8 of the U.S. Constitution gives the federal government the power to regulate interstate commerce, but this authority has been interpreted so broadly that the federal government can effectively control much of what happens at the state level. To this day, we see plenty of federal influence over even local criminal justice policies.

dual federalism
An interpretation of the U.S. Constitution that suggests a system in which the only powers vested in the federal government are those explicitly listed in the document, with the remaining powers being left to the states.

YOU DECIDE
The Leak

It is your first day on the job as an officer in a large urban police department. You witness a sergeant tell another officer about a federal undercover investigation that is taking place in the city. You also hear the sergeant grumbling about the fact that the feds kept the investigation secret for months and how upset he was that he and the department were kept in the dark for so long. You then witness that officer call someone and talk about the investigation. You think you hear the officer say "Get out of town" to the person on the other end of the line. What should you do? If you approach your sergeant directly and he tells you to drop it, what will you do then?

Federalism and Policing. Inherent in federalism is the concept of different levels of government. Consequently, American federalism effectively defines various levels of law enforcement. Our two-tiered governmental structure (states and the federal government) divides law enforcement within those levels. Further, federalism can affect relationships between the agencies at the various levels of government. For example, if the federal government grants money to local government, it can exercise a measure of control. Applying this to policing, the Office of Community Oriented Policing Services in the U.S. Justice Department gives various grants to local law enforcement agencies throughout the states, but typically with strings attached. One such string is that the money must be used to support community policing activities.

Federalism also adds to the dynamics of law enforcement because it creates relationships (and perhaps tensions) between levels of government. For example, "turf wars" sometimes occur between federal and state or local law enforcement agencies. In movies and television programs, such jurisdictional conflicts are often portrayed as some small-town police chief or sheriff laying claim to a particular criminal case before the "feds" get involved. Turf wars do indeed exist, but interagency (and interlevel) cooperation is now the word of the day, especially in the "war on terror." If it weren't for federalism, though, there would be neither tension nor cooperation across levels of government because different levels wouldn't exist in the first place.

THE POLICING ENVIRONMENT

Every organization operates within an environment that consists not just of the organization's physical surroundings, but also has human dimensions. In a democracy where the power of the people is emphasized, this is all the more apparent. Couple this with the highly visible nature of police organizations and it becomes clear that the police in the United States function within one of the most complex organizational environments imaginable. First, they serve and interact with citizens. Second, they are government organizations and, as such, regularly interact with other government entities, such as city councils and county boards of supervisors. Third, the media in the United States keep a close eye on the police, perhaps because we as citizens are intrigued by what the police do (or don't do). Police organizations are also influenced by the economic environment (which can impact funding), by the political and social environment (the community and cultural values), and by the physical environment (including terrain, weather, and climate). Finally, police organizations interact with other police organizations at all levels of government.

Citizen Support

By far the most significant environmental factor in law enforcement is the community. In sheer magnitude, the number of citizens dwarfs all other factors that influence the police. Not every citizen carries quite the same level of influence as, say, an evening newscaster, but given that there is roughly one sworn law enforcement officer for every 400 to 500 citizens in the United States, the voice of the citizenry must be reckoned with. Through the democratic process, citizens also influence the elected officials who speak for them. The president, members of Congress, county boards of supervisors, city mayors, and city councils, all of whom exert a measure of control over law enforcement activities, come to their posts with a mandate from their constituents.

Law enforcement officials have a vested interest in maintaining positive relationships with the communities they serve. The service element of the famous police mantra "protect and serve" all but requires a measure of concern for what community members think. But the protection function also requires citizen support. Much crime takes place behind closed doors, and police cannot always detect it without input from concerned citizens. A lack of citizen support can also influence law enforcement organizations through the political process. For example, public dissatisfaction with a local police department could prompt the mayor to seek a replacement for the chief.

Fortunately, the police rarely fight an uphill battle for public support. Studies reveal that the vast majority of citizens view police favorably.[10] One study revealed that about two-thirds of Americans felt their local police agencies and sheriff's departments were effective, friendly, and fair.[11] What about the other third? Some people regard authority figures with suspicion.[12] Moreover, a significant percentage of that one-third are minorities, and many minorities not only do not support police but view them with contempt.[13] Such perceptions are often an outgrowth of strained racial relations in some of America's high-crime, poor inner-city neighborhoods. Even that two-thirds majority is not unwavering in its support; various factors can affect whether police will be viewed favorably.

WEB PATROL 2-3

Public Opinions of the Police
http://www.mycrimekit.com

The importance of citizen support for the police is reflected in a vast literature. Scores of researchers have studied support for the police in an effort to identify who is supportive and who is not. A common thread running throughout most of the studies is a focus on four categories of factors thought to be associated with support for police: race, age, gender, and prior contact with the police. Some researchers have also looked beyond these to other factors, such as education, location, and various demographic and economic considerations. Such studies are important because knowing who is likely to be least supportive of police activities can give law enforcement administrators the information needed to target those groups for public relations efforts to improve the police image.

DOES IT WORK?

Citizen Contact Patrol

One approach to improving civilian attitudes toward the police—and thereby reducing crime—consists of door-to-door visits by police officers. Known as citizen contact patrol, this is where police officers knock on people's doors, introduce themselves, give out information, and otherwise try to make policing more personal in nature. This technique has been used by police to do everything from obtaining information about who is carrying guns on the street to providing citizens with tips about reducing burglaries.

The success of citizen contact patrol has been mixed. At least two studies found that door-to-door visits by police led to reductions in victimization.[1] Two other studies found reductions in victimization when door-to-door contacts were supplemented with either storefronts[2] or buy-bust operations.[3] On the other hand, three studies found that door-to-door contacts led to no reductions in victimization.[4] Needless to say, these findings make it difficult to draw conclusions about the effect on crime of citizen contact patrol.

To sift through these conflicting studies, it is useful to consider their specific findings. For example, one of the studies showed that door-to-door contacts reduced victimization, but largely for vehicular burglaries and minor property crimes.[5] Another researcher concluded that door-to-door contacts worked best in middle-class, predominantly white neighborhoods.[6] Referring to some of the positive outcomes associated with Houston's citizen contact patrol, researchers made the following observation:

> The darker side of these successes came to light in tests of the *generality* of the impact of the programs. Across a number of social indicators—most strongly in terms of race and class—those at the bottom of the local status ladder were severely underrepresented in terms of awareness and contact with the programs, and were unaffected by them. In short, the better-off got better off, and the disparity between area residents grew deeper.[7]

This suggests, on the one hand, that the "citizen contact" approach to the crime problem has a slim chance of succeeding where it is needed the most. On the other hand, though, it doesn't appear that citizens in more disadvantaged areas received the treatment to begin with, so we can't conclude with certainty that citizen contact patrol is a crime-control failure. We just can't conclude that it's a success, either.

---

[1]M. A. Wycoff and others, *Citizen contact patrol in Houston: Executive summary* (Washington, DC: Police Foundation, 1985); and W. Skogan, *Disorder and decline: Crime and the spiral decay in American neighborhoods* (New York: Free Press, 1990).

[2]A. M. Pate and W. Skogan, *Coordinated community policing: The Newark experience—Technical report* (Washington, DC: Police Foundation, 1985).

[3]C. D. Uchida, B. Forst, and S. O. Annan, *Modern policing and the control of illegal drugs: Testing new strategies in two American cities—Research report* (Washington, DC: National Institute of Justice, 1992).

[4]L. Sherman, J. W. Shaw, and D. P. Rogan, *The Kansas City gun experiment* (Washington, DC: National Institute of Justice, 1995); Uchida, Forst, and Annan, *Modern policing and the control of illegal drugs*; and R. C. Davis and B. G. Taylor, "A proactive response to family violence: The results of a randomized experiment," *Criminology* 35 (1997): 307–33.

[5]Wycoff and others, *Citizen contact patrol in Houston.*

[6]Skogan, *Disorder and decline.*

[7]Ibid., p. 107.

Police Sgt. Mike MacDonald answers questions during a Fullerton (California) Police Department press conference about a city high school teacher arrested on drug and weapons charges. How can police departments maintain positive relationships with the communities they serve? How does the flow of information, as represented by the press conference shown here, influence such relationships?

One problem with measuring support for the police is that support is a multidimensional concept. In other words, what do we mean by "support"? Are the police effective? Are they friendly? One researcher has identified five dimensions of support for the police.[14] Three of them address "efficacy," or effectiveness. They include the ability of police to protect citizens, solve known crimes, and prevent crime. The other two dimensions deal with "image," particularly the perceived friendliness and fairness of the police. It appears that race affects perceptions of the ability of police to solve crime but not to protect citizens or prevent crime. We will not go into more detail on these dimensions but rather present the "big picture" concerning support for the police.

WEB PATROL 2-4

Satisfaction with Police: What Matters?
http://www.mycrimekit.com

Race/Ethnicity. Race/Ethnicity is perhaps the most powerful predictor of support or lack of support for the police.[15] In general, Caucasians view the police far more favorably than non-Caucasians.[16] A Texas study revealed, for example, that Hispanics often express dissatisfaction with local law enforcement.[17] Minority perceptions of police also differ depending on what types of functions police engage in. Not surprisingly, use-of-force incidents tend to be regarded with less support than, say, police attendance at neighborhood meetings.[18] Moreover, race often works in conjunction with other factors to shape public opinions of the police. A minority resident from a poor, high-crime neighborhood who has had undesirable contact with police in the past will tend to maintain negative attitudes. In contrast, someone from a wealthy neighborhood where crime is not much of a concern will, in general, be more supportive.

Age. Like the relationship between race and support for the police, the relationship between age and support is not particularly surprising; young people tend to be much less supportive of police than the elderly.[19] The authors of one study found, for example, "a direct, almost linear relationship" between age and support for the police.[20] This means that as age increases, support for police increases in almost perfect parallel fashion. Why, then, are young people not supportive of police? For one thing, they value their freedom and like to buck authority from time to time. Another explanation is that young people commit more crimes than the elderly and therefore find themselves in unwelcome contact with authorities more often.[21] The same line of reasoning applies to young drivers; they receive more speeding tickets than the elderly and therefore find themselves on the receiving end of unwelcome contact with police. Yet another explanation is that young people are also the victims of more crime than the elderly. Some excessively victimized youth may believe that the police cannot effectively make a dent in the crime problem.

Gender. The relationship between gender and support for the police is much less clear. One team of researchers argued, for example, that men and women view the police similarly.[22] In another early study, the researchers found that women hold a more "idealized" image of the police and are therefore more supportive of them.[23] Further substantiating that finding, a later study revealed that younger males are less supportive of police than are women.[24] By no means is there consensus in the literature, however. Depending on who exactly is surveyed, the literature reveals contradictory findings.[25] It stands to reason, then, that at least in terms of gender, police agencies need to appeal to both men and women.

Prior Contact. Prior contact with the police can clearly influence support levels. Generally, involuntary contacts, such as a stop for speeding, are not linked with support for the police.[26] In fact, the more involuntary contacts a person has with officers, the less supportive of them he or she will be.[27] On that note, people who live in neighborhoods where most police contacts are involuntary (for example, officers responding to 911 calls) are less inclined to support the police than people in less crime-prone neighborhoods.[28] Importantly, though, it is not the sheer number of involuntary contacts that affects one's attitude toward police. If the experiences are regarded as favorable (if, for example, motorists feel they were treated fairly and with respect by officers), then people maintain relatively high levels of support for police.[29] Returning to the broader subject of this chapter, it behooves police officers to know what kinds of neighborhoods they serve, what their problems are, and what types of calls officers have gone on in the past. This knowledge can arm them with the information they need to reach out to historically unsupportive populations.

Other Factors Affecting Public Perceptions. Like gender, education's effect on police support is unclear.[30] On the one hand, less educated individuals might fail to appreciate the difficulties associated with police work and, as a result, hold them in lower regard. On the other hand, a highly educated person may be critical of police, perhaps through detailed knowledge of legal issues, department policies that are ignored or circumvented, and the like. One study on this subject, however, revealed no link at all between education levels and support for the police.[31]

Income levels and education go hand in hand, at least to a point. This has prompted some researchers to look at the links between income level and support for police. One study suggests, not surprisingly, that the wealthy are generally more supportive of the police than the poor are.[32]

Still other factors appear to predict support or lack of support for the police. People who perceive an excess of disorder in their neighborhoods tend to be less supportive of police.[33] Likewise, there is evidence that individuals who "dislike the characteristics of their neighborhoods" do not hold the police in high regard.[34] Other researchers have found that people's political beliefs and attitudes about the world in general are predictive of support; those with conservative leanings tend to be more supportive of police.[35]

DOES IT WORK?

Police Newsletters

Some police agencies publish newsletters that are distributed throughout the community. Unfortunately, research shows that such community newsletters rarely reduce crime rates.[1] Other forms of public education, particularly education about domestic violence, appear to be ineffective as well.[2]

One fairly comprehensive study on the use of crime-control newsletters focused on Evanston, Indiana; Houston, Texas; and Newark, New Jersey. While the researchers did not consider the effect of the newsletters on crime, they did reach this important conclusion:

> There is no evidence that disseminating crime prevention information and crime statistics has any sizable negative effects on the citizenry, at least none as measured by these evaluations. At the same time, there is some evidence that such newsletters may have positive effects in reinforcing citizen coproduction of community safety. In all three cities, those who received the newsletters were overwhelmingly enthusiastic about continuing the dissemination of this type of information.[3]

In other words, while newsletters may not be linked to crime rates per se, their public relations benefits might outweigh their costs.

[1] T. Pate and others, *Reducing the fear of crime in Newark and Houston* (Washington, DC: Police Foundation, 1986).

[2] R. C. Davis and B. G. Taylor, "A proactive response to family violence: The results of a randomized experiment," *Criminology* 35 (1997): 307–33.

[3] P. J. Lavrakas, "Evaluating police-community anticrime newsletters," in *Community crime prevention: Does it work?* ed. D. Rosenbaum, pp. 269–91 (Beverly Hills, CA: Sage, 1986). See also P. J. Lavrakas, D. P. Rosenbaum, and F. Kaminski, "Transmitting information about crime and crime prevention to citizens: The Evanston newsletter quasi-experiment," *Journal of Police Science and Administration* 11 (1983): 463–73.

Figure 2-4 • Factors Affecting Support for the Police

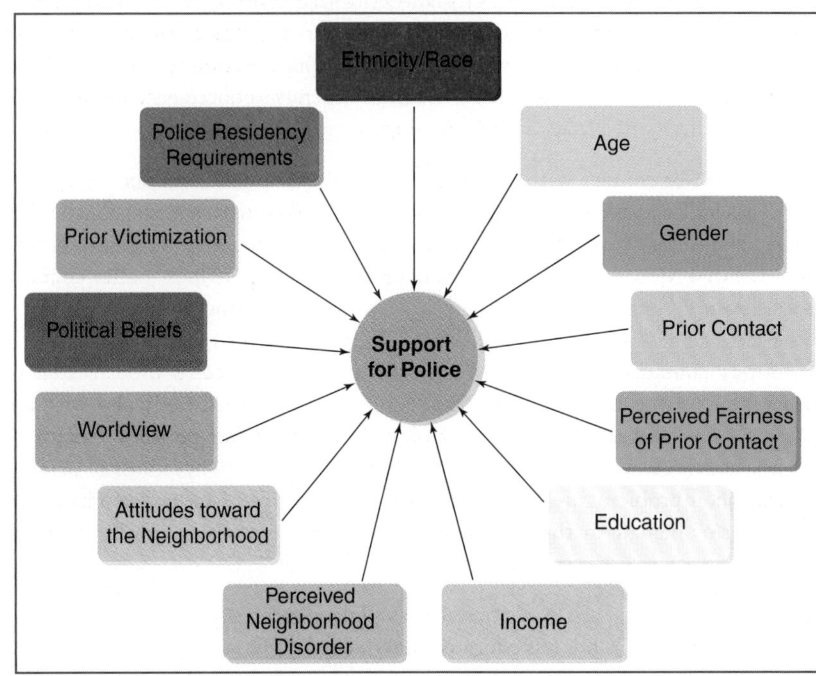

In addition, whether one lives in a rural or an urban area can affect support.[36] Whether one has been a crime victim is important, too. In particular, victims whose experience with the criminal justice system was perceived as unpleasant frequently hold the police in low regard.[37] When victims and other concerned citizens are empowered, however, their support levels improve.[38] For example, people who take charge of a problem in their neighborhood, such as by implementing block watch (perhaps in conjunction with the local police department), tend to be supportive of police. Finally, on the subject of police involvement, one study revealed that certain police residency requirements (those that require officers to live in the cities they serve) may positively affect support for the police.[39] See Figure 2-4 for a summary of the findings presented thus far.

WEB PATROL 2-5
The Public Image of the Police
http://www.mycrimekit.com

Sheriffs and the Electorate. Most of the research just discussed deals with people's impressions of municipal police agencies, and a few researchers have looked at citizen support for sheriff's deputies.[40] Although there is not much research on the subject of elected sheriffs, this much is true: Because sheriffs are elected, they must be more concerned than most police administrators with citizen support, especially voter support. Incumbent and would-be sheriffs owe much of their livelihood to the voting public.

Although sheriffs are elected, they are not all-powerful public officials. Like police chiefs, sheriffs generally have to answer to county boards of supervisors or their equivalent entities. One of the core functions of a county board of supervisors is setting the annual budget for all county agencies, including the sheriff's department. Moreover, board members are usually elected to their posts (often as nonpartisans) from various districts within a county. The result is that the sheriff answers not only to the voters but also to county supervisors, who themselves are elected.

Government Officials

Law enforcement agencies are government entities, but a host of non–law enforcement government officials—at the federal, state, and local levels—exercise significant control and influence over them. The president appoints the heads of federal law enforcement agencies. Governors set state policy and prioritize spending for certain projects. Courts issue decisions that affect the activities of officers on the street. Legislatures make funding decisions. Mayors hire and fire police chiefs. The list goes on, but the point is that one of the key environmental influences on law enforcement in America is governmental. In the sections that follow, we look at executive, legislative, and judicial influence. Although there are far more sources of influence than we can possibly cover here, there are a few standouts. For the executive, they are city councils, mayors, police commissions, and other appointing authorities. For the legislative, the roles of the U.S. Congress and the state legislatures in shaping America's law enforcement apparatus are most important. Finally, courts at all levels of government have a dramatic influence on policing.

Executive Influence. There are basically two forms of city government in the United States. The first, the **council-manager form**, which is the most common in cities of more than 12,000 people, consists of an elected city council of usually between five and 12 people. These individuals are responsible for all policy decisions for the city. Mayors under this form of municipal government generally perform ceremonial duties and serve as the voice, and often the leader, of the city council. Importantly, though, the mayor's vote on the city council carries no more or less weight than that of other council members. Thus council-manager systems significantly limit the power of the mayor. Under this system, city managers preside over the city's day-to-day operations and implement policy enacted by the council.

council-manager form
The most common form of city government in cities of more than 12,000 people. It consists of an elected city council (usually between five and 12 people) responsible for all policy decisions for the city. Mayors under this form of municipal government generally perform ceremonial duties and serve as the voice, and often the leader, of the city council.

In contrast to the council-manager form of government is the **mayor-council form**. The mayor-council form of municipal government can be broken down into two categories: strong mayor and weak mayor. The terms speak for themselves. The strong-mayor variation gives the mayor almost limitless authority over city operations, including the hiring and dismissal of key officials. More common in small towns is the weak-mayor variation, in which the mayor serves largely at the behest of the city council. The difference between the mayor-council and council-manager forms is the presence or absence of a city manager. City managers are supposed to be apolitical, but mayors are not. Both systems of municipal government have interesting implications for law enforcement.

mayor-council form
A form of municipal government that can be categorized in two ways. The strong-mayor variation gives the mayor almost limitless authority over city operations, including the hiring and dismissal of key officials. In the weak-mayor variation, which is more common in small towns, the mayor serves largely at the behest of the city council.

City Councils City councils do plenty to exercise control over municipal police agencies. For example, they enact policies that agencies underneath them must implement. Likewise, they can control the purse strings, deciding how much money is allocated to city agencies. They also get involved in dismissals in the event that a police chief fails to perform important functions. In some cities, councils do this directly. Other cities give the city manager authority to make personnel decisions for all city agencies. Still other council-manager cities give the city manager authority to make decisions with the council's approval. It obviously benefits the chief to know who makes key decisions under any system of municipal government.

The council-manager form of city government gives the impression that politics are removed from the process. Presumably, with several officials instead of one partisan mayor, it would be somewhat difficult to make drastic personnel decisions concerning the police department. That does not mean, however, that city councils sit on the sidelines while problems persist in law enforcement. Just recently, the council of Troy, Texas, a city about halfway between Dallas and Austin, fired not just the police chief but the entire department.[41] The city council cited poor performance and insubordination as key reasons for its decision. While replacements were being sought, the city was forced to rely on the local sheriff's department for law enforcement services.

Mayors As mentioned above, large cities tend to favor the council-manager system of government. At the beginning of 2006, the city of San Diego changed from a city manager to a strong-mayor form of government. (See the city's organizational chart in Figure 2-5.) The change was approved by the city's voters. According to the city, "Under the new system the Mayor is the City's chief executive officer, similar to the governor or the president. The Council is the legislative body, providing checks and balances to the Mayor's new authority."[42]

Mayors generally wield more authority in council-mayor systems. Nowadays, though, it is fairly rare for a mayor to exercise total authority over the hiring and firing of a city's first responders. This is true for San Diego, too, despite its move to a strong-mayor system. The city's new rules allow the mayor to nominate the police chief, but the nominee must be approved by the city council. Likewise, the mayor can dismiss the police chief, but such action is subject to review by the city council.

Figure 2-5 • City of San Diego Organizational Chart

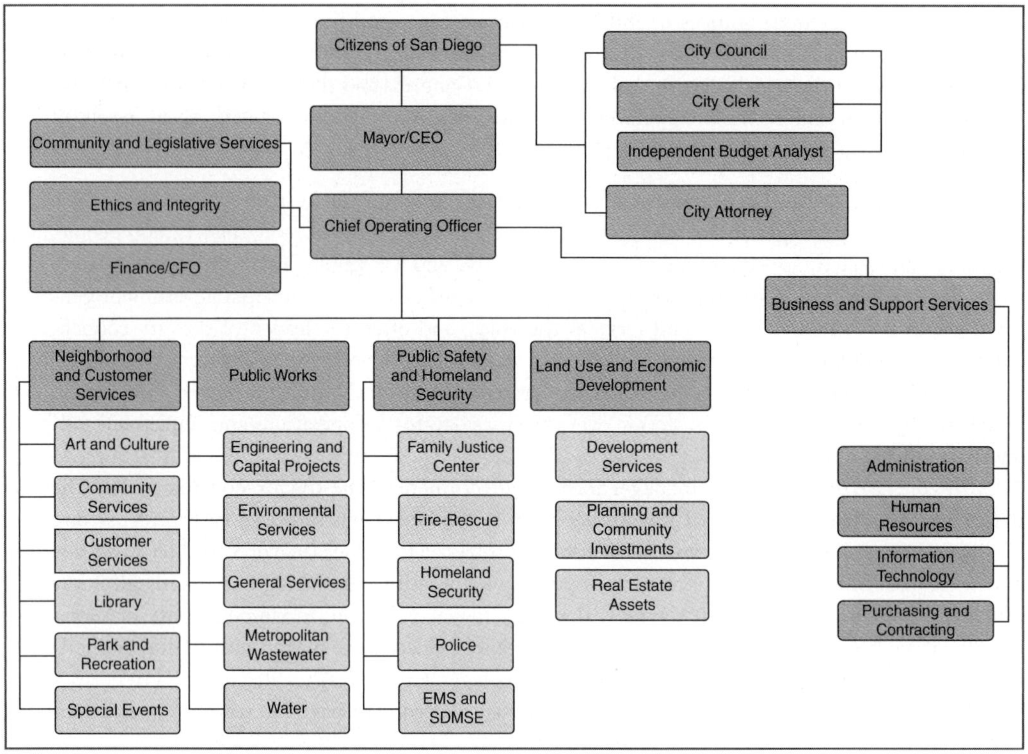

Source: Courtesy of the City of San Diego Police Department.

Not every police chief can take comfort in knowing that mayors are generally prohibited from dismissing them on a whim. Oftentimes, when a new mayor is elected, perhaps from an opposing political party, he or she makes a number of changes in the composition of the city's top management. The incoming mayor of Pittsburgh, for instance, recently fired the police chief because he wanted to take the agency in a different direction.[43] City councils often support such reorganizations when a new administration comes on board.

Police chiefs can sometimes make city mayors look bad. That is one of the alleged reasons why New York City's police commissioner, William J. Bratton (now the chief of the Los Angeles Police Department), was forced out of his position by Mayor Rudolph W. Giuliani in 1996. Bratton had appeared on the cover of *Time* magazine, and the accompanying article gave Bratton, rather than Giuliani, full credit for New York's precipitous drop in crime since the mid-1990s. There have also been rumors that the two men did not get along.

police commission
An agency maintained in some large cities that acts like a corporate board of directors, setting policy and overseeing the police department's operations.

Police Commissions Some large cities, regardless of their form of government, also maintain a **police commission**, which generally acts like a corporate board of directors, setting policy and overseeing the department's operations. The Los Angeles Police Commission, for example, consists of five civilian volunteers. The commissioners serving in 2008 were not just "average" citizens. Two

YOU DECIDE

The Mayor's Daughter

You handle recruiting and selection for your department. The mayor's daughter wants to enroll in the police academy, but she has failed the psychological exam your department has used for 12 years. On her own, she visits a nearby psychologist who sometimes consults for other police departments, but who also has a reputation for sometimes performing shoddy work and giving "contrary opinions" for a fee. She obtains from him a letter saying that she's now competent and mature enough to be a police officer. After getting off the phone with the mayor, the chief calls you into her office and says, "Put her in the next class." What should you do?

were prominent attorneys, two were successful corporate personalities, and one was a former president of the Los Angeles Urban League. The composition of a police commission can change, however, and tends to when a new mayor is elected.

The Los Angeles Police Commission is perhaps best known for its decision in 2002 to deny embattled police chief Bernard Parks' bid for a second five-year term. Parks asked the Los Angeles City Council to overturn the commission's decision, but it refused.[44] Hiring and firing decisions, though, are not usually the foremost responsibility of police commissions. Honolulu's police commission, while involved in such decisions, spends the bulk of its time reviewing department rules and regulations, reviewing the chief's annual proposed budget, and investigating charges of wrongdoing brought against the city's police department by members of the public and other police officers. It is critical for a police chief in a city with a police commission to understand the political process and the interplay between council, commission, and mayor.

Other Appointing Authorities Moving from the local to the federal level, there are other appointing authorities besides mayors, city managers, city councils, and police commissions who exercise control over top law enforcement officials. The heads of federal law enforcement agencies are appointed by the president and approved by the Senate. Interestingly, it is also generally much easier for a top federal law enforcement executive to be fired than it is for a local police chief. The president can simply urge a cabinet-level agency head to fire the head of a particular unit. That's what happened in 2004, when the Interior Department fired National Park Police Chief Teresa Chambers. She allegedly spoke about "taboo" topics with reporters from the *Washington Post* and acted with a lack of discretion in various areas: "improper budget communications, making public remarks regarding security on federal property, improper disclosure of budget deliberations, improper lobbying, failure to carry out a supervisor's instructions, and failure to follow the chain of command."[45]

Justice Department law enforcement agencies have also seen their share of administrative "replacements." Some readers may recall Attorney General Janet Reno's decision to fire FBI Director William Sessions in 1993 and replace him with Louis Freeh (who himself is no longer director). The point is that every law enforcement executive, whether federal or local, cannot get too comfortable in his or her position.

The tenure of the typical law enforcement administrator is generally pretty short. Although there are legitimate reasons for local police chiefs and their federal equivalents to leave their posts, such departures are often the result of political pressure or a firing decision. Fortunately, there are at least some checks and balances in place, but law enforcement executives are not unlike professional football coaches in that their jobs are tenuous, their futures are uncertain, and job security is a far cry from that of the lower-ranking street-level police officer. The successful law enforcement administrator *must* play politics.

Legislative Influence. Executive officials, such as mayors, are clearly important parts of the police environment. So are state legislatures and the U.S. Congress. While these bodies do not directly set local law enforcement agencies' budgets, they can exert influence in a number of key respects. Consider then-President Clinton's **Violent Crime Control and Law Enforcement Act of 1994**. It is the legislation that ushered in what is now known as the Office of Community Oriented Policing Services (the COPS Office) in the U.S. Justice Department. The COPS Office has dispensed billions of dollars in grant money to local law enforcement agencies to improve their community policing capabilities and hire 100,000 new officers. While the Violent Crime Control Act was one of Clinton's pet projects, it would not have succeeded were it not for Congress's decision to send the bill to the White House for that all-important signature.

Violent Crime Control and Law Enforcement Act of 1994
The legislation that established the Office of Community Oriented Policing Services (COPS Office) in the U.S. Justice Department.

Moving down from the federal level, nearly every state maintains an office that is responsible for grant funding of city and county law enforcement agencies. In California, the organization is called the Office of Emergency Services. It has no direct effect on local law enforcement, but it does have an indirect effect. It gives out competitive grants to local agencies provided that they implement a program, or add to an existing program, that is consistent with the funding program's mission. In other words, to get the grant, the agency must do what the state desires. Some grants reflect gubernatorial priorities, others reflect the legislature's desires, and still others reflect a measure of consensus over what is important to both governors and legislatures. One point is clear, however: Governors can do next to nothing in the name of crime control and prevention without the approval of the state legislature. For this reason, local law enforcement agencies need to be in tune with what is regarded as important in the state capital, especially if they want more money.

Judicial Influence. Judicial influence over local law enforcement also cannot be ignored. So influential is the judiciary, in fact, that we devote the better part of Chapters 11 and 12 to it. The U.S. Supreme Court decides important legal issues that trickle down to law enforcement at all levels of government, and state supreme courts often resolve issues that never make it to the U.S. Supreme Court. Lower appellate courts at both the state and federal levels, coupled with state supreme courts and the U.S. Supreme Court, decide criminal appeals that often bear on whether police employed proper procedures. If police officers act without regard to what the courts decide, they will be responsible for the embarrassing release of known criminals. Considering the importance of public opinion, as we have already seen in this chapter, legal mistakes that result in criminals going free are to be avoided at all costs.

The Media

A roll call training instruction from an actual urban police department reads as follows:

> We live in a media world! Everything and everyone is fair game for the roving video camera; there's profit in it! Whether it's a professional news station shooting some dramatic footage in order to win the ratings race or a home movie enthusiast selling his or her tape to the highest bidder, video pays! All one needs is a television to see how popular unstaged "video happenings" have become, and the evening news is only one of many venues for them. Today, shows like *World's Wildest Police Chases* proliferate on the airways. . . . As Police Officers, we must realize that the nature of our work makes us a natural and very attractive subject for reality-based television programs (news and otherwise). Therefore, it is more important than ever to maintain a professional demeanor. We simply do not have the luxury of letting our guard down. We owe it to ourselves, our fellow officers, our department and our families, not to become a negative story. There are cameras everywhere! Let them catch us doing the job the way we were trained.[46]

This communication to rank-and-file police officers speaks for itself. It summarizes the influence and importance of the media.

The "Fajitagate" story described at the beginning of this chapter also underscores the role of the media in modern-day law enforcement. The media, which include both print and television news sources, can be both the best friend and the worst enemy of every police organization. On the one hand, the media can provide favorable coverage of successful investigations, aid in the capture of fugitives, and encourage concerned citizens to call in crime tips.

Unfortunately, the media often get it wrong. This has prompted several large law enforcement agencies to hire media liaisons, some of whom are sworn officers. They assist in the preparation of press releases that present the agency's side of the story and do not give the press an opportunity to misconstrue the facts. On some occasions, though, as we saw in San Francisco, reporters take the initiative to investigate alleged wrongdoing in a police agency. Why? The answer should be pretty clear: Police agencies will not issue press releases that make themselves look incompetent or ineffective.

Media Portrayals of the Police. Most of us are familiar with how the media portray police. News reporters, who adhere to the "if it bleeds, it leads" philosophy, often make it look as though the police do nothing more than apprehend violent criminals. Televisions shows like *COPS* and *Dallas SWAT*, among others, highlight the most action-packed side of an occupation that is often anything but thrilling. As one researcher put it,

> these programs convey images of crime, criminals, law enforcement officials, and the criminal justice system which are incomplete, distorted, and inaccurate. . . . Viewers are led to believe policing is an action-packed profession, criminals frequently resist capture, crime is predominately violent, crime is the work of minorities, and the police regularly succeed in their endeavors to combat illicit activity.[47]

Additionally, the media have been criticized for increasing people's fear of crime, intensifying racist sentiments, and generally providing people with an incomplete picture of what police work is really like.[48]

WEB PATROL 2-6
Police and the Media
http://www.mycrimekit.com

Not all press coverage is inadequate. Press freedom, for better or for worse, is one of the key principles on which this country was founded. Even reality programs like *COPS* do not always get it wrong. Researchers have observed, for example, that "public display . . . plays an important function for citizen understanding of the criminal justice system."[49] Moreover, "police officers received overwhelmingly positive publicity, media networks corral a healthy bottom line, and interested viewers benefit from a few minutes of action and close-to-first-hand observation of police work."[50] Generally, though, there are several limitations associated with media coverage of police work in particular and crime in general.

With respect to the portrayal of criminals, the media give the impression that crime is almost exclusively a minority problem. One study of crime coverage in a New Orleans newspaper revealed that, in the newspaper stories, African Americans accounted for 93 percent of all robberies, a percentage well above their representation in the city's population.[51] Another study of reality-based shows revealed that African Americans were overrepresented as criminals in comparison to official crime statistics.[52] The footage in such programs also appears to be degrading, including "glowering mug shots or . . . footage of [black suspects] being led around in handcuffs, their arms held by uniformed white policemen."[53] Criminals are also portrayed as a violent lot. In their study of *America's Most Wanted*, for example, one team of researchers found that criminals acted violently in more than three of four altercations with officers.[54] Finally, the media tend to give more attention to traditional street crime than to white-collar crime, a pattern that seems to be changing to some extent in the wake of Enron, Tyco, and other highly publicized incidents of corporate crime in America over the past decade or two.[55]

A still image from the closing episode of *CSI Miami's* fifth televised season. The episode, entitled "Born to Kill," follows the action of a serial killer who is killing young women. How do the media portray police officers and criminal investigators? Are those portrayals realistic?

Do the media paint police officers in a balanced and objective light? Certainly not. The fictional media glorify the investigation aspect of policing and give the impression that scores of officers are routinely hurt and killed on the job.[56] Reality-based programs portray an arrest rate that is far in excess of official arrest rates.[57] Another study showed that crime dramas often portray the triumph of justice when, in reality, justice is not always served.[58] Fictional or not, the media also give an impression that many criminal apprehensions are resolved with the suspect's death.

How the media (whether via the evening news or reality police programming) portray law enforcement officials has important implications for how the police do their job. Citizen support is likely affected by media coverage. Even influential politicians can't be immune from the distorted images of police work presented on television and in newspapers. Media coverage of police work can lead to unrealistic expectations and misguided opinions about controversial incidents.

Impression Management. Smart police administrators do not let the media shape their image. Instead, they engage in what is known as **impression management**. As a police chief told the International Conference on Police-Media Relations,

> The future sees law enforcement becoming more and more transparent. We are sharing more and more information. We have to do this. We have to wake up and smell the roses. You have to really build media relations, formulate a plan, and provide other police with information on how to be prepared to deal with the media.[59]

impression management
A media relations concept that involves controlling the presentation of information to achieve a desired public perception.

According to one researcher, impression management best serves the public interest by reporting actual facts rather than by putting a "spin" on the information that police agencies release.[60] At the same time, though, the police are most definitely "performers" in the media relations game.

dramaturgical discipline
Achieving a balance between merely reporting facts and putting a "spin" on those facts to create a desired impression.

They generally strive to maintain a professional image. Thus there is a balance to be achieved between putting too much spin on reporting and simply reporting the essential facts in a given case. This has been called **dramaturgical discipline**. The term *dramaturgy* refers to dramatic composition. In short, the police have to "posture and perform."[61] As one officer notes,

> We can use drama to inform the public and still be accurate. . . . And if . . . cops [don't like] this, they had better go back to a time when TV didn't exist; like it or not, we live in a media/video/showbiz world. We can either understand and work with it or live in a bubble.[62]

The police, like the media, have an interest in the portrayal of a certain form of drama. For example, while the media often report the darkest side of crime, the police routinely publicize their successful apprehensions and investigations. This is dramaturgy. Too much of it, though, is regarded unfavorably by the public—and by the press. The "discipline" side of dramaturgical discipline is about finding the appropriate mix of facts and favorable police publicity.

The Public Information Officer: An Asset? In one of the most impressive media relations studies to date, Lovell surveyed and spent time at a number of city police departments in an effort to uncover the most successful practices those agencies engaged in to maintain a favorable public image.[63] He did not survey citizens but rather police chiefs and those in their departments who were charged with reporting to the media. Even so, the study yielded a veritable knowledge gold mine. One important finding is that crime has little bearing on media image, that is, police departments whose jurisdiction includes the most crime-prone cities are not regarded unfavorably by the press simply because crime rates are high.

public information officer
A police department's spokesperson. The media must go through the public information officer to gather information about the department.

Lovell also sought to determine whether having a dedicated **public information officer** was preferable over other approaches. A public information officer is basically the municipal police department's equivalent of the White House press secretary. He or she is the key point of contact through which the media must go to gather information. The public information officer also crafts press releases, holds news conferences, and otherwise serves as a department liaison to the press. Relatively few agencies have public information officers, however, relying instead on either departmental policies on how officers are supposed to interact with the media or training on how to handle media inquiries. Interestingly, Lovell found that departments with comprehensive media policies (Figure 2-6) or public information officers were *not* more likely to report a favorable media image than departments that allowed the press to speak with officers at all levels of the agency:

> It is not so much the presence of a media police [or a public information] officer but the content of the strategy within that contributes to effective impression management. One such strategy that emerged as significantly and positively associated with a favorable police image is best summarized as department "openness." Those departments that both authorized and encouraged its officers to communicate with news reporters were more likely to assess the quality of their department's image as favorable.[64]

Lovell also found that although media training (that is, teaching officers how to interact with the media) had a positive effect on a department's image, the effect was modest. Above all else, Lovell found that police administrators need to adopt a "media strategy" rather than a "media policy." In other words, one more entry in the typical police policy manual is not enough. Policy manuals tend to spell out what police officers *cannot* do. Lovell feels that while media policies are essential, such policies should also encourage officers to engage in proactive communications with the media when appropriate, to seek out the press if the circumstances merit it.

Interagency Communication

Every law enforcement agency—and in fact every organization or group—communicates with others like it. The chief, for example, might pick up the phone and call his or her counterpart in the next city over. Agencies also communicate with one another across radio frequencies. These varieties of communication are staples in modern law enforcement. There are two other key methods by which police agencies communicate with one another and learn what their colleagues are up to. The first is by participating in professional associations. The second is by reading research reports that highlight best practices, describe what does and doesn't work, and review recent trends in the field.

Figure 2-6 • Media Release Procedure for the Madison (Wisconsin) Police Department

Town of Madison Police Department	Title: Media Releases		
Effective Date: January 1, 2005	**Number:** 064	**Number of Pages:** 4	**Special Instructions:** Replaces P006, dated June 20, 2003
Reference: 005 Release of Records, 023 Juvenile Records, Media Release Template		**Distribution:** All Personnel	
Reevaluation Date: January 1, 2006		**Index as:** Media Releases	

I. Purpose

The purpose of this policy is to provide police officers with guidelines when releasing information to members of the media without harming the department's interests or the rights of the accused or suspects.

II. Policy

A well-informed public is imperative to the productive operation of any police department. This policy is intended to foster a professional working relationship between the police and members of the media so both may achieve their goals. Media members are encouraged to pursue their activities as long as they perform them within the boundaries of the law. Information will be released to the media without partiality for any one media organization. Police officers are encouraged to assist the media when possible.

III. Definitions

Formal press conference: A preannounced interview with media representatives for the purpose of releasing written or oral information and responding to questions.

Media: People who represent public print, radio, television, or film sources of news information, commentary, or entertainment.

IV. Procedures

A. Department Members

1. At all times, officers dealing with the media will be honest, fair, and impartial.
2. Officers will not display anger or frustration to the media, especially during interviews. Remember, the microphone is always on.
3. Officers may not seek publicity through the media for personal notoriety.
4. Officers will politely respond to media requests for information as soon as practical and within the parameters outlined in this policy.
   a. Officers will obtain the necessary facts surrounding a particular incident and prepare the information that can be released.
   b. Media releases can be in either written or verbal form.
   c. Officers will make every reasonable effort to return telephone calls from media personnel.

B. Chief of Police

1. If an incident involves a major crime, approval for any release must be obtained from the chief of police or his or her designee.
   a. See Policy P012 for further information.
2. Formal press conferences will be scheduled only with the approval of the chief or his or her designee.

C. Information That May Be Released

1. The following information about criminal matters can be released on request:
   a. Arrested person(s)
      (1) Name

(continued)

Figure 2-6 • *(continued)*

(2) Age
(3) Residence
(4) Race
(5) Sex
(6) Employment (optional)
(7) Marital status (optional)
(8) Similar biographical information (optional)

b. Text of the charge(s)
c. Identity of complainant (optional)
d. Amount or conditions of bail (optional)
e. Identity of arresting officer and agency (optional)
f. Duration of investigation (optional)
g. Circumstances of arrest, including
(1) Time
(2) Place
(3) Other information (optional)
h. Victim
(1) Age
(2) Sex
(3) General location (optional)
(4) Injuries to victim (optional)

2. Optional information may be released by the officer if deemed appropriate.
3. If media representatives inquire about information that is known by the officer but is deemed inappropriate for release, the officer may inform media representatives that the information will not be released at this time.

D. Information That May *Not* Be Released

Generally, it is not appropriate to disclose or report the following information because of the risk of prejudice to the rights of an accused for a fair trial.

1. Existence or contents of confessions, admissions, or statements given by the defendant, including any refusal to make such a statement
2. Opinions concerning guilt, reputation, or character of an accused
3. Results of any examinations or tests taken by an accused, including any refusal to take them
4. Information leading to discovery
5. Identity of witnesses or victims when clear danger to them or an ongoing investigation exists
6. Identity of victims of sexual assaults or other sex crimes
7. Prior criminal record
8. Identity of any critically injured or deceased person prior to the notification of the next of kin
9. Any "off the record" remarks or comments
10. Names of individuals who are merely suspects
11. Names of juvenile suspects or defendants
12. Social Security numbers
13. Medical records
14. Graphic descriptions of wounds or crime scenes

E. Photographs

The members of the media should recognize the need to ensure that both freedom of speech and a fair trial are allowed.

1. Law enforcement personnel may *not* pose a person in custody deliberately for purposes of media televising.
2. Media members may respond to the scene of incidents for coverage and freely photograph the scene as long as the investigation or its prosecution is not jeopardized.
3. Officers *may* take protective measures, such as securing a scene because of imminent danger or covering a body to prevent photographing or televising by the media or the public, if such measures are deemed necessary by the officer.

Figure 2-6 • *(continued)*

4. Officers will not dissuade victims or witnesses from speaking to the media. However, people in police custody shall not be allowed to discuss the situation with media members.

F. Media Releases (Format)

1. Generally, media releases may contain basic information about an event that answers questions concerning who, what, where, when, and how.
2. Specific information that should be part of all media releases includes:
   a. Date of media release
   b. Who prepared media release (name and rank)
   c. Type of incident
   d. Date, time, and location of incident
   e. Case number

By order of: ______________________________

Scott T. Gregory, Chief of Police

Source: Town of Madison (Wisconsin) Police Department, "Media release procedure" from the *Policy Manual* (Madison, 2005), pp. 183–86. Reprinted with permission.

Professional Associations. Every profession has at least one association for its members. Academics join associations that are unique to their fields and participate in those associations' annual meetings. Medical doctors join huge professional groups like the American Medical Association. Lawyers, whether prosecutors, defense attorneys, or others, have their respective associations. School teachers join associations. Even occupations that are not necessarily regarded as professions have their own associations. Law enforcement personnel are no different. There are far too many police associations to list and describe here, but four are quite prominent and well known. They are the International Association of Chiefs of Police, the National Black Police Association, the International Union of Police Associations, and the International Police Association. Each represents a different set of interests.

The International Association of Chiefs of Police The **International Association of Chiefs of Police** (IACP) is, hands down, the best-known law enforcement association. The organization's title suggests that membership is limited to police chiefs, but IACP uses the term *chief* somewhat loosely. Officers with executive authority are allowed to join as so-called active members. Associate memberships are available to anyone with sufficient background in law enforcement practice or study, including academics and trainers. The association also extends honorary and distinguished service memberships to other people, including a number of non–law enforcement personnel. All told, IACP boasts a membership of more than 20,000 people in 89 countries across the globe.

International Association of Chiefs of Police (IACP)
Founded in 1893, the best-known association for law enforcement professionals.

IACP was founded in 1893. (See Figure 2-7 for an overview of key developments in IACP history.) Its constitution describes the association's mission as follows:

> As a leadership organization the Mission of the International Association of Chiefs of Police is to advance professional police services; promote enhanced administrative, technical, and operational police practices; foster cooperation and the exchange of information and experience among police leaders and police organizations of recognized professional and technical standing throughout the world; champion the recruitment and training of qualified persons in the police profession; and, encourage all police personnel worldwide to achieve and maintain the highest standards of ethics, integrity, community interaction, and professional conduct.[65]

IACP facilitates interagency communication through several means. One is an annual meeting that convenes in a different city each year. At the meeting, there are panels, presentations, and training sessions. The meetings, which are generally organized around two subjects—law enforcement

WEB PATROL 2-7
Professional Associations in Law Enforcement
http://www.mycrimekit.com

Figure 2-7 • History of the International Association of Chiefs of Police

1893	Police chiefs from all parts of the country assemble in Chicago to form the National Chiefs of Police Union, primarily to apprehend and return wanted persons who flee local jurisdictions.
1897	The National Bureau of Criminal Identification becomes operational among association members.
1904	Fingerprint identification is encouraged through exhibits at the St. Louis World's Fair and in member communities.
1922	Work begins on a uniform crime records reporting system.
1924	IACP criminal identification files are used to create an FBI Identification Division.
1930	IACP's uniform crime records system is turned over to the FBI.
1934	IACP and the FBI establish the FBI National Academy for state and local police. Publication of the *Police Chiefs Newsletter* begins; this publication is the forerunner of *The Police Chief* magazine, which continues today as the "professional voice of law enforcement." IACP is recognized as a source of factual information for legislators, with 12 laws enacted by the U.S. Congress containing IACP recommendations.
1935	Field consulting services are initiated to assist local police departments.
1940	A headquarters office is established in Washington, DC, in order to create more organizational stability and to expand activities and services for members. This move also permits the association to begin a long period of cooperation with governments of the world that continues to this day.
1942	IACP's wartime mobilization plans provide guidelines for handling planned disorders, sabotage, and movement of troops and material in truck convoys.
1955	IACP provides police training for the International Cooperation Administration, developing the International Police Academy.
1960	Minimum training standards for all law enforcement officers are developed by IACP and urged upon state governments. To assist in meeting these standards, IACP develops training materials.
1970s	Worldwide training programs are established. A comprehensive testing program for police equipment is initiated. Police management studies are conducted around the world. The IACP Police Assessment Center is established. The United Nations confers consultative status on the association, recognizing IACP work performed in several member nations. A national bomb data center is established by IACP and is subsequently turned over to the FBI.
1980s	IACP opens its first World Regional Division in Europe. IACP conducts International Policing Executive Seminars in Europe and Asia. IACP and the Bureau of Justice Assistance establish a National Law Enforcement Policy Center. Along with the National Organization of Black Law Enforcement Executives, the National Sheriffs' Association and the Police Executive Research Forum, IACP helps establish the Commission on Law Enforcement Accreditation.
1990s	IACP efforts focus attention on international narcotics trafficking, drunk driving, police use of force, civil disorder and criminal aliens. A priority for the association is assisting departments in implementing community policing in their jurisdictions. IACP assists departments in implementing a host of programs, such as the Americans with Disabilities Act, less-than-lethal weapons training, and contemporary management techniques. IACP purchases a new headquarters building in Alexandria, Virginia. Highly successful summits on violent crimes and homicides are conducted by IACP; the results receive national visibility.
1993	IACP celebrates its centennial year.

Source: Adapted from International Association of Chiefs of Police, "About IACP," http://www.iacp.org/about/timeline.htm (accessed June 7, 2008). Copyright held by the International Association of Chiefs of Police, 515 North Washington St., Alexandria, VA 22314. Further reproduction without express written permission from the IACP is strictly prohibited.

technology and education—provide members ample opportunity to network with one another in both formal and informal settings. IACP also conducts various training programs throughout the year. The association's Research Center conducts a wide variety of police-related studies and disseminates the results, usually by posting them online. IACP also publishes *The Police Chief*, a print and online magazine that is widely read by law enforcement administrators throughout the United States. All in all, IACP provides a valuable interagency communication function for police administrators.

A Los Angeles Police Department honor guard stands at parade rest during the 111th International Association of Chiefs of Police (IACP) annual meeting in the Los Angeles Convention Center. What do organizations like the IACP do to enhance the status and effectiveness of the police profession in the United States?

Jeff Grace/*La Opinión*/NewsCom

The National Black Police Association Though far from being as large as IACP, the **National Black Police Association** was formed in 1972 as a parent association for local and regional black police associations.[66] According to the association, it "is a nationwide organization of African American Police Associations dedicated to the promotion of justice, fairness, and effectiveness in law enforcement." Basically, the National Black Police Association has succeeded in creating a network of minority police officers throughout the United States. Though the association's title suggests otherwise, membership is not restricted to African American police officers, although they do make up the bulk of the membership. Unlike IACP, the National Black Police Association does not hold an annual meeting for all members, but its regional affiliates hold their own meetings. There are five such regions.

National Black Police Association
The parent association, founded in 1972, for local and regional associations of African American police professionals.

The International Union of Police Associations The **International Union of Police Associations (IUPA)** represents rank-and-file police officers and their unions from across the country. IUPA describes itself as follows:

> The International Union of Police Associations is the only AFL-CIO union chartered exclusively for law enforcement and law enforcement support personnel. The AFL-CIO affiliation places I.U.P.A. in a position of strength within the labor movement. While I.U.P.A.'s officers, active and retired law enforcement officers, fight to improve the lives of their brothers and sisters in law enforcement, I.U.P.A. works to improve legislation that protects and affects public safety officers, as well as representing the needs of law enforcement officers and support personnel, whether that be for better equipment, more staff or a fair wage.[67]

International Union of Police Associations (IUPA)
An international police association, founded in 1954 and chartered by the AFL-CIO, that represents all rank-and-file officers and functions more as a lobbying group than as a professional association.

IUPA is more a lobbying organization than a professional association. It holds meetings but not on par with, for example, IACP. One of the marks of a lobbying organization is the use of us-versus-them language in its correspondence. For example, the National Rifle Association regularly battles those who would threaten Second Amendment rights, and the American Civil Liberties Union (ACLU) challenges people who threaten civil liberties. IUPA, not surprisingly, tends to not speak highly of police administrators, who are regarded as the "bad guys" in nearly every union contract negotiation. One can see an example of IUPA's us-versus-them language in its recent commentary on the rise in violent crime across America:

> The chiefs will get together and wring their hands. They will blame juvenile crime, money, the courts, and many other factors, all of which have contributed to the crime increase. What they

will not likely do, is have any representative of the rank and file officers in attendance. While they are the backbone of every department, and are the chiefs' eyes and ears in the neighborhoods they patrol, their opinions will not be asked. They will continue to answer their calls and conduct themselves in a manner that will not generate any complaints. They will be required to train new recruits who are less qualified than their predecessors. They will hope their pension is still there when they are eligible to retire.[68]

In addition to its lobbying efforts, IUPA facilitates communication among police officers and among the unions that represent them. Some agencies have their own unions, and police officers in other agencies join regional and state unions. IUPA is the body that represents *all* their interests in the nation's capital.

International Police Association (IPA)
Founded in 1950, the largest police professional association in the world.

The International Police Association The largest police association in the world is the **International Police Association (IPA)**, though it is less known to most Americans than IACP. The IPA boasts a membership of more than 300,000 people with national sections in some 60 countries around the globe. The IPA's core functions are, in its words, "to create bonds of friendship and to promote international cooperation."[69] Beyond that, the IPA describes its other concerns:

> It is committed to the principles set out in the *Universal Declaration of Human Rights* as adopted by the United Nations in 1948 and recognizes that any form of torture is absolutely inconsistent with these principles. Its aims include the development of cultural relations amongst its members, a broadening of their general knowledge and an exchange of professional experience. In addition, it seeks to foster mutual help in the social sphere and to contribute, within the limits of its possibilities, to the peaceful co-existence of different peoples and to the preservation of world peace.[70]

The IPA's national sections (those consisting of one country's members) hold annual meetings. The main annual meeting, known as the *IPA World Congress*, provides an opportunity for law enforcement professionals from around the world to meet one another, share information, and learn of operational "best practices" that have proved successful in other agencies. The IPA's role is especially important in the wake of September 11. International cooperation is the word of the day, and the IPA serves to promote such cooperation. We will look at other international cooperation efforts in Chapter 16.

Research Reports. We mentioned that IACP's Research Center generates reports and other publications for its members. There are, however, a number of organizations whose raison d'être is the provision of research-related services to the law enforcement or criminal justice profession. These include the National Institute of Justice, the Police Executive Research Forum, and the Police Foundation. These organizations promote interagency communication through the publication of research aimed at identifying "best practices" and learning what does and does not work in the realm of law enforcement.

National Institute of Justice (NIJ)
A research, development, and evaluation agency within the Office of Justice Programs in the U.S. Department of Justice.

The National Institute of Justice The **National Institute of Justice (NIJ)** is located within the Office of Justice Programs in the U.S. Department of Justice (DOJ). It is DOJ's research, development, and evaluation agency. NIJ is not concerned solely with policing, however, as the organization publishes research on a variety of criminal justice–related topics. Not only does NIJ conduct some of its own research, but it also funds universities, research organizations like the Urban Institute or the RAND Corporation, and qualified unaffiliated individuals to do some of the research for them. Research grants from NIJ are often regarded as the "holy grail" of research monies because they are intensely competitive. The upside is that the research that NIJ produces is high quality and rigorous. Whether it is completely objective, though, is unclear. The NIJ director is appointed by the president and serves at his pleasure.

NIJ provides a valuable communication function because it freely disseminates its research to all interested readers. A link on the agency's website provides instant access to many of the latest publications and findings in criminal justice and law enforcement research.[71] NIJ also provides an annual report to Congress that synthesizes the findings from many of the NIJ-funded research projects from the previous year. Finally, the *National Institute of Justice Journal* provides a less technical overview of interesting projects, research findings, and other relevant items. The journal can be accessed on the NIJ website, and print subscriptions are free. Anyone interested in a sample of the most current criminal justice and policing research should subscribe to the journal.

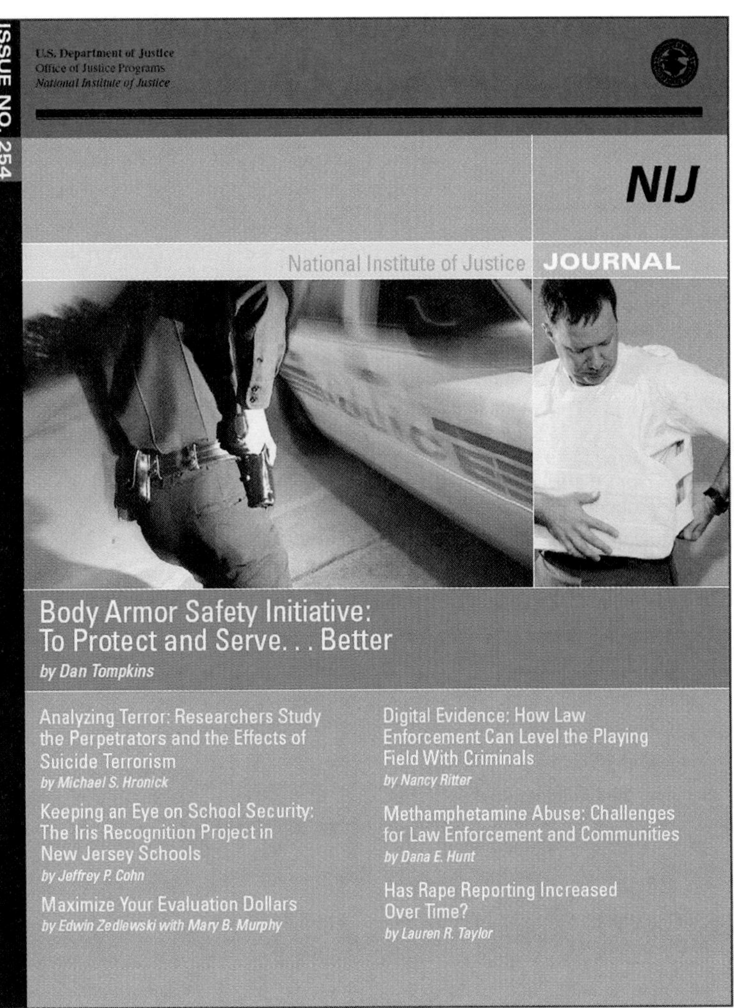

The *National Institute of Justice Journal*. What can you learn from reading the journal?

U.S. Department of Justice, Office of Justice Programs

The Police Executive Research Forum Unlike NIJ, the **Police Executive Research Forum (PERF)** is a research organization dedicated solely to police issues. As its title indicates, its main concern is with executive issues, though many of the organization's projects simply involve topics of interest to administrators (for example, what works and what doesn't). Also unlike NIJ, PERF is not a government entity. Headquartered in Washington, DC, it is a stand-alone nonprofit organization with no particular ideological stance on any subject. According to PERF:

> The Police Executive Research Forum is a national membership organization of progressive police executives from the largest city, county and state law enforcement agencies. PERF is dedicated to improving policing and advancing professionalism through research and involvement in public policy debate. Incorporated in 1977, PERF's primary sources of operating revenues are government grants and contracts, and partnerships with private foundations and other organizations.[72]

PERF members can access various publications, a few of which are available for free. The organization holds an annual meeting where members can network, be trained, and learn of cutting-edge research findings from around the country. PERF also maintains POPNet, a database of problem-oriented policing examples. (We discuss problem-oriented policing in greater detail in Chapter 10.) POPNet is invaluable from an interagency communication standpoint because it allows members from various agencies across the country to share their successes and failures in an educational forum accessible through the Internet.

Police Executive Research Forum (PERF)
A research organization, incorporated in 1977, dedicated solely to police administration issues.

The Police Foundation The **Police Foundation** is similar to PERF, but it is concerned with all facets of policing, not just administration. The Police Foundation also touts itself as a totally objective entity:

> Unconstrained by partisan imperatives, the Police Foundation speaks with a unique and objective voice. Its focus and perspective is the *whole* of American policing, rather than any single facet. . . . A guiding tenet of the foundation is that to advance, policing—like other public services—deserves the best of thorough, objective study, and the impetus of new ideas that have the widest possible dissemination. . . . Since its inception in 1970, the foundation has stressed the importance of helping to create a new body of knowledge about policing. The quality and quantity of its research reports have helped make the Police Foundation a catalyst for change in American policing. . . . By disseminating as widely as possible the publications that result from its work, the foundation seeks to ensure that the knowledge it has gained reaches the broader criminal justice community, including law enforcement practitioners, policy makers, and scholars.[73]

Police Foundation
A research agency, established in 1970, concerned with all facets of policing.

As this mission statement makes clear, one of the Police Foundation's core purposes is facilitation of communication between agencies. To that end, the foundation engages in a number of research projects and provides training, technical assistance, and other professional services. One of those services is the Crime Mapping and Problem Analysis Laboratory, whose mission is to promote police agencies' use of crime-mapping technologies (see Chapter 9) to aid in crime reduction and problem-solving efforts. The Police Foundation also pioneered the Risk Analysis Management System (RAMS), a computer system aimed at "ensuring proper training, accountability, quality service, and community satisfaction with police services."[74] The now-famous Kansas City Preventive Patrol Experiment was a Police Foundation project.

SUMMARY

- Democracy and federalism have contributed to the unique nature of policing in America. Democracy is the institutionalization of freedom. Among democracy's implications for policing is the need to balance due process against crime control. Federalism divides government power and decision-making capabilities between levels of government, and this has led to the creation of federal, state, and local law enforcement agencies in the United States.
- The environment of policing includes citizens, government officials, the media, and other law enforcement agencies. Citizen support for police is affected by factors like race, age, sex, and prior contact. Government influence over policing occurs through executive, legislative, and judicial channels. The media can both help and hurt law enforcement agencies, but skilled police administrators engage in impression management to ensure a favorable public image. Two methods of promoting interagency communication are participating in professional associations and keeping abreast of research.

COMING FULL CIRCLE

For Discussion

Return to the questions posed at the start of this chapter. Have any of your answers changed since you read the chapter? What portions of this chapter helped you answer these questions?

Writing Assignment

Using material from this chapter and additional resources, write a 500-word essay in response to one of the questions presented at the beginning of the chapter. Submit your essay to your instructor if asked to do so.

KEY TERMS AND NAMES

confederation
council-manager form
crime-control model
democracy
dramaturgical discipline
dual federalism
due process model
federalism
impression management
International Association of Chiefs of Police (IACP)
International Police Association (IPA)
International Union of Police Associations (IUPA)
mayor-council form
National Black Police Association
National Institute of Justice (NIJ)
police commission
Police Executive Research Forum (PERF)
Police Foundation
public information officer
Violent Crime Control and Law Enforcement Act of 1994

WEB INTERACTIVITY

Learn about a national plan for criminal intelligence sharing from the International Association of Chiefs of Police by visiting http://tinyurl.com/dhg45o.

Read the GLOBAL document that appears at that URL, and follow the links that it contains to read more about the initiative.

The third paragraph in the feature document says:

> The centerpiece of all summit recommendations was a call for a National Intelligence Plan. Elements of the plan include promoting intelligence led policing; providing critical counterbalance of civil rights; increasing opportunities for trust building; presenting a remedy for analytical and information deficits; and addressing training and technology issues. Summit participants called for the creation of a Criminal Intelligence Coordinating Council to support and improve intelligence sharing nationwide, in effect implementing the National Intelligence Plan. The Council's mandate was to "promote, ensure, and establish effective intelligence sharing and to address and solve, in an ongoing fashion, the problems that inhibit it".

When you have finished reading the featured document, write an answer to the question raised by the last sentence in the paragraph above; that is, what problems inhibit the effective sharing of intelligence by law enforcement agencies? How can they be overcome? Submit your answer to your instructor if asked to do so.

REVIEW QUESTIONS

1. What are the distinguishing features of policing in a democracy? How has our system of federalism affected policing in the United States?
2. What is the policing environment? Which aspect of the policing environment do you believe is most important?

chapter three

POLICE AND THE CRIMINAL JUSTICE SYSTEM

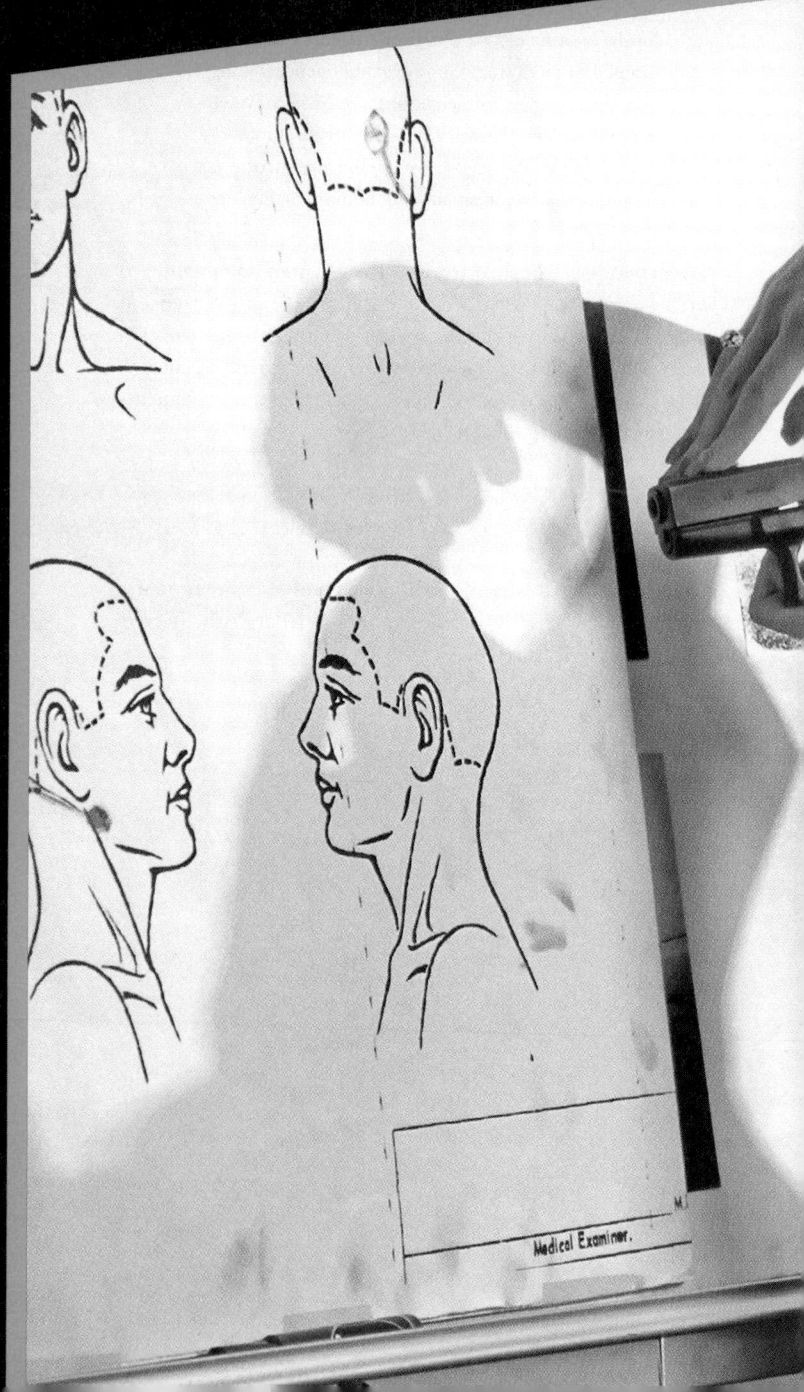

Learning Objectives

After reading this chapter, students should be able to:

1. Explain the police role in the criminal justice process, particularly during the pretrial, trial, and post-trial phases.
2. Provide specific examples of how police partner with other local criminal justice agencies.
3. Identify three popular federal-local partnerships.
4. Explain how the police collaborate with the military, and discuss the controversies associated with this practice.

POLICE
AUSTIN

THINK ABOUT IT

As in many other parts of the country, prosecutors in Fulton County, Georgia, routinely work with police officers to identify notorious "crack houses"—those with a history of at least five on-premises drug arrests or two previous occasions when drug search warrants were successfully served on the property. Once such a place is identified, prosecutors rely on state nuisance laws to initiate a forfeiture action against the property.

Before taking this action, prosecutors ensure that the value of the property relative to the drugs seized is roughly equal, as it would be unreasonable to forfeit an entire house because a small quantity of drugs was found there. Then, in accordance with Georgia law, they ensure that the person who owns the home knew about the criminal activity taking place there.

Emmanuel Awa, director of the Fresh Start drug rehabilitation program at Northern State Prison in Newark, New Jersey, talks about his program. New Jersey is expanding its comprehensive substance abuse initiative for incarcerated men. The Fresh Start program provides its participants with substance abuse treatment and education as well as with life skills training and mental health support. How does the New Jersey program appear to differ from the Atlanta Fresh Start program described at the start of this chapter?

Daniel Hulshizer/AP Wide World Photos

A recent report on this program, known as Neighborhood Fresh Start, details the process:

> Once a crack house has been identified for possible forfeiture, the chief of police sends the homeowner a "cease and desist" letter demanding an end to the illicit activity on the property. Next, the Police Department engages in heightened surveillance, conducts undercover drug buys and serves search warrants to determine if drug activity has stopped. If drug activity continues, the D.A.'s Office begins forfeiture proceedings.
>
> When the D.A.'s Office prevails at a bench trial, the house becomes the property of the State of Georgia and the Fulton County D.A.'s Office. Once the mortgage is paid off, the house is renovated, bringing it into compliance with the building code.[1]

After renovations are completed, an Atlanta police officer moves into the house and lives there for one year, paying a nominal amount of rent. In exchange, the officer is assigned to the neighborhood in which the house is located and serves as a community resource officer. He or she maintains a weekly log of criminal activity in the neighborhood and generates a neighborhood safety plan that is used to coordinate crime-prevention efforts in the neighborhood. After one year, prosecutors work with the United Way and a faith-based organization to move a low-income family into the house.

The program is somewhat controversial, as the following excerpt shows:

> During the first forfeiture, neighbors were sympathetic to the homeowner, who portrayed herself as an innocent victim. Some neighbors even circulated a petition calling for an end to the forfeiture proceedings. In addition, a newspaper suggested the forfeiture was an over-reaction to the problem. There were also community concerns about the placement of a police officer in the forfeited house.[2]

Neighborhood Fresh Start raises several interesting questions to keep in mind as you read this chapter:

1. Do the police generally enjoy favorable working relationships with other criminal justice agencies?
2. Should police departments work more closely with other criminal justice agencies?
3. What negative consequences might result from a closer working relationship?
4. Is the Fresh Start program fair?
5. Should criminal justice agencies take on the role of property managers?

INTRODUCTION

The police are but one part of a larger criminal justice system. Their interactions with other criminal justice agencies, at various levels of government, are important to consider. This is especially true of late, as *interagency collaboration* and *interagency cooperation* have become buzzwords in policing today. Indeed, government agencies at all levels are beginning to realize the benefits of teaming up to address difficult problems.

We begin this chapter by situating the police within the broader criminal justice system, by looking at their role in the criminal justice process, and by examining their relationships with local criminal justice agencies. We then discuss recent partnerships between the police and federal criminal justice agencies. Examples include Operation Ceasefire, the well-known Project Exile, and the Project Safe Neighborhoods program.

Many people do not know that the police in America have a close historical relationship with the military and that today many police units routinely train with military personnel. As this chapter will show, there is increasing interest in using the military to patrol the U.S.-Mexico border to block the flow of illegal immigrants. While the Reserves and the National Guard have for years assisted in border protection,[3] today's local police agencies are increasingly adopting military tactics and technology.

POLICE AS A PIECE OF THE CRIMINAL JUSTICE PUZZLE

The flowchart in Figure 3-1 was originally created in 1967 by the President's Commission on Law Enforcement and Administration of Justice and was later stylized with added color by the National Institute of Justice. It depicts a more or less linear and relatively smooth criminal justice process. The only reference to policing appears on the left side of the flowchart, suggesting that police are only involved in the investigation of crime and the apprehension of suspected lawbreakers. Modern-day police clearly continue to perform these functions, but the 1967 flowchart—even the stylized version shown here—is outdated and idealistic.[4]

Figure 3-1 • President's Commission Rendering of the U.S. Criminal Justice System

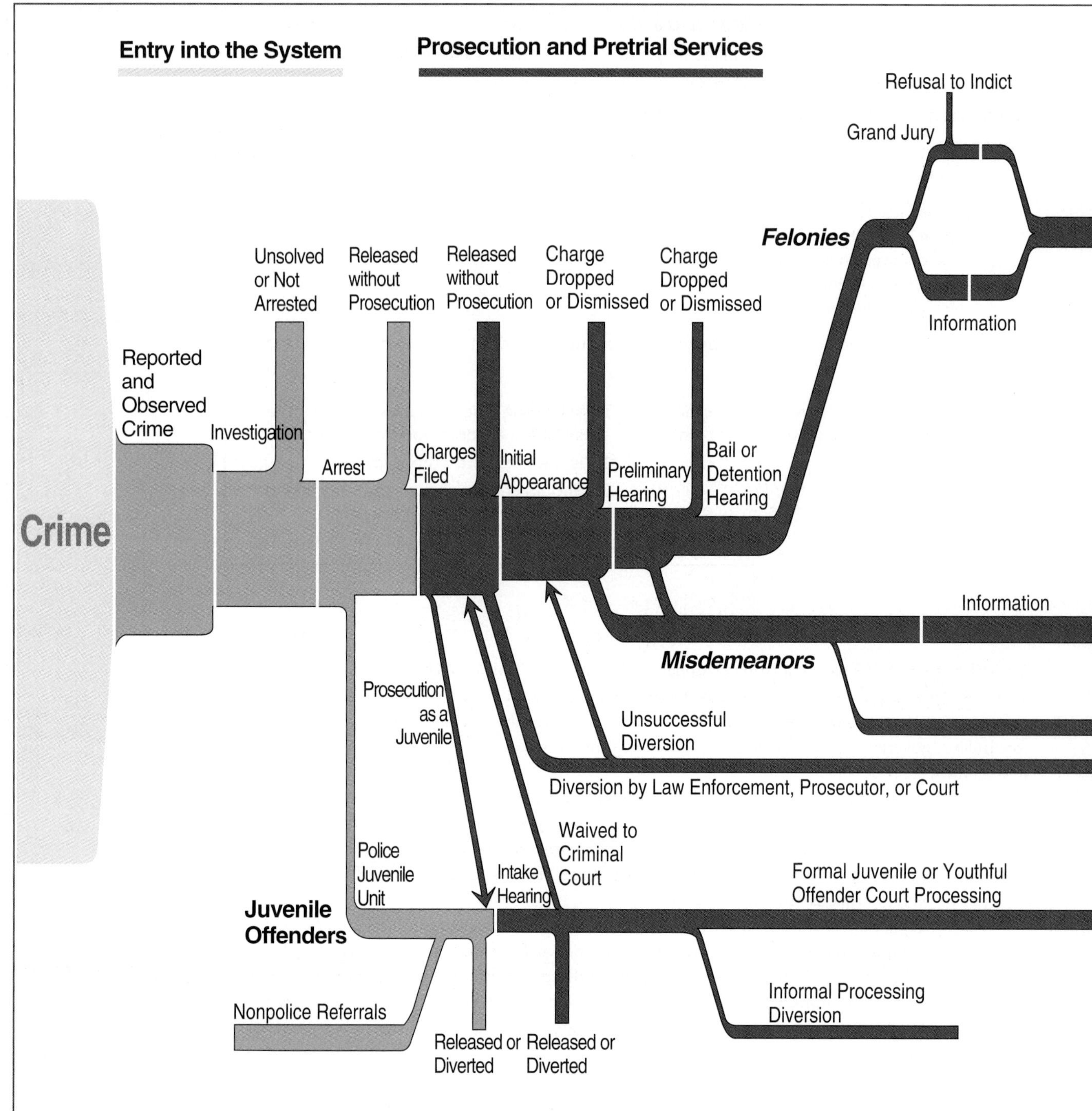

Note: This chart gives a simplified view of case flow through the criminal justice system. Procedures vary among jurisdictions. The weights of the lines are not intended to show the actual size of caseloads.

Source: Adapted from *The challenge of crime in a free society*. President's Commission on Law Enforcement and Administration of Justice, 1967. This revision, a result of the Symposium on the 30th Anniversary of the President's Commission, was prepared by the Bureau of Justice Statistics in 1997.

If today's criminal justice process were graphically depicted, the diagram would be circular. A significant number of offenders released from the system come right back in (Figure 3-2)—and in doing so, they cross paths with the police once again.

This "revolving door" notion requires that police agencies work with and collaborate with officials in other areas of the criminal justice system. Prosecutors, for example, know they will see the same offenders again if they don't receive the treatment or services they need. Parole officers know that the convicts under their watch will never lead law-abiding lives without adequate supervision

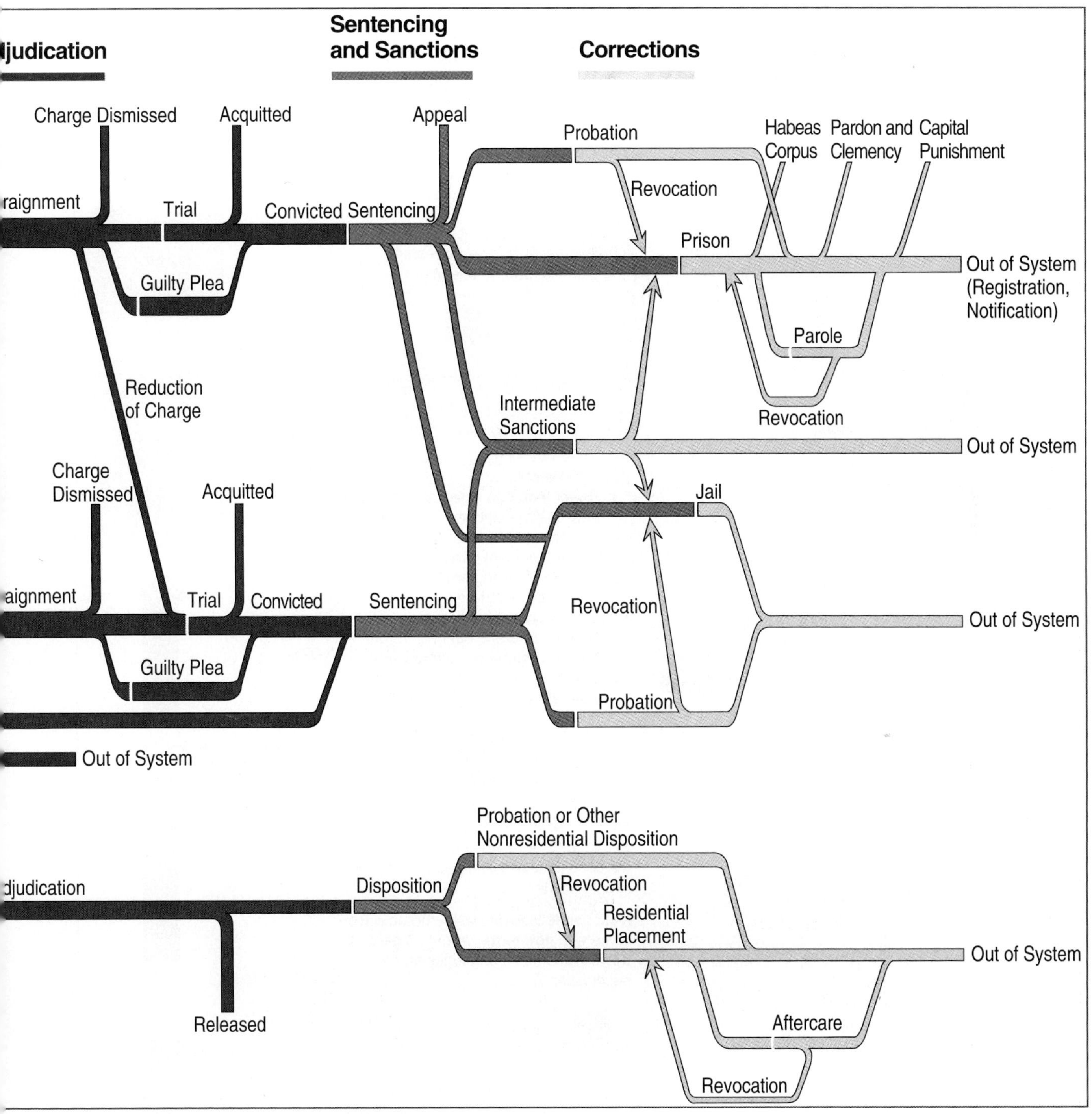

and guidance. Judges see the same offenders over and over. Police officers know they will see the same suspects time and again if, for example, the officers fail to build a sufficiently "prosecutable" case against them. All officials in the criminal justice system, whether they like it or not, work together for a common purpose.

Police work does not stop with an arrest. Police officers have duties to perform throughout the criminal justice process, even well after trial. Police have not always been too involved with after-trial affairs, but that is changing. Another profound change afoot in American criminal justice is

Figure 3-2 • The Flow of Inmates through the California Corrections System

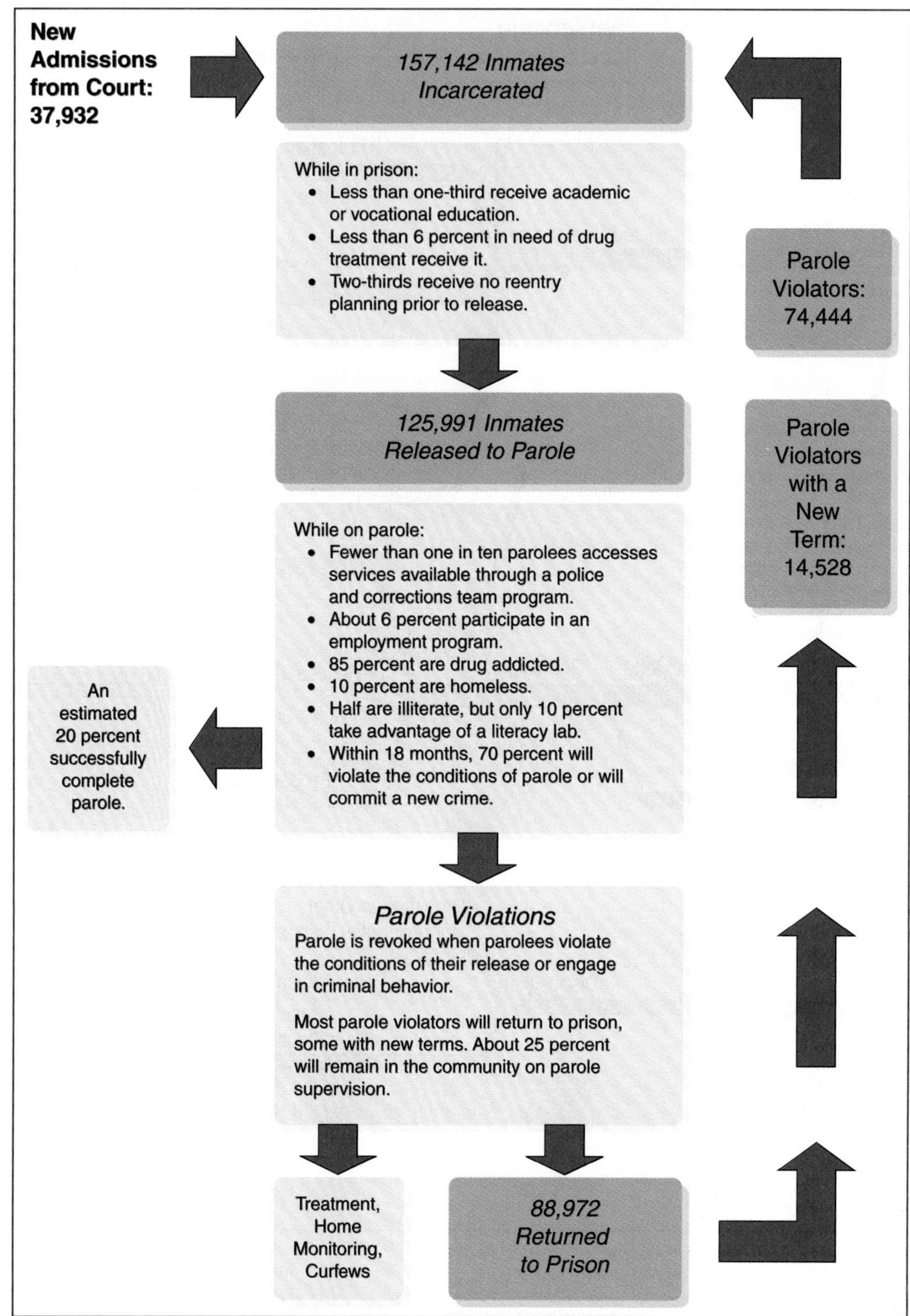

Source: Michael P. Jacobson, "Historical Trends, 1981–2001," written testimony to the Little Hoover Commission, January 23, 2003.

collaboration. Not only do police and other law enforcement agencies work together across jurisdictional boundaries, but they are also starting to work in greater numbers with prosecutors and various corrections officials, particularly parole officers, in the realization that these nontraditional partnerships are critical to safer streets in America.

The Criminal Justice Process

Police officers are involved in various stages of the criminal justice process. They are often called upon, for instance, to testify at trial. The following subsections provide an overview of the criminal justice process and point to stages where police officers may be called on to act or assist.

Police in the Pretrial Phase. A typical criminal case begins with a complaint, which may come in the form of a 911 call from a citizen, a report of victimization to the police, or an observation by a law enforcement officer of a crime in progress. If a citizen reports the crime, the police will usually follow up on the complaint by performing an investigation, taking steps to confirm the observations of the citizen. If an officer observes a crime, less investigation is necessary. In fact, when an officer witnesses a crime in progress, he or she will usually arrest the suspect on the spot. The arrest will then be subjected to judicial scrutiny in a hearing where a judge will decide if the officer had probable cause to arrest the suspect.

Once the police have identified a suspect in a crime reported by a citizen, they will approach a judge and seek either an arrest warrant or a search warrant. In either case, the police must be able to show probable cause that the suspect was the one who committed the crime or that the evidence they seek will be found in the place to be searched. If this burden is met, a warrant will be issued, and the police will locate and arrest the suspect or search the premises specified in the search warrant. The probable cause burden that is required for arrest and search warrants is not to be taken lightly; it has spawned a great deal of debate in the courts.

The role of the police during the pretrial process cannot be overemphasized. In the period between a police officer's first contact with a suspect until the suspect is arrested and detained, the police role is complex and multifaceted. The Constitution, particularly the Fourth Amendment, places significant restrictions on what the police can and cannot do when they investigate crime and interact with suspects. That is why courses on criminal procedure are found in many criminal justice curricula; these courses devote extensive attention to the role of the police in the criminal justice process and to the constitutional guidelines they must follow.

If a police officer arrests a suspect for a crime committed in his or her presence, no warrant is necessary. But it is also true that warrants are not always required for arresting suspects or searching their residences based on a citizen complaint. Many contingencies arise wherein the police are permitted to arrest or search without a warrant. Suspects who evade authorities, who seek to destroy evidence, or who seem likely to inflict harm on others create a situation requiring quick police action. Indeed, the police may be forced to make split-second decisions, to arrest or search, without the protection of a warrant.

Once a suspect has been arrested, he or she is searched. This is done for the protection of the officer as well as to discover any contraband in the suspect's possession. The suspect is then transported to the police station and booked. **Booking** is the process of fingerprinting, processing, and photographing the suspect, after which he or she is typically placed in a holding cell. The suspect may also be required to submit to a Breathalyzer or other test or be required to participate in a lineup.

booking
The process of fingerprinting, processing, and photographing a suspect, after which he or she is typically placed in a holding cell. The suspect may also be required to submit to testing (such as for alcohol) or be required to participate in a lineup.

After booking, the police present their case to the prosecutor (usually by filing a report of some sort or by contacting the prosecutor). If the prosecutor believes the evidence is persuasive enough, he or she will bring charges against the suspect, subject to certain restrictions specified in the Constitution and clarified by the Supreme Court. Once charges are brought, the suspect is then referred to as a *defendant*. If the charges are minor, the police may release the defendant rather than detaining him or her, in which case the defendant will be required to appear at court at some later date.

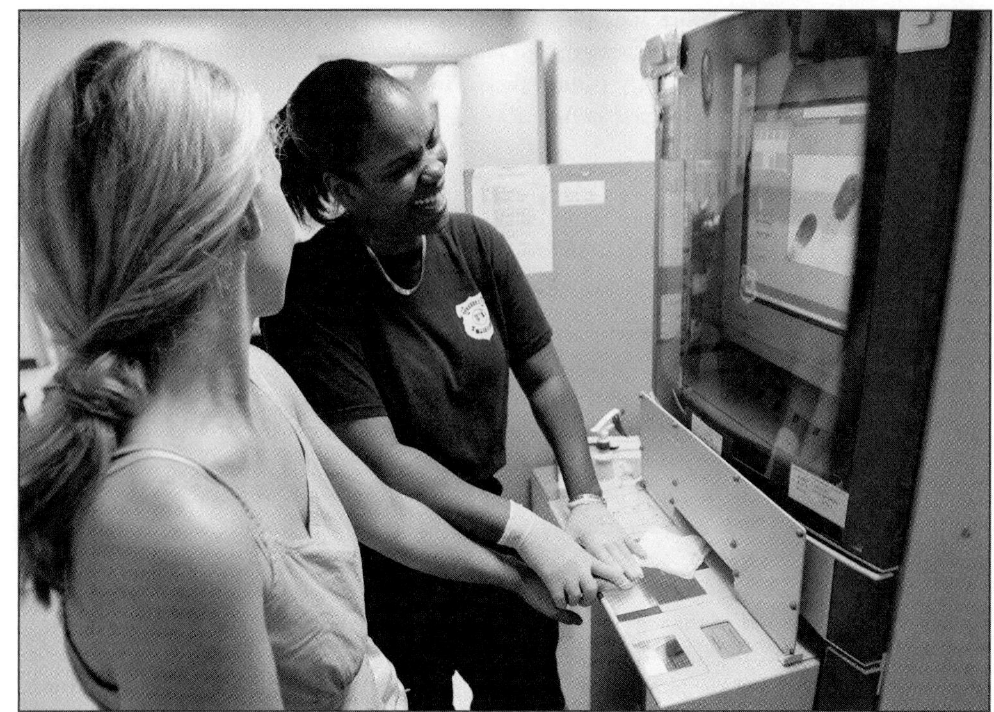

Bonnie Wherry, right, laughs with an arrestee to help keep her calm as she takes fingerprints at the Justice Center in Cleveland, Ohio. What happens during the booking process?

The Plain Dealer/Joshua Gunter/ AP Wide World Photos

arraignment
The hearing before a court having jurisdiction in a criminal case, during which the defendant is identified, informed of his or her rights, and required to enter a plea. Also, in some jurisdictions, any appearance in criminal court prior to trial.

guilty
A plea entered in response to a criminal charge whereby the accused acknowledges responsibility for the charged offense. Also, a finding rendered by a judge or jury following the completion of a criminal trial.

not guilty
A plea entered in response to a criminal charge whereby the accused denies responsibility for the charged offense. Also, a finding rendered by a judge or jury following the completion of a criminal trial.

nolo contendere
A plea of "no contest" entered in response to a criminal charge whereby the accused declines to contest the charged offense.

Through their investigations, police effectively "build" criminal cases for prosecutors. Without this assistance, prosecutors would be going into trial blind. When the process breaks down, particularly when the police forward weak cases to the prosecutor, a conviction is difficult to secure.

Some jurisdictions rely on a grand jury rather than allowing prosecutors to determine whether charges are appropriate. When a grand jury is used, it often works closely with the prosecutor, who presents the information that the grand jury needs to make its decision. Police officers often testify before grand juries in order to help make the case against a possible criminal defendant. The police role in grand jury investigations can be an important one because the suspects who are being investigated—and possibly indicted—do not enjoy the right to be present at the hearing or to offer evidence in their own defense.

Suspects who are booked, placed in detention, and charged with a crime then face a number of different court hearings, depending on the seriousness of the crime. Misdemeanors, because of their not-so-serious nature, tend to be fast-tracked. A misdemeanor defendant may only appear at one court hearing where the judge will decide guilt or innocence. Felony defendants, in contrast, face a longer road. If, as we have seen already, the suspect was arrested without a warrant, he or she is granted a hearing where the judge will decide whether the arresting officer had appropriate justification to make the arrest. This hearing may be merged with other hearings.

The next step in the criminal justice process is **arraignment.** At the arraignment, the defendant appears before a judge and is informed of the charges. The defendant is notified of his or her right to counsel, to remain silent, and other important rights and is required to enter a plea. Common pleas are **guilty, not guilty,** and ***nolo contendere***, the latter being akin to a plea of "no contest." A public defender may be assigned at this stage if the defendant is unable to afford representation. Probable cause may also be determined at the arraignment if a separate hearing is not required, and a **bail** determination may be made as well. Finally, the trial may take place at the arraignment, but only for misdemeanors. Generally, there is little police involvement at this step, but an officer may be called on to testify.

If the bail determination is not made at the arraignment, a separate hearing may be warranted. In deciding whether bail should be granted, the judge will consider the seriousness of the crime, the defendant's prior record, his or her likelihood of flight and level of dangerousness, and other factors. Police officers sometimes testify to these issues. The defendant's financial status may also be taken into account in deciding whether bail should be granted. If granted, **bail** is generally set at an amount that ensures the defendant's appearance at trial. If the defendant cannot afford bail, a bail bond agent may supply a bond for a fee. Bail can also be denied; the Eighth Amendment does not guarantee the *right* to bail, only that it cannot be "excessive."

bail
The money or property pledged to the court or actually deposited with the court to effect the release of a person from legal custody.

Police at Trial. Once the pretrial process has concluded and the charges stand, a trial may or may not take place. If the defendant pleads guilty at arraignment, then a trial is not necessary. In this case, special steps must be taken to ensure that the defendant's guilty plea is valid. The defendant may agree to plead guilty in exchange for leniency from the prosecutor or the court. Plea bargaining of this nature can occur at any stage of the criminal justice process, that is, the defendant can reach a plea agreement with the prosecutor as early as the pretrial stage and, in fact, well into jury deliberations. Regardless of when it occurs, the plea bargain must be accepted by the court.

If the defendant pleads not guilty, the case is set for trial. Trials are usually scheduled for some date well after arraignment. This allows both the prosecution and the defense time to prepare their cases. A balance must be achieved between providing enough time for both sides to develop effective arguments and protecting the defendant's Sixth Amendment right to a speedy trial. During the preparation stage, discovery takes place. **Discovery** is the process through which each side in a criminal case learns what evidence the other side will present. Although strategies that the parties intend to use in court need not be shared, the identities of witnesses who will testify, the physical evidence in possession of both parties, and other items are all fair game in the discovery process.

discovery
The process through which each side in a criminal case learns what evidence the other side will present.

At trial, the prosecutor bears the burden of proving that the defendant is guilty beyond a reasonable doubt. This often entails calling on one or more investigative or arresting police officers to provide testimony. Once the prosecution presents its case, the defense steps in and presents its case. In doing so, it seeks to cast doubt on the prosecutor's evidence, and this may involve the cross-examination of police officers who have testified for the prosecution. Criminal trials bounce back and forth in this fashion until each side rests its case.

Once the prosecution and the defense have finished presenting their cases, a verdict must be reached. Depending on the seriousness of the offense, the verdict is decided by either a judge or a jury. Judges decide the defendant's fate in bench trials, but only for offenses that are likely to result in less than six months' imprisonment. In either case, police officers need to be prepared to be put under oath and provide testimony, usually for the prosecution, depending on the nature of the charges.

WEB PATROL 3-1
New York State Unified Court System, Criminal Justice Handbook.
http://www.mycrimekit.com

Police after Trial. The criminal justice process does not necessarily end once the verdict has been read. Sentencing usually takes place at a separate hearing. The guilty party may be sentenced to death (for a capital crime), committed to prison, fined, placed on probation, or subjected to a host of other possible sanctions. Probation is the most common sanction, but imprisonment and, of course, death are much more serious. When a person is committed to prison or sentenced to death, it may appear that the criminal justice process has been completed. In actuality, it has just begun. The appeals process can drag out for years beyond the criminal trial. Even when all appeals have been exhausted, it is possible for a convicted criminal to seek relief through other means, such as invoking a writ of habeas corpus.

Generally, police officers have little to no role during the sentencing hearing or appellate phase. They do, however, continue to work the same streets to which convicted criminals are eventually released. Clearly, many police officers thrive on putting away bad guys, but there is little excitement in arresting the same person over and over. It is therefore advantageous for police officers to work with officials whose responsibility involves the supervision of convicted criminals. Not only does such cooperation promote successful reintegration of offenders into society, but it can also assist the law enforcement function. Police officers who team with probation officers, for instance, can creatively circumvent the Fourth Amendment and search probationers with relative ease. Collaborative methods like this are taken up in the next two sections.

Relationships with Prosecutors

Whether they like it or not, and whether they know it or not, police officers work closely with prosecutors. They may have almost no direct contact with prosecutors, save, perhaps, for testifying against a defendant in a criminal trial. But prosecutors depend on police officers to bring them cases. Were it not for police officers, few prosecutors would be employed. It is generally not their responsibility to go find suspected criminals and press charges. The police take the first step. Likewise, the police depend on prosecutors. Prosecutors present the government's case against criminal defendants. When they fail in this regard, criminals are released back into society and become police officers' problem all over again. It is in the interest of both officials to work together, whether one-on-one or otherwise.

Throughout most of this country's recent history, prosecutors have been reactive, that is, they have waited until police officers brought them cases to prosecute. To a large extent, this model persists today; a number of prosecutors thrive on taking serious offenders to court and sending them to prison for long periods of time. These prosecutors rely on the police for the preparation of key aspects of the cases, such as documenting a confession. This traditional prosecutorial role has been described as follows:

> The traditional . . . prosecutor likes to think of himself as the consummate carnivore: a learned lawyer, a compelling oral advocate, a relentless pursuer of the truth who fights crime by putting "bad guys" in jail. His allies in this fight are the . . . investigative agencies. Those agencies identify trends in criminal behavior and "bring" the prosecutor the significant cases.[5]

It would be inaccurate to say that prosecutors are totally dependent on police officers for the preparation of their cases. Many prosecutors' offices have commissioned peace officers who serve as investigators. California is one state that follows this model. There is also much to be said about knowing the law and crafting an argument. Prosecutors cannot rely on police officers in this regard. Being lawyers, they know the law better than the typical police officer. A skilled prosecutor will take the evidence that the police present and use it creatively to mount an argument before a judge or jury.

The traditional prosecutors, then, act more or less reactively. They are not concerned with preventing crime, reaching out to other agencies, and collaborating with their law enforcement colleagues. Recently, though, prosecution has changed. Collaboration, especially with police, is gaining momentum. Prosecutors are becoming more receptive to partnering and collaboration with various entities inside and outside the criminal justice system. Police-prosecution partnerships are also becoming quite popular. We look at some of these later in this chapter.

Relationships with Corrections Officials

It is perhaps easier to conceive of close working relationships between police and prosecutors than between police and corrections officials. This may be because, in terms of the criminal justice process, police and prosecutors work more closely together in time than police and corrections officials. In other words, a case moves directly from the police department to the prosecutor's office, but not from the police to, say, a parole officer. With few exceptions, corrections officials usually enter the picture after the criminal trial and sentencing stages.

When we talk about "corrections officials" in this chapter, we are not referring to jail or prison officers. Rather, our concern is with relationships between police officers and both probation officers and parole officers. Police officers have learned that such relationships can be quite helpful.

Parole officers do much of the same work as police; for efficiency's sake alone, it just makes sense to collaborate. While parole officers supervise individuals who were recently released from prison, they cannot supervise their clients perfectly, partly because of the high caseloads some parole officers oversee. Consequently, police officers often encounter parolees. When parole officers and police officers work together, however, duplication of effort can be minimized. Also, some police departments are actively involving themselves in the reentry process, especially in the days right after the parolee is released from prison.

PARTNERSHIPS WITH OTHER LOCAL AGENCIES

Partnering is a hot topic in criminal justice today. It is happening through all stages of the criminal justice process, across all levels of government, and between agencies inside and outside the criminal justice system. Police, in particular, are partnering in unprecedented ways with prosecutors, corrections officials, and a host of other stakeholders. As a component of this partnering movement, police are also looking to the future and trying to prevent additional crimes before they occur. They are getting involved in the reintegration of parolees back into neighborhoods, for example. In short, law enforcement officials are getting tired of the revolving door that has all too often characterized criminal justice in the past and are doing their best to close it. Here we consider police-prosecutor partnerships, police-corrections partnerships, and the participation of police in reentry programs for parolees.

Police-Prosecution Partnerships

American prosecution is in the throes of change.[6] In a word, prosecution is becoming more strategic. **Strategic prosecution** is intended to shift prosecutors' attention from individual criminal cases brought to them by the police to an overall concern with preventing and reducing crime. Here is one author's take on strategic prosecution:

> Because it is the prosecutor who has the direct connections with . . . investigative agencies, it . . . falls on the prosecutor to determine whether there are intersections between the case on which the police have focused and cases that other . . . investigative agencies might be working in the same neighborhood.[7]

strategic prosecution
A prosecutorial tactic that shifts emphasis away from individual criminal cases brought by the police to an overall concern with preventing and reducing crime.

In other words, under strategic prosecution the prosecutor acts as one piece in a larger crime-control puzzle. Strategic prosecution emphasizes an awareness of crime trends, communication, creativity, and cooperation.

Another term used to describe this shift in how prosecutors do their jobs is **community prosecution**, which is to prosecutors what community policing is to police officers. (We will discuss community policing in Chapter 10.) Community prosecution is an approach intended to improve cooperation and collaboration between prosecutors and individuals outside the criminal justice system, such as community members and business leaders. Barbara Boland, one of the first authors to write about this emerging law enforcement strategy, gives this definition of community prosecution:

community prosecution
A prosecutorial approach intended to improve cooperation and collaboration between prosecutors and individuals outside the criminal justice system, such as community members and business leaders.

> More than anything else, community prosecution is an organizational response to the grassroots public safety demands of neighborhoods, as expressed in highly concrete terms by the people who live in them. They identify immediate, specific crime problems they want addressed and that the incident-based 911 system is ill suited to handle.[8]

All of this means that police officers and prosecutors are starting to collaborate more than ever before. Prosecutors, like police, are coming to realize that making a dent in the crime problem requires cooperation, such as prosecutors meeting one-on-one with police officers and training them on what it takes to make a solid case against a suspected criminal. Another example of such cooperation puts prosecutors out in the field with police officers. One of this text's authors spent a fair amount of time observing one such partnership in San Bernardino, California. There, a deputy district attorney and two city police officers worked together in a substation and drove around the neighborhood together, with the intent of reducing drug dealing, prostitution, vagrancy, and other quality-of-life problems.

Other examples of police-prosecution partnerships have been seen in Maine, Oregon, New Hampshire, New York City, and other places.[9] In 1987, Maine enacted a law that mandated cooperation between investigators and prosecutors to more effectively address the drug problem. The law led to the creation of the Maine Bureau of Intergovernmental Drug Enforcement, an office staffed by 50 law enforcement agents and eight prosecutors. In Multnomah County, Oregon, the Regional Organized Crime Narcotics Task Force brought together 12 investigators from several agencies in the area as well as two prosecutors. Their job was to work together to reduce the county's illegal narcotics problem.

A more recent example of a police-prosecutor team in action is Indianapolis's ROAD Team, which stands for Rub Out Aggressive Driving. Working together, police and prosecutors in Marion County, Indiana, have stepped up their efforts to combat reckless and dangerous driving. Among the tactics used in the ROAD program are strict enforcement of traffic laws and a media campaign intended to spread the word that dangerous driving will not be tolerated.[10] Police need to work collaboratively with other criminal justice agencies because they, like other agencies, are just part of a larger crime-control puzzle.

A police officer and a probation officer converse outside San Fernando High School in San Fernando, California. How can police and probation/parole officers join together to prevent crime?

A. Ramey/PhotoEdit Inc.

Police-Corrections Partnerships

police-corrections partnership
A collaboration between police officers and either probation officers or parole officers (mostly the former) that seeks to reduce crime by increasing the supervision of probationers or parolees.

Police-corrections partnerships are collaborations between police officers and either probation officers or parole officers (mostly the former). A recent government report describes police-corrections partnerships in this way:

> In recent years, police and correctional agencies in many jurisdictions have formed a variety of partnerships in which their staff collaborate to share information or jointly perform services in ways that benefit both agencies. Some of these partnerships are formalized—they are the product of a detailed planning process, have multiagency advisory and oversight boards, and operate pursuant to written procedures. Other partnerships are informal, having evolved because a handful of staff in the two or more agencies involved began talking about better ways to do their jobs. Some partnerships are mainly known only to those directly involved. Others have been widely publicized and have served as prototypes for new programs.[11]

Operation Nightlight
A police-corrections partnership in San Bernardino, California, that deployed two-person teams, each staffed by one probation officer and one police officer, to conduct home visits to juveniles newly placed on probation and to enforce curfew and truancy rules.

An example of one such partnership was San Bernardino's **Operation Nightlight** program, patterned after the Operation Night Light program in Boston, Massachusetts. California's program consisted of five two-person teams, each staffed by one probation officer and one police officer. These teams worked in the field to conduct home visits to juveniles just placed on probation. The teams enforced curfew and truancy rules and rewarded well-behaved probationers with trips to sporting events and other activities. What made Operation Nightlight unique from other police and probation practices is that officials from both agencies worked together in teams to enforce the conditions of probation.

Operation Nightlight in San Bernardino was basically an enhanced supervision program. In other words, it ensured that juveniles placed on probation received more supervision than they would under normal circumstances.[12] In some jurisdictions around the country, it is not uncommon for probation officers to have caseloads in excess of one or two hundred. Obviously, this makes the supervision of probationers somewhat difficult.

Other enhanced supervision programs like Operation Nightlight have been implemented in Minneapolis, Minnesota (Minneapolis Anti-Violence Initiative); Clark County, Washington (Clark County Anti-Gang Unit); New Haven, Connecticut (Project One Voice); Bellevue and Redmond, Washington (Smart Partners); and Maricopa County, Arizona (Neighborhood Probation).[13] In each of these five locations, police officers pair up with corrections officials, including probation and pa-

DOES IT WORK?

Police-Corrections Partnerships

While police-corrections partnerships appear promising, there are very few published studies examining their effectiveness. The best available evidence suggesting that these partnerships may reduce crime comes from Boston. During the heyday of Boston's Operation Night Light program, which began in 1992, there was a substantial reduction in homicides. The number of homicides in Boston dropped from 93 in 1993 to just 39 between January 1 and November 30, 1997. And between early 1995 and late 1997, there were no homicides at all among juveniles.[1] These numbers appear to support the program's effectiveness, but there were several other crime-control measures in place in the city during the same period. (Operation Ceasefire, which we discuss in this chapter, was one of them.)

Researchers recently completed a study looking at the effects on juvenile arrests of San Bernardino's police-corrections partnership.[2] They found that the program led to citywide reductions in arrests for assault, burglary, and theft, but they also found some increases in crime in surrounding areas, suggesting that the city's Operation Nightlight program may have displaced the juvenile crime problem to some extent.

In perhaps the most recent look at police-corrections partnerships, one of this book's authors teamed up with a colleague to examine the possible "dark side" of this approach to crime. We called it *mission distortion*:

> Mission distortion refers to situations where the definition of one's professional mission (or role) orientation becomes blurred. For instance, actively working with the police makes it convenient for some community corrections officers to gravitate toward a greater emphasis on law enforcement priorities at the expense of their responsibilities to provide services to their clients. Moreover, police-probation partnerships threaten to increase the likelihood of community corrections officers serving as stalking horses for police officers.[3]

Interestingly, mission distortion seems to work mostly in one direction and rarely results in the taking on of a community corrections role by police officers.

---

[1]D. Parent and B. Snyder, *Police-corrections partnerships* (Washington, DC: National Institute of Justice, 1999), p. 5.

[2]L. K. Gaines and J. L. Worrall, *Evaluation report: San Bernardino County Probation Department's Project Impact/Nightlight Program* (San Bernardino: California State University, San Bernardino, 2003). See also J. L. Worrall and L. K. Gaines, "The effect of police-probation partnerships on juvenile arrests," *Journal of Criminal Justice* 34 (2006): 579–89.

[3]D. W. Murphy and J. L. Worrall, "The threat of mission distortion in police-corrections partnerships," *Policing: An International Journal of Police Strategies and Management* 30 (2007): 132–49, quote on p. 133.

role officers, jail personnel, and sometimes other individuals. Figure 3-3 describes the target populations, features, and partners in each of these five police-corrections partnerships.

Aside from providing enhanced supervision, the police-corrections partners engage in other activities, such as apprehending fugitives and dealing with serious habitual offenders.[14] Still other teams have been organized for the purposes of sharing information, promoting sex-offender registration, reducing prison gang problems, revitalizing neighborhoods, providing services to offenders, and so on.[15]

Police and Parole Reentry

In his 2004 State of the Union address, then-President George W. Bush proposed a four-year, $300 million prisoner reentry initiative to expand job training and placement services for parolees, among other things. The anticipated availability of this level of funding encouraged criminal justice agencies and allied organizations, including police departments, to develop innovative reentry initiatives. This is a most interesting development because, historically, reentry was a parole concern, not a policing concern.

While most reentry monies have been allocated to departments of corrections and similar entities, many of these agencies have entered into partnerships with police. For example, Boston's Reentry Initiative draws on the services of the Boston Police Department to educate parolees about what they need to know when they reenter society.[16] Marion County, Indiana, held one-time reentry meetings with returning offenders to inform them (1) that the police were aware they were returning to the community, (2) what their likelihood of reoffending was, and (3) the types of support services that were available to help them stay straight.[17] A number of similar examples hail from around the United States.[18]

Boston's Operation Ceasefire program (which is discussed in the next section) included meetings with parolees as well as the aggressive enforcement of parole conditions. Washington State utilizes partnering in this fashion:

> [The program] uses community-based storefront locations, staffed by community volunteers and providing office space for police and parole officers. A beat officer is partnered with a

Figure 3-3 • Features of Five Police-Corrections Partnerships

Probation Projects

Program	Year Started	Target Population									Features						Partnering Agencies						
		Adults	Juveniles	Probationers	Parolees	Pretrial Relapse	Gangs/Gang Leaders	Violent Offenders	Sex Offenders	High-Risk/Habitual Offenders	Information Sharing	Colocated Staff	Joint Training	Joint Patrol	Joint Home Visits	Police Report Observed Violations	Community Boards	Law Enforcement	Probation/Parole	Jails	Other Criminal Justice Agencies	Created with New Funds	Program Has Been/Is Being Evaluated
Minneapolis Anti-Violence Initiative Minneapolis, MN	1995	√	√	√			√	√		√	√		√	√	√			√	√			√	√
Clark County Anti-Gang Unit Vancouver, WA	1996	√		√	√		√	√		√	√	√	√	√	√	√	√	√	√		√	√	
Project One Voice New Haven, CT	1997	√	√	√	√	√	√	√		√	√	√		√	√	√		√	√		√		
Smart Partners Bellevue/Redmond, WA	1995	√		√	√			√	√	√	√	√				√		√	√	√	√		
Maricopa County Community Probation Phoenix, AZ	1996	√		√							√					√	√	√	√				√
Totals		5	2	5	3	1	3	4	1	4	5	3	2	3	3	4	2	5	5	1	3	2	2

Source: Dale Parent and Brad Snyder, *Police-corrections partnerships* (Washington, DC: National Institute of Justice, 1999), p. 13.

parole officer in an effort to better understand the community context facing ex-offenders and facilitating more timely and effective intervention if problems arise.[19]

Another program in Spokane, Washington, has police officers working with corrections officers to enforce curfew laws and couples their efforts with the work of volunteer guardians who help parolees gain access to services like job training.[20] In another example, Vermont police officers serve on community review boards that evaluate treatment plan options and monitor parolees before they enter the community, so as to steer them in the right direction on release.

The Project Safe Neighborhoods program, which was begun by the Bush administration, is primarily aimed at curbing gun violence but also has a reentry component. An overview of that aspect of the program is provided in Figure 3-4.

A recent report describes police involvement in the reentry process this way:

> While still maintaining separation among agencies and mission, law enforcement agencies are enhancing their role in reentry by receiving and transmitting intelligence about reentering offenders. In addition, law enforcement personnel may meet with offenders before or after prison release to deliver a strong deterrence message. In states including Alabama and Iowa, videotapes have been developed by police, prosecutors, and corrections officials to deliver deterrence messages focused particularly on the sanctions available for felons caught in possession of or using a gun.[21]

WEB PATROL 3-2

The U.S. Department of Justice Prisoner Reentry Initiative
http://www.mycrimekit.com

Figure 3-4 • The Reentry Process

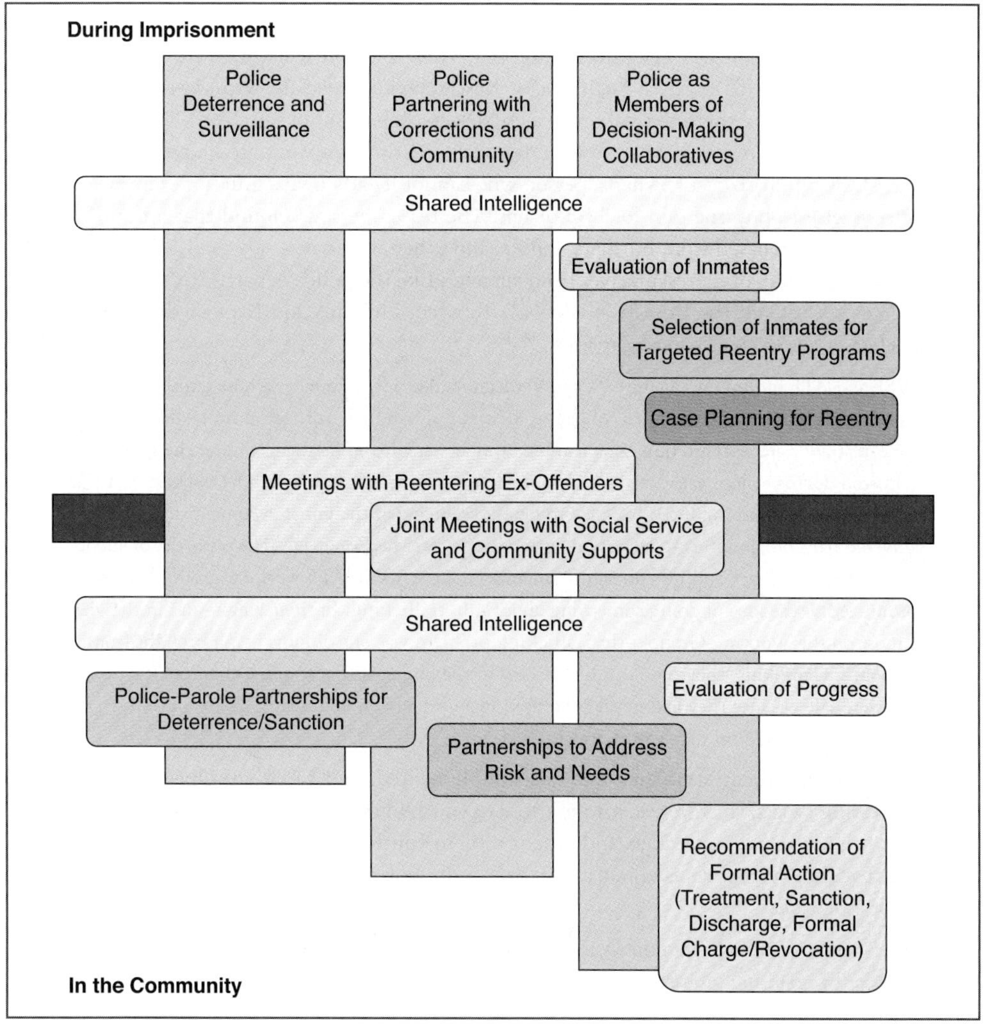

Source: E. F. McGarrell, C. R. Zimmerman, N. K. Hipple, N. Corsaro, and H. Perex, "The roles of the police in the offender reentry process," in *Prisoner reentry and community policing: Strategies for enhancing public safety*, (Washington, DC: Urban Institute, 2004), p. 37. Reprinted with permission.

PARTNERSHIPS WITH FEDERAL AGENCIES

Local police are teaming up with federal officials, partnering with such law enforcement agencies as the Drug Enforcement Administration. Police also partner with federal prosecutors, as in the recently developed Project Safe Neighborhoods program. More often than not, though, the partnerships involve local departments and federal officials from several agencies. It is not uncommon for municipal police departments, county sheriff's deputies, local prosecutors, federal prosecutors, and others to meet on a regular basis to formulate creative solutions to the problems of crime and disorder. One of the most noteworthy and celebrated examples of this approach is Boston's Operation Ceasefire program, which has since spawned other innovative programs throughout the country. Each is briefly addressed in the following subsections.

Operation Ceasefire
An initiative designed to disrupt the illegal gun market in the city of Boston. The initiative, originally called the Boston Gun Project, has achieved significant reductions in gun violence in the city.

Operation Ceasefire

Operation Ceasefire began as the Boston Gun Project. Its intent, simply, was to disrupt the illegal gun market in Boston. Like many large cities, Boston experienced a surge in youth gun violence during the late 1980s and early 1990s. The problem increased on the order of 230 percent, from 22 victims in 1987 to 73 in 1990. Since Operation Ceasefire began in 1995, evaluations have attributed significant reductions in gun violence to the intervention.[22]

Prior to the program, if a youth was caught with an illegal gun, he or she was charged with a crime, but little attention was given to finding out where the youth acquired the weapon. Operation Ceasefire turned this practice on its head. Researchers teamed up with various enforcement agencies and encouraged them to track gun sales back to their point of purchase. They began to notice, for instance, that many guns were illegally obtained through what are known as **straw purchases.** A straw purchase occurs when a person who cannot legally own a gun (for example, a youth) asks someone else to buy the gun for him or her. The researchers also found that a number of the guns were being purchased from burglars, fences, and other criminals.

straw purchase
An illegal gun purchase that occurs when a person who cannot legally own a gun (for example, a youth) asks someone else to buy the gun for him or her.

A working group of representatives from agencies like the police department's Youth Violence Strike Force (YVSF) and the Bureau of Alcohol, Tobacco, Firearms and Explosives (ATF) was also formed. Here is one of their success stories:

> YVSF and ATF built a case against a Cape Verdean named Jose Andrade, whose family lived on Wendover Street and who went to college in Mississippi. Andrade turned out to be using a network of straw purchasers to buy guns while he was at school, and he was bringing the guns back to Boston during school vacations to sell to the loose street crew with which he associated. YVSF arrested Andrade and...induced his crew to hand over many of the guns; in some instances, they delivered bags of handguns to officers at the Warren Street headquarters. The outbreak of shooting stopped and Joyce and his colleagues [members of the YVSF/ATF working group] became committed to the idea of doing something about gun trafficking. In their view—and in the view of most on the Working Group—the trafficking problem was one of guns being brought from the South. Gang kids, they thought, liked "new in the box," .380 or 9mm semiautomatic pistols that were safe because they had never been used in a crime before. Figuring out a solution to this problem became a Working Group priority.[23]

Various enforcement strategies were also implemented, and in one of Operation Ceasefire's more interesting twists, they were communicated to youth in the area. The working group convened meetings with active gang members and other problem youth (such as probationers) to drive home the point that they were serious about rooting out gun violence and to inform them of the consequences for violations.

> Gangs would be brought into the Dorchester courthouse, either through the Streetworkers' good offices or by requiring probationers to attend, and given a clear message about how violence would be treated in the future. These "forums," as they came to be called, were intended to make a graphic show of the new reality in Boston: A variety of agencies were working together and sharing information, with an enormous range of capacities to deploy and with violence as their only target.[24]

The enforcement strategy was multifaceted, creative, and complex. It consisted of a mix of the following:

- The focus of local, state, and federal authorities on intrastate firearms trafficking within Massachusetts in addition to interstate trafficking.
- Special enforcement attention on traffickers of those makes and calibers of handguns favored by gang members.
- Special enforcement attention on traffickers of handguns that had short time-to-crime intervals and thus were most likely to have been trafficked.
- Special enforcement attention on traffickers of handguns used by the city's most violent gangs.
- Efforts to restore the obliterated serial numbers of confiscated handguns and to investigate trafficking based on these restorations.
- Support of these enforcement priorities through strategic analyses of data generated by the Boston Police Department and ATF's comprehensive tracking of crime guns, and through the development of leads from the systematic debriefing of gang-affiliated arrestees involved in violent crime.
- The communication of successful investigations and prosecutions of gun traffickers to deter others from diverting firearms from retail sources to criminals and youth in Boston.[25]

Exile Programs

Project Exile was conceived in Richmond, Virginia, in 1994, shortly after the city experienced a significant increase in gun-related homicides. Through a coordinated team effort involving several individuals, the city adopted a three-pronged approach to gun violence.[26] First, federal prosecution was pursued because federal laws provide stiffer penalties for the use of firearms than Virginia's state law. Next, local, state, and federal law enforcement officials, including both police and prosecutors, worked together to reduce the city's homicide rate. Finally, Project Exile employed extensive community outreach and an aggressive media campaign to send a message to criminals that gun violence would not be tolerated.

Project Exile
A program established in Richmond, Virginia, that involves local, state, and federal law enforcement officials, including both police and prosecutors, working together to reduce the city's homicide rate.

The dramatic impact of this effort was reflected in official crime statistics, which showed a 57 percent drop in Richmond's homicide rate, from a peak of 160 in 1994 to 69 in 2001. Project Exile has also resulted in a high conviction rate (nearly 75 percent) and the seizure of nearly 1,000 illegal guns. Of course, it is difficult to conclude with certainty that Project Exile was solely responsible for this decline, but it certainly didn't hurt. According to one recent study, "While academic studies are needed to evaluate the extent to which these results are due to Project Exile, a positive impact on the Richmond community seems clear."[27] But a recent rigorous evaluation of Project Exile suggests that the reason declines were so apparent is because Richmond began the project with an unusually high homicide rate.[28] The drop, the authors of this report conclude, would have occurred eventually anyway.

Texas adopted Richmond's Project Exile model in January 2000[29] for two reasons. First, there was an increase in violent crime in the state during the late 1990s. Second, nearly 70 percent of violent offenders were reoffending within three years of their release from incarceration. The project was launched with a $1.6 million grant from then-Governor George W. Bush to the state attorney general's office. As of this writing, Texas Exile is being implemented in ten cities throughout the state.

Texas Exile consists of a partnership between several agencies: the Criminal Justice Division of the governor's office; the attorney general of Texas; district and county attorneys; the local U.S. attorney's office; local and state law enforcement agencies; and ATF. Besides partnering, one of Texas Exile's key strategies is community outreach. Indeed, the Texas attorney general's office dedicated $360,000 to fund a public-awareness campaign. The advertising slogan, "Gun Crime Means Hard Time," was borrowed from Fort Worth's Safe Cities program. Various media were used to publicize the campaign, including billboards, radio ads, television commercials, newspapers, bus benches, grocery carts, hats, T-shirts, delivery trucks, posters, and flyers.

Like Richmond's Project Exile, Texas Exile has not been subjected to rigorous evaluation. It appears, however, that the project has had a significant impact. In its first two years of operation,

- The project has resulted in nearly 1,500 indictments and 1,000 convictions.
- Judges sentenced offenders to an average of 72 months in federal prison.
- There was a massive increase in the prosecution of federal gun cases.
- Two thousand illegal guns were taken off the street.[30]

Between 1996 and 1999, the Seattle, Washington, area faced an increase in firearms prosecutions, and rates of juvenile firearm crime increased during the same period. In the space of one year, incidents involving the use of firearms by juveniles doubled.[31] In response to these developments, the Fire Arm Crime Enforcement (FACE) Coalition was established in 1999.

FACE operates within the borders of King County, Washington—a large metropolitan county with Seattle as its largest city. The program relies on collaboration between numerous agencies, including every local police department in the county; the King County Sheriff's Office; the King County prosecutor's office; the Washington State Crime Lab; ATF; the Washington Department of Fish and Game; and the Federal Bureau of Investigation. The program's two key elements are (1) coordinated prosecution of gun violence and (2) increased supervision and tracking of repeat offenders once they are released from prison. FACE, which has received accolades from the International Association of Chiefs of Police, has five goals:

1. To improve the quality of police investigations and case reports.
2. To increase the effectiveness of criminal prosecution.
3. To expedite the processing of firearms cases by police officers and prosecutors.
4. To identify "armed career criminal" cases for federal prosecution.
5. To increase the level of cooperation and information exchange between all agencies within the criminal justice system.[32]

Surprisingly, FACE has not been formally evaluated, even though elements of the program have been in place since as early as 1992. Thus it is difficult to comment with certainty on the effect of the program, but given the lengths to which agencies have gone to work together and the positive reputation the program has established, it cannot be worsening the gun violence situation in King County, Washington.

In 1998, Baltimore County, Maryland, ranked as the second most violent out of the 30 most populated counties in America. It witnessed a decade-long string of some 300 homicides annually. And while national figures showed an overall decline in homicide throughout most of the 1990s, Baltimore County's homicide rate actually increased. In response to these alarming figures, the Baltimore City State's Attorney's Office implemented an enhanced gun-prosecution program known as Project Disarm.[33] The project was implemented in 1994 and then expanded through the development of a specialized unit called the Firearms Investigation Violence Enforcement (FIVE) Division. This unit's purpose was to deal with gun cases that were eligible for federal prosecution.

Like the other partnerships discussed previously, Project Disarm relies on extensive interagency cooperation and coordination. It began as a joint venture of the U.S. attorney's office, the Baltimore Police Department, the Baltimore County State's Attorney's Office, and ATF. It has since been expanded to include county law enforcement officials and other federal, state, and local agencies. Project Disarm has resulted in a significant number of guns and gun criminals being removed from the streets,[34] but it is unclear whether the project has reduced the overall rate of gun violence in Baltimore.

Project Safe Neighborhoods

Project Safe Neighborhoods
A federal initiative that attempts to curb gun violence by linking existing local programs together and providing them with necessary tools.

In May 2001, President Bush announced that $901 million would be set aside over a three-year period to combat gun violence. The resulting program, **Project Safe Neighborhoods (PSN),** is designed to promote interagency (especially local-federal) coordination to find new and creative ways to deal with gun violence.[35] According to the program's website,

> Project Safe Neighborhoods is a comprehensive, strategic approach to reducing gun violence in America. The various crime reduction initiatives in the past decade have taught us that to have a truly significant impact, the federal government must do more than just increase its

U.S. Senator John Cornyn, R-TX, at a Judiciary Committee hearing on "Project Safe Neighborhoods: America's Network against Gun Violence." Some federally sponsored PSN programs incorporate a gun case referral system, where local and federal prosecutors screen gun cases to determine the most appropriate jurisdiction for prosecution. Cases that are prosecuted federally generally result in substantially higher sentences than state prosecutions, effectively removing gun predators from the streets. What other ways do you see to reduce gun violence in America?

Newscom

Figure 3-5 • The Five Prongs of the Project Safe Neighborhoods Program

1. Partnerships—Local gun crime task forces will include
   - U.S. attorneys
   - State and local prosecutors
   - Special agents in charge (ATF, FBI)
   - Chiefs of police
   - Other community and law enforcement leaders working together to
     - Develop district or statewide strategies to reduce gun violence
     - Prepare gun cases for prosecution in the most appropriate jurisdictions
     - Seek the most appropriate venue for firearm prosecutions
2. Strategic planning—a proactive approach
   - Intelligence gathering
     - Crime mapping
     - Identifying hot spots
     - Tracing
     - Ballistics technology
   - Enforcement policy
     - Where best to prosecute gun crimes
     - Let states do what states do best
     - Let feds do what feds do best
3. Training—coordinating interagency training and cross-training
   - Training at the National Advocacy Center
   - Regional gun crime training
   - Local gun crime training
4. Outreach—Promote aggressive enforcement publicly by showing criminals that they will do "Hard Time for Gun Crime."
   - The genius is in the deterrent message to would-be criminals and the supporting prevention message
   - Public service announcements
   - Educational literature
   - Crime prevention tool kits
   - Billboard advertisements
   - Press releases and news articles
   - Other community-engagement opportunities
5. Accountability
   - Success is based on "outcome" rather than "output."
   - The goal is to reduce the violent crime rate in our communities.

Source: Project Safe Neighborhoods, www.psn.gov.

> arrest and prosecution numbers. Our efforts must be comprehensive. We must build effective partnerships with our state and local counterparts. We must enhance our capacity to obtain and analyze crime and other data that should guide our strategies and afford us the opportunity to measure the impact of our efforts. We must maintain an edge in the attack on gun violence by providing expansive and comprehensive training for federal, state, and local law enforcement officers and prosecutors. We must convey the priorities, message, and results of our efforts to the media and community members. And we must build a powerful and lasting coalition with our citizens—one that empowers them to be agents of change in their own communities.[36]

Project Safe Neighborhoods prides itself on a five-pronged approach to gun violence. The five prongs—partnerships, strategic planning, training, outreach, and accountability—and their various constituent elements are presented in Figure 3-5. To get a feel for the breadth and depth of Project Safe Neighborhoods, consider this list of appropriations for a single fiscal year:

- \$39.3 million to U.S. attorney's offices.
- \$15 million in grants to combat juvenile gun crime.
- \$45 million in grants to the states for gun-violence-reduction efforts.
- \$25 million in grants to the states to provide safety locks for handguns.

- $35 million in grants to improve state criminal history records.
- $13 million to ATF for cooperative agreements for the Gang Resistance Education and Training (GREAT) program.[37]

One of the hallmarks of PSN is a careful review of gun cases. Training is conducted to ensure that cases presented to prosecutors are of the highest caliber. Local and federal prosecutors, along with police, then put their heads together and decide on the best approach for handling specific gun offenses. They decide, for instance, whether federal charges should be pursued in lieu of state charges. Local law enforcement gets involved in a number of respects. In the Western District of Tennessee, for instance, representatives from the U.S. attorney's office attend roll call meetings at the local police department.[38] In the Middle and Southern Districts of Alabama, U.S. attorneys visit local police departments and encourage officers to bring gun cases to them (in consultation with local prosecutors).[39] This is a most interesting and unprecedented development, as one team of researchers attests:

> For many in the local and state criminal justice systems, the U.S. Attorney's office has long been a source of isolation and not been actively involved in what were perceived to be "local" crime problems. In fact, in many jurisdictions the only experience local law enforcement has had with the U.S. Attorney was public corruption cases. Breaking down those barriers by making the U.S. Attorney's office and its staff more accessible and increasing knowledge about the federal process are important indirect benefits of the case review process.[40]

WEB PATROL 3-3

Project Safe Neighborhoods
http://www.mycrimekit.com

MILITARY PARTNERSHIPS AND MILITARIZATION

Most of us are familiar with the federal government's announced wars on drugs and on crime. To some, these connote nothing more than serious stances with respect to law-breaking. To others, the war metaphor means much more. For better or worse, it signals a blurring of the lines between the military and the police. Should this be cause for alarm? The **Posse Comitatus Act,** passed in 1878, generally prohibits federal military personnel and the National Guard (under federal authority) from engaging in local law enforcement activities. (Note the "under federal authority" language; it is quite appropriate and common for state governors to rely on the National Guard for enforcement functions in times of emergency and crisis.) Thus anything that looks like active collaboration between the military and local police raises some eyebrows.

Posse Comitatus Act
U.S. legislation passed in 1878 that generally prohibits federal military personnel and the National Guard (under federal authority) from engaging in local law enforcement activities.

While there are no apparent signs of the military replacing local police, the two are certainly working together closely. According to Peter Kraska and Victor Kappeler, two researchers who have studied this progression closely, "By the early 1990s, all branches of the military, including most state national guards, were becoming 'socially useful' by involving themselves in both domestic and international drug law enforcement."[41] This pattern, they note, has become more obvious since the end of the cold war because, in their view, the military has almost been searching for a purpose. Whether this is true today, in light of the "war on terror," is not totally clear. On the one hand, the various branches of the military certainly have their hands full in the Middle East; on the other hand, the "war on terror" begs for collaboration between police and the military.

Even before September 11, however, there were plenty of other signs of police-military partnerships. At the height of the "war on drugs" during the late 1980s, for instance, the Bush administration created several Department of Defense–sponsored joint task forces that included military personnel and local law enforcement agencies. Their role was to coordinate drug interdiction efforts at the borders and abroad—and interdiction efforts here in the States.[42] "This arrangement required substantial overlap and cooperation between the military and civilian police forces," Kraska and Kappeler note.[43]

The Police-Military Connection

If the links between the police and the military are not clear, here is an eloquent observation that brings the point home:

> Perhaps the most striking feature of the modern epoch is the homogeneity of forms of physical coercion. Armed forces, police forces, paramilitary forces around the world make use of the same

> type of military technology. . . . With the help of advisors and training courses, forms of command, patterns of operations, methods of recruitment also bear a global resemblance. For the first time in history, soldiers and policemen from different societies have more in common with each other than the societies from which they come.[44]

Perhaps the most concrete example of police-military partnering is that of **police paramilitary units (PPUs)**, also known as *special weapons and tactics (SWAT) teams*, *tactical units*, *special operations units*, *strike teams*, and so forth. While these are distinctly law enforcement tools and disconnected from any command relationship with the military, PPUs operate much like military units. Indeed, it is not uncommon for PPU members to train with one or more branches of the military. Kraska and Kappeler found that 43 percent of the officers in PPUs they surveyed trained with active military personnel, and some were members of the Army reserve.[45] This, they argue, is changing the face of American policing:

police paramilitary unit (PPU)
A specially trained and equipped law enforcement unit that trains with one or more branches of the military and uses military tactics and techniques.

> Initially these units constituted a small portion of police efforts and were limited to large urban police departments. The constructed and publicly understood role of PPUs was confined to rare situations involving hostages, terrorism, or the "maniac sniper." Despite the camouflage of these common assumptions, there have been recent unmistakable signs of intensifying military culture in police departments. Although these units are highly secretive about their operations, obvious expressions of militarism are found throughout contemporary policing in the form of changing uniforms, weaponry, language, training, and tactics.[46]

Police Paramilitary Units

Most of us don't have occasion to see PPUs except in the movies and on television. It is worth pointing out, then, the distinguishing features of these units. Kraska and Kappeler point to several such features[47]:

- Military-style equipment and technology.
- Common use of the Heckler & Koch MP5 submachine gun.
- Deployment of sophisticated weaponry, including tactical semiautomatic shotguns, M16 automatic rifles, sniper rifles, and automatic shotguns known as *street sweepers*.
- Deployment of less-than-lethal technology, such as percussion grenades.
- Use of tools for "dynamic entries," such as during the service of high-risk warrants.
- Use of battering rams, hydraulic door spreaders, and even C-4 explosives.
- Deployment of armored or military personnel carriers and specially equipped "tactical cruisers."
- Organizational structures that parallel those of military special operations groups.
- Deployment of officers dressed in black or "urban camouflage" and wearing Kevlar helmets, body armor, and so on.
- A tactical focus on "high-risk" work, including serving warrants, managing civil riots, responding to terrorism, and dealing with hostage situations and barricaded suspects.

Kraska and Kappeler conducted a survey to gauge the extent and use of police paramilitary units and found a growing reliance on PPUs in cities with more than 50,000 people. "In 1982, about 59 percent of the police departments surveyed had a PPU. By 1990, this figure had increased to 78 percent, and by 1995 it reached 89 percent."[48]

They also found increasing "normalization" of PPUs, meaning that the PPUs are taking on less traditional roles, focusing on more than just "high-risk" situations. More than 20 percent of the agencies that responded to the researchers' survey reported using PPUs for proactive patrol work, such as suppressing gang violence, the illicit drug trade, and other problems. One commander of a large city police department reported how his chief bought a "SWAT bus" that could carry upwards of 30 tactical officers in military gear out into the town to do patrol work.[49] And in a somewhat ironic twist of events, one department that touted community policing reported this about using PPUs for patrol:

> We're into saturation patrols in hot spots. We do a lot of our work with the SWAT unit because we have bigger guns. We send out two, two-to-four man cars, we look for minor violations and

> do jump-outs, either on people on the street or automobiles. After we jump out, the second car provides periphery cover with an ostentatious display of weaponry. We're sending a clear message: If the shootings don't stop, we'll shoot someone.[50]

This police department even used some community policing money for these patrols. Some would call this creative patrol. Others would say it's antithetical to the ideals of community policing. It is interesting to note that while there is all this talk of relationship building, community justice, citizen interaction, and the like, police departments in many American cities are adopting a very militaristic stance with respect to crime. We discuss this issue further when we cover the "war on terror" and international collaboration in Chapter 16. For now, though, we close with yet another interesting observation from frontline personnel on collaboration between the police and the military. This came straight from an officer involved in a large city police department's PPU:

> We've had special forces folks who have come right out of the jungles of Central and South America. . . . All branches of the military service are involved in providing training to law enforcement. U.S. Marshals act as liaisons between the police and the military to set up the training—our go-between. They have an arrangement with the military through JTF-6 (Joint Task Force Six). . . . I just received a piece of paper from a four-star general who tells us he's concerned about the type of training we're getting. We've had teams of Navy Seals and Army Rangers come here and teach us everything. We just have to use our judgment and exclude the information like: "at this point we bring in the mortars and blow the place up."[51]

SUMMARY

- The police are central participants in the overall criminal justice system. They participate in the criminal justice process during the pretrial, trial, and post-trial stages, and they interact regularly with prosecutors and corrections officials.
- Partnerships are becoming increasingly common in criminal justice, and police agencies frequently partner with prosecutors and corrections officials to prevent and solve crimes.
- Local police also partner with federal agencies. The best-known federal-local partnerships are Operation Ceasefire, Exile, and Project Safe Neighborhoods.
- Police agencies frequently work with military units for training. Police paramilitary units are increasingly adopting military technology and tactics for law enforcement.

COMING FULL CIRCLE

For Discussion

Return to the questions posed at the start of this chapter. Have any of your answers changed since you read the chapter? What portions of this chapter helped you answer these questions?

Writing Assignment

Using material from this chapter and additional resources, write a 500-word essay in response to one of the questions presented at the beginning of the chapter. Submit your essay to your instructor if asked to do so.

KEY TERMS AND NAMES

arraignment
bail
booking
community prosecution
discovery
guilty
nolo contendere
not guilty
Operation Ceasefire
Operation Nightlight
police-corrections partnership
police paramilitary unit (PPU)
Posse Comitatus Act
Project Exile
Project Safe Neighborhoods
strategic prosecution
straw purchase

WEB INTERACTIVITY

Visit Project Safe Neighborhoods on the Web at http://psn.gov. As the site notes, the U.S. Department of Justice recently sponsored the Project Safe Neighborhoods Anti-Gang Training pilot in Dover, Delaware. According to PSN, "Approximately 160 law enforcement agents and criminal justice practitioners attended the training, which presented the gang expertise of DOJ law enforcement and criminal justice professionals in a comprehensive curriculum." Intervention, prevention, suppression, and reentry strategies were presented to attendees, who also received a briefing on national and regional gang trends. A community gang problem-assessment strategy was offered, and tips for working with cooperating witnesses and confidential informants were provided.

Next, visit the PSN Anti-Gang Training page at http://www.iir.com/psnagt, and view the list of national partners that participate in the training program. How does that list illustrate the kinds of relationships between state, local, and federal agencies that are discussed in this chapter? Explore the site, and describe those relationships in as much detail as you can. Submit your description to your instructor if asked to do so.

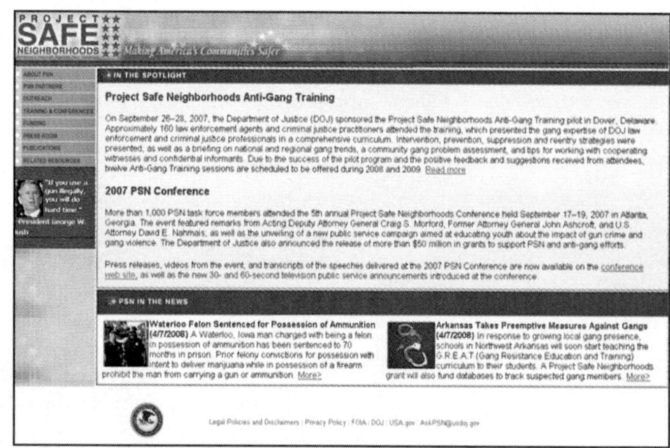

U.S. Department of Justice

REVIEW QUESTIONS

1. Describe the police role in the criminal justice process.
2. How do police agencies partner with other local criminal justice agencies? Why do they?
3. What are federal-local partnerships as they pertain to policing? Give three examples.
4. How do the police partner with the military? Discuss the pros and cons of such partnerships.

chapter four

LAW ENFORCEMENT AGENCIES AND THEIR ORGANIZATION

LEARNING OBJECTIVES

After reading this chapter, students should be able to:

1. Identify a number of important federal law enforcement agencies and their roles and distinguish between two models of state law enforcement, providing examples of each.
2. Identify differences between police departments and other types of organizations and describe both traditional and contemporary approaches to organization.

ENT – CITY OF LOS ANGELES

THINK ABOUT IT

Joe Arpaio, the controversial sheriff of Maricopa County, Arizona, is well known for his desert jail's "tent city," where inmates sometimes live outside in 110-degree heat. Arpaio is also famous for the pink underwear that he requires male inmates to wear (and that is sold to them to raise revenue for the county) and for the chain gangs that he reinstituted. On one occasion, Arpaio even had his inmates marched down public streets wearing only their pink underwear.

Although the sheriff has some supporters, he has also attracted criticism, both internationally and locally. In 2005, a Scottish judge decided not to extradite a Catholic priest back to Arizona to face molestation charges because Arpaio, he said, takes "a chillingly sadistic pleasure in his role as incarcerator. It [is] the duty of any Irish court to see that no citizen [is] handed over to such a regime."[1]

Some residents of Maricopa County became so critical of Arpaio's policies that a recall petition got under way in 2007. The petition was set into motion, in part, due to the suspicious death of inmate Scott Norberg in 1996. Arpaio was cleared of any personal wrongdoing, but Norberg's family filed a civil lawsuit, which the county settled for $8.25 million. In 2008, recall efforts targeting Arpaio fell by the wayside as supporters failed to get enough signatures to have it placed on the county's ballot.

Sheriff Arpaio represents an "extreme case" in the world of law enforcement executives—a phrase that he applied to himself in a book he coauthored with Len Sherman, *America's Toughest Sheriff: How We Can Win the War against Crime*. Arpaio has been reelected three times since he first took office in 1992.

The case of Joe Arpaio raises a number of important questions to keep in mind as you read this chapter:

1. If voters are dissatisfied with the performance of an elected sheriff, should they recall the sheriff or simply allow him or her to serve out the term?
2. Are Sheriff Arpaio's policies outrageous?
3. Would an appointed city police chief be allowed to adopt policies similar to Arpaio's?

INTRODUCTION

How many police agencies are there? What are the key federal law enforcement agencies? Where is most law enforcement concentrated? How are federal, state, and local agencies organized? How do law enforcement agencies differ from other types of organizations? How are they run? How are they structured? This chapter provides answers to all these questions. We begin with a look at the many organizations of law enforcement. Then we consider how these agencies are organized, or structured, and how their structures differ from that of other organizations.

There are three key points to keep in mind as you read this chapter. First, the events of September 11, 2001, drastically changed the organization of the federal law enforcement apparatus. Had this book been written before 2001, this chapter would look very different. Second, each agency (and each *type* of agency) has its own mission, domain, issues, and relationships with other agencies. As our chapter's opening story makes clear, sheriffs sometimes act quite differently—perhaps due to their elected status—than their municipal counterparts. Finally, in light of recent reform efforts, traditional approaches to organizing law enforcement agencies may be becoming outmoded.

LAW ENFORCEMENT AGENCIES

The federal government has a number of its own enforcement agencies, as does each state government. Additionally, county- and municipal-level agencies can be all across the country, including specialized agencies that don't necessarily fit neatly into any government category.

A prisoner in ankle chains walks out of the federal building in Albany, New York, after federal agents and local police raided the Masjid As-Salam mosque on Central Avenue in Albany. The arrestee, a Bangladeshi immigrant and owner of a pizza shop, was taken into custody after he and another man allegedly agreed to a request by an FBI informant to launder money to be used in support of a terrorist attack. How can different kinds of law enforcement agencies work together to prevent terrorism and other crimes?

Syracuse Newspapers/Dennis Net/The Image Works

How Many Are There?

Counting the number of law enforcement agencies in America is not unlike counting the number of citizens. The decennial census of people living in the United States always falls short on some level because the number of residents does not remain constant. Some people die; others are born. Not surprisingly, police agencies follow similar patterns. New agencies are created when newly incorporated cities need their own police force. Merging municipalities and shrinking towns can lead to the combination or elimination of police departments. This makes counting cops a difficult task at best.

Determining how many police agencies are out there is also difficult because there is no central directory of such agencies. Researchers have been forced to offer up estimates of how many law enforcement agencies—and law enforcement personnel—are at work in America. They have sometimes relied on the Uniform Crime Reporting (UCR) Program of the Federal Bureau of Investigation (FBI) to count police agencies because UCR Program data are submitted to the FBI by individual police agencies. Other researchers have based their estimates on federal databases used to track local agencies that have received public safety grants.

These and other sources of data have yielded widely varying estimates of the number of law enforcement agencies in the United States today. Some researchers have identified as few as 15,000 agencies, others as many as 40,000. What's the actual number? One of the more rigorous studies in this area relied on various sources of data and came up with a very defensible estimate of a little more than 20,000 federal, state, and local agencies.[2] The study's authors also estimated that these agencies employ some 680,000 sworn personnel.[3] That translates into roughly one sworn law enforcement officer for every 440 people.[4]

Federal Agencies

There are many federal law enforcement agencies, especially if we define them as any agency charged with the enforcement of federal laws. Most arms of the federal government have at least some enforcement component. The Internal Revenue Service, for example, has its own criminal enforcement division. Likewise, the U.S. Fish and Wildlife Service's Office of Law Enforcement ensures that relevant statutes are upheld. Even the various branches of the military have their own law enforcement arms. A comprehensive list of federal law enforcement agencies is provided in Figure 4-1. These enforcement agencies don't exactly come to mind, however, when we think about federal law enforcement. Instead, it is the familiar agencies like the FBI and the Drug Enforcement Administration that come to mind. A focus on these well-known agencies shortens the list considerably.

Figure 4-1 • Federal Law Enforcement Agencies

Department of Agriculture

U.S. Forest Service

Department of Commerce

Bureau of Export Enforcement

National Marine Fisheries Administration

Department of Defense

Air Force Office of Special Investigations

Army Criminal Investigation Division

Defense Criminal Investigative Service

Naval Investigative Service

Department of Energy

National Nuclear Safety Administration

Office of Mission Operations

Office of Secure Transportation

Department of Health and Human Services

Food and Drug Administration, Office of Criminal Investigations

Department of Homeland Security

Federal Law Enforcement Training Center

Federal Protective Service

Transportation Security Administration

U.S. Coast Guard

U.S. Customs and Border Protection (CBP)—includes U.S. Border Patrol

U.S. Immigration and Customs Enforcement (ICE)

U.S. Secret Service

Department of the Interior

Bureau of Indian Affairs

Bureau of Land Management

Fish and Wildlife Service

National Park Service

U.S. Park Police

Department of Justice

Bureau of Alcohol, Tobacco, Firearms and Explosives

Bureau of Prisons

Drug Enforcement Administration

Federal Bureau of Investigation

U.S. Marshals Service

Department of Labor

Office of Labor Racketeering

Department of State

Diplomatic Security Service

Department of Transportation

Federal Air Marshals Program

Department of the Treasury

Internal Revenue Service–Criminal Investigation Division

Treasury Inspector General for Tax Enforcement

Department of Veterans Affairs

Office of Security and Law Enforcement

U.S. Postal Service

Postal Inspection Service

Other Offices with Enforcement Personnel

Administrative Office of the U.S. Courts

AMTRAK Police

Bureau of Engraving and Printing Police

Environmental Protection Agency–Criminal Investigations Division

Federal Reserve Board

Tennessee Valley Authority

U.S. Capitol Police

U.S. Mint

U.S. Supreme Court Police

Washington, DC, Metropolitan Police Department

Source: Frank Schmalleger, *Criminal Justice Today*, 10th ed. (Upper Saddle River, NJ: Prentice Hall, 2008).

Homeland Security Act of 2002
U.S. legislation enacted after the terrorist attacks of September 11, 2001, that created the cabinet-level Department of Homeland Security.

Before the September 11, 2001, attacks on the United States, it was somewhat difficult to succinctly describe the organization of federal law enforcement. Agencies were housed in a number of different cabinet-level departments, including Justice, Treasury, Agriculture, Energy, and Health and Human Services. After September 11, America witnessed one of the most significant efforts to restructure the federal government in generations.

The **Homeland Security Act of 2002** created what is now known as the Department of Homeland Security (DHS), a cabinet-level department. Homeland Security now houses a number of law enforcement agencies that, prior to September 11, used to be found scattered throughout the federal government. The names of some of these agencies also changed. It has been a few years now since these changes were ushered in, but people are still sometimes confused about the names and parent agencies of various federal law enforcement agencies. To make sense out of the new organization, we will build our discussion of these agencies around two categories. We will begin with the law enforcement agencies found within Homeland Security and then discuss those found within the U.S. Department of Justice (DOJ).

WEB PATROL 4-1

U.S. Department of Homeland Security
http://www.mycrimekit.com

Homeland Security Agencies. The Department of Homeland Security now houses the U.S. Secret Service. The Secret Service used to be located within the Department of the Treasury. The move to DHS became effective on March 1, 2003. DHS also houses what used to be called the U.S. Customs Service. It is now called Customs and Border Protection (CBP). Finally, what used to be called the Immigration and Naturalization Service (INS) has basically been split into two separate entities, Immigration and Customs Enforcement (ICE) and Citizenship and Immigration Services (CIS). The first of these is of special interest to us here.

The Secret Service The U.S. **Secret Service** performs two functions: protection and criminal investigation. Its mission statement reads:

U.S. Secret Service
The federal law enforcement agency tasked with providing executive protection to specific federal officials and with investigating violations of laws relating to counterfeiting of obligations and securities of the United States; financial crimes including access device fraud, financial institution fraud, identity theft, and computer fraud; and computer-based attacks on our nation's financial, banking, and telecommunications infrastructure.

> The Secret Service protects the President and Vice President, their families, heads of state, and other designated individuals; investigates threats against these protectees; protects the White House, Vice President's Residence, Foreign Missions, and other buildings within Washington, D.C.; and plans and implements security designs for designated National Special Security Events. The Secret Service also investigates violations of laws relating to counterfeiting of obligations and securities of the United States; financial crimes that include, but are not limited to, access device fraud, financial institution fraud, identity theft, computer fraud; and computer-based attacks on our nation's financial, banking, and telecommunications infrastructure.[5]

The Secret Service is perhaps best known for its role in protecting the president and other government officials and their families. Tourists to the White House also see the Secret Service's uniformed officers protecting the president's residence. These individuals are members of the Secret Service's Uniformed Division. The agency was first created, though, to suppress counterfeit currency (Figure 4-2). From its beginnings in 1865, that has been one of the agency's primary functions (Figure 4-3). That is why, prior to September 11, the Secret Service was housed in the Treasury Department. The Counterfeit Division, however, is only one of several nonprotection divisions within the Secret Service.

> The Financial Crimes Division engages in a wide range of enforcement functions. It plans, reviews, and coordinates criminal investigations involving Financial Systems Crimes, including bank fraud; access device fraud; telemarketing; telecommunications fraud (cellular and hard wire); computer fraud; automated payment systems and teller machines; direct deposit; investigations of

Figure 4-2 • History of the U.S. Secret Service

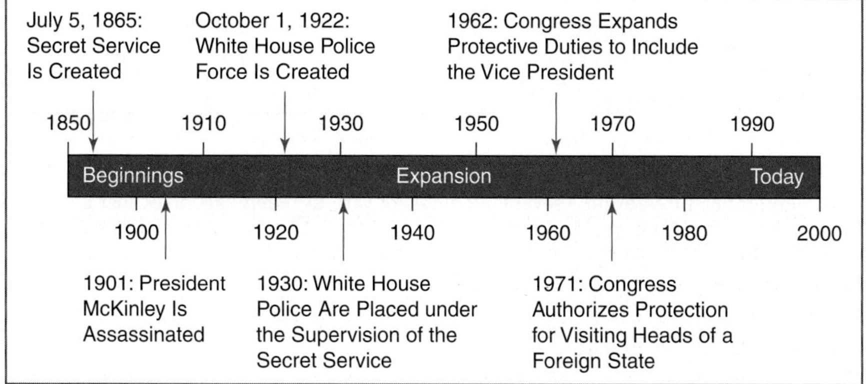

Source: U.S. Secret Service, "Secret Service History," http://www.secretservice.gov/history.shtml.

Figure 4-3 • Techniques for Detecting Counterfeit Money

Portrait

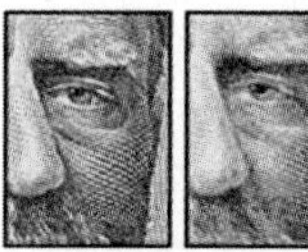

The genuine portrait appears lifelike and stands out distinctly from the background. The counterfeit portrait is usually lifeless and flat. Details merge into the background which is often too dark or mottled.

Federal Reserve and Treasury Seals

On a genuine bill, the saw-tooth points of the Federal Reserve and Treasury seals are clear, distinct, and sharp. The counterfeit seals may have uneven, blunt, or broken saw-tooth points.

Border

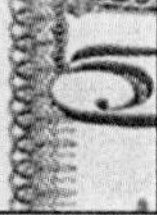

The fine lines in the border of a genuine bill are clear and unbroken. On the counterfeit, the lines in the outer margin and scrollwork may be blurred and indistinct.

Serial Numbers

Genuine serial numbers have a distinctive style and are evenly spaced. The serial numbers are printed in the same ink color as the Treasury Seal. On a counterfeit, the serial numbers may differ in color or shade of ink from the Treasury seal. The numbers may not be uniformly spaced or aligned.

Paper

Genuine currency paper has tiny red and blue fibers embedded throughout. Often counterfeiters try to simulate these fibers by printing tiny red and blue lines on their paper. Close inspection reveals, however, that on the counterfeit note the lines are printed on the surface, not embedded in the paper. It is illegal to reproduce the distinctive paper used in the manufacturing of United States currency.

Source: U.S. Department of Homeland Security, "Know Your Money," http://www.secretservice.gov/money_detect.shtml.

money laundering
The process by which criminals or criminal organizations seek to disguise the illicit nature of their proceeds by introducing them into the stream of legitimate commerce and finance.

Customs and Border Protection (CBP)
The U.S. law enforcement agency, established after the terrorist attacks on September 11, 2001, that combined the entire U.S. Border Patrol with portions of the U.S. Customs Service, U.S. Immigration, and the Animal and Plant Health Inspection Service. CBP was given the mission of controlling and protecting America's borders and ports of entry, including international airports and international shipping ports.

> forgery, uttering, alteration, false personation, or false claims involving U.S. Treasury Checks, U.S. Savings Bonds, U.S. Treasury Notes, bonds, and bills; electronic funds transfer (EFT) including Treasury disbursements and fraud within Treasury payment systems; fraud involving U.S. Department of Agriculture Food Coupons and Authority to Participate (ATP) cards; Federal Deposit Insurance Corporation investigations; Farm Credit Administration violations; fraud and related activity in connection with identification documents and fraudulent commercial, fictitious instruments, foreign securities.[6]

The Financial Crimes Division also investigates organized crime and **money laundering.** The Secret Service's Forensic Services Division assists with these and counterfeit currency investigations. As of this writing, the Secret Service employs several thousand agents in more than 125 offices worldwide.

Customs and Border Protection The establishment of U.S. **Customs and Border Protection (CBP)** after September 11 combined several elements of various federal agencies that had previously been separate. The entire U.S. Border Patrol was combined with portions of the U.S. Customs Service, U.S. Immigration, and the Animal and Plant Health Inspection Service. Today, the agency consists of more than 41,000 employees whose mission is, simply, to control and protect America's borders and ports of entry, including international airports and international shipping ports. Because CBP is part of the Department of Homeland Security, one of its foremost concerns is combating terrorism. The agency claims dual goals, however: fighting terrorism and "facilitating legitimate trade and travel."[7]

Figure 4-4 • Typical Activities of U.S. Customs and Border Protection

On a typical day in fiscal year 2006, U.S. Customs and Border Protection accomplished the following:

Processed

- 1.1 million passengers and pedestrians, including 680,000 aliens
- 70,900 truck, rail, and sea containers
- 240,737 incoming international air passengers
- 71,151 passengers/crew arriving by ship
- 327,042 incoming privately owned vehicles
- 85,300 shipments of goods approved for entry
- $84 million in fees, duties, and tariffs

Executed

- 63 arrests at ports of entry
- 2,984 apprehensions between ports for illegal entry

Seized

- 1,769 pounds of narcotics in 63 seizures at ports of entry
- 3,788 pounds of narcotics in 20 seizures between ports of entry
- $157,800 in undeclared or illicit currency and $646,900 worth of fraudulent commercial merchandise at ports of entry
- 4,462 prohibited meat, plant material, or animal products, including 147 agricultural pests at ports of entry

Refused entry of

- 574 noncitizens at ports of entry
- 63 criminal aliens attempting to enter the United States

Intercepted

- 71 fraudulent documents
- 20 smuggled aliens
- One or two travelers for terrorism or national security concerns

Rescued

- Eight illegal crossers in distress or dangerous conditions between ports of entry

Deployed

- 1,264 canine enforcement teams
- 8,075 vehicles, 260 aircraft, 215 watercraft, and 202 equestrian patrols

Protected more than

- 5,000 miles of border with Canada
- 1,900 miles of border with Mexico
- 95,000 miles of shoreline

Employed approximately 42,000 employees, including

- 18,000 officers
- 12,300 Border Patrol agents
- 2,000 agriculture specialists
- 650 air and marine officers

Managed

- 326 ports of entry
- 20 sectors with 35 border checkpoints between ports of entry

Source: Adapted from U.S. Customs and Border Protection, "This is CBP," http://www.cbp.gov/xp/cgov/about/mission/cbp_is.xml.

CBP relies on a number of sophisticated technological tools aimed at furthering its mission. These include the Advance Passenger Information System, the U.S. Visitor and Immigrant Status Indication Technology (US-VISIT), and the Student and Exchange Visitor System. The US-VISIT system records entry and exit of non-U.S. citizens who travel in and out of the United States, and provides officials with information about individuals who are in the U.S. in violation of their immigration status. Besides identifying potentially dangerous people, CBP is also concerned with cargo entering and leaving the United States. The Automated Targeting System, the Automated Export System, and regulations contained in the Trade Act of 2002 (Advance Electronic Information) help officials identify potentially threatening cargo.

Realizing that combating terrorism and maintaining the security of our borders is a complex task, CBP partners with other countries to screen potentially dangerous cargo before it leaves foreign ports. The agency also has an ambitious plan to partner with the private sector in an effort to promote security. The Customs-Trade Partnership against Terrorism program has seen the formation of partnerships between CBP and more than 6,000 private companies with an interest in border security. Inspection technologies, such as those involving shipping containers, are also being used and developed by and for CBP.

The most well-known component of CBP is the Border Patrol. The agents that make up this division number more than 10,000. Border Patrol agents, combined with every other official in CBP, make it one of the largest uniformed law enforcement agencies in the United States.[8] The Border Patrol reports having made more than 1.2 million arrests during 2005.[9] For a typical day's activity for CBP, see Figure 4-4.

Immigration and Customs Enforcement (ICE)
The largest investigative component of the federal Department of Homeland Security. ICE focuses specifically on illegal immigration.

Immigration and Customs Enforcement Closely connected to but independent of CBP is **Immigration and Customs Enforcement (ICE).** Whereas CBP is more concerned with border protection and customs checks, ICE focuses on investigation and is particularly concerned with illegal immigration. Indeed, it is the largest investigative component of the Department of Homeland Security. There are four main branches of ICE: the Office of Investigations, the Office of Detention and Removal Operations, the Federal Protective Service, and the Office of Intelligence. Of these, the second and third are of the most interest to us. The Office of Detention and Removal Operations enforces immigration laws by ensuring the departure from the United States of "removable aliens." The Federal Protective Service (FPS) is responsible for securing more than 8,800 federal facilities worldwide. There are nearly 2,000 FPS officers and more than 15,000 people in ICE altogether. Some of ICE's other key functions include these:

> [Dismantling] gang organizations by targeting their members, seizing their financial assets and disrupting their criminal operations; [targeting] illegal workers who have gained access to critical infrastructure worksites (like nuclear and chemical plants, military installations, seaports and airports); [identifying] fraudulent immigration benefit applications and fraudulent illegal document manufacture . . . ; [investigating] the illegal export of U.S. munitions and sensitive technology; [combating] criminal organizations that smuggle and traffic in humans across [the] borders; [and reducing] the number of fugitive aliens in the U.S.[10]

WEB PATROL 4-2
U.S. Department of Justice
http://www.mycrimekit.com

Justice Department Agencies. With the exception of the Secret Service, the Department of Homeland Security agencies discussed above are relatively new and unfamiliar. More accurately stated, their names are new and unfamiliar. The agents and staff who do the work have been around for some time—in one position or another. Some of the Justice Department agencies discussed in this section are, in contrast, quite familiar. Even people with no criminal justice education will recognize agencies like the Federal Bureau of Investigation or the U.S. Marshals Service (USMS). Because there is much misinformation about these agencies, we will cover them in some detail. We will also discuss the Bureau of Alcohol, Tobacco, Firearms and Explosives (ATF) and the Drug Enforcement Administration (DEA).

It should be clear why the Homeland Security agencies we have just discussed are housed where they are: Each has a unique opportunity to target terrorists and otherwise break up terrorist plots. Why are the FBI, DEA, ATF, and USMS in the Justice Department? This placement owes much to the 1870 Act to Establish the Justice Department.[11] As a result of this legislation, the Justice Department was tasked with handling the legal business (especially via prosecutions of criminal activity) of the United States and was given full control over all federal law enforcement. Of course, things have changed since 1870, and there are now law enforcement agencies, bureaus, and officials throughout the federal government. Through thick and thin, the agencies we are about to discuss have remained in the Justice Department for decades, and they will likely remain there for the foreseeable future.

Federal Bureau of Investigation (FBI)
The investigative arm of the U.S. Department of Justice.

Federal Bureau of Investigation The **Federal Bureau of Investigation (FBI)** remains in the U.S. Department of Justice, but its mission has changed to some extent as a result of September 11. Its mission is now to "protect and defend the United States against terrorist and foreign intelligence threats, to uphold and enforce the criminal laws of the United States, and to provide leadership and criminal justice services to federal, state, municipal, and international agencies and partners."[12] To be sure, the FBI had a role in terrorism investigation before September 11, but that was not one of the agency's foremost concerns. The September 11 attacks moved terrorism to the front of the line. Indeed, the FBI's "most wanted" list now includes known terrorists like Osama bin Laden.

Although the FBI is now heavily involved in investigating terrorism, its primary function is enforcing federal laws. It is to the federal government what state police agencies are to states, sheriff's departments are to counties, and municipal police agencies are to cities. It is, in short, the investigative arm of the U.S. Department of Justice. Its statutory authority can be found in Title 28, Section 533, of the U.S. Code. A number of other statutes, including the Congressional Assassination, Kidnapping, and Assault Act (Title 18, Section 351, U.S. Code), also name the FBI as the

FBI agents training with shotguns on a firing range at the FBI Academy in Quantico, Virginia. What is the mission of the FBI?

Newscom

agency charged with enforcement. Moreover, the FBI has jurisdiction to enforce more than 200 categories of federal law that proscribe all sorts of criminal activity.

The FBI has two main investigation/enforcement branches. One is the National Security Branch. Within this branch are four divisions concerned with preserving national security. The other, larger, branch—Criminal Investigations—investigates cybercrime, public corruption, civil rights violations, organized crime, white-collar crime, and a number of major thefts and violent crimes. Serious crimes of concern to the FBI include crimes against children, crimes on American Indian land, art theft, and violent gang activity. One of the FBI's main priorities today is dismantling the infamous MS-13, or Mara Salvatrucha, gang that took root in Los Angeles during the late 1980s and has since spread to many other parts of the country.

As of early 2006, the FBI employed more than 30,000 people, including about 12,500 special agents and 18,000 support staff.[13] The agency's budget for fiscal year 2003 was just shy of $4.3 billion. FBI officials can be found all around the globe. The headquarters is in Washington, DC, housed in the J. Edgar Hoover Building on Pennsylvania Avenue. But there are 56 field offices located in major cities, more than 400 resident agencies in smaller cities, and 50 international offices. The international offices are called *legal attachés* and are housed in U.S. embassies worldwide. The chain of command and various components of the FBI can be seen in the agency's organizational chart (Figure 4-5).

WEB PATROL 4-3

Federal Bureau of Investigation
http://www.mycrimekit.com

U.S. Marshals Service As we pointed out in Chapter 1, the **U.S. Marshals Service (USMS)** is America's oldest law enforcement agency. Marshals were key law enforcement officials in the Old West, but at the turn of the twentieth century, their responsibilities started to shift. For example, when Francisco Madero commenced his revolt—on U.S. soil—against Mexican President Porfirio Diaz in 1910, the marshals protected the U.S.-Mexico border against Diaz's supporters, who were attempting to harm Madero. When the Eighteenth Amendment was ratified in 1920, making the manufacture, sale, and transportation of intoxicating beverages illegal, the marshals were the key enforcement agents. Between 1920 and 1960, they also started to perform bailiff functions in U.S. courts. In 1971, the Witness Security Program was established and overseen by the U.S. Marshals Service. In 1979, the USMS took charge of apprehending federal fugitives. In the 1980s, the USMS assumed responsibility for managing and disposing of assets seized by all federal law enforcement agencies.[14] The federal Asset Forfeiture Program is housed in the USMS and manages more than $1.2 billion in cash, conveyances, and real property.

U.S. Marshals Service (USMS)
The oldest American law enforcement agency. Its mission includes judicial security and fugitive investigation and apprehension.

Figure 4-5 • Organizational Chart of the Federal Bureau of Investigation

Chief of Staff
Special Agent in Charge
Director
Deputy Director
Office of Public Affairs
Office of Congressional Affairs
Office of the General Counsel
Office of Equal Employment Opportunity
Office of Professional Responsibility
Office of the Ombudsman
Associate Deputy Director
Resource Planning Office
Inspection
Executive Assistant Director for National Security Branch
Associate Executive Assistant Director for National Security Branch
Counterterrorism
Counterintelligence
Directorate of Intelligence
Weapons of Mass Destruction Directorate
Executive Assistant Director for Criminal Investigations Branch
Criminal Investigative
Cyber
Critical Incident Response Group
Office of International Operations
Office of Law Enforcement Coordination
Executive Assistant Director for Science and Technology Branch
Operational Technology
Laboratory
Criminal Justice Information Services
Special Technologies and Applications Office
Chief Information Officer
Office of Information Technology Program Management
Office of Information Technology Systems Development
Information Technology Operations
Office of Information Technology Planning and Policy
Executive Assistant Director for Human Resources Branch Donald Packham
Training and Development
Human Resources
Facilities and Logistics Services
Finance
Records Management
Security

Source: Federal Bureau of Investigation.

Today, there are more than 3,000 deputy marshals throughout the United States.[15] They work for 94 presidentially appointed U.S. Marshals (one for each federal district). When staff are added to the mix, the USMS employs nearly 4,500 people in more than 200 offices both in the United States and abroad. The agency's main responsibilities are judicial security and fugitive investigation. Marshals protect federal judicial officials, including judges, attorneys, and jurors. The USMS arrests more federal fugitives than all other federal agencies combined. In fiscal year 2005, for instance, marshals arrested more than 35,000 federal fugitives.

Marshals work in task forces alongside local law enforcement agencies to apprehend fugitives. Less familiar are USMS units like the Special Operations Group, which is similar to a local police agency's special weapons and tactics (SWAT) team. As for witness security, the agency has protected, relocated, and given new identities to nearly 8,000 individuals. The USMS has also joined up with customs enforcement and immigration officials to more efficiently deport criminal aliens. Marshals are also responsible for housing more than 50,000 federal detainees.

Bureau of Alcohol, Tobacco, Firearms and Explosives (ATF)
A tax-collection, enforcement, and regulatory arm of the U.S. Department of Justice.

Bureau of Alcohol, Tobacco, Firearms and Explosives Unlike the USMS and the FBI, the **Bureau of Alcohol, Tobacco, Firearms and Explosives (ATF)** has not been housed in the Justice Department for very long. On January 24, 2003, it was transferred from the Department of the Treasury to Justice, in accordance with the Homeland Security Act. Vestiges of ATF remain in the Treasury Department, however. Specifically, the Treasury Department is still responsible for certain tax and trade functions associated with ATF. The move from the Treasury Department to the Justice Department included a name change for the agency, from simply the Bureau of Alcohol, Tobacco, and Firearms to the Bureau of Alcohol, Tobacco, Firearms, and Explosives. The *ATF* acronym remains in place, however, even though explosives are now one of the agency's key concerns.

ATF is basically a tax-collection, enforcement, and regulatory arm of the Justice Department. The Gun Control Act of 1968 required that every manufacturer, importer, and dealer of firearms obtain a Federal Firearms License. ATF screens the applications and issues the licenses. Dealers are required to comply with applicable federal laws and to keep records of all firearms sales, and ATF conducts inspections of gun dealerships to ensure compliance. This task is rather demanding because, as of late 2007, there were approximately 109,000 Federal Firearms License holders in the United States.[16] ATF also targets illegal firearms trafficking.

As for explosives, ATF investigates explosions and cases of arson. It has been particularly involved, for instance, with investigations of arson and bombings at abortion clinics throughout the United States.

Finally, the agency regulates distilleries, wineries, breweries, and tobacco manufacturers and retailers. Its National Laboratory Center ensures that the labels on alcoholic beverages do not contain misleading information. ATF states that the goals of its alcohol program are

> to ensure the collection of alcoholic beverage excise taxes; to provide for accurate deposit and accounting for these taxes; to prevent entry into the industry by criminals or persons whose business experience or associations pose a risk of tax fraud; and to suppress label fraud, commercial bribery, diversion and smuggling, and other unlawful practices in the alcohol beverage marketplace.[17]

Besides staff, ATF employs both special agents and inspectors. The agents are the criminal investigators and enforcement officials. Inspectors' responsibilities do not include investigation and enforcement per se. Rather, they help people start new businesses, such as firearms dealerships, liquor stores, and the like. Inspectors also visit dealerships and retail establishments to ensure compliance with the law. ATF also employs a number of lawyers, auditors, chemists, and computer experts. The agency is headquartered in Washington, DC, where the majority of the agency's roughly 5,000 employees work. The remainder staff about 25 field offices located throughout the United States and in a handful of foreign nations.

WEB PATROL 4-4
Bureau of Alcohol, Tobacco, Firearms and Explosives
http://www.mycrimekit.com

Drug Enforcement Administration The **Drug Enforcement Administration (DEA)** is tasked with enforcing controlled substance laws and regulations. The agency brings to justice people and organizations involved in the illegal growing, manufacture, and distribution of controlled substances. To accomplish these tasks, the DEA

Drug Enforcement Administration (DEA)
The U.S. law enforcement agency tasked with enforcing controlled substance laws and regulations.

- Investigates and prepares for the prosecution of major violators of controlled substance laws operating at interstate and international levels.
- Investigates and prepares for the prosecution of criminals and drug gangs who perpetrate violence and terrorize citizens through fear and intimidation.
- Manages a national drug-intelligence program in cooperation with federal, state, local, and foreign officials to collect, analyze, and disseminate strategic and operational drug-intelligence information.
- Seizes and effects forfeiture of assets derived from, traceable to, or intended to be used for illicit drug trafficking.
- Enforces the provisions of the Controlled Substances Act as they pertain to the manufacture, distribution, and dispensing of legally produced controlled substances.
- Coordinates and cooperates with federal, state, and local law enforcement officials on mutual drug enforcement efforts and enhancement of such efforts through exploitation of potential interstate and international investigations beyond local or limited federal jurisdictions and resources.
- Coordinates and cooperates with federal, state, and local agencies, and with foreign governments, in programs designed to reduce the availability of illicit abuse-type drugs on the U.S. market through nonenforcement methods such as crop eradication, crop substitution, and training of foreign officials.[18]

The DEA is one of the larger federal law enforcement agencies. In 2006, it employed nearly 11,000 people, including more than 5,000 special agents. The agency has 227 domestic offices in 20 divisions throughout the United States and in 86 foreign countries. Agents have accomplished some impressive feats in recent years, including the seizure in 2007 of more than 96,000 kilograms of cocaine, 600 kilograms of heroin, and 356,000 kilograms of marijuana.[19] The DEA routinely gets press attention through some of its focused efforts to target specific networks of criminals. The recently publicized Operation Black Gold Rush is featured in Exhibit 4-1. The agency's organizational chart is shown in Figure 4-6.

WEB PATROL 4-5
U.S. Drug Enforcement Administration
http://www.mycrimekit.com

Exhibit 4-1 • Operation Black Gold Rush

On August 15, 2006, DEA administrator Karen P. Tandy and Assistant Attorney General Alice S. Fisher of the Criminal Division announced that the agency had made more than 130 arrests as part of an international operation targeting the trafficking of black tar heroin in the United States.

The multistate investigation, called Operation Black Gold Rush, included arrests in 15 U.S. cities and 10 indictments in eight federal judicial districts, along with state charges. More than 17 kilograms of black tar heroin—a potent form of heroin that is dark and sticky in appearance—were also seized in the operation.

"Operation Black Gold Rush exposed a network of over 100 illegal aliens who controlled a pipeline of heroin operating from Nayarit, Mexico, to Nashville, Tennessee, and at least 14 cities in between," said DEA administrator Karen P. Tandy. "Today, DEA ruptured that pipeline, stopping the flow of heroin to our streets."

A total of 138 people were arrested on federal and state charges in connection with the operation. In Indiana, an indictment charged 13 defendants with conspiracy to distribute one kilogram or more of heroin. Fifteen individuals were charged in Indiana, 28 were arrested and indicted in Ohio, 47 in Tennessee, seven in Colorado, and 11 in North Carolina. A federal grand jury in South Carolina returned two indictments charging 26 individuals with drug-related offenses.

"As this operation demonstrates, the Department of Justice is as committed as ever to eradicating the flood of illegal and dangerous narcotics like black tar heroin," said Assistant Attorney General Alice S. Fisher of the Criminal Division.

Operation Black Gold Rush started with a single seizure of heroin. This DEA-led investigation, which began in November 2005, involved the cooperative efforts of federal, state, and local law enforcement agencies. Members of the trafficking organization charged in the indictments are alleged to have been responsible for importing and distributing 10 to 15 kilograms of black tar heroin monthly from Mexico into the United States; the heroin could be sold at an estimated street value of more than $3 million. The organization allegedly used illegal aliens as couriers; they were part of a "call and deliver" system of drug distribution whereby a customer could have heroin literally delivered to the front door. The illicit proceeds were allegedly laundered by the organization's financial managers using a combination of wire remitters and bulk currency transport.

The government seized more than $500,000 in cash representing illegal proceeds from this operation—$250,000 of that amount was seized in a single day.

Operation Black Gold Rush was a joint investigation involving operations in 15 cities. The investigation also involved eight U.S. attorney's offices; the Criminal Division's Narcotic and Dangerous Drug Section, Special Operations Division; and the Justice Department's Organized Crime and Drug Enforcement Task Force; along with ICE, the Internal Revenue Service, ATF, and various state and local law enforcement agencies.

Source: Adapted from Drug Enforcement Administration Office of Public Affairs, "International Black Tar Heroin Trafficking Group Dismantled," press release, August 15, 2006, http://www.dea.gov/pubs/pressrel/pr081506p.html.

State Agencies

Most state police agencies were initially created for a specific purpose. The Texas Rangers, for example, were established in 1835, even before Texas attained statehood, and functioned largely as a military organization responsible for patrolling the republic's borders. Massachusetts was the second state to create a law enforcement agency. It was developed with the intent of targeting vice crimes. Today, numerous state policing agencies exist. Table 4-1 shows that the number of personnel employed by state law enforcement agencies is significantly less than the number employed in local police departments.

Figure 4-6 • Organizational Chart of the Drug Enforcement Administration

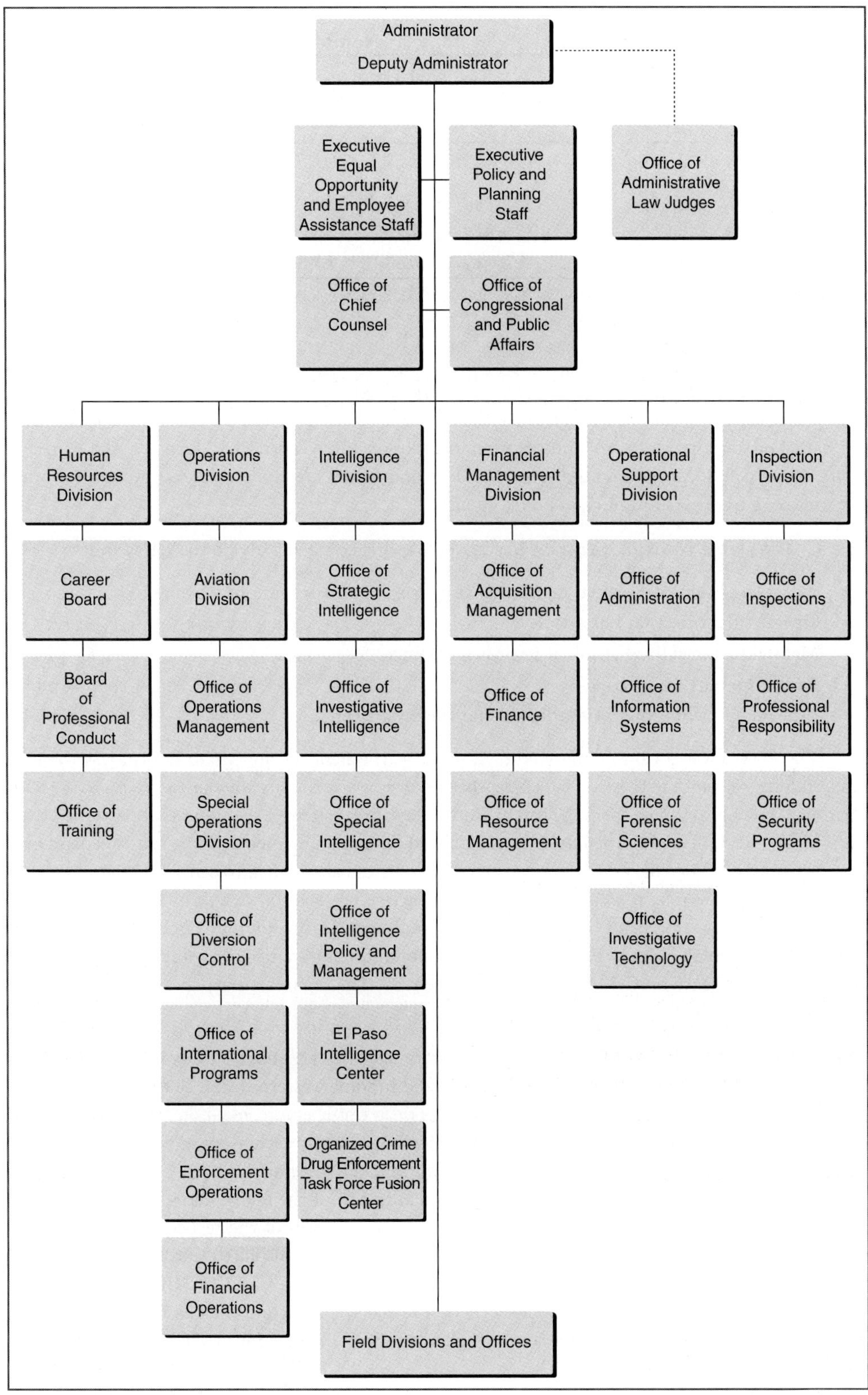

Source: Drug Enforcement Administration.

Table 4-1 • State and Local Law Enforcement Agencies and Employees in the United States, by Type of Agency, 2003

Type of Agency	Number of Agencies	Number of Employees					
		Full-Time			Part-Time		
		Total	Sworn	Civilian	Total	Sworn	Civilian
Total	15,766	993,442	683,599	309,843	75,958	35,152	40,806
Local police	12,656	580,749	451,737	129,013	51,281	25,614	25,667
Sheriff	3,061	330,274	174,251	156,022	23,884	9,498	14,386
State police	49	82,419	57,611	24,808	793	40	753

Source: Sourcebook of Criminal Justice Statistics Online, Table 1.0001.2003, http://www.albany.edu/sourcebook/pdf/t100012003.pdf.

centralized policing model
The less-prevalent model of state police organization, in which the tasks of major criminal investigations are combined with the patrol of state highways.

decentralized policing model
A model of policing in which central governments exercise relatively few police powers and in which the majority of police services are provided by separate local and regional agencies.

local agency
One of the three levels of law enforcement activity in the United States—the other two being state and federal—which encompasses organizations like municipal police departments, sheriff's departments, and other lesser-known agencies, including campus police, transit police, and specialized agencies at public schools, airports, state capitols, medical facilities, state parks, certain prosecutor's offices, and others. Together, the personnel in these local agencies far outnumber all state and federal law enforcement officials combined.

State law enforcement agencies are usually organized according to one of two models. In the first, a **centralized policing model,** the tasks of major criminal investigations are combined with the patrol of state highways. A number of states rely on these centralized agencies, the names of which often include *state police* or *state patrol*. The second model, the **decentralized policing model,** is more like a traditional municipal police agency.

The Centralized Model. Centralized state police agencies generally do the following:

- Assist local law enforcement departments in criminal investigations when asked to do so.
- Operate identification bureaus.
- Maintain a centralized criminal records repository.
- Patrol the state's highways.
- Provide select training for municipal and county officers.

The Pennsylvania Constabulary, known today as the Pennsylvania State Police, was the first modern force to combine these duties. It has been described as the first modern state police agency. Michigan, New Jersey, New York, Vermont, and Delaware are a few of the states that patterned their state-level enforcement activities after the centralized Pennsylvania model. Some state agencies give greater emphasis to one or more of the responsibilities listed above than to others. The Washington State Patrol, for example, is well known for its very active presence on state highways, but through its investigative and forensics bureaus, it assists local agencies in solving crimes throughout the state. The California Highway Patrol is also known foremost as a traffic enforcement agency because of its obvious presence on California roads and freeways. The organizational chart of the Washington State Patrol is shown in Figure 4-7.

The Decentralized Model. Decentralized state agencies are most prevalent in the southern United States. They are also found in the Midwest and in some western states. The decentralized approach to state policing draws a clear distinction between traffic enforcement on state highways and other state-level law enforcement functions by either creating two separate agencies or multiple divisions within a single agency. The structure varies from state to state.

North Carolina, South Carolina, and Georgia are a few of the many states that employ both a highway patrol and a state bureau of investigation. The names of the respective agencies may vary, however, even though their functions are largely the same. In North Carolina, for example, the two major state-level law enforcement agencies are the North Carolina Highway Patrol and the State Bureau of Investigation. Georgia fields a highway patrol and the Georgia Bureau of Investigation, and South Carolina operates a highway patrol and the South Carolina Law Enforcement Division.

States that use the decentralized model usually have a number of other adjunct state-level law enforcement agencies. North Carolina, for example, has created a State Wildlife Commission with enforcement powers, a Board of Alcohol Beverage Control with additional agents, and a separate En-

Figure 4-7 • Organizational Chart of the Washington State Patrol

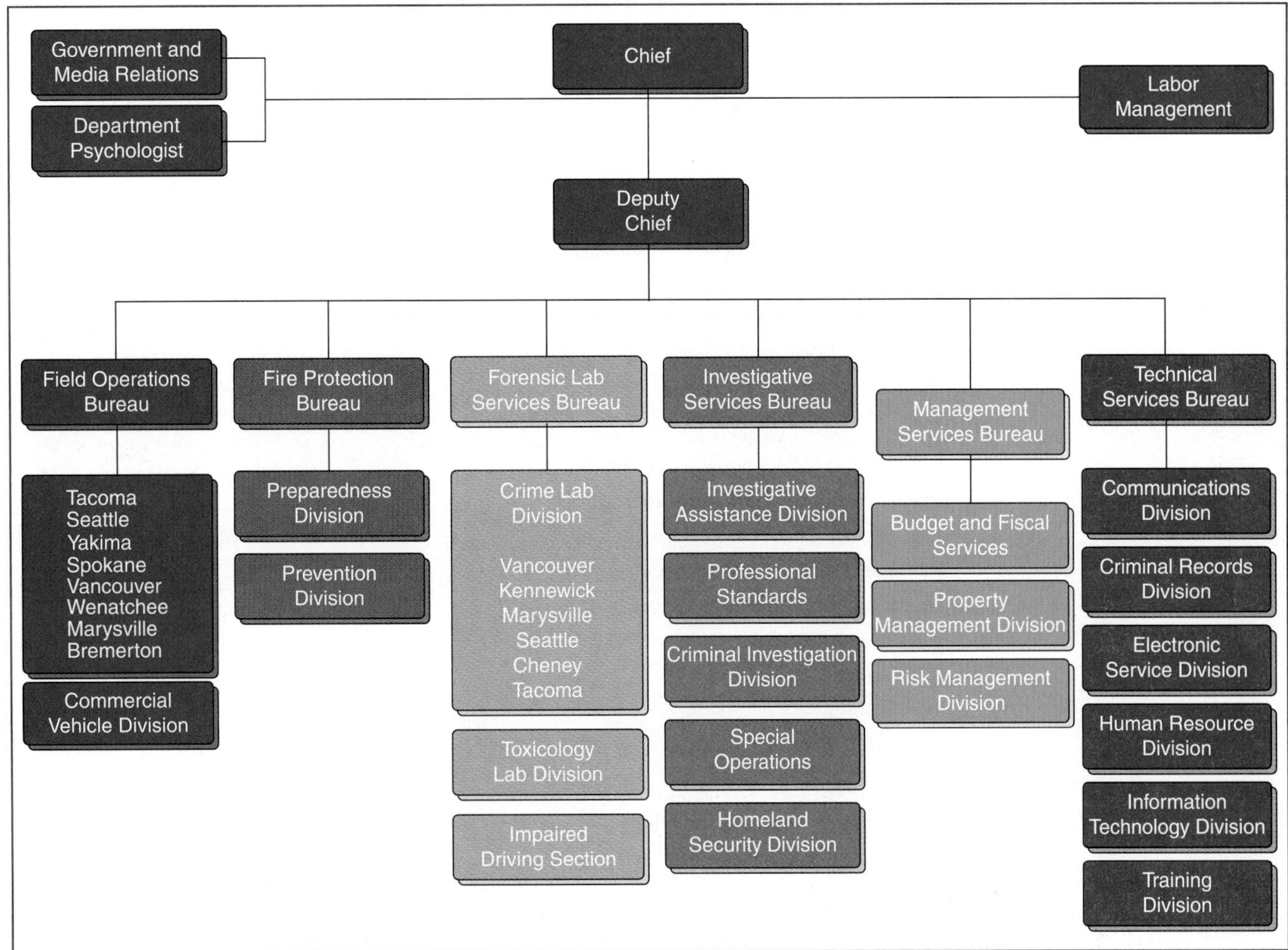

Source: Washington State Patrol, "WSP 2007 Organizational Chart," April 1, 2007, http://www.wsp.wa.gov/reports/orgchart.htm.

forcement and Theft Bureau for enforcing certain motor vehicle and theft laws. Other states have merged historically separate agencies into one parent organization. Oregon's State Police is an example. In 1993, the legislature in that state approved a law that merged the Oregon State Fire Marshal's Office, Oregon Emergency Management, the Law Enforcement Data System, and the Oregon Boxing and Wrestling Commission into the State Police.

Local Agencies

Local police agencies, including city and county agencies, make up the third level of law enforcement in the United States—the other two being federal and state. The term **local agencies** encompasses a wide variety of organizations. **Municipal police departments** and **sheriff's departments** are most familiar. Other lesser-known agencies, such as campus police departments and transit police, are also categorized as "local." Even some public schools have a police presence, as do airports, state capitols, medical facilities, state parks, certain prosecutor's offices, and other organizations. (See Table 4-2 for a list of some of these special jurisdiction agencies.) Viewed together, the personnel in these local agencies far outnumber all federal and state law enforcement officials combined.

Some local police departments are highly visible because of their size, huge budgets, innovative programs, and—perhaps above all else—the attention they receive from the press, television producers, and moviemakers. The nation's largest law enforcement agency, the New York City Police

municipal police department
One of the types of local law enforcement agencies in the United States. Specifically, the law enforcement agency that serves a municipality.

sheriff's department
One of the types of local law enforcement agencies in the United States. Specifically, the law enforcement agency that serves a county or parish.

Table 4-2 • Special Jurisdiction Law Enforcement Agencies, by Type of Jurisdiction and Number of Full-Time Sworn Personnel, 2004

Type of Special Jurisdiction	Agenices	Number of Full-Time Sworn Personnel
Total	1,481	49,398
Public buildings/facilities	1,011	19,247
Four-year universities/colleges	488	10,167
Public school districts	183	3,517
Two-year colleges	254	2,438
State capitol/government buildings	18	1,289
Medical schools/campuses	22	732
Public housing	12	411
Public hospitals/health facilities	30	399
Courts	4	294
Natural resources/parks and recreation	205	14,322
Fish and wildlife	50	4,937
Parks and recreational areas	95	4,212
Multifunction natural resources	25	3,550
Environmental laws	6	700
Waterways and boating	17	663
Water resources	5	129
Sanitation laws	2	97
Forest resources	5	44
Transportation systems/facilities	130	9,073
Mass transit systems/railroads	18	3,094
Airports	90	2,900
Transportation—multiple types	5	2,200
Port facilities	11	333
Commercial vehicles	2	285
Bridges, tunnels	4	261
Criminal investigations	103	4,739
County/city	62	1,756
State bureau	16	1,702
Fire marshal	17	454
Other	8	827
Special enforcement	32	2,007
Alcohol enforcement	17	1,219
Agricultural law enforcement	5	340
Gaming/racing law enforcement	6	225
Drug enforcement	4	223

Source: Brian A. Reaves, *Census of state and local law enforcement agencies, 2004* (Washington, DC: Bureau of Justice Statistics, 2007).

Department (NYPD), for example, has about 45,000 full-time employees, including about 36,000 full-time sworn officers.[20] Likewise, the police departments in Los Angeles, Chicago, Houston, and other large cities employ thousands of sworn officers. These agencies are routinely featured in television shows and "cop" movies, but far greater in number, albeit less visible, are small-town police and county sheriff's departments.

WEB PATROL 4-6

Law Enforcement Agency Directory
http://www.mycrimekit.com

There are approximately 12,700 municipal police departments and 3,100 sheriff's departments in the United States (out of the roughly 20,000 law enforcement agencies in the country).[21] These numbers are only estimates, given the difficulty associated with counting cops, but the point is that there are many of them. Most areas are patrolled and served by officials from one or both of these types of agencies.

Municipal Police. Every incorporated municipality in the country has the authority to create its own police force. Some very small communities hire only one officer to fill the roles of chief, investigator, and night watch—as well as everything in between. The majority of local agencies employ fewer than ten full-time officers, and about three of every eight agencies (more than 7,000 in all) employ fewer than five full-time officers. These smaller agencies include 2,245 (or 12 percent) with just one full-time officer and 1,164 (or 6 percent) with only part-time officers.[22]

A few communities contract with private security firms for police services, and still others have no active police force at all, depending instead on local sheriff's departments to deal with law violators. Some cities also contract with county sheriff's departments to provide law enforcement services. Whether a city has a police force, or any police presence at all, depends on funding, as well. Hiring a police officer, putting the person through training, paying benefits, and so on can cost hundreds of thousands of dollars.

City police chiefs are typically appointed by the mayor or selected by the city council. Their departments' jurisdictions are limited by convention to the geographic boundaries of their communities. Municipal police departments are all organized in a fairly similar fashion. Larger agencies have many more personnel and divisions, of course, but they still follow a fairly ordinary bureaucratic structure. Typically, the chief is near the top, followed by deputy chiefs, captains, lieutenants, sergeants, and so forth. How many of these ranks there are varies from one agency to the next. To illustrate, see Figures 4-8 and 4-9. The first presents the organizational chart of the Los Angeles Police Department, while the second shows the organization of the Allen (Texas) Police Department.

Sheriff's Departments. Sheriff's departments are responsible for law enforcement throughout the counties in which they function. Sheriff's deputies mostly patrol the unincorporated areas of the county, or those that lie between municipalities. They do, however, have jurisdiction throughout the county, and in some areas they routinely work alongside municipal police to enforce laws within towns and cities. If a traffic accident occurs within city limits, for example, a sheriff's deputy may appear on the scene first and take control.

Sheriff's departments are also generally responsible for serving court papers, including civil summonses, and for maintaining security within state courtrooms. They run county jails and are responsible for more detainees awaiting trial than any other type of law enforcement department in the country.

The Los Angeles County Jail System, operated by the Los Angeles County Sheriff's Department (LASD), is the largest in the world.[23] In 2003, with eight separate facilities, it had an average daily population of 18,423 inmates—considerably larger than the number of inmates held in many state prison systems. More than 2,200 uniformed officers and 1,265 civilian employees work in the Custody Division of the LASD, and that division alone operates with a yearly budget in excess of $200 million.[24]

Sheriff's departments remain strong across most of the country, although in parts of New England, deputies mostly function as court agents with limited law enforcement duties. One report reveals that most sheriff's departments are small; nearly two-thirds employ fewer than 25 sworn officers.[25] Only 12 departments employ more than 1,000 officers. Even so, sheriffs in southern and western states are still considered the chief law enforcement officers in their respective counties.

Figure 4-8 • Organizational Chart of the Los Angeles Police Department

Executive Director R. Tefank
Commission Investigation Division Lt. Dawson

BOARD OF POLICE COMMISSIONERS
Robert Saltzman Commissioner
Andrea Sheridan Ordin Commissioner
Anthony Pacheco Commissioner President
John W. Mack Commissioner Vice President
Alan J. Skobin Commissioner

Inspector General A. Birotte
Police Permit Review Panel

CHIEF OF POLICE William J. Bratton
Community Relations Section Lt. II Doug Miller
Chief's Adjutant Cpt. Snell
Administrative Section
Officer of The Chief of Police Scheduling Section
Officer of The Chief of Police Security Detail
Executive Administrative Assistant Mary Helen Ayala

CHIEF OF STAFF 1st Assistant Chief Jim McDonnell (*)
EMPLOYEE RELATIONS GROUP Commander Perez
PUBLIC INFORMATION OFFICE Public Information Director Grady
Governmental Liaison Section
Use of Force Review Division Cpt Sargent

OFFICE OF OPERATIONS Assistant Chief Earl Paysinger
ASSISTANT TO THE DIRECTOR, OFFICE OF OPERATIONS Commander Albanese
Jail Division Cpt Findley
Special Assistant Cpt W. Scott
Evaluation and Administration Section
Duty Officer Commander Gray

SPECIAL OPERATIONS BUREAU Deputy Chief Richard Roupoli
Assistant Commanding Officer Commander Kroeber
Air Support Division Cpt. M. Williams
Emergency Operations Division Cpt. T. Chamberlain
Metropolitan Division Cpt Greer Cpt. Kato

CENTRAL BUREAU Deputy Chief Sergio Diaz
Assistant Commanding Officer Commander Doan
Central Area (1) Cpt Wakefield Cpt. R. Wall
Rampart Area (2) Cpt Egan Cpt. P. Hernandez III
Hollenbeck Area (4) Cpt B. Chow Cpt. Nieto
Northeast Area (11) Cpt W. Murphy Cpt. L. Smith
Newton Area (13) Cpt M. Overa Cpt. J. Eisenberg
Central Traffic Division Cpt. Marbrey

SOUTH BUREAU Deputy Chief Kenneth Garner
CRIMINAL GANG HOMICIDE GROUP Commander A. Smith
Assistant Commanding Officer Commander K. Jackson
77th Street Area (12) Cpt. R. Green Cpt. G. Allen
Southwest Area (3) Cpt. Craig Cpt. Fontanetta
Harbor Area (5) Cpt. B. Hayes Cpt. Lindsay
Southeast Area (18) Cpt. Tingirides Cpt. McDonald
South Traffic Division Cpt. Schwartzer

VALLEY BUREAU Deputy Chief Michel Moore
Assistant Commanding Officer Commander Szymanski Commander Ward
Van Nuys Area (9) Cpt. Miller Cpt. Mulldorfer
West Valley Area (10) Cpt Zipperman Cpt. D.Baca
North Hollywood Area (15) Cpt. S. Buck Cpt. J. Peters
Foothill Area (16) Cpt. Curreri Cpt. Minsal
Devonshire Area (17) Cpt. Kane Cpt. S. Ruiz
Mission Area (19) Cpt. Villegas Cpt. Hayakawa
Topanga Area (21) Cpt John Sherman Cpt. M. Ryan
Valley Traffic Division Cpt. P. Trotter

WEST BUREAU Deputy Chief Terry Hara
Assistant Commanding Officer Commander Debra McCarthy
Wilshire Area (7) Cpt. E. Davis Cpt. Nathan
Hollywood Area (6) Cpt. Farrell Cpt. B. Girmala
West Los Angeles Area (8) Cpt. Eaton Cpt. J. West
Olympic Area (20) Cp. Blake Cpt. Hundshamer
Pacific Area (14) Cpt. J. Hiltner Cpt. R. De La Torre
LAX Field Services Division Cpt. Sutton
West Traffic Division Cpt. Lauer

DETECTIVE BUREAU Deputy Chief Charles Beck
COMPSTAT Det Godown
Investigative Analysis Section
Tactical Technology Unit
Assistant Commanding Officer Commander Patrick Gannon
Robbery-Homicide Division Cpt. D. Cremins
Commercial Crimes Division Cpt. B. Williams
Detective Support and Vice Division Cpt. A. Young
Juvenile Division Cpt. F. Lizarraga
Narcotics Division Cpt. K. McCarthy
Gang and Operations Support Division Cpt. R. Scott
RACR Division Cpt. J. Justice

INCIDENT MANAGEMENT AND TRAINING BUREAU Deputy Chief Sandy Jo Macarthur
TRAINING GROUP Commander Rick Jacobs
Continuing Education Division Cpt. Incontro
Training Division Cpt. Veenstra
POLICE TRAINING AND EDUCATION Dr. Pannell

PROFESSIONAL STANDARDS BUREAU Deputy Chief Mark Perez
INTERNAL AFFAIRS GROUP Commander Webb
Criminal Investigation Division Cpt.T. Brascia
Administrative Investigation Division Cpt. Moriarty
Force Investigation Division Cpt. Pitcher
Special Operations Division Cpt. R. Romero

CONSENT DECREE BUREAU Police Administrator III Gerald Chaleff
RISK MANAGEMENT GROUP Commander Maislin
Civil Rights Integrity Division Cpt. McClure
Audit Division Cpt. Schick

TEAMS II DEVELOPMENT BUREAU Police Administrator III Maggie Goodrich

COUNTER TERRORISM AND CRIMINAL INTELLIGENCE BUREAU Deputy Chief Michael Downing
Assistant Commanding Officer Commander McNamara
Major Crimes Division Cpt.Hall
Emergency Services Division Cpt. Frank

OFFICE OF SUPPORT SERVICES Assistant Chief Sharon Papa
OMBUDS OFFICE Cpt Weinstein
EXECUTIVE OFFICER Commander W. Fierro
Planning and Research Division Cpt Abom-Khoury

INFORMATION AND COMMUNICATIONS SERVICES BUREAU Chief Information Officer Tim Riley
Assistant Commanding Officer Police Administrator II Grube
Communications Division Cpt. Ortega
Emergency Command Control Communications System Dir Sys Hart
Information Technology Division Dir Sys Jantz
Records and Identification Division Police Administrator I Markley

ADMINISTRATIVE AND TECHNICAL SERVICES BUREAU Police Administrator III Rhonda Sims-Lewis
Assistant Commanding Officer Police Administrator II DiCarlo
Facilities Management Division Police Administrator I Brennan
Fiscal Operations Division Police Administrator I Filatoff
Assistant Commanding Officer Police Administrator II Gennusa
Property Division Police Administrator I Johnson
Motor Transport Division Director of Transportation Tagawa
Scientific Investigation Division Police Administrator I Sanchez-Owens
PERSONNEL GROUP Commander Carsler
Personnel Division Police Administrator I Gordon
Recruitment and Employment Division Cpt. Mariani
Officer Representation Section
BEHAVIORAL SCIENCE SERVICES Chief Psychologist Jablonski

*Chairman of the Use of Force Review Board or Designee
Sworn commanding officers of the rank of assistant chief
Sworn commanding officers of the rank of deputy chief
Civilian commanding officers comparable to the rank of deputy chief
Sworn commanding officers of the rank of commander
Civilian commanding officers comparable to the rank of commander

Source: Los Angeles Police Department, "LAPD Organization Chart," July 1, 2008, http://lapdonline.org/inside_the_lapd/pdf_view/5056. Reprinted by permission.

Figure 4-9 • Organizational Chart of the Allen (Texas) Police Department

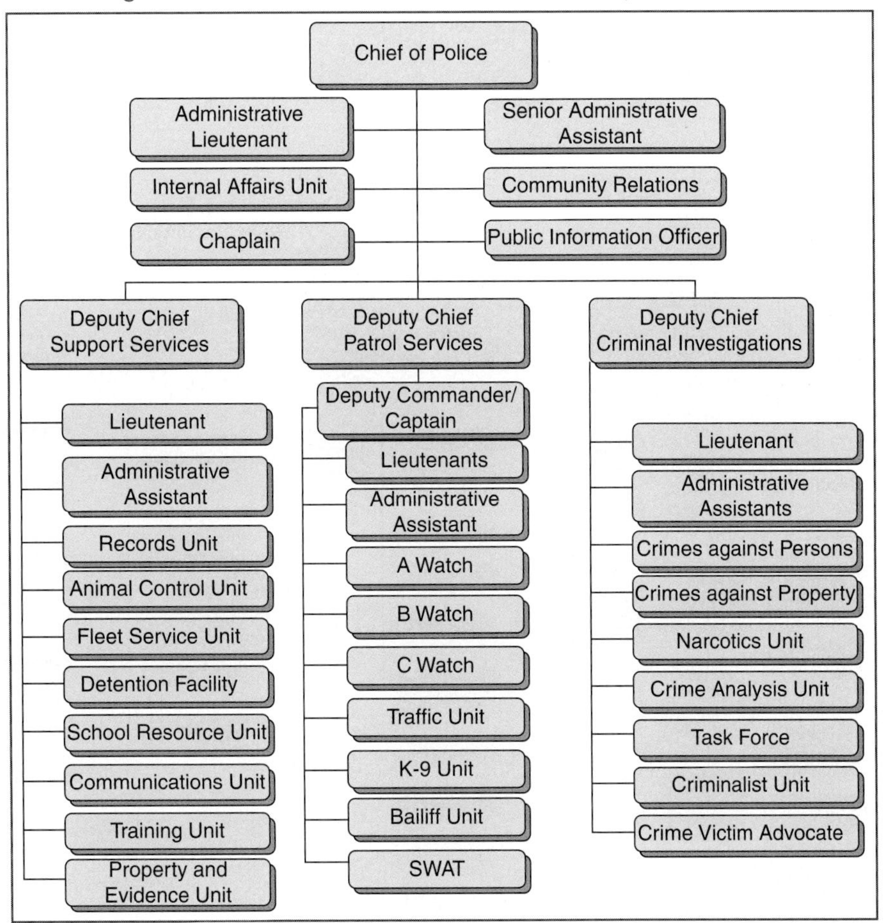

Source: Courtesy of Chief Bill Rushing, Allen (Texas) Police Department. Reprinted with permission.

Sheriffs are usually elected officials,[26] unlike city police chiefs. This creates a somewhat different set of priorities for them. Police chiefs answer to city officials, but sheriffs answer to voters. If the voters are displeased with a sheriff's performance, come election time they can move a new sheriff into office. As researchers have pointed out, this situation has its advantages and disadvantages:

> On one hand, this expresses the independence of the sheriff from other political offices or executives within local governmental structure. On the other hand, it means that the sheriff is subject directly to the approval of the community and to the power of public opinion. Since terms of office are often fairly short—usually two or four years—the sheriff is dependent on good relationships with voting members of the community who may remove him/her from office at the next available election. In these terms, the sheriff is less insulated from the public than the police chief, lacking the administrative buffer from the general public that most municipal departments have in the mayor, police commission, or city board who oversee them and appoint their chief executive.[27]

In most jurisdictions, not just anyone can run for the position of sheriff. Ohio, for example, requires not only past law enforcement experience, but experience in law enforcement administration.[28] The law ensures that all unqualified candidates are screened out in advance of elections.

Sheriff's departments are organized in a similar fashion to municipal police departments. Figure 4-10 shows the organization of the Chesterfield County (Virginia) Sheriff's Office. Figure 4-11 shows the organization of the Nevada County (California) Sheriff's Office.

Figure 4-10 • Organizational Chart of the Chesterfield County (Virginia) Sheriff's Office

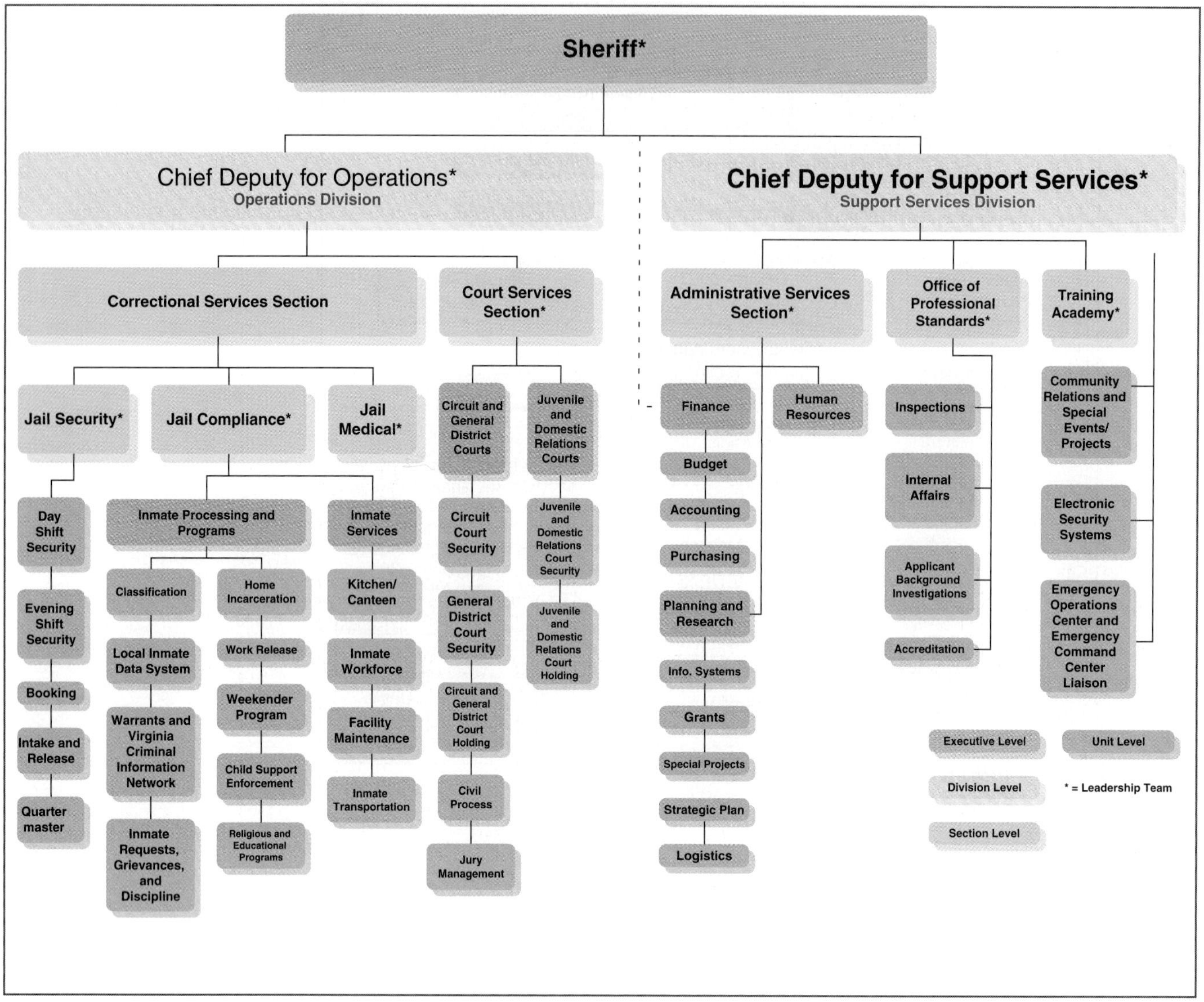

Sheriff*

Chief Deputy for Operations*
Operations Division

Chief Deputy for Support Services*
Support Services Division

Correctional Services Section

Court Services Section*

Administrative Services Section*

Office of Professional Standards*

Training Academy*

Jail Security*
Day Shift Security
Evening Shift Security
Booking
Intake and Release
Quarter master

Jail Compliance*
Inmate Processing and Programs
Classification
Local Inmate Data System
Warrants and Virginia Criminal Information Network
Inmate Requests, Grievances, and Discipline
Home Incarceration
Work Release
Weekender Program
Child Support Enforcement
Religious and Educational Programs

Jail Medical*
Inmate Services
Kitchen/ Canteen
Inmate Workforce
Facility Maintenance
Inmate Transportation

Circuit and General District Courts
Circuit Court Security
General District Court Security
Circuit and General District Court Holding
Civil Process
Jury Management

Juvenile and Domestic Relations Courts
Juvenile and Domestic Relations Court Security
Juvenile and Domestic Relations Court Holding

Finance
Budget
Accounting
Purchasing
Planning and Research
Info. Systems
Grants
Special Projects
Strategic Plan
Logistics

Human Resources

Inspections
Internal Affairs
Applicant Background Investigations
Accreditation

Community Relations and Special Events/ Projects
Electronic Security Systems
Emergency Operations Center and Emergency Command Center Liaison

Executive Level
Division Level
Section Level
Unit Level
* = Leadership Team

Source: Chesterfield Connections, "Sheriff's Office Organizational Chart," http://www.co.chesterfield.va.us/ConstitutionalOfficers/Sheriff/orgchart.asp.By permission of Chesterfield County Sheriff's Office, Chesterfield County, Virginia.

THE ORGANIZATION OF LAW ENFORCEMENT AGENCIES

organization
A group in which individuals work together to accomplish specified tasks or goals.

An **organization** can be defined as "a consciously coordinated social entity, with a relatively identifiable boundary, that functions on a relatively continuous basis to achieve a common goal or set of goals."[29] To be "consciously coordinated" means that someone (or perhaps a group of people) is managing the organization. The notion of "social entity" refers to the fact that organizations are groups of people. Finally, "identifiable boundary" refers to an organization's service population. By this definition, police departments are organizations, as are schools, businesses, and nonprofit groups. However, police departments, and nearly all law enforcement agencies in general, differ from other types of organizations in a number of key respects.

How Police Departments Differ from Other Organizations

WEB PATROL 4-7
Police: Organization and Management
http://www.mycrimekit.com

Police organizations differ from other types of organizations, most obviously, because usually only the police have both legitimate arrest power and authority to use force. The National Guard has been activated in various places and from

Figure 4-11 • Organizational Chart of the Nevada County (California) Sheriff's Office

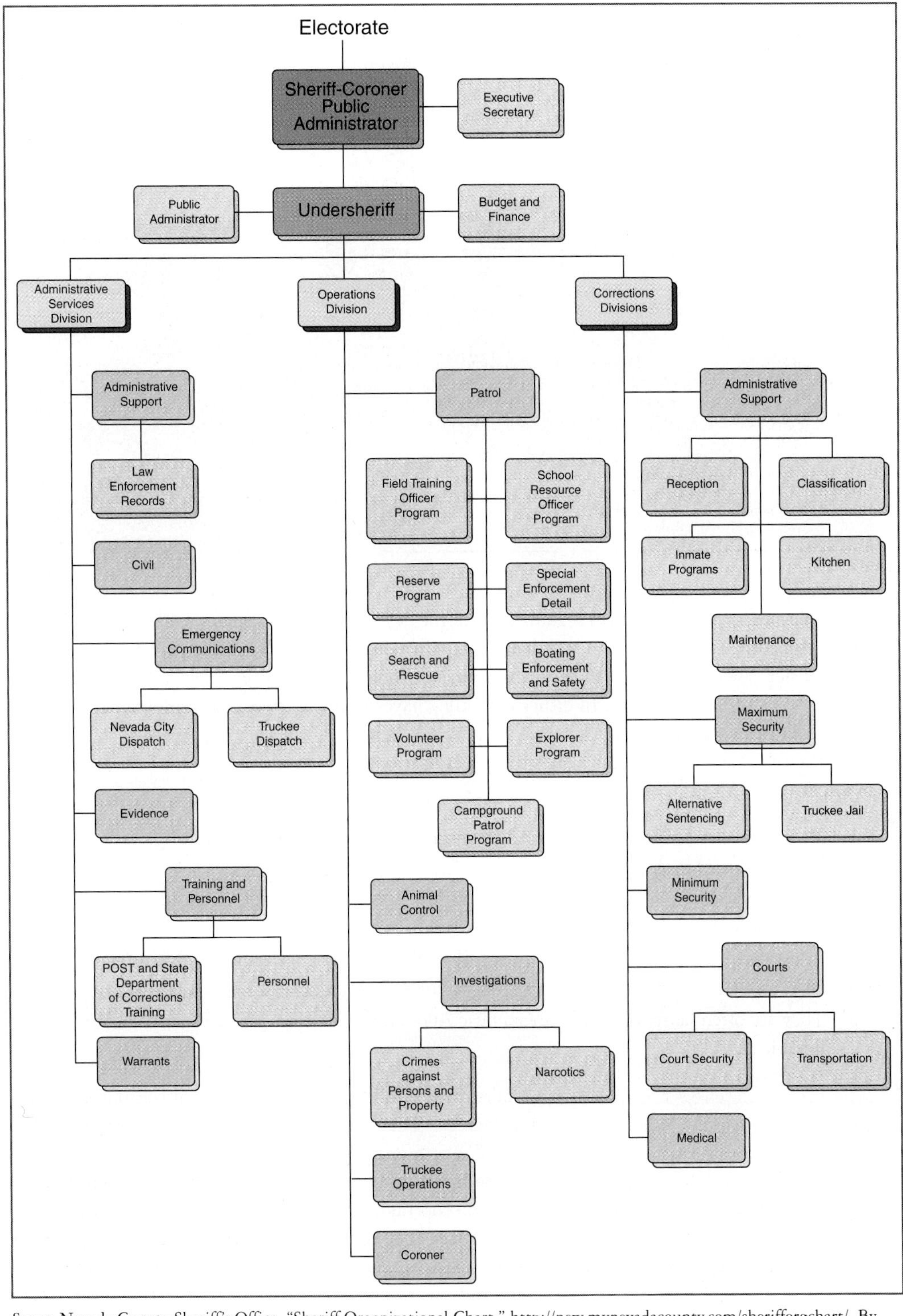

Source: Nevada County Sheriff's Office, "Sheriff Organizational Chart," http://new.mynevadacounty.com/sherifforgchart/. By permission of Nevada County Sheriff's Department.

time to time has been given arrest authority, such as in the wake of Hurricane Katrina. The Posse Comitatus Act prohibits the military from engaging in domestic law enforcement functions, but if Congress so allows, the act can be circumvented. In any case, the National Guard and the military are still connected with the government, not unlike the typical police agency. Perhaps it is useful, then, to distinguish between government and civilian law enforcement organizations.

Two deputies use snowmobiles while on patrol for the Onondaga County (New York) Sheriff's Department Special Enforcement Unit. How do sheriff's departments differ from other law enforcement agencies? In what ways are they the same?

Steve Ruark/*Syracuse Newspapers*/The Image Works

The closest parallel civilian organization to the modern law enforcement agency is a private security company. Such companies may look like police departments, but most private security officials are not sanctioned to use force in the course of their duties, nor are they authorized to make arrests in the traditional sense. In either case, they have to rely on sworn law enforcement officials to take over at a certain point.

Police organizations differ from other organizations in more than just arrest powers and use of force:

1. Their status as *public* agencies makes them quite distinct from the realm of private business.[30]
2. Unlike private organizations, they exist within a political environment, as do other public organizations, such as prosecutor's offices and universities.
3. They work in the public eye and must follow all the rules applicable to government agencies.
4. They are not run for profit, as are private security agencies and some private prisons.
5. They are often hamstrung by bureaucratic rules and regulations that can stifle creativity and flexibility.

WEB PATROL 4-8

Police Organization and Management Issues for the Next Decade
http://www.mycrimekit.com

Like most public agencies, police organizations have limited resources. They often have to pursue grants and other sources of "soft money" (that is, funding apart from their year-to-year budgets) just to make ends meet. Many private companies have no shortage of cash in the bank, and when they don't have the money they need, they can take out loans. This is not a luxury available to public-sector organizations, although parent governments can borrow, typically through the issuance of bonds. Finally, whereas many businesses answer to the shareholders, police organizations have to answer to the public. They may not have to answer *directly*, but as we have already seen, some law enforcement executives (such as sheriffs) do answer to the voters.

Law enforcement organizations also differ from other types of public and private organizations because the people who work in them generally fall into one of two categories: staff and line officials. A distinct "chain of command" is usually established in most law enforcement agencies.

nonsworn personnel
Support staff members of a law enforcement agency who are not empowered to make arrests.

sworn personnel
Members of a law enforcement agency who are empowered to make arrests.

Staff versus Line Duties. Staff (**nonsworn personnel**) assist line officials (**sworn personnel**). In some organizations, there are as many or more staff than line personnel. Secretaries and administrative assistants, human resources personnel, crime analysts, 911 dispatchers, record keepers, and a host of other functional specialists tend to fall into this category. The chief in most large agencies has a secretary or an office manager. This person is usually nonsworn. In very large agencies, the office manager may have additional assistants under his or her command. Likewise, crime analysts are often nonsworn, but the units they work in tend to be headed by sworn officials, such as sergeants. By contrast, sworn personnel consist of all the commissioned peace officers within the organization, from the chief or sheriff all the way down to the frontline officers or deputies. Small rural police agencies are not always organized in this fashion, but the typical agency has at least some mix of staff and sworn personnel. This is not the case in most other public agencies.

Chain of Command. Every organization, public or private, follows a chain of command. Private companies tend to have a chief executive officer (CEO), a president, or both at the helm. Schools have principals. Most prosecutor's offices are run by an elected district attorney. In this respect, police agencies, sheriff's departments, and other law enforcement agencies are no different; someone is in charge. Where law enforcement agencies part ways with other organizations, though, is in the **chain of command.**

WEB PATROL 4-9

How Police Supervisory Styles Influence Patrol Officer Behavior
http://www.mycrimekit.com

The chain of command is the unbroken line of authority that extends through all levels of an organization, from the highest to the lowest. More specifically, the chain of command clarifies who answers to whom. Most often, police departments follow a military chain of command. The rank structure in a municipal police department may begin with the chief, who supervises a number of captains, who in turn supervise a number of lieutenants, who in turn supervise a number of sergeants, who in turn supervise the frontline officers.

chain of command
The supervisory channel within a law enforcement organization.

The functional structure of a command chain incorporates the notion of **span of control,** which refers to the number of subordinates supervised by one person. The bigger the organization and the higher up the ladder a person ascends, the greater that person's span of control.

span of control
The number of subordinates supervised by one person.

Command structures differ from one police agency to the next, but they share much in common with the military command structure. This also makes law enforcement agencies different from most other organizations. While this command structure has its advantages, it is also significantly limited, as we will see shortly.

quasi-military
An organizational structure that follows the military model to some extent, but with subtle differences.

The Traditional Approach

The traditional approach to police organization hails from Sir Robert Peel's recommendation that agencies follow the military model. One of the first principles Peel espoused was that "the police must be stable, efficient, and organized along military lines."[31] As we just saw, Peel's legacy lives on. But because few police organizations follow the military model in every detail, they are often said to be **quasi-military** in structure. The leaders of law enforcement agencies are not called generals, for instance. Also, there tend to be fewer distinct ranks in the typical police organization than in the military. Even so, there is much similarity to the military model in terms of how most police agencies are organized.

Frederick W. Taylor (1856–1915)
A classical organizational theorist who posited that worker productivity could be increased through careful attention to how work was allocated and who performed what functions.

Classical Organizational Theory. Peel's advocacy of the military model for policing was echoed by O. W. Wilson and other influential figures in early American policing. But what is the logic for this model of organization? What makes the quasi-military model so desirable? To answer these questions, we need to look beyond policing to the realm of organizational theory—particularly to the legacy of two key individuals, **Frederick W. Taylor** and **Max Weber.**

Max Weber (1864–1920)
A classical organizational theorist, widely acknowledged as the father of bureaucracy, who identified five principles that he suggested are characteristic of an effective bureaucratic organization.

Taylor studied organizations for the purpose of improving worker productivity. During his time, people often worked to the point of exhaustion. People were assigned tasks they were unfamiliar with or were incapable of performing adequately. In a word, they worked ineffectively. Taylor's contribution was in the area of increasing worker productivity through careful attention to how work was allocated and who performed what functions. Weber, on the other hand, studied the features of successful organizations. Together, Weber and Taylor ushered in an era of scientific management. They believed that scientific principles should be applied to workplaces so that workers could be as productive as possible with the least amount of effort. Perhaps above all else, Taylor stressed the role of managers in ensuring a smooth-running workplace.

Another influential figure during these early years was **Henry Fayol,** who believed that a universal science of management was applicable to all organizations. He noted that greater technical

Henry Fayol (1841–1925)
A classical organizational theorist who posited that a universal science of management was applicable to all organizations and that greater technical knowledge was needed at higher organizational levels.

knowledge was needed at higher organizational levels. To this end, he developed five principles that he felt were essential for an organization to be effective:

1. A program of action prepared by means of annual and ten-year forecasts.
2. An organizational chart to guarantee order and to assure each person a definite place; careful recruiting; and technical, intellectual, moral, and administrative training of personnel of all ranks to facilitate finding the right person for each position.
3. Directing the activities of subordinates.
4. Meetings of the department heads of every division; conferences of the division heads presided over by the managing director to ensure coordination.
5. Universal control, based on clear accounting data made rapidly available.[32]

bureaucracy
The administrative structure of a large or complex organization, typically employing task-specialized bureaus or departments.

Max Weber is widely recognized as one of the first people to study **bureaucracy.** He did not *invent* bureaucracy, nor is he responsible for all the negative connotations the term takes on today. But Weber did identify five principles that he suggested are characteristic of an effective bureaucratic organization.[33] These principles can be applied to law enforcement:

1. *Well-defined hierarchy of authority.* In every traditional police organization, superior-subordinate relationships are based on authority, from the patrol officer up to the chief. Each person at a higher position or rank has more authority than do his or her subordinates.
2. *Specialization.* Every person's job is broken into precise, routine, and well-defined tasks. By dividing tasks among several work groups, the organization becomes more efficient.
3. *Formalization.* There must be a well-established system of rules and regulations detailing workers' duties to ensure uniformity and reduce discretion.
4. *Impersonality of management.* Decisions should be made without regard to personalities or individuals. Decision making should be based on the goals and objectives of the agency.
5. *Personnel decisions based on merit.* Positions should be filled and promotions made according to merit—that is, based on the experience and qualifications of the individual. The agency must strive to put the best qualified individuals in each position.

Does this sound like the typical police agency? The answer is most certainly yes. Every agency today has clearly defined levels of authority, specialization, and formalization. Authority is accomplished via the rank structure. Specialization is evident not just in levels of supervision (the vertical dimension), but also within the agency's various divisions (the horizontal dimension). These two features can be seen in the organizational charts presented earlier in this chapter. Concerning formalization, every law enforcement agency has a policy manual that employees must follow. In Chapter 1, we saw that policing in the political era was plagued by corruption and favoritism. Weber's principle of impersonality of management is intended to avoid these sorts of problems. Finally, merit-based personnel decisions are standard in modern police agencies. For example, to rise to the level of sergeant in a municipal police department, one must take a test that screens out unqualified applicants. At a glance, these principles of scientific management seem desirable and essential. But they have also been criticized extensively, as the following section attests.

Problems with the Classical Approach. Policing today is immersed in the so-called community era, which evolved from a number of events. We will discuss here the limits of the quasi-military bureaucratic structure that characterizes most modern law enforcement organizations.

In 1979, Dorothy Guyot, a management analyst with the Yonkers (New York) Police Department, conducted three national surveys of police agencies to assess their management issues. She found that there were five sets of problems associated with the traditional form of bureaucratic police management: lack of management flexibility in personnel decisions; lack of incentives within the rank of police officer; militarism; communication blocked by a tall organizational structure; and insularity.[34] The authors of a similar study reached this conclusion:

> Police organizations in our sample did have relatively greater communications problems; there were relatively greater amounts of distrust, particularly of higher echelons in police departments; there were relatively low levels of morale associated with these phenomena and there were lower perceived levels of organizational performance associated with all these factors.[35]

Weber's principles are also limited on other fronts. A key limitation of the traditional police organizational structure is authoritarianism. The mission and goals of the organization are often set by top-level officials without soliciting or considering input from subordinates. For example, changing a department's mission statement to espouse community policing principles without seeking or considering input from line officers often creates an atmosphere of resistance. Scores of researchers have found that this sort of authoritative management style is associated with worker frustration, alienation, and low productivity.[36]

Critics of traditional police organization claim that the complex bureaucratic structure stifles innovation. In a department of a thousand sworn personnel, imagine what it would take for a line officer to bring an innovative idea to the chief. The officer would have to work his or her way up the rank structure, a process that typically takes excessive time and often distorts the original message. Related to this is a common problem within big bureaucratic organizations: poor information flow. Most students are familiar with the game of telephone, in which you line up a number of people, whisper something in the first person's ear, and tell them to "pass it on." By the time the last person in line repeats what he or she was just told, it is often at odds with the original message. Even if the original message makes its way to the top unchanged, bureaucratic organizations are notorious for resisting change.[37]

Perhaps the most significant criticism of traditional police organization is lack of motivation. Some researchers have found that the police officer in a traditional organization lacks motivation because of psychological deprivation. That is, the organizational setting places police officers in a position where they have very little control over their job and are not involved in the day-to-day operation of the department. In contrast, officers who *are* given job autonomy and decision-making authority tend to be remarkably more content with their job.[38] Findings like these have given birth to contemporary theories of organizational management.

Is there a better way to organize a law enforcement organization than relying on the quasi-military model? According to some reformers, the answer is a resounding yes. Contemporary approaches to organization turn the traditional model on its head.

Contemporary Organization

As previously discussed, the classical structure is typical of most police organizations. It is also clear that this model has its limitations. Critics feel that the classical approach is, in a word, "mechanistic."[39] A contrasting view of organizations is that they are "organic," like living, breathing entities made up of real human beings. The mechanistic view of organizations separates the people element from the command structure. The organic view does the opposite; it allows employees greater input and responsibility in decision making, especially at the lower levels. Applying this thinking to policing, an organic organizational structure would elevate the status of the line officers by giving them some control over the organization's mission, day-to-day operations, and key decisions. Advocates believe that this is a more flexible and adaptive method of organization.[40]

Human Relations. The **human relations** approach to organization hails from the view that all organizations are organic entities. Formally defined, the human relations philosophy refers to "management engaged in a social process that combines techniques and people to mutually benefit the organization and the employee."[41] This definition can be better understood with reference to three important studies that are credited with its emergence. First, between 1927 and 1932, the Western Electric Company conducted a series of experiments in its Hawthorne facilities, near Chicago, particularly to determine whether the level of lighting or the pattern of employee breaks affected productivity. These **Hawthorne experiments** revealed that it was not the lighting or the breaks that affected productivity as much as it was the attention that employees received.

Maslow's hierarchy of needs is also credited, to some extent, with ushering in a new way of thinking about organization (Figure 4-12). His research revealed that people need more than just security, such as a stable job. They need higher-level emotional satisfaction. Douglas McGregor's **Theory X** and **Theory Y** were also important contributors. He identified two types of workers. First, there are the Theory X workers, people who lack ambition, are indolent by nature, are self-centered, and so on. Then there are Theory Y workers, those who are motivated and who fail only when management fails to provide a supportive working environment. The Hawthorne experiments, coupled with Maslow's and McGregor's contributions, gave rise to key principles of human

human relations
An organizational philosophy that contends that all organizations are organic entities and that management should engage in a social process that combines techniques and people to benefit both the organization and the employee.

Hawthorne experiments
A series of experiments conducted between 1927 and 1932 by the Western Electric Company at its Hawthorne facilities to determine whether the level of lighting or the pattern of employee breaks affected productivity. The experiments revealed that it was not the lighting or the breaks that affected productivity as much as it was the attention that employees received.

Maslow's hierarchy of needs
A psychological theory proposed by Abraham Maslow in his 1943 paper entitled "A Theory of Human Motivation." Maslow's theory holds that once people have achieved their basic needs, they will strive for higher-level emotional satisfaction and personal fulfillment.

Theory X
One of two types of workers posited by Douglas McGregor as lacking ambition, being indolent by nature, being self-centered, and so on.

Theory Y
One of two types of workers posited by Douglas McGregor as being motivated and failing only when management fails to provide a supportive working environment.

Figure 4-12 • Abraham Maslow's Hierarchy of Needs

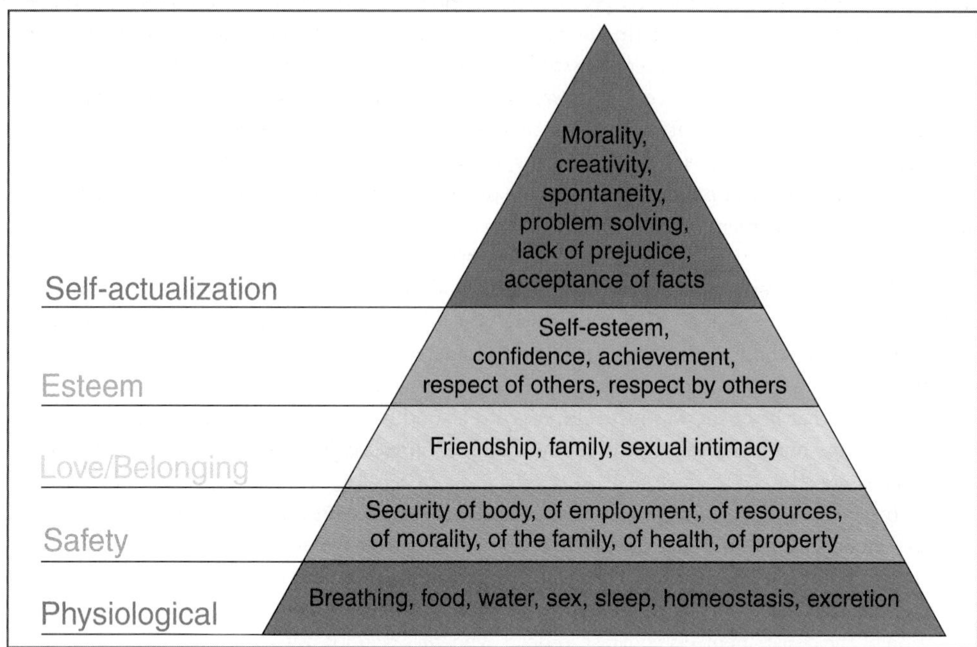

Source: Abraham H. Maslow; Robert D. Frager (Editor); James Fadiman (Editor), *Motivation and personality*, 3rd, © 1987. Electronically reproduced by permission of Pearson Education, Inc., Upper Saddle River, New Jersey.

relations theory. They guided the development of several policies and procedures in contemporary organizations:

1. Workers are viewed as whole individuals, not just as people who perform certain tasks for the organization, but as people with feelings and desires that go beyond the work environment.
2. Higher productivity and greater human satisfaction require employee participation in the organization.
3. Communication is the nervous system of the organization.
4. Cooperation in the form of teamwork is an indispensable management practice if the organization is to survive.
5. Employees are diversely motivated. Satisfaction comes from job accomplishment, recognition, and participation, as well as from economic and monetary rewards.[42]

participatory management
A form of leadership that allows subordinates to participate in decision making and planning, especially with regard to the manner in which their own units are operated.

quality circle
A group of qualified employees from all ranks who work together, often around one table, to solve organizational problems.

Applying this thinking to policing, there have been two key periods when advocates urged police agencies to adopt human relations principles. First, during the 1970s, when the police were initially immersed in the movement toward improving community relations, many people believed that agencies should shed their quasi-military structure and adopt a more open, employee-centered environment. It was believed that such a structure would facilitate better relations between officers and the public. More recently, during the second period, many of the changes we are witnessing in the community policing and problem-solving movements are consistent with human relations theory. **Participatory management** is an important concept in police management circles today. It refers to a form of leadership that allows subordinates to participate in decision making and planning, especially with regard to the manner in which their own units are operated. Related to this is the use of **quality circles,** groups of qualified officers from all ranks who work together (often around one table) to solve organizational problems.

Contingency and Systems Perspectives. The classical view of organizations is at the opposite end of the spectrum from the human relations perspective. In reality, though, the typical organization can enjoy the benefits of both. Bureaucratic structures will not disappear. It is difficult to conceive of a police department that would abandon its rank structure altogether and treat everyone on the payroll as equals. Likewise, trying to cater to everyone's individual needs is all but impossible. A mixture of both elements, though, may be an effective approach to organization. This is the idea behind contingency theory.

Contingency theory recognizes that there are often different types of tasks within a single organization: repetitive and nonrepetitive tasks. The former call for standardization and control. The latter call for flexibility and participatory management. How is this manifested in the typical police agency? On the one hand, consider the traffic enforcement division. Its tasks are repetitive, and it can easily be managed via a traditional organizational model; there is little need for flexibility in writing tickets. On the other hand, a problem-solving unit within the same agency may need to be structured to allow team members to be creative and do what it takes within the limits of the law to effectively target certain crimes. This is the very definition of contingency theory; organizational strategies are contingent on the tasks at hand.

contingency theory
A management theory that recognizes that there are often different types of tasks within a single organization, including repetitive tasks that call for standardization and control and nonrepetitive tasks that call for flexibility and participatory management.

The final approach to organizational style considered in this chapter is the **systems perspective,** which is rooted in biology. This view posits that organizations are living organisms that strive for a state of equilibrium, or balance, and that affect or are affected by their environment.[43] The last element is most telling. Nowadays, it is very clear that police organizations do not operate in a vacuum. They affect their surroundings through officers' actions and inactions. They are also affected by the environment (that is, the media, public opinion, relationships with other government officials, relationships with private business, and so on). They are, to use some organizational terminology, "open systems." Systems theory differs from the other approaches in its concern with organizational parts, and their relationships to one another, more than the whole being. The systems view of organizational design takes the same approach—making sure all the pieces of the whole work together to ensure survival.

systems perspective
A view of organizational style, rooted in biology, that posits that organizations are living organisms that strive for a state of equilibrium, or balance, and that affect or are affected by their environment.

SUMMARY

- The roughly 20,000 law enforcement agencies in the United States are found at the federal, state, and local levels. Most federal law enforcement agencies are located in the Department of Homeland Security and the Department of Justice. Most state police agencies follow either a centralized or decentralized model. Local law enforcement agencies consist mostly of municipal police departments and county sheriff's offices. Other agencies operate at the local level, but they are the exception.
- Law enforcement organizations differ from other organizations in several respects, but there are two *key* differences: Law enforcement organizations have line and staff personnel, and most follow a quasi-military command structure. The quasi-military organizational model is not without its faults, which led to the emergence in police agencies of modern organizational theories and designs (for example, human relations and contingency theories).

COMING FULL CIRCLE

For Discussion

Return to the questions posed at the start of this chapter. Have any of your answers changed since you read the chapter? What portions of this chapter helped you answer these questions?

Writing Assignment

Using material from this chapter and additional resources, write a 500-word essay in response to one of the questions presented at the beginning of the chapter. Submit your essay to your instructor if asked to do so.

KEY TERMS AND NAMES

bureaucracy
Bureau of Alcohol, Tobacco, Firearms and Explosives (ATF)
centralized policing model
chain of command
contingency theory
Customs and Border Protection (CBP)
decentralized policing model
Drug Enforcement Administration (DEA)
Federal Bureau of Investigation (FBI)
Frederick W. Taylor
Hawthorne experiments
Henry Fayol
Homeland Security Act of 2002
human relations
Immigration and Customs Enforcement (ICE)
local agency
Maslow's hierarchy of needs
Max Weber
money laundering
municipal police department
nonsworn personnel

organization
participatory management
quality circle
quasi-military
Secret Service
sheriff's department
span of control
sworn personnel
systems perspective
Theory X
Theory Y
U.S. Marshals Service (USMS)

WEB INTERACTIVITY

Visit the FBI at www.fbi.gov, and familiarize yourself with the resources available through the site. Then enter the following URL in your browser: http://www.fbi.gov/page2/jan08/shotspotter012308.html. (In the event that the URL is not working, search for "A Weapon against Crime" on the FBI's homepage.) Read and summarize the story, describing the FBI's role in the incident. What is the ShotSpotter system described in the article? Where does the article say that it was used? Is the technology applicable only to federal agencies? Submit your work to your instructor if asked to do so.

Federal Bureau of Investigation

REVIEW QUESTIONS

1. Identify and describe a number of key federal law enforcement agencies, and explain their roles.
2. How do police organizations differ from other types of organizations?

PERSONNEL ISSUES

SECTION II

chapter five

BECOMING A COP

LEARNING OBJECTIVES

After reading this chapter, students should be able to:

1. Discuss what it takes to become a police officer.
2. Explain the importance of diversity and the problem of discrimination in policing.
3. Identify at least two caveats that police applicants should be aware of before entering the profession.

OFFICER
WALK IN AN OFFICER'S SHOES
THE ACADEMY
TACTICAL TRAINING

THINK ABOUT IT

On March 16, 1996, Robert Jordan took a test for the position of entry-level police officer with the Law Enforcement Council of Connecticut, a consortium of fourteen different cities in the eastern part of the state. The test, like many of its kind, contained questions intended to assess applicants' cognitive and scholastic abilities. Jordan was informed, along with all of the other test takers, that the test "will generate an eligibility list for distribution to the participating police departments for possible future employment."

The test, developed by Wonderlic Personnel Test, Inc. (WPT), came with an official user's manual for each exam, including a table of recommended minimum scores for a number of occupations.[1] The company recommended a score of 22 as the minimum for a police officer. Further, Wonderlic recommended hiring people who scored at most four points below and eight points above 22.

In the fall of 1996, Jordan learned that the city of New London was going to be hiring police officers, so he requested a meeting with Keith Harrigan, the assistant city manager in charge of personnel decisions. Jordan was told he was ineligible to become a police officer because he had scored too high on the written test. New London set a test score range of 20 to 27 for police officers, and Jordan had scored above 27. Jordan promptly filed a lawsuit against the city, claiming that his equal protection rights, under the Fifth Amendment to the U.S. Constitution, had been violated. The national media picked up the story, and the headline of the day declared "Too Smart to Be a Cop."

While Jordan felt that he had been discriminated against for scoring well on the exam, the city was concerned with ensuring employment longevity for its officers and minimizing turnover. City officials felt that, given Jordan's apparently extraordinary level of intelligence, he would not have been happy as a police officer and would have quickly left his post, leaving the city with little return on its investment in his selection and training. At issue in the lawsuit, then, was whether there is a justifiable relationship between high cognitive ability and job satisfaction/longevity and, if so, whether a jurisdiction can base its hiring practices on such a relationship.

Jordan's case was heard in the U.S. District Court for the District of Connecticut.[2] Interestingly, the court sided with the city of New London, finding that the city

> followed the instructions accompanying the WPT test, on which they rationally could have relied as authoritative. Additionally, a body of professional literature concludes that hiring overqualified applicants leads to subsequent job dissatisfaction and turnover. While such studies have been challenged, it cannot be said that their conclusions have been refuted.[3]

Most equal protection lawsuits have been brought by people claiming to be victims of illegitimate discrimination. If African Americans are hired significantly less often than whites, for example, then there may be a basis for a lawsuit claiming discrimination because race is not a legitimate hiring criterion. Jordan's case was different, not only because he was not a member of any historically protected group but because the city reached its hiring decision by paying attention to what the court recognized as legitimate concerns. This raises several interesting questions to keep in mind as you read this chapter:

1. Was New London's hiring decision fair in this case?
2. How many other cities throughout the United States base their hiring decisions almost exclusively on test scores?
3. Is it really possible to be too smart to be a cop?
4. How effective are written tests at screening candidates for law enforcement positions?

INTRODUCTION

This chapter is about becoming a cop. We begin by taking a critical look at the hiring process. Then we move on to the academy experience and describe field training following graduation. This chapter also looks at the important issues of diversity and discrimination in law enforcement. The demographics of the typical police agency have changed in recent years, as more women and minorities are on the job than ever before. We consider the implications of this trend.

Most people are drawn to policing out of a desire to help people and catch bad guys. But policing, like any career, can have its downside. This chapter concludes with a look at two issues that sometimes surprise uninformed applicants: sexual harassment in the workplace and residency requirements. In Chapter 7, we look at other difficulties that go along with the job, such as stress and fatigue. We believe that it is important to identify these and other "caveats" in police work so those who enter the profession can do so with realistic expectations.

BECOMING AN OFFICER

Becoming a police officer involves much more than just taking an exam and spending a few weeks in the police academy. For many, it is a lifelong pursuit. First, of course, candidates need to apply for police work and be hired. In addition to test scores, the applicant's interview performance, character, and medical and drug history all factor into the hiring decision. Hiring is only the first step, however. Academy training comes next, followed by field training. The performance of police officers is measured throughout their careers. Those officers who hope for promotion must demonstrate, through their job performance, that they have the ability and qualifications to take on greater responsibilities.

Law enforcement is generally regarded as a **civil service** job. Civil service is a system in which employees are hired, retained, advanced, disciplined, and discharged on the basis of merit, or their abilities and qualifications. Civil service is in contrast to the **patronage system** of old. You may recall from Chapter 1 that during the political era, police hiring decisions were based more on an individual's political support for whomever was in charge than on the applicant's individual qualifications.

civil service
A system in which employees are hired, retained, advanced, disciplined, and discharged on the basis of merit (that is, their abilities and qualifications).

patronage system
A system of hiring in which decisions are based more on an individual's political support for an officeholder than on his or her abilities and qualifications. Patronage was common in police agencies during the political era.

An LAPD recruitment poster. What are the advantages and disadvantages of a career in law enforcement?

JoinLAPD.com © Copyright 2004. The Los Angeles Police Department.

civil service commission
A federal, state, or local agency charged with ensuring that employees in civil service positions receive specific protections.

Civil service was implemented to enhance police professionalism. Many states, local governments, and even the federal government have **civil service commissions** that ensure that employees in civil service positions receive specific protections such as job security and equal pay for equivalent work. Knowing that policing is a civil service job provides an appreciation for the intricacies and nuances of the hiring process; because people who become police officers tend to stay in their positions for a long time, considerable attention must be given to hiring the right people.

The Hiring Decision

Whether a person will be hired as a police officer depends on a number of conditions. Generally, candidates are evaluated on the basis of their test score, interview performance, personal background, performance on a polygraph exam, medical history, and past drug use. First, though, how do law enforcement agencies attract applicants? Quite simply, they recruit by running advertisements in newspapers, on the Internet, on TV, and so on. The problem, as police specialist Ken Peak has observed, is that agencies are often made to feel as though they have to find people who can "walk on water."[4] Early police reformer August Vollmer once said that candidates for the position of police officer should

WEB PATROL 5-1
A Police Officer's Mission
http://www.mycrimekit.com

> have the wisdom of Solomon, the courage of David, the patience of Job and leadership of Moses, the kindness of the Good Samaritan, the diplomacy of Lincoln, the tolerance of the Carpenter of Nazareth, and, finally, an intimate knowledge of every branch of natural, biological, and social sciences.[5]

Suffice it to say, that's a tall order!

Recruitment. Jobs in policing can be quite competitive, depending on the position and the timing. For positions regarded as prestigious, such as those with the federal government, getting a job can be quite difficult. Timing can be important. One applicant for the Seattle Police Department during the early 1990s took the exam with roughly a thousand other people in a lecture hall at the University of Washington, but the department had a mandate to hire only about a dozen officers.

Fortunately for those looking for police work, such stories are now the exception. In fact, police departments around the country are increasingly having to come to grips with a somewhat shallow hiring pool.[6] Recently, the National Association of Police Organizations put recruitment at the top of a list of problems facing police departments today.[7]

The hiring crisis in law enforcement is not to be taken lightly. The Los Angeles Police Department saw a 50 percent reduction in applications over the course of three years.[8] The Chicago Police Department had 25,000 applicants in 1993 and only 1,900 in 2000.[9] Why the sudden decline?

There are many reasons for today's lack of qualified applicants. One has been the war in the Middle East, which has drained young men and women from the U.S. civilian workforce. Another explanation has been the relative strength of the economy; police departments have a hard time competing with higher-paying private-sector jobs. An increasing (though relatively small) number of agencies are also requiring that their applicants have at least a few college credits, if not an actual degree. This further restricts the pool of eligible applicants. Unfavorable press coverage of scandals and corruption can further discourage people from applying.

In response, agencies are going to great pains to offer attractive schedules, benefits, and job perks and are aggressively recruiting applicants. Larger departments have officers who do nothing but travel around the country to recruit. Others have conducted studies to determine how best to attract applicants.

Testing Requirements. An applicant usually takes two tests to become an officer: a written test and a physical agility test. Written tests are intended to gauge general intelligence as well as reading and writing skills. To ensure that their tests are valid (that is, able to measure what they intend to measure) and reliable (the results don't vary markedly from one test to the next), most agencies use exams prepared by companies that specialize in creating exams for various occupations. One of those companies, WPT, was mentioned at the beginning of this chapter.

Some departments also use the written exam as an opportunity to determine an applicant's personality type. Personality tests like the Minnesota Multiphasic Personality Inventory and the California Personality Inventory are routinely used in the hiring process. They consist of numerous, sometimes odd and repetitive, questions that result in scores that agencies can then use to weed out the psychologically unfit.[10]

The city of New London, Connecticut, mentioned in this chapter's opening story, was not alone in its decision to deny employment to very smart candidates. A study of police hiring and retention in Tucson, Arizona, revealed that the IQ scores of officers who dropped out of the academy were significantly higher than those who stayed in.[11] In contrast, though, another study of sheriff's deputies revealed that those who scored highest were most likely to have successful law enforcement careers.[12] The jury appears to still be out, then, in terms of whether test scores alone can be used to determine future success in policing.

As for physical testing, every applicant must meet certain criteria. Physical agility tests vary widely from agency to agency. Some focus specifically on the candidates' ability to perform the job. State trooper applicants in Washington, for example, are required to lift a tire onto the mock hub of an automobile—among other tasks. Other departments ensure that their applicants can perform a certain number of push-ups and sit-ups and run a specified distance within a limited time period. The challenge for those involved in hiring police officers is to ensure that any exam is truly job-related. In fact, tests *have* to be job-related to avoid discrimination complaints. Some agencies therefore survey their officers to determine what physical work they engage in regularly, and then they tailor the physical agility exams to meet those tasks.[13]

The Interview. About 90 percent of all police agencies also use oral interviews for hiring decisions.[14] The vast majority of candidates, however, are screened out during the written and physical testing phase, leaving relatively few labor-intensive, time-consuming interviews. Oral interviews are often conducted by a board of officials, including active police officers from the jurisdiction and some civilians. Psychologists or psychiatrists might serve on such boards or might conduct separate interviews. To save time and resources, it is in the interest of hiring authorities to do as much screening as possible before the interviewing phase.

A candidate can get a stellar score on a test and yet be a lousy police officer. Consequently, oral interviews are intended to pick up where the written and agility tests leave off. They gauge factors like confidence, poise, reasoning abilities, oral skills, memory, and observational prowess. Candidates are often asked questions about what they would do in a specific situation. These questions can sometimes be difficult because candidates who have no background in law enforcement may be unsure of how to respond.

To assess observational skills, some elements of the interview may be staged (for example, there may be a phrase written on a board in the interview room). Candidates may be asked later to recall certain features of the room. Officers on patrol need to be observant; hence, this interview component might be especially useful in hiring officers seeking to work patrol.

Background Investigations. By far, the most expensive and time-consuming phase of the hiring process is the background investigation, sometimes called a *character investigation*, in which an investigator will peer into all conceivable elements of the applicant's life. The investigator will draw on official records and will conduct in-depth interviews with friends, family members, coworkers, acquaintances, and even former acquaintances. In short, the background investigation is intended to discover those skeletons, if any, in the applicant's closet that are not revealed during other phases of the hiring process. Here is what happens in a background investigation for police officer applicants in the city of San Diego:

> The Police Department will conduct a thorough investigation of your background. You will be requested to authorize organizations and individuals who know you to release and verify relevant information about you. The Background Investigator will contact prior employers, relatives, and references. Information provided during these contacts may result in other individuals being contacted. The investigator will check into your employment history, credit status, driving record, and other pertinent information. A criminal history check will also be made. Next, you will be scheduled for an in-depth background interview with the Police Department Investigator. During this appointment, you will be fingerprinted.[15]

Polygraph Exam. About two-thirds of America's law enforcement agencies rely on polygraph exams as part of the employment screening process.[16] Polygraphs are used to encourage honesty during questioning. The examiner begins by asking a number of reference questions, such as, "Is your name John Smith?" Then questioning about prior criminal history, drug use, and the like begins. Polygraphs are not without their faults. Evidence from polygraph exams is not allowed in court to prove guilt, for instance. On the other hand, polygraphists feel that their devices are very difficult to fool.[17] Polygraph exams continue to be used in many police hiring decisions because many law enforcement officials believe in the polygraph's usefulness.

As evidence of the need for polygraphs, Richard Arther, CEO of Scientific Lie Detection, Inc., and director of the National Training Center of Polygraph Science, has identified some of the following "discoveries" as a result of polygraph testing of police applicants:

1. An applicant with the Wichita, Kansas, Police Department admitted to the polygraphist that he had been involved in many burglaries. The detective division was able to clear eight unsolved crimes as a result of the applicant's confession.
2. An applicant for the San Diego Sheriff's Department admitted to that agency's polygraphist that on weekends he would go from bar to bar pretending to be a drunk. He would then seek out people to pick fights with, since he could only become sexually stimulated when inflicting pain on others. He also admitted that he got rid of his frustrations by savagely beating people.[18]

WEB PATROL 5-2

American Polygraph Association
http://www.mycrimekit.com

Medical and Drug Screening. One of the last steps in the hiring process is medical and drug screening. Although polygraphs and background checks can indicate past drug use, formal drug screening provides results that are difficult to dispute. Besides detecting past or current drug use, screening also assesses medical fitness to perform the job. A person with a serious heart condition, for instance, probably wouldn't be a good fit in any police agency, considering that officers have to physically exert themselves from time to time.

Medical screening is also used to check applicants' vision and weight, among other factors. Most agencies will not hire candidates who fail to meet some uncorrected vision requirement. Likewise, many agencies will not hire overweight people. This may seem discriminatory on one level, but there are certain bona fide job requirements that an obese or legally blind individual cannot perform. The Pittsburgh, Pennsylvania, Police Department describes its medical screening procedure this way:

> The medical exam . . . evaluates a candidate's health and physical capacity for work as a police officer. It may include such tests as the combined cardiovascular-pulmonary stress test (treadmill test), hearing test, vision test, and blood test. Aerobic exercise is essential in developing the cardiovascular-pulmonary levels required. If you have not done so already, we suggest that you begin some sort of physical conditioning or fitness training program in order to prepare for the medical examination. . . . The medical standards include having distant vision of at least 20/70, uncorrected, in the stronger eye, correctable to 20/20, and at least 20/200, uncorrected, in the weaker eye, correctable to at least 20/40. In addition, candidates shall have normal depth and color perception, and must be free of any significant visual abnormality.[19]

Note that the Pittsburgh Police Department does not have a maximum weight requirement.

The Academy

Once a candidate successfully passes through all of the steps involved in the hiring process and is offered employment, he or she will go to an academy for training. The teaching methods and curricula of academies differ depending on the student's anticipated future position and the hiring agency. A common thread runs through all police academies, however: They all strive to teach candidates how to be effective officers and how to develop the all-important "sixth sense" needed for successful police work. Students must "pass" through the academy without incident, or they will be terminated.

Types of Academies. Academy training is regarded as one of the most important elements of the police hiring process. In this era of heightened civil liability, it is critical that recruits learn the limits of the law as it applies to police work. In addition, they need to learn proper procedures, including how and when to use force, how to drive a vehicle aggressively, how to make felony stops, how to deal with belligerent suspects, how to make arrests, how to document incidents, and how to investigate accidents. Needless to say, adequate coverage of these and other pertinent topics takes a great deal of time. The typical academy, in fact, trains recruits for approximately 400 hours.[20] This number varies considerably from place to place, however (Table 5-1).

There are generally three types of academies: in-house, regional, and state. Candidates for the position of trooper with the Washington State Patrol, for instance, are trained at the agency's academy in Shelton, Washington. In California, the Commission on Peace Officer Standards and Training (POST) certifies city, county, and regional academies throughout the state. More than 600 agencies in California voluntarily participate in POST. There are nearly 40 different academies cer-

Table 5-1 • Training Requirements for New Officer Recruits in Local Police Departments in the United States, by Size of Population Served, 2003

	Average Number of Hours Required							
	New Officer Recruits						Nonprobationary Officers, in Service	
	Academy			Field				
Population Served	Total	State-Mandated	Other Required	Total	State-Mandated	Other Required	State-Mandated	Other Required
All sizes	628	588	40	326	147	179	24	23
1,000,000 or more	1,016	689	327	513	153	360	23	7
500,000 to 999,999	920	588	332	561	104	456	20	18
250,000 to 499,999	950	620	330	652	200	452	20	14
100,000 to 249,999	815	642	173	624	253	371	24	23
50,000 to 99,999	721	657	64	598	268	330	18	32
25,000 to 49,999	702	657	46	527	210	317	21	28
10,000 to 24,999	672	642	30	442	164	279	20	31
2,500 to 9,999	630	597	32	314	151	162	28	25
Less than 2,500	577	542	35	199	106	93	23	16

Source: U.S. Department of Justice, Bureau of Justice Statistics, *Local Police Departments, 2003* (Washington, DC: U.S. Department of Justice, 2006), p. 9.

tified by POST, for all different types of agencies. In other states, Florida for example, police academies are often run through community colleges and other institutions of higher learning.

In a growing trend, civilians are paying their own way through police academies in the hopes of gaining employment as an officer after completing the program.[21] This saves agencies not only the expense of paying for academy training, but also the salaries that the newly hired trainees would be earning while going through their training. Some states, like New York, follow a hybrid model, allowing interested applicants to complete basic training requirements before seeking employment; once they are sworn officers, they complete additional training.[22]

Curricular Issues. Police training academies vary in terms of their curricula, but most are similar in the sense that they teach recruits the technical aspects of police work. A range of topics are usually covered, including the criminal justice system, law, patrol, investigation procedures, job proficiency (for example, using a firearm), administration, and problems likely to be encountered on the

Baltimore Police Officer Angel Santana, top, takes down fellow officer Dane Hicks during a training session at the Baltimore Police Academy in Baltimore on October 27, 2006. Why does police training vary from place to place? What topics do you think are especially important in such training?

Chris Gardner/AP Wide World Photos

Figure 5-1 • The Los Angeles Police Department Academy Curriculum

Academics encompasses arrest and booking procedures, preliminary investigation techniques, radio and communications, report writing, traffic investigation, and traffic enforcement. (230 hours)

Driving includes the Emergency Vehicle Operations Course, which covers defensive driving, pursuit policy, and safe vehicle handling. (40 hours)

Firearms Training includes weapon care and safety, marksmanship, tactical manipulation with the sidearm and shotgun, and chemical agents handling. (113 hours) Police candidates are strongly discouraged from seeking firearms instruction prior to entering the Police Academy. Poor marksmanship habits may be developed that are difficult or impossible to overcome.

Human Relations includes cultural sensitivity training, sexual harassment issues, media relations, stress management, disability awareness, community relations, tactical communications, hate crimes, missing persons, and domestic violence. (100 hours)

Law covers search and seizure, evidence, laws of arrest, crimes against persons and property, sex crimes, crimes against children, and other general criminal statutes falling under the California Penal Code, Los Angeles Municipal Code, Welfare and Institutions Code, and Federal Laws. (105 hours)

Physical Training builds strength and endurance through physical conditioning while promoting a positive attitude toward a fitness lifestyle. It also encompasses training in physical arrest techniques, controls, and weaponless defense. (142 hours)

Tactics covers patrol techniques and procedures, crimes in progress, building searches, vehicle stops, use of deadly force, and shooting policy. (98 hours)

LAPD Specific Training includes advanced tactical training, mobile field force tactics, patrol ride-along, mobile digital computer (in-car computer) training, alcohol abuse, administration of discipline, cultural diversity, K-9 operations, air support operations, bomb squad, community policing and problem solving, Spanish language, civil liabilities, and sexual harassment training.

Source: Los Angeles Police Department, "Academy Training," http://www.joinlapd.com/academy.html.

plebe system
A police academy model that closely parallels a military-style boot camp and that aims to produce well-groomed and disciplined officers.

technical training model
A police academy training model that emphasizes the technical aspects of police work and provides little or no training in such nontechnical areas as stress management, interaction with difficult people, problem solving, and sensitivity to marginalized groups.

college system
A police academy training model intended to enhance the professional aspects of police training curricula by exposing trainees to problem solving, sensitivity to marginalized groups, and other valuable topics in addition to required technical knowledge.

job.[23] More recently, topics like diversity, sexual harassment, dispute resolution, victim awareness, technological applications, stress management, and courtroom demeanor have made their way into academies, as well. What we have seen is something of a move away from the traditional **plebe system**, an academy model that closely parallels a military-style boot camp and that aims to produce well-groomed and disciplined officers, to a model that stresses twenty-first-century problems.[24]

Modern police academy curricula have also moved somewhat beyond the **technical training model**[25] insofar as they expose trainees more to the less familiar dimensions of their jobs, such as managing stress, interacting with difficult people, and so on. The **college system** of training is gaining in popularity today.[26] This doesn't mean that the academy is run by a college. Rather, the academy's intent is to train budding officers to be professionals. To this end, besides gaining the needed technical knowledge, trainees learn problem solving, sensitivity to marginalized groups, and other valuable skills.

Research reveals that the college system approach to police academy training is still largely the exception rather than the rule. One study revealed that less than 3 percent of basic academy training is spent on topics other than the technical aspects of the job.[27] This concern is particularly serious in light of the recent movement toward community-oriented policing, which prides itself on relationship building, communication, and problem solving.

An overview of one of the nation's cutting-edge police academy curricula, that of the Los Angeles Police Department (LAPD), can be seen in Figure 5-1. Note that the LAPD's officers receive more than 800 hours of academy training.

Learning the Sixth Sense. Academy training also teaches recruits the so-called **sixth sense,** namely a heightened sense of suspicion. As Peak has observed, "A suspicious nature is as important to the street officer as a fine touch is to a surgeon. The officer should not only be able to visually recognize but also be able to physically sense when something is wrong or out of the ordinary."[28] Understood differently, teaching officers to be suspicious is like teaching them to be observant. They are taught how to develop knowledge of the area they work in, the people they come into contact with, and the ordinary conditions of the area. With that knowledge, they can more capably identify things that are amiss. A person who doesn't "belong" in a certain area, for instance, may be cause for suspicion. A Chicago Police Department bulletin described the need to be suspicious in this way:

> Actions, dress, or location of a person often classify him as suspicious in the mind of a police officer. Men loitering near schools, public toilets, playgrounds and swimming pools may be sex perverts. Men loitering near ... any business at closing time may be robbery suspects. Men or youths walking along looking into cars may be car thieves or looking for something to steal. Persons showing evidence of recent injury, or whose clothing is disheveled, may be victims or participants in an assault or strong-arm robbery.[29]

WEB PATROL 5-3

The New York City Police Department Home Page
http://www.mycrimekit.com

WEB PATROL 5-4

The Los Angeles Police Department Home Page
http://www.mycrimekit.com

There is a fine line between being an effective, inquisitive officer and being too suspicious. Too much suspicion can have a number of unfortunate consequences. For example, an officer who is overly suspicious of people who fit a certain profile or social or demographic category runs the risk of infringing on their constitutional rights. Profiling, as we will see in Chapter 8, is an important topic in modern law enforcement and, according to its critics, something to be avoided at all costs. At the same time, though, there is a clear need for healthy suspicion; even the most apparently innocuous traffic stop could turn into a violent encounter in a matter of seconds. New officers need to be prepared.

sixth sense
A healthy sense of suspicion; the experience-based ability to intuit when something is amiss.

Field Training and Development

Field training is not unique to policing. It is just like the on-the-job training that comes with learning any other occupation. The first formal police field training program was implemented in San Jose, California, in the late 1960s.[30] Since then, field training programs have evolved and moved in various directions. Most, however, assign a field training officer (a veteran officer) to a recent academy graduate. But as Bob Dylan so eloquently put it, "The times, they are a-changin'." The traditional field training officer program is quickly being replaced by a new model: the police training officer model.

The Field Training Officer Approach. The traditional approach to field training typically consists of three distinct phases[31]: (1) introduction, in which the new officer learns agency policies and rules; (2) training and evaluation, in which the recruit spends the most time learning the complicated tasks police officers perform regularly; and (3) the final portion, involving first-hand observation of the new officer's actions by the **field training officer (FTO).** The duration of FTO programs varies, but they typically range from one to 12 weeks.[32] A probationary period extending beyond that allows additional interactions between FTOs and trainees. The National Institute of Justice recommends the following guidelines for this system of training new police officers[33]:

field training officer (FTO)
A veteran police officer tasked with providing on-the-job training and performance critique during a rookie police officer's initial assignment following graduation from the academy.

1. The FTO program should be considered a normal part of the selection and training process and should be designed to provide the organization with the best possible police officers.
2. In large organizations, patrol should be given administrative control over the FTO program because of the close interrelation between the FTO program and the patrol function.
3. The recruit should be assigned to several FTOs during the field training program to reduce the possibility of bias and personality conflicts and to allow several experienced trainers to evaluate the recruit.
4. All FTO training should be planned, standardized, and logically sequenced.
5. Each skill should be demonstrated and explained to the recruit by his or her assigned FTOs. The training guide should clearly separate and state the elements necessary for mastery of

YOU DECIDE

The Freebie

It's your first week on the job, and you go out to lunch with several of your senior colleagues. After everyone finishes and gets ready to leave the table, you pull out a $20 bill. One of the senior officers says, "What are you doing? It's on the house. Why else would we eat here?" You say, "I was taught in the academy *not* to accept free meals." The other officers at the table burst into laughter. What should you do?

the skill. The recruit should be required to consistently and satisfactorily perform a skill before the FTO certifies his or her competence in the skill.

6. The FTO should evaluate the recruit daily using a standardized, checklist-style evaluation form.
7. A job task analysis for the patrol officer position should be the basis for the recruit's performance evaluation.
8. The FTO position should be clearly defined, preferably by a job task analysis for the position of FTO, and should include the responsibilities of the FTO as a trainer and as a patrol officer.
9. The FTO should be selected from a pool of highly motivated volunteers. Upon selection, the FTO should receive a minimum of 40 hours of training before being allowed to act in the official capacity of FTO.
10. Some form of extra compensation should be offered to FTOs to ensure that the most qualified officers are attracted to and retained in the FTO position.
11. Agencies should perform annual evaluations of their FTO programs.

police training officer (PTO) program
A police training method that focuses on developing an officer's learning capacity, leadership, and problem-solving skills.

Toward a Police Training Officer Approach. In 1999, the Office for Community Oriented Policing Services (COPS) provided a $300,000 grant to the Reno (Nevada) Police Department to collaborate with the Police Executive Research Forum to study police training and to develop a new field training model. The collaboration produced the so-called **police training officer (PTO) program.** According to the authors of a recent report on the PTO program, "This approach is very different from traditional police training methods that emphasize mechanical repetition skills and rote memory capabilities; rather, the focus is on developing an officer's learning capacity, leadership, and problem-solving skills."[34] Such skills are needed because

> today police need to think on their feet, work in partnership with neighborhoods to solve problems, and be sensitive to the ethnic and cultural difference[s] in communities. They need to be able to use new technologies such as the Internet and computerized crime mapping to diagnose crime patterns. Field trainers and police executives repeatedly told us that traditional training methods did not work to help recruits learn those skills. The Police Training Officer program was created in response to this dilemma.[35]

The PTO model is built around John Dewey's philosophy of learning,[36] namely that there is much more to learning than can be gleaned from a lecture. The model incorporates such concepts as Malcolm Knowles's principles of self-directed learning,[37] Howard Barrows's idea of problem-based learning,[38] and Benjamin Bloom's concern with intellectual outcomes of learning.[39] The PTO model emphasizes:

1. Knowledge: Remembering or recalling previously learned material.
2. Comprehension: Understanding meaning well enough to be able to explain and restate ideas.
3. Application: Applying learned material in new and different situations.
4. Analysis: Categorizing material into segments and demonstrating their relationships.
5. Synthesis: Grouping or combining separate ideas to form a new whole and to establish new relationships.
6. Evaluation: Assessing the material for appropriate outcomes based on established criteria.[40]

The Reno PTO program's architects offer this concrete example:

> A trainee may be asked to explain how to handle a robbery-in-progress call. If the trainee could explain how to handle a robbery response as required by policies and procedures, he or she has reached the general knowledge comprehension level. If the trainee could further explain how to control the scene; use proper tactics; coordinate with other units; and make proper notifications to forensics, supervisors, and detectives, he or she will have reached the application level. . . . If, however, the trainee could go further and elaborate on the differences between bank robberies and strong armed robberies, and possibly robbery trends and analysis in the area, he or she has attained the levels of analysis, synthesis, and possibly even evaluation.[41]

Reno's PTO trainees progress through seven phases: (1) integration, during which trainees learn to acclimate to their new environments; (2) phase A, which emphasizes nonemergency incident response; (3) phase B, which emphasizes emergency response; (4) midterm evaluation, in which the trainee's performance is examined by a trainer other than the assigned PTO; (5) phase C, which emphasizes patrol activities; (6) phase D, which emphasizes criminal investigation; and (7) final phase evaluation, in which the trainee's performance is again examined by another training evaluator.

This approach may not seem that dissimilar to the traditional FTO model, but its main difference lies in the manner through which material is taught and knowledge is evaluated. Problem-based learning exercises are used throughout the process. In each phase, the recruit is tasked with a structured problem. Trainees will also develop a neighborhood portfolio, which is a detailed overview of the beat in which they work. Finally, throughout the process, trainees must demonstrate competence in a number of areas, not all of which are unique to police work. Examples include problem solving, leadership, community problems, cultural diversity, ethics, safety, and report writing. The PTO model is being developed in jurisdictions across the United States and in Canada. The new model has even given rise to the Police Society for Problem Based Learning.[42]

WEB PATROL 5-5

Would You Be a Good Cop?
http://www.mycrimekit.com

DIVERSITY AND DISCRIMINATION

Diversity and discrimination both have important implications for human resources. They are of great importance to administrators in terms of how they staff their agencies, and they are important to officers in lower ranks, too. New recruits, as we have just seen, are trained extensively in these areas so that they understand the importance of diversity and the avoidance of discrimination. Things were not always this way, however. It was not until the civil rights movement of the 1960s that diversity and discrimination were brought to the attention of politicians and the public.

Equal Employment Opportunity

The notion of **equal employment opportunity** has a plain meaning: Everyone should receive an equal chance at employment. The goal of equal employment opportunity did not just emerge on its own; it was legislatively mandated. Title VII of the Civil Rights Act of 1964 provides the legal basis for fair employment practices as we know them today. Section 703A of the act, for example, makes it unlawful for any employer to fail to hire, refuse to hire, discharge, or otherwise discriminate in any other manner against any individual with respect to employment compensation, terms, conditions, or privileges because of race, color, religion, sex, age, pregnancy, or national origin, among other factors.

equal employment opportunity
Fair employment practices mandated by Title VII of the Civil Rights Act of 1964.

In 1972, Title VII was revised to create the **Equal Employment Opportunity Commission (EEOC).** The EEOC was given authority to "intervene on behalf of affected individuals" and to "file suit against businesses or governmental entities in cases of discrimination." What this means is that individuals no longer need to shoulder the burden of proving a discrimination claim; they can turn to the federal government for help.

Equal Employment Opportunity Commission (EEOC)
The federal agency that is empowered by Title VII of the Civil Rights Act of 1964 to "intervene on behalf of affected individuals," to "file suit against businesses or governmental entities in cases of discrimination," to intervene in cases of alleged sexual harassment, and to investigate cases of employer retaliation.[i]

The EEOC can also intervene in cases of alleged sexual harassment. According to Title VII, in fact, sexual harassment is a form of sex discrimination, not unlike denying employment to female candidates in favor of male candidates. Finally, the EEOC can also step in to investigate cases of employer retaliation: "An employer may not fire, demote, harass or otherwise 'retaliate' against an individual for filing a charge of discrimination, participating in a discrimination proceeding, or otherwise opposing discrimination."[43]

The push for equal employment opportunity has had interesting implications for the law enforcement profession. Policing remains, by and large, a white male-dominated occupation, but women and minorities have started to make significant inroads in terms of achieving parity in the ranks with their white male counterparts. The law enforcement profession is also in the strange position of requiring a certain physical condition for job candidates while not being allowed to discriminate based on disability.

Why is diversity essential in the police ranks? In general, it is felt that a diverse organization will be more capable of effectively addressing community needs. It is also felt that a diverse police force will be regarded more favorably by citizens, especially those in minority-dominated neighborhoods. The research supports some of these claims, but only to a modest extent. For example, researchers in Detroit found that African American citizens had more support for black than white officers.[44] Research has also revealed that New York residents had higher regard for the police department after coming into greater contact with female police officers.[45] In contrast, a study from Washington, DC, revealed little benefit resulted from assigning same-race officers to neighborhoods.[46]

Affirmative Action. Closely associated with equal employment opportunity is the practice of **affirmative action.** This is the practice of taking proactive steps to boost the presence of historically marginalized groups (typically minorities and women) in the ranks of an organization by giving preference to members of those groups. It is easy to see how affirmative action can further the goals of providing equal employment opportunity, but it is not part of Title VII.

affirmative action
The practice of taking proactive steps to boost the presence of historically marginalized groups (typically minorities and women) in the ranks of an organization by giving preference to members of those groups.

There have been many court cases addressing the constitutionality of affirmative action programs. In the policing context, one researcher found that affirmative action plans played a significant role in police hiring in America's 50 largest cities.[47] It is noteworthy, however, that 23 of the affirmative action plans in these 50 cities were court-mandated, not voluntary.

Minorities in Policing. It would be inaccurate to suggest that policing was exclusively a white male occupation before the 1960s. There were black police officers in Washington, DC, as early as 1861,[48] for example, but by 1940 black officers represented less than 1 percent of the nation's police forces.[49] The African Americans who did obtain work as police officers often faced discrimination on the job. For example, a study from 1959, right before the dawn of the civil rights era, revealed that several southern cities required black officers to call on white officers when they needed to arrest a white suspect.[50] Some black officers were only allowed to drive cars marked "Colored Police" and could only arrest black suspects.[51] Additionally, job assignments for black officers were not particularly desirable, dismissals were often arbitrary, there was little integration within the ranks,[52] and promotions were few and far between. For example, a study revealed that during the 1960s, only 22 police departments had promoted black officers beyond patrol positions.[53] Times have since changed, of course. Studies now show little connection between race and promotion or disciplinary decisions.[54]

double marginality
A situation in which black officers treat black suspects harshly to gain the respect of their white counterparts and to avoid giving the impression that they are biased toward members of their own race.

While there is little direct evidence that being a minority makes one a better cop, that claim was made during the 1960s. In the wake of various race riots during that decade, the President's Commission on Law Enforcement and Administration of Justice observed:

> Police officers have testified to the special competence of Negro officers in Negro neighborhoods. The reasons given include: they get along better and receive more respect from Negro residents; they receive less trouble; . . . they can get more information; and they understand Negro citizens better.[55]

Similarly, some studies have revealed that black residents wanted to see more black officers patrolling the streets because they believed that understanding would improve and that abuses would decrease.[56] On the other hand, some early studies showed that black officers either felt a need to be more forceful with black suspects[57] or were actively challenged by suspects of their own race.[58] One influential author even coined the term **double marginality** to refer to a situation in which black officers treat black suspects harshly to gain the respect of their white counterparts and to avoid giving the impression that they are biased toward members of their own race.[59]

Washington, DC, Metropolitan Police Department Chief Cathy L. Lanier. Appointed by District of Columbia Mayor Adrian Fenty, Lanier assumed the chief's job on January 2, 2007. What special skills and traits might women bring to policing?

Metropolitan Police Department Headquarters

Women in Policing. Women have faced much the same fate as minorities in terms of seeking law enforcement jobs. They remain significantly underrepresented in police departments to this day. Some researchers have attributed this situation to the idea that policing requires aggression, physical exertion, and "stable" emotions, supposedly masculine traits.[60] In contrast, traits often associated with women, such as compassion, empathy, and nurturing, may not find much of a home in the law enforcement world.[61] Obviously, there are exceptions to these generalities.

Historically speaking, police departments didn't start to hire women until the early twentieth century. Lola Baldwin was the first woman to hold police powers. Hired in 1905 by Portland, Oregon, Baldwin was mostly engaged in social work–like functions. Other police departments followed Portland's example: "Once the police began to think in terms of preventing juvenile delinquency, they responded to the traditional argument that women had a special capacity for child care."[62]

Alice Stebbins-Wells was hired by the Los Angeles Police Department in 1910. Even though her job also resembled social work, she led a movement for more female hiring, and by 1925, more than 200 cities had women working in police positions and even in jails.[63] In the ensuing years, women made some progress, but not much. By the mid-1960s, there were only around 1,700 female police officers in America's largest cities,[64] and most female officers were excluded from patrol duties.

It was not until 1968 that the first women were assigned to patrol work.[65] Indianapolis was the first city to put women on patrol, but other large cities like New York, Philadelphia, Miami, Washington, DC, and St. Louis quickly followed suit. By the end of the 1970s, nearly 90 percent of large police agencies employed female patrol officers.[66] That growth has continued at an impressive pace. Nearly all cities of more than 50,000 now have women working in the police ranks.[67] The growth is partially attributed to the fact that female and male officers perform similarly, as evidenced by some early studies on the subject.[68]

More recently, the same reasons that were once used to exclude women from the ranks of police agencies are now being used to recruit women in larger numbers. A study of patrol in New York City, for example, revealed that women are less likely than men to use firearms, to get into violent confrontations, and to become injured.[69] Some say that this means female officers are actually more emotionally stable than male officers, disavowing one of the earlier arguments that was used to keep them out of police positions.[70] A reason male and female police officers appear to perform similarly may not be so much that both sexes are equally competent, but that policing may attract a certain group of women, by either self-selection, department screening, or the recruit socialization process.[71]

Diversity in the Ranks Today. So far, we have addressed only female and African American police officers. Other minority groups have made advances, as well. This can be seen clearly in Figure 5-2. Between 1987 and 2003, both women and minorities increased their presence in the ranks of America's police departments, although it appears there are more minority than female police officers. This may be due to the possibility that fewer women than men are drawn to policing.

Table 5-2 provides a breakdown of what we mean by "minorities." The Bureau of Justice Statistics regularly surveys police agencies around the country to determine their demographic characteristics, among other things. There are obviously more minority groups than those reported in Table 5-2, but the percentages of other groups are almost too small to be meaningful. In any case, it is clear that African American officers make up the largest group of minority officers. They are followed by women, Hispanics, Asians/Pacific Islanders, and American Indians, respectively.

Figure 5-2 • Female and Minority Officers in Local Police Departments, 1987–2003

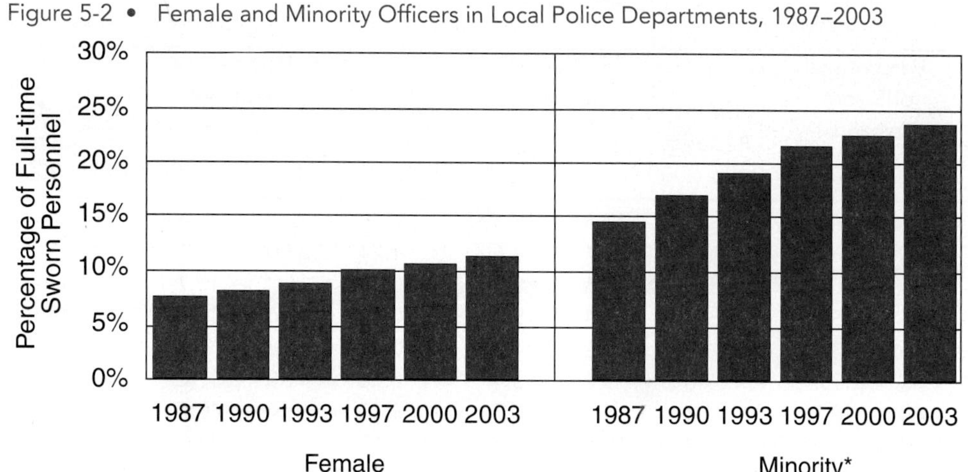

*Includes blacks or African Americans, Hispanics or Latinos, Asians, Native Hawaiians or other Pacific Islanders, American Indians, Alaska natives, and other racial and ethnic minorities.

Source: M. J. Hickman and B. A. Reeves, *Local police departments, 2003* (Washington, DC: Bureau of Justice Statistics, 2006).

Table 5-2 • Female and Minority Full-Time Sworn Personnel in Large City Police Departments in the United States, by Size of Population Served, 1990 and 2000

	Percent of Full-Time Sworn Personnel Who Were:											
	Female		Any Minority		Black, Non-Hispanic		Hispanic, Any Race		Asian/Pacific Islander		American Indian	
Population Served	1990	2000	1990	2000	1990	2000	1990	2000	1990	2000	1990	2000
Total	12.1%	16.3%	29.8%	38.1%	18.4%	20.1%	9.2%	14.1%	2.0%	2.8%	0.3%	0.4%
1,000,000 or more	12.3	16.8	27.6	37.6	15.1	16.9	11.4	17.5	0.9	2.1	0.2	0.3
500,000 to 999,999	12.6	16.1	35.8	41.1	25.2	27.0	5.0	7.7	5.3	5.3	0.3	0.5
350,000 to 499,999	10.9	14.4	30.7	36.4	18.9	20.4	10.2	12.7	1.0	2.1	0.6	1.0
250,000 to 349,999	10.5	15.8	24.0	32.7	17.4	20.9	6.2	10.4	0.3	0.7	0.2	0.4

Source: U.S. Department of Justice, Bureau of Justice Statistics, *Police departments in large cities, 1990–2000* (Washington, DC: U.S. Department of Justice, May 2002), p. 3.

These numbers carry little meaning, however, without some idea of how each group is represented in the general population. Table 5–3 addresses this concern for cities with populations greater than 1 million. Ratios greater than one suggest overrepresentation by minority groups.

Americans with Disabilities Act (ADA) U.S. legislation passed in 1990 that forbids discrimination against the disabled.

Disabled Cops. In 1990, Congress passed the **Americans with Disabilities Act (ADA),** which forbids discrimination against the disabled. How does this apply to policing? It doesn't necessarily mean that disabled individuals can become police officers. Rather, the ADA prohibits discrimination against applicants for any position if the applicant is able to perform the essential functions of the job.

The ADA is part of the reason why medical screening occurs during the final phase of the hiring process; it prevents applicants from being rejected early on because of physical disabilities. Moreover, the ADA has required police departments (and other organizations) to develop sophisticated selection procedures that mirror the job to the fullest extent possible. Selection cannot be a haphazard process.

Table 5-3 • Female and Minority Full-Time Sworn Personnel and Ratio of Minority Officers to Minority Residents in Cities of 1 Million or More

	Female		Any Minority			Black or African American			Hispanic or Latino		
	Percentage of Sworn Personnel		Percentage of Sworn Personnel		Officer-to-Resident	Percentage of Sworn Personnel		Officer-to-Resident	Percentage of Sworn Personnel		Officer-to-Resident
City	1990	2000	1990	2000	Ratio, 2000	1990	2000	Ratio, 2000	1990	2000	Ratio, 2000
New York	12.3%	15.5%	25.5%	34.7%	0.53	12.6%	13.3%	0.50	12.1%	17.8%	0.66
Los Angeles	12.5	18.4	37.5	53.9	0.77	13.4	13.6	1.21	21.0	33.1	0.71
Chicago	13.0	21.3	30.4	40.3	0.59	23.6	25.9	0.70	6.3	12.7	0.49
Houston	9.6	12.4	26.3	39.7	0.57	14.4	19.4	0.77	11.4	17.9	0.48
Philadelphia	14.7	24.2	26.5	41.1	0.71	23.2	34.5	0.80	2.8	5.6	0.66
Phoenix	8.1	15.0	15.5	17.9	0.40	3.6	3.9	0.76	11.0	12.0	0.35
San Diego	12.7	14.5	24.0	30.7	0.61	7.7	8.7	1.10	11.4	15.9	0.63
Dallas	13.3	15.8	22.7	36.8	0.56	15.5	21.4	0.83	6.2	13.5	0.38
San Antonio	5.7	6.0	43.9	48.0	0.70	5.8	5.8	0.85	37.9	41.7	0.71
Las Vegas	10.2	10.9	13.4	19.3	0.48	7.5	9.3	1.02	3.7	7.3	0.33

Source: U.S. Department of Justice, Bureau of Justice Statistics, *Police departments in large cities, 1990–2000* (Washington, DC: U.S. Department of Justice, May 2002), p. 11.

The term *disabled* may conjure up images of wheelchairs and significant physical limitations, but disabilities can sometimes be less visible. For example, the ADA protects people with human immunodeficiency virus (HIV); a positive test is not an outright bar to employment.[72] Indeed, a sheriff's department was ordered to pay damages to a reserve officer who was discharged after testing positive for HIV.[73] The ADA also protects diabetics. In one case, an insulin-dependent diabetic was denied employment with the Toledo (Ohio) Police Department, but the court held that a blanket policy denying employment to such individuals violates the ADA.[74]

Departments have a little more leeway, though, with serious physical disabilities. For example, a court sided with a department that put an officer on disability leave after he lost his arm in a motorcycle accident.[75] The court concluded that the department was justified in its decision because the officer could no longer perform one of the key functions of the job: making an arrest.

Reverse Discrimination: A Backlash?

The push for diversity in policing, like the push for diversity in other organizations, has sometimes gone too far. **Racial quotas,** for instance, are requirements for hiring and promoting a specified number of minorities. When minorities are hired and promoted based more on race than on any other criterion, allegations of **reverse discrimination** emerge—usually from white male officers. Reverse discrimination has also been described as entailing a "white backlash."

racial quota
A requirement for hiring and promoting a specified number of minorities.

reverse discrimination
Discrimination against nonminorities that occurs when the hiring and promotion of minorities are based more on race than on any other criterion.

Reverse discrimination appears to be more than a distant concern for white officers. A study from the late 1970s revealed that white officers felt that affirmative action was a threat to their careers.[76] Twenty years later, another study found marked resentment and bitterness on the part of white officers toward several of their black supervisors.[77] Reverse discrimination appears to be a real phenomenon. During the 1970s, for example, the Detroit Police Department adopted a policy that provided for the promotion to sergeant of one black officer for every white officer. While a court struck the policy down,[78] the U.S. Supreme Court later sanctioned temporary racial quotas in police hiring.[79]

Even in the face of conflicting court decisions, claims of reverse discrimination continue. Organizations like Adversity.net have emerged to shed light on egregious abuses of racial preference and quotas. In fact, the organization recently highlighted the case of a former Dayton (Ohio) Police Department major, a white woman, who was bypassed for promotion to chief in favor of a black man. In a surprising turn of events, she was then fired so more black officers could be promoted (the department, to this day, is overwhelmingly white). The city eventually agreed to a settlement of more than $1 million.[80]

The Dayton case came on the heels of another from Milwaukee, Wisconsin, in which a jury awarded $2.2 million to 17 white police officers who, the jury felt, had been systematically bypassed for promotion in favor of minority officers.[81] Twenty of 41 officers promoted to lieutenant were black, when the pool of applicants was more than 80 percent white.

WEB PATROL 5-6
Policewomen: Their First Century and the New Era
http://www.mycrimekit.com

SOME CAREER DECISION CAVEATS

Many factors must be considered when deciding on a career. In the policing context, applicants should ask themselves several questions, including these:

1. Can you handle boredom?
2. Can you handle adrenaline-pumping excitement coupled with the potential for loss of life?
3. Can you handle long hours away from your family, and would you be willing to work weekends and holidays?
4. Can you deal with people who do not like you?
5. Can you follow rules to the letter and adhere to a well-defined chain of command?

This list of questions could go on. Researchers have pointed out two other considerations for potential police applicants. The first, particularly relevant for female applicants, is the prospect of facing sexual harassment on entering the profession. Second, many applicants are not aware that their agencies sometimes require residency within a particular area. Residency requirements are the exception, but many agencies still have them.

Sexual Harassment

sexual harassment
Unwelcome sexual advances, requests for sexual favors, and other verbal or physical conduct of a sexual nature.

***quid pro quo* harassment**
A form of sexual harassment that generally involves a demand for sexual favors in exchange for some perk or benefit, such as a promotion or a favorable job assignment.

hostile work environment
A form of sexual harassment involving situations in which unwelcome sexual contact and comments have the effect of "unreasonably interfering with an individual's work performance or creating an intimidating environment."[ii]

Sexual harassment, which consists of unwelcome sexual advances, requests for sexual favors, and other verbal or physical conduct of a sexual nature, is a sad reality in many of America's workplaces. Sexual harassment has occurred for generations, but the practice attracted national attention in 1991, when University of Oklahoma law professor Anita Hill testified at Clarence Thomas's Supreme Court confirmation hearing. Hill described Thomas's conduct as constituting sexual harassment, and it prompted many people to question the way women are treated in the workplace.

Sexual harassment is a form of discrimination under Title VII, as decided in 1977.[82] In 1986, the Supreme Court defined sexual harassment as falling into two categories: (1) ***quid pro quo* harassment** and (2) **hostile work environment.**[83] *Quid pro quo* harassment occurs when sexual favors are demanded in exchange for some perk or benefit, perhaps a promotion or a favorable job assignment. Viewed differently, *quid pro quo* sexual harassment occurs when there is a tangible economic detriment associated with refusing to succumb to sexual advances. A hostile work environment is said to exist when unwelcome sexual contact and comments have the effect of "unreasonably interfering with an individual's work performance or creating an intimidating environment."[84]

Because of the prevalence of male officers, police work has seen its share of sexual harassment. In 1993, the state of California enacted legislation requiring all peace officers to undergo sexual harassment training. The law followed several large judgments against police agencies for their officers' unscrupulous actions. In the early 1990s, the New York City Police Department went to great lengths to cover up sexual harassment allegations by a female probationary police officer. The woman alleged that she was raped and sodomized by a male officer who threatened to kill her if she reported the incident. When the facts eventually came to light, she was awarded $264,242 in damages.[85]

To this day, sexual harassment still occurs in police departments at alarming rates.[86] The author of a 1996 study interviewed 187 female police officers and found that 62 percent of them had seen or experienced sexual harassment during their careers as officers.[87] More recently, the National Center for Women and Policing concluded that "law enforcement agencies have tolerated workplace environments that are openly hostile and discriminatory toward female employees."[88]

Residency Requirements

Many police officers do not live in the communities they serve.[89] For example, one study found that as many as 80 percent of police personnel working in Washington, DC, live outside the city.[90] The American Civil Liberties Union of Southern California reached a similar conclusion when researching the Los Angeles Police Department.[91] It appears that the overwhelming majority of police officers avoid living in the areas they serve, perhaps because they don't want to live there, because it's too expensive, or both.

residency requirement
A requirement that officers reside within the community they serve as a condition of employment.

The tendency for police officers to live outside their city of employment has received a fair degree of attention in the literature. Research on police officer **residency requirements** has indicated that individual officers typically oppose such requirements for reasons including high housing costs, safety and privacy concerns, and inferior educational opportunities for their children.[92] Many police departments have voiced concerns related to residency requirements and recruitment. Specifically, such requirements are feared to result in an overall diminishment of the quality and competence of law enforcement personnel because of the inability of police agencies, particularly those serving dangerous urban areas, to attract highly qualified applicants from outside their jurisdictions.[93] On the contrary, however, some research has shown that increased commuting distances can have a substantial negative impact on recruiting and retention, thus highlighting the need for reconsideration of residency requirements where practical.[94]

YOU DECIDE

The Harasser

You are fresh out of the academy and on probationary status. Your training officer repeatedly makes inappropriate comments to your colleague, another recent academy graduate, saying she is "hot" and has "a body to die for." You even overhear the training officer say to your colleague, "You will never make it in this line of work unless you go out on a date with me." Your colleague files a sexual harassment report, as she should, but what should you do as the person who observed the exchanges? What if she asks you to support her claims against the training officer?

Historically, support for police residency requirements has been couched in terms of their benefits to the community. For example, support has stemmed from a belief that such regulations presumably lower the unemployment rate, add to the local tax base,[95] and make neighborhoods safer. In the context of modern community policing efforts, residency requirements are believed to increase the attentiveness of officers to the unique problems and needs of the communities in which they serve.[96] Furthermore, this notion is based on the presumption that officers will be more capable of responding to the needs of the community, especially if the same issues affect their own families. Residency requirements may even enhance citizen attitudes toward the police. In the end, though, residency requirements are still very much the exception.

SUMMARY

- To enter the police force, candidates must move through the hiring decision, the police academy, and field training. The hiring decision follows recruitment and is based on performance in several areas, including written and physical agility tests, an interview, a background investigation, a polygraph, and medical and drug screening. Academies vary in their organization and curricular requirements. Each, however, strives to teach new hires the "sixth sense." The traditional model of postacademy training is that of the field training officer. The FTO system is gradually being replaced by a new police training officer model.
- Police departments are becoming increasingly diverse, due to the Civil Rights Act of 1964, equal employment opportunity, and affirmative action—and because departments are learning the value of hiring women and minorities. However, allegations of reverse discrimination, mostly by white male police officers, have surfaced in recent years.
- Police applicants should be aware of occasional sexual harassment problems in police agencies, particularly for female applicants, and that some agencies have residency requirements mandating that police officers live within certain boundaries.

COMING FULL CIRCLE

For Discussion

Return to the questions posed at the start of this chapter. Have any of your answers changed since you read the chapter? What portions of this chapter helped you answer these questions?

Writing Assignment

Using material from this chapter and additional resources, write a 500-word essay in response to one of the questions presented at the beginning of the chapter. Submit your essay to your instructor if asked to do so.

KEY TERMS AND NAMES

affirmative action
Americans with Disabilities Act (ADA)
civil service
civil service commission
college system
double marginality
equal employment opportunity
Equal Employment Opportunity Commission (EEOC)
field training officer (FTO)
hostile work environment
patronage system
plebe system
police training officer (PTO) program
quid pro quo harassment
racial quota
residency requirement
reverse discrimination
sexual harassment
sixth sense
technical training model

WEB INTERACTIVITY

Visit the home page of the FBI Academy at http://www.fbi.gov/hq/td/academy/academy.htm. Take note of the information provided on that page. Then examine the menu items along the left-hand side of the page, and click on "New Agents' Training Unit." Summarize the information found there, and then return to the FBI Academy home page. Click on "FBI National Academy" on the left-hand side of the page, and again summarize the information found there. Submit your report to your instructor if asked to do so.

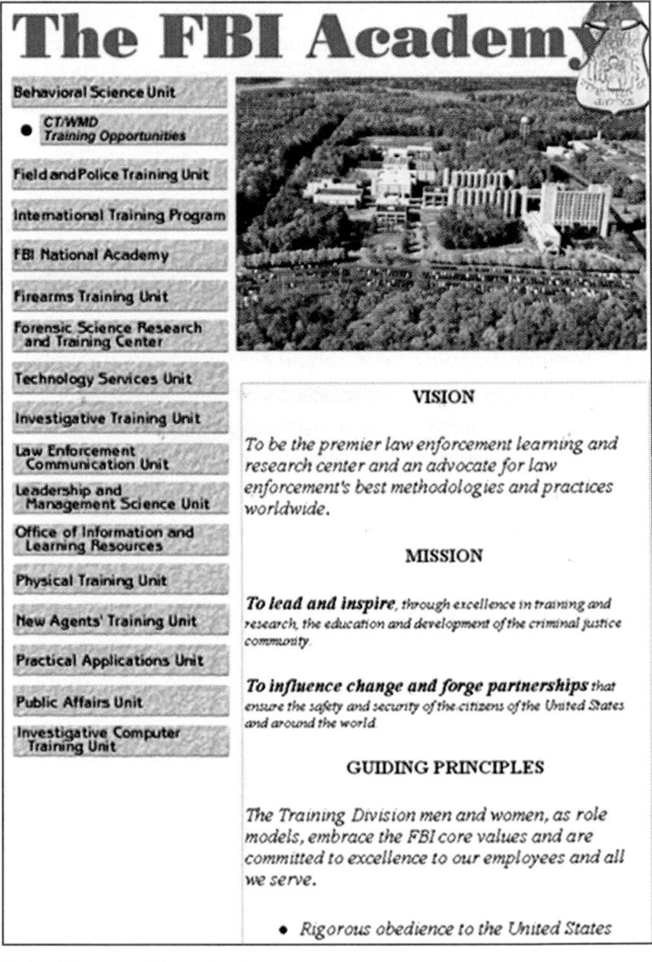

Federal Bureau of Investigation

REVIEW QUESTIONS

1. What does it take to become a police officer? Explain hiring, the police academy, and field training.
2. How are diversity and discrimination relevant in policing? How have these issues changed over time?
3. What are some caveats that police applicants should be aware of?

chapter six

POLICE SUBCULTURE

LEARNING OBJECTIVES

After reading this chapter, students should be able to:

1. Define *culture* and distinguish between culture and subculture.
2. Describe the various sources of police subculture.
3. Discuss the components of police subculture.

J. OLIVEIRA

THINK ABOUT IT

Sergeant Eileen Barry became supervisor of a New York City Police Department (NYPD) truancy unit on November 30, 1998. After assuming her post, she learned that one of the officers under her command was falsifying truancy reports. She informed her bosses, there was an investigation, and four officers were suspended. But Barry was then demoted and assigned to undesirable shifts. She was also accused of failing to supervise the officers in her unit.

An investigative hearing revealed that the officers who were suspended had falsified their reports *before* Barry came on the job. Accordingly, Barry was exonerated, but she sued the NYPD, alleging that her First Amendment rights were compromised and that she suffered retaliation for speaking out against misconduct that was occurring in her unit. Other cops in the department allegedly called her a "rat."

Barry also claimed in her lawsuit that the actions taken against her were part of a longstanding "blue wall of silence," the unwritten practice of protecting one's fellow officers, of not cooperating with investigators, and of taking whatever steps are necessary to preserve the "secrecy" of certain aspects of police work, whether right or wrong. A judge decided her lawsuit could go forward, saying:

> On balance, in light of the evidence before the court, a reasonable jury could find that a widespread custom of retaliating against officers who expose police misconduct, with officials willfully ignoring if not facilitating the practice, pervades the NYPD.[1]

Police executives, who are routinely called on by the press to comment on investigations of their officers, sometimes claim that the "blue wall of silence" is imaginary. A few years ago in Toronto, for example, a number of police officers were being investigated for theft and for offering perjured testimony. They were uncooperative and downright hostile to investigators, but the chief of the department supported his force, saying, "I don't think there is a blue wall of silence, and I can't speak to the hostility. . . . The way things have been portrayed—as if there is widespread corruption—that's not the case at all."[2]

Sergeant Barry's experience, along with the comments made by the Toronto police chief, raises several interesting questions:

1. Did Barry collide head on with the "blue wall of silence"?
2. Who is right about the existence of the "blue wall"—Barry or the Toronto police chief? Can they both be right?
3. Do police officers tend to "protect their own" in cases like this?
4. Is there anything inherently wrong with looking out for one's colleagues? If not, when does it go too far?
5. Does Barry's experience reveal the negative side of police work? What other elements might be part of that "underbelly"?

INTRODUCTION

culture
A set of shared values, norms, and behaviors that form a way of life.

value
A standard of goodness, desirability, behavior, beauty, or interaction that serves as a guideline for living within a particular culture.

norm
A rule or expectation for behavior that characterizes a particular social group.

Cops hang out with other cops. They run in the same circles. They work out together, vacation together, party together, go to "cop bars" together, and associate with one another when off duty. There is a tendency among most police officers to stick together. But cops are not the only people who work in the same field and associate with one another. Teachers often associate with other teachers, office workers relax with other office workers, and construction workers hang out with other construction workers. Yet policing is different from other occupations. Policing is, at its core, a potentially dangerous line of work, and this makes its occupational culture quite unique.

CULTURE: WHAT IS IT?

Culture refers to a shared set of **values, norms,** and behaviors that form a particular way of life. Values are standards of goodness, or those things that are perceived to be important. Norms re-

Members of the 159th Oakland Police Basic Academy celebrate after their graduation ceremony at the Scottish Rite Center in Oakland, California, on Friday, February 9, 2007. What is police subculture? How does it develop?

Sean Connelley/ZUMA Press

fer to rules and expectations about which forms of behavior are acceptable and which are not. Any discussion of culture should also consider social **institutions.** Institutions can be found in organizational structures—like schools, families, and churches. Social institutions communicate values and norms throughout society and over time contribute to cultural stability. In the policing context, significant research has shown that the nature of police organizations, like other social institutions, shapes police behavior. America is considered a multicultural melting pot because there are many different cultures within our borders, organized by all manner of shared sentiments.

institution
An organizational structure through which values and norms are transmitted over time and from one location to another within a society.

Culture versus Subculture

The term **subculture** refers to cultural patterns that distinguish some segment of a society's population from the rest of that population. Consequently, individuals who share values and norms that differ from those of the larger culture can be said to be members of a subculture. The term **police subculture** (sometimes called *police culture*) has been used to describe the shared values and norms and the established patterns of behavior that are found among police officers. It describes the fact that police officers generally adhere to a set of values and beliefs that differ in certain crucial respects from those held by members of the wider American culture. Some of the values that characterize police subculture, like patriotism and a dedication to creating a better society, are positive values that many Americans share. Others, like suspicion and cynicism, are not always prized by others but may be necessary for effective (and safe) police work. It is important to understand that the values and norms that characterize police subculture are not unique when taken individually. It is their occurrence together that gives policing its distinctive nature. Police corruption and deviance, insofar as they stem from the subculture of policing, are taken up in Chapter 14. Our concern in this chapter is with the broader nature of police subculture in general.

subculture
Cultural patterns that distinguish some segment of a society's population.

police subculture
The shared values and norms and the established patterns of behavior that tend to characterize policing. Also called *police culture*.

The section that follows looks at the generic elements of any culture. After covering the basics, we then turn our attention to the sources of police subculture and to the specific components of police subculture.

Elements of Culture

Cultures are characterized by themes, or shared commonalities. Consider NASCAR racing. Some would say that there is not only a racing subculture in America, but that there are a number of themes running through it, including fan loyalty to specific drivers, respect for the rules of racing, and a desire to own brand-name products associated with NASCAR winners. Themes tend to be shared by members of a particular culture. Culture also promotes the expression of norms and shared values in ways that are defined as acceptable. Let's look briefly at each of these concepts in greater detail.

Various Themes. John Crank, who has written extensively on the subject of police subculture,[3] refers to a "confluence of themes":

> The word "confluence" is a metaphor suggesting the emptying of streams and rivers into a common body of water. At a confluence, the particular contributions of the individual creeks and rivers are no longer clearly recognizable—the flow is a blend of them all.[4]

Hence culture might best be understood as the blending of various themes. If by "culture" we mean professional culture, then the concern is with how the various aspects of a particular profession mix together to create a common set of beliefs, behaviors, and reactions to particular sets of circumstances. According to Crank, "Police culture is like this: Diverse aspects of organizational activity merge into a whole united by commonly held values and shared ways of thinking."[5]

Consider another type of culture: academia. The wider American culture often sees universities as places of learning dominated by liberal thinkers. But to characterize the culture of academia, and all academics, as "liberal" would be inaccurate. Not only do many of today's professors characterize themselves as politically conservative, but liberalism in university settings is tempered by other factors. One of those other factors is skeptical positivism (the essence of science), a theme running through academia that combines with liberal beliefs and countless other factors to create a relatively unique set of beliefs, values, and behavioral patterns. Skeptical positivism rejects beliefs based on faith or tradition alone and demands rigorous scientific proof before an idea can be accepted.

Institutional Values. Our definition of *culture* highlights the role of shared values and norms. Recall that values are what people consider to be important, but they can also reflect an impression of how certain things should be done. This is what is meant by **institutional values**, or a sense of agreement within a particular culture on how to accomplish valued objectives.

institutional value
A sense of agreement within a particular culture about how to accomplish a valued objective.

There is a moral dimension to institutional values that suggests the norms we talked about earlier. Cultures contain beliefs not only about the best way to go about accomplishing tasks, but also about the moral superiority of one approach over another. For example, consider how a scientific approach to a problem might differ from a faith-based approach to the same problem.

It is useful to think of organizations as promoting their particular institutional values. The traditional police department, for example, has a hierarchical, quasi-military structure, and an established formal chain of command with rigid bureaucratic structure. It is probably safe to say that most law enforcement personnel at one time felt that this was the best way to go about the business of enforcing the law.[6] An opposing view says that the traditional approach to managing police organizations is slow to adapt to new problems (such as the challenges of terrorism and homeland security) and is resistant to change.[7] Some progressive police administrators feel that decentralization, one of the hot topics in policing today, is a more effective approach. (Note that the word *progressive* is itself value-laden and that "progressive" ideas should not be accepted in place of more traditional ones unless their true "value" can be demonstrated.)

Preference for centralization or decentralization may actually represent two subcultural perspectives within the larger culture of policing. What, then, would be an example of an institutional value that is ubiquitous in policing? Returning again to Crank's observations, we note the idea of personal responsibility, one of the bedrock (though unwritten) principles on which the American system of criminal justice is built:

> Our society carries a deep-seated belief in the free will of individuals, and it is widely thought that people will use a pleasure-pain calculus before they do something—they will do things that bring them pleasure, and avoid things that bring them pain. The criminal justice system in the United States embodies this powerful belief in the form of what is called *deterrence*, a way of thinking about people that includes policies and punitive strategies that seek to increase some sort of pain associated with wrongdoing.[8]

This belief in personal responsibility is clearly manifested throughout criminal justice agencies, including police departments. There is an almost unshakable faith among police administrators in preventive patrol as useful for deterring would-be criminals, even though much of the research does not necessarily support this approach. The belief seems to be that the *threat* of punishment, resulting from being caught in the act of committing a crime, serves to restrain those who would otherwise choose to break the law.

This point also illustrates the interconnectedness between cultures. Crank's observation refers to a general set of beliefs characteristic of American culture that is not limited to criminal justice. But these beliefs have clearly shaped policing—and police subculture. What makes police subculture different from the broader American culture is the many additional themes that have been grafted onto it.

Emotional Expression. Businesspeople and other workers "vent" from time to time with some of their colleagues. They complain about everything from annoying or incompetent coworkers to the direction their company is headed. Likewise, college students share with their peers concerns about college life, their professors, tests they have to take, papers they are asked to write, and even their books. Indeed, everyone expresses themselves in one way or another. Accordingly, another key element of culture is the expression (as well as the mode of expression) of that culture's shared norms and values.

Expression can occur through several media. In the police context, "war stories" told in the academy serve to build and reinforce cultural beliefs and preferences. Off-duty conversations between fellow officers provide a means for release. Even if an officer's feelings are not openly shared, they can still affect the officer's perception of the world and thus his or her behavior.

To summarize, culture is complex, deeply entrenched, and shared. It is complex in the sense that it comprises various themes. Several sets of beliefs and values intersect to create individual cultures. Finally, culture is shared through a host of verbal and nonverbal channels: openly, subtly, and sometimes tacitly.

One does not need to venture far (geographically or professionally) in this country to discover how rapidly culture can change. This recognition enables us to present a more accurate, complete, and practical definition of *culture*. Crank's definition is useful in this regard:

> Culture is a body of knowledge that emerges through the shared application of practical skills to concrete problems encountered in daily routines and the normal course of activities. This body of knowledge contains both information and values; and behavior tends to flow from this body of knowledge in ways that are self-confirming.[9]

In closing, we should remark on the self-confirming nature of culture. This means that culture is self-reinforcing. It sustains itself and propagates itself largely intact from one generation to the next. It is no mystery why police officers share many of the same sentiments in different places, and even over time. The beliefs they carry emanate from shared training and common experiences and, as such, tend to transcend time and location. To be sure, cultures change and adapt, but this change does not occur quickly.

SOURCES OF POLICE SUBCULTURE

Our discussion of culture to this point has been generic, without much reference to the unique nature of American policing. Now it is time to get more specific. What is police subculture? What does it look like? Where does it come from? This section is concerned primarily with the last question, the sources of police subculture. After we ascertain what it is that has given rise to police subculture, we will be in a better position to grasp exactly what its components are.

Organizational Factors

Although police departments are certainly not unique in this regard, police work is usually divided into at least three shifts. In larger police departments, there are often several squads of officers working each shift. In the largest agencies, these squads are organized into platoons of 25 or more officers. Platoons might be divided up based on geographic criteria.[10] Police agencies today often use terms other than *platoon* or *squad*, but the organizational makeup remains more or less the same.[11] The result, regardless of name, is a group of officers who work the same schedule.

Perhaps the most unusual shift in policing is the one stretching from midnight or so until shortly after daybreak. Officers who work this shift generally have difficulty associating with people who work normal nine-to-five jobs because they tend to sleep during daylight hours. What's more, less senior officers are often required to work weekends and holidays, which further interferes with their ability to socialize with and establish friendships with people outside their professional circle.

No matter what the hours, the period at the end of a shift provides ample opportunity to rehash the day's activities, further reinforcing common bonds among police officers. Two researchers who observed a Colorado police department highlighted the importance of these end-of-shift discussions, noting that the period at the end of a shift

> provided an opportunity to discuss department policies, politics, and personalities. Rumors made their rounds at this time—with a few being squelched, several being started, and many being embellished.[12]

Of course, rumors and stories do not stay confined to specific squads or platoons. With daily interaction and transfers, which are common, they spread from one group of officers to the next, as criminologist Ted Rubinstein notes:

> Occasionally a man transfers from one squad to another, bringing with him knowledge of ex-colleagues which he offers to his new colleagues, enriching their knowledge about co-workers who are frequently seen, greeted, chatted with, but rarely known in the personal way as are the [members of the] squad.[13]

This illustrates shift work's impact on the development of police subculture. Many other features of police organizations also work together to breed a relatively unique group of individuals. We will consider the influence of administrators on subordinates, for example, but for now let's shift gears and focus on the environment as a source of police subculture.

The Street Environment

Policing is a people profession. The daily work of most police officers involves interacting with ordinary citizens and with other professionals in the criminal justice system. No other encounters have as many culture-shaping implications as those between the police and citizens.

Crank has identified two types of encounters that are especially significant in shaping police subculture. The first of these is the **street environment**. Here, an officer's personal beliefs, the circumstances of the encounter (for example, within view of others or not), and the attitudes each party brings to the encounter (hostility, cooperation, respect, and so on) can influence behavior in ways that are enduring and reinforcing.

street environment
One of two settings identified by John Crank (the other is the traffic stop) in which police officers perform daily tasks that involve interaction with ordinary citizens and with other criminal justice professionals.[i]

Younger officers who have aspirations (some cynical older officers might say "delusions") of changing the world and of engaging in exciting crime-fighting activities are often soon disillusioned by the routine and even frustrating nature of many calls for service, especially those dealing with property crime. In this context, much attention usually focuses on the victim's experience. But the satisfaction that police officers get from taking property crime reports is usually quite low, as Crank recognizes:

> The likelihood of solving [most property crimes] is remote. . . . Consequently, these encounters tend to be dispiriting for police and citizens alike; they tend to be perfunctory and ceremonial, satisfying the record-keeping requirements of crime reporting and the needs of insurance companies.[14]

Violent crimes can also prove less than exciting. Random acts of violence between total strangers are often the exception. Although the media may suggest otherwise, the typical violent encounters that officers respond to are those between friends and acquaintances,[15] and high on the list are domestic incidents. As Crank notes,

> Instead of providing police with a satisfactory sense of work accomplished, [these encounters] reveal the seamy, coarse, and destructive side of ordinary human relations. They tend to be repetitive, involving assailants and victims the police have been in contact with before and who are involved in violence [about] which the police can do little. Far from satisfaction, these contacts tend to breed cynicism and disillusionment among officers.[16]

These observations show how the environment—especially the typical kind of contact between police and citizens—bodes ominously for police subculture. Such job frustrations, coupled with other environmental elements, lead to a unique worldview and to a characteristic set of beliefs about how to deal with most members of the public and with offenders.

The street environment is an influential shaper of police subculture, but the traffic stop is at least equally influential. Since nearly every traffic stop is involuntary (that is, drivers would rather *not* be stopped by the police), any hopes of a positive encounter between the officer and the driver are doomed from the start. As a result, traffic stop interactions negatively shape police subculture.

Administration

The administrative arrangements in the typical police department cannot help but inform police subculture. Interactions with superiors and the routine steps taken at the beginning and end of each shift work together with social and physical environments, organizational factors, and other factors to set policing apart from other professions.

The typical officer usually reports for duty at roll call. This may take place in a briefing room where officers are given their assignments, activities of the previous shift are recounted, new policies are discussed, and anything else of importance is brought up. Roll calls are usually presided over by sergeants or their equivalents. From a culture-forming standpoint, roll call is important because it

> may contain mild rebukes of officers. During roll call, particular officers may be singled out for unpleasant duty, may be given disagreeable temporary partners, or otherwise be the recipient of administrative "bullshit." . . . [And] the time periods before and after roll call, when officers are on their way to or from their cars, provide time to talk and exchange information.[17]

At shift end, officers return to the briefing room or equivalent locations to finish their paperwork, change back into civilian attire, and prepare to head home. Debriefing also occurs at this time, particularly if a critical incident, such as a shooting or use of force, occurred during the shift. No matter the arrangement, this stage of the typical officer's day also shapes police subculture:

> Officers often spend more time than necessary here, relaxing and exchanging stories about shift activities. Shift end is consequently an environment for the types of interaction and story-telling that contribute to the generation of local cultural knowledge. Officers also may extend the end of the shift to the local pub or to an officer's house, furthering interaction and story-telling.[18]

As for interactions with supervisors, one would suspect that sergeants (and other higher-ups) would have an influential role in the shaping of police subculture. Research reveals, interestingly, that this tends not to be the case. For example, police researchers David Allen and Michael Maxfield studied the arrest, citation, and warrant activities of police officers and found that sergeants had virtually no direct effects on their subordinates' activities—particularly the quantity of those activities:

> The influence of first-line supervisors in directing the behavior of officers is seriously limited. Even though supervisors emphasize a particular performance criterion or suggest that a certain level of performance be met, officers under their command do not seem to respond positively to these cues.[19]

Although supervisors may not directly influence the culture of line officers, there are other administrative factors that surely do. One of them, according to Crank, is the process of internal review, which encompasses everything from investigating officers whose activities are called into question to reviewing the performance of new and seasoned officers alike. Internal review activities, which are generally not openly welcomed by line officers, surely shape their worldviews, interactions with one another, and, ultimately, police subculture.

YOU DECIDE
Cover My Back

You and your partner are called to the scene of a burglary in progress. On arriving at the scene, you witness someone running away from the house, down a dark alley. Both of you give chase, splitting up in an effort to apprehend the fleeing suspect. As you are running, you hear a gunshot. You turn and run in the direction of the sound. Shortly, you come upon your partner. The suspect is on the ground, obviously dead from a gunshot wound to the back of the head. Your partner says, "I need you to back me up. No matter who asks, tell them you were with me and it looked like the guy was about to draw a gun." You can see that the suspect did not have a gun. Later that day, an investigator from internal affairs asks you to explain what happened. What do you do?

Finally, policies and procedures, sometimes known as *standard operating procedures*, also shape police subculture. Rules are put in place to protect citizens and to protect police organizations from undue scrutiny, complaints, criticisms, and lawsuits. Such rules are written by administrators, attorneys, or high-level officials, often with little input from the rank and file. Most people can sympathize with the resentment that this can breed. Students often have to follow various school procedures that may seem arcane and irrelevant. This, in turn, shapes their attitudes toward administrators, possibly their instructors, and maybe their entire educational experience. The same is true in police work.

Other Criminal Justice Agencies

Police officers' interactions with other criminal justice agencies also shape police subculture. If a prosecutor rejects a case that the investigating officer perceives to be strong, for example, this can lead to disillusionment and frustration, which the officer will likely communicate to his or her peers. The more often this occurs, the more police officers may feel that they stand alone in their crime-fighting efforts and are not being supported by other criminal justice professionals.

On the other hand, if the prosecutor elects to take a case forward, this can take a significant amount of an officer's time, including his or her off-duty time. The defense will be entitled to discovery, which usually includes examination of the police report. The defense will scrutinize the report to ensure that proper procedures were followed and may even call into question the officer's integrity and worthiness—especially if the report was poorly written. All of this can be quite stressful for the officer, thus contributing to a unique set of perceptions, beliefs, and values that characterize police subculture.

The Media

The media have perhaps the most influence on police subculture. Some members of the media are supportive of the police and represent what Crank has called the "inner circle." These are often reporters who have worked with police officers for years and have come to appreciate the difficulties involved in policing. Police officers can usually work constructively with these reporters to manage the release of information and to ensure that investigations proceed unfettered. But not all reporters are supportive, and at least a minority, it seems, are bent on casting law enforcement agencies in an unfavorable light.

An example can be seen in a recent incident from Houston, Texas. In 2006, the *Houston Chronicle* (a traditionally liberal newspaper) published a series of articles criticizing the Houston Police Department for its use of Tasers.[20] The department's Tasers were equipped with cameras, not unlike the cameras found in patrol cars around the country. The cameras help to ensure that officers act properly and within the law. At the same time, though, there is nothing pleasant about watching a person on the receiving end of a Taser shock. They frequently yell, howl, flail, and appear to be in great pain. The *Chronicle* posted on its website the Taser videos that it had obtained. The newspaper criticized the police department, claiming that officers were using Tasers not only to defuse hostile situations but often when use of the devices was inappropriate. The paper failed to report on any successful incidents where Taser use resulted in the apprehension of dangerous suspects without loss of life. This episode, which some saw as intentionally biased reporting, shows that the police are sometimes "damned if they do, and damned if they don't."

A police department's relationship with the media can be a double-edged sword. The media can aid in investigations, for example, by publicizing composite sketches of suspects. But they can also paint police departments in a less-than-favorable light. This is particularly true in the case of scandals. A scandal involving a small group of officers can tarnish the reputation of an entire department for years. This, in turn, takes its toll on officers who work in that department and who might come to regard members of the press skeptically. Crank notes,

> The impact of scandal is massive and dramatic loss of legitimacy of the police. Such events are periods of *uncontrolled articulation*, chaos personified, formal relations between the police and other groups yielding confusing and poorly regulated communications. Departments are swamped by persons seeking information, officers in different circumstances, ranks, and degrees of involvement provide inconsistent accounts of the department, and the veil of secrecy is widely breached, as managers and line personnel alike seek to strategically cover their butts.[21]

In summary, there are five factors that have been linked to the formation of police subculture: organizational matters, the street environment, administration and administrative styles, relationships with other criminal justice agencies, and relationships with the media. This, of course, is not an exhaustive list. It would be impossible to identify all of the elements that shape police subculture in America. All of these factors interact in complex and sometimes unpredictable ways to produce a set of values and norms not found in any other occupation. What exactly are these values and norms? What is police subculture? We answer these questions in the rest of this chapter.

POLICE SUBCULTURE: ITS COMPONENTS

In this section, we look at the values and norms that characterize police subculture in America. We examine control and territoriality; use of force; danger, unpredictability, and suspicion; solidarity; and other components of police subculture.

Control and Territoriality

It is the use of coercion—or at least the *authority* to use coercion—that ultimately defines police work. Sociologist Egon Bittner once described the coercive authority of policing as the distinguishing feature that sets law enforcement apart from other professions. He called it the capacity to use force.[22] The power that officers have when it comes to the potential use of force is awesome because force can be used to deny people their freedom or even to take their lives. The ability to be coercive and to use force shapes the attitudes of police officers and sets them apart from other professionals.

Of course, force is not necessary most of the time, nor is coercion, but the maintenance of control is critical. Combined with the notion of control is territoriality, or the sense of responsibility a police officer feels for a particular area. Police officers must establish control over crime scenes and maintain social control over the neighborhoods they patrol.

Control. The term *control* sounds ominous. It suggests that police officers actively take steps to place limits on people's actions. Certainly, this does occur, especially when criminal suspects do not cooperate; however, there is more to the element of control than this. As Crank observes, "Cops may strategically use symbolic elements of their authority as coercive devices . . . displaying their weaponry in an intimidating way, for example."[23] Simply maintaining a police presence can do wonders in the furtherance of control.

Control is somewhat synonymous with order maintenance, one of the principal police functions we identify in Chapter 8. The issue also comes up in Chapter 13, where we discuss police behavior and decision making. Viewed together, these chapters make it clear that a police officer's identity and effectiveness rest significantly on his or her ability to take control, whether that control is direct (at a crime scene, for example) or indirect (by simply maintaining a presence in the community).

Territoriality. People, like animals, are all territorial to some extent. Whether we are protecting our homes, our cars, or our personal possessions, each of us takes steps to ensure "ours" does not become "theirs" without our consent. Police officers are also territorial. Instead of using the term *territoriality*, however, Crank calls this aspect of police work **dominion**, as the term "captures the divine responsibility over secular human activity that characterizes the special relationship cops have with a piece of earthly terrain."[24] Dominion has also been described in this way:

> [The officer] learns the names and directions of the streets, and he knows each intersection by its buildings. His knowledge of the streets is dictated by his concern to achieve maximum visibility with his car. . . . He pays careful attention to the little connecting streets and alleys. He examines, in time, every empty space to see if he can drive his car through it. He carefully checks empty lots and fields to see whether he can drive his car over them.[25]

dominion
John Crank's substitute for the term *territoriality*, which refers to an officer's sense of personal ownership over the area for which he or she is responsible.

John Van Maanen, professor of organization studies at MIT, makes this observation about territoriality:

> [Officers] come to know, in the most familiar and penetrating manner, virtually every passageway—whether alley, street, or seldom used path—located in their sector. From such knowledge of this social stage comes the corresponding evaluations of what particular conditions are to be

considered good or bad, safe or unsafe, troubled or calm, usual or unusual, and so on. . . . These evaluations are also linked to temporal properties associated with the public use of a patrolman's area of responsibility. . . . The territorial perspective carried by patrolmen establishes the basic normative standard for the proper use of space.[26]

Use of Force

William Wesley was among the first police researchers to cite the importance of force as a crucial element of police culture. Others, like Bittner, also focused much of their attention on the role of force in policing. As one author notes, the very possibility of having to use or to face force, and the emotions that accompany the use or threat of force, is a powerful contributor to police subculture:

> A policeman understands the meaning of fear, the loosening of muscles in the midriff and the vision of terrible things happening to your body, and he does not condemn men for being afraid, but he does not want them when he is working. They are only a danger and a burden.[27]

The role force plays in shaping police culture is further magnified by the war metaphor we use to refer to crime fighting. The phrases "war on crime" and "war on drugs" are commonly used, often without much conscious thought, but the war metaphor effectively shapes police subculture. As Crank puts it, "The metaphor 'war' has had explosive mobilizing potential. It provided a way to view the police as protectors of society (read 'your wives and children'), and to view criminals as amoral enemies—less than human."[28] Villanova philosophy professor Joseph Betz has gone a step further in illustrating the powerful effects of the war metaphor:

> Thinking of themselves as soldiers and crime fighters, all the police carry guns, even when working in the radio room or the juvenile division. They wear uniforms with badges of rank, like soldiers. They have military inspections and sometimes march as units in parades. They expect violence from the enemy and are ready to respond to violence in its own coin. . . . The policeman is tainted by his Janus-like position. He has one foot planted in decent society and one in the criminal underworld. He crystallizes and focuses the hate of respectable society for the criminal, but he learns to think like the criminal and to make counter-moves in the criminal's own game. . . . If his coercive force crosses the line to become violence, no one watches, or watching, no one objects.[29]

It is not just force that shapes police subculture; it is specific types of force. Consider guns, perhaps the most familiar symbols of policing next to white sedans with light bars. "In the culture of policing, guns transform police work into a heroic occupation, providing both a bottom line and an unquestionable righteousness that pervades all police-citizen encounters,"[30] Crank notes. The ready availability of handguns, rifles, shotguns, and semiautomatic weapons combines with the war metaphor to create a special type of work environment, one that cannot help but mold police subculture:

> Policing in the United States is very much like going to war. Three times a day in countless locker rooms across the land, large men and a growing number of women carefully arm and armor themselves for the day's events. They begin by strapping on flak jackets. . . . Then they pick up a wide, heavy, black leather belt and hang around it the tools of their trade: gun, mace, handcuffs, bullets. When it is fully loaded, they swing the belt around their hips with the same practiced motion of the gun-fighter in Western movies, slugging it down and buckling it in front. Many officers slip an additional small-caliber pistol into their trouser pocket or a leg holster just above the ankle. Inspecting themselves in a full-length mirror, officers thread their night sticks into a metal ring on the side of their belt.[31]

Of all the items in a police officer's arsenal, though, it is the sidearm that is most apparent, most influential, and most significant in its contribution to occupational identity. The prospect of a deadly encounter, as Crank observes, is "etched into the personality of the police officer forever—an unrequested rite of passage that leaves a stain on the personality of the officer."[32]

There is an interesting paradox that arises with respect to guns. They shape police subculture perhaps more than any other factor, but (other than at practice ranges) police officers rarely fire their weapons. In their study of police firearm usage, William Geller and Michael Scott drew this conclusion:

> To take a single example, the average police officer working Jacksonville, Florida (a city with a high rate of police-citizen violence), would have to work 139 years before he or she would be sta-

> tistically expected to shoot and kill a civilian . . . , 42 years before non-fatally shooting a civilian . . . , and probably about 10 years before discharging a firearm at a civilian. Observational studies of New York police note similar patterns of infrequent use of guns, with guns used against civilians only in five of 1,762 police-citizen encounters.[33]

To be sure, there are some police duties that require more frequent weapons usage, such as serving on a special weapons and tactics (SWAT) team. And there are some cities (and areas of those cities) that are far more dangerous than others. On the whole, though, gun use by police officers is infrequent.

Some officers clearly bring an appreciation of and familiarity with guns to their training, but *all* trainees leave their academies with a similar sense of the power they possess through firearms. That power, whether it be real or symbolic, deadly or nondeadly, coupled with the concepts of control and territoriality, is a critical and powerful component of police subculture.

Danger, Unpredictability, and Suspicion

Chapter 5 touched on academy training and recruits' learning of the so-called sixth sense, the police officer's somewhat intuitive feelings of skepticism and suspicion. Skepticism and suspicion are essential in policing because the job can sometimes be very unpredictable. Much of police work is routine and predictable, but there is the potential, at any moment, for a violent altercation that could lead to the taking of a life, be it a suspect's life or the officer's. This section looks at how danger and unpredictability shape police subculture. Together they breed skepticism and suspicion at levels largely unmatched in other professions.

Danger. Former NYPD Officer Paul Ragonese's book, *The Soul of a Cop*, captures better than most the dangerous nature of police work. Here is a chilling segment from that book:

> I reached the doorway, peeked in, and the apartment was pitch black. . . . Fear surged through me when a shot rang out in the apartment. Then I saw a flash as another shot was fired. The four housing cops came crawling out of there as fast as they could, and one dove right between my legs.
>
> I reached with my left hand to close the door, and a shot rang out. I got hit by a bullet between my thumb and index finger, in the fleshy part. It felt like a burn. A fourth shot hit the door jamb before I got the door closed. A fifth shot passed through it and struck the metal frame on the door across the hall.[34]

The potential for danger sets policing apart from other occupations. It may not be the most objectively dangerous job (timber cutters and taxi drivers, for instance, die on the job considerably more often than police officers do), but this does not discount the prominent position that perceptions of danger hold in policing (Figure 6-1). Learning about the prospect of danger begins at the

Figure 6-1 • Rate of Fatal Occupational Injuries for Selected Occupations, 2003

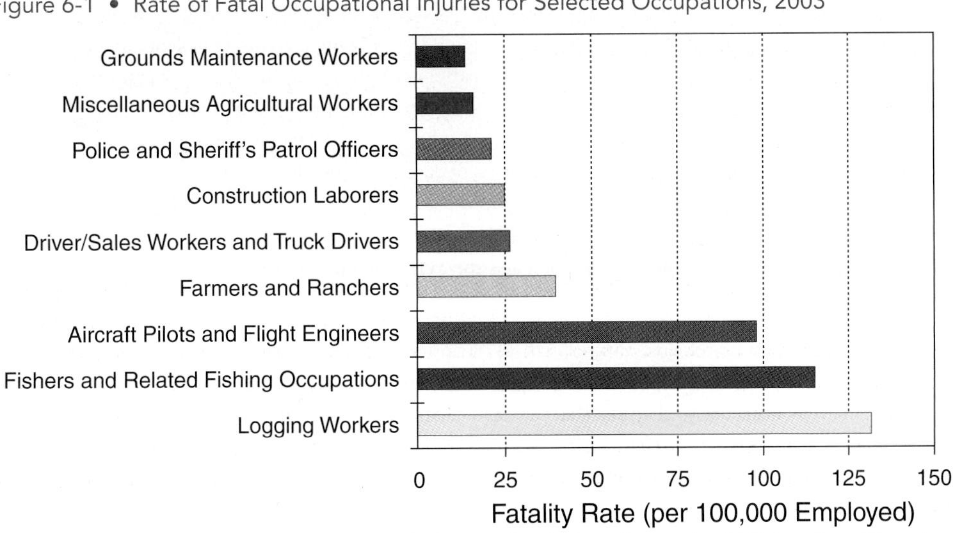

Source: Bureau of Labor Statistics, U.S. Department of Labor, *Fatal work injuries by occupation, 2003*, http://stats.bls.gov/opub/ted/2004/oct/wk1/art05.htm (accessed June 18, 2008).

academy and continues through field training, where "police vicariously experience, learn, and relearn the potential for danger through 'war stories'" told by veteran officers.[35] As Crank observes,

> Evocative symbols of danger—a razor hidden on the side of a driver's license, a .22 caliber weapon that looks like a pen knife—are common training fare. Officers are constantly reminded that in citizen encounters they can trust no one. A popular training film shows an officer murdered during a vehicular stop on a Texas highway. Training instructors provide stories of dangerous encounters and personal experiences convey a focus for occupational danger.[36]

paradox of policing
A phenomenon in which a police officer's fear of being injured or killed is stronger than is justified by actual rates of injury or death within the profession.

In the study of victims (known as *victimology*), there is a concept called the *victimization paradox*. It refers to the fact that some people, especially women, tend to be more fearful of crime than is justified by the likelihood of actually being victimized. A similar phenomenon has been identified in policing and has been called the **paradox of policing.** University of Cincinnati criminologist Francis Cullen and his colleagues found that while the potential for danger pervades police work, policing is not particularly hazardous compared with a number of other occupations. Officers who were interviewed felt that their personal chance of being injured or killed was slim, but they still perceived policing as a dangerous occupation.[37] In other words, policing carries a high *potential* for danger, even if the chances for *actual* danger are not all that high.

A problem with the Cullen study and other studies of the relative dangerousness of police work is that they often focus on officer deaths. Deaths are relatively rare, especially in light of modern medical care, training, and personal protection equipment, such as bulletproof vests. So, if deaths are not a good measure of dangerousness, what is? Crank offers this thought:

> A more realistic measure of danger experienced by police officers, I think, is a count of the number of assaults on officers in the line of duty. This number might more accurately reflect danger in the presence of real bodily threat because it includes injuries of all types.[38]

Some researchers *have* looked at assaults against police officers. The Federal Bureau of Investigation, for example, found that 58,634 officers were assaulted throughout the United States in 2006.[39] This number vastly exceeded the number of killings of police officers; when limited to homicides, such killings tend to number below 50 in any given year. Crank also observes that the indicated number of assaults may be low due to underreporting; some officers may not report minor injuries because of the paperwork that they would have to file, the air of machismo that pervades police work, or various other reasons. But how does police work compare with other occupations in terms of the potential for assault? Researchers have not fully answered this question. Even so, it is a safe bet that few other occupations carry as much potential for employee assault as does policing.

Certain elements of police work are far more dangerous than others. Consider the paramilitary units known as *SWAT teams*, for example. These groups are charged with the riskiest activities, such as serving high-risk warrants or dealing with hostage situations. Such work has interesting implications for police subculture, as Peter Kraska and Derek Paulsen have observed:

> The military weapons, tactics, training, and drug raids generate an intense feeling of "danger" among the officers. There exists, of course, a universal fear of being a victim of violence among regular police officers. . . . However, the preoccupation with danger in this special operations team, and the fear of being a victim of violence is heightened. All the [SWAT] officers expressed an extreme fear of the worst happening to them, emphasizing the "real possibility" that every call-out could end in tragedy. . . . The perception of danger and death serves to create a military-like camaraderie among [SWAT] officers. Just as the fear of danger involved in [SWAT] is more intense than in normal policing, the camaraderie formed is also more intense. Officers emphasize that they must rely on fellow officers more, and their close bonding functions to protect each other's "backsides."[40]

Unpredictability. The relative dangerousness of policing can be debated. Some researchers would say perceptions of dangerousness are overplayed, and officers on the streets would likely argue the opposite. But it is difficult to dispute that levels of unpredictability are high, no matter what one's perspective. In her book *What Cops Know*, Loyola University of Chicago journalism professor Connie Fletcher paints this image of uncertainty in describing an account that might have ended quite differently:

> Practically *anything* can happen on the street. My partner and I stopped a fellow speeding down Lake Shore Drive; the ceiling's forty-five; the guy must have been doing a hundred.

Fifth graders Dana Childs, 10, (left) and Simone Taylor, also 10, view the photographs of two of six California Highway Patrol officers who had been recently killed in the line of duty. The display is part of the California Peace Officers Memorial. Other than threats from violent criminals, what kinds of threats to life do officers face?

Rich Pedroncelli/AP Wide World Photos

> "Stop that son of a bitch!" So we turn on the blue lights, pull him over to the side. And he ran back to the car—we didn't even get a chance to look out, this is how fast he came back to the car. He says, "Please don't—I don't have time to get a speeding ticket. You see that girl in my car?" We say, "Yeah." "That is the greatest sexual experience I've ever had. She lives at the YWCA at Oak and Dearborn. If I don't get her back in five minutes, she's never gonna be able to go out with me again. I'd love to talk to you—if you stay here, I'll be back in ten minutes, you can write me up then, but I don't have time for this now"—he runs back, jumps back in his car, and *zoom*!—off he goes at a hundred miles an hour.[41]

There are pros and cons to the unpredictability that is inherent in policing. For one thing, danger can erupt at any moment. Unpredictability, on the other hand, lends meaning and excitement to the job. A common saying in the police literature is some variation of this: "Police work is hours of sheer boredom punctuated by moments of sheer terror." Others have referred to the "huff and puff of the chase."[42] Indeed, a number of researchers have argued that it is those unpredictable moments of terror, the adrenaline-pumping seconds, that make policing an attractive job to many people.[43]

Unpredictability need not equate with danger. It can simply give rise to the bizarre, as E.W. McNulty found:

> The officer responded to a call regarding a cab driver with a fare who wouldn't pay. In the parking lot, the cabby was standing outside his cab yelling at two prostitutes. In the front seat of the prostitute's car was a third prostitute who was naked, except for a red leather jacket that she somewhat used as covering, although as she got angry and got out of the car to scream at the cab driver, she didn't bother with the jacket. The cabby had picked up the naked prostitute and now she claimed she couldn't pay. All four of them were screaming at each other. The cabby was screaming for his money, the naked prostitute was screaming that she had been raped by a john, and the other two prostitutes were yelling that the cabby should have known that she had no money when he picked her up naked.[44]

Unpredictability can also take on an air of unpleasantness, and officers need a strong stomach to deal with some of what they encounter. Consider this fairly graphic account of a suicide:

> One time we had a jumper; this guy jumped out of the 19th floor of the YMCA. He hit the ground, and his head hit, and the top of his head popped off, and his brain fell out. And it was perfectly intact. I'm walking all around it; I can't get over how it's just a brain laying there, complete and perfect as can be. It's laying right on the gutter. It didn't splatter—it wasn't icky

> or anything. It was like somebody just *placed* a brain on the gutter. Like an egg yolk. It was just perfect. . . . So now the paramedics come. And this one paramedic goes, "Look at this brain! Do you think we should put it in a chest with ice?" I'm looking at him like "Sure, pal, go ahead and transplant this on somebody."[45]

Suspicion. A simple equation characterizes much of police work: danger + unpredictability = suspicion. Cops know that given the potential for danger around any turn and the inherent uncertainty that go along with police work, a sense of suspicion is essential. The problem is that suspicion can creep into an officer's private life and into his or her associations with others—such as neighbors and strangers—who are not employed in the same line of work. In this vein, suspicion is more than good police work or part of the working personality. Rather, it is a key factor that defines police subculture.

There are several sources of suspicion. Obviously, the potential for danger and unpredictability rank high on the list, but we can also add certain characteristics of our legal system. In Chapter 11, we discuss levels of justification for searches and seizures. One of them is reasonable suspicion, the requisite standard for conducting so-called stop-and-frisk activities. In Chapter 11, as you will learn, we place reasonable suspicion on a continuum of justification falling somewhere between a hunch and probable cause. Crank, however, feels this legal definition of *suspicion* is at odds with what policing is really like:

> The idea that there is a legal basis for suspicion is wholly inconsistent with cultural dimensions of suspicion, what I will call the *sixth sense suspicion*. The skill of *sixth sense suspicion* lies not in the ability to gather enough evidence to make an arrest, but in the ability to identify wrongdoers from the most meager of clues. . . . Suspicion is the special craft of policing.[46]

By outsiders, suspicion is regarded as an unfortunate by-product of policing that slowly takes over an officer's whole personality, not just his or her working persona. Some feel that the lack of trust police officers exhibit toward others (apart from other officers) explains why they do not associate much with civilians while off the clock.

Police officers regard suspicion in quite a different way. They understand that they have been *trained* to be suspicious:

> During his training period, the recruit is encouraged to patrol with his windows open, alert for any unusual sounds and smells. Under the common law he is considered a sight officer who may arrest for any crimes he sees being committed. The law interprets his sight to include all of his natural senses. If he smells something he feels reveals evidence of criminal activity—a still or drugs—it is sufficient cause for him to investigate without a warrant.[47]

Suspicion can be combined with powerful psychological tactics to make for effective crime prevention. An example is what Crank calls the *suspicious stare*. Wild animals often gain superiority over rivals with eye contact. The power of the stare is equally important in human culture. A stare by a police officer is just that, a display of power. Consider Rubinstein's observations on this subject:

> Instead of stopping and staring or riding on past, he [the officer] drives the car toward the suspects, openly displaying his interest in them. . . . As he comes even with them, he turns his head to look at them, not concealing his interest in any way. He does not halt nor does he stop looking. If he is successful, they will be following his actions intently. He is making a play and they are responding to it. . . . When he has gone past them, he suddenly hits the brake, causing the car's wheels to screech, and shifts the wheels into reverse. When he does this, he is watching closely for any movements in the group, someone throwing something to the ground or a person moving to block off his direct view.[48]

Suspicion is thus healthy, but we cannot divorce it from the legal requirements we talked about earlier. This is because if an officer is going to *act* on his or her suspicion, there must be some articulable reason for stopping or seizing someone. Regarding certain individuals as suspicious simply because they look different can translate into unequal treatment. Sometimes this is called *profiling*, a topic more fully discussed in Chapter 8.

drug courier profiling
A crime-detection process that makes use of what is known about the likely and observable characteristics of drug couriers. Drug courier profiling often occurs in stop-and-frisk situations.

An interesting type of law enforcement, in which the intersection between suspicion and profiling is apparent, concerns identifying drug couriers who transport illegal narcotics. The practice is called **drug courier profiling,** and it clearly illustrates the important role of suspicion in law enforcement.

Almost without exception, drug courier profiling occurs in stop-and-frisk situations—that is, when a person is stopped and questioned because he or she appears suspicious in some way. Drug courier profiling is most common in airports, but it is also used on our nation's highways and elsewhere. Indeed, profiling suspects for other offenses occurs as well. Law enforcement officials have developed profiles of a number of other varieties of offenders, including car thieves,[49] child abusers,[50] child batterers,[51] and sexual abusers.[52] All of these profiles are premised on suspect behaviors and characteristics that can be regarded as suspicious.

The carrying of controlled substances by airline passengers is a common way for drugs to enter the United States from a foreign country. Law enforcement agents *could* conceivably search every person who passes through an airport, but such an effort would be costly, time-consuming, unacceptable to passengers, and almost certainly unconstitutional. This is because warrantless searches that are based on no articulable justification are always unreasonable under the Fourth Amendment unless one of a few "specifically established and well-delineated exceptions" applies.[53]

Identifying drug couriers is controversial because the practice of smuggling drugs is inherently surreptitious. As the U.S. Supreme Court has observed, "Much . . . drug traffic is highly organized and conducted by sophisticated criminal syndicates. . . . And many drugs . . . may be easily concealed. As a result, the obstacles to detection . . . may be unmatched in any other area of law enforcement."[54] Rarely do officers observe overt actions that would give them the necessary justification to stop, search, or arrest someone. Instead, they have to rely on their sense of suspicion and on an ability to identify certain characteristics that drug couriers tend to exhibit. Figure 6-2 lists some common characteristics of drug couriers.

Perhaps a more innocuous description of suspicion is a concern with what is amiss:

> Police officers base action decisions, such as whether to stop someone, on *incongruity*—things out of place. . . . The focus on incongruity was especially evident in the strategies that the [police academy] staff recommended for initiating action. . . . For example, they taught the recruits to avoid the abstract question, "Where does the truth lie?" Instead, they posed a more concrete question, "What's wrong with this picture?" as a means for recognizing whether things were "out of place." The class sergeant told the recruits that looking for something *suspicious* was less effective than looking for the *unusual*, because *suspicious* was so hard to define. One instructor

Figure 6-2 • Drug Courier Characteristics

1. Use of small denominations of currency for ticket purchase.
2. Travel to and from major drug import centers.
3. Absence of luggage or use of empty suitcases on trips that normally require extra clothing.
4. Travel under an alias.
5. Unusual itinerary, such as a rapid turnaround time for a very lengthy airplane trip.
6. Unusually large amounts of currency (many thousands of dollars).
7. Unusual nervousness beyond that ordinarily exhibited by passengers.
8. The almost exclusive use of public transportation upon departing the airport.
9. Immediate placement of a phone call after deplaning.
10. False or fictitious call-back telephone number left with the airline.
11. Unusual dress.
12. Age between 25 and 35.
13. Paleness consistent with extreme nervousness.
14. Failure to use identification tags on luggage.
15. Purchase of tickets on the day of the flight.
16. Exiting first or last from the plane.
17. Walking quickly through the terminal while checking over one's shoulder.
18. Quick departure from the airport on arrival.

Source: John L. Worrall, *Criminal procedure: From first contact to appeal*, 2nd ed., © 2007. Reprinted by permission of Pearson Education, Inc., Upper Saddle River, New Jersey.

used the analogy of a black and white picture to demonstrate the importance of contrasting the usual and the unusual. He explained that he began investigations of crime scenes by taking black and white photographs to establish contrast, highlighting the relative positions of items without the distraction that details provide.[55]

split-second syndrome
A condition confronting police officers that involves three central features of policing—the urgency of police-citizen encounters, the involuntariness of such encounters, and a public setting—all of which combine to place officers in the position of having to make quick on-the-spot decisions.[ii]

The Split-Second Syndrome. If danger and unpredictability breed suspicion, then this is because of what criminologist James Fyfe has called the **split-second syndrome.**[56] Fyfe has argued that three features of policing—urgency of police-citizen encounters, the involuntariness of such encounters, and the public setting in which they take place—combine to put officers in the position of having to make quick on-the-spot decisions.

Sometimes officers' decisions are appropriate; other times they are not. If a bad decision is made, Fyfe says, it was partly due to the need to make decisions in the heat of the moment. When, for example, a police officer shoots a suspect who turns out not to be a danger, we must put ourselves in the shoes of the officer. Then it becomes a little more apparent how such decisions come to be made:

> The split-second syndrome is based on several assumptions. First, it assumes that, since no two police problems are precisely alike, there are no principles that may be applied to the diagnosis of specific situations. Thus, no more can be asked of officers than that they respond as quickly as possible to problems, devising the best solutions they can on the spur of the moment. This, of course, places an extraordinary burden upon officers, who must make life-or-death decisions under the most stressful and time-constrained conditions.[57]

Fyfe goes on to list other assumptions underlying the split-second syndrome. One of them is that inappropriate decisions should be expected given the demands placed on officers to choose a course of action in a short amount of time, and "any subsequent criticism of officers' decisions—especially by those outside the police, who can have no real appreciation of the burdens upon officers—is an unwarranted attempt to be wise after the event."[58] Finally, if judgments are to be made about officers' decisions in split-second situations, then they need to be judged from the position of the officers, particularly what was going on in their head at the time: "Thus, should police receive a report of an armed robbery in a crowded supermarket, they should be granted great leeway in their manner of response, because no two armed-robbery calls are precisely alike."[59]

Solidarity

solidarity
The tendency among police officers to stick together and associate with one another.

There is a tendency among police officers to stick together and to associate with one another. In terms of police subculture, this is known as **solidarity.** Solidarity itself consists of several elements, each of which is covered in the next few subsections. We will look at moral superiority, common sense, the masculine environment, the us-versus-them mentality, and secrecy. Again, we draw on John Crank's informative examination of police subculture for guidance.

YOU DECIDE

The Eleventh Commandment

You are a sergeant assigned to community and media relations. Your lieutenant made a big show in the media last week about how the police department has lowered crime in your city, in spite of being the most poorly funded agency in the county. He promised a follow-up news conference this week but has been called out of town for specialized training. He has asked you to hold the news conference in his absence.

Before the conference, you receive a call from the department's civilian crime analyst, who tells you that the lieutenant ignored several reports and that serious crime is actually up 3 percent compared with last year. Then you see a six-month-old published survey showing that your department is the third best funded of seven agencies in the county. The chief is on vacation in Hawaii, the news conference is in an hour, and you are mindful of your department's eleventh commandment: Thou shalt not embarrass a senior officer. How will you run the news conference? How will you handle reporters' questions?

Moral Superiority. Moral superiority is concerned with a belief on the part of police officers that they represent a higher moral order. In discussing police morality, Crank points out that "police see themselves as representatives of a higher morality embodied in a blend of American traditionalism, patriotism, and religion. As moral agents, police view themselves as guardians whose responsibility is not simply to make arrests but to roust out society's trouble-makers."[60] In other words, they see themselves as morally superior in some sense. This may sound pompous, but remember that policing is about enforcing the law. Laws reflect people's perceptions of right and wrong, and those who break them are on the "wrong side," at least most of the time.

There is a darker side to the police moral sense, too. It leads to a tendency to regard ordinary citizens as different and even inferior. For example, people who get speeding tickets are often admonished by the citing officer, who might conclude by saying, "Please watch your speed now." Such statements are usually offered up out of genuine concern for the driver's safety, but they can also be said with thick sarcasm laden with an air of superiority. It is these latter tendencies that Crank points to in his discussion of the "moral mandate" inherent in police work.

Related to the moral mandate is the concept of **dramaturgy.** The simple definition of *dramaturgy* is "the art of theater, or theatrics." Applied to policing, dramaturgy refers to putting on a display of high-mindedness. This display further reinforces beliefs—on the part of police *and* citizens—that law enforcement is doing the right thing and that those who work in it are the "good guys":

> The thin art of high-minded rhetoric is often present in public descriptions of the police and their adversaries. It typifies the often uncritical way in which the police are presented to the outside world as good guys, waging a war against the bad guys, criminals, or whoever fails to unequivocally support the police. The common-place term "bad guy" reveals this high-mindedness. Lawbreakers are rarely perceived to be ordinary people that have committed bad behavior: they are themselves wicked. The label is harsh and uncompromising.[61]

dramaturgy
In the law enforcement context, the act of putting on a display of high-mindedness.

Perhaps the classic study of this higher moral sense is John Van Maanen's 1978 paper called "The Asshole."[62] Although some people may find the title of Van Maanen's paper offensive, the paper is well known in academic circles, and we use it here in order to be true to his original presentation. Van Maanen found that police officers would brand difficult people with this quite negative term, stigmatizing them.

According to Van Maanen, the identification of an "asshole" proceeds in three steps. First, the **affront** is when an officer's authority is questioned. The second stage, **clarification,** occurs when the officer attempts to ascertain what kind of person he or she is dealing with. Finally, the **remedy** consists of the officer's response. "Assholes," according to Van Maanen, are the people most likely to be on the receiving end of some "street justice."

affront
According to John Van Maanen, the first of three steps police officers use in identifying an "asshole." It occurs when an officer's authority is questioned.

clarification
According to John Van Maanen, the second of three steps police officers use in identifying an "asshole." It occurs when the officer attempts to ascertain what kind of person he or she is dealing with.

remedy
According to John Van Maanen, the last of three steps police officers use in identifying an "asshole." It consists of the officer's response to an affront.

In reflecting on Van Maanen's work, Crank observes that the term "contained a great deal of meaning for the police. The label emerged from the need to maintain control in street encounters, and from a moral imperative to assert the authority of the state when it was questioned."[63] A problem, though, is that too many people can be branded with this label or, at best, viewed as untrustworthy. This is the result of an unfortunate reality in everyday police work:

> People lie to us eight hours a day. Everybody lies to us: offenders, victims, witnesses. They all lie to the police. It gets so bad, you go to a party, somebody comes up to talk to you. You're thinking, "Why is this guy saying this to me? What's his game?" You can't turn it off.[64]

There are other terms besides "asshole" that police use to describe criminal suspects, other officers, citizens in general, superiors, and scores of other people and issues. Indeed, there is a police vocabulary that is unique and sometimes humorous. Figure 6-3 provides a snapshot of police slang.

Common Sense. According to Crank, common sense is "the lifeblood of the police culture."[65] What is common sense? "Common sense arises from the doing of police work, what officers see and how officers act on and react to their working environment. It is the practical knowledge they use to do their work."[66]

The use of the term *common sense* in this context distinguishes between book learning and the ways in which actual police work is done:

> Officers take great pride in their common sense. But their common sense does not come from the world as given. To the contrary, police common sense is expressed in their ability to see the world unseen. Common sense derives from an officer's skills in recognizing the hidden danger in the seemingly safe world inhabited by ordinary citizens.[67]

Figure 6-3 • Police Slang and Abbreviations

100-yard hero: A member of the public who shouts obscenities at a police officer from a safe distance.

admission: A person's acknowledgment of involvement in crime that is not, in itself, sufficient to establish guilt. For example, a suspect acknowledges having been at the crime scene but does not confess to having committed the crime.

Alabama lie detector: A police baton.

angler: A thief who uses a rod or pole to steal from ground-floor windows.

A/O: Arresting officer. This abbreviation is often used in case reporting.

assist: A call for help from a police officer in trouble.

backup: A call to stop by another police officer's location or to aid another officer as a secondary unit.

beat: A geographic area assigned to specific officers for patrol.

beat car: A police car assigned to patrol a specific beat.

blues and twos: Driving very fast on an emergency call.

BOLO: Be on the lookout.

brew: A hot beverage, usually but not always coffee.

bus: An ambulance.

can: A jail or prison.

canteen cowboy: A police officer, generally young in service, who likes to advise other, even younger, officers.

cash in: To die.

Central: Central Dispatch.

check-by: A call for minor assistance from a police officer.

chip: The girlfriend or mistress of a police officer. Also called *chippie*.

choir practice: A party or social event for police officers.

chop shop: A place where stolen cars are disassembled for parts, which are then sold.

clink: A prison or jail; or a cell in a prison or jail.

complaint: A statement under oath in which a witness accuses an individual of criminal behavior. Although a complaint may trigger an arrest, it is not in itself sufficient in most jurisdictions to bring the offender before a criminal court.

con: A convict; or a confidence trick.

confession: A person's admission of enough facts to establish his or her guilt of a particular crime.

cooking the books: The art of making an area appear safer to the public than it actually is.

cop a plea: To plead guilty to a lesser charge to avoid standing trial for a more serious charge.

CSI: Crime scene investigator.

CSU: Crime scene unit.

data streaming: A growing crime in which a hacker obtains credit card details to create counterfeit cards.

deck: A packet of narcotics.

dee wee: Driving while intoxicated.

DOA: Dead on arrival. This abbreviation is applied to a person who dies before reaching a medical facility.

dog call: A distasteful or boring police assignment to respond to a nonserious call.

drop: To take a drug by mouth.

drop a dime: To make a telephone call, especially to the police to inform on or betray someone.

DT: A detective.

EDP: Emotionally disturbed person.

flash message: An informally broadcast message, transmitted via police radios, sent by an officer at the scene of a crime or incident to alert other officers in the vicinity. It is not a distress call. For example, following a hit-and-run traffic accident, the first officer at the scene may send out a flash message regarding the offender's vehicle, description, and direction of flight so other officers in the area can watch for the offender.

FLUB: Fat lazy useless bastard.

front: A person with a clean criminal record who provides an acceptable face for a known criminal who is the real owner of a club or business.

gate fever: The emotion shown by a prisoner nearing the end of his or her sentence.

get pulled: To be stopped by police; or to be taken aside by a senior officer and spoken to about something.

go down: To get arrested; or to be sent to prison.

good call: The very rare occasion where police presence is required. The term may also be used by fellow officers in reply to an attempt to point out a particularly attractive member of the public. The opposite is *bad call* or worse.

grass: An informer.

gun run: A search for a weapon reported sighted in the hands of a perp.

hit: A tactical assault on a criminal location.

hobbit: A prisoner who complies with the system.

house: The station house.

IAB: Internal Affairs Bureau; the branch of the police that investigates officers within the agency.

IR number: Individual record number; the number assigned to an individual upon his or her arrest. The IR number is used in any subsequent arrests of the same individual.

juice: Influence.

ker-ching: A sound like that of a cash register, usually made after giving a traffic ticket or when working extended shifts for overtime pay.

lawyering up: A suspect's decision to stop answering questions and request legal counsel.

LKA: Last known address.

lockup: A temporary detention facility; a jail.

MO: Modus operandi; the way in which a criminal commits a crime.

monkey: A person who is mocked, duped, or made to appear a fool; or a drug addiction: to have a monkey on one's back.

mope: A criminal perpetrator or criminal suspect; a perp.

muppet: Most useless police person ever trained. *Muppet* is generally used as a term of endearment.

mutt: A criminal perpetrator or criminal suspect; a perp.

obbo: Police observation of suspected criminals.

OC: Organized crime.

padding: The unscrupulous police practice of adding to a drug haul to upgrade an arrest or to ensure a conviction.

paying the rent: Handing out a specified number of traffic summonses and moving violations.

perp: A criminal perpetrator or criminal suspect. Also called *mope* or *mutt.*

pig: Polite, intelligent gentleman.

pop: An arrest.

PPO: Probationary police officer; a sworn member who has been employed as a police officer for less than one year. Informally referred to as a *rookie.*

rabbit: A fleeing subject.

rat squad: Officers and detectives assigned to the Internal Affairs Bureau.

rip: A loss in pay due to a disciplinary infraction, such as unauthorized moonlighting.

R/O: Responding officer. This abbreviation is used in police case reporting.

roll call: The first half hour of a watch, which is reserved for attendance, inspection, briefings, and training.

shoulder-surfing: Stealing personal identification numbers at automated teller machines for use later with copied cards.

skel: Skeleton; a derogatory term used to describe a junkie or a homeless vagrant.

slammer: Prison.

snitch: An informer.

stick: A truncheon. The term is now rarely used. Also, to hit with a truncheon for failing to do what you're told.

suit: A person who spends his or her time at a desk on the phone or using a computer.

supergrass: A very important informer.

tactical officer: A police officer who works in plainclothes and concentrates on vice and narcotics arrests.

ten-one: An officer's radio call for emergency assistance. A ten-one call is a matter of the utmost urgency and is responded to by any available unit nearby. Also called a *code eight.*

uniform carrier: A useless or ineffective police officer. Also called a *clothes hanger.*

white shirt: A lieutenant or other superior officer. The term comes from the white uniform shirt these officers wear.

youth: A person under the age of 17. Also called a *juvenile.*

Sources: SlangSearch.com, "Crime Slang," http://www.slangsearch.com/crime.html; "Police Glossary," http://members.aol.com/Welts23/PoliceGlossary.html; Police Oracle, www.policeoracle.com, Redhill, Surrey, UK. Copyright NSI Group. Reprinted by permission; and Sentinel Studio.com, "Commonly Used Police Abbreviations and Police Terminology," http://www.sentinelstudio.com/blogtopia/2004/11/commonly-used-police-abbreviations-and.html.

The Masculine Environment. Police officers work in a largely masculine environment. This is partly due to the fact that the profession has historically been dominated by males. Invariably, this has caused police subculture to be dominated by masculine values and orientations:

> From the outset, recruits are expected to confirm their masculine images to others and to themselves by exaggerating the characteristics associated with manhood. . . . Training emphasizes physical conditioning, fighting, weaponry, all skills that are associated with traditional male roles and are practiced as play in the early childhood of American males. . . . From crude slurs against women to the demonstration of an officer's willingness to put his or her life on the line for a fellow officer, themes of masculinity are pervasive to police culture.[68]

Female police scholars have taken notice of the masculine environment of the job. The book *Breaking and Entering: Police Women on Patrol*, by Maryland professor Susan Martin, contains several examples of the masculine environment. Here is one:

> Officers must adjust to the values of the citizens they police in order to work effectively and thus come to be influenced by the "focal concerns" of the members of the lower classes. One of these concerns is "toughness," a composite of physical prowess demonstrated by strength, endurance, and athletic skills; the absence of sentimentality and the conceptualization of women as conquest objects; and bravery in the face of physical threats.[69]

WEB PATROL 6-1

Contacts between Police and the Public
http://www.mycrimekit.com

The Us-versus-Them Mentality. Anthony Bouza, noted police scholar and former chief of the Minneapolis Police Department, vividly captured another defining component of police culture—the us-versus-them mentality:

> The sense of "us vs. them" that develops between cops and the outside world forges a bond between cops whose strength is the stuff of fables. It is called the *brotherhood in blue*, and it inspires a fierce and unquestioning loyalty to all cops, everywhere. It is widened by the dependence cops have on each other for safety and backup. The response to a summons to help is a cop's life-line. An "assist police officer" is every cop's first priority. The ultimate betrayal is for one cop to fail to back up another.[70]

A number of other researchers have also highlighted this important component of police culture:

> The way the police view the world can be described as a "we/they" or "us/them" orientation. The world is seen as composed of insiders and outsiders—police and citizens. Persons who are not police officers are considered outsiders and are viewed with suspicion. This "we/they" police worldview is created for a variety of reasons: the techniques used to select citizens for police service; the normative orientation police bring to the profession; an exaggeration of occupational danger; the special legal position police hold in society; and the occupational self-perception that is internalized by people who become police officers.[71]

The us-versus-them mentality is also reflected in the points we have already made about officers associating with one another. It spills over into (and is influenced by) other components of police subculture. The notion of moral superiority that we touched on earlier goes hand in hand with a perception that it is "us," the cops, against "them," everyone else: "It is important to bear in mind that being a member of the police fraternity is also a highly gratifying emotional experience in which the officer sees himself as belonging to an exclusive group of men who are braver, smarter, stronger, and more self-reliant than the civilian population they serve."[72]

Not only does the job itself breed an us-versus-them mentality, but there are other factors that could explain it. Crank identifies three of them.[73] One explanation lies in so-called cop families. Police work often runs in families. When there is an intergenerational connection, this fuels sentiments that it is "us against the world." Crank also points out that people from small towns often aspire to law enforcement due to limited employment prospects, and they bring with them to the job a shared set of beliefs about crime, society's problems, and "outsiders." Finally, some police officers have prior military experience. The military mind-set of "us versus the enemy" easily transfers to policing and is further exacerbated by the war metaphor described earlier in this chapter.

As mentioned earlier, police culture knows few parallels in other occupations or walks of life. To some extent, however, the us-versus-them component that characterizes police subculture may also exist to some degree among members of the military, outdoors men and women, gun-rights proponents, cop families in general, and even conservative political groups. Consequently, there may be segments of our society that gravitate toward police work not just because the job has attractions for them but because it puts them side by side with like-minded individuals. As Crank observes, "Many police recruits are drawn from the culture of policing [or to it], and by the time they decide to go into police work, their loyalties and values are already aligned with the police."[74]

WEB PATROL 6-2

Police Culture and the Code of Silence
http://www.mycrimekit.com

Secrecy. Researchers have found that secrecy goes hand in hand with solidarity. But one doesn't need to be a researcher to get a feel for how secrecy is important in police work. First, the public does not have access to much of what happens in the world of law enforcement. Information tends to be given out on a need-to-know basis. Secrecy also insulates officers from intensive scrutiny from supervisors and the community. The veil of secrecy that tends to pervade law enforcement has been readily revealed in high-profile investigations of police corruption. The Mollen Commission's investigation of the New York City Police Department during the 1990s reached this conclusion:

> [Secrecy and solidarity] facilitate corruption primarily in two ways. First, they encourage corruption by setting a standard that nothing is more important than the unswerving loyalty of officers to one another—not even stopping the most serious forms of corruption. Second, these attitudes thwart efforts to control corruption. They lead officers to protect or cover up for others' crimes—even crimes of which they heartily disapprove.[75]

Eastern Kentucky University police studies professor Victor Kappeler and his colleagues have identified a series of what they call "postulates shaping the ethos of secrecy." By "postulates" they mean statements that reflect the overall sentiments expressed by perhaps the majority of police officers. Here are some examples:

> *"Don't give up another cop."* As perhaps one of the most important factors contributing to secrecy and to a sense of solidarity, this postulate admonishes officers to never, regardless of the seriousness or nature of a case, provide information to either superiors or nonpolice that would cause harm to a fellow police officer. . . .
>
> *"Watch out for your partner first and then the rest of the guys working that tour."* This postulate tells police officers they have an obligation to their partners first, and then to other officers working the same shift. "Watching out," in this context, means that an officer has a duty not only to protect a fellow officer from physical harm, but also to watch out for their interests in other matters.
>
> *"If you get caught off base, don't implicate anybody else."* Being caught off base can involve a number of activities, ranging from being out of one's assigned sector to engaging in prohibited activities. This postulate teaches officers that if they are discovered in proscribed activities, they should accept the punishment, not implicate others.[76]

Not everyone has run up against this "blue wall of silence." A researcher who studied the Boston Police Department made this observation:

> The unwritten code of silence I had heard so much about was not the obstacle I had expected it to be. Maybe they were not entirely representative, but most of the cops that consented to be interviewed were gregarious. A number of them were downright charming. They seemed to enjoy talking.[77]

YOU DECIDE

A Few Too Many

On patrol at two in the morning, you observe a car being driven erratically, weaving in and out of the lane. You pull the car over and determine that the driver has been drinking. You examine the driver's identification and discover that she is a fellow police officer. What do you do?

But this example may not be representative. Crank ran up against police secrecy in his research into police agencies:

> I once visited a chief in an agency in a small community in Illinois, and had been given a tour of the department. The demeanor of everyone with whom I talked was courteous and friendly. As I finished, I stopped to look at a plaque on the wall that contained photos, badges, and insignia of fallen officers. Suddenly I sensed a presence behind me. Turning around, I saw three officers staring at me. . . . The clear sense I carried from that encounter was as if they had said to me *in this aspect of our lives you are not permitted entry*.[78]

Other Components of Police Subculture

Control and territoriality, use of force, suspicion, and solidarity are key components of police culture. There are a few others, though, that do not fit neatly into any of these categories. They include isolation, bravery, and the creative use of deception.

Isolation. Police work is characterized by at least two forms of isolation. First, the job often requires officers to literally work in isolation. Consider sheriff's deputies in rural counties. They can effectively be on their own most of the time. Perhaps more important, though, is the prospect of isolation from the community. Not only are officers somewhat physically removed from the communities they serve, but they can feel isolated in terms of relationships, as well. This is especially true of relationships with nonpolice:

> Social isolation becomes both a consequence and a stimulus. . . . Police officers find that constraints of schedule, of secrecy, of group mystique, and of growing adaptive suspiciousness and cynicism limit their friendships and relationships in the nonpolice world.[79]

Kappeler and his colleagues have identified a series of postulates describing this notion of isolation:

> *"Protect your ass."* As perhaps one of the most important postulates leading to a sense of isolation, this rule teaches police to be wary of everyone, including citizens and superiors. At the simplest level, the rule informs police that anyone who wants to cause trouble for an officer probably can. . . .
>
> *"Don't trust the new guy until you have him checked out."* Rookie police and officers who are new to a work group are not accorded status automatically. Instead, outsiders are treated cautiously until information about them can be obtained. . . .
>
> *"Don't talk too little or too much; don't tell anybody more than they have to know."* The themes of "don't talk too much" and "don't reveal more than necessary" inform new police officers that others including citizens and supervisors are not to be trusted.
>
> *"Don't trust bosses to look out for your interests."* This maxim informs new police officers that when forced to make a choice, managers and administrators will look out for their own best interests rather than those of the officer.[80]

Bravery. Police officers need to possess the attribute of bravery before entering the profession. A person who does not feel comfortable in confrontational, perhaps dangerous situations (or who cannot be taught to act bravely) probably won't make a very good officer. Bravery is thus one more key component of police subculture. New officers are taught the importance of not backing down, and veteran cops are constantly reminded not to appear "soft." Again, Kappeler and his colleagues have identified some postulates summarizing the "ethos of bravery." Two are relevant here:

> *"Show balls."* The police characterize their work as dangerous and fraught with hazards. This postulate counsels police that they are never to back down from a situation; backing down signals weakness. All police are harmed by the cowardice of an individual officer.
>
> *"Be aggressive when you have to, but don't be too eager."* This postulate reflects the idea that while officers should always be alert, they should not go out of their way to seek trouble. This is partly because overeagerness, or having a "chip" on one's shoulder, will bring unneeded complications.[81]

The Art of Deception. There is a clear dark side to deception. For one thing, most people do not enjoy being lied to. For another, deception can be criminal, such as in the case of providing perjured testimony. There is more to deception in the policing context, though, and it is not necessarily all bad. Indeed, some people regard it as none other than good policing or creative detective work. Viewed differently, to do their jobs, police officers either have to *or want to* bend the rules to get the job done. As Crank observes,

> Cops develop strategies for circumventing the legal rigors of due process. Consider consent. Consent is one of the exceptions to the warrant requirement. Consent is a common defense by officers when they have not received a warrant.[82]

The investigative process provides another illustration. Say detectives have two suspects in custody. The detectives tell one suspect that the other has implicated him—and vice versa—in order to elicit a confession. Assuming that neither suspect has ratted the other out, is this bad police work or just creative investigation? From a legal standpoint, nothing automatically prohibits admission into court of confessions elicited as a result of lies and deception. Thus, deception, or as Crank calls it, the "truth game," is probably just good police work.

What kinds of lies are appropriate? Thomas Barker, R. N. Friery, and David L. Carter identified three types of lies and then surveyed officers concerning their perceptions of each.[83] The first were so-called **accepted lies**, those that are necessary in furthering the police mission. Second were **tolerated lies**, those that are used to defend questionable discretionary decisions. Finally, **deviant lies** expressly violate the rules and legal requirements. Interestingly, 58 percent of the officers felt deviant lies were acceptable if the end result was satisfactory. The percentages were much higher for the other types of lies.

accepted lie
A lie that is necessary in furthering the police mission.

tolerated lie
A lie that is used to defend a questionable discretionary decision.

deviant lie
A lie that expressly violates the rules and legal requirements.

To further illustrate the "truth game" in law enforcement, New York University criminologist Jerome Skolnick discussed a New York study in which police descriptions of how evidence was secured varied before and after the U.S. Supreme Court's decision in *Mapp v. Ohio* (see Chapter 12). *Mapp* made the exclusionary rule binding on the states, thus giving some teeth to the Fourth Amendment by making an enforcement mechanism available to people who were wrongfully searched or seized.

In a look at the narcotics bureau in New York, police reported before *Mapp* that 28 percent of defendants threw evidence to the ground, but that percentage went up to 72 percent after the Supreme Court's decision. Why is this interesting? A criminal with half a brain is not going to throw his or her contraband down in front of police and increase the chances of getting caught. Skolnick argues that, instead, the increase in incidents of "dropped" evidence resulted from untruthful testimony on the part of police. If the evidence was "dropped," then it could be seized. He speculated that police used this argument even though no more defendants *actually* dropped the evidence after *Mapp* than before.

Carl Klockars, another well-known police scholar, sums up the art of deception in this way:

> The core of the police role in sting operations is packed with behaviors which go against conventional norms of respectable behavior: lies, deceptions, concealments, and betrayals. At the conclusion of the sting operation these behaviors require a public accounting.[84]

Consider the usual buy-bust operation in which an undercover officer sells a willing buyer a quantity of illegal narcotics. This operation is commonplace in police agencies throughout the United States and is conducted in an effort to control a number of different types of crime. Buy-bust activities rely completely on the art of deception. For obvious reasons, buy-busts would not succeed if they were conducted by uniformed officers.

Deception may not exactly pervade law enforcement, but it is certainly an important component of police subculture. It is but one element in a long list of values and beliefs that tend to characterize the law enforcement profession in America. Although a distinct culture characterizes many, if not all, occupations, it is safe to say that police subculture is clearly unique.

SUMMARY

- Culture is a shared set of values, norms, and behaviors that form a way of life. Cultures are characterized by similar themes, institutional values (that is, beliefs about how things should get done), and means of expression. A segment of a larger culture that shares particular values and norms is called a *subculture*.
- The sources of police culture include organizational factors, the street environment, administration, other criminal justice agencies, and the media. Values within police subculture are not necessarily foreign to the wider culture, but their close association with one another and the exclusion of other wider norms and values are what give police subculture its characteristics.
- Police subculture is characterized by several factors, including control and territoriality; use of force; danger, unpredictability, and suspicion; and solidarity. Control refers not just to control over a particular area, but also to an officer's sense of territoriality. Police work is potentially dangerous, and work situations are commonly unpredictable. These factors lead to suspicion and force officers to make split-second decisions. Solidarity is about sticking together. It has a number of components: moral superiority, common sense, masculine values, an us-versus-them mentality, and an aura of secrecy. Policing can be isolating; officers can be physically and socially isolated from the citizens they serve. Bravery is another essential component of police subculture. Finally, police subculture is sometimes characterized by the creative use of deception.

COMING FULL CIRCLE

For Discussion

Return to the questions posed at the start of this chapter. Have any of your answers changed since you read the chapter? What portions of this chapter helped you answer these questions?

Writing Assignment

Using material from this chapter and additional resources, write a 500-word essay in response to one of the questions presented at the beginning of the chapter. Submit your essay to your instructor if asked to do so.

KEY TERMS AND NAMES

accepted lie
affront
clarification
culture
deviant lie
dominion
dramaturgy
drug courier profiling
institution
institutional value
norm
paradox of policing
police subculture
remedy
solidarity
split-second syndrome
street environment
subculture
tolerated lie
value

WEB INTERACTIVITY

Visit Northeastern University's College of Criminal Justice on the Web at http://www.cj.neu.edu/index.php, and look for the Faculty Experts page entitled "Why Study Police Culture?" (You can find it d irectly at http://www.cj.neu.edu/about_the_college/faculty_expertise/police_culture/.) Why is the study of police culture important to the faculty experts at Northeastern University? Is there anything that you might add to the reasons they give for studying police culture? Submit your work to your instructor if asked to do so.

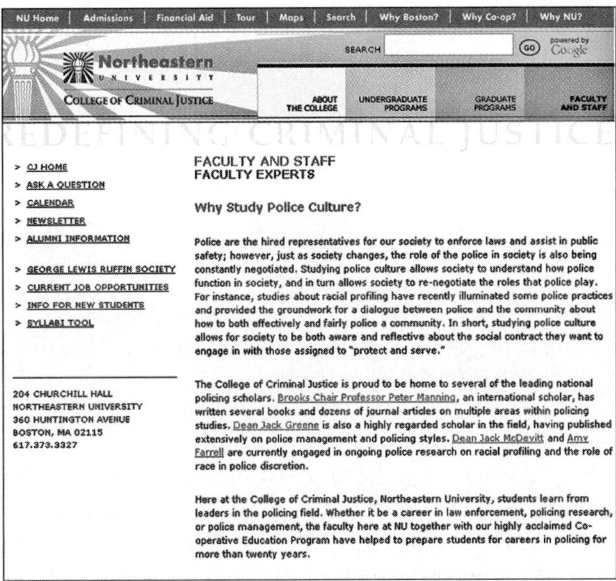

NU Home | Admissions | Financial Aid | Tour | Maps | Search | Why Boston? | Why Co-op? | Why NU?

SEARCH GO powered by Google

Northeastern University
College of Criminal Justice

ABOUT THE COLLEGE | UNDERGRADUATE PROGRAMS | GRADUATE PROGRAMS | FACULTY AND STAFF

REDEFINING CRIMINAL JUSTICE

- CJ HOME
- ASK A QUESTION
- CALENDAR
- NEWSLETTER
- ALUMNI INFORMATION
- GEORGE LEWIS RUFFIN SOCIETY
- CURRENT JOB OPPORTUNITIES
- INFO FOR NEW STUDENTS
- SYLLABI TOOL

204 CHURCHILL HALL
NORTHEASTERN UNIVERSITY
360 HUNTINGTON AVENUE
BOSTON, MA 02115
617.373.3327

FACULTY AND STAFF
FACULTY EXPERTS

Why Study Police Culture?

Police are the hired representatives for our society to enforce laws and assist in public safety; however, just as society changes, the role of the police in society is also being constantly negotiated. Studying police culture allows society to understand how police function in society, and in turn allows society to re-negotiate the roles that police play. For instance, studies about racial profiling have recently illuminated some police practices and provided the groundwork for a dialogue between police and the community about how to both effectively and fairly police a community. In short, studying police culture allows for society to be both aware and reflective about the social contract they want to engage in with those assigned to "protect and serve."

The College of Criminal Justice is proud to be home to several of the leading national policing scholars. Brooks Chair Professor Peter Manning, an international scholar, has written several books and dozens of journal articles on multiple areas within policing studies. Dean Jack Greene is also a highly regarded scholar in the field, having published extensively on police management and policing styles. Dean Jack McDevitt and Amy Farrell are currently engaged in ongoing police research on racial profiling and the role of race in police discretion.

Here at the College of Criminal Justice, Northeastern University, students learn from leaders in the policing field. Whether it be a career in law enforcement, policing research, or police management, the faculty here at NU together with our highly acclaimed Co-operative Education Program have helped to prepare students for careers in policing for more than twenty years.

Northeastern University College of Criminal Justice

REVIEW QUESTIONS

1. What is culture, and what are the differences between a culture and a subculture?
2. From what sources does the police subculture arise?
3. What are the key components of the police subculture? Which is most important in your view?

chapter seven
CAREER CONCERNS

LEARNING OBJECTIVES

After reading this chapter, students should be able to:

1. Discuss the effects of stress, fatigue, and labor relations on police work.
2. Explain the process of career advancement and discuss related issues.

THINK ABOUT IT

Many of the soldiers serving in Iraq are reservists who are also police officers back at home. Some of them are now returning from Iraq, sometimes with unanticipated consequences. Consider the case of Wayne Williamson, who returned from an 11-month deployment in Iraq as an army reservist. When Williamson returned to his job with the Austin Police Department, he didn't tell anyone, not even his supervisors, that he was jumping at nearly every unexpected sound. Shortly after being on the job again, he opened fire on an unarmed suspect whom he had been chasing on foot. The suspect was not hit, but the bullets from Williamson's gun hit a parked van, just missing two children seated inside. The incident cost Williamson his job.

Williamson's attorney told reporters, "His assessment of the threat level was wrong. He was assessing [the incident] as if he was back in the military, not from a police officer's side of it."[1] The problems facing police officers who are returning from military duty as reservists are not new. Many soldiers who served in Vietnam, for example, were also police officers. The situation today is different in a couple of ways. First, today there is an unprecedented reliance on the army reserves for the war in Iraq (in lieu of the draft), and that war is being waged in an urban combat environment. Most reservists do not anticipate combat service when they enlist in the military, and the exposure of these soldiers to almost constant gunfire and explosions can have serious and lasting effects.

In an effort to address these concerns, the Los Angeles County Sheriff's Department has launched a "repatriation" program to ease soldiers' transition back into law enforcement activities. The four-day program requires returning police officers to meet with department psychologists, who then monitor them for a full year. Other agencies, like the Tucson (Arizona) Police Department, have established similar programs. The need for such programs is clear. As one psychologist said, "You can't just put people back in these jobs, give them their badge and gun and expect that things are going to be fine. . . . Getting back into the flow of things is a challenge [for returning officers]. Most make it, but there are others who come back with problems."[2] This raises several important questions to keep in mind as you read this chapter:

1. To what extent has the war in Iraq exacerbated an already stressful occupation for those officers who served there?
2. Should we anticipate a surge in the use of excessive force and police violence as more police officers return home from military service and reenter the police profession?
3. Is stress the most serious problem in law enforcement today?
4. What are the causes of police stress?
5. Which critical incidents, whether at home or abroad, affect police officers the most?
6. What can be done about stress in policing?

INTRODUCTION

Chapter 5 described what it takes to get a job working in law enforcement. Chapter 6 examined the process by which police officers are absorbed into a distinctive policing culture. This chapter continues our focus on personnel issues with a look at what happens once police officers are on the job. We begin with a discussion of a few of the undesirable realities of police work. These include stress, fatigue, and labor disputes. To be sure, there are other unfortunate aspects of the job, just as there are rewarding and fulfilling ones. As this chapter's opening vignette makes clear, though, stress is of paramount concern in policing, and it is discussed at length in this chapter.

We also examine issues related to career advancement, particularly performance appraisal, the benefits of higher education, promotion, and leadership responsibilities. Along the way, we consider various options for advancement, what it takes to get promoted, and what happens to officers as they ascend to the highest position, that of chief (or equivalent). You are most likely read-

U.S. Army Sgt. Krista Ihde talks to an Iraqi girl during a visit to the provincial Iraqi police headquarters in Diwaniyah, Iraq, on Dec. 20, 2006. Ihde is a team leader with the 984th Military Police Company. Many soldiers who served in Iraq and Afghanistan are reservists who are also police officers back home. How might their military experience impact their return to policing in America?

Department of Defense photo by Tech. Sgt. Dawn M. Price, U.S. Air Force

ing this book because it is required as part of a college course. This raises several questions: How useful is a college education in the policing context? What effect does it have on people who enter the policing profession?

REALITIES OF THE JOB

Once a police officer begins working, he or she is almost instantly confronted with several important "realities" of the job that may not have been made clear early on. First, police work is a stressful occupation. Stress can take its toll over the course of an officer's career. Second, fatigue is a common problem in policing, though it has historically taken a backseat to stress. Only recently have researchers started to focus their attention on the problems that can result when officers are spread too thin and forced to work long hours. Finally, many officers are members of unions that negotiate contracts with their employing cities, counties, and states. Contract disputes "go with the territory" in policing and are yet another reality of the job that police officers are forced to deal with.

Stress

Stress is a fact of life in many occupations, but policing has its own unique brand of stress. The nature of the job, particularly the potential for violence at any turn, takes it toll on even the most emotionally hardened officer. This toll might be manifested in the form of health-related problems,[3] family breakdown,[4] and alcoholism, to name just a few.

stress
Anything that places a positive or negative adjustive demand on an organism.

Nature and Symptoms of Stress. **Stress** has been broadly defined as anything that places an adjustive demand on the organism.[5] In other words, stressful situations require some behavioral response, and that response is usually one intended to reduce the stress being experienced. Some people thrive on what others might consider stressful situations, and stress can have both negative and positive elements. Positive stress has been called **eustress**, and negative stress has been called **distress**.[6]

eustress
A positive form of stress that does not threaten or harm the individual but is pleasurable, challenging, or exciting.

distress
A harmful form of stress that can threaten an individual's functioning or overload his or her capacity to cope with environmental stimuli.

Eustress is a positive form of stress that does not threaten or harm the individual but is pleasurable, challenging, or exciting. For example, the stress created by beginning a new job or a challenging assignment could qualify as eustress. The new police officer experiences eustress when going on patrol for the first time. Experienced officers usually experience eustress when beginning a new assignment, such as criminal investigation. This form of stress is generally described as positive and can actually result in higher levels of motivation.

Distress is the harmful variety of stress. It threatens the individual's functioning or can overload his or her capacity to cope with environmental stimuli. Distress may result from such things as an extraordinarily high caseload, assignment to a high-crime area, inadequate equipment, or an unsupportive supervisor. All police organizations contain job assignments or situations that are perceived as threatening by most individuals, and it is these assignments or situations that create the greatest demands.

Perhaps more than anything, stress is a problem of incompatibility between a person and his or her environment. It occurs when the individual is overwhelmed by negative environmental factors or when the environment fails to provide for or meet the individual's needs. Every person has a unique set of skills, abilities, experiences, and personality traits, and every job, within the context of the environment, requires the employee to possess a certain set of skills, abilities, experiences, and personality traits. When the employee's characteristics do not match the job's requirements, a potential result is heightened stress.

Effective stress management requires that the symptoms of stress be recognized. Within a police organization, no one party should be burdened with the responsibility for recognizing these symptoms. Rather, it is vital that everyone in administrative and management positions be able to spot the signs of stress and identify possible methods for alleviating the distress. The symptoms must be acknowledged and ameliorated before they develop into excessive problems for both the stressed person and those who must associate with him or her.

There are five generally recognized categories in which stress symptoms may appear. From the least serious to the most serious, these are (1) physical, (2) intellectual, (3) emotional, (4) social, and (5) spiritual. Police personnel are regularly exposed to environmental stimuli that may bring about stress reactions in these categories. Individually, or in conjunction with one another, these symptoms can lead to burnout, which is discussed in the next subsection.

Physical symptoms of stress are usually the first to be recognized. Ulcers, headaches, backaches, frequent colds, sexual problems, and a general reduction of energy are the typical physical symptoms associated with stress. The first symptom to appear is fatigue, a general all-around tiredness. Officers who display physical symptoms of stress seldom engage in any systematic exercise or nutrition program.

Intellectual symptoms include a general loss of sharpness in thinking and problem solving. Creativity may diminish. There may be cynicism toward innovative or differing strategies for accomplishing work. Statements like "That will never work" or "We've tried something like that already" reflect cynicism that is symptomatic of stress. Officers who are manifesting intellectual symptoms of stress seldom have a hobby or any other means of intellectual relaxation, such as reading, playing poker, or listening to music.

Emotional symptoms are recognized by examining the general positive or negative aspects of the officer's emotional life. Is the officer's basic approach to life optimistic or pessimistic? Is the officer generally happy or unhappy? One of the common emotional symptoms is the overinvestment of energy in one's job with very little interest in anything outside of work. When the dreams and expectations for work are lost, feelings of helplessness may result, and symptoms of depression may be displayed. Officers who have varied interests apart from work appear to have a built-in buffer against these symptoms reaching a severe state. When problems arise at work, such officers are able to derive satisfaction or fulfillment from other aspects of their lives.

Social symptoms are connected to the officer's feelings of isolation versus feelings of involvement. There are several key questions to ask in attempting to recognize these symptoms. Do others understand this officer's feelings of fatigue, frustration, anger, or disillusionment? Is the officer free to share these feelings with others, or does such behavior seem inappropriate? What type of support system does the person perceive as being available? Is there someone outside of work who will listen? Officers suffering from serious social symptoms may not want to burden someone else with their problems; they may feel it is an imposition or may fear rejection. The net result is self-imposed isolation.

Spiritual symptoms are related to the degree of meaning one feels or perceives is present in life. Many officers have noble expectations when they enter the profession. If and when they realize that these expectations will never be fulfilled, there may be a void in their lives. A large part of who they are and what they have dreamed of being is now missing. One way to overcome the spiritual symptoms of stress is to create new meaning for the officer's life. This process begins by developing meaningful interests outside of work. The officer needs to ask this question (and implement the answer): What can be changed in my job to make it more meaningful for me? If the meaning for life is lost, the officer is left in a critical stress condition referred to as *burnout*.

burnout
The progressive loss of idealism, energy, purpose, and concern that results from the conditions of work.

Burnout. **Burnout** is the progressive loss of idealism, energy, purpose, and concern that results from the conditions of work. According to one team of researchers, burnout is "a debilitating psychological condition brought about by unrelieved work stress."[7] Burnout can also be understood as the final stage of mental or physical exhaustion, in which the individual is no longer able to cope with his or her job.[8]

There are five basic stages through which the symptoms of burnout manifest themselves: (1) the honeymoon/enthusiasm stage, (2) the fuel shortage/stagnation stage, (3) the chronic symptoms/frustration stage, (4) the crisis/apathy stage, and (5) the hitting the wall/intervention stage.[9] In the first stage, the officer reacts enthusiastically to the challenges of the job. This is followed by the realization that the job is not as exciting as he or she anticipated; routine sets in, and the officer may come to view the job as boring. This may be followed by feelings of intense and seemingly irresolvable apathy and frustration. Pessimism may emerge, and the officer may be plagued by feelings of self-doubt. In the "hitting the wall stage," the officer may reach his or her wits' end, perhaps turning to alcohol and drugs to relieve the feelings of failure and anger that have built up over time.

WEB PATROL 7-1
Rekindling Police Burnout: Implications for the Motivation and Retention of Personnel
http://www.mycrimekit.com

Sources of Stress. Police officers are required to provide the public with a wide variety of services. Many of these services are rendered in areas that are threatening to the officers. The tasks themselves frequently are dangerous, and the circumstances surrounding the delivery of the service might be unpleasant or undesirable. A number of researchers have examined police stress, and four general categories of police stress have been observed: (1) organizational and administrative practices, (2) the criminal justice system, (3) the public, and (4) stressors intrinsic to police work.[10]

Organizational and administrative practices are a two-way street as sources of stress. As noted in Chapter 4, administrators face stress when implementing new policies and effectuating change. This is because administrators often encounter resistance when they disrupt the status quo. Lower-ranking police officials must respond to changes and mandates imposed from above, and this becomes especially problematic when tension exists between superiors and subordinates. One researcher found, for example, that criticism, rejection, or derogation by their sergeants was a significant source of stress for officers.[11]

For police officers, stress also emanates from excessive paperwork, red tape, lack of participation in decision-making processes that directly affect them, antiquated promotional policies, disciplinary regulations that require them to maintain significantly higher personal and moral standards than are expected of civilians, irregular duty hours, departmental management policies that are unfair or unreasonable, insufficient opportunity for advancement, inadequate direction from supervisors, and conflicts between articulated expectations and the factors on which officers are evaluated.[12] Even agency size affects stress; there tends to be more stress in larger agencies.[13]

The criminal justice system can also be a source of stress. For example, researchers interviewed 100 police officers in Cincinnati and found that 56 percent of the respondents noted that courts were stressful.[14] Having to testify in court can be particularly stressful.[15] Corrections is also bothersome to some police officers.[16] Officers are concerned about the inability of the corrections system to rehabilitate criminals, and they are bothered that offenders serve only a small portion of their sentences. Lax or overly tolerant parole officers who allow parolees to commit numerous infractions before revoking parole are another source of concern to the average police officer. Officers often express the sentiment that criminals are back out on the street before the police officers can finish the arrest report.

Dealing with the public can also be stressful. As one officer observed, "Anytime you deal with the public they have certain images, stereotypes, and expectations of you. . . . Most people aren't happy to see the police, as it is usually some sort of negative contact."[17] This lack of approval is a

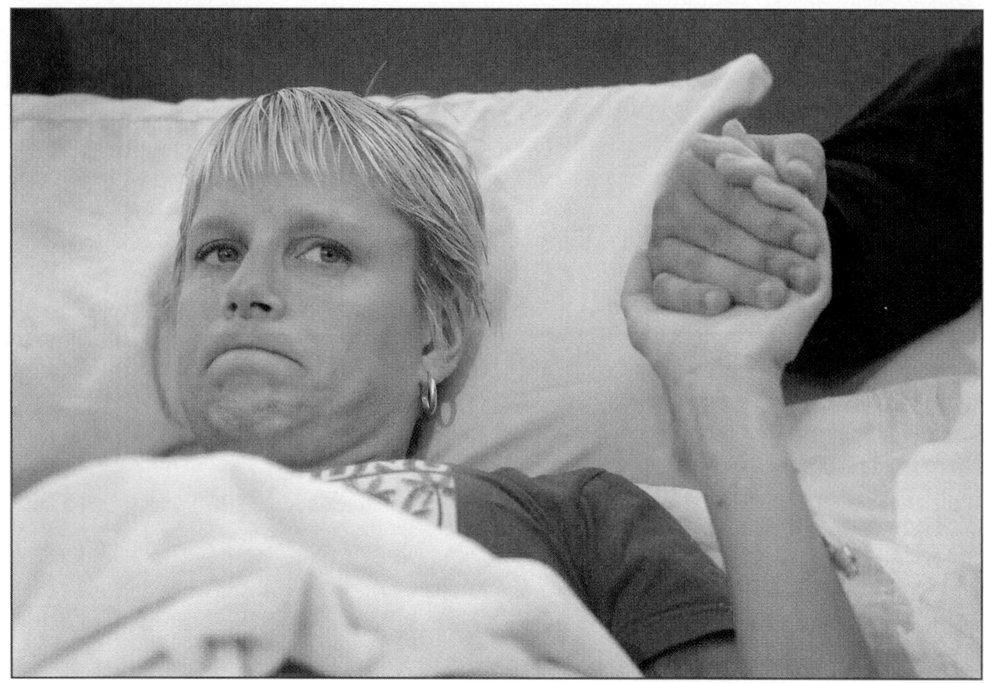

LAPD Officer Kristina Ripatti, who was shot and partially paralyzed while patrolling with the city's Southwest Division's gang enforcement detail in 2006, holds the hand of partner Joe Myer in a California hospital. Officer Ripatti's partner returned fire and killed the suspect. How do danger and stress impact police officers?

Hans Kutknecht/*LA Daily News*/Reportage.com/ZUMA Press

source of stress to many police officers. One study revealed that 22 percent of the officers interviewed were bothered by the public's apathy and lack of support for the police, while 16 percent identified the police officer's negative image as stressful.[18] As we saw in Chapter 2, stress on officers may be exacerbated by the media's occasional (or even frequent) tendency to portray the police and their actions in a negative light.

Police officers are required to make decisions that may result in serious negative consequences for the lives and the property of others. They are frequently placed in a work environment in which they consistently must deal with pain, crime, poverty, and citizens in despair. This environment can be seen as a significant source of stress for police officers.[19] They must deal with the worst problems and worst elements of society, and all the while they are expected to relate in a positive manner to everyone with whom they come in contact. The emotional toll of such stress is further compounded by the fact that many of their life-affecting decisions must be made instantly. This creates such intense situations that the police officer can become emotionally crippled. Even the mere anticipation of danger can have detrimental effects.[20]

Other features of the police job can contribute to stress. Shift work, boredom on the job, and performance of nonpolice duties can cause disillusionment and frustration, precursors to stress and burnout. In addition, the threat of civil liability is a significant source of stress for many police officers. This is especially true today, as many people seem to resort to litigation at the drop of a hat. The paradox for police officials is that they must work tirelessly to control crime but must also avoid stepping over the line that separates appropriate conduct from misconduct.

critical incident
An emergency situation that evokes immediate police response and that takes priority over all other police work.

Critical Incidents. A major source of stress in police work concerns the possibility of becoming involved in critical or traumatic incidents. A **critical incident** is an emergency situation (a crime in progress, a traffic accident with serious injuries, a natural disaster, a terrorist attack, an officer's request for assistance, and other situations in which human life may be in jeopardy) that evokes immediate police response and that takes priority over all other police work. Examples of critical-incident stressors may include apprehending a disturbed person, serving a warrant against a dangerous person, providing riot control, or dealing with a hostage taker or a barricaded suspect. Figure 7-1 ranks 14 critical-incident stressors in order of their seriousness, according to a sample of police officers.

One of the most stressful events that a police officer can experience is a shooting in which the officer critically wounds or kills another person or where a fellow officer is killed or critically

Figure 7-1 • Officers' Ranking of 14 Critical-Incident Stressors

1. The harming or killing of an innocent person
2. The harming or killing of another officer
3. The killing of another officer by a citizen
4. Hate groups and terrorists
5. Riot control
6. Barricaded suspects
7. Hostage takers
8. Disturbed offenders
9. High-risk warrants
10. Sniper incidents
11. The killing of a criminal
12. Hot pursuit
13. The use of excessive force
14. The protection of VIPs

Source: D. J. Stevens, "Stress and the American police officer," *Police Journal* 72 (3) (1999): 247–59. Reprinted by permission of Vethek Publishing.

wounded. Most experts agree that many good officers leave policing because of postshooting trauma; such trauma can have long-lasting effects on the police officer. However, not every officer who is involved in a shooting has a traumatic reaction. The postshooting trauma reactions are almost equally divided among mild reactions, moderate reactions, and severe reactions.[21] Research reveals that officers involved in shootings experience emotional or psychological numbing.[22] Five phases have been identified for coping with critical incidents:

1. *Denial.* The officer does not want to believe what has happened. This stage is usually very brief in officer-involved shootings.
2. *Anger and resentment.* Anger and resentment are usually nonspecific or vaguely directed at the person who was shot. This stage is usually short-lived, though it may return at various times during the adaptation process.
3. *Bargaining.* This stage involves the officer wishing the shooting had never happened. It may also be due to the officer's worry about reprisals from the department.
4. *Depression.* This stage lasts the longest. The severity of the depression depends on the basic personality of the officer, the amount of trauma involved in the incident, the agency's response to the incident, the officer's social network, and other factors.
5. *Acceptance.* This stage has been reached when the officer begins to integrate the event into his or her life or makes the transition from being totally preoccupied with the event to merely acknowledging that it took place.[23]

The symptoms of postshooting trauma are usually most intense for the first 48 to 72 hours following the incident, but the various reactions to such events can come and go for some time. For example, the officer may experience a heightened sense of danger or vulnerability, fear and anxiety about future encounters, anger or rage, nightmares, sleep difficulties (insomnia, sleep disturbances, or escaping through sleep), guilt, emotional numbing, emotional withdrawal from others, sexual difficulties, physical problems (headaches, indigestion, muscle aches, diarrhea, or constipation), or anxiety reactions (difficulty concentrating, excessive worry, irritability, or nervousness).[24] The officer may continually think about the incident and may have frequent flashbacks.

Occasionally, stress arising from critical incidents can lead to a condition known as **post-traumatic stress disorder (PTSD)**. PTSD has been defined as "a condition which sets in following a traumatic event with which the sufferer cannot cope. It has been described as an event outside the usual human experience, one which is experienced in a markedly distressing way, with intense fear, terror, bewilderment and a sense of helplessness."[25] Symptoms of PTSD can include (1) persistent and recurring memories of the event, (2) loss of interest and feelings, (3) problems sleeping and concentrating, and (4) hypervigilance.[26] In the wake of particularly traumatic incidents, it is advisable to treat potential PTSD problems before they get out of control. If early treatment is offered and utilized, many of the long-term negative effects of PTSD can be prevented and eliminated.

post-traumatic stress disorder (PTSD)
A condition which sets in following a traumatic event with which the sufferer cannot cope. It has been described as an event outside the usual human experience, one which is experienced in a markedly distressing way, with intense fear, terror, bewilderment and a sense of helplessness.[i]

Career Stages and Stress. Over time, the stress intrinsic to police work can take a toll. It appears that police officers go through a series of four stages during their careers[27]:

1. *Alarm stage.* In the alarm stage, the young police officer is exposed to the realities of police work. All recruits have preconceptions about what police work is about, and usually police work turns out to be something other than what they imagined.
2. *Disenchantment stage.* Eventually, officers realize and accept that they are unable to do anything about the problems of society and the bureaucratic inner workings of the police and criminal justice systems. Officers become extremely cynical and tend to distrust everyone around them. This cynicism is one of the primary coping tools used during the disenchantment stage.
3. *Personalization stage.* In the personalization stage, officers tend to focus outward, away from the police department and police work, allowing job stress to begin to subside. Personal goals, rather than police work, tend to dominate the individual's interests. The officer no longer fears failure, and the demands of being a police officer are taken in stride.
4. *Introspection stage.* After 20 years of service, police officers tend to be relatively secure in their jobs. They have experienced most of the undesirable situations and problems associated with police work and are able to cope with them with relatively little difficulty. Officers know that retirement is close, and they can leave just about any time they choose.

Fortunately, most police agencies are now aware of the potential harmful effects of stress. Proactive strategies like training, careful selection of recruits, career development, programs for spouses, and physical fitness programs help prevent stress or at least mitigate its effects. Reactive strategies like counseling, debriefing after critical incidents, and wellness programs are helpful, as well.

WEB PATROL 7-2

Evaluating the Effects of Fatigue on Police Patrol Officers
http://www.mycrimekit.com

Fatigue

Everybody gets tired on the job from time to time. Some of us can safely doze off for a few minutes without too much concern, but others work in professions in which a nap could lead to disaster. The last thing anyone would want is for an air traffic controller to snooze on the job. The same can be said of surgeons, truck drivers, and of course police officers.

Police officers, like some other workers, sometimes work lengthy shifts at odd hours. While they have more or less fixed schedules, it is sometimes impractical for police officers to just walk away at quitting time. An accident, an emergency, or a high-profile arrest could require an officer to work several extra hours, contributing to a long and unpredictable workweek. As two well-known police stress researchers point out, "It is totally reprehensible that the cops we expect to protect us, come to our aid, and respond to our needs when victimized should be allowed to have the worst fatigue and sleep conditions of any profession in our society."[28]

Tired Cops. Researchers have only recently turned their attention to police fatigue.[29] Reporters, too, have expressed concern.[30] The *Boston Globe* investigated one police agency and found that 16 officers worked more than 80 hours each week. Two averaged more than 100 hours per week over a 12-month period.[31] One even worked 130 hours in a single week, which translates into less than six hours off on any given day. Researchers identified some officers in Florida and Massachusetts who

YOU DECIDE
Sleeping on the Job

You are dispatched to the scene of a robbery. You find an elderly woman lying in a pool of blood on the ground, surrounded by a group of onlookers. As you survey the scene, you spot an unmarked police car nearby. The officer inside, your close friend, is sound asleep. None of the onlookers know another officer is nearby. You know he suffers from a sleep disorder and takes a prescription pain reliever. Naturally, you wonder what would have happened at the scene if your friend had not been sleeping. What should you do?

moonlighted (for example, as security guards) for 3,000 hours each year, above and beyond the hours spent performing their official duties.[32]

To further gauge the extent of police fatigue, criminologists Bryan Vila and Dennis Kenney surveyed a number of police agencies around the country and visited several more. Their survey revealed that while most officers work only a few overtime hours each month, some logged more than 100 hours of overtime.[33] What caused the overtime?

> On average, officers attributed 35 percent of the overtime they worked to off-duty court appearances; 20 percent to making late arrests or writing reports; 11 percent to taking extra shift assignments to fill in for someone who was sick, on vacation, or disabled; and 9 percent to covering special circumstances, such as crowd control, parades, or missing children.[34]

Nobody can blame police officers for wanting to increase their pay by working extra hours. Some, though, are forced to do so because of job demands. Either way, too much fatigue can lead to disaster. Vila and Kenney summarized some of the more serious incidents:

> A Michigan police officer working nearly 24 hours straight crashes his cruiser while chasing a fleeing motorist. He is critically injured. In California, a sheriff's deputy working alone drifts off a deserted highway and is killed instantly when his patrol car crashes into a tree. An officer in Florida, who has had trouble staying awake, runs a red light in her patrol car and crashes into a van driven by a deputy sheriff, injuring him severely. A police officer driving home from work in Ohio nods off at the wheel, begins swerving in and out of traffic, and runs off the road, striking and killing a man jogging down the sidewalk.[35]

WEB PATROL 7-3

Tired Cops: The Prevalence and Potential Consequences of Police Fatigue
http://www.mycrimekit.com

Scheduling and Workload. We have looked at the most obvious cause of police fatigue: too many hours on the job. Police fatigue may also stem from shift length and shift-assignment policies. Researchers have found that police departments that use compressed work schedules (that is, fewer than five eight-hour days) see less fatigue among their officers.[36] It appears that four ten- to 12-hour shifts result in less fatigue than five eight-hour shifts. Indeed, the Los Angeles Police Department recently switched to a three-day schedule for the bulk of its patrol officers (three 12-hour shifts). The schedule is especially appealing to the department's officers, many of whom commute long distances to work. The city was less supportive, however. It conducted a study that showed more money going to overtime pay, longer emergency response times, and fewer traffic citations and arrests.[37]

Shift assignments, in addition to shift length, may have implications for police fatigue, as well. Vila and Kenney note that people are less able to cope with fatigue as they grow older. They found that older officers who can select their own shifts were less fatigued than their counterparts who had no say over scheduling matters.[38] The predictability (or unpredictability) of work hours also appears to be linked to fatigue. Surprisingly, officers who work unpredictable schedules report less fatigue. According to Vila and Kenney, "One possible interpretation of this finding could be that the officers who were having problems with fatigue were actually avoiding or minimizing overtime work—perhaps by making fewer arrests or court appearances."[39] The same officers could also have had off-duty obligations (for example, caring for young children) that forced them to keep regular hours but that also contributed to fatigue.

Managing Fatigue. Administrators can minimize officer fatigue with attention to scheduling and overtime limitations. Vila and Kenney offer four specific recommendations for managing police fatigue. They encouraged administrators to[40]

WEB PATROL 7-4

Sleep and Job Performance in Law Enforcement
http://www.mycrimekit.com

1. Review the policies, procedures and practices that affect shift scheduling and rotation, overtime, moonlighting, the number of consecutive hours allowed, and the way in which the department deals with overly tired employees.
2. Assess how much of a voice officers are given in work-hour and shift-scheduling decisions. The number of hours officers work and the time of day they are assigned to work affect their personal, social, family, and professional lives. Excluding officers from decisions affecting this arena increases stress, which in turn reduces their ability to deal with fatigue and tends to diminish their job performance and ability to deal with stress.

3. Assess the level of fatigue officers experience, the quality of their sleep, and how tired they are while on the job, as well as their attitudes toward fatigue and work-hour issues.
4. Review recruit and in-service training programs to determine if officers are receiving adequate information about the importance of good sleep habits, the hazards associated with fatigue and shift work, and strategies for managing them. Are officers taught to view fatigue as a safety issue? Are they trained to recognize drowsiness as a factor in vehicle crashes?

Labor Relations

union
An organization that represents dues-paying workers for the purpose of negotiating with employers concerning issues of importance to the workers.

labor relations
The relationship between management and labor within an organization.

Each year in San Bernardino, California, the Professional Police Association collects information about police salaries throughout the state. Of interest to the association are beginning salaries, salary steps, and the maximum pay that officers receive. Once the information is compiled, the association writes a report and distributes it to its members, the press, government leaders, and politicians. The association uses the report as one of its primary tools for securing higher wages and better benefits for its members. The association is basically a union for the officers of San Bernardino. A **union** is an organization that represents dues-paying workers for the purpose of negotiating with employers concerning issues of importance to the workers.

The term **labor relations** can carry a negative connotation. Some union members regard administrative and executive officials as the "enemy." Likewise, some top-level officials view unions as the banes of their existence. Labor relations can also describe a largely peaceful process through which solutions can be found to the mutual problems of employers and employees. Not everyone can get what they want; compromise is necessary. This is especially true in government agencies where resources are often in short supply. Today, police unions can only go so far to improve their working conditions.[41] They cannot strike because in most states they are legally barred from doing so. But that was not always the case. The police labor movement has had a tumultuous history.

The Police Labor Movement. The police labor movement began during the Civil War era. Fraternal organizations emerged primarily to ensure death benefits, welfare insurance, and other forms of assistance to employees. Between 1890 and 1915, police officers in a number of cities formed organizations aimed at improving their working conditions. They did not formally unionize, however, until police work gained civil service protection, well into the reform era. Prior to that, the police were more involved in political affairs than they were in trying to obtain benefits and resources for themselves. By 1917, police officers aligned themselves with the American Federation of Labor (AFL). Some 40 chapters with more than 4,000 members soon appeared throughout the United States. One of the early charters was issued to police officers in Boston.

Boston is especially interesting in terms of the police labor movement because more than 1,100 police officers there went on strike in 1919. Not surprisingly, when the officers went on strike, crime soared. Lives were lost as a result of rioting, looting began almost immediately, and property damage ran into the millions of dollars. The Massachusetts State Guard was called in on the second day of the strike to provide security. The *New York Times*, in its September 10, 1919, edition, reported that "after twenty-four hours of lawlessness following the police strike Boston is under military rule. . ., with 5,000 soldiers of the State Guard in the streets, with orders at any cost to restore order and protect life and property, fierce rioting continues in several sections."[42]

Why did the Boston officers strike? One of the key reasons was that Police Commissioner E. V. Curtis refused to recognize the union, and had even prohibited officers from joining the union. The strike lasted four days, and all the officers involved lost their jobs. What's more, the AFL revoked the local charter, effectively stalling police unionization in Boston for years. Eventually, though, police unions gained a foothold and are commonplace today—but strikes are not.[43] Now there are enough police unions that they have their own representative body housed in Washington, DC, the National Association of Police Organizations (NAPO). And while police don't strike today, they do sometimes stage "blue flu" events, one of which is detailed in Figure 7-2.

Figure 7-2 • The "Blue Flu" in Wilmington, Delaware

NEWS
from the Office of Mayor James M. Baker

For Immediate Release
Tuesday, July 13, 2004

Contact:
John Rago
Communications Director
for Mayor Baker
(302) 576-2109
(302) 420-7928 (cell)
E-mail John Rago

City Hit with "Blue Flu"

Mayor Baker said this morning the city is experiencing a sick-out as more than 70 Wilmington police officers, members of FOP Lodge #1, have called out sick as part of what the mayor said is an improper and illegal protest over the lack of a new contract.

The mayor is assuring citizens that public safety is being maintained and that city streets are being patrolled by city police officers at the moment. He urged the FOP to direct its members to follow the law and follow their duty by returning to work.

"I strongly urge the FOP to settle their differences with the city over a new contract at the bargaining table and not hold the citizens of our city hostage in order to gain what they want concerning a contract. We offered the FOP a reasonable wage package, they rejected it, and we are now in mandatory mediation. We also have binding arbitration that is available by law if necessary to settle these contract differences. I simply cannot offer a wage package that the city cannot afford to pay. Dramatic and dangerous actions such as staging a 'blue flu' will not change the fact that the city only has so much money that it can offer the FOP. There is simply no reasonable or logical reason to endanger the public safety of our citizens through an illegal work action. It will have no bearing whatsoever as far as negotiations are concerned."

Here are other details of this "blue flu" situation as released this morning by Mayor Baker:

- Of the 20 to 25 officers scheduled to work the first shift of today beginning at 7 a.m. this morning, only four supervisory officers (three sergeants and one lieutenant) reported for duty.
- Through the assignment of other officers on duty from specialized units such as the Detective Division and the Office of Professional Standards, Chief Szczerba was able to staff this morning's day work patrol shift with a total of 18 Wilmington police officers.
- The next scheduled shift for today begins at 3 p.m., and we are monitoring to determine how many officers are calling out sick on this shift so we can prepare for the proper public safety patrols and staffing.
- To maintain public safety, the public safety director and police chief directed that officers from last night's midnight shift be held over to work this morning until an emergency coverage plan could be implemented.
- In addition, the city requested assistance from the Delaware State Police and the New Castle County Police Department. These officers will be placed on duty as needed throughout the day.
- Once the state and county officers became available to the city this morning, the Wilmington Police Department officers who were being held over from the midnight shift were relieved of their duties.
- The mayor is urging the FOP to direct its members to return to their duty as responsible officials. The mayor said that if necessary the city will seek to have a court direct the FOP to order its members back to work to fulfill their responsibilities as police officers.

City officials will update this situation throughout the day.

Source: Mayor's Communications Office, Wilmington, Delaware, "City hit with 'blue flu,'" news release, July 13, 2004, http://www.ci.wilmington.de.us/mayorpress/2004/0713_blueflu.htm (accessed June 25, 2008). Reprinted with permission.

collective bargaining
The process through which an employer and its employees, represented by their union, negotiate a formal written agreement over wages, hours, benefits, and other conditions of employment.

Collective Bargaining. Key to unions' success in improving working conditions is **collective bargaining**. This is the process through which an employer and its employees, represented by their union, negotiate a formal written agreement over wages, hours, benefits, and other conditions of employment. Not just any organization can bargain on behalf of its members; it must be the one organization with authority to do so. An authorized union receives certification as the duly recognized bargaining unit for a group of members. The union gains exclusive rights to represent the group when it receives authorization, usually through an election of the members, to represent the group. Once an authorized bargaining unit is identified, then the contract negotiation process commences. This can turn into a complicated affair that goes back and forth between the union and administrators over the course of many months. If an impasse is reached, resolution may involve a mix of fact-finding, arbitration, and mediation with a third party.

Police Contracts. What do police contracts look like? One team of researchers examined the content of police collective bargaining agreements (contracts) and found the following[44]:

- 84 percent of the contracts contained provisions dealing with management's rights and responsibilities.
- 89 percent contained clauses that identified grievance procedures.
- 24 percent contained a police officer's bill of rights.
- 90 percent contained a disciplinary appeals procedure.
- 72 percent gave management the authority to make staffing changes.
- 84 percent contained language concerning layoffs and the procedures for them.
- 61 percent required officers to provide the department with notice of sick leave.
- More than half required documentation for sick time.
- Some provided for college tuition benefits.

Every contract had some provision for pay details, possibly an increase. Indeed, the simple act of unionization in policing appears to have a beneficial effect on police salaries.[45] The point is that most of the contracts are not *just* about employee benefits; bargaining agreements lay down the rules and guidelines by which personnel actions and human resource decisions take place.

Nowadays, police administrators *must* be attuned to and involved in the collective bargaining process. Their job is to abide by and enforce the terms of the contracts signed by the parties to the agreement.

CAREER ADVANCEMENT

Advancement through the typical police department is based on a combination of three factors: performance, experience (years on the job and sometimes credits for training), and education. Once officers assume their positions, they are evaluated frequently. This is accomplished through performance appraisal. Those who perform satisfactorily gain the experience necessary to move up through the ranks. Some officers also pursue additional education, such as undergraduate and graduate degrees. Not all departments require specific degrees for promotion, but the well-educated officer certainly has a leg up over competitors.

After we look at performance appraisal and the role of college education in policing, we will look at the specific ranks and positions that are available to those seeking promotion. We wrap this section up with a detailed look at police chiefs, particularly (1) what it takes to get promoted to chief, (2) what happens throughout the chief's career, (3) how long chiefs stay on the job, and (4) the leadership styles chiefs employ. We limit the discussion mainly to police chiefs, instead of other law enforcement executives, simply because researchers have not focused much attention on management outside of municipal police departments.

Performance Appraisal

performance measurement
A formal process through which supervisors provide subordinates with feedback on their job performance.

Performance measurement refers to a formal process through which supervisors provide subordinates with feedback on their job performance. In the policing context, it is used to identify and evaluate officers' strengths and weaknesses and may also serve as the basis for a variety of human resource and personnel decisions. Promotions, for instance, are often based—in large part—on past performance.

Performance appraisals are used in several distinct areas: They provide formalized feedback to officers, assist in training, help supervisors decide issues of pay and benefits, and can be used for commendation or discipline. Researchers have identified eight core elements for an acceptable performance appraisal system[46]:

1. Appraisals must focus on performance standards as identified by a job analysis.
2. Performance standards must have been communicated to and understood by employees.
3. Ratings must be based on specific, clearly defined dimensions as opposed to undefined global dimensions.
4. The rated dimensions must be behaviorally anchored, and these ratings must be supported by objective, observable behaviors.
5. Abstract dimensions like loyalty or honesty must be avoided unless they can be defined in actual observable behavior.
6. Rating scale anchor statements must be logical and brief.
7. The appraisal system and the ratings of the individual raters must be reliable and valid.
8. The system must contain an appeal mechanism for employees who disagree with their ratings.

The last of these elements for a successful performance measurement protocol is most critical; civil protections exist to ensure that employees cannot be dismissed for arbitrary reasons. A performance measurement procedure that falls short on any of these elements can become the basis for a wrongful dismissal complaint and possibly even a lawsuit. Also, performance standards need continual adjustment to reflect new law enforcement priorities and to address past deficiencies.[47]

Policing and Higher Education

Police organizations, like other organizations inside and outside the public sector,[48] have started to impose education requirements beyond the commonly required high school diploma or equivalent.[49] While relatively few police departments require that police officers have four-year degrees before assuming their positions (Table 7-1), college education is often regarded favorably for promotion purposes.

As early as 1973, the National Advisory Commission on Criminal Justice Standards stated,

> Police agencies have lost ground in the race for qualified employees because they have not raised standards. College graduates look elsewhere for employment. Police work has often come to be regarded by the public as a second class occupation, open to anyone with no more than a minimum education, average intelligence, and good health.[50]

Table 7-1 • Minimum Educational Requirements for New Officer Recruits in Local Police Departments

		Percent of Agencies Requiring a Minimum Of			
Population Served	Total with Requirements	High School Diploma	Some College	Two-Year College Degree	Four-Year College Degree
All Sizes	98%	81%	8%	9%	1%
1,000,000 or more	98	72	18	7	1
500,000 to 999,999	99	72	13	9	5
250,000 to 499,999	99	84	8	4	3
100,000 to 249,999	98	81	13	3	2
50,000 to 99,999	100	76	17	6	1
25,000 to 49,999	99	77	10	11	1
10,000 to 24,999	99	82	7	9	1
2,500 to 9,999	99	83	7	9	(0)
Less than 2,500	97	82	6	9	0

Source: Sourcebook of criminal justice statistics online, Table 1.39.2003, http://www.albany.edu/sourcebook/pdf/t1392003.pdf.

Police officers in a criminal justice class in Garden Grove, California. How important is a college education for those seeking a policing career?

Spencer Grant/Photo Researchers, Inc.

The commission found it strange that education requirements for the police were not increased while, at the same time, other professions were beginning to adopt stringent education requirements. What is the argument supporting college degrees for police officers? How might a college degree improve police performance? In a study published by the Police Executive Research Form (PERF), researchers identified the following advantages of college education for police officers[51]:

1. College develops a broader base for decision making.
2. College ingrains responsibility and appreciation for people's rights.
3. College creates an ability to flexibly handle difficult situations.
4. College engenders tolerance and empathy.
5. College-educated officers are likely to be less rigid in their decision making.
6. College helps officers better communicate with people and better respond to the demands of the job.
7. College-educated officers are more professional.
8. The college experience makes officers less authoritarian in their demeanor.

Strangely, very few researchers have tried to validate these claims. The research that is available either is inconclusive or suggests that higher education for police officers makes virtually no difference in terms of job performance. For example, police researchers Lawrence W. Sherman and Mark Blumberg studied the impact of higher education on police use of force. They concluded, "In short, the present study is far from conclusive about higher education and the use of deadly force. It is even less conclusive about the value of higher education for improving police performance, the many components of which are not necessarily consistent for individual officers."[52] Several related studies show support for Sherman and Blumberg's findings.[53] Others conclude that the relationship between college education and job performance in policing is practically impossible to understand.[54] At least one study suggests, however, that college education for police officers may reduce their risks of being sued civilly.[55] Beyond that, we cannot conclude with any measure of certainty that higher education for police officers is necessarily critical.

Promotion

Some police officers are content to remain on patrol for their whole careers; others desire promotions and reassignments. There was a time when promotions were based on political factors, but today's police promotion process is complicated and multilayered. Equal Employment Opportunity Com-

YOU DECIDE

A Promotion Dilemma

You are studying to take the sergeant's exam—in addition to taking college classes, working full time, and raising two children as a single parent. A friend of yours who has already passed the exam has a sample copy and offers to share it with you. You know that accepting it is not just unethical, but also forbidden. What should you do?

mission (EEOC) requirements have further affected the promotion process to the point that, according to some critics, too many agencies promote inferior candidates simply to maintain an image of political correctness.[56]

Promotions, like the initial hiring decision, proceed through several stages. The first stage generally is a written exam. Patrol officers aspiring for sergeant positions, for instance, must take an exam, the results of which are then used to decide who advances to the next stage. The exams vary depending on the position sought. Some are more situationally based than knowledge based. An exam for the position of captain may test candidates on their knowledge in key administrative areas, such as human resources, budgeting, training techniques, data evaluation, scheduling, and, most importantly, supervision. Some sample questions from a police sergeant's examination can be found in Figure 7-3.

Performance appraisals, as we already mentioned, also factor into the promotion process; candidates with checkered pasts are less likely to be promoted than are those whose records are above reproach. Officers seeking promotion typically participate in oral interviews similar to those that new job applicants face, and a candidate's seniority will also be taken into account (there are few chiefs in their 30s, for instance). Other factors, such as education or training points, may also affect the promotion decision.

Management Levels. The 20,000 or so law enforcement agencies in the United States vary considerably in their structure and organization. Even so, most departments have four management levels: (1) sergeant, (2) lieutenant, (3) captain, and (4) chief. Officers who apply for and move into detective positions are effectively promoted, but the detective position is not generally regarded as supervisory (see Chapter 8). Some departments do use detectives to supervise patrol officers in the absence of a sergeant, however.

The police department of Upland, California, a suburb east of Los Angeles, is fairly typical of most municipal police departments. Its rank structure is as follows:

1. *Sergeant.* "[Sergeants] serve as front line supervisors of the patrol officers. They are responsible for guidance and the ongoing training of the officers assigned to their respective shifts. These sergeants report to the lieutenant assigned to their respective shifts. One sergeant is assigned to the Detective Bureau as the supervisor. He is responsible for the day to day operations of the Detective Bureau. The Detective Bureau sergeant reports to the Administration Division Commander which is staffed by a captain. The last sergeant is assigned to Special Services. This sergeant supervises the Code Enforcement Unit and DARE [Drug Abuse Resistance Education]. The Special Services sergeant conducts all department internal investigations such as complaints of misconduct. Additionally, this sergeant serves as the press information officer for the department. The Special Services sergeant reports directly to the Chief of Police."[57]

YOU DECIDE

A Shortcut to Promotion

You and ten other officers took the sergeant's exam and just received the results. Your score was the third highest. The person with the highest score was promoted and is now your supervisor, but you saw him stealthily refer to handwritten notes during the exam. What should you do?

Figure 7-3 • Sample Police Sergeant's Examination Questions

1. Which of the following individuals can *not* file a search warrant application in court?
   a. a police officer
   b. a district attorney
   c. a public servant acting in his or her official capacity
   d. a private school teacher
2. You are employed as a police officer in the city of Paradise. While on patrol and with what you believe to be reasonable suspicion, you stop a man who you believe has committed a misdemeanor. You ask the suspect for identification and an explanation of his actions. He fails to cooperate and becomes belligerent. What can you do?
   a. Arrest the suspect.
   b. Detain the suspect until a supervisor arrives.
   c. Release the suspect if there is no probable cause to arrest.
   d. Arrest the suspect if you have reasonable suspicion a felony has been committed.
3. John, a clerk at a convenience store, sold liquor to Frank who was 20 years old, but provided fraudulent identification showing he was 25. Under the circumstances, John
   a. committed no mistake.
   b. committed the offense of unlawful sale of liquor to a minor.
   c. committed the offense of endangering a minor.
   d. has a defense of good faith.
4. You arrest a suspect with probable cause to believe that she committed a felony. While you are booking the suspect you learn that she could not have committed the crime because she was in jail. Based on this information, you should:
   a. Ask a colleague for advice.
   b. Take the suspect to court and advise the judge.
   c. Release the suspect immediately.
   d. Serve the suspect with a summons ordering her to appear in court.
5. As a patrol supervisor you notice that two officers, each whom work in different sectors, respond to a dispatcher's assignment. Only one of them should have. In this situation, you should:
   a. Ignore the situation.
   b. Advise both officers as to which assignments require more than one officer to appear.
   c. Advise the officer who should not have responded and warn him that disciplinary action will follow if the practice continues.
   d. Refer the matter up the chain of command.
6. A new officer asks you, her supervisor, what she should do if she is the first to arrive at the scene of a bomb threat inside a building. You should:
   a. Tell her that the building should be evacuated immediately.
   b. Tell her to immediately begin searching for the explosive device.
   c. Tell her to ask the person in charge of the building whether he or she wants the property evacuated.
   d. Tell her about which devices she can disarm.
7. A 14-year-old male engages in sexual intercourse with a 10-year-old male. The age of majority in your state is 16. The 14-year-old should be
   a. processed in criminal court.
   b. processed in family court.
   c. found guilty of 1st degree sodomy.
   d. found guilty of sexual misconduct.
8. Sometimes it is necessary to engage in "selective enforcement" of traffic laws because the practice can
   a. reduce the potential for serious accidents.
   b. allow collection of accident investigation data.
   c. promote public awareness.
   d. reduce the potential for *all* traffic accidents.
9. The key element to a successful police-community relations program is
   a. a formal unit within the department that is tasked with improving police-community relations.
   b. the officers' conduct while on patrol.
   c. the hiring of police-community relations specialists.
   d. cooperation between top officials and members of the press.
10. Which of the following statements is incorrect regarding encounters with emotionally disturbed individuals?
    a. Police officers' main duty is to protect human life.
    b. Physical force will be used only if it is necessary to transport the subject to a hospital or detention facility.
    c. If the subject is armed, it is necessary to contact a supervisor before taking action.
    d. If the subject is unarmed and not dangerous, he or she can be taken into custody without the need to contact a supervisor.

2. *Lieutenant.* "The lieutenants are all assigned to the Operations Division. Each lieutenant serves as a watch commander for a patrol shift. As watch commanders, they are responsible for the day to day operation of their respective shifts. The lieutenants report to the Operations Division Commander which is staffed by a captain."[58]
3. *Captain.* "The captains each command a division within the department. They are responsible for the day to day operations of their divisions as well as long range planning. In order to promote to the rank of captain a lieutenant must have a bachelor's degree. The captains report directly to the Chief of Police."[59]

YOU DECIDE
The Lazy Subordinate

You are a lieutenant in a large municipal police department. One of the sergeants beneath you is the son of the chief. He and the chief are especially close, and the chief was influential in getting him hired. The sergeant has begun to arrive late for work and exhibits considerable laziness. The other sergeants—and some patrol officers—are starting to complain. What should be done?

4. *Chief.* "The Chief of Police is the highest authority within the department. He is responsible for the overall management of the police department to insure conformity to the highest standards. The Chief of Police develops and implements administrative policies, coordinates all department functions, prepares the annual budget and makes presentations to the City Council. The Chief of Police reports to the City Manager and, ultimately to the City Council."[60]

Taking on a Leadership Role

Not everyone is cut out to be a leader. Only an elite group of law enforcement officials makes it to the top positions in the profession. Given the power and influence of law enforcement executives, a number of researchers have studied them over the years. They have looked at the means by which they ascend to their posts, what happens to them once they are on the job, how long they stay there, and what leadership styles they tend to employ. Most of this research, however, has been concentrated on municipal police chiefs. This is not surprising considering how many municipal police departments there are relative to other types of law enforcement agencies.

WEB PATROL 7-5

The Los Angeles Police Department's West Point Leadership Program
http://www.mycrimekit.com

Ascending to the Top. Research reveals that there are at least five paths by which one can ascend to the position of chief of a municipal police agency.[61] The first path is that of the "Ultimate Outsider A," who has had experience in military or federal law enforcement before becoming chief. Only about 2 percent of chiefs appear to fit this mold. The "Ultimate Outsider B" has had experience in another criminal justice agency, such as a prosecutor's office. Only about 2 percent of chiefs fall into this category. The third path is the "Multi-Agency Career Path." About 5 percent of chiefs have had experience in a variety of police and nonpolice agencies. Next, the "Insider" is promoted through the ranks of a single agency. The vast majority of chiefs follow this path. Finally, the "Outsider" has had a career with two or more police agencies. About 28 percent of chiefs fit this category.

Police Chief Career Stages. Changing a job can be traumatic, and once one is in a new position, much can change. So it goes with police executives. In two separate studies, researchers identified several career stages through which long-term police chiefs progress.[62] From the initial appointment through their first two years, new chiefs go through a *crisis stage* in which they attempt to define their authority and gain the respect of their subordinates. During the third and fourth years, chiefs go through an *interregnum stage* in which they attempt to identify their power base and begin to take charge of the department and its operations. During years five through nine, chiefs who are still on the job go through what has been termed the *institutional stage*, becoming entrenched and continuing to pursue their program and policy plans. In years ten through 14, long-term chiefs continue to gain support from their subordinates and from the community, continue to fine-tune their programs, but generally do not adopt new ones. That stage is referred to as *concretion*. Chiefs don't stay on the job forever, of course, and if they serve long enough, they appear to go through a *demise stage* at some point after their fifteenth year. At this stage they realize that there is not much else they can do, so they more or less count the days until retirement. This model of career stages may characterize the *average* long-term chief, but there are, of course, many exceptions.

Police Chief Tenure. Most police chiefs do not serve for the long term and are in office for only short periods of time. In one study, a researcher examined police chief tenure in the nation's largest agencies. He found only one chief who had been in that position for more than five years.[63] In a fairly typical case, he found that Cleveland had fired three chiefs in a four-year period. The vast majority of police chiefs in an earlier study had held their posts for well under six years.[64]

Does the relatively short tenure of most police chiefs mean that they are ineffective? The answer appears to be no. Police chief terminations are generally not the result of incompetence, corruption, and other problems. Rather, police departments today must answer to many constituencies. When police fail to attend to the needs of constituents (even if they cannot possibly do so), this becomes a factor in the political process. Over time, such failures reduce public support, and mayors and city councils often replace the chief as a means of regaining public support. This is not unlike the routine firing of professional football coaches. A coach may be excellent, but if the team loses repeatedly, the coach will be held to answer.

To say that politics fully explains short police chief tenure is perhaps too simplistic. Why, exactly, do chiefs leave their posts? A study of police chief tenure in Kentucky revealed that 26.5 percent of chiefs left for personal reasons, 17.7 percent retired following successful service, another 17.7 percent were fired by government officials, 16.8 percent resigned due to political pressure, 9.7 percent retired due to political pressure, 8.8 percent were demoted, and 2.7 percent had died. If we treat termination as a political act, then this study suggests that more than 44 percent of chiefs leave their posts for political reasons.[65]

As mentioned in an earlier chapter, there are different selection methods for law enforcement executives. Sheriffs are generally elected. Federal law enforcement executives are appointed by the president and serve at his pleasure. Municipal police chiefs are usually appointed by the mayor or city council. The appointment method surely spells a shorter fate for most executives, but the real explanation for dismissals for political reasons may be something else entirely. A former superintendent of police in Chicago explains:

> The chief's ability to serve as a major municipal policy maker—and even his ability to run a police department free from the most outrageous kinds of partisan political incursions—is largely dependent on local idiosyncrasies rather than on the scientific application of immutable principles concerning the police chief-mayor relationship.[66]

Leadership Styles. As Joseph A. Schafer, at Southern Illinois University's Center for the Study of Crime, Delinquency and Corrections, notes, "Leadership represents a crucial determinant of police organizational efficacy."[67] Four leadership styles have been identified for law enforcement executives. They are administrator, top cop, politician, and statesman[68]:

1. *Administrator.* Administrators are executives who turn their attention inward. They concentrate on the inner workings of the department, generally adhere to classical organizational tenets, and expend a great deal of energy planning, directing, staffing, controlling, and organizing the internal workings of the department. Because they see autonomy as an important ingredient in success, they generally fail to read some of the problems within the environment as they occur.
2. *Top cop.* Top cops, somewhat like administrators, turn their attention inward. The difference is that top cops emphasize leadership rather than management. They see leadership as being actively involved in police operations. They are more likely to take charge of situations and make their presence known in the field. Top cops are generally well liked by the rank-and-file officers because of their involvement in field activities, but they are often neglectful of the department's management requirements. They do not spend a great deal of time on planning, controlling, staffing, or organizing.
3. *Politician.* Politicians turn their attention outward. Like top cops, they often do not attend to the managerial aspects of the department because they prefer to interject themselves into community and political affairs. While expending a great deal of energy acquiring personal

power through affiliation with community leaders, they typically abdicate management responsibilities to lower-level subordinates and seldom give such responsibilities adequate attention.

4. *Statesman.* Statesmen are attentive to both internal and external affairs. They understand the importance of working with community leaders, but they do not see doing so as their consuming responsibility because they also acknowledge the importance of managing the department through planning, directing, staffing, controlling, and organizing. They can delegate both internal and external responsibilities and are skilled at evenhandedly running their departments while working with community and political leaders.

Arguably, the last of these leadership styles would seem to be preferred, as it reflects something of a balance. However, one study of police chief leadership styles suggests that such a balance is almost impossible to achieve.[69] The recommended model, according to the study, is one that delegates management of internal affairs to an assistant chief. With internal affairs under control, the chief can turn his or her attention more fully to external matters, such as meeting with political officials and others. This is not unlike the model most universities follow; the provost or vice president presides over most internal affairs, while the president serves as the public face of the organization.

WEB PATROL 7-6

Effective Police Leadership
http://www.mycrimekit.com

SUMMARY

- Some of the realities of police work include stress, fatigue, and labor relations. Stress can be both positive (eustress) and negative (distress). Distress, the most destructive form of stress, can lead to numerous job-related and personal problems, including burnout. There are several sources of stress, including organizational and administrative practices, the criminal justice system, the public, stressors intrinsic to police work, and critical incidents. Fatigue is another problem for police officers. Police organizations, it would appear, should guard against scheduling- and workload-related fatigue.
- Career advancement is based on performance appraisal, experience, and education. Police chiefs arrive in their positions through a variety of channels, and they exhibit a number of different leadership styles. The typical tenure of a police chief is not particularly long.

COMING FULL CIRCLE

For Discussion

Return to the questions posed at the start of this chapter. Have any of your answers changed since you read the chapter? What portions of this chapter helped you answer these questions?

Writing Assignment

Using material from this chapter and additional resources, write a 500-word essay in response to one of the questions presented at the beginning of the chapter. Submit your essay to your instructor if asked to do so.

KEY TERMS AND NAMES

burnout
collective bargaining
critical incident
distress
eustress
labor relations
performance measurement
post-traumatic stress disorder (PTSD)
stress
union

WEB INTERACTIVITY

Visit CopCareer.com (http://www.copcareer.com), which describes itself as a site intended to help those "seeking police jobs, federal law enforcement jobs, and state trooper jobs as well as police job employers." Scan the clickable options listed on the home page. Although CopCareer.com is a commercial site, it offers a number of features useful to anyone seeking a career in law enforcement. One of those features is a résumé builder, which links to online tools at CareerBuilder.com.

Use the online tools to build your own résumé or to create a sample résumé. You can also upload an existing résumé that was created in Microsoft Word. (If your connection is lost during your résumé-building session, remember that both uploading and building make use of the online tools at http://www.careerbuilder.com/JobSeeker/Resumes/PostResumeNew/PostResumeStart.aspx. You can return directly to this page.) Submit your completed personal or sample résumé to your instructor if asked to do so.

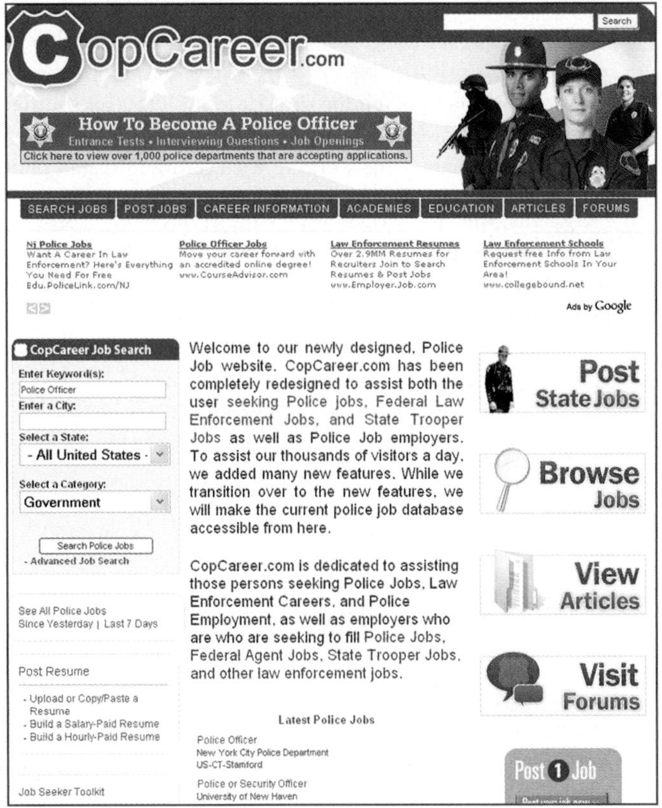

CopCareer.com, Inc.

REVIEW QUESTIONS

1. What are some of the realities of police work? Which one of the issues discussed in this chapter do you feel is most significant? Why?
2. What career advancement options are available in policing? What's required for advancement?

SECTION III

LEARNING OBJECTIVES

After reading this chapter, students should be able to:

1. Identify the elements of preventive patrol, incident response, and traffic enforcement.
2. Distinguish between directed patrol and proactive policing.
3. Describe elements of the peacekeeping and order maintenance function.
4. Identify investigative goals and explain the investigative process.
5. List and describe some significant issues associated with undercover work.

THINK ABOUT IT

The human body emits a broad spectrum of electromagnetic radiation, which can be detected with the proper equipment. Inanimate objects carried on one's person do not emit such radiation and tend to stand out against the body's electromagnetic background. Using technology based on these facts, Millivision Technologies has developed a weapons-detection device that uses radiometric millimeter wave–based sensors for passive threat detection. The device, called the concealed threat detection (CTD) system, is portable, can be used from a distance, and, according to the company, does not reveal intimate anatomical information. A press release from Millivision says,

> The automatic and effective detection of metal and non-metal weapons, plastic explosives, and other contraband concealed under people's clothing is a fundamental necessity in combating terrorism.
>
> Millivision's passive millimeter wave imaging technology is uniquely suited for this application. Metal and non-metal contraband objects concealed by multiple layers of clothing are revealed by Millivision detectors that are completely passive, i.e., they emit no man-made radiation, but instead produce images from the millimeter waves emitted naturally by the various objects within the scene. Images of contraband objects also aid in their location and identification.[1]

Millivision Technologies is but one of many companies currently developing innovative law enforcement applications. Whereas most high-tech consumer electronics tend not to be controversial, when law enforcement gets its hands on new detection and surveillance equipment, some people become alarmed. Critics of the Millivision device, for example, have charged that it reveals intimate anatomical information about people viewed with it—although the company has repeatedly denied such charges. This raises several important questions to keep in mind as you read this chapter:

1. Do threat detectors like those manufactured by Millivision unduly threaten individual privacy?
2. What other currently available law enforcement technologies might be of concern to privacy advocates?
3. Do advanced threat and surveillance technologies effectively deter criminals?
4. Can technology ever replace good old-fashioned police work?
5. Will we ever see the day when traditional preventive police patrol is completely replaced by advanced surveillance and threat-detection technologies?

INTRODUCTION

The police mission in this country is essentially fivefold: (1) to enforce and support the law, (2) to investigate crimes and apprehend offenders, (3) to prevent crime, (4) to help ensure domestic peace and tranquility, and (5) to provide local communities, states, and the nation as a whole with needed enforcement-related services.

The first police mission is the one that comes immediately to mind for most people. The police operate under an official public mandate to enforce the law. Not surprisingly, police officers see themselves as crime fighters, a view generally shared by the public and promoted by the popular media. Although it is the job of the police to enforce the law, it is not their *only* job. Most officers spend the majority of their time answering nonemergency public-service calls,[2] controlling traffic, or writing tickets. Most are not involved in intensive, ongoing crime-fighting activities. Research shows that only about 10 to 20 percent of all calls to the police involve situations that actually require a law enforcement response—that is, situations that might lead to arrest and eventual prosecution.[3]

Second, police are charged with investigating crimes and apprehending offenders. Some offenders are apprehended during the commission of a crime or immediately afterward. Fleeing Oklahoma City bomber Timothy McVeigh, for example, was stopped by an Oklahoma Highway Patrol officer on routine patrol only 90 minutes after the destruction of the Alfred P. Murrah Federal Building for driving a car with no license plate.

The third police mission, crime prevention, refers to a proactive approach to the problem of crime. Crime prevention involves "the anticipation, recognition and appraisal of a crime risk and initiation of action to remove or reduce it."[4] In preventing crime, police agencies seek to act before a crime happens, thus preventing victimization from taking place. Although the term *crime prevention* is relatively new, the idea is not. Securing valuables, limiting access to sensitive areas, and monitoring the activities of suspicious people are techniques used long before Western police forces were established in the 1800s. Modern crime-prevention efforts aim not only to reduce crime and criminal opportunities and to lower the potential rewards of criminal activity but also to lessen the public's fear of crime.[5]

Enforcing the law, apprehending offenders, and preventing crime are all daunting tasks for police departments because there are many laws and numerous offenders. Still, crimes are clearly defined by statute and are therefore limited in number. Peacekeeping, the fourth element of the police mission, is a virtually unbounded police activity involving not only the control of activities that violate the law (and hence the community's peace) but many others as well. Law enforcement officers who supervise parades, public demonstrations, and picketing strikers, for example, attempt to ensure that the behavior of everyone involved remains "civil" and does not unduly disrupt community life. Robert H. Langworthy, who has written extensively about the police, says that keeping the peace is often left up to individual officers.[6] Basically, he says, departments depend on patrol officers "to define the peace and decide how to support it," and an officer is doing a good job when his or her "beat is quiet, meaning there are no complaints about loiterers or traffic flow, and commerce is supported."

Then there is service, perhaps the most extensive and far-reaching police mission. As writers for the National Institute of Justice note, "Any citizen from any city, suburb, or town across the United States can mobilize police resources by simply picking up the phone and placing a direct call to the police."[7] "Calling the cops" has been described as the cornerstone of policing in a democratic society.[8] About 70 percent of the half-million daily calls to 911 systems across the country are directed to the police, although callers can also request emergency medical and fire services.[9] Calls received by 911 operators are prioritized and then relayed to patrol officers, specialized field units, or other emergency personnel. For example, the Hastings (Minnesota) Police Department handled a total of 687 calls for service from August 16 to August 31st, 2008.[10] A breakdown of those calls shows that there were 68 calls related to serious crimes like arson, assault, auto theft, burglary, larceny, rape, and robbery. The remaining 619 calls were nonemergency calls about lost and found articles, minor motor vehicle accidents, barking dogs, suspicious persons, and parking and traffic law violations.

There is much more to enforcement, investigation and apprehension, crime prevention, order maintenance, and community service than we have presented thus far. Enforcement, for example, can be accomplished through several means, such as preventive patrol, broken windows law enforcement, and emergency response. Investigation can be, and often is, performed by trained detectives, but traffic cops also perform this role, such as when they investigate traffic accidents. The police service mission is extensive and includes many functions that most people are not aware of. Thus, our goal in this chapter is to present these and other police functions in more detail.

WEB PATROL 8-1

Mission Statement of the Philadelphia Police Department
http://www.mycrimekit.com

PATROL

Most of us are familiar with policing because of the patrol function. Movies and television dramas like *CSI* and its spin-offs seem to focus more heavily on the investigation function, but in real life most of us see patrol officers far more often than we see detectives. That is because patrol officers are perhaps the most visible aspect of the police department, engaging in preventive patrol, incident response, and traffic enforcement.

Preventive Patrol

Police officers work to prevent crime in at least two ways: (1) crime-prevention programs and (2) preventive patrol. Crime-prevention efforts led by law enforcement include both techniques and programs. **Crime-prevention techniques** include access control, including barriers to entryways and exits; surveillance, including video systems; theft-deterrence devices like locks, alarms, and tethers;

crime-prevention technique

A technique designed to prevent criminal activity, such as access control with physical barriers to entryways and exits, surveillance (including video systems), theft-deterrence devices (locks, alarms, tethers), security lighting, and visibility landscaping.

An LAPD vehicle responding to an emergency call. Why are patrol officers the "most visible aspect of the police department"?

John Powell/911 Pictures

crime-prevention program
An organized effort that focuses resources on reducing a specific form of criminal threat.

security lighting; and visibility landscaping. **Crime-prevention programs** are organized efforts that focus resources on reducing a specific form of criminal threat. The Philadelphia Police Department's Operation Identification, for example, is designed to discourage theft and to help recover stolen property.[11] The program educates citizens on the importance of identifying, marking, and listing their valuables to deter theft (because marked items are more difficult to sell) and to aid in their recovery. Through Operation Identification, the police department provides engraving pens, suggests ways of photographing valuables, and provides window decals and car bumper stickers that identify citizens as participants in the program. Other crime-prevention programs typically target school-based crime, gang activity, drug abuse, violence, domestic abuse, identity theft, vehicle theft, and neighborhood crimes like burglary.

preventive patrol
The practice of canvassing neighborhoods in an effort to discourage people from committing crime.

deterrence theory
A perspective that holds that crime will be less likely to occur when the potential for getting caught outweighs any likely benefits from breaking the law.

Preventive patrol, in contrast, refers to the practice of canvassing (that is, scrutinizing) neighborhoods in an effort to discourage people from committing crime. **Deterrence theory,** a perspective holding that crime will be less likely when the potential for getting caught outweighs any likely benefits from breaking the law, underlies this practice. Preventive patrol can occur through a number of other means, several of which we will consider here. We will also consider two interesting questions: How much patrol is really preventive, and is preventive patrol effective?

foot patrol
The oldest method of police patrol, which entails officers walking through neighborhoods. Foot patrol tends to enhance rapport between citizens and officers, but it clearly limits an officer's ability to give chase if the need arises.

Types of Patrol. **Foot patrol** is the oldest method of patrol, predating the invention of the automobile. Foot patrol was how policing was accomplished in America's early cities. It continues to be practiced in a number of areas, especially in strip malls, downtown shopping districts, tourist destinations, and other areas where many people are concentrated in a limited space. Foot patrol's advantages lie in the close proximity it provides to citizens, which tends to enhance rapport between people and officers. Being on foot, though, can clearly limit an officer's ability to give chase if the need arises. Even so, criminologist and author John Fuller has this to say about foot patrol: "An aggressive, street-smart police officer, working an active post, can develop as many (or more) quality cases and arrests working foot patrol as he can working motorized patrol."[12]

Today, automobile patrol has effectively replaced foot patrol. The shift was inevitable once the automobile was invented and people began to spread out and move away from downtown areas. Automobile patrol reverses the advantages and disadvantages of foot patrol. On the one hand, it improves officer mobility. On the other hand, it distances officers from the people they serve. The act of driving itself can be a distraction, possibly diminishing even the most well-trained officer's ability to detect crimes in progress. Automobile patrol is also expensive; it requires not just an officer but a fully equipped vehicle (with all the attendant maintenance costs) for him or her to drive.

DOES IT WORK?

One- or Two-Officer Patrols?

We have looked at several varieties of patrol in this chapter, but we have not yet looked at the number of officers engaged in such patrol. Some departments employ one-officer patrols; others employ two-officer patrols. Which is more effective?

A department's decision to adopt one- versus two-officer patrol is usually dictated by concerns like officer safety. In late 2006, for example, the Mesa (Arizona) Police Department changed from one- to two-officer patrols,[1] in part because of a high-profile killing of a Phoenix police officer who was on patrol by himself. (Incidentally, Phoenix also uses two-officer patrols now, as do many other large cities like Los Angeles and New York City.)

Officer safety is obviously important. Some would say it's more important than crime control, but it is also interesting to look at one- versus two-officer patrols from a crime-control standpoint. What does the research show? There has been a good deal of research on the relationship between one- and two-officer patrols and crime, though much of it is now dated. The findings from several published studies[2] can be summarized as follows:

1. The patrol staffing mode has virtually no effect on police effectiveness.
2. Single-officer staffing increases patrol visibility, but the effect on crime is almost nonexistent.
3. Two-officer patrols are, not surprisingly, twice as costly as single-officer patrols.
4. Patrol activity levels are comparable between both staffing methods.

Only a minority of these observations are expressly concerned with crime. Still, we should ask, does one- versus two-officer patrol make a difference in terms of crime? In particular, can police prevent crime with the added visibility of one-officer patrols? One researcher notes, "As to the issue of prevention, the limited mathematical data . . . suggest that since visibility is only marginally improved by single-officer patrol, the concurrent deterrent effects should be minimal."[3] The answer, then, is that we don't know for sure.

---

[1]S. Scarborough, "Mesa police praise two-officer teams," *Arizona Republic*, http://www.azcentral.com/community/tempe/articles/1209mr-twomanpatrol1208Z10.html (accessed December 12, 2006).

[2]Examples include L. E. Boydstun, M. E. Sherry, and N. P. Moelter, *Patrol staffing in San Diego: One- or two-officer units* (Washington, DC: Police Foundation, 1977); S. H. Decker and A. E. Wagner, "The impact of police patrol staffing on police-citizen injuries and dispositions," *Journal of Criminal Justice* 10 (1982): 375–82; E. H. Kaplan, "Evaluating the effectiveness of one-officer versus two-officer patrol units," *Journal of Criminal Justice* 7 (1977): 325–55; D. A. Kessler, "One- or two-officer cars? A perspective from Kansas City," *Journal of Criminal Justice* 13 (1985): 49–64; and National Institute of Justice, *Performance measures for evaluating one- versus two-person cars* (Washington, DC: National Institute of Justice, 1986).

[3]C. Wilson, *Research on one- and two-person patrols: Distinguishing fact from fiction,* Australasian Centre for Policing Research, report series no. 94 (1990), http://www.acpr.gov.au/pdf/ACPR94.pdf (accessed June 30, 2008).

A number of other patrol methods are common and familiar. Bicycle patrol, for example, can be found in a number of relatively small towns and areas with fair weather. Bicycles give officers much more mobility than foot patrol. As police cyclist instructor Kathleen Vonk notes, "Officers on bike patrol have pursued and caught armed robbers, home invasion criminals, car thieves, criminals breaking into cars and criminals in possession of stolen property. . . . They have assisted in searches for missing children. . . . [And] housing officers have used bicycles in the areas where both stealth and speed are essential, pursuing and arresting many drug dealers, street thugs, and trespassers."[13] Bicycle patrol can also be advantageous from the standpoint of community relations: "The bicycle officer is an important public relations tool and is instrumental in bringing the citizenry closer to the police. An officer on bicycle, wearing the more casual 'uniform' of a polo-type shirt and shorts, is far more approachable than an officer zipping by in an air-conditioned cruiser with the windows up."[14]

Mounted patrol is also common in some areas. As one researcher recalls, "Folklore of the frontier lawman on horseback in the American Old West evokes an image of peace and justice. . . . That image of an officer on horseback remains a part of modern law enforcement. In the United States today, more than 600 organized mounted police patrol units form a visible pedestal and serve citizens throughout their jurisdiction. . . . An officer on horseback invites constructive community contact in its own unique way."[15] Like bicycle patrol, mounted patrol puts officers in closer contact with citizens. In addition, mounted patrol provides effective crowd control. Horses are large and heavy and put officers well above the crowd, thereby permitting them to push unruly groups back if the need arises. As one scholar has observed, "The horse gives the police a more visible presence in a crowd, and the horse gives the officer a better view of problems."[16] Mounted patrol is also relatively economical compared to automobile patrol.

Other methods of patrol are (1) air patrol, (2) water patrol, (3) K-9 assisted patrol, (4) special-terrain vehicle patrol, and even (5) Segway patrol. Air patrol is done for everything from traffic enforcement in rural areas to investigation of possible marijuana-growing operations (with thermal imagery) in inner cities. Water patrol can be found on lakes and waterways throughout the United States. Police officers who work with K-9 units (police dogs) do everything from searching

Deputy Troy Sella from the new technology department of the Los Angeles Sheriff's Department (LASD) prepares the SkySeer Unmanned Aerial Vehicle (UAV) for launch during a demonstration flight in Redlands, California. In what ways can police and sheriff's departments benefit from the use of UAVs?

Robyn Beck/Agence France Presse/Getty Images

for elusive suspects to detecting drugs, bombs, and other threats to public safety. Finally, terrain sometimes dictates a need for specialized vehicles. Some all-terrain vehicle (ATV) parks, for instance, are patrolled by officers on off-road motorcycles. ATV patrol is advantageous for a number of reasons: "Some of the typical offenses found while patrolling are noise violations, fire hazards, illegal dumping, illegal shooting, trespassing with motor vehicles, illegal hunting, abandoning stolen vehicles and undocumented alien trafficking."[17]

How Much Patrol Is Really Preventive?

The public has something of a romanticized image of preventive patrol, that of police officers diligently scanning up and down every side street, alleyway, and lot as they drive through their beat. Then there is the real world, which unfortunately does not bode particularly well for the prospects of preventive patrol. Consider, for instance, the number of police officers on patrol vis-à-vis crime rates: Several large cities across the country have approximately the same number of police officers per citizen, but very different levels of crime. As Table 8-1 shows, St Louis had 597 police officers per 100,000 residents in 2000, while Seattle had 340. At first glance, one may be inclined to conclude that St. Louis is a safer city, but not according to the Uniform Crime Reports. St. Louis routinely ranks near the top of the rankings for the 25 most dangerous cities in America (Camden, New Jersey, was number one in 2008), while Seattle doesn't even make the list.[18]

There are more reasons why preventive patrol may not do a good job of disrupting crime. First, the police presence in America is spread very thin. Even if we could double the size of our nation's police force, the number of police officers per 10,000 citizens would remain quite small. Next, according to Sam Walker, a prominent criminal justice professor, "many actual or potential offenders do not perceive police patrol as a meaningful threat."[19] Even with a substantial and visible police presence, some people cannot be deterred from committing crimes. Walker draws this conclusion: "Many crimes are inherently not 'suppressible' by patrol. . . . Because they usually occur indoors and in the heat of passion, the amount of police patrol out on the street is not going to affect them."[20]

Consider, for instance, the crime of burglary. If a burglar has at least a glimmer of intelligence, he or she will try to operate out of view of the police. Consequently, it is likely that police officers on patrol would not even notice that a burglary is taking place or has taken place. Likewise, consider both parties to an abusive relationship. How many domestic violence incidents take place in view of the police? Certainly very few. The very term *domestic* suggests that the abuse takes place in a private residence, out of view of authorities. It makes intuitive sense, therefore, that a heightened police presence cannot reduce all crime.

WEB PATROL 8-2

The Patrol Officer: America's Intelligence on the Ground
http://www.mycrimekit.com

Incident Response

Perhaps one of the reasons why preventive patrol may not be the most effective approach to law enforcement is that officers are routinely responding to calls, which may limit the time they have to patrol neighborhoods and prevent crime.

Routine Incident Response. Police officers on patrol frequently respond to routine incidents, such as minor traffic accidents. Routine incident response is the second most common activity of patrol officers.[21] Responding officers must collect information and, typically, file a written report. As noted by the National Institute of Justice, "The specific police objective will . . . vary depending on

Table 8-1 Police Staffing Levels in America's Big Cities

Number and rate (per 100,000 residents) of full-time employees and sworn personnel in large city police departments, by size of population served and city, United States, 1990 and 2000.

	Full-Time Employees						Full-Time Sworn Personnel					
	Total Number			Per 100,000 Residents			Total Number			Per 100,000 Residents		
Population Served and City	1990	2000	Percent Change	1990	2000	Percent Change	1990	2000	Percent Change	1990	2000	Percent Change
1,000,000 or more												
New York (NY)	39,398	53,029	34.6%	538	662	23.1%	31,236	40,435	29.4%	427	505	18.4%
Los Angeles (CA)	10,695	12,409	13.2	315	336	6.8	8,295	9,341	12.6	238	253	6.2
Chicago (IL)	14,909	16,466	10.4	536	569	6.2	11,837	13,466	13.8	425	465	9.4
Houston (TX)	5,579	7,440	33.4	342	381	11.3	4,104	5,343	30.2	252	273	8.7
Philadelphia (PA)	7,354	7,928	7.8	464	522	12.6	6,523	7,024	7.7	411	463	12.5
Phoenix (AZ)	2,584	3,394	31.3	263	257	−2.2	1,949	2,626	34.7	198	199	0.3
San Diego (CA)	2,498	2,746	9.9	225	224	−0.2	1,816	2,022	11.3	164	165	1.1
Dallas (TX)	3,487	3,586	2.8	346	302	−12.9	2,635	2,862	8.6	262	241	−8.0
San Antonio (TX)	1,912	2,387	24.8	204	209	2.1	1,576	1,882	19.4	168	164	−2.4
Las Vegas (NV)	1,782	3,286	84.4	289	322	11.4	1,162	2,168	86.6	189	213	12.7
Other cities												
Detroit (MI)	5,203	4,804	−7.7	506	505	−0.2	4,595	4,154	−9.6	447	437	−2.3
St. Louis (MO)	2,244	2,078	−7.4	566	597	5.5	1,544	1,489	−3.6	389	428	9.9
Honolulu (HI)	2,220	2,270	2.3	265	259	−2.4	1,781	1,792	0.6	213	205	−4.0
San Francisco (CA)	2,566	2,520	−1.8	354	324	−8.5	1,777	2,227	25.3	245	287	16.8
Indianapolis (IN)	2,113	2,402	13.7	299	313	4.5	1,436	1,592	10.9	203	207	1.9
Jacksonville (FL)	2,080	2,541	22.2	327	345	5.5	1,181	1,530	29.6	186	208	11.9
Columbus (OH)	1,724	2,144	24.4	272	301	10.6	1,381	1,744	26.3	218	245	12.3
Austin (TX)	1,082	1,656	53.0	232	252	8.5	795	1,144	43.9	171	174	2.1
Baltimore (MD)	3,414	3,649	6.9	464	560	20.8	2,861	3,034	6.0	389	466	19.9
Memphis (TN)	2,092	2,791	33.4	343	429	25.3	1,382	1,904	37.8	226	293	29.3
Charlotte (NC)	1,201	1,864	55.2	261	298	14.1	930	1,442	55.1	202	231	14.0
Milwaukee (WI)	2,274	2,472	8.7	362	414	14.4	1,866	1,998	7.1	297	335	12.7
Boston (MA)	2,741	3,046	11.1	477	517	8.3	2,053	2,164	5.4	357	367	2.7
Washington (DC)	5,259	4,468	−15.0	867	781	−9.9	4,506	3,612	−19.8	742	631	−15.0
Nashville (TN)	1,319	1,693	28.4	258	297	15.0	1,020	1,249	22.5	200	218	9.8
El Paso (TX)	928	1,351	45.6	180	240	33.1	738	1,057	43.2	143	188	30.9
Seattle (WA)	1,775	1,918	8.1	344	340	−1.0	1,271	1,261	−0.8	246	224	−9.1
Denver (CO)	1,558	1,802	15.7	333	325	−2.5	1,318	1,489	13.0	282	268	−4.8
Fort Worth (TX)	1,255	1,510	20.3	280	282	0.7	950	1,196	25.9	212	224	8.4
Portland (OR)	955	1,347	41.0	218	255	16.6	769	1,007	30.9	176	190	8.2
Oklahoma City (OK)	1,158	1,269	9.6	260	251	−3.7	863	1,011	17.1	194	200	2.9

Source: U.S. Department of Justice, Bureau of Justice Statistics, *Police departments in large cities, 1990–2000* (Washington, DC: U.S. Department of Justice, May 2002), p. 10.

the nature of the situation, but generally, the objective is to restore order, document information or otherwise provide some immediate service to the parties involved."[22]

One important measure of police success that is strongly linked to citizen satisfaction is **response time:** the time it takes for police officers to respond to calls for service. It is measured from the time a call for service is received by a dispatcher until an officer arrives on the scene. In 2001, for example, police response time in New York City averaged 7.2 minutes for all types of calls, 29 percent faster than the previous year and the quickest response time in a decade.[23] The average response time for critical calls in New York City decreased 20 percent, to 4.8 minutes. Response times

response time
The time it takes for police officers to respond to a call for service.

DOES IT WORK?

Preventive Patrol

How effective is preventive patrol? This is not an easy question to answer because it is difficult to get into the heads of would-be criminals to determine whether the police presence affects their decision making. However, researchers have examined the effects on crime of putting more officers on the streets. They began in Kansas City, Missouri, and then expanded their research to hundreds of other cities and counties throughout the United States.

One of the most important policing studies relevant to police hiring is the now-famous Kansas City Preventive Patrol Experiment.[1] Conducted during 1972 and 1973 in Missouri, the experiment divided the South Patrol District of Kansas City into three groups of patrol beats. *Proactive beats* received two to three times the normal level of patrol. *Reactive beats* received no patrol, only responses to calls for service. *Control beats* had normal police patrol levels.

The experiment revealed that the level of patrol had no effect on crimes suppressible by patrol. These included burglaries, auto thefts, larcenies involving auto accessories, robberies, and vandalism. Public safety was neither improved nor worsened in any of the three beats. What's more, citizens weren't even aware of the differences. Specifically, citizens' attitudes toward the police, their feelings of security, and their decisions to report crime did not vary noticeably from one beat to the next. The lessons of Kansas City, therefore, are often touted as evidence that more police will not reduce crime,[2] but they should not be construed as indisputable. For example, the authors of the experiment's final report pointed out that their findings may have been misinterpreted, that there was more to the experiment than just an examination of whether additional hiring is necessary.[3] Also, some academics have been highly critical of the experiment.[4]

Since the results of the Kansas City Experiment were published, multiple studies have examined the police-crime relationship,[5] that is, they have sought to determine whether there is a relationship between the police presence and crime. Whether a police-crime relationship exists is actually one of the most significantly researched questions in criminal justice.

In 1998, a researcher reviewed 22 studies of the police-crime relationship.[6] He concluded that 18 of the 22 studies found either no relationship between police and crime or a positive relationship. A "positive relationship" means that as the police presence increases, so does crime. A similar review published in 1996 looked at 36 previous studies.[7] The authors of that review reported that only 10 of the 36 previous studies found a decrease in crime accompanying an increase in police presence. In short, both reviews appear to show that there is *very little* research concluding that it is desirable to hire more police officers.

In recent years, as more sophisticated research techniques have been developed, some researchers have concluded that previous work in this important area of criminal justice was flawed. For example, criminologists Thomas Marvell and Carl Moody claim that previous researchers failed to address the possibility that not only may an enhanced police presence affect crime, but that crime may affect the police presence.[8] Clearly, this is a plausible possibility. We know, for example, that voters commonly express frustration when public safety is threatened, thereby calling on politicians to allocate more resources to law enforcement. In a sophisticated analysis that controlled for this possibility, Marvell and Moody were able to show that a heightened police presence does reduce crime. They conclude, "Higher police levels reduce most types of crime, particularly at the city level. The size of the impact is often substantial."[9]

Former President Bill Clinton signed the Violent Crime Control and Law Enforcement Act in September 1994. Title I of the act, known as the Public Safety Partnership and Community Policing Act of 1994, permitted the use of $8.8 billion to fund local law enforcement agencies in the fight against crime and to help improve their community policing capabilities. To spend this massive sum of money, the U.S. Department of Justice created a new agency known as the **Office of Community Oriented Policing Services** (the COPS Office). Its job was to administer and supervise the spending.[10]

Since its creation, the COPS Office has awarded grants to law enforcement agencies throughout the United States. More than $7 billion has been spent. These grant awards have included funds for the hiring of additional police officers,[11] for innovative community policing programs,[12] and for improvement of law enforcement technology.[13] COPS funds have also been used to fund regional community policing institutes, research, and training and technical assistance. All in all, the COPS Office has provided funding for the hiring of more than 100,000 new police officers throughout the United States. All of this spending has led researchers to ask whether it has reduced crime. One important study answered the question with a yes.[14] A few others have followed suit, but at least one study, one of the more sophisticated studies to date, revealed that COPS grants have made virtually no dent in the crime problem.[15] Thus, police officers may prevent some crimes, but certainly not all of them.

---

[1]G. L. Kelling and others, *The Kansas City Preventive Patrol Experiment: A summary report* (Washington, DC: Police Foundation, 1974).
[2]S. Walker, *Sense and nonsense about crime and drugs: A policy guide*, 5th ed. (Belmont, CA: Wadsworth, 2001), p. 81.
[3]Kelling and others, *The Kansas City Preventive Patrol Experiment*, p. 49, cited in D. H. Bayley, *What works in policing* (New York: Oxford University Press, 1998).
[4]R. C. Larson, "What happened to patrol operations in Kansas City? A review of the Kansas City Preventive Patrol Experiment," *Journal of Criminal Justice* 3 (1975): 267–97.
[5]Illustrative examples include D. H. Bayley, *Patterns of policing: A comparative international analysis* (New Brunswick, NJ: Rutgers University Press, 1985); C. Cornwell and W. M. Trumbell, "Estimating the economic model of crime with panel data," *Review of Economics and Statistics* 72 (1994): 360–66; D. F. Greenberg, R. C. Kessler, and C. Loftin, "The effect of police employment on crime," *Criminology* 21 (1983): 375–94; S. Hakim, "The attraction of property crimes to suburban localities: A revised economic model," *Urban Studies* 17 (1980): 265–76; C. R. Huff and J. M. Stahura, "Police employment and suburban crime," *Criminology* 17 (1980): 461–70; S. Levitt, "Using electoral cycles in police hiring to estimate the effect of police on crime," *American Economic Review* 87 (1997): 270–91; and T. V. Kovandzic and J. J. Sloan, "Police levels and crime rates revisited: A county level analysis from Florida (1980–1998)," *Journal of Criminal Justice* 30 (2002): 65–76.
[6]S. Cameron, "The economics of crime deterrence: A survey of theory and evidence," *Kyklos* 41 (1988): 301–23.
[7]Marvell and Moody, "Specification problems, police levels, and crime rates," *Criminology* 34 (1996): 609–43.
[8]Ibid.
[9]Ibid., p. 640.

[10]J. Roth and J. Ryan, "Overview," in *National evaluation of the COPS Program, Title I of the 1994 Crime Act*, ed. J. Roth and others, p. 1 (Washington, DC: U.S. Department of Justice, 2000).
[11]The Universal Hiring Program (UHP); the Accelerated Hiring, Education, and Deployment (AHEAD) program; the Funding Accelerated for Smaller Towns (FAST) program; and the Police Hiring Supplement (PHS) program were used to this end.
[12]These grant programs include the Advancing Community Policing Program, Organizational Change Demonstration Centers, and the Distressed Neighborhoods Program.
[13]The Making Officer Redeployment Effective (MORE) program was used to this end.
[14]J. S. Zhao, M. C. Scheider, and Q. Thurman, "Funding community policing to reduce crime: Have COPS grants made a difference?" *Criminology and Public Policy* 2 (2002): 7–32.
[15]See J. L. Worrall and T. V. Kovandzic, "COPS grants and crime revisited," *Criminology* 45 (2007): 159–90; but also see W. N. Evans and E. Owens, "COPS and crime," *Journal of Public Economics* 91 (2007): 181–201.

in 2001 were cut by an average of nearly three minutes over the previous year, even in the face of an increased number of calls and budget cutbacks that resulted in fewer officers on patrol.

Office of Community Oriented Policing Services (COPS Office) An agency within the U.S. Department of Justice tasked with administering and supervising federal funds allocated to improve community policing capabilities.

Emergency Response. In May 2003, Pomona, California, police officers on routine patrol responded to a dispatcher's instructions to assist in an emergency at a local coin-operated laundry.[24] On arrival, they found a two-year-old girl trapped inside an industrial-size washing machine. The officers used their batons to smash the locked glass-paned door. The girl, unconscious and nearly drowned when pulled from the machine, was taken to a local hospital, where she was expected to recover. Her mother, 35-year-old Erma Osborne, was arrested at the scene and charged with child endangerment when the on-site video surveillance cameras showed her placing her daughter in the machine and shutting the door. This is but one disturbing example of the many emergencies police officers throughout the United States respond to.

DOES IT WORK? Rapid Response

A common assumption is that if the police could reach crime scenes more quickly, they would have a better chance of apprehending lawbreakers. This is the essence of rapid response. The possible advantages of rapid response have been summarized as follows:

> [It is assumed] that the shorter the police travel time from assignment to arrival at a crime scene, the more likely it is that police can arrest offenders before they flee. This claim is then extended to rapid response producing three crime prevention effects. One is a reduction in harm from crimes interrupted in progress by police intervention. Another, more general benefit of rapid response time is a greater deterrent effect from the threat of punishment reinforced by response-related arrests. The third hypothesized prevention effect comes from the incapacitation through imprisonment of offenders prosecuted more effectively with evidence from response-related arrests.[1]

Are these "advantages" borne out in reality? Is rapid response effective at deterring criminals and apprehending them? Most of the research on this subject was published during the 1960s and 1970s. The author of one early study selected 265 police responses to citizen calls for service by the Los Angeles Police Department.[2] He found, as did researchers in a subsequent study,[3] that the probability of arrest increased when police travel time to the crime scene decreased. These findings were refuted, however, by later research.[4]

Another fairly rigorous study hails from Kansas City during the 1970s.[5] The researchers focused on "reporting time" (the amount of time between the criminal act and the call to 911), "dispatch time" (the amount of time between the 911 call and when an officer was dispatched), and "travel time" (the amount of time from dispatch to arrival at the crime scene). The researchers found virtually no relationship between reporting time and the probability of arrest. Cutting travel time was ineffective, as well.

More recently, the National Institute of Justice commissioned response time studies in four cities.[6] The results from the four studies reaffirmed the Kansas City experiences; response time had virtually no effect on crime. Why is it that rapid response doesn't work particularly well? There are two easy explanations. First, people tend to be slow when it comes to reporting crime. Second, most crimes are discovered well after the fact rather than while the crime is in progress.[7]

[1]L. W. Sherman, "Policing for crime prevention," in *Preventing crime: What works, what doesn't, what's promising*, ed. L. W. Sherman and others, p. 143 (Washington, DC: National Institute of Justice, 1998).
[2]H. Isaacs, "A study of communications, crimes, and arrests in a metropolitan police department," Task Force Report: Science and Technology, *A report to the President's Commission on Law Enforcement and Administration of Justice* (Washington, DC: U.S. Government Printing Office, 1967).
[3]C. Clawson and S. K. Chang, "The relationship of response delays and arrest rates," *Journal of Police Science and Administration* 5 (1977): 53–68.
[4]J. M. Chaiken, "What is known about deterrent effects of police activities," in *Preventing crime*, ed. James A. Cramer, pp. 109–35 (Beverly Hills, CA: Sage, 1978).
[5]W. Bieck and D. A. Kessler, *Response time analysis* (Kansas City, MO: Board of Police Commissioners, 1977). See also T. Pate and others, *Police response time: Its determinants and effects* (Washington, DC: Police Foundation, 1976).
[6]W. Spelman and D. K. Brown, *Calling the police: A replication of the citizen reporting component of the Kansas City response time analysis* (Washington, DC: Police Foundation, 1981).
[7]For a look at the relationship between response time and citizen perceptions of the police, see S. Percy, "Response time and citizen evaluation of police," *Journal of Police Science and Administration* 8 (1980): 75–86.

Although police respond to emergencies far less frequently than to routine incidents,[25] emergency response is a vital aspect of what police agencies do. Emergency response, often called *critical incident response,* is used for crimes in progress, traffic accidents with serious injuries, natural disasters, terrorist attacks, officer requests for assistance, and other situations in which human life may be in jeopardy. Emergency responses take priority over all other police work, and until order is restored, the officers involved will not turn to other tasks. An important part of police training involves emergency response techniques, including first aid, hostage rescue, and the physical capture of suspects. Perhaps the ultimate critical incident these days is a terrorist attack. We discuss terrorism in greater detail in Chapter 16.

Traffic Enforcement

Most civilians are more familiar with the traffic enforcement function of police work than with any other dimension of the job—often because they've been on the receiving end of the enforcement. Traffic enforcement is generally concerned with enforcing laws pertaining to motor vehicles and their operation. It also involves the relief of congestion and the reduction of accidents. To do each of these tasks, officers may run radar surveillance, conduct checkpoints to apprehend drunk drivers, perform license and safety checks, direct traffic, enforce anticruising ordinances, ensure that people wear their seatbelts, target illegal street racers, nab red light runners, and keep an eye out for road rage. According to one writer, "Among the most common problems facing law enforcement today are those relating to traffic issues in their community. Citizens may call to complain about speeding cars in their neighborhood or voice concern over a nearby school crosswalk."[26] Perhaps the most controversial aspect of traffic enforcement these days involves stopping a motorist for reasons *other* than legitimate law violations, a practice known as *profiling*.

Pretext Stops and Profiling. The U.S. Supreme Court has held that police officers can stop cars based on the belief that a crime has been committed, which includes any traffic violation.[27] Once a motorist has been stopped, the officer can order him or her to stand outside of the vehicle without any justification,[28] search the vehicle with consent,[29] seize items that are in "plain view,"[30] frisk the driver and search the passenger compartment of the vehicle out of concerns for safety,[31] and search the entire car if probable cause to arrest or search is developed.[32] In other words, there are numerous opportunities for the police to detect contraband during the course of a vehicle stop. And since almost every driver commits traffic law violations at some point, there is usually ample justification for stopping motorists.

WEB PATROL 8-3

An Examination of Racial Profiling Data in a Large Metropolitan Area
http://www.mycrimekit.com

Whether every motorist is stopped for a legitimate reason, though, is sometimes questionable. What's more, even if an officer has legal grounds to stop a motorist, the question of pretext presents itself: Should police with other motivations in mind (for example, to gain consent to search) be allowed to use traffic laws to stop people? In other words, should officers be able to conduct **pretext stops,** which are stops based on more than one motive? In a pretext stop, the officer stops the vehicle for a legitimate reason but is also suspicious about the driver. To the extent that pretext stops occur, too many of them can amount to **racial profiling,** which as been defined as "the use of discretionary authority by law enforcement officers in encounters with minority motorists, typically within the context of a traffic stop, that results in the disparate treatment of minorities."[33]

pretext stop
A traffic stop based on more than one motive. For example, an officer stops a vehicle for a legitimate reason but is also suspicious about the driver.

racial profiling
"The use of discretionary authority by law enforcement officers in encounters with minority motorists, typically within the context of a traffic stop, that results in the disparate treatment of minorities."[i]

A driver's race obviously does not create justification to stop. Yet there are many people who have argued that the police use existing traffic laws, which are many and easy to violate, to single out certain drivers based on their race.[34] The Supreme Court has yet to decide directly on the constitutionality of this type of conduct, but at least one of its decisions has come close. In *Whren v. United States*,[35] Washington, DC, police made a traffic stop and observed two bags of crack cocaine in the hands of a passenger who was seated in the front of the car. The police testified that they stopped the driver because he violated traffic laws. In contrast, the defendants claimed that the stop was made based on their race and that the police used alleged traffic violations as a reason to stop them.

The Supreme Court concluded that the "constitutional reasonableness of traffic stops" does not depend "on the actual motivations of the individual officers." The Court also concluded that the only relevant inquiry is whether the officer has cause to stop the car. It rejected the argument that the Fourth Amendment requires a court to consider whether "the officer's conduct deviated materially from usual police practices, so that a reasonable officer in the same circumstances would not have made the stop for the reasons given." Simply put, the Supreme Court has stated that officers' individual motivations—whether racial or otherwise—are irrelevant. The only question worth answering, according to the Court, is whether the officer has cause to stop the vehicle. Needless to say, this decision did not satisfy critics of racial profiling.

Justice Anthony Kennedy's dissent in *Whren* summarizes the position of critics of racial profiling:

> The practical effect of our holding in *Whren,* of course, is to allow the police to stop vehicles in almost countless circumstances. When *Whren* is coupled with today's holding, the Court puts tens of millions of passengers at risk of arbitrary control by the police. If the command to exit were to become commonplace, the Constitution would be diminished in a most public way. As the standards suggested in dissent are adequate to protect the safety of the police, we ought not to suffer so great a loss.

Is racial profiling really a problem? Some studies suggest that it is. For example, in a study of drivers' characteristics during traffic stops, Robin Engel and Jennifer Calnon reached this conclusion: "The findings show that young black and Hispanic males are at increased risk for citations, searches, arrests, and use of force after other extralegal and legal characteristics are controlled."[36] Their findings are supported by other researchers:

> The small but growing research literature on racial profiling has produced several common findings regarding race and ethnic differences in police stops, searches, and arrests. Including the present study, the accumulated research indicates that Black motorists are more likely than Whites, and in some studies Hispanics, to be pulled over by the police. The racial difference in the probability of being stopped is small but consistent across local and national-level investigations employing different methods of data collection and analysis. In addition, Black and Hispanic drivers who have been stopped by the police are about twice as likely as Whites to be searched and arrested.[37]

There is some concern that conclusions like these are difficult to make sense of without first considering the demographic composition of the area studied. We might expect, for example, that more blacks than whites will be stopped in an area with a large percentage of black residents. Most of us would agree that such an apparent disparity could be explained by the demographics of the area. The problem, though, is settling on the appropriate base for comparison. For example, we could look at census data to ascertain the racial composition of a particular neighborhood, but just because someone is stopped in their vehicle in that area doesn't mean they live there. The mobility of automobiles makes it difficult to find something with which to compare police traffic stop data. An alternative is driver's license databases, but even they are limited because not every driver has a license. There are ways around these types of research problems. For example, researchers can look at different officers within the same department. If one stops significantly more minorities than others, then arguably something other than legitimate enforcement is going on.

WEB PATROL 8-4

Traffic Stop Information and Biased Enforcement
http://www.mycrimekit.com

Assuming that racial profiling does occur, what explains it? Here is one observer's answer: "The use of profiles in law enforcement is thought to increase the efficiency of officers and, consequently, the police organization as a whole. . . . The 'war on drugs' has certainly heightened the use of profiles in law enforcement."[38] Similarly, University of Missouri-Kansas City criminologist Kenneth Novak has pointed out that "police officers have suggested disproportionate contacts between officers and citizens may be an unanticipated byproduct of the war on drugs, the get-tough-on-crime movement, zero-tolerance policing or perhaps efficient operational tactics."[39] Some police officers are quick to defend what would appear, on its face, to be biased policing:

> Police have a mandate to battle crime. They use the tools they know work and profiling is one of them. . . . This nation's war on drugs is the No. 1 culprit behind the accusations of "racial

> profiling." It's an unpleasant fact that blacks are disproportionately involved in the drug trade. . . . Cops aren't out to get blacks so much as to get drug dealers, creating collateral damage for black motorists. . . . To allow political correctness to disarm police of an important law enforcement tool on the grounds of unfounded claims of racism is criminal.[40]

As most of us are aware, profiling has become a hot topic in the war on terror. Before September 11, 2001, critics were up in arms over the profiling of black motorists. Now the focus has shifted to people of Middle Eastern descent. But surprisingly, there is now a measure of support for profiling: "After years of enduring harsh criticism and suspicion from the public for alleged racial profiling practices, law enforcement in the aftermath of the World Trade Center disaster has suddenly found itself on the high road, as some who once considered the practice taboo are now eager for police to bend the rules when it comes to Middle Easterners."[41] One researcher reported on a *Los Angeles Times* poll, conducted after September 11, which found that more than two-thirds of those questioned favored "randomly stopping people who may fit the profile of suspected terrorists."[42]

Despite a possible new public attitude in favor of profiling, whether for the enforcement of drug laws or to target terrorists, law enforcement agencies have taken great strides to bring it to a halt. Some have revised their mission statements and policy manuals to discourage the practice. Others train their officers on how to *not* make decisions based on race and other illegitimate criteria. Law enforcement accreditation bodies (see Chapter 12) have started to take evidence of profiling into account when reviewing police departments that have applied for accreditation. The Police Executive Research Forum (see Chapter 2) has released a detailed report that calls for improved data collection, oversight, accountability, and training in the area of profiling.[43]

WEB PATROL 8-5

Characteristics of Drivers Stopped by Police
http://www.mycrimekit.com

WEB PATROL 8-6

Citizens' Views on Biased Policing
http://www.mycrimekit.com

It is interesting that through all the ups and downs of the racial profiling debate, the Supreme Court, in *Whren*, effectively continues to condone the practice. The Court does not have a problem with pretext stops (and, by extension, profiling) as long as police officers have legitimate reasons for stopping people.

Durham, North Carolina, police evidence technician D. F. King examines the wreckage of a vehicle involved in a three-car accident on the Durham Freeway, where a car crossed the median, cutting one car in half and severely damaging another. How can police accident investigators help lower the likelihood of future crashes?

AP Wide World Photos

Accident Investigation. The traffic function involves much more than enforcement. Officers also respond to accidents. Motor vehicle crashes are all too common and exceedingly costly: "Although the traffic fatality rate has dropped dramatically since the mid-1960s, traffic crashes account for 95 percent of all transportation-related deaths and 99 percent of transportation-related injuries. Traffic crashes are the leading cause of death for people ages 4 to 34. The total economic costs of motor vehicle crashes in the United States exceeds $230 billion annually."[44] In addition, traffic crashes are the leading cause of line-of-duty deaths for police officers.[45]

Accident investigation begins, of course, with a response to the incident. Once an accident occurs, the officer must do the following:

- Take immediate steps to stabilize the accident scene, provide for life safety, and establish traffic control; establish a perimeter for the scene; and evacuate the injured, if required.
- Evaluate the situation and call for needed assistance.
- Triage the injured and provide appropriate field treatment and emergency care transportation.
- Extend the area of operation to ensure safe and orderly traffic flow through and around the accident scene.
- Provide for the safety, accountability, and welfare of personnel, a responsibility that continues throughout the incident.
- Restore the roadway to normal operations after the accident has been cleared.[46]

After victims' needs have been met and the scene secured, officers turn to investigating the accident. The causes of some accidents are immediately apparent and require little investigation. Some even occur in plain view of an officer. The causes of many accidents, though, may not be immediately apparent. To ascertain the cause, the officer takes statements from witnesses, physically examines the vehicles involved, measures the skid marks, takes note of the final positions of vehicles on the roadway, and so on. The officer takes photographs and notes in an effort to carefully document all pertinent aspects of the accident scene. All of this helps the officer "reconstruct" the accident in order to determine who, if anyone, was at fault.

One difficult situation is the investigation of "staged" accidents, which are intentionally caused for insurance fraud purposes. A number of telltale signs indicate that a group of claimants might be staging accidents. Here are just a handful:

- The accidents occur right after the claimants become insured.
- Relatively minor accidents result in excessive medical costs.
- The claimants list a suspect address, such as a post office box.
- The claimants, their doctors, and attorneys belong to the same ethnic group.
- The vehicles used by the claimants are old and often have previous damage.
- The same auto body shop works on the damaged vehicles.
- All of the claimants go to the same health care provider.[47]

Pursuits. Every now and then suspects flee the police, and pursuits ensue. In some areas of the country, pursuits seem to be a frequent occurrence in light of all the media attention they receive. Some characteristics of police pursuits are listed in Table 8-2. The public seems to thrive on "the chase." There is a thrill in it for police officers, too, but there is also a dark side: Every pursuit carries with it the potential for danger to third parties. When innocent motorists or pedestrians are injured or killed in the course of a pursuit, lawsuits are often filed and sometimes the plaintiffs prevail. In Washington, DC, a jury awarded $1 million to a woman who was seriously injured when her car was struck during a high-speed police pursuit.[48] Virtually all police administrators are committed to avoiding the costs associated with such litigation.

Before initiating a high-speed pursuit, the officer must weigh two competing objectives. As Geoffrey Alpert, one of the nation's leading authorities on police pursuits, puts it, "The basic dilemma associated with high-speed pursuit of suspects is deciding whether the benefits of potential apprehension outweigh the risks of endangering police officers, the public, and suspects in the chase."[49] This dilemma becomes especially pronounced in the context of minor offenses. Research reveals that the majority of violators who flee from the police were suspected of committing offenses for which arrest would not be customary.[50]

Table 8-2 • Characteristics of Police Pursuits

	Number (Percentage) of Incidents		
Reason for Pursuit	Metro-Dade (Miami) Florida	Omaha, Nebraska	Alken County, South Carolina
Traffic Violation	**448 (45%)**	**112 (51%)**	**5 (36%)**
DUI/Reckless driving		8 (4%)	1 (7%)
"Suspect" vehicle		7 (3.5%)	2 (14%)
Driver known from previous incident		3 (1.5%)	
Felonies	**344 (35%)**	**89 (40%)**	**6 (43%)**
Armed robbery	117		2
Vehicular assault	67		
Aggravated assault	37		
Stolen vehicle	37	36	3
Burglary	24		
Other felonies	62	53	1
Accidents			
Personal injury	428 (41%)	31 (14%)	2 (12%)
Property damage	213 (20%)	91 (40%)	4 (24%)
Arrests	**784 (75%)**	**118 (52%)**	**14 (82%)**

Source: G. P. Alpert, *Police pursuit: Policies and training* (Washington, DC: National Institute of Justice, 1997), p. 3.

Most police agencies have some sort of policy governing police pursuits, and these policies have a direct impact on the incidence of pursuits. A study revealed, for instance, that when the Metro-Dade (Florida) Police Department adopted a "violent felony only" pursuit policy, the number of pursuits declined markedly.[51] In contrast, Omaha adopted a more lax pursuit policy and witnessed an increase in pursuits of 600 percent in the space of one year.[52] Clearly, then, agencies can manage the incidence of police pursuits by altering their policies.

Assuming the officer decides to engage in a pursuit, what are the likely outcomes? First, research reveals that injuries are more likely to occur when people suspected of violent felonies flee the police.[53] Injuries are also likely when pursuits occur on surface streets (rather than highways) in urban and suburban (rather than rural) areas.[54] An in-depth analysis of pursuits involving the Metro-Dade Police Department revealed that four factors affect the likelihood of injury:

1. The greater the number of police cars, the greater the likelihood of injury.
2. The involvement of other police agencies also increases the likelihood of injury.
3. High-speed chases result in more injuries than low-speed pursuits.
4. Chases in residential areas result in more injuries than those conducted in nonresidential areas.[55]

Researchers have also looked at factors affecting the likelihood of suspect escape:

> In Omaha, the likelihood of escape was related to supervisory assistance (the lack of supervisory assistance increased the likelihood of escape), the number of police cars involved in the chase (pursuits with one police car resulted in more escapes than chases with more than one police car), the speed of the chase (chases conducted at higher speeds resulted in more escapes than those at lower speeds), the location of the pursuit (chases in residential areas resulted in more escapes than those in rural areas), and the level of traffic congestion (chases in light traffic resulted in more escapes than those in heavy traffic).[56]

Police agencies must train their officers and adopt policies that take these research findings into account.

The Washington, DC, case described at the beginning of this section might not have occurred but for apparent negligence on the part of the pursuing officer. The DC police department has one of the most restrictive pursuit policies in the country, permitting officers to chase only those suspected of committing violent felonies, but the officer gave chase through a residential area after a suspect with expired license plates. Was the jury's decision a just one? Perhaps it would help to know that the woman who was injured lost three fingers and other parts of her left hand—and she was an innocent bystander to the chase.

Numerous technologies have been developed to assist police with interrupting high-speed pursuits. Most readers are probably familiar with spike strips. Recent versions of these feature hollow spikes that slowly release the air from the fleeing suspect's tires to bring the vehicle to a safe stop. The spikes can be retracted remotely so pursuing vehicles can pass over them safely.

The Auto-Arrestor, another device that is currently being developed, disrupts the fleeing vehicle's electronics, kills the ignition, and brings it safely to a stop. The manufacturer explains how it works:

> For the growing problem of high-speed vehicle pursuit, Titan is refining and miniaturizing the Auto-Arrestor™ system, which uses electromagnetic pulses to disrupt a fleeing automobile's sensitive electronics and safely stop it. The system can be deployed as a permanent or temporary barrier across a road. The electrical energy injected onto the vehicle's frame couples to the ignition system and disables the engine, bringing it to a safe, controlled stop.[57]

DIRECTED PATROL AND PROACTIVE POLICING

Directed patrol is, as the term suggests, patrol with direction. Unlike random patrol, directed patrol involves concentrating the police presence in areas where certain crimes are a significant problem. Two terms used in conjunction with directed patrol are **hot spots** and **hot times.** Hot spots are concentrated areas of significant criminal activity, such as a street corner well known for its prostitution traffic. Hot times are those times of day when crime is particularly problematic, such as after dark on a Friday night.

Other terms that frequently arise with reference to directed patrol include **crime peaks,** or those times of day when certain crimes increase; **saturation patrol,** which occurs when several police officers flood a certain area in an effort to catch criminals and to deter would-be offenders; and **focused patrol,** in which police focus their efforts on certain problems, locations, or times.

Police departments today are able to identify hot spots and hot times with crime mapping. Using dispatch data, for example, police departments can plot the concentration of certain offenses on a map, including the times during which they occur. This allows officials to see firsthand where the problems are so they can allocate personnel to the areas where they are needed the most. Directed patrol is one way of making the most out of a police department's limited resources.

Proactive policing relies heavily on police-initiated arrests, as opposed to arrests made after someone calls for police assistance. When a police department makes most arrests *after* a call for service, this is referred to as *reactive policing*. As we have already seen, the effectiveness of the reactive approach is not well supported by the literature. In other words, when the police wait around for calls for service, the resulting arrests do not appear to affect the crime rate. By contrast, research suggests that proactive policing may have beneficial effects on crime rates.

The proactive policing strategy does not involve arresting people based on the mere *possibility* that they may commit a crime. When the police arrest someone without probable cause to believe that person has committed a crime, they violate the Fourth Amendment to the U.S. Constitution. Instead, proactive arrests follow increased police attention to specific types of criminals and crimes.

Proactive policing differs from directed patrol. Whereas proactive policing focuses heavily on particular criminals and types of crime, directed patrol is more concerned with increasing the law enforcement presence in specific geographic areas. Directed patrol researchers commonly refer to hot spots of criminal activity, which reinforces the notion that directed patrol is geographic, not targeted against specific individuals or types of criminal activity.

directed patrol
A form of patrol that involves concentrating the police presence in areas where certain crimes are a significant problem.

hot spot
A concentrated area of significant criminal activity, such as a street corner known for its prostitution traffic.

hot time
A period during the day when crime is particularly problematic, such as after dark on a Friday night.

crime peak
A time of day when a particular crime increases in frequency.

saturation patrol
A form of patrol that involves concentrating the police presence in a certain area in an effort to catch criminals and to deter would-be offenders.

focused patrol
A form of patrol that focuses police efforts on certain problems, locations, or times.

proactive policing
A policing method that relies heavily on police-initiated arrests, as opposed to arrests made after someone calls for police assistance.

DOES IT WORK?

Directed Patrol

Directed patrol refers to patrol with direction—that is, patrol targeted at specific areas and problems. Is this approach effective? Research by Lawrence Sherman,[1] Patrick Gartin and Michael Buerger[2] is among the most cited in the directed patrol literature. These researchers found that aggressive enforcement of the laws in crime hot spots, areas plagued by a disproportionate amount of crime and disorder, causes crime to decline. Their efforts have spawned an extensive body of hot spots research,[3] most of which has concentrated on areas with drug problems and excessive gun violence. We begin with drugs.

In 1989, the National Institute of Justice initiated the Drug Market Analysis (DMA) Program. The DMA Program was designed in an effort to develop strategies that could be used to address street-level drug crime and to effectively target the areas plagued by drug activity.[4] More importantly, the DMA Program was intended to help researchers determine what policing strategies prove effective for combating drug problems.

In one DMA study, two researchers reported on the effect of an innovative drug enforcement strategy in Jersey City, New Jersey.[5] Using computer mapping technology, they identified 56 drug hot spots.[6] These 56 hot spots were randomized into experimental and treatment groups. Then police officers took various steps to target drug activity. These ranged from minor tactics to major coordinated efforts carried out by a large number of officers. The researchers found that focusing on hot spots significantly reduced disorder-related emergency calls for service.

The Jersey City study is one of the few criminal justice *experiments*—complete with treatment and control groups as well as random assignment. Accordingly, the findings should be taken seriously. In addition, other research suggests that targeted drug enforcement efforts can reduce crime.[7]

One problem with directed patrol at drug hot spots is that the effects of such patrol can be short-lived. A recent study of the use of police raids for dealing with illegal drug selling at nuisance bars serves as proof positive.[8] The authors concluded that "police intervention suppresses levels of drug dealing during periods of active enforcement, but the effects largely disappear when the intervention is withdrawn."[9] The same study suggests that authorities need to give careful attention to the areas targeted by proactive enforcement; some target areas respond to aggressive enforcement better than others do.[10]

We turn now to violent crime. In the early 1990s, the Kansas City (Missouri) Police Department studied the effect of a directed patrol strategy on violent crime. The department placed some officers in patrol cars, freed them of their responsibility of responding to calls for service, and instructed them to proactively patrol the neighborhood with a special emphasis on locating and seizing illegally possessed firearms. Findings from the study were impressive. There was a 65 percent increase in gun seizures and a 49 percent decrease in gun-related crime in the target area.[11]

In a study patterned after the Kansas City gun experiment, researchers examined the effects of an initiative implemented by the Indianapolis Police Department.[12] In July 1997, the department implemented directed patrol in two target areas for a total of 90 days. The strategy was summarized as follows:

> The goal was to maximize vehicle stops and thereby create a sense of significantly increased police presence. The theory was that offenders would be deterred by this increased police presence. Additionally, the police anticipated that the large number of vehicle stops would yield seizures of illegal weapons.[13]

What did the research show? Apparently, crime was reduced in one of the target areas but not the other. The researchers concluded that "the impact of directed patrol on gun crime, homicide, aggravated assault with a gun, and armed robbery in the north target beat was similar to that observed in Kansas City."[14] These outcomes did not carry over into the other target area, a result possibly attributable to lower directed patrol "dosage levels" in that area. The researchers argued that reductions occurred in the north target beat because there the police maximized stops for suspicious activities and conducted more thorough investigations than in the east beat.

Taken together, the results from the Kansas City and Indianapolis studies suggest that directed patrol for the purpose of taking guns out of circulation can have a desirable effect. The Indianapolis study suggests, in particular, that the police can have a specific deterrent effect on gun violence when they target suspicious individuals and activities. The researchers claim that this "targeted offender approach sends a message of increased surveillance and removes firearms from those individuals most likely to engage in violent crime."[15]

---

[1]L. Sherman, "Police crackdowns: Initial and residual deterrence," in *Crime and justice: A review of research*, vol. 12, ed. M. Tonry and N. Morris, pp. 1–48 (Chicago: University of Chicago Press, 1990).
[2]L. Sherman, P. Gartin, and M. Buerger, "Hot spots of predatory crime: Routine activities and the criminology of place," *Criminology* 27 (1989): 27–55.
[3]L. Sherman and D. Rogan, "Effects of gun seizures on gun violence: Hot spots patrol in Kansas City," *Justice Quarterly* 12 (1995): 673–94; D. Weisburd and L. Green, "Policing drug hot spots: The Jersey City drug market analysis experiment," *Justice Quarterly* 12 (1995): 711–35; and A. Braga and others, "Problem-oriented policing in violent crime places: A randomized controlled experiment," *Criminology* 37 (1999): 541–79.
[4]National Institute of Justice, *Program plan* (Washington, DC: National Institute of Justice, 1989).
[5]Weisburd and Green, "Policing drug hot spots," pp. 711–35.
[6]For a thorough discussion of the characteristics of the hot spots, see D. Weisburd and L. G. Mazerolle, "Crime and disorder in drug hot spots: Implications for theory and practice in policing," *Police Quarterly* 3 (2000): 331–49.
[7]See, for instance, L. G. Mazerolle, C. Kadleck, and J. Roehl, "Controlling drug and disorder problems: The role of place managers," *Criminology* 36 (1998): 371–404.
[8]J. Cohen, W. Gorr, and P. Singh, "Estimating intervention effects in varying risk settings: Do police raids reduce illegal drug dealing at nuisance bars?" *Criminology* 41 (2003): 257–92.
[9]Ibid., p. 257.
[10]Ibid.
[11]Sherman and Rogan, "The effects of gun seizures on gun violence," pp. 673–93; L. W. Sherman, J. W. Shaw, and D. P. Rogan, *The Kansas City Gun Experiment* (Washington, DC: National Institute of Justice, 1995).
[12]E. F. McGarrell and others, "Reducing firearms violence through directed police patrol," *Criminology and Public Policy* 1 (2001): 119–48.
[13]Ibid., p. 130.
[14]Ibid., p. 142.
[15]Ibid., p. 143.

There are many proactive policing strategies. One consists of keeping tabs on high-risk repeat offenders in the hope of catching them in the act. Another involves prioritizing arrests for certain types of offenders, such as drunk drivers or drug dealers. A third makes use of enhanced supervision and interrogation of known and suspected criminals.

PEACEKEEPING AND ORDER MAINTENANCE

Peacekeeping and order maintenance are also critical police missions. The mere thought that police officers might be close can discourage crime and deviance, thereby fostering peace and order. On the other hand, it is sometimes necessary to take visible steps to maintain peace and order. Police officers dressed in riot gear during a high-profile public protest are an example of this. The presence of police officers at sporting events, such as on the sidelines in a football game, is another. In either case, police officers take *proactive* steps to maintain peace and order. There is also a *reactive* element to peacekeeping and order maintenance, such as when neighborhood disorder and quality-of-life problems surface in the wake of civil disobedience and during crisis situations.

Managing Disorder and Quality-of-Life Issues

Many police departments focus on quality-of-life offenses as a crime-reduction and peacekeeping strategy. **Quality-of-life offenses** are minor law violations, sometimes called *petty crimes,* that demoralize residents and businesspeople by creating disorder. Examples of petty crimes include excessive noise, graffiti, abandoned cars, and vandalism. Other quality-of-life offenses reflect social decay and include panhandling and aggressive begging, public urination, prostitution, roaming youth gangs, public consumption of alcohol, and street-level substance abuse.[58] Homelessness, while not necessarily a violation of the law unless it involves some form of trespass,[59] is also typically addressed under quality-of-life programs. Through police interviews, the homeless may be relocated to shelters or hospitals or arrested for some other offense. Some researchers claim that reducing the number of quality-of-life offenses in a community can restore a sense of order, reduce the fear of crime, and lessen the number of serious crimes that occur. However, quality-of-life programs have been criticized by those who say that the government should not be taking a law enforcement approach to social and economic problems.[60]

quality-of-life offense
A minor law violation that demoralizes residents and businesspeople by creating disorder. Sometimes called *petty crime.*

broken windows model
A model of policing based on the notion that physical decay in a community (for example, litter and abandoned buildings) can breed disorder and lead to crime by signaling that laws are not being enforced.

The Broken Windows Model. A similar approach to keeping the peace can be found in the **broken windows model** of policing.[61] This model is based on the notion that physical decay in a community, such as litter and abandoned buildings, can breed disorder and can lead to crime by signaling that laws are not being enforced (Figure 8-1).[62] Such decay, the theory

Figure 8-1 • An Overview of the Broken Windows Model

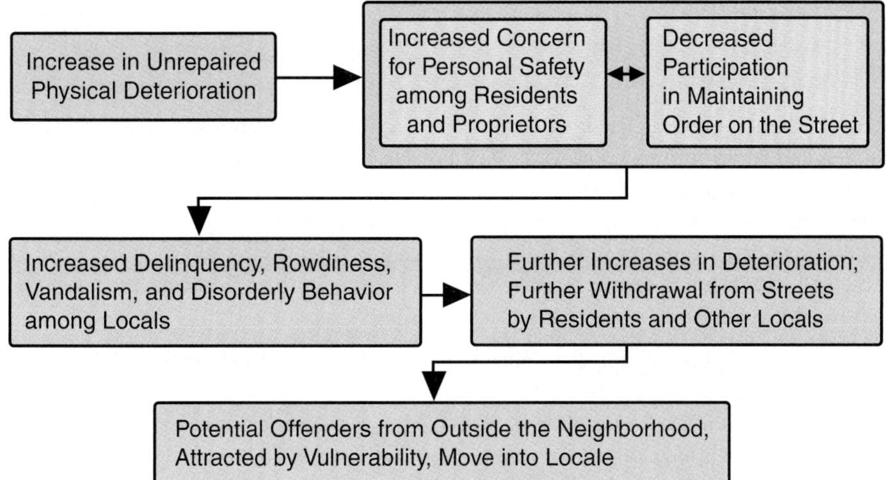

Source: R. B. Taylor and A. V. Harrell, *Physical environment and crime* (Washington, DC: U.S. Department of Justice, Office of Justice Programs, 1996).

DOES IT WORK?

Broken Windows Policing

As explained in the text, the broken windows theory is concerned with targeting low-level offenses and quality-of-life problems in an effort to prevent more serious crimes from occurring later. The authors of one study examined a community's attempt to deal with two quality-of-life offenses: street drinking and joyriding.[1] The enforcement strategy undertaken consisted, first, of assigning extra undercover liquor-control agents to the target area and instructing them to make arrests and to issue citations for open containers of alcohol. Second, the local police department allocated several patrol cars to the areas where joyriding was prominent. The researchers evaluated this approach in terms of its effect on the serious crimes of robbery and aggravated burglary, but they found that the interventions had no effect on these more serious crimes. They judged successfulness from the standpoint of robbery and burglary because, if the broken windows model is true, both would probably decline in the wake of a policing strategy that focuses on low-level offenses.

A recent evaluation of quality-of-life policing also paints the broken windows theory in an unfavorable light. Charles Katz and his colleagues studied the effect of the Chandler (Arizona) Police Department's quality-of-life initiative on police calls for service in several categories.[2] These included calls for personal crime, property crime, drug crime, suspicious persons, assistance, public morals, physical disorder, nuisance, disorderly conduct, and traffic.[3] They found that quality-of-life policing reduces physical disorder and public morals offenses (for example, prostitution), but little else. This is not a surprising conclusion considering that a major component of the Chandler initiative involved policing physical disorder (mainly through code enforcement) and public morals offenses. Another recent study, arguably the most sophisticated to date, suggests that failure to address low-level problems like litter and unkempt lawns leads to future increases in serious crime.[4]

[1]K. Novak, J. Hartman, A. Holsinger, and M. Turner, "The effects of aggressive policing of disorder on serious crime," *Policing: An International Journal of Police Strategies and Management* 22 (1999): pp. 171–90.

[2]C. M. Katz, V. J. Webb, and D. R. Schaefer, "An assessment of the impact of quality-of-life policing on crime and disorder," *Justice Quarterly* 18 (2001): 825–76.

[3]Ibid., p. 844.

[4]B. Brown, D. D. Perkins, and G. Brown, "Crime, new housing, and housing incivilities in a first-ring suburb: Multilevel relationships across time," *Housing Policy Debate* 15 (2004): 301–45. See also R. Taylor, *Breaking away from broken windows: Baltimore neighborhoods and the nationwide fight against crime, grime, fear, and decline* (New York: Westview, 2001).

WEB PATROL 8-7
"Broken Windows" and Police Discretion
http://www.mycrimekit.com

WEB PATROL 8-8
Is Broken Windows Policing Broken?
http://www.mycrimekit.com

postulates, pushes law-abiding citizens to withdraw from the streets, which then sends a signal that lawbreakers can operate freely.[63] The broken windows model suggests that by encouraging the repair of rundown buildings and controlling disorderly behavior in public spaces, police agencies can create an environment in which serious crime cannot easily flourish.[64] While desirable, public order has its own costs. Noted police author Charles R. Swanson says, "The degree to which any society achieves some amount of public order through police action depends in part upon the price that society is willing to pay to obtain it."[65] Swanson describes the price to be paid in terms of (1) police resources paid for by tax dollars, and (2) "a reduction in the number, kinds, and extent of liberties" that are available to members of the public.[66]

Civil Disobedience and Crisis Situations

civil disobedience
Law-breaking used as a political tactic to prove a point or to protest against something.

Civil disobedience involves law-breaking to prove a point or to protest against something. As Karen Hess and Henry Wrobleski observe, "Civil disobedience occurs daily around the world, from the fight against apartheid in South Africa, to the quest for autonomy of ethnic groups in Europe, to demonstrations in Washington, DC, against racism or for a more responsive government."[67] Examples can include refusing to move for police officers who are trying to establish crowd-control lines to serious law-breaking such as setting fires and looting. Police officers need to be equipped to deal with such situations:

> The need to train law enforcement command and line officers to manage crowds and respond to civil disobedience has never been clearer. Large protests have accompanied such planned events as the World Trade Organization (WTO) meeting in Seattle, the national political conventions in Philadelphia and Los Angeles, and the Group of Eight summit in Genoa, Italy.[68]

A problem with policing civil disobedience is that much of it is based on a desire to protest some perceived inequity, a right protected by the First Amendment. When managing civil disobedience, police have to be cautious that they don't trample people's constitutional rights to free expression and assembly. The same problem is posed in cases where crowds gather to celebrate, perhaps because their baseball team won the World Series. There is a fine line that police officers must walk between maintaining order and permitting gatherers to enjoy the moment. As the *New York Times* reported, "The death of a 21-year-old college student outside Fenway Park on October 21, [2004,] the night the Red Sox beat the Yankees for the American League pennant, is only the latest reminder that crowd control has reemerged as one of the toughest challenges for police."[69]

Protestors and celebrators are sometimes permitted to gather; other times they are ordered to disperse. What happens when they don't disperse? One department approached the problem in this way:

> Metro entered the scene like something from an epic movie. Down the hill came 25 mounted officers in a column of two, with helmets, face shields, the whole works. And behind them were four Suburbans with our guys on the side wearing tac vests, helmets and face shields, and carrying less-lethal weapons. They were followed by a big blue jail bus.[70]

London Metropolitan Police officers dressed in riot gear practice moving in formation down a street that's on fire from simulated Molotov cocktails. In what other ways do the police help to maintain social order?

John Powell/911 Pictures

Depending on the incident, some agencies use high-tech equipment. Consider the New York City Police Department's approach to crowd control outside the 2004 Republican National Convention:

> Plainclothes police officers on stylish Italian motor scooters herded bicycle riding demonstrators into thick orange nets stretched across intersections. Airborne spy cameras on blimps and helicopters monitored the crowd. Digital video cameras were used to tape arrest scenes and collect evidence for later use in court. A military-inspired sound device was ready to disperse crowds with shouted orders or painful blasts of noise.[71]

Civil disobedience keeps officers busy, and so do crisis situations. Among the common crisis situations are hostage taking, barricaded suspects, and suicide attempts. Ever wonder why the police don't just swarm a building where a person is being held hostage? The obvious answer is that doing so would be dangerous, but why? Because an assault by police threatens the lives of hostages as well as the hostage takers. Hostages could be killed by those holding them before they can be rescued, or they might be killed or injured in the battle between police and the hostage takers. An assault, of course, can also result in loss of life or injury to police personnel. Often, time is on the side of hostage negotiators. Cecil Pearson points out that

> the first two hours of any hostage incident are the most dangerous. Tension, stress, and anxiety are all extremely high in the hostage-taker, hostage, and rescue personnel. As time progresses, the hostage and his captor have the opportunity to emotionally bond and, in general, calm down.[72]

The hostage-captor bonding phenomenon is known as the **Stockholm syndrome**.

Stockholm syndrome
The phenomenon in which a person held as a hostage for some time develops an emotional bond with his or her captor.

INVESTIGATIONS

Criminal investigation is one of the most important police functions—and certainly the most romanticized. Investigation is largely carried out by detectives, sworn officers who have moved up from patrol to something of a "glamour" job wherein they spend their days solving crimes. Detective work would be unnecessary if patrol officers were able to catch all crimes in progress. Of course, they hardly ever do this, in part because they are spread so thin. Hence the need for a dedicated criminal investigations division.

WEB PATROL 8-9
Criminal Investigations
http://www.mycrimekit.com

Large police agencies often have hundreds of detectives in various divisions covering offenses that run the gamut from homicide to check fraud. Indeed, a study by the RAND Corporation revealed that police departments in every city with a population of more than 250,000 people, and 90 percent of those in smaller cities, have dedicated detectives.[73]

The Evolution of Investigations

criminalistics
The use of technology in the service of criminal investigation; the application of scientific techniques to the detection and evaluation of criminal evidence.

trace evidence
Minute, nearly invisible evidence of a crime that would escape all but the most skilled investigators.

anthropometry
A technique developed by Alphonse Bertillon in 1882 for identifying people based on their body measurements. Also called *Bertillon measurements*.

dactylography
An early name for fingerprinting.

At the heart of any investigation is the practice of **criminalistics,** which refers to the scientific study and evaluation of evidence associated with the commission of a crime. Today this term carries connotations of recent technological advancements that detect nearly invisible **trace evidence** (for example, blood stains that someone tried to clean up) or other evidence of a crime that would escape all but the most skilled investigator. But criminalistics is about as old as policing itself. Henry Fielding's Bow Street Runners and Sir Robert Peel's bobbies experienced some early investigative success. The bobbies, for instance, were occasionally removed from their patrol duties to perform investigations.

Anthropometry and Dactylography. Some fundamentals of detective work were developed well over 100 years ago. **Anthropometry** (also known as *Bertillon measurements*), a technique for identifying people based on their body measurements, was developed in 1882. Alphonse Bertillon, who developed this technique, concluded that if just eleven measurements were taken on a person, the odds of finding someone with similar measurements were 4,191,304 to 1.[74] The problem, though, was in attempting to use these measurements to identify those who would be most likely to commit crime.

Bertillon successfully identified some criminals, but his ideas fell out of favor because they were inaccurate and a bit complicated. They were replaced with the more accurate identification practice of **dactylography,** or fingerprinting. Dactylography was proposed for criminal investigation around 1880 in England,[75] but knowledge of fingerprints far predated the routine use of such prints to identify criminals. In the first century, for example, a Roman lawyer by the name of Quintilianus used a bloody fingerprint from what was apparently a crime scene to defend a child who was accused of murdering his father.[76]

Throughout the 1880s, fingerprinting continued to gain popularity as a valid technique for identifying criminal perpetrators. Once it was accepted practice (in the mid-1890s), it was successfully used in a number of high-profile contexts. For example, in 1904, Detective Sergeant Joseph Faurot of the New York City Police Department went to England to study fingerprinting. On his return, he used his newfound knowledge to successfully identify a man accused of burglarizing a suite in the Waldorf-Astoria Hotel. The man claimed to be a respected businessman by the name of James Jones, but Faurot learned, as a result of fingerprints, that he was actually Daniel Nolan, a man with 12 prior convictions for similar crimes.[77]

In another high-profile case, as Will West was being processed into the federal prison in Leavenworth, Kansas, a guard noted that there was already a photograph on file for him. West claimed to have never been in the prison before. After measurements and fingerprints were taken, it became clear that he had been mistaken for another man, William West, who had been in the same prison for some time. The concern was that Will West had tried to change his name to avoid harsh punishment for being a repeat offender, which was, of course, not the case. The two were so close in both physical appearance and Bertillon measurements—not to mention the similarity of their names—as to be virtually indistinguishable. Ultimately, it was their fingerprints that permitted authorities to distinguish one man from the other. This case earned fingerprinting a permanent place in the criminal investigator's toolkit.

WEB PATROL 8-10

The History of Fingerprinting
http://www.mycrimekit.com

Firearms Identification and Beyond. Firearms identification, or ballistics, burst onto the criminalistics scene during the mid-1800s. In 1835, Henry Goddard, who was one of the last Bow Street Runners, was the first to successfully identify a murderer from a spent bullet removed from the victim's body. He noticed that the bullet had similar characteristics as bullets fired from the suspect's gun. When confronted with the evidence, the suspect quickly confessed.[78] Near the turn of the twentieth century, Paul Jeserich, a German chemist, testified against a murder defendant on the grounds that the bullet pulled from the victim matched those fired from the defendant's gun.[79] Firearms identification gained popularity in the early 1900s. The first permanent crime laboratory was established at the Northwestern University Law School and was headed by a former army physician, Calvin Goddard, who is credited with making firearms identification a science through his development of the bullet comparison microscope.[80]

August Vollmer is credited with helping initiate the police professionalism movement, but he also made his mark in early criminal investigations. Vollmer teamed up with a chemist from the University of California, Berkeley, to help identify a poison that was allegedly used to murder someone. He also trained his officers in the identification and preservation of evidence and established a forensics lab in Los Angeles. Vollmer's partnership with the university prompted a number of scientists to become interested in criminal investigations.

Other influential figures of the early twentieth century included Albert Osborn, who wrote *Questioned Documents,*[81] an important work intended to assist in the identification of fabricated and falsified papers and records, and Leone Lattes, who pioneered a blood-typing procedure that assisted in the identification of criminals.[82]

Investigative Goals and Process

In the world of mystery novels and television shows, the goal of investigations is to discover "whodunit." In the real world, though, the goals of detective work are much more complex. They include the following:

- *Determining whether a crime has been committed.* The reporting of an alleged crime and the completion of a report by the responding officer does not necessarily mean that a crime has actually been committed. Consider, for instance, a reported sexual assault. Has it actually occurred, or is it a falsified claim made by a vindictive lover? Thorough investigations are often needed to sort out the truthfulness of such reports when the credibility of the victim is in doubt.
- *Obtaining information and evidence.* This is perhaps the most labor-intensive and least glamourous aspect of detective work. Untold hours of interviewing and questioning can lead to a dead end.
- *Apprehending suspects.* Detectives, as sworn police officers, may elect to arrest the individual they feel was responsible for the crime. Alternatively, they may seek a warrant that would permit any duly authorized peace officer to make the arrest.
- *Recovering stolen property.* In cases of theft, detectives may spend a great deal of time recovering stolen property so it can be used as part of a criminal prosecution before being returned to its rightful owner.
- *Successfully presenting the case to the prosecutor.* One of the detective's foremost responsibilities is presenting an airtight case to the prosecutor so that the correct person can be held to answer for the offense in question.

Criminal investigations typically progress through two stages: (1) the preliminary investigation and (2) the follow-up investigation. The preliminary investigation is the investigation that plays out immediately after the incident is reported. The typical steps include these:

- Attending to emergencies, such as a fleeing suspect
- Securing the scene
- Measuring, photographing, and videotaping the crime scene
- Searching for evidence
- Identifying, collecting, and examining physical evidence (for example, suspected weapons, bloodstains, fingerprints, hair samples)
- Questioning victims, witnesses, possible witnesses, and suspects
- Recording all statements given for later inclusion in the written report[83]

forensic evidence
Physical evidence whose usefulness in a court of law may not be immediately apparent to an untrained observer but can be demonstrated through the application of accepted scientific techniques.

In the vast majority of police departments, either line officers or detectives do all this work. In larger agencies, though, dedicated crime scene investigators get involved, especially in the search for **forensic evidence**. Generally speaking, *evidence* is anything useful in a court of law that tends to prove or disprove the facts at issue. *Physical evidence* is evidence that consists of physical material or traces of physical activity. The term *forensic* refers to that which (1) is of interest to the legal system or (2) must be adapted or suited to use through argumentation—that is, something that is not self-evident. For purposes of policing, forensic evidence, therefore, is physical evidence whose usefulness in a court of law would not be immediately apparent to an untrained observer. Argument, usually through the application of accepted scientific techniques, is necessary to demonstrate the legal value of forensic evidence. This is where crime scene investigators come on board. They often take trace evidence to a laboratory, where further testing is performed with the intent of identifying the perpetrator.

Lisa M. Bilby, 29, is arrested by undercover officers from the Canton (Ohio) Police Department's vice unit during a prostitution sting in October 2006. Bilby was charged with soliciting for prostitution, cocaine possession, and possession of drug paraphernalia. What kinds of crimes do undercover officers investigate?
Michael S. Balash/*The Repository*

The job of crime scene investigators has of course been prominently featured on television programs like *CSI*. The show and its progeny portray the crime scene investigator's life as something of an exciting frontline occupation. In reality, it is often anything but exciting. Much of the work is tedious and plays out behind the scenes. It is also performed more often by trained scientists than by police officers. These individuals, often labeled *forensic experts,* are adept at linking nearly all conceivable forms of evidence to an alleged perpetrator. Examples of such experts include forensic pathologists, toxicologists, anthropologists, odontologists, psychiatrists, and serologists, to name just a few.

The follow-up investigation proceeds through a few more steps, each with a common theme:

- *Continuing the investigation.* This stage, which begins when preliminary work is done, includes conducting follow-up interviews; developing a theory of the crime; analyzing the significance of information and evidence; continuing the search for witnesses; contacting crime lab technicians and assessing their analyses of the evidence; conducting surveillance, interrogations, and polygraph tests, as appropriate; and preparing the case for the prosecutor.
- *Reconstructing the crime.* The investigator seeks a rational theory of the crime, using inductive reasoning. The collected information and evidence are carefully analyzed to develop a theory. Often, a rational theory of a crime is developed with some assistance from the careless criminal. *Verbrecherpech,* or "criminal's bad luck," is an unconscious act of self-betrayal. One of the

major traits of criminals is vanity; their belief in their own cleverness is the key factor in their leaving a vital clue. Investigators look for mistakes.

- *Focusing the investigation.* When this stage is reached, all investigative efforts are directed toward proving that one suspect or group of suspects is guilty of the crime. This decision is based on the investigator's analysis of the relationship between the crime, the investigation, and the habits and attitudes of the suspect or suspects.[84]

WEB PATROL 8-11

American Academy of Forensic Sciences
http://www.mycrimekit.com

UNDERCOVER WORK

Undercover work is closely aligned with investigations. Indeed, many detectives might as well be working undercover because they usually dress in street clothes. For the most part, though, undercover work is common in the investigation and detection of vice crimes, particularly those involving the illicit drug trade.

For obvious reasons, effective drug enforcement would be impossible if it were performed solely by uniformed officers. Police need to infiltrate the criminal underworld in order to successfully nab high-profile criminals. This is seductive work for a number of officers because of the thrill and autonomy it provides. As police scholar Ken Peak has observed, "Since only a few officers are actually selected for undercover assignments, these officers enjoy a professional latitude in their roles, minimal departmental supervision, the ability to exercise greater personal initiative, and a higher degree of professional autonomy than regular patrol officers."[85] What attracts police officers to undercover work, though, can also be their undoing. Several potential problems are associated with working undercover.

Problems with Undercover Work

The lack of supervision and the procedural flexibility that go with undercover work can diminish some officers' respect for procedural rules or tempt them with a number of criminal "perks." The money that changes hands in the illegal drug trade, for example, can be all too enticing to civil servants who aren't necessarily well paid. Undercover work also calls for long and unpredictable hours, which can place not just a physiological strain on officers but also a strain on their personal relationships. One study revealed, for instance, that a high number of undercover assignments over the course of an officer's career was associated with problems like drug use, alcohol abuse, and disciplinary actions.[86] While many officers emerge from undercover work unscathed, not all do:

> A good example of this is the case of a Northern California police officer who participated in a deep-cover operation for eighteen months, riding with the Hell's Angels. He was responsible for a very large number of arrests, including previously almost untouchable higher-level drug dealers. But this was at the cost of heavy drug use, alcoholism, brawling, the break-up of his family, an inability to fit back into routine police work, resignation from the force, several bank robberies, and a prison term.[87]

One of the more celebrated examples of undercover work of late is the partnership between NBC's *Dateline,* the activist group Perverted Justice (an organization based in Portland, Oregon, that is dedicated to identifying adults who involve themselves in sexual chat room conversations with children), and various law enforcement agencies. NBC has aired a number of "To Catch a Predator" *Dateline* episodes featuring the arrests of men who troll Internet chat rooms looking for children to molest. The programs have shown the apprehension of a number of sex offenders, and Perverted Justice continues to rack up an impressive track record of apprehensions on its own. In July 2008, the organization achieved its 279th conviction and reported averaging two arrests per week. Its volunteers continue to pose as children in Web chat rooms and then relay the information that they acquire to local police detectives. They sometimes post chat logs on the organization's website at www.perverted-justice.com.

SUMMARY

- Preventive patrol refers to the practice of canvassing neighborhoods in an effort to discourage people from committing crime. Incident response, which often involves patrol units, includes both emergency response and routine incident response. Traffic enforcement consists of enforcing applicable traffic laws, relieving congestion, and reducing accidents.
- Directed patrol addresses crime in hot spots. Crackdowns, where police officers target a particular area, are the most common example of this. Proactive patrol refers to targeting specific offenses or offenders. Examples include targeting drunk drivers or identifiable repeat offenders.
- Peacekeeping and order maintenance policing involve the management of disorder, quality-of-life policing, and the management of civil disobedience and crisis situations.
- Investigative goals include determining whether a crime has actually been committed, gathering information and evidence, apprehending suspects, recovering stolen property, and successfully presenting the case to the prosecutor. Criminal investigations typically progress through two stages: (1) the preliminary investigation and (2) the follow-up investigation—each of which has its own substages.
- Undercover work is common in policing today, but as this chapter notes, it is especially challenging because it may tempt officers to break the law and can strain personal relationships.

COMING FULL CIRCLE

For Discussion

Return to the questions posed at the start of this chapter. Have any of your answers changed since you read the chapter? What portions of this chapter helped you answer these questions?

Writing Assignment

Using material from this chapter and additional resources, write a 500-word essay in response to one of the questions presented at the beginning of the chapter. Submit your essay to your instructor if asked to do so.

KEY TERMS AND NAMES

anthropometry
broken windows model
civil disobedience
crime peak
crime-prevention program
crime-prevention technique
criminalistics
dactylography
deterrence theory
directed patrol
focused patrol
foot patrol
forensic evidence
hot spot
hot time
Office of Community-Oriented Policing Services (COPS Office)
pretext stop
preventive patrol
proactive policing
quality-of-life offense
racial profiling
response time
saturation patrol
Stockholm syndrome
trace evidence

WEB INTERACTIVITY

Read Amnesty International's publication *Understanding Police: A Resource for Human Rights Activists,* available on the Web at http://www.amnesty.nl/documenten/phrp/Understanding%20policing%20Part%201.pdf. The report begins by saying that the "[p]olice can be violators of human rights, but at the same time they play an essential role in the protection of human rights." Thus, says the report, "[p]olicing is . . . at the heart of a broad spectrum of human rights discourses." After you have read the report, summarize what it says about how the police can be human rights protectors, and submit your findings to your instructor if asked to do so.

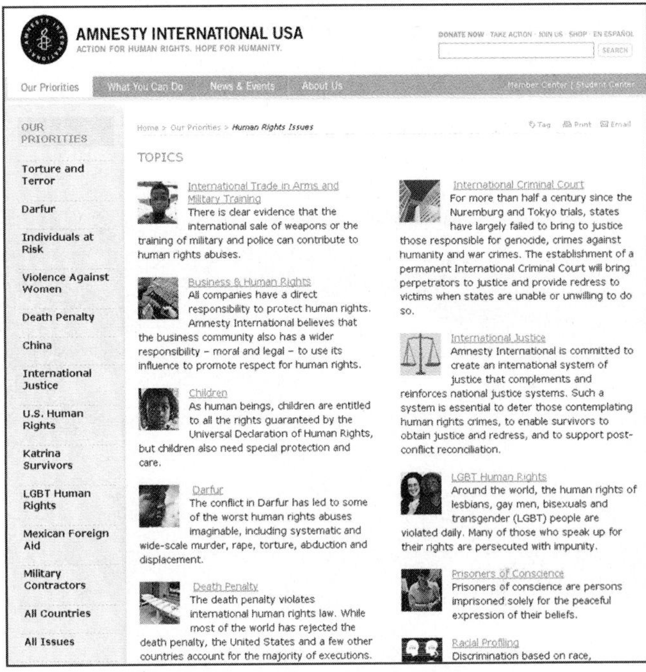

Source: Amnesty International USA

REVIEW QUESTIONS

1. Distinguish between preventive patrol, the response role, and the traffic function. Summarize the leading issues associated with each.
2. Distinguish between directed patrol and proactive policing. In your opinion, which approach is better?
3. How does the peacekeeping and order maintenance role frequently manifest itself?
4. What are the investigative goals identified by this chapter? What is involved in the investigative process?
5. What are the possible problems associated with undercover work?

chapter nine

INTELLIGENCE, INFORMATION, AND SPECIAL PROBLEMS

LEARNING OBJECTIVES

After reading this chapter, students should be able to:

1. Define *intelligence-led policing* and provide examples of it.
2. Discuss advances in information and communications technology as they apply to policing.
3. Identify five special groups or problems that the police must increasingly deal with.

LAMBETH PALACE
RD
PALL MALL / WATERLOO PLACE
1020234
0547452
0410555
PAS Westminster 3
OXFORD ST / REGENT ST
POD
14
SOR 3
1010212
MILTON SECOND ON GRID FOR TOMORROW'S FRENCH GRAND PRIX
SPORT
SKY NEWS

THINK ABOUT IT

Every week, [Los Angeles Police Department (LAPD)] Chief William Bratton shows up at one of his police stations, demanding answers to the city's crime problems. . . . Every week, division captains step up to the microphone and tell the chief which crimes are up, and which are down—and offer their best explanations as to why. Every week, Bratton's commanders are dressed down, expected to have the answers or incur his wrath. . . . Welcome to Bratton's Compstat crime-tracking meetings, his way of making division bosses more accountable for crimes on their turf.[1]

Chief Bratton brought Compstat to Los Angeles from his years as commissioner of the New York City Police Department (NYPD). The strategy has been credited with reducing crime, but some critics have alleged that something other than good policing is at work. In 2007, the *LA Voice* published an article asking, "Is LAPD fudging our crime stats?"[2] The article alleged that *crime* was not actually down, but that *crime reporting* was. The *Voice* pointed to an anecdotal account of LAPD officers who had allegedly refrained from arresting a drunk driver, instead asking him not to drive until he sobered up. Why? So they wouldn't have to make an arrest and file an official report of the incident. These kinds of claims infuriate Detective Jeff Godown, the officer in charge of the LAPD's Compstat unit, who says,

> I can assure you that no Captain, Commander, or Chief level staff officer is "cooking the books" to reduce crime in his area to make themselves look good. . . . I know of no LAPD command or staff officer who would "risk" their career by encouraging, or participating in, the "fudging" of crime statistics. . . . The anecdotal evidence of LAPD personnel attempting to artificially impact the accurate reporting of crime, as may be occurring in other jurisdictions, does not wash.[3]

The *LA Voice* article and Detective Godown's response to it represent a clash of perspectives and interests in the ongoing struggle to reduce crime. Throughout America, police departments are continually being pressured to reduce crime. They are also increasingly pressured to make decisions based on timely intelligence and careful analysis of crime trends. Crime statistics have been falling for over a decade, but it may be that crime numbers can only decline so far before hitting an impenetrable floor. As one critic said, "When you finally get a real handle on crime, you eventually hit a wall where you can't push it down any more. Compstat does not recognize that wall so the commanders have to get 'creative' to keep their numbers going down."[4] These kinds of observations raise several questions to keep in mind as you read this chapter:

1. What is Compstat, and is it an effective crime-reduction technique?
2. Compstat is just one example of the movement to make policing more effective. Is there a potential downside to this effort?
3. To what extent can information and intelligence be abused?
4. How have increased amounts of technology-generated information affected policing in America?
5. Has enhanced technology affected policing for better or for worse? How?

INTRODUCTION

Police departments, like other public agencies, have limited resources. They are almost wholly dependent on taxpayer funds for their continued existence, and budgets dictate their daily activities. Although they can always ask for more money, departments everywhere must make the most of available resources. Consequently, there can be only so many officers on the ground, and only limited funds are available to pay for overtime and to hire additional officers. Through experience and research, police departments have also come to realize that traditional responses to crime, such as preventive patrol, have met with limited success. Fortunately, relatively inexpensive and widely available technological advances are aiding police departments today in their crime-fighting efforts, especially in the areas of information gathering and communications.

This chapter begins by introducing the concept of intelligence-led policing. Not to be confused with evidence-based policing, which we have featured throughout this book, intelligence-led policing is about gathering information, analyzing it, and using the results to target specific crime problems. Next, we look at various advances in information and communications technology, including crime-mapping programs and Compstat. Finally, the chapter concludes with a look at the police response to several special groups and problems, including youthful offenders, the mentally ill, the illegal drug trade, gangs, and domestic violence.

INTELLIGENCE-LED POLICING

In 2005, the U.S. Department of Justice embraced **intelligence-led policing (ILP)** as an important technique that American law enforcement agencies can employ in the battle against terrorism.[5] ILP can also be used to target other pressing problems, such as property crime, narcotics violations, and organized crime. Not every agency has the staff or resources needed to create a dedicated intelligence unit. Even without an intelligence unit, however, a law enforcement organization should have the ability to effectively utilize the information and intelligence products that are developed and disseminated by organizations at all levels of government. In other words, even though a police agency may not have its own resources for analyzing all the information it acquires, it should still be able to mount an effective response to credible threat information that it receives. The following sections take a closer look at the nature of intelligence, why it is important, the intelligence process, and the nature of intelligence-led policing, especially in comparison to some other approaches we discuss elsewhere in this book.

intelligence-led policing (ILP)
The collection and analysis of information to produce an intelligence end product designed to inform police decision making at both the tactical and strategic levels.[i] Also called *intelligence-driven policing*.

Intelligence

What is intelligence? It is tempting to liken it to information, but they are not the same. Rather, **intelligence** has been defined as the sum of information and analysis.[6] Another definition is "a formal process of taking information and turning it into knowledge while ensuring that the information is collected, stored, and disseminated appropriately."[7] Police expert David Carter's *Law Enforcement Intelligence: A Guide for State, Local, and Tribal Law Enforcement Agencies* defines criminal intelligence as "a synergistic product intended to provide meaningful and trustworthy direction to law enforcement decision makers about complex criminality, criminal enterprises, criminal extremists, and terrorists."[8]

intelligence
Information that has been analyzed and integrated into a useful perspective.

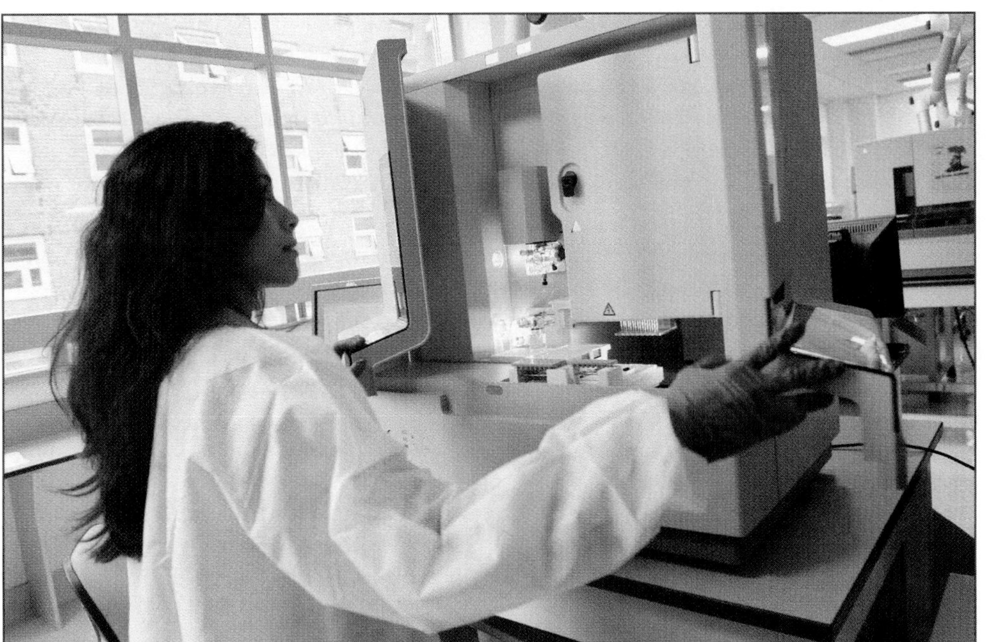

A crime lab technician operates a genetic analyzer at the office of the Chief Medical Examiner in New York City. How is her work an essential part of the intelligence-gathering process that is necessary for effective policing?
Tina Fineberg/AP Wide World Photos

criminal intelligence
"A synergistic product intended to provide meaningful and trustworthy direction to law enforcement decision makers about complex criminality, criminal enterprises, criminal extremists, and terrorists."[ii] A "process that evaluates information collected from diverse sources, integrates the relevant information into a cohesive package, and produces a conclusion or estimate about a criminal phenomenon by using the scientific approach to problem solving."[iii]

Intelligence is information that has been analyzed and integrated into a useful perspective. The information used in the development of effective intelligence is typically gathered from many sources, such as newspapers, surveillance, covert operations, financial records, electronic eavesdropping, interviews, and interrogations. Law enforcement intelligence, or **criminal intelligence,** is the result of a "process that evaluates information collected from diverse sources, integrates the relevant information into a cohesive package, and produces a conclusion or estimate about a criminal phenomenon by using the scientific approach to problem solving."[9] While criminal investigation is typically part of the intelligence-gathering process, the intelligence function of a police department is more exploratory and more broadly focused than a single criminal investigation.[10]

Key to these definitions is the idea that, without analysis, there is no intelligence. What, then, is analysis? It is not just information processing by trained crime analysts. Instead, "analysis requires thoughtful contemplation that results in conclusions and recommendations."[11] With this in mind, it is useful to distinguish between various types and levels of intelligence.

Tactical and Strategic Intelligence. Carter points out that there are two types of intelligence: tactical and strategic. **Tactical intelligence** "includes gaining or developing information related to threats of terrorism or crime and using this information to apprehend offenders, harden targets, and use strategies that will eliminate or mitigate the threat."[12] **Strategic intelligence,** in contrast, provides information to decision makers about the changing nature of threats for the purpose of "developing response strategies and reallocating resources"[13] to accomplish effective prevention.

WEB PATROL 9-1
The Law Enforcement Intelligence Function
http://www.mycrimekit.com

tactical intelligence
A type of intelligence that "includes gaining or developing information related to threats of terrorism or crime and using this information to apprehend offenders, harden targets, and use strategies that will eliminate or mitigate the threat."[iv]

strategic intelligence
A type of intelligence that provides information to decision makers about the changing nature of threats, enabling them to develop response strategies and reallocate resources for effective threat prevention.

Levels of Intelligence. There are four levels of intelligence. Level 1 intelligence is the highest. According to one study, "the law enforcement agency at [level 1] employs an intelligence manager, intelligence officers, and professional intelligence analysts."[14] The secretive Financial Crimes Enforcement Network (FINCEN) fits into this category. "Level 2 intelligence includes police agencies that produce tactical and strategic intelligence for internal consumption. . . . These agencies generally use intelligence to support investigations rather than to direct operations."[15] The typical agency at this level is a state police agency that may have intelligence units or officers on the payroll. Level 3 intelligence, the second most common form, includes local law enforcement agencies with anywhere from a few dozen to hundreds of sworn personnel. These agencies sometimes produce their own intelligence but often rely on other higher-level (state or federal) agencies that specialize in intelligence gathering. Level 3 agencies should not always rely on outside help, however. According to one study,

> While smaller agencies may not be able to devote a full-time position to the criminal intelligence function . . . [they] need to understand the proactive concept of criminal intelligence and recognize that most law enforcement agencies, regardless of size, are susceptible to organized criminal activity that may extend beyond jurisdictional boundaries. Their personnel should be trained to recognize and report indications of organized crime, gang activity, and criminal extremist and terrorist activity. The information should be shared with intelligence-trained personnel from neighboring agencies.[16]

Finally, level 4 intelligence characterizes the vast majority of law enforcement agencies in the United States. "If they assign someone to intelligence operations, that person generally has multiple responsibilities and is often a narcotics officer, gang officer, or counter-terrorism officer."[17]

The Importance of Intelligence

Law enforcement agencies at all levels depend on intelligence and cannot function adequately without it. The following subsections elaborate on the importance of intelligence for decision making, planning, strategic targeting, and crime prevention.

Decision Making. It is common for law enforcement agencies to gather information and to decide what to do with it. The problem is that the abundance of information, especially in large agencies, can lead to decisions that are based on less-than-perfect information. Having the most accurate and complete intelligence aids in decision making. Indeed, "experience shows that intelligence and analyses must be strengthened to meet the threat of terrorism against the United States."[18]

Planning. Planning also depends on intelligence. Unfortunately, though, planning in many agencies is done without sufficient intelligence, such as the nature of specific crime problems facing an area. The United Kingdom's **National Intelligence Model** stresses that police planners should adopt a business model:

> The law enforcement *business* is about the successful management and reduction of crime and other law enforcement problems. . . . The vital central ingredient in successful planning is identification and understanding, [including] an accurate picture of the business, what is actually happening on the ground, the nature and extent of the problem, the trends, and where the main threats lie.[19]

National Intelligence Model
The United Kingdom's law enforcement planning model, which stresses a business approach to the management and reduction of crime.

Strategic Targeting. As noted at the beginning of the chapter, resources are in scarce supply in most public agencies, including police organizations. Intelligence enables administrators to carefully target their efforts to achieve the best results with limited funds. Marilyn Peterson gives this example:

> To help fight terrorism and domestic extremism, the California Department of Justice examines group characteristics, criminal predicates, target analyses, and intervention consequences to determine which groups pose the greatest threat to the state. By reviewing and comparing this information, the agency can prioritize which groups require the earliest intervention.[20]

In other words, strategic targeting is about focusing on the individuals, groups, or locations where success is most likely.

Crime Prevention. Every police agency hopes to prevent crime rather than just respond to it. Intelligence from previous crimes, for instance, may arm decision makers with the information they need to prevent similar crimes from occurring. Also, "comparing the indicators from local neighborhoods, analysts can anticipate crime trends and agencies can take preventive measures to intervene or mitigate the impact of those crimes."[21] With no information, the best police agencies can hope for is to respond to crime, certainly something community members would prefer less than prevention.

WEB PATROL 9-2
Stopping Crime in Real Time
http://www.mycrimekit.com

The Intelligence Process

The Global Intelligence Working Group, consisting of approximately 30 intelligence professionals, met throughout 2003 to come up with a plan for intelligence sharing. The final product was called the **National Criminal Intelligence Sharing Plan (NCISP).** It was approved and released by the U.S. attorney general in October 2003. Several recommendations for improved intelligence gathering were offered, and the group also organized the process into six steps (Figure 9-1). Note that the process is circular and that it starts with planning and direction. According to a recent report, *planning and direction* require

> an agency to identify the outcomes it wants to achieve from its collection efforts. This identification directs the scope of the officers' and agents' investigations—for example, a straightforward inquiry to identify crime groups operating in a jurisdiction or a more complex inquiry to determine the likelihood that criminal extremists will attack a visiting dignitary.[22]

Next, *collection* refers to gathering and processing information. This can be accomplished through several strategies, including physical surveillance, electronic surveillance (for example, wiretapping), confidential informants, newspaper reports, and so on. Third, *processing* consists of sifting through all this information to organize and collate it. *Analysis* converts the information to intelligence. As one official put it, "Without the explicit performance of this function, the

National Criminal Intelligence Sharing Plan (NCISP)
"A formal intelligence sharing initiative that addresses the security and intelligence needs recognized after the tragic events of September 11, 2001. It describes a nationwide communications capability that will link together all levels of law enforcement personnel, including officers on the streets, intelligence analysts, unit commanders, and police executives, for the purpose of sharing critical data."[v]

Figure 9-1 • The Intelligence Process

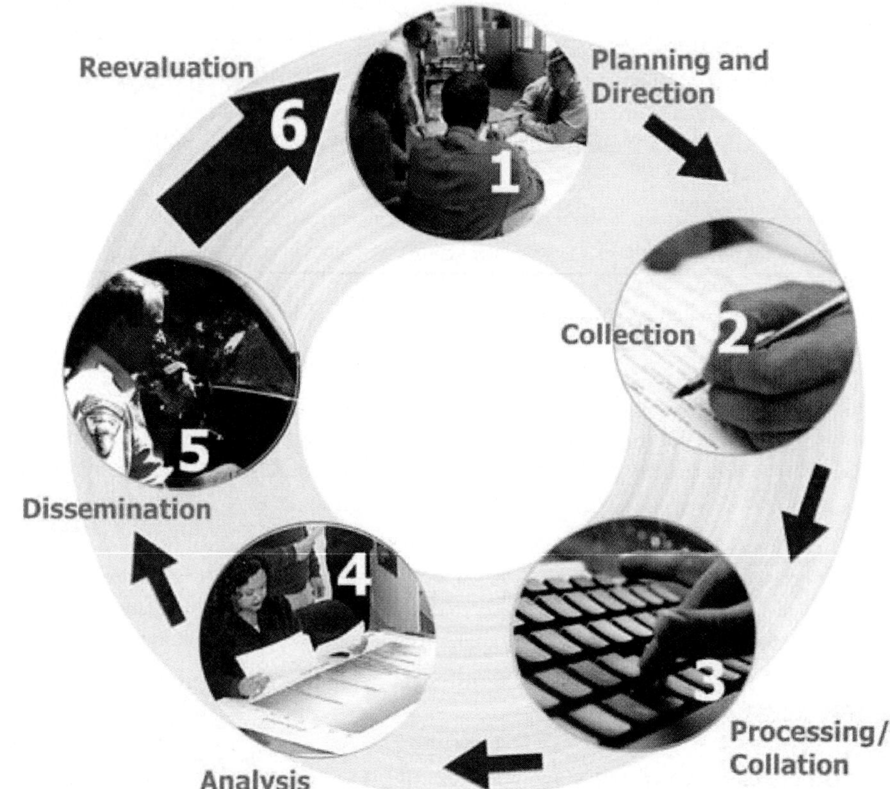

Source: Office of Justice Programs, *National criminal intelligence sharing plan* (Washington, DC: U.S. Department of Justice, 2003), p. 6.

intelligence unit is nothing but a file unit."[23] Analysis includes crime analysis (for example, crime-pattern analysis with mapping software), but it also includes investigative analysis (bank record analysis) and strategic analysis (risk assessment). The next step is *dissemination,* which is the process of getting intelligence to the decision makers who need it. Finally, *reevaluation* is concerned with reanalysis of intelligence products to determine their accuracy and effectiveness. According to a report on the subject, "One way to reevaluate intelligence is to include a feedback form with each product that is disseminated."[24]

In the Maryland fusion center's "watch section" outside of Baltimore, watch commander Jeffrey L. Wobbleton, right, speaks with one of the center's working specialists. What is a fusion center?

Robert A. Reeder/*The Washington Post*/Pictopia.com

The Nature of Intelligence-Led Policing

We have spent significant time discussing intelligence in general, but what *exactly* is intelligence-led policing? The term originated in the United Kingdom.[25] Specifically, the Kent Constabulary came up with the concept in response to a rise in property crime—a rise that occurred while police resources were being cut. Originally called the *Kent Policing Model*, this approach prioritized calls for service and referred nonemergency calls to other agencies, when appropriate. This freed up resources so that officers could focus on the property crimes that were on the rise. The result was a property crime drop of 24 percent over three years. According to one assessment of this effort,

> [I]ntelligence-led policing focuses on key criminal activities. Once crime problems are identified and quantified through intelligence assessments, key criminals can be targeted for investigation and prosecution. Because the groups and individuals targeted in Kent were those responsible for significant criminal activity, the ultimate reduction in crime was considerable.[26]

Since it has been imported into the United States, intelligence-led policing has remained largely the same, with some minor twists. For example, it has benefited from so-called **fusion centers.** These are essentially intelligence-gathering units, often collaborative efforts that serve various agencies. As Peterson explains, fusion centers

fusion center
An intelligence-gathering unit, often constituted as a collaborative effort, that serves various agencies.

> may support anti-terrorism and other crime-specific objectives. The centers may search numerous public and private databases to gather and analyze information. They may also generate intelligence products of their own, providing overviews of terrorist or other crime groups, analysis of trends, and other items of information for dissemination to participating agencies.[27]

Intelligence-Led versus Problem-Oriented Policing. Intelligence-led policing sounds similar to problem-oriented policing (see Chapter 10), but the two are somewhat different. Problem-oriented policing seeks to control crime through the study of problems. Common to problem-oriented policing, too, is the scanning, analysis, response, assessment (SARA) model.

Intelligence-led policing basically takes problem-oriented policing to the next level; it does the same for community-oriented policing. These strategies "have been used for crime analysis, which is statistical and incident-based, rather than strategic intelligence analysis, which looks at large-scope problems or models."[28] In other words, intelligence-based policing takes problem-oriented policing beyond the level of a single police agency.

Intelligence-led policing may also sound something like Compstat. As Table 9-1 shows, they are similar but not quite the same.

Table 9-1 • Comparison of Compstat and Intelligence-Led Policing

Compstat	Commonalities	Intelligence-Led Policing
• Single jurisdiction • Incident driven • Street crime and burglary • Crime mapping • Time sensitive (24-hour feedback and response) • Disrupt crime series (e.g., burglary ring) • Drives operations: – Patrol – Tactical unit – Investigators • Analysis of offender MOs	• Both have a goal of prevention. • Both require – Organizational flexibility – Consistent information input – A significant analytic component • Both are driven from the bottom up with respect to operational needs.	• Multiple jurisdictions • Threat driven • Criminal enterprises and terrorism • Commodity flow; trafficking and transiting logistics • Strategic • Disrupt enterprises • Drives operations: – JTIF – Organized crime investigations – Task forces • Analysis of enterprise MOs

Source: Office of Community-Oriented Policing Services, *Intelligence-led policing: The integration of community policing and law enforcement intelligence, Part 4* (Washington, DC: COPS Office, n.d.), p. 43. Web available at http://www.cops.usdoj.gov/pdf/e09042536_Chapter_04.pdf. Accessed July 24, 2008.

Examples of Intelligence-Led Policing. A recent Bureau of Justice Assistance report offers some examples of how intelligence-led policing could be further utilized throughout the United States. Here are three of them:

- A county sheriff's office identifies narcotics control as its top priority and develops strategies accordingly. The office targets known offenders and groups, shuts down open-air drug markets and crack houses, and participates in school-based drug-awareness programs to help prevent drug use.
- A statewide agency identifies vehicle insurance fraud as a top area for enforcement. The agency targets those involved in staged accidents, identifies communities in which insurance fraud is prevalent, looks for similar methods of operation that may indicate ongoing fraudulent activity, and mounts a public education campaign.
- A police agency in a small city makes safe streets a priority. The agency focuses on directed enforcement in identified hot spots. It also targets career criminals whose apprehension will significantly reduce the number of crimes being committed. Preventive measures include enhanced patrols, improved street lighting, and crime watch programs.[29]

Law Enforcement Assistance and Partnership (LEAP) Strategy
A plan introduced in the U.S. Congress that called for the establishment of a national center for intelligence-led policing.

As recently as December 2006, U.S. Representative Bennie G. Thompson (D-MS) released a plan called the **Law Enforcement Assistance and Partnership (LEAP) Strategy,** in which he called for the establishment of a national center for intelligence-led policing. Initiatives proposed by others include providing funding for police chiefs to help defray the costs of intelligence gathering, improving border intelligence, providing funding for tribal participation, establishing a national counterterrorism center to include law enforcement officers in intelligence gathering, issuing security clearances to law enforcement executives who need them, and tracking the progress of intelligence-led policing efforts.[30] It will be most interesting to follow these developments over time.

INFORMATION AND COMMUNICATIONS TECHNOLOGY

WEB PATROL 9-3
Gunshot Location Systems for Public Safety
http://www.mycrimekit.com

Advances in information and communications technology have worked wonders for law enforcement. From helping investigators reconstruct crime scenes to facilitating information sharing between agencies, they have transformed the way police do business. This section briefly examines some of the more interesting developments in this area.

Computer-Aided Drafting

computer-aided drafting (CAD)
A technology, adapted to meet the needs of police officers and criminal investigators, that facilitates the drafting of crime scenes on a computer so that they can be viewed three-dimensionally.

Computer-aided drafting (CAD) is not a law enforcement technology per se, but it has been adapted to meet the needs of police officers and criminal investigators. Basically, CAD permits drafting of crime scenes on a computer that can then be viewed three-dimensionally. Gone are the days of convincing jury members to convict based on tedious one-dimensional drawings and photographs. A three-dimensional image puts jurors at the crime scene almost as if they were actually there.

CAD software has also been developed for animation purposes, enabling viewers to get a feel for the perpetrators' movements, as well. As this technology continues to develop, it is becoming more portable. For example, the Department of Energy has been working on a device that officers in the field can use to beam the information they gather (via pictures, laser range finders, Global Positioning System devices, etc.) to the crime lab for instant expert advice and accurate recording of the crime scene.[31]

CAD programs offer several advantages. First, they create images that are professional in their appearance, an improvement over traditional methods of drafting crime scene images by hand and relying on simple photographs. This is of great importance if the images are to be shared with jurors in a criminal trial. In this vein, the next CAD advantage is that the software minimizes duplication of effort; there is no need to draft separate images for investigators and jurors. With a few keystrokes, a large image can be printed for sharing with a jury.

The software makes crime scene investigation much cheaper, too. Gone are the days when draftspeople or engineers needed to take precise measurements of every detail of a crime scene. Delays in crime-scene reconstruction are now largely a thing of the past. Perhaps most important, it is easy to alter images as new information becomes available, thus eliminating the need to redraw the entire image.

Computer-Assisted Training

Computers also enhance the training of law enforcement officers. Veteran officers may have had the opportunity to participate in one of the old "shoot/don't shoot" training exercises in front of a television screen with a noninteractive video. Those days are largely over; computers have helped make such exercises much more realistic and dramatic.

One of the new technologies in this area, the **firearms training system (FATS)**, is about as realistic as shooting a simulated firearm can get. It is a full-size, fully interactive device, not unlike flight and driving simulators. Moreover, it fully encases trainees in a particular surrounding rather than simply putting them in front of a television screen. This makes the training more realistic, as threats can come from any direction on the job. The technology is also relatively affordable and portable.

firearms training system (FATS)
A full-size, fully interactive training device, not unlike flight and driving simulators, that exposes police trainees to realistic shooting scenarios. The realism is enhanced by fully encasing the trainees in a particular surrounding rather than simply putting them in front of a television screen.

VirTra Systems, which markets FATS devices, describes one of its training simulators in this way:

> The IVR 360™ series training system is a projection-based 360-degree simulator with integrated tracking developed for high-fidelity "fourth-generation" warfare, situational awareness, judgmental use-of-force, and marksmanship training. The IVR 360™ enables users to experience a 360-degree *immersive virtual reality*™ training simulation utilizing state-of-the-art projection technology. The system's features include precision-tracking for up to six trainees (or up to 24 trainees in reconfigurable marksmanship mode), instructor's station, special effects, optional motion system, and 360-degree high-quality digital imagery.[32]

Another company has gone so far as to develop a simulator that actually pelts the trainee with large-caliber nylon balls when he or she makes a mistake, further approximating reality. One such device, the Professional Range Instruction Simulator (PRISim), has been described as "training so real, you will not call it a simulator."[33] AIS Solutions, the company behind the device, says this:

> PRISim™ puts trainees into the middle of an interactive theatre to cause responses to potentially deadly mistakes, indecision, sudden fear, partial understanding, blindside surprise, eye-blink response and life or death choices. The PRISim™ system gives trainees the coaching they could never get in actual field operations and provides situational experiences far beyond the capability of conventional training. . . . The PRISim™ ShootBack cannon is a devastatingly effective tool to train effective use of cover. An instructor-aimed cannon is mounted above the centre of the screen to fire 17mm caliber nylon projectiles synchronized with the video scenario. The cannon fires accurate single, 3-round burst or full auto hostile fire.[34]

WEB PATROL 9-4
Development of Crime Forecasting and Mapping Systems for Use by Police
http://www.mycrimekit.com

Crime Mapping

It used to be that patterns of criminal activity were identified on **pin maps.** Colored stick pins would literally be stuck in various places on a map of a city, county, district, precinct, or other area. Different colors corresponded to different types of crimes. This approach, while crude, permitted police to identify problem areas and patterns of criminal activity. The problem was that the maps were one-dimensional and could easily get crowded with pins, especially in the case of minor crimes that occurred with great frequency. The maps were also static, meaning that they could not easily be manipulated to serve different purposes, such as tracking certain types of crime over time. Pin maps were large and could take up significant wall space. Enter crime-mapping software.

pin map
An early crime-mapping technique that used colored pins to track criminal events on a map of the police department's jurisdictional area.

Figure 9-2 • A Geographic Information System Crime Map Created with Maptitude Mapping Software Showing Motor Vehicle Thefts in Newtown, MA

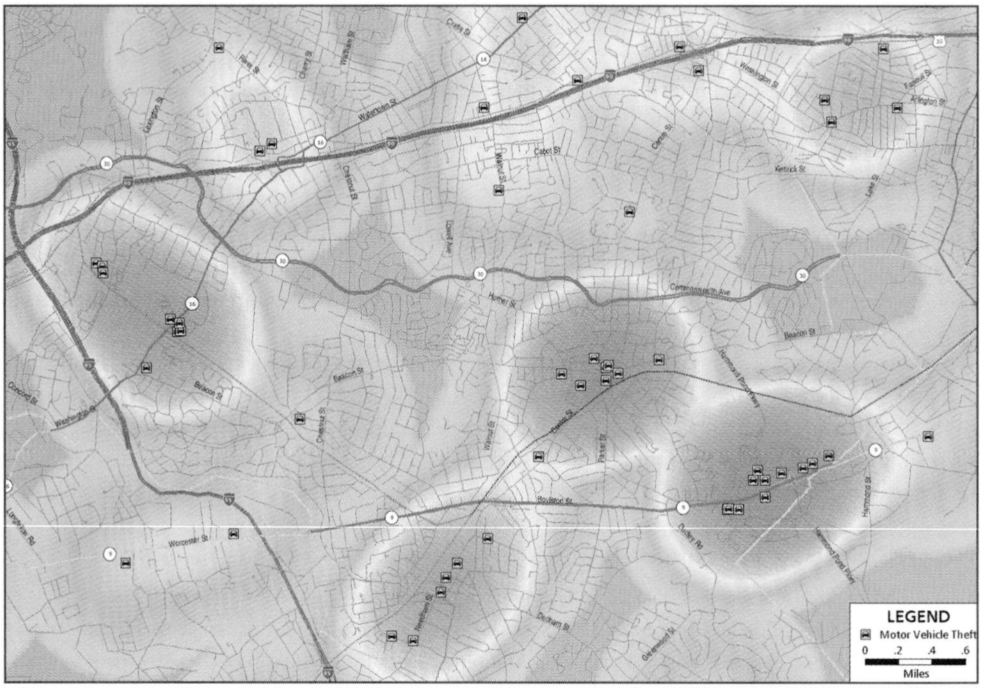

Source: Produced by the Maptitude mapping software, © 2008 Caliper Corporation. Reprinted with permission.

computerized crime mapping
A computer-based system that combines a geographic information system with crime statistics generated by a police department, allowing crime data to be plotted on a map.

Crime Mapping Research Center (CMRC)
A U.S. Justice Department agency that promotes research, training, and technical assistance for police agencies around the country and assists them in their crime-mapping efforts. Also called the *Mapping and Analysis for Public Safety (MAPS) Program.*

Computerized crime mapping combines geographic information systems with crime statistics generated by a police department so that the crimes can be plotted on a map (Figure 9-2). The result is a clean image with details concerning the frequency with which certain crimes take place in given areas. This is advantageous because it provides a cleaner image than a dense cluster of pins can. More importantly, though, computerized crime maps can be overlaid with other information, such as demographic or law enforcement data (for example, unemployment levels or known gang territories).

Crime mapping has become so commonplace that the National Institute of Justice (an agency of the U.S. Justice Department) has created the **Crime Mapping Research Center (CMRC).** The center promotes research, training, and technical assistance for police agencies around the country and assists them in their mapping efforts. CMRC is an enthusiastic supporter of computerized crime mapping for some simple reasons:

> Mapping crime can help law enforcement protect citizens more effectively in the areas they serve. Simple maps that display the locations where crimes or concentrations of crimes have occurred can be used to help direct patrols to places [where] they are most needed. Policy makers in police departments might use more complex maps to observe trends in criminal activity, and maps may prove invaluable in solving criminal cases. For example, detectives may use maps to better understand the hunting patterns of serial criminals and to hypothesize where these offenders might live.

WEB PATROL 9-5
LAPD Crime Maps
http://www.mycrimekit.com

Geographic Profiling

geographic profiling
The use of crime-mapping technology to identify the likely whereabouts or residences of repeat or serial offenders.

Geographic profiling, which makes use of crime-mapping technology, allows investigators to identify the likely whereabouts or residences of repeat or serial offenders. Environmental Criminology Research, Inc. (ECRI), a company that develops and supplies software for this purpose, describes geographic profiling in this way:

> Geographic profiling is an investigative methodology that uses the locations of a connected series of crimes to determine the most probable area of offender residence. It is generally ap-

plied in cases of serial murder, rape, arson, and robbery, though it can be used in single crimes (auto theft, burglary, bombing, etc.) that involve multiple scenes or other significant geographic characteristics.[35]

Geographic profiling can be made particularly effective when it is combined with databases used to track serial offenders. For example, the Washington State Attorney General's Office uses the **Homicide Investigation and Tracking (HITS) System,** which ties various databases together, including gang files, sex offender registries, parole records, and department of motor vehicle records, so that they can be searched simultaneously. According to University of Nevada at Reno criminologist Ken Peak,

Homicide Investigation and Tracking System (HITS)
A geographic profiling system that ties various databases together (gang files, sex offender registries, parole records, and department of motor vehicle records) to facilitate simultaneous database searches.

> When an agency in the state has a major crime in its jurisdiction, the case is loaded into a central system, which scans every database and linking file for connections by comparing eyewitness descriptions of a suspect and vehicle. It then builds a dataset containing profiles of the offender, the victims, and the incidents. The dataset then goes into a geographic information system, where the program selects and maps the names and addresses of those suspects whose method of operation fits the crime being investigated.[36]

WEB PATROL 9-6
Mapping and Analysis for Public Safety
http://www.mycrimekit.com

Crime Intelligence Systems

Nowadays, nearly every patrol officer has a laptop computer in his or her car that is linked to various databases, such as vehicle registration records and criminal history information. Recently, though, the databases have become increasingly sophisticated. One of them, known as **CalGang** (in California) or GangNet (in other states) contains detailed information on known gang members that officers in the field can quickly access. SRA International, a provider of such software, explains the need for it:

CalGang
A sophisticated software database of known gang members that field officers in California can access quickly. *GangNet* is a modified version of the software that is used nationwide.

> For much of the country, violent, gang-related crimes are a growing trend. Solving these cases is complicated by gang members' mobility and growing realm of influence. SRA's GangNet solution is a browser-based investigative, analysis, and statistical resource for recording and tracking gang members and their activities. The database system enables information sharing on relationships between individuals involved in gangs. GangNet gives law enforcement officials a tool to identify individuals, vehicles, tattoos, gang symbols, and locations, and to facilitate work on gang-related cases. Additional features, such as mapping and facial recognition, are continuously being added to the system.[37]

A civilian police photographer takes photographs outside of London's City Hall on May 2, 2008. What role does photography play in policing today? How can it help in the development of actionable intelligence?

Photo by Marc Vallee/marcvallee.co.uk/© Marc Vallee 2008

DOES IT WORK?

Compstat

The effect of Compstat on crime has not received much research attention. Some researchers have attributed drops in crime to Compstat and similar managerial approaches,[1] but to date, no one has conducted an experiment to conclusively determine whether Compstat directly affects crime. As one researcher observes, "It is too early to tell if Compstat can sustain the claims of its supporters that it is responsible for falling crime rates."[2]

Recently, one team of researchers worked to examine the effects of Compstat on crime in New York City.[3] They found that New York's downward trend in homicide was consistent with similar trends in other cities around the country during the same time period, so they concluded that Compstat could not have been responsible for the drop. Theirs is certainly not the last word, however, because their research design had limitations. For example, it did not compare New York City to a control city. We will have to wait to see what other researchers find. At least one other study suggests that the mere implementation of Compstat may be easier said than done.[4]

[1]E. Silverman, *NYPD battles crime: Innovative strategies in policing* (Boston: Northeastern University Press, 1999).
[2]W. F. Walsh, "Compstat: An analysis of an emerging police managerial paradigm," *Policing: An International Journal of Police Strategies and Management* 24 (2001): 347–62, quote on p. 356.
[3]R. Rosenfeld, R. Fornango, and E. Baumer, "Did Ceasefire, Compstat, and Exile reduce homicide?" *Criminology and Public Policy* 4 (2005): 419–50.
[4]J. J. Willis, S. D. Mastrofski, and D. Weisburd, "Compstat and bureaucracy: A case study of challenges and opportunities for change," *Justice Quarterly* 21 (2004): 463–96.

Compstat

During the early years of his tenure as police commissioner of New York City, William Bratton called for weekly meetings with representatives from each of the NYPD's eight bureaus. Deputy Commissioner Jack Maple, in conjunction with other high-ranking officials, placed pressure on the bureaus to generate crime statistics, which had not been kept up-to-date at the time. Precincts began to measure criminal activity more carefully; then the results were computerized and assembled into a document known as the *Compstat book*.[38] The crime figures reported in the Compstat book were eventually used to hold precinct commanders responsible for the crime rates in their areas.

Compstat
A goal-oriented police management process that relies heavily on computer technology and accountability of top-level administrators.

Compstat is an acronym for "computer statistics" or, in some locations "compare statistics." The NYPD program has been widely imitated around the country,[39] and the programs have several different designations (Figure 9-3). One researcher has defined Compstat as "a goal-oriented strategic management process that uses computer technology, operational strategy and managerial accountability to structure the manner in which a police department provides crime-control services."[40]

Generally speaking, Compstat emphasizes four important elements: (1) accurate and timely intelligence; (2) effective tactics; (3) rapid deployment; and (4) relentless follow-up and assessment.[41] The logic behind the intelligence aspect is that "information describing how and where crimes are committed, as well as who criminals are, must be available to all levels of policing."[42] "Tactics are designed to respond directly to facts discovered during the intelligence gathering process."[43] Rapid deployment is important and often involves quick and ef-

WEB PATROL 9-7
The Compstat Pathway
http://www.mycrimekit.com

Figure 9-3 • Names of Compstat-Like Programs in Various Locations

Location	Program
Baltimore	CrimeStac
El Paso	Strategic Analysis of Crime (SAC)
Los Angeles County Sheriff	Sheriff's Critical Issues Forum (SCIF)
Los Angeles Police Department	CompStat (was called FASTRAC before Bratton)
Minneapolis	Computer-Optimized Deployment (CODEFOR)
New Orleans	Comstat
New York	CompStat
San Antonio	Management Accountability Program (MAP)

Figure 9-4 • General Elements of the Compstat Model

1. *Accurate, timely intelligence that is communicated to all relevant parties.* Intelligence includes providing commanders, supervisors, and other officers with information identifying the types of crimes that are occurring, pinpointing where they are occurring, and identifying the types of offenders committing those crimes.
2. *Effective tactics and strategies based on intelligence to achieve desired outcomes.* Tactics and strategies must be based on facts—that is, on the intelligence developed via the program.
3. *Rapid deployment of tactics that are synchronized and focused.* Rapid deployment will likely require several different units working together, and the best results are likely to be achieved when patrol officers, investigators, and support personnel bring their capabilities to focus in a coordinated effort.
4. *Relentless follow-up and assessment of tactics to ensure that desired outcomes are being achieved.* Follow-ups will assess the results from the tactics employed; assess the usefulness of various tactics; identify the tactical elements that worked best; and allow for the redeployment of assets to the next crime problem.

Source: J. J. Willis, S. D. Mastrofski, and D. Weisburd, *Compstat in practice: An in-depth analysis of three cities* (Washington, DC: Police Foundation, 2004). Reprinted by permission.

fective coordination because "the most effective plans require that personnel from several units and enforcement functions work together as a team."[44] Relentless follow-up is necessary to ensure desired outcomes. Figure 9-4 lists the general elements of the Compstat model.

New Orleans has had promising results with its version of Compstat, which it calls *Comstat.* During 1996, the New Orleans Police Department undertook a major reorganization and philosophical change. All crime-fighting responsibilities were placed under eight district commanders. New resources were also allocated to assist them in accomplishing their mission to reduce crime and violence in one of the most dangerous cities in the country.

The last step, relentless accountability, is extremely important and is usually accomplished most effectively in intensive management meetings. According to Jack Maple, former deputy commissioner of the NYPD, "the first step to crime reduction itself—the gathering and analyzing of accurate, timely intelligence—has to be quickened by the heat of accountability."[45] The New Orleans Comstat program maintains a similar philosophy: "Accountability is paramount in this procedure. Each District Commander is expected to be fully aware of the crimes that take place in his or her area of responsibility and is expected to not only react to these offenses but to take proactive measures to reduce and deter them. In addition, each District Commander must prepare an extensive weekly report on the activity in his or her district."[46]

One important aspect of Compstat is crime mapping. Because crime data must be portrayed clearly and rapidly, computer technology is essential. According to one source, "A powerful software tool, MapInfo 94, became the NYPD's crime radar screen, with attention-grabbing colors and shapes. Red dots indicated drug complaints from the public, blue dots showed drug arrests, green triangles represented shooting incidents, and yellow dots indicated homicides."[47] Computerized images generated by MapInfo 94 brought together all the data in the Compstat books. Previously, crime statistics had not been kept or presented in any single source. As another researcher observed, "These visual presentations are a highly effective complement to the Compstat report, since they permit precinct commanders and executive staff members to instantly identify and explore trends, patterns, and possible solutions for crime and quality-of-life problems."[48]

Crime statistics are the most popular measure of success for precinct commanders. However, Sam Houston State University criminologists Randall Garner and Larry Hoover question the appropriateness of crime statistics as the sole measure of success.[49] They cite quality-of-life issues and citizen complaints as barometers of police performance that agencies experimenting with Compstat may wish to consider. The appropriate measure of success, they suggest, "communicates what issues are valued most in the department."[50] They also raise concerns about the NYPD version of Compstat, which they regard as confrontational. While NYPD's program has established greater accountability, increased awareness, improved problem-solving

WEB PATROL 9-8

Compstat Implementation
http://www.mycrimekit.com

A Miami Police Department Compstat presentation at the annual 2006 International Association of Chiefs of Police conference in Miami Beach, Florida. What is Compstat? How can it help police departments in the fight against crime?

David Hathcox

endeavors, and increased managerial control, they caution that weekly meetings may be too shortsighted and aggressive an approach to reducing crime and may overemphasize outcomes rather than underlying causes of problems. Indeed, one researcher has observed that "Compstat's approach ignores decades of expert research that has shown that crime levels are determined by vast social forces beyond police control—poverty, racism, [and] demographics."[51]

SPECIAL GROUPS AND SPECIAL PROBLEMS

For some particular groups and crime problems, the traditional policing approach may not work. Children, the mentally ill, drug addicts, gangs, and domestic violence are but a few examples of areas where traditional routine incident response and preventive patrol (among other time-honored tactics) may not be the most desirable approach. Special knowledge and tactics are necessary.

Children

Children (or *juveniles,* in legal parlance) are generally all persons under the age of 18, although a few states set 17 or even 16 as the age of adulthood. Children of all ages come into contact with police for all manner of reasons, from young children exposed to violence all the way up through teenagers who violate curfew laws or commit major felony crimes. Collectively, children can keep law enforcement officers quite busy. At the least, police officers need to be aware of the legal procedures governing the treatment of children by the criminal justice system. In the case of juvenile offenders, for example, the U.S. Supreme Court has held in *In re Gault* that juveniles should be provided with

> (1) written notice of the specific charge or factual allegations, given to the child and his or her parents or guardian sufficiently in advance of the hearing to permit preparation;
> (2) notification to the child and his or her parents of the child's right to be represented by counsel retained by them, or if they are unable to afford counsel, counsel appointed by the court to represent the child;
> (3) application of the constitutional privilege against self-incrimination; and
> (4) absent a valid confession, a determination of delinquency and an order of commitment based only on sworn testimony subjected to the opportunity for cross-examination in accordance with constitutional requirements.[52]

When we speak of juveniles and police, the tendency is to think of juvenile delinquency. But although it is true that juvenile crime is a problem, police often deal with children who are not criminal but who simply need help. Additionally, police often encounter children who are just "hanging out" and acting rowdy but not necessarily breaking any laws. Thus it is useful to distinguish between children in need of help, troublemakers, status offenders, and violent offenders.

Children in Need of Help. Many children need police help or protection, whether they ask for it or not. For example, there are uncountable numbers of poverty-stricken, neglected, and abused children in this country. Between 12 and 15 percent of children live in households below the poverty level[53]; millions of others are abused each year, and more than 1,000 die from such abuse.[54] There is only so much police officers can do (or be expected to do) for poor and poverty-stricken children. Abuse, however, is clearly criminal, so detecting signs of abuse and enforcing relevant laws are important aspects of police work. Add to that missing children, runaways, and so-called throwaways (those who have been told to leave by their parents or guardians), and it is clear why dealing with juveniles is an important function of police work. Fortunately, resources like **Amber alerts,** or voluntary partnerships between police and the news media, assist police in locating children in danger. Announcements on television, the radio, and electronic billboards are most popular.

Amber alert
A voluntary partnership program between police and the news media involving saturation notices on radio, television, and electronic billboards to elicit widespread and immediate public assistance in locating a child or children thought to be in danger.

Beyond these somewhat "traditional" juvenile issues, researchers are coming to realize that when children are exposed to violence, its effects can be harmful over the long term. Some police agencies have teamed up with mental health professionals in an effort to intervene with children who experience traumatic incidents. An example can be had in the former Police Action Counseling Team (PACT) program in Palm Desert, California. Licensed clinical psychologists accompanied sheriff's deputies to incidents where children were exposed to violence. The deputies dealt with the heads of household while the psychologist counseled any children involved in the incident at the scene. Follow-ups were also conducted in an effort to minimize lasting traumatic effects. Palm Desert's PACT program has ended, but similar programs continue to operate throughout the United States.

Troublemakers. Encounters with disorderly and rowdy youth who are just "hanging out" are also common in police work. Sometimes youth just associate with one another in public places and are mistaken for troublemakers when, in fact, they are not. Other times, youth can bother and make trouble for passersby. It falls to police officers to make the distinction.

There is nothing wrong with public assembly, but certain steps must be taken if the youth begin to act improperly. In some situations, though, no amount of assembly is permissible. This is true in the context of **curfew laws,** which are statutes that require juveniles to remain indoors during specific hours, usually late evening through early morning, unless accompanied by an adult. Hundreds of cities in the United States now have curfew laws.[55] They can be an annoyance for police officers because, as some officers see it, they shift parental responsibility to law enforcement. Other officers view curfew laws as a useful tool for breaking up a suspicious assembly of youth.

curfew law
A statute or ordinance that requires juveniles to remain indoors during designated time periods (usually late evening through early morning) unless accompanied by an adult.

A number of researchers have started to question whether curfew laws are effective. In one study, researchers conducted a sophisticated time-series analysis of the New Orleans curfew law on juvenile victimization and arrests. They found that the law had no effect:

> The findings show that the juvenile curfew law in New Orleans, although restrictive, was ineffective for reducing victimizations [overall], victimizations of juveniles, and juvenile arrests. All changes found in victimizations were small, half were temporary, and four of the six significant changes were increases.[56]

Status Offenders. **Status offenses** are acts or conduct that is declared by statute to be an offense only if committed by or engaged in by a juvenile. Examples of status offenses include truancy, incorrigibility, underage drinking or smoking, and running away from home (Figure 9-5). Truancy is enough of a problem that many jurisdictions have enacted programs intended to make sure youth do not skip school; these programs have had varying levels of success. Incorrigibility refers to youths who habitually fail to obey their parents or guardians. Drinking and smoking are only legal if the

status offense
An act or conduct that is declared by statute to be an offense only if committed by or engaged in by a juvenile. Such offenses can be adjudicated only by a juvenile court.

Figure 9-5 • Selected Status Offenses under California's Welfare and Institutions Code

601. (a) Any person under the age of 18 years who persistently or habitually refuses to obey the reasonable and proper orders or directions of his or her parents, guardian, or custodian, or who is beyond the control of that person, or who is under the age of 18 years when he or she violated any ordinance of any city or county of this state establishing a curfew based solely on age is within the jurisdiction of the juvenile court which may adjudge the minor to be a ward of the court.

(b) If a minor has four or more truancies within one school year as defined in Section 48260 of the Education Code or a school attendance review board or probation officer determines that the available public and private services are insufficient or inappropriate to correct the habitual truancy of the minor, or to correct the minor's persistent or habitual refusal to obey the reasonable and proper orders or directions of school authorities, or if the minor fails to respond to directives of a school attendance review board or probation officer or to services provided, the minor is then within the jurisdiction of the juvenile court which may adjudge the minor to be a ward of the court. However, it is the intent of the Legislature that no minor who is adjudged a ward of the court pursuant solely to this subdivision shall be removed from the custody of the parent or guardian except during school hours.

Source: Sections 601(a) and 601(b) of the California Welfare and Institutions Code.

person is "of age," hence their classification as status offenses. Running away from home, too, can be considered a status offense, but it isn't always treated as such. Indeed, for all of these offenses, the officer might take an informal approach, returning the child to his or her home with a warning. Other times, though, status offenses are taken as seriously as some violent offenses. It depends on agency and community priorities.

The so-called rave party is linked to the problem of status offenses (and even to some serious offenses). "Rave parties—or, more simply, raves—are dance parties that feature fast-paced, repetitive electronic music and accompanying light shows."[57] The rave phenomenon has been explained in this way:

> Word of the parties usually starts on campuses, where slick, lurid handbills, often promising sex, illicit drugs and alcohol, are distributed. Raves are the focus of rave culture, a youth-

DOES IT WORK?

Cops in Schools

While there is much anecdotal evidence suggesting that putting police officers in schools can reduce crime and deviance,[1] there is a dearth of scientific evidence showing that this law enforcement approach can make a difference. A researcher in the United Kingdom recently examined the placement in local elementary schools of full-time uniformed police officers.[2] Preliminary evaluation findings suggest that the officers were able to reduce truancy and bullying, but the evaluation had not been completed as of this writing.

Another study suggests that school-police partnerships are helpful in terms of improving school behavior. The study focused on a truant recovery program in the West Contra Costa Unified School District in California.[3] The program placed some police officers in schools, and others worked with the schools to find and recover truant children. A group of 178 juveniles were randomly selected for an 18- to 21-month follow-up. Results revealed that the youths who were recovered during truancy sweeps were more civilized while in school, but they were arrested more frequently than other youths during the follow-up period.

The most recently published study in this area was concerned with a program known as Community Outreach through Police in Schools. The program, implemented by the Child Development–Community Policing Program at Yale University, is "a short-term, prevention-oriented, school-based group intervention that brings together community police officers and child clinicians as group coleaders to provide weekly sessions for middle school students who are at risk of being exposed to violence in the community."[4] Preliminary evaluation results suggest that the program helps youth cope with exposure to violence, but the program's effects on crime and deviance among schoolchildren have not been examined.

[1]See, e.g., R. L. Paynter, "Policing the schools," *Law Enforcement Technology* 26 (1999): 34–36, 38–40; National Crime Prevention Council, "Police station in a school," *Catalyst* 16 (May 1996): 1–2; M. L. West and J. M. Fries, "Campus-based police/probation teams: Making schools safer," *Corrections Today* 57 (August 1995): 144, 146, 148; and W. C. Torok and K. S. Trump, "Gang intervention: Police and school collaboration," *FBI Law Enforcement Bulletin* 63 (May 1994): 13–16.

[2]A. N. Briers, "School-based police officers: What can the UK learn from the USA?" *International Journal of Police Science and Management* 5 (2003): 129–42.

[3]M. D. White and others, "School-based partnership: Identifying at-risk youth through a truant recovery program," *Evaluation Review* 25 (2001): 507–32.

[4]U.S. Department of Justice, *Community outreach through police in schools* (Washington, DC: Office for Victims of Crime, U.S. Department of Justice, August 2003), p. 1.

> oriented subculture that blends music, art, and social ideals (e.g., peace, love, unity, respect, tolerance, happiness). Rave culture also entails the usage of a range of licit and illicit drugs. Drug use is intended to enhance ravers' sensations and boost their energy, so they can dance for long periods.[58]

Some raves are far from criminal in the traditional sense, but youth who participate in them may be guilty of one or more status offenses, such as violating curfew. But when drug use crosses over from licit to illicit, status offenses take a backseat to criminal violations of controlled substance laws.

Violent Offenders. Status offenders rarely get much attention. Rather, it is the violent juvenile offenders who seem to capture the headlines. The infamous Columbine shooting is perhaps the best example. According to the surgeon general, "For every youth arrested in any given year in the late 1990s, at least 10 were engaged in some form of violent behavior that could have seriously injured or killed another person. . . . Confidential surveys find that 13 to 15 percent of high school seniors report having committed an act of violence in recent years. The best available evidence from multiple sources indicates that youth violence is an ongoing national problem."[59] It is tragic that so many juveniles commit violent acts. At the same time, though, violent offenses are typically criminal, which permits law enforcement to take a tougher stance with respect to the problem. Interestingly, some jurisdictions have taken a direct approach to targeting juvenile violence through the enactment of **juvenile waiver** statutes.

The term **juvenile waiver** refers to a legal maneuver is which juveniles are waived to adult court, where they are tried as adults. Waivers have been around for some time and have been used on occasion when a juvenile commits a particularly harsh crime and the prosecutor wants to charge him or her in the adult justice system. What has changed recently, though, are the criteria for juvenile waivers. Recent changes have made it easier to try juvenile offenders as adults, a significant departure from the original intent of having a separate juvenile justice system. A number of states have effectively had their own versions of juvenile waivers for some time; they simply define "juvenile" differently. In Connecticut, North Carolina, and New York, the jurisdiction of the juvenile court ends after age 15. Offenders who are 16 years of age and older are processed by the adult courts. A number of other states, including Georgia, Illinois, Louisiana, Massachusetts, Michigan, Mississippi, New Hampshire, South Carolina, Texas, and Wisconsin, extend the jurisdiction of the juvenile court up to a youth's seventeenth birthday.

juvenile waiver
A legal maneuver in which jurisdiction over a juvenile offender is waived by the juvenile court to permit criminal prosecution of the offender in an adult court.

The Mentally Ill

Historically, the criminal justice system and mental health agencies have acted independently of one another.[60] This is a significant problem because there are many mentally ill offenders who cross paths with authorities regularly, many of whom simply "slip through the cracks" because their issues and needs go unidentified or unnoticed.[61] In fact, by some estimates there are more than a quarter million mentally ill offenders in America's prisons and jails.[62] Prisons and jails are not generally equipped to treat mentally ill offenders or even to identify their needs, nor are the police, who represent the first point of contact. On top of that, there is significant pressure nowadays to do *something* about people, the mentally ill included, who commit minor offenses, threaten public order, and make citizens feel uncomfortable. This creates an unpleasant predicament for police.

The term *mentally ill* refers to "all diagnosable mental conditions characterized by alterations in thinking, mood or behavior (or some combination thereof) associated with distress or impaired functioning."[63] As one concerned critic observed,

> In recent years there has been a marked shift in responsibility for the untreated mentally ill from the mental health system to the criminal justice system. It is becoming increasingly clear that any hope of alleviating the burden of untreated mental illness rests with those who are impacted the most, our nation's law enforcement officials.[64]

Fortunately, police agencies are becoming increasingly aware of the mental health problem that besieges our justice system. Some have responded by training officers to identify mentally ill individuals so as to avoid arresting them for disturbing the peace and for other offenses when they could just as easily be referred to service providers and treated.

The Illicit Drug Trade

America has a drug problem. It is estimated that enforcing America's drug laws costs the federal government about $14 billion annually.[65] State and local governments spend almost as much, resulting in a "drug war" whose costs are approaching $40 billion annually.[66] America's drug problem is also evident in the obscene amounts of money people make from supplying illicit substances to customers. One study estimates that drugs generate approximately $60 billion in annual income to those who supply the product to consumers. This equates to roughly 1 percent of total personal consumption expenditures in America.[67] Then there is drug use itself. According to the Office of National Drug Control Policy (ONDCP), drugs cost the United States approximately $181 billion annually in lost productivity, associated criminal activity, medical costs, death, and so on.[68] Two noteworthy surveys that have been used to measure drug use, the **National Survey on Drug Use and Health (NSDUH)** and the **Monitoring the Future (MTF) Survey,** make it clear that the majority of the adolescent population experiments with drugs, marijuana being the substance of choice.[69] The NSDUH shows that nearly half of all Americans between the ages of 18 and 34 experiment with illicit drugs.

National Survey on Drug Use and Health (NSDUH)
A national survey program that measures drug use in the United States.

Monitoring the Future (MTF) Survey
A national survey program that measures drug use among adolescents in the United States.

asset forfeiture
The governmental seizure of property (homes, automobiles, boats, aircraft, and so on) that has been illegally obtained with the profits from drug sales. The proceeds from these seizures sometimes go to the seizing agencies to fund continuing efforts in the "war on drugs."

In response to the drug problem, law enforcement officials have adopted a number of strategies. Buy-bust operations, for instance, place officers undercover to buy drugs and then "bust" (arrest) the sellers. Other officers go undercover and infiltrate drug markets, seeking to make high-profile arrests, close down shipping routes, and otherwise make dents in the problem. In drug raids, a number of officers serve warrants on properties whose residents are suspected of manufacturing and selling illicit substances. Some agencies make liberal use of **asset forfeiture:** Various laws at the federal and state levels permit governmental seizure of property obtained illegally (such as through drug sales). The proceeds from these seizures sometimes go right back to the seizing agencies to further assist their efforts in the "war on drugs." For example, cash seized from a drug bust can, in some states, go right back into the seizing officer's department to be used for various law enforcement purposes.

Task Forces. Some police agencies have experimented with **multijurisdictional drug task forces.** In these efforts, law enforcement agencies from several jurisdictions, and often several levels of government, work together to interdict and eradicate drugs. A well-known example of such a task force is California's longstanding Campaign against Marijuana Planting (CAMP). Headed by the California Department of Justice, the CAMP

WEB PATROL 9-9
National Survey on Drug Use and Health
http://www.mycrimekit.com

Undercover narcotics agents with the North Little Rock, Arkansas, police force arrest a man for production of crystal methamphetamine—a synthetic stimulant drug which induces a strong feeling of euphoria and can be highly addictive. Can the fight against illicit drugs ever be won? If so, how?

Robert King/ZUMA Press

DOES IT WORK?

Proactive Arrests for Drug Offenders

Proactively targeting drug offenders for arrest is a popular law enforcement strategy. It is often accomplished through crackdowns, in which authorities raid an area known for drug problems in an effort to remove criminals from the area.

The evidence is mixed concerning the effectiveness of drug crackdowns. There are more studies supporting this practice than not, but they do not amount to a significant majority. In fact, researchers have become increasingly critical of drug crackdowns because of their tendency to ignore the underlying root causes of crime, to push crime into surrounding areas,[1] and to fix the problem only temporarily.[2] Others have claimed that crackdowns increase the health risks to those who are addicted to drugs and increase fear and uncertainty among members of the community.[3]

Even so, some researchers have concluded that drug crackdowns are necessary and effective. One study showed that violence was reduced following a crackdown on heroin.[4] Another study on heroin crackdowns also supported the strategy.[5] A third study showed that raids of crack houses led to a decline in crime, but only for 12 days,[6] and a final study of a crackdown on drugs in seven Virginia neighborhoods in 1999 showed a 92 percent reduction in reported crime during the crackdown period, with no apparent displacement of the problem into surrounding neighborhoods.[7]

But just as many, if not more, studies do not find reductions in drug problems in the wake of crackdowns. For example, one study showed that a police crackdown on the crack cocaine market had no effect on violence.[8] Another set of researchers concluded that there were no consistent, desirable changes in the period following an aggressive antidrug arrest strategy.[9] Other studies show that buy-bust operations do not affect the illicit drug market[10] and that drug crackdowns in public housing had no measurable effect on crime.[11] It is likely that many crackdowns appear to be ineffective because they do not target the demand side of America's drug problem. As one researcher has observed, the drug market rapidly adapts to its new conditions following proactive arrest strategies.[12]

[1]For some commentary to this effect, see L. Zimmer, "Proactive policing against street-level drug trafficking," *American Journal of Police* 9 (1990): 43–74.
[2]C. Aitken and others, "The impact of a police crackdown on a street drug scene: Evidence from the street," *International Journal of Drug Policy* 13 (2002): 189–98.
[3]L. Maher and D. Dixon, "The cost of crackdowns: Policing Cabramatta's heroin market," *Current Issues in Criminal Justice* 13 (2001): 5–22.
[4]M. Kleiman, *Crackdowns: The effects of intensive enforcement on retail heroin dealing* (Washington, DC: National Institute of Justice, 1988).
[5]Zimmer, "Proactive policing against street-level drug trafficking."
[6]L. Sherman and D. P. Rogan, "Deterrent effects of police raids on crack houses: A randomized, controlled experiment," *Justice Quarterly* 12 (1995): 755–81.
[7]M. R. Smith, "Police-led crackdowns and cleanups: An evaluation of a crime control initiative in Richmond, Virginia," *Crime and Delinquency* 47 (2001): 60–83.
[8]M. Sviridoff and others, *The neighborhood effects of street-level drug enforcement: Tactical narcotics teams in New York* (New York: Vera Institute of Justice, 1992).
[9]C. D. Uchida, B. Forst, and S. O. Annan, *Modern policing and the control of illegal drugs: Testing new strategies in two American cities* (Washington, DC: National Institute of Justice, 1992).
[10]Ibid.
[11]S. Annan and W. Skogan, *Drug enforcement in public housing: Signs of success in Denver* (Washington, DC: Police Foundation, 1993).
[12]Aitken and others, "The impact of a police crackdown on a street drug scene."

program involves agencies like the California National Guard, the U.S. Forest Service, the Bureau of Land Management, the U.S. Drug Enforcement Agency, and dozens of county and local law enforcement agencies. Officials involved in the CAMP program are lowered by helicopter into marijuana "gardens" to eradicate the crops. In 2006 alone, the CAMP program destroyed 1,675,681 marijuana plants worth an estimated $6.7 billion.

multijurisdictional drug task force
A drug interdiction and eradication team composed of members from law enforcement agencies from multiple jurisdictions and often several levels of government.

Prevention and Education. There is more to combating illicit drugs than enforcement. Prevention through education is important as well, and it is a key component of our country's drug-control strategy. Perhaps the most familiar example of this approach is **Drug Abuse Resistance Education (DARE).** The DARE program began in 1983 as a joint venture between the Los Angeles Police Department and the Los Angeles Unified School District. It is now the most visible drug-prevention program in America, with the majority of school districts in all 50 states participating.[70] DARE's primary component is classroom visits by police officers, and the core curriculum consists of 17 lessons presented to students in fifth and sixth grades (Figure 9-6). Students learn about social pressures to use drugs, strategies to overcome such pressures, and consequences of drug use. In addition, they are taught about alternatives to drugs, responsible decision making, self-esteem issues, and other topics. The bulk of DARE education takes place in fifth and sixth grades, but variations on the 17-lesson curriculum are now appearing in kindergarten, high school, and every grade in between.[71] Unfortunately, however, almost all published evaluations of DARE show that the program has little to no effect on drug use.[72]

Drug Abuse Resistance Education (DARE)
A collaborative effort between local police departments and schools involving police visits to fifth- and sixth-grade classrooms to present a drug-abuse-prevention curriculum.

Figure 9-6 • Drug Abuse Resistance Education Curriculum

The DARE curriculum is continually enhanced and expanded to more effectively meet the needs of children. Following are the current DARE components.

Core Curriculum

Delivered by a DARE officer to fifth- and sixth-grade students, the core curriculum includes one lesson each week for 17 consecutive weeks. A number of teaching techniques are used, including question-and-answer sessions, group discussions, role playing, and workbook exercises.

Kindergarten through Fourth Grade Visitation Lessons

As time permits, officers teaching the core curriculum can visit students in each of the lower grades to introduce younger students to the DARE concept. The 15- to 20-minute lessons cover such topics as obeying laws, personal safety, and the helpful and harmful uses of medicines and drugs.

Junior High Curriculum

The DARE junior high curriculum emphasizes information and skills that enable students to resist peer pressure and negative influences in making personal choices. The ten lessons concentrate on helping students manage their feelings of anger and aggression and on showing them how to resolve conflicts without resorting to violence or to the use of alcohol or drugs.

Senior High Curriculum

The DARE senior high curriculum focuses on the everyday situations that high school students encounter. For the first five lessons, a DARE officer and a high school teacher use the technique of team teaching. They emphasize information and skills that enable students to act in their own best interests when facing high-risk, low-gain choices and to handle feelings of anger properly without causing harm to themselves or others. Five follow-up lessons, presented by the teacher, serve to reinforce the initial lessons.

Special Education Curriculum

The DARE Midwestern Regional Training Center, administered by the Illinois State Police, has adapted the DARE curriculum for special populations. DARE officers receive specialized training that prepares them to teach the 17-week core curriculum in special classrooms to children with learning disabilities and behavioral disorders.

Parent Component

The DARE parent component was developed to address the growing need for comprehensive family support and involvement in school programs. It is intended for any adult interested in ensuring health, safety, and development of life skills for children. The program provides information on communication and self-esteem building, risk factors associated with young children, basic facts on drug usage and the stages of adolescent chemical dependency, protective factors and sources of pressure, violence and conflict resolution, and agency networking in the community. The sessions offer participants the opportunity to become more involved in DARE and give them access to community resources. The program consists of six 2-hour sessions, usually held in the evening, that are conducted by a certified DARE officer.

DARE Plus Component

This component was initiated in 1993 on a pilot basis at Marina del Rio School in Los Angeles, California. It was created as an extension of the successful DARE program and is designed to help sixth, seventh, and eighth graders stay involved in school and away from gangs, drugs, and violence. DARE Plus provides students with a wide range of educational, vocational, and recreational after school activities in a safe and well-supervised campus setting.

Source: C. Ringwalt, J. Greene, S. Ennett, R. Lachan, R. R. Clayton, and C. G. Leukefeld, *Past and future directions of the DARE program: An evaluation review—Draft final report* (Washington, DC: National Institute of Justice, 1994). Reprinted by permission of RTI International and R. R. Clayton.

Gangs

According to official estimates, there are approximately 785,000 active gang members and 26,500 gangs in the United States.[73] Given their size and the potential behavioral impact of their members, gangs pose their share of problems for the police. On the one hand, since a number of gang members commit traditional crimes like robbery and murder, they can be arrested and prosecuted just like anyone else. On the other hand, the organized aspect of gang activity requires something other than a traditional approach to the problem. Several strategies have been undertaken to deal with gangs, beyond law enforcement. These include social interventions, community mobilization, and the provision of opportunities to steer people away from gang life. Even so, the law enforcement/suppression approach is perhaps most familiar. Its tactics include

> tactical patrols by law enforcement, vertical prosecution by district attorneys [one prosecutor handling the case from beginning to end], and intensive supervision by probation departments. Generally, suppression involves the arrest, prosecution, and incarceration of gang members. Although suppression is the primary strategy used in many jurisdictions, it is also frequently viewed as the least effective.[74]

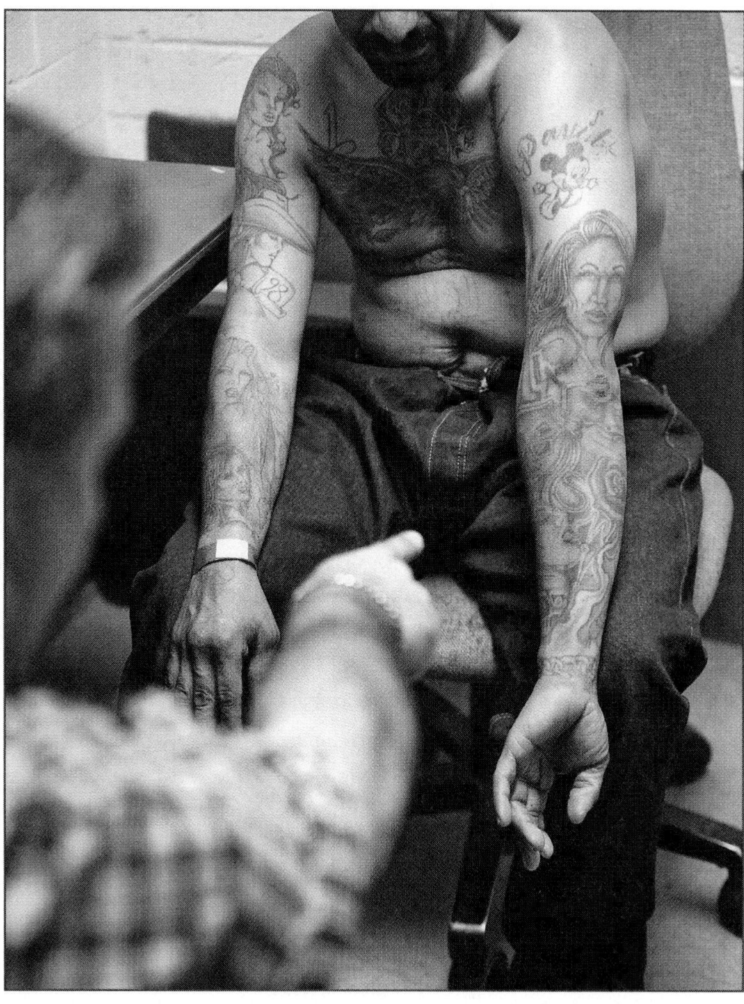

A captured offender with the MS-13 gang from El Salvador is interrogated and his tattoos recorded. What special challenges do gangs like MS-13 represent to police departments across the United States?

Knox Merrill/Getty Images, Inc./*Christian Science Monitor*

To further the enforcement/suppression approach, many police agencies rely on specialized gang units. Generally, these are made up of a group of officers who participate in a mix of enforcement, intervention, and prevention activities. By and large, though, gang units adopt an enforcement stance,[75] though they sometimes team up with other city or county officials to adopt creative approaches aimed at stemming the tide of gangs. One such approach involves **street closures.**

street closure
An anticrime/antigang tactical measure designed to control traffic flow so as to deny easy or undetected movement through a neighborhood or business district.

The reasoning behind street closures is that when gangs cannot easily access their targets, they will commit fewer crimes. Street closures can also trap suspects, and they are used for more than just disrupting gangs. As one author explains,

> Closing streets makes escaping more difficult. In the case of prostitution cruising and drive-by shootings, the offenders are likely to follow a circular driving pattern in their search for targets. By making circular driving patterns harder and increasing the chances that offenders will find themselves at the end of a dead-end street, criminal behavior may be thwarted.[76]

The LAPD's Operation Cul-de-Sac is a successful example of closing streets to target gangs. Put into effect in 1990, the initiative saw the placement of traffic barricades on 14 streets in a South Central Los Angeles neighborhood that had experienced significant gang-related drug activity as well as a number of shootings. An evaluation compared the target area with surrounding neighborhoods and revealed a 65 percent decline in crime in the treatment area.[77] Even more importantly, during the two years when the barriers were in place, there was only one killing in the target area.[78] Unfortunately, though, once the barricades were removed, homicides rose 800 percent in comparison to the surrounding areas.[79]

antigang injunction
A judicial order, often obtained at the request of a prosecutor, that bars gang members from associating with one another. Also called *civil gang injunction.*

Another creative approach to targeting gangs involves **antigang injunctions.** An injunction is a judicial order requiring that a certain form of conduct cease. In the case of gang injunctions, a court will issue an injunction—often at the request of a prosecutor—that bars gang members from associating with one another. The legal theory behind injunctions of this sort is that gangs, as unincorporated associations, engage in criminal and other activities that constitute a public nuisance. Usually, specific gang members are named in the injunctions and are barred from associating with one other within specific locations. To ensure that the injunction is publicized, law enforcement officials will sometimes contact gang members to make them aware of the order.[80] Violation of the court's order can result in a number of different penalties. According to one study, there were some 32 separate injunctions issued in Southern California alone during the 1990s,[81] but whether they were effective remains unclear.

As mentioned earlier, there is more to managing the gang problem than enforcement. Afterschool programs, for instance, are intended to keep youth busy, and some are aimed at discouraging kids from joining gangs. Other programs provide opportunities for both at-risk youth and active gang members, such as job training and mentoring. The prevention angle is also popular. We already mentioned the DARE program in the drug context. There is a roughly equivalent program aimed at preventing gang membership. Known as **Gang Resistance Education and Training (GREAT)**, this program relies on uniformed police officers who introduce students to conflict-resolution skills, cultural sensitivity, and the dark side of gang membership. The program began in 1992 as a joint venture between the Phoenix Police Department and the Bureau of Alcohol, Tobacco, Firearms and Explosives. It has since expanded to schools in all 50 states.[82] The curriculum consists of eight weekly lessons for middle school students:

Gang Resistance Education and Training (GREAT)
An educational program that uses uniformed police officers to introduce students to conflict-resolution skills, cultural sensitivity, and the dark side of gang membership.

1. Introduction to the program and the officer(s) doing the instruction
2. Crimes and crime victims, including the consequences of crime for communities
3. Cultural sensitivity and the harmful effects of prejudicial attitudes and behavior
4. Conflict-resolution skills
5. How to satisfy needs without joining a gang
6. How drugs affect schools and communities
7. Personal responsibilities
8. Goal setting[83]

Is GREAT really that great? Perhaps the most sophisticated evaluation of GREAT reported to date was conducted by researchers at the University of Nebraska at Omaha.[84] After following program participants for several years, the researchers found that GREAT improved prosocial attitudes but did not affect participants' decision to join gangs. However, because the research was based on student surveys rather than official data (such as arrest histories), it is difficult to gauge the program's effect on criminal behavior. Overall, though, GREAT appears to show more promise than DARE.

WEB PATROL 9-10
Into the Abyss: A Personal Journey into the World of Street Gangs
http://www.mycrimekit.com

Domestic Violence

domestic violence
Generally, any violence that takes place in the home. The term has recently been expanded to include violence between domestic partners and violence directed at or occurring between children. Also called *family violence.*

Domestic violence generally refers to all violence in the home. Historically, it has been defined in terms of a physical confrontation between husband and wife. More recently, however, the term has been expanded to include violence of all sorts, including physical disputes between domestic partners. The term today even encompasses violence directed at or occurring between children. *Child abuse,* though, is the term used when parents or guardians use unacceptable physical violence with their children. Some use the term *family violence* in place of domestic violence. Regardless of the term used, violence within the home is a big problem. More than 1,100 women and nearly 400 men were killed by an intimate partner in 2005.[85] Numbers like these probably underestimate the true extent of the problem. As some experts have noted, "Victims of domestic violence are less likely than victims of other types of violence to call the police because of their privacy concerns, their fear of reprisal, and their desire to protect offenders."[86]

DOES IT WORK?

Mandatory Arrests for Domestic Violence

In response to the problem of domestic violence, some police agencies have implemented mandatory arrest policies. The logic behind these policies is simple: By removing one of the parties from the scene through an arrest, the problem stops—at least in the short term. The question, however, is whether mandatory arrest has long-term consequences. Several researchers have sought to answer this question.

The first noteworthy study in this area, known as the Minneapolis Domestic Violence Experiment, was conducted during the 1980s.[1] Minneapolis officers responding to domestic violence calls were required either to arrest the offender, to separate both parties, or to counsel both parties but not arrest or separate them. Officers were not given the choice of which course of action to take; the required course of action was based on random assignment (one of the hallmarks of a rigorous study). The researchers then tracked the frequency and severity of domestic violence involving the parties for a period of six months after first contact. Interestingly, they found that arrest stemmed the tide of domestic violence. The study's findings led police departments throughout the country to adopt mandatory arrest policies, but the research also set off a firestorm of controversy.[2]

The consensus in the literature now is that mandatory arrest is ineffective, that is, most of the research published after the Minneapolis study either does not support mandatory arrest for domestic violence or suggests that the arrest/no arrest dilemma is far from clear-cut. Other researchers have argued that mandatory arrest policies can be easily circumvented,[3] that victims' desires should not be discounted in domestic violence situations,[4] and that short- versus long-term arrests can affect repeated violence.[5] One study, though, suggests that arrest can reduce future acts of domestic violence, but it appears to be the exception.[6]

[1]L. Sherman and R. Berk, *The Minneapolis domestic violence experiment* (Washington, DC: Police Foundation, 1984).The academic version of this report can be found in L. Sherman and R. Berk, "The specific deterrent effects of arrest for domestic assault," *American Sociological Review* 49 (1984): 261–72. See also L. Sherman, *Policing domestic violence* (New York: Free Press, 1992).

[2]At least two academic journals devoted symposia to this topic. See *American Behavioral Scientist* 36 (1993) and *Journal of Criminal Law and Criminology* 83 (1992).

[3]For an example, see T. N. Ho, "Domestic violence in a southern city: The effects of a mandatory arrest policy on male-versus-female aggravated assault incidents," *American Journal of Criminal Justice* 25 (2000): 107–18.

[4]R. C. Davis, B. E. Smith, and B. Taylor, "Increasing the proportion of domestic violence arrests that are prosecuted: A natural experiment in Milwaukee," *Criminology and Public Policy* 2 (2003): 263–82.

[5]L. W. Sherman and others, "From initial deterrence to long-term escalation: Short custody arrest for poverty ghetto domestic violence," *Criminology* 29 (1991): 821–50.

[6]C. D. Maxwell, J. H. Garner, and J. A. Fagan, "The preventive effects of arrest on intimate partner violence: Research, policy, and theory," *Criminology and Public Policy* 2 (2002): 51–80.

Domestic violence calls are among the most risky for law enforcement personnel for a number of reasons. If police respond to the scene, it is likely because someone in the home or close by called for assistance. This level of attention indicates that the incident is probably quite serious. Next, a number of domestic incidents are fueled by the use of alcohol or drugs, which puts the parties in a less than rational state of mind. Tempers flare and people are typically quite agitated during these incidents. Weapons may also be present. Together, these elements can create a violent (or at least very tense) confrontation even after authorities arrive on the scene. Fortunately, officers can take steps in advance to promote their safety. For example, as one researcher observed, "Greater awareness of the events in relationships and communities that precede domestic homicides can improve police policies, inform police intervention, and lessen the likelihood of officer injury and death."[87]

One of the most difficult problems for law enforcement in the domestic violence context is what to do once the violence has been stopped and the parties have been separated. Is arrest the best option? What about counseling? On the one hand, an arrest can be helpful in the sense that once at least one party is removed from the scene, the incident cannot continue. On the other hand, arrest can have its downside, including possible retaliation against the victim. But officers who fail to make arrests may expose themselves to liability for failing to protect the victim. This has prompted several agencies to adopt mandatory arrest policies when there is clear evidence of an assault. Beyond policing, other common approaches to domestic violence include batterer intervention programs and dedicated domestic violence courts.

WEB PATROL 9-11

Police Knowledge of Older Populations
http://www.mycrimekit.com

SUMMARY

- Intelligence-led policing is a method of policing that focuses resources on key criminal activities. Once crime problems are identified and quantified through intelligence assessments, key criminals can be targeted for investigation and prosecution.
- Advances in information and communications technology that have affected police agencies include computer-aided drafting, computer-assisted training, crime mapping, geographic profiling, and crime intelligence systems. Compstat, a controversial police management strategy, stresses intelligence gathering, rapid deployment of police resources, effective tactics, and follow-up.
- Children, the mentally ill, drug addicts, gangs, and domestic violence are but a few examples of special groups and problems where traditional routine incident response and preventive patrol may not be the most effective or desirable approach. Special and innovative policing strategies are necessary for the management of these problems.

COMING FULL CIRCLE

For Discussion

Return to the questions posed at the start of this chapter. Have any of your answers changed since you read the chapter? What portions of this chapter helped you answer these questions?

Writing Assignment

Using material from this chapter and additional resources, write a 500-word essay in response to one of the questions presented at the beginning of the chapter. Submit your essay to your instructor if asked to do so.

KEY TERMS AND NAMES

Amber alert
antigang injunction
asset forfeiture
CalGang
Compstat
computer-aided drafting (CAD)
computerized crime mapping
Crime Mapping Research Center (CMRC)
criminal intelligence
curfew law
domestic violence
Drug Abuse Resistance Education (DARE)
firearms training system (FATS)
fusion center
Gang Resistance Education and Training (GREAT)
geographic profiling
Homicide Investigation and Tracking System (HITS)
intelligence
intelligence-led policing (ILP)
juvenile waiver
Law Enforcement Assistance and Partnership (LEAP) Strategy
Monitoring the Future (MTF) Survey
multijurisdictional drug task force
National Criminal Intelligence Sharing Plan (NCISP)
National Intelligence Model
National Survey on Drug Use and Health (NSDUH)
pin map
status offense
strategic intelligence
street closure
tactical intelligence

WEB INTERACTIVITY

Search the Internet and visit various police department Compstat pages. You might, for example, review Compstat information from the Los Angeles Police Department (http:// www.lapdonline.org/crime_maps_and_compstat), the Philadelphia Police Department (http://www.ppdonline.org/hq_compstat.php), and the New York City Police Department (http://home2.nyc.gov/html/nypd/downloads/pdf/crime_statistics/cs041pct.pdf). Some police departments even provide location-specific crime maps that allow viewers to see up-to-date statistical overviews of crimes that have recently occurred in particular neighborhoods. (See, for example, the LAPD crime-mapping page at http://www.lapdcrimemaps.org.) For this assignment, you should visit three or four police department Compstat sites of your choosing and write down your impressions of the sites, including the kinds of information they offer, the history of each program (if provided), and so on. Determine which site is, in your opinion, the most useful for members of the community, and submit the material to your instructor if asked to do so.

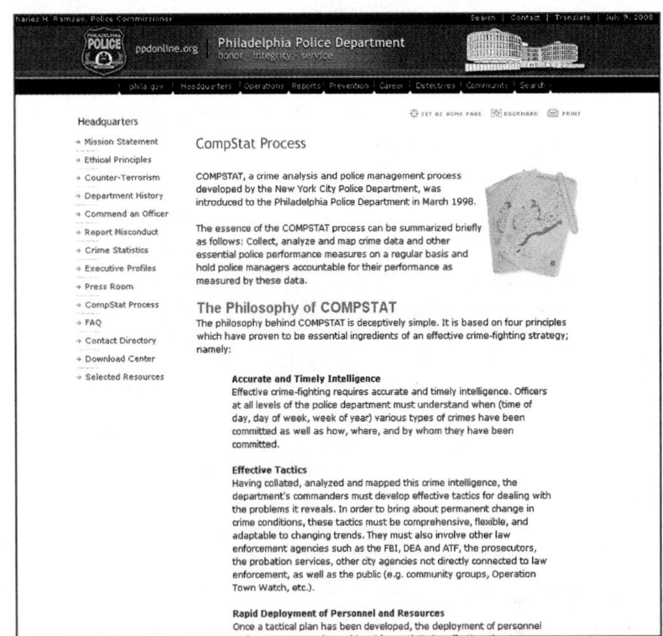

Philadelphia Police Department

REVIEW QUESTIONS

1. What is intelligence-led policing? Provide some examples.
2. How has information and communications technology improved law enforcement?
3. Which special groups or problems pose unique challenges for law enforcement today? Explain.

THINK ABOUT IT

Some years ago, the Washington (DC) Metropolitan Police Department launched an online crime bulletin service. The department is making use of crimereports.com, a free online service that allows police agencies to keep their communities up-to-date about criminal incidents in their areas. "Through this new digital partnership, we are able to provide the community with the type of information it needs to be full and active partners," said the department's chief, Charles H. Ramsey.[1]

One view of DC's crime bulletin service is that it embodies the spirit of community policing and, as the chief said, brings members of the community and the police into close contact. An opposing view is that the effort is largely symbolic—meaning that the department is giving the *appearance* of working closely with the community when in fact it is simply making use of a Web service that is readily available. These competing views raise some interesting questions to keep in mind as you read this chapter:

1. Is a Web-based approach to community policing sufficient? Is it meaningful and useful reform?
2. Is community policing an honest effort to improve police-community relations, or is it merely a symbolic gesture?
3. Where is the line between real and symbolic community policing drawn?
4. Is it realistic to expect the police and the community to work together in the name of crime prevention?
5. Is community policing effective, or is its actual intent something other than crime reduction?

INTRODUCTION

The last two or three decades have seen a powerful movement to bring police officers closer to the communities they serve and to get citizens more involved in policing.[2] Police officers have gone out into the community to build relationships and to establish rapport with citizens through a number of innovative programs and interventions. Citizens have sought out police agencies, as well, to learn what it's like to be an officer and to peek into the world of law enforcement. Some agencies have even hired civilians in place of sworn officers for certain jobs in an effort to cut costs. There are also signs of increased reliance by police departments on third parties, like landlords and apartment managers, to engage in policing-related functions.

It is important to understand why these kinds of things are happening in policing today. Accordingly, we begin this chapter with a background section that puts recent developments in context. The rest of the chapter is organized into three key sections on community policing, citizen involvement in policing, and third-party policing. Whereas Chapter 8 covered the traditional aspects of policing, this chapter continues Chapter 9's focus on innovative, creative, and otherwise nontraditional forms of police work.

BACKGROUND

It is tempting to view current trends in policing as unique to policing. They are not. The idea of reaching out to the community in an effort to improve relationships with citizens and to put citizens in closer touch with criminal justice professionals is part of a larger community justice movement that has been under way for some time now. Prosecutors, for example, have begun to pursue many of the same proactive, preventive, and creative crime-control strategies as those in which the police are engaged. In "community prosecution," as attorneys call it, prosecutors do much more than just charge suspected criminals and bring them to court.

Closely connected to community involvement and community policing is the idea of problem-oriented policing, which emerged at roughly the same time as the strategies we cover in this chapter. It is worth discussing separately, however, because it is the glue that holds a number of recent developments together. The idea that policing (and criminal justice in general) should be geared toward the identification and solution of root problems in the community is a relatively recent one.

Still, it explains why police want to strengthen ties with the communities they serve and why police departments want to provide citizens with a window into the law enforcement world.

Community Justice

Community justice is a relatively new and innovative set of ideas about how the goals of the criminal justice system can be achieved. It favors original, nontraditional approaches to crime control that draw heavily on input and cooperation from members of the community. A recent book on the topic points to two fundamental assumptions underlying community justice:

> First, it is assumed that within existing jurisdictions, such as states or large cities, there are critically important differences from one community to another, and these differences suggest that criminal justice strategies need to be tailored to fit those differences."[3]

community justice
A relatively new and innovative set of ideas about how the goals of the criminal justice system can be achieved. It favors original, nontraditional approaches to crime control that draw heavily on input and cooperation from the community.

In other words, a significant assumption underlying community justice is that custom-fit crime control is better than the traditional approach, which is increasingly criticized as unimaginative.

> The second assumption is that formal systems of social control, such as the criminal justice system, are not the main mechanisms of public safety. Rather, informal social controls—families, neighbors, social organizations, and friendship relations—form the most important foundation for public safety.[4]

Community justice emphasizes that criminal justice agencies (police, courts, corrections) cannot accomplish crime control alone; community participation is essential. Together, these assumptions define the essence of community justice. It is an innovative and cooperative effort to deal with America's crime problem. Its hallmark is collaboration between the justice system and the community.

Community policing is simply a part of this larger community justice movement. Outside of the policing context, community justice has manifested itself in our nation's courts, particularly through the creation of so-called community courts and other problem-solving courts, including drug courts, domestic violence courts, teen courts, and reentry courts. Corrections agencies are also doing community justice as we have just defined it. Approaches like restorative justice fit the community justice model, as do partnerships between probation, parole, and private companies, such as treatment facilities.

WEB PATROL 10-1
Brennan Center for Justice at New York University School of Law
http://www.mycrimekit.com

Problem-Oriented Policing

Problem-oriented policing (POP) is, as the term suggests, policing that is oriented toward problem solving. This method of policing is geared toward identifying and solving particular and specific problems—from serious ones, such as gang shootings in one part of town, to minor ones, such as panhandlers bothering visitors at a local park. POP involves identifying areas, times of days, specific crimes, individuals, and the like that are particularly troublesome and then crafting a creative solution to these problems.[5]

problem-oriented policing (POP)
A method of policing that is geared toward identifying and solving problems within a community that are particularly troublesome and then crafting creative solutions to them. Also called *problem-solving policing.*

Problem-oriented policing is the brainchild of law professor (emeritus) Herman Goldstein and shares much in common with some of the policing strategies discussed in earlier chapters.[6] For example, problem-oriented policing resembles directed patrol because it emphasizes direction and purpose, not just random and reactive patrol. Problem-oriented policing also resembles community policing because it usually relies on input from citizens to help identify problems. Indeed, some of the time the terms *community policing* and *problem-oriented policing* are used interchangeably. Much of the time, though, problem solving is viewed as a separate strategy unto itself.

WEB PATROL 10-2
Center for Problem-Oriented Policing
http://www.mycrimekit.com

There are at least two ways to distinguish between community policing and problem-oriented policing. First, problem-oriented policing focuses on innovation and is independent of contact with citizens. In contrast, for policing to be truly community oriented, it must include some degree of citizen involvement. Another, perhaps more controversial, way to distinguish between both approaches is to say that community policing focuses on citizen involvement and satisfaction as an end in itself, and problem-oriented policing is concerned with achieving a swift reduction in crime.

WEB PATROL 10-3
Interview with Herman Goldstein
http://www.mycrimekit.com

WEB PATROL 10-4

Community Building Measures: How Police and Neighborhood Groups Can Measure Their Collaboration
http://www.mycrimekit.com

Despite POP's differences from community policing and community justice, it is still useful to think of it as a part of both movements because problem solving is a central feature of community policing and community justice. All three approaches necessitate an understanding of the geographic area, an in-depth understanding of the problems, and some degree of familiarity with the people in the areas where the problems occur. It is possible, of course, for POP to have no community involvement (direct or indirect), but true problem-oriented policing almost requires some outreach and relationship building with the community. See Figure 10-1 for a summary of the relationships between community justice, community policing, and problem-oriented policing.

Figure 10-1 • Relationships between Community Justice, Community Policing, and Problem-Oriented Policing

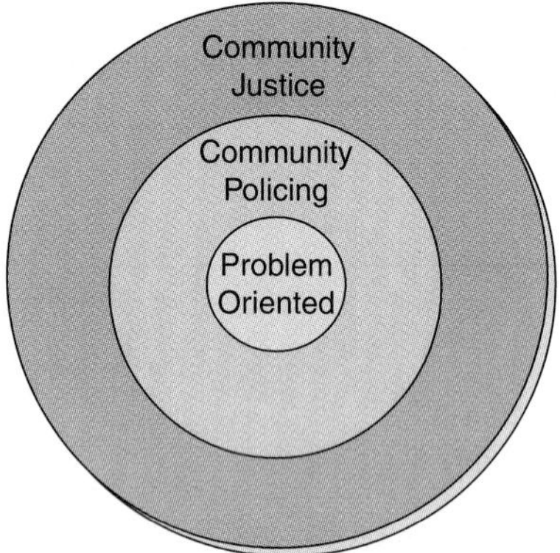

Source: J. L. Worrall, *Crime control in America: An assessment of the evidence* (Upper Saddle River, NJ: Pearson Education, Inc., 2006), p. 87. Reprinted by permission.

COMMUNITY POLICING

Community policing emerged in the wake of the reform era discussed in Chapter 1. The reform era hasn't disappeared; there is much that occurs in the world of policing that is consistent with the ideas set forth by August Vollmer, O. W. Wilson, and others. Some not-so-desirable aspects of police professionalism, however, have been replaced with something new.

What were some of the not-so-desirable aspects of reform era policing? First, police research revealed that preventive patrol wasn't particularly effective (see Chapter 8). Also, as we have already seen, the 1960s witnessed a great deal of strain in relationships between the police and the public. At the same time, the police came to realize that they couldn't reduce crime by their own efforts alone. Community-era reformers sought authorization from community members and extensive citizen support; a broad mandate that stressed the provision of services; a decentralized, responsive organizational structure; and improved relationships with citizens. These strong ties would be achieved through foot patrol, problem solving, quality-of-life preservation, and a host of other tactics—all of which were designed to ensure citizen satisfaction.

community policing
"A collaborative effort between the police and the community that identifies problems of crime and disorder and involves all elements of the community in the search for solutions to these problems."[i]

The sentiments of the community era were perhaps most clearly expressed in an important article authored by John Angell, a community policing innovator, during the early 1970s.[7] He argued that traditional police departments, and particularly their paramilitary organization and structure, are culture bound, that police bureaucracy is inconsistent with the humanistic democratic values of the United States, that it demands that employees demonstrate "immature" personality traits, and that it cannot cope with environmental pressures. The community model, he said, would (1) improve community relations, which suffered under the bureaucratic paramilitary model of law en-

Nampa City (Idaho) police gather near a neighborhood watch sign at the entrance to a subdivision. How can the effectiveness of programs like neighborhood watch be assessed?

Joe Rowley/AP Wide World Photos

forcement; (2) improve officers' morale by allowing them a measure of flexibility in the performance of their duties; and (3) improve interagency coordination.

There is more to the emergence of community policing than we have presented thus far. Some have argued, for instance, that it has emerged for less-than-noble purposes. It is also important to define community policing and, from a research standpoint, to gauge its true extent. We conclude by exploring the various forms of community policing and looking at the compatibility of community policing and the "war on terror."

WEB PATROL 10-5

Office of Community Oriented Policing Services
http://www.mycrimekit.com

The Birth of Community Policing

The history of community policing is rich and nuanced. There has been a tendency to assume that community policing has emerged for simple reasons, such as poor police-citizen relations, but there is a great deal more to the origins of the new policing paradigm. Together, the explanations fall into two categories: (1) those concerned directly with crime control and (2) those involving other intentions.

WEB PATROL 10-6

Policing.com: Community Policing Headquarters
http://www.mycrimekit.com

Crime Control. A few writers have called attention to the many noble reasons for the present community policing era. In a discussion concerning the "drive for change," one researcher identifies three reasons for the changes that have occurred and those that are taking place now.[8] The first reason, not surprisingly, is citizen disenchantment with police services. "Minority citizens in inner cities continue to be frustrated by police who whisk in and out of their neighborhoods with little sensitivity to community norms and values."[9]

The second reason concerns social science research undertaken in the 1970s. Specifically, "research about preventive patrol, rapid response to calls for service, and investigative work—the three mainstays of police tactics—was uniformly discouraging."[10] The third reason for reform suggests that "patrol officers have been frustrated with their traditional role"[11] and that they began to demand improved methods of interacting with citizens. It is sometimes felt that such an approach improves police officer morale.

Other authors have suggested that community policing can be traced to two interrelated problems: the isolation of police officers in patrol cars from citizens and the public's fear of victimization and perceptions of a rising crime rate.[12] More specifically, the authors claim that community policing "rose like a phoenix from the ashes of burned cities"[13] for seven reasons:

> (1) the isolation of officers in police cars; (2) the narrowing of the police mission to crime fighting; (3) an over-reliance on the scientific approach to management that stressed efficiency and effectiveness; (4) increased reliance on high-tech gadgetry instead of human interaction; (5) insulation of police administration from community input and accountability; (6) a long-standing concern about police violation of human rights; and (7) failed attempts by the police to reach the community, such as PCR [police-community relations], crime prevention, and team policing units.[14]

WEB PATROL 10-7

Origins and Evolution of Community Policing
http://www.mycrimekit.com

Other Intentions. Is there more to the community policing movement than meets the eye? Some scholars believe there is. For example, some have argued that police organizations may have adopted community policing for selfish reasons, such as to make rank-and-file officers more content with their jobs.[15] A professional ethic, or a desire to emulate progressive police agencies, could also be responsible for the current and widespread diffusion of community policing.

Perhaps more cynically, community policing may be a means of changing the goals of police work (from crime control to service, for example), of shaping public opinion instead of responding to it,[16] or of deflecting attention away from law enforcement officials.[17] Fiscal constraints may have served as a powerful motivator. Political culture and community characteristics could also explain the origins of community policing.[18]

How might community policing shape public opinion? By presenting officers in a favorable light, by making them look good in the eyes of citizens, historically strained relationships can improve. What about deflecting attention? Part of community policing puts crime control at least *partly* in the hands of citizens (as in neighborhood watch). Some have said, therefore, that community policing

Figure 10-2 • Twenty Reasons to Initiate Community Policing Services

1. Citizen disenfranchisement with police services
2. Research showing the ineffectiveness of random patrol and quick response times
3. Patrol officers' frustration with the traditional reactive police role
4. Isolation of officers from citizens, largely owing to increased use of patrol vehicles
5. Narrow crime-fighting police image
6. Overreliance on bureaucratic and paramilitary structure
7. Overreliance on high-tech gadgetry that diminishes personal interactions
8. Insulation of police administration from community input and accountability
9. Concern about human rights
10. Failure of police to reach out to the community
11. Desire to appear "with it" and professional
12. Desire to emulate other agencies
13. Need to change the goal of police work from crime control to service
14. Need to reduce police officers' workloads
15. Desire to deflect attention from the police department to the community
16. Need to save money
17. Needs or wants of the community
18. Political culture of the surrounding area
19. Desire to improve the police image
20. Desire to increase control over the community by adopting multiple strategies

Source: J. L. Worrall, *Crime control in America* (Upper Saddle River, NJ: Pearson Education, Inc., 2006), p. 89. Reprinted by permission.

passes the buck. And what about fiscal constraints? Some have argued that community policing is a cheap alternative to more expensive innovations because, at its core, it is a philosophy, and a philosophical change is free. These and many other reasons to initiate community policing are summarized in Figure 10-2. Whatever the reasons for its present popularity, community policing owes its origins to multiple demands and historical contingencies.

Definitions of Community Policing

We are guilty of having talked about community policing without really defining it, but that is for good reason: It is difficult to define. Community policing is a relatively new approach to law enforcement that is premised on the assumption that the police and citizens must work together to control crime.[19] Unfortunately, this short definition fails to adequately capture all of the various aspects of community policing.

One source defines community policing as

> a new philosophy of policing, based on the concept that police officers and citizens working together in creative ways can help solve contemporary community problems related to crime, fear of crime, social and physical disorder, and neighborhood decay.[20]

Other writers define community policing as

> a reorientation of policing philosophy and strategy away from the view that police alone can reduce crime, disorder and fear. The strategy is based on the view that police don't help their communities very much by placing primary reliance on random preventive patrolling, rapid response to calls for service irrespective of their urgency, post-incident investigations to identify offenders, and other primarily reactive criminal justice system tactics.[21]

Community Policing Perspectives. According to the Police Executive Research Forum (PERF), community policing consists of five different "perspectives."[22] The first is the *deployment perspective,* which emphasizes the fact that police officers are deployed in a way that moves them closer to citizens. The second is *community revitalization,* which emphasizes the importance of the police and citizens working closely together to improve neighborhoods and make them safer places. Next is the *problem-solving perspective,* an approach in which citizens and police work together to identify and respond to neighborhood problems. The fourth perspective is that of the *customer.* This emphasizes the importance of the police listening to citizens and serving their needs. Finally, *legitimacy* emphasizes bolstering the credibility of the police through police-citizen partnerships.

Community Policing Dimensions. Eastern Kentucky University professor Gary Cordner has identified the philosophical, strategic, tactical, and organizational dimensions of community policing and has described some of the common elements within each.[23] The *philosophical dimension* includes the ideas and beliefs surrounding a new paradigm of policing. Three ideas underlying community policing are citizen input, an enhanced and broadened police function, and personal service.[24] The *strategic dimension* consists of "the key operational concepts that translate philosophy into action."[25] Community policing strategies include reoriented operations (for example, from cruiser patrol to foot patrol), geographic permanency (assigning patrol officers to the same areas for extended periods of time), and an emphasis on crime prevention (for example, police officers acting as mentors and role models).

WEB PATROL 10-8

Determinants of Citizen and Police Involvement in Community Policing
http://www.mycrimekit.com

Cordner's *tactical dimension* is best understood as the inevitable outcome of the successful implementation of the first two dimensions. "The tactical dimension of community policing ultimately translates ideas, philosophies, and strategies into concrete programs, practices, and behaviors."[26] This dimension stresses constructive interactions between the police and citizens, improved partnerships between law enforcement officials and the public, and problem solving. Finally, the *organizational dimension,* though not necessarily a fundamental part of community policing, is essential to its development. The structure of police agencies and their management and information services need to be adjusted to accommodate community policing through such changes as decentralization, strategic planning, and program evaluation.

The Extent of Community Policing

The rhetoric of community policing has become more or less institutionalized in American policing. Elsewhere we have discussed the Violent Crime Control Act of 1994, the creation of the COPS Office in the U.S. Department of Justice, and the billions of dollars in grants to local law enforcement agencies to enhance their community policing capabilities. These and other developments in American policing over the past two decades have put the term *community policing* in nearly every police officer's vocabulary. But is there more to community policing than the term itself? Is community policing really being done, or do police departments just *say* they're doing it? Two research focuses help us answer these questions: (1) research on structural changes to police departments and (2) research on whether the rank and file are buying into community policing.

WEB PATROL 10-9

Community Policing: A Critical Analysis of a Small Police Department
http://www.mycrimekit.com

Structural Change. Researchers have questioned whether police departments have actually changed their structure in ways that are consistent with the spirit of community policing. A recent study on trends in police agencies' implementation of community policing from 1995 to 2000 is particularly revealing.[27] The authors of that study conclude, "Among organizational changes to support community policing activities, the most rapidly growing were those intended to signal change: revised mission statements and new performance review criteria for community police officers."[28] In other words, the study found that police departments were focusing on the form of change by making mostly symbolic changes to show their acceptance of community policing.[29]

The author of another recent study reached the same conclusion: "The police still cling to an institutional definition that stresses crime control and not prevention."[30] He also concludes that "by all available evidence, police organizations (their structures, division of labor, and the like) have not been radically or even significantly altered in the era of community and problem-oriented policing."[31] In short, many police agencies have adopted the cosmetic tenets of community policing but without altering their basic organizational structure in a meaningful way that actually changes the substance of their performance.[32] Additional research appears to confirm the discouraging news that structural change linked to community policing is frustratingly slow and is failing to result in functional change.[33]

Attitudinal Change. If American police agencies are slow to change in response to community policing, what about police officers themselves? Here is one author's answer to this important question:

> Police have a remarkable ability to wait out efforts to reform them. Important aspects of police culture mitigate against change. Police resist the intrusion of civilians (who "can't really understand") into their business. They fear that community troublemakers will take over the program and that people will seek to use police for their private purposes or for personal revenge. When police dislike changes proposed from within, they snort that the top brass are "out of touch with the street."[34]

In short, police officers are resistant to change and, as the preceding passage suggests, will actively take steps to thwart change. In fairness to law enforcement officials, other types of agencies—especially public agencies—also respond slowly to change. Nevertheless, it seems that community policing is being resisted by police officers themselves.

Two researchers recently described the efforts to do community policing in two mid-sized U.S. cities.[35] Those cities' police departments attempted four types of community policing: participatory management, community policing training, the decentralization of certain police operations, and the creation of special community policing units. The authors then tracked the opinions of the officers in both cities over a six-year period. They found that (1) a specialized community policing unit, not full-scale implementation of community policing, is desirable because not all officers will buy in, and (2) despite the presence of different community policing approaches, much law enforcement business proceeded as it always had (for example, routine patrol remained unchanged).

In another related study, researchers sought to determine whether community policing affects police officers' decisions to use coercion during encounters with suspected criminals.[36] Studying two cities, they focused in particular on whether community policing assignments, community policing training, and community partnerships affected officers' patterns of using coercion. Their analysis showed that none of these variables had much effect on officers' decisions to use coercion, again lending support to previous studies that showed that police are resistant to change. In yet another study concerning alleged resistance to community policing, the researchers concluded:

> The current transitional period in urban policing in America has left police departments a legacy of fragmented organizational cultures, with a variety of approaches to police work pulling in contradictory directions. . . . Given recent evidence for the effectiveness of community policing practices, widespread reports of implementation difficulties suggest that this morass may quickly become quicksand, suffocating reform efforts.[37]

Critical Views of Community Policing

Some authors note that "community policing has become the dominant theme of contemporary police reform in America,"[38] yet problems have plagued the movement since its inception.[39] For one thing, the range, complexity, and evolving nature of community policing programs make their effectiveness difficult to measure.[40] Moreover, "citizen satisfaction" with police performance can be difficult to conceptualize and quantify. Most early studies examined how citizens' attitudes developed through face-to-face interaction with individual police officers. They generally found a far higher level of dissatisfaction with the police among African Americans than among most other groups. Recent findings continue to show that the attitudes of African Americans toward the police remain poor. The wider reach of these studies, however, led evaluators to discover that this dissatisfaction may be rooted in overall quality of life and type of neighborhood.[41] Because most African Americans continue to experience a lower quality of life than most other U.S. citizens and because they often live in neighborhoods characterized by economic problems, drug trafficking, and street crime, recent studies conclude that it is these conditions of life, rather than race, that are most predictive of citizen dissatisfaction with the police.

Those who study community policing have often been stymied by ambiguity surrounding the concept of community.[42] Sociologists, who sometimes define a community as "any area in which members of a common culture share common interests,"[43] tend to deny that a community needs to be limited geographically. Police departments, on the other hand, tend to define communities "within jurisdictional, district or precinct lines, or within the confines of public or private housing developments."[44] Robert Trojanowicz, a well-regarded community policing scholar, once cautioned police planners that "the impact of mass transit, mass communications and mass media have widened the rift between a sense of community based on geography and one [based] on interest."[45]

Researchers who follow the police definition of *community* recognize that there may be little consensus within and between members of a local community about the community's problems and about appropriate solutions. Robert Bohm and colleagues at the University of Central Florida have found, for example, that while there may be some "consensus about social problems and their solutions . . . the consensus may not be community-wide." It may, in fact, exist only among "a relatively small group of 'active' stakeholders who differ significantly about the seriousness of most of the problems and the utility of some solutions."[46]

Finally, there is continuing evidence that not all police officers or managers are willing to accept nontraditional images of police work. One reason is that the goals of community policing often conflict with standard police performance criteria (such as arrests), leading to a perception among officers that community policing is inefficient at best and, at worst, a waste of time.[47] Similarly, many officers are loathe to take on new responsibilities as service providers whose role is defined more by community needs and less by strict interpretation of the law.

Some authors have warned that police subculture (see Chapter 6) is so committed to a traditional view of police work, which is focused almost exclusively on crime fighting, that efforts to promote community policing can demoralize an entire department, rendering it ineffective at its basic tasks.[48] As the Christopher Commission found following the Rodney King riots, "Too many . . . patrol officers view citizens with resentment and hostility; too many treat the public with rudeness and disrespect."[49] Some analysts warn that only when the formal values espoused by today's innovative police administrators begin to match those of rank-and-file officers can any police agency begin to perform well in terms of community policing.[50]

Some public officials, too, are unwilling to accept community policing. Ten years ago, for example, New York City Mayor Rudolph W. Giuliani criticized the police department's Community Police Officer Program, saying that it "has resulted in officers doing too much social work and making too few arrests."[51] Similarly, many citizens are not ready to accept a greater involvement of the police in their personal lives. Although the turbulent, protest-prone years of the

DOES IT WORK?

Foot Patrol

We looked at several varieties of patrol in Chapter 8. One of these, foot patrol, has been closely aligned with community policing. But is it effective?

The notion of putting officers in close contact with citizens is desirable not just because of today's preference for community policing, but because foot patrol is useful in some areas where car patrol is impossible. To determine whether foot patrol "works," though, we have to give some careful thought to where it is used. Indeed, it is quite likely that foot patrol works in some areas better than others. For example, pedestrian malls and downtown areas lend themselves more readily to foot patrol than suburban and rural areas do. Clearly, it would be impractical to put officers on foot patrol in rural areas where they have to cover thousands of square miles.

Given the modern-day appeal of foot patrol, a number of researchers have evaluated it, but the results are mixed. The good news: A number of studies have shown that citizens are more likely to notice police when they patrol on foot,[1] and some studies have shown that citizens are more satisfied with police following the implementation of foot patrol.[2]

These are interesting outcomes, but they do not answer the question of whether foot patrol reduces crime. In particular, do foot patrol interventions reduce crime in areas previously patrolled by officers in cars? The bad news: While one study showed that foot patrol was associated with a reduction in such public-order offenses as vagrancy, disorderly conduct, and vandalism,[3] many other studies suggest that its effect on crime is virtually nonexistent.[4] This is discouraging news, but it shouldn't be taken as evidence that *no* foot patrol is effective. There are places that can only be patrolled on foot, and thus this form of patrol surely helps, to some extent, in keeping crime at bay.

[1]A. M. Pate, "Community-oriented policing in Baltimore," in *Police and policing: Contemporary issues,* ed. D. J. Kenney, pp. 112–35 (New York: Praeger, 1989); and Police Foundation, *The Newark foot patrol experiment* (Washington, DC: Police Foundation, 1981).

[2]G. Kelling, *Foot patrol* (Washington, DC: National Institute of Justice, 1987); but see F. Esbensen, "Foot patrols: Of what value?" *American Journal of Police* 6 (1987): 45–65. Also see A. M. Pate, "Community-oriented policing in Baltimore," in *Police and policing: Contemporary issues,* ed. D. J. Kenney, pp. 112–35 (New York: Praeger, 1989); and Police Foundation, *The Newark foot patrol experiment.*

[3]Esbensen, "Foot patrols."

[4]J. Q. Wilson, *Thinking about crime* (New York: Basic Books, 1975); W. J. Bowers and J. H. Hirsch, "The impact of foot patrol staffing on crime and disorder in Boston: An unmet promise," *American Journal of Police* 6 (1987): 17–44; J. E. McElroy, C. A. Cosgrove, and S. Sadd, *Community policing: The CPOP in New York* (Newbury Park, CA: Sage, 1993); A. M. Pate, "Experimenting with foot patrol: The Newark experience," in *Community crime prevention: Does it work?* ed. D. Rosenbaum, pp. 137–56 (Beverly Hills, CA: Sage, 1986); and D. Rosenbaum, ed., *Community crime prevention: Does it work?* (Beverly Hills, CA: Sage, 1986).

1960s and early 1970s are long gone, some groups remain suspicious of the police. No matter how inclusive community policing programs become, it is doubtful that the gap between the police and the public will ever be entirely bridged. The police role of restraining behavior that violates the law will always produce friction between police departments and some segments of the community.

Examples of Community Policing

Community policing is practiced in more forms than we can possibly list here. The majority of community policing programs, though, can be placed into one of three categories. First, some are intended to encourage citizens to take an interest in crime control. Others seek to communicate with and inform citizens. Finally, some programs expand police presence in the community, such as putting police in schools or on specialized patrols. These three categories are discussed in this section.

WEB PATROL 10-10

The Chicago Police Department's Community Policing Page
http://www.mycrimekit.com

Mobilizing Citizens. The police in some areas host meetings with community members in an effort to identify and deal with specific crime problems and locations. These community meetings must be distinguished from neighborhood watch programs. (See the "Does It Work?" box on neighborhood watch and community meetings.) Community meetings are different because, unlike neighborhood watch, they are not surveillance oriented. Instead, they bring together police officers and community members so they can hash out ideas about crime prevention and control. In addition, the meetings are usually more formal and are typically held in public places, such as a police station, a community center, or a city hall. Neighborhood watch, on the other hand, tends to be less formal and is usually organized in neighborhoods.

crime-control newsletter
A newsletter published by a police department that typically contains information on recent developments at the police department, crime statistics for the area, tips for avoiding victimization, and so on.

Informing Citizens. Some police departments have also experimented with disseminating **crime-control newsletters** to community members. These newsletters often contain information on recent developments at the police department, crime statistics for the area, tips for avoiding victimization, and so on. The intent of the newsletter is to improve the police agency's communication with citizens.

Another easy way for police departments to improve their communication with citizens and to foster closer relations is to develop a website. With the proliferation of home computers and

A young male volunteer with the North Miami Beach Police Department parking enforcement division writing a ticket. What role do volunteers serve in police departments?

Jeff Greenberg/Alamy Images

Franklin (Massachusetts) Police Officer Brian Johnson with a computer showing the surveillance tape he uploaded in 2007 to YouTube.com, in hopes of solving a crime. Johnson posted a 32-second clip from a security camera on the video-sharing website and then e-mailed about 300 people and organizations to say the department was seeking information on the suspects. How else can police departments involve the public when seeking information about crimes?

Stew Milne/AP Wide World Photos

the increasing number of people who are connected to the Web, this strategy can benefit both the police and the community. The police can benefit by giving citizens an opportunity to report problems in their neighborhood. In fact, some departments allow citizens to complete hot-spot reports of criminal activity online and to submit noncriminal complaints electronically. At the same time, citizens can learn about new approaches taken by the department, see pictures of dangerous fugitives, view active warrants, and otherwise develop familiarity with their local police department.

It is safe to say that the development of a police website is consistent with the spirit of community policing. One author argues that police websites improve communication, generate leads, increase awareness, and can lead to the apprehension of criminal suspects.[52] A similar approach is to use television as a medium to get closer to the community. Some police departments—mostly in the largest jurisdictions—actually have their own community-access channel that broadcasts programs like "John TV," which shows the faces and names of men suspected of soliciting prostitutes. Other programming includes television shows and TV advertisements designed to improve public relations and public attitudes toward the local police force.

Engaging with Citizens. Community policing prides itself on an improved police presence. Some of the nontraditional patrol tactics discussed in Chapter 8 exemplify this. Another example is the police storefront, or substation, which is the subject of a "Does It Work?" box in this section. Police officers are also coming to occupy a significant position in our nation's schools. Police who work in schools are often called **school resource officers.**[53] They are represented by the National Association of School Resource Officers.[54] Police are also collaborating more with schools, and some schools are opting to hire private security personnel to patrol campuses in an effort to preserve a safe learning environment.

school resource officer
A police officer whose duty assignment is to patrol inside a specific school.

The presence of police officers or private security personnel in schools can be attributed, in part, to the diffusion of community policing; officers interacting with students may help by improving police-citizen relationships: "Children get to know their community police officers better, develop an understanding of the impact of violence and trauma, and learn adaptive means of dealing with the consequences of exposure to violence and trauma."[55] Police officers are also present in schools to provide security in response to incidents like the infamous Columbine High School shooting.

Some Community Policing Successes. Seattle's Community Crime Prevention Program (CCPP) integrated several of the strategies discussed thus far.[56] Mostly in response to a rise in burglaries, police officials began by contacting community organizations to alert them of their intentions to target burglary. Focusing on specific locations in the city where burglary was a problem,

DOES IT WORK?

Neighborhood Watch and Community Meetings

Neighborhood watch programs are a very popular example of community policing. Throughout suburban neighborhoods across the country, one encounters signs announcing "Block Watch" and similar programs. These and other neighborhood watch programs are sometimes started by neighborhood residents and sometimes at the urging of local police departments. Most of the research in this area is concerned with the ability of the police to organize neighborhood watch programs for the purpose of reducing criminal activity.

The literature devoted to neighborhood watch almost uniformly does not support this approach to America's crime problem. One study in Minneapolis sought to determine whether neighborhood watch (with and without police participation) reduced crime, but researchers found that the program had no apparent effect on crime.[1] An earlier study showed a link between neighborhood watch and a reduction in burglary for a period of 18 months,[2] but this study appears to be isolated. More typically, researchers in Cincinnati found that neighborhood watches and other community-based organizations had no effect on crime.[3]

Researchers have attributed these findings to reluctance among citizens to organize neighborhood watch programs in poor, high-crime areas.[4] This reluctance might stem from paranoia or fear of the police or from distrust between neighbors.[5] To make matters worse, researchers have found that in those areas where neighborhood watch programs flourish (usually middle-class neighborhoods), the programs *increase* rather than decrease fear of crime. This effect was also witnessed in a study of an "apartment watch" program.[6]

Community meetings, like neighborhood watch, are also popular. Community meetings differ from neighborhood watch in the sense that they are organized more often by police than by citizens themselves. Community meetings are also less surveillance-oriented than neighborhood watch. Surprisingly, the effectiveness of community meetings as a crime-control mechanism has been subjected to virtually no research. One study of community meetings in Madison, Wisconsin, sponsored by the National Institute of Justice, suggests that community meetings had no effect on crime whatsoever.[7] Another study of community meetings, this time in Chicago, suggests that this approach to the crime problem may or may not be effective.[8] The Chicago study showed that community meetings led to reductions in certain types of crime and victimization but not others. Before making any claims concerning the effectiveness of community meetings for crime control, it would be helpful to see additional research.

---

[1]A. M. Pate, M. McPherson, and G. Silloway, *The Minneapolis community crime prevention experiment: Draft evaluation report* (Washington, DC: Police Foundation, 1987).

[2]B. Lindsay and D. McGillis, "Citywide community crime prevention: An assessment of the Seattle program," in *Community crime prevention: Does it work?* ed. D. Rosenbaum, pp. 46–67 (Beverly Hills, CA: Sage, 1986).

[3]B. W. Smith, K. J. Novak, and D. C. Hurley, "Neighborhood crime prevention: The influences of community-based organizations and neighborhood watch," *Journal of Crime and Justice* 20 (1997): 69–86. See also D. P. Rosenbaum, "The theory and research behind neighborhood watch: Is it a sound fear and crime reduction strategy?" *Crime and Delinquency* 33 (1987): 103–34.

[4]D. Rosenbaum, D. A. Lewis, and J. A. Grant, "Neighborhood-based crime prevention: Assessing the efficacy of community organization in Chicago," in *Community crime prevention: Does it work?* ed. D. Rosenbaum, pp. 109–33 (Beverly Hills, CA: Sage, 1986).

[5]See, e.g., T. Bennett, *Evaluating neighborhood watch* (Basingstoke, England: Gower, 1990).

[6]C. Meredith and C. Paquette, "Crime prevention in high-rise rental apartments: Findings of a demonstration project," *Security Journal* 3 (1992): 161–68.

[7]M. A. Wycoff and W. G. Skogan, *Community policing in Madison: Quality from the inside out—An evaluation of implementation and impact—Technical report* (Washington, DC: Police Foundation, 1993).

[8]W. Skogan and others, *Community policing in Chicago, year two* (Chicago: Criminal Justice Information Authority, 1995).

they then contacted neighborhood residents. They sent out mailings alerting residents of their intentions and then started a door-to-door contact campaign. The intention of the mailings and the contacts was to secure citizen support for the program.

After contacts were made, the CCPP began several primary services, including the organization of a block watch program, the initiation of an operation ID program so residents could mark their property for identification purposes, and the conduct of home security inspections to inform residents about vulnerabilities to burglary. Seattle's CCPP was different from other community policing programs, however, because it combined these three services—along with additional approaches—into a single, uniform, and very deliberate community policing strategy.

Officials in Seattle also took careful steps to maintain the program so that public interest didn't wane, and they provided advisory services to those who wanted them. In summary, what made the CCPP somewhat unique is that it targeted a single problem: burglary. This singular focus, officials' use of several different community policing strategies, and continuing citizen contacts have been highly effective in keeping the program alive and vibrant. Three subsequent victimization surveys of people involved in and *not* involved in the CCPP showed modest reductions in burglary in the program area, suggesting that an integrated community policing strategy can be effective.[57]

A very different integrated approach was taken in Hartford, Connecticut.[58] There, police began by assessing the nature of criminal activity in the Asylum Hill area of the city. They paid special attention to the way in which the physical environment contributed to criminal activity. From their analysis of the area's geography, they decided to target the northern half of the area. They then implemented a three-pronged approach to crime control that was tailored to that area.

First, proposals were developed for changing the physical environment to make the area less vulnerable to criminal activity. Ultimately, several changes were made to the physical environment, such as restricting traffic flow on certain streets to residential traffic only. Then efforts were made to organize the community. Before the program, there was one citizen group in the north Asylum Hill area. Over a period of six months, two more organizations were formed. Next, a group of police officers was permanently assigned to the area, and these officers were given a fair degree of autonomy to make their own decisions. This decentralized approach was taken in order to build lasting relationships and trust between police officers and neighborhood residents.

After the program had been up and running for some time, an evaluation showed that these integrative community policing strategies had some beneficial effects. For example, the evaluators concluded that "[t]here is no doubt that the people in the North Asylum Hill were significantly less fearful and concerned about crime after the program was implemented than one would have expected given the trends in the rest of the city."[59] Examining victimization data, they concluded that "burglary dropped significantly below its expected levels immediately after the program was implemented, but then rose significantly during the following two years."[60] While this latter finding was not wholly desirable, at least it showed an initial reduction in one prevalent type of crime.

Recently, an experimental evaluation of the Redlands, California, Risk-Focused Policing at Places (RFPP) program showed that the program had little effect on rates of self-reported delinquency, perceptions of risk, and perceived police legitimacy.[61] RFPP combined community-oriented and problem-solving policing strategies into a public health crime-control model that led to a focus on a 26-block area of the city that exhibited higher risk factors for delinquency and crime. The program, which is still in operation, attempts to target risk factors that are associated with delinquency and seeks to enhance protective factors that reduce such risks.

Community Policing and Antiterrorism

Community policing stresses improved relationships between police and citizens. The ongoing "war on terror," however, seems to place a strain on those relationships. The typical response to terrorism, particularly high terrorist alert levels, is to put more police on the streets, make more liberal use of searches, and otherwise inconvenience people in the name of national security. These tactics are somewhat at odds with building relationships and improving police-community bonds and contacts. Some have argued, though, that community policing is *not* at odds with antiterrorism efforts. According to Chuck Wexler, director of the Police Executive Research Forum,

> The events of September 11, 2001, have changed the role of local police in America—perhaps forever. Local law enforcement faces the challenges of assuming more responsibility in countering domestic terrorism threats while continuing to address crime and disorder. Success will depend on their ability to build on strong community policing networks for information exchange and to maintain a collaborative problem-solving approach to crime amid high anxiety and crisis. Now more than ever, departments need to adhere to community problem-solving principles to decrease crime and disorder in their communities, increase their departments' efficiency and strengthen their relationships with citizens.[62]

Not everyone is so convinced, however. In fact, some have argued that police departments that haven't historically favored community policing are using the "war on terror" as a reason to scrap it.[63] But they also argue that even in the face of resistance, community policing is needed to succeed against terrorism:

> Few people outside the field know about the pitched battle for the heart and soul of policing that has raged over the past decade [the traditional bureaucratic model versus community policing]. It is said that people get the police they deserve. If we are to maintain recent reductions in violent crime and uncover the terrorists living among us, while preserving the civil rights that make our society special, we must insist on community policing now more than ever.[64]

DOES IT WORK?

Police Storefronts and Substations

Most of us have happened upon a police information booth in a shopping mall or have seen police officers working out of a building in a strip mall. These storefronts and substations are consistent with the spirit of community policing; they bring police officers in closer contact with citizens. The logic is that members of the public may be more likely to talk with police officers if they find them in a place that they frequent rather than having to go to the police station, which may be located out of the way. Here is one researcher's description of a storefront in action:

> [Substation] personnel took crime reports and gave and received information, and the police provided a place for people to meet with police. [Substation] officers were freed from routine patrol. . . . The office was to be their base of operations for getting acquainted with neighborhood residents and business people, identifying local problems and helping solve them, seeking ways of delivering better service to the area, and developing programs to draw the police and community closer together.[1]

Somewhat discouragingly, most research suggests that the presence of police offices in storefronts and strip malls does not affect crime.[2] According to one study,

> The lack of positive effects for those at the bottom of the social ladder may be related to their more limited awareness of the programs. In many instances, blacks and renters were less familiar with the programs, and recalled fewer contacts with them. For example, the community station was recognized by 43 percent of blacks and 77 percents of whites. . . . Merely making opportunities available for informal contact with the police, and participation in their programs, . . . was not enough.[3]

And there is little convincing evidence that such police substations are necessary to begin with; they tend to pop up in the areas where they are needed the least. Placing police officers in strip malls and storefronts may improve public perceptions of the police,[4] but there is no evidence that much else is accomplished. Part of the reason for this may be that substations are largely informational and passive, that is, they are most often concerned with providing crime-control information to the public; comparatively little attention is given to proactive crime control. Some substations are staffed by civilian personnel or volunteers, making it doubtful that they could do much to affect crime rates.

[1]W. Skogan, *Disorder and decline: Crime and the spiral decay in American neighborhoods* (New York: Free Press, 1990), p. 96.
[2]M. A. Wycoff and W. G. Skogan, *Community policing in Madison: Quality from the inside out—An evaluation of implementation and impact—Technical report* (Washington, DC: Police Foundation, 1993); C. D. Uchida, B. Forst, and S. O. Annan, *Modern policing and the control of illegal drugs: Testing new strategies in two American cities—Research report* (Washington, DC: National Institute of Justice, 1992); and A. M. Pate and W. Skogan, *Coordinated community policing: The Newark experience—Technical report* (Washington, DC: Police Foundation, 1985).
[3]Skogan, *Disorder and decline,* pp. 107–9.
[4]See, e.g., W. G. Skogan and M. A. Wycoff, "Storefront police offices: The Houston field test," in *Community crime prevention: Does it work?* ed. D. Rosenbaum, pp. 179–99 (Beverly Hills, CA: Sage, 1986).

Many other experts agree, too, that community policing and antiterrorism tactics are compatible:

> Any remaining doubts about the efficacy of community policing should have been dispelled [in September 2001] when such programs provided law enforcement not only with a vehicle for communicating a reassuring message to fearful residents, but a means for gathering information that may yet help further the federal investigations into the terrorist attacks on the World Trade Center and the Pentagon.[65]

According to Wexler,

> In order to truly protect our communities from terrorism we must enlist them as partners in our fight to prevent the next attack. If we are to be successful, it is imperative that we have the full cooperation of the communities we are trying to serve. The onus is on law enforcement to expand our community policing capabilities and continue to build relationships with our citizens, so that we can work together to reduce crime, violence, and fear.[66]

WEB PATROL 10-11
Situational Policing
http://www.mycrimekit.com

WEB PATROL 10-12
Community Policing and Homeland Security
http://www.mycrimekit.com

CITIZEN INVOLVEMENT AND CIVILIANIZATION

Thus far we have examined community policing strategies that are operated largely by the police. The strategies covered are best considered one-way because the police develop or coordinate them. Moreover, they are one-way in the sense that the police are the ones who go out into the community to work with citizens in numerous ways. An alternative to these approaches is to bring citizens to the police. While programs of this type are still run and coordinated by the police, they are different in that they allow citizens to view and participate in the world of law enforcement.

Citizen Patrol and Citizen Police Academies

There are hundreds, if not thousands, of **citizen patrols** around the United States.[67] Typically, citizen patrols comprise volunteers who engage in preventive patrol. These volunteers are often provided with some type of government vehicle and patrol the streets during daylight hours. Sometimes, however, citizens volunteer to drive their own vehicles and operate independently of the police. In this section, we will focus on police-sponsored citizen patrols.

citizen patrol
A preventive patrol program staffed by citizen volunteers.

An example of citizen patrol that has received some attention is the Neighborhood Patrol Officers Program in Fort Worth, Texas.[68] Started in 1991, the program provided eight hours of training to volunteers on such topics as rules of conduct, liability issues, and legal considerations. Once training was completed, volunteers were issued an identification badge, a T-shirt, a hat, and a jacket. They also received police radios. Once trained and equipped, the volunteers used their own vehicles to patrol neighborhoods, looking for evidence of criminal activity.

Many police departments also operate so-called **citizen police academies.**[69] Although the programs differ to some extent, they all possess a common element: Citizens are given an opportunity to learn about the policing profession and even to experience some of the same sensations that uniformed officers experience.[70] This is usually accomplished through a watered-down version of a police academy where citizens are taught the nature, operations, and complexity of the policing profession.[71] Sometimes citizens even learn to use firearms and otherwise defend themselves from victimization. See Figure 10-3 for an overview of the Concord (California) Citizen Police Academy program and curriculum.

citizen police academy
A training experience that offers citizens an opportunity to learn about the policing profession and even to experience some of the same sensations that uniformed officers experience.

It is tempting to ask whether citizen police academies work, but in order to answer this question, we must first understand their purpose. While some critics find it difficult to fathom any

Figure 10-3 • A Citizen Police Academy Curriculum

About the Citizen Academy

The academy provides community members with an inside look at local law enforcement. During the academy, students will be introduced to a variety of topics, as described under the curriculum outline.

The 13-week academy is designed to give citizens an overview of the police department's function and operational procedures. The curriculum and teaching methods are similar to the traditional police academy, but the weekly sessions are not designed to train the participant as a police officer.

Academy classes are taught by police executives and veteran police officers. Participants will have the opportunity to meet with the chief of police and staff members. They are encouraged to ask questions and express ideas and concerns to police employees.

Applications for the citizen academy may be submitted at any time.

For additional information about the Citizen Police Academy, please call the Community Action and Awareness Unit.

Weeks 1 and 2

- Chief of Police—Introduction to Community Policing
- Criminal Justice System
- Laws of Arrest
- Legal Issues

Weeks 3 and 4

- Narcotics Enforcement
- Reserves and Volunteers
- Patrol Procedures
- Traffic Investigations

Weeks 5 and 6

- Criminal Investigations
- Police Facility Tour
- Police Vehicle Operations
- Pursuit Driving Exercise

Weeks 7 and 8

- Use of Force Issues
- Communications—911
- Youth Crimes
- K-9

Weeks 9 and 10

- Firearms Simulation
- Use of Deadly Force
- SWAT Operations
- Hostage Negotiations

Weeks 11, 12, and 13

- Gang Investigations
- Crime Scene Investigations
- Practical Scenarios
- Graduation

Source: Courtesy of the Concord (California) Police Department, "Citizen Police Academy," http://www.ci.concord.ca.us/police/m-227-1-citizen-academy.pdf (accessed July 5, 2008).

crime-reduction benefits due to citizen police academies, that is not their direct goal. Rather, the academies are intended to affect citizens' perceptions of the police rather than to reduce crime, and that is what the research suggests they accomplish. The authors of one recent study found that citizen police academy participants viewed the police more favorably after completing the program.[72] Similar findings were reported in at least two other studies.[73]

Other researchers have been critical of citizen police academies. One researcher found that academy participants tend to be mostly community "elites" and that minorities are drastically underrepresented.[74] The argument has also been raised that citizen police academies—like citizen patrol programs—perpetuate a traditional law enforcement strategy and may in fact be antithetical to the spirit of community policing.[75] This argument becomes quite convincing when police departments teach civilians many law enforcement "tricks of the trade," such as self-defense techniques.

What can be gleaned from the literature on citizen police academies? They appear to improve public perceptions of and attitudes toward the police, but people who participate in the academies may already be more prone to viewing the police favorably prior to enrolling in the curriculum. As far as the effect of citizen police academies on crime, there is no evidence that there is any. In fact, there is a total lack of research on the subject. Regardless of this, the practice of giving citizens a window into the law enforcement world is intended to do little more than improve the image of the police, and while there is nothing particularly wrong with that, an improved police image has no effect on crime.

WEB PATROL 10-13

National Citizens Police Academy Association
http://www.mycrimekit.com

WEB PATROL 10-14

The Los Angeles Police Department's E-Policing home page
http://www.mycrimekit.com

Civilianization

civilianization
A "law enforcement agency's hiring of nonsworn personnel to replace or augment its corps of sworn officers" in an effort to reduce costs and improve service.[ii]

Civilianization has been defined as a "law enforcement agency's hiring of nonsworn personnel to replace or augment its corps of sworn officers, typically with the aims of reducing costs and improving service."[76] In some agencies, "civilians are employed as communications specialists, criminalists (crime scene technicians, forensic laboratory scientists, etc.), computer specialists, lawyers, and a host of other support positions."[77] This definition makes it clear that civilianization is something distinct from private security, private policing, and privatization in general.

Citizen patrol and citizen police academies have largely different motivations than civilianization. They both get citizens involved in policing-related functions, by having them either actively patrol neighborhoods or experience policing life through a short mock academy. Civilianization, in contrast, is largely done because it saves money. It is more expensive to have a sworn officer handle department communications when a civilian could just as easily be hired. A civilian doesn't need to go through the police academy or use the expensive specialized equipment that a sworn officer needs.

At the same time, civilianization may not be *all* about cost savings. The hiring of civilians is, first, the sign of a progressive, change-oriented agency. As American University professor Brian Forst has observed, "While some tradition-bound police executives have been reluctant to transfer a variety of support functions to civilians, it has become increasingly clear that civilians tend to perform certain specialized roles more effectively than sworn officers."[78] Dispatch functions were largely performed by sworn officers during the 1960s; now dispatch is almost exclusively performed by nonsworn personnel. Hiring more civilians also creates an air of openness consistent with the community policing ideals of involving more and more citizens in crime-control functions.

third-party policing
A recently coined term that describes "police efforts to persuade or coerce nonoffending persons to take actions which are outside the scope of their routine activities, and which are designed to indirectly minimize disorder caused by other persons or to reduce the possibility that crime may occur."[iii]

civil law
The branch of modern law that governs relationships between parties.

THIRD-PARTY POLICING

We introduced private policing and security in Chapter 1. One could conceive of these approaches as policing by third parties—that is, by parties other than citizens or the police. When we talk about third-party policing, however, we are referring to something entirely different. **Third-party policing** is a recently coined term that describes "police efforts to persuade or coerce nonoffending persons to take actions which are outside the scope of their routine activities, and which are designed to indirectly minimize disorder caused by other persons or to reduce the possibility that crime may occur."[79] Basically, it amounts to formal methods of policing that invoke the use of the **civil law** rather than the criminal law. A criminal law approach to policing has officers arresting people for the commission of crimes. A civil law approach, by contrast, has not just the police but other officials relying on civil process, such as nuisance abatement and code enforcement, to reduce crime and disorder.

Michael Buerger and Lorraine Mazerolle, the scholars who first conceived the term *third-party policing,* distinguish it from community policing and problem-oriented policing because of its intended targets: "In community- and problem-oriented policing, the police assume an active quasi-enforcement and managerial role in addition to their more established, hortatory [encouraging] role as dispensers of expert advice."[80] They go on to argue that community policing and problem-oriented policing are simply augmented versions of traditional policing that rely heavily on citizens and guardians (those responsible for places, like landlords) for influence and control over criminals and would-be criminals. Third-party policing is different from this because "it focuses on the places that the guardians control by promoting certain collective responses as a way of controlling individual behavior."[81] In other words, third-party policing is more place oriented than person oriented.

Third-party policing should not be confused with environmental criminology, which is concerned with designing "places" to make them less vulnerable to crime (for example, access control with a tall security gate). Third-party policing is place oriented, but it is not concerned with design. Instead, it is about providing guardians with the information and tools they need to take a certain element of law enforcement into their own hands.

There is a possible "dark side" to third-party policing, however. It is not just about encouraging guardians to target problems at the places they are responsible for. It is also about coercing them to do so. Once again according to Buerger and Mazerolle, "Third-party policing constitutes a return to a compliance model of policing, although the police do not resume inspectorial functions. . . . Rather, these functions are performed by nominal partners of the police, or remain an implied threat behind police negotiations with guardians."[82]

In our definition of *third-party policing,* the "nonoffending" persons are the guardians. They are basically persuaded by police to do something about identified problems "or else." Simply put, "third-party policing establishes a control over nonoffending persons and persuades (or coerces) them to engage in activities thought to control crime."[83]

At its core, some would say that third-party policing is about turning certain enforcement functions over to those who haven't traditionally done them. Others, though, would argue that this is simply good law enforcement and that it is intended to bring guardians out of the shadows to take control over their properties. The police might, for instance, coerce a slumlord to fix a problem at one of his or her apartment complexes or face possible civil consequences.

Beyond the Criminal Law

Police routinely use the criminal law, local ordinances, curfew statutes, and the like to target crime. Third-party policing goes beyond the criminal law, primarily invoking civil law provisions. These, according to Buerger and Mazerolle, are "controls imported from the regulatory wing of the civil law [that] include provisions that allow the police to target deviant places, typically crackhouses, blighted homes, and false-front stores (such as 'bodegas') that sell drugs or traffic in black-market food stamps."[84] In truth, the civil law has always been available to the police, but the recent proliferation of problem-oriented and community policing has caused police officials to use more creative methods of crime control.

Civil law provisions, like those governing building codes, have been used periodically in law enforcement and, indeed, throughout the public sector to target problems. A dilapidated building that is replete with code violations can be shut down or condemned, something officials have done for years. Recently, though, scores of cities have capitalized on existing civil ordinances and created more of their own. An example is San Diego's creative ordinances aimed at the problem of illegal street racing.

Illegal street racing is a very real social problem, not just the stuff of Hollywood. Indeed, movies like *The Fast and the Furious* were based, at least to some extent, on reality. Between 1998 and 2001, the National Highway Traffic Safety Administration reported that 315 fatal crashes resulted from illegal street racing.[85] The California Office of Traffic Safety reported that more than 800 citations were issued for illegal street racing in 2001.[86] In San Diego, illegal street racing has been described as "epidemic."[87] Sixteen deaths and 31 injuries were related to street racing in 2001.[88] The city attorney's office prosecuted 147 illegal street-racing cases in 1999, 161 in 2000, and 290 in 2001.[89] Concerned about these numbers, San Diego enacted a forfeiture ordinance, which says, in part, that

> a motor vehicle shall be declared a nuisance and forfeited subject to this division if . . . [i]t is used in violation of California Vehicle Code sections 23109(a) or (c); and . . . it is being driven by the registered owner of the vehicle, the registered owner is a passenger, the registered owner's immediate family member is driving or riding in the car, or the driver or passenger lives at the same address as the registered owner.

The San Diego ordinance offers this reason for forfeiture:

> Streets and highways within the City of San Diego have been the site of continuing and escalating illegal street-racing over the past several years. Such street-racing threatens the health and safety of the public, interferes with pedestrian and vehicular traffic, creates a public nuisance, and interferes with the right of private business owners to enjoy the use of their property within the City of San Diego.[90]

Interestingly, some recent research has revealed that the forfeiture ordinance significantly reduced street-racing casualties.[91] And, perhaps more importantly, it is an ordinance that uses a civil process to target an underlying problem. It is not an example of third-party policing per se, as police officers are the ones who first come into contact with the racers, but it illustrates an out-of-the-box approach to crime control. The next subsection briefly considers the use of civil process in the third-party policing context.

Examples of Third-Party Policing

Beat Health Program
A third-party policing program in Oakland, California, that uses civil remedies to prevent and reduce drug and disorder problems.

The **Beat Health Program** in Oakland, California, is a good example of third-party policing. This still-thriving program was highlighted in Buerger and Mazerolle's study, which we cited earlier. What puts the program in the third-party policing category is the fact that police officers make the first contacts with the targeted nonoffending parties:

> The Beat Health team will open a case (1) after preliminary site visits to a zone that is identified as a potential problem, owing to a high number of narcotic arrests, citizen complaints, or (2) at the request of community groups. Beat Health teams try to establish relationships with place managers (landlords, managers, owners, or tenants of properties) or with others who hold a stake in improving the conditions of the case location. During the intervention, police communicate landlords' rights and tenants' responsibilities, provide ideas for crime prevention measures, and assist civilians in contacting city or community agencies (for legal, ordinance, and rental information). Officers maintain contact with property owners and place managers for [six] months afterward. Beat Health officers also coordinate site visits with the Specialized Multi-Agency Response Team (SMART), composed of a group of city inspectors. Based on initial assessments made by the police, representatives from various agencies such as housing, fire, public works, gas, and electric or vector control are invited to inspect, enforce city codes, and offer solutions to related issues.[92]

WEB PATROL 10-15
Oakland's Beat Health Program
http://www.mycrimekit.com

Initial contacts are as collegial as possible. The teams attempt to build rapport with the property owners. Any owners who fail to cooperate, however, quickly encounter the more coercive arm of third-party policing. Mazerolle, who was one of the evaluators of this program, found that the most effective means of precipitating change was the identification of sewer and fire violations, which landlords were required to fix.[93] Additionally, the program appeared to have been more successful in commercial rather than residential facilities, and third-party policing coupled with traditional enforcement (such as targeting drug offenders) appeared to be the most effective approach.[94]

Minneapolis Repeat Call Address Policing
A third-party policing program in Minneapolis, Minnesota, that used a small, detached, developmental unit working on a diverse set of "problems" derived from a computer analysis of addresses with high levels of calls for police service.

Another third-party policing program that continues today is the **Minneapolis Repeat Call Address Policing** (RECAP) program. It began with police officers presenting call histories to the owners and managers of problem properties. Not surprisingly, a number of them knew about the problems; others, though, did not. Officers then explained that improvements would be mutually beneficial. For example, businesses would attract more customers and thereby increase profits if police weren't routinely called to—and seen arresting people on—the property. Owners of rental properties were told that better tenants would be more likely to pay their rent and increase the profitability of the property.

The program began without an official mandate from the city and was thus forced to operate only out of the police department. It eventually grew into something larger, however, and to partner with other officials, such as those in the city housing inspector's office.[95] The police department's licensing division was also revived from a period of dormancy to target problem bar owners: "When RECAP succeeded in having the licenses of the two most notorious bars revoked (an action unprecedented in recent Minneapolis history), city officials took note of the benefits to be derived from demanding responsible ownership."[96]

The Minneapolis and Oakland stories represent the proverbial tip of the iceberg. Police departments are increasingly wising up to the idea that, in some instances, civil law can work just as well for crime control as does the criminal law. Beyond the policing realm, other criminal justice officials, particularly prosecutors, are coming to the same realization. Prosecutors sometimes work closely with the police because they bring to the table the legal knowledge and ability to pursue appropriate actions in court. Although third-party policing is catching on, it hasn't been subject to extensive evaluation. We cited a few examples of research in this area, but much more remains to be done in order to identify best practices.

SUMMARY

- The contemporary notion of community justice encompasses community policing and several other recent law enforcement innovations, such as citizen patrol. Problem-oriented policing is best viewed as part of community policing. Both policing styles rely on citizen involvement.
- Community policing is often promoted as an effective crime-control technique, but it exists for several other reasons as well. For example, it serves to address citizen dissatisfaction, and it saves money. *Community policing* can be defined in various ways, but the essence of community policing is a partnership in which the police and the community work together to reduce crime.
- Citizen involvement in policing is commonplace today and occurs largely through citizen patrol and citizen police academies. Civilianization refers to the hiring of nonsworn personnel to perform certain limited functions within police departments.
- In third-party policing, the police apply pressure to nonoffending third parties (such as landlords) to improve their properties and thereby promote crime control and crime prevention.

COMING FULL CIRCLE

For Discussion

Return to the questions posed at the start of this chapter. Have any of your answers changed since you read the chapter? What portions of this chapter helped you answer these questions?

Writing Assignment

Using material from this chapter and additional resources, write a 500-word essay in response to one of the questions presented at the beginning of the chapter. Submit your essay to your instructor if asked to do so.

KEY TERMS AND NAMES

Beat Health Program
citizen patrol
citizen police academy
civilianization
civil law
community justice
community policing
crime-control newsletter
Minneapolis Repeat Call Address Policing (RECAP)
problem-oriented policing (POP)
school resource officer
third-party policing

WEB INT

Visit the federal Office
Services (the COPS Of
usdoj.gov. Click on "W
the site's home page, a
fice describes the comm
the core elements of co
the home page, and cli
Topics" menu item. Li
that appear there, and
Submit the informatio
structor if asked to do

REVIEW

1. What is commun
policing? How ar
2. What is commun
widely promoted

chapter eleven POLICING AND THE LAW

LEARNING OBJECTIVES

After reading this chapter, students should be able to:

1. Discuss when Fourth Amendment provisions apply to activities undertaken by law enforcement officers, and describe existing rules governing the conduct of searches and seizures.
2. Discuss existing rules concerning interrogations undertaken by law enforcement officers and the in-court admissibility of obtained confessions, especially as established under the Fifth, Sixth, and Fourteenth Amendments.

GOD BLESS AMERICA
589

THINK ABOUT IT

In 1991, Agent William Elliott of the U.S. Department of the Interior suspected that Danny Kyllo was growing marijuana in his home, which was part of a triplex in Florence, Oregon, a town close to the ocean and west of Eugene. At 3:20 a.m. on January 16, 1992, Elliott and a colleague used an Agema Thermovision 210 thermal imager (an infrared heat detector about the size of a digital camera) to scan the triplex. The scan, conducted from the passenger seat of Elliott's vehicle, took only seconds, and the imager revealed unusual signs of high heat in part of Kyllo's home. The heat signature was consistent with the type of heat that would be emitted by an active marijuana-growing operation.

Elliott correctly concluded that Kyllo was using bright halide lights (a relatively common practice known to law enforcement officers at the time) to grow marijuana inside the house. He took the results of the scan, tips from informants, and copies of Kyllo's unusually high electric bills to a judge, who issued a warrant to search Kyllo's home. The search uncovered more than 100 marijuana plants under cultivation in the home.

Kyllo's attorney attempted to exclude the marijuana plants from evidence at his trial for marijuana manufacturing by arguing that the thermal imager scan was an unconstitutional search within the meaning of the Fourth Amendment. The attorney argued that Elliott shouldn't have been allowed to scan the house without first showing that he had probable cause to do so and obtaining a warrant permitting the scan. His attorney's motion to suppress the results of the scan was unsuccessful. Following conviction, Kyllo appealed to the Ninth Circuit Court of Appeals. After considering the fact that Kyllo had made no effort to conceal the heat escaping from his home, the court sided with the agents. Moreover, the court concluded that the scan did not "expose any intimate details of Kyllo's life," only "amorphous hot spots on the roof and exterior wall."

Kyllo continued appealing his conviction until he reached the U.S. Supreme Court. The Court issued its decision in 2001, reversing the findings of the lower courts. The justices held, "Where, as here, the Government uses a device that is not in general public use, to explore details of a private home that would previously have been unknowable without physical intrusion, the surveillance is a Fourth Amendment 'search,' and is presumptively unreasonable without a warrant."[1]

Court watchers find the *Kyllo* case to be especially interesting because it deals with the intersection of today's technology and our 220-year-old Constitution. Significantly, in *Kyllo*, the Supreme Court did not limit its decision to thermal imagers. The justices talked about devices "not in general public use," a phrase that seems to cover many modern technologies, including those that are on the horizon. Constitutional interpretations of the applicability of today's technology to law enforcement raise several questions to keep in mind as you read this chapter:

1. What can we expect to keep private?
2. Should people enjoy privacy in the "waste heat" emanating from their homes?
3. Was the Supreme Court's *Kyllo* decision reasonable?
4. Why didn't the Court specifically reference thermal imagers in its decision?
5. Is existing Supreme Court precedent sufficient to address future technological developments in the law enforcement context?

WEB PATROL 11-1

Kyllo v. United States Full Text Opinion
http://www.mycrimekit.com

INTRODUCTION

Police officers must be aware of how the law governs their everyday activities.[2] When they make arrests, search suspects, and interrogate them—and even when they make simple observations and draw certain actionable conclusions—various constitutional considerations come into play. Those constitutional issues, which are sometimes collectively referred to as *the law of search and seizure*, are the focus of this chapter. Here we will examine the rules governing searches and seizures, as well as those pertaining to confessions and interrogations. The rules we will be discussing stem largely from court interpretations of the Fourth and Fifth Amendments to the U.S. Constitution, and it would be a good idea to review both amendments before proceeding. While the language in these amendments may seem to be relatively straightforward, it has been scrutinized in scores of federal court cases.

SEARCH AND SEIZURE

Of all the important legal issues in law enforcement today, the issue of how to properly conduct searches and seizures ranks as among the most important. Serving search warrants, arresting suspects, making traffic stops, stopping suspicious individuals on foot, inventorying impounded vehicles, and a host of other activities require an intimate knowledge of the Fourth Amendment. Fourth Amendment violations can result in lawsuits, complaints, difficulty convicting defendants, the release of criminals into the community, and even criminal charges against law enforcement officers.

When the Fourth Amendment Applies

The **Fourth Amendment** states:

> The right of the people to be secure in their persons, houses, papers, and effects, against unreasonable searches and seizures, shall not be violated, and no Warrants shall issue, but upon probable cause, supported by Oath or affirmation and particularly describing the place to be searched, and the persons or things to be seized.

The Fourth Amendment applies when a search or seizure is being contemplated (search warrants are discussed later in this chapter) or takes place. **Searches** are, as the term suggests, activities performed in order to find evidence to be used in a criminal prosecution. To define when a *Fourth Amendment search* takes place, however, two important elements must be considered: (1) whether the search is a product of **government action** and (2) whether the government action infringes upon the individual's **reasonable expectation of privacy**. We will return to this topic shortly.

The term **seizure** has a dual meaning in policing. First, property can be seized, and a search often results in the seizure of evidence. For example, if the police successfully serve a search warrant to look for illegal weapons at 345 Oak Street, any illegal weapons they find there will be seized. But people can also be seized. Seizures of people can occur almost anywhere and at any time. An arrest, for example, is considered a seizure within the meaning of the Fourth Amendment.

The next stage in the Fourth Amendment analysis requires that we focus on the **reasonableness** of the search or seizure. Once Fourth Amendment protections have been triggered, we must ask whether the officers acted in line with Fourth Amendment requirements. If a person has been arrested, for example, the question is whether the police had adequate reason to believe that the person arrested in fact committed the crime. When courts focus on the reasonableness of a search or seizure, they speak in terms of **justification.** If the police engage in searches or seizures without justification, they violate the Fourth Amendment.

The only justification mentioned in the Fourth Amendment is probable cause. Consequently, lay readers may be inclined to think that any search or seizure based on a lesser degree of certainty than probable cause would violate the Fourth Amendment. For a time this was the case, but in recent decades the U.S. Supreme Court has carved out exceptions to the Fourth Amendment's probable cause requirement. The Court has ruled that there are certain situations in which the police can seize people or look for evidence with a lesser degree of certainty than probable cause. These situations are described later in this chapter.

Defining Search and Seizure

Not every act of looking for evidence can be considered a search within the meaning of the Fourth Amendment, nor is every act of "grabbing" something or someone considered a seizure. For example, private citizens may look for evidence, but their actions are not bound by the Fourth Amendment because private citizens are not government actors. The Fourth Amendment protects citizens from *government* action. As such, one requirement in determining when a search occurs is to ascertain *who* is looking for evidence. And although the Fourth Amendment restricts government action, it is not

Fourth Amendment
The amendment to the U.S. Constitution that governs search and seizure.

search
An activity performed in order to find evidence to be used in a criminal prosecution.

government action
In the context of search and seizure law, one of two elements that must be considered when defining a Fourth Amendment search. (The other element is a reasonable expectation of privacy.) Government actions consist of measures to effect a search undertaken by someone employed by or working on behalf of the government.

reasonable expectation of privacy
In the context of search and seizure law, one of two elements that must be considered when defining a Fourth Amendment search. (The other element is government action.) A reasonable expectation of privacy means that people who speak or act in private can reasonably expect that what they say or do will not be seen or heard by someone else.

seizure
The confiscation of one's person (arrest) or property by a government agent.

reasonableness
The elements of a situation that serve to justify a search or seizure.

justification
The focus of a court's examination of the reasonableness of a search or seizure.

the case that government actors always engage in searches when looking for evidence. There are many things the police can do to look for evidence, such as looking in open fields and public areas, examining items that have been discarded, observing people and things in public view, and so on, without being bound by the Fourth Amendment.

What Is a Search? The Fourth Amendment's protection against unreasonable searches and seizures has been limited by the courts to conduct that is governmental in nature. When a private individual seizes evidence or otherwise conducts a search, Fourth Amendment protections are not triggered.[3] One requirement for a Fourth Amendment search, then, is that it be conducted by a government actor.

Government Action The inapplicability of the Fourth Amendment to searches or seizures carried out by private individuals was first recognized by the U.S. Supreme Court in 1921.[4] Some private individuals entered a man's business office and seized records. The records were later turned over to the U.S. attorney general, who planned to use them against the man in court. The Supreme Court concluded that there was nothing wrong, from a constitutional standpoint, with the conduct in question: "[O]rigin and history clearly show that it was intended as a restraint upon the activities of sovereign authority, and was not intended to be a limitation upon other than governmental agencies."[5]

Who are government actors? Clearly, a uniformed police officer working in his or her official capacity is a government actor. Numerous other officials are responsible for enforcing the law, however. Even those whose actions will never result in a criminal prosecution are bound by Fourth Amendment restrictions. For example, in *Camara v. Municipal Court* (1967),[6] the Supreme Court held that regulatory officials conducting health and safety inspections can be considered government actors for purposes of the Fourth Amendment. This ruling has been expanded to apply to numerous other government officials, including fire inspectors,[7] Occupational Safety and Health Administration (OSHA) inspectors,[8] federal mine inspectors,[9] and even public school teachers.[10]

The situation is decidedly less clear for individuals who perform law enforcement–like functions but are not employed by the government per se. An example is a store security guard. In general, when a private security officer is used deliberately in place of the police, Fourth Amendment protections are triggered, that is, the officer is said to be acting in a government capacity.[11] Private actors can also become government actors when they are acting at the behest of police. For example, if an officer doesn't have authority to conduct a search but asks a private party to do so simply to skirt the Fourth Amendment, that private party would be considered a government actor.[12]

Reasonable Expectation of Privacy In a Fourth Amendment search, the government actor infringes on a person's reasonable expectation of privacy. What is a reasonable expectation of privacy? Prior to 1967, the definition of *search* was closely tied to property interests. Police action was only deemed a search if it physically infringed on an individual's property. Essentially, the activity had to

YOU DECIDE
A Search?

The ethical decision scenarios presented so far in this book have asked the question, What would you do? We adopt a slightly different focus in light of this chapter's concern with legal issues. Here, our focus is on whether a particular police action conformed to constitutional requirements. Here is the first scenario.

An electrical meter reader employed by a utility under contract with the city observes through a window near the meter a significant number of marijuana plants growing under several rows of bright lights. She returns to her vehicle and reports her observations to the police. Armed with this new information, as well as information from an ongoing stakeout, the police obtain a warrant, search the house, and seize the plants. The plants are then entered into evidence against the homeowner at trial. May he move to have the plants excluded on the grounds that the meter reader was a government actor whose actions triggered the protections of the Fourth Amendment?

You may search the Internet for additional information that will help you answer this question.

amount to what would otherwise be considered common law trespass for it to be considered a search. Any police activity that was not trespassory in nature was not considered a search. This definition became outdated in the landmark decision in *Katz v. United States* (1967).[13]

In *Katz*, federal agents placed a listening device outside a phone booth in which Katz was having a conversation. Katz made incriminating statements during the course of his conversation, and the Federal Bureau of Investigation (FBI) sought to use the statements against him at trial. The lower court ruled that the FBI's activities did not amount to a search because there was no physical entry into the phone booth. The U.S. Supreme Court reversed the lower court's decision, holding that the Fourth Amendment "protects people, not places," so its reach "cannot turn upon the presence or absence of a physical intrusion into any given enclosure."[14] Instead, the Fourth Amendment definition of *search* turns on the concept of privacy. In the Court's words: "The Government's activities in electronically listening to and recording words violated the privacy upon which [Katz] justifiably relied while using the telephone booth and thus constituted a 'search and seizure' within the meaning of the Fourth Amendment."[15]

Despite the seemingly profound change in the *search and seizure* definition following *Katz*, several subsequent decisions have interpreted the *Katz* ruling rather narrowly. For example, the Supreme Court has since ruled that a Fourth Amendment search or seizure occurs only when there has been an infringement on an expectation of privacy that society (through the eyes of a court) is willing to accept as reasonable.[16] It further stated that "[w]hat a person knowingly exposes to the public, even in his own home or office, is not subject to Fourth Amendment protection."[17] Protection is only afforded for "what he seeks to preserve as private."[18]

WEB PATROL 11-2

Katz v. United States Full Text Opinion
http://www.mycrimekit.com

What Is a Seizure? The Supreme Court has concluded that the seizure of tangible property occurs "when there is some meaningful interference with an individual's possessory interest in that property."[19] A seizure of a person occurs when a police officer, by means of physical force or show of authority, intentionally restrains an individual's liberty in such a manner that a reasonable person would believe that he or she is not free to leave.[20] Another way to understand a Fourth Amendment seizure is by asking the question: Would a reasonable person believe that he or she is free to decline the officer's requests or otherwise terminate the encounter?[21] If the answer is no, a seizure has occurred.

There can be several types of seizures of a person, just as there can be many different types of searches. For example, a person can be arrested, perhaps the most significant form of seizure. But a stop-and-frisk situation also amounts to a seizure, as we will see later. A seizure can also occur without

Lt. Timothy Navarre, of the Harris County (Texas) Sheriff's Department stands guard near a huge pile of seized marijuana. What is a "seizure" for purposes of the law?

Houston Chronicle, Brett Coomer/AP Wide World Photos

probable cause
A set of facts and circumstances that would induce a reasonably intelligent and prudent person to believe that another particular person has committed a specific crime. Probable cause is the only justification for search and seizure mentioned in the Fourth Amendment.

reasonable suspicion
A belief, based on a consideration of the facts at hand and on reasonable inferences drawn from those facts, that would induce an ordinarily prudent and cautious person under the same circumstances to conclude that criminal activity is taking place or that criminal activity has recently occurred. Reasonable suspicion is the standard for less intrusive stop-and-frisk searches; it is less than probable cause but more than a hunch.

administrative justification
The standard for an administrative search based on the fact that government entities occasionally conduct searches in circumstances other than criminal investigations, such as a sobriety checkpoint set up for the purpose of apprehending drunk drivers. Sometimes called *special-needs* or *regulatory searches*, such searches attempt to achieve a balance between protecting individuals' privacy interests and protecting public safety.

any physical contact; for example, an officer can block a person's path, which could amount to a seizure. Add to that the number of possible search scenarios, including searches with and without warrants, and things get even more complex.

Justification

To this point we have only addressed the threshold question of whether the Fourth Amendment applies, that is, has a search or a seizure occurred? If the answer is no, the matter would go no further, and justification would not matter because a search or seizure did not occur. However, if, in the case of a search, the government's action infringes upon a person's reasonable expectation of privacy, the next issue involves deciding whether the police acted within the limits of the Fourth Amendment.

The police must have justification, or cause, before they can conduct a search or a seizure. Justification must be in place *a priori,* that is, before a person or evidence is sought in an area protected by the Fourth Amendment. The police cannot conduct illegal searches to obtain evidence and then argue *after the fact* that what they did was appropriate.

Justification can be viewed as something of a sliding scale that hinges on the type of intrusion the police make. Generally, the more intrusive the police action, the higher the level of justification required. Likewise, the lower the level of intrusion, the lower the justification the police need. Three primary levels of justification recognized by the courts are considered in this chapter: (1) **probable cause**—the standard for searches and seizures; (2) **reasonable suspicion**—the standard for stop-and-frisk activities; and (3) **administrative justification**—the standard for administrative searches.

Probable Cause. *Probable cause* has been defined by the U.S. Supreme Court as more than bare suspicion; it exists when "the facts and circumstances within [the officers'] knowledge and of which they [have] reasonably trustworthy information [are] sufficient to warrant a prudent man in believing that the [suspect] had committed or was committing an offense."[22] The Court had noted in an earlier case, "The substance of all the definitions of probable cause is a reasonable ground for belief of guilt."[23] A more practical definition of probable cause is that it consists of more than 50 percent certainty. Probable cause lies somewhere below absolute certainty and proof beyond a reasonable doubt (the latter is necessary to obtain a criminal conviction), but above a hunch or reasonable suspicion (the latter is required to conduct a stop and frisk). See Figure 11-1 for an overview of the components of probable cause.

Reasonable Suspicion. While the justification required to conduct a search or a seizure is probable cause, much police activity does not reach the level of intrusion that occurs when a search or seizure is carried out. For example, the police routinely confront people on the street to question them or pull over automobiles to enforce traffic laws. If probable cause were required under such circumstances, there would be very little the police could do in terms of investigating suspicious activity.

Recognizing how essential these lesser intrusions are to the police mission, the Supreme Court established a different level of justification for such activities in *Terry v. Ohio* (1968).[24] The standard the Court created was "reasonable suspicion," something below probable cause but above a hunch.

YOU DECIDE
Probable Cause to Arrest?

An observant police officer on foot patrol notices a "suspicious" person standing at the counter in a convenience store. The man, who has one hand in his coat pocket, appears to be carrying on a conversation with the clerk, who is nervously reaching into the cash register. On a hunch that he is witnessing a robbery in progress, the officer quickly enters the store, surprises the person talking to the clerk, arrests him, and, upon searching him incident to the arrest, finds a handgun in his coat pocket. The defendant later moves in court to suppress the handgun on the grounds that the officer did not have probable cause to arrest him. What would you do if you were the judge?

Figure 11-1 • The Components of Probable Cause

1. Prior record
   a. A man suspected of operating a meth lab had a prior conviction for the same activity (*People v. Wilson*, 182 Cal. App. 3d 742, 754 [1986]).
   b. A man suspected of murdering two boys "had a record for physical abuse of a nine-year-old" (*People v. Memro*, 11 Cal. 4th 786, 843 [1995]).
   c. A man suspected of robbery was "known as a burglar" (*People v. Franklin*, 171 Cal. App. 3d 627, 631 [1985]).
   d. A man suspected of possessing stolen property "had been active as a receiver of stolen property" (*People v. Martin*, 9 Cal. 3d 687, 693 [1973]).

2. Flight from the scene
   a. The suspect fled from an apartment known for drug dealing, coupled with an anonymous tip (*United States v. Lane*, 909 F.2d 895 [6th Cir. 1990]).
   b. Upon seeing the police, the suspects rose and ran away (*People v. Britton*, 91 Cal. App. 3d 1112, 1118–19 [2001]).
   c. Two men fled the scene of a jewelry store robbery (*People v. Dolliver*, 181 Cal. App. 3d 49 [2986]).
   d. A man approached a stolen car as if to open the door; then he spotted officers and ran away (*People v. Superior Court*, 83 Cal. App. 3d 609, 615 [1978]).

3. Suspicious conduct
   a. A suspect failed to make eye contact with officers (*United States v. Montero-Camargo*, 208 F.3d 1122, 1136 [9th Cir. 2000]).
   b. A suspect exhibited extreme inattention to officers (*United States v. Arvizu*, 534 U.S. 266).
   c. A suspect exhibited extreme attention to officers (*Flores v. Superior Court*, 17 Cal. App. 3d 219, 224 [1971]).
   d. A suspect appeared startled by police and quickly looked away (*People v. Fields*, 159 Cal. App. 3d 555, 564 [1984]).
   e. A suspect appeared to be nervous (*People v. Guajardo*, 23 Cal. App. 4th 1738, 1743 [1994]).
   f. A suspect appeared to be casing the premises (*Terry v. Ohio*, 392 U.S. 1, 23 [1968]).

4. Admission
   a. A suspect told an informant that he "could do a small thing of boy (sell a small amount of heroin)" (*People v. Veasey*, 98 Cal. App. 3d 779, 784–85 [1979]).
   b. While investigating an illegal bookmaking operation, an officer overheard two men talking about "point spreads" for professional football (*People v. Rooney*, 175 Cal. App. 3d 634, 648 [1985]).
   c. An officer arrived at a suspect's home to discuss graffiti vandalism, and the suspect said, "Take me to jail" (*In re Trinidad V.*, 212 Cal App. 3d 1077, 1080 [1989]).
   d. As an officer approached two burglary suspects, one told the other, "I told you not to do it" (*People v. Stokes*, 224 Cal. App. 3d 715, 721 [1990]).

5. Incriminating evidence
   a. A suspect was found in possession of the fruits or instrumentalities of a crime (*People v. Hagen*, 6 Cal. App. 3d 35, 43 [1970]).
   b. Two burglary suspects were found with pillowcases full of loot (*People v. Valdez*, 138 Cal. App. 3d 995, 1001 [1983]).
   c. A man suspected of possessing drugs was carrying a "big stack or wad of bills" (*People v. Brueckner*, 223 Cal. App. 3d 1500, 1505 [1990]).
   d. Inside a robbery suspect's car, police find live shotgun shells and a ski mask (*People v. Jardine*, 116 Cal. App. 3d 907, 913 [1981]).

6. Unusual hour
   a. 2:35 a.m.: An officer saw a man "exiting from darkened private property where valuable merchandise was located" (*People v. Allen*, 50 Cal. App. 3d 896, 901 [1975]).
   b. 3:00 a.m.: An officer saw a man riding a bicycle to which was attached a large axe (*People v. Foranyic*, 64 Cal. App. 4th 186, 190 [1998]).
   c. 3:30 a.m.: Two men walking in a business area started running when they saw police (*Crofoot v. Superior Court*, 121 Cal. App. 3d 717, 724 [1981]).
   d. 4:00 a.m.: A suspect was standing alone next to a business in which a silent burglar alarm was triggered (*People v. Lloyd*, 4 Cal. App. 4th 724, 733–34 [1992]).

(continued)

Figure 11-1 • The Components of Probable Cause (*continued*)

7. Suspect resembling perpetrator
   a. A suspect was wearing clothes similar to those of the perpetrator (*People v. Anthony*, 7 Cal. App. 3d 751 [1970]).
   b. A suspect was in a car similar in appearance to the car used by the perpetrator (*People v. Hill*, 89 Cal. App. 4th 48 [2001]).
   c. A suspect was with one or more other people who matched a general description of the perpetrators (*In re Brian A.*, 173 Cal. App. 3d 1168 [1985]).
   d. The number of suspects in a vehicle was the same as the number of perpetrators of the crime (*People v. Soun*, 34 Cal. App. 4th 1499 [1995]).

8. Evasive and untruthful responses to questions
   a. A suspect was caught in a lie about where he was coming from (*People v. Suennen*, 114 Cal. App. 3d 192, 199 [1980]).
   b. A suspect gave a false name or date of birth (*People v. Superior Court*, 137 Cal. App. 3d 90, 97 [1982]).
   c. A suspect was using an alias (*United States v. Sokolow*, 490 U.S. 1, 9 [1989]).
   d. A suspect denied owning a car that was registered to him (*People v. Carrillo*, 37 Cal. App. 4th 1662, 1668–71 [1995]).
   e. A suspect gave vague and confusing answers to questions (*People v. Adams*, 175 Cal. App. 3d 855, 861 [1985]).
   f. A suspect told unbelievable stories (*People v. Fields*, 159 Cal. App. 3d 555, 564 [1984]).

9. Obvious attempt to hide something
   a. When officers arrived to serve a search warrant, they heard a toilet flushing (*People v. Clark*, 262 Cal. App. 2d 471, 475 [1968]).
   b. A suspect pushed something under the seat of a car (*People v. Superior Court*, 272 Cal. App. 2d 383, 387 [1969]).
   c. Officers observed a group of men looking at a TV set in the trunk of a car; then the men slammed the trunk lid when they saw the officers (*People v. Gravatt*, 22 Cal. App. 3d 133, 137 [1971]).

10. Presence in a high-crime area or near the crime scene
    a. An officer witnessed a car leaving the scene of a burglary; no other vehicles or people were around (*People v. Conway*, 25 Cal. App. 4th 385, 390 [1994]).
    b. A suspect was the only pedestrian near the scene of the burglary (*People v. Juarez*, 35 Cal. App. 3d 631, 635 [1973]).
    c. A suspect was the only person found riding a motorcycle near the scene of a reckless motorcycling incident (*In re Frank V.*, 233 Cal. App. 3d 1232, 1238, fn. 2 [1991]).
    d. An officer witnessed an apparent drug transaction in an area known for narcotics activity (*People v. Souza*, 9 Cal. 4th 224, 240 [1994]).

11. Furtive gestures
    a. Officers spotted a suspect car, and one person ducked from view (*In re Jonathan M.*, 117 Cal. App. 3d 530, 535 [1981]).
    b. A suspect made a quick "hand-to-mouth" movement, as though secreting drugs (*People v. Johnson*, 231 Cal. App. 3d 1, 12 [1991]).
    c. A suspect turned away from officers when they announced their presence (*People v. Valdez*, 196 Cal. App. 3d 799, 806 [1987]).
    d. A driver reached under the seat of a car (*People v. Clayton*, 13 Cal. App. 3d 335 [1970]).

12. Knowing too much
    a. A suspect volunteered information that only the perpetrator would know (*People v. Spears*, 228 Cal. App. 3d 1 [1991]).

Source: Alameda County District Attorney's Office, *"Probable cause," point of view* (Oakland, CA: District Attorney's Office, 2002). Reprinted by permission.

The facts of the *Terry* case are interesting: An officer's attention was drawn to two men on a street corner who appeared to the officer to be "casing" a store for a robbery. The officer approached the men and asked them to identify themselves and then proceeded to pat the men down. Finding a gun on each man, he placed the men under arrest. They later sought to have the guns excluded as evidence from trial (the exclusionary rule is discussed in the next chapter), but the U.S. Supreme Court eventually held that the officer's actions were valid in the interests of

Figure 11-2 • A Fourth Amendment Checklist

The following checklist will help you determine whether the Fourth Amendment applies and whether a search or seizure is reasonable.

1. Did a search or seizure take place?
   a. For a search, did a governmental actor violate a reasonable expectation of privacy?
   b. For a seizure, would a reasonable person believe he or she is not free to leave?

If the answer to either *a* or *b* above is no, the Fourth Amendment does not apply.

2. Was the search or seizure justified?
   a. Identify the level of intrusion, seizure, stop, nonstop, and so on.
   b. Identify the level of justification appropriate to the intrusion.

Inappropriate justification leads to an unreasonable search or seizure.

3. Was the search or seizure conducted in accordance with constitutional guidelines?

Source: Adapted from J. L. Worrall, *Criminal procedure: From first contact to appeal,* 2nd ed. (Upper Saddle River, NJ: Pearson Education, Inc., 2007), p. 95. Reprinted by permission.

"effective crime prevention and detection."[25] It also stated that because "street encounters between citizens and police officers are incredibly rich in diversity,"[26] a lower standard than probable cause is required.

As a level of justification lying below probable cause, reasonable suspicion is "considerably less than proof of wrongdoing by a preponderance of evidence"[27] but more than a mere hunch. Think of reasonable suspicion as more than 0 percent certainty (that is, more than a mere hunch) and less than 51 percent certainty (that is, less than probable cause).

Administrative Justification. A third level of justification has arisen by virtue of the fact that government entities occasionally conduct searches in circumstances other than criminal investigations. There are occasions where some sort of search is necessary, but that search is not conducted in an effort to detect evidence of a crime, such as a cache of illegal weapons. We have seen that searches and seizures aimed at obtaining evidence intended to be used in a criminal proceeding cannot occur without appropriate justification: probable cause for a search or seizure; reasonable suspicion for a stop and frisk. The Supreme Court has created a different level of justification for noncriminal, or administrative, searches.

Administrative searches attempt to achieve a balance between protecting individuals' privacy interests and protecting public safety. Where public-safety concerns outweigh individual privacy interests, an administrative search may be permissible. One such search that has routinely been sanctioned by the courts is a sobriety checkpoint set up for the purpose of protecting the public by removing drunk drivers from roadways. Other examples of permissible administrative searches are discussed later in this chapter. For a summary of the Fourth Amendment discussion presented thus far, see Figure 11-2. For a summary of the various levels of proof, see Figure 11-3.

Figure 11-3 • A Comparison of the Levels of Proof

Proof beyond a reasonable doubt = around 95 percent certainty

Probable cause = more than 50 percent certainty

Preponderance of the evidence = civil equivalent of probable cause

Reasonable suspicion = between 1 and 50 percent certainty

Administrative justification = balancing approach

Hunch = no justification or certainty at all

The Rules of Search and Seizure

Assuming that a case arises wherein the Fourth Amendment applies and officers have proper justification, what's next? The answer depends on whether the action in question is a search, a seizure, a stop, or an administrative search. It also depends on whether a warrant is required.

Arrest Warrant Requirements. The Fourth Amendment does not *require* an arrest warrant for all arrests, but the U.S. Supreme Court has adopted the view that arrest warrants are preferable. They can be obtained when the police know who they want to arrest, but the person is not immediately available (for example, he or she has escaped confinement). In contrast, if a police officer observes a person rob a bank, then it would obviously be impractical to require the officer to obtain an arrest warrant before arresting the suspect.

When are arrest warrants required? Essentially, the rule is this: An arrest made in a public place does not require an arrest warrant (but does require probable cause); an arrest made in a private place usually requires a warrant, unless special circumstances exist. In its landmark decision in *Payton v. New York* (1980),[28] the U.S. Supreme Court held that the Fourth Amendment prohibits warrantless, nonconsensual entries into private homes for the purpose of making an arrest. The Court has also required that arrests made in third-party homes require a warrant to search the property for the person to be arrested. To enter without a warrant could amount to a search without proper justification, in violation of the Fourth Amendment.[29]

Assuming that an arrest warrant is required, it must conform to certain requirements. First, a neutral and detached magistrate must authorize the warrant. Second, a showing of probable cause must be made. Finally, the warrant should be sufficiently particular so as to minimize the possibility of arresting the wrong person.

Neutral and Detached Magistrate The U.S. Supreme Court has said,

> The point of the Fourth Amendment . . . is not that it denies law enforcement the support of the usual inferences reasonable men draw from evidence. Its protection consists in requiring that those inferences be drawn by a neutral and detached magistrate instead of being judged by the officer engaged in the often competitive enterprise of ferreting out crime.[30]

Most judges are considered neutral and detached. Even so, the Supreme Court has focused on this first critical warrant requirement in a number of cases. For example, the Court has declared that a state attorney general cannot issue a search warrant.[31] State attorneys general are chief prosecutors and thus inclined to side with law enforcement officers. Similarly, in another case the Court decided that the president, acting through the attorney general of the United States, cannot authorize electronic surveillance without judicial approval.[32]

Probable Cause The probable cause showing in an arrest warrant is not particularly complex. The officer applying for the warrant must simply show probable cause that the person to be arrested committed the crime but not that the suspect will be found at a particular location. The Court has stated, "If there is sufficient evidence of a citizen's participation in a felony to persuade a judicial officer that his arrest is justified, it is constitutionally reasonable to require him to open his doors to the officers of the law."[33]

Particularity There are two ways to satisfy the Fourth Amendment's particularity requirement with regard to arrest warrants. First, if the suspect's name is known, then simply supplying the suspect's name is enough to meet the particularity requirement. There are some situations, however, where the suspect's name is *not* known. In such situations, a sufficiently specific description of the suspect supports issuance of a "John Doe" warrant. As long as other officers may locate the suspect with reasonable effort, the suspect's name is not required.

Search Warrant Requirements. Search warrants have the same three requirements as arrest warrants. The neutral and detached magistrate requirement remains the same, but there *are* differences in terms of probable cause and particularity. The probable cause showing in a search warrant is twofold. First, the officer applying for the search warrant must show probable cause that the items to be seized are connected with criminal activity. Second, the officer must show probable cause that the items to be seized are in the location to be searched. If a warrant does not par-

Figure 11-4 • A Typical Search Warrant Form

SUPERIOR COURT OF CALIFORNIA
County of ______________

SEARCH WARRANT
♦ Special Instructions ♦

THE PEOPLE OF THE STATE OF CALIFORNIA to: **Warrant No. __________**
Any peace officer in ______________________ County
The affidavit filed herewith by ______________________________, sworn to and subscribed before me, has established probable cause for this warrant which you are ordered to execute as follows:

Place(s) to be searched: Described in Exhibit 1A, *attached* hereto and incorporated by reference.

Property to be seized: Described in Exhibit 1B, attached hereto and incorporated by reference.

Disposition of property: All property seized pursuant to this search warrant shall be retained in the affiant's custody pending further court order pursuant to Penal Code §§ 1528(a), 1536.

♦ SPECIAL INSTRUCTIONS ♦

The Statement of Probable Cause, filed herewith, has demonstrated legal justification for the following special procedures which are authorized if checked:

☐ **Night Service:** This warrant may be served at any hour of the day or night.

☐ **No Knock Authorization:** Compliance with Penal Code § 1531 is excused *unless* a change in circumstances negates the need for non-compliance.

☐ **Special Master:** The search shall be conducted by a Special Master pursuant to Penal Code §§ 1524(c)-(g). The Special Master shall be ______________________________.

☐ **Sealing Order:** The following documents shall be sealed and delivered into the custody of the Clerk of the Superior Court pending further court order: ☐ All documents filed herewith. ☐ Documents listed in Exhibit 2. Grounds for sealing: ☐ Informant protection (Evid. Code § 1041) ☐ Official information (Evid. Code § 1040)

☐ **Nondisclosure Order:** The financial institution served with this warrant, including its employees and agents, shall not disclose any information regarding its content, existence, or execution pending further court order.

☐ **BloodDraw:** (Not for HIV testing per Penal Code § 1524.1): A blood sample shall be drawn from the person described in Exhibit 1A by trained medical personnel in accordance with accepted medical practices.

☐ **Anticipatory Warrant:** Having determined that probable cause for this search will exist upon the occurrence of the triggering event(s) described in Exhibit 3, and that there is probable cause said triggering event(s) will occur, this warrant shall be executed promptly after said triggering event(s) occur. Exhibit 3 is *attached* hereto and incorporated by reference.

☐ **Covert Warrant:** The property described in Exhibit 1B shall not be removed from the premises. An inventory shall be prepared showing the location of all such property discovered on the premises. Said property shall be photographed or videotaped to show its location when discovered. Compliance with the receipt requirements of Penal Code § 1535 is excused until ____________________ unless an extension is granted by this court. [Initial compliance date must not be more than 7 days following execution of the warrant.] Within two days after executing this warrant, the following shall be filed with this court: (1) the inventory, and (2) the original or copy of all photographs and/or videotape recordings made during the execution of this warrant.

☐ **Additional Instructions:** Additional instructions pertaining to this search warrant are contained in Exhibit 4, *attached* hereto and incorporated by reference.

Date and time warrant issued ______________ Judge of the Superior Court ______________

Source: Alameda County (California) District Attorney Office, "Multi-functional search warrant," *Point of view*. Reprinted by permission.

ticularly describe the place to be searched and the items to be seized, then it is not automatically deemed in violation of the Fourth Amendment. If there is a reasonable basis for the officers' mistaken belief, then the warrant will most likely be upheld.[34] For an example of a search warrant special instructions form, see Figure 11-4.

Searches and Seizures without Warrants. Searches without warrants are far more common than those with warrants. Police can, for example, rely on the hot pursuit doctrine to chase a fleeing suspect into a private area and make an arrest without a warrant. Requiring officers to secure warrants in all such instances would be impractical. Similarly, it would endanger the public's safety if police were required to obtain a warrant in the face of a clear and sudden threat to public safety. Warrantless searches thus come in several varieties: (1) searches incident to arrest, (2) searches based on exigent circumstances, (3) automobile searches, (4) plain-view searches, and (5) consent searches.

Searches Incident to Arrest The first type of permissible warrantless search is known as a **search incident to arrest.** The U.S. Supreme Court has said that a warrantless search incident to arrest is permitted "to remove any weapons that the [arrestee] might seek to use in order to resist arrest or effect his escape" and to "seize any evidence on the arrestee's person in order to prevent its concealment or destruction."[35] A search incident to arrest is basically a search made at the time of or shortly following an arrest, and it is done out of a concern for the safety of the arresting officer and others.

search incident to arrest
A warrantless search made at the time of or shortly following an arrest, conducted out of a concern for the safety of the arresting officer and others.

arm-span rule
A doctrine established by the U.S. Supreme Court that limits a search incident to arrest to the area "within [the] immediate control" of the person arrested—that is, "the area from within which he might have obtained either a weapon or something that could have been used as evidence against him."[i]

protective sweep
A permissible cursory visual inspection of places in which a person might be hiding. A protective sweep may be conducted by police up to the point of an arrest but must be supported by reasonable suspicion.

exigent circumstances
A situation that makes a warrantless search constitutionally permissible, such as hot pursuit, the likelihood of a suspect's escaping or presenting a danger to others, and evanescent evidence.

hot pursuit exception
One exception to the Fourth Amendment's warrant requirement, recognized by the U.S. Supreme Court in *Warden v. Hayden* (1967).[ii] The hot pursuit doctrine provides that police officers may enter the premises where they suspect a crime has been committed, or a perpetrator is hiding, without a warrant when delay would likely endanger their lives or the lives of others and possibly lead to the escape of the alleged perpetrator.

Probable cause to arrest must always precede a search incident to arrest.[36] This is to restrict officers from engaging in "fishing expeditions," searches based on less than probable cause that could potentially result in establishing the probable cause needed to make an arrest.

If probable cause to arrest is in place, the officer is not required to formally arrest the suspect before engaging in the search,[37] but the search should take place *soon* after the arrest if one is made. In other words, the search must be *contemporaneous* to the arrest. In *Preston v. United States* (1964),[38] the case that established this rule, Justice Hugo Black observed that the "justifications [for the search incident to arrest] are absent where a search is remote in time or place from the arrest."[39] In *Preston,* police officers arrested the occupants of a car and took them to jail. After this, the officers searched the car, which had been towed to an impound lot. In reversing the lower court's ruling, the Supreme Court noted that the possibilities of destruction of evidence or danger to the officers were no longer in place, as the suspects were no longer present to pose a threat.[40]

What is the scope of a search incident to arrest? In *Chimel v. California* (1969),[41] the Court held that "a warrantless search 'incident to a lawful arrest' may generally extend to the area that is considered to be in the 'possession' or under the 'control' of the person arrested."[42] It went on to create the so-called **arm-span rule.** In the Court's words, a search incident to arrest is limited to the area "within [the] immediate control" of the person arrested, that is, "the area from within which he might have obtained either a weapon or something that could have been used as evidence against him."[43]

In *Maryland v. Buie* (1990),[44] the Court further expanded the scope of the incident search in two ways. It held that the police may, as part of a search incident to arrest, look in areas immediately adjoining the place of arrest for other individuals who might attack the officers; no justification is required. The key is that such a search must occur incident to arrest. Next, the Court held that at any point up to the time the arrest is completed, the police may engage in a **protective sweep** (that is, "a cursory visual inspection of those places in which a person might be hiding"), but reasonable suspicion must exist for such a sweep to be justified. No justification is required *after* arrest, but reasonable suspicion is required to engage in a sweep up to the point of the arrest.

Searches Based on Exigent Circumstances Searches (and, by extension, arrests) based on **exigent circumstances** are permissible without warrants. Generally, three types of exigencies (emergencies) have been recognized: (1) hot pursuit, (2) the likelihood of a suspect's escaping or presenting a danger to others, and (3) evanescent evidence.

The Supreme Court established a **hot pursuit exception** to the Fourth Amendment's warrant requirement in *Warden v. Hayden* (1967).[45] In that case, the police were called by taxicab drivers who reported that their taxi company had been robbed. The police then located and followed the suspect to a house and were granted entry by the suspect's wife. When they entered, they found the suspect upstairs, pretending to be asleep. However, as they were searching the house for the suspect, the police found and seized clothing, a shotgun, and a pistol which were used as evidence against the suspect at trial. The Court found that the warrantless entry was "reasonable" because the "exigencies of the situation made that course imperative."[46] Several reasons were offered for the decision. First, as Justice William Brennan stated, "The Fourth Amendment does not require police officers to delay in the course of an investigation if to do so would gravely endanger their lives or the lives of others."[47] Second,

WEB PATROL 11-3
Revoking Consent to Search
http://www.mycrimekit.com

"[s]peed . . . was essential, and only a thorough search of the house for persons and weapons could have insured that Hayden was the only man present and that the police had control of all weapons which could be used against them or to effect an escape."[48]

Despite its sweeping language in the *Hayden* decision, the Supreme Court has imposed a number of restrictions on searches and seizures premised on hot pursuit. First, hot pursuit permits warrantless entry only when the police have probable cause to believe that the person they are chasing has committed a crime and is on the premises entered.

Second, the police must have reason to believe that the suspect will escape or that further harm will occur, either to evidence or to other people, if the suspect is not immediately apprehended. One court has observed that "[a] hot pursuit, by itself, creates no necessity for dispensing with a warrant."[49] Similarly, the Ninth Circuit has stated that police officers must reasonably believe (1) "that the suspect either knows or will learn at any moment that they are in immediate danger of apprehension"; (2) that "evidence is being currently removed or destroyed and it is impractical to avert the situation without immediately arresting the suspects or seizing the evidence"; or (3) that "a suspect is currently endangering the lives of themselves or others."[50]

Third, the police must begin hot pursuit from a lawful starting point. If officers are unlawfully on someone's private property, they will not succeed in claiming hot pursuit to justify any further warrantless action. However, in *United States v. Santana* (1976),[51] the Supreme Court upheld the warrantless arrest of a woman in her house when the police *observed* a crime on private property from a public vantage point. In that case, police officers observed Santana standing in the open doorway of her house with a brown paper bag, which they believed to contain narcotics. They pursued her into the house and arrested her. This decision suggests that the police can pursue from a public vantage point a suspect whom they observe on private property.

Fourth, the hot pursuit doctrine only applies to "serious" offenses. These include felonies and some serious misdemeanors.[52] This is perhaps the most important restriction on the hot pursuit doctrine—and, indeed, on exigent circumstance searches in general.

A fifth restriction on hot pursuits concerns the scope of the search. Generally, the scope of a search based on hot pursuit is broad. In *Hayden,* the Supreme Court stated, "The permissible scope of search must, at the least, be as broad as may reasonably be necessary to prevent the dangers that the suspect at large in the house may resist or escape."[53] However, the search must be "prior to or immediately contemporaneous with" the arrest of the suspect. Also, officers may only search where the suspect or weapons might reasonably be found.

WEB PATROL 11-4

Special-Needs Searches
http://www.mycrimekit.com

Moving beyond hot pursuit, it is also permissible for police officers to dispense with the warrant requirement when it is likely that a suspect could escape or endanger others, even in the absence of hot pursuit.[54] Finally, **evanescent evidence** refers to evidence that is likely to disappear if the officers took the time to obtain a warrant.[55] An example of evanescent evidence is alcohol in a person's bloodstream.

evanescent evidence
Evidence that is likely to disappear quickly.[iii]

Automobile Searches The warrantless search of an automobile is permissible when (1) there is probable cause to believe that the vehicle contains evidence of a crime and (2) securing a warrant is impractical.[56] This rule resulted from a Prohibition-era case involving the vehicle stop of a suspect who was known to have previously engaged in the sale of bootleg whiskey. A warrantless search of the car revealed 68 bottles of illegal liquor. The Supreme Court upheld the warrantless search on the grounds that the evidence would have been lost if the officers had been required to secure a warrant. It pointed out that the inherent mobility of motor vehicles made it impractical to obtain a warrant, that people enjoy a lesser expectation of privacy in their vehicles, and that vehicles are subject to extensive government regulation, essentially making driving a privilege.

Several subsequent decisions have dealt with the definition of an automobile, the role of probable cause, whether warrants are required, and the scope of automobile searches. Concerning the first of these issues, any vehicle that serves a transportation function is considered to be an automobile. Four factors are used to determine whether a vehicle serves a transportation function: (1) whether it is mobile or stationary, (2) whether it is licensed, (3) whether it is connected to utilities, and (4) whether it has convenient access to the road. If, for example, a trailer is on blocks, unlicensed, connected to utilities, and in a trailer park, then it will almost certainly be treated as a residence for Fourth Amendment purposes.

Next, despite the fact that a vehicle search is permissible without a warrant, the search must still be based on probable cause. Even when probable cause to search exists, this does not automatically create probable cause to arrest; likewise, probable cause to arrest may not give rise to probable cause to search.

Given the circumstances surrounding most vehicle stops, it would seem foolish to require that the police obtain warrants before engaging in automobile searches. In *Husty v. United States* (1931),[57] a police officer, acting on a tip from an informant, found contraband in Husty's unattended car. Given that the car was unattended, one can argue that a warrant should have been secured, but the Court ruled that the officer "could not know when Husty would come to the car or how soon it would be removed."[58] Contrast *Husty* with *Coolidge v. New Hampshire* (1971).[59] In the *Coolidge* case, the Court ruled that the automobile exception did not apply to a warrantless search and seizure of two cars located on the defendant's property because the police had probable cause to act more than two weeks before the search.

Finally, what about the scope of an automobile search? In *United States v. Ross* (1982), the Supreme Court declared that as long as the police have justification to conduct a warrantless vehicle search, they may conduct a search "that is as thorough as a magistrate could authorize in a warrant."[60] The only limitation is "defined by the object of the search and the places in which there is probable cause to believe that it may be found."[61] Accordingly, if the contraband sought is small (for example, a syringe), the scope of the vehicle search exception is almost limitless.

WEB PATROL 11-5
The Motor Vehicle Exception
http://www.mycrimekit.com

Plain-View Searches Plain-view searches can also be conducted without a warrant. In *Coolidge v. New Hampshire*,[62] the Supreme Court held that seizure of an item found in **plain view** is authorized when (1) the police are lawfully in the area where the evidence is located, (2) the item is "immediately apparent" as being subject to seizure, and (3) the discovery of the evidence is "inadvertent."[63] Police are lawfully in the area where the evidence is located when they have a warrant or are otherwise authorized to be there (for example, due to a hot pursuit exigency). "Immediately apparent" means that the police must have probable cause that the item of interest is subject to seizure.[64] The inadvertency requirement was eliminated by the Court's subsequent ruling in *Horton v. California* (1990).[65]

plain view
A doctrine articulated by the U.S. Supreme Court that permits the warrantless seizure of objects that are readily visible.

Texas Department of Public Safety officers arrest a young man after finding stolen goods in his car. What is required for a warrantless search of a vehicle?

Bob Daemmrich, The Image Works

Consent Searches Consent searches are also permissible without a warrant—and even without probable cause. If a person gives consent to search, he or she effectively waives Fourth Amendment protection. While the general rule is that validly obtained consent justifies a warrantless search with or without probable cause, it is important to note that only voluntary consent is valid. This means that consent cannot be "the result of duress or coercion, express or implied."[66] When does duress or coercion take place? There is no clear answer to this question. Instead, the Supreme Court has opted for a "totality of circumstances" test. This requires considering factors such as whether a show of force was made; whether the person's age, mental condition, or intellectual capacities inhibited understanding; whether the person was in custody; and whether consent was granted.

WEB PATROL 11-6

Protecting Personal Privacy
http://www.mycrimekit.com

Importantly, consent to search may be valid even if the consenting party is unaware of the fact that he or she can refuse consent.[67] As the Court stated in *Ohio v. Robinette* (1996),[68] "[J]ust as it 'would be thoroughly impractical to impose on the normal consent search the detailed requirements of an effective warning,' so too would it be unrealistic to require police officers to always inform detainees that they are free to go before a consent to search may be deemed involuntary."[69] Nevertheless, the issue of one's awareness of the right to refuse consent is still factored into the totality of circumstances of analysis,[70] although ignorance of the right to refuse is not enough in and of itself to render consent involuntary.

To err on the side of constitutionality, many police departments have suspects complete consent-to-search forms. An example of one such form, from the Alabama Court of Criminal Appeals, is reprinted in Figure 11-5.

The scope of a consent search is limited to the terms of the consent. In other words, the person giving consent defines the limits of the search. This was the decision reached in *Florida v. Jimeno* (1991).[71] For example, if a person says "you may look around," that does not necessarily mean that the police can look *anywhere* for evidence of criminal activity.

WEB PATROL 11-7

"Knock and Talk" Searches
http://www.mycrimekit.com

Another issue concerning the scope of a consent search is whether the consent can be withdrawn once given. In *State v. Brochu* (1967),[72] the Maine Supreme Court held that a defendant's consent to search his house for evidence of his wife's murder did not extend to another search carried out the day after he was arrested as a suspect. Thus, although the man did not expressly request that the search end, the Maine court still decided that consent had been terminated.

WEB PATROL 11-8

"knock and Announce" Violations
http://www.mycrimekit.com

"Knock and talk" consent searches are popular with law enforcement officers because of the difficulty of securing a warrant in particular instances. In the typical "knock and talk" scenario, police officers approach someone's house, knock on the front door, and request consent to search the home. The North Carolina Supreme Court described the procedure as follows:

"knock and talk"
A police tactic used to obtain consent to search, in which police officers approach a home, knock on the door, and request consent to search the premises.

> The "knock and talk" procedure is a tactic used by law enforcement . . . when they get information that a certain person has drugs in a residence but the officers don't have probable cause for a

Figure 11-5 • A Consent-to-Search Form

I, ____________________, having been informed of my constitutional right not to have a search made of the premises hereinafter mentioned without a search warrant and of my right to refuse consent to such a search, hereby authorize Officers ___________________ and _______________ of the city of ____________, state of Alabama, to conduct a complete search of ____.

These officers are authorized by me to take from this location any property that they may desire. This written permission is being given by me to the above-mentioned officers voluntarily and without threats or promises of any kind.

Dated, signed, and witnessed

____

Source: Reprinted by permission of Institute for Criminal Justice Education, Inc. (ICJE) search warrant. The officers then proceed to the residence, knock on the door, and ask to be admitted inside. Thereafter gaining entry, the officers inform the person that they're investigating information that drugs are in the house. The officers then ask for permission to search and apparently are successful in many cases in getting the occupant's "apparent consent."[73]

"Knock and talk" searches are controversial because they are not predicated on either warrants or probable cause. Such searches strike at the cardinal Fourth Amendment principle that "physical entrance into the home of another without a warrant is the chief evil the Fourth Amendment has sought to alleviate."[74] What makes "knock and talk" legal in the strictest sense, however, is that the subsequent search is based on consent, although the extent to which ordinary people are aware of their right to *refuse* consent is not altogether clear.

A police sergeant with a drug-sniffing dog checks bags and lockers in a Nebraska high school. What restrictions have been placed on these kinds of searches?

Mikael Karlsson/Arresting Images

Other Search and Seizure Issues

Earlier we talked about standards of justification, including reasonable suspicion. We pointed out that reasonable suspicion, which is a lesser standard of proof than probable cause, permits stop-and-frisk activities by police.[75] In this section, we look first at what constitutes a **stop and frisk.** Then we examine a few special-needs searches that must be based on administrative justification, which was also introduced earlier.

stop and frisk
The detaining of a person by a law enforcement officer for the purpose of investigation, accompanied by a superficial examination by the officer of the person's body surface or clothing to discover weapons, contraband, or other objects relating to criminal activity.[iv]

Stop and Frisk. In *Terry v. Ohio*,[76] the famous stop-and-frisk case mentioned earlier, the U.S. Supreme Court failed to provide a clear definition of a stop, but it did offer one in a later case, *United States v. Mendenhall* (1980):

> [A] person has been "seized" within the meaning of the Fourth Amendment only if, in view of all the circumstances surrounding the incident, a *reasonable person would have believed that he was not free to leave*. Examples of circumstances that might indicate a seizure, even where the person did not actually attempt to leave, would be the threatening presence of several officers, the display of a weapon by an officer, some physical touching of the person of the citizen, or the use of language or tone of voice indicating that compliance with the officer's request might be compelled.[77]

The Court's decision in this case stemmed from a confrontation between plainclothes Drug Enforcement Administration agents and a 22-year-old woman named Mendenhall in the Detroit airport. They had asked the woman for her ticket and identification. The name on the ticket did not match the name on the woman's identification, so the agents asked her to accompany them into a nearby private room. The Court did not actually decide whether Mendenhall had been "stopped," but it nevertheless articulated the "free to leave" test cited in the above quote.

The duration of a stop must also be given consideration. Sometimes a stop is drawn out until it evolves into an arrest, which would require probable cause rather than reasonable suspicion. At the other extreme, so-called nonstops, or consensual encounters, require no justification at all. See Figure 11-6 for a list of factors used to distinguish between a stop and a consensual encounter.

Frisks are often associated with stops. A frisk is a pat-down of a person's outer clothing done out of a concern for the officer's safety. The officer is not permitted to reach into the person's pockets at the outset or to grope or manipulate the target area.[78] In one relevant case,[79] police officers observed an individual driving a vehicle with expired plates. The officers stopped the vehicle in order to issue the driver a traffic summons. When the officers asked the driver to step out of the car, they observed a large bulge in the pocket of his jacket. Fearing that the bulge might be a weapon, one of

Figure 11-6 • Factors Used to Distinguish between a Stop and a Consensual Encounter

1. Degree of threatening behavior on the part of the officer.
2. Number of officers present.
3. Display of a weapon by the officer.
4. Physical touching of the person by the officer.
5. Orders by the officer, as opposed to requests.
6. Intimidating language or tone of voice used by the officer.
7. Length of time involved.
8. Intrusive actions (such as a full body search).
9. Use of lights or siren.
10. Blocking of the person's path.
11. Coercive police behavior.
12. Location of the encounter away from public view.

Source: J. L. Worrall, *Criminal procedure: From first contact to appeal,* 2nd ed. (Upper Saddle River, NJ: Pearson Education, Inc., 2007), p. 172. Reprinted by permission.

the officers frisked the driver. It turned out that the bulge was a .38-caliber revolver. The driver claimed at his trial that the gun was seized illegally, but the U.S. Supreme Court upheld the frisk. Even though a bulge in one's pocket is not necessarily indicative of a weapon, the Court felt that under these particular circumstances it was.

Terry has also been expanded to include **plain touch.** In one case, a police officer exceeded the bounds of *Terry* while frisking a man who had a suspicious packet in his clothing because the officer "squeezed, slid, and otherwise manipulated the packet's content" before learning that it was cocaine.[80] Despite the Court's decision in this case, it is considered by many to be the case that officially recognized the possibility that a search could be supported by plain touch. The Supreme Court has long recognized that items in plain *view* fall outside Fourth Amendment protections because they are plainly visible to the police. This case represents something of a cross between a *Terry*-type frisk and the plain-view doctrine.

plain touch
A doctrine articulated by the U.S. Supreme Court that permits an expansion of a stop-and-frisk search "if the officer, while staying within the narrow limits of a frisk for weapons, feels what he has probable cause to believe is a weapon, contraband or evidence."[v]

person inventory
The search of an arrestee and his or her personal items, including containers found in his or her possession, as part of a routine inventory that is incident to the booking and jailing procedure. Often called *arrest inventory*.

vehicle inventory
A warrantless inventory of a vehicle that is permissible on administrative or regulatory grounds. Vehicle inventories must follow a lawful impoundment, must be of a routine nature, must follow standard operating procedures, and must not be a pretext that attempts to conceal an investigatory search.

checkpoint
A location at which a warrantless, suspicionless search is constitutionally permissible in furtherance of an overriding national or public safety interest. National border entry points and sobriety checkpoints are examples.

Special-Needs Searches. Special-needs searches (sometimes called *regulatory or administrative searches*) are those whose primary purpose is noncriminal. They are based on administrative justification, which was introduced earlier. Because such searches nonetheless intrude on people's privacy and can lead to the discovery of evidence, the Fourth Amendment is implicated. However, instead of focusing on probable cause or reasonable suspicion, the courts use a "balancing test" that weighs citizens' privacy interests with public-safety interests. When the latter outweighs the former, administrative searches are allowed, subject to certain limitations, such as department policy. There are many types of special-needs searches. We consider two that are most relevant in the policing context: inventories and checkpoints.

Inventories There are two types of inventories: **person inventories** and **vehicle inventories.** The general rule is that the police may search an arrestee and his or her personal items, including containers found in his or her possession, as part of a routine inventory incident to the booking and jailing procedure. Neither a search warrant nor probable cause is required.[81] As for vehicle inventories,[82] the U.S. Supreme Court held that warrantless inventories are permissible on administrative or regulatory grounds; however, they must (1) follow a *lawful* impoundment, (2) be of a routine nature and follow standard operating procedures, and (3) not be a "pretext concealing an investigatory police motive."

Checkpoints Many types of **checkpoints** have been authorized. First, brief border detentions are constitutionally permissible.[83] That is because it is in the interest of "national self-protection" to permit government officials to require "one entering the country to identify himself as entitled to come in, and his belongings as effects which may be lawfully brought in."[84] Second, the U.S. Supreme Court has upheld the establishment of roadblocks near the Mexican border designed to discover illegal aliens.[85] Third, warrantless, suspicionless sobriety checkpoints have also been authorized.[86]

The administrative search rationale is *not* acceptable for detecting evidence of criminal activity. This was the decision reached in *City of Indianapolis v. Edmond* (2000),[87] in which the Court examined whether a city's suspicionless checkpoints for detecting illegal drugs were constitutional. Here is how the Supreme Court described the checkpoints:

> The city of Indianapolis operated a checkpoint program under which the police, acting without individualized suspicion, stopped a predetermined number of vehicles at roadblocks in various locations on city roads for the primary purpose of the discovery and interdiction of illegal narcotics. Under the program, at least one officer would (1) approach each vehicle, (2) advise the driver that he or she was being stopped briefly at a drug checkpoint, (3) ask the driver to produce a driver's license and the vehicle's registration, (4) look for signs of impairment, and (5) conduct an open-view examination of the vehicle from the outside. In addition, a narcotics-detection dog would walk around the outside of each stopped vehicle.[88]

The Court held that stops like those conducted during Indianapolis's checkpoint operations require individualized suspicion. In addition, "because the checkpoint program's primary purpose [was] indistinguishable from the general interest in crime control,"[89] it was deemed to violate the Fourth Amendment.

In *Illinois v. Lidster* (2004),[90] the Supreme Court decided that officers at checkpoints are also authorized to ask questions related to crimes occurring at the same area earlier. In that case, police briefly detained motorists to ask them if they had any information about a hit-and-run accident between a vehicle and a bicycle that took place at the same location a week earlier. A driver entered the checkpoint, swerved, and nearly hit an officer. He was stopped and subjected to a field sobriety test. He was eventually convicted of drunk driving but challenged the constitutionality of the checkpoint. The Court rejected the challenge, thus permitting yet another type of checkpoint.

CONFESSIONS AND INTERROGATIONS

Just as the police need to be cognizant of Fourth Amendment requirements, they also need to be aware of the rules governing confessions and interrogations. It is possible to violate a suspect's rights by failing to adhere to legal requirements spelled out in the Constitution and interpreted by the courts. Accordingly, this section briefly reviews the leading constitutional rules governing confessions and interrogations.

Fifth Amendment
An amendment to the U.S. Constitution that establishes due process rights, including the right to remain silent in the face of criminal accusations.

due process voluntariness approach
A means for determining the admissibility of a suspect's self-incriminating statement based on whether it was made voluntarily. Involuntariness is held to occur when, under the "totality of circumstances that preceded the confessions," the defendant is deprived of his or her "power of resistance."[vi]

Three Approaches to Confession Law

The primary focus in this section is on the **Fifth Amendment,** but for the sake of placing Fifth Amendment confession law into context, it is important to briefly consider the extent to which confessions are protected by other constitutional provisions. Indeed, the very fact that three constitutional amendments place restrictions on how the government can obtain confessions suggests that our country places a high degree of value on the people's right to be free from certain forms of questioning.

The Due Process Voluntariness Approach. One approach to confessions and admissions is the Fifth Amendment **due process voluntariness approach.** In general, a suspect's involuntary statement is not admissible in a criminal trial (or in any other criminal proceeding) to prove guilt. A confession is involuntary when, under the "totality of circumstances that preceded the confessions," the defendant is deprived of his or her "power of resistance."[91] This statement, unfortunately, does not provide any uniform criteria for determining voluntariness. Instead, courts take a case-by-case approach to determine voluntariness. This usually requires focusing on two issues: (1) the police conduct in question and (2) the characteristics of the suspect. For example, if

YOU DECIDE
A Valid Confession?

A man walks up to a police officer on the street and says that he once killed someone and wants to talk about it. He confesses to an unsolved murder that occurred several years earlier. Prior to trial, the man's attorney seeks to have his confession excluded, arguing that it was involuntarily given. At the trial a psychiatrist testifies for the defense, saying that the man suffers from "command auditory hallucinations," a condition that renders him unable to resist what "voices in his head" tell him to do. If you were the judge, would you rule that his confession was voluntary? Explain.

the suspect is a minor and the police act with brutality, any subsequent confession will be deemed involuntary.

The Sixth Amendment Approach. The U.S. Supreme Court's decision in *Massiah v. United States* (1964)[92] led to the rule that the Sixth Amendment's guarantee to counsel in all "formal criminal proceedings" is violated when the government "deliberately elicits" incriminating responses from a person. The two key elements are thus (1) **deliberate elicitation** and (2) **formal criminal proceedings.** The first element is defined as an effort by a government actor to draw incriminating statements from a suspect who is not represented by counsel in violation of the Sixth Amendment right to counsel. Formal criminal proceedings, the second element, include the formal charge, preliminary hearing, indictment, information, and arraignment.[93] So, for example, if a police officer questions a person who has already been indicted and counsel is not present, the officer violates the person's Sixth Amendment rights.

deliberate elicitation
An effort by a government actor to draw incriminating statements from a suspect who is not represented by counsel, in violation of that person's Sixth Amendment right to counsel.

formal criminal proceedings
Following *Escobedo v. Illinois* (1964), any official action by a government actor that occurs once the accused becomes the focus of an investigation by the police.

The *Miranda* Approach. In *Miranda v. Arizona* (1966), the Supreme Court announced the following important rule:

> [T]he prosecution may not use statements, whether exculpatory or inculpatory, stemming from *custodial interrogation* of the defendant unless it demonstrates the use of procedural safeguards effective to secure the privilege against self-incrimination.[94]

The ***Miranda*** **rights,** which are often read by police to an arrestee, sound something like this:

> You have the right to remain silent. Anything you say can and will be used against you in a court of law. You also have the right to an attorney. If you cannot afford an attorney, one will be provided to you at no cost. Do you understand these rights as they have been read to you?

***Miranda* rights**
The set of rights that a person accused or suspected of having committed a specific offense has during interrogation and of which he or she must be informed prior to questioning, as stated by the U.S. Supreme Court in *Miranda v. Arizona* (1966) and related cases.

Many people believe that *Miranda* rights apply whenever the police begin to question a person. This is not the case; if the person being questioned is not in custody, *Miranda* rights do not apply. Simple police questioning—even full-blown interrogation—is not enough to trigger the protections afforded by the Fifth Amendment. The person subjected to such questioning must be in police custody.

What is custody? The Court announced that *Miranda* applies when "a person has been taken into custody or otherwise deprived of his freedom of action in any significant way." An arrest is a clear-cut case of police custody, but what about a lesser intrusion such as an order not to leave the scene? Unfortunately, there is no easy answer to this question. Instead, courts focus on the circumstances surrounding each individual case. The Supreme Court has stated, however, that "the only relevant inquiry [in analyzing the custody issue] is how a reasonable man in the suspect's position would have understood his situation."[95]

The second major component of *Miranda* is interrogation. Custody by itself is not enough to require that *Miranda* warnings be given. For a person to be afforded Fifth Amendment protection—and particularly to be advised of his or her right to remain silent—then that person must be subjected to interrogation.

Miranda defined *interrogation* as "questioning initiated by law enforcement officers." Then, in *Rhode Island v. Innis* (1980), the Court noted that interrogation "must reflect a measure of compulsion above and beyond that inherent in custody itself."[96] Thus, any questions that tend to incriminate,

A police officer reads *Miranda* warnings to a man who has been arrested. When are *Miranda* warnings required?

Paul Coklin/PhotoEdit Inc.

functional equivalent of a question

"[A]ny words or actions on the part of the police (other than those normally attendant to arrest and custody) that the police should know are reasonably likely to elicit an incriminating response from the suspect."[vii]

18 U.S.C. Section 3501

The U.S. Code designation assigned to the Crime Control Act of 1968, which among other things, attempted to invalidate the *Miranda* decision.

that is, those that are directed toward an individual about his or her suspected involvement in a crime, are considered interrogation.

Unfortunately, many "questions" are not always readily identifiable as such. In *Innis,* the Supreme Court noted that in addition to "express questioning," the "functional equivalent" of a question is also possible. The **functional equivalent of a question,** according to the Court, includes "any words or actions on the part of the police (other than those normally attendant to arrest and custody) that the police should know are reasonably likely to elicit an incriminating response from the suspect."[97] Figure 11-7 lists some factors that are considered when distinguishing between interrogations and general questioning.

The *Miranda* decision was not without controversy. Shortly after the *Miranda* decision, Congress passed the Crime Control Act of 1968, which, among other things, attempted to overrule the *Miranda* decision. The statute, codified as **18 U.S.C. Section 3501,** states that in any federal prosecution a confession "shall be admissible in evidence if it is voluntarily given." Under the law, suspects need not be advised of their right to counsel, their right not to incriminate themselves, and so on.

For several years, Section 3501 remained dormant, but critics of *Miranda* continued to look for ways to bring it before the Court. That opportunity arose in 2000. The case involved Charles Dickerson, who had been indicted for bank robbery and related crimes. He moved to suppress a statement he made to agents from the Federal Bureau of Investigation on the ground that he had not received his *Miranda* warnings. The district court granted Dickerson's motion to suppress but also noted that the confession was voluntary, despite the apparent *Miranda* violation. The Court of Appeals for the Fourth Circuit held (in a 2–1 decision) that "Congress, pursuant to its power to establish the rules of evidence and procedure in the federal courts, acted well within its authority in enacting Section 3501, [and] Section 3501, rather than *Miranda,* governs the admissibility of confession in federal court."[98] The case then went before the U.S. Supreme Court.[99] In a 7–2 opinion for the Court, Chief Justice Rehnquist wrote,

> We hold that *Miranda,* being a constitutional decision of this Court, may not be in effect overruled by an Act of Congress, and we decline to overrule *Miranda* ourselves. We therefore hold

Figure 11-7 • Distinguishing between Interrogation and General Questioning

Interrogation
- Guilt-seeking questions
- Conversation intended to elicit a response

General Questioning
- Information-gathering questions
- Conversation not intended to elicit a response

Source: J. L. Worrall, *Criminal procedure: From first contact to appeal,* 2nd ed. (Upper Saddle River, NJ: Pearson Education, Inc., 2007), p. 243. Reprinted by permission.

> that *Miranda* and its progeny in this Court govern the admissibility of statements made during custodial interrogation in both state and federal courts.[100]

The Court further noted, "We do not think there is such justification for overruling *Miranda*. *Miranda* has become embedded in routine police practice to the point where the warnings have become part of our national culture."[101]

The Importance of *Miranda*

Subsequent Supreme Court cases have hinged on the substance and adequacy of the *Miranda* warnings and waivers. For example, if *Miranda* rights are not given "adequately," then the police risk having a confession thrown out of court. Also, like many rights, *Miranda* rights can be waived, that is, suspects can elect *not* to remain silent. Finally, suspects need not be advised of their *Miranda* rights when doing so could compromise public safety.

Substance and Adequacy of the Warnings. There is a long line of cases involving people who have sought to have their confessions excluded at trial because all or some of the *Miranda* warnings were not read adequately. For example, in *California v. Prysock* (1981), a juvenile was told, "You have the right to talk to a lawyer before you are questioned, have him present with you while you are being questioned, and all during the questioning." The defendant was then told that he had the right to a court-appointed lawyer, but not that one would be provided for him if he was indigent. Prysock challenged his conviction, but the Court concluded that the warnings given him were sufficient and that "*Miranda* itself indicates that no talismanic incantation was required to satisfy its strictures."[102]

In another case, *Duckworth v. Eagan* (1989), the following warnings were given:

> Before we ask you any questions, you must understand your rights. You have the right to remain silent. Anything you say can be used against you in court. You have the right to talk to a lawyer for advice before we ask you any questions, and to have him with you during questioning. You have this right to the advice and presence of a lawyer even if you cannot afford to hire one. We have no way of giving you a lawyer, but one will be appointed for you, if you wish, if and when you go to court. If you wish to answer questions now without a lawyer present, you have the right to stop answering questions at any time. You also have the right to stop answering at any time until you've talked to a lawyer.[103]

Interestingly, even though the warnings in this version suggested that counsel would only be provided at court, the U.S. Supreme Court held, in a 5–4 decision, that these warnings "touched all the bases required by *Miranda*."[104] Thus, simple departures from *Miranda*—as long as all the essential information is communicated—will not render confessions thereby obtained inadmissible in a criminal trial.

To ensure that *Miranda* warnings are read properly, most police departments have policies describing how the rights should be read. One such policy, from the Kansas City (Missouri) Police Department, is reprinted in Figure 11-8.

Waiver of Miranda. In *Miranda,* the Supreme Court stated that if a person talks after being read the warnings, "a heavy burden rests on the government to demonstrate that the defendant knowingly and intelligently waived his privilege against self-incrimination and his right to retained or appointed counsel."[105] Furthermore, "a valid waiver will not be presumed simply from the silence of the accused after warnings are given or simply from the fact that a confession was in fact eventually obtained."[106] According to the Court,

> Whatever the testimony of the authorities as to waiver of rights by an accused, the fact of lengthy interrogation or incommunicado incarceration before a statement is made is strong evidence that the accused did not validly waive his rights. In these circumstances the fact that the individual eventually made a statement is consistent with the conclusion that the compelling influence of the interrogation finally forced him to do so. It is inconsistent with any notion of a voluntary relinquishment of the privilege. Moreover, any evidence that the accused was threatened, tricked, or cajoled into a waiver will, of course, show that the defendant did not voluntarily waive his privilege.[107]

Figure 11-8 • Sample *Miranda* Advisement and Waiver Policy

A. When a law enforcement officer takes a person into police custody, or otherwise deprives them of their freedom of action in any significant way, that person shall be issued the following *Miranda* warning *before any questioning takes place.*
   1. You have the right to remain silent.
   2. Anything you say can and will be used against you in a court of law.
   3. You have the right to talk to a lawyer and have him present with you while you are being questioned.
   4. If you cannot afford to hire a lawyer, one will be appointed to represent you before any questioning, if you wish.
   5. You can decide at any time to exercise these rights and not answer any questions or make any statements.

B. The following questions should be asked after the specific warning and an affirmative reply is secured to each question in order to secure a waiver.
   1. Do you understand each of these rights I have explained to you?
   2. Having these rights in mind, do you wish to talk to us now?

Note: If a person indicates prior to or during custodial questioning that they wish to remain silent or wish to consult with a lawyer, the questioning must stop.

Questioning *will not* begin or continue until the person has consulted with a lawyer or voluntarily reinitiates communication with the police which leads to reinterrogation and voluntarily, knowingly, and intelligently waiving their rights.

C. When a formal interrogation is contemplated and the person wants to waive their rights, a typewritten or department printed waiver, i.e., Miranda Waiver, Form 340 P.D., shall be completed and signed by the person before any questioning. A witness shall be present through the signing of the waiver by the person. The typewritten waiver shall have the following minimum content:

> Before being asked any questions, I have been told of my right to remain silent, that anything I say can and will be used against me in court, that I have the right to talk with a lawyer and to have the lawyer with me during questioning. I have also been told that if I cannot afford a lawyer that one will be appointed for me, at no cost to me, before I am questioned. I have also been told that I can stop talking at any time. I understand all of these rights and I am willing to talk to you.
>
> Signed

____

1. If a person understands the warning and still wishes to talk without consulting a lawyer and/or having them present, the statement should be taken immediately. It should be the discretion of the investigative element whether to audiotape, videotape, or type the statement. The names of all persons present and the time should be set forth in the statement. The person shall be requested to date and sign the statement.
2. If a person wants to give a statement but refuses to sign the Miranda Waiver, Form 340 P.D., the officer should write "refused" in the signature space and complete the remainder of the form.
3. Anytime an officer gives the *Miranda* warning it should be stated in the officer's report. The officer should also verbally notify the detective handling the investigation that the *Miranda* warning was given.
4. In cases where an officer takes a confession, admission, or statement, to eliminate any question of admissibility of the utterance or writing, they should state in their report(s):
   a. The circumstances of the utterance or writing.
   b. The location where made.
   c. The length of time the individual has been in custody.
   d. The individual's ability to understand their own actions, e.g., education level, physical and mental condition, criminal background, age, experience, or anything else that would tend to show that the suspect knew what they were doing when they agreed to talk to the officer. This evidence indicates a knowing and intelligent waiver.

Source: Kansas City (Missouri) Police Department, Procedural Instruction 06-6, August 10, 2006.

In recent years, the courts have interpreted this language loosely, that is, where *Miranda* declared that a waiver is to be viewed with considerable caution, later decisions have suggested that the burden of demonstrating a valid waiver is not difficult to meet. For example, in *Colorado v. Connelly* (1986),[108] the Court held that the government need only show the validity of a waiver by a "preponderance of evidence." In a related case, the Court held that the "totality of the circumstances approach is adequate to determine whether there has been a waiver."[109] This latter test is not unlike the due process voluntariness test discussed earlier in this chapter.

Must the waiver be expressed, that is, must a person affirmatively state something to the effect that "I am willing to answer questions" for a waiver of *Miranda* to take place? The answer to this question is no. In the past, the Court preferred an expressed waiver; in *Miranda*, the Court noted that "a valid waiver will not be presumed." Similarly, in *Westover v. United States* (1966), the Court stated that an "articulated waiver" is required before a confession will be considered admissible.[110]

However, in *North Carolina v. Butler* (1979),[111] the Court decided otherwise. According to Justice Potter Stewart, "The question [of a waiver] is not one of form, but rather whether the defendant in fact knowingly and voluntarily waived his rights delineated in the *Miranda* case."[112] Further, a "course of conduct indicating waiver" (such as the suspect's decision to converse with the police) is sufficient for a valid waiver to take place. Based on this decision, the current rule is that the government must show a valid waiver based on "the particular facts and circumstances surrounding [the] case, including the background, experience, and conduct of the accused."[113] In other words, courts now take a case-by-case approach in determining whether *Miranda* waivers have been obtained legally.

To be safe, many police departments require that suspects complete a *Miranda* waiver before interrogation commences. This helps ensure that the waiver is documented. A sample *Miranda* waiver form is included in Figure 11-8.

The Public-Safety Exception to *Miranda*. On some occasions, custodial interrogation is permissible without *Miranda* warnings. Specifically, if public safety is in jeopardy, no warnings are required. This was the decision reached in *New York v. Quarles* (1984),[114] in which the Court held that the warnings need not be given if taking the time to do so would endanger public safety.

The facts from *Quarles* are as follows: After receiving information that a man with a gun had just entered a supermarket, Officer Kraft, along with three other officers, entered the store. Kraft spotted the defendant, drew his gun, and ordered the man to stop and put his hands over his head. The officers found an empty shoulder holster on the man when they frisked him. They asked him where he had put the gun. He replied, "The gun is over there." Officer Kraft retrieved the revolver, placed the man under arrest, and read him his *Miranda* warnings. The trial court and the lower appellate courts excluded the gun on the grounds that it was obtained in violation of *Miranda,* since the man had not yet been advised of his right to remain silent.

The U.S. Supreme Court disagreed. Justice William Rehnquist wrote the majority opinion, arguing that rigid application of *Miranda* is not always warranted, particularly when public safety is a concern:

> [T]he need for answers to questions in a situation posing a threat to public safety outweighs the need for the prophylactic rule protecting the Fifth Amendment's privilege against self-incrimination. We decline to place officers such as Officer Kraft in the untenable position of having to consider, often in a matter of seconds, whether it best serves society for them to ask the necessary questions without the *Miranda* warnings and render whatever probative evidence they uncover inadmissible, or for them to give the warnings in order to preserve the admissibility of evidence they might uncover but possibly damage or destroy their ability to obtain that evidence and neutralize the volatile situation confronting them.[115]

The Court also made it clear that the appropriate test for determining whether a threat to public safety exists is an objective one, that is, one based on what a reasonable person in the same circumstances would believe: "[W]here spontaneity rather than adherence to a police manual is necessarily the order of the day, the application of the [public safety] exception . . . should not be made to depend on *post hoc* findings at a suppression hearing concerning the subjective motivation of the arresting officer."[116] The majority in *Quarles* apparently believed that an objective threat to public safety existed. Insofar as the officers did not know where the gun was located, not knowing "obviously posed more than one danger to the public safety: an accomplice might make use of it [or] a customer or employee might later come upon it."[117]

The Importance of Documenting a Confession

This section has been mainly concerned with the methods by which the police can extract incriminating information from criminal suspects. Assuming that the police are successful in terms of eliciting an incriminating response, it is not enough for the suspect to say, "I did it," or to offer some other form of a verbal confession. In fact, if the police hand the suspect a pencil and paper and say, "Write down your confession," this will not be enough, either. Instead, the police must follow specific procedures for documenting and reporting a confession.

The police should document every interrogation and even keep an interview log, which is a document containing information about the individuals involved in the interrogations and actions taken by both sides.[118] A list of topics to be recorded in an interview log can be found in Figure 11-9.

Figure 11-9 • Contents of a Typical Interview Log

Interview Log

1. Identity of person interviewed
2. Identity of officers conducting interview
3. Location of interview
4. Date of interview
5. Time of arrest, if applicable
6. Location of arrest
7. Identity of officers making arrest
8. Time interview began
9. Time officers informed subject or suspect of his rights, and if more than one officer, name of officer advising subject or suspect
10. Time subject or suspect waived his rights
11. Time interview concluded
12. Time preparation of statement commenced
13. Identity of person preparing statement
14. Time statement completed
15. Time subject or suspect reviewed statement
16. Time subject or suspect signed written statement
17. A record of requests and complaints of subject and the action taken thereon, such as the time a subject requests permission to call an attorney, the time he made a call to his attorney, the time subject complained of illness, the time and action taken on this complaint, the time subject requested food, the time and action taken on this request, and the details as to how this request was handled

Source: T. T. Burke, "Documenting and reporting a confession with a signed statement: A guide for law enforcement," *FBI Law Enforcement Bulletin* (February 2001): 21.

Also, the police should secure a signed statement from the accused. The statement should identify the suspect, the investigators, and the crime involved and should describe, in language that the suspect can understand, the details of the crime, what the suspect did, and how he or she did it. The statement should then be carefully reviewed with the suspect, even read aloud, so that its contents are clear. Finally, it should be signed by the suspect, the officer conducting the interrogation, and at least one witness, preferably another officer. Figure 11-10 shows a sample statement form for securing a written confession from a criminal suspect.

WEB PATROL 11-9

Applying Criminological Theory to Interrogation
http://www.mycrimekit.com

Figure 11-10 • Sample Form for Securing a Written Confession

Signed Statement Format: White-Collar Crime Sample

I, [*subject's name and address*], hereby make the following free and voluntary statement to [*officer's official name and title*], who has identified himself/herself as a [*title of officer and name of department or agency*]. I have been advised that I have been interviewed concerning my involvement in [*phrase describing scheme or nature of crime and victim, such as "the misappropriation and theft of $100,000 from the First National Bank while I was employed there during 1999"*].

I was born on [*subject's date of birth*] at [*subject's place of birth*]. I attended [*last school attended*] and completed [*last grade or graduation date*]. I read and write the English language.

Officers should use the next few paragraphs to summarize what the subject did and how the subject did it, in the subject's own words. Because this statement occurs after the subject's confession, officers can assist the subject in formulating the statement, using information previously provided. Officers should include any information the subject provides regarding what happened to the stolen money, how it was spent, items purchased, and other related details.

I knew that what I was doing was wrong, and I regret my actions. I wish to cooperate with the [*name of agency*] investigation and get this matter resolved. [*Optional paragraph, depending on circumstances and subject's remorse*]

I have read this [*number of pages*] page statement, I have initialed all corrections, and I am signing it because it is true and correct. [*The subject writes this after reading the statement aloud and accepting its contents.*]

____

[subject's signature and date]

First witness: ______________________________

[officer taking statement, title, agency, location, and date]

Second witness: ______________________________

[third-party individual, title, agency, location, and date]

[*NOTE: Officers should always have the subject read the statement aloud to them and initial any corrections. Also, they should avoid blank lines between sentences and paragraphs in the statement.*]

Source: T. T. Burke, "Documenting and reporting a confession with a signed statement: A guide for law enforcement," *FBI Law Enforcement Bulletin* (February 2001): 19.

SUMMARY

- A Fourth Amendment violation occurs when a government actor infringes on a person's reasonable expectation of privacy during a search or seizure. Seizures can be of people or property. Probable cause is more than 50 percent certainty; reasonable suspicion is between 1 and 50 percent certainty. Administrative justification balances society's interest in protecting public safety against individuals' privacy concerns. Search and arrest warrants must be issued by a neutral and detached magistrate and require a showing of probable cause and particularity. Searches that can be conducted without a warrant include searches incident to arrest, searches based on exigent circumstances, automobile searches, plain-view searches, and consent searches. Stop and frisk stems from the U.S. Supreme Court's decision in *Terry v. Ohio,* which permits police to briefly detain someone to determine whether criminal activity is afoot. Special-needs searches include inventories and checkpoints.
- The due process voluntariness approach to confessions and interrogations holds that all confessions must be voluntary. The Sixth Amendment applies to confessions and interrogations when officers deliberately elicit incriminating information from an accused person after the initiation of criminal proceedings. The *Miranda* approach to confessions and interrogations requires that an attorney be provided to an accused person who is in custody *and* is being interrogated. *Miranda* warnings must be read carefully; critical information should not be omitted. *Miranda* rights can be waived, and the warnings can be dispensed with, for a short time, if there is an imminent threat to public safety that would be worsened if the warnings were read.

COMING FULL CIRCLE

For Discussion

Return to the questions posed at the start of this chapter. Have any of your answers changed since you read the chapter? What portions of this chapter helped you answer these questions?

Writing Assignment

Using material from this chapter and additional resources, write a 500-word essay in response to one of the questions presented at the beginning of the chapter. Submit your essay to your instructor if asked to do so.

KEY TERMS AND NAMES

18 U.S.C. Section 3501
administrative justification
arm-span rule
checkpoint
deliberate elicitation
due process voluntariness approach
evanescent evidence
exigent circumstances
Fifth Amendment
formal criminal proceedings
Fourth Amendment
functional equivalent of a question
government action
hot pursuit exception
justification
"knock and talk"
Miranda rights
person inventory
plain touch
plain view
probable cause
protective sweep
reasonable expectation of privacy
reasonableness
reasonable suspicion
search
search incident to arrest
seizure
stop and frisk
vehicle inventory

WEB INTERACTIVITY

Visit the Fourth Amendment page of the Cornell University Law School at http://www.law.cornell.edu/anncon/html/amdt4toc_user.html. Once there, review the various topics under the various "Search and Seizure" headings. Determine which of these topics are relevant to the discussion in this chapter. Review each of your selections, and make note of any information that supplements this chapter. Summarize what you have learned, and submit your report to your instructor if asked to do so.

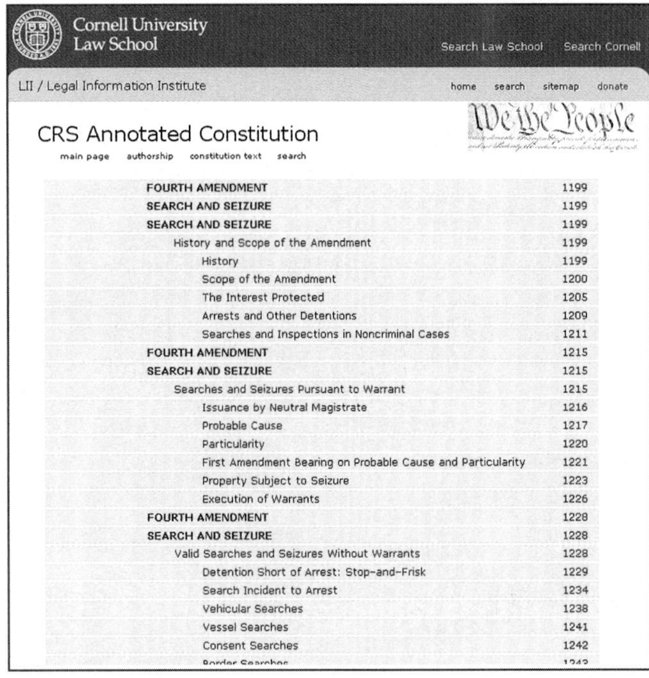

Cornell University Law School

REVIEW QUESTIONS

1. When does the Fourth Amendment apply? What are the rules governing search and seizure that are most relevant in the policing context?
2. What confessions and interrogations rules should the police be aware of? What Supreme Court decisions are most relevant?

LEARNING OBJECTIVES

After reading this chapter, students should be able to:

1. Identify the two main avenues available to aggrieved parties seeking to sue for police civil liability, and list some of the defenses against civil liability that law enforcement officers and their supervisors and departments might employ.
2. List and explain five external measures, other than litigation, for promoting police accountability.
3. Discuss procedures for promoting accountability from within police agencies.

AUSTIN
POLICE
4202

THINK ABOUT IT

Some years ago, at around 6:45 in the morning, a group of deputy federal marshals and local sheriff's deputies invited a newspaper reporter and a news photographer to accompany them as they served an arrest warrant. The team arrived at a private residence where they expected to find Dominic Wilson, a fugitive who had violated his probation following convictions for assault, robbery, and theft. The officers did not know, however, that the house they were about to enter belonged to Dominic's parents, Charles and Geraldine Wilson. The officers forcibly entered the home while the two were still in bed. Charles, dressed only in his underwear, ran into the living room to investigate the noises he heard. When he discovered five men in street clothes armed with guns, he demanded that they state their business.

The officers initially thought that Charles was Dominic, and they quickly subdued him. Meanwhile, Geraldine, dressed only in a nightgown, stepped out of the bedroom to find her husband handcuffed on the floor. The officers conducted a sweep of the residence, found no sign of Dominic Wilson, and quickly left.

The Wilsons were emotionally shaken by the experience, but what infuriated them was the presence of the reporter, who had been taking notes, and the photographer, who snapped several pictures. The news crew, *Washington Post* staffers, never wrote a story or published an account of what had occurred, but the Wilsons nevertheless sued the officers involved, alleging that the early-morning intrusion had violated their Fourth Amendment right to be free from unreasonable searches and seizures.

The officers who served the warrant made a mistake, but no one was physically harmed and they left the premises as soon as they realized that Dominic Wilson was not there. Would it be fair to hold the officers liable for their actions? If so, which of their actions were inappropriate?

This case eventually reached the U.S. Supreme Court, which declared that the officers violated the Fourth Amendment[1] by bringing members of the media with them into a private home. But the Court also decided that because the officers didn't know any better, they should not be required to pay damages. This case raises several questions to keep in mind as you read this chapter:

1. Did the officers go too far in bringing the reporters with them? After all, the *Washington Post* staffers did not *participate* in the service of the search warrant. They were simply observers, and other people (like neighbors) might also have observed what transpired.
2. Do lawsuits promote police accountability? Why or why not?
3. What mechanisms other than lawsuits can help ensure that the police are held accountable to the law?
4. Do we hold police officers and their departments to excessively high standards with respect to liability?
5. Is America too "litigious," that is, do people sue too often? If so, what might be done about it?

WEB PATROL 12-1

Wilson v. Layne Full Text Court Opinion
http://www.mycrimekit.com

INTRODUCTION

One of the core principles of the democratic system of government is public accountability. The American system of government is designed to ensure that public officials ultimately answer to the people, whom they serve. Making elected officials accountable is relatively easy; they can be voted out of office. This is less true for workers in civil service positions; they answer to the public through a complex chain of relationships. The police have not always been held closely accountable to the public. Times have changed, however, and the mechanisms for ensuring public accountability of police activity are the focus of this chapter.

While holding public officials accountable is certainly important, those officials enjoy many of the same legal protections that the rest of us do. Police officers who are sued, for example, can assert a number of defenses. Likewise, officers who are investigated by their departments for alleged misconduct enjoy a number of procedural protections. Bills of rights for police officers have emerged in an effort to preserve the due process rights of accused officers and to reduce the potential for wrongful firings, demotions, and transfers. This chapter examines efforts to balance the need for police accountability against the need to preserve due process protections for everyone, including the police.

WEB PATROL 12-2
Liability for Failure to Train
http://www.mycrimekit.com

CIVIL LIABILITY

Whenever a person's constitutional or other federal civil rights are violated, a lawsuit can be filed. Even if a person merely *believes* that his or her rights have been violated, litigation is still an option. Litigation is also an option for tort violations, or civil wrongs that do not rise to the level of a constitutional rights violation. In either case, the worst that can happen for the plaintiff (the person bringing the lawsuit) is that the lawsuit will be dismissed and the plaintiff may be stuck with the attorney's bill.

What is the purpose of civil litigation? Aside from sometimes being the only remedy available to those who have been wronged, civil lawsuits are attractive because they sometimes result in monetary awards. Lawsuits in which people seek monetary compensation are called *damages suits*, and the money paid is called **damages**. In such suits, the plaintiff seeks payment for perceived or actual injuries. In addition to damages, plaintiffs can seek **injunctive relief**, which means that the plaintiff wants the court to bring the injurious or offensive action to a halt.

damages
Monetary compensation awarded to the plaintiff in a successful civil lawsuit.

injunctive relief
A court order to bring injurious or offensive action to a halt.

The Effect of Civil Liability on Police

Today, the "heavy machinery of law is being wheeled out to deal with an expanding array of personal disputes."[2] As one researcher reported, "Americans in all walks of life are being buried under an avalanche of lawsuits."[3] Even a former U.S. Supreme Court justice has complained about the tendency of many people to resort to litigation rather than other less formal methods of resolving disputes:

> One reason our courts have become overburdened is that Americans are increasingly turning to the courts for relief from a range of personal distresses and anxieties. Remedies for personal wrongs that once were considered the responsibility of institutions other than the courts are now boldly asserted as legal "entitlements." The courts have been expected to fill the void created by the decline of church, family, and neighborhood unity.[4]

Law enforcement officials feel this trend perhaps more than most. As part of one of the most visible branches of the executive arm of government, police officers occupy a precarious position with respect to liability. This is complicated by the often confrontational nature of police work. Police officers must sometimes use force, which can upset people or injure them.

The prospect of civil liability—of being sued for misconduct—affects all law enforcement officials at all levels of government, especially administrators. One reason is that lawsuits are costly in terms

Police officers using force in making an arrest. What civil liability issues must be recognized by officers in situations like the one depicted here?

Mikael Karlsson, Arresting Images

of both time and, potentially, money. Even baseless lawsuits can affect the insurance premiums that police officials have to pay. Lawsuits can also tarnish a department's image, reduce morale, and instill fear and paranoia in frontline police officers. Administrators (and the people *they* work for) have much to be worried about, too, because they can be held liable for the misconduct of their subordinates.

Section 1983 Liability

42 U.S.C. Section 1983 The federal statute that provides a remedy in federal court for the "deprivation of any rights . . . secured by the Constitution and laws" of the United States.

A portion of the U.S. Code, 42 **U.S.C. Section 1983**, provides a remedy in federal court for the "deprivation of any rights . . . secured by the Constitution and laws" of the United States. Section 1983 states:

> Every person who, under color of any statute, ordinance, regulation, custom, or usage, of any State or Territory or the District of Columbia, subjects, or causes to be subjected, any citizen of the United States or other persons within the jurisdiction thereof to the deprivation of any rights, privileges, or immunities secured by the Constitution and laws, shall be liable to the party injured in an action at law, suit in equity, or other proper proceeding for redress.

This statute was originally enacted as part of the Civil Rights Act of 1871, but it was largely ignored for nearly 100 years. It experienced a resurgence of interest, however, in the 1961 case of *Monroe v. Pape*.[5] In that case, a group of police officers allegedly entered the home of James Monroe without warning and then forced the occupants to stand naked in the living room while the house was searched and ransacked. Monroe brought a Section 1983 action against the police officers and the city of Chicago. The case eventually reached the U.S. Supreme Court, where eight justices held that Section 1983 could be used to sue the police. The Court disagreed with the city of Chicago's argument that its officers could not be held liable under Section 1983 for performing their official duties.

Since *Monroe*, Section 1983 litigation has become quite popular. In 1978 Chief Justice William Rehnquist referred to *Monroe* as "the fountainhead of the torrent of civil rights litigation of the last 17 years."[6] One team of researchers called Section 1983 the "cornerstone of police federal liability litigation" and observed that "[t]he increased use of the 1871 Civil Rights Act may be attributable to expanded interpretation of the legislation by the Supreme Court."[7] More importantly, "Section 1983 is extremely controversial because of its widespread impact on criminal justice personnel, particularly police officers."[8]

color of law The condition that exists when an individual acts in an official government capacity and with the appearance of legal power. Police officers, mayors, and a number of other government officials perform their duties under color of law.[i]

constitutional rights violation Conduct that violates a specific constitutional provision.

culpability The state of deserving blame or being morally or legally responsible. Under the Section 1983 culpability requirement, plaintiffs generally must prove that the defendant officer intended for the violation to occur.

Color of Law. One of the requirements for a successful Section 1983 lawsuit is that the defendant, the person being sued, must have acted under color of law. The U.S. Supreme Court has said that someone acts under **color of law** when he or she acts in an official government capacity and with the appearance of legal power. This includes police officers, mayors, and a number of other government officials.[9] For example, a police officer who is on duty acts under color of law. Police officers also act under color of law when they (1) identify themselves as officers, (2) perform criminal investigations, (3) file official police documents, (4) make arrests, (5) invoke police powers in or outside their jurisdiction, (6) settle personal vendettas with police power, or (7) display weapons or police equipment.[10] By contrast, someone acting in a private capacity (for example, an ordinary citizen) cannot be said to have acted under color of law.

Constitutional Violation. The second requirement for a successful Section 1983 lawsuit is that a federal or constitutional rights violation must have taken place. In the law enforcement context, the concern is almost exclusively over constitutional rights violations. In determining whether a **constitutional**

YOU DECIDE

An Off-Duty Fight

The "You Decide" boxes in earlier chapters asked the question, What should you do? The boxes in the last chapter asked whether the conduct in question was constitutional. This chapter takes a slightly different approach. In light of its civil liability/accountability focus, we ask whether the officer should be held liable. Here is the first scenario, based on an actual case.

While off duty, Officer Smith patronized a bar, where he got into a fight, drew his gun, and shot and killed James Henry. Smith claimed that he was trying to arrest Henry at the time for drunk and disorderly conduct. Henry's heirs filed a Section 1983 lawsuit against the city, alleging that the city had failed to adequately train Smith about how to react during off-duty altercations. Furthermore, Henry's heirs alleged that this failure caused Smith, acting under color of law, to deprive them of their constitutional rights. Should the city be held liable?

YOU DECIDE
A Pursuit

Seventeen-year-old Danny Johnson stole a van from Bob's Fancy Cars by driving it through a showroom window. Almost immediately, members of the local police department began to pursue him. After a dangerous, lengthy, high-speed chase, the van was stopped. When Johnson emerged from the van, unarmed, Officers Jones and Sechrest began to hit him and pull his hair. In the scuffle, Officer Jones's pistol discharged, striking Johnson in the head and hand. Johnson died as a result of these wounds. His parents brought suit under Section 1983, seeking damages from the city, the police department, and the officers. They argued that the city had a custom of using excessive police force and that this caused Johnson's death. Assuming this unfortunate incident was isolated, should Jones be held liable?

---

rights violation has taken place, the plaintiff (the suing party) must establish that the conduct of the defendant (or defendants) violated a specific constitutional provision, such as the Fourth Amendment's prohibition against unreasonable searches and seizures (see Chapter 11), that is, "in any given Section 1983 suit, the plaintiff must still prove a violation of the underlying constitutional right."[11]

Recently, the courts have begun to require that constitutional rights violations alleged under Section 1983 be committed with a certain level of **culpability**, that is, plaintiffs generally have to prove that the defendant officer *intended* for the violation to occur. The practical result of this is that Section 1983 is now reserved for the most serious of constitutional rights violations. The level of culpability required for a constitutional rights violation depends on the type of unconstitutional conduct alleged by the plaintiff.[12]

Theories of Liability. The term **theory of liability** refers essentially to reasons offered as to why a particular person ore entity should be held answerable under civil law for some action. A typical Section 1983 lawsuit will target an individual officer, that officer's supervisor, the city or municipality for which the officer works, or some combination of these. Besides suing the officer who may have been responsible for a constitutional rights violation, it is often attractive for plaintiffs to go after the "bigger fish" because that is where the money is. Cities and counties tend to have deeper pockets than the average police officer and are therefore more attractive targets for civil litigation. To date, cities and counties have only been held liable for failing to train officers[13] and for adopting unconstitutional policies and customs.[14] For the latter, the plaintiff must prove that the city or county adopted and implemented a policy or custom that led to the injury. Isolated incidents are not sufficient to hold a city or county liable.

Suing Federal Officials. Before 1971, it was not clear whether federal officials could be sued under Section 1983. In the 1971 case of ***Bivens v. Six Unknown Named Agents***,[15] however, the U.S. Supreme Court held that federal law enforcement officers *can* be sued for Fourth Amendment violations. The decision has since been expanded to include liability for violations of constitutional rights embodied in other relevant amendments.[16]

Bivens claims are primarily limited to law enforcement officers, as many other federal officials enjoy absolute immunity. **Absolute immunity** means that the official cannot be sued under any circumstances. Federal officials who enjoy absolute immunity include judges[17] and prosecutors, among others.[18] By contrast, heads of federal agencies,[19] presidential aides,[20] and federal law enforcement officers *can* be sued. However, these and other federal officials enjoy qualified immunity, the same defense that applies to state officials in the Section 1983 context.

Defenses. There are two defenses to Section 1983 liability: **sovereign immunity** and **qualified immunity**. Sovereign immunity is based on the Eleventh Amendment to the U.S. Constitution. In contrast, qualified immunity is found nowhere in the Constitution; it is an outgrowth of various U.S. Supreme Court decisions.

The Eleventh Amendment states that "[t]he judicial power of the United States shall not be construed to extend to any suit in law or equity, commenced or prosecuted against one of the United States by citizens of another State, or by citizens or subjects of any foreign state." In simple terms, this means that states and state officials acting in their official capacities cannot be sued in federal court. However, lawsuits against other government employees as well as employees of lower levels of government, such as cities and counties, are still permissible. Also, the Eleventh Amendment only limits the jurisdiction of the federal courts, which means that lawsuits against state officials can be

theory of liability
Reasons offered as to why a particular person or other entity should be held answerable under law for some action.

Bivens v. Six Unknown Named Agents
The 1971 U.S. Supreme Court ruling that held that federal law enforcement officers can be sued for Fourth Amendment violations. The decision has since been expanded to include liability for violations of constitutional rights embodied in other relevant amendments.[ii]

absolute immunity
Protection from lawsuits enjoyed by federal officials when acting in their official capacities.

sovereign immunity
A liability defense based on the Eleventh Amendment that shields states and state officials who are acting in their official capacities from being sued in federal court.

qualified immunity
A liability defense that shields a police officer who has acted in an objectively reasonable fashion as long as he or she did not violate clearly established rights that a reasonable person would have known. Qualified immunity is an outgrowth of various U.S. Supreme Court decisions.

YOU DECIDE

Another Pursuit

Officer Lewis was in pursuit of a motorcycle carrying a passenger. During the pursuit, the motorcycle crashed in the road, directly in front of Lewis. Despite his attempt to stop his cruiser in time, it slid into the back of the motorcycle, killing the passenger. The passenger's family brought a Section 1983 lawsuit against Lewis and the county, alleging that the passenger's substantive due process rights had been violated. The case worked its way up to a federal district court, which decided that the appropriate standard for Section 1983 civil liability for a substantive due process violation is deliberate indifference and that the deputy in this case acted in a deliberately indifferent fashion. In the words of the court, "[T]he appropriate degree of fault to be applied to high-speed police pursuits is deliberate indifference to, or reckless disregard for, a person's right to life and personal security."[1]

Do you agree that Lewis should have been held liable for what happened? In other words, do you think that he acted in a deliberately indifferent fashion?

When Lewis's appeal reached the U.S. Supreme Court, the Court sided with the officer, holding that "a police officer does not violate substantive due process by causing death through deliberate or reckless indifference to life in a high-speed automobile chase aimed at apprehending a suspected offender."[2] The Court went on to say that "in such circumstances only a purpose to cause harm unrelated to the legitimate object of arrest will satisfy the element of arbitrary conduct shocking to the conscience, necessary for a due process violation."

[1] *Lewis v. Sacramento County,* 98 F.3d 434 (9th Cir. 1996). Reversed in *County of Sacramento v. Lewis,* 523 U.S. 833 (1998).
[2] *County of Sacramento v. Lewis*, 323 U.S. 833 (1998).

---

heard in state courts, but Section 1983 lawsuits cannot.[21] Finally, the Eleventh Amendment does not prevent federal courts from issuing injunctions against state officers who act unconstitutionally.[22]

objective reasonableness
A standard, used to determine whether qualified immunity applies, that looks at how a reasonable person would have acted under a given set of circumstances.[iii]

As we have already mentioned, qualified immunity is a judicially created defense. It emerged in response to two conflicting policy concerns: effective crime control and the protection of people's civil liberties. On the one hand, Section 1983 lawsuits are intended to deter police misconduct. But on the other hand, the U.S. Supreme Court has recognized that it is not fair to hold officials liable for lapses in judgment and honest mistakes.[23]

Similar to the Fourth Amendment's test for reasonableness, the courts have applied an **objective reasonableness** standard in order to determine whether qualified immunity should bar a successful lawsuit. In other words, a defendant police officer is said to have acted in an objectively reasonable fashion if he or she did not violate clearly established rights of which a reasonable person would have known. In some Section 1983 cases, police have benefited from qualified immunity even when they violated clearly established constitutional rights, as long as the mistake was a reasonable one.[24]

WEB PATROL 12-3
The Doctrine of Sovereign Immunity
http://www.mycrimekit.com

state tort liability
An important avenue of redress for plaintiffs whose minor injuries, allegedly resulting from negligent acts or misconduct by the police, are not serious enough to make Section 1983 litigation a viable option.

In *Baker v. Putnal* (1996),[25] the Fifth Circuit Court of Appeals developed a two-pronged test for determining whether qualified immunity should be granted: "First, the court must determine whether the plaintiff has alleged a violation of a clearly established constitutional right. If the plaintiff fails at this step, the defendant is entitled to qualified immunity. If she is successful, the issue becomes the objective legal reasonableness of the defendant's conduct under the circumstances."[26] Qualified immunity thus affords protections to defendant criminal justice officials for reasonably mistaken beliefs. In essence, it offers a defense for ignorance, provided that the ignorance in question is reasonable.

intentional tort
An action that is highly likely to cause injury or damage.

negligence tort
A liability claim that must demonstrate that a legal duty existed between the officer and the plaintiff, that a breach of that duty occurred, that a proximate (direct) causation between the officer's actions and the alleged harm resulted, and that actual damage or injury occurred.

State Tort Liability

State tort claims are an alternative for aggrieved people who do not choose to sue under Section 1983. Moreover, **state tort liability** is an important avenue of redress because negligent acts or misconduct by the police that results in minor injuries is usually not serious enough to make Section 1983 litigation a viable option. State tort claims tend to be reserved mostly for less serious claims. There are exceptions, however, such as tort lawsuits for wrongful death, an admittedly serious act.

Types of Torts. There are two types of state tort claims that matter in the law enforcement context. First, **intentional torts** consist of actions that are highly likely to cause injury or damage. For a plaintiff to successfully sue for an intentional tort, he or she must also show that the defendant officer knowingly engaged in the behavior. To be liable for an intentional tort, an officer need not intend to harm; it need only be shown that the officer intended to engage in the behavior that *led* to the harm. Common forms of intentional torts that are applicable to policing include wrongful death, assault and battery, false arrest, and false imprisonment.

A second and more far-reaching tort claim involves negligence. In a **negligence tort**, the mental state of the defendant officer is not at issue. Plaintiffs need only demonstrate the presence of four elements to succeed with a negligence claim: (1) a legal duty between the officer and the plaintiff, (2) a breach of that duty, (3) proximate (direct) causation between the officer's actions and the alleged harm, and (4) actual damage or injury.

public-duty doctrine
A doctrine stating that police protection (like any other government function) is owed to the general public, not to individuals. Police officers have used the public-duty doctrine as a liability defense.

Defenses. Police officers who are sued for tort violations benefit from the so-called **public-duty doctrine**. It states that police protection (like any other government function) is owed to the general public, not to individuals. This means that if a police officer is not present to thwart a criminal act, the officer cannot be held liable for failure to protect. The reason for this barrier to liability is clear: It would be unreasonable to hold law enforcement officials liable every time they do not intervene in criminal activity.

contributory negligence
A liability defense that holds that if an officer can show that the plaintiff or someone else was also negligent in an event, the officer should not be held liable. Contributory negligence can arise not only from the actions of a criminal suspect, but also from the actions of third parties.

There are situations, however, in which police officers owe a legal duty to an individual and, as such, can be held liable for failing to perform that legal duty. For example, if a police officer stops a motorist, confirms that he is drunk, but lets him go, a special relationship has been created; the officer should arrest the drunk driver or, at a minimum, ensure that he does not drive until he is sober. The officer could therefore be held liable under state tort law for negligent failure to protect.

However, even in situations in which a special relationship exists between a police officer and a private citizen, the officer may be able to assert one of several defenses to liability. The first such defense is known as **contributory negligence**. This defense holds that if an officer can show that the plaintiff was also negligent in, say, causing an accident, the officer should not be held liable. Contributory negligence can arise not only from the actions of a criminal defendant, but also from those of third parties. If, during the course of a high-speed pursuit, a third motorist runs a red light and is struck by the officer, the officer may not be found liable because the motorist contributed to the crash by running a red light.

comparative negligence
A partial defense against state tort liability that examines who is to blame and assigns liability accordingly.

Unlike contributory negligence, the **comparative negligence** defense is not a total bar to state tort liability. Comparative negligence looks at who is to blame and assigns liability accordingly. If it is found that the police officer is 20 percent liable and the plaintiff is 80 percent liable, damages would be awarded in accordance with these percentages. The comparative negligence defense permits courts to determine fault and the extent to which each party contributed to an incident or injury.

assumption of risk
A defense against state tort liability that provides that if a plaintiff voluntarily engaged in a dangerous activity that led to his or her injury, then the police officer should not be held liable.

The **assumption of risk** defense against state tort liability provides that if a plaintiff voluntarily engaged in a dangerous activity that led to his or her injury, then the police officer should not be held liable. If a suspect is injured during the course of a high-speed pursuit and sues the officer, the court may decide that the suspect assumed the risk of injury by fleeing from the police.

Protestors march down 125th Street in East Harlem during a 2008 demonstration in New York City over the acquittals of the NYPD detectives involved in the shooting of Sean Bell. How can officers and departments best limit their civil liability when force must be employed?

Chris McGrath/Getty Images, Inc.

sudden peril
A defense against state tort liability that is used for cases in which police officers were required to make split-second decisions.

Finally, police defendants in state tort claims enjoy a defense referred to as **sudden peril**. This is basically an "emergency" defense for situations in which officers were required to make split-second decisions. This defense only applies in situations in which the injury or death is *clearly* attributed to the heat of the moment. If the officer asserting such a defense contributed in any way to the creation of the emergency situation, courts (and juries) may be inclined to find in favor of the plaintiff.

OTHER EXTERNAL ACCOUNTABILITY MEASURES

Lawsuits serve as a powerful check on police misconduct. The problem, however, is that litigation is not always a viable or desirable alternative. Other measures have been put in place to pick up where litigation leaves off. This section looks at what we call *external accountability measures*, those stemming from outside law enforcement agencies. A later section looks at internal measures that police agencies employ to deal with complaints of misconduct and impropriety.

There is some debate over whether police accountability should be internal or external. Some feel that the police themselves are most capable of reviewing allegations against them. Others feel that a balance between internal and external review is necessary. For example, one researcher observed that "the departmental administrative structure has by far the greatest potential for efficient, effective action to prevent, to investigate, to adjudicate, or to punish police misconduct"[27] but that external review allows outside scrutiny of the process and thereby lends credibility to internal review. Others feel that external review of police agencies is critical, arguing that true control occurs only when civilians have the primary responsibility for investigating misconduct.

A more comprehensive view recognizes that the issue of control must be examined as a partnership between the police *and* the community. From this perspective, external accountability mechanisms are essential. We will look at several such mechanisms: citizen oversight, citizen complaints, agency accreditation, the exclusionary rule, and criminal prosecution for serious misconduct.

Citizen Oversight

During the 1980s, one researcher found that the vast majority of police departments used an internal process to handle disciplinary actions.[28] His survey of police agencies revealed that only about 15 percent of them allowed "outsiders" into the review process. Today, however, a host of police agencies have established external (citizen) complaint review procedures.[29] There are a number of reasons for these changes:

> Citizen involvement in the complaint process will produce (1) more objective and more thorough investigations; (2) a higher rate of sustained complaints and more disciplinary actions against guilty officers; (3) greater deterrence of police misconduct (through both general and specific deterrence); and (4) higher levels of satisfaction on the part of both individual complainants and the general public.[30]

There is little consistency in the way external review is structured,[31] but three distinct approaches have been identified:[32] **civilian review, civilian input**, and **civilian monitor**.

civilian review
One of the stronger models of citizen oversight of a police agency in which a group of citizens investigates complaints against the police, adjudicates the complaints, and recommends punishment.

civilian input
A model of civilian oversight of a police agency in which civilians receive and investigate complaints, but the next steps are taken by the police department.

civilian monitor
A model of civilian oversight of a police agency that is similar to an ombudsman approach in which complaints are received by the police department and the process, from beginning to end, is monitored by civilians.

Civilian Review. The civilian review model is one of the stronger models of citizen oversight. It occurs when a group of citizens investigates complaints against the police, adjudicates the complaints, and recommends punishment. This approach has been taken in cities like Washington, D.C., Philadelphia, Rochester, New York City, and Berkeley. The strongest argument against the civilian review model is that it vests responsibility and authority for police discipline in the hands of individuals who have no expertise in police work and who likely do not have the capacity for investigating and understanding the issues involved in a disciplinary problem.[33] On the other hand, the civilian review model represents almost everything that critics of traditional internal review mechanisms desire.

Civilian Input. The civilian input model puts the reception and investigation of complaints in the hands of civilians, but the next steps are taken by the police department. In Kansas City, Missouri, the Office of Community Complaints (OCC) serves as the central clearinghouse for receiving complaints.[34] The OCC reviews all complaints and assigns them, as needed, to the police department's internal affairs unit for investigation. The internal affairs unit is staffed by sworn officers who investigate allegations of wrongdoing in the ranks. Once the investigation has been completed, the

OCC reviews the results and makes recommendations to the chief. In Chicago, the Office of Professional Standards (OPS) is located in the police department but is staffed by nonsworn personnel. The OPS handles all citizen complaints involving excessive force, deadly force, and nondeadly force, while the department's internal affairs division is responsible for all other disciplinary issues.

Civilian Monitor. The civilian monitor model is similar to an ombudsman approach. With the civilian monitor model, complaints are received by the police department, and the process, from beginning to end, is monitored by the external unit. The key feature of this model is that the civilians *monitor* but do not *make* decisions. The monitoring consists of scrutinizing the internal process for inconsistencies or problems. For example, in San Jose, California, the Independent Police Auditor (IPA) receives and investigates complaints (as does the police department's internal affairs division). The IPA's mission consists of the following:

> (a) Reviewing Police Department investigations of complaints against police officers to determine if the investigation was complete, thorough, objective and fair.
> (b) Making recommendations with regard to Police Department policies and procedures based on the Independent Police Auditor's review of investigations of complaints against police officers.
> (c) Conducting public outreach to educate the community on the role of the Independent Police Auditor and to assist the community with the process and procedures for investigation of complaints against police officers.[35]

Other Citizen Oversight Models. The three models we just mentioned are not the only methods of providing citizen oversight. One team of researchers identified *four* classes of citizen review.[36] They overlap to some extent with the three just described. The first involves independent citizen review bodies in which nonsworn investigators conduct investigations and make recommendations to the police executive. Citizen review bodies are found, for example, in New Orleans and Cincinnati.[37] The second approach involves initial investigations by sworn police officers, followed by a review of the officers' reports by an individual or board that contains at least some nonsworn people. The individual or board then makes recommendations to the chief. Procedures of this type have been used in Kansas City (Missouri), Portland (Oregon), and Albuquerque.[38]

In the third approach, an internal affairs department investigates complaints and makes recommendations to the chief. Citizens who are not satisfied with the final disposition can appeal to a board containing at least some nonsworn individuals. The board reviews the case and may make different recommendations to the chief. In the fourth approach, auditors investigate citizen complaints. In both Seattle and San Jose, for example, an auditor reviews the department's complaint procedure and recommends changes as necessary. Also, the auditor often contacts complainants to assess their satisfaction with the complaint process.[39]

It is also important to distinguish between the independent review of citizen complaints and citizen oversight.[40] Independent review occurs when a civilian review body investigates complaints filed against law enforcement officers and then forwards its recommendations to the chief or sheriff. Citizen oversight, in contrast, stresses community outreach, review of complaint policies by a civilian group, audits of complaint investigation procedures, information dissemination, and the like.

Citizen oversight represents an important step in promoting accountability, but its effectiveness in reducing or eliminating misconduct is unclear. This is because most of the mechanisms only provide for disciplinary recommendations, that is, most oversight groups can only make advisory recommendations to the chief police.[41] As two noted researchers observed, "The powers of citizen review procedures are far more limited than those of judges in the criminal process."[42] Nevertheless, certain cities vest citizens with the ability to make disciplinary decisions. Examples include the San Francisco Office of Citizen Complaints, the Milwaukee Fire and Police Commission, the Chicago Police Board, and the Detroit Police Commission.[43]

Citizen Complaints

In general, citizen oversight is concerned with investigations of police misconduct, including investigations of citizen complaints. **Citizen complaints** are documents filed by people who feel they have been wronged by one or more police officers in a department. An example of a citizens' complaint form is provided in Figure 12-1.

citizen complaint
A document filed by someone who believes that he or she has been wronged by one or more police officers in a department.

Figure 12-1 • Citizens' Complaint Form

Abilene Police Department
Citizen Complaint/Commendations Form

File complaints or commendations about Police Department employees on this form. Return the completed form to the desk duty officer, 1st floor at the Police Department, 450 Pecan, or hand deliver to the City Manager's Office, 555 Walnut, Room 203, or by mail to P.O. Box 60 Abilene, Texas 79604.
Complaints will not be investigated until a Police Supervisor has contacted the Complaining Party.

Involved Officer/Employee(s) Information:			
Name:			
Name:			
Person Making the Complaint/Commendation:			
Name:		Phone:	
Address:		Phone:	

Information
Please provide as much information about the reason you were contacted by the officer/employee. Specific information about the date, time and location will help in locating computer-based information if you do not know the officer/employee's name.

Date of Contact:		Approximate Time:	AM/PM
Location Contacted:			

Reason For The Complaint/Commendation: (attach additional pages if needed)

Witness Information:			
Name:		Phone:	
Address:		Phone:	
Name:		Phone:	
Address:		Phone:	

Submitted by_______________________________Date_______________________________

Source: Abilene (Texas) Police Department. Reprinted by permission.

Citizen complaints are sometimes seen by administrators as "a barometer of police performance."[44] Complaints can indicate how officers are behaving on the street, which is useful because police officers are not always directly supervised by their superiors. Agencies should not have to *rely* on complaints to understand how they are doing, but complaints can often send important messages that would not otherwise be clear.

Many police agencies have centralized areas where all citizen complaints about police misbehavior or ill-treatment of citizens must be reported. Complaints are confidentially received and permanently logged in chronological order of receipt. The complainant's information is also recorded, and an investigation is set into motion. Some agencies actively publicize their citizen complaint procedures. Visitors to the Los Angeles Police Department's website, for example, can find a link to a complaint form. Some agencies have even distributed citizen complaint forms to civic organizations and neighborhood groups. Still others require any police employee who is approached by a citizen with a complaint to report the complaint to the internal investigation registration desk within a set period of time after receiving the information.

The Disposition of Complaints. While many agencies have taken steps to ensure that it is easier for citizens to complain, a great deal of research suggests that it is much more difficult to have a complaint sustained, that is, resolved in favor of the person filing the complaint. One study revealed that only about 10 percent of complaints against the police are decided in the complainant's favor.[45] In another study, a researcher examined how the frequency of citizen complaints, the origin of the complaint, and the type of complaint affected its disposition.[46] He found that the frequency of complaints had no bearing on dispositions, but that complaints filed by police officers (as opposed to citizens) were more likely to be sustained. Moreover, complaints of excessive force were less likely than other complaints to be sustained, regardless of who filed the complaint. Both of these conclusions suggest that citizens face an uphill battle when filing complaints and that the most serious complaints are the least likely to be resolved favorably for the complainant.

Similar findings emerged in another study by David Demers and his colleagues,[47] but they also looked at the race of the complainer. They found that the "police were nearly twice as likely to sustain complaints filed against police officers by white citizens than by nonwhites." This finding is especially troubling because "nonwhite citizens, especially blacks, [are] more often the victims of police misconduct,"[48] and nonwhite citizens are responsible for the majority of complaints against the police in many jurisdictions.[49] Another study reveals that citizens in areas characterized by higher unemployment rates were less likely to have their complaints substantiated.[50] The study's author found that nonwhites are less likely to have their complaints resolved satisfactorily and that complaints of excessive force were among the least likely to be resolved in favor of the complainant.

Agency Accreditation

Accreditation refers to certification for having met all applicable requirements put in place by an accrediting body. Accreditation is a big issue in the academic world. Universities have to satisfy their accrediting bodies' requirements, or they risk losing their accreditation, which is akin to losing credibility. Accreditation has spilled over into law enforcement, as well. It is a process intended to ensure that agencies remain accountable to the public and that they abide by the highest standards of conduct in the field.

accreditation
Certification for having met all applicable requirements put in place by an accrediting body.

The Commission on Accreditation for Law Enforcement Agencies (CALEA) was established in 1979 by the International Association of Chiefs of Police (IACP), the National Sheriffs' Association, the Police Executive Research Forum, and the National Organization of Black Law Enforcement Executives. Their goal was to evaluate and accredit police agencies that meet the commission's accreditation standards. CALEA has developed standards designed to do the following:

1. Increase the ability of law enforcement agencies to prevent and control crime.
2. Increase agency effectiveness and efficiency in the delivery of law enforcement services.
3. Increase cooperation and coordination with other law enforcement agencies and with other agencies of the criminal justice system.
4. Increase citizen and employee confidence in the agency's goals, objectives, policies, and practices.[51]

The standards set forth by CALEA address nine major law enforcement subjects: (1) role, responsibilities, and relationships with other agencies; (2) organization, management, and administration; (3) personnel structure; (4) personnel process; (5) operations; (6) operational support; (7) traffic operations; (8) prisoner and court-related activities; and (9) auxiliary and technical services.[52] These subjects are then broken into 38 content areas consisting of (as of this writing) 439 standards.[53]

A police agency seeking accreditation must pass through five phases: application, self-assessment, on-site assessment, commission review and decision, and maintenance of compliance and reaccreditation. The accreditation process is a voluntary one, so only agencies interested in being accredited apply. Once eligibility has been confirmed, the agency and the commission both sign an agreement that identifies what is expected of each party. Then the agency completes an agency profile questionnaire. The responses to the questionnaire provide important information to the accreditation manager and facilitates interaction between the agency and the commission. Next, the agency conducts a self-assessment in which it determines whether it complies with standards set forth by the commission. Proof of compliance is required. The on-site assessment consists of a visit by commission officials during which the agency's compliance with commission standards is determined. The assessors' final report is then forwarded to the commission for review. If, during the review period, the commission is satisfied that the agency meets all relevant standards, accreditation is granted. Accredited agencies then submit annual reports to the commission attesting to their continued compliance with relevant standards.

Accreditation may also provide additional benefits besides accountability and the maintenance of high standards. One is a reduction in insurance premiums.[54] This is not unlike a reduction in auto insurance premiums for drivers who take a safe-driving course. A person who has taken the course is presumably at less risk for getting in an accident or filing a claim. So it goes with police agencies. Those who maintain the highest standards are presumably the least likely to be sued. Evidence also suggests that accredited law enforcement agencies may be more likely to receive grant funds.[55]

WEB PATROL 12-4

The Commission on Accreditation for Law Enforcement Agencies
http://www.mycrimekit.com

Despite the apparent benefits associated with national accreditation, there has been a great deal of debate and controversy over the accreditation process.[56] Some state law enforcement associations have vocally opposed national accreditation standards, arguing that state-level accreditation is preferable. This has resulted in an increase in state-level accreditation.[57] For example, the Washington Association of Sheriffs and Police Chiefs (WASPC) was directed by the state legislature to develop accreditation standards during the 1970s. The result was the WASPC Law Enforcement Accreditation Program.[58] Figure 12-2 depicts WASPC's outline of the benefits of state-level accreditation.

Another area of controversy concerning agency accreditation is its compatibility with community-oriented policing (COP).[59] Much of the debate revolves around the apparent formal administrative and bureaucratic characteristics of accreditation and the decentralized, flexible characteristics of community policing. Not everyone is concerned, however. Police specialists Gary Cordner and Gerald Williams reported that accreditation and community policing are not incompatible, in part because accreditation standards do not necessarily encourage or require formal rules, centralization of authority, increased specialization, or more hierarchy.[60] They also found that conflict between community policing and accreditation, if any, depends on administrators' organization and management philosophies. In short, they found "little evidence of conflict between accreditation and COP."[61]

Figure 12-2 • Benefits of Participating in the WASPC Accreditation Program

- Improved morale within the police agency
- Increased credibility with the agency's governing body
- Increased pride in the agency
- Systemized self-assessment
- Broadened perspectives
- Intensified administrative and operational effectiveness
- Confidence that recruitment, selection, and promotion processes are fair and equitable
- Strengthened understanding of agency policies and procedures by all police personnel
- Decreased susceptibility to litigation and costly civil court settlements
- Potential reduction in premiums for liability insurance
- Greater public confidence in the agency
- State and local acknowledgment of professional competence

Source: Washington Association of Sheriffs and Police Chiefs, "Accreditation," http://www.waspc.org/index.php?c=accreditation (accessed July 10, 2008).

The Exclusionary Rule

Another important mechanism for ensuring the accountability of police agencies is the **exclusionary rule**, which mandates that evidence obtained in violation of the U.S. Constitution cannot be admitted in a criminal trial to prove guilt.[62] In the Supreme Court case of *Elkins v. United States*, Associate Justice Tom C. Clark provided eloquent reasoning for such a rule: "The criminal goes free, if he must, but it is the law that sets him free. Nothing can destroy a government more quickly than its failure to observe its own law, or worse, its disregard of the charter of its own existence."[63]

exclusionary rule
A rule mandating that evidence obtained in violation of the U.S. Constitution cannot be admitted in a criminal trial. The exclusionary rule is an important mechanism for ensuring the accountability of police officials.[iv]

The so-called **fruit of the poisonous tree doctrine** has expanded the scope of the exclusionary rule to include evidence derived from materials that were unconstitutionally obtained. Suppose, for example, that a police officer illegally arrests someone. The fruit of the poisonous tree doctrine would not only require the exclusion of the evidence obtained in the search of the arrestee following that arrest but, potentially, any other evidence (such as a confession) obtained after that initial illegal act.[64] The question of what is considered "fruit," however, has become complicated over the years. This is partly due to the emergence of a number of exceptions to the fruit of the poisonous tree doctrine.

fruit of the poisonous tree doctrine
An expansion of the scope of the exclusionary rule that requires the exclusion of any secondary evidence (such as a confession) that derives from evidence originally obtained in violation of the U.S. Constitution.[v]

The intentions of the exclusionary rule are to promote accountability and to deter misconduct. Some would say, though, that the rule does not serve the same deterrent effect today that it perhaps once did. Its deterrent effect may have been diminished as the U.S. Supreme Court has become more conservative in its decisions. A variety of subsequently established exceptions to the rule helps to ensure that the criminal does not go free when reasonable mistakes are made. The deterrent effect is probably minimal, too, because the time elapsed between illegal police conduct and the decision to exclude evidence is usually rather lengthy.[65]

There is evidence, however, that many police organizations, fearful of losing criminal cases on technicalities, have instituted programs designed to teach trainees about constitutional guidelines. To that end, the exclusionary rule plays at least a minimal role in promoting accountability; when the police violate the Constitution, criminals go free. When criminals go free, the public demands answers. Thus law enforcement officials recognize the importance of operating within established constitutional and legal boundaries.

WEB PATROL 12-5
The Exclusionary Rule
http://www.mycrimekit.com

Arguments for and against the Exclusionary Rule. It is worth giving a little more attention to the arguments for and against the exclusionary rule. Critics and supporters of the rule tend to invoke at least one of three concerns: whether the rule deters police misconduct, whether the rule imposes unnecessary costs on society, and whether alternative remedies are effective and should be pursued.

With regard to deterrence, critics argue that the exclusionary rule does not deter police misconduct. They claim that most constitutional rights violations are unintentional and that such mistakes are undeterrable. As for police officers who act in bad faith, critics of the rule argue that such officers will commit perjury to mask a constitutional rights violation. Supporters of the deterrence argue, in contrast, that the rule is not intended to deter individual officers (specific deterrence), but rather that it is intended to have a broader, systemic deterrent effect (general deterrence). This perspective is well supported; since the exclusionary rule was applied to the states in *Mapp v. Ohio* (1961),[66] many police departments have amended their policies and encouraged their officers to adhere to constitutional safeguards.

Critics make a number of claims regarding the social costs of the exclusionary rule. First, they believe that the rule requires the exclusion of some of the most reliable forms of evidence (for example, confessions), resulting in guilty people going free. Second, they believe that innocent people have nothing to gain from the exclusionary rule because they have nothing to be seized by law enforcement officers who would infringe on constitutional protections. They also believe that the exclusionary rule creates public cynicism because some guilty individuals escape prosecution. Finally, they believe that the exclusionary rule is too extreme. In other words, a relatively trivial violation by a police officer may result in the exclusion of significant evidence.

Supporters of the exclusionary rule, in contrast, do not believe that the social costs of the rule outweigh its benefits. For example, they argue that the exclusionary rule is rarely applied. Indeed, this is true; motions to exclude evidence because of alleged constitutional rights violations are relatively uncommon, and when they are made, they rarely succeed. Second, supporters believe that the rule is beneficial because it *does* help innocents. Supporters of the exclusionary rule argue that public cynicism, to the extent that it exists, should be directed at wayward government officials, not at the exclusionary rule. Finally, they argue that the exclusionary rule is not disproportionate in terms of its consequences, but rather is intended to serve as a general deterrent.

Opinions about the exclusionary rule are also divided around the notion of alternative remedies. Critics of the rule claim that there are effective alternatives that should be pursued. These include civil litigation, criminal prosecution, and internal discipline. Their view is that overzealous law enforcement officers can be deterred from violating the constitution by these enforcement mechanisms. Others do not believe that the alternatives are likely to prove effective. They claim, for example, that juries are more likely to favor police officers in civil trials, that immunity is often extended to police officers in civil litigation cases, and that internal police discipline is something of a sham, that is, disciplinary decisions tend to favor the officer, not the citizen filing the complaint.

Those on both sides of the exclusionary rule debate make interesting points, and their arguments are persuasive. However, given the relatively low number of cases in which serious criminals have gone free, the exclusionary rule is probably more beneficial than it is harmful. In addition, the exclusion of specific evidence because of police misconduct does not automatically mean that the defendant will avoid conviction because the prosecutor often has sufficient additional evidence to support conviction. For example, if a defendant's confession is excluded but several witnesses are willing to testify that she committed the crime, she will likely be convicted. Figure 12-3 summarizes the scholarly research on the effect of the exclusionary rule on policing.

Criminal Prosecution

Various statutes at the state and federal levels provide criminal remedies for police misconduct. Some states make it a crime for police officers to trespass or to falsely arrest people. In fact, most criminal sanctions that apply to ordinary citizens also apply to police officers. Likewise, there are various statutes at the federal level that make it not only improper but criminal for police officers to engage in certain types of conduct.

18 U.S.C.A. Section 242
The most common federal statute used to hold police officers criminally liable.

Federal Prosecution. At the federal level, the most common statute for holding police officers criminally liable is **18 U.S.C.A. Section 242**. Section 242 is to criminal liability what Section 1983 (discussed earlier) is to civil liability. It can be used to prosecute either a state or a federal law enforcement officer. Section 242 states:

> Whoever, under color of any law, statute, ordinance, regulation, or custom, willfully subjects any inhabitant of any State, Territory, or District to the deprivation of any rights, privileges, or immunities secured or protected by the Constitution or laws of the United States, or to different punishments, pains, or penalties, on account of such inhabitant being an alien, or by reason of his color, or race, than are prescribed for the punishment of citizens, shall be fined not more than $1,000 or imprisoned not more than one year, or both; and if death results shall be subject to imprisonment for any term of years or for life.

To be held liable under Section 242, a law enforcement officer must act with specific intent to deprive a person of important constitutional or other federal rights.[67] A finding of criminal liability under Section 242 also requires that a constitutional right be clearly established.[68] These restrictions have resulted in relatively few Section 242 cases. In fact, criminal liability under Section 242 is reserved for the most egregious forms of police misconduct.

Despite its relatively infrequent application, there have been a few cases in which Section 242 was invoked. For example, in *Miller v. United States* (1968),[69] a police officer was held criminally liable for allowing his canine unit to bite a suspect. In *Williams v. United States* (1951),[70] a defendant had been beaten, threatened, and physically punished for several hours, and the police officer was held criminally liable. Section 242 has also been applied in cases involving assault and battery of criminal defendants.[71]

Additional federal statutes make it a criminal act to unlawfully search and seize individuals (18 U.S.C.A. Section 2236), although applications of this statute are rare. For example, 18 U.S.C.A. Section 2235 makes it a crime to maliciously procure a warrant, and Section 2234 makes it a criminal offense to exceed the authority of a warrant. Regardless of which criminal statute applies, an important distinction between the various criminal statutes and 42 U.S.C. Section 1983 is that officers

Figure 12-3 • Summary of Empirical Research on the Exclusionary Rule

The question of whether the exclusionary rule is beneficial or harmful has been subjected to a fair amount of empirical research. Of particular interest to researchers has been the effects of the rule on the police and the outcomes of criminal cases. Most of the research can be organized around two topics: (1) the impact of the rule on the police and (2) the incidence of cases where the rule resulted in the suppression of evidence or the extent to which search and seizure concerns dictated the decision to prosecute.

The following is a list of leading studies. The main research findings are reported here. Citations are also provided so readers can examine the findings and research designs in more detail.

The Effects of the Rule on Police and Prosecutors

1. Following *Mapp*, arrests declined for Narcotics Bureau detectives but increased for other detectives: "Effect of *Mapp v. Ohio* on police search and seizure practices in narcotics cases," *Columbia Journal of Law and Social Problems* 4 (1968): 87.
2. The exclusionary rule has virtually no effect on police arrest behavior: D.H. Oaks, "Studying the exclusionary rule in search and seizure," *University of Chicago Law Review* 37 (1970): 665.
3. The exclusionary rule has no deterrent effect on illegal search practices and exacts a high cost on society because of its potential to free guilty criminals: J. Spiotto, "Search and seizure: An empirical study of the exclusionary rule and its alternatives," *Journal of Legal Studies* 2 (1973): 243.
4. Law enforcement search and seizure practices changed significantly following *Mapp*—police officers were more likely to comply with search warrant procedures: B.C. Canon, "Is the exclusionary rule in failing health? Some new data and a plea against a precipitous conclusion," *Kentucky Law Journal* 62 (1974): 681.
5. Interviews with narcotics detectives in Chicago led a researcher to conclude that the exclusionary rule had "significant deterrent effects. . . . [It] changed police, prosecutorial, and judicial procedures. . . . It educated police officers in the requirements of the Fourth Amendment and punished them when they violated requirements": M. Orfield, "The exclusionary rule and deterrence: An empirical study of Chicago narcotics officers," *University of Chicago Law Review* 54 (1987): 1016.

Research on the Incidence of Lost Cases and Related Issues

1. Of 2,804 cases analyzed between July 1 and August 31, 1978, successful motions for the exclusion of evidence were made in only 1.3 percent of prosecuted cases. That is 1.3 percent of the 16 percent whose cases were accepted for prosecution: General Accounting Office, *Report of the comptroller general of the United States: Impact of the exclusionary rule on federal criminal prosecutions* (Washington, DC: USGPO, 1979).
2. Of cases rejected for prosecution, 4.8 percent were rejected because of search and seizure problems. Approximately 50 percent of those released because of the exclusionary rule were rearrested within two years of their release: National Institute of Justice, *The effects of the exclusionary rule: A study in California* (Washington, DC: U.S. Dept. of Justice, 1983).
3. In a reanalysis of the preceding study, one researcher found that prosecutors rejected only 0.8 percent of felony arrests because of Fourth Amendment concerns. He concluded further that "only about 2.35% of felony arrests are lost because of illegal searches": T.Y. Davies, "A hard look at what we know (and still need to learn) about the 'costs' of the exclusionary rule: The NIJ study and other studies of 'lost' arrests," *American Bar Foundation Research Journal* 3 (1983): 611.
4. A nine-county study of 7,500 felony court cases revealed that motions to suppress were filed in less than 5 percent of all cases. The success rate of such motions was reported to be 0.69 percent. The study's conclusion was that less than 0.6 percent of all cases were lost due to the exclusion of evidence: P.F. Nardulli, "The societal cost of the exclusionary rule: An empirical assessment," *American Bar Foundation Research Journal* 3 (1983): 585.
5. Craig D. Uchida and Timothy S. Bynum reported that "motions to suppress were successful in only 0.9% of the primary warrants (15 of 1,748). Judges sustained motions for 2% of all defendants (27 of 1,355) in our warrant-based sample. Few cases were 'lost' as a result of the exclusionary rule in seven jurisdictions when police used search warrants. Twenty-one of 1,355 defendants (1.5%) were 'allowed to go free' as a result of a successful motion to suppress physical evidence": C.D. Uchida and T.S. Bynum, "Search warrants, motions to suppress, and 'lost cases': The effects of the exclusionary rule in seven jurisdictions," *Journal of Criminal Law and Criminology* 81 (1991): 1034.

Source: J. L. Worrall, *Criminal procedure: From first contact to appeal*, 2nd ed. (Upper Saddle River, NJ: Pearson Education, Inc., 2007), p. 58. Reprinted by permission.

who are held *criminally* liable receive criminal convictions and can even go to prison; Section 1983, by contrast, is civil, meaning that it is used independently of the criminal process. A successful Section 1983 lawsuit will never result in the imprisonment of the defendant.

State Prosecution. The same laws that apply to ordinary citizens also apply to police officers. For example, if a police officer knowingly and intentionally kills someone and is not legally justified in doing so (that is, it was not a justifiable killing that occurred in conjunction with the officer's official police duties), the officer can be held criminally liable for murder. Similarly, if a police officer trespasses on private property without appropriate justification, he or she can be held criminally liable. Criminal liability can extend to police officers for virtually any conceivable offense.

Three categories of offenses have been identified[72]: (1) violent and sex crimes, (2) drug crimes, and (3) other crimes. Examples of officers accused of violating state law include the so-called Miami River Cops, who were charged with murdering drug smugglers, and the police officer in Fort Myers, Florida, who was charged with sexual assault against a 19-year-old woman. Indeed, as of this writing, U.S. Border Patrol agents along the Arizona-Mexico border have become the targets of almost daily *criminal* complaints for a variety of actions.

Given the staggering amounts of money associated with the illegal drug trade, it is no wonder that some police officers cross the "thin blue line" and attempt to profit from illegal drugs. This appears to be the case with the infamous Rampart scandal in the Los Angeles Police Department. Officers in other cities have faced similar charges. In 1996, seven officers on the Chicago Police Department's Tactical Unit were charged with stealing and extorting drug money; seven officers in Atlanta were arrested in 1995 on drug charges; and a deputy in Tucson was arrested in 1999 for conspiracy to distribute drugs. The list, unfortunately, goes on.[73]

Police officers have also been held liable for such offenses as burglary, fabrication of evidence, perjury, and shoplifting. One report revealed that federal agents arrested three city police officers in Detroit who were planning a home invasion to steal $1 million in cash.[74]

public-duty defense
A legal defense that shields a police officer from criminal liability in situations in which he or she is legally performing an assigned or implied public duty and engages in a necessary and reasonable action that, for ordinary citizens, would be considered a crime.

This is not to suggest that police officers frequently engage in criminal activity, only that it does happen. No one is above the law, not even police officers. However, when officers break the law in order to protect the innocent or to prevent some greater harm, then they can claim a "law enforcement" or **public-duty defense.** Such a defense would, for example, be useful by an officer who finds the use of force necessary in effecting an arrest, but is later accused of assault by the person arrested. The public-duty defense is meant to shield police officers from criminal liability when they act reasonably in such situations.

New York City Police Sgt. Robert Patelli testifies in the Albany County Courthouse in Albany, New York in the trial of the three New York City police officers who were accused in the shooting death of Amadou Diallo. What was the outcome of the trial?

Philip Kamrass/AP Wide World Photos

ACCOUNTABILITY FROM THE INSIDE

The preceding section may give the impression that there is something wrong with internal accountability mechanisms, the organizational steps that police departments take to address wrongdoing. Nothing could be further from the truth. Internal affairs divisions and codes of ethics are effective methods for promoting the accountability of those charged with serving the public.

Internal Affairs

Many police agencies have developed innovative and highly regarded internal complaint review units, most commonly known as **internal affairs (IA)** divisions. The IA division in Oakland, California, for instance, is respected throughout the country.[75] According to one source, the "Internal Affairs Section of the Oakland Police Department works closely with the chief of police, who sets the tone for its rigorous investigations." Officers who have worked in IA "help to pass on [the unit's] knowledge about citizens' complaints and educate the everyday cop about how IA works. Ideally these dynamics combine to make IA respected, understood, and feared by the cops it polices."[76]

internal affairs (IA)
An investigative agency within a police department that is tasked with investigating allegations of misconduct or criminality by members of the department.

In its police misconduct policy, which is meant to serve as a model policy for departments throughout the nation, the Police Executive Research Forum lists three ways that the police themselves can implement effective complaint procedures:

> (1) Through the provision of meaningful and effective complaint procedures, citizen confidence in the integrity of police increases and this engenders community support and confidence in the police department; (2) through disciplinary procedures that permit police officials to monitor officers' compliance with departmental procedures; and (3) by clarifying rights and ensuring due process protection to citizens and officers alike.[77]

Some police departments utilize a citizen oversight process that asks community members to review the activities of police officers whose performance has been called into question on legal or ethical grounds. This kind of *external* review differs significantly from *internal* investigations. Some writers have suggested that citizen oversight procedures suffer from a number of drawbacks: (1) They ignore existing legal resources at citizens' disposal; (2) it is difficult for people disconnected from the police department to have an adequate understanding of its internal operations; (3) citizen review damages morale; (4) citizen review invites abdication of authority by line supervisors; (5) they weaken the ability of top management to achieve conformity through discipline; and (6) they are tantamount to admitting that the police are incapable of policing themselves.[78] To the extent that any of these observations is accurate, there is clear merit in maintaining internal investigations of police misconduct and complaints.

Functions and Procedures. The functions of internal investigation units have evolved to include the following:

1. Receiving, recording, and investigating complaints concerning police misconduct
2. Investigating other indications of misconduct by police
3. Investigating incidents involving police use of deadly force that resulted in homicide or serious injury, or possible breach of integrity or ethical standards by a member of the police agency
4. Evaluating policies related to police ethics and behavior
5. Providing administrative trial mechanisms for reviewing instances and accusations of police misconduct
6. Prosecuting employees who are revealed by evidence to be responsible for serious misbehavior
7. Providing commanders with intelligence on deviance and misbehavior occurring within the agency
8. Informing complainants and victims of police misconduct of actions on their behalf by the police agency

The effectiveness of internal investigations of police misconduct depends on the accurate receipt and recording of all relevant information of improper personnel or organizational behavior, regardless of its source. Administrative efforts to minimize the potential for manipulating complaints have led to the designation of specifically identified individuals or offices as the point for registering employee misconduct complaints.

Internal investigation units receive complaints that are filed in various manners: verbally or in writing, openly or anonymously, by civilians or sworn police officers, in person or by telephone, or by other means. Complaints must be investigated regardless of the manner of filing or the type of incident involved. The following three types of complaints are critical to effective managerial control and must be fully investigated: (1) a citizen complaining about the police department or one of its employees, (2) a police employee complaining about another police employee, and (3) a police employee complaining about the police agency or its practices.[79]

Once they are recorded, complaints and reports must be managed in such a fashion as to ensure prompt, thorough, confidential investigation. Only the chief executive officer and police officials with a need to know are normally permitted access to information about the complainant, the complaint, or the investigation, at least during the initial investigative phase. Time limits for completing various aspects of the investigation and reporting to complainants are essential for the effective operation of internal affairs.

Another matter deserving careful consideration by the chief is the selection of staff investigators for internal affairs. Role conflicts are created when line police officers are assigned to investigate other line officers with whom they must work or when investigative officers are shifted back and forth between the internal affairs unit and operational units that are subject to investigations. In each of these instances, investigators may be tempted to be lenient with those officers accused of misconduct.

Although there is no universal agreement on this matter, internal investigations may be best served by police personnel who will never be reassigned to work under officers who have been the subject of their investigations. To prevent this situation from occurring, small police agencies sometimes use high-level staff commanders or investigators from other nearby police agencies or sheriff's departments. Larger organizations usually have the option of developing separate career paths for those who specialize in the investigation of other police officers. Such separate career routes have the advantage of permitting the use of rewards for vigorous, competent, and objective investigations.

Together, all of these concerns have led to sophisticated procedures for tracking and investigating complaints against the police through internal affairs. To illustrate one such process, Figure 12-4 shows how complaints are reviewed internally within the Claremont (California) Police Department. The Police Review Ad Hoc Committee referenced in the figure consists of no more than three commissioners drawn at random from the city's police commission.

The Trial Board. Internal investigations are conducted only to determine the facts surrounding a question of employee misconduct. Internal affairs officers have no authority to initiate or carry out corrective actions against employees. Since IA is an administrative tool of the chief, the unit is responsible for advising the chief on the general state of the organizational discipline and the adequacy of the personnel-control efforts of field commanders and supervisors. The IA registration data and information from personnel investigations can be used as a basis for staff reports that the chief and top commanders can rely on in managerial decision making. Even cases that result in inconclusive or unfounded outcomes produce information that may be valuable in the administration of the police agency.

Where the information accumulated by internal investigations produces evidence of police conduct that is in violation of formal departmental standards and expectations, the evidence is subjected to further review and assessment by supervisors or to a decision-making process called a **trial board**. The trial board is operated in conjunction with the internal investigation unit and is staffed on an ad hoc basis when the need arises for thorough, impartial evaluation of alleged employee misconduct. The trial board is modeled after the military court-martial. If the offense substantiated by an internal affairs investigation so merits (that is, if it is serious enough to warrant dismissal from the police agency) or if the accused officer so requests, the chief may appoint a trial board. The board, consisting of three to five sworn officers, none of whom are below the rank of the accused officer, proceeds in a fashion parallel to a civil trial. The accused employee is tried on a specific formally drafted accusation; witnesses are called, examined, and cross-examined; evidence is introduced; and the board renders a decision based on a preponderance of evidence, as in civil proceedings. The board is responsible for rendering a judgment after hearing the case presented by internal affairs and compiling its findings and conclusions in an advisory report to

trial board
An agency within a police department that operates in conjunction with the internal investigation unit and is staffed on an ad hoc basis when the need arises for thorough and impartial evaluation of alleged employee misconduct.

Figure 12-4 • Citizen Complaint Process in Claremont, California

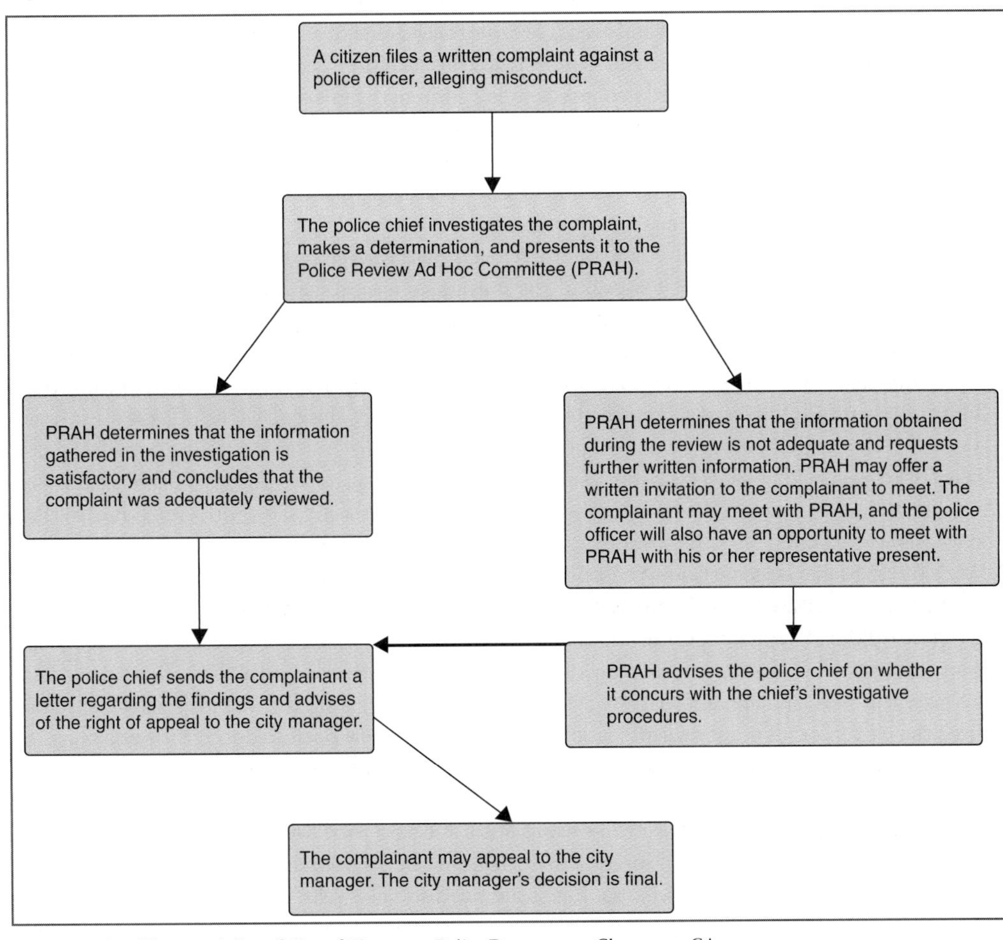

Source: Reprinted by permission of City of Claremont Police Department, Claremont, CA.

the chief. Most police trial boards are expected to recommend one of five courses of action to the chief:

1. Further investigation, with specific suggestions for how the reopened investigation should proceed
2. Dismissal of the accusation
3. Written reprimand
4. Suspension
5. Dismissal of the accused officer

A trial board serves to protect citizens, the police agency, and the accused by bringing the results of the police investigation before a deliberating body of experienced police personnel to permit organized challenges and rational consideration of all available information. Careful selection of the board members serves to ensure sound, objective judgments. The final decision is made by the chief, who benefits from a thorough exploration of the evidence and issues.

Officers' Rights during Investigations. Vigorous personnel investigations sometimes neglect employees' rights to privacy and due process. Internal investigations officers may assume that accused officers are guilty until proven innocent. Given this fact, it should not be surprising that line police officers tend to be suspicious and fearful of police internal investigation personnel and units, sometimes referring to them disparagingly as "God Squads" or the "Hatchet Details." Administrators must therefore ensure that internal investigations are performed in a thorough, objective, and impersonal manner.

A number of court cases have addressed the issue of police officers' rights during the course of internal investigations. In *Garrity v. New Jersey* (1967),[80] the U.S. Supreme Court ruled that information gained from the interrogation of a police officer could not be used in a criminal trial because it was not voluntary. In that case, a state deputy attorney general was asking police officers about ticket fixing. The officers were read their rights and then told that if they failed to answer the questions, they would be dismissed. Subsequent criminal convictions based on the officers' admissions were deemed unconstitutional because the admissions were not voluntary. Similarly, in *Gardner v. Broderick* (1967),[81] the Supreme Court ruled that police officers could not be fired for invoking their constitutional rights against self-incrimination. In *Gardner*, a police officer refused to answer questions from a grand jury on the grounds that the answers might incriminate him. The department fired the officer, but the Court held that this termination was unconstitutional.

Gardner and *Garrity* are often misinterpreted as granting total protection to officers during the investigation stage. This is not the case; if the purpose of an internal investigation is disciplinary rather than criminal, then the officer *can* be compelled to answer questions.

The Supreme Court stated in *Gardner* and *Garrity* that officers can be required to answer questions (in essence, waiving their Fifth Amendment privilege), but the questions asked of the officers must be specifically, directly, and narrowly related to the officers' duties *and* the officers must be advised that the answers they provide will not be used in a criminal proceeding. The Court felt that it was fair to require that officers answer questions regarding their duties because of the need to protect the state and to ensure that officers perform their duties faithfully. The Fifth Amendment, then, only applies when the responses to the questions are to be used in a criminal prosecution.

In 1998, the Supreme Court consolidated six internal investigations cases and rendered its decision in *LaChance v. Erickson*.[82] The *LaChance* case involved the issue of whether police officers who gave untruthful statements during the course of an internal investigation could be dismissed. The lead case concerned an officer who allegedly made harassing telephone calls. The officer denied any involvement in the phone calls, despite evidence to the contrary from the investigation. The agency fired the officer for giving untruthful statements. A merit review board reduced the punishment to a 15-day suspension, and a federal circuit court basically agreed with the decision, stating that if officers were not allowed to make inaccurate statements, they might be coerced into admitting misconduct. The Supreme Court disagreed unanimously, holding that "willful falsehoods" made by an employee during the course of an internal investigation can be grounds for dismissal.

The disciplinary aspect of internal investigations also raises issues about the rights that police officers enjoy. If, for example, an internal investigation results in a recommendation for suspension or dismissal, due process issues come into play. Both types of due process—procedural and substantive—that we introduced earlier in the litigation context are also relevant here.

Procedural due process cases have been rather frequent in the area of public employment. In *Cleveland Board of Education v. Loudermill* (1985), the Supreme Court ruled that public employees are "entitled to oral or written notice of the charges against [them], and explanation of the employer's evidence, and an opportunity to present [their] side of the story."[83] In the more recent *Gilbert v. Homar* (1997), however, the Court interpreted *Loudermill* to mean that a public employee is only entitled to a "very limited hearing prior to his termination, to be followed by a more comprehensive post-termination hearing."[84] The definitions of *very limited* and *more comprehensive* remain elusive.

A substantive due process case involving police personnel matters is *Bence v. Breier* (1974).[85] In that case, the Seventh Circuit Court of Appeals held that a Milwaukee Police Department rule that prohibited "conduct unbecoming a member and detrimental to the service" lacked "inherent, objective content from which ascertainable standards defining the proscribed conduct could be fashioned."[86] The court noted that the rule permitted "unfettered discretion" to those charged with enforcing it. This decision is important on an administrative level because it suggests that departmental policies and regulations need to be clear and specific, leaving very little room for interpretation.

A Police Officers' Bill of Rights. To reduce the temptation for internal investigators to proceed against police employees in an insensitive fashion, some police agencies have formally adopted a statement of the rights of police officers who are accused of misconduct. Sometimes such conditions are contained in labor contracts; other times they are mandated by law. The most widely discussed **police officers' bill of rights** includes the following:

police officers' bill of rights
A police agency's formal statement of the rights of officers who are accused of misconduct.

1. A ban on the use of polygraphs and alcohol-detection devices on officers.
2. Clearly established hours describing when an investigator may interrogate a suspected officer.
3. Advance notice to an officer who is being investigated, which includes the accusation and the name and address of any complainant.

4. Accusation and trial procedures that ensure an officer's right to counsel, cross-examination of accusers and witnesses, and established penalties.
5. The right of an accused officer to choose some members of any review panel or trial board that will sit in judgment of the officer upon completion of the investigation.[87]

Although the individual components of this list can be debated, fairness requires that officers deserve reasonable protection from inappropriate investigative practices. Procedures for ensuring that officers receive fair and appropriate treatment at the hands of specialized IA investigators and their supervisors should be observed in the investigative process. The following guidelines have been suggested:

1. Assign the complaint to be investigated to an IA investigator following registration with the central intake position.
2. Have the investigating officer review the details of the complaint and check with the complainant as required to obtain an accurate understanding of the accusation or report.
3. Present the accused employee with a summary of the accusation and provide the employee an opportunity to respond in writing. Unless exercising constitutional rights related to criminal prosecution, an accused can be expected to provide information about job-related actions and behavior. Further, in cases where serious criminal behavior is alleged, the investigator should proceed as one would in handling a criminal investigation. Policy should prevent accused employees from engaging in any actions that can be construed as being intended to influence complainants or others regarding matters under investigation.
4. Conduct IA investigative activities thoroughly and confidentially on the authority and behalf of the chief.
5. Upon completion of an investigation, have the investigator prepare a summary report of findings and recommendations. The report should specify whether the complaint was deemed to be unfounded, inconclusive, or founded.
6. Prohibit notations or records in an employee's personnel file that refer to investigations that produced unfounded or inconclusive findings.
7. When misconduct is found, make a recommendation for action directly to the chief (when serious misbehavior is found) or to the appropriate lower-level supervisor (when less serious violations merit such a referral).
8. Afford employees the opportunity for an appeal of supervisory action or, in serious matters, a departmental trial for complete hearing before a decision by the chief executive.

Several states have adopted bills of rights for police officers,[88] beginning with Florida in 1974. Portions of the Delaware police officers' bill of rights appear in Figure 12-5. Supporters of such legislation argue that "the bill of rights merely ensures [that] the officer under investigation knows the subject of the investigation and is afforded rights and protections against certain interrogation techniques subject to abuse."[89] Critics claim that "the basic premises of such legislation only confound an already complex area of public police without substantially improving police labor-management relations."[90]

Codes of Ethics

Another mechanism for promoting accountability from within the law enforcement agency is a **code of ethics**, a statement of principles concerning the behavior of those who subscribe to the code. According to Joycelyn Pollock,[91] a leading police ethicist, these codes consist of several standard elements: "legality (enforcing and upholding the law), service (protecting and serving the public), honesty and integrity (telling the truth, being honest in action), loyalty (to other police officers), and the Golden Rule (treating people with respect or the way one would like to be treated)."[92]

code of ethics
A statement of principles concerning the behavior of those who subscribe to the code.

The development of a code of ethics for law enforcement can be traced back to early movements to professionalize policing. During the 1930s, the International Association of Chiefs of Police (IACP) created a committee to make recommendations designed to promote professionalism. The committee agreed that one of the criteria for accomplishing this goal was the creation of a code of ethics. It was not until 1957, however, that the Law Enforcement Code of Ethics was unanimously approved by delegates attending the sixty-fourth IACP conference in Honolulu. Then, in 1989, IACP voted to replace the 1957 code with a newer version that reflects concern over a wider range of issues.

WEB PATROL 12-6
Gratuities: Pay Now or Later
http://www.mycrimekit.com

Figure 12-5 • The Delaware Law Enforcement Officers' Bill of Rights

Title 11

Crimes and Criminal Procedure

Victims of Crimes

Chapter 92. Law Enforcement Officers' Bill of Rights

§9203. Hearing—Required on suspension or other disciplinary action.

If a law enforcement officer is (1) suspended for any reason, or (2) charged with conduct alleged to violate the rules or regulations or general orders of the agency that employs the officer, or (3) charged with a breach of discipline of any kind, which charge could lead to any form of disciplinary action (other than a reprimand) which may become part of the officer's permanent personnel record, then that officer shall be entitled to a hearing which shall be conducted in accordance with this chapter unless a contractual disciplinary grievance procedure executed by and between the agency and the bargaining unit of that officer is in effect, in which case the terms of that disciplinary grievance procedure shall take precedence and govern the conduct of the hearing. (65 Del. Laws, c. 12, §1; 65 Del. Laws, c. 139, §3; 70 Del. Laws, c. 186, §1.)

§9204. Hearing—Scheduling; notice.

In the event an officer is entitled to a hearing, a hearing shall be scheduled within a reasonable period of time from the alleged incident, but in no event more than 30 days following the conclusion of the internal investigation, unless waived in writing by the charged officer. The officer shall be given written notice of the time and place of the hearing and the issues involved, including a specification of the actual facts that the officer is charged with having committed; a statement of the rule, regulation or order that those facts are alleged to violate; and a copy of the rule, regulation or order. The charge against the law-enforcement officer shall advise the officer of the alleged facts and that the violation of the rule constituted a basis for discipline, and shall specify the range of applicable penalties that could be imposed. (65 Del. Laws, c. 12, §1; 70 Del. Laws, c. 186, §1.)

§9205. Hearing—Procedure.

(a) An official record including testimony and exhibits shall be kept of the hearing.

(b) The hearing shall be conducted within the department by an impartial board of officers. The prosecuting party and the officer and/or the officer's representative shall be given an opportunity to present evidence and argument with respect to the issues involved. Both the department and the officer may be represented by legal counsel. In the event an impartial board cannot be convened, then a board of three officers or more shall be convened under the auspices of the Delaware Criminal Justice Council. Any officer appointed under this subsection, either within the department or under the auspices of the Criminal Justice Council, shall not be liable for civil damages from any acts or omissions arising out of such officer's service on the board as long as the member of the board of officers acted in good faith and without malice in carrying out his or her responsibilities or duties. A member of the board of officers is presumed to have acted in good faith and without malice unless proven otherwise.

(c) Evidence which possesses probative value commonly accepted by reasonable and prudent persons in the conduct of their affairs shall be admissible in evidence and given probative effect. The tribunal conducting the hearing shall give effect to the rules of privilege recognized by law and may exclude incompetent, irrelevant, immaterial and unduly repetitious evidence. All records and documents which any party desires to use shall be offered and made a part of the record. Documentary evidence may be received in the form of copies of excerpts or by incorporation by reference.

(d) Every party shall have the right of cross-examination of witnesses who testify and may submit rebuttal evidence.

(e) The tribunal may take notice of judicially cognizable facts and in addition may take notice of general, technical or scientific facts within its specialized knowledge. Parties shall be notified beforehand of the materials so noticed by the trial board. No law enforcement officer may be adjudged guilty of any offense unless the hearing tribunal is satisfied that guilt has been established by substantial evidence. (65 Del. Laws, c. 12, §1; 65 Del. Laws, c. 139, §4; 70 Del. Laws, c. 186, §1; 71 Del. Laws, c. 166, §1.)

Source: Delaware Code, Title 11, Chapter 92, "Law Enforcement Officers' Bill of Rights," http://delcode.delaware.gov/title11/c092/index.shtml (accessed July 10, 2008).

Among the issues covered in the 1989 code of ethics are (1) the responsibilities of police officers, (2) the performance of police duties, (3) discretion, (4) use of force, (5) confidentiality, (6) integrity, (7) cooperation with other agencies, (8) personal and professional responsibilities, and (9) private life. For example, with respect to an officer's private life, the code states, "Police officers will behave in a manner that does not bring discredit to their agencies or themselves." With respect to use of force, the code states, "A police officer will never employ unnecessary force or violence and will use only such force in the discharge of duty as is reasonable in all circumstances."[93] The IACP code of ethics is reproduced in Chapter 1. The ethical dilemmas presented throughout this book also reinforce this ethics focus.

WEB PATROL 12-7

Gratuities: There Is No Free Lunch
http://www.mycrimekit.com

SUMMARY

- Police can be held liable for monetary and other damages under 42 U.S.C. Section 1983 and state tort law. For a Section 1983 lawsuit to succeed, the plaintiff must show that the defendant acted under color of law and violated an applicable constitutional provision. Defenses to Section 1983 liability include absolute and qualified immunity. Common state tort claims against police include intentional and negligent misconduct. There are several defenses to state tort liability, including the public-duty doctrine, contributory negligence, comparative negligence, assumption of risk, and sudden peril.
- External mechanisms for promoting police accountability in addition to civil liability include citizen oversight, citizen complaint procedures, agency accreditation, the exclusionary rule, and criminal prosecution. Citizen oversight refers to the oversight of police actions and the investigation of complaints by nonsworn personnel. Citizen complaints promote accountability, but the fate of a complaint depends on who files it. Police agencies, like universities, seek accreditation to demonstrate that they meet critical professional standards. The exclusionary rule requires that evidence obtained in violation of the U.S. Constitution be inadmissible in a criminal trial. The rule has been expanded with the fruit of the poisonous tree doctrine. There are several arguments for and against the exclusionary rule. Ultimately, however, it is rarely applied. Police officers, like ordinary citizens, can be held *criminally* liable for egregious misconduct.
- Accountability from inside police agencies is promoted via internal affairs divisions and professional codes of ethics. Internal affairs (IA) refers to either a division within a police agency or one or more officers who are tasked with investigating allegations of misconduct. The targets of IA investigations enjoy a number of protections today. Codes of ethics encourage officers to abide by various professional standards.

COMING FULL CIRCLE

For Discussion

Return to the questions posed at the start of this chapter. Have any of your answers changed since you read the chapter? What portions of this chapter helped you answer these questions?

Writing Assignment

Using material from this chapter and additional resources, write a 500-word essay in response to one of the questions presented at the beginning of the chapter. Submit your essay to your instructor if asked to do so.

KEY TERMS AND NAMES

18 U.S.C.A. Section 242
42 U.S.C. Section 1983
absolute immunity
accreditation
assumption of risk
Bivens v. Six Unknown Named Agents
citizen complaint
civilian input
civilian monitor
civilian review
code of ethics
color of law
comparative negligence
constitutional rights violation
contributory negligence
culpability
damages
exclusionary rule

fruit of the poisonous tree doctrine
injunctive relief
intentional tort
internal affairs (IA)
negligence tort
objective reasonableness
police officers' bill of rights
public-duty defense
public-duty doctrine
qualified immunity
sovereign immunity
state tort liability
sudden peril
theory of liability
trial board

WEB INTERACTIVITY

Visit the Internal Affairs Bureau of the Philadelphia Police Department on the Web at http://www.ppdonline.org/hq_misconduct.php. Take note of the bureau's mission statement and of the three groups that the bureau says it works to protect. How can the bureau minimize the conflicts that might arise as it attempts to protect members of those groups? Submit your notes and analysis to your instructor if asked to do so.

REVIEW QUESTIONS

1. What are the two main avenues available to aggrieved parties seeking to sue for police civil liability? What are some of the defenses against civil liability that law enforcement officers and their supervisors and departments might employ? How can civil liability promote accountability?
2. Discuss five external measures, other than litigation, for promoting police accountability.
3. How do police agencies promote accountability from within?

CHALLENGES

SECTION V

CHAPTER 13
Police Discretion and Behavior

CHAPTER 14
Deviance, Ethics, and Professionalism

CHAPTER 15
The Use of Force

chapter thirteen

POLICE DISCRETION AND BEHAVIOR

LEARNING OBJECTIVES

After reading this chapter, students should be able to:

1. Define police discretion and identify some of its pros and cons.
2. Summarize the findings of several classic studies of police behavior.
3. Explain the differences between the universalistic and particularistic perspectives on police behavior.
4. Identify four categories of factors that affect police decision making and provide examples of each.

YORK CITY

THINK ABOUT IT

In late 2003, the manager of a White Castle restaurant in Cincinnati called the fire department at about 6:00 a.m. to report that a patron was unconscious on the floor. Paramedics arrived and found Nathaniel Jones, age 41, passed out. Jones, an African American, regained consciousness, but then he started acting strangely, so the paramedics called the police. Two white officers from the Cincinnati Police Department arrived. Their cruiser's video camera captured what happened next. One of the officers, who was out of view of the camera, was heard saying to Jones, "You gotta tell me what's going on." Jones then said, "White boy, redneck," at which point the camera caught Jones, who weighed 350 pounds, lunging at one of the officers and attempting to put him in a headlock. The two officers took Jones to the ground and tried to subdue him, but he resisted.

Soon four more officers arrived and joined the fray with their colleagues, who were using metal nightsticks to subdue a still-struggling Jones. When the video ended, Jones was on the ground and seemed to be saying, "Help!" At 6:06 a.m., an officer could be seen administering CPR to Jones. One minute later, and barely ten minutes after contact was first made, one of the officers was heard asking another if he turned his cruiser's camera off. He responded that he turned off the microphone; then seconds later the camera went blank. Jones was later pronounced dead at a local hospital. The coroner handling the case told CBS's *60 Minutes* that Jones was probably suffering from "excited delirium"—a controversial condition with a long history but no single definition—and that his heart had simply given out during the struggle.[1] The video of the encounter, taken by a parked police cruiser's dashboard camera, eventually wound up on the YouTube website,[2] where it was viewed by tens of thousands of people.

The Jones story raises several interesting questions to keep in mind as you read this chapter:

1. Was Jones treated fairly by the responding officers?
2. Would the officers likely have acted differently if they had known for certain that their actions were being recorded and would be posted on the Internet and broadcast on national news programs?
3. What factors generally affect police decision making in cases like the one described here?

INTRODUCTION

Police officers have the authority to make decisions that can affect individuals in profound and lasting ways. One officer might decide to arrest someone for the first time, giving that person a criminal record. Another officer in the same situation might feel that arrest is unnecessary and might use an informal tactic instead. All criminal justice officials, including prosecutors, exercise discretion, but police are the gatekeepers to the criminal justice process, and without the decisions they make to begin the process, prosecutors and other criminal justice officials would never have the opportunity to decide the fate of criminal suspects.

In previous chapters, we described what police do—or should and should not do. But what *explains* police action—the choices that individual officers make when faced with varying situations? Is there something about the job that causes police officers to behave in certain ways? Are there different kinds of officers, and might differing personalities shed some light on these questions? What about factors other than the officers themselves, such as the characteristics of the communities they serve? In this chapter we explore how considerations like these help explain and even predict police behavior.

DEFINING DISCRETION

George Kelling, known for his "broken windows" perspective on crime prevention, once described the observations he made while walking with a Newark, New Jersey, police officer who was patrolling a neighborhood:

> As he saw his job, he was to keep an eye on strangers, and make certain that the disreputable regulars observed some informal but widely understood rules. Drunks and addicts could sit on the stoops, but could not lie down. People could drink on side streets, but not at the main intersection. Bottles had to be in paper bags. Talking to, bothering or begging from people waiting at the bus stop was strictly forbidden. Persons who broke the informal rules, especially [the latter], were arrested for vagrancy. Noisy teenagers were told to keep quiet.[3]

This observation captures the essence of police discretion more than any formal definition can. Although it is from a study that took place more than 25 years ago, the theme remains the same. Every community has its share of problems and priorities. Police officers must respond to those priorities and manage problems as best they can. Priorities may be assigned by residents and may have little to do with serious crime. Problems may need to be addressed in one way for some people and in another way for others. Or, in the case of Kelling's observations, *where* a problem occurs—and *how* it occurs—helps officers decide on the proper course of action.

Kelling's observations describe what discretion is, but we would be remiss to ignore more formal definitions of *police discretion*. Put simply, discretion consists of a two-part decision made by a police officer in a particular situation: (1) whether to intervene, and if the decision to intervene is made, (2) how best to intervene. But this definition is anything but simple when examined closely. Consider the typical traffic stop. Researchers have identified about ten different kinds of action that officers can take once a vehicle is stopped (for example, order the driver out of the car), seven strategies that could be used during the stop (for example, administer a field sobriety test), and 11 exit strategies (for example, arrest). These three factors alone present a total of 770 possible action combinations.[4] Needless to say, deciding whether and how to intervene can take an officer in *many* different directions, and he or she must be prepared for and trained to handle each one effectively.

Another way to conceive of discretion is to consider the distinction between the *letter* of the law and the *spirit* of the law. A police officer who follows the letter of the law issues a citation for every infraction, no matter how minor, and arrests every criminal suspect for all manner of criminal activity. In contrast, an officer who follows the spirit of the law looks at what the law intends and realizes that, from time to time, arrests and citations may not meet with the law's intent. The reality of policing is that officers frequently *must* make decisions, and often the law and an officer's decision correspond, but not always. Indeed, as we will see shortly, the two can be completely at odds with one another.

Note that we are not talking about police deviance, which is discussed in the next chapter. Perhaps it sounds a bit deviant that a police officer would ignore the letter of the law or let outside considerations enter into his or her decision-making process. And yes, it can be deviant—and possibly criminal—for an officer to overlook certain activities. But it can also be necessary. There are many occasions when it is simply not practical or advisable to arrest all suspects. We see this particularly in the war on drugs. Is it advisable to arrest every person caught with a modest amount of marijuana for personal consumption? Some readers may feel the answer is yes, but the practical answer is certainly no. There is just not enough room in jail to arrest everyone who *could* be arrested. In this sense, police officers are de facto policymakers. They decide, in some respects, what is and is not right. According to one scholar,

> The police are among the most important policy makers of our entire society. And they make far more discretionary determinations in individual cases than does any other class of administrators; I know of no close second.[5]

WEB PATROL 13-1

Police Officers' Decision Making and Discretion
http://www.mycrimekit.com

A uniformed officer talks to young people in a housing project. How might the opportunity for the officer to exercise discretion influence her future interaction with these youth?

Peter Casolino/Alamy Images

The Pros and Cons of Police Discretion

One of the clear advantages associated with police discretion is that it gives law enforcement officers a measure of job satisfaction. Indeed, research reveals that job satisfaction improves with job conditions like autonomy.[6] Autonomy and discretionary decision making go hand in hand. Discretion is also advantageous because without it the wheels of justice would grind to a halt. The system is just not equipped to deal with the massive influx of people that would result if officers arrested every identifiable lawbreaker. On a related note, discretion allows officers to treat each situation differently, in accordance with realistic goals and humanitarian principles (Figure 13-1). Some people favor "throwing the book" at every offender, but for those who favor mercy from time to time, police discretion is the best solution.

The negative aspects of police discretion probably outweigh the positive ones, mainly because the public's attention is drawn to discretionary decisions when something goes wrong. Incidents of police abuse and corruption generally lead people to call for reforms aimed at reining in police behavior. As we saw in Chapter 8, many police departments have adopted policies restricting pursuit driving. These are intended to limit officer discretion in the name of preserving public safety and minimizing injuries to innocent third parties. Policies restricting the use of deadly force also limit what officers can do in terms of apprehending resistant suspects. In fact, the bulk of a po-

WEB PATROL 13-2

"Broken Windows" and Police Discretion
http://www.mycrimekit.com

Figure 13-1 • The Pros and Cons of Police Discretion

Pros	Cons
Promotes job satisfaction	Potential for abuse
Promotes autonomy	Potential for corruption
Necessary for criminal justice system efficiency	Potential for needless death/injury (for example, if no pursuit-driving policy)
Promotes realistic goals	Possible citizen complaints of unequal treatment
Promotes humanitarian principles	Possible litigation when things go awry

lice department's policy manual is aimed at telling officers what they can and cannot do. When discretion runs amok, things can go wrong, resulting in needless injury or death, civil litigation, and other problems.

Discretion and Seniority

We have been discussing discretion as though it were used in the same manner by officers of all ranks. Nothing could be further from the truth. There is, as University of Nevada (Reno) professor Ken Peak has observed, an inverse relationship between discretion and seniority.[7] As an officer's rank increases, he or she is able to make fewer discretionary decisions. How is this so? The officer on the street has the greatest authority to decide who to arrest, pursue, stop, and so forth. The discretion of chiefs of police and other high-level administrators, in contrast, is limited by two factors. First, they do less ordinary police work, thus limiting the number of occasions when they may be able to employ discretion as we have defined it. Second, administrators tend to be limited by budget constraints, union pressures, governing boards, influential politicians, and others. In deciding who to hire, for instance, the chief (or whoever makes this decision) must be cognizant of diversity issues. This limits the pool of prospective officers to some extent.

This is not to say that administrators can't make decisions on their own or think outside the box. They do, but in different ways than patrol officers. For example, since money is often in short supply in some agencies, top executives have to act creatively to drum up needed revenue. The chief who sells advertising space on his department's cruisers (and some have) may be seen as a creative, forward-thinking, entrepreneurial manager. Others might regard this as unethical behavior and criticize the chief for pandering to certain interests, such as the owners of the business who buy the space. Either way, the initial decision to sell the advertising space is a discretionary one. It is safe to say, then, that while an administrative position limits one's discretionary latitude, it certainly opens the door to new types of decisions that the beat cop or frontline officer ordinarily does not get to make.

CLASSIC STUDIES OF POLICE BEHAVIOR

Before we can look at what factors influence police decision making, it is important to review the classic studies of police behavior. Scholars have for years offered a wide range of insights and theoretical perspectives pertaining to police work in America. This section provides a brief overview. Note the dates of the various studies. Some of the research was published decades ago, when law enforcement was a very different profession.

Westley's *Violence and the Police*

In 1949, in Gary, Indiana, William Westley conducted one of the first scientific studies of police behavior.[8] He found that socialization was a critical factor in shaping police behavior; "old-timers" worked with recruits, teaching them how to take charge of the situations they were confronted with. He also noted that recruits would come to be respected by the community if they took charge capably. Respect was, in his view, the be-all and end-all of police work; without it, officers could not do their jobs. It was considered appropriate for officers to respond with force to citizens' challenges to police authority. While it is risky for officers in this day and age to respond forcibly to every threat to their authority, in 1949 it was regarded as quite acceptable—and necessary.

Westley was perhaps the first researcher to call attention to the isolated nature of police work, that is, he found that most officers viewed themselves as not having the support of the majority of the citizens. They felt that the public could not be trusted. This, in turn, led officers to develop a tight-knit culture characterized by secrecy and looking out for one another. Indeed, nearly every study of police culture since Westley's has cited this pattern of behavior.

Skolnick's *Justice without Trial*

Another important classic was Jerome Skolnick's *Justice without Trial,* first published in 1966.[9] The title of Skolnick's book speaks volumes. It suggests that, in policing, decisions concerning what to do with suspects can be made with no trial at all—that is, by police officers themselves.

symbolic assailant
According to Jerome Skolnick, a person whom a police officer thinks is potentially dangerous.

danger signifier
A factor, such as a person's behavior, location, race, dress, age, or sex, that can be a signal of danger.

Skolnick also identified the concept of the **symbolic assailant.** This refers to a person whom a police officer thinks is potentially dangerous. Perceptions of a person's relative dangerousness can come from past experience but also from so-called war stories told by other police officers. Factors such as a person's behavior, location, race, dress, age, and sex can be signals of danger, or **danger signifiers.** These signifiers, whether they translate into actual danger or not, are often perceived as challenges to an officer's authority, which must be responded to verbally or physically. The fact that even today some police officers view particular groups, such as racial minorities, as more dangerous than others may be tied to this socialization process.

Skolnick also focused heavily on how the conflicts of democratic society can undermine police enforcement of the rule of law. One of these conflicts is the tension between law and order. We hear both terms used together all the time. But Skolnick argues that law sets forth the rules by which police must abide. Order, though, cannot always be accomplished within the limits of the law. Consider this observation:

> Five features of the police officer's occupational environment weaken the conception of the rule of law as a primary objective of police conduct. One is the social psychology of police work—that is, the relation between occupational environment, working personality, and the rule of law. Second is the police officer's stake in maintaining a position of authority, especially an interest in bolstering accepted patterns of enforcement. Third is police socialization, especially as it influences the police officer's administrative bias. A related factor is the pressure put on individual police to "produce"—to be efficient rather than legal when the two norms are in conflict. Finally, there is the police officer's opportunity to behave inconsistently with the rule of law as a result of the low visibility of much of police conduct.[10]

WEB PATROL 13-3
Explaining Police Behavior
http://www.mycrimekit.com

Manning and the Management of Appearances

Peter Manning, another well-known police scholar, has argued that the police have staked out a large and unmanageable domain and that their job has an impossible mandate.[11] His argument is not unlike Skolnick's: "Because their mandate automatically entails mutually contradictory ends—protecting both public order and individual rights—the police resort to managing their public image and the indexes of their accomplishment."[12] How do police manage their public image? According to Manning, one answer lies in the professionalism movement: "The guise of professionalism embodied in a bureaucratic organization is the most important strategy employed by the police to defend their mandate and thereby to build self-esteem, organizational autonomy, and occupational solidarity and cohesiveness."[13]

Another answer lies in the collection of crime statistics. It is the police, of course, who collect crime statistics, and Manning has argued that this is no accident: "In spite of their inability to control the commission of illegal acts (roughly, the actual rate), since they do not know about all crime, the police have claimed responsibility for crime control, using the crime rate as an index of their success."[14] This may sound somewhat conspiratorial, but it raises the question of how accurately crime statistics are recorded. Another question is whether statistics can be manipulated to serve a particular agenda. The old adage, "You can prove anything with statistics," is very true. Whether there is deliberate manipulation of crime statistics to serve particular agendas is probably unknowable, but it is at least possible. In Manning's view, then, crime statistics give police an opportunity to make themselves look good in the eyes of the public.

Wilson's Varieties of Police Behavior

As noted in Chapter 1, the history of American policing can be divided into roughly four eras,[15] each distinguishable by the relative dominance of a particular approach to police operations. The influence of each of the first three historical phases survives today in what noted social commentator and Presidential Medal of Freedom recipient James Q. Wilson[16] calls "policing styles."[17] A style of policing describes how a particular agency sees its purpose and chooses the methods it uses to fulfill that purpose. Wilson's three policing styles—which he does not link to any particular historical era—are the watchman style (characteristic of what was described in Chapter 1 as the political era), the legalistic style (professional crime fighting of the reform era), and the service style (which is becoming more common today). These three styles characterize nearly all municipal law enforcement agencies now operating in the United States, although some departments adopt a mixture of two or more styles.

The Watchman Style. Police departments marked by the **watchman style** are chiefly concerned with achieving what Wilson calls "order maintenance" through control of illegal and disruptive behavior. Compared to the legalistic style, the watchman style makes liberal use of discretion. Watchman-style departments keep order through informal police "intervention," which may include persuasion, threats, or even "roughing up" disruptive people. Some authors condemn this style of policing, suggesting that it is typically found in lower- or lower-middle-class communities, especially where interpersonal relations include a fair amount of violence or physical abuse.

watchman style
A style of policing that is focused on achieving order maintenance through the control of illegal and disruptive behavior.

The watchman style was typified by the white Los Angeles police officers who took part in the infamous beating of African American motorist Rodney King. After the riots which followed their initial acquittal in a state trial, the Christopher Commission, the independent commission on the Los Angeles Police Department (LAPD), found that the LAPD "placed greater emphasis on crime control over crime prevention, a policy that distanced cops from the people they serve."[18]

The Legalistic Style. Departments operating under the **legalistic style** enforce the letter of the law. For example, an officer who tickets a person going 71 mph in a 70-mph speed zone may be enforcing the law, but she is likely a member of a department that adheres to the legalistic style of policing. Conversely, legalistic departments routinely avoid community disputes arising from violations of social norms that do not break the law. Police expert Gary Sykes calls this enforcement style "*laissez-faire* policing" in recognition of its hands-off approach to behaviors that are not illegal but simply bothersome or inconsiderate of community principles.[19]

legalistic style
A style of policing that is focused on enforcing the letter of the law.

service style
A style of policing that is focused on meeting the needs of the community and serving its citizens.

The Service Style. In service-oriented departments, which strive to meet the needs of the community and to serve its members, the police see themselves more as helpers than as soldiers in a war on crime. This type of department works with social services and other agencies to provide counseling for minor offenders and to assist community groups in preventing crimes and solving problems. Prosecutors may support the **service style** by agreeing not to prosecute law violators who seek psychiatric help or who voluntarily participate in programs like Alcoholics Anonymous, family counseling, or drug treatment. The service style is supported, in part, by citizens who seek to avoid the embarrassment that might result from a public airing of personal problems, thereby reducing the number of criminal complaints filed, especially in minor disputes. While the service style of policing may seem more appropriate to wealthy communities or small towns, it can also exist in cities whose police departments actively seek citizen involvement in identifying issues that the police can help address.

A police car displaying a "to protect and to serve" motto. How is the service style of policing reflected in this slogan? How would you describe the service style of policing?

Ablestock/Alamy Images Royalty Free

Rubinstein's *City Police*

Jonathan Rubinstein's *City Police* stands out as another classic in the annals of law enforcement scholarship.[20] Rubinstein, unlike some of the other scholars we have cited, actually worked as a patrol officer in Philadelphia and was thus in a unique position to report on police activity and behavior. His findings echoed Skolnick's observations concerning officers' perceptions of danger on the job. Rubinstein also concluded, however, that of paramount concern in any police-citizen encounter is physical control over the scene. He observed that officers must maintain alertness, watch a suspect's hands closely, remain alert to the possible presence of weapons, and stand close to suspects so they cannot lash out easily.

Wilson emphasized the role of organizational factors in shaping police behavior. Rubinstein, in contrast, emphasized the officer's working environment as being most influential. He found that officers learn various features of the job, such as what is and is not important or who is and is not a possible threat, from their veteran peers. In short, Rubinstein concluded that the socialization of officers, the process of being influenced by others around them, shapes police behavior more than other factors like organizational structure or managerial preferences.

preentry
John Van Maanen's first stage of police recruit socialization, in which the recruit chooses to pursue a job in law enforcement, having been attracted by the idea that policing is an elite occupation that offers an opportunity to do something important for society, such as serve people.

admittance
John Van Maanen's second stage of police recruit socialization, in which the recruit enters the academy and learns the importance of abiding by the rules and regulations of the department.

change
John Van Maanen's third stage of police recruit socialization, in which the recruit completes academy training, enters the field, is partnered with a training officer, and is continually tested and evaluated on several criteria.

continuance
John Van Maanen's fourth stage of police recruit socialization, in which the recruit moves through the field training period and comes to accept the reality of police work.

perspective
The dimension of police ethical development that indicates the extent to which an officer understands human suffering and is inclined to show compassion.

passion
The dimension of police ethical development that indicates how comfortable an officer is in using coercive means to carry out his or her responsibilities.

Van Maanen's "Observations on the Making of Policemen"

In 1973, John Van Maanen published "Observations on the Making of Policemen," one of the first studies of police socialization as it plays out in the academy.[21] He, like Rubinstein, immersed himself in his object of study by going through an academy and serving as a police officer for a period of time in California. He identified four stages through which recruits are socialized into the police department. The first stage is **preentry,** which Van Maanen explained sets police recruits apart from applicants for other careers. He found that those who aspire to a career in policing are attracted by the idea that policing is an elite occupation that offers an opportunity to do something important for society, such as serve people.

Van Maanen's second stage is called **admittance.** Admittance occurs when the recruit enters the academy, where he or she learns the importance of abiding by the rules and regulations of the department. As remains true today, recruits live in a military-like environment resembling a boot camp, study hard, and are punished for violating the rules. They are also regaled with war stories from seasoned officers that serve more than an entertainment function; they inform trainees about the values of their job, of sticking together, and of what it means to be a "good" cop.

The third stage is known as **change.** This occurs once academy training comes to a close and the new officer enters the field. Typically partnered with a training officer, the new hire is continually tested and evaluated on several criteria. Can the officer control encounters with suspects? Does the officer exercise common sense? Is he or she sufficiently careful? Van Maanen found that new officers are also continually tested on their abilities to back up other officers, further reinforcing the cultural solidarity that characterizes police work. This, of course, requires helping other officers when they are in trouble.

Van Maanen called the last stage **continuance.** It occurs as officers move through the field training period and come to accept the reality of police work. While the potential for danger and excitement remains, much of the romanticized image of the job fades away as officers learn the bureaucratic dimensions of their chosen profession, such as following orders and completing paperwork. Officers also develop a sense of disillusionment, insofar as they learn that much of the public is unsupportive of what they do or has no clear understanding of what police work is really like. Van Maanen found that officers employ a strategy of "lie low and hang loose" to avoid getting in trouble and to make the job tolerable.

Muir's *Police: Streetcorner Politicians*

William Ker Muir, Jr., authored another important study, which was published in 1977. Its title, *Police: Streetcorner Politicians,*[22] speaks volumes. Muir identified two dimensions of police ethical development: **perspective** (the extent to which an officer understands human suffering and is inclined to show compassion) and **passion** (how comfortable the officer is in using coercive means to carry out his or her responsibilities). Then, based on these dimensions, he identified four types of officers. First are the *professional-style officers,* those who are both compassionate and comfortable using their authority when the need arises. *Enforcers,* who use force whenever the opportunity arises, lack the compassion that goes along with the professional style. *Reciprocators,* the third type of officer, are compassionate and somewhat uncomfortable with their authority role. These officers use communication to defuse volatile situations and avoid using force unless

Figure 13-2 • A Summary of Policing Classics

Brown: Aggressiveness and selectivity used as criteria to identify several types of officers.

Manning: Police manage their image (for example, with crime statistics).

Muir: Stages of ethical development and types of officers.

Rubinstein: Officers need to establish control; organizational factors shape behavior.

Skolnick: Symbolic assailant; tension between law and order.

Van Maanen: Stages of police socialization.

Westley: Officers experience isolation; socialization is important.

Wilson: Three policing styles (watchman, legalistic, service).

it is absolutely necessary. Finally, *avoiders,* not surprisingly, are officers who avoid using force but are also devoid of compassion. Avoiders do as little as possible to maintain their positions and avoid risk-taking behavior.

Brown's *Working the Street: Police Discretion*

One of the classics aimed specifically at police discretion is Michael Brown's *Working the Street: Police Discretion,* first published in 1981.[23] His study focused on three policing styles found in three different southern California cities. Like Muir, Brown identified various officer types that depended, in his view, on their aggressiveness and selectivity. Aggressiveness, Brown said, refers to officers' willingness to actively seek out problems. Selectivity is the extent to which officers are concerned only with serious crime problems. Using these two variables, Brown identified four police styles. *Old-style crime fighters* are aggressive officers who concentrate on serious felony-type crimes. These are also the officers who use coercion and are inclined to bend the rules to obtain the best results. Next, *clean-beat crime fighters* emphasize following proper police procedures. These officers are proactive but also follow the letter of the law. *Service-style officers* generally avoid coercion and aggression while focusing on the most serious problems. They also avoid enforcement unless a crime is sufficiently serious to warrant it. Finally, *professional-style officers* are neither overly aggressive nor selective. Brown used the term "professional" for this officer because this is how he hoped the typical officer would be. Such officers enforce the law when necessary but don't focus on any particular types of offenders, nor do they seek out trouble simply for the thrill of it.

The works of these eight scholars (see Figure 13-2 for a summary) provide interesting insights into the world of policing. These studies show us, generally, that there are features of police work that make officers different from people who work in other occupations and that there are different types of police officers. They also provide a glimpse of police culture—what makes police officers tick. We look more closely at these ideas in the remainder of this chapter. We begin with an overview of the theoretical perspectives in this area and then look at some of the research aimed at uncovering factors that influence police decision making.

EXPLAINING POLICE BEHAVIOR

Police behavior can be explained from either a **universalistic perspective** or a **particularistic perspective.** The universalistic perspective is simply the view that all police officers are similar and that they exhibit some of the same characteristics and behavior patterns. The particularistic perspective, in contrast, considers how individual officers differ from one another. Similarly, we can ask whether law enforcement officers behave the way they do because of personal values and patterns of behavior they have acquired through socialization and introduction into police subculture or because of individual predispositions toward certain ways of thinking and acting.

universalistic perspective
The view that all police officers are similar and that they exhibit some of the same characteristics and behavior patterns.

particularistic perspective
The view that individual officers differ from one another in various ways, including values, role orientation, and preferred styles of policing.

The Universalistic Perspective

To say that all police officers are similar in some respects requires some attention to sociology, psychology, and organizational theory. Sociology, in this case, is concerned with the influence of peers and coworkers. Psychology is concerned with whether there is a distinct police personality. Organizational factors can influence police behavior as well.

Police officers are selected and trained in a very unique environment.[24] It is unlike that found in almost any other occupation. Academy training indoctrinates recruits into the world of policing and teaches trainees to view others in a particular way (that is, with a measure of suspicion). The sociological perspective is also important from a demographic standpoint. To this day, the typical police officer is a white male. Women and minorities have made great strides in terms of gaining representation in the law enforcement profession, but they are not represented in the profession in accordance with their numbers in the population as a whole. Research reveals that female officers are socialized to adapt to a largely male-dominated work environment.[25] In other words, traditional police training (in the academy and on the job) has encouraged female recruits to act in a masculine fashion.

Does policing draw a particular personality type? If so, this is an example of how psychological factors may yield common bonds among police officers. There is surprisingly little research on what types of personalities are drawn to police work. Much more accepted is the view that socialization is more influential than any degree of predisposition. Not everyone agrees, however, so we will revisit the predisposition versus socialization issue shortly. It is the law enforcement equivalent of the nature-versus-nurture argument that plays out in the criminology literature and elsewhere in human development studies.

In addition, there are organizational factors that make all officers alike. The quasi-military structure of most police agencies requires a certain pattern of behavior among all employees. Everything from chain of command to rules of dress ensures that one officer closely resembles the others.

Community policing may be creating suborganizations within specific police departments. Ask a special weapons and tactics (SWAT) or narcotics officer in any large urban police department what he or she thinks of the officers who work in the community policing division. Some will answer that those officers are somewhat different; some may even say that they are not doing real police work. The point is that, *traditionally,* organizational factors may have led to similarities among all officers. It is quite probable that all of this is changing in contemporary policing—and that a particularistic perspective is starting to take hold.

The Particularistic Perspective

In contrast, the particularistic perspective is concerned with how specific officers differ from one another. We just suggested that narcotics officers may be (and almost certainly are) different in a number of respects from community police officers, although there are some officers who work both assignments at some point in their careers.

Studies of police culture and personality point to a number of characteristics that police officers share, including suspiciousness, cynicism, loyalty to colleagues, and pessimism. Particularistic perspectives, however, suggest that there is no one personality or set of traits that typifies all police officers. Robert Worden at SUNY Albany has identified several means by which police officers differ from one another:

> Officers' occupational attitudes might predispose them toward one "style" of policing rather than another. For example, they may choose to be more or less proactive; or they may lean toward formal or informal dispositions, or toward one particular informal disposition rather than another.[26]

Worden has identified five attitudinal dimensions that can be used to explain differences between individual police officers. They include role orientations, perceptions of legal restrictions, perceptions of citizen respect and cooperation, perceptions of legal institutions, and views on selective enforcement.

Role orientation refers to an officer's individual conception of what constitutes proper and good police work. As might be expected, police officers differ in this regard. As Worden observes, "Some officers believe that the police role is defined wholly by the mandate to fight crime and enforce the law; they believe in the utility of an aggressive style of patrol, and they regard order maintenance and service tasks with distaste."[27] At the other extreme are officers who favor a broader police role that includes more than crime fighting. Some officers see order maintenance and service provision as higher callings than crime control and see themselves as positive rather than negative influences on people's lives.[28]

The officer who views his or her role as consisting mainly of crime control will be inclined to behave in a manner consistent with that view. This might translate into frequent stops of suspicious individuals, punitive responses to disputes (for example, arresting the parties to a domestic dispute rather than counseling them), and zealous criminal investigations. Because these officers see crime control as most important, "minor disputes fall outside of their definition of police responsibilities, and more serious disputes are police business only insofar as they constitute crimes."[29] Officers with this narrow role orientation would not have an interest in mediating disputes to settle them verbally instead of with force or by arresting someone. By contrast, officers who see themselves as having a broad role orientation will use an approach that best serves the needs of the people they serve.

All police officers are bound by various legal requirements, whether they agree with them or not. This does not mean, however, that they necessarily *like* operating under these legal limitations. In fact, there are clear differences between police officers in terms of their perceptions of legal restrictions. Some officers have total respect for the law, for department policy, and for the influence of the courts on their duties. These officers may be the exception,[30] however. According to Worden, "The stereotypical police officer chafes under due process provisions in the single-minded pursuit of criminal offenders. This officer bitterly resents legal and departmental restrictions concerning search and seizure, interrogation, and the use of force."[31]

An officer's perceptions of legal restrictions may also be indicative of his or her overall ideological stance. For example, some officers may occasionally bend the rules when it comes to accosting pedestrians or stopping motorists. If the justification for doing so is not in place in advance, these officers may fabricate a reason to justify their actions in hindsight. This resembles a conservative law-and-order mentality with a clear focus on crime control in lieu of due process. Indeed, studies of on-the-job performance have revealed numerous examples of this behavior.[32] At the other extreme, of course, are officers who both are cognizant of and strictly adhere to legal restrictions.

If a suspect physically resists police intervention, the officer will surely respond in kind, that is, uncooperative suspects will be dealt with accordingly. We will see some more evidence of this toward the end of the chapter. For now, it is also important to note that there are differences between police officers in terms of their perceptions of citizen respect and cooperation. Some officers think that the public is mostly supportive. It would be easy to get this sense if one is a recruiter, a Drug Abuse Resistance Education (DARE) program officer, or an officer who works closely with citizens in a positive sense. Other officers sometimes feel that they are held in somewhat low regard by citizens, and still others feel—rightly, much of the time—that they enjoy little respect and are viewed with nothing short of hostility and animosity.

These differences may be traced to a more fundamental characteristic, such as the officer's view of human nature:

> Officers with a cynical outlook may be disinclined to believe that citizens are respectful and cooperative. . . . In particular, officers who believe that citizens fail to accord police the respect they are due, and/or that citizens are hostile and even abusive to police, might be especially reluctant to stop traffic law violators because they either find such encounters exceedingly unpleasant or fear that an irate motorist might file a complaint.[33]

Other officers, of course, thrive on such encounters and relish the opportunity to deal with a belligerent and uncooperative citizen. These officers may even take pride in "punishing" those who do not afford them the proper respect.

Law enforcement is an institution, not unlike a religion. As an institution, it views itself somewhat differently, perhaps, than other institutions. Police officers themselves have their own divergent perceptions of legal institutions. Consider the courts, for example. Some officers view the courts as supportive and helpful. Others regard them as being soft on crime or totally out of

Table 13-1 • The Universalistic versus Particularistic Perspective on Police Behavior

Universalistic Perspective	Particularistic Perspective
Officers are socialized.	Officers take on different role orientations.
Officers are psychologically similar.	Officers act differently based on legal restrictions.
Police organizations force all officers to act similarly.	Officers act differently based on their perceptions of citizens.
Officers act differently based on their views of the criminal justice system.	Officers act differently based on their views of certain laws.

Source: Adapted from R. Roberg, K. Novak, and G. Cordner, "The universalistic versus the particularistic," *Police and society,* 4th ed. (New York: Oxford University Press, 2008), p. 272. Reprinted by permission.

touch with the realities of police work. In a recent case, for example, the U.S. Supreme Court decided that it is not unconstitutional for a police officer to arrest someone for a traffic violation.[34] While police officers generally applauded this clarification (and seeming expansion) of their powers, the decision did not change police work very much. It does not mean that the police will begin an aggressive campaign of arresting people for not wearing their seatbelts. Police agencies have bigger fish to fry. Decisions like this, then, seem to officers to be concerned with legal minutia and do little to help the police on a practical level. Officers' perceptions of courts can be extended to include attitudes toward judges and prosecutors:

> Officers who believe that prosecutors and judges do not support them may thus be less likely to take legal action, since in their eyes an arrest is likely to be of little consequence. The failure of other actors in the justice system to follow through on criminal proceedings initiated against abusive spouses, for example, is sometimes offered as an explanation for officers' reluctance to make arrests in domestic cases.[35]

Some officers are more proactive in their duties than others. This may also owe to their perceptions of other criminal justice institutions—including even prisons. If an officer feels that the prosecutor will reject his or her case, or that the judge will hand down a lenient decision, or there is not enough room in the local jail or nearby prison, this may influence the arrest decision. Research on traffic enforcement makes this more clear. Forty years ago, J. A. Gardiner set out to explain why police in one city issued more traffic tickets than their counterparts in a nearby city. He traced this to the fact that the first city did not require its officers to appear in court until after a not guilty plea was entered.[36] This suggests a degree of collaboration between the police and the court that influenced police behavior. In contrast, the officers in the other city, where the court was not as supportive of their efforts, were inclined to make fewer traffic stops because it would be a burden. (See Table 13-1 for a summary of the discussion in this section.)

Research reveals—and common sense suggests—that police officers also vary in terms of their selectivity—that is, their willingness to enforce the law.[37] In the case of a murder, few would argue that any officer would not want to arrest the perpetrator. But what of less serious offenses like public intoxication, prostitution, and vagrancy? Do all officers enforce laws against these behaviors equally? Of course not. To the extent that selectivity varies between individual police officers, it is reasonable to conclude that this could affect their decisions in any number of disputes:

> Officers who believe that they should be selective in enforcing the law might be expected seldom to invoke the law in resolving disputes and instead avail themselves of informal methods; officers who are non-selective might be expected to make arrests more frequently and to adopt extra-legal strategies less frequently.[38]

Socialization or Predisposition?

We earlier raised the question of whether law enforcement officers are socialized into the perspectives they hold or whether they bring with them certain predispositions in terms of their values and behavior. The socialization perspective holds that police officers are socialized formally and informally into their occupations. Formal socialization usually plays out in the academy and during the field training period. Informal socialization results from the new hires' interactions with seasoned officers and their colleagues. It is not always the case that formal socialization and informal socialization get the same points across. For example, instructors at the academy may say, "Do it this way," but officers on the streets may say, "Okay, here's how we *really* do it." It is a safe bet that socialization is powerful in law enforcement and affects every officer to some extent. Although some are more susceptible to peer influence and pressure than others, it would be impossible for any officer to completely ignore his or her colleagues, superiors, and instructors.

Recently, there has been renewed interest in whether police officers are somehow predisposed either to accept a law enforcement position or to act a certain way once employed. If one were to ask the political affiliation or views of any sworn officer, the odds are good that the vast majority would be conservative. Research has for decades backed up this point.[39] Research also reveals that those who enter law enforcement believe in the importance of authority and seek fulfillment in their careers. A more recent study confirms these findings, leading the authors to conclude that "individual value systems are more important than occupational socialization."[40] This means that police officers' values are somewhat entrenched before they even enter the force.[41] Chances are, though, that there is a mix of predisposition and socialization that actually takes place.

POLICE DECISION MAKING

Scores of researchers have sought to identify predictors of police decision making. We can place their findings into four general categories: organizational factors, neighborhood factors, situational factors, and individual officer characteristics. Within each of these categories are several subcategories, which we explore in this section.

WEB PATROL 13-4
Emotional Intelligence in Policing
http://www.mycrimekit.com

Organizational Factors

The organization for which an officer works can shape his or her decision-making patterns. The bureaucratic structure of the typical police organization requires that its employees jump through certain hoops. Whether they like it or not, officers must follow the rules. This is true of any organization; people must follow the rules or risk losing their job.

Bureaucratic Structure. The typical police department adheres to a fairly rigid bureaucratic model of administration. This is done primarily to guide employee behavior and to direct and control it.[42] Part of this is accomplished through written policies. Policy manuals seek to control police decision making, such as pursuit or arrest decisions.

Several researchers have criticized the bureaucratic control principle. Proponents of the community policing movement suggest that there may be a better way to run police departments, such as by decentralizing them and giving line officers more latitude in their decision making. More than one researcher has argued, for instance, that written policy manuals do little to affect the quality of police service.[43] Such controls can have undesirable side effects:

> Bureaucratic controls can backfire, contributing to police secrecy and undermining bureaucratic control. For these reasons, the effectiveness of bureaucracy as a way to stimulate some behaviors and dampen others is certainly limited. Highly bureaucratic departments also tend to be impersonal and may overemphasize punitive discipline in an attempt to control officers' behavior. This tendency may result in officers doing as little as possible in an effort to avoid getting into trouble.[44]

Beats and Scheduling. An officer's beat can also influence his or her behavior. In general, the larger the patrol beat, the more impersonal the relationship will be between officer and citizen.[45] In contrast, officers who patrol relatively smaller areas, such as small towns, tend to adopt more of a service orientation in their daily activities.[46] This does not mean, however, that all small areas will see a service style of policing. Some officers work dangerous beats in high-crime downtown areas on bicycle or on foot. In these places, an enforcement stance may prevail over a service orientation. Somewhat related to this is the finding that officers in larger departments are less prone to making arrests for drunk driving than their counterparts in smaller agencies.[47]

We all know that work can get boring, especially if it is routine, totally predictable, and unchanging. This extends to policing, too, but not necessarily in the way one would expect. Researchers have found that police departments that routinely rotate their officers into different beats, units, or shifts affect the relationships between their officers and citizens. In particular, frequent rotation puts distance between officers and the people they serve.[48] This has been called "stranger policing,"[49] and it is not unlike what occurs when a person frequently moves from one city or state to the next; it becomes difficult to form close relationships.

When a police officer routinely works the same beat, he or she can come to form close relationships with citizens. As one researcher puts it, "An officer's continued presence in a neighborhood increases the likelihood of repeated contact with citizens and helps officers develop empathy through an understanding of problems."[50] In fact, research also reveals that officers who routinely patrol the same area develop a sense of obligation to the area and even a desire to be protective of it. This has been called the **territorial imperative**,[51] and police departments appear to be taking advantage of it.

territorial imperative
The sense of obligation, even protectiveness, that develops in officers who routinely patrol the same area.

Neighborhood Factors

Police officers who patrol America's affluent communities rarely encounter problems. They often enjoy good relationships with the vast majority of the law-abiding citizens they see daily. Then there are the officers who patrol the worst run-down neighborhoods, which are plagued by drug problems, gang violence, and serious crime. These officers are regarded with suspicion, insulted, and even shot at periodically. It goes without saying, then, that the nature of the neighborhood that an officer patrols surely has some effect on his or her behavior.

Consider, again, the broken windows theory. It argues for a certain type of law enforcement, depending on the problems a particular neighborhood faces. James Q. Wilson and George L. Kelling argue that if signs of physical and social disorder affect a neighborhood, then officers should concentrate their efforts on those problems because failure to address quality-of-life matters like these will surely invite serious crime. The broken windows theory thus provides another illustration of how neighborhood conditions can affect police strategies, decisions, and discretion.

WEB PATROL 13-5
Policing a Diverse Community
http://www.mycrimekit.com

Racial Composition and Heterogeneity. Several researchers have looked at neighborhood racial composition and its effects on police decision making. Findings reveal a greater demand for police services in minority-dominated neighborhoods.[52] This, some have argued, has been due to a greater number of incidents as well as "a belief in the appropriateness of calling the police."[53] The relationship between neighborhood racial composition and police activity can also be understood in this way:

> Research tends to support the view that the police write more reports, make more arrests, engage in more abusive behavior, and receive more citizen requests for police intervention in minority areas. . . . Police tend to view minority areas as places where violent crimes are more likely to occur and where they are more likely to have their authority challenged. As a result, police are more suspicious and alert and more concerned for their own safety. Data consistently show that police arrest more individuals in minority areas than in other areas.[54]

YOU DECIDE
The Favor

You are an officer on traffic patrol in an affluent part of the city. As you are running radar in a school zone, you see a late-model SUV sail past you at 50 mph in a 20-mph zone. You turn into traffic, follow the vehicle, and pull it over. When you check the license plate, the name listed rings a bell. As you approach the vehicle, you realize that the driver is the mayor, your chief's boss. What should you do?

A police officer talks with a young girl sitting on the steps of a building in New York City. How might the socioeconomic status of a neighborhood influence the style of policing it receives? Should it?

Richard Lord/The Image Works

Although it is not clear why, research also suggests that the police are more active in neighborhoods characterized by extensive racial heterogeneity.[55] Heterogeneous neighborhoods are those with ethnic or racial diversity.

Socioeconomic Status. Minority-dominated neighborhoods also tend to be comparatively less well-off. Numerous studies back this up and also show that police tend to make more arrests in poorer areas.[56] Interestingly, research also reveals that police are more likely to listen to a request for arrest in wealthier neighborhoods. For example, if one of the parties to a domestic dispute insists that an officer not make an arrest, the officer would apparently be more inclined to listen to a wealthy person's views on this subject than a poor person's. This is assuming, of course, that the officer's department does not follow a mandatory arrest policy.

Crime. Informed readers know that racial composition, socioeconomic status, and crime go hand in hand. There is more crime where there are more people. Conversely, there is much less crime in rich areas. It should be no surprise, then, to find that police make more arrests in densely populated, poor, high-crime areas. Where there is no crime, there is little need to make arrests. But there are *some* mixed findings in this area. For example, at least one author has argued that where crime is common, this may stretch police resources, forcing them to respond less vigorously than they otherwise would.[57] At the least, extensive research reveals that neighborhood crime rates can influence officer attitudes.[58]

Situational Factors

Every police-citizen encounter is different. Some occur behind closed doors, such as when an arrest warrant is served in a private residence. Others occur in full view of bystanders and even cameras. Some suspects are docile and cooperative; others put up a fight. Offenses vary, too. A person facing the prospect of life in prison for his third violent felony may have little to lose if he resists arrest, but the juvenile who is arrested for the first time may not cause any trouble. Even the means by which the police arrive at the scene can have an effect on the outcome of the situation. The point is that situational factors, in addition to community-level factors, can influence an officer's decision making.

Scene and Suspects. Whether an officer arrives at the scene on his or her initiative or as a result of a call is the first important factor in determining how the officer will act. As might be expected, if someone calls the police, it generally means that the person *wants* officers there. In contrast, if officers initiate contact with people on their own, such as by engaging in preventive patrol, the contacts can be somewhat more antagonistic. Moreover, police are more likely to make arrests and treat people harshly in the second situation.[59]

Research has also cited examples of retaliation by officers who feel offended by a suspect's behavior. For example, people who are not respectful to an officer during a traffic encounter receive more traffic citations than those who show respect.[60] This also extends to other types of police-citizen encounters. In fact, the evidence is very clear that suspect demeanor is one of the most significant predictors of police behavior: Disrespectful and uncooperative people are more likely to be arrested or cited.[61] Even studies on police corruption and brutality reveal that both occur more often when a lack of respect is displayed toward the officer.[62]

One of the research problems in this area concerns the proper measurement of suspect demeanor. Many researchers have measured demeanor in terms of criminal activity (for example, assaulting the arresting officer), but one researcher found that legal forms of resistance (such as insulting the officer) did not lead to a higher probability of arrest.[63] Not everyone is in agreement with these findings, however.[64]

It is important to note that we are looking at all these predictors of police decision making in isolation. In reality, these factors occur together. Race combined with demeanor may have a stronger influence on an officer's decision. Socioeconomic status may interact with the crime rate—and even race—and also exert a substantial influence.

Suspect demographic characteristics, notably race, gender, and age, have also been shown to influence police decision making. The effects of race are consistent with the neighborhood factors we have already touched on: Minorities tend to be treated differently from whites.[65] "Some researchers contend that this situation is the result of the fact that African-Americans, and possibly other minorities, may be more likely to resist police authority or display a 'bad' attitude or outright hostility, from an officer's point of view."[66] One recent study reveals, interestingly, that race is more important in shaping an officer's level of suspicion toward someone than his or her initial decision to stop or arrest the person.[67]

Consider racial profiling. Although it is difficult to measure accurately whether profiling actually occurs, many believe it is rampant, and at least a few studies support such claims.[68] To the extent that profiling occurs, it provides perhaps the clearest evidence that race can influence officer decision making. But is that because police officers are racially biased? Is it misguided stereotyping, or is it just good policing? The answers to these questions remain somewhat elusive. Some law enforcement officials say more minorities appear to be stopped because they are where crime is; civil libertarians argue otherwise.

Gender has also been considered as a possible predictor of police decision making, although researchers have not been drawn to it as much as race. Who is more likely to be arrested, men or women? At least one study reveals, not too surprisingly, that women are less likely to be arrested than men, particularly when they display ladylike characteristics or behaviors.[69] In contrast, when women step outside the bounds of what is considered proper behavior, they are arrested more often.

Controversially, some researchers have studied police sexual violence, finding that it may be more common than once expected.[70] Others have explained this as resulting from the greater opportunities (for example, isolation from others, such as during a traffic stop) and the power and authority of police work. Indeed, some researchers have even found that attractive women are more likely to be stopped for traffic violations, mainly so the officer can make personal contact.[71]

Finally, the suspect's age may be associated with police decision making, as well. In general, young people tend to be rebellious and thus disrespectful toward police. The research bears this out,[72] particularly as it influences officer behavior. In general, younger people are more likely than older people to be arrested or dealt with harshly.[73] This may create a two-way relationship, that is, if young people are dealt with more harshly because they are disrespectful, then disrespect may be exacerbated by the fact that young people are treated harshly.[74] Of course, these are generalizations.

There are different types of officers out there, as we have already made clear. Research reveals, in fact, that community police officers may be more inclined than their traditional counterparts to deal with young people informally.[75]

Relationships between Parties. The evening news makes it appear as though most crime is violent and that it occurs between strangers. Neither is correct. Most crime is nonviolent, and much of it occurs between people who know each other to some extent. When thinking about police decision making, it is also important to consider the relationship between both parties to the incident: victims and offenders. If two people know each other, does it always make sense to arrest one of the parties when, perhaps, the matter could be settled informally? The answer is often no. Several studies reveal that as relational distance between the parties increases, arrest is more likely.[76] Research also reveals that when the victim prefers that no arrest be made, officers are often influenced by such sentiments.[77]

Offense Seriousness. For obvious reasons, the seriousness of the offense will bear significantly on officer behavior. A serious crime, such as a homicide, will surely result in an arrest if a suspect is identified and located. Minor offenses and infractions are more often dealt with informally, perhaps with just a warning. An interesting question has arisen in this context, however. Do police officers make more arrests in cases of serious crime simply because the crime is serious, or is something else at work? The answer lies in what constitutes proper legal justification, or probable cause, to make an arrest. Probable cause is more likely to be present in cases of serious crime, especially violent crime, because there may be signs of physical injury, a weapon that can be located, witness accounts, and so forth. In contrast, minor offenses like shoplifting a trivial amount of merchandise may be more difficult to prove, thus making it harder for an officer to justify an arrest.[78]

Location. Consider this hypothetical scenario. An officer stops a motorist for drunk driving. He then administers a field sobriety test in broad daylight in view of several pedestrians. The driver has apparent difficulty passing the exam, but the officer lets her drive away. Would this happen? Certainly not, for two reasons. First, it would dangerous to allow an intoxicated motorist to drive off. It would also be against department rules for a police officer to allow a visibly intoxicated motorist to drive home on her own. Second, the presence of bystanders would make it even more controversial to send the motorist on her way. The location of this incident in plain view of other people would be sure to influence the officer's decision to some extent. Step outside this scenario to any other high-profile public contact between a police officer and a citizen. Officers know in these moments that they must be careful to follow proper policy to avoid complaints, litigation, and so forth. Alternatively, when police-citizen contacts take place behind closed doors, or out of public view, there is more of an opportunity to treat the matter informally. Here is what one team of authors has said with respect to public versus private interactions:

> Police are more likely to respond harshly in public settings than in private settings. This difference is the result of several factors: the type of crime (usually perceived as more serious crimes), the need to appear in control of the situation in public, the ambiguous role of the police in situations that occur in private places, and the fact that there are more police-initiated, or proactive, calls in public.[79]

YOU DECIDE
A Minor Incident?

You are called to the scene of an alleged shoplifting incident at the local grocery store. As you walk through the door, the manager sees you and says, "Officer, this woman just tried to steal two gallons of milk and a dozen eggs. I want her arrested and prosecuted." After you question the woman, you find that she paid for everything else in her cart with food stamps. She says she has no more food stamps and no other money. She also says that she needs the food to feed her four children at home and that she only took as much as was absolutely necessary. What should you do?

YOU DECIDE

No One Around

You are an off-duty officer and are spending a day golfing with your friends. As you are driving along the cart path, you notice a wallet lying in the grass. You pick it up, determine whom it belongs to, and find $500 cash inside. No one saw you pick up the wallet. What should you do?

Bystanders. Closely related to the public-private distinction is the issue of whether bystanders are present. Bystanders are, of course, more likely to be present in public places. Thus, when they are under citizen scrutiny, officers will act differently than when they are not. A different sort of situation arises when the observers are other police officers, in which case an officer's decision making will likely be influenced differently. The motivation to look good in the eyes of one's peers, for instance, may prompt an officer to act differently than he or she would otherwise behave. Researchers have found that officers who work together, as opposed to alone, are sometimes more prone to make arrests or to treat citizens harshly.[80] The combination of working in public and having bystanders present can have a profound influence on police decision making.

Individual Officer Characteristics

Thus far we have focused only on how neighborhood and situational factors affect officers' decisions. What about the officers themselves? How do differences between them affect their decision making? A number of individual officer characteristics have been linked to police decision making. These include factors such as education, age, experience, gender, ambition, and attitude toward the job.

Education, Age, and Experience. Does a well-educated officer act differently than, say, an officer with just a high school diploma? Unfortunately, researchers have yet to determine whether ed-

A Miami marine officer patrols one of the city's wealthy waterfront neighborhoods. Do the wealthy receive special treatment from the police?

Jeff Greenberg/Alamy Images

ucation affects an officer's decision to behave one way over another. The same can be said of age and experience, which tend to go hand in hand:

> In general, younger officers may work harder and are more aggressive and more punitive than older officers. However, the quality of the older officers' work may be superior. While some older, more seasoned officers may do less work and become less punitive, others may actually become more punitive if they become excessively cynical. Older police officers may become frustrated with the department and the legal system and engage in illegal behavior, including the use of excessive force.[81]

Gender. Few researchers have looked recently at gender as a possible predictor of police decision making. Some studies from the late 1980s, when women were first beginning to gain a significant presence in law enforcement, revealed that female officers tend to act less aggressively than their male counterparts.[82] On the whole, women tend to be less aggressive than men, which probably explains the differences in their decision making in the law enforcement context.

Ambition and Attitudes. An officer's ambition can clearly affect his or her decision making. One study revealed, for example, that officers who made the most arrests felt they needed to do so in order to gain a promotion.[83] Some of the officers who made more than their share of arrests were also motivated by the possibility of making more money from the overtime they needed to work to process all of their arrestees.

Attitudes toward the job, and particularly toward different types of police work, have also been linked to decision making. Researchers have found that an officer's perception of community policing can affect his or her arrest patterns.[84] In general, officers who view community policing favorably tend to be more selective in their arrest decisions. Circumstances, preferences, and neighborhood characteristics can call for an intervention other than arrest. Figure 13-3 summarizes the explanations of police decision making discussed in this section.

Figure 13-3 • Factors Affecting Police Decision Making

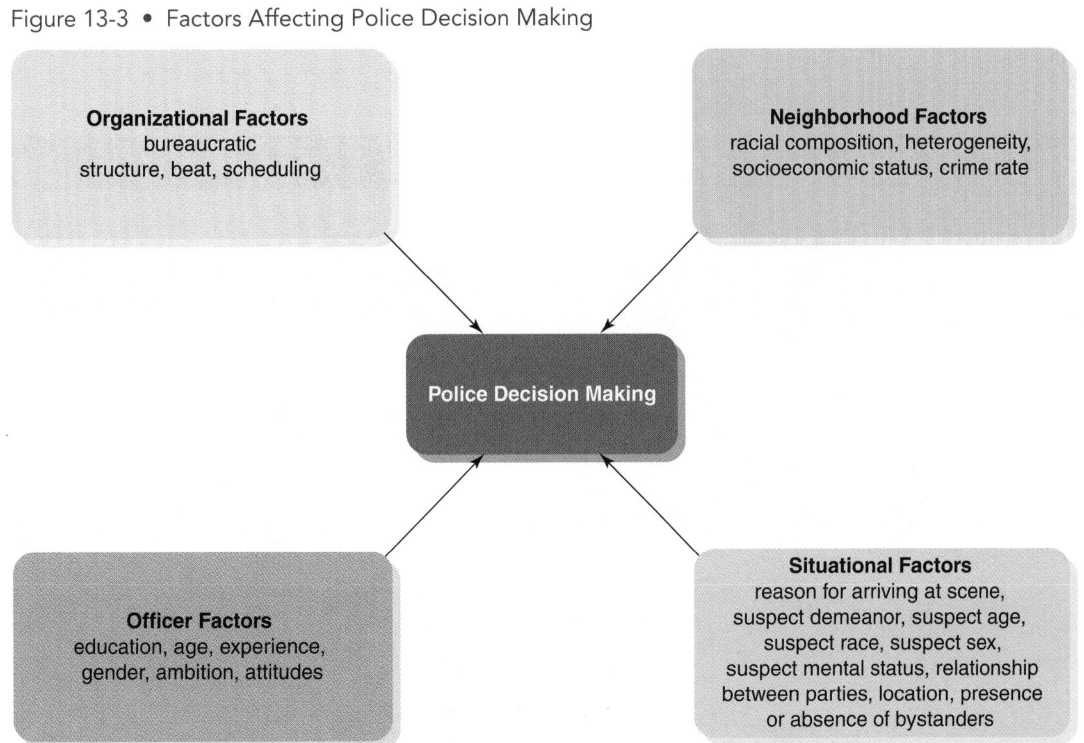

SUMMARY

- Police discretion is the latitude an officer has in making the decision to act one way instead of another. Discretion is helpful because the police cannot be everywhere and arrest every offender. It is risky because it can lead to unequal treatment, favoritism, and even corruption.
- Several early studies provide insight into officer behavior and decision making. The most influential thinkers include Westley, Skolnick, Manning, Wilson, Rubinstein, Van Maanen, Muir, and Brown.
- Police behavior can be perceived as being either universalistic (all officers share some of the same characteristics and attitudes) or particularistic (officers differ from one another in various respects). It is likely that officers are socialized to behave in certain ways (the socialization perspective), but there is also evidence that policing attracts a certain kind of person (the predisposition perspective).
- Police decision making can be understood in terms of organizational factors, neighborhood factors, situational factors, and officer characteristics. Organizational factors that can influence officer decision making include the bureaucratic structure of an agency, beats, and scheduling. Neighborhood factors include racial composition, heterogeneity, socioeconomic status, and crime. Situational factors include the reason the officer arrives at the scene (on his or her initiative or following a call for assistance), the suspect's demeanor and demographic characteristics, the relationship between the parties, the seriousness of the offense, the location of the contact, and the presence or absence of bystanders. Individual characteristics that can influence officer decision making include the officer's education, age, experience, gender, ambition, and attitudes toward the job.

COMING FULL CIRCLE

For Discussion

Return to the questions posed at the start of this chapter. Have any of your answers changed since you read the chapter? What portions of this chapter helped you answer these questions?

Writing Assignment

Using material from this chapter and additional resources, write a 500-word essay in response to one of the questions presented at the beginning of the chapter. Submit your essay to your instructor if asked to do so.

KEY TERMS AND NAMES

admittance
change
continuance
danger signifier
legalistic style
particularistic perspective
passion
perspective
preentry
service style
symbolic assailant
territorial imperative
universalistic perspective
watchman style

WEB INTERACTIVITY

Visit the website of the United Kingdom's Judicial Studies Board, and view their Discretion and Decision Making page at http://www.jsboard.co.uk/magistrates/nacro/mf_03.htm. Review the eight discretionary exercises provided on that page, and identify any important differences between the American and British justice systems in the area of discretion. Submit your findings to your instructor if asked to do so.

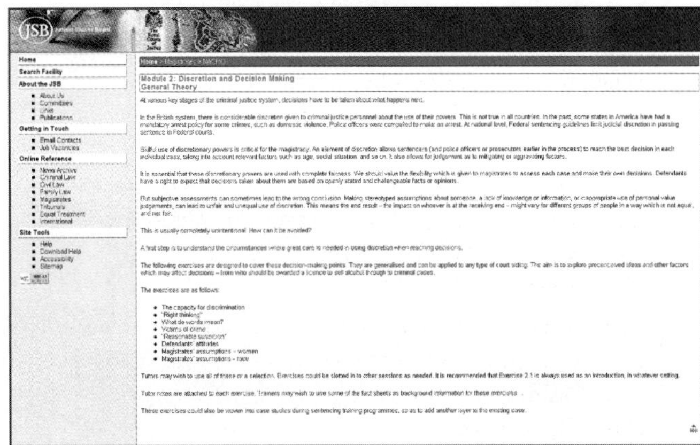

The United Kingdom's Judicial Studies Board

REVIEW QUESTIONS

1. What is police discretion? Is it beneficial or harmful? Explain your response.
2. Which do you feel is the most influential of the classic studies of police behavior? Why?
3. What are the differences between the universalistic and particularistic perspectives on police behavior? Which do you believe is more important in predicting police behavior: socialization or predisposition?
4. List the four categories of factors that researchers have identified as possible predictors of police decision making.

chapter fourteen

DEVIANCE, ETHICS, AND PROFESSIONALISM

LEARNING OBJECTIVES

After reading this chapter, students should be able to:

1. Discuss how various commissions established to examine police misconduct in the United States have uncovered deviance.
2. Identify several typologies of police deviance that scholars have proposed.
3. Discuss some infamous instances of police deviance.
4. Discuss explanations for police deviance, its incidence, and methods of controlling it.

THINK ABOUT IT

In 2007, police officers in California's Laguna Beach confronted a man and a woman who were apparently having a domestic dispute at a luxury oceanfront resort. Callers to the 911 emergency operators reported that the woman was running around the expensive hotel naked, waving a gun. When officers arrived at the couple's room, the pair passed the gun back and forth between them, and then the woman pointed it at the officers. At that point, the officers fired into the room, killing the couple.

Without knowing more about what actually happened, one might be inclined to criticize the police shooting of *both* the man and the woman. After all, only one of them could hold the gun at a time, and the officers might have taken better aim. Still, the officers who responded to the call were clearly in danger, and they may have thought that they had no choice but to shoot both people. What's interesting about this case, however, is the media's reaction to the shooting. It seemed as if reporters were *hoping* that the officers had acted improperly and that they *wanted* to inflame the public. The following day, for example, an MSNBC story based on details provided by the Associated Press recounted the incident in an article titled "Cops Kill Couple at Luxury Oceanfront Resort."[1] The story described the shootings as "the first homicides in Laguna Beach in nearly four years." The language used by the media raises several questions that bear on the subject of police deviance:

1. Was the use of the phrase "cops kill" in the Associated Press headline unnecessarily inflammatory?
2. Was *homicide* a good choice of words, or should the reporter have made it clear that the police officers fired in self-defense?
3. Did the MSNBC story pass judgment on the officers too quickly?
4. Is there a preexisting bias in this country's media against the police?
5. What might explain the apparent desire by at least some members of the press to paint the police as deviant or even criminal?
6. Is police deviance a real problem in this country, or is it largely a creation of the media?

INTRODUCTION

With the enormous power afforded to law enforcement officials comes the potential for abuse of that power. As in any job, when employees are given a large amount of autonomy coupled with a significant degree of control over others, it is not surprising that some will step outside the bounds of acceptable conduct. Police training, supervision, professionalism, ethical standards, and legal constraints may deter some inappropriate behavior, but even the most effective controls do not work all the time or for all officers.

corruption
Dishonest or fraudulent conduct by public officials in a position of power.

When talk of police improprieties comes up, the term **corruption** inevitably surfaces. Corruption can be defined as dishonest or fraudulent conduct by public officials in a position of power. One researcher says that corruption occurs

> when an official receives or is promised significant advantage or reward (personal, group or organizational) for doing something that he is under a duty to do anyway, that he is under a duty not to do, for exercising a legitimate discretion for improper reasons, and for employing illegal means to achieve approved goals.[2]

Another researcher notes, "Police officers act corruptly when, in exercising or failing to exercise their authority, they act with the primary intention of furthering private or departmental/divisional advantage."[3]

deviance
Any behavior that is at odds with socially expected or accepted behavior.

Corruption, though, is but one example of improper conduct. Perhaps a better term to apply to the material discussed in this chapter is **deviance.** *Deviance* is a broad term that applies to any behavior that is at odds with socially expected or accepted behavior. *Police deviance* thus refers to police behavior that is not regarded as appropriate by those in a position to make such determinations. Usually, this means training authorities, supervisors, the authors of professional standards, and the like, but it also means members of the wider society. Viewed in this way, police deviance can take a number of forms. It can range from the most flagrant physical abuses to seemingly innocuous behaviors that probably wouldn't catch the eye of any but the most ardent police critics.

WEB PATROL 14-1

Measuring the Professionalism of Police Officers
http://www.mycrimekit.com

UNCOVERING DEVIANCE

Varying degrees of deviance and corruption have characterized societies everywhere and are certainly not new. Criminal justice historian Samuel Walker describes police corruption during the eighteenth century:

> With few books and even less legal training available, many constables and justices of the peace simply did not know the law. Corruption was also a problem, as officials gave favored treatment to friends, relatives, and influential people. . . . [There were] also accounts of sheriffs and constables taking bribes to release prisoners or fix juries and assaulting citizens without any cause. In short, police corruption and brutality appeared at the very outset of American criminal justice history.[4]

We mentioned Tammany Hall in Chapter 1. It provides a flagrant example of police (and political) deviance. Around the turn of the twentieth century, according to Walker,

> [C]orruption flourished because the criminal law created irresistible opportunities through restrictions on drinking, gambling, and sex. . . . Small entrepreneurs arose to provide the forbidden pleasures in the vice district. The saloon and its allied enterprises constituted an important avenue for entry into business careers for the recent immigrant with little capital. Illegal activities, of course, could survive only if protected by law enforcement, and the result was systematic corruption.[5]

Other historians have remarked that not only did early urban police protect the criminal element, they practically encouraged crime:

> The police did not suppress vice; they licensed it. From New York . . . to San Francisco, and from Chicago . . . to New Orleans . . . they permitted gamblers, prostitutes, and saloon keepers to do business under certain well understood conditions. These entrepreneurs were required to make regular payoffs [to the police].[6]

The Wickersham Commission

As patterns of misconduct were being revealed and policing entered the professional era, accounts of police deviance became even more commonplace. This was partly due to the work of various crime commissions. The first of these to tackle the issue of improper police conduct was the 1929 Wickersham Commission (known officially as the *National Commission on Law Observance and Enforcement*). Its report, *Lawlessness in Law Enforcement*, provided a blistering critique of police corruption around the country. Its authors found that the "third degree," or "the inflicting of pain, physical or mental, to extract confessions or statements," was "extensively practiced across the country."[7]

WEB PATROL 14-2

Bad Cops: A Study of Career-Ending Misconduct among New York City Police Officers
http://www.mycrimekit.com

Walker notes,

> San Francisco police would beat a suspect in the patrol wagon to give him a "foretaste of things to come if he does not incriminate himself." Detectives in one city suspended a suspect out a second-story window by his ankles until he confessed. Cleveland detectives interrogated suspects in teams working in relays. Suspects were denied sleep and food and "kept standing, clear of a wall, for many hours."[8]

One of the Wickersham report's authors, Walter Pollak, went on to argue successfully for the defense in 1932 in ***Powell v. Alabama***,[9] in which the U.S. Supreme Court held that a defendant facing the death penalty is entitled to an attorney at trial. *Powell* arose from the famous Scottsboro case,

Powell v. Alabama
A 1932 case in which the U.S. Supreme Court held that a defendant facing the death penalty is entitled to an attorney at trial.

Knapp Commission
A commission to investigate police corruption that was appointed by New York City Mayor John V. Lindsay in 1970 in response to a *New York Times* article that reported widespread corruption in the New York City Police Department.

grass eater
A police officer who accepts small gifts and engages in minor acts of deviance but does not actively pursue opportunities for corruption.

meat eater
A police officer who actively seeks out and plans opportunities to exploit his or her position for personal gain.

in which eight African American youth in Alabama were convicted of raping two white women and sentenced to die—without the assistance of counsel. This and some other successful cases that Pollak argued pointed to examples of questionable police conduct, shaky evidence, race discrimination, and other police misconduct.

The Knapp Commission

The formation of the **Knapp Commission** in 1970 marked another significant milestone in the investigation of police deviance. It was established in May of that year under the auspices of Mayor John V. Lindsay of New York in response to an article published by the *New York Times* that reported widespread corruption in the New York City Police Department (NYPD). Judge Whitman Knapp was appointed to chair the commission and investigate the extent to which the *New York Times* accurately portrayed the behaviors of the department. Here is a summary of one of the commission's findings:

> The investigation found corruption to be widespread in the police department and many officers, both investigators and patrol officers, to be involved. Corruption was most extensive among investigators (what the commission called plainclothes officers) in the area of gambling. The plainclothes officers participated in what was known as a "pad." For example, each illegal gambling establishment in a precinct would contribute a certain amount of money (as much as $3,500 per establishment once or twice a month) to the officers. The total amount collected would be divided among the officers, each one receiving his "nut" (which was usually $300 to $400 per month, but at least one precinct had a "nut" of $1,200 per officer).[10]

Former NYPD officer Frank Serpico as he looks today. What was Serpico's role in uncovering police corruption? Is it likely that the kind of corruption he uncovered exists in some American police departments today?

Billy Tompkins/RETNA Ltd.

The authors of the Knapp Commission report identified two types of corrupt police officers: **grass eaters** and **meat eaters.** Grass eaters, the commission said, are the police officers who accept small gifts and engage in minor deviance, mostly in response to peer pressure. Meat eaters, by contrast, are the officers who actively seek out opportunities to exploit their positions, in a proactive and planned fashion, and who may be involved in large-scale and far-reaching corrupt activities.

The problem of meat-eating corruption is, of course, more serious. The difficulty facing police reformers is that while meat-eating corruption is much more serious, grass-eating corruption is far more commonplace. This is not unlike the media's apparent obsession with violent crime; while there are almost constant media demands that something be done about it, property crimes are far more common and, by many accounts, more costly, but the media pay little attention to property crime.

The Knapp Commission's reference to grass- and meat-eating corruption has since been expanded to include other types of police behaviors. Police expert Tom Barker, for example, expanded the commission's typology.[11] **White knights,** he argued, are the honest and upstanding officers who never step over the line between accepted and deviant conduct, no matter how great the pressure. **Straight shooters** are officers who, for the most part, are honest but will overlook some of the misconduct committed by their peers. Next are the grass eaters and meat eaters identified by the Knapp Commission. Finally, **rogues** are the most seriously deviant officers, according to Barker. In 2005, for example, a federal grand jury in Brooklyn indicted retired NYPD officers Stephen Caracappa and Louis Eppolito, saying that in the 1980s the two had routinely passed confidential law enforcement information to members of organized crime and had worked as hitmen for the mob, killing rival gangsters.[12] Even meat eaters view rouges, who engage in serious criminal activity, as extraordinarily corrupt.

white knight
An honest and upstanding officer who never steps over the line between accepted and deviant conduct, no matter how great the pressure to do so.

TYPOLOGIES OF DEVIANCE

The Wickersham and Knapp crime commissions uncovered several varieties of police deviance. Since then, still other corrupt and deviant practices have come to light. This has prompted researchers to classify, or construct typologies of, police deviance. There are several such noteworthy efforts. We begin with one of the better-known typologies and then consider some others. The last part of this section looks at other forms of police deviance that do not fit neatly into any one category or set of categories.

straight shooter
An honest police officer who will overlook some misconduct committed by peers.

rogue
A seriously deviant officer.

The Dark Side of Policing

Victor Kappeler, Richard Sluder, and Geoffrey Alpert's popular book *Forces of Deviance: Understanding the Dark Side of Policing*[13] identifies four types of police deviance: police crime, occupational deviance, police corruption, and abuse of authority. Each is discussed below. The order in which they appear is not intended to suggest that one is any more serious than the other.

Police Crime. In Chapter 12, we discussed different mechanisms for preserving the accountability of law enforcement officials. One of those is the criminal law. Generally, when police officers break the criminal law, they do so during the course of their legitimate duties and thus cannot be prosecuted as the rest of us can. Indeed, there are a number of so-called affirmative defenses that police officers can assert, which immunize them from charges of criminal activity, when they engage in activities that would be considered criminal for the rest of us. These include entering private property without permission, using physical force to complete an arrest, and even shooting a person. The key for ensuring that an officer is not held criminally liable is that he or she performs in accordance with accepted law enforcement standards and within the limits of department policy and established legal guidelines. When officers step outside these constraints, they can be held criminally liable. This is what Kappeler and his colleagues meant by **police crime.** They defined police crime as an "officer's use of the official powers of his or her job to engage in criminal conduct."[14] Researchers have uncovered several examples of police criminal behavior.[15]

police crime
An "officer's use of the official powers of his or her job to engage in criminal conduct."[i]

Occupational Deviance. **Occupational deviance** refers either to behavior that does not conform to accepted standards of conduct or that is not part of normal patrol work and is committed under the guise of police authority. Almost anyone can engage in occupational deviance. Consider embezzlement, an offense that nearly anyone can commit during the course of legitimate employment. It basically amounts to using one's position for personal (usually financial) gain. Embezzlement is basically theft without a trespassory element. The occupational deviance Kappeler and his colleagues refer to, however, is behavior that is facilitated by virtue of serving as a police officer, and it can include much more than just deviance for personal gain. By this definition, occupational deviance can include conduct ranging from committing theft from the evidence locker to helping a friend get a speeding ticket removed from his or her driving record. Occupational deviance is perhaps the most intractable problem for police administrators because it's common, it's difficult to detect, and it does not always rise to the level of a criminal offense.

occupational deviance
Behavior performed under the guise of police authority that either does not conform to accepted standards of conduct or is not part of normal patrol work.

WEB PATROL 14-3
Measurement of Police Integrity
http://www.mycrimekit.com

Police Corruption. Remember that our definition of deviance *includes* corruption. Knowing that, it should come as no surprise that Kappeler and his colleagues liken police corruption to deviance. They defined **police corruption** as the misuse of police authority for personal gain. Another scholar states, "Whatever the officer receives through the misuse of his or her authority must be of some material reward or gain. Material reward or gain must be some tangible object, either cash, service, or goods that have cash value."[16]

police corruption
The misuse of police authority for personal or organizational gain.

More often, the term *police corruption* connotes serious and even criminal conduct committed by law enforcement officers. Thus to minimize confusion, it is useful to put deviance in the *inappropriate but not necessarily flagrant* category. Corruption is a bit more serious, but if corruption is for personal gain, then simply accepting a free cup of coffee fits the term. Can we logically argue that an officer who accepts a free cup of coffee is the same as one who routinely skims drugs or cash from big busts? Probably not.

Abuse of Authority. Abuse of authority is basically the catchall category for other inappropriate conduct that does not necessarily amount to crime, deviance, or corruption. Kappeler and his colleagues identify three elements of **abuse of authority**:

abuse of authority
A catchall category for various forms of inappropriate police conduct that do not necessarily amount to crime, deviance, or corruption.

- Officers may physically abuse a citizen through the use of excessive force.
- Officers may psychologically abuse a citizen through the use of verbal assault, harassment, or ridicule.
- Officers may violate a citizen's constitutional, federal, or state rights.[17]

Physical abuse and brutality are arguably the most serious forms of police misconduct, but they can also overlap with some of the other behaviors we have already discussed. Police crime, for example, can contain physical elements. If a police officer wrongfully (and intentionally) kills someone, then what we have is police crime and abuse of authority all wrapped up in a single case. Given the serious nature of physical force, and particularly abuses of it, we return to this topic in Chapter 15.

Classifying Corruption

Some researchers have been content to use the term *corruption* to refer to all manner of police misconduct. For example, in his popular book *Conduct Unbecoming: The Social Construction of Police Deviance and Control*,[18] Maurice Punch identifies four categories of behavior that he considers to be corruption: straightforward corruption, predatory corruption, combative corruption, and the perversion of justice. The order in which they are presented here does not relate to their seriousness.

Straightforward Corruption. According to Punch, **straightforward corruption** is simply any form of misconduct that provides a direct financial benefit to the officer. An officer who is in cahoots with organized crime figures and receives money for "looking the other way," for example, is said to engage in straightforward corruption.

straightforward corruption
Any form of police misconduct that provides direct financial benefit to police officers.

Predatory Corruption. **Predatory corruption** refers to the actions of police officers who actively promote and engage in criminal and other wrongful activities. For example, instead of "looking the other way" and ignoring organized crime, the police *are* the organized criminals. Predatory corruption is arguably more serious than straightforward corruption.

predatory corruption
A form of police corruption that consists of more than just passive participation (for example, looking the other way while a fellow officer commits a crime). In predatory corruption, officers actively promote and engage in criminal and other wrongful activities.

Combative Corruption. Combative corruption refers to making arrests, gaining convictions, and ensuring lengthy sentences at whatever the cost. Here are several examples of combative corruption:

- Flaking: Planting evidence on a suspect
- Padding: Adding evidence to strengthen a case against a suspect
- Using verbals, or words, to describe and incriminate a suspect
- Intimidating a witness
- Scoring on an informant: Shaking down an informant for money, drugs, and other items
- Burning: Revealing an informant's identity
- Paying an informant with illegally obtained drugs[19]

It is not difficult to see how combative corruption may be among the most common forms of police misconduct. There is pressure in any organization to perform. This is as true in the public sector as it is in the private sector, both inside and outside of criminal justice. The infamous Duke lacrosse team sexual assault scandal in 2007 highlighted what happens when prosecutors seek convictions at all costs. Police officers who want to impress their supervisors and get promotions are sometimes tempted to step over the line, whether it be for their own personal gain or out of genuine concern with getting dangerous criminals off the streets.

Perversion of Justice. Punch's **perversion of justice** consists of serious actions by a police officer, such as lying under oath (perjury), intimidating a witness, and performing other activities that resemble combative corruption. The difference between the two lies in the officer's motivations. Where combative corruption was concerned with "doing justice" (in the police officer's view), the perversion of justice refers to acting vengefully, of using one's position as a police officer to exact revenge on others. There is, of course, some overlap between these categories. The common thread running throughout each is behavior that is at odds with accepted standards.

perversion of justice
A kind of police corruption that consists of serious actions by a police officer, such as lying under oath (perjury), intimidating a witness, and performing other activities that resemble combative corruption.

There have been many examples of police officers offering false testimony either to obtain a conviction or to satisfy vengeful motives. Officer Mark Fuhrman's perjured testimony during the famous O. J. Simpson trial is one example.[20] Then there are the findings of the **Mollen Commission,** which investigated allegations of police corruption in the NYPD during the 1990s. The commission drew this conclusion about the pervasiveness of police perjury:

Mollen Commission
A commission appointed by New York City Mayor David N. Dinkins in 1992 to investigate allegations of police corruption in the New York City Police Department.

> Officers reported a litany of manufactured tales. For example, when officers unlawfully stop and search a vehicle because they believe it contains drugs or guns, officers will falsely claim in police reports and under oath that the car ran a red light (or committed some other traffic violation) and that they subsequently saw contraband in the car in plain view. To conceal an unlawful search of an individual who officers believe is carrying drugs or a gun, they will falsely assert that they saw a bulge in the person's pocket or saw drugs and money changing hands. To justify unlawfully entering an apartment where officers believe narcotics or cash can be found, they pretend to have information from an unidentified civilian informant or claim they saw the drugs in plain view after responding to the premises on a radio run. To arrest people they suspect are guilty of dealing drugs, they falsely assert that the defendants had drugs in their possession when, in fact, the drugs were found elsewhere where the officers had no lawful right to be.[21]

If the commission's observations seem inaccurate or troubling, or even a little biased, then consider the findings from Myron Orfield's famous study of police perjury.[22] He interviewed prosecutors, judges, and defense attorneys and found that 52 percent believed that at least "half of the time" the prosecutor "knows or has reason to know" that police fabricate evidence at suppression hearings, where judges decide whether evidence should be excluded due to inappropriate police actions. More shocking still is the finding that more than nine of the ten prosecutors surveyed had knowledge of police perjury "at least some of the time." In fairness to police officers, Orfield's study also revealed that much of the perjured testimony given by police at suppression hearings was encouraged by prosecutors who would often say something like, "If this happens, we win. If this happens, we lose."[23]

Police Misconduct

Barker has argued that not only should deviance be couched in terms of corruption, but also that any focus on corruption should be limited to those activities for which there is a monetary reward for the officers.[24] Here we briefly consider eight examples of this form of corruption.

Corruption of Authority. According to Barker, **corruption of authority** occurs when an officer agrees to accept free meals, discounts, and rewards by virtue of his or her position as a police officer. This type of corruption is perhaps the most innocuous and does not require any significant degree of organization. An officer who receives a free cup of a coffee from a restaurant owner fits into this category.

corruption of authority
A level of police corruption that consists of receiving free meals, discounts, and rewards.

The old saying "There is no free lunch" may come to mind. An officer who accepts a free meal is not being given a "reward" for a job well done. Instead, it is likely that the restaurant owner is attempting to curry favor with the police and possibly benefit from some added attention and/or surveillance of the restaurant that other business owners in the area would not necessarily receive. Free meals and such are an example of gratuities, a topic we will come back to shortly.

kickback
An illegal payment for a service performed.

Kickbacks. **Kickbacks** are illegal payments for services performed. An example of this form of corruption hails from Illinois.[25] In January 2001, the public safety director of Cicero, Illinois, Emil Schullo, was indicted in a kickback scheme. He was accused of contracting out town investigative work to a private investigative firm in exchange for kickbacks amounting to 10 percent of the contracted billings. To Schullo's chagrin, the investigator was working with federal law enforcement officials and tape-recorded their conversations. Surprisingly, Schullo was the *ninth* Cicero official to be indicted for corruption. In 2003, Schullo was sentenced to more than nine years in prison.[26]

opportunistic theft
A theft that occurs when an opportunity presents itself.

Opportunistic Theft. **Opportunistic theft** is theft that occurs when an opportunity presents itself. Examples include theft from arrestees, crime victims, crime scenes, and unprotected places. Sometimes this form of theft can be quite lucrative, as this story from Michigan illustrates:

> In Detroit, former police officer Donald Hynes, 43, was convicted . . . of being part of a ring that stole more than 80 kilos of cocaine from the Detroit Police evidence room. Hynes was accused of making more than $336,000 from his share of the stolen coke. In a plot that continued from 1995 to 2000, Hynes and civilian police employee John Earl Cole, who worked in the evidence room, stole the coke over the years. Hynes was found guilty of conspiracy to distribute cocaine, distribution of cocaine, conspiracy to embezzle police property, conspiracy to launder money, and making false declarations to a grand jury. He faces a mandatory minimum 10 years in prison when he is sentenced June 19.[27]

In fact, Hynes received a sentence of 220 months—18 and a third years!

shakedown
A demand by a corrupt police officer for money, goods, or something of value from a citizen in exchange for lenient treatment, protection, or some other illegitimate "service."

Shakedowns. **Shakedowns** consist of corrupt officers demanding money, goods, or other valuables from people in exchange for lenient treatment, protection, or some other illegitimate service. Basically, shakedowns are extortion. Shakedowns are less common today than they were in the past, so we have to look back in time for examples. During the 1960s, for instance, Seattle police officers were paid $200 each month in exchange for protecting a gay bathhouse called the Atlas Club.[28]

There is some recent evidence of shakedowns of a different kind. Reporters at the *Boston Globe* found examples of prosecutors giving drug defendants favorable treatment (for example, reduced charges) if they surrendered the cash received from buying and selling drugs. The prosecutors shared the money they obtained with police.[29]

Protecting Illegal Activities. The protection of illegal activities is not unlike a shakedown in the sense that police receive money for their services. Here, though, instead of seeking payment for protection, they seek payment for turning a blind eye to criminal activity. It is safe to say that the police protection of criminal activity is very much the exception these days. It was perhaps most frequent during the Prohibition era, when corrupt officers would routinely protect establishments that continued to serve liquor. Many of these so-called speakeasies could not have operated without police protection.

Fixes. Fixes occur when police officers fix a speeding ticket or other infraction or charge—that is, remove it from someone's record. Examples of ticket fixing are commonplace. For example, during the late 1980s, an NYPD officer, Robert Hanes, was fired for a ticket-fixing scheme in Queens traffic court.[30] As recently as 2006, a police chief and city councilperson in Edwardsville, Kansas, were charged in a driving under the influence (DUI) ticket-fixing scheme.[31]

no-fix law
A law that requires police officers to account for every ticket that is issued, even the voided ones, in an effort to prevent favoritism and unequal treatment.

In response to these sorts of problems, a number of states have implemented so-called **no-fix laws**—with varying degrees of success. Massachusetts has had one such law in place since 1962. It requires officers to account for every ticket they issue, even the voided ones, in an effort to prevent favoritism and unequal treatment. An article in the *Boston Globe* described how the law operates (or, perhaps more accurately, how it does not operate):

> The law requires each police chief to return audit sheets to the Registry of Motor Vehicles, listing every citation which [was] written out, voided, destroyed, or lost. All voided citations are supposed to be returned to the Registry and explained. Failing to follow the no-fix law is official misconduct, a misdemeanor punishable by a fine of up to $500, and imprisonment up to a year. . . . In practice, most of the state's police departments provide only a sketchy accounting for their

> tickets. Others don't provide even that much. Boston, Cambridge, and Lowell police departments are among about 200 that do not send in the audit forms. Even when police departments file their lists of tickets, voided ones are almost never returned or explained.[32]

Crimes. We have talked about crimes committed by police officers already. Obviously, these are among the most serious forms of misconduct. Opportunistic theft is, of course, a type of crime, but Barker was referring mostly to serious criminal activity, including burglary, robbery, rape, and murder. These actions are very much the exception, as the vast majority of police officers are law-abiding and professional, but there are numerous accounts of egregious criminal activity nevertheless. Additional examples are presented later in the chapter.

Internal Payoffs. Finally, **internal payoffs** refer to the "sale" of anything within a police department, from work assignments and time off to evidence and promotion. The sale of work assignments is not particularly serious, at least not in comparison to criminal activity and other egregious forms of misconduct. In some departments, for example, officers can sell their scheduled shifts to colleagues who are happy to earn pay for the time worked, plus a little extra. This kind of practice may raise some ethical concerns, but it certainly is not criminal. At the other extreme, though, offering money in exchange for promotion or, worse, offering to sell evidence, including contraband, is a serious action that can lead to dismissal and even criminal charges.

internal payoff
The "sale" of anything within a police agency, from work assignments and time off to evidence and promotion.

Other Forms of Deviance

There are other forms of deviance that either don't fit neatly into the categories we have already covered or overlap those categories. We wrap up our introduction to various forms of police deviance by exploring each of these problems: gratuities, police sexual misconduct, and temptations arising from the illicit drug trade.

Gratuities. **Gratuities** occur when officers accept something of value. Traditional examples of gratuities include a free cup of coffee, a free lunch, or a "police price" discount on a meal or other service. But gratuities can extend into other realms and include everything from free admission to sporting events to lavish gifts.

gratuity
Something of value that is freely given to police officers simply because they are police officers. Examples include a cup of coffee, a lunch, or a "police price" discount on a meal or other service.

A person who simply gives a gift to a police officer may not expect anything in return, but there is always the possibility that it could *appear* otherwise. In other words, it just looks bad to accept free goods and services, whether the gift is an expression of someone's genuine thanks or is given with a more sinister motive in mind. The International Association of Chiefs of Police agrees; it considers gratuities to be unethical, but this does not stop officers from accepting them. In fact, the practice is actually quite common.

It is even a little risky to describe the acceptance of gratuities as a form of deviance. There are arguments for and against the practice. Stephen Coleman, a police ethics expert, has offered a series of arguments against the acceptance of gratuities[33]:

> - The slippery slope to corruption: . . . It could be argued that although there seems to be a big difference between accepting a cup of coffee and accepting a six-figure bribe to look the other way while a murder is carried out, this is not really the case. For there is a logical

YOU DECIDE

No Free Lunch

You are a veteran officer patrolling a new beat. On your previous beat, you would frequent a convenience store and buy something to drink. You once accepted free drinks from the clerk, but you quickly learned that there is no such thing as a "free lunch"; people always expect something in return. On your new beat, you stop by a convenience store for a drink. The clerk refuses to accept payment. When you insist on paying, the clerk becomes visibly upset and accuses you of trying to be "better than the others." He says he is going to call your supervisor, who he says has no problem with accepting free drinks. What should you do?

YOU DECIDE
Quid Pro Quo?

Early in the morning, you are patrolling a stretch of freeway when you come upon a vehicle that is broken down by the side of the road. You learn that the driver lives only a short distance away, so you take him home so that he can arrange to have the vehicle towed. The man is very appreciative and offers you a $20 bill for your kindness. What should you do?

slippery slope here, given that there is only a small difference between accepting a cup of coffee, and accepting a cup of coffee and a doughnut, and only a small difference between accepting a cup of coffee and a doughnut, and accepting a free meal. . . .

- The democratic ethos of policing: Given that, in a democracy, public services should be equally available to all, allowing a fee-for-service system for policing would be "anti-democratic."
- The public perception: A public perception that police are corrupt, whether or not true, will have a deleterious effect on police performance. To avoid this problem, police need to avoid even the appearance of corruptibility.[34]

There are, of course, two sides to every story. Coleman goes on to call attention to some reasons why police *should* accept freebies. One is that they are the building blocks of positive relationships. Second, some people draw on police services more than others. Why shouldn't they be allowed to tip those who serve them? It happens elsewhere in the service sector, some would say, so why not in public service?

For the most part, police departments, training academies, and law enforcement associations discourage the practice of accepting gratuities, mainly due to the slippery slope argument: Given the stigma attached to the acceptance of gratuities, an officer who accepts them might *feel* corrupt, thus greasing the slippery slope toward more serious misconduct. As Coleman puts it, "If officers feel that they are already compromised, they might find it easier to make more significant compromises later, because they feel that they have nothing to lose."[35] See Table 14-1 for a summary of the arguments for and against accepting gratuities.

Police reformers, perhaps most notably August Vollmer, have almost unanimously rallied against gratuities:

> Gratuities often lead to things like kickbacks (bribery) for referring business to towing companies, ambulances, or garages. Further up the scale comes pilfering, or stealing (any) company's supplies for personal use. At the extreme, opportunistic theft takes place, with police officers skimming items of value that won't be missed from crime scenes, property rooms, warehouses, or any place they have access to.[36]

A number of police departments have responded by either prohibiting, or at least discouraging, the acceptance of gratuities. The Philadelphia Police Department discourages gratuities by raising the integrity argument:

> The public demands that the integrity of its law enforcement officers be above reproach. The dishonesty of just one officer may impair public confidence and cast suspicion upon the Department as a whole. Succumbing to even minor temptations can generate a malignancy which will ultimately destroy an individual's effectiveness and which may well contribute to the corruption of fellow officers.[37]

YOU DECIDE
The Gift

You are a community police officer who lives in a high-crime inner-city neighborhood in exchange for cheap rent (not unlike Neighborhood Fresh Start, featured at the beginning of Chapter 3). Most of your neighbors are deeply appreciative that the city has moved an officer into the neighborhood. During the holidays, they take up a collection and present you with a $200 gift certificate to a local store. Should you accept the gift? Does it make any difference that you live in the neighborhood?

Table 14-1 • Arguments for and against Accepting Gratuities

Arguments in Support of Acceptance	
Appreciation	Natural and reasonable to show appreciation to those providing a public service. Rude to refuse.
Not significant	Gratuities are not significant enough to buy or cultivate favor.
Officially offered	When offered officially by a company or corporation, no personal sense of obligation can develop.
Links with the community	Part and parcel of fostering close links with the community, including businesspeople. In turn, a fundamental of "good policing."
Police culture	An entrenched part of police culture. Any attempt to end it will result in displeasure and cynicism.
Trust and discretion	Attempts to prohibit acceptance imply that officers cannot be trusted to exercise discretion and are incapable of making sensible moral judgments to guide their behavior.
Arguments against Acceptance	
Sense of obligation	Even the smallest gift inevitably creates a sense of obligation if it becomes regularized.
"Slippery slope"	Gratuities lead to a "slippery slope" where the temptations become imperceptibly greater and refusal increasingly difficult.
Remove temptation	Not all officers can exercise proper judgment on what is reasonable to accept. More sensible for the organization to remove temptation altogether.
Purchase preferential treatment	Businesses that offer gratuities are, in essence, seeking to purchase preferential treatment (e.g., encourage greater police presence in the vicinity of their business).

Source: T. Newburn, *Understanding and preventing police corruption: Lessons from the literature* (London: Home Office, Policing and Reducing Crime Unit, 1999), p. 10. Reproduced under the terms of the Click-Use Licence.

Police Sexual Misconduct. The position of authority a police officer enjoys provides ample opportunity for stepping over the line. Recently, researchers have called attention to another type of police misconduct: police sexual misconduct, or **police sexual violence**.[38] If we use the term *sexual misconduct*, we can identify two forms. First, there is consensual on-the-job sex. One study from the 1970s found that 32 percent of 43 officers surveyed in a southern police department reported having sex with women while on duty.[39] The study's author noted,

police sexual violence
A sexually degrading, humiliating, violating, damaging, or threatening act committed by a police officer against a (usually female) citizen through the use of force or police authority.[ii]

> The police officer comes into contact with a number of females during his routine patrol duties. These contacts occur under conditions which provide enormous opportunities for illicit sex. . . . The officer also has the opportunity to stop a number of women coming home after a night of drinking. An intoxicated female may decide that here *sexual favors* are a small price to pay in order to avoid arrest for driving while intoxicated.[40]

Other researchers have chosen to focus on what they call *police sexual harassment*. This seems to fit somewhere between consensual encounters and violent or nonconsensual ones. One study presented this officer's observation:

> You bet I get [sex] once in a while by some broad who I arrest. Lots of times you can just hint that if you are taken care of, you could forget about what they did. One of the department stores here doesn't like to prosecute. . . . If it's a decent looking woman, sometimes I'll offer to take her home and make my pitch. Some of the snooty, high class broads turn on real quick if they think their friends and the old man doesn't have to find out about their shoplifting.[41]

Both of these studies were conducted some years ago, but it is a safe bet that neither of these forms of sexual misconduct has vanished from the law enforcement landscape. More disturbing still are nonconsensual, sometimes violent attacks by police officers. Not only are these inappropriate, they are also potentially criminal.

Pete Kraska and Victor Kappeler, who authored perhaps the most comprehensive study of police sexual violence, defined the problem as "those situations in which a female citizen experiences a sexually degrading, humiliating, violating, damaging, or threatening act committed by a police officer through the use of force or police authority."[42] They went on to develop a "continuum of sexual violence." It begins with "unobtrusive behavior," such as watching victims, viewing private photographs or videos, and otherwise invading a citizen's privacy. Next, "obtrusive behavior" consists of custodial strip searches, cavity searches, deception to gain sexual favors, and similar actions. Finally, "criminal behavior" is just that: harassment, involuntary sexual contact, sexual assault, and even rape. While most sexual victimization by police may be of women, the sexual abuse of power by policewomen has yet to be explored.

How common is police sexual violence? Kraska and Kappeler examined news sources from January 1991 to June 1993 and identified 124 cases.[43] Most of the cases were actual court cases, not just news accounts. Ninety-one of the cases were from the federal courts. Nine of these involved "unobtrusive" behaviors, 67 involved "obtrusive" behavior, and 15 were criminal.[44] The vast majority of the court cases involved allegations of improper strip searches, but there were a few violations of privacy, sexual assaults, and rapes, as well. Following are some excerpts from three of the cases that Kraska and Kappeler uncovered, ranging from unobtrusive behavior to criminal behavior. (Note that even though the search in the second case was performed by a female officer, a lawsuit was still filed.)

> *James v. City of Douglas*.[45] Celeste James and George Lee owned and operated a floral and bridal store in Douglas, Georgia. In February 1988, the store was destroyed by fire. The Douglas Police Department suspected that the fire was intentionally started in order to collect insurance proceeds. During the ensuing investigation, Claude Jones, then a captain in the Detective Division of the Douglas Police Department, was told by James that Lee was attempting to extort her portion of the insurance proceeds. She reported that Lee threatened to show James's family a videotape of James and Lee engaged in sexual activity unless James gave him her share of the insurance money. Lee videotaped this activity without the knowledge or consent of James. James told Captain Jones that she was unwilling to cooperate in the investigation and prosecution of Lee because of the embarrassing nature of the tape. Jones assured James that if she cooperated the police would handle the tape discreetly. . . . James assisted the police in their investigation; and in March 1988, the Douglas police arrested Lee. The police searched Lee's home and seized several videotapes, including the tape which depicted James and Lee engaging in sexual activity. All the police officers involved in the search of Lee's home viewed the tape on Lee's videotape player. The tape was then given to Jones but never logged in as evidence.[46]
>
> *Timberlake v. Benton*.[47] Both Stewart and Timberlake (two women who were stopped while driving a truck) were wearing T-shirts and "short shorts" which apparently left little room for concealing dangerous weapons. Nevertheless, Stewart had brought a pistol with her in the truck that evening and when Benton stopped them, Timberlake attempted to hide the gun in her shorts. Benton [the officer] claims he observed Timberlake walking stiff-legged with a suspicious bulge in her shorts. Surprisingly, however, neither Stewart nor Timberlake was frisked at any time, nor was Timberlake ever asked about the bulge. Oddly enough, despite his alleged suspicions about Timberlake, Benton ordered Stewart searched first. . . . In accordance with instructions given by Gregory (another officer who arrived at the scene), Stewart sat in the back seat of the patrol car and removed her clothes while Gregory stood in the open doorway of the car with a flashlight in her hand and the dome light of the car on. After removing all of her clothes, Stewart was ordered onto her hands and knees in the back seat with her posterior facing the open doorway and the highway. With rubber gloves, Gregory inspected Stewart's anal and genital areas by spreading Stewart's buttocks. Gregory went through the clothing and shoes as well, but no drugs or weapons were found. Benton then sent Timberlake to be searched. Before she removed her clothes, she handed a pistol to Gregory and said, "you're going to find it anyway." The strip search was then completed in the same manner as before. As with Stewart, no drugs or other weapons were found. During the search, cars would pass within six to ten feet from the open door, and it is alleged by Plaintiff that others at the scene could see into the car while the search was conducted. Ac-

cording to Plaintiff, she was detained for nearly three hours. At no time were the women placed under arrest or informed of their rights.[48]

Parrish v. Lukie.[49] Officer Lukie drove a female detainee to an isolated portion of North Little Rock and forced her to perform oral sex. The police were aware of Lukie's history of sexually assaulting women on the job, but no action was ever taken. The court ruled: "[W]e find overwhelming evidence to support the jury's finding that North Little Rock police officers operated in a system where reports of physical or sexual assault by officers were discouraged, ignored, or covered up."[50]

Drug War Temptations. Before the start of the "war on drugs" in the 1960s, police deviance was mostly connected with the protection of illegal gambling, prostitution, and other vice crimes. Officers were not faced with too many overt temptations to break the law. Since this country has sought to eradicate illicit drug use, however, those temptations have become quite pronounced.

Michigan State University police expert David Carter has identified two types of drug-related police corruption, both of which he says "have notably increased" in recent years.[51]

> ***Type 1 drug corruption:*** This "occurs when an officer seeks to use his or her position simply for personal gain. This type of drug corruption includes the following: giving information to drug dealers about investigations, names of informants, planned raids, and so forth; accepting bribes from drug dealers in exchange for nonarrest, evidence tampering, or perjury; theft of drugs from the police property room for personal consumption; 'seizure' of drugs for personal use without arresting the person possessing the drugs; taking the profits of drug dealers' sales or their drugs for resale; extorting drug traffickers for money or property in exchange for nonarrest or nonseizure of drugs."[52]

> ***Type II drug corruption:*** This "involves the officer's search for legitimate gains and may not even be universally perceived as being corrupt. 'Gain' may involve organizational benefit—perhaps a form of 'winning' or 'revenge.' Included are such actions as giving false statements to obtain arrest or search warrants against suspected or known drug dealers; perjury during hearings and trials of drug dealers; 'planting,' or creating evidence against known drug dealers; entrapment; and falsely spreading rumors that a dealer is a police informant in order to endanger that person."[53]

Victor Kappeler and his colleagues have come up with their own classification scheme for drug-related police corruption. It includes **use corruption, economic corruption, police violence,** and **subjugation of defendants' rights.** Use corruption refers to the personal use of illicit drugs. Two researchers found, for example, that 20 percent of the officers they surveyed reported using marijuana *on duty*.[54] Economic corruption is like Carter's Type I corruption cited above: Officers seek personal gain by stealing drugs, selling drugs, or extorting money from drug dealers. Police violence involves the use of improper physical force to extract confessions. Finally, the subjugation of defendants' rights refers to committing perjury or telling other lies or fabricating evidence in an attempt to secure drug convictions. The latter of these has also been called **noble-cause corruption,**[55] which has been defined as any corruption that occurs in connection with the goal of getting criminals off the streets and protecting the community.

There have been cases of serious police corruption in connection with the "war on drugs." Earlier in this chapter, we mentioned the Mollen Commission's investigation of the NYPD. Here is another account from the commission's report:

> Witnesses told the commission of systematic corruption that was strikingly similar to the Buddy-Boys case [of the mid 1980s]. Michael Dowd, a former officer in the 75th precinct, bluntly described how he and his peers routinely robbed crime victims, drug dealers, and arrestees of money, drugs, and anything else of value. Dowd revealed that many officers were receiving substantial sums for protecting illegal drug operations; Dowd's share amounted to $4,000 each week. Dowd told of officers routinely using drugs and alcohol while on duty, informing the commission that he regularly snorted lines of cocaine off the dashboard of his police cruiser.[56]

The **Buddy Boys** scandal that the commission referred to broke out in the NYPD's Brooklyn precinct in 1986. Thirteen officers were indicted for a number of criminal activities,

Type I drug corruption
Drug-related police corruption that "occurs when an officer seeks to use his or her position simply for personal gain."[iii]

Type II drug corruption
Drug-related police corruption that involves the officer's desire for legitimate gain (for example, winning a conviction). The officer's actions may not even be universally perceived as corruption.[iv]

use corruption
Drug-related police corruption that consists of an officer's personal use of illicit drugs.

economic corruption
Drug-related police corruption in which an officer seeks personal gain by stealing drugs, selling drugs, or extorting money from drug dealers.

police violence
In the context of drug investigations, the use of improper physical force to extract a confession or to obtain evidence.

subjugation of defendants' rights
In the context of drug investigations, an officer lying or committing perjury or fabricating evidence in the name of securing a conviction.

noble-cause corruption
Any corruption that occurs in connection with the goal of getting criminals off the streets and protecting the community.

Buddy Boys
A New York City Police Department scandal that occurred in the Brooklyn precinct in 1986 and resulted in the indictment of 13 officers for a number of criminal activities, including stealing and selling drugs.

including stealing and selling drugs. The group was called the Buddy Boys because the officers knew each other well, ran in the same circles, and stuck together. Before the indictments, the officers were difficult to catch. They had connections within the department who tipped them off when internal investigations were being launched. Department administrators also experimented early on with a job-rotation plan that would have separated most of the officers by placing them in different areas or on different shifts, but then a work slowdown occurred, forcing the administrators to abandon the plan.

SOME INFAMOUS EXAMPLES OF POLICE DEVIANCE

Police deviance, and especially crime, is very much the exception, as we have said repeatedly. Even so, it would be impossible to detail all of the high-profile cases in which police stepped over the line. We will focus on just five significant examples from cities around the country.

The Miami Police Department

Miami River Cops
A Miami Police Department scandal that occurred in the 1980s and resulted in the indictment of a number of officers for criminal acts ranging from stealing cash from motorists stopped for traffic violations to major thefts and murder.

Past corruption in the Miami Police Department (MPD) has received widespread attention. In the 1980s, seven officers known as the **Miami River Cops** were indicted for a variety of criminal acts. They began by stealing cash from motorists whom they stopped for traffic violations, and they worked their way up to major thefts. Informants would alert the officers to the whereabouts of large drug caches, and they would steal the drugs instead of arresting the dealers. A jury deadlocked in their first criminal trial. After that, more officers were accused of being involved, and ultimately 19 officers were convicted.

What made the Miami River Cops scandal so notorious? Apparently it was the officers' audacity and the seriousness of their crimes. They were charged with everything from theft to murder, but stealing from drug dealers was their bread and butter:

> In September, 1984, K-9 Officer Rodolfo "Rudy" Arias, acting on a tip from a major drug trafficker named Luis Rodriguez, stopped and searched a vehicle. Inside, Arias found a small amount of cocaine and $16,000 in cash, which never made it to the MPD evidence lock-up. A month later, Arias and two other River Cops, Armando Lopez and Felix Beruvides, raided a poker game in Little Havana, where they seized $3,500 in cash. In April of 1985, Officers Coello and Garcia stopped motorist Menelao Estevez, who was carrying $11,000 in cash. The officers arrested Estevez for carrying an unregistered gun, and at booking Estevez was given a receipt for about half of the money.[57]

Allegations of misconduct at the MPD were by no means limited to the Miami River Cops. The U.S. attorney for the Southern District of Florida noted in 1987 that "the Miami Police Department has an extraordinarily serious problem, equal or surpassing anything I've seen anywhere. Unfortunately, our probe is mushrooming and we could end up with the largest police corruption case in United States history."[58] John Dombrink offers this recounting of events in Miami:

> An FBI agent pled guilty to accepting cocaine kickbacks, and three Miami police officers were each charged with three counts of first-degree murder for their roles in a drug execution. Authorities have yet to catch the person(s) who stole $150,000 from the safe at the headquarters office of the Miami police vice squad, as well as the theft of a quarter of a ton of marijuana from a supposedly secure place in the Miami Police Department Compound. In February 1986, a police officer in nearby North Bay Village was arrested for allegedly selling protection to FBI agents posing as drug dealers.[59]

Rampart Division scandal
A Los Angeles Police Department scandal in the late 1990s that resulted in the convictions of numerous police officers for a wide variety of serious crimes. Because of the scandal, the Los Angeles City Council was forced to accept the terms of a federal consent decree through which federal officials took over the supervision of the department's daily operations.

The Los Angeles Police Department

Nowhere in recent history has police corruption and deviance been more apparent than in the infamous scandal that unfolded in the late 1990s in the Los Angeles Police Department (LAPD) Rampart Division. The **Rampart Division scandal** became one of the most significant scandals in the department's history, if not the biggest scandal in the history of law enforcement.

The events that set the Rampart Division scandal into motion began in late 1997, when three suspects robbed a Los Angeles branch of Bank of America. The investigation into the robbery led to the arrest of West Los Angeles area officer David Mack. A second incident in February of 1998 involved the false imprisonment and subsequent beating of a handcuffed arrestee at the Rampart substation. The officer responsible for the beating was Brian Hewitt. Hewitt was a member of the Rampart Division's Community Resources against Street Hoodlums (CRASH) unit, the LAPD's elite street crime enforcement unit. Two other CRASH officers admitted to being involved in the beating. A month later, six pounds of cocaine were checked out from a property room at LAPD headquarters, supposedly to be used as evidence in a trial. When the cocaine was not returned to the property room, police officials initiated an internal investigation to ascertain its whereabouts. On August 25, Rampart Division Officer Rafael A. Perez was arrested on suspicion of stealing the cocaine.

The investigations of all three incidents revealed that the suspect officers were associated with one another. They either worked as partners or were close friends. Hewitt and Perez were assigned to the Rampart Division, and Mack had previously been assigned to that division. This established a clear connection between the three officers. This information led Chief Bernard Parks to launch a special criminal task force in May 1998 to further investigate the incidents.

Ultimately, the CRASH unit officers involved in the beating at the Rampart substation were terminated, and Mack was convicted in federal court of bank robbery. Perez was prosecuted on drug charges, but his first trial resulted in a hung jury in December of 1998.

Nothing else of note occurred (or at least became publicized) until September 1999 when, during jury selection for his second trial, Perez pleaded guilty to stealing the cocaine from the LAPD storage facilities. He then entered into a confidential plea agreement to receive a reduced sentence on the theft charges in exchange for identifying other Rampart Division police officers involved in illegal activities. This agreement marked the beginning of public exposure of the Rampart Division scandal.

On September 15, 1999, Chief Parks called a press conference to announce that Perez had implicated himself and another Rampart officer in the shooting of an unarmed man. Parks went on to state that 12 officers had been either placed on leave or fired in connection with covering up the shooting. One day later, Javier Francisco Ovando, the unarmed man who was shot and framed for assaulting the two officers, was freed from prison after serving three years of a lengthy term. At that point, the Federal Bureau of Investigation (FBI) began an investigation into civil rights violations in the LAPD.

In an interview from jail on September 20, Perez called corruption in the LAPD a cancer. The next day, Chief Parks convened a board of inquiry (BOI) to investigate the scope of the Rampart Division scandal. Ultimately, more than 300 people were involved in the investigation, and special subcommittees were established to examine issues like personnel, work product, supervision and management, risk management, operations, corruption, and integrity.

In October 1999, two LAPD officers linked to the Rampart corruption scandal were subpoenaed to testify before a grand jury focusing on two allegedly unjustified shootings by Rampart Division officers. In ensuing court actions, a judge overturned the convictions of four men and dismissed the case against a fifth, and then the Rampart Division scandal ballooned out of control.

On February 29, 2000, the board of inquiry gave its 362-page report to Los Angeles Mayor Richard Riordan and members of the LAPD Police Commission (Parks's supervisors). The report cited numerous factors that were responsible for the scandal, including the failure to check the backgrounds of new recruits, to monitor officer misconduct, and to supervise officers in the field. In a letter accompanying the board's report, Chief Parks wrote that "we as an organization provided the opportunity."[60] The BOI report's executive summary noted that, "had the Department and the Rampart management team exercised more vigorous and coordinated oversight of area operations, and its CRASH unit in particular, the crimes and misconduct that occurred may have been prevented, discouraged, or discovered much earlier."[61] The scandal was made possible, the BOI noted, because supervision suffered and the department's internal accountability mechanisms proved ineffective.

Essentially, the Rampart scandal revealed a couple of problems. First, it showed that it is difficult to ensure accountability in large police departments. Total supervision is difficult, if not

The new LAPD Rampart division headquarters building. How might the Rampart division's problems have been averted? Are they likely to reoccur today?

Stephen Friday/LAPD Rampart Station

impossible, in departments that employ thousands of officers and are spread across a substantial geographic area, as is definitely the case with the Los Angeles Police Department. Second, the scandal showed what can happen when administrators fail to take significant steps to tackle police corruption.

On September 19, 2000, federal officials essentially took over the LAPD when the Los Angeles City Council voted (10–2) to accept a consent decree that appointed a federal judge to act on behalf of the U.S. Justice Department to oversee reforms in the LAPD for a period of five years. The consequences of not entering into the decree would have been a federal lawsuit against the LAPD.[62]

In 2006, a Blue Ribbon Panel created to examine the consequences of the Rampart scandal and ensuing problem-solving actions by the LAPD issued its report. The report, titled *Rampart Reconsidered: The Search for Real Reform Seven Years Later*, concluded that the new Rampart leadership currently in place, and the crime-fighting model adapted after the crisis, could today successfully defuse a crisis similar to the one that led to so many problems for the division and the department.[63] According to the panel, supervisors under the new "model do not indulge LAPD's traditional 'us versus them' and 'ends justify the means' paranoia that excuses misconduct and excessive force."[64] Nor, said the panel, does the current leadership "tolerate the silencing of whistle-blowers or share LAPD's historic disdain for laws and policies viewed as obstacles to tough policing."[65]

WEB PATROL 14-4

Rampart Reconsidered: The Search for Real Reform Seven Years Later
http://www.mycrimekit.com

The Philadelphia Police Department

The Philadelphia Police Department has also seen its share of scandal. In the 1980s, more than 30 officers were convicted of criminal charges stemming from federal prosecutions for what has been labeled "systemic corruption."[66] Among those charged was the second in command, making it clear that the problem was not just limited to a few rogue officers. As one of the prosecutors who tried several of the officers said, "I think we [revealed] the depth and prevalence of corruption at the department, and this led the city to reexamine the department and begin an extensive reform to prevent the recurrence of institutionalized corruption."[67]

The Philadelphia Police Study Task Force was commissioned to investigate the department. Headed by Professor Gerald Caplan, the task force issued its report in March 1987 and called the department "unfocused, unmanaged, under-trained, underequipped and unaccountable."[68] The report claimed that "the dead hand of past traditions guides the department rather than the challenge of the future. A history of favoritism, corruption, and brutality hangs over it."[69]

According to Dombrink, most of the department's problems could be traced to illegal gambling:

> Beginning in the 1970s, vending machine companies began buying video poker machines and placing them in bars and taverns in Philadelphia. A patron who played the games would win free games by beating the programmed odds and would be paid off in cash for the free games won, with the bar owner and the vendor splitting equally the profits from the machine.[70]

Because it was a crime to operate the machines, corrupt officers began to extort money by threatening bar owners with arrest; payment, of course, allowed the bar owners to continue their illegal gambling operations. They were effectively paying for police protection by sharing some of their profits with officers of the Philadelphia Police Department.

The problems became more serious when a new mayor, Wilson Goode, was elected in November 1983. Goode appointed a new police commissioner, Gregor J. Sambor, whose decisions further paved the way for a department-wide corruption scandal that ultimately led to the indictments and convictions mentioned earlier. For example, Sambor consolidated all of the vice enforcement units into a single Major Investigations Unit and then made the commander of that unit answer directly to Deputy Commissioner James Martin. This enabled Martin to launch a citywide extortion ring that ultimately led to his federal conviction on charges of racketeering, extortion, and conspiracy.

Once higher-ups were aware of what was going on, the department took several steps toward reform. The mayor replaced ineffective Commissioner Sambor with retired U.S. Secret Service agent Kevin M. Tucker in 1986. Tucker was brought in as an "outsider" in an effort to force change. He had no interest in protecting corruption in the ranks and owed no particular allegiance to his subordinates. Among other measures, his reform efforts included the following:

- Formation of review boards to oversee promotions and to remove politics and favoritism from the process
- Departmental reorganization that reassigned scores of officers
- Establishment of foot patrols
- Mandate that the Internal Affairs Division investigate *all* injuries sustained by citizens at the hands of the police
- Requirement that all candidates for command-level promotions fully disclose their finances
- Limited tenure in specialized vice and narcotics units
- Prosecution of everyone involved in corruption, including officers, public officials, and citizens
- Lenient treatment of officers cooperating with official investigations in regard to their own misconduct
- Arousal of public concern
- Establishment of field associates
- Establishment of proactive instead of reactive probes of possible corruption.[71]

Following the criminal convictions in the late 1980s, some 80 additional officers were dismissed as a result of internal affairs investigations between 1990 and 1995. Another scandal erupted during the mid-1990s, when several officers from the 39th District in the northern part of the city were convicted of various crimes.

WEB PATROL 14-5

Enhancing Police Integrity
http://www.mycrimekit.com

The Boston Police Department

Boston is no stranger to police corruption. A report by Professor Herman Goldstein, author of *Problem-Oriented Policing*, pointed out that "corruption has been part of the culture of Boston for a long time. . . . It's more accurate to view these things as the ebb and flow of officialdom's willingness to investigate corruption."[72] According to Dombrink, it was the conviction of reputed mob boss Gennaro Angiulo that broke the Boston Police Department scandal of the early 1980s. During Angiulo's 1983 trial, evidence surfaced of police indifference to illegal gambling and loan sharking.

One reason corruption recurred in Boston, Dombrink said, is that Boston police officers inspected bars for compliance with liquor-related regulations as official agents of the Boston Licensing Board. That gave them ample opportunity to look the other way or to work with bar owners to violate the law. Dombrink also pointed to other examples of corruption in Boston, including

> charges of illegal shakedowns, bribes, drug trading, vice operations, and harassment. . . . Another . . . string of allegations involved Boston police officers taking bribes for overlooking violations of liquor license laws at bars. Several bar owners describe[d] situations where officers threatened to cite bar owners for liquor license violations if they did not pay off the officer.[73]

The San Francisco Police Department

The Chapter 2 opening story described San Francisco's infamous "Fajitagate" scandal, but that is not the only such scandal hailing from the Golden Gate City. As Dombrink points out,

> The city of San Francisco has weathered decades of political conflict resulting from the diversity of the city's population, no more so than in [the late 1980s] when Bohemians, hippies, commune members, activist groups, gay and lesbian communities, and various influxes of immigrants have made San Francisco a unique melting pot.[74]

Police brutality has plagued the San Francisco Police Department more than financial corruption. One explanation for this is that historically many police officers in San Francisco have come from a conservative Irish-American background and adhered to values that tended to be at odds with the more liberal culture of the Bay Area.[75] To counteract this kind of potential conflict, personnel evaluations are now taken very seriously and are performed on a more regular basis. In addition, the department has gone beyond the state requirements for ethics and professionalism training and also requires extensive sensitivity training. Leaders of gay and lesbian communities have even been invited to meetings at police stations in the city in an effort to promote tolerance and improve police-community relations. Moreover, a gay officer was hired to serve as a liaison between the police and these special-interest communities.[76] Despite such reforms, allegations of abuse have continued. These three cases were summarized by Human Rights Watch:

1. *Officer Daniel Yawczak:* The killing of Michael Acosta was a case where an officer put himself in harm's way against departmental guidelines and then successfully defended his use of a firearm on that basis. On November 2, 1991, Officer Daniel Yawczak shot and killed Acosta. With his gun drawn, Yawczak had chased two suspected purse-snatchers to an idling car in the Pacific Heights neighborhood, where he twice shot Acosta, who was sitting in the driver's seat; the men were unarmed.
2. *Sgt. John Haggett:* The Police Commission apparently violated disciplinary guidelines after finding Sgt. John Haggett guilty of four offenses that should have led to dismissal, but instead giving him a six-month suspension. Prior to this case, Haggett had an extensive history of misconduct, according to press reports and a local police abuse monitor. Press reports stated that he had received two previous 90-day suspensions for excessive force and was involved in the fatal shooting of an unarmed man, Edwin Sheehan, in 1995, which was being investigated by the FBI.
3. *Officer William Wohler:* On July 15, 1993, Brian Sullivan was shot and killed by Officer William Wohler, at Sullivan's parents' home in San Francisco's Excelsior District. Sullivan had an unloaded shotgun on his bike when Wohler responded to an emergency call about him. Riding away from Wohler on a bicycle as Wohler sat in his car, Sullivan rode into his parents' garage and closed the garage door. Wohler reportedly opened fire through the closed garage door. He then followed Sullivan to a side yard, and as Sullivan started up a ladder to the roof, unarmed, Wohler reportedly fired twice; one bullet entered Sullivan's buttocks and traveled to his heart, killing him.[77]

WEB PATROL 14-6

Principles for Promoting Police Integrity
http://www.mycrimekit.com

What became of the officers involved in these cases? Yawczak was convicted of excessive force, and the city was required to pay the victim's family $259,358. The city called the shooting justified. Haggett was neither convicted nor charged with a criminal offense, but he was sued several times, and the city settled several of the lawsuits against him for hundreds of thousands of dollars. Finally, Wohler was not charged, but the city paid $295,000 to settle a wrongful death lawsuit.

EXPLANATIONS, INCIDENCE, AND CONTROLS

Criminological theory tells us why criminals offend. In much the same way, theories of police deviance explain what makes a law enforcement officer cross over to the dark side. There are far more theories of crime, however, than there are theories of police deviance. In addition to considering explanations of police deviance, it is also important to gauge the extent of the problem. The stories we have presented hardly capture the reality of police deviance. We described some of the more notorious cases, but what about the more mundane cases of police deviance—just how common are they? Finally, and perhaps most importantly, we need to consider what can be done to stop police deviance. It is not enough to wait around until something goes wrong. Administrators want to know what they can do to prevent police deviance before it becomes a problem.

WEB PATROL 14-7
Developing and Sustaining a Culture of Integrity
http://www.mycrimekit.com

Explaining Police Deviance

There are two main theories of police deviance. One explains deviance in terms of the isolated behavior of individual officers, while the other attributes deviance to the influence of environmental factors that could affect all police officers. These explanations roughly parallel classical and positivist theories of crime. Classical theories look at individual factors like personality; positivist theories look at environmental factors, including socialization and temptations in the environment.

The Rotten Apple Theory. The **rotten apple theory** attributes police deviance to a few individuals who should not have become police officers and whose propensity toward corruption was not recognized during the recruitment and hiring phases. The implication of this theoretical perspective is that police agencies must continue to refine and improve their hiring procedures. The hope is that adequate screening for candidates of the highest moral character will prevent deviance from taking root in the department.

rotten apple theory
A perspective that attributes police deviance primarily to a few individuals whose propensity toward corruption was not recognized during the recruitment and hiring phases.

Identifying "rotten apples"—that is, officer candidates with a propensity for deviance—is difficult. Skilled liars will not be screened out during hiring. Psychological exams can only do so much, usually identifying only the most unfit of applicants. In response to these problems, some researchers have studied citizen complaints against the police in an effort to determine which officers receive the most complaints, hoping to discern the most common characteristics of "problem" officers. The authors of one study found that 7 percent of the officers in one department were responsible for more than one-third of all the complaints. The officers were younger and had less experience, and the complaints against them were more likely to arise from their proactive (as opposed to reactive) contacts with citizens.[78] These findings suggest that it is important to monitor police-citizen encounters and to focus on less seasoned officers.

Environmental Factors. Positivist criminologists explain crime in terms of environmental factors like peer influence, family conditions, and neighborhood characteristics. Applying this line of thinking to police deviance, it may be that some officers become deviant as a result of either a corrupt political environment or the socialization process. If a city or its police department shows a pattern of problem behavior, then it is understandable that some officers will fall victim to it. Some of the examples discussed earlier revealed cultures of corruption within a department or city, making it pretty clear why police deviance spread.

Cases of systemic corruption are rare, especially these days. This forces us to look at other environmental explanations of police deviance, namely those stemming from the socialization process. It is easier to conceive of a few officers working together and reinforcing one another's behavior through graft and corruption than it is to conceive of a whole police department doing the same. In Chapter 6's discussion of police subculture, we saw, for instance, that the code of silence pervades police work.

Table 14-2 • Factors Affecting the Development of Police Deviance

Constant Factors	
Discretion	The exercise of discretion is argued to have both legitimate and illegitimate bases.
Low managerial visibility	A police officer's actions are often low in visibility as far as line management is concerned.
Low public visibility	Much of what police officers do is not witnessed by members of the public.
Peer group secrecy	Police subculture is characterized by a high degree of internal solidarity and secrecy.
Managerial secrecy	Police managers have generally worked themselves up from the beat and share many of the values held by those they manage.
Status problems	Police officers are sometimes said to be poorly paid relative to their powers.
Association with lawbreakers, contact with temptation	Police officers inevitably come into contact with a wide variety of people who have an interest in police not doing what they have a duty to do. Such people may have access to considerable resources.
Variable Factors	
Community structure	Refers to the degree of "anomie," the political "ethos," and the extent of culture conflict.
Organizational characteristics	Levels of bureaucracy, integrity of leadership, solidarity of work subcultures, moral career stages of police officers, and the perception of legitimate opportunities.
Legal opportunities for corruption	Moral: so-called victimless crimes associated with the policing of vice. Regulative: the exploitation of minor or trivial regulations, such as those associated with construction, traffic, and licensing.
Corruption controls	How the guardians are themselves "guarded."
Social organization of corruption	Two basic forms: arrangements and events.
Moral cynicism	Association with lawbreakers and contact with temptation are inevitable in police work, inclining officers toward moral cynicism.

Source: T. Newburn, *Understanding and preventing police corruption: Lessons from the literature* (London: Home Office, Policing and Reducing Crime Unit, 1999), p. 17. Reproduced under the terms of the Click-Use Licence.

The code certainly presents problems for administrators who are intent on rooting out corruption and deviance. This, in turn, allows problems to persist because they are difficult to bring to light.

Some researchers have attributed police deviance to a mixture of constant and variable factors unique to police work. Examples of these factors appear in Table 14-2. Some would also say that the explanations of corruption that we have covered are too simple and that corruption is a nasty and complex self-reinforcing cycle. This idea can be seen in Figure 14-1. Note that the flowchart is not limited specifically to policing, but addresses public service in general.

How Common Is Police Deviance?

Noted police researcher Lawrence Sherman offered this enlightening commentary on the incidence of police corruption in 1978: "Most police departments have members who commit corrupt acts from time to time. Only some police departments, however, become corrupt police departments."[79] In other words, corruption was—and still is—relatively rare. The vast majority of law enforcement officers are law-abiding, upstanding professionals. Even so, it is important to consider just how common police deviance is. We also need to look beyond the high-profile cases and consider the whole gamut of police deviance, most of which is not as serious as the stories from New York, Los Angeles, and Miami would have us believe.

Figure 14-1 • The Self-Reinforcing Cycle of Corruption

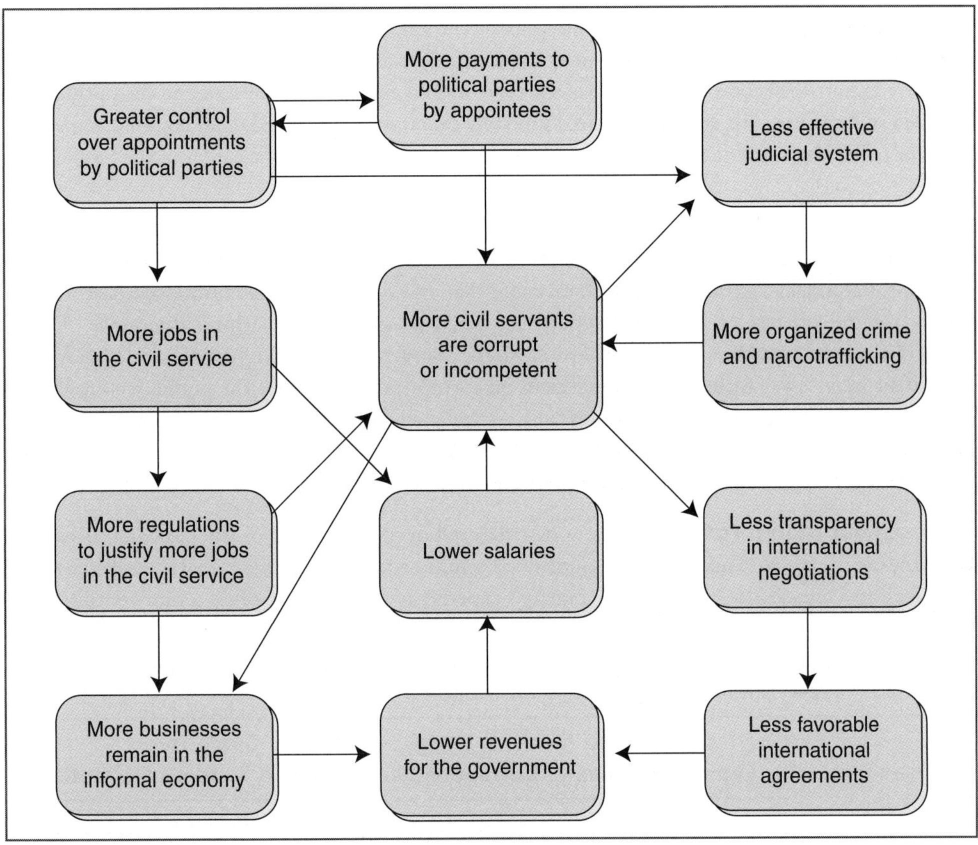

Source: L. Cobb and M. Gonzalez, *Corruption as a system of interlocking vicious cycles: Lessons from NationLab* (Louisville, CO: Aetheling Consultants, 2005). Reprinted by permission of Loren Cobb.

Unfortunately, just as it is difficult to estimate the true extent of crime (the so-called dark figure of crime), it is also difficult to estimate the true prevalence of police deviance. Corrupt officers try to keep their activities private, just as criminals try to hide theirs. As a result, researchers have had to get creative. One researcher surveyed officers in a police department that he called South City. They were asked to estimate how frequently they thought officers engaged in five behaviors: sleeping on duty, using excessive force, having sex on duty, committing perjury, and drinking on duty. Sleeping on duty, brutality, and sex on duty were, surprisingly, considered the most common (40, 39, and 32 percent, respectively). In other words, officers estimated that nearly four in ten officers slept on duty or used excessive force and that more than three in ten had sex on duty.

Researchers have also looked at the frequencies of racial and sexual harassment by police.[80] The results are not too encouraging. According to one review of this research, racial harassment is common:

> One out of every four officers in Illinois (26.2%) and one in six in Ohio (14.9%) stated that they had [witnessed racial harassment]. If one extrapolates these percentages back to the base populations from which they were drawn, one can appreciate the magnitude of the harassment and its potential for the alienation of minority citizens.[81]

Sexual harassment was not reported as often:

> Six percent of the officers surveyed in Ohio stated that they had witnessed sexual harassment, and 8.6 percent of the respondents in Ohio agreed. These percentages sound relatively small until one recognizes that they are incidents where one officer (1) witnesses another officer display this behavior, and (2) is willing to tell an interviewer he or she witnessed the behavior. In other words, situations where officers won't come forward, and incidents where officers acted alone—more likely occurrences—aren't reported.[82]

These studies are important because they look at police deviance from a realistic perspective. Cases of officers selling drugs, stealing evidence, and committing crimes are relatively rare in comparison to less extreme examples of police deviance. Sleeping on the job, sexual misconduct, harassment, and similar behaviors are perhaps easier to commit without getting caught. In addition, they may be viewed as relatively minor when compared to some of the more serious examples of deviance and corruption cited earlier in this chapter. The studies just cited probably cannot be generalized to all law enforcement officials or police departments, but they provide some needed insight into the extent of the problem.

Controlling Police Deviance

Perhaps the best control for police deviance is to screen out applicants who are unfit for the job. Obviously, though, this approach has failed on more than one occasion. A remaining option is to constantly remind officers of how they should act when presented with ethical dilemmas. This is accomplished through the promotion of professional standards and through police codes of ethics.

If we move away from policing and focus on corruption throughout the public sector, we find a large body of literature about prevention.[83] One scholar advocates treating corruption as a disease.[84] First, the disease has to be identified (Stage One). Once the disease has been identified, so-called Stage Two and Stage Three responses can be crafted (Table 14-3).

Professional Standards. As policing has matured over time, most of the rampant corruption we witnessed in the past has subsided. Continued reinforcement of professional standards, however, is critical. Joycelyn Pollock, one of the country's experts on police ethics, offers a number of sugges-

Table 14-3 • The "Medical" Response to Corruption

	Stage Two: Fighting "Ordinary" Corruption	Stage Three: Fighting Systemic Corruption
Key metaphor	Controlling corruption.	Subverting corruption.
Medical analogy	Strengthen the body to prevent the disease from taking hold. Examples: exercise, nutrition, lifestyle.	Attack the disease itself. Examples: antibiotics, chemotherapy, surgery.
Use analysis to find out	Where healthy systems are vulnerable and how to strengthen them.	Where organized corruption is itself vulnerable and how to weaken it.
Some key analytical questions	How are agents selected? How is the principal-agent-client relationship structured? What are the incentives? How can discretion be clarified and circumscribed? How can accountability be enhanced? How can the moral costs of corruption be increased?	How are corrupt deals made and kept secret? How are corrupt goods and services delivered? How are members recruited and disciplined? What "footprints" are there from corrupt activities? How can risks and penalties be created or enhanced? How can corrupt activities be carried out with impunity, and where are they vulnerable?
Draw inspiration from	Best practices in business management; public health programs.	Best practices in fighting organized crime: pathology and medicine.
Key functions in the fight against corruption	Audit, systems design, incentive and personnel systems, control, citizen oversight.	All of these, *plus* undercover agents, infiltrators, turncoats and key witnesses, "dirty tricks."
Key actors in the fight against corruption	People who run the system. The "principal" (metaphorically, the people; in practice, the people in charge).	People who can influence and, if necessary, subvert the corrupt system. Citizens, professional associations, the press, business groups, some government agencies or levels of government.

Source: R. Klitgaard, "Stages two and three in the fight against corruption," *Finance and development* (June 2000), 37 (2), http://www.imf.org.

Former NYPD Commissioner Bernard Kerik leaves the U.S. District Courthouse in White Plains, New York, in late 2007 after being indicted on federal tax fraud and corruption charges related to his business dealings. Why is it necessary for police leaders to keep their personal lives unsullied?

Reuters/Mike Segar/Landov Media

tions in this regard.[85] She couches these in terms of some simple questions for officers to answer. The first is the so-called **first-page test**. The question is, "How would you feel if your action appeared on the front page of the newspaper?" The second question is, "How will you feel about your action when looking back on it?" Finally, "Would you consider your action fair if you were each of the other parties involved?" Or, put differently, "Did you treat others the way you would want to be treated?"[86] Pollock goes on to note:

first-page test
A series of questions proposed by Joycelyn Pollock that police officers can ask themselves to reinforce professional ethical standards.[v]

> These questions are sometimes overlooked when making day-to-day decisions. Thoughtful policing involves being sensitized to the ethical nature of decision-making and, if being egotistic at times, at least recognizing such actions for what they are.[87]

Pollock also points out that police officers, as professionals, need to distinguish between good police work and what it means to be a good person. The two do not always go hand in hand. "Good" police officers are those who make many arrests, catch criminals, and so on. But Pollock notes that "being a 'good' officer may be contradictory to being a 'good' person, and the good people who become officers may be distressed to find that being a good person is not 'good enough.'"[88] So police officers must be constantly aware that being a good person is part of being a good officer. It is not all about making good busts at all costs. Indeed, one of the hallmarks of a profession is abiding by certain standards of conduct, and that means following the rules and upholding the law.

WEB PATROL 14-8
Education, Training, and Ethical Dilemmas
http://www.mycrimekit.com

WEB PATROL 14-9
Law Enforcement Ethics
http://www.mycrimekit.com

Codes of Ethics. Those police departments that do not train their officers how to act when presented with ethical dilemmas can at least adopt appropriate codes of ethics. The professional associations that many officers are affiliated with (such as the Fraternal Order of Police) have them.

In fact, most professions have ethical codes of one form or another. Doctors, nurses, and attorneys have them. Even the authors of this textbook have to abide by ethical codes either established through their place of employment or promulgated by the professional associations with which they are affiliated (such as Academy of Criminal Justice Sciences).

Police codes of ethics come in various forms, but they are similar to some extent. All emphasize providing service to the community, respecting people's legal rights, maintaining an unsullied private life, and preventing personal feelings and biases from entering into decision making, among other things. See the first ethics box in Chapter 1 for a sample police code of ethics.

SUMMARY

- The Wickersham (1929) and Knapp Commissions were credited with uncovering police deviance. The Wickersham Commission, in its report, *Lawlessness in Law Enforcement*, found that the "third degree," or "the inflicting of pain, physical or mental, to extract confessions or statements," was "extensively practiced across the country."
- Scholars have proposed several typologies of police deviance. Some focus on forms of corruption, while others focus on types of deviance. Gratuities (that is, gifts) are perhaps the most minor form of deviance. Some people don't regard them as deviance at all but rather as relationship builders. Police sexual misconduct includes everything from consensual sex on duty to rape. The ongoing "war on drugs" presents significant temptations to officers to step over the line.
- Incidents in Miami and Los Angeles provide some of the best-known examples of police corruption, but Philadelphia, Boston, San Francisco, and other large cities have seen their share of similar problems.
- Two theories of police deviance were offered in this chapter. The rotten apple theory argues that deviance is primarily the result of a few rogue officers. Environmental theory attributes deviance to peer pressure and other organizational factors. The true extent of police corruption remains elusive, rather like the dark figure of crime. Police deviance, however, can be controlled through rigorous hiring procedures, professional standards and training, and codes of ethics.

COMING FULL CIRCLE

For Discussion

Return to the questions posed at the start of this chapter. Have any of your answers changed since you read the chapter? What portions of this chapter helped you answer these questions?

Writing Assignment

Using material from this chapter and additional resources, write a 500-word essay in response to one of the questions presented at the beginning of the chapter. Submit your essay to your instructor if asked to do so.

KEY TERMS AND NAMES

abuse of authority
Buddy Boys
corruption
corruption of authority
deviance
economic corruption
first-page test
grass eater
gratuity
internal payoff
kickback
Knapp Commission
meat eater
Miami River Cops
Mollen Commission
noble-cause corruption
no-fix law
occupational deviance
opportunistic theft
perversion of justice
police corruption
police crime
police sexual violence
police violence
Powell v. Alabama
predatory corruption
Rampart Division scandal
rogue
rotten apple theory
shakedown
straightforward corruption
straight shooter
subjugation of defendants' rights
Type I drug corruption
Type II drug corruption
use corruption
white knight

WEB INTERACTIVITY

Visit John Jay College's journal, *Criminal Justice Ethics*, on the Web at http://www.lib.jjay.cuny.edu/cje/html/cje.html. Click on "Sample Articles," and read the articles that are available. Identify those articles that relate to the materials covered by this chapter. Submit your observations to your instructor if asked to do so.

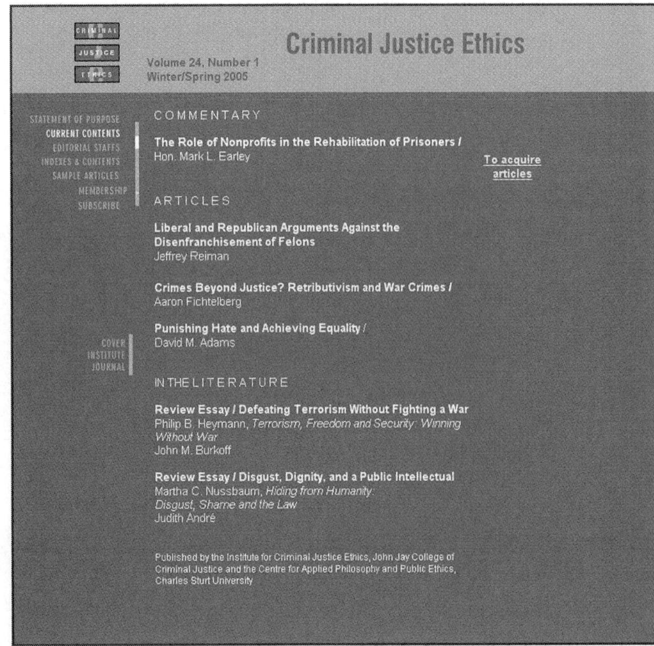

Institute for Criminal Justice Ethics, John Jay College/CUNY

REVIEW QUESTIONS

1. What did the Wickersham and Knapp Commissions investigate? What did they find? What sources of information were especially important to commission members?
2. Describe the typologies of police deviance discussed in this chapter, and give examples of each.
3. List and describe some infamous instances of police deviance.
4. What explains police deviance? How common is it? How can it be controlled?

chapter fifteen
THE USE OF FORCE

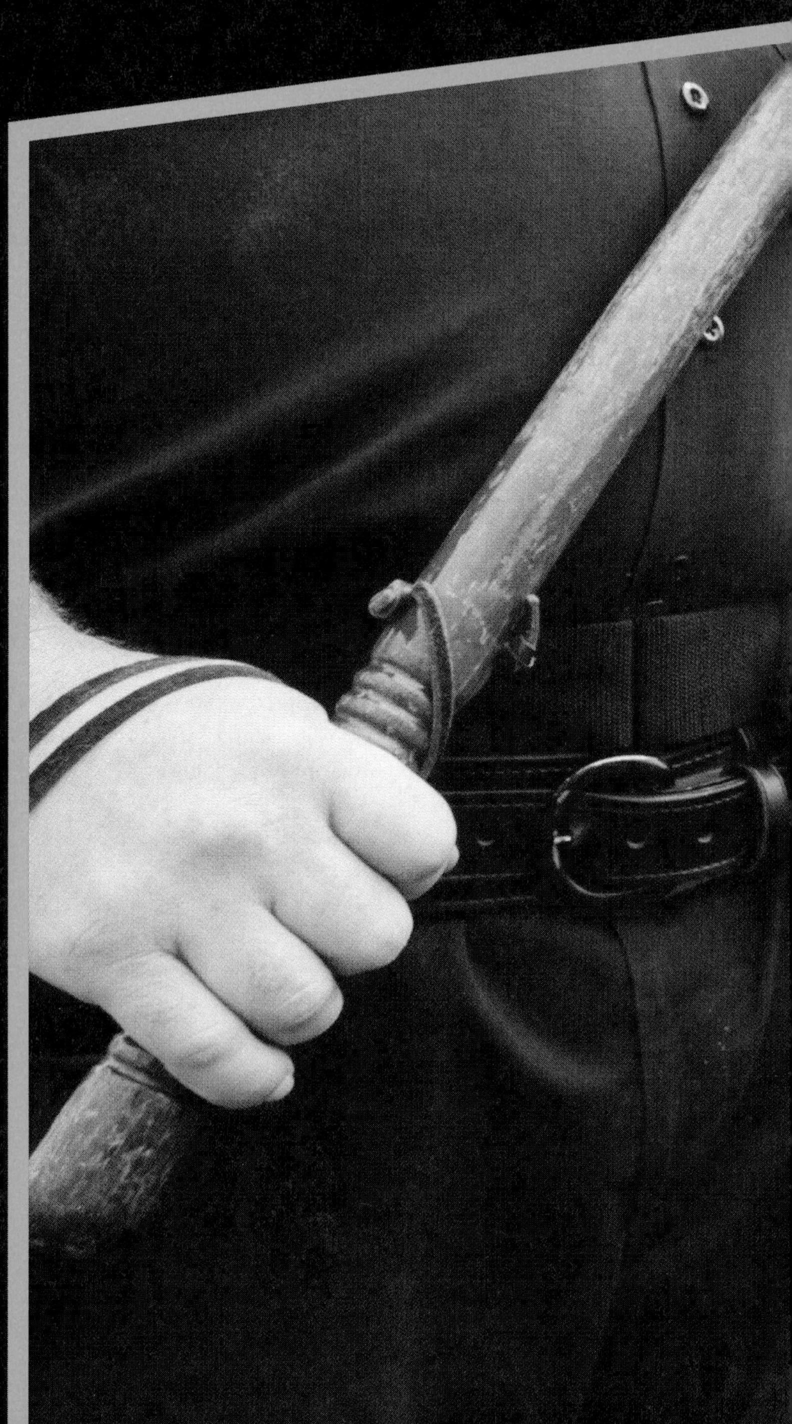

LEARNING OBJECTIVES

After reading this chapter, students should be able to:

1. Identify the various levels of force, explain how they are controlled by policy, and describe their applications in police work.
2. Describe legal standards associated with the use of deadly force by law enforcement officers, explain the patterns of deadly force, and describe the problem of suicide by cop.
3. Describe legal standards governing nondeadly force, including less-lethal weapons.
4. List three types of excessive force and describe perspectives on the frequency of excessive force.

THINK ABOUT IT

Police brutality cases have been on the rise since the terrorist attacks of September 11, 2001, and federal prosecutors are targeting an increasing number of abusive officers. Brooklyn, New York, tops the list, with 11 criminal prosecutions of police officers during the first 10 months of fiscal year 2007.[1] Several other cities, including Milwaukee; Jackson, Mississippi; New Orleans; Chicago; and Cleveland, have seen a similar upsurge in uncalled for police violence. On the whole, U.S. Justice Department statistics show a 25 percent increase in the incidence of police brutality between 2001 and 2007. The vast majority of police abuse cases are never prosecuted, so the real numbers could be even higher.

One explanation that has been offered for this trend is the growing difficulty that police departments face in finding qualified police officer applicants, partially because of the war in the Middle East. Throughout the country, many agencies have been forced to revise their recruitment policies or lower their standards to fill vacancies. Age, height, and weight requirements have been relaxed; test standards have been revised; hiring bonuses are being offered; and some agencies have become more tolerant of recruits' past drug use.[2] Since many police officers and applicants are steadily being drawn into military service, agencies have had to ramp up their hiring efforts. This raises some interesting questions to keep in mind as you read this chapter:

1. Does a nationwide increase of 25 percent in police brutality cases over a six-year period seem significant?
2. If police brutality has risen substantially since the terrorist attacks of September 11, can those events somehow be blamed?
3. To what extent have relaxed recruitment standards affected police brutality?
4. If it is necessary to relax police hiring standards to meet the realities of police recruiting today, then at what point do we draw the line?

INTRODUCTION

use of force
The use of physical restraint by a police officer when dealing with a member of the public.[i]

Police **use of force** is defined as the use of physical restraint by a police officer when dealing with a member of the public.[3] Law enforcement officers are authorized to use the amount of force that is reasonable and necessary given the circumstances. Most officers are trained in the use of force and typically encounter numerous situations during their careers when the use of force is appropriate—for example, when making some arrests, restraining unruly combatants, or controlling a disruptive demonstration. Force may involve hitting; holding or restraining; pushing; choking; threatening with or using a baton, a flashlight, or chemical or pepper spray; restraining with a police dog; using a Taser or a similar energy weapon; or threatening with or using a gun.

WEB PATROL 15-1
Analysis of Police Use-of-Force Data
http://www.mycrimekit.com

excessive force
"The application of an amount and/or frequency of force greater than that required to compel compliance from a willing or unwilling subject."[ii]

A more complex issue is the use of *excessive* force. The International Association of Chiefs of Police defines **excessive force** as "the application of an amount and/or frequency of force greater than that required to compel compliance from a willing or unwilling subject."[4] When excessive force is employed, the activities of the police often come under public scrutiny and receive attention from the media and legislators. A police officer's use of excessive force can also result in lawsuits by members of the public who feel that they have been treated unfairly. Whether the use of excessive force is aberrant behavior on the part of an individual officer or is the practice of an entire law enforcement agency, both the law and public opinion generally condemn it.

Kenneth Adams, an expert in the use of force by police, notes that there is an important difference between the terms *use of excessive force*, such as shoving or pushing when simply grabbing a suspect would be adequate, and the *excessive use of force*, which refers to the phenomenon of force being used unacceptably, often on a department-wide basis. The distinction "deals with relative comparisons among police agencies, and there are no established criteria for judgment."[5] The *use of excessive force* and the *excessive use of force* may also be distinguished from the *illegal use of force*, which refers to situations in which the use of force by police violates a law or statute.[6]

Excessive force can be symptomatic of **problem police officers.** Problem officers are those who exhibit problem behavior, as indicated by a large number of citizen complaints, frequent involvement in use-of-force incidents, and other evidence.[7] The **Christopher Commission,** which studied the structure and operation of the Los Angeles Police Department (LAPD) in the wake of the **Rodney King** beating, found a number of "repeat offenders" on the force.[8] According to the commission, approximately 1,800 LAPD officers were alleged to have used excessive force or improper tactics between 1986 and 1990. Of these officers, more than 1,400 had only one or two allegations against them. Another 183 officers had four or more allegations, 44 had six or more, 16 had eight or more, and one had 16 such allegations. The commission also found that, generally speaking, the 44 officers with six complaints or more had received positive performance evaluations that failed to record "sustained" complaints or to discuss their significance.

problem police officer
An officer who exhibits problem behavior, as indicated by a large number of citizen complaints, frequent involvement in use-of-force incidents, and other evidence.[iii]

Christopher Commission
The commission that studied the structure and operation of the Los Angeles Police Department in the wake of the Rodney King beating incident.

Rodney King
A suspect whose videotaped beating by members of the Los Angeles Police Department led to civil unrest across the nation.

THE USE OF FORCE

Recall that *use of force* and *use of excessive force* are not one and the same. Most of this chapter is concerned with the legitimate use of force. We save the discussion of improper force for the end of the chapter. What, then, are the types of force? When can force be used? How often do officers use force? What distinguishes deadly force from nondeadly force? What are the rules governing an officer's use of force? We answer these and related questions in the next few sections.

Levels of Force

Whether police officers use force properly or improperly, seven levels of force have been identified:

WEB PATROL 15-2
Early Detection of the Problem Officer
http://www.mycrimekit.com

1. *Mere presence.* It is believed that the simple presence of an officer, the embodiment of the authority of the state, will deter dangerous and criminal behavior.
2. *Verbalization.* When officers speak, they are taught to do so persuasively. If verbalization doesn't work, officers move on to more forcible options.

A protestor is arrested in New York City during the 2004 Republican National Convention. When is police use of force legitimate?

3. *Command voice.* An officer's command voice is more vibrant than his or her speaking voice, and the officer's request takes the form of an order: "Sir, I asked you for your vehicle papers once. Now I'm *telling* you to give them to me *now*."
4. *Firm grips.* These are physical grips on the body directing a suspect when and where to move. They are not intended to cause pain.
5. *Pain compliance.* These tactics seek the suspect's compliance by causing pain. They should not cause lasting physical injury.
6. *Impact techniques.* Impact techniques may involve physical contact or the use of chemical spray or stunning weapons.
7. *Deadly force.* This is force that is capable of killing the suspect. Examples include the "sleeper hold" (a choke-hold which can interfere with a person's breathing), the "bar arm control hold" (in which the forearm is squeezed against the neck to cut off the flow of air), and the use of guns.[9]

Our concern in this chapter is primarily with the last two types of force. These are the most likely to result in the injury or death of a suspect. Moreover, of all of the levels of force, they attract the most attention. All too often, it seems, bystanders record what they perceive to be police brutality. Sometimes such recordings *do* reveal brutality. Other times, though, untrained bystanders may fail to understand that what an officer did to apprehend a resistant suspect followed the police agency's policy to the letter.

WEB PATROL 15-3

Citizen Complaints about Police Use of Force
http://www.mycrimekit.com

Use-of-Force Policy

force continuum
The spectrum of force available to a police officer, from the absence of physical force to the use of a deadly weapon.

Justifiable force is not applied arbitrarily. Police officers are trained to use only the necessary level of force to gain control over a situation or to subdue an unruly suspect. Sometimes they are taught a **force continuum**, or use-of-force continuum. Other times their policy manuals contain elaborate descriptions of proper and improper force. Some agencies combine both approaches. Figure 15-1 contains some force-related terminology that will help you work through this section.

Figure 15-1 • Force-Related Terminology

Suspect resistance

No resistance. Suspect was cooperative and followed all verbal instructions given by the officer.

Slight resistance. Suspect resisted the officer's actions, and the officer had to use strong directive language or minimal force (skills) to encourage suspect to cooperate and follow directions.

Moderate or high resistance. Suspect impeded officer's movement or resisted cuffing or placement in a car This level of resistance required the officer to use arm/wrist locks or distraction techniques or fighting skills to gain compliance and control.

Violent or explosive resistance. In this, the most extreme, level of resistance, the suspect struggled or fought violently and required the officer to (1) use fighting skills to disengage, (2) use a chemical agent, baton, or firearm, or (3) continue fighting to gain control. In some cases in this resistance category, the officer decided that he or she needed to use weapons or other special tactics to gain control instead of engaging the suspect directly.

Officer force

No force. Officer used typical verbal commands.

Slight force. Officer had to use strong directive language or minimal physical force to encourage the suspect to cooperate and follow directions.

Forcibly subdued suspect with hands. Officer used an arm/wrist lock, takedown, block, punch, or kick, or struck or wrestled the suspect.

Forcibly subdued suspect using methods other than hands. Officer used chemical agent, baton, gun, or other special tactics or weapons.

Source: G. P. Alpert and R. G. Dunham, "The force factor: Measuring police use of force relative to suspect resistance," in *Use of force by police: Overview of national and local data* (Washington, DC: Bureau of Justice Statistics, 1999), p. 55. Full report available at http://www.ojp.usdoj.gov/bjs/abstract/ufbponld.htm (accessed July 21, 2008).

Figure 15-2 • Use-of-Force Continuum

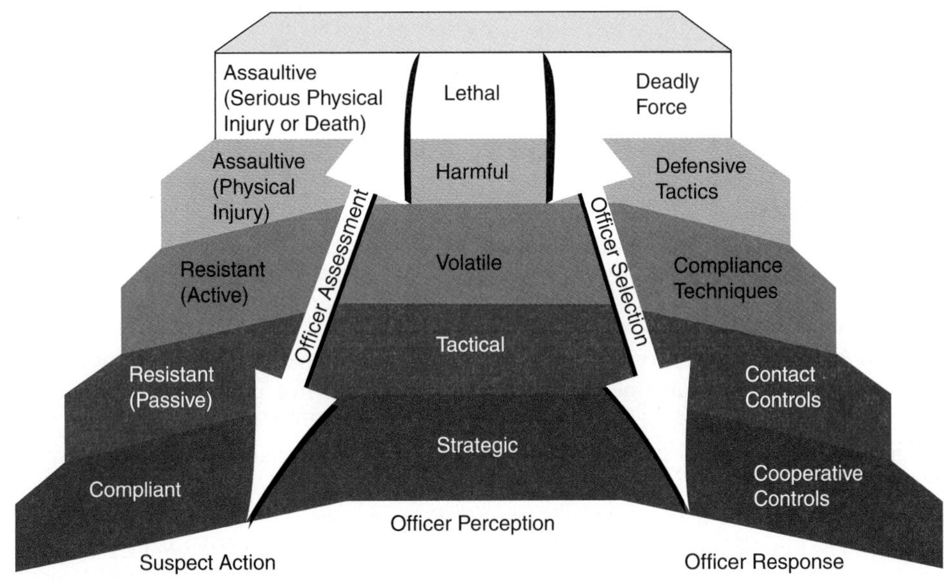

Source: Federal Law Enforcement Training Center, Department of Homeland Security.

An example of a use-of-force continuum, this one from the Federal Law Enforcement Training Center (FLETC), appears in Figure 15-2. The left side looks at the suspect's action. The right side looks at the appropriate response the officer should use. So, for example, if the suspect is compliant, an officer should only use "cooperative controls." These include verbal commands. At the other end of the continuum, if the officer perceives that the suspect is assaultive and likely to inflict serious injury or death, deadly force is justified.

Another force continuum appears in Table 15-1. This one is from the Phoenix (Arizona) Police Department. Seven categories of suspect behavior are listed alongside seven categories of police response. No resistance should equate with no force. Passive resistance, such as laying down and obstructing a road or entrance to a facility, should be met with control and restraint, sometimes coupled with arrest and use of handcuffs. Finally, a suspect who wields a firearm could very likely be shot—and justifiably so.

More often than not, law enforcement agencies adopt use-of-force policies that are far more detailed and restrictive than the force continuums just presented. The Allegan County (Michigan) Sheriff's Office, for example, limits use of force as follows:

> It is the policy of the Sheriff's Office to employ in all situations only those levels of force that are reasonable and necessary to control behavior of the offender. Reasonable and necessary levels of force are those levels that permit the officer to restrain or control the offender while maintaining

Table 15-1 • Phoenix Police Department Force Continuum

Police	Suspects
0. No force	0. No resistance
1. Police presence	1. Psychological intimidation
2. Verbal commands	2. Verbal noncompliance
3. Control and restraint (handcuffs)	3. Passive resistance
4. Chemical agents	4. Defensive resistance
5. Tactics and weapons[a]	5. Active aggression
6. Firearms/deadly force	6. Firearms/deadly force

[a]Includes all physical tactics and weapons except chemical agents and firearms.

Source: J. Garner and others, *Understanding the use of force by and against the police* (Washington, DC: National Institute of Justice, 1996), p. 5.

a high level of safety for themselves, their fellow officers, and the public. Reasonable physical force may be used in the following situations:

1. Self-defense.
2. To protect, defend or aid fellow officers.
3. To protect, defend or aid civilians or prisoners.
4. To prevent a person from harming themselves whether intentionally, recklessly or accidentally.
5. To prevent a crime or escape.
6. To effect an arrest.
7. To maintain public order or stop a disturbance.
8. To protect or preserve evidence or a crime scene.[10]

Additionally, the agency's policy manual explains in detail what type of force can be used and when. A list of suspect actions is provided, along with proper responses deputies can use. This portion of the Allegan County (Michigan) Sheriff's Office policy manual appears in Figure 15-3.

force factor
The level of force used by a police officer relative to the suspect's level of resistance.

In a study reported in 2001, police experts Geoffrey Alpert and Roger Dunham found that the **force factor**—the level of force used by the police relative to the suspect's level of resistance—is a key element to consider in attempting to reduce injuries to both the police and suspects.[11] The force factor is calculated by measuring both the suspect's level of resistance and the officer's level of force on an equivalent scale and by then subtracting the level of resistance from the level of police force used. Results from the study indicate that, on average, the level of force that officers use is closely related to the type of training that their departments emphasize.

Applications of Force

The National Institute of Justice estimates that nearly 45 million people nationwide have face-to-face contact with the police over a typical 12-month period and that approximately 700,000 of them are subjected to the use of force or the threat of force.[12] When handcuffing is included in the definition of force, the number of people subjected to force increases to 1.2 million, or slightly more than 2.5 percent of those having contact with the police. Other studies show that police use weaponless tactics in approximately 80 percent of use-of-force incidents and that half of all use-of-force incidents involve merely grabbing or holding the suspect.[13]

Studies show that police use force in fewer than 20 percent of adult custodial arrests. Even in instances where force is used, the police primarily use weaponless tactics. For example, a study of more than 7,000 police arrests in Phoenix revealed that no weapon was displayed, much less used, in about 95 percent of the arrests (see Table 15-2).[14] In addition, female officers are less likely to use physical force and firearms and are more likely to use chemical weapons (mostly pepper spray) than are their male counterparts. The use of weapons by suspects, a decidedly different issue, is detailed in Table 15-3.

Who is most likely to experience police force? Perhaps not surprisingly, males, African Americans, and younger people are most likely to experience force:

> Blacks (4.4%) and Hispanics (2.3%) were more likely than whites (1.2%) to experience use of force during contact with police in 2005. Blacks accounted for 1 out of 10 contacts with police but 1 out of 4 contacts where force was used. Persons age 16 to 29 (2.8%) who had contact with police were more likely than those over age 29 (1.0%) to have had force used against them. Persons age 16 to 29 made up a smaller percentage of persons who had a police contact (34.5%) compared to the percentage of persons experiencing force during a contact (60.3%). The median age of those experiencing force was 26.[15]

The nature of the contact is also associated with whether force is used. People whose contact was initiated by the police were much more likely to see force used. Indeed, about 80 percent of the contacts involving use of force were initiated by the police. This, too, is not surprising because police-initiated contacts are those where officers generally witness a criminal act or a person they suspect of having committed a crime. Sometimes these suspects flee, and force is required to stop them.

Figure 15-3 • Sample Use-of-Force Policy

INACTIVE RESISTANCE

Subject Action: Inactive Resistance

Resistance may include psychological intimidation or verbal resistance (blank stares, clenching of fists, verbal disagreement, for example). The subject complies, however, with verbal attempts to control.

Officer Response: Presence or Verbal Direction

The presence of a uniformed officer or verbal direction alone may control the incident.

PASSIVE RESISTANCE

Subject Action: Passive Resistance

The subject does not attempt to defeat the officer's attempts to touch or control but will not voluntarily comply with verbal or physical attempts to control (dead weight, does not listen to verbal commands).

Officer Response: Compliance Controls

The officer responds with soft empty-handed techniques. They may inflict pain and are used to gain control (joint locks, pressure points). They are used when verbal orders have not been effective and the subject does not comply with lawful orders. Selection of a reasonable control method is critical in this situation.

ACTIVE RESISTANCE

Subject Action: Active Resistance

The subject attempts to prevent an officer from gaining control (pulling or pushing away, blocking). This is not an attack against the officer, but an overt attempt to keep the officer from gaining control.

Officer Response: Physical Controls

The officer responds with hard empty-handed techniques, chemical agents, or electromuscular disruption (strikes, takedowns, chemical agents, Advanced Taser). Based on the totality of circumstances, controls available, and officer's ability, the control response may vary.

ACTIVE AGGRESSION

Subject Action: Active Aggression

The subject initiates physical actions or assaults against an officer or another person with less than deadly force (challenging, punching, kicking). The resistance is aimed specifically against another person or the officer.

Officer Response: Intermediate Controls

The officer responds with an intermediate weapon like an impact weapon or less-than-lethal munitions (baton, 12-gauge less-than-lethal munitions).

DEADLY FORCE ASSAULT

Subject Action: Deadly Force Assault

The subject uses deadly force against an officer or another person, which may result in great bodily harm or the loss of human life.

Officer Response: Deadly Force

The officer responds with deadly force, which may result in great bodily harm or the loss of life. A deadly force assault leaves little room for officer response options; he or she must act immediately to stop the assault and to neutralize the threat.

Source: Allegan County (Michigan) Sheriff's Office, "Use of force," February 11, 2004, http://www.less-lethal.org/docs/30/Policy (accessed July 21, 2008).

Table 15-2 • Weapons Threatened, Displayed, or Used by Police in 7,512 Arrests

	Used		Displayed or Used		Threatened, Displayed, or Used	
	Arrests	Percentage of Arrests	Arrests	Percentage of Arrests	Arrests	Percentage of Arrests
No weapon involved	7,354	97.9	7,151	95.2	7,130	94.9
Weapon involved	158	2.1	361	4.8	382	5.1
All arrests	7,512	100.0	7,512	100.0	7,512	100.0
Type of weapon[a]						
None	7,354	97.9	7,151	95.2	7,130	94.9
Baton	15	0.2	39	0.5	43	0.6
Flashlight	41	0.5	72	1.0	73	1.0
Handgun	11	0.1	202	2.7	204	2.7
Chemical agent	88	1.2	118	1.6	130	1.7
Rifle/shotgun	7	0.1	31	0.4	32	0.4
Motor vehicle	15	0.2	21	0.3	21	0.3
Canine	20	0.3	31	0.4	37	0.5
Other	19	0.3	19	0.3	19	0.3

[a]Because some arrests involved the use, display, or threatened use of more than one weapon, the percentages under Type of weapon do not add up to 100 percent.

Source: J. H. Garner and C. D. Maxwell, "Measuring the amount of force used by and against the police in six jurisdictions," *Use of force by police: Overview of national and local data* (Washington, DC: Bureau of Justice Statistics, 1999), p. 31, http://www.ncjrs.gov/pdffiles1/nij/176330-2.pdf (accessed July 21, 2008).

Table 15-3 • Weapons Threatened, Displayed, or Used by Suspects in 7,512 Arrests

	Used		Displayed or Used		Threatened, Displayed, or Used	
	Arrests	Percentage of Arrests	Arrests	Percentage of Arrests	Arrests	Percentage of Arrests
No weapon involved	7,460	99.3	7,411	98.7	7,367	98.1
Weapon involved	52	0.7	101	1.3	145	1.9
All arrests	7,512	100.0	7,512	100.0	7,512	100.0
Type of weapon[a]						
None	7,460	99.3	7,411	98.7	7,367	98.1
Stick	17	0.2	31	0.4	56	0.7
Knife	18	0.2	34	0.5	42	0.6
Handgun	12	0.2	29	0.4	47	0.6
Chemical agent	5	0.1	5	0.1	7	0.1
Rifle/shotgun	5	0.1	14	0.2	16	0.2
Motor vehicle	14	0.2	14	0.2	15	0.2
Canine	4	0.1	4	0.1	6	0.1
Other	9	0.1	14	0.2	17	0.2

[a]Because some arrests involved the use, display, or threatened use of more than one weapon, the percentages under Type of weapon do not add to 100 percent.

Source: J. H. Garner and C. D. Maxwell, "Measuring the amount of force used by and against the police in six jurisdictions," in *Use of force by police: Overview of national and local data* (Washington, DC: Bureau of Justice Statistics, 1999), p. 32, http://www.ncjrs.gov/pdffiles1/nij/176330-2.pdf (accessed July 21, 2008).

DEADLY FORCE

Generally speaking, **deadly force** is force that is likely to cause death or significant bodily harm. *Black's Law Dictionary* adopts a more general definition, namely "force that may result in the death of the person against whom the force is applied."[16] According to a report released by the Bureau of Justice Statistics in 2001, the number of justifiable homicides by police averages nearly 400 per year.[17]

deadly force
Force that is likely to cause death or significant bodily harm.

The use of deadly force by law enforcement officers, especially when it is *not* considered justifiable, is one area of potential civil liability that has received considerable attention in recent years. Historically, the "fleeing-felon rule" applied to most U.S. jurisdictions. It held that officers could use deadly force to prevent the escape of a suspected felon, even when that person represented no immediate threat to the officer or to the public. This, as we will see, has changed.

WEB PATROL 15-4
Excessive Force 101
http://www.mycrimekit.com

Legal Standards

The 1985 U.S. Supreme Court case of ***Tennessee v. Garner***[18] specified the conditions under which deadly force can be used to apprehend a suspected felon. Edward Garner, a 15-year-old suspected burglar, was shot to death by Memphis police after he refused their order to halt and attempted to climb over a chain-link fence. In an action initiated by Garner's father, who claimed that his son's constitutional rights had been violated, the Court held that the use of deadly force by the police to prevent the escape of a fleeing felon could be justified only where the suspect could reasonably be thought to represent a significant threat of serious injury or death to the public or to the officer and where deadly force is necessary to effect the arrest. In reaching its decision, the Court declared that "[t]he use of deadly force to prevent the escape of *all* felony suspects, whatever the circumstances, is constitutionally unreasonable."

Tennessee v. Garner
The 1985 U.S. Supreme Court case that specified the conditions under which deadly force could be used to apprehend suspected felons.

More specifically, the Court ruled that deadly force may be used when two criteria are present: (1) It is necessary to prevent the suspect's escape, and (2) the officer has probable cause to believe that the suspect poses a serious threat of death or serious physical injury to others. Given the nature of the *Garner* case, one would think the Court would have handed down a unanimous decision, but three justices dissented, noting that the statute struck down by the majority "assist[s] the police in apprehending suspected perpetrators of serious crimes and provide[s] notice that a lawful police order to stop and submit to arrest may not be ignored with impunity."[19] In any case, to further grasp the reach of *Garner*, it is important to consider the notion of what kind of offender poses a "serious threat." Courts will generally consider present and/or past dangerousness.

Present Dangerousness. According to Victor Kappeler of Eastern Kentucky University, "[A] dangerous suspect is, generally, an armed suspect who can inflict serious physical harm."[20] As such, suspects who are armed with a deadly weapon, be it a gun, knife, or other object, can safely be considered dangerous. Moreover, the weapon must be capable of inflicting death or serious bodily harm. Fingernail clippers, for example, cannot be considered a deadly weapon.

It is not enough that the suspect be merely armed for deadly force to be justifiably used. In addition, the danger posed by the suspect must be *immediate*. If, for example, the suspect is armed with a gun, the gun must be pointed at a police officer or some other individual. Deadly force may not be considered justified if the suspect's hand is not raised (or being raised) into the shooting position. In one illustrative case, one of the federal district courts concluded that the police used deadly force inappropriately in killing a woman (Hegarty) when

> Hegarty repeatedly asked the officers to leave, but she neither threatened them nor did she fire any shots while the officers were present. In fact, the officers decided to enter Hegarty's home forcibly only after it appeared that she had put down her rifle. Hegarty did not threaten injury to herself at any time, nor were there other individuals in danger.[21]

WEB PATROL 15-5
Curbing Police Brutality: What Works?
http://www.mycrimekit.com

Past Dangerousness. A suspect can also pose a serious threat based on his or her past conduct or based on the nature of the crime in question. It is easier to defend deadly force against suspects who have committed murder, armed robbery, and similar offenses, in contrast to less serious offenses like burglary or motor vehicle theft. These less serious offenses, in general, do not enhance the police authority to use deadly force.

It should be emphasized that only a handful of courts have permitted deadly force based solely on past dangerousness, and the U.S. Supreme Court has never sanctioned such action. In fact, a federal circuit court of appeals has held that the use of deadly force to apprehend a suspect charged with a serious crime is unconstitutional.[22] For example, if a suspect committed robbery but was then confronted by the police and, following their orders, raised his hands, he could not then be shot.

Finally, if police are going to defend deadly force based on past dangerousness, then the serious offense that the suspect is alleged to have committed must have been committed in the recent past. In other words, officers should avoid deadly force if too much time has elapsed between the crime and the use of deadly force. For example, if a police officer used deadly force based solely on the fact that a suspect committed homicide several months ago, the officer's actions would probably be considered unconstitutional. This is especially true if the officer could have used other methods besides the use of deadly force to apprehend the suspect.

Federal Policy. In 1995, following investigations into the actions of federal agents at the deadly siege of the Branch Davidian compound at Waco, Texas, and the tragic deaths associated with a 1992 FBI assault on antigovernment separatists in Ruby Ridge, Idaho, the federal government announced that it was adopting an "imminent danger" standard for the use of deadly force by federal agents. The imminent danger standard restricts the use of deadly force to situations in which the lives of agents or others are in danger. When the new standard was announced, federal agencies were criticized for not adopting it sooner. The federal deadly force policy, as adopted by the FBI, contains the following elements[23]:

> *Defense of life.* Agents may use deadly force only when necessary—that is, only when they have probable cause to believe that the subject poses an imminent danger of death or serious physical injury to the agent or to others.
>
> *Fleeing subject.* Deadly force may be used to prevent the escape of a fleeing subject if there is probable cause to believe that the subject has committed a felony involving the infliction or threatened infliction of serious physical injury or death and that the subject's escape would pose an imminent danger of death or serious physical injury to the agents or to others.
>
> *Verbal warnings.* If feasible, and if doing so would not increase the danger to the agent or to others, a verbal warning to submit to the authority of the agent should be given prior to the use of deadly force.
>
> *Warning shots.* Agents may not fire warning shots.
>
> *Vehicles.* Agents may not fire weapons solely to disable moving vehicles. Weapons may be fired at the driver or other occupant of a moving motor vehicle only when the agent has probable cause to believe that the subject poses an imminent danger of death or serious physical injury to the agent or to others and when the use of deadly force does not create a danger to the public that outweighs the likely benefits of its use.

Patterns of Deadly Force

Studies of killings by the police have often focused on claims of discrimination—that is, that African American and minority suspects are more likely to be shot than whites. But research has not provided solid support for such claims. While individuals shot by police are more likely to be minorities, an early study by criminologist James Fyfe found that police officers will generally respond with deadly force when mortally threatened and that minorities are considerably more likely to use weapons in assaults on officers than are whites.[24] Complicating the picture further, Fyfe's study showed that minority officers are involved in the shootings of suspects more often than other officers, a finding that may be due to the assignment of minority officers to poor inner-city areas. However, a later study by Fyfe, which analyzed police shootings in Memphis, Tennessee, found that African American property offenders were twice as likely as whites to be shot by police.[25]

Although relatively few police officers ever fire their weapons at suspects during the course of their careers, those who do may become embroiled in social, legal, and personal complications. It is estimated that in an average year, 600 suspects are killed by police officers in America, while another 1,200 are shot and wounded, and 1,800 are shot at and missed.[26] The personal side of police shootings is well summarized in the title of an article that appeared in *Police Magazine*. The article, "I've Killed That Man Ten Thousand Times," demonstrates how police officers who have to use their weapons may be haunted by years of depression and despair.[27] According to author Anne Cohen, all departments did to help officers who had shot someone was to "give him enough bullets to reload his gun." The stress and trauma that police officers suffer from having shot someone are now being realized, and many departments have developed mechanisms for dealing with them.[28]

Suicide by Cop

Police officers have particular difficulty dealing with instances of **suicide by cop**, in which individuals who are determined to die engage in behavior that causes responding officers to resort to deadly force. On March 10, 2005, for example, John T. Garczynski, Jr., a father of two preteen boys, died in a hail of 26 police bullets fired by officers who had surrounded his vehicle in a Boca Raton, Florida, condominium parking lot.[29] Garczynski, a Florida Power and Light Company employee, appeared to have been despondent over financial problems and the breakup of his marriage. The night before his death, Garczynski met his wife at a bowling alley and handed her a packet containing a suicide note, a typed obituary, and a eulogy to be read at his funeral. After he left, Garczynski's wife called police, and officers used the help of a cell phone company to locate Garczynski. As deputies surrounded Garczynski's 2003 Ford Explorer, he attempted to start the vehicle. One of the officers yelled "Freeze," and then "Let me see your hands." It was at that point, deputies said, that Garczynski pointed a gun at them and they fired.

suicide by cop
An incident in which an individual who is determined to die engages in behavior meant to provoke responding officers to resort to deadly force.

Rebecca Stincelli, author of the book *Suicide by Cop: Victims from Both Sides of the Badge*,[30] says that an incident like the one involving Garczynski can be devastating for police officers. "In the past, people have used rope, a gun, gas, jumped off a building. A police officer is just another method," says Stincelli. "They say it's nothing personal. [But] they are wrong. It's very personal" for the officers involved.[31] The FBI notes that "suicide-by-cop incidents are painful and damaging experiences for the surviving families, the communities, and all law enforcement professionals."[32]

A study of fatal shootings by Los Angeles police officers found that an astonishingly large number—more than 10 percent—could be classified as suicide by cop.[33] Recently, researchers have identified three main categories of suicide by cop: direct confrontations, in which suicidal subjects instigate attacks on police officers for the purpose of dying; disturbed interventions, in which potentially suicidal subjects take advantage of police intervention in their suicide attempt in order to die; and criminal interventions, in which criminal suspects prefer death to capture and arrest.[34]

Several steps for managing suicide-by-cop scenarios have been suggested:

- Contain the area, while remaining aware that too close a containment may allow the precipitator [the suicidal person] to provoke a deadly confrontation.
- If time and circumstances allow, make a clear demand for compliance—a demand that will usually be ignored.
- Ask the person what he or she wants (specifically, ask if they are trying to die).
- If family, friends, or acquaintances of the subject are present, ask if they are aware of the subject's mental health history, chemical dependency or any criminal record.
- Remain a good listener, while avoiding making promises or committing to anything.
- Use a less-than-lethal weapon only as a diversionary tactic before making a planned attempt to apprehend but never as a stand-alone tactic, as the use of such devices without an immediate attempt to apprehend may in fact escalate the situation.[35]

It may seem silly to ask the apparently suicidal individual about his or her intentions, but failure to do so can result in needless death:

> While the individual shot by police may have committed a suicidal act, he may not have been suicidal. In fact, the offender's physical survival probably did not enter his thought processes at the moment he made his fateful decision. Instead, this person was momentarily indifferent to the consequences of his threatening behavior. Rather than suicide by cop, he committed "death by indifference."[36]

WEB PATROL 15-6

Understanding the Prevalence and Severity of Force Used by and against the Police
http://www.mycrimekit.com

NONDEADLY FORCE

nondeadly force
Force that is unlikely to cause death or significant bodily harm.

We defined *deadly force* as force that is likely to cause death or significant bodily harm. **Nondeadly force** is basically the opposite: force that is *unlikely* to cause death or significant bodily harm. We cannot safely say that nondeadly force will always prevent injury or preserve loss of life because sometimes—rarely—people die as a result of injuries suffered from nondeadly force. This is more true of so-called less-lethal weapons, which we will introduce shortly, than physical force, although people sometimes die or suffer long-term injury from physical force, too.

Legal Standards

Graham v. Connor
The 1989 U.S. Supreme Court case in which the Court declared that claims of excessive nondeadly force must be judged under the Fourth Amendment's reasonableness clause.

In the 1989 case of ***Graham v. Connor***,[37] the U.S. Supreme Court declared that claims of excessive nondeadly force must be judged under the Fourth Amendment's reasonableness clause:

> [A]ll claims that law enforcement officers have used excessive force—deadly or not—in the course of an arrest, investigatory stop, or other "seizure" of a free citizen should be analyzed under the Fourth Amendment and its "reasonableness" standard.[38]

The Court also said that whether deadly force has been used appropriately should be judged from the perspective of a reasonable officer on the scene and not with the benefit of 20/20 hindsight. The justices wrote, "The calculus of reasonableness must embody allowance for the fact that police officers are often forced to make split-second judgments—in circumstances that are tense, uncertain, and rapidly evolving—about the amount of force that is necessary in a particular situation."[39]

In helping to decide what a reasonable police officer would do, courts need to consider three factors: the severity of the crime, whether the suspect poses a threat, and whether the suspect is resisting or attempting to flee the scene. Generally, if the crime in question is a serious one and the suspect is dangerous or resists arrest, the suspect will have difficulty prevailing with a claim of excessive force.

WEB PATROL 15-7

Understanding the Use of Force by and against the Police in Six Jurisdictions
http://www.mycrimekit.com

WEB PATROL 15-8

Early Warning Systems: Responding to the Problem Police Officer
http://www.mycrimekit.com

YOU DECIDE

Back Me Up

You and your partner are on patrol when a car roars through a red light at a high speed. You give chase. The driver does not pull over right away, yet he does not appear to be evading you. He is just continuing to drive, as if looking for a place to stop. Your partner is getting increasingly agitated and mutters that when he gets his hands on the driver, "He's going to get what he deserves." You know your partner is on edge anyway, as he just went through a nasty divorce and has been having problems at work. As the vehicle finally pulls over, your partner jumps out and says, "Back me up!" He then draws his gun and shouts to the driver, "Get out of the car with your hands up!" The driver, a juvenile, gets out of the vehicle and appears visibly scared. Your partner then yells, "Get on the ground, facedown!" The driver appears confused and does not immediately respond. Your partner takes out his nightstick and, with one hit to the legs, brings the driver to the ground. The driver never fights back or resists, but your partner looks as though he is about to strike another blow. What should you do?

Less-Lethal Weapons

Less-lethal weapons offer what may be a problem-specific solution to potential incidents of suicide by cop, as well as a generic solution to at least some charges of use of excessive force. Less-lethal weapons are designed to disable, capture, or immobilize, rather than kill.

less-lethal weapon
A weapon that is designed to disable, capture, or immobilize, rather than kill.

Efforts to provide law enforcement officers with less-lethal weapons like stun guns, Tasers, rubber bullets, beanbag projectiles, and pepper spray began in 1987.[40] More exotic types of less-lethal weapons are available today. They include snare nets fired from shotguns, disabling sticky foam that can be sprayed from a distance, microwave beams that heat the tissue of people exposed to them until they desist or lose consciousness, and high-tech guns that fire bolts of electromagnetic energy at a target, causing painful sensory overload and violent muscle spasms. The National Institute of Justice says, "The goal is to give line officers effective and safe alternatives to lethal force."[41]

As their name implies, however, less-lethal weapons are not always safe. On October 21, 2004, for example, 21-year-old Emerson College student Victoria Snelgrove died hours after being hit in the eye with a plastic pepper-spray-filled projectile. Police officers had fired the projectile at a rowdy crowd celebrating after the Red Sox won the American League championship. Witnesses said that officers fired into the crowd after a reveler near Fenway Park threw a bottle at a mounted Boston police officer.[42] The following sections look at three families of less-lethal weapons. There are others besides those we discuss here, but these are some of the most widely used.

WEB PATROL 15-9
Less-Lethal Weaponry Case Study (Long Beach, California)
http://www.mycrimekit.com

Conducted Energy Devices. The most popular **conducted energy device (CED)** is the familiar Taser. The most common Taser models are the X26 and M26. The Taser International website explains how the X26 works (the M26 performs similarly):

conducted energy device (CED)
A device that uses electrical shock to incapacitate a suspect. Examples are the Taser and the Sticky Shocker. Also called *electromuscular disruption technology*.

> The Taser X26 uses a replaceable cartridge containing compressed nitrogen to deploy two small probes that are attached to the Taser X26 by insulated conductive wires with a maximum length of 35 feet (10.6 meters). The Taser X26 transmits electrical pulses along the wires and into the body affecting the sensory and motor functions of the peripheral nervous system. The energy can penetrate up to two cumulative inches of clothing, or one inch per probe.[43]

Some Tasers have two modes: "probe" and "touch stun." In the "probe" mode, a cartridge projects and attaches to a suspect's clothing or penetrates the skin with barbs. Between the barbs and the pistol-like Taser unit are two small wires. An electrical charge is then sent down the wires, disabling the suspect. The "touch stun" mode requires the officer to touch the suspect with the unit (similar to a stun gun); wires are not used. For obvious reasons, the "probe" mode is safer for the officer.

Another recently developed conducted energy device is the so-called Sticky Shocker. Developed by Titan, the device is intended to fill the gap between a Taser or pepper spray and impact munitions. (We will discuss pepper spray and impact munitions shortly.) According to its developer,

> The Sticky Shocker idea evolved in response to the need for a nonlethal weapon bridging the gap between kinetic rounds (e.g., rubber bullets, beanbags, wooden batons) and devices designed for use at close-in range, such as electric stun devices with darts and pepper spray (effective only within 5 m) or stun guns (arms-length range). The Sticky Shocker concept puts stun gun technology on a wireless self-contained projectile, allowing temporary incapacitation of a human target at safe, stand-off distance, using a widely accepted 40 mm or 37 mm projectile configuration and conventional launchers. The Sticky Shocker can extend the range of electrical stun technology out to 10 m and potentially further. The projectile contains a battery pack and associated electronics that will impart a short burst of high-voltage pulses. Pulse amplitudes are near 50 kV with pulse widths of a few microseconds and repetition rate between 10 to 15 pulses per second. The pulse characteristics are similar to those of commercial stun guns. The pulses are not lethal but will disable a human target temporarily, with full recovery from impact within a few minutes.[44]

There are some concerns over the use and safety of conducted energy devices. Chapter 6 discussed a *Houston Chronicle* article that criticized the Houston Police Department for its allegedly excessive use of Tasers. Researchers, too, have fixed their sights on CEDs. A recent Police Executive Research Forum study called attention to the need for national guidelines governing their use, particularly the use of Tasers, and the organization offered more than 50 recommendations for proper and safe operation of the devices.[45] Their recommendations included the following:

1. CEDs should only be used against suspects who are actively resisting or exhibiting active aggression or to prevent individuals from harming themselves or others. CEDs should not be used against passive suspects.
2. No more than one officer at a time should activate a CED against a person.
3. When activating a CED, law enforcement officers should use it for one standard cycle (five seconds) and stop to evaluate the situation. If subsequent cycles are necessary, agency policy should restrict the number and duration of those cycles to the minimum activations necessary to place the subject in custody.
4. Training protocols should emphasize that multiple activations and continuous cycling of a CED appear to increase the risk of death or serious injury and should be avoided where practical.
5. Officers should be trained to recognize the limitations of CED activation and should be prepared to transition to other force options as needed.[46]

The need for such guidelines is critical because despite their supposedly nonlethal nature, conducted energy devices *have* been implicated in some deaths. In fact, Amnesty International, the well-known human rights group, has called for a moratorium on Taser use until its risks can be properly assessed. According to the Amnesty International report, which was published in 2006, the number of Taser-related deaths has passed 150.[47] Here is a story of one Taser death from the Amnesty International report:

> Russell Walker, aged 47, died after being tasered by Las Vegas police officers on 7 June 2005. Officers were called to a hotel at 8 p.m. when Walker was reported as creating a disturbance. Officers tasered him when he began to struggle with them, and they then placed him in handcuffs. Once handcuffed, Russell Walker again began struggling and the taser was used again. The taser was used a third and final time when Walker had been placed on a gurney, and he then stopped breathing. He was pronounced dead at hospital at 9 p.m. Although the Las Vegas policy on tasers stipulates that they may not be used on handcuffed suspects, and may not be used multiple times, a grand jury inquest into the death of Russell Walker found that the actions of the officers were justified. The coroner in the case ruled that Russell Walker died of "heart arrhythmia during restraint procedures" and commented that the struggle with officers together with the amount of cocaine Walker had ingested was a "recipe for disaster."[48]

excited delirium
A condition in which a suspect experiences an overdose of adrenaline during a heated confrontation with the police.

weapons continuum
The array of nonlethal and lethal weaponry available to police officers, the selection of which depends on the situation.

impact munitions
Munitions designed to stun or otherwise temporarily incapacitate a suspect or a dangerous individual so that law enforcement officers can subdue and arrest that person with less risk of injury or death to themselves and to others.[iv]

Amnesty International attributes deaths like that described here primarily to the use of Tasers. In the vast majority of cases, however, it appears that the suspects were under the influence of illicit drugs or had heart conditions, and the Taser apparently exacerbated an existing condition. Medical examiners have also attributed some Taser-related deaths (and other deaths in police custody) to a condition known as **excited delirium**, an overdose of adrenaline that can occur in heated confrontations with the police.

Impact Munitions. Earlier in this chapter, we mentioned a force continuum. There is also a **weapons continuum**. Traditional less-lethal technologies require that officers be in close proximity to suspects. Whether employing a baton, a can of pepper spray, or a Taser in "touch stun" mode to get the job done, an officer has to be a few feet from the suspect. Lethal weapons, especially guns, by contrast, do not require close proximity. These devices can be put on a continuum that moves the threat of injury to the officer from low to high. Guns generally present a low risk to officers, whereas batons present a fairly high risk. In response to this problem, less-lethal technologies have been developed that can be used from a distance. Such devices are most commonly called **impact munitions**. According to the National Institute of Justice,

A Taser demonstration gone awry. A Dane County (Wisconsin) sheriff's department sergeant rushes to catch deputy Krist Boldt after Boldt was stunned by an M26 Taser during a demonstration. Boldt, who was expected to fall forward, fell backward instead, injuring his head. When might the use of conducted energy devices like the Taser be appropriate?

Wisconsin State Journal/Craig Schreiner/AP Wide World Photos

> These devices can be fired at a greater distance from the target, thus reducing the risk to officers and the likelihood they will resort to lethal force. . . . Impact munitions are designed to stun or otherwise temporarily incapacitate a suspect or dangerous individual so that law enforcement officers can subdue and arrest that person with less danger of injury or death for themselves and others.[49]

WEB PATROL 15-10

Use of Force, Civil Litigation, and the Taser
http://www.mycrimekit.com

Impact munitions include foam rubber bullets, wooden dowels, beanbags, and other projectiles that are usually fired from 12-gauge shotguns or 37/40-millimeter gas grenade launchers. For example, the 12-gauge launching cap produced by Combined Tactical Systems (CTS) can fire a large rubber projectile from a distance of 75 to 100 meters. Beanbags can also be fired from these types of devices.

The company's 12-gauge point round is another example of a less-lethal technology. According to CTS, "The point target cartridge round delivers a strong blow to the body with the capability to stun individuals without penetrating the body. The round is designed to be fired at the center mass of an adult subject at distances between 10 and 20 meters."[50]

So-called area rounds are 12-gauge shotgun shells full of rubber pellets that deliver strong blows to people without penetrating the body (although they can break the skin). Sponge point grenades and similar projectiles, fired from grenade launchers, also function to subdue unruly individuals. Even rubber pellet–filled hand grenades have been developed. Finally, flash grenades or flash-bang stun hand grenades are available in the law enforcement arsenal. All of these devices pose minimal risk of death, though they can certainly cause injury.

Law enforcement officers need to be careful to use impact munitions from proper distances. When employed from too great a distance, less-lethal weapons can be ineffective. On the other hand, when fired from less than 30 or so feet, these devices can cause serious injury, including broken bones. Death can even occur if the devices are not used as intended. A National Institute of Justice study of 373 incidents involving impact munitions found that eight individuals died as a result of injuries sustained from the weapons.[51] Most of the deaths were caused by broken ribs that pierced the heart or lungs. At least one suspect died as a result of being hit in the neck with a beanbag round. Additional findings from this study appear in Figure 15-4.

Figure 15-4 • Findings from a Study of 373 Incidents Involving Impact Munitions

The Targets

The study found that 181, or nearly half, of the reported 373 incidents involved emotionally disturbed individuals who were armed and showed signs of suicidal intent. The reported incidents also included

- Nonsuicidal but armed individuals in open areas who had refused police orders to drop their weapons (70 incidents)
- Individuals barricaded inside buildings or vehicles (48 incidents)
- Hostage takers (nine incidents)

The data showed the characteristics of those who were shot by law enforcement officers firing impact munitions:

- Most individuals were in their 30s, though ages ranged from 14 to 83.
- Nearly all were men (291 of 315 cases in which gender was recorded).
- Nearly two-thirds were white (200 out of 301 where information on race or ethnic group was included), followed by Hispanics (49) and African Americans (40).

Armed and Dangerous

Subjects were armed in almost 90 percent of the 306 cases for which weapons data were available. (In the few instances where suspects possessed multiple weapons, the researchers counted only the most dangerous one.)

- Cutting instruments (knives, swords, axes, machetes)—50 percent of the 306 cases
- Firearms (handguns, shotguns, rifles)—29 percent
- Blunt instruments (bats, clubs, sticks)—6 percent
- Other objects (rocks, bottles, Molotov cocktails)—4 percent
- No weapon—11 percent

Number of Shots Fired

Law enforcement officers fired one to 141 shots at individual targets. Often, multiple shots were needed to subdue an individual because a single hit by an impact munition was not always immediately effective. In the overwhelming number of cases, however, the number of shots fired was few.

Ten or fewer rounds were fired in 98 percent of the 316 cases for which information was available, five or fewer in 93 percent, and one shot in 38 percent of the cases.

Respondents in 313 of the cases reported on the number of shots that struck their intended target, with the number of hits ranging from one to 13. In one case, the individual being fired at surrendered after the shots missed. Others surrendered when follow-up shots missed but the initial shots hit their target.

Type of Munition Used

The type of impact munition used was identified in 962 of the 969 reported discharges of devices. Of the 21 different types of munitions used, beanbags shot from 12-gauge shotguns were the most common, accounting for 65 percent of all the projectiles fired. Plastic baton rounds were the second most common, used in 28 percent of the cases.

Where Struck

Most often, targets were struck in the abdomen (34 percent) or the chest (19 percent), followed by the legs (15 percent), arms (14 percent), and back (11 percent). Only 2 percent of the impacts were on the head, and only 1 percent each in the groin and neck, the more vulnerable parts of a person's body. Of the 969 reported discharges of impact munitions, 782 resulted in injuries. Of those, more than 80 percent were bruises and abrasions, both relatively minor injuries that may not require medical treatment. Bruises accounted for 51 percent of the injuries, and abrasions added another 31 percent. More serious lacerations accounted for 5.5 percent of the injuries; broken bones accounted for 3.5 percent. Of the 782 injuries, there were 14 instances (1.8 percent) in which the impact munition penetrated the target's skin and caused a more serious injury.

Impacts to the head produced a greater proportion of nonfatal serious injuries than other areas struck. Of the 19 head impacts reported, 14 resulted in a laceration, bone fracture, or penetration wound.

Source: National Institute of Justice, *Impact munitions use: Types, targets, effects* (Washington, DC: National Institute of Justice, 2004), pp. 4–5, http://www.ncjrs.gov/pdffiles1/nij/206089.pdf (accessed July 21, 2008).

pepper spray
A so-called lachrymatory (inflammatory) agent that causes irritation to the eyes and skin. Also called *oleoresin capsicum (OC)*.

Pepper Spray (Oleoresin Capsicum). **Pepper spray**, or oleoresin capsicum (OC), is a so-called lachrymatory (inflammatory) agent that causes irritation to the eyes and skin. Pepper spray, like tear gas, causes the eyes to close tightly and tear up, and it may even cause temporary blindness. It also causes the mucous membranes of the nose, throat, and sinuses to burn and swell, making breathing difficult. OC spray is very effective when used to subdue a resistant suspect. Note that pepper spray is not the same as tear gas. There are two forms of tear gas: chlorobenzylidenemalononitrile (CS) gas and chloroacetophenone (CN) gas. These gases are irritants and are used more often than pepper spray to control unruly crowds, rather than to gain compliance from an individual.

The active ingredient in pepper spray is capsaicin, a derivative of the fruit from plants in the *Capsicum* genus, which includes certain peppers, notably the cayenne pepper—hence the term *pepper spray*. The spray is usually packaged in small pressurized canisters that are carried on the person and can be dispensed quickly to subdue a suspect or for self-defense. The spray is most effective when sprayed in the eyes. Pepper spray, unlike some of the other less-lethal technologies, can be acquired legally by non–law enforcement personnel, but not in all states. Most states that permit its sale have laws that penalize improper use of the spray.

Pepper spray is aptly called a less-lethal weapon because some people *have* died as a result of its use.[52] A study of pepper spray's effectiveness was conducted by researchers at the University of North Carolina.[53] They examined injuries to officers and suspects and complaints of excessive force before and after police departments adopted the use of pepper spray. The researchers found an overall decline in officer injuries, but the decline apparently preceded the introduction of pepper spray, and the effect varied across police departments. The researchers found fewer suspect injuries due to the introduction of pepper spray. Finally, complaints of excessive force declined markedly after pepper spray came into use.

Another study looked at in-custody deaths following the use of pepper spray. Researchers at the University of Texas Southwestern Medical Center identified 63 such cases and concluded, for the most part, that pepper spray was not the culprit. According to one summary of this research,

> For pepper spray to cause death, it would have to make breathing difficult by closing or narrowing the bronchial tubes. The subject would have to struggle to both inhale and exhale. These effects would be noticeable shortly after the application of pepper spray. Yet, except for the two cases in which the subjects were classified as asthmatics, comments regarding breathing (other than "ceased breathing") were found in only five case reports, none of which referred to a struggle to breathe. In none of these cases did death immediately follow pepper spray application.[54]

The researchers went on to conclude that pepper spray did not cause *or* contribute to death in 61 of the 63 identified cases. The two remaining deaths were of asthmatics whose conditions were exacerbated by pepper spray. Table 15-4 contains a summary of the causes of death in these 63 cases.

Table 15-4 • Causes of Death in 63 Cases Where Pepper Spray Was Used

Category	Number of Cases
Category I: clear cut	23
IA: Drugs alone	12
IB: Drugs and disease	4
IC: Positional asphyxia	7
Category II: combined effects	32
IIA: Confrontational situation + drugs	23
IIB: Confrontational situation + disease	5
IIC: Confrontational situation + drugs and disease	4
Category III: outliers (uncategorizable)	6
Category IV: asthma	2
Total cases examined in study	**63**

Source: National Institute of Justice, *The effectiveness and safety of pepper spray* (Washington, DC: National Institute of Justice, 2003), p. 9.

Positional asphyxia, which is mentioned in the table, sometimes occurs when suspects are placed, usually with handcuffs behind their backs, in a prone position. The position sometimes makes breathing more difficult.

On the subject of positional asphyxia, researchers at the University of California, San Diego, measured the effects of both pepper spray and a placebo spray on police recruits who were then placed in either a sitting position or in the "hogtie" (feet and hands bound behind the back) position.[55] The study found that pepper spray alone does not cause respiratory problems in either position. It should be noted, however, that the study participants were healthy police recruits and that they were allowed to wear goggles to minimize the harmful effects of the pepper spray. Even so, it is safe to say that pepper spray is likely the safest less-lethal weapon, especially when compared to some of the other weapons we have discussed in this chapter.

Indirect Force

We touched on issues related to pursuit driving in Chapter 8. They are worth revisiting here because questions sometimes arise about whether officers went too far in their efforts to apprehend a suspect. Injury could occur to the suspect, but also to innocent bystanders. Either way, one could allege that an officer's decision to pursue effectively amounted to excessive force. This is best understood as **indirect force**, however. It is indirect in the sense that if injury or death occurs, it is not directly at the hands of a police officer, as it would be in the case of a shooting.

indirect force
Actions by an officer that indirectly expose a suspect or an innocent bystander to potential injury but that do not involve the intentional application of direct physical force. A high-speed automobile pursuit is an example.

Some U.S. Supreme Court cases are illustrative. In *Brower v. County of Inyo* (1989),[56] for example, Brower stole a vehicle and led the police on a high-speed chase over a 20-mile stretch of highway. Officers used an 18-wheeler to block both lanes of the highway on which Brower was driving. They also pointed the headlights of their police cars in Brower's direction, hoping to blind him. Brower crashed into the roadblock and was killed, and the police were subsequently sued by Brower's family members, who alleged that the roadblock violated Brower's Fourth Amendment rights. The U.S. Supreme Court ruled that "Brower's independent decision to continue the chase can no more eliminate [the officers'] responsibility for the termination of his movement effected by the roadblock than Garner's independent decision to flee eliminated the Memphis police officer's responsibility for the termination of his movement effected by the bullet."

WEB PATROL 15-11
Police Attitudes toward Abuse of Authority
http://www.mycrimekit.com

In other words, the Court found that the law enforcement officers involved in setting up the roadblock had seized Brower within the meaning of the Fourth Amendment.

In *County of Sacramento v. Lewis* (1998),[57] a patrol officer witnessed a motorcycle approaching at breakneck speed. A sheriff's deputy gave chase. During the pursuit, the motorcyclist lost control and tipped over. The pursuing deputy was unable to bring his cruiser to a halt before running into the crashed motorcycle and killing its operator. Representatives of the motorcyclist's estate brought a lawsuit against the police, but the U.S. Supreme Court did not see the indirect force applied in this case as excessive:

> Respondents' allegations are insufficient to state a substantive due process violation. Protection against governmental arbitrariness is the core of due process . . . , including substantive due process . . . , but only the most egregious executive action can be said to be "arbitrary" in the constitutional sense . . . ; the cognizable level of executive abuse of power is that which shocks the conscience. . . . In the circumstances of a high-speed chase aimed at apprehending a suspected offender, where unforeseen circumstances demand an instant judgment on the part of an officer who feels the pulls of competing obligations, only a purpose to cause harm unrelated to the legitimate object of arrest will satisfy the shocks-the-conscience test. Such chases with no intent to harm suspects physically or to worsen their legal plight do not give rise to substantive due process liability.

In other words, the pursuing officer could not be held responsible for the motorcyclist's death because the officer did not intend for the man to die, nor could he have reasonably foreseen the outcome of the pursuit.

In a decision welcomed by police officers everywhere, the U.S. Supreme Court recently held, in the case of *Scott v. Harris* (2007),[58] that police officers cannot be sued for their decision to chase fleeing motorists, even if such a chase results in serious injury to the suspect. As the Court put it,

"[A] police officer's attempt to terminate a dangerous high-speed car chase that threatens the lives of innocent bystanders does not violate the Fourth Amendment, even when it places the fleeing motorist at risk of serious injury or death."

EXCESSIVE FORCE AND ABUSE OF AUTHORITY

Recall that excessive force is not the same as use of force. Excessive force is *inappropriate* force. To clarify even further, consider the distinction between ends and means. In our democratic system of government, we are very concerned with process. Applied to policing, *process* refers to the means or procedures police use to perform their jobs. We are nervous about the prospect of giving police unlimited authority. On the other hand, we don't like to ignore the ends either—in other words, crime control. We want police to control crime *and* preserve our liberty. But when the ends become more of a concern than the means, inappropriate or excessive force is a likely result.

Excessive force is not the only form of inappropriate police conduct. It is also possible to abuse one's authority. We saw some examples of this in the preceding chapter. We also looked at the consequences of violating people's legal rights in Chapters 11 and 12. It is important here, however, to point out that in addition to excessive force, abuse of authority is also inappropriate. Abuse of authority, which was defined in the last chapter, can be thought of as something of an umbrella under which excessive force falls. An officer can abuse his or her authority without resorting to physical force. In either case, the end result is a person who is improperly and unjustly made to suffer in one way or another.

Types of Excessive Force

Excessive force and abuse of authority take at least three distinct forms. Neither is quite the same as, say, accepting a gratuity or receiving a kickback (see Chapter 14). Each leads to a measure of discomfort, if not pain or even death, on the part of a criminal suspect—or even an innocent person. Physical brutality, verbal and psychological abuse, and other so-called rights violations are discussed in this section. Think of these as appearing on a continuum that moves from most to least serious.

Physical Brutality. Perhaps the most notorious example of police brutality in recent years is the infamous 1991 Rodney King incident, which was mentioned at the beginning of this chapter. King was stopped for speeding and for fleeing from police. He did not cooperate once he was stopped, and officers applied force to subdue him, but a bystander's video recording of the incident revealed something else. King was hit and kicked more than 50 times, as 27 officers from various agencies stood by. What's more, the beating continued even after King appeared to be under control. King received 11 fractures to his skull, a broken ankle, and several other serious injuries. So serious was the incident that an independent commission, the Christopher Commission (named for Warren Christopher, former deputy attorney general and deputy secretary of state for the United States), was appointed to investigate it—along with other alleged problems in the Los Angeles Police Department. Three officers who were criminally charged in the incident were acquitted in 1992, inciting one of the largest riots in Los Angeles history.

In 2008, LAPD officers were once again criticized by the press for their handling of another incident, an immigration rally. Two officers were reassigned after the incident, but this has not stopped people from trying to connect the dots—from Rodney King to the Rampart Division scandal, to the crackdown at the 2000 Democratic National Convention which took place at Los Angeles' Staples Center. Critics argue that the LAPD is plagued by a warrior culture that, like an ocean liner, is difficult to turn around.[59]

According to Michigan State University criminologist David Carter, physical brutality and excessive force go hand in hand:

> Operationally, this classification [excessive force] includes (1) any officer behavior involving the use of more force than is necessary to effect an arrest or search, and/or (2) the wanton use of any

> degree of physical force against another by a police officer under the color of the officer's office. The key test is whether there was any physical force directly used against an individual with no distinction between injurious and noninjurious incidents with the proposition that the causal variables are the same.[60]

In other words, physical brutality is concerned with the force used, *not* with the end result. This makes sense because some people are more resistant to injury than others, so it would be unfair to ignore applications of excessive force simply because they do not result in injury to the suspect.

Verbal and Psychological Abuse. The old idiom "Sticks and stones may break my bones, but words will never hurt me" couldn't be further from the truth. We know from some high-profile school shootings that words definitely hurt. Any child of a dysfunctional family, even one where physical abuse was never a problem, knows that communication problems and insults can take their toll. There is no reason why police officers should be excused when they engage in verbal abuse. When the things they say and do exclusive of the application of physical force go beyond standards of acceptability, they can be considered abusive. Such actions include everything from insulting suspects to denying them basic necessities during the course of an aggressive interrogation. As Carter observed,

> These are incidents where police officers verbally assail, ridicule, or harass individuals and/or place persons who are under the actual or constructive dominion of an officer in a situation where the individual's esteem and/or self-image [is] threatened or diminished. Also included in this category [verbal and psychological abuse] is the threat of physical harm under the supposition that a threat is psychologically coercive and instills fear in the average person.[61]

There is a fine line between psychological pressure and abuse. Consider police interrogation. Assume that a detective lies to a suspect by saying that an accomplice has implicated him. Is this abuse or just good detective work? On the one hand, it is not a verbal assault, ridicule, harassment, or even a threat of harm. It is, however, something that could instill fear. What if, to take it one step further, the detective *indirectly* threatened the suspect, perhaps by claiming that a jury would surely find him guilty? This type of deception is increasingly common, especially in the wake of the U.S. Supreme Court's famous *Miranda* decision (see Chapter 11). *Miranda* has, for better or for worse, made it more difficult for police to secure confessions. As such, they have had to resort to creative means of doing so, including deception.

Richard Leo, a researcher who has documented this trend, summarized one exchange between a detective and a suspect that illustrates the point:

> Detective: If you take this to a jury trial, they're going to hit you hard. They're going to slam you real hard. He's trying to lie to us, he must think we're stupid. Ladies and gentlemen of the jury, we have the evidence that shows he broke the window. He says "no, I didn't do it." Now do you want to be lenient with this guy?
>
> The suspect interjects: No, I'm not going to go for this one.
>
> Detective: Fine, we'll take it to a jury trial, but they're going to say he's guilty, he's guilty. You had a chance to tell the truth. They'll say: he had a chance. The sergeants talked to him and gave him an opportunity to explain how it happened, to give his side of the story, and what did he do? He lied. That's what he's going to say. He's going to say you lied. You had a chance to tell the truth but you lied. That's exactly what he's going to say.[62]

We are not suggesting that this exchange amounts to abuse, but at what point does deception go too far? This is not an easy question to answer. Gone are the days where psychological pressures were combined with physical force in a mix commonly called the **third degree**, but words alone can go pretty far toward directly harming an individual.

third degree
A formerly common coercive interrogation technique that combined psychological pressures with physical force.

Other Rights Violations. If an officer physically and unnecessarily abuses a suspect during an arrest, there is a clear rights violation that might enable the suspect to claim a violation of the Fourth Amendment right to be free from unreasonable seizures. Likewise, a detective who coerces a suspect into confessing or who violates the suspect's *Miranda* rights also commits a rights violation. Specifically, the detective violates the suspect's Fifth Amendment right to be free from compelled self-incrimination. There are other rights, however, that can also be violated without physical abuse and in the absence of verbal or psychological abuse. David Carter calls this **legal abuse**:

legal abuse
Any violation of a person's constitutionally, federally, or state-protected rights.[v]

> This form of abuse occurs with greater frequency than the other categories. Legal abuse is defined as any violation of a person's constitutional, federally or state-protected rights. Although the individual may not suffer any apparent psychological damage in the strictest sense, an abuse of authority has nonetheless occurred. In all cases of physical abuse and in many cases of verbal abuse, there will also be a legal question. However, legal abuse can—and does—occur frequently without the other forms.[63]

What if, for example, a police officer pushes a suspect up against a brick wall before conducting a pat-down search, and the suspect bumps his head, causing it to bleed? The injury is by no means serious, and we would probably be remiss to call it brutality. A bystander may not even take notice. But what if the force is unnecessary? If it is not abuse and it is not psychological pressure, what can the suspect do? If the seizure in this case is not justified, what remedies are available? There are not too many (see Chapter 11), but this doesn't make the incident any more acceptable than a full-on physical assault.

Perspectives on the Frequency of Excessive Force

Excessive force and abuse of authority are the exception, not the norm, in police work. This may not have rung true before the civil rights era, when abuses were serious and commonplace, but much has happened since then. The courts have handed down important decisions clarifying constitutional protections. Police departments have changed their policies and training procedures in response to these court rulings and to the rising tide of litigation. The police professionalism movement has also served to rein in misbehavior and to screen out the unfit. There are, of course, exceptions, and just as we have seen police abuses in the past, we will see them again in the future. This raises an important question: Is there cause for concern? We will wrap this chapter up with some yes and no answers to this question.

Perspective 1: Brutality Is Still a Problem. Human Rights Watch asserts that police corruption and brutality are anything but behind us. The organization's report, *Shielded from Justice: Police Brutality and Accountability in the United States*, although published nearly a decade ago, is still available on the organization's website.[64] The report discusses 14 large American cities and presents several noteworthy examples of police officers run amok. Its authors were very critical of big-city policing:

> Police officers engage in unjustified shootings, severe beatings, fatal chokings, and unnecessarily rough physical treatment in cities throughout the United States, while their police superiors, city officials, and the Justice Department fail to act decisively to restrain or penalize such acts or even to record the full magnitude of the problem. Habitually brutal officers—usually a small percentage of officers on a force—may be the subject of repeated complaints but are usually protected by their fellow officers and by the shoddiness of internal police investigations. A victim seeking redress faces obstacles at every point in the process, ranging from overt intimidation to the reluctance of local and federal prosecutors to take on brutality cases. Severe abuses persist because overwhelming barriers to accountability make it all too likely that officers who commit human rights violations escape due punishment to continue their abusive conduct.[65]

Human Rights Watch also criticized the lack of effective accountability mechanisms. We discussed accountability in Chapter 12. While there may seem to be several methods of ensuring police accountability, most apply only in limited circumstances and are reserved for the most egregious of civil rights violations. According to *Shielded from Justice*,

> Victims of police brutality have many options for reporting abusive treatment by officers but little chance of seeing those officers punished or prosecuted. Citizen review agencies are often overwhelmed and understaffed; reporting an abuse to such an agency may, eventually, lead to an investigation, but it is unlikely to result in the offending officer's being appropriately punished. Filing an abuse complaint with a police department's internal affairs unit can be

> intimidating, and police departments' excessive secrecy usually means that the complainant learns nothing about any disciplinary action that may have been taken against the accused officer. Filing a civil lawsuit is an option for some victims, but success rates vary widely from city to city, and typically it is the municipality rather than the officer that is held financially responsible. Also, most victims of abuse correctly perceive that criminal prosecution, either locally or federally, is rarely an option—except in highly publicized cases. As a result, resentment and frustration often exacerbate the original abusive treatment. Because it is an open secret that oversight procedures for police abuse do not function effectively, many abuse victims do not even bother to pursue a complaint at all. This series of factors results in violent officers remaining on the job.

Perspective 2: Brutality Is the Exception. Human Rights Watch, like Amnesty International, has traditionally adopted a liberal political orientation. Since the vast majority of law enforcement officials tend to adopt a more conservative stance, it is no surprise that many disagree with the *Shielded from Justice* report. Although the incidents described in the report did happen, critics feel that Human Rights Watch may have exaggerated the extent of police brutality in the United States, giving the misleading impression that it is somehow rampant. One researcher has argued that it is impossible to put police brutality into context without some attention to how often officers are assaulted or killed. In other words, violent physical altercations between police and citizens are often a two-way street; officers will respond with force if they are attacked. While the following observation was made more than 10 years ago, its message still rings true today:

> While the FBI's civil rights division reports 2,450 complaints involving law enforcement officers in 1989, during the same period, 62,712 law enforcement officers were the victims of assaults. In 1990, there were more than 71,794 assaults against law enforcement officers nationwide, according to the Uniform Crime Reports. Sixty-five officers were killed.[66]

What, then, explains perceptions that police brutality is rampant? These are a few of the possible explanations:

1. The media are responsible. Media accounts of police violence unduly emphasize the exceptional and fail to report on the vast majority of police-citizen encounters where there is no physical altercation. In addition, some media have a liberal bias and seem intent on casting the police in an unfavorable light.
2. Reports of police brutality tell only part of the story. A person who files a complaint of excessive force, for instance, may be airing a contrived complaint against the police. For this reason, many reports of police brutality are found to be unsubstantiated.
3. Citizens and the media are not trained in the use of force and thus cannot discern what is and is not excessive. It may seem abusive to an observer to see a police officer hit a suspect with a nightstick, but the officer may have been trained to do just that under the circumstances.

Some critics have alleged that the media take isolated incidents and spin them into something much bigger. Consider one author's account of the Rodney King incident in Los Angeles:

> When a videotape of LAPD officers raining blows on King filled television screens across the country in March 1991, the news pages began to fill with claims that police brutality had long been rampant in Los Angeles. But police misconduct had not been an important issue for the city's premier news organization, the *Los Angeles Times*. In fact, the *Times* had marginalized the issue for years. Yet when the King video was released to a local television news station, the *Times* helped build the story into a serious crisis for LAPD chief Daryl Gates and played a major role in constructing the brutality problem that would drive Gates from office.[67]

In other words, the *Los Angeles Times* took what was arguably a shameful display of police brutality and made an agenda out of it. It used the incident to move brutality to center stage. In doing so, it gave the impression that the problem pervaded the LAPD when, in fact, the incident was quite isolated given the size of the department, which today employs nearly 10,000 sworn officers. Morale suffered for the whole organization following the Rodney King incident.

SUMMARY

- Use of force and excessive force are not the same thing. Police officers are authorized to use force when necessary, but excessive force is *unnecessary* force. Levels of force range from an officer's mere presence all the way up to deadly force. Use-of-force policies usually refer to a force continuum that describes the appropriate levels of force to use in response to the level of resistance or force used by the suspect. Force is applied infrequently. For example, force is used in less than 20 percent of custodial arrests, to say nothing of encounters that do not result in arrest. The use of excessive force may be symptomatic of problem police officers.
- Deadly force is force that is likely to cause death or significant bodily harm. Strict legal standards govern the use of deadly force. In general, it is unconstitutional for an officer to shoot an unarmed fleeing felon. Such shootings are permissible, however, if the officer has probable cause to believe that the suspect poses a serious risk of danger to others. Roughly 3,600 suspects are shot at by police officers each year. Of these, about 600 die from injuries they receive. Suicide by cop refers to situations in which individuals who are determined to end their lives engage in behavior that causes responding officers to resort to deadly force.
- Nondeadly force is the opposite of deadly force; it is force that is unlikely to cause death or significant bodily harm. Claims of excessive force are judged under the Fourth Amendment's reasonableness clause. Nondeadly force would be excessive if a "reasonable person" would feel it was unreasonable to employ such force in a given situation. Less-lethal weapons, including conducted energy devices, impact munitions, and pepper spray, have been developed as alternatives to (but not replacements for) deadly force. Indirect force, or actions by an officer that indirectly expose a suspect or an innocent bystander to potential injury but that do not involve the intentional application of direct physical force—as in the case of a high-speed automobile pursuit—was also discussed in this chapter.
- Excessive force falls into three general categories: (1) physical abuse, (2) verbal and psychological abuse, and (3) other rights violations. The latter includes constitutional rights violations that result from police actions besides abuse. An example would be a push. There are differing views on whether excessive force is still a problem today. Human Rights Watch and other liberal-minded groups feel that it is. Law enforcement groups and conservative thinkers feel that it is not.

COMING FULL CIRCLE

For Discussion

Return to the questions posed at the start of this chapter. Have any of your answers changed since you read the chapter? What portions of this chapter helped you answer these questions?

Writing Assignment

Using material from this chapter and additional resources, write a 500-word essay in response to one of the questions presented at the beginning of the chapter. Submit your essay to your instructor if asked to do so.

KEY TERMS AND NAMES

Christopher Commission
conducted energy device (CED)
deadly force
excessive force
excited delirium
force continuum
force factor
Graham v. Connor
impact munitions
indirect force
legal abuse
less-lethal weapon
nondeadly force
pepper spray
problem police officer
Rodney King
suicide by cop
Tennessee v. Garner
third degree
use of force
weapons continuum

WEB INTERACTIVITY

Visit the Bureau of Justice Statistics on the Web, and view the page "Use of Force by Police: Overview of National and Local Data," which can be found at http://www.ojp.gov/bjs/abstract/ufbponld.htm. The findings available through that page constitute a joint report by the National Institute of Justice and the Bureau of Justice Statistics. Read through the findings and summarize what they reveal about the extent and nature of police use of force and the circumstances under which force is applied. Submit your summary to your instructor if asked to do so. If the URL doesn't work, try http://www.ncjrs.gov/pdffiles1/nij/176330-1.pdf.

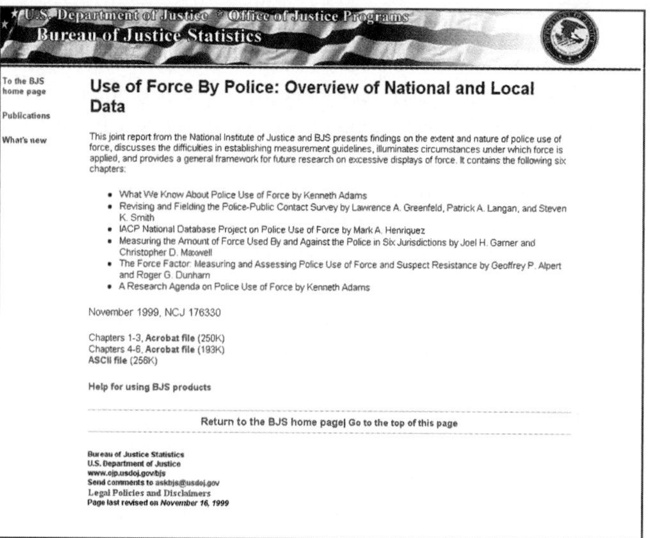

U.S. Department of Justice, Bureau of Justice Statistics

REVIEW QUESTIONS

1. What are the levels of police use of force that this chapter discusses? Which level is most commonly used by police officers?
2. What legal standards govern the use of deadly force by police officers?
3. What legal standards govern the use of nondeadly force by police officers? How might today's less-lethal weapons be effectively employed in place of deadly force?
4. Identify three types of excessive force, and provide examples of each. Do you believe that excessive force is a serious problem in policing today? Explain.

THE FUTURE

SECTION VI

THINK ABOUT IT

In April 2005, three British nationals were charged with plotting to bomb five financial buildings in New York City, New Jersey, and Washington, D.C. The men allegedly served as al-Qaeda scouts and performed reconnaissance on the buildings.[1] The three had been arrested by British authorities in August 2004. Information gathered during the arrest led Homeland Security officials in the United States to convene a press conference at the Citigroup tower in Midtown Manhattan.

The nation was told that known al-Qaeda operatives had conducted surveillance at several large New York financial centers, including the New York Stock Exchange.[2] Officials said that the terrorists may have been planning to use truck bombs targeting Wall Street in an effort to disrupt world financial markets. Tom Ridge, secretary of the Department of Homeland Security, stressed the seriousness of the threat when he told reporters, "This is the most significant, detailed piece of information about any particular region that we have come across in a long, long time, perhaps ever."[3]

In response to the announcement, the New York City Police Department set up barricades and vehicle checkpoints in the financial district and mobilized heavily armed officers who were specially trained in antiterrorism tactics to patrol the area. Downtown city streets took on the embattled look of a city at war. This example of the terrorist threat and the police response to it raises several questions to keep in mind as you read this chapter:

1. Have government officials, including the police, occasionally overreacted to perceived terrorist threats?
2. To what extent should police in America be involved in the "war on terror"?
3. How has American policing been affected by the threat of terrorism?
4. Are the police in the United States adequately equipped to prevent and preempt emerging terrorist threats?

INTRODUCTION

It is difficult to escape the burgeoning worldwide specter of terrorism. For a time, it was tempting to regard terrorism as an international problem of little concern to those of us living in the United States. The events of September 11, 2001, of course, changed that belief forever. Today, the threat of terrorism is real—and ongoing. Few days go by when we don't hear about the latest terror plot or the death of a U.S. soldier in the Middle East. The Department of Homeland Security's terror alert level has remained at or above "Elevated" for years now. This creates a situation that requires law enforcement—and the general public—to maintain a heightened level of vigilance.

Beyond terrorism, there are other emerging problems that local, federal, and international law enforcement organizations must be ready to address. Computer technologies, for example, facilitate criminal collaboration around the globe, leading to an expanding transnational crime problem. The future no doubt holds complex problems in store for law enforcement agencies and their administrators, who must be prepared to address them.

WEB PATROL 16-1

Twenty-First-Century Reality and Law Enforcement
http://www.mycrimekit.com

TERRORISM AND HOMELAND SECURITY

Terrorism is a type of criminal activity that is not unlike other violent crimes that occur in all developed societies. Terrorists who kill are murderers, just like the criminal who kills a victim during a robbery. But terrorism differs from "typical" cases of homicide and property destruction because it tends to have a religious or political motivation, is often international in scope or origin, and is carried out with what the perpetrators consider to be "higher" (not self-centered) goals.

A North Miami Beach (Florida) Police Department dive team member prepares to enter the ocean. Why are special police units, like a scuba diving team, needed in the fight against terrorism?

Jeff Greenberg/Alamy Images

The Problem of Terrorism

Most of us know terrorism when we see it; the events of September 11 were prime examples of terrorism. Even so, there is no single definition of *terrorism*. The Foreign Relations Authorization Act defines terrorism in terms of four main characteristics: premeditation, political motivation, violence, and the fact that it generally targets noncombatants (that is, nonmilitary personnel).[4] An alternative definition has been offered by the Federal Bureau of Investigation (FBI), which defines *terrorism* as

> a violent act or an act dangerous to human life in violation of the criminal laws of the United States or of any state to intimidate or coerce a government, the civilian population, or any segment thereof, in furtherance of political or social objectives.[5]

These definitions are fairly concise. An even more detailed definition, this one from the Immigration and Nationality Act, appears in Figure 16-1.

Criminologist Gwynn Nettler proposes a definition of *terrorism* that consists of six characteristics:

1. *No rules.* There are no moral constraints or standards of what is considered acceptable. In other words, anything goes.
2. *No innocents.* Terrorists do not distinguish between innocents and noninnocents, or civilians and soldiers.
3. *Economy.* The concern is with inflicting as much damage as possible while at the same time scaring even more people (for example, kill one person, terrify 10,000 more).
4. *Publicity.* All terrorist incidents are highly publicized. Terrorists seek publicity in an effort to heighten people's fear levels, weaken economies, and so forth.
5. *Meaning.* Violent acts and the infliction of mass casualties give meaning to terrorists' lives.
6. *No clarity.* The long-term goals of terrorism are either delusional or impossible to implement (for example, Islamic dominance).[6]

Domestic versus International Terrorism. The two main types of terrorism are domestic and international. **Domestic terrorism** is "homegrown" terrorism, or terrorism carried out by an individual or a group that is based in and operating within the country being attacked. Moreover, domestic terrorism is not planned and directed by international actors. The most notorious example of domestic terrorism in the United States is the infamous 1995 bombing of the Oklahoma City federal building by the "homegrown" terrorist Timothy McVeigh.

domestic terrorism
Terrorism carried out by an individual or a group that is based in and operating within the country being attacked.

Figure 16-1 • Terrorist Activity under the Law

(i)

"Terrorist activity" defined

... the term "terrorist activity" means any activity which is unlawful under the laws of the place where it is committed (or which, if committed in the United States, would be unlawful under the laws of the United States or any State) and which involves any of the following:

(I) The hijacking or sabotage of any conveyance (including an aircraft, vessel, or vehicle).

(II) The seizing or detaining, and threatening to kill, injure, or continue to detain, another individual in order to compel a third person (including a governmental organization) to do or abstain from doing any act as an explicit or implicit condition for the release of the individual seized or detained.

(III) A violent attack upon an internationally protected person (as defined in section 1116(b)(4) of title 18) or upon the liberty of such a person.

(IV) An assassination.

(V) The use of any—

(a) biological agent, chemical agent, or nuclear weapon or device, or
(b) explosive or firearm (other than for mere personal monetary gain), with intent to endanger, directly or indirectly, the safety of one or more individuals or to cause substantial damage to property.

(VI) A threat, attempt, or conspiracy to do any of the foregoing. . . .

(iii)

"Engage in terrorist activity" defined

As used in this chapter, the term "engage in terrorist activity" means to commit, in an individual capacity or as a member of an organization, an act of terrorist activity or an act which the actor knows, or reasonably should know, affords material support to any individual, organization, or government in conducting a terrorist activity at any time, including any of the following acts:

(I) The preparation or planning of a terrorist activity.

(II) The gathering of information on potential targets for terrorist activity.

(III) The providing of any type of material support, including a safe house, transportation, communications, funds, false identification, weapons, explosives, or training, to any individual the actor knows or has reason to believe has committed or plans to commit a terrorist activity.

(IV) The soliciting of funds or other things of value for terrorist activity or for any terrorist organization.

(V) The solicitation of any individual for membership in a terrorist organization, terrorist government, or to engage in a terrorist activity.

Source: Immigration and Nationality Act, Public Law 82-414.

international terrorism
The unlawful use of violence by an individual or a group that has some connection to a foreign power or organization.

International terrorism refers to the unlawful use of violence by an individual or a group that has some connection to a foreign power or organization. International terrorism is sometimes mistakenly called *foreign terrorism,* but the latter refers to terrorism that takes place in another country outside the United States. The most prominent example of international terrorism in recent years occurred at various American sites on September 11, 2001. While the acts took place within our borders, they clearly had international origins. A list of State Department–designated foreign terrorist organizations is provided in Figure 16-2.

The events of September 11 tend to overshadow many of the lesser-known and foiled terrorist plots, domestic and otherwise, that have been uncovered in recent years. Domestic cases include the following:

- In Tennessee, the FBI arrested a man whom agents say hated the federal government and was attempting to acquire chemical weapons and explosives to blow up a government building. Demetrius "Van" Crocker, 39, of McKenzie, Tennessee, pleaded not guilty on November 5, 2004. He was found guilty of the charges against him in 2006 and was sentenced to 30 years in prison.[7]

Figure 16-2 • Foreign Terrorist Organizations

1. Abu Nidal Organization (ANO)
2. Abu Sayyaf Group
3. Al-Aqsa Martyrs Brigade
4. Ansar al-Islam
5. Armed Islamic Group (GIA)
6. Asbat al-Ansar
7. Aum Shinrikyo
8. Basque Fatherland and Liberty (ETA)
9. Communist Party of the Philippines/ New People's Army (CPP/NPA)
10. Continuity Irish Republican Army
11. Gama'a al-Islamiyya (Islamic Group)
12. HAMAS (Islamic Resistance Movement)
13. Harakat ul-Mujahidin (HUM)
14. Hizballah (Party of God)
15. Islamic Jihad Group
16. Islamic Movement of Uzbekistan (IMU)
17. Jaish-e-Mohammed (JEM) (Army of Mohammed)
18. Jemaah Islamiya organization (JI)
19. al-Jihad (Egyptian Islamic Jihad)
20. Kahane Chai (Kach)
21. Kongra-Gel (KGK, formerly Kurdistan Workers' Party, PKK, KADEK)
22. Lashkar-e Tayyiba (LT) (Army of the Righteous)
23. Lashkar i Jhangvi
24. Liberation Tigers of Tamil Eelam (LTTE)
25. Libyan Islamic Fighting Group (LIFG)
26. Moroccan Islamic Combatant Group (GICM)
27. Mujahedin-e Khalq Organization (MEK)
28. National Liberation Army (ELN)
29. Palestine Liberation Front (PLF)
30. Palestinian Islamic Jihad (PIJ)
31. Popular Front for the Liberation of Palestine (PFLP)
32. PFLP-General Command (PFLP-GC)
33. Tanzim Qa'idat al-Jihad fi Bilad al-Rafidayn (QJBR) (al-Qaida in Iraq) (formerly Jama'at al-Tawhid wa'al-Jihad, JTJ, al-Zarqawi Network)
34. al-Qa'ida
35. al-Qaida in the Islamic Maghreb (formerly GSPC)
36. Real IRA
37. Revolutionary Armed Forces of Colombia (FARC)
38. Revolutionary Nuclei (formerly ELA)
39. Revolutionary Organization 17 November
40. Revolutionary People's Liberation Party/Front (DHKP/C)
41. Shining Path (Sendero Luminoso, SL)
42. United Self-Defense Forces of Colombia (AUC)

Source: U.S. Department of State, "Foreign terrorist organizations (FTOs)," http://www.state.gov/s/ct/rls/fs/37191.htm (accessed June 23, 2008).

- In April 2004, agents raided a storage facility rented by William Krar and his common-law wife, Judith Bruey. The Noonday, Texas, facility housed enough sodium cyanide to kill everyone inside a 30,000-square-foot building. Krar, described by federal prosecutors as a white supremacist, also had nine machine guns, 67 sticks of explosives, and more than 100,000 rounds of ammunition. He was sentenced to 11 years in prison.
- In 2004, two Utah men described by the U.S. attorney there as "domestic terrorists" pleaded guilty to setting separate arson fires related to ecoterrorism. Justus Ireland, 23, admitted to starting a fire that caused $1.5 million in damage at a West Jordan lumber company and spray-painting "ELF" at the site. (The Earth Liberation Front is discussed in more detail later in this section.)
- In May 2004, the FBI's domestic terrorism unit charged seven members of an animal rights group with terrorism after investigating what they said was a marked increase in crimes to stop the use of animals for product testing. The activists, arrested in New York, New Jersey, California, and Washington, were members of Stop Huntington Animal Cruelty. The group sought to shut down Huntington Life Sciences, a New Jersey product-testing company. In 2008, one of the activists, Diane Jamieson, 60, pleaded guilty to six counts of interference with contractual relationships and was sentenced to 51 weeks in jail on each count but had her sentence suspended and was placed on two years probation.[8]

WEB PATROL 16-2
Psychological Warfare and Terrorism
http://www.mycrimekit.com

WEB PATROL 16-3
A Basis for Middle East Islamic Extremism
http://www.mycrimekit.com

WEB PATROL 16-4
Hostage Taking and Kidnapping in Terrorism
http://www.mycrimekit.com

Examples of international terrorism include the following:

- In 1988, Pan American flight 103 from London to New York was destroyed over Lockerbie, Scotland, by a powerful bomb. All 259 passengers and crew members, and eleven other people on the ground, were killed.
- In 1996, a truck bomb exploded next to a U.S. military barracks in Dhahran, Saudi Arabia, killing 19 U.S. Air Force personnel.
- The first World Trade Center bombing, in 1993, killed four people and blasted a 100-foot-wide hole through four subfloors beneath the towers. Two years later, Sheik Omar Abdel-Rahman and eight other Muslim fundamentalists were convicted on charges of plotting a holy war and planning to commit assassinations and bombings in the United States.

Other Forms of Terrorism. The typical terrorist incident is international rather than domestic. In addition to international and domestic terrorism, there are three other, lesser-known forms of terrorism: **cyberterrorism, narcoterrorism,** and **ecoterrorism**.

cyberterrorism
The use of computers and the Internet to carry out terrorist attacks.

narcoterrorism
The collaboration between drug traffickers and terrorist groups.

ecoterrorism
Terrorism that "involves extremist views on environmental issues and animal rights, and is a fringe-issue form of terrorism aimed primarily at inflicting economic damage on those seen as profiting from the destruction and exploitation of the environment."[i]

Cyberterrorism uses computers and the Internet to carry out attacks. Barry Collin, a senior research fellow at the California-based Institute for Security and Intelligence, first coined the term *cyberterrorism* in the 1980s.[9] The term was later made popular in a report by the RAND Corporation that warned of "new terrorism."[10] The FBI subsequently defined *cyberterrorism* as "the premeditated, politically motivated attack against information, computer systems, computer programs, and data which results in violence against noncombatant targets by subnational groups or clandestine agents."[11]

No major cyberterrorist incidents have occurred to date, but it is easy to imagine some possibilities. An attack against the nation's air traffic control system, for example, could wreak havoc by causing planes to collide in midair, and attacks on power grids could threaten the storage of valuable data. Technological advances appear to have kept these threats contained thus far.

In September 2002, the President's Critical Infrastructure Protection Board published *The National Strategy to Secure Cyberspace,*[12] and in 2003, the National Infrastructure Advisory Council (NIAC) was created pursuant to a presidential directive. According to its charter, the NIAC "shall draw on the expertise of its members so as to provide advice and make recommendations on the following":[13]

1. Enhancing cooperation between the public and private sectors in protecting information systems supporting critical infrastructures in key economic sectors and providing reports on the issue to the President, as appropriate;
2. Enhancing cooperation between the public and private sectors in protecting critical infrastructure assets in other key economic sectors and providing reports on these issues to the President, as appropriate; and
3. Proposing and developing ways to encourage private industry to perform periodic risk assessments of critical information and telecommunications systems.[14]

WEB PATROL 16-5
A Homeland Security Model for Assessing U.S. Domestic Threats
http://www.mycrimekit.com

Narcoterrorism is concerned with the collaboration between drug traffickers and terrorist groups. For example, during 2005, Afghan drug lord Bashir Noorzai was arrested in New York on charges that he attempted to smuggle $50 million worth of heroin into the United States. People have also used the term *narcoterrorism* to refer to attacks by drug traffickers against their governments and law enforcement authorities. These insurgent operations, like that of the Colombia-based Nineteenth of April Movement (M-19), make enforcement of a nation's antinarcotics laws difficult, at best. The true extent of the problem remains unknown, due in part to the clandestine nature of the illicit drug trade. Narcoterrorism also raises a number of questions, such as those posed by noted drug researcher James Inciardi:

- What is the full threat posed by narcoterrorism?
- How should narcoterrorism be dealt with?

- Is narcoterrorism a law enforcement problem or a military one?
- How might narcoterrorism be affected by changes in official U.S. policy toward drugs and drug use?
- Is the international drug trade being used as a tool by anti-American and other interests to undermine Western democracies in a calculated way?[15]

According to one official's testimony before the Senate Foreign Relations Subcommittee on Terrorism, Narcotics, and International Operations, our country is ill prepared to address the problem of narcoterrorism:

> We must recognize that the rules of the crime game have changed. . . . International criminal organizations are challenging governments, permeating societies. They're running roughshod over weak institutions and exploiting gaps in the U.S. and international response. They have the upper hand at the moment and they know it.[16]

While cyberterrorism and narcoterrorism can have a strong international component, this is less true of ecoterrorism. According to one source, "Ecoterrorism involves extremist views on environmental issues and animal rights, and is a fringe-issue form of terrorism aimed primarily at inflicting economic damage on those seen as profiting from the destruction and exploitation of the environment."[17] One well-known ecoterrorist group goes by the name **Earth Liberation Front** (ELF). A website that uses ELF's name but specifically disavows any connection to the unstructured organization states that ELF has no leadership, no membership, and no official spokesperson.[18] The site describes ELF as an underground movement by autonomous and anonymous individuals who use sabotage and guerrilla warfare to stop what it calls the "exploitation and destruction of the natural environment."

Earth Liberation Front (ELF)
An ecoterrorist group.

Readers may recall the 1998 arson attack against a Vail, Colorado, ski resort. On December 15, 2006, Chelsea Dawn Gerlach and Stanilas Gregory Meyerhoff pleaded guilty to setting the fire (as well as several other fires in several western states) that led to some $12 million in damages. Some observers have noted the irony inherent in destroying the Earth to save the Earth. Even Gerlach herself noted that the attacks that she and her colleagues in "the family" (a Eugene-based ELF cell) carried out probably did more harm than good. The ELF movement has by no means been quashed, and the group remains a significant concern to law enforcement officials.

Causes of Terrorism. According to the federal government, the actions of international terrorist organizations can be explained in terms of the five-step process depicted in Figure 16-3.[19] The **National Strategy for Combating Terrorism (NSCT)**,[20] from which Figure 16-3 is drawn,

National Strategy for Combating Terrorism (NSCT)
The U.S. national plan for combating terrorism.

Figure 16-3 • International Terrorist Organizations: The Building Process

Source: National strategy for combating terrorism (Washington, DC: White House, 2003), p. 6.

begins with so-called underlying conditions, which can include everything from poverty and political corruption to religious conflict and civil war. These conditions give terrorists the motivation to act and, in their minds, legitimize violent action. The ongoing war in Iraq continues to fuel terrorists' desire to inflict harm on Americans and their allies, both here and abroad. Terrorists cite certain conditions that the U.S. occupation has brought about as the source of their continuing displeasure with the U.S. presence and their determination to expel all international forces from within Iraq.

The next level on the figure is the international environment. This refers to the fact that terrorist activities like training camps flourish in countries whose borders are free and open. According to the NSCT,[21] "As a result of freer, more open borders, this environment unwittingly provides access to havens, capabilities, and other support to terrorists." Next, terrorism is explained in part by state support:

> Terrorists must have a physical base from which to operate. Whether through ignorance, inability, or intent, states around the world still offer havens—both physical (e.g., safe houses, training grounds) and virtual (e.g., reliable communication and financial networks)—that terrorists need to plan, organize, train, and conduct their operations. Once entrenched in a safe operating environment, the organization can begin to solidify and expand.[22]

Once underlying conditions, the international environment, and state-related conditions become supportive, all that is necessary is proper organization and leadership. The NSCT reports that, "at the top of the structure, the terrorist leadership provides the overall direction and strategy that links all these factors and thereby breathes life into a terror campaign."[23] Part of the U.S. strategy for combating terrorism is, of course, to target terrorist leaders. The ongoing pursuit of Osama bin Laden is a case in point. Some terrorist groups collapse after their leadership is lost, but it would be naïve to assume that groups like al-Qaeda will whither and die in the absence of their leader, when that day comes to pass.

Combating Terrorism. The U.S. government has adopted a so-called 4D strategy for combating terrorism: defeat, deny, diminish, and defend.[24] *Defeat* refers to defeating terrorists and their organizations. *Deny* refers to denial of "sponsorship, support, and sanctuary" to terrorists:

> The strategy to deny sponsorship, support, and sanctuary is three-fold. First, it focuses on the responsibilities of all states to fulfill their obligations to combat terrorism both within their borders and internationally. Second, it helps target U.S. assistance to those states [that] are willing to combat terrorism, but may not have the means. And finally, when states prove reluctant or unwilling to meet their international obligations to deny support and sanctuary to terrorists, the United States, in cooperation with friends and allies, or if necessary, acting independently, will take appropriate steps to convince them to change their policies.[25]

Diminish refers to altering the underlying conditions that terrorists use to justify their attacks. U.S. efforts to resolve regional disputes, foster development, and encourage democracy fall into this category. *Defend* refers to all strategies, both in the United States and abroad, designed to protect our country's interests. We will see shortly how some of this work is being carried out by federal, state, and local law enforcement officials. The military, intelligence agencies, and other entities also combine their efforts to round out the government's concern with defending the United States from (and preventing) future terrorist attacks.

The government has also taken many deliberate, particularly legislative, steps in addition to forming a national strategy to combat terrorism. In the wake of the 1995 Oklahoma City bombing, for example, the **Antiterrorism and Effective Death Penalty Act (AEDPA)** became law. The act's key provisions are as follows:

Antiterrorism and Effective Death Penalty Act (AEDPA)
U.S. legislation enacted in the wake of the 1995 Oklahoma City bombing to combat terrorism.

- Within the United States, it banned fund-raising for and financial support of international terrorist organizations.
- It provided $1 billion for enhanced fighting of terrorism by federal and local officials.
- It allowed foreign terrorist suspects to be deported or to be kept out of the United States *without* disclosure of the evidence against them.

- It sanctioned the use of the death penalty against anyone who commits an international terrorist incident within the United States.
- It made it a federal crime to use the United States as a base for planning terrorist attacks.
- It required that so-called taggants, or chemical markers, be added to certain explosives during their manufacture.
- It ordered a feasibility study on marking other explosives (other than gun powder).[26]

Readers may be more familiar with the USA PATRIOT Act, which is much broader than the AEDPA. We turn our attention to the USA PATRIOT Act now.

WEB PATROL 16-6

Responding to Coordinated Terrorist Attacks
http://www.mycrimekit.com

The USA PATRIOT Act. On September 14, 2001, in response to the September 11 attacks on the World Trade Center and the Pentagon, President George W. Bush declared a state of emergency, which permitted him to invoke certain presidential powers. These powers included the ability to summon reserve troops, marshal military units, and issue executive orders for the implementation of such things as military tribunals. Congress also took action to empower the Justice Department to respond to terrorism by passing the **USA PATRIOT Act** on October 26, 2001, which President Bush signed into law the following day.

USA PATRIOT Act

A federal law (Public Law 107-56) enacted in response to terrorist attacks against the United States on September 11, 2001. The law, officially titled the Uniting and Strengthening America by Providing Appropriate Tools Required to Intercept and Obstruct Terrorism Act, substantially broadened the investigative authority of law enforcement agencies throughout America and is applicable to many crimes other than terrorism. The law was slightly revised and reauthorized by Congress in 2006. Also called the *Antiterrorism Act.*

The act's full title is the Uniting and Strengthening America by Providing Appropriate Tools Required to Intercept and Obstruct Terrorism Act. It is a very long and complex piece of legislation, consisting of ten parts and more than 300 single-spaced pages. Given its staggering size and breadth, the act is a testament to the fact that Congress *can* move quickly when it must.

The USA PATRIOT Act made several important changes to past law and practice:

- It centralized federal law enforcement authority in the U.S. Department of Justice. For example, Section 808 of the act reassigned the authority for investigating several federal crimes of violence from law enforcement agencies like the U.S. Secret Service and the Bureau of Alcohol, Tobacco, Firearms and Explosives to the U.S. attorney general.
- It provided for Central Intelligence Agency (CIA) oversight of all domestic intelligence gathering. Before the USA PATRIOT Act, the CIA was primarily concerned with gathering foreign intelligence.
- It expanded the definition of the terms *terrorism* and *domestic terrorism* to include activities that (1) involve acts dangerous to human life that are a violation of the criminal laws of the United States or of any state; (2) appear to be intended to intimidate or coerce a civilian population, to influence the policy of a government by mass destruction, assassination, or kidnapping, or to effect the conduct of a government by mass destruction, assassination, or kidnapping; and (3) occur primarily within the territorial jurisdiction of the United States.[27]

There were also several noteworthy changes in criminal procedure attributable to the USA PATRIOT Act. Before describing these changes, some background will be informative. First, the U.S. Supreme Court has held that the Fifth and Sixth Amendment rights of due process and access to jury trials apply to all "persons," not just citizens of the United States.[28] In addition, the Court has held that all undocumented aliens living inside U.S. borders are entitled to the protections enunciated in the Bill of Rights.[29] Specifically, the Court has stated that

> the Fifth Amendment, as well as the Fourteenth Amendment, protects every one of these persons from deprivation of life, liberty, or property without due process of law. Even one whose presence in this country is unlawful, involuntary, or transitory is entitled to constitutional protection.[30]

These rights also applied to the exclusion of aliens from within U.S. borders, that is, proceedings for the deportation of aliens had to conform to constitutional requirements, especially due process.[31] In short, legal, illegal, resident, and temporary aliens have historically enjoyed the same constitutional protections as ordinary U.S. citizens. Why does all this matter? In several ways, the USA PATRIOT Act alters and even abolishes constitutional protections historically

Figure 16-4 • Main Titles of the USA PATRIOT Act

Title I—Enhancing Domestic Security against Terrorism—deals with measures that counter terrorism.

Title II—Enhanced Surveillance Procedures—gives increased powers of surveillance to various government agencies and bodies. There are 25 sections, with one of the sections (section 224) containing a sunset clause.

Title III—International Money Laundering Abatement and Anti-Terrorist Financing Act of 2001—creates special measures to deal with terrorist funding.

Title IV—Protecting the Border—ensures adequate personnel for northern and southern borders.

Title V—Removing Obstacles to Investigating Terrorism—provides the U.S. Attorney General with the authority to pay rewards for information on terrorist activities.

Title VI—Providing for Victims of Terrorism, Public Safety Officers and Their Families— expedites payments to public-safety officers involved in responding to terrorist attacks.

Title VII—Increased Information Sharing for Critical Infrastructure Protection—expands of regional information-sharing systems.

Title VIII—Strengthening the Criminal Laws against Terrorism—makes punishable acts of terrorism against mass transportation vehicles and systems.

Title IX—Improved Intelligence—clarifies the role of the director of central intelligence.

Title X—Miscellaneous—authorizes investigations of civil rights violations brought by members of the U.S. Department of Justice.

available to people under the jurisdiction of the United States, including aliens. Space constraints prevent full coverage of all of the relevant changes (see Figure 16-4 for an overview of the act's main sections), but we consider some of them here.

The USA PATRIOT Act also has implications for investigative detentions. Section 412 of the act requires the U.S. attorney general to take into custody any alien whom he or she has "reasonable grounds to believe" is "engaged in any other activity that endangers the national security of the United States."[32] The alien can then be held for seven days, at the end of which he or she must be released, charged criminally, or deported. However, if an alien is detained for purposes related to immigration, rather than suspected criminal activity, he or she can be detained indefinitely. This has been one tool in the war on terrorism; authorities can indefinitely detain illegal immigrants, which obviously raises serious due process concerns.

It is also worth pointing out that the USA PATRIOT Act permits the seizure of certain assets without due process protections. Specifically, Section 106 of the act increases the president's power over the property and assets of foreign persons and organizations. This portion of the USA PATRIOT Act permits the president to "confiscate any property, subject to the jurisdiction of the United States, of any foreign person, foreign organization, or foreign country that he determines has planned, authorized, aided, or engaged in such hostilities or attacks against the United States."[33] The act also allows the president to direct other agencies and individuals to use or transfer such property as he deems necessary.

The USA PATRIOT Act has also given enhanced authority to law enforcement in the name of intelligence gathering. For example, the act modified portions of the Electronic Communications Privacy Act that govern access to stored electronic communications, like email correspondence and voice mail. Wiretap orders, which traditionally were difficult to secure, are now only required to intercept real-time phone communications. As another example of improved intelligence gathering, Section 206 creates so-called roving wiretap authority. This basically abandons a previous requirement that a government eavesdropper make sure the target was actually using the device being monitored. This means that if a suspected terrorist switches cell phones, the government can continue to listen.

The act also amended Title 18, Section 3103, of the U.S. Code to authorize courts to issue search warrants that delay notification of an impending search and that can be executed in the absence of the suspect. This is very different than the typical search warrant scenario, where an announcement is made before the warrant is served, and the occupant is usually present during the search. These "sneak and peek" warrants can be obtained, pursuant to the USA PATRIOT Act, if a court finds "reasonable cause" that by providing advance notification, even right before the search, an "adverse result" could occur. Several other such changes were authorized by the act, all with a common theme of giving investigative authorities broader power to investigate terrorism and related forms of criminal activity.

The USA PATRIOT Act was set to expire at the end of 2005. In March 2006, then-President Bush signed into law a "renewal" of the act that incorporated some changes. On the one hand, various civil liberties protections were written into the new version. Many of these addressed so-called Section 215 requests, which permitted the government to access business and library records. Here are a few examples:

- *Requiring high-level approval and additional reporting to Congress for Section 215 requests for sensitive information like library or medical records.* Without the personal approval of the FBI director, the deputy director, or the official in charge of intelligence, the 215 order for these sensitive categories of records may not be issued.
- *Statement of facts showing relevance to a terrorism or foreign spy investigation required for Section 215 requests.* The conference report requires that a Section 215 application must include a statement of facts demonstrating that the records sought are "relevant" to an authorized investigation to obtain terrorism or foreign intelligence information. This "statement of facts" civil liberty safeguard does *not* exist under current law.
- *Explicitly allowing a U.S. Foreign Intelligence Surveillance Act (FISA) court judge to deny or modify a Section 215 request.* The USA PATRIOT Act conference report explicitly provides a FISA court judge the discretion not only to approve or modify a Section 215 application but also to deny an application.
- *Requiring minimization procedures to limit retention and dissemination of information obtained about U.S. persons from Section 215 requests.* The USA PATRIOT Act conference report requires that the U.S. attorney general create minimization procedures for the retention and dissemination of these data and that the FBI use these procedures.[34]

On the other hand, the act also expanded law enforcement capabilities, especially through the **Combat Methamphetamine Epidemic Act of 2005**. According to the White House,

> This bill introduces commonsense safeguards that will make many ingredients used in methamphetamine manufacturing more difficult to obtain in bulk and easier for law enforcement to track. For example, the bill places limits on large-scale purchases of over-the-counter drugs that are used to manufacture methamphetamines and requires stores to keep these ingredients behind the counter or in locked display cases. It increases penalties for smuggling and selling methamphetamines.[35]

Combat Methamphetamine Epidemic Act of 2005
U.S. legislation that introduced commonsense safeguards that made many ingredients used in methamphetamine manufacturing more difficult to obtain in bulk and easier for law enforcement to track and that increased penalties for smuggling and selling methamphetamine.[ii]

Policing in an Age of Terrorism

September 11, 2001, and the events in its wake have made clear the changed role of American police agencies in a new era of international terrorism. While the core mission of American police departments has not changed, law enforcement agencies at all levels now devote an increased amount of time and other resources to preparing for possible terrorist attacks and to gathering the intelligence necessary to thwart them.

Local police departments play an especially important role in responding to the challenges of terrorism. They must help prevent attacks and respond when attacks occur, offering critical evacuation, emergency medical, and security functions to help stabilize communities following an incident. A recent Police Executive Research Forum (PERF) survey of 250 police chiefs found that the chiefs strongly believe that their departments can

WEB PATROL 16-7
Police Innovation and Crime Prevention
http://www.mycrimekit.com

make valuable contributions to terrorism prevention by using community policing networks to exchange information with citizens and to gather intelligence.[36]

The Council on Foreign Relations, headquartered in New York City and Washington, D.C., agrees with PERF that American police departments can no longer assume that federal counterterrorism efforts alone will be sufficient to protect the communities they serve. Consequently, says the council, many police departments have responded by

- Strengthening liaisons with federal, state, and local agencies, including fire departments and other police departments
- Refining their training and emergency response plans to address terrorist threats, including attacks with weapons of mass destruction
- Increasing patrols and shoring up barriers around landmarks, places of worship, ports of entry, transit systems, nuclear power plants, and so on
- More heavily guarding public speeches, parades, and other public events
- Creating new counterterrorism divisions and reassigning officers to counterterrorism from other divisions, such as drug enforcement
- Employing new technologies such as X-ray-like devices to scan containers at ports of entry and sophisticated sensors to detect a chemical, biological, or radiological attack[37]

The extent of local departments' engagement in such preventive activities depends substantially on budgetary considerations and is strongly influenced by the assessed likelihood of attack. The New York City Police Department (NYPD), for example, which has firsthand experience in responding to terrorist attacks (23 of its officers were killed when the World Trade Center towers collapsed), has created a special bureau headed by a deputy police commissioner responsible for counterterrorism training, prevention, and investigation.[38] One thousand officers have been reassigned to antiterrorism duties, and the department is training its entire 39,000-member force in how to respond to biological, radiological, and chemical attacks.[39] The NYPD has assigned detectives to work abroad with law enforcement agencies in Canada, Israel, Southeast Asia, and the Middle East to track terrorists who might target New York City,[40] and it now employs officers with a command of the Pashto, Farsi, and Urdu languages of the Middle East to monitor foreign television, radio, and Internet communications. The department has also invested heavily in new hazardous materials protective suits, gas masks, and portable radiation detectors.

In November 2004, in an effort to provide the law enforcement community and policymakers with guidance on critical issues related to antiterrorism planning and critical-incident response, the International Association of Chiefs of Police (IACP) announced its **Taking Command Initiative**. The IACP describes the initiative as "an aggressive project to assess the current state of homeland security efforts in the United States and to develop and implement the actions necessary to protect our communities from the specter of both crime and terrorism."[41] Initial deliberations under the initiative led IACP to conclude that "the current homeland security strategy is handicapped by a fundamental flaw: It was developed without sufficiently seeking or incorporating the advice, expertise, or consent of public safety organizations at the state, tribal or local level."[42] Building on that premise, the IACP identified five key principles that it says must form the basis of any effective national homeland security strategy:

Taking Command Initiative
A project undertaken by the International Association of Chiefs of Police to assess the current state of homeland security efforts in the United States and to develop and implement the actions needed to protect American communities from the specter of both crime and terrorism.

- Homeland security proposals must be developed in a local context, acknowledging that local, not federal, authorities have the primary responsibility for preventing, responding to, and recovering from terrorist attacks.
- Prevention, not just response and recovery, must be paramount in any national, state, or local security strategy. For too long, federal strategies have minimized the importance of prevention, focusing instead on response and recovery.
- Because of their daily efforts to combat crime and violence in their communities, state and local law enforcement officers are uniquely situated to identify, investigate, and apprehend suspected terrorists.
- Homeland security strategies must be coordinated nationally, not federally.
- A truly successful national strategy must recognize, embrace, and value the vast diversity among state and local law enforcement and public-safety agencies. A one-size-fits-all approach will fail to secure our homeland.[43]

As IACP recognizes, workable antiterrorism programs at the local level require the effective sharing of critical information between agencies. FBI-sponsored **Joint Terrorism Task Forces (JTTFs)** facilitate this by bringing together federal and local law enforcement personnel to focus on specific threats. The FBI currently has established or authorized JTTFs in each of its 56 field offices. In addition to the JTTFs, the FBI has created Regional Terrorism Task Forces (RTTFs) to share information with local enforcement agencies. Through the RTTFs, FBI special agents assigned to terrorism prevention and investigation meet twice a year with their federal, state, and local counterparts for common training, discussion of investigations, and intelligence sharing. The FBI says that "the design of this non-traditional terrorism task force provides the necessary mechanism and structure to direct counterterrorism resources toward localized terrorism problems within the United States."[44] Six RTTFs are currently in operation: the Inland Northwest, South Central, Southeastern, Northeast Border, Deep South, and Southwest.

Joint Terrorism Task Force (JTTF)
An FBI-sponsored group comprised of federal, state, and local law enforcement personnel who are brought together to focus on a specific threat.

Given the changes that have taken place in American law enforcement since the terrorist attacks of September 11, 2001, some say that traditional distinctions between crime, terrorism, and war are fading and that, at least in some instances, direct military action and civil law enforcement are becoming integrated. The critical question for law enforcement administrators in the near future may be one of discerning the role that law enforcement is to play in the emerging global context.

Federal Agencies and Antiterrorism. The FBI's counterterrorism efforts became especially important following the September 11, 2001, attacks on American targets. Two months after the attacks, then-U.S. Attorney General John Ashcroft announced a major reorganization and mobilization of the FBI and other federal agencies, such as the Immigration and Naturalization Service. Speaking at a press conference in Washington, D.C., Ashcroft said,

> Our strategic plan mandates fundamental change in several of the most critical components of American justice and law enforcement, starting with the organization that is at the center of our counterterrorism effort, the Federal Bureau of Investigation. In its history, the FBI has been many things: the protector of our institutions when they were under assault from organized crime; the keeper of our security when it was threatened by international espionage; and the defender of our civil rights when they were denied to some Americans on the basis of their race, color or creed. Today the American people call upon the Federal Bureau of Investigation to put prevention of terrorism at the center of its law-enforcement and national-security efforts.[45]

Following the attorney general's lead, the FBI reshaped its priorities to focus on preventing future terrorist attacks. This effort is managed by the Counterterrorism Division at FBI headquarters and is emphasized at every field office, resident agency, and legal attaché (Legat) office. Headquarters administers a national threat warning system that allows the FBI to instantly distribute important terrorism-related bulletins to law enforcement agencies and public-safety departments throughout the country. "Flying Squads" provide specialized counterterrorism knowledge and experience, language capabilities, and analytic support as needed to FBI field offices and Legats. To combat terrorism, the FBI's Counterterrorism Division collects, analyzes, and shares information and critical intelligence with various federal agencies and departments—including the CIA, the National Security Agency, and the Department of Homeland Security—and with law enforcement agencies throughout the country.

An essential weapon in the FBI's battle against terrorism is the JTTF. A national JTTF, located at the FBI's Washington headquarters, includes representatives from the Departments of Defense and Energy, the Federal Emergency Management Agency, the CIA, U.S. Customs and Border Protection, the U.S. Secret Service, and U.S. Immigration and Customs Enforcement. In addition, through 66 local JTTFs, representatives from federal agencies, state and local law enforcement personnel, and first responders coordinate efforts to track down terrorists and to prevent acts of terrorism in the United States.

In testimony before Congress in 2005, FBI Director Robert S. Mueller III identified three areas of special concern relative to the bureau's ongoing antiterrorism efforts. First, said Mueller, "is the threat from covert operatives who may be inside the U.S. who have the intention to facilitate or conduct an attack."[46] The very nature of trained covert operatives is that they are difficult to detect.

"I remain very concerned about what we are *not* seeing," Mueller said. Second, Mueller identified a concern "with the growing body of sensitive reporting that continues to show al-Qaeda's clear intention to obtain and ultimately use some form of chemical, biological, radiological, nuclear or high-energy explosives (CBRNE) material in its attacks against America." Finally, said Mueller, "[W]e remain concerned about the potential for al-Qaeda to . . . exploit radical American converts and other indigenous extremists."

Information Sharing and Antiterrorism. The need to effectively share criminal intelligence across jurisdictions and between law enforcement agencies nationwide became apparent with the tragic events of September 11, 2001. Consequently, governments at all levels are today working toward the creation of a fully integrated criminal justice information system.

According to a recent task force report, a fully integrated criminal justice information system is "a network of public safety, justice and homeland security computer systems which provides to each agency the information it needs, at the time it is needed, in the form that it is needed, regardless of the source and regardless of the physical location at which it is stored."[47] The information that is provided should be complete, accurate, and formatted in whatever way is most useful for the agency's tasks. In such a system, information would be made available at the practitioner's workstation, whether that workstation is a patrol car, desk, laptop, or judge's bench. Each agency shares information not only with other agencies in its own jurisdiction but with multiple justice agencies on the federal, state, and local levels. In such an idealized justice information system, accurate information is also available to nonjustice agencies with statutory authority and a legal obligation to check criminal histories before licensing, employment, weapons purchase, and so on.

Although a fully integrated nationwide criminal justice information system does not yet exist, efforts to create one began with the 2003 National Criminal Intelligence Sharing Plan (NCISP). The NCISP was developed under the auspices of the U.S. Department of Justice's Global Justice Information Sharing Initiative and was authored by its Global Intelligence Working Group.[48] Federal, local, state, and tribal law enforcement representatives all had a voice in the development of the plan. The NCISP provides specific steps that can be taken by law enforcement agencies to participate in the sharing of critical law enforcement and terrorism prevention information. Plan authors note that not every agency has the staff or resources needed to create a formal intelligence unit. Even without a dedicated intelligence unit, however, the plan says that every law enforcement organization must have the ability to effectively consume the intelligence available from a wide range of organizations at all levels of government.[49]

boundaryless policing
Any of various technology-based intelligence efforts designed to combat crime and terrorism.

Efforts to share crime- and terrorism-related intelligence can result in what some have called **boundaryless policing.**[50] Examples of boundaryless policing can be found today in the Regional Information Sharing Systems Anti-Terrorism Information Exchange (RISS ATIX) Program and the State and Local Anti-Terrorism Training (SLATT) program, both of which are supported through grants from the Bureau of Justice Assistance.[51] A similar program, the Multistate Anti-Terrorism Information Exchange (MATRIX), ceased operation in 2005 after fielding almost 2 million queries from law enforcement investigators during the two years of its existence.[52]

RISS, a nationwide communications and information-sharing network, serves more than 6,300 law enforcement member agencies from the 50 states, the District of Columbia, the U.S. territories, Canada, Australia, and England. A private, secure intranet (riss.net) connects six RISS centers and their participating law enforcement member agencies.[53] The RISS ATIX, a special aspect of the RISS Program that began operating in 2003, allows for the secure exchange of information between government and nongovernment officials who are responsible for planning and implementing terrorism-related prevention, response, mitigation, and recovery efforts.

The MATRIX project was an Internet-based proof-of-concept pilot program, jointly funded by the Departments of Justice and Homeland Security, to increase and enhance the exchange of sensitive information about terrorism and other criminal activity between enforcement agencies at the local, state, and federal levels. MATRIX used the Factual Analysis Criminal Threat Solution (FACTS) software application, which provides a technology-based investigative tool to facilitate free-form searches of available state and public records. FACTS analyzes and integrates disparate data from many different types of storage systems.[54] The MATRIX system combined data from various sources to which agencies already had access into a single searchable database of 4 billion records. Available records included criminal histories, driver's license data, vehicle registration data, prison/corrections records, digitized photographs, and public data. Using FACTS, investigators were able to conduct searches using incomplete information, such as a portion of a vehicle license number. At the conclusion of the MATRIX pilot program, a number of participating states continued to use the FACTS application.[55]

Finally, the federally funded SLATT Program provides specialized training for active state and local law enforcement personnel in combating terrorism and extremist criminal activity.[56] The SLATT Program has been central to antiterrorism research and training since the bombing of the Alfred P. Murrah Federal Building in Oklahoma City in 1995. SLATT focuses on the prevention of terrorism by training state and local law enforcement officers to understand, detect, deter, and investigate acts of terrorism in the United States by both international and domestic terrorists. Following the attacks of September 11, 2001, SLATT increased its training in the area of international terrorism.

WEB PATROL 16-8

The FBI's Field Intelligence Groups and Police: Joining Forces
http://www.mycrimekit.com

TRANSNATIONAL CRIME AND INTERNATIONAL COOPERATION

Transnational crime is simply crime that crosses international borders. For such crimes to be effectively targeted, governments and law enforcement organizations must band together and collaborate and cooperate with one another. One high-ranking U.S. official explained,

> The United States recognizes that we cannot confront crime in isolation. . . . It is clear crime does not respect international boundaries. It is clear that crime is global. As recent economic trends demonstrate, what happens in one part of the world impacts all the rest. And crime problems and trends are no different.[57]

In this post–cold war era, there is a measure of instability in certain areas around the globe. The fall of the Soviet Union created something of a power vacuum in some regions. Add to that the growing problems throughout the Middle East and what is left is a situation that can easily be exploited by the criminal element. Another U.S. official said,

> The main threat now is transnational organized crime. It comes in many forms: drug trafficking, money laundering, terrorism, alien smuggling, trafficking in weapons of mass destruction, [human trafficking, especially children, and often involving forced prostitution], fraud and other forms of corruption. These problems all have one critical element in common. . . . They threaten the national security of all states and governments.[58]

Toward Multinational Criminal Justice

Most of our understanding of criminal justice, and of the police in particular, is limited to what happens in the United States. But as the previous section made clear, it is critical that we turn our attention beyond U.S. borders. The events of September 11 force us to look outward, but transnational crime is by no means limited to terrorist activity. Just as there is extensive legitimate trade in legal products between nations, so too is there a vast international marketplace in *illegal* goods and services.

In fairness, criminal justice and police scholars have not *ignored* developments abroad. A number of researchers have specialized in what can be called **comparative criminology** or comparative criminal justice. This field, which involves comparing and contrasting the criminal justice institutions and processes between various nations, gives rise to thoughtful reflection on the various approaches to crime taken in this country. Comparative research has yielded valuable insights for decades, but it is as important now as ever. For its continued success, we must overcome ethnocentrism.

comparative criminology
Research that compares and contrasts the criminal justice institutions and processes of various nations.

ethnocentrism
The belief that one's own ethnic group or culture is superior. Also, the tendency to view other ethnicities and cultures through the lens of one's own culture.

Overcoming Ethnocentrism. Many of us are guilty of being ethnocentric with respect to criminal justice. **Ethnocentrism** generally refers either to the belief that one's own ethnic group or culture is superior or to the tendency to view other ethnicities and cultures through the lens of one's own perspective. It is easy to see how ethnocentrism occurs. We are socialized from our birth into a particular culture, and our tendency throughout life—for the most part—is to prefer our culture to others. We consider our native patterns of conduct and behavior to be "natural." This can be extended to our religious practice.

Overcoming ethnocentrism is important for a number of reasons. In terms of law enforcement and criminal justice, we must become receptive and open to the approaches to crime that other countries take. Some approaches we would not want to emulate, but others may be quite attractive. For example, some people feel that the Dutch approach to treating drug abuse as a public health problem, rather than a crime problem, is wise.

Unfortunately, some countries are not always as open as ours is to sharing information and data, and some are downright hostile to researchers. Other countries, while perhaps receptive to academic scrutiny, do not have sufficient data to allow for meaningful research. This can make it difficult to learn of—and from—the approaches to crime that other countries take.

globalization
The internationalization of trade, services, investment, information, and other forms of human social activity.

The Globalization of Crime. We have yet to offer an in-depth definition of transnational crime, but for now it is useful to think of it as being a *product* of **globalization,** which is "the internationalization of trade, services, investment, information, and other forms of human social activity."[59] In other words, there is nothing criminal about globalization, but it is making it easy for both legitimate *and* illegitimate activities to flourish. Boundaries, both geographic and technological, continue to be broken down.

Today's tool of globalization is technology, but globalization occurred long before the advent of computers and telecommunications. Early on, as some nation-states sought to expand their influence, they sent trading expeditions to other nations. Sometimes they would effectively take over, or conquer, those places. Then came rapid travel, which made it easier still to cross national boundaries. The multinational corporations of today are evidence of the continued march toward full globalization. Many a foreign company operates subsidiaries inside U.S. borders—and vice versa.

Thomas Friedman's popular book *The World Is Flat*[60] offers perhaps the most insightful look at the globalization trend. The book's title refers to the fact that the business playing field has been effectively leveled with the advent of technology. The laying of fiber-optic cables across the globe, for example, has made it possible for customer service representatives to answer calls from India. U.S. companies have outsourced at record levels, due in large part to cheaper labor costs in other countries. Turning an eye outward improves a business's competitive advantage. And so it is for the criminal element. Criminals, too, know full well the benefits of an international focus.

WEB PATROL 16-9
Human Trafficking
http://www.mycrimekit.com

transnational crime
Crime that crosses international borders.

Transnational Crime. **Transnational crime** consists of "offenses whose inception, prevention, and/or direct or indirect effects involve more than one country."[61] Throughout the 1980s, for example, during the height of the "war on drugs," trafficking in illegal narcotics between South America and the United States was rampant (and, of course, still is). But more recently, the face of transnational crime has changed so that it now includes *much* more than just the illegal drug trade.[62] As one report put it,

> The world has gotten smaller due to better transportation and the ever-increasing reach of communication technology, and new types of crime that reach across borders have appeared: high tech money laundering; trafficking in weapons, identity papers or cultural artifacts or exotic animals; trafficking in human beings; and terrorism.[63]

What's more, "The enormous resources of transnational organized crime and greater expansion beyond major metropolitan and border areas mean that citizens increasingly are susceptible to their activities."[64]

We now turn our attention to four of the more noteworthy transnational crimes: human trafficking, weapons trafficking, identity theft, and money laundering. The trafficking crimes, because they involve moving people or products illegally from place to place, can clearly be transnational. Identity theft and money laundering, however, need not be transnational, but they are increasingly becoming so.

Human Trafficking The Victims of Trafficking and Violence Protection Act of 2000[65] defines **human trafficking** as follows:

> a) Sex trafficking in which a commercial sex act is induced by force, fraud, [or] coercion, or in which the person induced to perform such act has not attained 18 years of age; or, b) the recruitment, harboring, transportation, provision or obtaining of a person for labor or services, through the use of force, fraud, or coercion for the purpose of subjection to involuntary servitude, peonage, debt bondage or slavery.[66]

human trafficking
"a) Sex trafficking in which a commercial sex act is induced by force, fraud, [or] coercion, or in which the person induced to perform such act has not attained 18 years of age; or, b) the recruitment, harboring, transportation, provision or obtaining of a person for labor or services, through the use of force, fraud, or coercion for the purpose of subjection to involuntary servitude, peonage, debt bondage or slavery."[iii]

How serious is the human trafficking problem? The U.S. government estimates that no fewer than 700,000 people, mostly women and children, are trafficked *each year* into the United States.[67] Of those, some 50,000 people are trafficked for purposes of sexual exploitation.[68] One study in the late 1990s estimated that trafficked women were working in more than 250 brothels in cities across the United States.[69] The second part of the act's definition includes trafficking of agricultural migrant workers and sweatshop workers.

Weapons Trafficking Weapons trafficking is another serious form of transnational crime. The U.S. Department of State has estimated that more than 60 countries produce illegal small arms and light weapons, such as machine guns and shoulder-fired rockets.[70] Moreover, according to the State Department, 4 million people have been killed worldwide with these weapons, in either regional or intrastate warfare.[71] According to the report,

> These weapons are part of the trafficking in goods that make up the large illegal trade internationally. They are sold or bartered into the hands of criminals and terrorists and are often part of trafficking in other illegal goods such as drugs, diamonds, and timber. Small lightweight weapons are in great demand worldwide as a wide range of customers use them: armed groups, militia, and individuals. They are small and relatively easy to conceal in smuggling.[72]

Identity Theft Most of us are familiar with **identity theft,** the unauthorized use of someone else's personal identification information (for example, a Social Security number) to establish new credit lines or for other fraudulent purposes, such as stealing money from the victim's bank account by accessing debit card numbers and pass codes. Identity theft is certainly a serious domestic problem. Increasingly, though, it has taken on an international focus.

identity theft
The unauthorized use of someone else's personal identification information (such as a Social Security number) to establish new credit lines or for other fraudulent purposes, such as stealing money from the victim's bank account.

The reason identity theft is growing in popularity among international criminal groups is because it is a high-profit, low-risk crime. Most victims do not even know that they have been targeted until *after* they are denied credit, are billed for goods or services they did not purchase, or receive calls from collection agencies. Most identity thieves are never caught. The average arrest rate for identity theft is under 5 percent, according to a recent report.[73] When the criminal works in another country, the odds of apprehension become slimmer still.

Not only is identity theft profitable, but it provides a means for terrorists and other criminals to travel in and out of the United States without much difficulty. Fake driver's licenses are commonly secured with stolen information because "with driver's licenses the primary source of identification by Americans, the existence of numerous fraudulent licenses makes movement of criminals and/or terrorists far easier through such things as airport checkpoints."[74] Ongoing changes to passport policies are helping curb this problem to some extent, but much work remains to be done.

Money Laundering Like identity theft, money laundering is not inherently international in scope. Increasingly, though, money laundering has close ties to transnational criminal organizations. Money laundering is basically the conversion of cash generated through illegal channels into legal assets by moving it through financial institutions:

> The purpose in this activity is to conceal the profits generated and to obscure any connection between the criminal activity and the funds. The money launderer deposits illegally gained funds into legal financial systems in multiple deposits and then moves those funds from one institution, company, or even country quickly to dissociate them from the source in a complicated web of difficult to follow transactions.[75]

The money-laundering problem is extensive. In 2001, for example, the Treasury Department seized more than $500 million in laundered money.[76] The International Monetary Fund has estimated that between 2 and 5 percent of the world's gross domestic product is laundered![77] These estimates may even be conservative because many of the deposits are not large enough to trigger mandatory reporting to regulatory agencies like the Internal Revenue Service.

A serious problem for law enforcement officials, both in the United States and abroad, is that of the "shell" bank or corporation, an entity set up to look like a legitimate business but whose sole purpose is to launder illegally obtained cash. Law enforcement faces an uphill battle. The transactions are complex and sophisticated, and financial institutions—especially in other countries—are not always willing to open their doors to investigators.

Policing Transnational Crime. Transnational crime is difficult to police because it is increasingly sophisticated, complicated, and sometimes indistinguishable from traditional crime. As one recent report put it,

> The tools needed to address the threat of transnational crime are more complex than those needed to fight local street crime. Some aspects of organized transnational crime can, on the surface, look like traditional, domestic criminal activity. For example, international prostitution rings involving trafficked women may operate next to local prostitutes, and be indistinguishable to vice officers not trained to recognize a wider criminal enterprise. Similarly, agencies processing non-U.S. citizens may find themselves investigating a forged visa that could lead to identity fraud, money laundering and schemes involving foreign terrorist organizations.[78]

What, then, can law enforcement do? One approach is to rely on international police and crime-fighting organizations, such as Interpol. Another approach, perhaps the most promising, is one we have looked at repeatedly in this book: collaboration. The problem, as one report puts it, is that basic institutional barriers remain: "For example, police agencies have relied historically on information communication channels between departments or with other agencies . . . and may see external agencies as competitors or part of 'turf battles' in an investigation—attitudes and practices that may be difficult to change."[79]

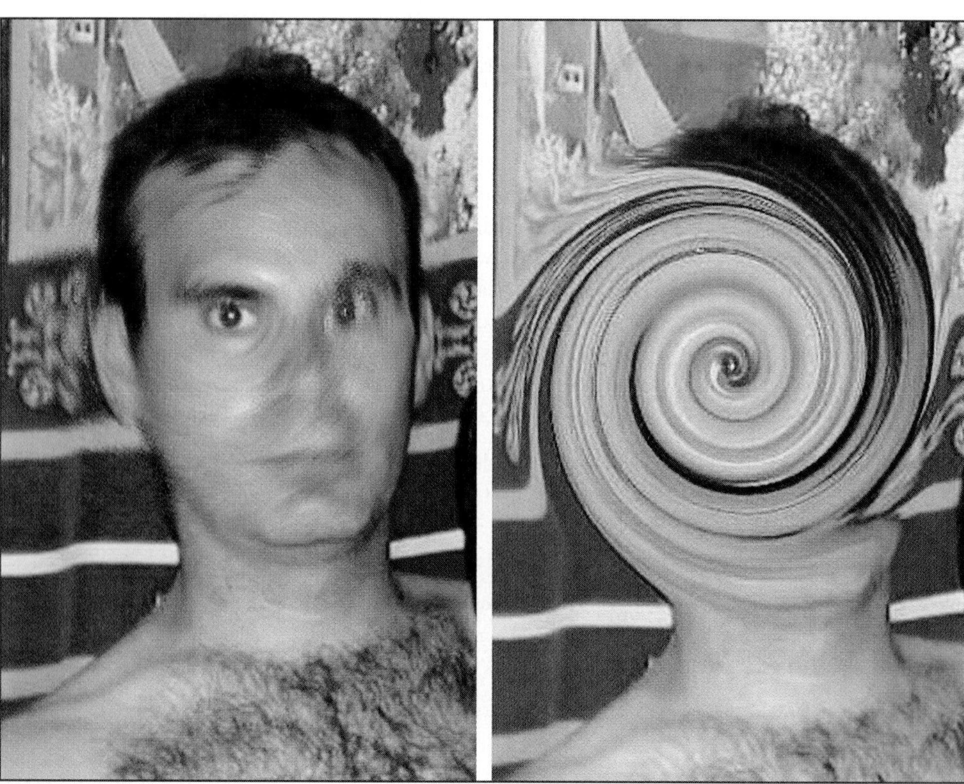

Christopher Paul Neil, a 32-year-old Canadian man, was arrested by Royal Thai Police in 2007 and charged with the sexual abuse of a child. Neil's arrest came ten days after Interpol used advanced computer technology to unscramble the Web-posted photo on the right to reveal Neil's face (left photo). What is transnational crime? Why is it becoming increasingly important?

Interpol/AP Wide World Photos

James Finckenauer, former director of the National Institute of Justice's International Center, has argued, first, that research and evaluation are critical to identifying best practices.[80] Then he advocates knowledge dissemination. The old saying "Knowledge is power" could not ring more true with respect to transnational crime. If law enforcement cannot understand the problem, how is it going to be prepared to tackle it? Finally, it is necessary to arm law enforcement agencies with the resources they need to combat transnational crime. A recent survey of local agencies revealed that most agencies need funding for equipment, training, and personnel.[81]

WEB PATROL 16-10

Investigating International Cybercrimes
http://www.mycrimekit.com

International Police and Crime-Fighting Organizations

It is one thing for a local law enforcement agency to think about (or even target) transnational crime. It is quite another, though, for a local agency to turn its attention outside U.S. borders and work hand in hand with an international police or crime-fighting organization. In this section, we briefly introduce the leading international police organizations, and we wrap up the discussion with some attention to the United Nations (UN) and the International Criminal Court (ICC).

WEB PATROL 16-11

The Spread of Identity Theft
http://www.mycrimekit.com

Interpol. **Interpol,** the International Criminal Police Organization, is headquartered in Lyons, France. Interpol can be traced back to 1914, when the first International Criminal Police Congress met in Monaco.[82] The goal of that meeting was to encourage international cooperation in criminal investigation and fugitive apprehension. It was not until 1946, however, that Interpol officially began its operations.

Interpol
The International Criminal Police Organization, an international police organization comprised of 182 member countries.

Today, 182 countries belong to Interpol. Each member country, in turn, has some entity that serves as the point of contact for Interpol. In the United States, that entity is the U.S. National Central Bureau (USNCB), an agency within the U.S. Justice Department that is staffed with personnel from several other federal agencies. According to USNCB, its mission is to facilitate international law enforcement cooperation as the U.S. representative to Interpol. It functions to:

- Transmit information of a criminal justice, humanitarian, or other law enforcement–related nature between the national central bureaus of Interpol member countries and law enforcement agencies of the United States.
- Respond to requests by law enforcement agencies and legitimate organizations, institutions, and individuals when in agreement with the Interpol constitution.
- Coordinate and integrate information for investigations of an international nature, and identify those involving patterns and trends of criminal activities.[83]

USNCB does not provide investigative assistance to private parties or to non–law enforcement sources. Its sole responsibility is to other law enforcement agencies.

Through USNCB, Interpol is linked with all the major computerized criminal records that the U.S. government maintains. These include the FBI's National Crime Information Index, the State Department's Advanced Visa Lookout System, and the Department of Homeland Security's Master Index. After the events of September 11, Interpol adopted the Budapest Anti-Terrorism Resolution, which calls for greater international law enforcement cooperation in the "war on terror." Interpol continues to expand its activities in this regard because it is now clear to law enforcement officials across the planet that openness and communication are essential to fight terrorism effectively.

Interpol is thus different from other law enforcement organizations because of its information-gathering and information-sharing focus. In one sense, it is not really a law enforcement organization at all, as it has no arrest powers and it does not employ field investigators. It owes much of its livelihood to the willingness of member nations to lend law enforcement support for its efforts. Although the 250 or so employees of Interpol are not law enforcement officials in the traditional sense, many of them have been employed as officers, agents, or investigators at one point or another. They gather data from around the world, facilitate the sharing of information, and alert interested agencies to the whereabouts and movements of known criminals and their confederates.

WEB PATROL 16-12

Interpol
http://www.mycrimekit.com

Europol
The European Police Office, an integrated police-intelligence gathering and dissemination group comprised of member countries of the European Union.

Europol. Europol, like Interpol, has several countries as its members, but in this case, the member countries are those of the European Union. **Europol,** the European Police Office, is based in The Hague, the Netherlands. Its mission is to improve the effectiveness of law enforcement efforts within the member nations:

> Europol is the European Union law enforcement organisation that handles criminal intelligence. Its aim is to improve the effectiveness and cooperation between the competent authorities of the Member States in preventing and combating serious international organised crime and terrorism. The mission of Europol is to make a significant contribution to the European Union's law enforcement action against organised crime and terrorism, with an emphasis on targeting criminal organisations.[84]

Europol further supports its member countries by

- Facilitating the exchange of information, in accordance with national law, between Europol liaison officers, who are sent to Europol by the member states as representatives of their national law enforcement agencies.
- Providing operational analysis in support of operations.
- Generating strategic reports (for example, threat assessments) and crime analysis on the basis of information and intelligence supplied by Member States and third parties.
- Providing expertise and technical support for investigations and operations carried out within the European Union, under the supervision and the legal responsibility of the member states concerned.[85]

Europol success stories are numerous. The organization recently assisted numerous countries in shutting down an illegal printing operation in Colombia..[86] The operation was printing counterfeit U.S. dollars and euros. It also helped member agencies shut down an international credit card fraud ring. According to Europol, "The criminals were skimming credit card data at manipulated payment terminals inside of several shopping centres in Italy for the purpose of subsequent illegal cash withdrawals at ATMs within Italy and other European countries."[87] Italy, Spain, Sweden, France, and Romania were among the countries involved.

WEB PATROL 16-13
Europol
http://www.mycrimekit.com

United Nations (UN)
An international agency comprised of 192 member countries.

The United Nations. We must not overlook the important role of the **United Nations (UN)** in international law enforcement efforts. The UN, which is based in New York City, consists of 192 member countries and is the largest, most inclusive international member body in the world. Formed in 1945, the UN has a number of responsibilities:

> The United Nations is central to global efforts to solve problems that challenge humanity. Cooperating in this effort are more than 30 affiliated organizations, known together as the UN system. Day in and day out, the UN and its family of organizations work to promote respect for human rights, protect the environment, fight disease and reduce poverty. UN agencies define the standards for safe and efficient air travel and help improve telecommunications and enhance consumer protection. The United Nations leads the international campaigns against drug trafficking and terrorism. Throughout the world, the UN and its agencies assist refugees, set up programmes to clear landmines, help expand food production and lead the fight against AIDS.[88]

The UN is well known for its various charters and agreements. Examples include its Standard Minimum Rules for the Treatment of Prisoners; its Code of Conduct for Law Enforcement Officials; its Convention against Transnational Organized Crime; and the Vienna Declaration on Crime and Justice, portions of which are reprinted in Figure 16-5. The UN also conducts the World Crime Survey, which reports official crime statistics from almost 100 countries, and the International Victim Survey, which is conducted in about 50 countries. The UN is not concerned solely with law enforcement and criminal activity, as we have seen, but these concerns rank high on its list of priorities.

International Criminal Court (ICC)
A permanent criminal court that tries individuals (not countries) who commit the most serious crimes against humanity: genocide and other war crimes.

The International Criminal Court. On April 12, 2000, the **International Criminal Court (ICC)** was formed. Operating in association with the United Nations, the ICC is intended to be a per-

Figure 16-5 • Vienna Declaration on Crime and Justice

We the Member States of the United Nations.

Concerned about the impact on our societies of the commission of serious crimes of a global nature and convinced of the need for bilateral, regional, and international cooperation in crime prevention and criminal justice.

Concerned in particular about transnational organized crime and the relationships between its various forms.

Convinced that adequate prevention and rehabilitation programs are fundamental to an effective crime-control strategy, and that such programs should take into account social and economic factors that may make people more vulnerable to, and likely to engage in, criminal behavior.

Stressing that a fair, responsible, ethical, and efficient criminal justice system is an important factor in the promotion of economic and social development and of security.

Aware of the promise of restorative approaches to justice that aim to reduce and promote the healing of victims, offenders, and communities.

Having assembled at the Tenth United Nations Congress on the Prevention of Crime and the Treatment of Offenders in Vienna from 10 to 17 April 2000 to decide to take effective concerted action, in a spirit of cooperation, to combat the world crime problem.

Declare as follows:

- We emphasize the responsibility of each State to establish and maintain a fair, responsible, ethical, and efficient criminal justice system.
- We recognize the necessity of closer coordination and cooperation among States in combating the world crime problem, bearing in mind that action against it is a common and shared responsibility. . . .
- We undertake to strengthen international cooperation in order to create a conducive environment for the fight against organized crime, promoting growth and sustainable development and eradicating poverty and unemployment.
- We also commit ourselves to the development of action-oriented policy recommendations based on the special needs of women as criminal justice practitioners, victims, prisoners, and offenders.
- We commit ourselves to the development of more effective ways of collaborating with one another with a view to eradicating the scourge of trafficking in persons, especially women and children, and the smuggling of migrants. . . .
- We also commit ourselves to the enhancement of international cooperation and mutual legal assistance to curb illicit manufacturing of and trafficking in firearms, their parts and components, and ammunition, and we establish 2005 as the target year for achieving a significant decrease in their incidence worldwide.
- We reaffirm that combating money laundering and the criminal economy constitutes a major element of the strategies against organized crime. . . .
- We decide to develop action-oriented policy recommendations on the prevention and control of computer-related crime. . . . We also commit ourselves to working towards enhancing our ability to prevent, investigate, and prosecute high-technology and computer-related crime.
- We note that acts of violence and terrorism continue to be of grave concern. In conformity with the Charter of the United Nations and taking into account all the relevant General Assembly resolutions, we will together, in conjunction with our other efforts to prevent and to combat terrorism, take effective, resolute, and speedy measures with respect to preventing and combating criminal activities carried out for the purpose of furthering terrorism in all its forms and manifestations. . . .
- We also note that racial discrimination, xenophobia, and related forms of intolerance continue, and we recognize the importance of taking steps to incorporate into international crime-prevention strategies and norms measures to prevent and combat crime associated with racism, racial discrimination, xenophobia, and related forms of intolerance.
- We affirm our determination to combat violence stemming from intolerance on the basis of ethnicity and resolve to make a strong contribution, in the area of crime prevention and criminal justice. . . .
- We also recognize the importance of prison reform, the independence of the judiciary and the prosecution authorities, and the International Code of Conduct for Public Officials. . . .
- We shall endeavor, as appropriate, to use and apply the United Nations standards and norms in crime prevention and criminal justice in national law and practice. . . .
- We further recognize with great concern that juveniles in difficult circumstances are often at risk of becoming delinquent or easy candidates for recruitment by criminal groups, including groups involved in transnational organized crime, and we commit ourselves to undertaking countermeasures to prevent this growing phenomenon. . . .
- We recognize that comprehensive crime-prevention strategies at the international, national, regional, and local levels must address the root causes and risk factors related to crime and victimization through social, economic, health, educational, and justice policies. . . .
- We commit ourselves to according priority to containing the growth and overcrowding of pretrial and detention prison populations, as appropriate, by promoting safe and effective alternatives to incarceration.
- We decide to introduce, where appropriate, national, regional, and international action plans in support of victims of crime, such as mechanisms for mediation and restorative justice. . . .
- We encourage the development of restorative justice policies, procedures, and programs that are respectful of the rights, needs, and interests of victims, offenders, communities, and all other parties.

Source: Excerpted from the Tenth U.N. Congress on the Prevention of Crime and the Treatment of Offenders, *Vienna Declaration on Crime and Justice: Meeting the Challenges of the Twenty-first Century,* Vienna, April 10–17, 2000. Reprinted by permisssion.

manent criminal court that tries individuals (not countries) who commit the most serious crimes against humanity: genocide and other war crimes. More than 100 UN member countries approved the creation of the court in the Rome Statute of the International Criminal Court. In April 2003, the court's first official prosecutor, Luis Moreno Ocampo of Argentina, was elected. The court is based in The Hague, the Netherlands, but cases can be tried anywhere.

Readers may be familiar with past efforts, especially in the wake of World War II, to try offenders in international courts. Prior to the ICC, military tribunals were used, such as those held in Nuremberg, Germany, and Tokyo, Japan. It would be nearly 50 more years before an actual standing court would be developed. The delay was partially due to U.S. resistance because of a concern that members of the U.S. military could come under the court's jurisdiction. In 2004, however, the United States dropped demands to exempt members of its military from ICC jurisdiction.[89]

The ICC has not been used to prosecute criminals as we know them, not even the most high-profile international drug, arms, and human traffickers. It has, however, taken some significant steps toward improving the treatment of people across the planet. For example, in 2005, a panel of ICC judges decided to allow Dutch investigators to perform forensic tests in the Democratic Republic of the Congo as part of an ongoing investigation into the genocidal deaths of scores of people. In late 2006, charges were brought against several individuals, and some 18 decisions were issued.[90] The court has since turned some of its attention to the situations in Darfur, Sudan, Uganda, and the Central African Republic.

WEB PATROL 16-14
The International Criminal Court
http://www.mycrimekit.com

POLICING THE FUTURE

No one can accurately predict the future, but this does not mean that we should abandon the effort. Forward-thinking law enforcement officials can, if nothing else, be *prepared* for what lies ahead by examining crime trends, keeping abreast of emerging crime problems, and looking beyond narrow jurisdictional boundaries. This section is thus about policing the future. We look at some emerging crimes that law enforcement agencies will have to deal with in the future. Then we look at professional groups whose mission is to anticipate future developments. We close this chapter with a review of some of the leading methods for forecasting future developments.

WEB PATROL 16-15
The Policing Profession in 2050
http://www.mycrimekit.com

Emerging Crimes

Advances in the areas of genetic mapping, nanotechnology, computer technology, the Internet, wireless communications, artificial intelligence, and satellite positioning systems have all done wonders for humankind, but they have also created problems for law enforcement. Just as they can be used legitimately by law-abiding citizens, they can also be used *illegitimately* by the criminal element. Here, we look at two categories of criminal behavior that probably would not exist but for recent advances in the technology.

WEB PATROL 16-16
Child Pornography Websites: Techniques Used to Evade Law Enforcement
http://www.mycrimekit.com

biocrime
A "criminal offense committed through the use of biologically active substances, including chemicals and toxins, disease-causing organisms, altered genetic material, and organic tissues and organs."[iv]

Biocrime. Biocrime, or biological crime, is a "criminal offense committed through the use of biologically active substances, including chemicals and toxins, disease-causing organisms, altered genetic material, and organic tissues and organs."[91] What's more, "Biocrimes unlawfully affect the metabolic, biochemical, genetic, physiological, or anatomical status of living organisms."[92] Biocrimes come in many varieties. Unleashing a poison in a crowded park or shopping center qualifies, but so does the harvesting of human organs.

Readers may be familiar with reports of kidney thefts in the United States and abroad. Some observers are convinced that the thefts are an urban legend,[93] as no victims have come forward. But if we turn our attention abroad, a different story sometimes emerges. Just recently in China, the Coalition to Investigate the Persecution of the Falun Gong commissioned a report to explore whether illegal organ harvesting has taken place in China.[94] The Fulan Gong is a religious sect whose practitioners have allegedly been persecuted by the Chinese government. According to the report,

> The government of China and its agencies in numerous parts of the country, in particular hospitals but also detention centres and people's courts, since 1999 have put to death a large but unknown number of Falun Gong prisoners of conscience. Their vital organs, including kidneys, livers, corneas and hearts, were seized involuntarily for sale at high prices, sometimes to foreigners, who normally face long waits for voluntary donations of such organs in their home countries. . . . It appears to us that many human beings belonging to a peaceful voluntary organization made illegal eight years ago by President Jiang because he thought it might threaten the dominance of the Communist Party of China have been in effect executed by medical practitioners for their organs.[95]

We cannot say with any measure of certainty whether the report's conclusions are correct, but we can safely say that there is some cause for concern. If organ harvesting is not a serious problem and there is no black market in the trade of harvested organs right now, this does not mean there never will be. If criminals can figure out a way to make money by illegally harvesting organs, they will surely do it.

Regarding other types of biocrime, we know there is potential for serious incidents. Readers may recall the release of poisonous gas on a Tokyo subway in 1995. The incident killed 12 people and sickened thousands.

Cybercrime. We introduced the concept of cyberterrorism earlier in this chapter; cybercrime is essentially the same thing but without the terrorist motive. **Cybercrime,** or computer crime, is "any crime perpetrated through the use of computer technology."[96] This includes any violation of federal or state computer crime statutes. Many readers may be familiar with computer crime through their receipt of fradulent email messages requesting that they update their bank account or become a fiduciary of some important person's fortune. Cybercrime can include everything from software piracy to flagrant attacks with viruses, Trojan horses, and malware programs to those annoying phishing email messages that seek to acquire our personal information.

cybercrime
"Any crime perpetrated through the use of computer technology."[v]

Criminals often go further by posing as other individuals in an effort to obtain passwords and other privileged information. This practice, known as **social engineering,**

> involves persuading administrators or telephonists to give details of passwords or other things by pretending to be staff, suppliers or trusted individuals—even police officers. They could be even masquerading as a computer repair man to get access to the premises.[97]

social engineering
A nontechnical kind of cyberintrusion that relies on human interaction and often involves tricking people into breaking normal security procedures.

Kevin Mitnick, who was once the FBI's most wanted hacker, agrees. In an interview after his release from prison, Mitnick said that

> malicious hackers don't need to use stealth computer techniques to break into a network. . . . Often they just trick someone into giving them passwords and other information. . . . People are the weakest link. . . . You can have the best technology, firewalls, intrusion-detection systems, biometric devices . . . and somebody can call an unsuspecting employee . . . [and] they [get] everything.[98]

These and other computer crimes have taken on a transnational flavor. Also, terrorists are increasingly exploiting computer technology to do everything from raising money through credit card fraud to communicating with one another.

WEB PATROL 16-17
ePolicing at the LAPD
http://www.mycrimekit.com

While these problems are difficult for law enforcement officials to target effectively, these officials have certainly not been left behind. Technological advances have helped law enforcement, as well. Law enforcement access to high-technology investigative tools has produced enormous amounts of information on crimes and suspects, and the use of innovative investigative tools like DNA fingerprinting, keystroke captures, laser and night vision technologies, digital imaging, and thermography are beginning to shape many of the practical aspects of the twenty-first-century criminal justice system.[99]

Table 16-1 contains a list of specific cybercrimes, mostly hacking, fraud, and Internet-related crimes. It also presents a list of the federal agencies most likely to investigate such acts.

WEB PATROL 16-18
Defending against Cybercrime and Terrorism
http://www.mycrimekit.com

Table 16-1 • Computer Hacking, Fraud, and Internet-Related Crimes and the Agencies that Investigate Them

Type of Crime	Federal Investigative Law Enforcement Agencies
Computer intrusion (hacking)	• FBI local office • U.S. Secret Service • Internet Crime Complaint Center
Password trafficking	• FBI local office • U.S. Secret Service • Internet Crime Complaint Center
Counterfeiting of currency	• U.S. Secret Service • FBI local office
Child pornography or exploitation	• If imported, U.S. Immigration and Customs Enforcement • Internet Crime Complaint Center
Child exploitation and Internet fraud matters that have a mail nexus	• U.S. Postal Inspection Service • Internet Crime Complaint Center
Internet fraud and spam	• FBI local office • U.S. Secret Service (Financial Crimes Division) • Federal Trade Commission (online complaint) • If securities fraud or investment-related spam emails, Securities and Exchange Commission (online complaint) • Internet Crime Complaint Center
Internet harassment	• FBI local office
Internet bomb threats	• FBI local office • Bureau of Alchol, Tobacco, Firearms and Explosives (ATF) local office
Trafficking in explosive or incendiary devices or firearms over the Internet	• FBI local office • ATF local office

Source: U.S. Department of Justice, Computer Crime and Intellectual Property Section, "Reporting computer, Internet-related, or intellectual property crime," http://www.usdoj.gov/criminal/cybercrime/reporting.htm (accessed July 25, 2008).

Police Futurists

Throughout this book, we have introduced various professional law enforcement organizations, as well as various police agencies at the federal, state, and local levels. But there are other organizations whose sole concern is what lies ahead. Two such groups stand out: the Society of Police Futurists International and the Futures Working Group.

Society of Police Futurists International (PFI)
An organization of forward-thinking law enforcement professionals.

The **Society of Police Futurists International (PFI)** is an organization whose members are forward-thinking law enforcement professionals. The group uses prediction techniques developed by futures researchers in other fields to forecast the future for law enforcement. Here is what PFI says about its role in the law enforcement arena:

> Futures Research (long-range planning and forecasting) is the pivotal discipline that constitutes the philosophical underpinnings of PFI. The tools and techniques of this field are applied in order to more accurately anticipate and prepare for the evolution of law enforcement ten, twenty, and even fifty years into the future. Futures Research offers both philosophical and methodological tools to analyze, forecast, and plan in ways rarely seen in policing in the past.[100]

PFI recently joined forces with the Federal Bureau of Investigation to form the Futures Working Group (FWG). The mission of the FWG is "to develop and encourage others to develop forecasts

Members of the Futures Working Group, shown during a 2008 meeting. The Futures Working Group is a collaborative effort between the FBI and the Society of Police Futurists International. What does the future hold for policing?

Courtesy of Police Futurists International

and strategies to ethically maximize the effectiveness of local, state, federal, and international law enforcement bodies as they strive to maintain peace and security in the 21st century."[101]

Both the PFI and FWG have generated a number of informative reports. PFI publishes a free newsletter, operates a listserv, and has produced several extensive reports on what the future likely holds for law enforcement in America. One of the reports, *Policing 2020,* considers how demographic shifts, cultural changes, information technology, emerging crime problems, and other developments will affect law enforcement over the next several years.

WEB PATROL 16-19

Society of Police Futurists International
http://www.mycrimekit.com

Forecasting the Future

How exactly is the future forecast? Believe it or not, there is a science behind it. The whole field of **futures research** is concerned with developing and refining techniques for accurately predicting what lies ahead. Futures research includes "any activity that improves understanding about the future consequences of present developments and choices."[102] The authors of this definition describe forecasting as a progression:

futures research
Research that is concerned with developing and refining techniques for accurately predicting what lies ahead.

- A statement about the future
- A probabilistic statement about the future
- A probabilistic, reasonably definite statement about the future
- A probabilistic, reasonably definite statement about the future based on an evaluation of alternative possibilities[103]

This is not the stuff of shady fortune-tellers and crystal balls—it is real science. At the risk of oversimplification, there are four methods of forecasting the future: (1) the Delphi method, (2) trend extrapolation, (3) historical analogy, and (4) scenarios.

The Delphi Method. The **Delphi method** of forecasting the future relies on the systematic solicitation of expert opinion. Developed by the RAND Corporation several decades ago, this method proceeds as follows:

Delphi method
A forecasting method that relies on the systematic solicitation of expert opinion.

> A questionnaire designed by a monitor team is sent to a select group of experts. After the responses are summarized, the results are sent back to the respondents who have the opportunity to re-evaluate their original answers, based upon the responses of the group. By incorporating a second and sometimes third round of questionnaires, the respondents have the opportunity to defend their original answers or change their position to agree with the majority of respondents.[104]

In other words, the Delphi method is concerned with obtaining consensus about likely future developments from a group of recognized experts. The rub is that the accuracy of the forecast is directly tied to the quality of the opinions offered by the experts. Some people have expressed concerns that relying on expert opinion may be misguided.[105]

trend extrapolation
A forecasting method that involves "observing a change through time in the character of something and projecting or extrapolating that change into the future."

Trend Extrapolation. **Trend extrapolation** involves "observing a change through time in the character of something and projecting or extrapolating that change into the future."[106] It requires a look into the past and confidence that past events will repeat themselves—in more or less the same way—if the conditions are correct. Growth curves are often useful for trend extrapolation. Just as changes in a person's height and weight can be plotted on a graph, so too can historical developments.

In the crime-control context, trend extrapolation is fraught with difficulty. A steady growth rate in a particular type of crime carries with it no guarantee that the trend will continue into the future. At the same time, some offenses, especially emerging ones that are expanding at unprecedented rates (such as identity theft), are likely to continue to grow in the foreseeable future.

historical analogy
A forecasting method that looks at past events that seem to be repeating themselves.

Historical Analogy. **Historical analogy** is concerned less with trends over time than with past events that seem to be repeating themselves. Consider the situation in Iraq. In early 2007, White House Press Secretary Tony Snow reported at a press conference that President Bush expected that the situation in Iraq would continue to develop along the lines of the "Korean model," meaning that U.S. troops would maintain a presence for some time and would act as a "force of stability" in the region.[107] Whether this analogy is a good one, however, is debatable. This leads to the number one problem with historical analogy:

> Historical analogies can helpfully inform policy. Many policy-makers, however, are historically illiterate, and most that are well read make policy decisions, just like their untutored brethren, primarily on the basis of considerations having nothing to do with the perceived lessons of past experience.[108]

Let's consider a historical analogy specific to policing. Chapter 1 followed the development of policing in America over time, beginning with the political era. During the next period, the professional era, there was an effort to separate policing from politics and corruption. The community policing era followed, presumably to overcome the impersonal nature of professional policing. Some critics of community policing, however, claim that it represents a return to the past and may put police officers in too close contact with citizens, thus encouraging the favoritism and, possibly, corruption found during the political era.[109] Others have said that community policing involves officers too much in service work rather than crime control, just like at the turn of the twentieth century.[110]

scenarios
A forecasting method that involves "a series of events that we imagine happening in the future."[vi]

Scenarios. The use of **scenarios** for forecasting the future has been described in this way: "It is simply a series of events that we imagine happening in the future."[111] Stated differently, it is "making up stories about the future."[112] Scenarios can come in a number of forms. The common theme is that a scenario be a description of "a hypothetical, likely or unlikely, development or situation; a development which is described as caused to some extent by the actions and reactions of various actors: a desirable or nondesirable development or situation."[113]

Scenario-based assessments of likely future trends, especially in law enforcement, can readily use worst-case scenarios to plan for either possible or eventual developments. Mock terrorist attack drills, for example, are conducted based on someone's belief that such an incident could very well take place at some point in the future. In one sense, scenarios are almost an alternative to forecasting because they do not rely on looking into the past or even soliciting expert opinions. Also, scenarios do not pretend to predict the future. Rather, they just present a series of possibilities about it.[114]

SUMMARY

- An act is terrorism if it is premeditated, politically motivated, violent, and committed against noncombatants. Domestic terrorism is carried out by an individual or a group that is based in and operates within the target country. International terrorism refers to the unlawful use of violence by a group or an individual that has some connection with a foreign power or group. Other forms of terrorism include cyberterrorism, narcoterrorism, and ecoterrorism. Terrorism usually builds on underlying conditions, which can include everything from poverty and political corruption to religious conflict and civil war. The U.S. government has adopted a so-called 4D strategy for combating terrorism: defeat, deny, diminish, and defend. Other noteworthy federal efforts to combat terrorism include the Antiterrorism and Effective Death Penalty Act (AEDPA) and the USA PATRIOT Act.
- Ethnocentrism generally refers either to the belief that one's own ethnic group or culture is superior to others or to the tendency to view other ethnicities and cultures through the lens of one's own culture. Globalization is the internationalization of trade, services, investment, information, and other forms of human social activity. Transnational crime consists of offenses whose inception, prevention, or direct or indirect effects involve more than one country. Examples includes human trafficking, weapons trafficking, identity theft, and money laundering. Transnational crime is difficult to police because it is increasingly sophisticated and complicated, and it is sometimes indistinguishable from traditional crime. International police and crime-fighting organizations include Interpol, Europol, certain components of the United Nations, and the International Criminal Court.
- Emerging crimes include biocrime and cybercrime. Biocrime, or biological crime, is a criminal offense committed through the use of biologically active substances, including chemicals and toxins, disease-causing organisms, altered genetic material, and organic tissues and organs. Cybercrime, or computer crime, is any crime perpetrated through the use of computer technology. The Society of Police Futurists and the Futures Working Group are concerned with predicting future developments in the world of law enforcement. Approaches to forecasting future developments include the Delphi method, trend extrapolation, historical analogy, and scenarios.

COMING FULL CIRCLE

For Discussion

Return to the questions posed at the start of this chapter. Have any of your answers changed since you read the chapter? What portions of this chapter helped you answer these questions?

Writing Assignment

Using material from this chapter and additional resources, write a 500-word essay in response to one of the questions presented at the beginning of the chapter. Submit your essay to your instructor if asked to do so.

KEY TERMS AND NAMES

Antiterrorism and Effective Death Penalty Act (AEDPA)
biocrime
boundaryless policing
Combat Methamphetamine Epidemic Act of 2005
comparative criminology
cybercrime
cyberterrorism
Delphi method
domestic terrorism
Earth Liberation Front (ELF)
ecoterrorism
ethnocentrism
Europol
futures research
globalization
historical analogy
human trafficking
identity theft
International Criminal Court (ICC)
international terrorism
Interpol
Joint Terrorism Task Force (JTTF)
narcoterrorism
National Strategy for Combating Terrorism (NSCT)
scenarios
social engineering
Society of Police Futurists International (PFI)
Taking Command Initiative
transnational crime
trend extrapolation
United Nations (UN)
USA PATRIOT Act

WEB INTERACTIVITY

Visit the Society of Police Futurists International on the Web at http://www.policefuturists.org, and click the "Futures Research" tab at the top of the organization's home page. How does the PFI site describe futures research? What futures research techniques are discussed? How is futures research applicable to the law enforcement profession? Submit your conclusions to your instructor if asked to do so.

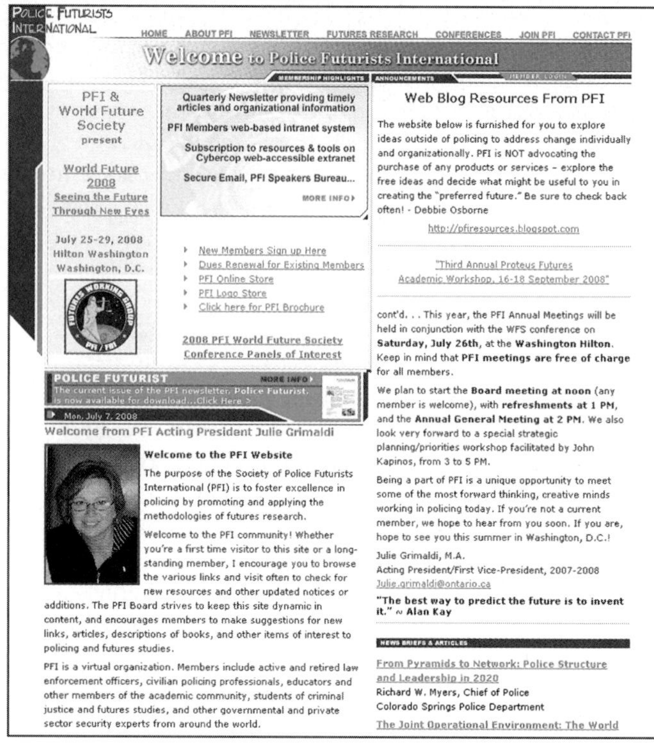

Police Futurists International

REVIEW QUESTIONS

1. Explain the problem of terrorism and its impact on policing today.
2. What are some of the difficulties associated with the policing of transnational crime, and how might international police cooperation be enhanced?
3. What new forms of crime are emerging? Who are police futurists? What techniques do they use in their attempts to predict the law enforcement landscape of the future?

GLOSSARY

18 U.S.C. Section 3501 The U.S. Code designation assigned to the Crime Control Act of 1968, which, among other things, attempted to invalidate the *Miranda* decision.

18 U.S.C.A. Section 242 The most common federal statute used to hold police officers criminally liable.

311 system A public-access municipal services call network reserved for nonemergency calls.

42 U.S.C. Section 1983 The federal statute that provides a remedy in federal court for the "deprivation of any rights . . . secured by the Constitution and laws" of the United States.

absolute immunity Protection from lawsuits enjoyed by federal officials when acting in their official capacities.

abuse of authority A catchall category for various forms of inappropriate police conduct that do not necessarily amount to crime, deviance, or corruption.

accepted lie A lie that is necessary in furthering the police mission.

accreditation Certification for having met all applicable requirements put in place by an accrediting body.

administrative justification The standard for an administrative search based on the fact that government entities occasionally conduct searches in circumstances other than criminal investigations, such as a sobriety checkpoint set up for the purpose of apprehending drunk drivers. Sometimes called *special-needs* or *regulatory searches*, such searches attempt to achieve a balance between protecting individuals' privacy interests and protecting public safety.

admission A confession to having committed a crime, but without written documentation.

admittance John Van Maanen's second stage of police recruit socialization, in which the recruit enters the academy and learns the importance of abiding by the rules and regulations of the department.

affirmative action The practice of taking proactive steps to boost the presence of historically marginalized groups (typically minorities and women) in the ranks of an organization by giving preference to members of those groups.

affront According to John Van Maanen, the first of three steps police officers use in identifying an "asshole." It occurs when an officer's authority is questioned.

aggressiveness A police officer's willingness to actively seek out problems.

Amber alert A voluntary partnership program between police and the news media involving saturation notices on radio, television, and electronic billboards to elicit widespread and immediate public assistance in locating a child or children thought to be in danger.

Americans with Disabilities Act (ADA) U.S. legislation passed in 1990 that forbids discrimination against the disabled.

anthropometry A technique developed by Alphonse Bertillon in 1882 for identifying people based on their body measurements. Also called *Bertillon measurements.*

antigang injunction A judicial order, often obtained at the request of a prosecutor, that bars gang members from associating with one another. Also called *civil gang injunction.*

Antiterrorism and Effective Death Penalty Act U.S. legislation enacted in the wake of the 1995 Oklahoma City bombing to combat terrorism.

apparent authority A doctrine established by the U.S. Supreme Court that permits the warrantless entry of a residence if entry is based on the consent of a person whom the officers reasonably believe has authority to grant consent, even if their belief is erroneous.

arm-span rule A doctrine established by the U.S. Supreme Court that limits a search incident to arrest to the area "within [the] immediate control" of the person arrested—that is, "the area from within which he might have obtained either a weapon or something that could have been used as evidence against him."[1]

arraignment The hearing before a court having jurisdiction in a criminal case, during which the defendant is identified, informed of his or her rights, and required to enter a plea. Also, in some jurisdictions, any appearance in criminal court prior to trial.

asset forfeiture The governmental seizure of property (homes, automobiles, boats, aircraft, and so on) that has been illegally obtained with the profits from drug sales. The proceeds from these seizures sometimes go to the seizing agencies to fund continuing efforts in the "war on drugs."

assumption of risk A defense against state tort liability that provides that if a plaintiff voluntarily engaged in a dangerous activity that led to his or her injury, then the police officer should not be held liable.

August Vollmer (1876–1955) An early and especially effective advocate of police reform whose collaboration with the University of California established the study of criminal justice as an academic discipline.

avoider An officer who avoids using force, is devoid of compassion, does as little as possible to maintain his or her position, and avoids risk-taking behavior.

bail The money or property pledged to the court or actually deposited with the court to effect the release of a person from legal custody.[2]

Beat Health Program A third-party policing program in Oakland, California, that uses civil remedies to prevent and reduce drug and disorder problems.

behavioral perspective One of two traditional approaches to motivating subordinates—the other is the *humanistic perspective*—that assumes that people are not by nature self-motivated, that they need reinforcement for their endeavors, and that the organization needs to be structured so that otherwise unmotivated individuals can gain a sense of accomplishment in their work.

biocrime A criminal offense committed through the use of biologically active substances, including chemicals and toxins, disease-causing organisms, altered genetic material, and organic tissues and organs.

Bivens v. Six Unknown Named Agents The 1971 U.S. Supreme Court ruling that held that federal law enforcement officers can be sued for Fourth Amendment violations. The decision has since been expanded to include liability for violations of constitutional rights embodied in other relevant amendments.[3]

bobby The popular British name given to a member of Sir Robert Peel's Metropolitan Police Force.[4]

booking The process of fingerprinting, processing, and photographing a suspect, after which he or she is typically placed in a holding cell. The suspect may also be required to submit to testing (such as for alcohol) or be required to participate in a lineup.

boundaryless policing Any of various technology-based intelligence efforts designed to combat crime and terrorism.

Bow Street Runners An early English police unit formed under the leadership of Henry Fielding, magistrate of the Bow Street region of London. Also referred to as *thief takers*.[5]

broken windows model A model of policing based on the notion that physical decay in a community (for example, litter and abandoned buildings) can breed disorder and lead to crime by signaling that laws are not being enforced. Such decay is thought to push law-abiding citizens to withdraw from the streets, which signals that lawbreakers can operate freely. The model suggests that by encouraging the repair of run-down buildings and by controlling disorderly behavior in public spaces, police agencies can create an environment in which serious crime cannot easily flourish.

Buddy Boys A New York City Police Department scandal that occurred in the Brooklyn precinct in 1986 and resulted in the indictment of 13 officers for a number of criminal activities, including stealing and selling drugs.

budgeting The creation of a fiscal plan for an organization.

bureaucracy The administrative structure of a large or complex organization, typically employing task-specialized bureaus or departments.

Bureau of Alcohol, Tobacco, Firearms and Explosives (ATF) A tax-collection, enforcement, and regulatory arm of the U.S. Department of Justice.

burnout The progressive loss of idealism, energy, purpose, and concern that results from the conditions of work.

CalGang A sophisticated software database of known gang members that field officers in California can access quickly. GangNet is a modified version of the software that is used nationwide.

centralized policing model The less prevalent model of state police organization, in which the tasks of major criminal investigations are combined with the patrol of state highways.

chain of command The supervisory channel within a law enforcement organization.

change John Van Maanen's third stage of police recruit socialization, in which the recruit completes academy training, enters the field, is partnered with a training officer, and is continually tested and evaluated on several criteria.

checkpoint A location at which a warrantless, suspicionless search is constitutionally permissible in furtherance of an overriding national or public-safety interest. National border entry points and sobriety checkpoints are examples.

Christopher Commission The commission that studied the structure and operation of the Los Angeles Police Department in the wake of the Rodney King beating incident.

citizen complaint A document filed by someone who believes that he or she has been wronged by one or more police officers in a department.

citizen contact patrol A community policing technique in which police officers knock on people's doors, introduce themselves, give out information, and otherwise try to make policing more personal in nature.

citizen patrol A preventive patrol program staffed by citizen volunteers.

citizen police academy A training experience that offers citizens an opportunity to learn about the policing profession and even to experience some of the same sensations that uniformed officers experience.

civil disobedience Law-breaking used as a political tactic to prove a point or to protest against something.

civilian input A model of civilian oversight of a police agency in which civilians receive and investigate complaints, but the next steps are taken by the police department.

civilianization "A law enforcement agency's hiring of nonsworn personnel to replace or augment its corps of sworn officers" in an effort to reduce costs and improve service.[6]

civilian monitor A model of civilian oversight of a police agency that is similar to an ombudsman approach in which complaints are received by the police department and the process, from beginning to end, is monitored by civilians.

civilian review One of the stronger models of citizen oversight of a police agency in which a group of citizens investigates complaints against the police, adjudicates the complaints, and recommends punishment.

civil law The branch of modern law that governs relationships between parties.

civil service A system in which employees are hired, retained, advanced, disciplined, and discharged on the basis of merit (that is, their abilities and qualifications).

civil service commission A federal, state, or local agency charged with ensuring that employees in civil service positions receive specific protections.

clarification According to John Van Maanen, the second of three steps police officers use in identifying an "asshole." It occurs when the officer attempts to ascertain what kind of person he or she is dealing with.

clean-beat crime fighter An officer who emphasizes following proper police procedures.

code of ethics A statement of principles concerning the behavior of those who subscribe to the code.

collective bargaining The process through which an employer and its employees, represented by their union, negotiate a formal written agreement over wages, hours, benefits, and other conditions of employment.

college system A police academy training model intended to enhance the professional aspects of police training curricula by exposing trainees to problem solving, sensitivity to marginalized groups, and other valuable topics in addition to required technical knowledge.

color of law The condition that exists when an individual acts in an official government capacity and with the appearance of legal power. Police officers, mayors, and a number of other government officials perform their duties under color of law.[7]

Combat Methamphetamine Epidemic Act of 2005 U.S. legislation that introduced commonsense safeguards that made many ingredients used in methamphetamine manufacturing more difficult to obtain in bulk and easier for law enforcement to track and that increased penalties for smuggling and selling methamphetamine.[8]

common authority A basis for third-party consent to search, based on mutual use of the property by persons generally having joint access or control for most purposes.

community era By most accounts, the contemporary era of U.S. law enforcement, which stresses service and an almost customer-friendly approach to police work.

community justice A relatively new and innovative set of ideas about how the goals of the criminal justice system can be achieved. It favors original, nontraditional approaches to crime control that draw heavily on input and cooperation from the community.

community policing "A collaborative effort between the police and the community that identifies problems of crime and disorder and involves all elements of the community in the search for solutions to these problems."[9]

community prosecution A prosecutorial approach intended to improve cooperation and collaboration between prosecutors and individuals outside the criminal justice system, such as community members and business leaders.

comparative criminology Research that compares and contrasts the criminal justice institutions and processes of various nations.

comparative negligence A partial defense against state tort liability that examines who is to blame and assigns liability accordingly.

Compstat A goal-oriented police management process that relies heavily on computer technology and accountability of top-level administrators.

computer-aided drafting (CAD) A technology, adapted to meet the needs of police officers and criminal investigators, that facilitates the drafting of crime scenes on a computer so that they can be viewed three-dimensionally.

computerized crime mapping A computer-based system that combines a geographic information system with crime statistics generated by a police department, allowing crime data to be plotted on a map.

conducted energy device (CED) A device that uses electrical shock to incapacitate a suspect. Examples are the Taser and the Sticky Shocker. Also called *electromuscular disruption technology*.

confederation A system of government that lacks a strong central authority.

confession A written document in which a person admits having been involved in criminal activity.

constitutional rights violation Conduct that violates a specific constitutional provision.

contingency theory A management theory that recognizes that there are often different types of tasks within a single organization, including repetitive tasks that call for standardization and control and nonrepetitive tasks that call for flexibility and participatory management.

continuance John Van Maanen's fourth stage of police recruit socialization, in which the recruit moves through the field training period and comes to accept the reality of police work.

contributory negligence A liability defense that holds that if an officer can show that the plaintiff or someone else was also negligent in an event, the officer should not be held liable. Contributory negligence can arise not only from the actions of a criminal suspect, but also from the actions of third parties.

cooperative federalism A form of federalism in which the lines between federal and state power are sometimes blurred or, at least, have fluctuated over time.

corruption Dishonest or fraudulent conduct by public officials in a position of power.

corruption of authority A level of police corruption that consists of receiving free meals, discounts, and rewards.

council-manager form The most common form of city government in cities of more than 12,000 people. It consists of an elected city council (usually between five and 12 people) responsible for all policy decisions for the city. Mayors under this form of municipal government generally perform ceremonial duties and serve as the voice, and often the leader, of the city council.

crime control Policing policies and activities undertaken to reduce the incidence of crime in a community.

crime-control model One of two competing perspectives—the other is the *due process model*—described by Herbert Packer that embody the inherent tension in contemporary U.S. society regarding government's role in response to criminal behavior.

Crime-control advocates argue that protecting the public is the government's primary duty, even at the expense of individual rights.

crime-control newsletter A newsletter published by a police department that typically contains information on recent developments at the police department, crime statistics for the area, tips for avoiding victimization, and so on.

Crime Mapping Research Center (CMRC) A U.S. Justice Department agency that promotes research, training, and technical assistance for police agencies around the country and assists them in their crime-mapping efforts. Also called the *Mapping and Analysis for Public Safety (MAPS) Program*.

crime peak A time of day when a particular crime increases in frequency.

crime prevention Policing policies and activities undertaken to prevent crime in a community.

crime-prevention program An organized effort that focuses resources on reducing a specific form of criminal threat.

crime-prevention technique A technique designed to prevent criminal activity, such as access control with physical barriers to entryways and exits, surveillance (including video systems), theft-deterrence devices (locks, alarms, tethers), security lighting, and visibility landscaping.

criminal intelligence "A synergistic product intended to provide meaningful and trustworthy direction to law enforcement decision makers about complex criminality, criminal enterprises, criminal extremists, and terrorists."[10] A "process that evaluates information collected from diverse sources, integrates the relevant information into a cohesive package, and produces a conclusion or estimate about a criminal phenomenon by using the scientific approach to problem solving."[11]

criminalistics The use of technology in the service of criminal investigation; the application of scientific techniques to the detection and evaluation of criminal evidence.

criminal proceeding In the context of the Fifth Amendment's self-incrimination clause, any grand jury hearing, trial, or other official questioning proceeding—whether civil or criminal, formal or informal—in which the answers provided might incriminate the person being questioned. The Fifth Amendment not only protects the individual against being involuntarily called as a witness against himself in a criminal prosecution, but also privileges him not to answer official questions put to him in any other proceeding, civil or criminal, formal or informal, where the answers might incriminate him in *future* criminal proceedings."[12]

critical incident An emergency situation that evokes immediate police response and that takes priority over all other police work.

culpability The state of deserving blame or being morally or legally responsible. Under the Section 1983 culpability requirement, plaintiffs generally must prove that the defendant officer *intended* for the violation to occur.

culture A set of shared values, norms, and behaviors that form a way of life.

curfew law A statute or ordinance that requires juveniles to remain indoors during designated time periods (usually late evening through early morning) unless accompanied by an adult.

custody The legal or physical control of a person or a thing. Also, the legal, supervisory, or physical responsibility for a person or a thing.

Customs and Border Protection (CBP) The U.S. law enforcement agency, established after the terrorist attacks on September 11, 2001, that combined the entire U.S. Border Patrol with portions of the U.S. Customs Service, U.S. Immigration, and the Animal and Plant Health Inspection Service. CBP was given the mission of controlling and protecting America's borders and ports of entry, including international airports and international shipping ports.

cybercrime Any crime perpetrated through the use of computer technology.

cyberterrorism The use of computers and the Internet to carry out terrorist attacks.

dactylography An early name for fingerprinting.

damages Monetary compensation awarded to the plaintiff in a successful civil lawsuit.

danger signifier A factor, such as a person's behavior, location, race, dress, age, or sex, that can be a signal of danger.

deadly force Force that is likely to cause death or significant bodily harm.

decentralized policing model A model of policing in which central governments exercise relatively few police powers and in which the majority of police services are provided by separate local and regional agencies.

deliberate elicitation An effort by a government actor to draw incriminating statements from a suspect who is not represented by counsel, in violation of that person's Sixth Amendment right to counsel.

Delphi method A forecasting method that relies on the systematic solicitation of expert opinion.

democracy A form of government that vests supreme authority in the people, usually through their freely elected representatives.

deterrence theory A perspective that holds that crime will be less likely to occur when the potential for getting caught outweighs any likely benefits from breaking the law.

deviance Any behavior that is at odds with socially expected or accepted behavior.

deviant lie A lie that expressly violates the rules and legal requirements.

directed patrol A form of patrol that involves concentrating the police presence in areas where certain crimes are a significant problem.

discovery The process through which each side in a criminal case learns what evidence the other side will present.

distress A harmful form of stress that can threaten an individual's functioning or overload his or her capacity to cope with environmental stimuli.

domestic terrorism Terrorism carried out by an individual or a group that is based in and operating within the country being attacked.

domestic violence Generally, any violence that takes place in the home. The term has recently been expanded to include violence between domestic partners and violence directed at or occurring between children. Also called *family violence*.

dominion John Crank's substitute for the term *territoriality*, which refers to an officer's sense of personal ownership over the area for which he or she is responsible.

double marginality A situation in which black officers treat black suspects harshly to gain the respect of their white counterparts and to avoid giving the impression that they are biased toward members of their own race.

dramaturgical discipline Achieving a balance between merely reporting facts and putting a "spin" on those facts to create a desired impression.

dramaturgy In the law enforcement context, the act of putting on a display of high-mindedness.

Drug Abuse Resistance Education (DARE) A collaborative effort between local police departments and schools involving police visits to fifth- and sixth-grade classrooms to present a drug-abuse-prevention curriculum.

drug courier profiling A crime-detection process that makes use of what is known about the likely and observable characteristics of drug couriers. Drug courier profiling often occurs in stop-and-frisk situations.

Drug Enforcement Administration (DEA) The U.S. law enforcement agency tasked with enforcing controlled-substance laws and regulations.

dual federalism An interpretation of the U.S. Constitution that suggests a system in which the only powers vested in the federal government are those explicitly listed in the document, with the remaining powers being left to the states.

due process model One of two competing perspectives—the other is the *crime-control model*—described by Herbert Packer that embody the inherent tension in contemporary U.S. society regarding government's role in response to criminal behavior. Due process advocates argue that protecting individual rights is the government's primary duty, even at the expense of increased threats to public safety.

due process of law A right guaranteed by the Fifth, Sixth, and Fourteenth Amendments and generally understood, in legal contexts, to mean the due course of legal proceedings according to the rules and forms established for the protection of individual rights. In criminal proceedings, due process of law is generally understood to include the following basic elements: a law creating and defining the offense, an impartial tribunal having jurisdictional authority over the case, accusation in proper form, notice and opportunity to defend, trial according to established procedure, and discharge from all restraints or obligations unless convicted.

due process voluntariness approach A means for determining the admissibility of a suspect's self-incriminating statement based on whether it was made voluntarily. Involuntariness is held to occur when, under the "totality of circumstances that preceded the confessions," the defendant is deprived of his or her "power of resistance."[13]

Earth Liberation Front (ELF) An ecoterrorist group.

economic corruption Drug-related police corruption in which an officer seeks personal gain by stealing drugs, selling drugs, or extorting money from drug dealers.

ecoterrorism Terrorism that "involves extremist views on environmental issues and animal rights and is a fringe-issue form of terrorism aimed primarily at inflicting economic damage on those seen as profiting from the destruction and exploitation of the environment."[14]

enforcer An officer who uses force whenever the opportunity arises and who lacks the compassion that goes along with the professional style of policing.

equal employment opportunity Fair employment practices mandated by Title VII of the Civil Rights Act of 1964.

Equal Employment Opportunity Commission (EEOC) The federal agency that is empowered by Title VII of the Civil Rights Act of 1964 to "intervene on behalf of affected individuals," to "file suit against businesses or governmental entities in cases of discrimination," to intervene in cases of alleged sexual harassment, and to investigate cases of employer retaliation.[15]

ethnocentrism The belief that one's own ethnic group or culture is superior. Also, the tendency to view other ethnicities and cultures through the lens of one's own culture.

Europol The European Police Office, an integrated police intelligence-gathering and dissemination group comprised of member countries of the European Union.

eustress A positive form of stress that does not threaten or harm the individual but is pleasurable, challenging, or exciting.

evanescent evidence Evidence that is likely to disappear quickly.[16]

evidence-based policing "The use of the best available research on the outcomes of police work to implement guidelines and evaluate agencies, units, and officers; the use of research to guide practice and evaluate practitioners."[17]

excessive force "The application of an amount and/or frequency of force greater than that required to compel compliance from a willing or unwilling subject."[18]

excited delirium A condition in which a suspect experiences an overdose of adrenaline during a heated confrontation with the police.

exclusionary rule A rule mandating that evidence obtained in violation of the U.S. Constitution cannot be admitted in a criminal trial. The exclusionary rule is an important mechanism for ensuring the accountability of police officials.[19]

exigent circumstances A situation that makes a warrantless search constitutionally permissible, such as hot pursuit, the likelihood of a suspect's escaping or presenting a danger to others, and evanescent evidence.

fair examination rule The procedural rule that ensures that witnesses at either a trial or a grand jury hearing can be compelled to answer questions once they waive their Fifth Amendment privilege and begin to testify.[20]

"Fajitagate" A violent altercation that occurred in 2002 between three off-duty San Francisco police officers and two civilians carrying bags of fajitas.

Federal Bureau of Investigation (FBI) The investigative arm of the U.S. Department of Justice.

federalism A political doctrine holding that power is divided (often constitutionally) between a central governing body (the federal government, for example) and various constituent units (the states).

field training officer (FTO) A veteran police officer tasked with providing on-the-job training and performance critique during a rookie police officer's initial assignment following graduation from the academy.

Fifth Amendment An amendment to the U.S. Constitution that establishes due process rights, including the right to remain silent in the face of criminal accusations.

firearms training system (FATS) A full-size, fully interactive training device, not unlike flight and driving simulators, that exposes police trainees to realistic shooting scenarios. The realism is enhanced by fully encasing the trainees in a particular surrounding rather than simply putting them in front of a television screen.

first-page test A series of questions proposed by Joycelyn Pollock that police officers can ask themselves to reinforce professional ethical standards.[21]

focused patrol A form of patrol that focuses police efforts on certain problems, locations, or times.

foot patrol The oldest method of police patrol, which entails officers walking through neighborhoods. Foot patrol tends to enhance rapport between citizens and officers, but it clearly limits an officer's ability to give chase if the need arises.

force continuum The spectrum of force available to a police officer, from the absence of physical force to the use of a deadly weapon.

force factor The level of force used by a police officer relative to the suspect's level of resistance.

forensic evidence Physical evidence whose usefulness in a court of law may not be immediately apparent to an untrained observer but can be demonstrated through the application of accepted scientific techniques.

formal criminal proceeding Following *Escobedo v. Illinois* (1964), any official action by a government actor that occurs once the accused becomes the focus of an investigation by the police.

Fourth Amendment The amendment to the U.S. Constitution that governs search and seizure.

frankpledge system The ultimate outgrowth of the night watch system of social control, dating to the twelfth century, in which ten households were grouped into a tithing, and each adult male member of the tithing was held responsible for the conduct of the others.

Frederick W. Taylor (1856–1915) A classical organizational theorist who posited that worker productivity could be increased through careful attention to how work was allocated and who performed what functions.

fruit of the poisonous tree doctrine An expansion of the scope of the exclusionary rule that requires the exclusion of any secondary evidence (such as a confession) that derives from evidence originally obtained in violation of the U.S. Constitution.[22]

functional equivalent of a question "[A]ny words or actions on the part of the police (other than those normally attendant to arrest and custody) that the police should know are reasonably likely to elicit an incriminating response from the suspect."[23]

fusion center An intelligence-gathering unit, often constituted as a collaborative effort that serves various agencies.

futures research Research that is concerned with developing and refining techniques for accurately predicting what lies ahead.

Gang Resistance Education and Training (GREAT) An educational program that uses uniformed police officers to introduce students to conflict-resolution skills, cultural sensitivity, and the dark side of gang membership.

geographic profiling Using crime-mapping technology to identify the likely whereabouts or residences of repeat or serial offenders.

globalization The internationalization of trade, services, investment, information, and other forms of human social activity.

Global Positioning System (GPS) A system that uses global positioning satellite technology to track the exact locations of offenders who wear tracking devices.

government action In the context of search and seizure law, one of two elements that must be considered when defining a Fourth Amendment search. (The other element is a reasonable expectation of privacy.) Government actions consist of measures to effect a search undertaken by someone employed by or working on behalf of the government.

Graham v. Connor The 1989 U.S. Supreme Court case in which the Court declared that claims of excessive nondeadly force must be judged under the Fourth Amendment's reasonableness clause.

grass eater A police officer who accepts small gifts and engages in minor acts of deviance but does not actively pursue opportunities for corruption.

gratuity Something of value that is freely given to police officers simply because they are police officers. Examples include a cup of coffee, a lunch, or a "police price" discount on a meal or other service.

guilty A plea entered in response to a criminal charge whereby the accused acknowledges responsibility for the charged offense. Also, a finding rendered by a judge or jury following the completion of a criminal trial.

Hawthorne experiments A series of experiments conducted between 1927 and 1932 by the Western Electric Company at its Hawthorne facilities to determine whether the level of lighting or the pattern of employee breaks affected productivity. The experiments revealed that it was not the lighting or the breaks that affected productivity as much as it was the attention that employees received.

Henry Fayol (1841–1925) A classical organizational theorist who posited that a universal science of management was applicable to all organizations and that greater technical knowledge was needed at higher organizational levels.

Henry Fielding (1707–1754) An English magistrate who founded what some have called London's first police force, the Bow Street Runners.

historical analogy A forecasting method that looks at past events that seem to be repeating themselves.

Homeland Security Act of 2002 U.S. legislation enacted after the terrorist attacks of September 11, 2001, that created the cabinet-level Department of Homeland Security.

Homicide Investigation and Tracking System (HITS) A geographic profiling system that ties various databases together (gang files, sex offender registries, parole records, and department of motor vehicle records) to facilitate simultaneous database searches.

horizontal communication Organizational communication that flows out through the ranks.

hostile work environment A form of sexual harassment involving situations in which unwelcome sexual contact and comments have the effect of "unreasonably interfering with an individual's work performance or creating an intimidating environment."[24]

hot pursuit exception One exception to the Fourth Amendment's warrant requirement, recognized by the U.S. Supreme Court in *Warden v. Hayden* (1967).[25] The hot pursuit doctrine provides that police officers may enter the premises where they suspect a crime has been committed, or a perpetrator is hiding, without a warrant when delay would likely endanger their lives or the lives of others and possibly lead to the escape of the alleged perpetrator.

hot spot A concentrated area of significant criminal activity, such as a street corner known for its prostitution traffic.

hot time A period during the day when crime is particularly problematic, such as after dark on a Friday night.

house In the context of search and seizure law, a broadly construed term meaning any structure that a person uses as a residence (and frequently a business) on either a temporary or a long-term basis.

humanistic perspective One of two traditional approaches to motivating subordinates—the other is the *behavioral perspective*—which focuses on human relationships, employee potential, and people's internal drive. This perspective contends that motivation comes from within,[26] so there is nothing police organizations necessarily need to do to motivate subordinates other than to attract and retain motivated individuals.

human relations An organizational philosophy that contends that all organizations are organic entities and that management should engage in a social process that combines techniques and people to benefit both the organization and the employee.

human trafficking (a) Sex trafficking in which a commercial sex act is induced by force, fraud, [or] coercion, or in which the person induced to perform such act has not attained 18 years of age; or (b) the recruitment, harboring, transportation, provision or obtaining of a person for labor or services, through the use of force, fraud, or coercion for the purpose of subjection to involuntary servitude, peonage, debt bondage or slavery."[27]

hundred See parish.

identity theft The unauthorized use of someone else's personal identification information (such as a Social Security number) to establish new credit lines or for other fraudulent purposes, such as stealing money from the victim's bank account.

Illinois Crime Survey A series of influential reports, published in 1929, on homicide, juvenile justice, and justice operations in Chicago that criticized the corrupt political influence on the justice system.[28]

Immigration and Customs Enforcement (ICE) The largest investigative component of the federal Department of Homeland Security. ICE focuses specifically on illegal immigration.

impact munitions Munitions designed to stun or otherwise temporarily incapacitate a suspect or a dangerous individual so that law enforcement officers can subdue and arrest that person with less risk of injury or death to themselves and to others.[29]

impression management A media relations concept that involves controlling the presentation of information to achieve a desired public perception.

indirect force Actions by an officer that indirectly expose a suspect or an innocent bystander to potential injury but that do not involve the intentional application of direct physical force. A high-speed automobile pursuit is an example.

individual liability Section 1983 liability that arises from an individual officer's actions that violate a specific constitutional right.

injunctive relief A court order to bring injurious or offensive action to a halt.

Innocence Project A private initiative that uses DNA technology to exonerate individuals who have been wrongfully convicted and imprisoned.

inspection Any one of numerous examinations conducted by a government actor that are held to be permissible without a warrant or probable cause. Examples include a welfare compliance inspection and a wide array of business inspections to ensure compliance with tax or regulatory requirements.

institution An organizational structure through which values and norms are transmitted over time and from one location to another within a society.

institutional value A sense of agreement within a particular culture about how to accomplish a valued objective.

intelligence Information that has been analyzed and integrated into a useful perspective.

intelligence-led policing (ILP) The collection and analysis of information to produce an intelligence end product designed to inform police decision making at both the tactical and strategic levels.[30] Also called *intelligence-driven policing*.

intentional tort An action that is highly likely to cause injury or damage.

intergroup conflict Conflict between two or more groups within an organization.

internal affairs (IA) An investigative agency within a police department that is tasked with investigating allegations of misconduct or criminality by members of the department.

internal payoff The "sale" of anything within a police agency, from work assignments and time off to evidence and promotion.

International Association of Chiefs of Police (IACP) Founded in 1893, the best-known association for law enforcement professionals.

International Criminal Court (ICC) A permanent criminal court that tries individuals (not countries) who commit the most serious crimes against humanity: genocide and other war crimes.

International Police Association (IPA) Founded in 1950, the largest police professional association in the world.

international terrorism The unlawful use of violence by an individual or a group that has some connection to a foreign power or organization.

International Union of Police Associations (IUPA) An international police association, founded in 1954 and chartered by the AFL-CIO, that represents all rank-and-file officers and functions more as a lobbying group than as a professional association.

interorganizational conflict Conflict between two or more agencies.

interpersonal conflict Conflict between individual members of an organization.

Interpol The International Criminal Police Organization, an international police organization comprised of 182 member countries.

interrogation "Questioning initiated by law enforcement officers."[31]

intragroup conflict Conflict within a particular group in an organization.

Joint Terrorism Task Force (JTTF) An FBI-sponsored group comprised of federal, state, and local law enforcement personnel who are brought together to focus on a specific threat.

justification The focus of a court's examination of the reasonableness of a search or seizure.

juvenile waiver A legal maneuver in which the jurisdiction over a juvenile offender is waived by the juvenile court to permit criminal prosecution of the offender in an adult court.

Kansas City Preventive Patrol Experiment A study of the effects of various methods of police patrol conducted in Missouri in 1972 and 1973.

kickback An illegal payment for a service performed.

Knapp Commission A commission to investigate police corruption that was appointed by New York City Mayor John V. Lindsay in 1970 in response to a *New York Times* article that reported widespread corruption in the New York City Police Department.

"knock and talk" A police tactic used to obtain consent to search, in which police officers approach a home, knock on the door, and request consent to search the premises.

labor relations The relationship between management and labor within an organization.

Law Enforcement Assistance and Partnership (LEAP) Strategy A plan introduced in the U.S. Congress that called for the establishment of a national center for intelligence-led policing.

leadership The process of directing and influencing the task-related activities of group members.

legal abuse Any violation of a person's constitutionally, federally, or state-protected rights.[32]

legalistic style A style of policing that is focused on enforcing the letter of the law.

less-lethal weapon A weapon that is designed to disable, capture, or immobilize, rather than kill.

local agency One of the three levels of law enforcement activity in the United States—the other two being state and federal—which encompasses organizations like municipal police departments, sheriff's departments, and other lesser-known agencies, including campus police, transit police, and specialized agencies at public schools, airports, state capitols, medical facilities, state parks, certain prosecutor's offices, and others. Together, the personnel in these local agencies far outnumber all state and federal law enforcement officials combined.

Maslow's hierarchy of needs A psychological theory proposed by Abraham Maslow in his 1943 paper titled "A Theory of Human Motivation." Maslow's theory holds that once people have achieved their basic needs, they will strive for higher-level emotional satisfaction and personal fulfillment.

mass private property Large shopping malls and other properties that attract large numbers of consumers but have little or no public police protection. It can be argued that private policing evolved to meet the protection needs of mass private property.

Max Weber (1864–1920) A classical organizational theorist, widely acknowledged as the father of bureaucracy, who identified five principles that he suggested are characteristic of an effective bureaucratic organization.

mayor-council form A form of municipal government that can be categorized in two ways. The strong-mayor variation gives the mayor almost limitless authority over city operations, including the hiring and dismissal of key officials. In the weak-mayor variation, which is more common in small towns, the mayor serves largely at the behest of the city council.

meat eater A police officer who actively seeks out and plans opportunities to exploit his or her position for personal gain.

Metropolitan Police Act The legislation adopted by the British Parliament in 1829 that established the world's first large-scale organized police force in London.

Miami River Cops A Miami Police Department scandal that occurred in the 1980s and resulted in the indictment of a number of officers for criminal acts ranging from stealing cash from motorists stopped for traffic violations to major thefts and murder.

Minneapolis Domestic Violence Experiment A study conducted in the 1980s of the effects of various police responses to domestic violence calls.

Minneapolis Repeat Call Address Policing A third-party policing program in Minneapolis, Minnesota, that used a small, detached, developmental unit working on a diverse set of "problems" derived from a computer analysis of addresses with high levels of calls for police service.

***Miranda* rights** The set of rights that a person accused or suspected of having committed a specific offense has during interrogation and of which he or she must be informed prior to questioning, as stated by the U.S. Supreme Court in *Miranda v. Arizona* (1966) and related cases.

mission distortion "Situations where the definition of one's professional mission (or role) orientation becomes blurred."[33]

Mollen Commission A commission appointed by New York City Mayor David N. Dinkins in 1992 to investigate allegations of police corruption in the New York City Police Department.

money laundering The process by which criminals or criminal organizations seek to disguise the illicit nature of their proceeds by introducing them into the stream of legitimate commerce and finance.

Monitoring the Future (MTF) Survey A national survey program that measures drug use among adolescents in the United States.

motivation The set of processes that arouse, direct, and maintain human behavior toward attaining some goal.

multijurisdictional drug task force A drug interdiction and eradication team composed of members from law enforcement agencies from multiple jurisdictions and often several levels of government.

municipal/county liability Section 1983 liability that arises from adopted customs or implemented policies that lead to constitutional rights violations.[34]

municipal police department One of the types of local law enforcement agencies in the United States. Specifically, the law enforcement agency that serves a municipality.

narcoterrorism The collaboration between drug traffickers and terrorist groups.

National Black Police Association The parent association, founded in 1972, for local and regional associations of African American police professionals.

National Criminal Intelligence Sharing Plan (NCISP) "A formal intelligence sharing initiative that addresses the security and intelligence needs recognized after the tragic events of September 11, 2001. It describes a nationwide communications capability that will link together all levels of law enforcement personnel, including officers on the streets, intelligence analysts, unit commanders, and police executives for the purpose of sharing critical data."[35]

National Institute of Justice (NIJ) A research, development, and evaluation agency within the Office of Justice Programs in the U.S. Department of Justice.

National Intelligence Model The United Kingdom's law enforcement planning model, which stresses a business approach to the management and reduction of crime.

National Strategy for Combating Terrorism (NSCT) The U.S. national plan for combating terrorism.

National Survey on Drug Use and Health (NSDUH) A national survey program that measures drug use in the United States.

negligence tort A liability claim that must demonstrate that a legal duty existed between the officer and the plaintiff, that a breach of that duty occurred, that a proximate (direct) causation between the officer's actions and the alleged harm resulted, and that actual damage or injury occurred.

neighborhood watch Formal and informal crime-prevention programs in which citizen volunteers patrol communities and report suspicious activities to the local police.

noble-cause corruption Any corruption that occurs in connection with the goal of getting criminals off the streets and protecting the community.

no-fix law A law that requires police officers to account for every ticket that is issued, even the voided ones, in an effort to prevent favoritism and unequal treatment.

nolo contendere A plea of "no contest" entered in response to a criminal charge whereby the accused declines to contest the charged offense.

nondeadly force Force that is unlikely to cause death or significant bodily harm.

nonsworn personnel Support staff members of a law enforcement agency who are not empowered to make arrests.

nonverbal communication Gestures, behavior, and bodily and facial expressions that can convey a message.

norm A rule or expectation for behavior that characterizes a particular social group.

not guilty A plea entered in response to a criminal charge whereby the accused denies responsibility for the charged offense. Also, a finding rendered by a judge or jury following the completion of a criminal trial.

objective reasonableness A standard, used to determine whether qualified immunity applies, that looks at how a reasonable person would have acted under a given set of circumstances.[36]

occupational deviance Behavior performed under the guise of police authority that either does not conform to accepted standards of conduct or is not part of normal patrol work.

Office of Community Oriented Policing Services (COPS Office) An agency within the U.S. Department of Justice tasked with administering and supervising federal funds allocated to improve community policing capabilities.

old-style crime fighter An aggressive officer who concentrates on serious felony crimes.

Operation Ceasefire An initiative designed to disrupt the illegal gun market in the city of Boston. The initiative, originally called the Boston Gun Project, has achieved significant reductions in gun violence in the city.

Operation Fresh Start A program in Atlanta, Georgia, that moves officers into homes within their patrol areas to provide service to a very small and specific target area.[37]

Operation Nightlight A police-corrections partnership in San Bernardino, California, that deployed two-person teams, each staffed by one probation officer and one police officer, to conduct home visits to juveniles newly placed on probation and to enforce curfew and truancy rules.

opportunistic theft A theft that occurs when an opportunity presents itself.

organization A group in which individuals work together to accomplish specified tasks or goals.

Orlando Winfield "O. W." Wilson (1900–1972) A progressive era reformer, professor of police administration, and protégé of August Vollmer whose writings and teachings continue to influence contemporary U.S. law enforcement.

papers and effects In the context of search and seizure law, nearly all personal items.

paradox of policing A phenomenon in which a police officer's fear of being injured or killed is stronger than is justified by actual rates of injury or death within the profession.

parish Under the frankpledge system, a group of ten tithings. Also referred to as a *hundred.*

participatory management A form of leadership that allows subordinates to participate in decision making and planning, especially with regard to the manner in which their own units are operated.

particularistic perspective The view that individual officers differ from one another in various ways, including values, role orientation, and preferred styles of policing.

passion The dimension of police ethical development that indicates how comfortable an officer is in using coercive means to carry out his or her responsibilities.

patronage system A system of hiring in which decisions are based more on an individual's political support for an officeholder than on his or her abilities and qualifications. Patronage was common in police agencies during the political era.

pepper spray A so-called lachrymatory (inflammatory) agent that causes irritation to the eyes and skin. Also called *oleoresin capsicum (OC).*

performance measurement A formal process through which supervisors provide subordinates with feedback on their job performance.

person In the context of search and seizure law, the individual as a whole, both internally and externally.

person inventory The search of an arrestee and his or her personal items, including containers found in his or her possession, as part of a routine inventory that is incident to the booking and jailing procedure. Often called *arrest inventory.*

perspective The dimension of police ethical development that indicates the extent to which an officer understands human suffering and is inclined to show compassion.

perversion of justice A kind of police corruption that consists of serious actions by a police officer, such as lying under oath (perjury), intimidating a witness, and performing other activities that resemble combative corruption.

physical evidence Tangible property and the like.

pin map An early crime-mapping technique that used colored pins to track criminal events on a map of the police department's jurisdictional area.

plain touch A doctrine articulated by the U.S. Supreme Court that permits an expansion of a stop-and-frisk search "if the officer, while staying within the narrow limits of a frisk for weapons, feels what he has probable cause to believe is a weapon, contraband or evidence."[38]

plain view A doctrine articulated by the U.S. Supreme Court that permits the warrantless seizure of objects that are readily visible.

plebe system A police academy model that closely parallels a military-style boot camp and that aims to produce well-groomed and disciplined officers.

police commission An agency maintained in some large cities that acts like a corporate board of directors, setting policy and overseeing the police department's operations.

police-corrections partnership A collaboration between police officers and either probation officers or parole officers (mostly the former) that seeks to reduce crime by increasing the supervision of probationers or parolees.

police corruption The misuse of police authority for personal or organizational gain.

police crime An "officer's use of the official powers of his or her job to engage in criminal conduct."[39]

Police Executive Research Forum (PERF) A research organization, incorporated in 1977, dedicated solely to police administration issues.

Police Foundation A research agency, established in 1970, concerned with all facets of policing.

police officers' bill of rights A police agency's formal statement of the rights of officers who are accused of misconduct.

police paramilitary unit (PPU) A specially trained and equipped law enforcement unit that trains with one or more branches of the military and uses military tactics and techniques.

police sexual violence A sexually degrading, humiliating, violating, damaging, or threatening act committed by a police officer against a (usually female) citizen through the use of force or police authority.[40]

police subculture The shared values and norms and the established patterns of behavior that tend to characterize policing. Also called *police culture.*

police training officer (PTO) program A police training method that focuses on developing an officer's learning capacity, leadership, and problem-solving skills.

police violence In the context of drug investigations, the use of improper physical force to extract a confession or to obtain evidence.

political era The period of American policing during the late nineteenth and early twentieth centuries during which police forces served more to regulate crime pursuant to the wishes of corrupt politicians (who used patronage to give police jobs to handpicked loyalists) than to control crime in the interests of the public good.

Posse Comitatus Act U.S. legislation passed in 1878 that generally prohibits federal military personnel and the National Guard (under federal authority) from engaging in local law enforcement activities.

post-traumatic stress disorder (PTSD) A condition which sets in following a traumatic event with which the sufferer cannot cope. It has been described as an event outside the usual human experience, one which is experienced in a markedly distressing way, with intense fear, terror, bewilderment, and a sense of helplessness.[41]

Powell v. Alabama A 1932 case in which the U.S. Supreme Court held that a defendant facing the death penalty is entitled to an attorney at trial.

predatory corruption A form of police corruption that consists of more than just passive participation (for example, looking the other way while a fellow police officer commits a crime). In predatory corruption, officers actively promote and engage in criminal and other wrongful activities.

preentry John Van Maanen's first stage of police recruit socialization, in which the recruit chooses to pursue a job in law enforcement, having been attracted by the idea that policing is an elite occupation that offers an opportunity to do something important for society, such as serve people.

pretext stop A traffic stop based on more than one motive. For example, an officer stops a vehicle for a legitimate reason but is also suspicious about the driver.

preventive patrol The practice of canvassing neighborhoods in an effort to discourage people from committing crime.

private policing The acquisition and use of security products and services, as well as the application of specialized knowledge in areas like crime control, investigation, and risk management, by nonsworn personnel.[42]

private security The industry that provides for-profit security products and services, which include three broad categories: the provision of guards, equipment, and investigative or consulting services.[43]

proactive policing A policing method that relies heavily on police-initiated arrests, as opposed to arrests made after someone calls for police assistance.

probable cause A set of facts and circumstances that would induce a reasonably intelligent and prudent person to believe that another particular person has committed a specific crime. Probable cause is the only justification for search and seizure mentioned in the Fourth Amendment.

problem-oriented policing (POP) A method of policing that is geared toward identifying and solving problems within a community that are particularly troublesome and then crafting creative solutions to them. Also called *problem-solving policing*.

problem police officer An officer who exhibits problem behavior, as indicated by a large number of citizen complaints, frequent involvement in use-of-force incidents, and other evidence.[44]

procedural due process A constitutional prohibition against "arbitrary and unfair deprivations of protected life, liberty, or property interests without procedural safeguards."[45]

professional-style officer An officer who is both compassionate and comfortable using his or her authority when the need arises.

programming The process of converting plans into action-oriented strategies.

Project Exile A program established in Richmond, Virginia, that involves local, state, and federal law enforcement officials, including both police and prosecutors, working together to reduce the city's homicide rate.

Project Safe Neighborhoods A federal initiative that attempts to curb gun violence by linking existing local programs together and providing them with necessary tools.

protective sweep A permissible cursory visual inspection of places in which a person might be hiding. A protective sweep may be conducted by police up to the point of an arrest but must be supported by reasonable suspicion.

public-duty defense A legal defense that shields a police officer from criminal liability in situations in which he or she is legally performing an assigned or implied public duty and engages in a necessary and reasonable action that, for ordinary citizens, would be considered a crime.

public-duty doctrine A doctrine stating that police protection (like any other government function) is owed to the general public, not to individuals. Police officers have used the public-duty doctrine as a liability defense.

public information officer A police department's spokesperson. The media must go through the public information officer to gather information about the department.

qualified immunity A liability defense that shields a police officer who has acted in an objectively reasonable fashion as long as he or she did not violate clearly established rights that a reasonable person would have known. Qualified immunity is an outgrowth of various U.S. Supreme Court decisions.

quality circle A group of qualified employees from all ranks who work together, often around one table, to solve organizational problems.

quality-of-life offense A minor law violation that demoralizes residents and businesspeople by creating disorder. Sometimes called *petty crime*.

quasi-military An organizational structure that follows the military model to some extent, but with subtle differences.

***quid pro quo* harassment** A form of sexual harassment that generally involves a demand for sexual favors in exchange for some perk or benefit, such as a promotion or a favorable job assignment.

racial profiling "The use of discretionary authority by law enforcement officers in encounters with minority motorists, typically within the context of a traffic stop, that results in the disparate treatment of minorities."[46]

racial quota A requirement for hiring and promoting a specified number of minorities.

Rampart Division scandal A Los Angeles Police Department scandal in the late 1990s that resulted in the convictions of numerous police officers for a wide variety of serious crimes. Because of the scandal, the Los Angeles City Council was forced to accept the terms of a federal consent decree through which federal officials took over the supervision of the department's daily operations.

reasonable expectation of privacy In the context of search and seizure law, one of two elements that must be considered when defining a Fourth Amendment search. (The other element is government action.) A reasonable expectation of privacy means that people who speak or act in private can reasonably expect that what they say or do will not be seen or heard by someone else.

reasonableness The elements of a situation that serve to justify a search or seizure.

reasonableness clause One of two basic clauses that make up the Fourth Amendment. The reasonableness clause proscribes "unreasonable searches and seizures."[47] See also *warrant clause*.

reasonable suspicion A belief, based on a consideration of the facts at hand and on reasonable inferences drawn from those facts, that would induce an ordinarily prudent and cautious person under the same circumstances to conclude that criminal activity is taking place or that criminal activity has recently occurred. Reasonable suspicion is the standard for less intrusive stop-and-frisk searches; it is less than probable cause but more than a hunch.

reciprocator An officer who is compassionate but somewhat uncomfortable with his or her authority role, who tends to use communication to defuse volatile situations, and who avoids using force unless it is absolutely necessary.

reform era The period of American policing during the early to mid-twentieth century, during which efforts were made to professionalize police forces and to eliminate the influence of corrupt politicians.

remedy According to John Van Maanen, the last of three steps police officers use in identifying an "asshole." It consists of the officer's response to an affront.

Repeat Offender Project A specialized crime-prevention unit that operated in the Washington, DC, area during the early 1980s and that targeted individuals with outstanding warrants and individuals thought to be criminally active.

residency requirement A requirement that officers reside within the community they serve as a condition of employment.

response time The time it takes for police officers to respond to a call for service.

reverse discrimination Discrimination against nonminorities that occurs when the hiring and promotion of minorities are based more on race than on any other criterion.

Rodney King A suspect whose videotaped beating by members of the Los Angeles Police Department led to civil unrest across the nation.

rogue A seriously deviant officer.

rotten apple theory A perspective that attributes police deviance primarily to a few individuals whose propensity toward corruption was not recognized during the recruitment and hiring phases.

saturation patrol A form of patrol that involves concentrating the police presence in a certain area in an effort to catch criminals and to deter would-be offenders.

scenarios A forecasting method that involves "a series of events that we imagine happening in the future."[48]

school resource officer A police officer whose duty assignment is to patrol inside a specific school.

search An activity performed in order to find evidence to be used in a criminal prosecution.

search incident to arrest A warrantless search made at the time of or shortly following an arrest, which is conducted out of a concern for the safety of the arresting officer and others.

Secret Service The federal law enforcement agency tasked with providing executive protection to specific federal officials and with investigating violations of laws relating to counterfeiting of obligations and securities of the United States; financial crimes including access device fraud, financial institution fraud, identity theft, and computer fraud; and computer-based attacks on our nation's financial, banking, and telecommunications infrastructure.

seizure The confiscation of one's person (arrest) or property by a government agent.

selectivity The extent to which officers are concerned only with serious crime problems.

service style A style of policing that is focused on meeting the needs of the community and serving its citizens.

service-style officer An officer who generally avoids coercion and aggression while focusing on the most serious problems that the community faces.

sexual harassment Unwelcome sexual advances, requests for sexual favors, and other verbal or physical conduct of a sexual nature.

shakedown A demand by a corrupt police officer for money, goods, or something of value from a citizen in exchange for lenient treatment, protection, or some other illegitimate "service."

sheriff The modern-day term for the Old English *shire-reeve*. In the United States today, the senior law enforcement official in a county.

sheriff's department One of the types of local law enforcement agencies in the United States. Specifically, the law enforcement agency that serves a county or parish.

shire Under the frankpledge system, a collection of several parishes.

shire-reeve The Old English term for *sheriff*. Literally, "the keeper of the shire."

Sir Robert Peel (1788–1850) A former British home secretary whose criticisms of the state of policing in London led to the passage of the Metropolitan Police Act and the establishment of the world's first large-scale organized police force in that city in 1829.

sixth sense A healthy sense of suspicion; the experience-based ability to intuit when something is amiss.

slave patrol A crude form of private policing, often carried out by citizen volunteers. Slave patrols were created in the eighteenth century to apprehend runaway slaves and to ensure that slaves did not rise up against their owners.

social engineering A nontechnical kind of cyberintrusion that relies on human interaction and often involves tricking people into breaking normal security procedures.

Society of Police Futurists International (PFI) An organization of forward-thinking law enforcement professionals.

solidarity The tendency among police officers to stick together and associate with one another.

sovereign immunity A liability defense based on the Eleventh Amendment that shields states and state officials who are acting in their official capacities from being sued in federal court.

span of control The number of subordinates supervised by one person.

split-second syndrome A condition confronting police officers that involves three central features of policing—the urgency of police-citizen encounters, the involuntariness of such encounters, and a public setting—all of which combine to place officers in the position of having to make quick on-the-spot decisions.[49]

state tort liability An important avenue of redress for plaintiffs whose minor injuries, allegedly resulting from negligent acts or misconduct by the police, are not serious enough to make Section 1983 litigation a viable option.

status offense An act or conduct that is declared by statute to be an offense only if committed by or engaged in by a juvenile. Such offenses can be adjudicated only by a juvenile court.

Stockholm syndrome The phenomenon in which a person held as a hostage for some time develops an emotional bond with his or her captor.

stop and frisk The detaining of a person by a law enforcement officer for the purpose of investigation, accompanied by a superficial examination by the officer of the person's body surface or clothing to discover weapons, contraband, or other objects relating to criminal activity.[50]

storefronts and substations A community policing initiative that places satellite police offices in locations that are readily accessible to community members.

straightforward corruption Any form of police misconduct that provides direct financial benefit to police officers.

straight shooter An honest police officer who will overlook some misconduct committed by peers.

strategic intelligence A type of intelligence that provides information to decision makers about the changing nature of threats, enabling them to develop response strategies and reallocate resources for effective threat prevention.

strategic prosecution A prosecutorial tactic that shifts emphasis away from individual criminal cases brought by the police to an overall concern with preventing and reducing crime.

straw purchase An illegal gun purchase that occurs when a person who cannot legally own a gun (for example, a youth) asks someone else to buy the gun for him or her.

street closure An anticrime/antigang tactical measure designed to control traffic flow so as to deny easy or undetected movement through a neighborhood or business district.

street environment One of two settings identified by John Crank (the other is the traffic stop) in which police officers perform daily tasks that involve interaction with ordinary citizens and with other criminal justice professionals.[51]

stress Anything that places a positive or negative adjustive demand on an organism.

subculture Cultural patterns that distinguish some segment of a society's population.

subjugation of defendants' rights In the context of drug investigations, an officer's lying or committing perjury or fabricating evidence in the name of securing a drug conviction.

substantive due process A constitutional prohibition against "the government's abuse of power or its use for the purpose of oppression."[52]

sudden peril A defense against state tort liability that is used for cases in which police officers were required to make split-second decisions.

suicide by cop An incident in which an individual who is determined to die engages in behavior meant to provoke responding officers to resort to deadly force.

supervisory liability A doctrine established by the U.S. Supreme Court in *Rizzo v. Goode* (1976)[53] requiring that for a Section 1983 lawsuit to succeed against a supervisor, there must be a clear link between the supervisor and the constitutional violation committed by a subordinate.

sworn personnel Members of a law enforcement agency who are empowered to make arrests.

symbolic assailant According to Jerome Skolnick, a person whom a police officer thinks is potentially dangerous.

systems perspective A view of organizational style, rooted in biology, that posits that organizations are living organisms that strive for a state of equilibrium, or balance, and that affect or are affected by their environment.

tactical intelligence A type of intelligence that "includes gaining or developing information related to threats of terrorism or crime and using this information to apprehend offenders, harden targets, and use strategies that will eliminate or mitigate the threat."[54]

Taking Command Initiative A project undertaken by the International Association of Chiefs of Police to assess the current state of homeland security efforts in the United States and to develop and implement the actions needed to protect American communities from the specter of both crime and terrorism.

Tammany Hall The corrupt Democratic Party political "machine" that operated in New York City in the late nineteenth and early twentieth centuries and that used patronage to control city operations.

technical training model A police academy training model that emphasizes the technical aspects of police work and provides little or no training in such nontechnical areas as stress management, interaction with difficult people, problem solving, and sensitivity to marginalized groups.

Tennessee v. Garner The 1985 U.S. Supreme Court case that specified the conditions under which deadly force could be used to apprehend suspected felons.

territorial imperative The sense of obligation, even protectiveness, that develops in officers who routinely patrol the same area.

testimonial evidence Verbal testimony given by a witness at trial.

Texas Rangers A militia originally formed by Stephen F. Austin in 1823 to protect the territory of Texas against American Indian raids, criminals, and intruders. Today, the Rangers serve as part of the Texas Department of Public Safety.

theory of liability Reasons offered as to why a particular person or other entity should be held answerable under law for some action.

Theory X One of two types of workers posited by Douglas McGregor as lacking ambition, being indolent by nature, being self-centered, and so on.

Theory Y One of two types of workers posited by Douglas McGregor as being motivated and failing only when management fails to provide a supportive working environment.

thief taker An alternative name for Henry Fielding's Bow Street Runners.

third degree A formerly common coercive interrogation technique that combined psychological pressures with physical force.

third-party policing A recently coined term that describes "police efforts to persuade or coerce nonoffending persons to take actions which are outside the scope of their routine activities, and which are designed to indirectly minimize disorder caused by other persons or to reduce the possibility that crime may occur."[55]

tithing Under the frankpledge system, a group of ten households.

tolerated lie A lie that is used to defend a questionable discretionary decision.

trace evidence Minute, nearly invisible evidence of a crime that would escape all but the most skilled investigators.

traffic stop One of two settings identified by Crank (the other is the street environment) in which police officers perform daily tasks that involve interactions with ordinary citizens and with other law enforcement professionals.[56]

transnational crime Crime that crosses international borders.

trend extrapolation A forecasting method that involves "observing a change through time in the character of something and projecting or extrapolating that change into the future."[57]

trial board An agency within a police department that operates in conjunction with the internal investigation unit and is staffed on an ad hoc basis when the need arises for thorough and impartial evaluation of alleged employee misconduct.

Type I drug corruption Drug-related police corruption that "occurs when an officer seeks to use his or her position simply for personal gain."[58]

Type II drug corruption Drug-related police corruption that involves the officer's desire for legitimate gains (for example, winning a conviction). The officer's actions may not even be universally perceived as corruption.[59]

union An organization that represents dues-paying workers for the purpose of negotiating with employers concerning issues of importance to the workers.

United Nations (UN) An international agency comprised of 192 member countries.

universalistic perspective The view that all police officers are similar and that they exhibit some of the same characteristics and behavior patterns.

USA PATRIOT Act A federal law (Public Law 107-56) enacted in response to terrorist attacks against the United States on September 11, 2001. The law, officially titled the Uniting and Strengthening America by Providing Appropriate Tools Required to Intercept and Obstruct Terrorism Act, substantially broadened the investigative authority of law enforcement agencies throughout America and is applicable to many crimes other than terrorism. The law was slightly revised and reauthorized by Congress in 2006. Also called the *Antiterrorism Act.*

use corruption Drug-related police corruption that consists of an officer's personal use of illicit drugs.

use of force The use of physical restraint by a police officer when dealing with a member of the public.[60]

U.S. Marshals Service (USMS) The oldest American law enforcement agency. Its mission includes judicial security and fugitive investigation and apprehension.

universalistic perspective The view that all police officers are similar and that they exhibit some of the same characteristics and behavior patterns.

value A standard of goodness, desirability, behavior, beauty, or interaction that serves as a guideline for living within a particular culture.

vehicle inventory A warrantless inventory of a vehicle that is permissible on administrative or regulatory grounds. Vehicle inventories must follow a lawful impoundment, must be of a routine nature, must follow standard operating procedures, and must not be a pretext that attempts to conceal an investigatory search.

verbal communication Face-to-face oral communications.

vertical communication Organizational communication that flows down through the ranks.

Violent Crime Control and Law Enforcement Act of 1994 The U.S. legislation that established the Office of Community Oriented Policing Services (the COPS Office) in the U.S. Justice Department.

warrant clause One of two basic clauses that make up the Fourth Amendment. The warrant clause requires that "no Warrants shall issue, but upon probable cause, supported by Oath or affirmation, and particularly describing the place to be searched, and the persons or things to be seized."[61] See also *reasonableness clause.*

watchman An early officer on foot patrol who, during the hours of darkness, watched for fires and criminal activities. Upon detecting such events, the watchman's role was to sound the "hue and cry" to evoke a defensive response from the citizenry. This style of policing dates back to the early to mid-eighteenth century in England.

watchman style A style of policing that is focused on achieving order maintenance through the control of illegal and disruptive behavior.

weapons continuum The array of nonlethal and lethal weaponry available to police officers, the selection of which depends on the situation.

weapons trafficking A serious form of transnational crime that involves the smuggling of illegal small arms and light weapons, such as machine guns and shoulder-fired rockets.[62]

white knight An honest and upstanding officer who never steps over the line between accepted and deviant conduct, no matter how great the pressure to do so.

Wickersham Commission A commission appointed by President Herbert Hoover in 1929 to investigate the operations and problems of the criminal justice system. Formally known as the *National Commission on Law Observance and Enforcement.*

William M. "Boss" Tweed (1823–1878) A corrupt American politician who became notorious as the powerful leader of New York City's Tammany Hall.

NOTES

Chapter One

i. D. H. Bayley, *Patterns of policing: A comparative international analysis* (New Brunswick, NJ: Rutgers University Press, 1985), pp. 31–32.
ii. F. Schmalleger, *Criminal justice today: An introductory text for the twenty-first century*, 9th ed. (Upper Saddle River, NJ: Prentice Hall, 2006), p. 162.
iii. Illinois Association for Criminal Justice, *Illinois crime survey* (1929; repr., Montclair, NJ: Patterson Smith, 1968), p. 359.
iv. E. E. Joh, "The paradox of private policing," *Journal of Criminal Law and Criminology*, 95 (2004): 67.

---

1. See the Minuteman Project website, http://www.minutemanproject.com
2. See http://www.vigilantewatch.org.
3. American Civil Liberties Union, "ACLU, advocacy groups fear anti-immigrant violence," press release, http://www.aclu.org/immigrants/gen/11742prs20050330.html (accessed June 4, 2008).
4. B. L. Berg, *Law enforcement: An introduction to police in society* (Boston: Allyn and Bacon, 1992), pp. 15–16.
5. W. Kunkel, *An introduction to Roman legal and constitutional history*, 2nd ed. (Oxford: Clarendon Press, 1973).
6. W. J. Bopp and D. D. Schultz, *A short history of American law enforcement* (Springfield, IL: Charles C. Thomas, 1972), pp. 9–10.
7. There are three "historical" Statutes of Westminster, dated 1275, 1285, and 1290 (they are known as 'First,' 'Second,' and 'Third'), relating to the government of the Kingdom of England. There is also a 1931 Statute of Westminster, relating to the British Empire and its dominions.
8. W. L. M. Lee, *A history of police in England* (repr., Montclair, NJ: Patterson Smith, 1971).
9. D. H. Bayley, *Patterns of policing: A comparative international analysis* (New Brunswick, NJ: Rutgers University Press, 1985), p. 29.
10. J. J. Tobias, "Police and public in the United Kingdom," *Journal of Contemporary History* (January–April 1972): 201–19.
11. G. Armitage, *The history of the Bow Street Runners, 1729–1829* (London: Wishart, n.d.), p. 123.
12. A. C. Germann, F. D. Day, and R. R. Gallati, *Introduction to law enforcement and criminal justice* (Springfield, IL: Charles C. Thomas, 1978).
13. S. Spitzer and A. T. Scull, "Social control in historical perspective: From private to public responses to crime," in *Correction and punishment*, ed. D. F. Greenberg, pp. 265–86 (Beverly Hills, CA: Sage, 1977).
14. Bayley, *Patterns of policing*, pp. 31–32.
15. Germann, Day, and Gallati, *Introduction to law enforcement and criminal justice*.
16. J. L. Lyman, "The Metropolitan Police Act of 1829: An analysis of certain events influencing the passage and character of the Metropolitan Police Act in England," *Journal of Criminal Law, Criminology, and Police Science*, vol. 55, no. 1 (March 1964), p. 141.
17. Roy Ingleton, "The early days of policing in Kent" (Part 6). The Kent Police Museum. Web available at http:// www.kent-police-museum.co.uk/core_pages/pasttimes_early_days_pt6.shtml. Accessed July 4, 2008.
18. L. Radzinowicz, *A history of English criminal law and its administration since 1750* (New York: Macmillan, 1957), p. 177.
19. E. L. Ayers, *Vengeance and justice: Crime and punishment in the nineteenth century American South* (New York: Oxford University Press, 1984), p. 181.
20. B. Chapin, *Criminal justice in colonial America, 1606–1660* (Athens: University of Georgia Press, 1983), p. 146.
21. F. Browning and J. Gerassi, *The American way of crime* (New York: G. P. Putnam's Sons, 1980).
22. L. H. Randolph, *Biographical sketches of distinguished officers of the army and navy* (New York: Henry E. Huntington, 1905), pp 82–88.
23. R. B. Fosdick, *American police systems* (New York: The Century Co., 1920), p. 62.
24. G. L. Lankevich, *American metropolis: A history of New York City* (New York: New York University Press, 1998), pp. 84–85.
25. Fosdick, *American police systems*, p. 82.
26. Others date the NYPD's official beginning as January 1, 1898—the day that the five boroughs of Manhattan, the Bronx, Brooklyn, Queens, and Staten Island joined together under a charter as the City of Greater New York. What should be clear, however, is that what was essentially a city-wide police force operated in the area prior to the 1898 charter.
27. Some of the information in this paragraph comes from Bernard Whalen, "The birth of the NYPD," Web

available at http://www.nycop.com/Aug_00/The_Birth_of_the_NYPD/body_the_birth_of_the_ nypd.html. Accessed July 5, 2008. The department was further expanded in 1995, when the city's housing and transit police were merged into the NYPD.

28. B. Vila and C. Morris, eds., *The role of police in American society: A documentary history* (Westport, CT: Greenwood Press, 1999), p. 25.
29. W. Miller, *Cops and bobbies* (Chicago: University of Chicago Press, 1977), p. 2.
30. Vila and Morris, eds., *The role of police in American society*.
31. Ibid.
32. R. Brown, *Strain of violence* (New York: Oxford University Press, 1975).
33. S. Walker, *Popular justice* (New York: Oxford University Press, 1998), p. 15.
34. B. Smith, *Police systems in the United States* (New York: Harper and Brothers, 1949).
35. Walker, *Popular justice*, p. 55.
36. G. L. Kelling and M. H. Moore, "The evolving strategy of policing," in *Perspectives on policing*, vol. 4 (Washington, DC: National Institute of Justice, 1988).
37. Walker, *Popular justice*, p. 57.
38. J. C. Schneider, *Detroit and the problem of order, 1830–1880* (Lincoln: University of Nebraska Press, 1980), pp. 26–27, 121.
39. Walker, *Popular justice*, p. 59.
40. A. von Hoffman, "An officer of the neighborhood: A Boston patrolman on the beat in 1895," *Journal of Social History*, vol. 26, no. 2 (Winter 1992), pp. 309–330.
41. E. H. Monkkonen, *Police in urban America, 1860–1920* (Cambridge: Cambridge University Press, 1981), pp. 87, 89.
42. Walker, *Popular justice*, p. 62.
43. "Thomas F. Byrnes," in *Wikipedia, The free encyclopedia*, revised May 18, 2008. Web available at http://en.wikipedia.org/w/index.php?title=Thomas_F._Byrnes&oldid=213279082. Retrieved June 19, 2008.
44. C. H. Parkhurst, *Our fight with Tammany* (1895; repr., New York: Arno Press, 1970), p. 5.
45. H. P. Jeffers, *Commissioner Roosevelt: The story of Theodore Roosevelt and the New York City Police, 1895–97* (New York: Wiley, 1994).
46. Walker, *Popular justice*, p. 65.
47. A. Vollmer, "Predelinquency," in *Proceedings, 1919*, ed. International Association of Chiefs of Police, pp. 77–80 (New York: Arno Press, 1971).
48. Walker, *Popular justice*, p. 131.
49. For more on Vollmer's legacy, see J. Liss and S. Schlossman, "The contours of crime prevention in August Vollmer's Berkeley," in *Research in law, deviance, and social control*, vol. 6 (Greenwich, CT: JAI Press, 1984); A. Vollmer and A. Schneider, "The school for police as planned at Berkeley," *Journal of Criminal Law and Criminology* 7 (1917): 877–98; and G. E. Carte and E. H. Carte, *Police reform in the United States: The era of August Vollmer* (Berkeley: University of California Press, 1975).
50. Illinois Association for Criminal Justice, *Illinois crime survey* (1929; repr., Montclair, NJ: Patterson Smith, 1968), p. 359.
51. Walker, *Popular justice*, p. 172.
52. O. W. Wilson and R. C. McLaren, *Police administration*, 4th ed. (New York: McGraw-Hill, 1977).
53. O. W. Wilson, *The distribution of police patrol forces* (Chicago: Public Administration Service, 1941).
54. Walker, *Popular justice*, p. 173.
55. J. E. Angell, "Toward an alternative to the classic police organizational arrangements: A democratic model," *Criminology* 9 (1971): 185–206.
56. See, e.g., M. K. Nalla and C. G. Heraux, "Assessing the goals and functions of private police," *Journal of Criminal Justice* 31 (2003): 237–47.
57. E. E. Joh, "The paradox of private policing," *Journal of Criminal Law and Criminology* 95 (2004): 49–131.
58. R. Behar, "Thugs in uniform," *Time* (March 9, 1992): 44.
59. W. C. Cunningham and J. J. Strauchs, "Security industry trends: 1993 and beyond," *Security Management* 36 (1992): 27–30, 32, 34–36.
60. P. S. Bailin and D. K. Cole, *Industry study 1244: Private security services* (Cleveland: Freedonia Group, 2000).
61. Cunningham and Strauchs, "Security industry trends," pp. 27–30, 32, 34–36.
62. D. A. Sklansky, "The private police," *UCLA Law Review* 46 (1999): 1165–1287, quote on p. 1166.
63. Joh, "The paradox of private policing," p. 67.
64. Ibid.
65. Ibid., p. 62.
66. C. D. Shearing and P. Stenning, "Modern private security: Its growth and implications," in *Crime and justice: A review of research*, ed. M. Tonry, pp. 193–246 (Chicago: University of Chicago Press, 1981). See also C. D. Shearing and P. C. Stenning, *Private policing* (Newbury Park, CA: Sage, 1987).
67. Joh, "The paradox of private policing," p. 62.
68. Shearing and P. Stenning, "Modern private security: Its growth and implications."
69. Joh, "The paradox of private policing," p. 62.
70. Ibid., p. 63.
71. For more detail, see M. K. Nalla, "Designing an introductory survey course in private security," *Journal of Criminal Justice Education* 12 (2001): 35–52; M. K. Nalla and M. A. Morash, "Assessing the scope of corporate security: Common practices and relationships with other business functions," *Security Journal* 15 (2002): 7–19; and M. Nalla and G. Newman, *A primer on private security* (New York: Harrow and Heston, 1990).

72. D. A. Sklansky, "The private police," *UCLA Law Review* 46 (1999): 1165–1287, especially pp. 1221–22.
73. Shearing and Stenning, *Private policing*.
74. Sklansky, "The private police," p. 1222.
75. See, e.g., D. Shichor and M. J. Gilbert, eds., *Privatization in criminal justice: Past, present, and future* (Dayton, OH: Lexis-Nexis, 2001).
76. Sklansky, "The private police," p. 1166.
77. Ibid., pp. 1230–31.
78. *Griffin v. Maryland*, 378 U.S. 130 (1964).
79. See, e.g., *Wade v. Byles*, 83 F.3d 902 (7th Cir. 1996); *Gallagher v. Neil Young Freedom Concert*, 49 F.3d 1442 (10th Cir. 1995); *United States v. Francoeur*, 547 F.2d 891 (5th Cir. 1977); *People v. Taylor*, 271 Cal. Rptr. 785 (Ct. App. 1990); *United States v. Lima*, 424 A.2d 113 (D.C. 1980) (en banc); *People v. Toliver*, 377 N.E.2d 207 (Ill. App. Ct. 1978); *People v. Holloway*, 267 N.W.2d 454 (Mich. Ct. App. 1978); and *State v. Buswell*, 460 N.W.2d 614 (Minn. 1990).
80. See, e.g., *United States v. Antonelli*, 434 F.2d 335 (2d Cir. 1970); and *City of Grand Rapids v. Impens*, 327 N.W.2d 278 (Mich. 1982).
81. See, e.g., *United States v. Cruz*, 783 F.2d 1470, 1473 (9th Cir. 1986); *State v. Garcia*, 528 So. 2d 76 (Fla. Dist. Ct. App. 1988); *Perez v. State*, 517 So. 2d 106 (Fla. Dist. Ct. App. 1987); *People v. Gorski*, 494 N.E.2d 246 (Ill. App. Ct. 1986); *State v. Farmer*, 510 P.2d 180 (Kan. 1973); and *Commonwealth v. Lindenmuth*, 554 A.2d 62 (Pa. Super. Ct. 1989).
82. Joh, "The paradox of private policing," p. 64.
83. See, e.g., J. Hall, "Legal and social aspects of arrest without a warrant," *Harvard Law Review* 49 (1935): 566.

Chapter Two

1. S. Sward, B. Wallace, and E. Fernandez, "The use of force: When SFPD officers resort to violence," *San Francisco Chronicle*, February 5, 2006, p. A1. See also, "3-off duty S.F. cops probed in beating," SFGage.com, November 21, 2002. Web posted at http://www.sfgate.com/cgi-bin/article.cgi?file=/chronicle/archive/2002/11/21/MN45560.DTL. Accessed June 20, 2008.
2. Wallace and Fernandez, "The use of force."
3. Ibid.
4. According to its website, "*The San Francisco Chronicle* is the second largest newspaper in California and operates the fourth largest newspaper website in the country. The *Chronicle* has a daily readership of 1,079,900; Sunday readership is 1,231,700." See SFGate Media Kit. Web available at http://www.sfgate.com/mediakit/stats. Accessed June 20, 2008.
5. H. G. Rainey, *Understanding and managing public organizations* (San Francisco: Jossey-Bass, 1991).
6. G. T. Marx, "Police and democracy," http://web.mit.edu/gtmarx/www/dempol.html (accessed June 6, 2008).
7. Robert F. Kennedy quotations from Memorable Quotations.com, http://www.memorablequotations.com/rfk.htm (accessed June 6, 2008).
8. H. L. Packer, *The limits of the criminal sanction* (Stanford, CA: Stanford University Press, 1968).
9. Ibid.
10. See, e.g., S. K. Ivkovich, "Shades of blue: A cross-national study of public support for the police," paper presented at the annual meeting of the American Society of Criminology, Toronto, June 20, 2008. Web available at http:// www.allacademic.com/meta/p34026_index.html; H. MacDonald, "At long last, South L.A. has a prayer: the police," *Los Angeles Times*, August 6, 2003. Web available at http://www.manhattan-institute.org/html/_latimes-at_ long_last.htm. Accessed June 20, 2008; S. G. Brandl, J. Frank, J. Wooldredge, and R. C. Watkins, "On the measurement of public support for the police: a research note, *Policing: An International Journal of Police Strategies & Management*, vol. 20, no. 3 (1997): 473–80; and E. Erez, "Self-defined desert and citizen's assessment of the police," *Journal of Criminal Law and Criminology* 75 (1984): 1276–99.
11. J. L. Worrall, "Public perceptions of police efficacy and image: The fuzziness of support for the police," *American Journal of Criminal Justice* 24 (1999): 47–66.
12. D. Bayley, *Forces of order: Police behavior in Japan and the United States* (Berkeley: University of California Press, 1976); and S. M. Lipset and W. Schneider, *The confidence gap: Business, labor, and government in the public mind* (New York: Free Press, 1983).
13. S. Albrect and M. Green, "Attitudes toward the police and the larger attitude complex: Implications for police-community relations," *Criminology* 15 (1977): 67–87; T. Jefferson and M. A. Walker, "Ethnic minorities in the criminal justice system," *Criminal Law Review* 28 (1993): 83–95; and R. B. Parks, "Linking objective and subjective measures of performance," *Public Administration Review* 44 (1984): 118–27.
14. Worrall, "Public perceptions of police efficacy and image."
15. F. Furstenberg and C. Wellford, "Calling the police: The evaluation of police service," *Law and Society Review* 7 (1973): 393–406; and I. Hadar and J. Snortum, "The eye of the beholder: Differential perceptions of police by the police and the public," *Criminal Justice and Behavior* 2 (1975): 37–54.
16. D. Smith and R. Hawkins, "Victimization, types of citizen-police contacts, and attitudes toward the police," *Law and Society Review* 8 (1973): 135–52.
17. D. L. Carter, "Hispanic perception of police performance: An empirical assessment," *Journal of Criminal Justice*, vol. 13, no. 6 (1985): 487–500.

18. R. Scaglion and R. Condon, "The structure of black and white attitudes toward the police," *Human Organization* 39 (1980): 280–83.
19. D. Walker and others, "Contact and support: An empirical assessment of public attitudes toward the police and the courts," *North Carolina Law Review* 51 (1972): 43–79.
20. R. G. Zevitz and R. J. Rettammel, "Elderly attitudes about police service," *American Journal of Police* 9 (1990): 25–39.
21. D. Sagi and C. Wellford, "Age composition and patterns of change in criminal statistics," *Journal of Criminal Law, Criminology, and Police Science* 59 (1968): 29–35.
22. Hadar and Snortum, "The eye of the beholder."
23. J. Preiss and H. Ehrlich, *An examination of role theory: The case of state police* (Lincoln: University of Nebraska Press, 1958).
24. J. Q. Wilson, *Thinking about crime* (New York: Vintage, 1985).
25. T. Winfree and C. Griffiths, "Adolescent attitudes toward law enforcement," in *Juvenile delinquency: Little brother grows up*, ed. T. Ferdinand, pp. 79–99 (Beverly Hills, CA: Sage, 1977); and M. E. Correia, M. D. Reisig, and N. P. Lovrich, "Public perceptions of state police: An analysis of individual-level and contextual variables," *Journal of Criminal Justice* 24 (1996): 17–28.
26. C. Vedder and O. Keller, "The police and middle class conflicts," *Police* 9 (1965): 6–8.
27. C. Wirths, "The development of attitudes toward law enforcement," *Police* 3 (1958): 50–52; and T. Bercal, "Calls for police assistance: Consumer demands for governmental service," *American Behavioral Scientist* 13 (1970): 681–91.
28. D. Bordua and L. Tifft, "Citizen interviews, organizational feedback, and police-community relations decisions," *Law and Society Review* 6 (1971): 155–82; and A. Schwartz and S. Clarren, *The Cincinnati team policing experiment: A technical report* (Washington, DC: U.S. Government Printing Office, 1978).
29. M. E. Correia, M. D. Reisig, and N. P. Lovrich, "Public perceptions of state police: An analysis of individual-level and contextual variables," *Journal of Criminal Justice* 24 (1996): 17–28.
30. Ibid.; and L. Cao, J. Frank, and F. Cullen, "Race, community context, and confidence in the police," *American Journal of Police* 15 (1996): 3–22.
31. Worrall, "Public perceptions of police efficacy and image."
32. O. Marenin, "Supporting the local police: The differential group basis of varieties of support," *Police Studies* 6 (1983): 50–56.
33. Cao, Frank, and Cullen, "Race, community context, and confidence in the police"; and D. Lewis and G. Salem, *Fear of crime: Incivility and the production of a social problem* (New Brunswick, NJ: Transaction Books, 1986).
34. P. Jesilow, J. Meyer, and N. Namazzi, "Public attitudes toward the police," *American Journal of Police* 2 (1995): 67–88.
35. Albrect and Green, "Attitudes toward the police and the larger attitude complex"; R. Chackerian, "Police professionalism and citizen evaluations: A preliminary look," *Public Administration Review* 34 (1974): 141–48; K. S. Larsen, "Authoritarianism and attitudes toward the police," *Psychological Reports* 3 (1968): 349–50; and E. Zamble and P. Annesley, "Some determinants of public attitudes toward the police," *Journal of Police Science and Administration* 15 (1987): 285–90.
36. See, e.g., H. Jacob, "Black and white perceptions of justice in the city," *Law and Society Review* 5 (1971): 69–89; and A. Mirande, "Fear of crime and fear of the police in a Chicano community," *Sociology and Social Research* 64 (1980): 528–41.
37. Hadar and Snortum, "The eye of the beholder"; and J. Garofalo, *The police and public opinion: An analysis of victimization and attitude data from 13 American cities* (Washington, DC: U.S. Government Printing Office, 1977).
38. Jesilow, Meyer, and Namazzi, "Public attitudes toward the police"; and Q. C. Thurman and M. Reisig, "Community-oriented research in an era of community-oriented policing," *American Behavioral Scientist* 39 (1996): 570–86.
39. D. W. Murphy and J. L. Worrall, "Residency requirements and public perceptions of the police in large municipalities," *Policing: An International Journal of Police Strategies and Management* 22 (1998): 327–42.
40. R. Weisheit, E. Wells, and D. Falcone, *Crime and policing in rural and small-town America: An overview of the issues* (Washington, DC: U.S. Department of Justice, 1995); and D. Falcone and L. Wells, "The county sheriff as a distinctive policing modality," *American Journal of Police* 14 (1995): 123–49.
41. Associated Press, "Town to police: 'You're fired,'" October 23, 2006, http://www.cbsnews.com/stories/2006/10/23/national/main2114983.shtml (accessed October 26, 2008).
42. City of San Diego, "Strong mayor form of governance," http://www.sandiego.gov/mayortransition/index.shtml (accessed October 26, 2008).
43. WTAE-TV, "Pittsburgh police chief fired by incoming mayor," December 29, 2005, http://www.thepittsburghchannel.com/news/5694973/detail.html (accessed October 26, 2008).
44. James Sterngold, "Police chief rebuffed in Los Angeles," *New York Times*, April 18, 2002. Web available at http://query.nytimes.com/gst/fullpage.html?res=9B04E3DE173FF93BA25757C0A9649C8B63. Accessed June 20, 2008.
45. GovernmentExecutive.com, "Park police chief fired," July 9, 2004, http://www.govexec.com/dailyfed/0704/070904a1.htm (accessed October 26, 2008).

46. J. S. Lovell, *Media power and information control: A study of police organizations and media relations* (Washington, DC: U.S. Justice Department, National Institute of Justice, 2002), p. 16.
47. J. L. Worrall, "Constitutional issues in reality-based police television programs: Media ride-alongs," *American Journal of Criminal Justice* 25 (2000): 41–64. Also see P. G. Kooistra, J. S. Mahoney, and S. D. Westervelt, "The world of crime according to 'COPS,'" in *Entertaining crime: Television reality programs*, ed. M. Fishman and G. Cavender, pp. 141–58 (New York: Aldine De Gruyter, 1998); and M. B. Oliver, "Portrayals of crime, race, and aggression in 'reality-based' police shows: A content analysis," *Journal of Broadcasting and Electronic Media* 38 (1994): 179–92.
48. J. M. Carlson, "Crime show viewing by preadults: The impact on attitudes toward civil liberties," *Communication Research* 10 (1983): 529–52; J. M. Carlson, *Prime time law enforcement: Crime show viewing and attitudes toward the criminal justice system* (New York: Praeger, 1985); R. M. Entman, "Modern racism and the images of blacks in local television news," *Critical Studies in Mass Communication* 7 (1990): 332–45; R. M. Entman, "Blacks in the news: Television, modern racism and cultural change," *Journalism Quarterly* 60 (1992): 341–61; G. Gerbner and L. Gross, "Living with television: The violence profile," *Journal of Communication* 26 (1976): 173–99; and R. P. Hawkins and S. Pingree, "Uniform messages and habitual viewing: Unnecessary assumptions in social reality effects," *Human Communication Research* 7 (1981): 291–301.
49. R. Costello and F. Biafora, "Just the facts ma'am: The supreme court says 'no' to media ride-alongs," *Journal of Criminal Justice and Popular Culture* 7 (1999): 15–25, quote on p. 15.
50. J. L. Worrall, "Constitutional issues in reality-based police television programs: Media ride-alongs," *American Journal of Criminal Justice* 25 (2000): 41–64, quote on pp. 42–43.
51. J. F. Sheley and C. D. Ashkins, "Crime, crime news, and crime views," *Public Opinion Quarterly* 45 (1981): 492–506.
52. Oliver, "Portrayals of crime, race, and aggression in 'reality-based' police shows."
53. Entman, "Modern racism and the images of blacks in local television news," p. 337.
54. G. Cavender and L. Bond-Maupin, "Fear and loathing on reality television: An analysis of America's Most Wanted and Unsolved Mysteries," *Sociological Inquiry* 63 (1993): 305–17.
55. S. Evans and R. Lundman, "Newspaper coverage of corporate price-fixing," *Criminology* 21 (1983): 521–41; and H. Molotch and M. Lester, "News as purposive behavior: On the strategic use of routine events, accidents, and scandals," in *Popular culture, crime, and justice*, ed. S. Cohen and J. Young, pp. 118–37 (Newbury Park, CA: Sage, 1981).
56. J. Livingston, "Crime and the media: Myths and reality," *USA Today Magazine* 122 (May 1994): 40–42.
57. J. R. Dominick, "Crime and law enforcement on prime-time television," *Public Opinion Quarterly* 37 (1973): 241–50; and Oliver, "Portrayals of crime, race, and aggression in 'reality-based' police shows."
58. D. Zillman and J. Wakshlag, "Fear of victimization and the appeal of crime drama," in *Selective exposure to communication*, ed. D. Zillman and J. Bryant, pp. 141–56 (Hillsdale, NJ: Lawrence Erlbaum, 1985).
59. J. S. Lovell, *Media power and information control*, p. 179.
60. Ibid.
61. Ibid.
62. Ibid.
63. Ibid.
64. Ibid., pp. 188–89.
65. International Association of Chiefs of Police, *Constitution* (Alexandria, VA: International Association of Chiefs of Police, 2006), http://www.iacp.org/about/IACPConstitution.pdf (accessed November 2, 2008).
66. The National Black Police Association website is at http://www.blackpolice.org/.
67. International Union of Police Associations, "What Is the International Union of Police Associations?" http://www.iupa.org/about/iupamission.html (accessed November 2, 2008).
68. International Union of Police Associations, http://www.iupa.org/index.php?option=com_content&task=view&id=8&Itemid=17 (accessed November 2, 2008).
69. International Police Association, "Aims of the International Police Association," http://en.ipa-iac.org/en_aims.htm (accessed November 2, 2008).
70. Ibid.
71. National Institute of Justice, http://nij.ncjrs.gov/publications/pubs_db.asp.
72. Police Executive Research Forum, "About the Police Executive Research Forum," http://policeforum.org/perf/overview.asp (accessed November 2, 2008).
73. Police Foundation, http://www.policefoundation.org/ (accessed November 2, 2008).
74. Ibid.

Chapter Three

1. R. V. Wolf and J. L. Worrall, *Lessons from the field: Ten community prosecution leadership profiles* (Alexandria, VA: American Prosecutors Research Institute, 2004), p. 19.
2. Ibid., p. 20.
3. See, e.g., G. A. Thomas, Posse comitatus *and the use of the military in denying terrorist access to the United States along the border with Mexico* (Carlisle Barracks, PA: U.S. Army War College, 2005), http://www.strategicstudiesinstitute.army.mil/Pubs/display-papers.cfm?q=216 (accessed January 9, 2008).
4. This section borrows liberally from J. L. Worrall, "Appendix A: An ultra-brief introduction to criminal justice

in the United States," *Crime control in America: An assessment of the evidence* (Boston: Allyn and Bacon, 2006).

5. E. Glazer, "Thinking strategically: How federal prosecutors can reduce violent crime," *Fordham Urban Law Journal* 26 (1999): 573–606.
6. J. L. Worrall and M. E. Nugent-Borakove, *The changing role of the American prosecutor* (Albany: State University of New York Press, forthcoming).
7. Ibid.
8. B. Boland, "What is community prosecution?" *National Institute of Justice Journal* (August 1996): 35–40.
9. J. Buchanan, "Police-prosecutor teams: Innovations in several jurisdictions," *Georgia Trooper* 4 (1990): 35, 37, 39, 41, 43.
10. Marion County Prosecutor's Office, "R.O.A.D. Team to target aggressive motorists: Marion County traffic safety partnership launches new initiative," press release, February 28, 2001.
11. D. Parent and B. Snyder, *Police-corrections partnerships* (Washington, DC: National Institute of Justice, 1999), p. 5.
12. See also Matthew J. Giblin, "Using police officers to enhance the supervision of juvenile probationers: An evaluation of the Anchorage CAN program," *Crime and Delinquency* 48 (2002): 116–37.
13. Ibid.
14. Ibid.
15. Ibid.
16. For more on this type of approach, see E. McGarrell, D. Banks, and N. Hipple, "Community meeting as a tool in inmate reentry," *Justice Research and Policy* 5 (2003): 5–32.
17. E. F. McGarrell and others, "The roles of the police in the offender reentry process," in *Prisoner reentry and community policing: Strategies for enhancing public safety*, ed. N. G. La Vigne and others, pp. 19–53 (Washington, DC: Urban Institute, 2004).
18. Ibid. See also J. M. Byrne, F. S. Taxman, and D. Young, *Emerging roles and responsibilities in the reentry partnership initiative: New ways of doing business* (Washington, DC: National Institute of Justice, 2000).
19. Ibid., pp. 35–36.
20. Ibid., p. 36. See also F. S. Taxman, J. M. Byren, and D. Young, *Targeting for reentry: Matching needs and services to maximize public safety* (Washington, DC: Bureau of Government Research, 2000).
21. Ibid., p. 37.
22. For a detailed list of such references, see Program in Criminal Justice Policy and Management, Kennedy School of Government, Harvard University, "Operation Ceasefire/Boston Gun Project," http://www.ksg.harvard.edu/criminaljustice/research/bgp.htm (accessed February 1, 2007).
23. D. M. Kennedy, A. A. Braga, and A. M. Piehl, *Reducing gun violence: The Boston Gun Project's Operation Ceasefire* (Washington, DC: National Institute of Justice, 2001), pp. 15–16.
24. Ibid., p. 30.
25. A. A. Braga and G. L. Pierce, "Disrupting illegal firearms markets in Boston: The effects of Operation Ceasefire on the supply of new handguns to criminals," *Criminology and Public Policy* 4 (2005): 717–48.
26. *Combating gun violence: An in-depth look at Richmond's Project Exile* (Alexandria, VA: American Prosecutors Research Institute, 2001), http://www.ndaa-apri.org/pdf/combating_ gun_violence_web.pdf (accessed July 4, 2008).
27. American Prosecutors Research Institute, *Combating gun violence: Promising practices for America's prosecutors* (Washington, DC: Bureau of Justice Assistance, 2001).
28. S. Raphael and J. Ludwig, "Prison sentence enhancements: The case of Project Exile," in *Evaluating gun policy: Effects on crime and violence*, ed. J. Ludwig and P. J. Cook, pp. 251–86 (Washington, DC: Brookings Institution Press, 2003).
29. Colorado has done the same. Its program, Colorado Exile, is similar in several ways to the exile programs in Virginia and in Texas.
30. American Prosecutors Research Institute, *Combating gun violence: Promising practices for America's prosecutors*, p. 33.
31. Ibid., p. 34.
32. Ibid., p. 35.
33. See Baltimore City State's Attorney Office, Media Release: "State's attorney Jessamy announces grant funding for 4 gun prosecutors to work with police in communities where violence has spiked," January 18, 2002. Web posted at http://www.stattorney.org/Press_Release/2002/Press140.htm. Accessed July 4, 2008.
34. Ibid., p. 37.
35. For further information on PSN, see Office of Justice Programs, *Project Safe Neighborhoods* (Washington, DC: Office of Justice Programs, U.S. Department of Justice, 2004); J. A. Calhoun, "Project Safe Neighborhoods: America's network against gun violence facilitating the work of outreach," *USA Bulletin* 50 (2002): 26–28; E. Dalton, "Targeted crime reduction efforts in ten communities: Lessons for the Project Safe Neighborhoods initiative," *USA Bulletin* 50 (2002): 16–25; and J. Donovan, "Project Safe Neighborhoods: A network to make America's communities safer," *USA Bulletin* 50 (2002): 1–5.
36. Project Safe Neighborhoods, www.projectsafeneighborhoods. com (accessed July 4, 2008).
37. Ibid.
38. S. Decker and J. McDevitt, "Project Safe Neighborhoods and the changing role of the U.S. attorney's office," in *The changing role of the American prosecutor,* ed. J. Worrall and M. E. Nugent-Borakove (Albany: State University of New York Press, forthcoming).

39. Ibid.
40. Ibid.
41. P. B. Kraska and V. E. Kappeler, "Militarizing American police: The rise and normalization of paramilitary units," *Social Problems* 44 (1997): 1–18.
42. P. B. Kraska, "Militarizing the drug war: A sign of the times," in *Altered states of mind: Critical observations of the drug war,* ed. P. B. Kraska, pp. 159–206 (New York: Garland, 2001).
43. Kraska and Kappeler, "Militarizing American police," p. 12.
44. R. Kothari and others, *Towards a liberating peace* (New York: New Horizons Press, 1988).
45. Kraska and Kappeler, "Militarizing American police," p. 11.
46. Ibid. See also P. B. Kraska, "Enjoying militarism: Political/personal dilemmas in studying U.S. police paramilitary units," *Justice Quarterly* 13 (1996): 405–29; and P. B. Kraska, "Militarizing Mayberry and beyond: Making sense of American paramilitary policing," *Justice Quarterly* 14 (1997): 607–29.
47. Kraska and Kappeler, "Militarizing American police," pp. 3–4.
48. Ibid., p. 6.
49. Ibid.
50. Ibid., p. 10.
51. Ibid., p. 12.

Chapter Four

1. J. T. Gilliland, "Ireland refuses to extradite alleged pedophile to Arizona," July 29, 2005, Cybercast News Service, http://www.cnsnews.com/news/viewstory.asp?Page=%5CNation%5Carchive%5C200507%5CNAT20050729c.html (accessed January 9, 2008).
2. E. R. Maguire and others, "Counting cops: Estimating the number of police departments and police officers in the USA," *Policing: An International Journal of Police Strategies and Management* 21 (1998): 109.
3. Ibid.
4. We divided 300 million (there are approximately this many people in the United States today) by 680,000.
5. U.S. Secret Service, "Mission Statement," http://www.secretservice.gov/mission.shtml (accessed June 12, 2008).
6. U.S. Secret Service, "Financial Crimes Division," http://www.secretservice.gov/financial_crimes.shtml (accessed June 12, 2008).
7. U.S. Customs and Border Protection, "This Is CBP," http://www.cbp.gov/xp/cgov/about/mission/cbp_is.xml (accessed July 5, 2008).
8. U.S. Customs and Border Protection, "Securing America's Border," http://www.cbp.gov/linkhandler/cgov/newsroom/publications/mission/cbp_securing_borders.ctt/cbp_securing_borders.pdf (accessed July 5, 2008).
9. Ibid.
10. U.S. Immigration and Customs Enforcement, "About us," http://www.ice.gov/about/index.htm (accessed June 12, 2008).
11. 16 Stat. 162.
12. Federal Bureau of Investigation, "About us—quick facts," http://www.fbi.gov/quickfacts.htm (accessed June 12, 2008).
13. Ibid.
14. More historical details can be found at U.S. Marshals Service, "Historical Perspective," http://www.usmarshals.gov/history/index.html (accessed June 12, 2008).
15. These and other facts draw from U.S. Marshals Service, *Fact sheet* (Washington, DC: U.S. Department of Justice, U.S. Marshals Service, Pub. No. 21-A, January 13, 2006).
16. ATF press release, "Decline in the number of federal firearms licenses," June, 2008. Web available at http://www.atf.gov/firearms/ffl/factsheets/0608-factsheet-decline_in_ffls-rev2.pdf. Accessed July 5, 2008.
17. Bureau of Alcohol, Tobacco, Firearms and Explosives, "Alcohol/Tobacco Programs," http://www.atf.treas.gov/about/programs/proal.htm (accessed June 12, 2008).
18. U.S. Drug Enforcement Administration, "DEA mission statement," http://www.dea.gov/agency/mission.htm (accessed June 12, 2008).
19. U.S. Drug Enforcement Administration, "Stats and Facts," http://www.dea.gov/statistics.html#seizures (June 12, 2008).
20. New York City Police Department website, http://www.nyc.gov/html/nypd (accessed June 11, 2005). See also, Magdalene Perez, "NYPD manpower at 'crisis proportions," *Newsday*, June 28, 2007. Web available at http://www.policeone.com/police-recruiting/articles/1284746-NYPD-manpower-at-crisis-proportions. Accessed July 5, 2008.
21. B. A. Reaves and M. J. Hickman, *Census of state and local law enforcement agencies, 2000* (Washington, DC: Bureau of Justice Statistics, 2002).
22. Ibid.
23. Note, however, that New York City jails may have daily populations that, on a given day, exceed those of Los Angeles County.
24. The Police Assessment Resource Center, *The Los Angeles County Sheriff's Department—17th semiannual report* (Los Angeles: Los Angeles County Sheriff's Department, 2003); and telephone communication with Deputy Ethan Marquez, Los Angeles County Sheriff's Department, Custodial Division, January 24, 2002.
25. Reaves and Hickman, *Census of state and local law enforcement agencies, 2000.*
26. This is not the case in every state.
27. D. N. Falcone and L. E. Wells, "The county sheriff as a distinctive policing modality," *American Journal of Police* 14 (1995): 127.

28. Ohio Revised Code, Section 3313.616 (2006).
29. S. P. Robbins, *Organization theory: Structure, design, and applications* (Englewood Cliffs, NJ: Prentice Hall, 1990).
30. H. G. Rainey, *Understanding the managing of public organizations* (San Francisco: Jossey-Bass, 1991).
31. A. Germann, F. Day, and R. Gallati, *Introduction to law enforcement and criminal justice* (Springfield, IL: Charles C. Thomas, 1978).
32. E. Dale, *Readings in management: Landmarks and new frontiers* (New York: McGraw-Hill, 1965), p. 148.
33. M. Weber, "Bureaucracy," in *Organizations*, vol. 1, ed. J. Litterer, pp. 29–31 (New York: Wiley, 1969).
34. D. Guyot, "Bending granite: Attempting to change the rank structure of American police departments," *Journal of Police Science and Administration* 7 (1979): 253–84.
35. V. Franz and D. Jones, "Perceptions of organizational performance in suburban police departments," *Journal of Police Science and Administration* 15 (1987): 153–61, quote on p. 161.
36. Ibid. See also R. Likert, *New patterns of management* (New York: McGraw-Hill, 1961); and J. Pfeffer, "The micropolitics of organizations," in *Environments and organizations*, ed. M. Meyer (San Francisco: Jossey-Bass, 1978).
37. C. Argyris, *Personality and organization: The conflict between system and the individual* (New York: Harper and Row, 1957).
38. J. Zhao, Q. Thurman, and N. He, "Job satisfaction and police work: A test of two competing models," *Justice Quarterly* 16 (1999): 153–73; and M. Reiner and J. Zhao, "The importance of work environment in job satisfaction research in Air Force Security Police," *Journal of Public Personnel Administration* 14 (1999): 5–18.
39. T. Burns and G. Stalker, *The management of innovation* (London: Tavistock, 1961).
40. J. Kuykendall and R. Roberg, *Police administration* (Los Angeles: Roxbury, 1997).
41. L. K. Gaines and others, *Police administration*, 2nd ed. (New York: McGraw-Hill, 2003), p. 145.
42. Ibid., p. 151.
43. L. Bertalanffy, "General systems theory: A new approach to the unity of science," *Human Biology* 23 (1951): 302–61.

Chapter Five

i. Equal Employment Opportunity Commission, "Retaliation," http://eeoc.gov/types.retaliation.html (accessed November 9, 2006).
ii. *Hall v. GHS Construction Co.*, 842 F.2d 101 (8th Cir. 1988)

---

1. For more information, see the Wonderlic website, http://www.wonderlic.com (accessed June 15, 2008).
2. *Jordan v. New London*, 1999 U.S. Dist. LEXIS 14289 (1999).
3. Ibid., pp. 6–7.
4. K. J. Peak, *Policing America: Methods, issues, challenges*, 5th ed. (Upper Saddle River, NJ: Prentice Hall, 2006), p. 69.
5. Quoted in V. A. Leonard and H. W. More, *Police organization and management*, 3rd ed. (Mineola, NY: Foundation Press, 1971), p. 128.
6. J. Nislow, "Is anyone out there?" *Law Enforcement News*, October 31, 1999, p. 1.
7. N. Z. Dizon, "Searching for police," June 3, 2000, Associated Press news service.
8. M. Lifsher, "State strains to recruit new police," *Wall Street Journal*, November 10, 1999, p. CA1.
9. Peak, *Policing America*, p. 72.
10. For a thorough review of studies in this area, see J. G. Varela and others, "Personality testing in law enforcement employment settings: A meta-analytic review," *Criminal Justice and Behavior* 31 (2004): 649–75. See also S. Daniels and E. King, "Predictive validity of MMPI-2 content scales for small-town police officer performance," *Journal of Police and Criminal Psychology* 17 (2002): 54–62; and W. U. Weiss and others, "Personality assessment inventory as a selection device for law enforcement personnel," *Journal of Police and Criminal Psychology* 19 (2004): 23–29.
11. W. H. Thweatt, "Improving police selection on a shoestring budget," *Police Chief* (November 1972): 60–63.
12. S. H. Marsh, "Validating the selection of deputy sheriffs," *Public Personnel Review* 23 (1962): 41–44.
13. K. Peak, D. Farenholtz, and G. Coxey, "Physical abilities testing for police officers: A flexible, job-related approach," *Police Chief* (January 1992): 51–56.
14. T. Eisenberg, D. A. Kent, and C. R. Wall, *Police personnel practices in state and local governments* (Gaithersburg, MD: International Association of Chiefs of Police, 1973), p. 15.
15. City of San Diego, *Police officer testing and selection process* (San Diego: City of San Diego, 2006), http://www.sandiego.gov/police/join/selection.shtml (accessed November 7, 2008).
16. F. Horvath, "Polygraphic screening of candidates for police work in large police agencies in the United States: A survey of practices, policies, and evaluative comments," *American Journal of Police* 12 (1993): 67–86.
17. See, for example, Truth or Lie Polygraph Lie Detector Examination Agency, "How can you beat the polygraph?" http://www.truthorlie.com/beatpoly.html (accessed July 8, 2008).
18. Quoted in C. R. Swanson, L. Territo, and R. W. Taylor, *Police administration*, 2nd ed. (New York: Macmillan, 1988), pp. 202–203.
19. Pittsburgh Personnel and Civil Service Commission, "Police Officer Examination and Selection," http://www.city.pittsburgh.pa.us/personnel/html/exam_and_selection.html (accessed November 8, 2008).
20. Peak, *Policing America*, p. 78.
21. Ibid.

22. See, e.g., New York State Division of Criminal Justice Services, "Pre-employment Police Basic Course," http://criminaljustice.state.ny.us/ops/training/bcpo/bcpo04.htm (accessed June 15, 2008).
23. See, e.g., D. Bradford and J. E. Pynes, "Police academy training: Why hasn't it kept up with practice?" *Police Quarterly* 2 (1999): 283–301; N. Marion, "Police academy training: Are we teaching recruits what they need to know?" *Policing: An International Journal of Police Strategies and Management* 21 (1998): 54–79; and R. F. Brand and K. Peak, "Assessing police training curriculums: 'Consumer reports,'" *Justice Professional* 9 (winter 1995): 45–58.
24. J. J. Broderick, *Police in a time of change*, 2nd ed. (Prospect Heights, IL: Waveland, 1987), p. 215.
25. Ibid.
26. Ibid.
27. Bradford and Pynes, "Police academy training."
28. Peak, *Policing America*, p. 81.
29. L. S. Wrightman, *Psychology and the legal system* (Monterey, CA: Brooks/Cole, 1987), p. 86.
30. M. S. McCampbell, *Field training for police agencies: The state of the art* (Washington, DC: U.S. Department of Justice, National Institute of Justice, 1986).
31. K. J. Peak, S. Pitts, and R. W. Glensor, "From 'FTO' to 'PTO': A contemporary approach to post-academy recruit training," paper presented at the annual meeting of the Western and Pacific Association of Criminal Justice Educators, Reno, NV, 2006.
32. R. G. Dunham and G. P. Alpert, *Critical issues in policing: Contemporary readings* (Prospect Heights, IL: Waveland Press, 1989), pp. 111–15.
33. McCampbell, *Field training for police agencies.*
34. Peak, Pitts, and Glensor, "From 'FTO' to 'PTO,'" p. 6.
35. Police Society for Problem Based Learning, *Program description* (Clayton, CA: Police Society for Problem Based Learning, 2006).
36. See, e.g., J. Dewey, *How we think: A restatement of the relation of reflective thinking on the educative process* (Boston: D. C. Heath, 1933).
37. M. Knowles, *Andragogy in action: Applying modern principles of adult learning* (San Francisco: Jossey-Bass, 1981).
38. H. Barrows and R. M. Tamblyn, *Problem-based learning: An approach to medical education* (New York: Springer, 1980).
39. B. S. Bloom, *Taxonomy of educational objectives, handbook I: The cognitive domain* (New York: David McKay, 1956).
40. Peak, Pitts, and Glensor, "From 'FTO' to 'PTO,'" pp. 8–9.
41. Ibid., p. 9.
42. The organization's website is http://www.pspbl.com/.
43. Equal Employment Opportunity Commission, "Retaliation," http://eeoc.gov/types/retaliation.html (accessed June 15, 2008).
44. J. Frank and others, "Reassessing the impact of citizens' attitudes toward the police: A research note," *Justice Quarterly* 13 (1996): 231–34.
45. J. L. Sichel and others, *Women on patrol: A pilot study of police performance in New York City* (New York: Vera Institute of Justice, 1978).
46. R. Weitzer, "White, black, or blue cops? Race and citizen assessments of police officers," *Journal of Criminal Justice* 28 (2000): 313–24.
47. S. Walker, *Employment of black and Hispanic police officers, 1983–1988: A follow-up study* (Omaha: Center for Applied Urban Research, University of Nebraska at Omaha, 1989).
48. C. S. Johnson, *Into the mainstream: A survey of best practices in race relations in the South* (Chapel Hill: University of North Carolina Press, 1947).
49. J. L. Kuykendall and D. E. Burns, "The black police officer: An historical perspective," *Journal of Contemporary Criminal Justice* 4 (1980): 5.
50. E. Rudwick, *The unequal badge: Negro policemen in the South—Report of the Southern Regional Council* (Atlanta: Southern Regional Council, 1962).
51. P. S. Sullivan, "Minority officers: Current issues," in *Critical issues in policing: Contemporary readings*, ed. R. G. Dunham and G. P. Alpert, pp. 331–45 (Prospect Heights, IL: Waveland, 1989).
52. H. F. Gosnell, *Negro politicians: The rise of negro politics in Chicago* (Chicago: University of Chicago Press, 1935).
53. S. Leinen, *Black police, white society* (New York: New York University Press, 1984).
54. M. J. Hickman and others, "Does race influence the police disciplinary process?" *Justice Research and Policy* 3 (2001): 97–113.
55. President's Commission on Law Enforcement and Administration of Justice, *Task force report: The police* (Washington, DC: U.S. Government Printing Office, 1967), p. 162.
56. L. W. Landrum, "The case of Negro police," *New South* 11 (1947): 5–6; and G. Myrdal, *An American dilemma: The Negro problem and modern democracy* (New York: Harper and Brothers, 1944).
57. W. M. Kephart, *Racial factors and urban law enforcement* (Philadelphia: University of Pennsylvania Press, 1957).
58. N. Alex, *New York cops talk back* (New York: Wiley, 1976).
59. N. Alex, *Black in blue* (Englewood Cliffs, NJ: Prentice Hall, 1969).
60. D. Parsons and P. Jesilow, *In the same voice: Women and men in law enforcement* (Santa Ana, CA: Seven Locks Press, 2001).
61. Ibid.
62. S. Walker, *A critical history of police reform* (Lexington, MA: Lexington Books, 1977), p. 85.
63. C. Owings, *Women police* (New York: F. H. Hitchcock, 1925).

64. G. E. Berkeley, *The democratic policeman* (Boston: Beacon, 1969).
65. C. Milton, *Women in policing* (Washington, DC: Police Foundation, 1972).
66. C. Sulton and R. A. Townsey, *Progress report on women in policing* (Washington, DC: Police Foundation, 1981).
67. Police Foundation, *Community policing: A binding thread through the fabric of our society* (Washington, DC: Police Foundation, 1990).
68. P. Bloch and D. Anderson, *Policewomen on patrol: Final report* (Washington, DC: Police Foundation, 1974); L. J. Sherman, "Evaluation of policewomen on patrol in a suburban police department," *Journal of Police Science and Administration* 3 (1975): 434–38; and J. L. Sichel and others, *Women on patrol: Pilot study of police performance in New York City* (New York: Vera Institute of Justice, 1978).
69. S. Grennan, "Findings on the role of officer gender in violent encounters with citizens," *Journal of Police Science and Administration* 15 (1988): 78–85.
70. Ibid. See also M. Morash and J. R. Greene, "Evaluating women on patrol: A critique of contemporary wisdom," *Evaluation Review* 10 (1986): 231–55.
71. Parsons and Jesilow, *In the same voice.*
72. D. A. Snyder, *The Americans with Disabilities Act* (Portland, OR: Labor Relations Information Systems, 1991).
73. *Tanberg v. Weld County Sheriff*, 787 F.Supp. 970 (D. Colo. 1992).
74. *Bombrays v. Toledo*, 849 F.Supp. (N.D. Ohio 1933).
75. *Champ v. Baltimore County*, 884 F.Supp. 991 (1995).
76. J. Jacobs and J. Cohen, "The impact of racial integration on the police," *Journal of Police Science and Administration* 6 (1978): 168–83.
77. R. N. Haarr, "Patterns of interaction in a police patrol bureau: Race and gender barriers to integration," *Justice Quarterly* 14 (1997): 53–85.
78. *Detroit Police Officers Association v. Young*, 446 F.Supp. 979 (1978).
79. *United States v. Paradise*, 107 U.S. 1053 (1987).
80. For more information, see Adversity.net, "Case 49: Dayton, Ohio Police Dept. Loses Reverse Discrimination Suit," http://www.adversity.net/Dayton_OH_PD/default.htm (accessed June 16, 2008).
81. For more information, see Adversity.net, "Milwaukee Police Reverse Discrimination," http://www.adversity.net/milwaukee_police/alexander_v_jones.htm (accessed June 16, 2008).
82. *Barnes v. Costle*, 561 F.2d 983 (D.C. Cir. 1977).
83. *Meritor Savings Bank v. Vinson*, 474 U.S. 1047 (1986).
84. *Hall v. GHS Construction Co.*, 842 F.2d 101 (8th Cir. 1988).
85. *Sorlucco v. New York City Police Department*, 971 F.2d 864 (2nd Cir. 1992).
86. S. C. Collins, "Sexual harassment and police discipline: Who's policing the police?" *Policing: An International Journal of Police Strategies and Management* 27 (2004): 512–38.
87. T. Mahoney, "Sexual harassment in California law enforcement: A survey of women police officers," *Journal of California Law Enforcement* 30 (1996): 82–87.
88. National Center for Women and Policing, *Equity denied: The status of women in policing, 1997* (Los Angeles: Feminist Majority Foundation, 1998), p. 5.
89. This section borrows from J. L. Worrall, *Crime control in America: An assessment of the evidence* (Boston: Allyn and Bacon, 2006).
90. A. Chase, "Residency laws: Should police be free to live where they choose?" *Police Magazine* 2 (1979): 62–65.
91. American Civil Liberties Union of Southern California, *From the outside in: Residency patterns within the Los Angeles Police Department* (Los Angeles: American Civil Liberties Union, 1994).
92. Chase, "Residency laws"; and S. Coleman, "Dilemma of police residency: Views from the street," *Journal of Police Science and Administration* 11 (1983): 194–99.
93. J. Dorschner, "Dark side of the force," in *Critical Issues in Policing*, ed. R. Dunham and G. Alpert, pp. 254–74 (Prospect Heights, IL: Waveland, 1989).
94. E. Aasted, *How will law enforcement adapt to the potential increase in commuting police employees by the twenty-first century?* (Rockville, MD: National Institute of Justice, 1991).
95. W. Hirsch and A. Rufolo, "Economic effects of residence laws on municipal police," *Journal of Urban Economics* 17 (1985): 335–48.
96. Chase, "Residency laws."

Chapter Six

i. J. P. Crank, *Understanding police culture* (Cincinnati: Anderson, 1998), p. 30. See also J. Van Maanen, "Observations on the making of policemen," *Human Organization* 32 (1973): 407–18.
ii. Adapted from J. J. Fyfe, "The split-second syndrome and other determinants of police violence," in *Critical issues in policing*, 4th ed., ed. R. G. Dunham and G. P. Alpert, pp. 583–98 (Prospect Heights, IL: Waveland, 2001).

---

1. R. Gearty, "Blue wall whistleblower gets day in court after demotion," *Daily News*, June 13, 2004, p. 27.
2. K. Makin, "Police chief denies 'blue wall of silence' in corruption probe," *National News*, January 21, 2004, p. A6.
3. J. P. Crank, *Understanding police culture* (Cincinnati: Anderson, 1998). His book was an invaluable resource in the organization of this chapter. We cite it in several places.
4. Ibid., p. 14.
5. Ibid., p. 15.
6. See, for example, D. Guyot, "Bending granite: Attempts to change the rank structure of American police depart-

ments," *Journal of Police Science and Administration* 7 (1979): 253–84.

7. See, J. E. Angell, "Toward an alternative to the classic police organizational arrangements: A democratic model," *Criminology* 9 (1971): 185–206.
8. Crank, *Understanding police culture*, p. 15.
9. Ibid., p. 17.
10. J. Rubinstein, *City police* (New York: Farrar, Strauss, and Giroux, 1973), pp. 32–43.
11. Note that *platoon* and *squad* are terms commonly used in the military.
12. M. R. Pogrebin and E. D. Poole, "Humor in the briefing room," *Journal of Contemporary Ethnography* 17 (1988): 183–210, quote on pp. 188–89.
13. T. Rubinstein, *City police*, p. 32.
14. J. Crank, *Understanding police culture*, p. 30. See also J. Van Maanen, "Observations on the making of policemen," *Human Organization* 32 (1973): 407–18.
15. M. Felson, *Crime and everyday life* (Thousand Oaks, CA: Pine Forge Press, 1994).
16. J. Crank, *Understanding police culture*, p. 30. See also A. Niederhoffer, *Behind the shield* (Garden City, NY: Doubleday, 1967).
17. Crank, *Understanding police culture*, p. 32.
18. Ibid., p. 32. See also Pogrebin and Poole, "Humor in the briefing room."
19. D. N. Allen and M. G. Maxfield, "Judging police performance: Views and behavior of patrol officers," in *Police at work: Policy issues and analysis*, ed. R. R. Bennett, pp. 65–86 (Beverly Hills, CA: Sage, 1983).
20. See *Houston Chronicle*, "Houston police Taser videos," http://www.chron.com/content/chronicle/special/07/taservids/ (accessed June 17, 2008).
21. Crank, *Understanding police culture*, p. 36.
22. E. Bittner, *The functions of police in modern society* (Washington, DC: National Institute of Mental Health, 1970).
23. Crank, *Understanding police culture*, p. 40.
24. Ibid., p. 44.
25. Rubinstein, *City police*, p. 137.
26. Van Maanen, "Observations on the making of policemen," p. 226.
27. Rubinstein, *City police*, p. 318.
28. Crank, *Understanding police culture*, p. 69.
29. J. Betz, "Police violence," in *Moral issues in police work*, ed. F. A. Elliston and M. Feldberg, pp. 177–96 (Totowa, NJ: Rowman and Allanheld, 1988), pp. 182–83.
30. Crank, *Understanding police culture*, p. 82.
31. J. H. Skolnick and D. H. Bayley, *The new blue line: Police innovation in six American cities* (New York: Free Press, 1986), pp. 141–42.
32. Crank, *Understanding police culture*, p. 86.
33. W. A. Geller and M. S. Scott, "Deadly force: What we know," in *Thinking about police*, 2nd ed., ed. C. Klockars and S. Mastrofski, pp. 446–76 (New York: McGraw-Hill, 1991), p. 449.
34. P. Ragonese, *The soul of a cop* (New York: St. Martin's Paperbacks, 1991), pp. 200–202.
35. V. E. Kappeler, R. D. Sluder, and G. P. Alpert, *Forces of deviance: The dark side of policing* (Prospect Heights, IL: Waveland, 1994), p. 100.
36. Crank, *Understanding police culture*, p. 107.
37. F. Cullen and others, "Paradox in policing: A note on perceptions of danger," *Journal of Police Science and Administration* 11 (1983): 457–62.
38. Crank, *Understanding police culture*, p. 109.
39. Federal Bureau of Investigation, *Law enforcement officers killed and assaulted, 2006,* Table 71; http://www.fbi.gov/ucr/killed/2006/table71.html (accessed September 9, 2008).
40. P. B. Kraska and D. J. Paulsen, "Grounded research into U.S. paramilitary policing: Forging the iron fist inside the velvet glove," *Police and Society* 7 (1997): 253–70, quote on p. 263.
41. C. Fletcher, *What cops know* (New York: Pocket Books, 1990), p. 6.
42. E. Bittner, *Aspects of police work* (Boston: Northeastern University Press, 1990).
43. P. K. Manning, *Police work: The social organization of policing.* (Cambridge: The MIT Press, 1977); J. Van Maanen, "Working the street: A developmental view of police behavior," in *The potential for reform in criminal justice*, vol. 3, ed. H. Jacob, pp. 83–129 (Beverly Hills, CA: Sage, 1974).
44. E. W. McNulty, "Generating common-sense knowledge among police officers," *Symbolic Interaction* 17 (1994): 281–94, quote on p. 285.
45. Fletcher, *What cops know*, p. 3.
46. Crank, *Understanding police culture*, p. 97.
47. Rubinstein, *City police*, p. 224.
48. Ibid., pp. 241–42.
49. *People v. Martinez*, 12 Cal. Rptr. 2d 838, 840 (Cal. Ct. App. 1992).
50. *Flanagan v. State*, 586 So.2d 1085, 1099 (Fla. Dist. Ct. App. 1991).
51. *Commonwealth v. Day*, 569 N.E.2d 397, 399 (Mass. 1991).
52. *State v. McMillan*, 590 N.E.2d 23, 31 (Ohio Ct. App. 1990).
53. *Katz v. United States*, 389 U.S. 347, 357 (1967).
54. *United States v. Mendenhall*, 446 U.S. 544 (1980), pp. 545–46.
55. McNulty, "Generating common-sense knowledge among police officers," p. 286.
56. J. J. Fyfe, "The split-second syndrome and other determinants of police violence," in *Critical issues in policing*, 4th ed., ed. R. G. Dunham and G. P. Alpert, pp. 583–98 (Prospect Heights, IL: Waveland, 2001).
57. Ibid., p. 593.

58. Ibid.
59. Ibid.
60. Crank, *Understanding police culture*, p. 151. See also G. W. Sykes, "Street justice: A moral defense of order maintenance policing," *Justice Quarterly* 3 (1986): 497–512.
61. Crank, *Understanding police culture*, p. 154.
62. J. Van Maanen, "The asshole," in *Policing: A view from the street*, ed. P. K. Manning and J. Van Maanen, pp. 221–38 (Santa Monica, CA: Goodyear, 1978).
63. Crank, *Understanding police culture*, p. 160.
64. C. Fletcher, *Pure cop* (New York: Pocket Books, 1991), p. 278.
65. Crank, *Understanding police culture*, p. 164.
66. Ibid., p. 170.
67. Ibid., pp. 172–73.
68. Ibid., p. 180.
69. S. Martin, *Breaking and entering: Police women on patrol* (Los Angeles: Univ. of California Press, 1980), p. 90.
70. A. Bouza, *The police mystique: An insider's look at cops, crime, and the criminal justice system* (New York: Plenum Press, 1990), p. 74.
71. V. E. Kappeler, R. D. Sluder, and G. P. Alpert, "Breeding deviant conformity: The ideology and culture of police," in *Critical issues in policing*, 4th ed., ed. R. G. Dunham and G. P. Alpert, pp. 290–316 (Prospect Heights, IL: Waveland, 2001), p. 295.
72. P. Bonifacio, *The psychological effects of police work: A psychodynamic approach* (New York: Plenum Press, 1991), p. 39.
73. Crank, *Understanding police culture*, pp. 192–93.
74. Ibid., p. 194.
75. *The Report of the City of New York Commission to Investigate Allegations of Police Corruption and the Anti-Corruption Procedures of the Police Department* (The Mollen Commission, 1994), pp. 51–52.
76. Kappeler, Sluder, and Alpert, "Breeding deviant conformity," pp. 308–9.
77. M. Baker, *Cops: Their lives in their own words* (New York: Pocket Books, 1985), p. 5.
78. Crank, *Understanding police culture*, p. 225.
79. C. Bahn, "Police socialization in the eighties: Strains in the forging of an occupational identity," *Journal of Police Science and Administration* 12 (1984): 390–94, quote on p. 392.
80. Kappeler, Sluder, and Alpert, "Breeding deviant conformity," pp. 310–11.
81. Ibid., p. 311.
82. Crank, *Understanding police culture*, p. 238.
83. T. Barker, R. N. Friery, and D. L. Carter, "After L.A., would your local police lie?" in *Police Deviance*, 3rd ed., ed. T. Barker and D. Carter, pp. 155–68 (Cincinnati: Anderson, 1994).
84. C. B. Klockars, "The modern sting," in *Thinking about policing*, 2nd ed., ed. C. Klockars and S. Mastrofski, pp. 258–67 (New York: McGraw-Hill, 1991).

Chapter Seven

i. C. McHenry, "Stress in the police service: Preventing the long-term effects of trauma," *Occupational Health Review* (July–August 1995): 17–20, quote on p.18.

---

1. K. Johnson, "Reservists back in police jobs raise concerns," *USA Today*, November 15, 2007, http://www.usatoday.com/news/nation/2007-11-15-reentry-inside_N.htm (accessed November 11, 2008).
2. Ibid., citing Maryland psychologist Stephen Curran.
3. See, e.g., J. Grencik, "Toward an understanding of stress," in *Job stress and the police officer: Identifying stress reduction techniques*, ed. W. Kroes and J. Hurrell (Washington, DC: U.S. Department of Health, Education, and Welfare, 1975), pp. 163–81.
4. See, e.g., J. Blackmore, "Are police allowed to have problems of their own?" *Police Magazine* 1 (1978): 47–55; and L. Territo and H. Vetter, *Stress and police personnel* (Boston: Allyn and Bacon, 1981).
5. J. Selye, *Stress without distress* (Philadelphia: Lippincott, 1981).
6. Ibid.
7. R. L. Veniga and J. Spradley, *How to cope with job burnout* (Englewood Cliffs, NJ: Prentice Hall, 1981), p. 6.
8. M. Silbert, "Job stress and burnout of new police officers," *Police Chief* 49 (1982): 46–48.
9. H. W. More, *Special topics in policing*, 2nd ed. (Cincinnati: Anderson, 1998). See also Veniga and Spradley, *How to cope with job burnout*.
10. S. Webb and D. Smith, "Stress prevention and alleviation: Strategies for police," *Criminal Justice Review* 5 (1980): 1–15. For a different perspective, see R. Lawrence, "Police stress and personality factors: A conceptual model," *Journal of Criminal Justice* 12 (1984): 247–63.
11. E. Stotland, "The effects of police work and professional relationships on health," *Journal of Criminal Justice* 19 (1991): 371–79.
12. J. E. Storch and R. Panzarella, "Police stress: State-trait anxiety in relation to occupational and personal stressors," *Journal of Criminal Justice* 24 (1996): 99–107; and V. B. Lord, D. O. Gray, and S. B. Pond III, "The police stress inventory: Does it measure stress?" *Journal of Criminal Justice* 19 (1991): 139–49.
13. R. Regoli, J. Crank, and R. Culbertson, "Police cynicism, job satisfaction, and work relations of police chiefs: An assessment of the influence of department size," *Sociological Focus* 22 (1989): 161–71; M. Morash and R. Haarr, "Gender, workplace problems, and stress in policing," *Justice Quarterly* 12 (1995): 113–40; and L. W. Brooks and N. L. Piquero, "Police stress: Does department size matter?" *Policing: An International Journal of Police Strategies and Management* 21 (1998): 600–17.

14. W. M. Kroes, B. Margolis, and J. Hurrell, "Job stress in policemen," *Journal of Police Science and Administration* 2 (1974): 145–55.
15. R. T. Sigler, C. N. Wilson, and Z. Allen, "Police stress and teacher stress at work and at home," *Journal of Criminal Justice* 19 (1991): 361–70; and Brooks and Piquero, "Police stress."
16. Brooks and Piquero, "Police stress."
17. J. P. Crank and M. Caldero, "The production of occupational stress in medium-sized police agencies: A survey of line officers in eight municipal departments," *Journal of Criminal Justice* 19 (1991): 341–52, quote on p. 345.
18. Kroes, Margolis, and Hurrell, "Job stress in policemen."
19. Crank and Caldero, "The production of occupational stress in medium-sized police agencies."
20. Ibid.
21. R. M. Solomon, "Post-shooting trauma," *Police Chief* 55 (1988): 40, 42, 44.
22. S. Carson, "Post-shooting stress reduction," *Police Chief* (October 1982): 66–68.
23. Ibid.
24. Solomon, "Post-shooting trauma."
25. C. McHenry, "Stress in the police service: Preventing the long-term effects of trauma," *Occupational Health Review* (July–August 1995): 17–20, quote on p.18.
26. Ibid.
27. A. Niederhoffer, *Behind the shield: The police in urban society* (New York: Doubleday, 1967). See also J. Violanti, "Stress patterns in police work: A longitudinal study," *Journal of Police Science and Administration* 11 (1983): 211–16.
28. Cited in B. Vila and D. J. Kenney, "Tired cops: The prevalence and potential consequences of police fatigue," *NIJ Journal* 248 (2002): 16–21, quote on p. 20.
29. B. Vila, *Tired cops: The importance of managing police fatigue* (Washington, DC: Police Executive Research Forum, 2000).
30. Vila and Kenney, "Tired cops," p. 18.
31. As cited in Vila and Kenney, "Tired cops," p. 17.
32. Ibid.
33. Ibid., p. 18.
34. Ibid.
35. Ibid., p. 17.
36. Ibid., p. 18.
37. Associated Press, "LAPD's three-day workweek popular with officers, study notes pitfalls," October 23, 2006, http://www.lapd.com/article.aspx?a=4329 (accessed November 14, 2006).
38. Vila and Kenney, "Tired cops," p. 18.
39. Ibid., p. 19.
40. Ibid., pp. 19–20.
41. See, e.g., H. LeVan, M. Katz, and C. Carley, "The arbitration of grievances of police officers and fire fighters," *Public Personnel Management* 22 (1993): 433–44; and J. Burpo, R. DeLord, and M. Shannon, *Police association power, politics, and confrontation* (Springfield, IL: Charles C. Thomas, 1997).
42. "Battle in Boston streets," *New York Times*, September 10, 1919.
43. Boston was not the only strike. See, e.g., W. Gentel and M. L. Handman, *Police strikes: Causes and prevention* (Gaithersburg, MD: International Association of Chiefs of Police, 1979); and D. J. Giacopassi and J. R. Sparger, "The Memphis police strike: A retrospective analysis," *Southern Journal of Criminal Justice* 6 (1981): 39–52.
44. D. Carter and A. Sapp, "A comparative analysis of clauses in police collective bargaining agreements as indicators of change in labor relations," *American Journal of Police* 12 (1992): 17–46.
45. J. Zhao and N. Lovrich, "Collective bargaining and the police: What consequences for supplemental compensation policies in large agencies?" *Policing: An International Journal of Police Strategies and Management* 20 (1997): 508–18. See also M. Connolly, "The impact of final-offer arbitration on wage outcomes of public safety personnel: *Michigan v. Illinois*," *Journal of Collective Negotiations,* 15 (1986): 251–62.
46. W. F. Cascio and J. Bernardin, "Implications of performance appraisal litigation for personnel decisions," *Personnel Psychology* 9 (1981): 211–26, list on pp. 211–12.
47. L. M. Coutts and F. W. Schneider, "Police officer performance appraisal systems: How good are they?" *Policing: An International Journal of Police Strategies and Management* 27 (2004): 67–81.
48. This section borrows heavily from J. L. Worrall, *Crime control in America: An assessment of the evidence* (Boston: Allyn and Bacon, 2006).
49. See T. J. Hawley III, "The collegiate shield: Was the movement purely academic?" *Police Quarterly* 1 (1998): 35–59.
50. National Advisory Commission on Criminal Justice Standards and Goals, *The police* (Washington, DC: U.S. Government Printing Office, 1973).
51. D. L. Carter, A. D. Sapp, and D. W. Stephens, *The state of police education: Police direction for the 21st century* (Washington, DC: Police Executive Research Forum, 1988).
52. L. Sherman and M. Blumberg, "Higher education and police use of deadly force," *Journal of Criminal Justice* 9 (1981): 317–31.
53. G. Griffin, *A study of the relationship between level of college education and police patrolmen's performance* (Saratoga, NY: Twenty One, 1980); A. Lewis, "Police halt push for college grads," *Washington Post*, December 17, 1970, D1; and J. Livermore, "Policing," *Minnesota Law Review* 55 (1971): 649–730. More recently, see C. W. Sherwood, "Job design, community policing, and higher education: A tale of two cities," *Police Quarterly* 3 (2000): 191–212.

54. T. Eisenberg and R. Reinke, "The use of written examinations in selecting police officers: Coping with the dilemma," *Police Chief* 40 (1973): 24–28.
55. D. Carter and A. Sapp, "The effect of higher education on police liability: Implications for police personnel policy," *American Journal of Police* 8 (1989): 153–66.
56. P. Glastris, "The thin white line: City struggles to mix standardized testing and racial balance," *U.S. News and World Report* (August 15, 1994): 53–54.
57. City of Upland, California, "Department Rank Structure," http://www.uplandpd.org/asp/Site/Police/Admin/Rank/index.asp (accessed January 11, 2008).
58. Ibid.
59. Ibid.
60. Ibid.
61. J. Enter, "The rise to the top: An analysis of police chief career patterns," *Journal of Police Science and Administration* 14 (1986): 334–46.
62. J. Crank and others, "Cynicism and career stages among police chiefs," *Justice Quarterly* 3 (1986): 343–52; and R. Regoli and others, "Career stages and cynicism among police chiefs," *Justice Quarterly* 7 (1990): 593–614.
63. C. Mahtesian, "Mission impossible," *Governing Magazine* (January 1997): 19–23.
64. D. C. Witham, *The American law enforcement chief executive: A management profile* (Washington, DC: Police Executive Research Forum, 1985).
65. K. Tunnell and L. Gaines, "Political pressures and influences on police executives: A descriptive analysis," in *Managing police organizations*, ed. G. Cordner and D. Kenney, pp. 5–18 (Cincinnati: Anderson, 1996).
66. R. J. Brzeczek, "Chief-mayor relations: The view from the chief's chair," in *Police leadership in America: Crisis and opportunity*, ed. W. Geller (New York: Praeger, 1985), p. 55.
67. J. A. Schafer, "Effective Police Leadership: Experiences and Perspectives of Law Enforcement Leaders," *FBI Law Enforcement Bulletin* (July 2008): 13.
68. R. Sheehan and G. W. Cordner, *Police administration*, 3rd ed. (Cincinnati: Anderson, 1995).
69. N. H. Stamper, *Removing managerial barriers to effective police leadership* (Washington, DC: Police Executive Research Forum, 1992).

Chapter Eight

i. C. Batton and C. Kadleck, "Theoretical and methodological issues in racial profiling research," *Police Quarterly* (March 2004): 30–64.

1. Millivision, "Technology," http://www.millivision.com/technology.html (accessed February 5, 2008).
2. C. D. Hale, *Police patrol: Operations and management* (Englewood Cliffs, NJ: Prentice Hall, 1994).
3. V. Kappeler and others, *The mythology of crime and criminal justice* (Prospect Heights, IL: Waveland Press, 1996).
4. This definition has been attributed to the National Crime Prevention Institute. See, for example, "Background: Crime Prevention and CPTED," web available at http://www1.brcc.edu/murray/research/cpted/background/CPTED/default.htm (accessed August 7, 2008).
5. See S. P. Lab, *Crime prevention at a crossroads* (Cincinnati: Anderson, 1997).
6. R. H. Langworthy and L. P. Travis III, *Policing in America: A balance of forces*, 2nd ed. (Upper Saddle River, NJ: Prentice Hall, 1999), p. 194.
7. L. Mazerolle and others, *Managing citizen calls to the police: An assessment of nonemergency call systems* (Washington, DC: National Institute of Justice, 2001), p. 1–1.
8. Ibid.
9. Terence Dunworth, "Criminal justice and the IT revolution," in *Criminal Justice 2000* (Washington, DC: National Institute of Justice, 2000), pp. 371–426. Web available at http://www.ncjrs.gov/criminal_justice2000/vol_3/03h.pdf. Accessed July 21, 2008.
10. Hastings (Minnesota) Police Department, "Bi-weekly statistical report," http://www.ci.hastings.mn.us/CityServices/PDStats.htm (accessed September 18, 2008).
11. See the Philadelphia Police Department's Operation Identification website at http://www.ppdonline.org/prev/prev_home_opid.php (accessed August 28, 2008).
12. J. Fuller, "Rethinking foot patrol," *Police and Security News* (May–June 2004): 63–66, quote on p. 63.
13. K. D. Vonk, "Bike patrol successes," *Law and Order* (April 2003): 82–86, quote on p. 85.
14. J. Bellah, "Low-speed ahead," *Law Enforcement Technology* (October 2001): 76–82, quote on p. 78.
15. J. C. Fine, "Police on horseback: A new concept for an old idea," *FBI Law Enforcement Bulletin* (July 2001): 6–7, quote on p. 6.
16. S. Slahor, "MEU: Mounted units for crowd control," *Law and Order* (October 2001): 234–37, quote on p. 237.
17. C. Streit, "Patrolling in an off-road environment," *Law Enforcement Technology* (July 2002): 16–20, quote on p. 17.
18. *City crime rankings*, 14th ed. (Washington, DC: CQ Press, 2008), available from http://www.cqpress.com/product/City-Crime-Rankings-14th-Edition.html.
19. S. Walker, *Sense and nonsense about crime and drugs: A policy guide*, 5th ed. (Belmont, CA: Wadsworth, 2001), p. 81.
20. Ibid.
21. Much of this material is adapted from Walker, *Sense and nonsense about crime and drugs*.
22. Ibid., p. 86.
23. W. K. Rashbaum, "Response time to police calls is 29% faster," *New York Times*, September 26, 2002, p. B1.

24. Details for this story come from K. Streeter, "Girl, 2, rescued from washer," *Los Angeles Times,* May 26, 2003, http://www.latimes.com/news/local/la-me-laundry 26may26,1,7334286.story (accessed May 27, 2008).
25. See M. S. Scott, *Problem-oriented policing: Reflections on the first 20 years* (Washington, DC: Office of Community Oriented Policing Services, 2000), p. 87, from which much of this material is adapted.
26. G. Carrick, "Traffic safety in the new millennium," *Law and Order* (April 2003): 44–50.
27. *Whren v. United States,* 517 U.S. 806 (1996).
28. *Maryland v. Wilson,* 519 U.S. 408, 410 (1997); and *Pennsylvania v. Mimms,* 434 U.S. 106, 111 (1977).
29. *Ohio v. Robinette,* 519 U.S. 33 (1996).
30. *Horton v. California,* 496 U.S. 128, 133–37 (1990).
31. *Michigan v. Long,* 463 U.S. 1032, 1035 (1983).
32. *New York v. Belton,* 453 U.S. 454, 460 (1981).
33. C. Batton and C. Kadleck, "Theoretical and methodological issues in racial profiling research," *Police Quarterly* (March 2004): 30–64.
34. See, for example, "Driving while Black: Study shows minorities more likely to question why police stopped them, how they were treated," *Ohio State Research,* February 10, 2003. Web available at http://researchnews.osu.edu/archive/dwbstudy.htm. Accessed July 22, 2008.
35. *Whren v. United States* (1996).
36. R. S. Engel and J. M. Calnon, "Examining the influence of drivers' characteristics during stops with the police: Results from a national survey," *Justice Quarterly* (March 2004): 49–90, quote on p. 49.
37. J. Rojek, R. Rosenfeld, and S. Decker, "The influence of driver's race on traffic stops in Missouri," *Police Quarterly* (March 2004): 126–47, quote on p. 143.
38. D. Tomaskovic-Devey, M. Mason, and M. Zingraff, "Looking for the driving while black phenomena: Conceptualizing racial bias processes and their associated distributions," *Police Quarterly* (March 2004): 3–29, quote on p. 12.
39. K. J. Novak, "Disparity and racial profiling in traffic enforcement," *Police Quarterly* (March 2004): 65–96, quote on pp. 65–66.
40. J. R. Labbe, "Get it straight! Profiling is not racism," *American Police Beat* (October 2001): 25, 37, quote on p. 25.
41. J. Nislow, "Are Americans ready to buy into racial profiling?" *Law Enforcement News,* October 15, 2001, p. 11.
42. Ibid.
43. L. A. Fridell, *By the numbers: A guide for analyzing race data from vehicle stops* (Washington, DC: Police Executive Research Forum, 2001).
44. O. Cox, "2003 traffic safety data," *Police Chief* (July 2004): 15.
45. Ibid.
46. E. M. Sweeney, "Managing highway incidents with NIMS," *Police Chief* (July 2004): 26.
47. N. Dyer, "Staged traffic collisions and automobile insurance fraud," *Police Chief* (July 1994): 51–54.
48. H. E. Cauvin, "D.C. ordered to pay in police chase: Woman maimed in crash is awarded almost $1 million," *Washington Post,* December 14, 2006, p. B1.
49. G. P. Alpert, *Police pursuit: Policies and training* (Washington, DC: National Institute of Justice, 1997), p. 1.
50. G. P. Alpert and others, *Police pursuits: What we know* (Washington, DC: Police Executive Research Forum, 2000).
51. Alpert, *Police pursuits,* p. 4.
52. Ibid.
53. Ibid., p. 3.
54. Ibid.
55. Ibid.
56. Ibid.
57. Titan National Security Solutions, "Less-Than-Lethal Technologies," http://www.jaycor.com/jaycor_main/web-content//eme_ltlt.html (accessed February 6, 2007).
58. Adapted from Bronx County (New York) District Attorney's Office, "Quality of Life Offenses," December 24, 2002, http://www.bronxda.net/fighting_crime/quality_of_life_offenses.html (accessed June 20, 2006).
59. Other violations may be involved, as well. On December 29, 2000, for example, Judge John S. Martin, Jr., of the Federal District Court in Manhattan, ruled that homeless people in New York City could be arrested for sleeping in cardboard boxes in public. Judge Martin held that a city sanitation department regulation barring people from abandoning cars or boxes on city streets could be applied to the homeless who were sleeping in boxes.
60. For example, Norman Siegel, executive director of the New York Civil Liberties Union, as reported in "Quality of life offenses targeted," *Western Queens Gazette,* November 22, 2000, http://www.qgazette.com/News/2000/1122/Editorial_pages/e01.html (accessed June 12, 2007).
61. The broken windows thesis was first suggested by G. L. Kelling and J. Q. Wilson in "Broken windows: The police and neighborhood safety," *Atlantic Monthly* (March 1982), http://www.theatlantic.com/politics/crime/windows.htm (accessed June 29, 2008).
62. For a critique of the broken windows thesis, see B. E. Harcourt, *Illusion of order: The false promise of broken windows policing* (Cambridge: Harvard University Press, 2001).
63. P. Schuler, "Law professor Harcourt challenges popular policing method, gun violence interventions," *Chicago Chronicle,* March 20, 2003.
64. G. L. Kelling, C. M. Coles, and J. Q. Wilson, *Fixing broken windows: Restoring order and reducing crime in our communities* (repr., New York: Touchstone, 1998).

65. C. R. Swanson, L. Territo, and R. W. Taylor, *Police administration: Structures, processes, and behavior,* 4th ed. (Upper Saddle River, NJ: Prentice Hall, 1998), p. 1.
66. Ibid.
67. K. M. Hess and H. M. Wrobleski, *Police operations: Theory and practice,* 4th ed. (Belmont, CA: Wadsworth, 2006), pp. 188–89.
68. C. A. Rohr, "Training for managing crowds and responding to civil disobediences," *Police Chief* (October 2001): 10–11, especially p. 10.
69. F. Butterfield, "Student's death returns crowd control to the fore," *New York Times,* November 1, 2004.
70. D. Griffith, "Policing dissent," *Police* (August 2003): 44–50, quote on p. 50.
71. M. Slackman and A. Baker, "With restraint and new tactics, March is kept orderly," *New York Times,* August 30, 2004.
72. C. Pearson, "What to do if you are taken hostage," *Police* (January 2001): 44–45, quote on p. 44.
73. P. W. Greenwood and J. Petersilia, *The criminal investigation process,* vol. 1, *Summary and policy implications* (Santa Monica, CA: RAND, 1975).
74. J. Thorwald, *The century of the detective* (New York: Harcourt, Brace, and World, 1965), pp. 9–10.
75. Ibid., p. 62.
76. A. L. Califana and J. S. Levkov, *Criminalistics for the law enforcement officer* (New York: McGraw-Hill, 1978), p. 20.
77. J. Thorwald, *The marks of Cain* (London: Thames and Hudson, 1965), pp. 78–79.
78. Ibid., pp. 87–88.
79. Ibid., p. 164.
80. C. R. Swanson, N. C. Chamelin, and L. Territo, *Criminal investigation,* 4th ed. (New York: Random House, 1988), p. 19.
81. A. S. Osborn, *Questioned documents: A study of questioned documents with an outline of methods by which the facts may be discovered and shown* (Rochester, NY: The Lawyers' Co-operative Publishing Co., 1910).
82. P. R. DeForest, R. E. Gaensslen, and H. C. Lee, *Forensic science: An introduction to criminalistics* (New York: McGraw-Hill, 1983), p. 19.
83. K. M. Hess and H. M. Wrobleski, *Police operations: Theory and practice,* 4th ed. (Belmont, CA: Wadsworth, 2006), p. 319.
84. P. B. Weston and K. M. Wells, *Criminal investigation: Basic perspectives,* 4th ed. (Englewood Cliffs, NJ: Prentice Hall, 1986), pp. 5–10.
85. K. J. Peak, *Policing America: Methods, issues, challenges,* 5th ed. (Upper Saddle River, NJ: Prentice Hall, 2006).
86. M. Girodo, "Drug corruption in undercover agents: Measuring the risk," *Behavioral Sciences and the Law* 3 (1991): 299–308.
87. G. T. Marx, "Who really gets stung? Some issues raised by the new police undercover work," in *Moral issues in police work,* ed. F. Ellison and M. Feldberg, pp. 99–128 (Totowa, NJ: Bowman and Allanheld, 1988).

Chapter Nine

i. This paragraph is adapted from A. Smith, ed., *Intelligence-led policing* (Richmond: International Association of Law Enforcement Intelligence Analysts, 1997), p. 1.
ii. D. L. Carter, *Law enforcement intelligence: A guide for state, local, and tribal law enforcement agencies* (Washington, DC: U.S. Department of Justice, 2004), p. 7.
iii. Ibid.
iv. Ibid.
v. U.S. Department of Justice, "Information Technology Initiatives," http://www.it.ojp.gov/topic.jsp?topic_id=93 (accessed November 14, 2007).

---

1. J. Kandel, "LAPD brass sing Compstat praise: New program highlights crime trends geographically," *Daily News,* May 18, 2003, http://www.thefreelibrary.com/lapd+brass+sing+compstat+praise+new+program+highlights+crime+trends...-a0101982874 (accessed January 13, 2008).
2. "Is LAPD fudging our crime stats?" LAVoice.org, http://lavoice.org/index.php?name=News&file=article&sid=2525 (accessed July 24, 2008).
3. J. Godown, "Compstat and crime reduction," January 25, 2007, http://lapdblog.typepad.com/lapd_blog/2007/01/compstat_and_cr.html (accessed January 13, 2008).
4. R. Zink, "The trouble with Compstat," *PBA Magazine,* http://www.nycpba.org/publications/mag-04-summer/compstat.html (accessed January 13, 2008).
5. The concept of intelligence-led policing appears to have been first fully articulated in A. Smith, ed., *Intelligence-led policing* (Richmond: International Association of Law Enforcement Intelligence Analysts, 1997).
6. M. Peterson, *Intelligence-led policing: The new intelligence architecture* (Washington, DC: Bureau of Justice Assistance, 2005), p. 3.
7. Ibid., p. 11.
8. I. D. L. Carter, *Law enforcement intelligence: A guide for state, local, and tribal law enforcement agencies* (Washington, DC: U.S. Department of Justice, 2004), p. 7.
9. Ibid.
10. Much of the information and some of the wording in this section is taken from Carter, *Law enforcement intelligence.*
11. Peterson, *Intelligence-led policing,* p. 3.
12. Carter, *Law enforcement intelligence,* p. 8.
13. Ibid.
14. Peterson, *Intelligence-led policing,* p. 12.
15. Ibid.

16. R. Wright, "Management of the intelligence unit," in *Intelligence 2000: Revising the basic elements,* ed. M. B. Peterson, R. Wright, and B. Morehouse, p. 69 (Lawrenceville, NJ: International Association of Law Enforcement Intelligence Analysts and Law Enforcement Intelligence Units, 2001).
17. Peterson, *Intelligence-led policing,* p. 13.
18. Ibid., p. 4.
19. National Criminal Intelligence Service, *The national intelligence model* (London: National Criminal Intelligence Service, 2000).
20. Peterson, *Intelligence-led policing,* p. 4.
21. Ibid.
22. Ibid., p. 6.
23. Ibid., p. 7.
24. Ibid.
25. This section draws from Peterson, *Intelligence-led policing,* p. 9.
26. Ibid.
27. Ibid.
28. Ibid., p. 11.
29. Ibid., p. 10.
30. International Association of Chiefs of Police, *IACP Capitol Report* 5:19 (December 14, 2006).
31. J. Raymond, "Forget the pipe, Sherlock: Gear for tomorrow's detectives," *Newsweek* (June 22, 1998): 12.
32. VirTra Systems, "IVR 360 Series," http://www.virtrasystems.com/tr_prd_360.htm (accessed February 7, 2007).
33. Advanced Interactive Solutions, "PRISim," http://www.ais-solutions.co.uk/prisim.php (accessed July 18, 2008).
34. Ibid.
35. Environmental Criminology Research, Inc., "Company Overview," http://www.ecricanada.com/about/index.html (accessed February 7, 2007).
36. K. J. Peak, *Policing in America: Methods, issues, challenges,* 5th ed. (Upper Saddle River, NJ: Prentice Hall, 2006), pp. 430–31.
37. SRA International, "Powering the attack on a nationwide gang problem," http://www.sra.com/gangnet (accessed July 18, 2008).
38. E. Silverman, *NYPD battles crime: Innovative strategies in policing* (Boston: Northeastern University Press, 1999).
39. D. Weisburd and others, *Compstat and organizational change: Findings from a national survey* (Washington, DC: Police Foundation, 2001). For a review of Compstat-like strategies in six cities, see also M. H. Moore and A. A. Braga, "Measuring and improving police performance: The lessons of Compstat and its progeny," *Policing: An International Journal of Police Strategies and Management* 26 (2003): 439–53.
40. W. F. Walsh, "Compstat: An analysis of an emerging police managerial paradigm," *Policing: An International Journal of Police Strategies and Management* 24 (2001): 347–62.
41. E. Brady, "Compstat: Mapping, accountability, equal less crime," *USA Today,* December 1, 1997, p. 18A.
42. K. Harries, *Mapping crime: Principle and practice* (Washington, DC: National Institute of Justice, 1999), p. 79.
43. Ibid.
44. Ibid.
45. J. Maple, *The crime fighter* (New York: Doubleday, 1999), p. 93.
46. New Orleans Police Department, *Comstat* (New Orleans: New Orleans Police Department, 1999), http://www.acadiacom.net/nopd/comstat.htm (accessed August 28, 2004).
47. Silverman, *NYPD battles crime,* p. 104.
48. Harries, *Mapping crime,* p. 80.
49. R. Garner and L. Hoover, "The Compstat craze: Emphasizing accountability in policing," paper presented at the annual meeting of the Academy of Criminal Justice Sciences in New Orleans, 2000.
50. Ibid., p. 11.
51. D. Pederson, "Bullets in the big easy," *Newsweek* (December 23, 1996), p. 29.
52. *In re Gault,* 387 U.S. 1 (1967).
53. U.S. Census Bureau, "Poverty: 2006 highlights," http://www.census.gov/hhes/www/poverty/poverty06/pov06hi.html (accessed July 25, 2008).
54. Administration for Children and Families, "Summary: Child maltreatment 2006," http://www.census.gov/hhes/www/poverty/poverty06/pov06hi.html (accessed July 25, 2008).
55. W. Ruefle and K. M. Reynolds, "Keep them at home: Juvenile curfew ordinances in 200 American cities," *American Journal of Police* 15 (1996): 63–84.
56. K. M. Reynolds, R. Seydlitz, and P. Jenkins, "Do juvenile curfew laws work? A time-series analysis of the New Orleans law," *Justice Quarterly* 17 (2000): 206–30, p. 219.
57. M. S. Scott, *Disorderly youth in public places* (Washington, DC: Office of Community Oriented Policing Services, 2004), p. 1.
58. R. Winton and E. Hayasaki, "LAPD considers new tactics to combat rave parties," *Los Angeles Times,* November 30, 2004.
59. "Surgeon general warns of 'hidden' violence by youths," *Criminal Justice Newsletter,* February 9, 2001, pp. 4–5, quote on p. 4.
60. For an introduction, see D. Denckla and G. Berman, *Rethinking the revolving door: A look at mental illness in the courts* (New York: Center for Court Innovation, 2001).
61. A. Watson and others, "Mental health court: Promises and limitations," *Journal of the American Academy of Psychiatry and the Law* 28 (2000): 476–82.

62. P. M. Ditton, *Mental health and treatment of inmates and probationers* (Washington, DC: Bureau of Justice Statistics, 1999).
63. R. Hill, G. Quill, and K. Ellis, "The Montgomery County CIT model: Interacting with people with mental illness," *FBI Law Enforcement Bulletin* (July 2004): 18–25, quote on pp. 18–19.
64. M. Zdanowicz, "A shift in care," *Community Links* (June 2001): 3–5, quote on p. 3.
65. Office of National Drug Control Policy, *National drug control strategy: 2008 annual report* (Washington, DC: ONDCP, 2008), p. 5.
66. R. J. MacCoun and P. Reuter, *Drug war heresies* (New York: Cambridge University Press, 2001), p. 24.
67. W. Rhodes and others, *What America's users spend on illegal drugs, 1988–1995* (Washington, DC: Office of National Drug Control Policy, 1997).
68. Office of Drug Control Policy, *The economic costs of drug abuse in the United States, 1992–2002* (Washington, DC: ONDCP, 2004).
69. D. B. Kandel, "The social demography of drug use," *Milbank Quarterly* 69 (1993): 365–414; and J. Shedler and J. Block, "Adolescent drug use and psychological health: A longitudinal inquiry," *American Psychologist* 45 (1990): 612–30.
70. "Truth or DARE: Washington cities shelve anti-drug curriculum," *Law Enforcement News* (New York: John Jay College of Criminal Justice, 1996).
71. C. Ringwalt and others, *Past and future directions of the DARE program: An evaluation review—Draft final report* (Washington, DC: National Institute of Justice, 1994).
72. For a short list, see S. T. Ennett and others, "Long-term evaluation of Drug Abuse Resistance Education," *Addictive Behaviors* 19 (1994): 113–25; M. A. Harmon, "Reducing the risk of drug involvement among early adolescents: An evaluation of Drug Abuse Resistance Education (DARE)," *Evaluation Review* 17 (1993): 221–39; C. Ringwalt, S. T. Ennett, and K. D. Holt, "An outcome evaluation of Project DARE (Drug Abuse Resistance Education)," *Health Education Research* 6 (1991): 327–37; and D. P. Rosenbaum and others, "Cops in the classroom: A longitudinal evaluation of Drug Abuse Resistance Education (DARE)," *Journal of Research in Crime and Delinquency* 31 (1994): 3–31.
73. Office of Juvenile Justice and Delinquency Prevention, *Highlights of the 2006 national youth gang survey* (Washington, DC: Office of Juvenile Justice and Delinquency Prevention, U.S. Department of Justice, 2008), p. 1.
74. E. J. Fritsch, T. J. Caeti, and R.W. Taylor, "Gang suppression through saturation patrol and aggressive curfew and truancy enforcement: A quasi-experimental test of the Dallas Anti-Gang Initiative," in *Policing gangs and youth violence*, ed. S. H. Decker, pp. 267–84 (Belmont, CA: Wadsworth/Thompson Learning).
75. C. M. Katz and V. J. Webb, *Policing gangs in America* (New York: Cambridge University Press, 2006), p. 25.
76. J. E. Eck, "Preventing crime at places," in *Evidence-based crime prevention,* ed. L. W. Sherman and others (New York: Routledge, 2002), p. 277.
77. J. R. Lasley, *Using traffic barriers to "design out" crime: A program evaluation of LAPD's Operation Cul-De-Sac—Report to the National Institute of Justice* (Fullerton: California State University, 1996).
78. Ibid.
79. Ibid.
80. For a description of the process, see B. J. Whitbread and S. Mazza, "Utilizing civil injunction to combat gangs: Part 2," *Law Enforcement Quarterly* 28 (1999): 34–37.
81. C. L. Maxson, K. Hennigan, and D. C. Sloane, "For the sake of the neighborhood? Civil gang injunction as a gang intervention tool in Southern California," in *Policing gangs and youth violence,* ed. S. H. Decker (Belmont, CA: Wadsworth, 2003).
82. F. Esbensen and others, "How great is GREAT? Results from a longitudinal quasi-experimental design," *Criminology and Public Policy* 1 (2001): 87–118.
83. Ibid., p. 88.
84. Ibid.
85. Bureau of Justice Statistics, *Intimate partner violence in the U.S.,* http://www.ojp.usdoj.gov/bjs/intimate/overview.htm (accessed July 26, 2008).
86. R. B. Felson and others, "Reasons for reporting and not reporting domestic violence to the police," *Criminology* (August 2002): 617–42, quote on p. 617.
87. N. Websdale, H. Moss, and B. Johnson, "Domestic violence fatalities reviews: Implications for law enforcement," *Police Chief* (July 2001): 65–74, quote on p. 70.

Chapter Ten

i. Community Policing Consortium, *What is community policing?* (Washington, DC: Community Policing Consortium, 1995).
ii. B. Forst, "The privatization and civilianization of policing," in *Boundary changes in criminal justice organizations,* ed. C. M. Friel, pp. 19–79 (Washington, DC: National Institute of Justice, 2000), p. 23.
iii. M. E. Buerger and L. G. Mazerolle, "Third-party policing: Theoretical analysis of an emerging trend," in *The police and society: Touchstone readings,* 2nd ed., ed. V. E. Kappeler, pp. 402–26 (Prospect Heights, IL: Waveland, 1999), p. 402.

---

1. Washington, DC, Metropolitan Police, "Neighborhood Crime Data," press release, July 20, 1999, http://newsroom.dc.gov/show.aspx/agency/mpdc/section/2/release/240/year/1999/month/7 (accessed January 8, 2008).
2. Several portions of this chapter borrow from Chapter 5 of J. L. Worrall, *Crime control in America: An assessment of the evidence* (Boston: Allyn and Bacon, 2006).
3. T. R. Clear and E. Cadora, *Community justice* (Belmont, CA: Wadsworth, 2003), p. 1.

4. Ibid., pp. 1–2.
5. V. G. Strecher, *Planning community policing* (Prospect Heights, IL: Waveland, 1997).
6. H. Goldstein, *Problem oriented policing* (New York: McGraw-Hill, 1990); and H. Goldstein, "Improving policing: A problem-oriented approach," *Crime and Delinquency* 25 (1979): 236–58.
7. J. E. Angell, "Toward an alternative to the classic police organizational arrangements: A democratic model," *Criminology* 9 (1971): 185–206.
8. G. L. Kelling, "Police and communities: The quiet revolution," in *Criminal justice in America: Theory, practice, and policy,* ed. B. W. Hancock and P. M. Sharp, pp. 134–44 (Upper Saddle River, NJ: Prentice Hall, 1996).
9. Ibid., p. 138.
10. Ibid.
11. Ibid.
12. R. Trojanowicz and others, *Community policing: A contemporary perspective,* 2nd ed. (Cincinnati: Anderson, 1988).
13. Ibid., p. 53.
14. Ibid.
15. D. Hayeslip and G. Cordner, "The effects of community-oriented patrol on police officer attitudes," *American Journal of Police-Special Issue on Foot Patrol and Community Policing* 4 (1987): 95–119.
16. P. K. Manning, "Community policing as a drama of control," in *Community policing: Rhetoric or reality?* ed. J. R. Greene and S. D. Mastrofski, pp. 27–45 (New York: Praeger, 1988).
17. D. Garland, "The limits of the sovereign state: Strategies of crime control in contemporary society," *British Journal of Criminology* 36 (1996): 445–71.
18. J. Zhao, *Why police organizations change* (Washington, DC: Police Executive Research Forum, 1996).
19. See, for instance, W. G. Skogan and S. M. Hartnett, *Community policing: Chicago style* (New York: Oxford University Press, 1997).
20. R. Trojanowicz and B. Bucqueroux, *Community policing: A contemporary perspective* (Cincinnati: Anderson, 1990).
21. W. A. Geller and G. Swanger, *Managing innovation in policing: The untapped potential of the middle manager* (Washington, DC: Police Executive Research Forum, 1995).
22. Police Executive Research Forum, *Themes and variations in community policing* (Washington, DC: Police Executive Research Forum, 1996).
23. G. W. Cordner, "Community policing: Elements an effects," in *Critical issues in policing: Contemporary readings,* 3rd ed., ed. R. G. Dunham and G. P. Alpert (Prospect Heights, IL: Waveland, 1997), p. 452.
24. Ibid.
25. Ibid., p. 454.
26. Ibid., p. 458.
27. J. A. Roth, J. Roehl, and C. C. Johnson, "Trends in the adoption of community policing," in *Community policing: Can it work?* ed. W. G. Skogan, pp. 3–29 (Belmont, CA: Wadsworth, 2003).
28. Ibid., p. 24.
29. See also J. Zhao, Q. Thurman, and N. Lovrich, "Community oriented policing across the U.S.: Facilitators and impediments to implementation," *American Journal of Police* 14 (1995): 11–28; and J. Zhao, N. Lovrich, and Q. Thurman, "The status of community policing in American cities," *Policing: An International Journal of Police Strategies and Management* 22 (1999): 152–70.
30. J. R. Greene, "Community policing and organization change," in *Community policing: Can it work?* ed. W. G. Skogan (Belmont, CA: Wadsworth, 2003), p. 49.
31. Ibid.
32. See, for example, D. Guyot, "Bending granite: Attempts to change the rank structure of American police departments," *Journal of Police Science and Administration* 7 (1979): 253–384.
33. E. R. Maguire, "Structural change in large municipal police organizations during the community-policing era," *Justice Quarterly* 14 (1997): 547–76. See also J. A. Roth, ed., *National evaluation of the COPS program: Title 1 of the 1994 Crime Act* (Washington, DC: National Institute of Justice, 2000).
34. W. G. Skogan, ed., *Community policing: Can it work?* (Belmont, CA: Wadsworth, 2003), p. xxviii.
35. D. P. Rosenbaum and D. L. Wilkinson, "Can police adapt? Tracking the effects of organizational reform over six years," in *Community policing: Can it work?* ed. W. G. Skogan, pp. 79–108 (Belmont, CA: Wadsworth, 2003). See also D. P. Rosenbaum, S. Yeh, and D. L. Wilkinson, "Estimating the effects of community policing reform on police officers," *Crime and Delinquency* 40 (1994): 331–53.
36. W. Terrill and S. D. Mastrofski, "Working the street: Does community policing matter?" in *Community policing: Can it work?* ed. W. G. Skogan, pp. 109–35 (Belmont, CA: Wadsworth, 2003). See also W. Terrill and S. D. Mastrofski, "Situational and officer based determinants of police coercion," *Justice Quarterly* 19 (2002): 101–34.
37. R. L. Wood, M. Davis, and A. Rouse, "Diving into quicksand: Program implementation and police subcultures," in *Community policing: Can it work?* ed. W. G. Skogan, pp. 136–61 (Belmont, CA: Wadsworth, 2003).
38. J. Zhao, N. P. Lovrich, and Q. Thurman, "The status of community policing in American cities: Facilitators and impediments revisited," *Policing* 22:1 (1999): 74.
39. For a good critique and an overview of community policing, see G. P. Alpert and others, *Community policing: Contemporary readings* (Prospect Heights, IL: Waveland Press, 1998).
40. Jack R. Greene, "Community policing in America: Changing the nature, structure, and function of the police," in U.S. Department of Justice, *Criminal justice 2000,* vol. 3 (Washington, DC: Department of Justice, 2000).

41. Michael D. Reisig and Roger B. Parks, "Experience, quality of life, and neighborhood context: A hierarchical analysis of satisfaction with police," *Justice Quarterly* 17:3 (2000): 607.
42. Mark E. Correia, "The conceptual ambiguity of community in community policing: Filtering the muddy waters," *Policing* 23:2 (2000): 218–33.
43. Adapted from D. R. Fessler, *Facilitating community change: A basic guide* (San Diego: San Diego State University, 1976), p. 7.
44. D. W. Flynn, *Defining the "community" in community policing* (Washington, DC: Police Executive Research Forum, 1998).
45. R. C. Trojanowicz and M. H. Moore, *The meaning of community in community policing* (East Lansing: Michigan State University's National Neighborhood Foot Patrol Center, 1988).
46. R. M. Bohm, K. M. Reynolds, and S. T. Holms, "Perceptions of neighborhood problems and their solutions: Implications for community policing," *Policing* 23:4 (2000): 439.
47. Ibid., p. 442.
48. M. K. Sparrow, "Implementing community policing," *Perspectives on policing,* no. 9 (Washington, DC: National Institute of Justice, 1988).
49. "L.A. police chief: Treat people like customers," *USA Today,* March 29, 1993, p. 13A.
50. R. Wasserman and M. H. Moore, "Values in policing," *Perspectives in policing,* no. 8 (Washington, DC: National Institute of Justice, 1988), p. 7.
51. "New York City mayor sparks debate on community policing," *Criminal Justice Newsletter,* January 18, 1994, p. 1.
52. M. Alvaro, "Online 'substations' enhance public safety efforts," *Police* 24 (2000): 44–47.
53. K. S. Trump, *NASRO school resource officer survey 2002: Final report on the 2nd annual national survey of school-based police officers* (Anthony, FL: National Association of School Resource Officers, 2002).
54. National Association of School Resource Officers, www.nasro.org (accessed July 5, 2008).
55. U.S. Department of Justice, *Community outreach through police in schools* (Washington, DC: Office for Victims of Crime, U.S. Department of Justice, August 2003), p. 1.
56. B. Lindsay and D. McGillis, "Citywide community crime prevention: An assessment of the Seattle program," in *Community crime prevention: Does it work?* ed. D. Rosenbaum, pp. 46–67 (Beverly Hills, CA: Sage, 1986).
57. Ibid., p. 65.
58. F. J. Fowler, Jr. and T. W. Mangione, "The three-pronged effort to reduce crime and fear of crime: The Hartford experiment," in *Community crime prevention: Does it work?* ed. D. Rosenbaum, pp. 87–108 (Beverly Hills, CA: Sage, 1986).
59. Ibid., p. 104.
60. Ibid., p. 105.
61. D. Weisburd, N. A. Morris, and J. Ready, "Risk-focused policing at places: An experimental evaluation," *Justice Quarterly,* 25 (1) (March 2008), pp. 163–99.
62. C. Wexler, "Foreword," in *Solving crime and disorder problems: Current issues, police strategies, and organizational tactics,* ed. M. Reuland, C. S. Brito, and L. Carroll (Washington, DC: Police Executive Research Forum, 2001), p. vii.
63. B. Bucqueroux and D. Diamond, "Community policing is our best bet against terror," *Subject to Debate* (January 2002): 1, 6, especially p. 6.
64. Ibid.
65. J. Nislow, "Secret weapon against terrorism? Chiefs say community policing is an ace in the hole," *Law Enforcement News,* October 15, 2001, p. 1.
66. C. Wexler, "Policing a multicultural community," *Subject to Debate* (July 2003): 2.
67. U.S. Department of Justice, *Citizen patrol projects: National evaluation program phase 1 summary report* (Washington, DC: U.S. Department of Justice, 1976).
68. J. Hilson, "Fort Worth's citizens on patrol program," *TELEMASP Bulletin* 1 (1994): full issue.
69. See, e.g., V. W. Bumphus, L. K. Gaines, and C. R. Blakely, "Citizen police academies: Observing goals, objectives, and recent trends," *American Journal of Criminal Justice* 24 (1999): 67–79.
70. See, e.g., G. A. Aryani and others, "Citizen police academy: Success through community partnership," *FBI Law Enforcement Bulletin* 69 (2000): 16–21.
71. E. M. Bonello and J. A. Schafer, "Citizen police academies: Do they just entertain?" *FBI Law Enforcement Bulletin* 71 (2002): 19–23.
72. M. J. Palmiotto and N. P. Unninthan, "Impact of citizen police academies on participants: An exploratory study," *Journal of Criminal Justice* 30 (2002): 101–6.
73. J. A. Schafer and E. M. Bonello, "Citizen police academy: Measuring outcomes," *Police Quarterly* 4 (2001): 434–48; and E. G. Cohn, "Citizen police academy: A recipe for improving police-community relations," *Journal of Criminal Justice* 24 (1996): 265–71.
74. W. T. Jordan, "Citizen police academies: Community policing or community politics," *American Journal of Police* 25 (2000): 93–118.
75. Ibid.
76. B. Forst, "The privatization and civilianization of policing," in *Boundary changes in criminal justice organizations,* ed. C. M. Friel (Washington, DC: National Institute of Justice, 2000), p. 23.
77. Ibid.
78. Ibid., p. 25.
79. M. E. Buerger and L. G. Mazerolle, "Third-party policing: Theoretical analysis of an emerging trend," in *The police and society: Touchstone readings,* 2nd ed., ed. V. E.

Kappeler (Prospect Heights, IL: Waveland, 1999), p. 402.

80. Ibid.
81. Ibid., p. 403.
82. Ibid.
83. Ibid., p. 408.
84. Ibid.
85. S. Knight, L. J. Cook, and L. M. Olson, "The fast and the fatal: Street racing fatal crashes in the United States," *Injury Prevention* 10 (2004): 53–55.
86. National Hot Rod Association, "Illegal Racing Stats," http://www.nhra.com/streetlegal/stats.html (accessed July 5, 2008).
87. City Council of the City of San Diego, supplemental docket number 2, October 15, 2002.
88. National Hot Rod Association, "Illegal Racing Stats."
89. L. Peter, personal communication with author, April 27, 2004. Linda Peter was the deputy city attorney in San Diego.
90. San Diego Municipal Code, chapter 5, article 2, division 52.5301.
91. J. L. Worrall and S. G. Tibbetts, "Explaining San Diego's decline in illegal street-racing casualties," *Justice Quarterly* 23 (2006): 530–44.
92. Helping America's Youth, "Oakland Beat Health Program," http://guide.helpingamericasyouth.gov/programdetail.cfm?id=454 (accessed July 5, 2008).
93. See, e.g., L. G. Mazerolle and J. Roehl, *Controlling drug and disorder problems: Focus on Oakland's Beat Health Program* (Washington, DC: National Institute of Justice, 1999); and L. G. Mazerolle, J. Price, and J. Roehl, "Civil remedies and drug control: A randomized field trial in Oakland, California," *Evaluation Review* 24 (2000): 212–41.
94. Ibid.
95. See, e.g., M. E. Buerger, ed., *The crime prevention casebook: Securing high crime locations* (Washington, DC: Crime Control Institute, 1992).
96. M. E. Buerger and L. G. Mazerolle, "Third-party policing: Theoretical analysis of an emerging trend," in *The police and society: Touchstone readings*, 2nd ed., ed. V. E. Kappeler (Prospect Heights, IL: Waveland, 1999), p. 414.

Chapter Eleven

i. *Chimel v. California*, 395 U.S. 752 (1969).
ii. *Warden v. Hayden*, 387 U.S. 294 (1967).
iii. *Breithaupt v. Abram*, 352 U.S. 432 (1957).
iv. F. Schmalleger, *Criminal Justice Today*, 10e (Upper Saddle River, NJ: Prentice Hall, 2009), p. G-22.
v. S. L. Emanuel and S. Knowles, *Emanuel Law Outlines:* Criminal Procedure (Larchmont, NY: Emanuel, 1998), p. 129.
vi. *Fikes v. Alabama*, 352 U.S. 191 (1957), p. 198.
vii. *Rhode Island v. Innis*, 446 U.S. 291 (1980), n. 8.

1. *Kyllo v. United States*, 533 U.S. 27 (2001).
2. This chapter borrows liberally from J. L. Worrall, *Criminal procedure: From first contact to appeal*, 2nd ed. (Boston: Allyn and Bacon, 2007).
3. Of course, other questions then arise, including whether the private citizen had the right to be in the place where the evidence was thought to be, how he or she gained access to that place, and so on. While the private seizure of evidence might not lead to its inadmissibility at court, it might provide grounds for a civil suit against the citizen or even for his or her arrest (in case of burglary or theft).
4. *Burdeau v. McDowell*, 256 U.S. 465 (1921).
5. Ibid., p. 475.
6. *Camara v. Municipal Court*, 387 U.S. 523 (1967).
7. *Michigan v. Tyler*, 436 U.S. 499 (1978).
8. *Marshall v. Barlow's, Inc.*, 436 U.S. 307 (1978).
9. *Donovan v. Dewey*, 452 U.S. 594 (1981).
10. *New Jersey v. T.L.O.*, 469 U.S. 325 (1985).
11. See, e.g., *People v. Mangiefico*, 25 Cal. App.3d 1041 (1972).
12. See, e.g., *Coolidge v. New Hampshire*, 403 U.S. 443 (1971), p. 487.
13. *Katz v. United States*, 389 U.S. 347 (1967).
14. Ibid., p. 353.
15. Ibid.
16. *California v. Greenwood*, 486 U.S. 35 (1988).
17. *Katz v. United States*, p. 351.
18. Ibid.
19. *United States v. Jacobsen*, 466 U.S. 109 (1984).
20. *Terry v. Ohio*, 392 U.S. 1 (1968); and *United States v. Mendenhall*, 446 U.S. 544 (1980).
21. *Florida v. Bostick*, 501 U.S. 429 (1991).
22. *Beck v. Ohio*, 379 U.S. 89 (1964), p. 91.
23. *Brinegar v. United States*, 338 U.S. 160 (1949), p. 175.
24. *Terry v. Ohio*, 392 U.S. 1 (1968).
25. Ibid., p. 22.
26. Ibid., p. 13.
27. *United States v. Sokolow*, 490 U.S. 1 (1989), p. 7.
28. *Payton v. New York*, 445 U.S. 573 (1980).
29. *Steagald v. United States*, 451 U.S. 204 (1981).
30. *Johnson v. United States*, 333 U.S. 10 (1948), pp. 13–14.
31. *Coolidge v. New Hampshire*, 403 U.S. 443 (1971).
32. *United States v. United States District Court*, 407 U.S. 297 (1972).
33. *Payton v. New York*, 445 U.S. 573 (1980), pp. 602–3.
34. *Massachusetts v. Sheppard*, 468 U.S. 981 (1981).
35. *Chimel v. California*, 395 U.S. 752 (1969), p. 763.
36. *Sibron v. New York*, 392 U.S. 40 (1968).
37. See *Rawlings v. Kentucky*, 448 U.S. 98 (1980).
38. *Preston v. United States*, 376 U.S. 364 (1964).

39. Ibid., p. 367.
40. See also *Chambers v. Maroney,* 399 U.S. 42 (1970).
41. *Chimel v. California,* 395 U.S. 752 (1969).
42. Ibid., p. 759.
43. Ibid., p. 768.
44. *Maryland v. Buie,* 494 U.S. 325 (1990).
45. *Warden v. Hayden,* 387 U.S. 294 (1967).
46. Ibid., p. 298.
47. Ibid., pp. 298–99.
48. Ibid., p. 299.
49. *State v. Wren,* 115 Idaho 618 (1989), p. 625.
50. *United States v. George,* 883 F.2d 1407 (9th Cir. 1989).
51. *United States v. Santana,* 427 U.S. 38 (1976).
52. See, e.g., *Welsh v. Wisconsin,* 466 U.S. 740 (1984).
53. *Warden v. Hayden,* 387 U.S. 294 (1967), p. 299.
54. *Minnesota v. Olson,* 495 U.S. 91 (1990).
55. *Breithaupt v. Abram,* 352 U.S. 432 (1957).
56. *Carroll v. United States,* 267 U.S. 132 (1925).
57. *Husty v. United States,* 282 U.S. 694 (1931).
58. Ibid., p. 701.
59. *Coolidge v. New Hampshire,* 403 U.S. 443 (1971).
60. *United States v. Ross,* 456 U.S. 798 (1982), p. 800.
61. Ibid., p. 824.
62. *Coolidge v. New Hampshire,* 403 U.S. 443 (1971).
63. Ibid.
64. *Arizona v. Hicks,* 480 U.S. 321 (1987).
65. *Horton v. California,* 496 U.S. 128 (1990).
66. *Schneckloth v. Bustamonte,* 412 U.S. 218 (1973).
67. Ibid.
68. *Ohio v. Robinette,* 519 U.S. 33 (1996).
69. Ibid., pp. 39–40.
70. *United States v. Mendenhall,* 446 U.S. 544 (1980).
71. *Florida v. Jimeno,* 500 U.S. 248 (1991).
72. *State v. Brochu,* 237 A.2d 418 (Me. 1967).
73. *State v. Smith,* 488 S.E.2d 210 (N.C. 1997), p. 212.
74. *Payton v. New York,* 445 U.S. 573 (1980), p. 585.
75. *Terry v. Ohio,* 392 U.S. 1 (1968).
76. Ibid.
77. *United States v. Mendenhall,* 446 U.S. 544 (1980), p. 554, emphasis added.
78. *Sibron v. New York,* 392 U.S. 40 (1968).
79. *Pennsylvania v. Mimms,* 434 U.S. 106 (1977).
80. *Minnesota v. Dickerson,* 508 U.S. 366 (1993).
81. *Illinois v. Lafayette,* 462 U.S. 640 (1983).
82. *South Dakota v. Opperman,* 428 U.S. 364 (1976).
83. *Carroll v. United States,* 267 U.S. 132 (1925).
84. Ibid., p. 154. See also *United States v. Montoya de Hernandez,* 473 U.S. 531 (1985), p. 538.
85. *United States v. Martinez-Fuerte,* 428 U.S. 543 (1976).
86. *Michigan Dept. of State Police v. Sitz,* 496 U.S. 444 (1990).
87. *City of Indianapolis v. Edmond,* 531 U.S. 32 (2000).
88. Ibid., p. 32.
89. Ibid., p. 44.
90. *Illinois v. Lidster,* 540 U.S. 419 (2004).
91. *Fikes v. Alabama,* 352 U.S. 191 (1957), p. 198.
92. *Massiah v. United States,* 377 U.S. 201 (1964).
93. *Kirby v. Illnois,* 406 U.S 682 (1972), p. 689.
94. *Miranda v. Arizona,* 384 U.S. 436 (1966), p. 444, emphasis added.
95. *Berkemer v. McCarty,* 468 U.S. 420 (1984), p. 442.
96. *Rhode Island v. Innis,* 446 U.S. 291 (1980), p. 300.
97. Ibid., p. 302, n. 8.
98. *United States v. Dickerson,* 166 F.3d 667 (4th Cir. 1999), p. 671.
99. *Dickerson v. United States,* 530 U.S. 428 (2000).
100. Ibid., p. 431.
101. Ibid., p. 443.
102. *California v. Prysock,* 453 U.S. 355 (1981), p. 359.
103. *Duckworth v. Eagan,* 492 U.S. 192 (1989), p. 198.
104. Ibid., p. 203.
105. *Miranda v. Arizona,* 384 U.S. 436 (1966), p. 475.
106. Ibid.
107. Ibid., p. 476.
108. *Colorado v. Connelly,* 479 U.S. 157 (1986).
109. *Fare v. Michael C.,* 442 U.S. 707 (1979), p. 725.
110. Joined with *Miranda v. Arizona,* 384 U.S. 436 (1966).
111. *North Carolina v. Butler,* 441 U.S. 369 (1979).
112. Ibid., p. 373.
113. Ibid., pp. 374–75.
114. *New York v. Quarles,* 467 U.S. 649 (1984).
115. Ibid., pp. 657–58.
116. Ibid., p. 656.
117. Ibid., p. 657.
118. T. T. Burke, "Documenting and reporting a confession with a signed statement: A guide for law enforcement," *FBI Law Enforcement Bulletin* (February 2001): 17.

Chapter Twelve

i. *Lugar v. Edmondson Oil Co.*, 457 U.S. 922 (1982), p. 937.
ii. See, e.g., *Davis v. Passman*, 442 U.S. 228 (1979); *Sonntag v. Dooley*, 650 F.2d 904 (7th Cir. 1981); and *Carlson v. Green*, 446 U.S. 14 (1980).
iii. *Tennessee v. Garner*, 471 U.S. 1 (1985).
iv. *Weeks v. United States*, 232 U.S. 383 (1914); and *Mapp v. Ohio*, 367 U.S. 643 (1961).
v. *Silverthorne Lumber Co. v. United States*, 251 U.S. 385 (1920).

---

1. *Wilson v. Layne*, 526 U.S. 603 (1999).
2. M. A. Glendon, *A nation under lawyers: How the crisis in the legal profession is transforming American society* (New York: Farrar, Straus, and Giroux, 1994), p. 268.
3. D. F. Pike, "Why everybody is suing everybody," *U.S. News and World Report* (December 4, 1978): 50–54.
4. W. E. Burger, "Isn't there a better way?" *American Bar Association Journal* 68 (1982): 274–77, quote on p. 275.

5. *Monroe v. Pape*, 365 U.S. 167 (1961).
6. *Monell v. New York City Dept. of Social Services*, 436 U.S. 658 (1978).
7. V. E. Kappeler, S. F. Kappeler, and R. V. del Carmen, "A content analysis of police civil liability cases: Decisions of the federal district courts, 1978–1990," *Journal of Criminal Justice* 21 (1993): 325–37, quote on p. 327.
8. M. S. Vaughn and L. F. Coomes, "Police civil liability under Section 1983: When do police officers act under color of law?" *Journal of Criminal Justice* 23 (1995): 395–415, quote on p. 396.
9. *Lugar v. Edmondson Oil Co.*, 457 U.S. 922 (1982), p. 937.
10. Vaughn and Coomes, "Police civil liability under Section 1983," p. 409.
11. *Daniels v. Williams*, 474 U.S. 327 (1986), p. 330.
12. J. L. Worrall, "Culpability standards in Section 1983 litigation against criminal justice officials: When and why mental state matters," *Crime and Delinquency* 47 (2001): 28–59.
13. See, e.g., *City of Canton v. Harris*, 489 U.S. 378 (1989).
14. See, e.g., *Monell v. Department of Social Services*, 436 U.S. 658 (1978).
15. *Bivens v. Six Unknown Named Agents*, 403 U.S. 388 (1971).
16. See, e.g., *Davis v. Passman*, 442 U.S. 228 (1979); *Sonntag v. Dooley*, 650 F.2d 904 (7th Cir. 1981); and *Carlson v. Green*, 446 U.S. 14 (1980).
17. *Bradley v. Fisher*, 80 U.S. 335 (1871).
18. *Yaselli v. Goff*, 275 U.S. 503 (1927).
19. *Butz v. Economou*, 438 U.S. 478 (1978).
20. *Harlow v. Fitzgerald*, 457 U.S. 800 (1982).
21. See, e.g., *Will v. Michigan Department of State Police*, 491 U.S. 58 (1989).
22. *Ex parte Young*, 209 U.S. 123 (1908).
23. See, e.g., *Harlow v. Fitzgerald*, 457 U.S. 800 (1982); and *Wood v. Strickland*, 420 U.S. 308 (1975).
24. See, e.g., *Anderson v. Creighton*, 483 U.S. 635 (1987); and *Malley v. Briggs*, 475 U.S. 335 (1988).
25. *Baker v. Putnal*, 75 F.3d 190 (5th Cir. 1996).
26. Ibid., p. 198. See also *Saucier v. Katz*, 121 S.Ct. 2151 (2001).
27. W. A. Kerstetter, "Who disciplines the police? Who should?" in *Police leadership in America*, ed. W. Geller (Chicago: American Bar Association, 1985), pp. 178, 188.
28. P. West, "Investigation of complaints against the police: Summary report of a national survey," *American Journal of Police* 7 (1988): 101–22.
29. S. Walker and B. Wright, *Citizen review of the police: A national survey of the 50 largest cities* (Washington, DC: Police Executive Research Forum, 1995).
30. S. Walker and B. Wright, "Varieties of citizen review: The relationship of mission, structure, and procedures to police accountability," in *Critical issues in policing: Contemporary readings*, 3rd ed., ed. R. G. Dunham and G. P. Alpert (Prospect Heights, IL: Waveland, 1997).
31. A. J. Goldsmith, *Complaints against the police: The trend toward external review* (Oxford: Clarendon Press, 1991).
32. Kerstetter, "Who disciplines the police?"
33. A. E. Wagner and S. H. Decker, "Evaluating citizen complaints against the police," in *Critical issues in policing: Contemporary readings*, 3rd ed., ed. R. G. Dunham and G. P. Alpert, pp. 302–18 (Prospect Heights, IL: Waveland, 1997); and Americans for Effective Law Enforcement, *Police civilian review boards*, AELE Defense Manual, Brief #82-3 (San Francisco: Americans for Effective Law Enforcement, 1982).
34. For more details, see the Kansas City (Missouri) Police Department home page, http://www.kcpd.org/ (accessed July 10, 2008).
35. City of San Jose, Office of the Independent Auditor, "Charter," http://www.sanjoseca.gov/ipa/Charter.html (accessed November 27, 2008).
36. S. Walker and V. W. Bumphus, *Civilian review of the police: A national survey of the 50 largest cities* (Omaha: University of Nebraska at Omaha, 1991).
37. S. Walker, *Citizen review resource manual* (Washington, DC: Police Executive Research Forum, 1995).
38. Ibid.
39. Ibid.
40. S. Walker, *Police accountability: The role of citizen oversight* (Belmont, CA: Wadsworth, 2001).
41. D. W. Perez, *Common sense about police review* (Philadelphia: Temple University Press, 1994).
42. S. Walker and B. Wright, "Varieties of citizen review: The relationship of mission, structure, and procedures to police accountability," in *Critical issues in policing: Contemporary readings*, 3rd ed., ed. R. G. Dunham and G. P. Alpert (Prospect Heights, IL: Waveland, 1997), p. 333.
43. Ibid.
44. A. E. Wagner and S. H. Decker, "Evaluating citizen complaints against the police," in *Critical issues in policing: Contemporary readings*, 3rd ed., ed. R. G. Dunham and G. P. Alpert (Prospect Heights, IL: Waveland, 1997), p. 310.
45. A. Pate and L. Fridell, *Police use of force*, vol. 1 (Washington, DC: Police Foundation, 1993).
46. D. B. Griswold, "Complaints against the police: Predicting dispositions," *Journal of Criminal Justice* 22 (1994): 215–21.
47. D. P. Demers and others, "The color of justice," *Twin Cities Reader* (March 1992): 8–11, 25–31.
48. Wagner and Decker, "Evaluating citizen complaints against the police," p. 306.
49. See, e.g., A. E. Wagner, "Citizen complaints against the police: The complainant," *Journal of Police Science and Administration* 8 (1980): 373–77; and City of Minneapolis, *Annual review of the civilian police review board* (Minneapolis: City of Minneapolis, 1996).
50. K. M. Lersch, "Police misconduct and malpractice: A critical analysis of citizens' complaints," *Policing: An*

International Journal of Police Strategies and Management 21 (1998): 80–96.
51. Commission on Accreditation for Law Enforcement Agencies, *Standards for law enforcement agencies*, 4th ed. (Fairfax, VA: Commission on Accreditation for Law Enforcement, 1999), p. xiii.
52. Commission on Accreditation for Law Enforcement Agencies, *Standards for law enforcement agencies*, 5th ed. (Fairfax, VA: Commission on Accreditation for Law Enforcement Agencies, 2006), http://www.calea.org (accessed August 15, 2008).
53. Ibid., p. xiv.
54. J. A. Conser and G. D. Russell, *Law enforcement in the United States* (Gaithersburg, MD: Aspen, 2000).
55. S. J. Hill, "The significance of police credentialing," *Police* 23 (March 1999): 40–42.
56. W. E. Eastman, "National accreditation: A costly, unneeded make-work scheme," in *Police management today*, ed. J. Fyfe, pp. 49–54 (Washington, DC: International City Managers Association, 1985); and J. Pearson, "National accreditation: A valuable management tool," in *Police management today*, ed. J. Fyfe, pp. 45–48 (Washington, DC: International City Managers Association, 1985).
57. J. W. Bizzack and V. Delacruz, "Demystifying police accreditation," *Law Enforcement News*, April 30, 1994, pp. 8, 11.
58. Washington Association of Sheriffs and Police Chiefs, *Accreditation program* (Olympia: Washington Association of Sheriffs and Police Chiefs, 1998).
59. C. J. Behan, "Allies, not adversaries: Accreditation and community policing," *Commission update: September 1* (Fairfax, VA: Commission on Accreditation for Law Enforcement Agencies, 1992), p. 1; and G. W. Sykes, "Accreditation and community policing: Passing fads or basic reforms?" *Journal of Contemporary Criminal Justice* 10 (1994): 1–16.
60. G. W. Cordner and G. L. Williams, "Community policing and police agency accreditation," in *Policing perspectives: An anthology*, ed. L. K. Gaines and G. W. Cordner, pp. 372–79 (Los Angeles, CA: Roxbury, 1999).
61. Ibid., p. 174.
62. *Weeks v. United States*, 232 U.S. 383 (1914); and *Mapp v. Ohio*, 367 U.S. 643 (1961).
63. *Elkins v. United States*, 364 U.S. 206 (1960).
64. *Silverthorne Lumber Co. v. United States*, 251 U.S. 385 (1920).
65. M. Wilkey, "Why suppress evidence?" *Judicature* 62 (1978): 214.
66. *Mapp v. Ohio*, 367 U.S. 643 (1961).
67. *Screws v. United States*, 325 U.S. 91 (1945).
68. *United States v. Lanier*, 520 U.S. 259 (1997).
69. *Miller v. United States*, 404 F.2d 611 (5th Cir. 1968).
70. *Williams v. United States*, 341 U.S. 97 (1951).
71. *Lynch v. United States*, 189 F.2d 476 (5th Cir. 1951).
72. M. L. Birzer, "Crimes committed by police officers," in *Police misconduct*, ed. M. J. Palmiotto, pp. 168–81 (Upper Saddle River, NJ: Prentice Hall, 2001).
73. Ibid.
74. M. W. Lyman, *The police: An introduction* (Upper Saddle River, NJ: Prentice Hall, 1999).
75. J. Douglas and J. Johnson, *Official deviance* (New York: Lippincott, 1977); and D. Guyot, *Policing as though people matter* (Philadelphia: Temple University Press, 1991).
76. D. W. Perez and W. K. Muir, "Administrative review of alleged police brutality," in *And justice for all: Understanding and controlling police abuse of force*, ed. W. A. Geller and H. Toch (Washington, DC: Police Executive Research Forum, 1995), pp. 207–8.
77. Police Executive Research Forum, *Police agency handling of officer misconduct: A model policy statement* (Washington, DC: Police Executive Research Forum, 1981), p. 1.
78. W. A. Geller, *Police leadership in America* (New York: Praeger, 1985), pp. 157–98.
79. J. Angell, "The adequacy of the internal processing of citizen complaints by police departments," master's thesis (Michigan State University, 1966).
80. *Garrity v. New Jersey*, 385 U.S. 483 (1967).
81. *Gardner v. Broderick*, 392 U.S. 273 (1967).
82. *LaChance v. Erickson*, 118 S.Ct. 753 (1998).
83. *Cleveland Board of Education v. Loudermill*, 470 U.S. 532 (1985), p. 546.
84. *Gilbert v. Homar*, 520 U.S. 924 (1997), p. 929.
85. *Bence v. Breier*, 501 F.2d 1185 (1974).
86. Ibid., p. 1190.
87. K. Krajack, "Internal affairs," *Police Magazine* (1979): 9–16.
88. M. Chiuchiolo, "The law enforcement officer's bill of rights: Panacea or problem?" *Police Chief* 68 (1981): 70–72.
89. H. Johnson, "A police officer's bill of rights: A needed protection for cops?" in *Controversial issues in policing*, ed. J. D. Sewell (Boston: Allyn and Bacon, 1999), p. 42.
90. M. Scott, "A police officer's bill of rights: A needed protection for cops?" in *Controversial issues in policing*, ed. J. D. Sewell (Boston: Allyn and Bacon, 1999), pp. 36–41.
91. J. M. Pollock, "Ethics in law enforcement," in *Critical issues in policing: Contemporary readings*, 4th ed., ed. R. G. Dunham and G. P. Alpert (Prospect Heights, IL: Waveland, 2001), p. 366.
92. J. Pollock and R. Becker, "Ethical dilemmas in police work," in *Justice, crime, and ethics*, ed. M. Braswell, B. McCarthy, and B. McCarthy, pp. 83–103 (Cincinnati, OH: Anderson, 1996).

93. L. K. Gaines, V. E. Kappeler, and J. B. Vaughn, *Policing in America*, 3rd ed. (Cincinnati: Anderson, 1999), pp. 344–45.

Chapter Thirteen

1. "Was it 'excited delirium' or police brutality?" CBS News, *60 Minutes,* December 10, 2003, http://www.cbsnews.com/stories/2003/12/09/60II/main587569.shtml (accessed August 6, 2007).
2. The video was posted at http://www.youtube.com/watch?v=NsR5CP1XQ6A (accessed August 6, 2007), but has been removed.
3. J. Q. Wilson and G. L. Kelling, "Broken windows: The police and neighborhood safety," *Atlantic Monthly* (March 1982): 28–29.
4. D. H. Bayley and E. Bittner, "Learning the skills of policing," in *Critical issues in policing: Contemporary readings,* ed. R. G. Dunham and G. P. Alpert, pp. 87–110 (Prospect Heights, IL: Waveland, 1989).
5. K. C. Davis, *Police discretion* (St. Paul: West, 1975), p. 73.
6. J. Zhao, Q. Thurman, and N. He, "Sources of job satisfaction among police officers: A test of demographic and work environment models," *Justice Quarterly* 16 (1999): 153–73.
7. K. Peak, *Policing America: Methods, issues, challenges,* 5th ed. (Upper Saddle River, NJ: Prentice Hall, 2006).
8. W. A. Westley, "Violence and the police," *American Journal of Sociology* 59 (1953): 34–42. See also W. A. Westley, *Violence and the police* (Cambridge, MA: MIT Press, 1970).
9. J. H. Skolnick, *Justice without trial,* 3rd ed. (New York: Macmillan, 1994).
10. Ibid., p. 226.
11. See P. K. Manning and J. Van Maanen, eds., *Policing: A view from the street* (Santa Monica, CA: Goodyear, 1978).
12. P. K. Manning, "The police: Mandate, strategy, and appearances," in *The police and society: Touchstone readings,* 2nd ed., ed. V. E. Kappeler (Prospect Heights, IL: Waveland, 1999), p. 101.
13. Ibid., p. 109.
14. Ibid., p. 108.
15. For more information on the first three categories, see F. X. Hartmann, "Debating the evolution of American policing," in *Perspectives on policing,* no. 5 (Washington, DC: National Institute of Justice, 1988).
16. To learn more about Wilson, see "Presidential Medal of Freedom Recipient James Q. Wilson," http://www.medaloffreedom.com/JamesQWilson.htm (accessed January 5, 2006).
17. J. Q. Wilson, *Varieties of police behavior: The management of law and order in eight communities* (Cambridge, MA: Harvard University Press, 1968).
18. Independent Commission on the Los Angeles Police Department, *Report of the Independent Commission on the Los Angeles Police Department* (Los Angeles: Independent Commission on the Los Angeles Police Department, 1991).
19. G. W. Sykes, "Street justice: A moral defense of order maintenance policing," *Justice Quarterly* 3(4) (December 1986): 505.
20. J. Rubenstein, *City police* (New York: Farrar, Straus, and Giroux, 1973).
21. J. Van Maanen, "Observations on the making of policeman," *Human Organization* 32 (1973): 407–18.
22. W. K. Muir, *Police: Streetcorner politicians* (Chicago: University of Chicago Press, 1977).
23. Michael Brown, *Working the street: Police discretion,* revised edition (New York: Russell Sage Foundation, 1988).
24. D. Black, *The manners and customs of the police* (New York: Academic Press, 1980).
25. S. E. Martin, *Breaking and entering: Policewomen on patrol* (Berkeley: University of California Press, 1980).
26. R. Worden, "Situational and attitudinal explanations of police behavior: A theoretical reappraisal and empirical assessment," *Law and Society Review* 23 (1989): 687.
27. Ibid.
28. S. O. White, "A perspective on police professionalization," *Law and Society Review* 7 (1982): 61; J. J. Broderick, *Police in a time of change* (Morristown, NJ: General Learning Press, 1977); and M. K. Brown, *Working the street: Police discretion and the dilemmas of reform* (New York: Russell Sage Foundation, 1981), pp. 223–37.
29. Worden, "Situational and attitudinal explanations of police behavior," p. 687.
30. White, "A perspective on police professionalization," p. 61; Broderick, *Police in a time of change*; and Brown, *Working the street.*
31. Worden, "Situational and attitudinal explanations of police behavior," p. 688.
32. See, e.g., Brown, *Working the street*, p. 162
33. Worden, "Situational and attitudinal explanations of police behavior," p. 688.
34. *Atwater v. City of Lago Vista* 121 S.Ct. 1536 (2001).
35. Worden, "Situational and attitudinal explanations of police behavior," p. 689.
36. J. A. Gardiner, *Traffic and the police: Variations in law enforcement policy* (Cambridge, MA: Harvard University Press, 1969).
37. See, e.g., Brown, *Working the street.*
38. Worden, "Situational and attitudinal explanations of police behavior," p. 690.

39. M. Rokeach, M. Miller, and J. Snyder, "The value gap between police and policed," *Journal of Social Issues* 27 (1971): 155–71.
40. M. Caldero and A. P. Larose, "Value consistency within the police: The lack of a gap," *Policing: An International Journal of Police Strategies and Management* 24 (2003): 162–80, quote on p. 162.
41. See also J. Crank and M. Caldero, *Police ethics: The corruption of noble cause* (Cincinnati: Anderson, 1999), for an examination of this issue.
42. G. Alpert and W. Smith, "Developing police policy: An evaluation of the control principle," in L. Gaines and G. Cordner (eds.), *Policing Perspectives: An Anthology*, pp. 353–362 (Los Angeles, CA: Roxbury, 1998). See also J. Auten, "Preparing written guidelines," *FBI Law Enforcement Bulletin* 57 (1988): 1–7.
43. G. Cordner, "Written rules and regulations: Are they necessary?" *FBI Law Enforcement Bulletin*, July (1989): 17–21. See also, T. Adams, *Police Field Operations* (Englewood Cliffs, NJ: Prentice-Hall, 1990).
44. R. Roberg, K. Novak, and G. Cordner, *Police and society,* 4th ed. (New York: Oxford, 2008).
45. Ibid., p. 285.
46. S. D. Mastrofski, "Policing the beat: The impact of organizational scale on patrol officer behavior in urban residential neighborhoods," *Journal of Criminal Justice* 9 (1981): 343–58.
47. S. D. Mastrofski, R. Ritti, and D. Hoffmaster, "Organizational determinants of police discretion: The case of drinking-driving," *Journal of Criminal Justice* 15 (1987): 387–402.
48. Brown, *Working the street*, p. 58; P. V. Murphy and T. Pate, *Commissioner* (New York: Simon and Schuster, 1977), p. 39.
49. Murphy and Pate, *Commissioner.*
50. L. W. Brooks, "Police discretionary behavior: A study of style," in *Critical issues in policing: Contemporary readings,*4th ed., ed. R. G. Dunham and G. P. Alpert (Prospect Heights, IL: Waveland, 1989), p. 123.
51. E. M. Davis, *Staff one: A perspective on effective police management* (Englewood Cliffs, NJ: Prentice Hall, 1978), p. 135.
52. S. Walker, *The police in America,* 2nd ed. (New York: McGraw-Hill, 1991); and P. F. Nardulli and J. M. Stonecash, *Politics, professionalism, and urban services: The police* (Cambridge, MA: Oelgeschlager, Gunn, and Hain, 1981).
53. Nardulli and Stonecash, *Politics, professionalism, and urban services,* pp. 86–88.
54. Roberg, Novak, and Cordner, *Police and society*, p. 286.
55. D. A. Smith, "The neighborhood context of police behavior," in *Crime and justice: An annual review of research,* vol. 8, ed. A. J. Reiss and M. Tonry (Chicago: University of Chicago Press, 1986).
56. E. C. Riksheim and S. M. Chermak, "Causes of police behavior revisited," *Journal of Criminal Justice* 21 (1993): 353–82; D. A. Smith, "The organizational aspects of legal control," *Criminology* 22 (1984): 19–38; Smith, "The neighborhood context of police behavior"; and D. A. Smith and J. R. Klien, "Police agency characteristics and arrest decisions," in *Evaluating performance of criminal justice agencies,* ed. G. D. Whitaker and C. D. Phillips (Beverly Hills, CA: Sage, 1984).
57. D. A. Klinger, "Negotiating order in patrol work: An ecological theory of police response to deviance," *Criminology* 35 (1997): 277–306.
58. L. W. Brooks, A. Piquero, and J. Cronin, "Workload rates and police officer attitudes: An examination of 'busy' and 'slow' precincts," *Journal of Criminal Justice* 22 (1994): 277–86.
59. L. W. Sherman, "Causes of police behavior: The current state of quantitative research," in *The Ambivalent Force,* 3rd ed., ed. A. S. Blumberg and E. Niederhoffer (New York: Holt, Rinehart, and Wilson, 1985), p. 187.
60. J. Van Maanen, "The Asshole," in *Policing: A view from the streets,* ed. P. K. Manning and J. Van Maanen, pp. 221–38 (Santa Monica, CA: Goodyear, 1978).
61. See, e.g., D. Black and A. Reiss, "Police control of juveniles," *American Sociological Review* 35 (1970): 63–77; R. Ericson, *Reproducing order: A study of police patrol work* (Toronto: University of Toronto Press, 1982); D. A. Smith, "The neighborhood context of police behavior," in *Crime and justice: An annual review of research,* vol. 8, ed. A. J. Reiss and M. Tonry (Chicago: University of Chicago Press, 1986); and C. A. Visher, "Gender, police arrest decisions, and notions of chivalry," *Criminology* 21 (1983): 5–28.
62. K. M. Lersch and J. R. Feagin, "Violent police-citizen encounters: An analysis of major newspaper accounts," *Critical Sociology* 22 (1996): 29–49.
63. D. Klinger, "Demeanor or crime: Why 'hostile' citizens are more likely to be arrested," *Criminology* 32 (1994): 475–93.
64. See, e.g., R. J. Lundman, "Demeanor or crime? The midwest city police-citizen encounter," *Criminology* 32 (1994): 631–56; and R. E. Worden and R. L. Shepard, "Demeanor, crime, and police behavior: A reexamination of the police services study data," *Criminology* 34 (1996): 83–105.
65. V. E. Kappeler, R. D. Sluder, and G. P. Alpert, *Forces of deviance: Understanding the dark side of policing* (Prospect Heights, IL: Waveland, 1994); W. Chambliss, "Policing the ghetto underclass: The politics of law and law enforcement," in *Public Policy: Crime and Criminal Justice,* ed. B. Handcock and P. Sharp, pp. 146–65 (Upper Saddle River, NJ: Prentice Hall, 1997); and M. Maurer, *Young black men and the criminal justice system: A growing national problem* (Washington, DC: Sentencing Project, 1993).

66. Roberg, Novak, and Cordner, *Police and society,* p. 288.
67. G. P. Alpert, J. M. Macdonald, and R. G. Dunham, "Police suspicion and discretionary decision making during citizen stops," *Criminology* 43 (2005): 407–34.
68. For some examples, see D. A. Harris, "The stories, the statistics, and the law: Why 'driving while black' matters," *Minnesota Law Review* 84 (1999): 265–326; and E. Spitzer, *The New York City Police Department's 'stop and frisk' practices: A report to the people of the state of New York from the office of the attorney general* (Albany: New York Attorney General's Office, 1999).
69. C. A. Visher, "Gender, police arrest decisions, and notions of chivalry," *Criminology* 21 (1983): 5–28.
70. P. B. Kraska and V. E. Kappeler, "To serve and pursue: Exploring police sexual violence against women," *Justice Quarterly* 12 (1995): 85–112.
71. Kappeler, Sluder, and Alpert, *Forces of deviance.*
72. See, e.g., D. Black, *The behavior of law* (New York: Academic Press, 1976).
73. K. J. Novak and others, "Revisiting the decision to arrest: Comparing beat and community officers," *Crime and Delinquency* 48 (2002): 70–98.
74. Y. G. Hurst and J. Frank, "How kids view cops: The nature of juvenile attitudes toward the police," *Journal of Criminal Justice* 28 (2000): 189–202.
75. See, e.g., S. D. Mastrofski, R. E. Worden, and J. B. Snipes, "Law enforcement in a time of community policing," *Criminology* 33 (1995): 539–63; and G. Cordner, "Community policing: Elements and effects," *Police Forum* 5 (1995): 1–8.
76. Black and Reiss, "Police control of juveniles"; D. Black, "The social organization of arrest," *Stanford Law Review* 23 (1971): 1087–1111; and R. J. Friedrich, "The impact of organizational, individual, and situational factors on police behavior," Ph.D. dissertation (Department of Political Science, University of Michigan, 1977).
77. Black and Reiss, "Police control of juveniles"; Black, "The social organization of arrest"; L. W. Brooks, "Determinants of police officer orientations and their impact on police discretionary behavior," Ph.D. dissertation (Institute of Criminal Justice and Criminology, University of Maryland, 1986); Friedrich, "The impact of organizational, individual, and situational factors on police behavior"; D. A. Smith, "Police response to interpersonal violence: Defining the parameters of legal control," *Social Forces* 65 (1987): 767–82; D. A. Smith and C. Visher, "Street level justice: Situational determinants of police arrest decisions," *Social Problems* 29 (1981): 167–78; C. A. Visher, "Gender, police arrest decisions, and notions of chivalry," *Criminology* 21 (1983): 5–28; and Worden, "Situational and attitudinal explanations of police behavior."
78. See, e.g., Black, *The manners and customs of the police.*
79. Roberg, Novak, and Cordner, *Police and society,* p. 291.
80. See, e.g., Brooks, "Police discretionary behavior, p. 126; and Sherman, "Causes of police behavior," pp. 189–92.
81. Roberg, Novak, and Cordner, *Police and society,* p. 292.
82. See, e.g., S. E. Martin, "Female officers on the move?" in *Critical issues in policing: Contemporary readings,* ed. R. G. Dunham and G. P. Alpert, pp. 312–30 (Prospect Heights, IL: Waveland, 1989), pp. 312–30; and S. A. Grennan, "Findings on the role of officer gender in violent encounters with citizens," *Journal of Police Science and Administration* 15 (1988): 78–85.
83. W. F. Walsh, "Police officer arrest rates," *Justice Quarterly* 3 (1986): 271–90.
84. Mastrofski and others, "Law enforcement in a time of community policing."

Chapter Fourteen

i. V. E. Kappeler, R. D. Sluder, and G. Alpert, *Forces of deviance: Understanding the dark side of policing* (Prospect Heights, IL: Waveland, 1994), p. 21.
ii. Adapted from P. B. Kraska and V. E. Kappeler, "To serve and pursue: Exploring police sexual violence against women," *Justice Quarterly* 12 (1995): 85–109.
iii. K. J. Peak, *Policing America: Methods, issues, challenges*, 5th ed. (Upper Saddle River, NJ: Prentice Hall, 2006), p. 307.
iv. Ibid.
v. J. M. Pollock, "Ethics and law enforcement," in *Critical issues in policing: Contemporary readings*, 4th ed., ed. R. G. Dunham and G. P. Alpert, pp. 356–73 (Prospect Heights, IL: Waveland, 2001).

---

1. Associated Press, "Cops kill couple at luxury oceanfront resort," April 23, 2007, http://www.msnbc.msn.com/id/18270556 (accessed January 15, 2008).
2. M. Punch, *Conduct unbecoming: The social construction of police deviance and control* (London: Tavistock, 1985).
3. J. Kleinig, *The ethics of policing* (Cambridge: Cambridge University Press, 1996), p. 166.
4. S. Walker, *Popular justice: A history of American criminal justice*, 2nd ed. (New York: Oxford University Press, 1998), pp. 26–27.
5. Ibid., pp. 61–62.
6. R. M. Fogelson, *Big-city police* (Cambridge, MA: Harvard University Press, 1977), p. 32.
7. National Commission on Law Observance and Enforcement, *Report on lawlessness in law enforcement* (1931; repr., Montclair, NJ: Patterson Smith, 1968), p. 4.
8. Walker, *Popular justice*, p. 155.
9. *Powell v. Alabama*, 287 U.S. 45 (1932).
10. R. Roberg, K. Novak, and G. Cordner, *Police and society*, 3rd ed. (Los Angeles, CA: Roxbury, 2005), p. 298.
11. T. Barker, *Police ethics: Crisis in law enforcement* (Springfield, IL: Charles Thomas, 1996).

12. "2 former N.Y. cops charged as Mafia hit men," CNN Law Center, March 11, 2005, http://www.cnn.com/2005/LAW/03/11/police.slayings/index.html (accessed August 23, 2008).
13. V. E. Kappeler, R. D. Sluder, and G. Alpert, *Forces of deviance: Understanding the dark side of policing* (Prospect Heights, IL: Waveland, 1994).
14. Ibid., p. 21.
15. For a fairly thorough account, see M. L. Birzer, "Crimes committed by police officers," in *Police misconduct: A reader for the 21st century*, ed. M. J. Palmiotto, pp. 168–81 (Upper Saddle River, NJ: Prentice Hall, 2001).
16. Barker, *Police ethics*, p. 25.
17. Kappeler, Sluder, and Alpert, *Forces of deviance*, p. 24.
18. Punch, *Conduct unbecoming*.
19. Roberg, Novak, and Cordner, *Police and society*, p. 295. See also P. Manning, *The narc's game* (Cambridge, MA: MIT Press, 1980).
20. "Mark Fuhrman's 10/2/96 plea agreement to felony perjury at O.J. Simpson's criminal trial," The 'Lectric Law Library, http://www.lectlaw.com/files/case63.htm (accessed August 23, 2008).
21. Cited in C. Slobogin, "Testifying: Police perjury and what to do about it," *University of Colorado Law Review* 67 (1996): 1037–60, quote on pp. 1042–43.
22. M. W. Orfield, Jr., "Deterrence, perjury, and the heater factor: An exclusionary rule in the Chicago criminal courts," *University of Colorado Law Review* 107 (1992): 75.
23. Ibid.
24. Barker, *Police ethics*.
25. M. O'Connor and R. Gibson, "U.S. indicts ex-Cicero police chief," *Chicago Tribune*, January 13, 2001, http://www.laborers.org/Tribune_cop_1-13-01.html (accessed July 15, 2008).
26. "Alleged mob boss in Cicero is sentenced," *Los Angeles Times*, January 8, 2003, http://articles.latimes.com/2003/jan/08/nation/na-briefs8.6 (accessed August 23, 2008).
27. Drug War Chronicle, "Newsbrief: This week's corrupt cops stories," April 8, 2005, http://stopthedrugwar.org/chronicle-old/381/thisweek1.shtml (accessed July 15, 2008).
28. HistoryLink.org, "Police Shake Down a Seattle Gay Bathhouse for Payoffs from 1965 to 1968," http://www. historylink.org/essays/output.cfm?file_id=1174 (accessed July 15, 2008).
29. For details and other examples of this, see E. Blumenson and E. Nilsen, "The drug war's hidden economic agenda," *The Nation* (March 9, 1998): 11–16.
30. "New York City police officer dismissed over ticket fixing," *New York Times*, April 8, 1987, http://query.nytimes .com/gst/fullpage.html?res=9B0DE5DA143EF93BA35757C0A961948260 (accessed July 15, 2008).
31. The Weird News Blog, "Edwardsville police chief Steve Vaughan and Kansas City Kansas police officer Bob Lane arrested, charged with ticket-fixing scandal," July 29, 2006, http://theweirdnewsblog.com/edwardsville-police-chief-steve-vaughan-and-kansas-city-kansas-police-officer-bob-lane-arrested-charged-with-ticket-fixing-scandal.html (accessed August 26, 2008).
32. B. Dedman, "Police flouting 'no-fix' law on tickets," *Boston Globe*, February 16, 2004, http://www.boston.com/news/local/massachusetts/articles/2004/02/16/police_flouting_no_fix_law_on_tickets (accessed July 15, 2008).
33. S. Coleman, "When police should say 'no!' to gratuities," *Police Ethics* (winter–spring 2004): 33–44.
34. Ibid, pp. 34–37.
35. Ibid., p. 39.
36. J. Ruiz and C. Bono, "At what price a 'freebie'? The real cost of police gratuities," *Police Ethics* (winter–spring 2004): 44–54, quote on p. 45.
37. Ibid.
38. See P. B. Kraska and V. E. Kappeler, "To serve and pursue: Exploring police sexual violence against women," *Justice Quarterly* 12 (1995): 85–109.
39. T. Barker, "An empirical study of police deviance other than corruption," *Journal of Police Science and Administration* 3 (1978): 264–72.
40. Ibid., p. 266.
41. A. D. Sapp, "Sexual Misconduct by Police Officers," in T. Barker and D. Carter (eds.), *Police deviance*, pp. 83–95 (Cincinnati: Anderson, 1986), p. 88.
42. See Kraska and Kappeler, "To serve and pursue."
43. Ibid.
44. Ibid.
45. *James v. City of Douglas, GA*, 941 F.2d 1539 (11th Cir. 1991).
46. Ibid.
47. *Timberlake by Timberlake v. Benton*, 786 F.Supp. 676 (M.D. Tenn, 1992).
48. Ibid.
49. *Parrish v. Lukie*, 963 F.2d (8th Cir. 1992).
50. Cited in Kraska and Kappeler, "To serve and pursue."
51. D. L. Carter, "Drug use and drug-related corruption of police officers," in *Policing perspectives: An anthology*, ed. L. K. Gaines and G. W. Cordner, pp. 311–23 (Los Angeles, CA: Roxbury, 1999).
52. K. J. Peak, *Policing America: Methods, issues, challenges*, 5th ed. (Upper Saddle River, NJ: Prentice Hall, 2006), p. 307.
53. Ibid.
54. P. B. Kraska and V. E. Kappeler, "Police on-duty drug use: A theoretical and descriptive explanation," *American Journal of Police* 7 (1988): 1–28.
55. J. Crank and M. Caldero, *Police ethics: The corruption of noble cause* (Cincinnati: Anderson, 1999).

56. Cited in Roberg, Novak, and Cordner, *Police and society*, p. 306.
57. K. M. Lersch, "Drug related police corruption: The Miami experience," in *Police misconduct: A reader for the 21st century*, ed. M. J. Palmiotto (Upper Saddle River, NJ: Prentice Hall, 2001), p. 139.
58. G. Volsky, "Wide Miami inquiry into police is seen," *New York Times*, December 13, 1987, p. 29.
59. J. Dombrink, "The touchables: Vice and police corruption in the 1980's," *Law and Contemporary Problems* 51 (1988): 201–32.
60. J. Newton, M. Lait, and S. Glover, "LAPD condemned by its own inquiry into Rampart scandal," *Los Angeles Times*, March 1 (2000) p. A1.
61. Board of Inquiry, *Board of inquiry report into the Rampart corruption incident: Executive summary* (Los Angeles, CA: Los Angeles Police Department, 2000), p. 4.
62. Additional details regarding the Rampart scandal are available on the PBS website at http://www.pbs.org/wgbh/pages/frontline/shows/lapd/scandal (accessed July 31, 2008).
63. Blue Ribbon Rampart Review Panel, *Rampart reconsidered: The search for real reform seven years later*, http://www.lapdonline.org/assets/pdf/Rampart%20Reconsidered-Full%20Report.pdf (accessed July 31, 2008).
64. Ibid., p. 12.
65. Ibid.
66. Dombrink, "The touchables," p. 209.
67. Ibid.
68. Ibid., p. 210.
69. Ibid.
70. Ibid., p. 212.
71. Ibid., p. 214.
72. Quoted in ibid., pp. 220–21.
73. Ibid., p. 223.
74. Dombrink, "The touchables," pp. 223–24.
75. Ibid., p. 224.
76. Ibid., pp. 225–26.
77. Human Rights Watch, *Shielded from justice: Police brutality and accountability in the United States*, http://www.hrw.org/reports98/police/uspo131.htm (accessed July 15, 2008).
78. K. Lersch and T. Mieczkowski, "Who are the problem-prone officers? An analysis of citizen complaints," *American Journal of Police* 15 (1996): 23–44.
79. L. W. Sherman, *Controlling police corruption: The effects of reform policies* (Washington, DC: U.S. Department of Justice, 1978), p. 32.
80. C. Martin, *Illinois municipal officer's perceptions of police ethics* (Chicago: Statistical Analysis Center, Illinois Criminal Justice Information Authority, 1994); and J. J. Knowles, *The Ohio police behavior study* (Columbus, OH: Office of Criminal Justice Services, 1996).
81. J. Crank, *Understanding police culture* (Cincinnati: Anderson, 1998), p. 212.
82. Roberg, Novak, and Cordner, *Police and society*, p. 303.
83. See, for example, R. Klitgaard, "Subverting corruption," *Finance and development* (June 2000), http://www.imf.org/external/pubs/ft/fandd/2000/06/klitgaar.htm (accessed July 15, 2008).
84. R. Klitgaard, "Subverting corruption," *Finance and development* (June 2000), http://www.imf.org/external/pubs/ft/fandd/2000/06/klitgaar.htm (accessed July 15, 2008).
85. J. M. Pollock, "Ethics and law enforcement," in *Critical issues in policing: Contemporary readings*, 4th ed., ed. R. G. Dunham and G. P. Alpert, pp. 356–73 (Prospect Heights, IL: Waveland, 2001).
86. Ibid., p. 369.
87. Ibid.
88. Ibid., p. 370.

Chapter Fifteen

i. Adapted from National Institute of Justice, *Use of force by police: Overview of national and local data* (Washington, DC: National Institute of Justice, 1999).
ii. International Association of Chiefs of Police, *Police use of force in America, 2001* (Alexandria, VA: International Association of Chiefs of Police, 2001), p. 1.
iii. S. Walker, G. P. Alpert, and D. J. Kenney, *Responding to the problem police officer: A national study of early warning systems* (Washington, DC: National Institute of Justice, 2000).
iv. National Institute of Justice, *Impact munitions use: Types, targets, effects* (Washington, DC: National Institute of Justice, 2004).
v. D. L. Carter, "Theoretical dimensions in the abuse of authority by police officers," in *Police deviance*, 3rd ed., ed. T. Barker and D. Carter (Cincinnati: Anderson, 1994), pp. 269–290.

---

1. K. Johnson, "Police brutality cases on rise since 9/11," *USA Today*, January 18, 2007, http://www.usatoday.com/news/nation/2007-12-17-Copmisconduct_N.htm (accessed August 16, 2008).
2. See, e.g., B. Taylor and others, *Cop crunch: Identifying strategies for dealing with the recruiting and hiring crisis in law enforcement* (Washington, DC: Police Executive Research Forum, 2006); A. Sharp, "Departmental divergences on marijuana use and new recruits," *Law and Order* 51 (2003): 80–84; S. F. Domash, "Who wants this job?" *Police* 26 (2002): 34–39; L. K. Decker and R. G. Huckabee, "Raising the age and education requirements for police officers: Will too many women and minority candidates be excluded?" *Policing: An International Journal of Police Strategies and Management* 25 (2002): 789–802; and T. Anderson and J. Kandel, "Wanted:

Cop recruits," *Los Angeles Daily News*, http://www.lapd.com/article.aspx?&a=2737 (accessed January 16, 2008).

3. Some of the material in this section is adapted or derived from National Institute of Justice, *Use of force by police: Overview of national and local data* (Washington, DC: National Institute of Justice, 1999).
4. International Association of Chiefs of Police, *Police use of force in America, 2001* (Alexandria, VA: International Association of Chiefs of Police, 2001), p. 1.
5. K. Adams, "Measuring the prevalence of police use of force," in William A. Geller and Hans Toch eds., *Police violence: Understanding and controlling police abuse of force* (New Hartford: Yale University Press, 2005), pp. 52–93.
6. *Police use of force in America, 2001*, op. cit.
7. S. Walker, G. P. Alpert, and D. J. Kenney, *Responding to the problem police officer: A national study of early warning systems* (Washington, DC: National Institute of Justice, 2000).
8. Some of the wording in this paragraph is adapted from Human Rights Watch, "The Christopher Commission report," http://www.hrw.org/reports98/police/uspo73.htm (accessed March 30, 2002).
9. J. P. Crank, *Understanding police culture* (Cincinnati: Anderson, 1998), p. 78. See also J. H. Skolnick and J. J. Fyfe, *Above the law: Police and the excessive use of force* (New York: Free Press, 1993).
10. Allegan County (Michigan) Sheriff's Office, "Use of force," February 11, 2004, www.less-lethal.org/docs/30/Policy (accessed May 18, 2007).
11. G. P. Alpert and R. G. Dunham, *The force factor: Measuring police use of force relative to suspect resistance—A final report* (Washington, DC: National Institute of Justice, 2001).
12. M. R. Durose, E. L. Smith, and P. A. Langan, *Contacts between police and the public* (Washington, DC: Bureau of Justice Statistics, 2007).
13. J. H. Garner and C. D. Maxwell, "Measuring the amount of force used by and against the police in six jurisdictions," in *Use of force by police: Overview of national and local data* (Washington, DC: Bureau of Justice Statistics, 1999), p. 41. Full report available at http://www.ncjrs.gov/pdffiles1/nij/176330-2.pdf (accessed July 21, 2008).
14. Ibid., p. 30.
15. Durose, Smith, and Langan, *Contacts between police and the public*, p. 8.
16. S. W. Lathrop, "Reviewing use of force: A systematic approach," *FBI Law Enforcement Bulletin* (October 2000): 18.
17. *Black's law dictionary*, 6th ed. (St. Paul, MN: West Publishing Co., 1990), p. 398.
18. *Tennessee v. Garner*, 471 U.S. 1 (1985).
19. Ibid., p. 28.
20. V. E. Kappeler, *Critical issues in police civil liability*, 3rd ed. (Prospect Heights, IL: Waveland, 2001), p. 72.
21. *Hegarty v. Somerset County*, 848 F.Supp. 257 (1994), p. 257.
22. *Hemphill v. Schott*, 141 F.3d 412 (1998).
23. J. C. Hall, "FBI training on the new federal deadly force policy," *FBI Law Enforcement Bulletin* (April 1996): 25–32.
24. J. Fyfe, *Shots fired: An examination of New York City Police firearms discharges* (Ann Arbor, MI: University Microfilms, 1978).
25. J. Fyfe, "Blind justice? Police shootings in Memphis," paper presented at the annual meeting of the Academy of Criminal Justice Sciences, Philadelphia, March 1981.
26. See W. Geller, *Deadly force study guide*, Crime File Series (Washington, DC: National Institute of Justice, no date).
27. A. Cohen, "I've killed that man ten thousand times," *Police Magazine* (July 1980).
28. For more information, see Joe Auten, "When police shoot," *North Carolina Criminal Justice Today*, 4:4 (Summer 1986): 9–14.
29. Details for this story come from S. Slater, "Suicidal man killed by police fusillade," *Palm Beach Post*, March 11, 2005, p. 1A.
30. R. Stincelli, *Suicide by cop: Victims from both sides of the badge* (Folsom, CA: Interviews and Interrogations Institute, 2004).
31. Slater, "Suicidal man killed by police fusillade."
32. A. J. Pinizzotto, E. F. Davis, and C. E. Miller III, "Suicide by cop: Defining a devastating dilemma," *FBI Law Enforcement Bulletin* 74:2 (February 2005): 15.
33. "Ten percent of police shootings found to be 'suicide by cop,'" *Criminal Justice Newsletter*, September 1, 1998, pp. 1–2.
34. R. J. Homant and D. B. Kennedy, "Suicide by police: A proposed typology of law enforcement officer–assisted suicide," *Policing: An International Journal of Police Strategies and Management*, 23:3 (2000): 339–55.
35. A. L. Honig, "Police-assisted suicide: Identification, intervention, and investigation," *Police Chief*, October (2001): 89–93, quote on p. 93.
36. G. T. Williams, "Death by indifference," *Law and Order* (December 2003): 66–69, quote on p. 67.
37. *Graham v. Connor*, 490 U.S. 386, 396–397 (1989).
38. Ibid, p. 490.
39. Ibid.
40. D. W. Hayeslip and A. Preszler, *NIJ initiative on less-than-lethal weapons,* NIJ Research in Brief (Washington, DC: National Institute of Justice, 1993).
41. Ibid.
42. T. Farragher and D. Abel, "Postgame police projectile kills an Emerson student," *Boston Globe*, October 22, 2004, http://www.boston.com/sports/baseball/redsox/

articles/2004/10/22/postgame_police_projectile_kills_an_emerson_student (accessed July 25, 2007).

43. Taser International, "Taser X26," http://www2.taser.com/products/law/Pages/TASERX26.aspx (accessed May 18, 2007).
44. Titan, "Sticky Shocker," http://www.jaycor.com/web-content/eme_ltl_sticky.html (accessed May 18, 2007).
45. J. M. Cronin and J. A. Ederheimer, *Conducted energy devices: Development of standards for consistency and guidance* (Washington, DC: Police Executive Research Forum, 2006), http://www.policeforum.org/upload/CED-Guidelines_414547688_2152007092436.pdf (accessed July 21, 2008).
46. Ibid., p. 23.
47. Amnesty International, *Amnesty International's continued concerns about Taser use* (New York: Amnesty International, 2006), http://web.amnesty.org/library/index/engamr510302006 (accessed July 21, 2008).
48. Ibid.
49. National Institute of Justice, *Impact munitions use: Types, targets, effects* (Washington, DC: National Institute of Justice, 2004).
50. National Institute of Justice, *Department of defense nonlethal weapons and equipment review: A research guide for civil law enforcement and corrections* (Washington, DC: National Institute of Justice, 2004), http://www.ncjrs.gov/pdffiles1/nij/205293.pdf (accessed July 21, 2008).
51. National Institute of Justice, *Impact munitions use,* p. 3.
52. For some research in this area, see R. J. Kaminski, S. M. Edwards, and J. W. Johnson, "Assessing the incapacitative effects of pepper spray during resistive encounters with police," *Policing: An International Journal of Police Strategies and Management* 22 (1999): 7–29; and R. J. Kaminski, S. M. Edwards, and J. W. Johnson, "The deterrent effects of oleoresin capsicum on assaults against police: Testing the velcro-effect hypothesis," *Police Quarterly* 1 (1998): 1–20.
53. National Institute of Justice, *The effectiveness and safety of pepper spray: Research for practice* (Washington, DC: National Institute of Justice, 2003), http://www.ncjrs.gov/pdffiles1/nij/195739.pdf (accessed July 21, 2008).
54. Ibid., p. 10.
55. Ibid., p. 11.
56. *Brower v. Inyo County,* 489 U.S. 593 (1989).
57. *County of Sacramento v. Lewis,* 523 U.S. 833 (1998).
58. *Scott v. Harris*, No. 05-1631 (2007).
59. See, e.g., http://www.cnn.com/2007/US/05/12/la.cops.ap/ index.html?eref=rss_us.
60. Cited in R. Roberg, K. Novak, and G. Cordner, *Police and society*, 3rd ed. (Los Angeles: Roxbury, 2005), p. 333. See also D. L. Carter, "Theoretical dimensions in the abuse of authority by police officers," in *Police deviance,* 3rd ed., ed. T. Barker and D. Carter, pp. 269–90 (Cincinnati: Anderson, 1994), p. 273.
61. Ibid.
62. R. A. Leo, "*Miranda's* revenge: Police interrogation as a confidence game," *Law and Society Review* 30 (1996): 259–88, quote on p. 278.
63. Cited in R. Roberg, K. Novak, and G. Cordner, *Police and society,* 3rd ed. (Los Angeles: Roxbury, 2005), p. 333. See also Carter, "Theoretical dimensions in the abuse of authority by police officers," p. 273.
64. See Human Rights Watch, *Shielded from justice: Police brutality and accountability in the United States,* http://www.hrw.org/reports98/police (accessed July 21, 2008).
65. Human Rights Watch, "Summary and Recommendations," *Shielded from justice: Police brutality and accountability in the United States, Summary and recommendations,* http:// www.hrw.org/reports98/police/uspo06.htm (accessed July 21, 2008).
66. L. B. Sulc, "Police brutality is not a widespread problem," in *Policing the police,* ed. P. Winters, pp. 79–85 (San Diego: Greenhaven, 1995), p. 80.
67. R. G. Lawrence, *The politics of force: Media and the construction of police brutality* (Berkeley: University of California Press, 2000), p. 62.

Chapter Sixteen

i. http://www.apsu.edu/oconnort/3410/3410lect05.htm (accessed August 16, 2008).
ii. White House, "USA PATRIOT Act," http://www.whitehouse.gov/infocus/patriotact/ (accessed July 25, 2008).
iii. Public Law 106–386.
iv. P. Turunen, "Hack attack: How you might be a target," CNN.com, April 12, 2002, http://archives.cnn.com/2002/TECH/ptech/04/12/hack.dangers/index.html (accessed June 27, 2007).
v. E. Cornish, *The study of the future* (Washington, DC: World Future Society, 1977), p. 108.
vi. Ibid., p. 11.

---

1. T. Locy, "Three men indicted on terror charges," *USA Today,* April 13, 2005, p. 1A.
2. Details for this story are taken from T. Valdmanis, "Wall Street stays on guard against terror attacks," *USA Today,* August 3, 2004, http://www.usatoday.com/money/markets/us/2004-08-03-wall-street_x.htm (accessed January 10, 2008).
3. Ibid.
4. In the words of the act: "The term 'terrorism' means premeditated, politically motivated violence perpetrated

against noncombatant targets by subnational groups or clandestine agents." 22 U.S.C. 2656 f(d)(2).

5. Federal Bureau of Investigation, *Counterterrorism section, terrorism in the United States, 1987* (Washington, DC: Federal Bureau of Investigation, 1987).
6. G. Nettler, *Killing one another* (Cincinnati: Anderson, 1982).
7. Alex Koppleman, "The terrorist you've never heard of," Salon.com (December 16, 2006), http://www.salon.com/news/feature/2006/12/18/tennessee_terrorist (August 16, 2008).
8. F. Schmalleger, *Criminal justice today: An introductory text for the twenty-first century*, 9th ed. (Upper Saddle River, NJ: Prentice Hall, 2007), pp. 677–78.
9. See B. Collin, "The future of cyberterrorism," *Crime and Justice International* (March 1997): 15–18.
10. J. Arquilla and D. Ronfeldt, *The advent of netwar* (Santa Monica, CA: RAND Corporation, 1996).
11. M. M. Pollitt, "Cyberterrorism: Fact or fancy?" *Proceedings of the Twentieth National Information Systems Security Conference* (October 1997): 285–89.
12. President's Critical Infrastructure Protection Board, *The national strategy to secure cyberspace* (Washington, DC: U.S. Government Printing Office, 2002).
13. U.S. Department of Homeland Security, *Charter of the National Infrastructure Advisory Council* (Washington, DC: 2003), http://www.dhs.gov/xlibrary/assets/niac/NIAC_Charter.pdf (accessed June 20, 2008).
14. Ibid.
15. J. A. Inciardi, "Narcoterrorism," paper presented at the annual meeting of the Academy of Criminal Justice Sciences, San Francisco, 1988, p. 8.
16. "U.S. government lacks strategy to neutralize international crime," *Criminal Justice International* 10 (September–October 1994): 5.
17. Tom O'Connor, "Special Interest and Single Interest Extremism," http://www.apsu.edu/oconnort/3410/3410lect05.htm (accessed June 20, 2008).
18. "Earth Liberation Front News," http://www.earthliberationfront.com/elf_news.htm (accessed July 25, 2008).
19. *National strategy for combating terrorism* (Washington, DC: White House, 2003).
20. Ibid.
21. Ibid.
22. Ibid.
23. Ibid.
24. Ibid.
25. Ibid.
26. Schmalleger, *Criminal justice today,* p. 684.
27. USA PATRIOT Act 802, 115 Stat. at 376.
28. *United States v. Verdugo-Urquidez,* 494 U.S. 259 (1990), pp. 264–66.
29. *Mathews v. Diaz,* 426 U.S. 67 (1976), p. 77.
30. Ibid.
31. *Shaughnessy v. United States ex rel. Mezei,* 345 U.S. 206 (1953), p. 212.
32. USA PATRIOT Act, Pub. L. No. 107–56, 412, 115 Stat. 272, 350 (2001).
33. USA PATRIOT Act 106, 115 Stat. at 277.
34. The full list can be found at Wikipedia, "USA PATRIOT Act," http://en.wikipedia.org/wiki/USA_PATRIOT_Act (accessed July 25, 2008).
35. White House, "USA PATRIOT Act," http://www.whitehouse.gov/infocus/patriotact/ (accessed July 25, 2008).
36. Police Executive Research Forum, *Local law enforcement's role in preventing and responding to terrorism* (Washington, DC: Police Executive Research Forum, October 2, 2001), http://www.policeforum.org/terrorismfinal.doc (accessed June 1, 2006). See also http://www.cops.usdoj.gov/files/RIC/Publications/e02021441.pdf (accessed August 28, 2008).
37. Council on Foreign Relations, "Terrorism questions and answers: Police departments," http://www.terrorismanswers.com/security/police.html (accessed April 19, 2006).
38. Ibid.
39. M. Weissenstein, "NYPD shifts focus to terrorism, long considered the turf of federal agents," Associated Press, March 21, 2003.
40. Ibid.
41. International Association of Chiefs of Police, *From hometown security to homeland security: IACP's principles for a locally designed and nationally coordinated homeland security strategy* (Alexandria, VA: International Association of Chiefs of Police, 2005).
42. Ibid.
43. J. G. Estey, International Association of Chiefs of Police, "President's message: Taking command initiative—An update," 2005, http://www.theiacp.org/documents/index.cfm?fuseaction5document&document_id5697 (accessed July 25, 2005).
44. R. J. Jordan, Federal Bureau of Investigation, Congressional statement on information sharing before the U.S. Senate Committee on the Judiciary, Subcommittee on Administrative Oversight and the Courts, Washington, DC, April 17, 2002, http://www.fbi.gov/congress/congress02/jordan041702.htm (accessed April 19, 2007).
45. U.S. Department of Justice, "Attorney General Ashcroft and Deputy Attorney General Thompson announce reorganization and mobilization of the nation's justice and law enforcement resources," press release, November 8, 2001.
46. R. S. Mueller III, Federal Bureau of Investigation, Testimony before the Senate Committee on Intelligence, February 16, 2005.
47. Governor's Commission on Criminal Justice Innovation, *Final report* (Boston: Governor's Commission on Crimi-

nal Justice Innovation, 2004), p. 57, from which much of the wording in the rest of this paragraph is taken.

48. The plan was an outgrowth of the IACP Criminal Intelligence Sharing Summit held in Alexandria, Virginia, in March 2002. Results of the summit are documented in International Association of Chiefs of Police, *Recommendations from the IACP intelligence summit, criminal intelligence sharing* (Washington, DC: COPS Office, 2002).
49. Office of Justice Programs, *The national criminal intelligence sharing plan* (Washington, DC: U.S. Department of Justice, 2003).
50. The term comes from Bud Levin, as quoted in Gene Stephens, "Policing the future: Law enforcement's new challenges," *The Futurist* (March–April 2005): 55.
51. Much of the information in this section comes from Bureau of Justice Assistance, *Promoting partnerships for public safety, annual report FY 2002* (Washington, DC: December 2003), http://www.ncjrs.org/html/bja/200252/sec2_b.html (accessed January 5, 2006).
52. MATRIX, "Background information for press releases/inquiries," press release, April 2005.
53. Visit RISS at http://www.riss.net/centers.aspx.
54. MATRIX, "FACTS defined," http://www.matrix-at.org/FACTS_defined.htm (accessed March 14, 2005).
55. MATRIX, "Background information for press releases/inquiries."
56. See Institute for Intergovernmental Research, "State and Local Anti-Terrorism Training (SLATT)," http://www.iir.com/slatt (accessed March 14, 2008).
57. L. Robinson, address given at the Twelfth International Congress on Criminology, Seoul, Korea, August 28, 1998.
58. R. S. Gelbard, "Foreign policy after the cold war: The new threat—transnational crime," address given at St. Mary's University, San Antonio, Texas, April 2, 1996.
59. Schmalleger, *Criminal justice today,* p. 673.
60. T. L. Friedman, *The world is flat: A brief history of the twenty-first century* (New York: Farrar, Straus, and Giroux, 2006).
61. M. Shively and others, *Survey of practitioners to assess the local impact of transnational crime: Task order final report* (Washington, DC: U.S. Department of Justice, 2007), p. 2.
62. J. O. Finckenauer, "Meeting the challenge of transnational crime," *National Institute of Justice Journal* (July 2000): 2–7.
63. Ibid., p. 2.
64. L. Shelley, "Transnational organized crime in the United States: Defining the problem," *Kobe University Law Review* 1 (1998): 77–91.
65. Public Law 106–386.
66. Ibid.
67. U.S. Department of State, International Information Programs, *Fact sheet: State department programs to combat trafficking in persons* (Washington, DC: U.S. Dept. of State, February 1, 2001).
68. J. G. Raymond, D. M. Hughes, and C. J. Gomez, *Sex trafficking of women in the United States: International and domestic trends—Report to Coalition against Trafficking in Women* (Amherst, MA: University of Massachusetts, Amherst, and University of Rhode Island, 2001).
69. A. O. Richard, *International trafficking in women to the United States: A contemporary manifestation of slavery and organized crime* (Washington, DC: U.S. Department of State, Bureau of Intelligence and Research, 1999).
70. Shively and others, *Survey of practitioners to assess the local impact of transnational crime,* p. 11.
71. Ibid., p. 12.
72. Ibid., p. 11.
73. Ibid., p. 16.
74. Ibid.
75. Ibid., p. 20.
76. Ibid., p. 21.
77. Ibid.
78. Ibid., p. 24.
79. Ibid., p. 5.
80. Finckenauer, "Meeting the challenge of transnational crime."
81. Shively and others, *Survey of practitioners to assess the local impact of transnational crime.*
82. Interpol, "A brief history of Interpol," http://www.interpol.com/public/ICPO/history.asp (accessed August 16, 2008).
83. U.S. National Central Bureau, http://www.usdoj.gov/jmd/mps/manual/usncb.htm (accessed June 26, 2008).
84. European Police Office, "Fact Sheet on Europol 2008," http://www.europol.europa.eu/index.asp?page=facts (accessed July 25, 2008).
85. Ibid.
86. See the Europol website at http://www.europol.europa.eu/ (accessed July 25, 2008).
87. Ibid.
88. United Nations, "Not So Well Known," http://www.un.org/Overview/uninbrief/ (accessed June 26, 2007).
89. Thalif Deen, "Facing humiliating defeat, US abandons move to exempt troops from war crimes," http://www.commondreams.org/headlines04/0623–08.htm (accessed August 16, 2008).
90. International Criminal Court, *Report on the activities of the court,* http://www.icc-cpi.int/library/asp/ICC-ASP-5-15_English.pdf (accessed June 26, 2007).
91. Schmalleger, *Criminal justice today,* p. 705.
92. Ibid.
93. See, e.g., About.com: Urban Legends, "The Kidney Thieves: An Urban Legend," http://urbanlegends.about.

com/od/horrors/a/kidney_thieves.htm (accessed July 25, 2008).

94. D. Matas and D. Kilgour, *Bloody harvest: Revised report into allegations of organ harvesting of Falun Gong practitioners in China,* January 31, 2007, http://organharvestinvestigation.net/report0701/report20070131-eng.pdf (accessed June 27, 2007).
95. Ibid., p. 58.
96. Schmalleger, *Criminal justice today,* p. 706.
97. P. Turunen, "Hack attack: How you might be a target," CNN.com, April 12, 2002, http://archives.cnn.com/2002/TECH/ptech/04/12/hack.dangers/index.html (accessed June 27, 2007).
98. E. Abreu, "Kevin Mitnick bares all," *Industry Standard,* September 28, 2000, http://www.networkworld.com/news/2000/0928mitnick.html (accessed June 27, 2007).
99. Schmalleger, *Criminal justice today,* p. 712.
100. Police Futurists International, "About PFI," http://www.policefuturists.org/about_pfi.htm (accessed June 27, 2007).
101. Federal Bureau of Investigation, "Futures Working Group," http://www.fbi.gov/hq/td/fwg/workhome.htm (accessed June 27, 2007).
102. R. Amara and G. Salanik, "Forecasting: From conjectural art toward science," *Technological Forecasting and Social Change* 3 (1972): 415–26, quote on p. 415.
103. Ibid.
104. D. Donnelly, "Forecasting methods: A selective literature review," http://mediafuturesarchive.org/forecasting.htm (accessed June 27, 2007).
105. See, e.g., G. Wise, "The accuracy of technological forecasts: 1890–1940," *Futures* 8 (1976): 411–19.
106. E. Cornish, *The study of the future* (Washington, DC: World Future Society, 1977), p. 108.
107. See, e.g., F. Kaplan, "Iraq is Korea? Bush's latest appalling historical analogy," Slate.com, May 31, 2007, http://www.slate.com/id/2167362/pagenum/all/#page_start (accessed June 27, 2007).
108. J. Record, *Perils of reasoning by historical analogy: Munich, Vietnam, and American use of force since 1945* (Alabama: Maxwell Air Force Base, Center for Strategy and Technology, Air War College, 1998).
109. For some elaboration on this point, see J. L. Worrall and O. Marenin, "Emerging liability issues in the implementation and adoption of community oriented policing," *Policing: An International Journal of Police Strategies and Management* 21 (1998): 121–36.
110. "New York City mayor sparks debate on community policing," *Criminal Justice Newsletter,* 25:2 (January 18, 1994): 1.
111. Cornish, *The study of the future,* p. 11.
112. Ibid.
113. B. Schwartz, U. Svedin, and B. Wittrock, *Methods in future studies* (Boulder: Westview Press, 1982), p. 28.
114. S. Schnaars, *Megamistakes: Forecasting and the myth of rapid technological change* (New York: Free Press, 1989).

Glossary

1. *Chimel v. California*, 395 U.S. 752 (1969).
2. *Dictionary of Criminal Justice Data Terminology* (Washington, DC: Bureau of Justice Statistics, 1982) p. G-2.
3. See, e.g., *Davis v. Passman*, 442 U.S. 228 (1979); *Sonntag v. Dooley*, 650 F.2d 904 (7th Cir. 1981); and *Carlson v. Green*, 446 U.S. 14 (1980).
4. F. Schmalleger, *Criminal justice today: An introductory text for the twenty-first century,* 9th ed. (Upper Saddle River, NJ: Prentice Hall, 2007), p. 162.
5. Ibid.
6. B. Forst, "The privatization and civilianization of policing," in *Boundary changes in criminal justice organizations*, ed. C. M. Friel, pp. 19–79 (Washington, DC: National Institute of Justice, 2000), p. 23.
7. *Lugar v. Edmondson Oil Co.*, 457 U.S. 922 (1982), p. 937.
8. White House, "USA PATRIOT Act," http://www.whitehouse.gov/infocus/patriotact/ (accessed June 5, 2008).
9. Community Policing Consortium, *What is community policing?* (Washington, DC: Community Policing Consortium, 1995).
10. D. L. Carter, *Law enforcement intelligence: A guide for state, local, and tribal law enforcement agencies* (Washington, DC: U.S. Department of Justice, 2004), p. 7.
11. Ibid.
12. *Lefkowitz v. Turley*, 414 U.S. 70 (1973).
13. *Fikes v. Alabama*, 352 U.S. 191 (1957), p. 198.
14. See http://www.apsu.edu/oconnort/3410/3410lect05.htm (accessed August 16, 2008).
15. Equal Employment Opportunity Commission, http://eeoc.gov (accessed November 9, 2008).
16. *Breithaupt v. Abram*, 352 U.S. 432 (1957).
17. L. W. Sherman, *Evidence-based policing* (Washington, DC: Police Foundation, 1998), pp. 3–4.
18. International Association of Chiefs of Police, *Police use of force in America, 2001* (Alexandria, VA: International Association of Chiefs of Police, 2001), p. 1.
19. *Weeks v. United States*, 232 U.S. 383 (1914); and *Mapp v. Ohio*, 367 U.S. 643 (1961).
20. See, e.g., *Brown v. United States*, 356 U.S. 148 (1958); and *Rogers v. United States*, 340 U.S. 367 (1951).
21. J. M. Pollock, "Ethics and law enforcement," in *Critical issues in policing: Contemporary readings*, 4th ed., ed. R. G. Dunham and G. P. Alpert, pp. 356–73 (Prospect Heights, IL: Waveland, 2001).

22. *Silverthorne Lumber Co. v. United States*, 251 U.S. 385 (1920).
23. Ibid., p. 302, n. 8.
24. *Hall v. GHS Construction Co.*, 842 F.2d 101 (8th Cir. 1988).
25. *Warden v. Hayden*, 387 U.S. 294 (1967).
26. See, e.g., A. Maslow, "A theory of human motivation," *Psychological Review* 50 (1943): 370–96; and F. Herzberg, "One more time: How do you motivate employees?" *Harvard Business Review* (January–February 1968): 27–35.
27. Public Law 106-386.
28. Illinois Association for Criminal Justice, *Illinois crime survey* (1929; repr. Montclair, NJ: Patterson Smith, 1968), p. 359.
29. National Institute of Justice, *Impact munitions use: Types, targets, effects* (Washington, DC: National Institute of Justice, 2004).
30. A. Smith, ed., *Intelligence-led policing* (Richmond, VA: International Association of Law Enforcement Intelligence Analysts, 1997), p. 1.
31. *Miranda v. Arizona*, 384 U.S. 436 (1966).
32. D. L. Carter, "Theoretical dimensions in the abuse of authority by police officers," in *Police deviance*, 3rd ed., ed. T. Barker and D. Carter (Cincinnati: Anderson, 1994), pp. 269–90.
33. D. W. Murphy and J. L. Worrall, "The threat of mission distortion in police-corrections partnerships," *Policing: An International Journal of Police Strategies and Management* (forthcoming).
34. *Monell v. Department of Social Services*, 436 U.S. 658 (1978).
35. U.S. Department of Justice, "Information Technology Initiatives," http://www.it.ojp.gov/topic.jsp?topic_id=93 (accessed November 14, 2008).
36. *Tennessee v. Garner*, 471 U.S. 1 (1985).
37. R. V. Wolf and J. L. Worrall, *Lessons from the field: Ten community prosecution leadership profiles* (Alexandria, VA: American Prosecutors Research Institute, 2004).
38. S. L. Emanuel and S. Knowles, *Emanuel law outlines: Criminal procedure* (Larchmont, NY: Emanuel, 1998), p. 129.
39. V. E. Kappeler, R. D. Sluder, and G. Alpert, *Forces of deviance: Understanding the dark side of policing* (Prospect Heights, IL: Waveland, 1994), p. 21.
40. Adapted from P. B. Kraska and V. E. Kappeler, "To serve and pursue: Exploring police sexual violence against women," *Justice Quarterly* 12 (1995): 85–109.
41. C. McHenry, "Stress in the police service: Preventing the long-term effects of trauma," *Occupational Health Review* (July–August 1995), p. 18.
42. E. E. Joh, "The paradox of private policing," *Journal of Criminal Law and Criminology* 95 (2004): p. 67.
43. Ibid.
44. S. Walker, G. P. Alpert, and D. J. Kenney, *Responding to the problem police officer: A national study of early warning systems* (Washington, DC: National Institute of Justice, 2000).
45. *Howard v. Grinage*, 82 F.3d 1343 (6th Cir. 1996), p. 1350.
46. C. Batton and C. Kadleck, "Theoretical and methodological issues in racial profiling research," *Police Quarterly* (March 2004): 30–64.
47. Fourth Amendment to the U.S. Constitution, http://www.law.cornell.edu/constitution/constitution.billofrights.html (accessed November 11, 2008).
48. E. Cornish, *The study of the future* (Washington, DC: World Future Society, 1977), p. 11.
49. J. J. Fyfe, "The split-second syndrome and other determinants of police violence," in *Critical issues in policing*, 4th ed., ed. R. G. Dunham and G. P. Alpert, pp. 583–98 (Prospect Heights, IL: Waveland, 2001).
50. Schmalleger, *Criminal justice today*, p. G-26.
51. Crank, *Understanding police culture*, p. 30. See also J. Van Maanen, "Observations on the making of policemen," *Human Organization* 32 (1973): 407–18.
52. Crank, *Understanding police culture*, p. 30.
53. *Rizzo v. Goode*, 423 U.S. 362 (1976).
54. David L. Carter, *Law enforcement intelligence: A guide for state, local, and tribal law enforcement agencies* (Washington, DC: U.S. Department of Justice, 2004), p. 8.
55. M. E. Buerger and L. G. Mazerolle, "Third-party policing: Theoretical analysis of an emerging trend," in *The police and society: Touchstone readings*, 2nd ed., ed. V. E. Kappeler (Prospect Heights, IL: Waveland, 1999), p. 402.
56. Crank, *Understanding police culture*, p. 30. See also Van Maanen, "Observations on the making of policemen."
57. Cornish, *The study of the future*, p. 108.
58. K. J. Peak, *Policing America: Methods, issues, challenges*, 5th ed. (Upper Saddle River, NJ: Prentice Hall, 2006), p. 307.
59. Ibid.
60. Adapted from National Institute of Justice, *Use of force by police: Overview of national and local data* (Washington, DC: National Institute of Justice, 1999).
61. Fourth Amendment to the U.S. Constitution.
62. M. Shively and others, *Survey of practitioners to assess the local impact of transnational crime: Task order final report* (Washington, DC: U.S. Department of Justice, 2007), p. 11.

INDEX

L

M

N

O

T

U

V